DISCARDED

COMMUNIST CHINA 1955–1959

Policy Documents with Analysis

Prepared at Harvard University under the Joint Auspices of
the Center for International Affairs and the East Asian Research Center

With a Foreword by
ROBERT R. BOWIE AND JOHN K. FAIRBANK

HARVARD UNIVERSITY PRESS
Cambridge, Massachusetts
1962

© Copyright 1962 by the President and Fellows of Harvard College

Distributed in Great Britain by
Oxford University Press
London

Preparation of this volume was aided by funds of the Rockefeller Foundation and the Ford Foundation granted to the sponsoring centers. This help is gratefully acknowledged. Neither foundation, however, is the author, owner, publisher, or proprietor of this publication and neither is to be understood as approving by virtue of its grants any of the statements made or views expressed therein.

Library of Congress Catalog Card Number 62-11394
Printed in the United States of America

FOREWORD

This volume of forty-eight documents from Communist China covers a five-year period of intense revolutionary change. It begins with 1955, which saw the publication, after a delay of two years, of the first Five-Year Plan. It closes during the months of stock-taking, some of it clearly painful, which followed the massive celebration of the regime's tenth anniversary in October 1959. In 1955 the period in which the institutions of the old "bourgeois" society were being abolished or gradually changed was nearly at an end. From 1955 on, new and radical programs were launched in steady progression to reorganize the entire structure of Chinese life and institutions.

The purpose of this volume is to present a documented and interpretive record of Chinese domestic policy during this period, a time in which the unfolding of radical designs for contemporary China may afford an opportunity for an understanding of the special features and qualities of Chinese Communism. Since the internal politics of Communist China are largely veiled in totalitarian secrecy, the attention of scholars naturally lodges on the regime's international conduct and foreign policies. Our conviction, however, is that external actions and policies cannot be adequately understood apart from domestic politics, in China as elsewhere.

Any selection of documents has its own character. This collection was developed by a visiting Fellow of the Center for International Affairs at Harvard University. He wrote the essay that introduces the volume, the introductions to the chapters, and the commentaries preceding the documents. Though several staff members of the two centers have reviewed the work and helped in the preparation of the book, the responsibility rests chiefly with the author-editor, who for various and necessary reasons must remain unnamed. Our belief that his selections and interpretations are of interest and value to serious students has overcome our normal reluctance to publish a work by a scholar who cannot publicly assume the responsibilities, as well as the rewards, for his own labors. We can assure those who use this volume that the author has had a background and experience which few can match in qualifying him for a work on this subject and period.

Among those who helped in the task of getting this manuscript ready were Mrs. Ellen Wood Barth, Mrs. Anne B. Clark, Edward Friedman, Roy Hofheinz, and John M. H. Lindbeck, of the East Asian Research Center, and Mrs. Lillian Christmas, Mrs. Stephanie Richardson Gaskins, Max Hall, and Mrs. Anne Freeman Mayo, of the Center for International Affairs. Still other staff members of the two centers were responsible for typing and other services in connection with the book.

Robert R. Bowie, Director
Center for International Affairs

John K. Fairbank, Director
East Asian Research Center

PREFACE
PURPOSE AND PLAN OF THE WORK

This volume is intended to provide a documentary introduction to the internal history of Communist China, 1955-1959. It is not a work of original research addressed to those who have access to the originals and can read Chinese; it is rather a work of digestion for the general student. The translations have not been specially made for this book. Many of the forty-eight documents included are taken from English-language books or pamphlets issued by the official Foreign Languages Press in Peking.* The texts of the rest are taken from other official Chinese publications or from mimeographed series issued by the U.S. Consulate General in Hong Kong. The first object of this work has been to furnish the student with a convenient and compendious selection of important documents.

Full texts have been given in all cases, for obvious reasons, in spite of their length and prolixity. The texts have not been altered by us, not even in those spots where the translations are awkward or ungrammatical. Usages with respect to punctuation, capital letters, italics, hyphens, and alternative forms of spelling (e.g., "plough" or "plow") have been left just as we found them in the source publications. This is not always true in the document *titles*, which in any case are sometimes variable and arbitrary, but as for the *texts*, our intention is to give the student the document just as it appears in our source, which in every case is clearly identified. However, in a few cases where perfectly obvious typographical errors occurred in the source, the errors have been silently corrected here.

Many—perhaps the majority—of these documents have selected themselves. It would be unthinkable to leave out of any collection, for example, Mao Tse-tung's speech of February 27, 1957, on "Contradictions," or that of Liu Shao-ch'i on the "Great Leap Forward." It is regrettable that the authors of such major items repeat themselves and one another so often; but any serious student of Communist policies must be prepared for this. In the selection of supporting material, such as Lu Ting-yi's article on education of May 1958, subjective judgments have of course played a greater part. The principle has been to choose material which most vividly illustrated the main themes of the period—the "leap forward" of 1955-56, the period of anxious consolidation which followed it, the "Hundred Flowers" and "rectification" campaigns, the change of course in 1957, the "Great Leap Forward" of 1958, the establishment of people's communes, and the second period of consolidation in 1959. The presentation is (with minor exceptions) chronological. Documents on foreign affairs have been included only when they seemed also to have an important bearing on domestic issues (e.g., Documents 7, 13, and 24).

A word of explanation about the treatment of one particular theme may be given in illustration of editorial difficulties. Policy toward the national minorities has been an important issue on the Chinese domestic scene and may be thought to merit extensive discussion; but in fact, only one document on the subject is included (Document 44). For one thing, we deliberately omitted items on Tibet, which are available elsewhere in convenient form. Also, it seemed impossible in the space available to give to the general theme more than the barest illustrative treatment. Even the choice of a single document has been difficult. More revealing single documents could be found, and some are listed in the notes to Document 44; but the one selected provides a convenient historical retrospect of the changes in Chinese policy over the period 1955-1959, and other possible choices would not fit in with the general chronological arrangement of the collection.

The documents are numbered continuously, 1 through 48, but grouped in eleven chapters. Each chapter begins with a commentary. In addition, there are in most cases some paragraphs of introductory comment to the individual documents. References to source material for further reading are there

---

*"Peking," rather than "Peiping," is used throughout this volume because that is the form used in the documents themselves.

provided. The references in all cases are to books or articles written in or translated into English. In the case of articles originating in China, the references include the series in which the translations may be found—e.g., CB (*Current Background*) or ECMM (*Extracts from China Mainland Magazines*). This procedure is for the convenience of the student who does not read Chinese, and who will not easily trace a single reference to Chinese periodicals, such as to *Study* of November 1, 1957, without further indication of where the translation is to be found.

The selection of subjects for annotation and of themes for further reading has also been a matter of some difficulty. The lists are of course intended to be typical, not exhaustive; in many cases there is a mass of further interesting material, on the subjects listed as well as others, in the various series of translations. No attempt has been made to turn this already bulky volume into an encyclopaedia of Communist China by comprehensive notes on all the personalities mentioned, or on all the Marxist texts cited. The student who is interested will have little difficulty in finding out what he needs to know about these. Cross references between the documents could have been innumerable, but have in fact been kept to a minimum. The notes provided by the Chinese official translators have been retained. All footnotes appearing on the same pages as the texts of the documents were present in the texts as we found them. (Our own notes in the eleven chapters containing the documents are incorporated in the commentaries preceding the texts, and not at the foot of the pages.)

The General Introduction following this preface is an interpretive essay, to which is given the rather comprehensive title "Domestic Policy Trends in Communist China, 1955–1959." The form of this General Introduction needs some explanation. The main body of it is divided into eleven parts (I–XI) corresponding to the eleven documentary chapters and bearing the same titles. It is, however, intended to be read straight through, and to suggest a political and economic pattern behind the events described or foreshadowed in the documents themselves. The intention has been to provide, not a judgment on the material progress made in Communist China, but some idea of how the political machine works in practice. In particular, the General Introduction attempts to trace the continuous interaction between the demands of ideology and of administrative practice, and also—a closely connected subject—to trace the play of forces within the Chinese Communist Party. This play of forces is a theme on which the Chinese leaders have themselves from time to time been remarkably frank. "Politics is in command," as the slogan runs, in Communist China. The political judgments of the dominant leaders, more than the technical judgments of the experts, determined the course of internal events over the years 1955–1959. Not surprisingly, however, the political judgments prevailed in many cases only after prolonged and bitter debate within the Party and have been continually, though usually not openly, corrected by the lessons of experience.

The General Introduction is designed to illustrate in a continuous narrative the tensions that have occurred between the Central Committee and what may be described as the two wings of the Chinese Communist Party. Tensions between the Central Committee and the "rightists" ("conservatives") within the Party have been frequent and considerable. Those between the Central Committee and the wild men (or "good-hearted but over-enthusiastic" comrades) have been less frequent and less bitter. The differences have in either case been treated as occurring between the Central Committee and lower levels rather than within the Central Committee itself. It is of course certain that in one case at least (the speed-up of cooperativization in 1955) the final decision was preceded by intense argument at the highest level. It is likely enough that none of the big decisions recorded in these documents was taken without similar argument. And it is possible that some members of the Politburo itself could be regarded as "rightists" (on the other hand, Khrushchev seems to have regarded some as "adventurists"). There is very little firm evidence on this subject, although it is a fascinating one for speculation. No attempt has therefore been made here to discuss the major differences of policy within the Chinese Communist Party in terms of opposition between the leading members of the Central Committee.

The conclusions in the General Introduction have been drawn both from the documents themselves and from the material cited in the notes to the General Introduction, which are placed in the back of the book. Some citations in those notes are repeated in the lists of additional reading given in the documentary chapters. The works referred to are, as already noted, very largely translations of newspaper articles or broadcasts from Communist China, a type of material about which there must be certain reservations which it is well to bear in mind. Chinese Communist press sources are often diffi-

PURPOSE AND PLAN OF THE WORK

cult to interpret, particularly when they are available to the student only in preselected English translations which force the reader to rely upon the judgment of the translator as to the meaning of the documents. Also, the articles themselves are likely to be heavily distorted to follow the momentary exigencies of the Party line, and it is not always possible to tell from an item in translation how much prominence was given to a particular broadcast or article. As the Chinese themselves are apt to exaggerate not only in their success stories but in their confessionals, it is sometimes difficult to judge how well official propaganda corresponds to facts. Again there is the temptation to find in a mass of raw materials from such sources only what one is looking for without stopping to balance evidence from the success story as well as from the confessional.

Yet when all due reservations are made, the Chinese Communist press, like other totalitarian presses, remains an extremely revealing indicator of the concerns of the Party. Assuming that everything is deliberate, one can often gather from official communications not only the Party line, but also anti-Party lines, or the intra-Party heresies, which are being confuted. The Chinese press is perhaps more susceptible to this sort of analysis than is the Russian, because the Chinese press makes more use of the dialectic of contradictions. Further, the press serves as the medium through which the general line must be propagated to the masses, and thus often takes the form of sermon notes for the cadres who sell the line at ground level. Objections to the line are therefore often met in detail, and from countercriticisms one can usually get a good idea of the nature of the original criticism. Moreover, sometimes, the countercriticism is aimed explicitly at "some comrades" (certain Party members) and from this there is a reflection of the tensions within the Communist Party itself.

The scheme of the commentaries in this volume is to move from the broad to the specific. The General Introduction ranges widely over the events from 1955 through 1959. The general comment at the outset of each documentary chapter contains detailed information on the chapter's main themes. In the specific comment at the head of an individual document, additional background information may be brought in which does not necessarily fall squarely within the main themes of the chapter. Thus, in connection with Document 15, there is a discussion of the history of propaganda for birth control, a topic that is extraneous to the principal subject matter of Chapter VI. Although this kind of arrangement results in some duplication, it serves the interest of students who wish to concentrate on one particular chapter or document without reconsulting the General Introduction.

List of Chinese Periodicals

Name in English Translation	Chinese Name (in Romanization)
Architectural Journal	Chien-chu Hsueh-pao
China Water Conservancy	Chung-kuo Shui-li
China Youth	Chung-kuo Ch'ing-nien-pao
Chinese Agriculture	Chung-kuo Nung-pao
Current Events	Shih-shih Shou-ts'e
Economic Research	Ching-chi Yen-chiu
Education Fortnightly	Chiao-yü Pan-yueh-k'an
Finance	Ts'ai-cheng
Financial and Economic Research	Ts'ai-ching Yen-chiu
Grain	Liang-shih
Industrial and Commercial Circles	Kung-shang Chieh
Liberation	Chieh-fang
Masses Daily	Ta-chung Jih-pao
New China Fortnightly	Hsin-hua Pan-yueh-k'an
New China Monthly	Hsin-hua Yueh-k'an
New Construction	Hsin Chien-she
New Observer	Hsin Kuan-ch'a
Outlook	Chan-wang
People's Daily	Jen-min Jih-pao (Renmin Ribao)
People's Education	Jen-min Chiao-yü
Planned Economy	Chi-hua Ching-chi
Political Study	Cheng-chih Hsueh-hsi
Red Flag	Hung Ch'i (Hongqi)
Science Journal	K'o-hsueh T'ung-pao
Soldier of the Liberation Army	Chieh-fang-chün Chan-shih
Statistical Work Bulletin	T'ung-chi Kung-tso T'ung-hsun
Study	Hsueh-hsi
Teaching and Research	Chiao-hsueh yü Yen-chiu
Theoretical Study	Li-lun Hsueh-hsi
Trumpet	Hao-chueh
Water Conservancy Journal	Shui-li Hsueh-pao
Women of China	Chung-kuo Fu-nü
Workers of China	Chung-kuo Kung-jen
World Culture	Shih-chieh Chih-shih

CONTENTS

Preface: PURPOSE AND PLAN OF THE WORK v
    List of Chinese Periodicals viii
    Abbreviations and Terms xii

General Introduction: DOMESTIC POLICY TRENDS IN COMMUNIST CHINA, 1955–1959 1

Chapter I: THE FIRST FIVE-YEAR PLAN 42
    Document 1. Li Fu-ch'un, *Report on the First Five-Year Plan, 1953–1957*, July 5–6, 1955 .. 42

Chapter II: THE SPEED-UP OF AGRICULTURAL COOPERATIVIZATION, 1955–56 92
    Document 2. Mao Tse-tung, *The Question of Agricultural Cooperation*, July 31, 1955 94
    Document 3. *Decisions on Agricultural Cooperation*, October 11, 1955 106
    Document 4. Mao Tse-tung, *Preface* to the book *Socialist Upsurge in China's Countryside*, December 27, 1955 117
    Document 5. *The Draft Program for Agricultural Development, 1956–1967*, submitted January 23, 1956 119

Chapter III: FLOWERS AND SCHOOLS 127
    Document 6. Chou En-lai, *On the Question of Intellectuals*, January 14, 1956 128
    Document 7. *On the Historical Experience of the Dictatorship of the Proletariat*, editorial in *People's Daily*, April 5, 1956 144
    Document 8. Lu Ting-yi, *Let a Hundred Flowers Blossom, a Hundred Schools of Thought Contend!* May 26, 1956 151

Chapter IV: THE EIGHTH PARTY CONGRESS 164
    Document 9. Liu Shao-ch'i, *Political Report of the Central Committee*, September 15, 1956 164
    Document 10. *Proposals for the Second Five-Year Plan (1958–1962)*, September 27, 1956 ... 204
    Document 11. Chou En-lai, *Report on the Proposals for the Second Five-Year Plan*, September 16, 1956 216
    Document 12. *On Strengthening Production Leadership and Organizational Construction of Agricultural Producer Cooperatives*, Party directive, September 12, 1956 242

Chapter V: CHINA AND THE SOCIALIST CAMP, 1956–57 256
    Document 13. *More on the Historical Experience of the Dictatorship of the Proletariat*, editorial in *People's Daily*, December 29, 1956 257

Chapter VI: "CONTRADICTIONS" AND "RECTIFICATION" 273
    Document 14. Mao Tse-tung, *On the Correct Handling of Contradictions among the People*, February 27, 1957 273

Document 15. Madame Li Teh-ch'üan, *Birth Control and Planned Families*, March 7, 1957 .. 295

Document 16. Chou En-lai, *Report on the Work of the Government*, June 26, 1957 299

Document 17. Lo Lung-chi, *My Preliminary Examination*, July 15, 1957................. 330

Document 18. Chang Po-chün, *I Bow My Head and Admit My Guilt before the People*, July 15, 1957... 337

Document 19. Teng Hsiao-p'ing, *Report on the Rectification Campaign*, September 23, 1957 341

Document 20. Chiang Hua, *Adhere to the Correct Line of the Party and Win Victory of the Rectification Campaign on Every Front*, December 9, 1957 363

Chapter VII: THE "GREAT LEAP FORWARD" 389

Document 21. Mao Tse-tung, *Speech at Moscow Celebration Meeting*, November 6, 1957 389

Document 22. Liu Shao-ch'i, *The Significance of the October Revolution*, November 6, 1957 393

Document 23. Chou En-lai, *The Present International Situation and China's Foreign Policy*, February 10, 1958 401

Document 24. *Resolution on the Moscow Meetings*, adopted by the Chinese Eighth Party Congress, May 23, 1958... 410

Document 25. Liu Shao-ch'i, *The Present Situation, the Party's General Line for Socialist Construction and Its Future Tasks*, May 5, 1958 416

Document 26. Lu Ting-yi, *Education Must Be Combined with Productive Labor*, July 1, 1958 438

Chapter VIII: PEOPLE'S COMMUNES: THE PHASE OF ENTHUSIASM 451

Document 27. Ch'en Po-ta, *New Society, New People*, July 1, 1958..................... 451

Document 28. *Resolution of the Central Committee on the Establishment of People's Communes in the Rural Areas*, August 29, 1958 454

Document 29. *Greet the Upsurge in Forming People's Communes*, editorial in *Red Flag*, September 1, 1958 457

Document 30. *Hold High the Red Flag of People's Communes and March On*, editorial in *People's Daily*, September 3, 1958 459

Document 31. *Tentative Regulations (Draft) of the Weihsing (Sputnik) People's Commune*, August 7, 1958 463

Document 32. *Directive of the Hopei Provincial Committee of the Party on the Building of People's Communes*, August 29, 1958 470

Chapter IX: PEOPLE'S COMMUNES: DISILLUSION AND CONSOLIDATION 478

Document 33. Hsu Li-ch'ün, *Have We Already Reached the Stage of Communism?* November 16, 1958 479

Document 34. *Communiqué of the Sixth Plenary Session of the Eighth Central Committee*, issued December 17, 1958 483

Document 35. *Decision Approving Comrade Mao Tse-tung's Proposal That He Will Not Stand as Candidate for Chairman of the People's Republic of China for the Next Term of Office*, adopted by Central Committee, December 10, 1958, and issued December 17 487

Document 36. *Resolution on Some Questions Concerning the People's Communes*, adopted by Central Committee, December 10, 1958, and issued December 17 488

CONTENTS

Document 37. Chou En-lai, *Report on Government Work*, April 18, 1959 503

Chapter X: ANTI-RIGHTIST CAMPAIGN 530

Document 38. *Overcome Rightist-Inclined Sentiment and Endeavor to Increase Production and Practice Economy*, editorial in *People's Daily*, August 6, 1959 531

Document 39. *Communiqué of the Eighth Plenary Session of the Eighth Central Committee*, issued August 26, 1959 533

Document 40. *Resolution on Developing the Campaign for Increasing Production and Practicing Economy*, adopted by Central Committee, August 16, 1959, and issued August 26 536

Document 41. Chou En-lai, *Report on Adjusting the Major Targets of China's 1959 National Plan and Further Developing the Campaign for Increasing Production and Practicing Economy*, August 26, 1959 540

Document 42. *Long Live the People's Communes!* editorial in *People's Daily*, August 29, 1959 550

Document 43. *The Great Call*, editorial in *Red Flag*, September 1, 1959 556

Chapter XI: CELEBRATION OF THE TENTH ANNIVERSARY 562

Document 44. Wang Feng, *The Great Victory in Our Nationalities Policy*, September 27, 1959 562

Document 45. Liu Lan-t'ao, *The Chinese Communist Party Is the Supreme Commander of the Chinese People in Building Socialism*, September 28, 1959 571

Document 46. Lin Piao, *March Ahead under the Red Flag of the General Line and Mao Tse-tung's Military Thinking*, September 27, 1959 577

Document 47. Li Fu-ch'un, *On the Big Leap Forward in China's Socialist Construction*, October 1, 1959 587

Document 48. Teng Hsiao-p'ing, *The Great Unity of the Chinese People and the Great Unity of the Peoples of the World*, October 1, 1959 596

Notes to General Introduction 603

Index 606

Abbreviations

CB—*Current Background*. A mimeographed series of translations from the China mainland press, issued several times a month by the U.S. Consulate General, Hong Kong. The items are selected for their special significance and grouped according to subject.

CCP—Chinese Communist Party.

ECMM—*Extracts from China Mainland Magazines*. A mimeographed series of translations from periodicals, issued several times a month by the U.S. Consulate General, Hong Kong. Name changed in 1960 to *Selections from China Mainland Magazines*.

JPRS—Joint Publications Research Service. A United States Government translation service which publishes from New York and Washington a number of items translated from foreign journals. The translations from Chinese publications generally do not duplicate those of the Hong Kong Consulate General.

NCNA—New China News Agency. The official news agency of the Chinese People's Republic, issuing releases both in Chinese and English.

SCMP—*Survey of the China Mainland Press*. A daily collection of translations assembled and issued in mimeographed form by the U.S. Consulate General, Hong Kong.

URS—*Union Research Service*. A twice-weekly mimeographed series issued at Hong Kong by the Union Research Institute, a nongovernmental organization. The reports include translations of Chinese press articles, often from provincial newspapers.

Statistical Terms

catty—0.5 kg. or 1.1023 lbs.

mou (mow)—.066 hectare or 0.1647 acre.

tan—50 kgs. or 110.23 lbs.

yuan, or ¥—U.S. $0.4246 (unofficial exchange rate).

GENERAL INTRODUCTION

DOMESTIC POLICY TRENDS IN COMMUNIST CHINA, 1955–1959

The history of the Chinese Communist Party from 1955 through 1959 may be viewed in terms of the major issues of "socialist construction"—that is, of remaking China into a socialist country. Perhaps the most characteristic political device of the Chinese Communist Party (or of any Leninist party in power) is the singling out of opinions (or "deviations") which the Party regards as dangerous at a given historical point. It is by means of careful and continual redefinition of deviations that the Party line is arrived at. Not far below the surface of official propaganda and unity it is possible to detect the outlines of a considerable debate on major questions of internal Chinese policy. During certain periods this debate was carried on without any check except the assumption of good faith. At certain junctures, however, the Party felt it necessary to lay down the line. The documents selected in this volume are for the most part summations of Party wisdom at such junctures.

I. THE FIRST FIVE-YEAR PLAN

A documentary history of Communist China in the second half of the 1950's can find no more significant starting point than the lengthy report delivered to the National People's Congress in July 1955 by Li Fu-ch'un, Chairman of the State Planning Commission. His speech qualifies as Document 1 in this collection for two major reasons. First, it marks the end of a period of makeshift year-to-year economic planning and the final adoption of a fully detailed Five-Year Plan which, since it appeared more than two years after it was originally promised, really amounted to a two-and-one-half-year plan. And, second, Li's report contains in embryonic form many of the key issues of "socialist construction" which led to divisions within the Chinese Communist Party and caused it to adopt alternatively enthusiastic and cautious policies.

One of the most sensitive issues was the applicability to China of the experience of the Soviet Union in economic growth. The speech of Li Fu-ch'un contains suggestions that the Chinese People's Government wished or felt bound to cut away from the Soviet economic model, and to content itself with more modest standards of capital investment. The mechanical application of Soviet experience to China was a fault apparent in various fields, from overly grandiose buildings to anti-religious propaganda. The extent of blind imitation was to become apparent later when intellectuals aired their grievances in May and June 1957, but it was in 1955 that the Chinese authorities began seriously to discourage it.

At the same time, material considerations were probably forcing the Government to think out new and in some ways less ambitious economic plans. Bad harvests in 1953 and 1954 had reduced the amount of agricultural produce available for exports, and in consequence less equipment could be imported from the Soviet Union (the great majority of imports had to be paid for on a basis of current trade). By 1955 the limits of aid from the Soviet Union, even in favorable years, must have been apparent to the most optimistic of the Chinese leaders. By the end of 1959 at the latest the second Soviet loan (of 1954) would be exhausted; and in the meantime its annual instalments of $26 million did not cover the annual amounts due from 1954 onwards in repayment of the first Soviet loan (of 1950). Valuable as Soviet aid certainly was in terms of visiting experts, blueprints, and the like, it could certainly not be reckoned as a major factor in China's "socialist construction." The Chinese People's Government would therefore have to rely on its own resources for the implementation of the first Five-Year Plan, to be content with less than the highest standards of physical construction, and to insist on thrift and economy in the standard of popular consumption as well as in the factories.

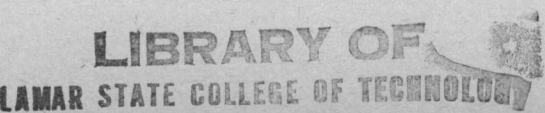

Despite the heavier burden which Soviet parsimony imposed on the Party leadership, the first Five-Year Plan was by no means a pessimistic or even sober one. Li Fu-ch'un's speech implied that although the consumer must reckon with continuing austerity and the bulk of investment should be devoted to heavy industry, light industrial production could also be increased considerably, and that both grain and industrial crops could be simultaneously increased. This optimism was based on a twofold policy, the contradictions of which were to provide fuel for later disputes: the demand for more efficient and rational management and the call for increased enthusiasm in production.

The administrative demands of the Plan were from the first recognized to be high. Li Fu-ch'un demanded intensive efforts to train new technical cadres, and to ensure that people who already had suitable technical and scientific training were properly placed to make their maximum contribution. The need for such persons was the basic need from which the "Hundred Flowers" policy sprang. Li also recognized that the tasks involved in the execution of the Plan required a new look within the Chinese Communist Party. The Party must be strong and devoted, but it must also command the confidence of the "masses." It must dispense with bureaucratic and dogmatic methods, and Party members must unlearn a "growing and extremely dangerous feeling of conceit." This is a theme of which much more was heard in 1956 and 1957.

Not the least of the Party's administrative tasks would be to reconcile the workers and peasants to very limited food supplies at a time when the growth of purchasing power, induced by the new construction plans, would outrun the production of consumer goods, especially in the country. It is worth noting that Li Fu-ch'un clearly anticpated the risk of inflation involved in the Plan—a risk which, as it happened, was not successfully avoided.

Hand in hand with the call for higher technical efficiency and for greater regard for the mood of the people went the call, probably contradictory in practice, for a "leap forward" in all forms of industry, a program implicit in Li's report and applied later in the campaigns of 1955-56 and with even greater vigor in the so-called "Great Leap Forward" of 1958. The similar pattern of these two drives, separated by more than two years, has been noted by Party leaders themselves. Li Fu-ch'un, in a speech of December 1957 setting the stage for the later campaign. made it clear that some of the campaign slogans which he prescribed for 1958 dated in fact from 1955-56.[1]*
It was, he said, in the winter of 1955-56 that the Party, opposing "conservatism," put forward the policy of simultaneously achieving "quantity, speed, quality and economy." From contemporary newspaper sources,[2] it is clear that, as early as the summer of 1955, workers were urged on to greater and greater production in "emulation campaigns," a technique also applied in 1958. A further similarity between the two drives was the attempt to create genuine backing for the new policy by means of a nationwide campaign against political laggards. In 1955 this took the form of a campaign against political counterrevolutionaries centered on the personality of Hu Feng; in 1957-1958 it was intellectuals such as Chang Po-chün and Lo Lung-chi who were "rectified." A final parallel is to be found in the wholesale and sudden conversion of remnants of the past bourgeois era into functioning parts of the new socialist society: in 1955 the vast majority of private enterprises which had been allowed to remain intact were suddenly "socialized"; in 1958 the "Democratic" parties and other non-Communist organizations staged processions and parades in order to "give their hearts" to the Chinese Communist Party.

Li Fu-ch'un in his report of July 1955 acknowledged that there was conservative opposition on technical grounds to certain aspects of the Five-Year Plan—especially the large scale of capital construction, involving heavy burdens on the peasants, and the high ratio of heavy-industry investment to all industrial investment. "Rightist conservatism" must be opposed, he said, no less than "leftist adventurism." The term "conservative," more explicitly defined in the 1958 leap, described those members of the Party who stuck to established techniques and economic conventions, did not recognize the power of political ideas to overcome economic obstacles, did not trust the initiative and inventiveness of the masses, and preferred to preserve the mystery of their own expertise. Conservatives were also defined as those who had their hearts in the right place with regard to "socialist construction" but were inclined to oppose Central Committee policy on technical grounds. Their opposition was due to wrong thinking, perhaps even to a certain "bourgeois" taint, but was not necessarily antagonistic to the rule of the Party.

* The notes for this General Introduction will be found beginning on page 603.

PART II

The first Five-Year Plan evoked in some degree the opposition between conservative and enthusiastic Communists which became so marked a feature of the next four years. But it was in connection with Mao Tse-tung's new policy on cooperatives that this opposition first became acute and obvious.

II. THE SPEED-UP OF AGRICULTURAL COOPERATIVIZATION, 1955-56

The various stages in the formation of "agricultural producers' cooperatives" from 1951 on are listed in the general comment at the beginning of Chapter II. The following is an attempt to analyze in more detail the motives behind the actions of the Chinese People's Government starting in the summer of 1955, and the tensions to which these actions gave rise within the Chinese Communist Party.

Until the summer of 1955, the Government had on the whole been wary in its advance toward the formation of agricultural producers' cooperatives. Of course, even a Government set on the speediest possible collectivization would not proclaim its goal too openly soon after land reform had created a large new class of peasant small holders. But there is little reason to doubt that, as the result of conviction or experience, the majority of the Central Committee was genuinely adhering to the often proclaimed principles of "gradualness" and "voluntariness." They were sufficiently aware of the terrible experiences of the 1930's in the Soviet Union. Teng Tzu-hui, a Vice-Premier, who often acted as official spokesman on agricultural matters, had put the matter tactfully in 1954. While agreeing with the U.S.S.R. on the goal of collectivization, he said:

> We differ from her about the steps and measures necessary for reform. We all know that in the agricultural reform movement in the U.S.S.R. 1930-1932, collectivism and mechanization were introduced simultaneously. As the U.S.S.R. possessed the various necessary conditions at the time, it was right for her to act thus. We, however, have not the necessary conditions ... Moreover, the Chinese peasant's conception of private ownership is relatively deep, while our rural task is heavy and we have not enough cadres.[3]

The policy of gradualism, however, had not been adopted without debate and tentative experiment in other directions. Attempts had been made in the spring of 1953, in the fall of 1954, and again in the spring of 1955, to increase the pace of collectivization. These had run into obstacles and been abandoned or modified. The debate continued, and seems to have been most confused in the spring of 1955. Against this background, at the end of July 1955, when it was clear that there would be a good harvest, Mao Tse-tung pronounced that the tempo of collectivization should be increased. Ch'en Yi said in November 1955 that Mao's report had "settled the debate of the past three years" on the question of cooperatives.[4]

Mao Tse-tung warned in his speech (Document 2) against two dangers, the "leftist mistake" of being drunk with success, and the "rightist mistake" of "resolute shrinking" which resulted from being afraid of success. It was the latter which was, in his view, the more dangerous at the time. Haste, "commandism," and "adventurism" must, of course, be eschewed. "Some comrades" (a phrase which is always worth careful attention in a Chinese official pronouncement) were no doubt right in thinking that the Russians had at one time been too hasty and "adventuristic" in their policy of collectivization. Such mistakes must be avoided. But (and this is the key passage), "What we should not do is allow some of our comrades to cover up their dilatoriness by quoting the experience of the Soviet Union" (Document 2, section VIII).

The objects of Mao's call to speed up collectivization are apparent. On the economic side, the gradual method had not led to brilliant results; the system of small peasant ownership was not leading to any decisive increase in agricultural production. The harvests of 1953 and 1954 had been disappointing and China's industrial superstructure was beginning to become too heavy for its agricultural base. The need to increase agricultural production was plainer than ever at a time when the grandiose first Five-Year Plan had just been formulated, and when there was no hope of much more substantial aid from the U.S.S.R. The whole economy depended greatly on the agricultural sector, which provided 90 percent of the raw materials for consumer goods industries, and 75 percent (either in raw or in manufactured form) of the exports with which the Government earned its industrial imports.[5] It did not require a Communist fanatic to think in 1955 that total production was unlikely to do worse under a cooperative regime than it had done to date.

The cooperative farm system made it easier for the Party to control labor and to collect grain taxes. It was no doubt for this reason that Mao insistently opposed the indiscriminate dissolution of agricultural producers' cooperatives, which in Chekiang had taken place as late as the spring of 1955 (Document 2, section III). Significantly, the drive toward cooperativization was accompanied or even preceded, in August 1955, by the new "Three Fix" system for determining the amount of grain to be collected by the state, and also by the introduction of grain rationing for the countryside. Thus far the process of speedy cooperativization was realistic and more closely related to the needs of the Five-Year Plan than the agricultural clauses of the Plan itself.

The political calculations behind Mao's decision were more complex. On the one hand there were indications that the Chinese peasant's "relatively deep sense of private ownership" was being strengthened under the system of private holdings, tempered by mutual aid and gradual collectivization. Teng Tzu-hui, in the 1954 speech quoted above, talked of a sharp class struggle already proceeding in the villages, and of exploitation by the rich peasants. Mao Tse-tung himself put the situation in more concrete terms (Document 2). If, he said, the poor peasants had gone on selling land at this time, there would have been increasingly serious class polarization in the villages. In such circumstances, even if production had increased, it would have been harder for the Government to maintain the proportion of grain collected.

The Party thus thought it important to stop the growth of a new "rich peasant" class—the sooner the better. Mao, in deciding to act decisively and push through complete cooperativization quickly (though the pace proved in fact hotter than he had envisaged in July), calculated on the support of the "masses" or "poor peasants." This involved an act of faith—that the poor peasants would be more interested in attaining equality with the rich peasants under the cooperative regime than in maintaining or increasing their own private property without it. In fact, Mao professed to believe that the poor peasants were ahead of the Party cadres in their zeal for the new system. This apparently was still believed eighteen months later when an authoritative survey of the shortcomings of the first Five-Year Plan criticized it for overestimating the backwardness of the peasants. The error, according to the survey, was due to a mechanical copying of the experience of the Soviet Union and was corrected only by the new collectivization policy.[6]

The process of rapid cooperativization initiated by Mao obviously involved new and difficult tasks for the Chinese Communist Party. Many existing Party members and cadres had to be sent down to the country to cope with the new situation; Mao said that the new cooperatives would have to be checked not once but two or three times a year, and that the process would be a "splendid schooling for cadres." In addition, large numbers of new Party members and cadres were being enrolled in order to force through rural reorganization (700,000 new rural members had been recruited in the winter of 1954).[7] Therefore political standards had to be relaxed at a time when firmness was necessary against peasants who resisted or perverted the new line. In Kwangtung province particularly there is evidence of difficulties in overcoming the cadres' sympathy with "rightist" elements in the countryside, and of a Party purge connected with the implementation of the Party directive of October 1955 (Document 3).

From the first, and even before the difficulties of execution were proved in practice, Mao's line on the cooperatives seems to have run into severe opposition within the Party. This is hardly surprising, since down to July 1955, whatever the arguments in the Central Committee, the cadres had fairly consistently been taught the virtues of gradualness and voluntariness. The suddenness of the latest change was illustrated by the fact that Li Fu-ch'un at the beginning of July (Document 1) was still preaching the old line. Ch'en Po-ta, a member of the Rural Work Department of the Central Committee and a prominent theoretician, in his explanatory notes on the Party directive of October, was still at pains to defend the leadership from the obvious charge of inconsistency. It was from July 1955 that the Communist leaders, in subsequent authoritative pronouncements, dated the appearance of "rightist" and "conservative" elements within the Chinese Communist Party, and the basic conflict between those in the Party who favored, and those who opposed, the policy of "more, better, faster, more economically." Li Fu-ch'un in *Red Flag* of October 1, 1959 (Document 47, section I) expounded the authorized version of events by saying that in the winter of 1955, Mao "scientifically foresaw" the possibility of a quick economic advance. He said the question of whether socialist construction could be carried out at still higher speed became the central and most

PART III

important question of those demanding a solution "in order to uphold resolutely the basic principle of integrating the universal truth of Marxism-Leninism with the actual practice of China's construction."

The rightist opposition within the Party is indicated by references in official documents throughout the winter of 1955-56. Thus the Central Committee's "Decisions on Agricultural Cooperation" (Document 3) contains a formal statement that "Rightist tendencies in the Party should be censured and overcome." The point was again elaborated by Mao Tse-tung himself in his preface (December 1955) to a collection of essays entitled *Socialist Upsurge in China's Countryside*. (The preface is reprinted as our Document 4.) Here, he said specifically:

> The problem today is that rightist conservatism is still causing trouble in many fields and preventing the work in these fields from keeping pace with the development of the objective situation.

Many people, he continued, thought impossible what was in fact possible "if they exerted themselves." Some more details of "conservative" opposition at this time are given in part IV of this General Introduction. In this connection it is worthwhile to anticipate one of the few personal charges advanced against Mao during the period of free criticism in the spring of 1957, when Ch'en Ming-shu accused him of being "very confident about the false reports and dogmatic analysis presented him by his cadres," and of being "impetuous in making decisions without first making a careful study of the facts."[8] Events again seem to foreshadow the Great Leap Forward and formation of people's communes in 1958, when considerable opposition within the Party was apparently overwhelmed by fanatical efforts on the part of some cadres and a flood of fantastic success stories which seemed to have fed the fires of the leaders' faith in miracles. By the end of 1956 there was much official criticism of the "blind optimism" displayed by the cadres in their rural work. And even by the late summer of 1956, it had become apparent to the Party leaders that something was still very wrong with the organization of Chinese agriculture. The conservatives within the Party might by then have claimed, not for the last time in the period under consideration, that they had been justified by events in their skepticism.

III. FLOWERS AND SCHOOLS

The publication of the first Five-Year Plan was followed, as has been seen, by intensive efforts to achieve a "leap forward" in agriculture and industry. Some political preparation was undertaken in the campaign against counterrevolutionaries and against the followers of Hu Feng. But more was needed. The Central Committee recognized that if they were to achieve socialist construction without massive aid from outside, all the resources of the Party and of the masses would have to be mobilized. Even this would not be enough. They had also to mobilize the technical and intellectual resources of China; and here was a delicate political task. A large proportion of China's scientists and technicians had been trained in the West or under Western auspices in China. They were therefore politically tainted in Communist eyes, even if they were genuinely anxious to cooperate with the Communist regime. Those employed by the Chinese People's Government had often been relegated to subordinate positions. Others, naturally enough, stood aloof. By the fall of 1955, if not earlier, the Central Committee set about the task of reclaiming this lost or underemployed talent and harnessing it to the task of socialist construction.

The history of the earlier stages of this campaign is summarized in the comments at the beginning of Chapter III. At this stage, and indeed until after Mao's speech of February 1957 (Document 14), the intellectuals themselves were on the whole cautious in taking advantage of the Party's invitations. At the end of 1955, the "Democratic" parties, which contained a number of intellectuals, discussed (under directive from the Party) the "unity and reform" of Chinese intellectuals as a whole, and dwelt more on their duties than on their rights.

On the Party's side, too, the first steps were cautious enough. Chou En-lai's main speech of January 1956 (Document 6) was made at a time when a "surging tide of socialism" was prevailing in both industry and agriculture. Private industry had just been brought almost completely under public control, and the 12-Year Agricultural Program (Document 5) was about to be published. It is therefore not surprising that Chou En-lai insisted on the limits of a socialist framework and did not commit himself far to any "liberalization." Chou's main points were that better use should be made of intellectuals, that they should be given more scope and initiative by the Party cadres, and that better working conditions (time, reference books, assistants, and wages) should be provided. At the same time, intellectuals should "remold" themselves, and a seven-year plan for re-educating them should be launched, culminating in the admission to the Party of one-third of the higher intellectuals by 1962.

The provisos about remolding and re-education seem at first sight highly restrictive. It should be remembered, however, that they imply what is, for a Communist leader, a fairly hopeful view of the intellectuals. Chou's suggestion is that they could without too much difficulty be converted to an entirely correct way of thinking and used in the meantime. By the fall of 1957 the official line was that remolding would be a very gradual process at best, that some of the old intellectuals were past repair, and that the Party would have to train its own new intellectuals, who would be simultaneously "red and expert" (see Chapter VII). In the meantime, the main task of the intellectuals in the early spring of 1956 was to give a lead toward socialism within their own professions and help to swell the "tide."

The next landmark in the campaign to win over the intellectuals was the launching of the slogan "Let a hundred flowers blossom, a hundred schools of thought contend." The first half of the slogan was used by Mao Tse-tung in 1951 to characterize the Party's policy for theatrical and literary reform. The second is a quotation from the classical "warring states" period of Chinese history. The composite phrase was apparently first used by Mao Tse-tung in an unrecorded statement to the Supreme State Conference, May 2, 1956.[9] The doctrine, as expanded later in the month, represented a distinctly more liberal policy toward the intellectuals than was implied in Chou's speech of January. The aim was still largely practical—to give intellectuals a greater sense of participation and, directly or indirectly, to stimulate a fresh flow of ideas which would hasten the progress of socialist construction. This was to be done partly by encouraging the use of Western as well as Russian technical literature.

The implications of the new policy were optimistic. The leaders felt that they could afford some relaxation of their former very tight grip on intellectual life, and that the intellectuals, given more freedom, would keep within reasonable bounds. These presuppositions were stated by Lu Ting-yi, head of the Propaganda Department of the Central Committee, in an address (Document 8) to a select gathering of scientists, social scientists, doctors, and writers in Peking on May 26, 1956, as follows:

"Socialist transformation" has already achieved a decisive victory; the political thought of intellectuals has undergone a fundamental change; there are still internal enemies, but they have been much weakened; there is virtual unanimity of political thought in the country.

On this basis, Lu Ting-yi put forward some guiding lines of thought:

1. *Natural sciences,* including *medicine,* have no "class character." Argument in these fields can be free, and intellectuals need not fear that unorthodox views will be considered as political heresies.

2. *Literature* and *art* must serve the workers. They should automatically criticize the old system and praise the new; but within these limits, there should be no restriction on subject matter.

3. In *philosophy* and *social sciences,* achievements have already been great, and the dangers of "sectarianism" (i.e., an over-rigid orthodoxy) on the part of the Chinese Communist Party have consequently been great also. Intellectuals should learn selectively from the U.S.S.R., and should not hesitate to learn also from enemy countries.

The Hundred Flowers policy had some effects. There is no doubt that the Academy of Sciences and the universities, for example, took advantage of the clause permitting them to import technical literature from Western sources. But, with respect to "blossoming" or "blooming" (self-expression), the intellectuals were mainly cautious, for two closely connected reasons. They were reluctant to try out the new freedom, when a misunderstanding of its limits could have very unpleasant consequences. Further, it appeared from criticism voiced by the "Democratic" parties in the spring of 1957 that many Communist Party cadres were unable to adapt themselves to the new line, or even doubted its wisdom (thus laying themselves open to charges of "dogmatism" and "subjectivism"). They could still point to many general reservations in the official line if they wished to justify restrictive behavior toward the intellectuals. It is not surprising, therefore, that the intellectuals were very cautious on most important political and economic subjects. There was, however, a good deal of subdued "blooming" in the field of publications and literature.

At this point it is impossible to divorce the Chinese scene from the dramatic events in the "Socialist Camp." It seems probable that an important factor in determining the switch to the Hundred Flowers policy was the Soviet Twentieth Party Congress at Moscow in February 1956, at which Khrushchev had criticized Stalin for his excessively dictatorial ways. The Chinese Communist Party took up its general position on Khrushchev's criticisms of Stalin and the cult of the individual in an authoritative article in the *People's Daily*, April 5, 1956 (Document 7). This emphasized the importance of the "mass line," i.e., the leaders should keep in touch with the masses, allow their initiative more play, and not order them about in a routine manner ("commandism").

It was the warning words about "commandism" and "dogmatism" among Party cadres which probably gained some new measure of freedom for the intellectuals. The gain was largely negative; material conditions were improved, and cadres were forced to be more careful in their behavior. There was a little blooming in the literary field. But in "intellectual" publications there was not much fundamental criticism of the main political and economic policies of the Chinese People's Government. In fact those policies seem to have been criticized in 1956 more by the rightists within the Party than by intellectuals outside it.

It may well be that the most important effect of the Hundred Flowers policy in its early stages was to puzzle the cadres, and arouse resentment among the left wing of the Party. By the fall of 1956 the Central Committee was faced with some trouble from two groups in the Party—from "rightists" who opposed the over-hasty leap forward and by "dogmatists" who disapproved of the Hundred Flowers policy.

IV. THE EIGHTH PARTY CONGRESS

The second half of 1956 was a time of disillusion for the Central Committee of the Chinese Communist Party. The Party cadres, spurred on by the desire to attain the targets set by the leaders, and accepting their estimate of the political reliability of the rural masses, had evidently been rash in the organization of new cooperatives. A Party directive of April 4 enjoining the strictest economy in investment, and moderation in target-setting, does not seem to have had much effect, according to later Chinese press accounts. These may have been exaggerated, in order to push the blame for a mistaken policy onto junior officers, but probably had a considerable basis of truth. On the one hand, peasants had been induced to join by false promises of increased income, and were correspondingly discontent when benefits did not materialize. On the other hand, cadres had misled their superior authorities about the results to be expected from reorganization. They had displayed "blind optimism" (an often repeated phrase) in their estimates of the harvests which would be achieved after collectivization, and the amount that would be made available by and to the peasants. The same "blind optimism" was illustrated at a higher level by failure to plan production, wasteful investment, and a premature attempt to mechanize Chinese farming by introducing the two-wheel, two-share plow, which proved to be thoroughly unsuitable.

As it turned out, the summer weather in 1956 was unfavorable in large areas of China. The grain harvest was officially said to be slightly above the figure for 1955, but results did not seem to bear out the claim. Local famine was later reported in Kwangsi province,[10] and there was widespread slaughter of draft animals in the countryside, either for lack of fodder or to avoid having to surrender them to the management of the agricultural producers' cooperatives. The peasants began to hoard grain, and the Party's attempt to draw it out of them by allowing them to open a limited free market further upset the official grain distribution system; a "controlled free market" was readily transformed into an uncontrolled black market. The grain supply of the cities became a major problem, and it was only solved at the expense of imposing a new and heavy burden on the rural standard of living.

"The peasants' burden" was a constant theme of official anxiety and propaganda by the fall of 1956. The obvious conclusion for the peasant was that the burden had been imposed upon him by the newly introduced or enlarged system of cooperatives, and he reacted against it accordingly. There was an unplanned migration to the cities which imposed further strain on supplies and housing. Incomplete figures, cited later in the *People's Daily*, revealed that 570,000 people had moved from rural areas between the fall of 1956 and the summer of 1957.[11] The Central Committee directive of September 12, 1956 (Document 12) was a sober document but could do no more than palliate the deficiencies of the cooperative system by emphasis on realistic targets, the avoidance of "commandism," and the importance of maintaining the peasants' standard of living.

It is plain, if only from Mao's speech of February 1957 (Document 14) that criticism of and opposition to the cooperative system continued throughout the winter of 1956-57, constituting in Mao's phrase a "small typhoon." Sales of grain from the state stores to maintain minimum standards of consumption rose in the second half of 1956 by 32.5 percent over sales for the same period in 1955. In some places, widespread withdrawal from cooperatives forced their dissolution. During the proceedings against the governor and some officials of Chekiang province in December 1957, for example, it was revealed that early in that year many cooperatives in Hsienchu county had been disbanded, and that by March the number of peasants in cooperatives there had fallen to 16 percent of the total number of peasants.[12]

Even more significant, perhaps, are the revelations in the Chinese technical press of routine administrative corruption in those cooperatives that stood up to the "small typhoon." At some Party levels at least, it was recognized that those in charge of cooperatives were quite capable of making false reports on output in order to avoid taxation. There is in the technical press at the end of 1956 an almost wistful recognition of the human weakness of localism: "Judging by the way in which tax was collected in isolated areas according to output, it would appear that production teams and agricultural producers' cooperatives generally conceal their actual output."[13] This is a far cry from the signals for a leap forward sounded so confidently earlier in the year.

There was similar disillusion over events on the industrial front, though the failure to attain the targets proposed had not been so marked there as in agriculture. By 1957, the defects of the first Five-Year Plan were being discussed fairly frankly, in accordance with the example set by Chou En-lai in section I of his September 1956 report to the Eighth National Congress of the Communist Party of China (Document 11). A particularly interesting article in *New Construction*, February 1957,[14] lists the main defects of the first Five-Year Plan as follows (the criticisms apply nominally to the whole period of the Plan from 1953 onward, but in fact most seriously to 1955-1956):

1. Agricultural production fell behind industrial production.
2. Light industry's production fell behind that of heavy industry.
3. Construction in nonproductive fields lagged behind, and the housing situation was especially serious.
4. Consumption fell behind capital accumulation.
5. Average wage increases did not keep pace with the increased efficiency of production. In 1954-55 in particular the standard of living was not maintained.

This list, however, reveals only partially what was recognized to be the main economic fault of the annual economic plan for 1956. The excessive rate of capital construction was admitted in 1957 by Li Hsien-nien (Minister of Finance) and Po I-po (Chairman of the State Economic Commission) in their reports to the National People's Congress.[15] New workers numbering 2,260,000 were enrolled in 1956 instead of the 840,000 originally envisaged. This meant that purchasing power for some time ran ahead of the supply of consumer goods. The situation was aggravated by the indiscriminate issue of loans for new agricultural construction— 2.03 billion *yuan* instead of 1.12 billion as originally planned. All this money came on the market at a period when food was short and consumer-goods industries were insufficiently developed. The inflationary experience of 1956 was one of the main reasons for the new form of labor mobilization adopted in 1958.

The standard of living was thus by the winter of 1956-57 a serious problem for the industrial workers as well as for the peasants. Local papers from Shanghai, Shansi, and Heilungkiang[16] show that problems of labor discipline were widespread in the early months of 1957. Even in January 1956, Lai Jo-yü, Chairman of the All-China Federation of Trade Unions, had warned against rightism within the unions. His general review of trade union work in December 1957[17]

PART IV

contains many significant warnings to "certain comrades who had displayed doubts and vacillations about the task of trade unions in the period of national construction." He made it clear that the primary function of Chinese trade unions was to increase production, not to improve living conditions; the standard of living could only be improved gradually on the basis of increased production, and there should not be too much stress on material incentive. This was a doctrine which neither the workers nor all the trade union officials would be expected to appreciate.[18] Mao Tse-tung, in his speech of February 1957 (Document 14), mentioned workers' and students' strikes during 1956 for material benefits (some details are given in the introduction to Chapter VI). It is clear from all this that the Eighth Party Congress, opening on September 15, 1956 (eleven years had passed since the Seventh Congress), was faced primarily with a task of consolidation and hanging on to any gains achieved during the advance earlier in the year.

Again it is necessary to compare the 1956 and 1958 situations. The pattern of events and general atmosphere foreshadow the aftermath of the Great Leap Forward of 1958, though in the 1956 case the advance had been less well prepared, and the immediate difficulties encountered had been greater. The industrial as well as the agricultural drive in early 1956 was carried out in an atmosphere of enthusiasm deliberately inspired by the Party. Later, Chou En-lai in his speech of June 1957 (Document 16) defended the leap forward of 1956 by saying that the "basic victory of the socialist revolution fired the enthusiasm of the working people in building socialism. They vied with one another in demanding an increase in production and raising their work quota." Another aspect of such a leap forward was the subsequent demand for more attention to the quality of workmanship (a point mentioned by both Liu and Chou in their reports to the Eighth Party Congress), accompanied by occasional admissions of too hard working hours and too high accident rates. Similar reactions appeared on a larger scale in the fall and winter of 1958.

Liu Shao-ch'i recognized the parallel between the two leaps when he talked in May 1958 (Document 25) about the "U-shaped development" (i.e., an upward surge in 1955-56, a slump in 1956-57, a further rise in 1958).

It remains to consider what was the effect of the 1956 leap forward—and the disillusion which followed it—on the balance of forces within the Party. At the level of the cadre in the field there had been some puzzlement at the change of line. For example, in Fukien during the preparations for the 1958 Great Leap, misgivings were expressed as follows: "We were very vigorous in the first half of 1956 and were censured in the second half of the year. This year we're asked to be even more vigorous. Is there a bigger censure waiting?"[19] And at the level of the intellectual struggling with the more obscure points of Marxism, a pertinent and awkward question had been raised: "In higher agricultural producers' cooperatives have production relations [i.e., the new, large-scale form of organization best adapted to highly mechanized and specialized agriculture] outstripped the material and technical conditions of the productive forces [i.e., the predominantly unmechanized and unspecialized type of farming still practiced in most of China]?"[20] Clearly those Party members who in the winter of 1955-56 had been accused of conservatism for opposing Mao's new line on cooperatives must have felt themselves amply justified by events.

The leaders were by no means ready to admit any misjudgments; but by September 1956 they were severe enough against the "commandism," "dogmatism," and "blind optimism" of the orthodox cadres. Such accusations served in part to excuse their own misjudgments, and the cadres concerned may have felt that they had been doing no more than observe the spirit of their instructions. But the Central Committee members were serious in trying to restrain their followers.[21] Indeed, a *People's Daily* editorial of December 29, 1956 (Document 13) was able to speak of "the present anti-doctrinaire tide" (p. 266, below). The phrase is sometimes translated "tide of anti-dogmatism." This development, partly the result of the fate of the 1956 leap forward, partly of the Hundred Flowers campaign to encourage Chinese intellectuals, represented in itself a considerable victory for the more moderate or conservative elements in the Party.

Liu Shao-ch'i, in his political report to the Eighth Party Congress (Document 9), laid down the Central Committee's course between Scylla on the right and Charybdis on the left:

> Any work that deviates from the general line, immediately lands itself in
> mistakes, either Rightist or "Leftist." In the last few years the tendency of

deviating... to the Right has manifested itself mainly in being satisfied merely
with what has been achieved in the bourgeois-democratic revolution, in wanting to
call a halt to the revolution, in not admitting the need for our revolution to pass on
into socialism, in being unwilling to adopt a suitable policy to restrict capitalism in
both town and countryside, in not believing that the Party could lead the peasantry
along the road to socialism, and in not believing that the Party could lead the people
of the whole country to build socialism in China. The tendency of deviating... to the
"Left" has manifested itself mainly in demanding that... some method of expropriation
be used in our country to eliminate the national bourgeoisie as a class, or some method
be used to squeeze out and bankrupt capitalist industry and commerce, in not admitting
that we should adopt measures for advancing, step by step, to socialism, and in not believing that we could attain the goal of socialist revolution by peaceful means (p. 167,
below).

Liu's definitions of right and left, in terms of outmoded issues such as expropriation, did not apply to what were probably the most heavily disputed issues between moderates and extremists at the time. The rightists could feel some satisfaction, after the attacks on them in 1955, at being treated so mildly. They have not again been accorded equality of treatment with what were described in the Wuhan Resolution of December 1958 (Document 36) as "good-hearted" but "overeager" comrades. September 1956 may therefore be regarded as the time of the greatest influence of the rightists within the Chinese Communist Party.

V. CHINA AND THE SOCIALIST CAMP, 1956-57

Though Chinese foreign policy in general falls outside the scope of this volume, the attitude of the Chinese People's Government toward the crisis in Eastern Europe in the fall and winter of 1956-57 was closely interrelated with its policy toward "doctrinaires" and "revisionists" at home.

The Government was faced at this time with the possibility of playing—even with the need to play—an unexpectedly and disproportionately important part in the "Socialist Camp." Events in Poland and Hungary in October and November 1956 revealed the full extent of those tensions within Eastern Europe to which the retreat from Stalinism, initiated by Khrushchev in the preceding February, had given play. Khrushchev's own leadership within the U.S.S.R. was far from secure, as was proved by the events of the next summer; in particular his comparatively light-handed policy in Eastern Europe had evidently provoked opposition among his own colleagues.

From the edge of the Camp, Tito, with whom Khrushchev had sought reconciliation only a year before, was uttering heresies which expanded dangerously the ideas of coexistence between the "socialist" and "imperialist" camps and of the inevitable evolution of socialism among the imperialist countries. Such ideas cast doubt on the need for any "dictatorship of the proletariat." Tito even went further in discrediting this key concept, suggesting by implication at least that it might inevitably lead to Stalinist bureaucracy. His ideas might thus have had dangerous effects throughout the camp and as far afield as within the ranks of the Chinese Communist Party.

In these circumstances the voice of China acquired more weight than it had had previously within the counsels of the Socialist Camp, and more than would normally have belonged to a country so distant, so backward industrially and so much preoccupied with internal problems. At the same time the Chinese People's Government probably felt it a duty—not just for reasons of prestige—to make its voice heard. More open repression by the Russians (e.g., in Poland) would further have discredited the Communist cause; and at the other extreme, any tendency toward disintegration of the Camp would not only have been of immense long-term harm to the Communist cause as a whole, but would also have immediately endangered Chinese imports from the U.S.S.R. and Eastern Europe, still essential for the task of "socialist construction."

The domestic circumstances of Communist China in the fall of 1956 have already been described. They were, to say the least, unfavorable. Although bad weather and the continued activity of "counterrevolutionary" saboteurs could still be blamed for the economic state of the country—in particular the shortage of consumer supplies and the low standard of living—the Party leaders were already openly dissatisfied with the performance of the cadres in 1956.

PART V

Already the cadres were being directed to give up "commandism," adopt a more persuasive working style, and keep more closely in touch with the masses. If the *leaders* were dissatisfied with the performance of the cadres, the masses themselves were no doubt critical not only of them but of the Party as a whole. Perhaps most important, the conservatives within the Party or among the cadres were critical of the type of policy pursued by the Central Committee over the last year, and could be suspected of wishing for a different type of leadership.

It was against this domestic background that the news from Hungary reached China in October and November 1956. The Chinese Communist Party realized that the Hungarian Communist Party, which had not until then been the subject of particular criticism by the Chinese, had not kept in touch with the masses. The results were obvious and deplorable; they seem to have raised doubts among junior Party members and students in China about some of the fundamentals of Communism as hitherto practiced, and consequently to have affected the thinking of the Chinese Communist leaders as well.

Months later, in June 1957, Chou En-lai talked to the National People's Congress (Document 16) of "dark clouds" which had at the time hovered over the Socialist Camp and had since been dispelled. Mao Tse-tung in his speech of February 1957 (Document 14) even talked of "certain people" who were "delighted when the Hungarian events took place" and "hoped that something similar would happen in China." This passage may have been specially inserted in the version published four months later, which was probably doctored to meet the situation created by the period of free criticism, and intended less as an historical record than as an awful warning of the measures which rightists could contemplate.

More significant as an index to reactions within the Party were the sorts of questions which the Chinese press found it necessary to answer. There seems to have been some sense of shock, among the younger Party members at least, at the apparent "great-nation chauvinism" of the Soviet Union in its forcible intervention in Hungary. In the major theoretical periodicals, this intervention was justified by the claim that otherwise the imperialists might establish a bridgehead in Eastern Europe. It was even alleged that Soviet action saved a major war.[22] A much more serious reaction, calling for immediate refutation, was that the Hungarians were perhaps in the right. This "revisionist" sentiment, which had in fact been encouraged by some of the early Chinese pronouncements on the Hungarian events, coincided with (and was perhaps stimulated by) some of Tito's arguments about the natural connection between the concept of proletarian dictatorship and Stalinism. And when the intellectuals were finally permitted to flower in May 1957, it was the ossification of Marxist categories such as proletarian dictatorship which bore the brunt of their attacks.

From January to March 1957, periodicals intended principally for the eyes of Party members treated the subject of "revisionism" rather defensively. It was admitted, that, since "de-Stalinization," there had been confused thoughts in China on the question of the dictatorship of the proletariat. The "creative use of Marxism-Leninism" had nothing to do with "revisionism"; mixed with guidance for the faithful in China are some obvious but not explicit digs at Yugoslav doctrines, which may have been thought to be infectious; thus the "clamor for broadening democracy in Hungary" and the idea that "State leadership in construction fosters bureaucracy" are specifically attacked.[23] As in the key *People's Daily* editorials (Documents 7 and 13), it was emphasized that it is not the whole socialist system which is proved wrong when Stalin or other individuals overstep the bounds; errors are the result of inevitable but comparatively superficial contradictions within the system.

In sum, the lessons of the Hungarian events for the leadership of the Chinese Communist Party were two. First, those events emphasized the need for the already existing campaign to eliminate commandism and keep the Party in touch with the masses. Secondly, they indicated the dangers that could arise when "anti-dogmatism" got out of hand and lapsed into revisionist demands for radical modification of the Chinese Party's political monopoly. It seems likely therefore that events in Hungary had an important influence in bringing about the Chinese decision to launch the "rectification" campaign of 1957, and perhaps even in putting forward the date of the campaign.

VI. "CONTRADICTIONS" AND "RECTIFICATION"

The last two parts have described the economic and international background of the "rectification" campaign. The Party cadres were held even by their own leaders to be partly responsible for the economic setbacks of 1956, owing to their dogmatism and commandist behavior. The example of Hungary proved that separation between the Party and the masses could have very dangerous results. The gap between the two could be bridged by educating the masses and educating the Party. In the fall of 1956, educating the Party seemed to be the more urgent and practicable task. It should have the indirect result of releasing new energies among the masses and the intellectuals for socialist construction.

The campaign for rectification of the working style of the Party and of intellectuals, in its earliest phase, was coupled to the Hundred Flowers policy and largely aimed at doctrinaire cadres who desired to stifle freedom of expression. But gradually its orientation swung about until by mid-1957 it became a part of the anti-rightist struggle. Thus rectification as such had no preconceived bias against right or left, but rather was aimed at either wing as the situation demanded.

The rectification campaign had been decided on by the Central Committee in November 1956. In January 1957 an article in *China Youth* said the campaign would start in 1958 only, 1957 being reserved for the preparatory study of texts. It seems possible that it was Mao himself who speeded up the program to go into effect in the spring of 1957, just as he had hastened the whole process of cooperativization in the summer of 1955. At least he was very much identified with the policy of seeking a solution to China's economic problems primarily by political action—the exposition of the theory of "contradictions" as a guiding line, the further encouragement of intellectuals to speed up socialist construction, and the instruction of the Party in a new working style. The connection of these leading ideas may be illustrated by a quotation at the end of section 1 of Mao's speech on contradictions, February 27, 1957 (Document 14):

> It is imperative that at this juncture we raise the question of distinguishing contradictions among the people from contradictions between ourselves and the enemy, as well as the question of properly handling contradictions among the people, so as to rally people of all nationalities in our country to wage a new battle—the battle against nature—to develop our economy and culture... and build up our new state.

There was little apparent recognition at this time that the economic recipes of September 1956 had encountered more than temporary obstacles, or that a radical change of economic policy, such as that adopted in the spring of 1958, might be necessary.

Mao's February 1957 speech was intended to encourage the intellectuals. In spite of the launching of the Hundred Flowers campaign in May 1956, and some blooming in the literary sphere, generally the intellectuals had been cautious, and the cadres had done little to change their behavior toward those outside the charmed circle. Liu Shao-ch'i, in his political report of September 15, 1956 (Document 9), had complained that not enough consideration was yet being paid to the intellectuals. He said: "There are still some members of our Party who hold that everything should absolutely be 'of one colour'; who are unwilling to see non-Party people work in state organs; who do not consult with them when circumstances require, and do not respect the authority that goes with their posts. This is a kind of sectarian viewpoint" (p. 189, below). Criticism of the Party cadres for an over-rigid orthodoxy and failure to understand their new duties was voiced by Mao Tse-tung himself in his speech on contradictions. In getting along with intellectuals, he said, many comrades "are stiff with them, lack respect for their work, and interfere in scientfic and cultural matters in a way that is uncalled for" (Document 14, section 5).

The intellectual tide was slow in rising, however, even though discussions and rectification meetings were being held for some time before the main rectification movement started at the end of April. At the sessions of the National Committee of the Chinese People's Political Consultative Conference, held in March, Lo Lung-chi, Minister of the Timber Industry, who was to become one of the main targets of anti-rightist criticism later in the year, said that many intellectuals were wrongly employed or underemployed, and that many primary school teachers were used for all sorts of office jobs by inconsiderate cadres, "who displayed a lack of correct recognition and comprehension." A number of cadres felt that, after the advancement of the Hundred Flowers slogan, "society had swarmed with heresies." They were, therefore, overeager in defending the faith. The reader may

PART VI

recall the phrase in the *People's Daily* editorial of December 29, 1956 (Document 13) about the "present anti-doctrinaire tide."

In the literary world, too, the atmosphere was not yet favorable to free expression. In January 1957 the *People's Daily* printed a warning by members of the Army Propaganda Bureau that certain writers had wandered beyond the proper limits of blooming. Not until April did the paper finally criticize the overzealous army commissars for unduly restricting freedom of discussion (though their stand had provoked considerable comment in the correspondence columns).[25] It was in this climate of uncertainty that Fei Hsiao-t'ung, the sociologist, made his famous remark about a feeling of "early spring" (which, though warm enough to encourage buds, threatens a returning frost). The periodical which quoted this remark said that the movement for blooming and contending did not become established practice until after April.[26] Even in May some people thought that the new Party policy was just a trick, and were correspondingly cautious.[27] Many artists and intellectuals, however, felt free at this time to voice complaints about their position and about the quality of output under the Communist regime.

The artistic "high tide" was of course submerged and finally reversed during that summer by the course of events in the more strictly political field during May and June. Briefly summarized, this happened as follows. The campaign to rectify the Party's working style was formally announced on April 27 and had in fact been initiated before then. Central Party and Government organs, as a sign of good faith, were cutting down their numbers, sending many cadres off to work in the country, and encouraging them to be less bureaucratic in their dealings with the general public. Professional men of various kinds were encouraged to hold discussion meetings and air their grievances. At the same time, the idea of "mutual supervision" between the Party and the "Democratic" parties was also revived, and took something more than a nominal form.

Up till then, the Democratic parties had been understandably cynical about their function, which they described, according to Lo Lung-chi, as "adding flowers to the brocade and oil to the fire; being free to find out the direction of the wind and to chart the weather."[28] In May, however, there seemed to be a genuine change in attitude of the Chinese Communist Party. A series of seven meetings was sponsored by the Party, at which leaders of Democratic political parties were asked to put forward their criticisms. Mao's speech of the preceding February (Document 14) had probably provided in its original form a framework rather more liberal than the "six criteria" which appear in the present version published in June. Nonetheless, there seems again to have been a slow start. At last, after some hesitation and reassurances, the Democratic party spokesmen let themselves go.

The main trends of the criticism uttered were to call in question the achievement of socialist construction; to call for an end to the political monopoly of the Communist Party and for the setting up of a "Political Planning Council" which would have destroyed the Party's "democratic dictatorship"; and to demand correction of the excesses of the anti-counterrevolutionary campaign and the establishment of a codified law.

These criticisms found an echo and amplification in academic and above all in student circles. There was talk of a repetition of the "May 4 movement" of 1919, and this may have caused genuine alarm to the Party leaders. Ko P'ei-ch'i, a lecturer at the People's University, Peking, was reported to have said: "The Party has committed mistakes and should submit itself to punishment...If Communist rule proves unsatisfactory, the masses may bring it down. The downfall of the Communist Party would not mean the downfall of China."[29] Most of the student criticism was also radical, to judge by examples quoted later at the time of "rightist confessions"; but little was printed at the time it was made (perhaps indication that newspapers were well under control). Later reports from the Chinese provincial press suggest that there was a good deal of student unrest, at least; and such behavior by the favored younger generation, who were meant to provide the most enthusiastic support for the Party, was particularly shaming. Here was sufficient justification for any previous doubts within the Party about the wisdom of the Hundred Flowers policy.

Effective counteraction was initiated from the beginning of June onward. A mass campaign of psychological pressure was organized against the rightist critics, and by the end of June 1957 the "rectification of the Party's working style" was submerged in a nationwide debate on whether the main lines of the Party's policy of socialist construction were correct (a question demanding the answer "yes"). It was in June that Mao's speech of February 27 was published. In its published form it laid down narrow limits for legitimate criticism, which must not be directed against the principles of socialist construction. It was implied that definitions in all cases would be made by the Party. At the beginning of July was held the fourth session of the first National People's Congress, in which "confessions" of the rightists featured prominently, and particularly of those who had led the criticism against the Communist Party at the May forum of Democratic parties. The chief scapegoats were Chang Po-chün, Minister of Communications, and Lo Lung-chi, whose arguments in favor of a less restricted version of blooming and contending have already been quoted.

Open political opposition and general criticism of the regime's policies, rather than excessive artistic license, were now the problems at issue. Criticism, especially of the Party's economic and agricultural policies, had of course been widespread within as well as outside the Party. But now it was held to imply political opposition; in the June and July counteroffensive any criticism was held to stem from the political designs of the old intellectual class, which Mao had intended to encourage by means of the Hundred Flowers campaign.

Everything was now done to discredit this class. Lo Lung-chi, for example, confessed to having conspired for the separation of the intellectuals from the Communist Party, and for the absorption of them together with other middle-of-the-road people into the "Democratic League." There was, he said, within the League an "invisible organization" of people who had undergone American or British education, an organization which had been crushed in 1952 and revived in 1957. Chang Po-chün brought the academics and students into the "conspiracy," talking in his confession about the role of certain Peking professors when the original rectification campaign was introduced in the institutes of higher learning in May. These professors, he said, had pronounced that the ferment among the students was serious, and that if students united with the surrounding city population, a Hungarian-type situation might arise. The evidence quoted in such confessional pieces may of course have been deliberately exaggerated. There is no doubt of the ends which it was designed to serve.

The new policy of the Party probably represented the disillusion of Mao himself, who had been the inspirer of the "blossoming" period, and possibly a triumph for his more dogmatic colleagues, some of whom had no doubt shared the doubts of junior cadres about the "anti-doctrinaire tide." The Hundred Flowers policy was based on an optimistic assumption—that "Marxist-Leninist thought has become the guiding principle of the state."[30] In other words, Mao seems to have been convinced at that time that even the Western-trained intellectuals and members of the Democratic parties accepted the main principles of his policy, including the need for the dictatorship of the proletariat. The alternative to this theory is that he was setting a deliberate trap, which goes against the bulk of the evidence. His conviction was now proved wrong. The Party leadership was therefore determined to inculcate as deeply and widely as possible the principles of socialism and to deal in quite a different way with the problem of Western-trained intellectuals and experts. No concessions would be made to conciliate them. Where their services were still necessary they would be under strict Party surveillance. There would now be no question of meeting one of the main demands of the intellectuals in May—that the Party committee system in schools should be relaxed. The working class must train its own ideologically irreproachable élite—the socialist men of the future who would be both "red and expert."

The various elements in this policy were evolved gradually: emphasis on each shifted with the passage of time, and there was no open abandonment of the Hundred Flowers doctrine. Chou En-lai in his speech to the National People's Congress (Document 16) insisted on firm Party leadership at all crucial points, but echoed previous warnings to Communist cadres not to interfere too much with specialists in the exercise of their functions, and in schools particularly to treat non-Communists with respect. By August, the emphasis was placed on the need for intellectuals to "remold themselves." Lu Ting-yi demanded publicly that "Chinese intellectuals should become intellectuals of the working class, through living and working with the masses, being supervised by the masses and guided by the Party."[31]

PART VI

In September, the General Secretary of the Central Committee, Teng Hsiao-p'ing, in his full report about rectification to the very important plenary session of the Eighth Central Committee (Document 19), dealt more fully with all these themes. He defended the Party's consistency in pursuit of the Hundred Flowers policy; weeds must be allowed to grow, in order to serve as "negative examples," to provide fertilizer and to give exercise to good Communist cadres (the half-meaningful use of metaphor is very typical). In the meantime, intellectuals could still be an important asset to the country and the Party must "make friends with them." But it had been proved that rightist activity was at its most virulent where intellectuals were concentrated. The speaker said they employed the dangerous arguments that Marxism was identical with dogmatism, that laymen should not be put into the position of trying to lead experts, and that history proved socialist countries to have neither science nor culture (the launching of the first Russian Sputnik in October 1957 was to provide a welcome counter to this latter argument). Chinese intellectuals must, therefore, be transformed; but the process would be a long one, and so party cadres on the cultural and ideological fronts must be strong, and "red experts" must be trained.

In the meantime the events of the summer of 1957 had done nothing to improve the economic and particularly the agricultural situation. At the September session of the Eighth Central Committee, Teng Hsiao-p'ing gave his audience a gloomy picture of the situation in the agricultual producers' cooperatives, admitting that "well-to-do" peasants were still withdrawing from them, that there was too great a flow of population from the country to the cities, that class warfare persisted in the countryside and that too many rural cadres were insufficiently aware of this. As at the Eighth Party Congress one year earlier, no economic remedies were proposed which seemed to measure up to the state of the country as described. Certain palliative measures were taken. The Central Committee directives on cooperatives, September 15 and 24, 1957, made some concessions designed to ease relations between cadres and peasants.[32] Agricultural taxes had previously been stabilized (at a rather higher figure than that laid down by Mao Tse-tung in February); an almost total prohibition had been applied to free markets in grain; and the foundations were laid in September for a mass campaign for irrigation and water conservancy ("as in 1955-56," according to Teng Hsiao-p'ing). As yet, however, no drastic change or intensification of economic policy was put in hand. The Party seemed still to be convinced that the economic situation must and could still be dealt with by primarily political means.

The political means which suggested themselves no longer had any connection with the Hundred Flowers campaign. They had one advantage from the practical point of view. They were simpler than Mao's proposals of February. Those proposals, it seems, had proved difficult for the normal cadres to understand. Mao himself remarked that "many think that the proposal to use democratic methods to resolve contradictions among the people raises a new question; but this is not so."[33] It was reported that young cadres found it hard to make contact with the masses, because both sides were occupied with hard work; "some comrades" wondered if, in order to practice methods of gentle persuasion, they would have to unlearn the lessons of the *People's Daily* editorial of December 29, 1956 (Document 13), which they had evidently been interpreting in a restrictive sense.

The primarily anti-rightist line pursued from the summer of 1957 onward gave rise to less doubt and ambiguity. On the other hand it demanded a genuine conviction and fervor among the cadres; and this demand in turn gave rise to a fresh set of problems. The Party, as shown in Teng Hsiao-p'ing's figures about its composition, had been considerably diluted in recent years, not least in 1955-56 when new members were required to implement the leap forward of cooperativization in the countryside. A bar on all new recruitment had been imposed in 1957. The Minister of Public Security, Lo Jui-ch'ing, gave a depressing picture at the beginning of 1958 of rightist tendencies prevalent in the Party after the spring of 1956 (when the Hundred Flowers policy was initiated).[34] A *People's Daily* editorial of September 11, 1957,[35] under the title "Handle Inner Party Rightists Sternly," remarked that it was not only the opportunists, who had joined the Party after "liberation," but also a number of veteran members who were affected. The class struggle against such people had been taken far too lightly. The policy had now changed, and the leaders were alerted to danger; but the basic problem of administration remained and had indeed been intensified. To make a success of the agricultural cooperative system, the cadres must make peasants work harder for the benefit of others, and surrender most of the fruits of their labor. Local cadres would in many ways be most suitable for this purpose; at least they would not be regarded as "foreigners" (regional feeling was particularly strong in Kwangtung). On the other hand, precisely the local cadres would be least likely to have their hearts in the right place from the "collective" point of view, and would be most ready to sympathize with local feeling.

Indeed, something of a genius in propaganda would have been needed to persuade peasants that the grain question in the countryside was largely ideological [36] and that tension about the grain supply was largely fictitious. It seems highly probable that the "class struggle" in the countryside was a Communist fiction to disguise or discredit by association the tension between "localist" and "collective" feeling that resulted from Party policies.

A typical illustration of this mixture was the pictorial exhibition devoted in late 1957 to the life history of the peasant Liu Cheih-mei.[37] He was depicted as having been a landless peasant before 1949. He had fought for the Communists against the landlords, and had become a model peasant; but in 1953 he had begun to be too much interested in his own land, and his interest in the affairs of the cooperatives waned steadily. By 1957 he was hoarding grain. In the summer of that year he was subjected to a massive psychological attack by his comrades; he eventually yielded to pressure, was reconverted, and devoted himself wholeheartedly to cooperative production. The purely psychological treatment of this case of economic man reverting to nature is of particular interest.

Liu Chieh-mei was saved by the good local cadres. Too frequently, however, problems of administration and conversion had to be solved by Party cadres whose sympathies could not be trusted. The account of the provincial Party congress in Chekiang, December 1957 (Document 20) contains many passages which are instructive in this connection; and, as will become clear in the next part of this General Introduction, the policies of the "Great Leap Forward" of 1958 would not be put into operation without further extensive political education and purges within the provincial branches of the Party.

In respect to policy dissensions among the Party leaders, the events of the first half of 1957 put the supporters of a "radical" line into a very strong position. There is some indirect evidence, from the articles on rightists in July and August 1957, that Mao was personally responsible for the period of free blooming from March to June and was opposed throughout by Liu Shao-ch'i and P'eng Chen.[38] If, as seems likely enough, they did not share Mao's faith in the efficiency of socialist education among Chinese intellectuals, it was their turn to be justified by events. The same events made it difficult for anyone in the Party to criticize radical policy in any way without incurring the charge of rightism. In 1957, as in 1955 and 1956, there was plenty to criticize on the economic side from a purely technical point of view. Conservatives could point to the existing muddle in the agricultural cooperatives in order to justify their previous doubts and criticisms. But in the summer of 1957 they were in danger of being considered guilty by association with more extreme rightists outside the Chinese Communist Party. Their position was correspondingly and gravely weakened.

VII. THE "GREAT LEAP FORWARD"

The first priority of the Central Committee's meeting in September 1957 seems to have been to lay new political foundations. Liu Shao-ch'i, in his November speech celebrating the fortieth anniversary of Russia's October Revolution (Document 22), assembled the slogans under which the "Great Leap Forward" was announced and conducted six months later—"more, better, faster and more economically," "thrift and conservatism," "red and expert." None of these were new, and the first two at least had been used to launch the 1955-56 leap forward. The only fresh battle-cry was "Mao's militant call" to overtake Britain in the main branches of industry within fifteen years. This seems to have been launched at the National Economic Planning Conference in December 1957 which worked out the 1958 Draft Economic Plan.[39]

The main political lines were thus laid down, but for various reasons the Central Committee did not translate them immediately into a new and full-scale economic drive. The season of course had something to do with this, and there was in any case plenty of activity in the Chinese countryside. Plans were laid in September for large-scale works of irrigation and water conservation to be undertaken during the winter months. Such work was useful in itself, providing the economic foundation for the agricultural leap in 1958. It also had financial advantages which attracted the Chinese People's Government after the inflationary experiences of 1956. No large capital investment was necessary, and there was little or no additional cost in wages involved for central or local authorities.

As for an industrial leap forward, it was natural to wait for the meeting of the National People's Congress in February 1958 to endorse a radically new plan. It seems likely, however, that there were other reasons for delay—political ones. The Party leaders probably had in mind the resistance in and outside the Party which had been encountered by the 1955-56 leap forward, as well as the events of the spring and summer of 1957. Before launching a total new economic drive, they wanted to ensure that the memory of the "blooming" period in May and June had been thoroughly wiped out and that the Party cadres were properly educated for the task which they had to undertake. The plenary session of the Central Committee in September 1957 evidently directed that the rectification campaign in the provinces should be intensively pursued. The very revealing series of reports by secretaries of provincial Party committees, published in the *People's Daily* during May 1958,[40] show that the task of educating the provincial cadres to undertake the Great Leap had been no light one.

It seems as if political education and the level of economic targets progressed together. The record of the decisions taken by the National People's Congress in February 1958 suggests that at that time no final determination had been made about the extent of the Great Leap Forward. Li Hsien-nien, in presenting the 1958 budget, made it clear that there would be a leap, and that it was being made from a firm political base. He said 1958 would be a year that would witness the amazing revolutionary power of the great nationwide rectification movement in all fields.[41] The National People's Congress finally called for a "Great Leap," demanding an increase of 19 percent in steel production, 18 percent in production of electricity, and 17 percent in that of coal; but the steel target in particular was successively raised from 6.2 million tons in February, to 7 million in March, to 8-8.5 million in May, and finally to 10.7 million in August. Targets for other main branches of industry were similarly raised, and as early as March 20 the New China News Agency was able to forecast an increase of Chinese total industrial production by 33 percent over 1957, instead of the comparatively modest 14.6 percent announced by the National People's Congress a month earlier.[42]

There was particular emphasis on increased targets for small and medium-sized industries to be financed and controlled by local authorities; measures were taken to devolve organizational and financial responsibility to local authorities, and to increase their tax receipts accordingly. Local industries had particular advantages; they spared expenditure of the state's money, they would absorb rural surplus population, and they could be regarded as favoring the initiative of the masses. "Targetry" for local industry and for all branches of national life continued throughout the summer and particularly after the speech of Liu Shao-ch'i on the Great Leap Forward (Document 25) had been published. *Reductio ad absurdum* was achieved by (among others) the Association of Chinese Paleontologists, who pledged themselves to cut thirteen years off their twenty-year targets, and in seven years to achieve a level of research above that of capitalist countries.[43]

From the reports of the provincial Party secretaries, it appears that from February onward the development of local industries, as well as of irrigation projects, was stimulated most energetically by the Party cadres. In Shansi, for example, following a provincial meeting on local industrial work, it was estimated that over 13,000 factories would be built within the year, and that over 90 percent of them would be small factories set up and run by *hsien* or *hsiang* authorities or by the agricultural producers' cooperatives.[44] Economy, thrift and frugality, and the do-it-yourself spirit were marked features of this campaign. There seem to have been extensive scrap drives in the provinces. In Kiangsu province, for instance, people were urged in April 1958 to contribute to the state all household hardware not in use, or for which substitutes could be found.[45]

The frenetic atmosphere of competition to overfulfill quotas produced some strange incidents. In Port Arthur and Darien during May, people had to be urged not to promote the scrap campaign by selling steam-heating installations from offices or breaking up municipal dustbins.[46] This is a typical instance of what has been called *nei-ti* (interior) Communism; the cadres in remoter districts overinterpret their instructions, in order to be on the safe side. Further economies, even less welcome, were made in the amount of money and energy devoted to safety measures. Po I-po himself urged that these measures should not receive too much attention, and cadres in the coal industry were exhorted not to take a "one-sided view" of safety in relation to increased production.[47] Sticking to the letter of an outmoded law could at this time be reckoned as "conservatism."

In the meantime the targets for agricultural production had remained more modest. The planned increase of grain production announced by Po I-po to the People's Congress in February was only 5.9 percent over 1957, which had not been a particularly good harvest year. Here no specific revised target was announced. The first indication of the extent of Party aims came in a speech on May 17, 1958, by Vice-Premier T'an Chen-lin explaining the second draft of the 12-Year Agricultural Program. (This program, the first draft of which is Document 5, had been passed in its revised form in October 1957.) T'an, addressing the Eighth Party Congress, Second Session, argued optimistically that "the targets for increasing production set by certain units appear to be very high and seem hardly realizable, but if we take a look at the measures they put forward to achieve them, we will find that there are good grounds for their realization."[48]

It is probable that one good reason for not raising agricultural targets immediately to correspond with industrial targets was that rural manpower was being transferred on a large scale to local industry. The organization of a rural labor reserve force in Shansi to cope with the unified labor needs of the province is an indication of this trend. Such diversion of manpower could be compensated for by the use of more womanpower in agriculture, and this seems to have taken place starting in the early spring of 1958. The more enthusiastic cadres may therefore have seen no reason why they should not indulge in an agricultural leap forward in excess of the People's Congress targets.

It seems likely that the situation of 1956 repeated itself. Within the Party there were certainly conservatives who were skeptical about the whole leap-forward policy, especially in agriculture; but in the enthusiastic atmosphere generated in the spring of 1958, and at a time when technical opposition was still likely to be attributed to bourgeois rightist influence, they could not lift up their voices. In the meantime the enthusiasts, or careerists, probably indulged in, or felt bound to simulate, "blind optimism" of the sort that had been castigated in the sober days of the fall of 1956. It was in this mood that targets were stepped up. The Kiangsu provincial committee, for example, committed itself to a 20-25 percent increase of grain and cotton production over 1957—much more than the target set by the People's Congress, much less than the typical increases eventually claimed in 1958, and somewhat less than the increases finally claimed in 1959.

The Great Leap in industry and agriculture required an intensification of work in the countryside by the Party. The spring and summer of 1958 saw a high tide in the movement "down to the country" which had taken place for administrative reasons in the winter of 1955-56 and had been continued as part of the rectification movement in 1957. The Mayor of Peking, P'eng Chen, for example, had called in August 1957 for the withdrawal of 30-50 percent of Peking municipal employees to work in factories and on farms.[49]

Subsidiary motives for this "down to the country" movement were numerous and varied. They included the need to reduce the population of the cities, also the advancement of literacy among peasants and of character-training among the cadres themselves, who would become, in the current phrase, "tempered by labor," would learn to appreciate the masses and would bridge the former gap between the Mandarin official and the manual worker. In any case, secondary schools, universities, and institutes of higher learning were overcrowded and it was all the more desirable to transfer boys straight to jobs in agricultural cooperatives after the minimum of secondary education. The mystical element in this mixture is brought out well in Lu Ting-yi's article in July 1958 on education and productive labor (Document 26), which contains an unusually large seasoning of quotations from the Marxist classics.

PART VII 19

The Great Leap of 1958 was thus planned on a larger scale and with greater publicity than that of 1956. Some attention must also be paid to its international setting, which again was very different. In the openly expressed view of the Chinese leaders (and there is no reason to suppose that they did not mean what they said), the balance of international power had since the fall of 1957 turned decisively in favor of the Socialist Camp. In the first place, the U.S.S.R. had conducted successful missile tests and had launched a Sputnik, thereby demonstrating in one important field technical superiority over America. In the second place, an economic recession had hit the United States in the winter of 1957-58, and the Chinese leaders were unwilling to see the signs that it was leveling off by May. It is difficult to estimate precisely what effect these portents had on the Party's domestic policy. At the least, however, it seems likely that they strengthened the leaders' belief in the possibility of miraculous short cuts to Communism on the internal front as well as in the field of foreign policy, and made them disinclined to accept more moderate internal policies proposed on technical grounds.

More debatable is the relation between the Party's violent anti-Yugoslav propaganda campaign, launched in May 1958 to confute the Yugoslav Party Program of March, and its attitude toward revisionists or other heretics at home. It seems unlikely that the Party would have given such publicity within China to the Yugoslavs if they had had no ulterior motive beyond embarking on a Sino-Yugoslav doctrinal argument. Again, even at this time the Chinese leaders perhaps thought that Khrushchev was pursuing too energetically a mirage of coexistence; the arguments against Yugoslav concepts of coexistence with and peaceful evolution of the "imperialist camp" may have been intended partly at least for his ears. It seems quite as likely, however, that the arguments against revisionism were intended as warnings to the weaker members of the Party. In early 1957 it had been thought worthwhile to counter, for the ears of the Chinese Communist Party, the main arguments advanced by Tito on the Hungarian question.[50] Since then it had been proved, in May and June 1957, that some highly revisionist ideas were current in China (if not directly among the Party). And, in 1958, conservative opposition to the Great Leap policies was by no means dead. On the whole, therefore, it seems likely that the violently anti-Yugoslav line of the Party leaders was intended as a warning to critics or would-be revisionists at home. It is on these grounds that Document 24, a Chinese resolution having to do with Yugoslavia, has been included in this collection.

Against this background, it is worthwhile to analyze in some detail the speech of Liu Shao-ch'i in May 1958 launching the Great Leap Forward (Document 25). It was in some ways no more than a logical development of what he had said on the anniversary of the October Revolution (Document 22). It represented, however, a much more specific call to action, and showed a fanatical faith in the possibility of a really speedy and revolutionary "transition to socialism." The principal themes of Liu's speech were as follows:

1. The international situation has reached a new turning point and is very favorable to the Socialist Camp. In particular, the United States is in the throes of an economic crisis which is shaking the whole capitalist world.

2. In China, the rectification campaign has brought a decisive victory for the socialist way over the capitalist way. The Party is now rid of rightist elements, and a Communist ideological movement among the masses is bringing about profound changes in the alignment of class forces. "This mighty torrent of communist ideas has swept away many stumbling blocks—individualism, departmentalism, localism and nationalism" (p. 422 below). Everywhere, he said, there is a spirit of self-sacrifice and socialist emulation. He spoke of the beginning of a change of world historical significance, and of a great revolutionary drive for socialist construction.

3. "Some comrades" opposed the line of rapid collectivization in 1955, and regarded the leap forward of 1956 as a reckless advance. They had misgivings about the principle of "more, faster, better, and more economically" as expressed in the 12-Year Agricultural Program. This dampened the initiative of the masses and hampered progress, particularly on the agricultural front, in 1957. However, the Central Committee's decision of October 1957 to readapt the 12-year program, Mao Tse-tung's "militant call" to overtake Britain, and the mass initiative evoked by the rectification and anti-rightist campaigns had led to an all-round Leap Forward.

4. Many of those comrades who expressed misgivings about the slogan "greater and faster"

have learned a lesson from all this. But some of them have not learned anything. "They say: 'We'll settle accounts with you after the autumn harvest.' Well, let them wait to settle accounts. They will lose out in the end!" (p. 427 below).

5. "Uninterrupted revolution" is necessary. This involves at present the simultaneous development of agriculture and industry, with priority for heavy industry, and the simultaneous development of large, medium, and small plants. To achieve the necessary technological and cultural revolutions, it is essential "to train new intellectuals and remould the old intellectuals in order to establish a gigantic force of tens of millions of working-class intellectuals" (p. 428 below).

6. "Some people" raise the following objections to the proposed general increase of tempo:

(a) It makes people feel tense. (But, replied Liu, they would feel more tense if left to continue in poverty.)

(b) The leaders crave greatness, and seek quick success and instant benefits. (But should they be looking for the opposite?)

(c) The policy of more, faster, better will lead to waste. (But the quality of production can be ensured.)

(d) Imbalance will result from the new policy. (But there is never complete balance; the Party is simply trying to achieve balance at a higher rather than a lower level.)

(e) Will not industrialization have to be slowed down, if agricultural production is to be speeded up? (This is not necessary, said Liu.)

(f) Expert authorities are quoted to prove that, given China's population, the increase in agricultural production can only be gradual. (But these authorities fail to see that men should be producers first and consumers only in the second place.)

(g) Ideological and political work can produce neither grain nor steel. (This is untrue, said the speaker. The Party at all levels must stop the "vulgar habit" of holding only technical discussions.)

7. Full scope, said Liu, must be given to mass initiative by encouraging light industries, and by decentralizing as far as possible.

As often with the major pronouncements of Chinese leaders, Liu's speech represented a summing-up of decisions already reached in laborious discussions, rather than a fundamentally new line designed to stimulate thought. Four aspects make the speech remarkable. The first is Liu's view of the international scene; the American recession bulks larger than in public pronouncements before or after, and the conclusions of the speech may have been based in part on a considerable misappreciation of what was happening in the world outside China. The second feature is the marked insistence on the "mass line." Here too Liu's speech simply reiterates, often in milder form, some of the expressions of blind faith in the masses that had been made before—for example, statements to the effect that people who cast doubt on the general line do not realize that this line, once understood and grasped by the masses, will work miracles. Thirdly, the practical deduction which Liu draws from his assumption of the eagerness of the masses is that the nation is prepared for an all-out spurt on agricultural and industrial fronts simultaneously (this is more than was demanded by the People's Congress in February). Lastly, and strangely in view of the other features, there is the extraordinary amount of attention devoted to critics—especially within the Party—of the policies announced. Liu's speech contains a specific challenge to conservatives within the Party on the official agricultural policy. They were challenged to await the harvest for the results of the new policy. By the end of the year, however, many of the criticisms mentioned by Liu had been borne out by events.

In fact, there is no need to refer to this speech of May 1958 for proof of major controversies within the Chinese Communist Party about some aspects of the policy embodied in the Great Leap Forward. After Liu's speech was delivered, but before its publication, the *People's Daily*, about mid-May, published a series of articles by the first secretaries of various provincial Party committees. These show clearly the scale of conservative opposition which had to be overcome early in 1958 by the supporters of an activist policy. The reports cover ten provinces, Fukien, Hopei, Hunan, Kansu, Kiangsu, Kirin, Kwangsi, Kwangtung, Shansi, and Shensi. They can be

PART VIII

supplemented by an earlier report from Chekiang (Document 20) and later ones from Anhwei, Honan, Liaoning, Shantung, and Yunnan. In most of these provinces, purges of the Party (often including the local Party secretary) were specifically mentioned. In most other cases, the Party secretaries talked of criticisms and a wide variety of "negative phenomena" within and outside the Party.

Some of the criticism (e.g., that attributed to P'an Fu-sheng, deposed secretary of the Honan provincial committee) implied fundamental opposition to Central Committee policies since 1955, and a strong element of "localism." More typical is perhaps the case of those Party elements in Shansi who doubted the possibility of a leap forward or of simultaneously developing agriculture and industry. They were accused of spending all their time on financial and distributional questions, and advocating the absolute equalization of living standards between workers and peasants (this would in practice involve more pay and less taxes for peasants). The Party secretary from Hunan said that in a conference of Party committees lasting from January to March, opposition was overcome from conservative-minded cadres who wanted to advance gradually. Similar instances were reported from all provinces (the Kansu cadres anticipated Liu's challenge and said that they would "reckon accounts with leaders after the fall").

Here is further proof of a repetition of the 1956 pattern. In spite of all the political preparation in the rectification campaign, the Great Leap Forward was initiated in February and March 1958 against the opposition of the Party conservatives. When it was announced by Liu in May, their arguments still had to be carefully met. It is surprising, perhaps, that after the rectification campaign they had ventured to speak so openly against the dominant views of the leaders. After Liu Shao-ch'i had laid down the general line and announced the Great Leap Forward, for some time there were few public allusions to it. The purges in Honan, Liaoning, and Shantung were all announced some time later; it was clear that rightist opposition within the Party had not been rooted out by the rectification campaign and the "great debate" on the main lines of Communist policy conducted in the autumn of 1957. On the contrary, it was likely *a priori* that rightist opposition would re-emerge in the Party if the Great Leap Forward landed among serious obstacles.

The Central Committee's problem can be illustrated by Liu's own figure of the "U-shaped development." The official line was that this represented "leap forward—conservative progress—leap forward," and that the stage of "conservative progress" had been due to a fundamentally different and mistaken policy, forced on the Party by "conservative subjectivism." The conservatives' own view was that the second stage in the "U-shaped development" followed inevitably from the mistaken policies of the first, and (by implication) that the second upward swing would be followed by a second downward swing.[51]

VIII. PEOPLE'S COMMUNES: THE PHASE OF ENTHUSIASM

The official reasons given from the end of August 1958 onward for the establishment of the people's communes were largely of a practical nature. The communes were township-wide (*hsiang*) or even county-wide (*hsien*) units of administration composed of a number of former agricultural producers' cooperatives (now renamed "production brigades"). In them were combined the administrative functions of the organs of local government and the economic functions of the cooperatives and local state-owned industries. They were necessary, it was said, to mobilize the labor for major public works in agriculture, to provide local finance for local industries, and to coordinate agricultural with industrial production. These tasks were all the more necessary in the light of the Great Leap Forward in local industry which was being made from February 1958.

A good deal had already been done in the direction of creating large-scale administrative units in the months before the people's communes were established. In fact two years before, in 1956, there had been a nationwide campaign to amalgamate cooperatives into "higher scale" farms,[52] and the formation of communes may be regarded as a further step in this amalgamation. In May of 1958 the press reported an experiment in Shansi which turned the entire province into huge, commune-like administrative areas based on the principle of rural-urban cooperation.[53] This experiment also provided for a "reserve labor army" to avoid rivalry in labor power between town and country. Various other elements of the commune system were also being tried out during the same period. The big movement for the construction of irrigation and water conservation works in the winter of 1957-58 had raised problems about how to mobilize labor effectively from the comparatively small units of agricultural producers' cooperatives (in fact the official policy as late as September 1957 had been to make them even smaller).[54] Further, the build-up of small-scale, local industry was already, as has been seen, an integral part of the Great Leap Forward, and had made great progress before the communes were created.

The first official account of the formation of communes said that the "Weihsing" (Sputnik) commune was set up in Honan during April 1958, and that its success determined the Party leaders in favor of establishing the communal system throughout the country. Other versions, not entirely consistent with this, are that from April on, communes were being set up throughout certain districts (e.g., throughout Suip'ing county, and the whole Hsinyang administrative district of Honan) from May to July; that after Mao Tse-tung had indicated his approval, in July, there was a wide popular demand (e.g., in Kirin) to set up communes; and finally, that the movement for communization rested primarily on a basis of popular demand (see Document 42).[55]

It seems certain that there was a period of genuine experimentation along definite general lines. The new form would presumably have to represent a step forward toward the collectivization of property and a step toward total mobilization of labor, but much initiative would be left to Party cadres, relying (in accordance with the millennial atmosphere of the time) on the "mass line." The movement was only launched on a nationwide scale when the experiments had proved reasonably successful, but it is unlikely that there was any popular demand for this form of reorganization. It is possible, as suggested by A. V. Sherman,[56] that the final goal was known well in advance, that a great deal of organization went on in the provinces, and that the final steps were rushed through in August 1958 in order to give the peasants no time to react against it. The coinciding of these steps with the Offshore Islands crisis of 1958 with its resulting mobilization of the "People's Militia" (which before long was serving largely agricultural purposes) speaks in favor of the last step in this argument. But the last step is not necessarily bound up with the others, and it seems unlikely that so much evidence of experiment should be manufactured after the event, or that so much experiment should be allowed if the main object was to surprise the peasant population. A more likely (but unsupported) explanation of the decision suddenly to universalize the commune system after a period of noncommittal experiment is that Mao Tse-tung himself may have pronounced the time ripe for a tempo quicker than had previously been determined—this would be exactly in line with what happened in 1955.

No full certainty is possible about origins and motives. In any case the attempt to analyze the proceedings of the Party in terms of purely rational calculation may be a waste of time or a fundamental mistake. Reference has been made to the enthusiastic prophecies about the coming age of Communism contained in the speech of Liu Shao-ch'i (Document 25) launching the Great Leap Forward. His very optimistic view of the international prospects of the Socialist Camp may have partly determined his ideas about what was practicable on the domestic front. Lu Ting-yi wrote (Document 26) as if the communal form had already been firmly decided upon as that of the bright future: "It can be imagined that when China enters into communism, our basic social organizations will be many communist communes. With few exceptions, each basic unit will have workers, peasants, traders, students and militia" (p. 447 below). The vision of the age of Communism is here, but any implication about timing is cautious; the communes must wait for Communism, rather than being introduced to herald it.

The theme of the advent of Communism was first explicitly developed by Ch'en Po-ta, whose words are never to be taken lightly, in *Red Flag*, July 1, 1958 (Document 27). The periodical had been founded in June as the most authoritative medium for discussion of theoretical issues. The relevant passage, referring to the Hsukuang No. 1 agricultural producers' cooperative in Hupeh, runs as follows:

> Can it be said that what this cooperative is doing is actually an indication that our country can develop the productive forces of society at a rate unknown in history, can quickly eliminate the distinction between industry and agriculture and the distinction be-

tween mental and physical labor, thereby to open a road on which our country can smoothly pass over from socialism to communism? I think it can be said... Can it be said that illuminated by the general line of our Party for building socialism more, faster, better and more economically, the Hsukuang No. 1 cooperative is concretely and gradually realizing ... an ideal of the founder of scientific communism? [Engels] I think it can be said.

Even when the decision was taken to establish communes throughout the country, the "transition to Communism" was treated cautiously in the texts of the major announcements and articles in August and September 1958, the most daring statement being a September 3 editorial in the *People's Daily* (Document 30), which fixes the timetable for transition in the rural areas to "ownership by the whole people" (full collective ownership by the state, with the minimum intermediate ownership by communes or higher units) at "three or four years, even five or six years." The transition to Communism ("from each according to his ability, to each according to his needs") would take place, the editorial said, "after another few years." (This phrase, appearing in the official translation, was later modified to read "after a number of years.") But official caution was belied by the more enthusiastic secondary propaganda which accompanied or followed the resolution of August 29 (the "Peitaiho Resolution," Document 28). A typical *People's Daily* article on August 6 (i.e., a month before the Peitaiho Resolution was published) contrasts the two world camps: "While American and British Imperialism is engaged in aggression against the Middle East, we are living in beautiful surroundings in a countryside where buds of Communism are sprouting everywhere... China is moving forward at the speed of space flight. Not long ago, peasants in their fifties were worried that they might not last long enough to see the good days of Communism. Now even octogenarians and nonagenarians firmly believe that they will enjoy the happiness of Communism. Indeed, some old men believe that they are already living in the Communist Age."

The official trumpeting of the coming era of Communism had interesting effects on the Party cadres, and also on the Soviet Union—effects that will be discussed presently. The immediate point is that an atmosphere of wild enthusiasm and optimism was being created. It was enhanced by a further spate of stories about new achievements in agriculture and local industry. These stories, in many cases fantastic in themselves, were particularly so in that they seemed to attribute to the new system much activity which had in fact been going on since the start of the Great Leap Forward. Another constant theme was the breakdown of barriers between town and country, and between office and manual work, in an unprecedented fit of enthusiastic "togetherness." The newspapers were full of material and psychological miracles, of which a charming anthology is presented by A. V. Sherman.[57] It is very hard to sift fact from fantasy here, and there is some temptation to ignore the probable achievements while absorbed in the fascinating study of Chinese propaganda technique. The most likely picture is that the industrial and agricultural drive initiated under the Great Leap Forward was accelerated with the formation of communes, and that a great deal was achieved without much coordination and at the cost of considerable duplication and muddle (some instances and evidence will be given in part IX of this General Introduction).

A more important question is how far the Central Committee was itself a victim of the propaganda which it had inspired. It is at least highly probable that local cadres felt themselves under pressure to put in claims for record outputs in various spheres, that the leaders were not sufficiently skeptical about this, and that achievements did not always live up to claims. The local press of Liaoning, for example, told in November the story of some cadres who in the desire to achieve publicity for themselves gave press correspondents a detailed account of their achievements in deep plowing.[58] This was so wildly optimistic as to attract attention and a visit of inspection from a Party team, who in five days' solid work knocked the bottom out of the claim. In the light of evidence about the cadres' "blind optimism" in 1956 and of the revision of 1958 output figures issued in 1959 (Document 39), it is probable that this was a typical case. At the same time, the fact that the Central Committee issued such extravagant claims for 1958 production, particularly in the agricultural field, suggests that they themselves may have been deceived in general by the propaganda which they issued or inspired.

Certain points about the first enthusiastic weeks in the life of the communes deserve some comment here. As before mentioned, the formation of the communes coincided, whether or not by intention of the Party leaders, with a new phase in the Offshore Islands conflict. This was used as the occasion for mobilizing the "People's Militia," much advertised at the time as representing the reaction of the masses to American imperialism and the threat of an invasion of the mainland.

It is not possible to assess thoroughly the reasons for reactivating the militia without going into the question of Chinese military aims and expectations during the Offshore Islands crisis; but a few words may be said here. The Government advertised the new militia, now organized as a part of the commune system, as an important defensive force and issued weapons to some of the units, to judge by various eyewitness accounts. They may have been frightened of a desperate stroke by Chiang Kai-shek. Beyond question, however, once the Offshore Islands crisis died down the main use of the militia was for agricultural "shock operations"; and it seems possible that a primary object all along had been to put agricultural mobilization on a military and securely disciplined basis. A pamphlet of "Questions and Answers about People's Communes" issued in Canton in October 1958[59] makes it clear that with "organization along military lines" (that is, with the entire population under tight discipline and with a clear line of command from the top) agricultural production can be carried out much more efficiently.

A further question which has been much argued is how far the commune was intended to abolish, or succeeded in abolishing, family life. This is a point on which the Party leaders subsequently showed themselves very sensitive to propaganda from outside. The latest facts available at this writing (e.g., a series of articles by a special correspondent in China published in the London *Times* of July 11-15, 1960) suggest that in reality the commune mess hall has provided the only serious encroachment on the old family arrangements. In September and October 1958, however, Chinese propagandists and officials did something to suggest that plans were being made for communal children's boarding schools and for architectural reduction of the facilities for private family life. *China Youth* discussed the need for primary school students to become boarders, and referred to some thoughts of Liu Shao-ch'i on this subject, voiced during an inspection of work in Honan and Kiangsu in September.[60] For future planning purposes, schools as well as factories were to be regarded as "units of Communism." There are references to the setting up of "collectivized school life" in Paoting, throughout one district of Honan, and in many other provinces. However, though the Chinese claimed that thousands of schools (primary, technical, and part-time) were set up in the communes, it is very doubtful that the boarding school system could be widely introduced, owing to the administrative difficulties of the building program involved.

The Communist leaders and propagandists were frank enough in their desire to abolish traditional family life, largely in order to emancipate women from household work and employ them in factories and agriculture. Some technical plans were evolved for the thorough realization of this end. Thus the *Architectural Journal*, starting from the premise that "the family no longer constitutes the basic developmental cell of social and economic structure," proceeded to explain how 80 percent of the new houses for the Suich'eng commune, Hsushui *hsien*, Hopei, were being designed with only one and a half rooms each.[61] But again it is likely that because of the low priority given to any new domestic architecture, such houses were not in fact built and most families continued to live much as before.

IX. PEOPLE'S COMMUNES: DISILLUSION AND CONSOLIDATION

By October 1958, an interesting situation had developed within the Party in relation to the communes.

On the one hand, the members of the Central Committee itself seemed to be persuaded that the process of communization could be pushed ahead very fast, in cities as well as in the countryside. They evidently gave a fairly free hand to the cadres at provincial and lower levels, and encouraged them to push ahead toward Communism. Presumably their assumption (or one of their assumptions) was that political education was succeeding this time, and that the masses of peasants were either converted to the new dispensation, or could at least be rushed into it by the cadres without raising serious difficulties.

On the other hand, administrative difficulties were beginning to appear in unmistakable form. Many of these were discussed at an important conference of officials from the northern and north-

PART IX

eastern provinces, held in October, and attended by Li Hsien-nien and T'an Chen-lin among others. Serious doubts seem to have arisen. While theoretical discussions proceeded at the lower levels— e.g., about the extension of the "free supply" system in the communes and the proper role in a socialist economy of "commodity exchange"—from the beginning of November there were almost continuous informal and formal consultations of the leaders of the Party. These talks resulted finally in the Wuhan communiqué and resolution.

The resolution itself (Document 36), adopted by the Central Committee on December 10, 1958, is a comparatively frank one. An examination of the issues on which the Central Committee felt bound to give general guidance in the Wuhan Resolution seems appropriate here, in order to give a picture of the problems confronting the Party in the fall and winter of 1958-59 and of the probable interaction of ideological and practical considerations in Party councils. These issues are not discussed here in the order of their appearance in the resolution; instead an attempt is made to deal with the themes in order of abstraction, starting with the most concrete and working up to the most theoretical.

1. *The militia and Communist Party Command organizations must be separate. There must be a "comradely" style of work, with no rudeness or "commandism." Cadres must not become "dizzy with success" and exaggerate* (especially sections VI and VII of the document).

"Commandism" is the form of deviation from current Party policy which favors forcing the populace against its will. Naturally in 1957 during the period of blooming and contending and at the beginning of the rectification campaign, it had been singled out as the main error. During the fanatical days of the summer of 1958 almost all reference to it was eliminated, and the exhortation to "get organized along military lines" offered encouragement to just those cadres who had been accused of "commandism" in 1957. In October 1958 a "National On-the-spot Militia Work Conference," held near Peking, actually ordered Party secretaries to take command of the movement to "turn the whole nation into soldiers."[62] Apparently this order was interpreted to mean that the Party need not worry about the fine distinction between communal and military chains of command, for just this mistake was attacked in the Wuhan Resolution. This would tend to confirm the idea discussed above that one of the main objects of the militia system had been to enforce strict discipline in agricultural production.

Military discipline seems to have led to other and less desirable aspects of the military "working style." A newspaper report in October talked of "sudden attacks" for the deep plowing of wheat fields.[63] It subsequently became clear that the militarization of work methods was a frequent popular complaint against the commune system (see Document 33). From a technical point of view, efficiency may have suffered from the attempt to apply military methods. Thus the *Masses Daily* of January 12, 1959,[64] talks of the indiscriminate use of "major troop units" (presumably shock brigades, rather than People's Liberation Army units), which were in the future to be employed only on emergency assignments and not to interfere with normal agricultural methods. The main theme of this article was the need for a unified production plan for each commune. At present, it said, most communes existed without production plans, and work was assigned day by day. Such slapdash methods may well have been encouraged by excessive reliance on the "military" style of shock work.

2. *Commune members should retain individual means of livelihood, including "odd trees around their houses, small farm tools, small instruments, small domestic animals and poultry"* (Document 36, section IV).

From August on, the retention of individual means of livelihood had been a theme of considerable public anxiety. This had been stimulated by public pronouncements in the early days of the commune system. Thus, in *Red Flag* of September 1, 1958 (Document 29), it was stated that in many communes the "last vestiges of private ownership" were removed, and "in certain respects" things had gone beyond the stage of collective ownership. That is, the state or people as a whole, not the commune itself, was the owner. The next number of *Red Flag* was much more specific and was no doubt designed to dispel fears:

> Residences of the members, land inside the courts of their houses, small strips of land by the side of houses, a certain small number of fruit trees, as well as the pigs, sheep, chickens and ducks raised by members, shall remain their private prop-

erty and shall not be touched. As to the members' bicycles, radio sets, house furniture, wrist watches, clothing, and bedsheets and such living needs, they shall all belong to the individuals themselves, for even in the Communist society these things shall remain private property.[65]

In spite of such detailed reassurances, it is clear that anxiety persisted. In the "Questions and Answers" pamphlet of October from Canton cited above, "some people" are quoted as saying that all private property will become public. They are duly refuted, again with specific reference to bicycles, watches, clothes, and bedding. Not the least of the Party's reasons for trying to allay fears on this subject was that these fears had spread beyond China and seriously affected the willingness of the overseas Chinese to send remittances on the former scale to mainland China. Directives on the treatment of the property of overseas Chinese, issued in December 1958, were at pains to emphasize respect for individual property and the continued financial priority for interest payments on loans from overseas.[66] Such anxieties probably resulted less from "imperialist" propaganda than from the behavior of certain cadres on the spot, who may have taken too literally the early propaganda about the rapid transition to Communism.

3. *The institution of communes in cities must be postponed for the present* (Document 36, section 1).

On this theme, there is comparatively little information in the main press sources. The first communes were organized in rural areas, and throughout 1958 the movement was largely a rural one. It is plain, however, from various items in the provincial press beginning in August (see p. 489 below) that communes were also set up in Shanghai, Kweiyang, Amoy, and Kaifeng. Urban communes could coincide with factory, school, and street units, but it is not clear what, if any, efforts were made to concentrate factory workers or students entirely at their place of work, thus virtually abolishing home life. The most important object seems to have been to "emancipate" women by providing communal mess halls, and thus to have extra labor available for new small factories. The inhabitants of Kaifeng were basically transformed, it was said, from "consumers to producers."

Opposition came, it was said in the case of Kweiyang, from workers who wanted freedom of movement to look for work elsewhere, from landlords who feared for their property, and from those who were "afraid of being put to work." In this connection, Bogunovic, the usually well-informed Yugoslav correspondent of *Politika* (Belgrade), in a dispatch of July 1959,[67] mentioned press items of October 1958 dealing with the transfer of workers en masse from an industrial section of one town to semimilitary settlements in another. This would fit in with the fears reported from Kweiyang. The report from Amoy mentioned that people were becoming afraid to bank their savings. It seems possible that fear of losing further remittances from overseas Chinese to one of the areas from which many of them originate, played some part in determining the Party leadership to go slow on the establishment of city communes. In any case the movement was officially halted by the Wuhan Resolution, and only resumed in April 1960.

4. *Communes must "go in for industry in a big way," and industrial production should first of all serve the development of agriculture but at the same time serve to meet the demands of commune members for staple consumer goods and serve the country's big industries. Communes must also develop commodity production and exchange commodities with other communes. Contrary to the views of "some people, attempting to 'enter communism' prematurely," commodities, commodity value, money and prices still have "positive roles"* to play (pp. 496-497 below).

The question of the industrialization of the communes raised very large issues. The establishment of local industries had been an important object of the Great Leap Forward from the spring of 1958, and the formation of communes was designed in part to accelerate the process. On the theoretical plane, it was thought desirable to introduce the peasants to simple factory work, to narrow the gap between town and country, and train a new generation with technological as well as agricultural skills. On the practical plane, the exodus to the cities had to be stopped, and production of all kinds had to be increased at minimum cost by maximum use of the communes' labor force. In these circumstances, it is likely enough that the cadres at commune level were, on material grounds alone, urged to set up their own industries without waiting for elaborate plans, and when possible with purely local supplies, relying on the "wisdom of the masses" to provide

PART IX

know-how and materials. The much publicized mass movement to make ball-bearings in small communal factories is a typical example of this activity.

Even in more sober days, there had been plenty of argument between the Party enthusiasts for speed and the conservatives who despised the "rural" or "guerilla" working style and thought it at best penny wise and pound foolish. This tension was likely to be increased in the extravagant atmosphere of the summer of 1958, when the "wisdom of the masses" was being given full play in industry. Some of the more ingenious economy plans would naturally meet with opposition from technicians within the Party. The Minister of Light Industry, Li Chu-ch'en, speaking one year later (*People's Daily*, Oct. 10, 1959) against rightists, quoted a typical instance of conflict in the paper industry, between the conservatives who wanted to wait for woodpulp, and those who wanted to carry on manufacture with a straw-fiber substitute.

The list of priorities for communal industry given in the Wuhan Resolution probably implies a minor victory for such conservatives, and an admission that many cadres had overambitiously tried to press ahead toward a form of self-sufficiency at communal level. This interpretation is confirmed negatively by the general propaganda line of the spring of 1959 ("Treat the whole country as a single chess board") and especially by Chou En-lai's survey of work given to the National People's Congress on April 18 of that year (Document 37). The period of coordination of industry and consolidation of communes will be discussed presently.

The argument about the degree of communal industrialization was pursued on an almost mystical level. There had been deep theoretical reasons for the enthusiasm of some of the cadres in the communes to set up their own industries. The idea of self-sufficiency had some fascination for the more advanced students of the Communist classics. The text of the Wuhan Resolution indicates that there were people (presumably among the left-wing Party theorists) anxious to advance from the economic stage of exchanging goods and using money as a means of exchange to a Communist system of local production for all needs, free distribution, and the minimum use or even abolition of money exchange. Indeed, after the adoption of the Resolution but before its publication, a technical periodical[68] stated that the disappearance of the circulation of merchandise and the function of money is an important condition for the realization of Communism, and added that the condition had yet to be created.

The heresy, or premature orthodoxy, of mooting such ideas at an early stage aroused the anxieties of the Government's financial officials, who, if these notions began to be put into effect, would be deprived of their important revenue from commodity and turnover taxes. The Wuhan Resolution takes a clear and pragmatic position. In March 1959, the State Council made this position even plainer when it approved the holding of commodity exchange meetings between city and countryside, to ensure proper distribution. The theoretical aspects of the question are closely linked with the problem of "free supply" or "wages."

5. *Any negation of the socialist principle "to each according to his work" at this stage will "dampen the working enthusiasm of the people." The system of wages paid according to work done must take first place for a "certain period" and an "important place over a long period." To replace this principle by that of "to each according to his needs" would be Utopian until the general supply situation is far more abundant; to do so would lower the standards of Communism and vulgarize its ideals* (Document 36, section II).

The choice or mixture between payment by wages and provision of free supplies evoked a great deal of discussion within the Party during the autumn and winter of 1958; this provides the clearest evidence available of the existence of a doctrinaire element in the Party which was anxious to exceed even the pace set by the Central Committee in the advance to Communism. The essential and practical issue underlying the discussion was how far workers in the communes should be paid in money wages and how far in free supplies of food, clothing, and so forth; but the discussion ranged much further to cover, for example, the political desirability of various forms of wage systems.

The issue did not arise at first. One of the earliest official commentaries indicated that even free supply of grain would have to be postponed to a distant future (*People's Daily*, September 4, 1958). The general pattern to be gathered from various news items of late August and early September is of an advance from the application of a sort of piece-wage system in agriculture (rates fixed per hour of various types of work, with bonuses for overfulfillment of norms or extra hours worked) to a system of regular wages supplemented by incentive pay. What commune members urgently demanded was a fixed wage income, as opposed to pay by the hour for the job. Free supply was, it seems, regarded as a secondary phenomenon.

By October, however, this was no longer the case. There was much enthusiastic propaganda on free supply of grain, in particular, as an epoch-making event in peasants' lives. Once the propaganda started, further attempts by the cadres at commune level to spread the "supply system" is easily explicable. *Political Study*, in an article on "The Outlook of Communism As Seen from the People's Communes," suggests how the impetus may have been given.[69] It talks of that fascinating slogan "Eat rice without pay," and quotes Mao as saying on a tour of Anhwei: "Since one commune can put into practice the principle of rice without pay, others can do the same. Since rice can be eaten without pay, clothing can also be had without pay in future." This was no formal directive, but a suggestion from Mao could be very powerful.

However this may be, the idea of "free supply" clearly caught on faster than the practical possibilities allowed. This conclusion is supported by a study of theoretical articles in the Party newspapers, especially the *People's Daily*, during October and November.[70] Three concurrent trends of opinion must be understood if the attitude of the "leftists" in the wages-vs.-free-supply controversy is to be appreciated.

First, there was the conviction that the transition to Communism was already being prepared, and that the principle to each according to his need would soon begin to replace the principle of the socialist state, that is, to each according to his work. The free-supply system was obviously an embodiment of the Communist principle, and thus appealed to the enthusiasts.

In the second place, there was a romantic yearning (perhaps shared by Mao himself) for the return of the simple Communism of wartime days in Yenan. It seems that the supply system had in certain cases persisted as a partial means of payment to Party and government employees at least down to the spring of 1957; and general wages were sometimes adjusted downward to allow for extra welfare services supplied. From the technical economic standpoint such practices were regarded as harmful to incentive, but the supply system still retained a certain moral prestige. This was typically expressed in an article from the Shanghai paper *Liberation* reproduced in the *People's Daily* of October 13, 1958. During the "liberation war," it stated, thousands of Communist militiamen lived on the supply system with no thought of wages, let along piece-wages in mind. After liberation, "military Communism" and the supply system persisted, and were very popular; but the system was gradually subjected to bourgeois influence and corrupted. People talked mockingly of "guerilla habits" or "rural working style," and the term "supply system" became almost one of abuse. Now, however, it should be recognized that those who oppose it are willing to "let money assume command" (this is an offensive perversion of the stock Party slogan, "let politics assume command").

The third trend of thought, somewhat less romantic but working initially in the same direction as the above, was the dislike of the piece-wage system and the feeling that it led to excessive inequalities between wage-earners and between town and country. Piece-wages had played an important part in the Chinese workers' life. In 1956, extension of the system was being urged, and from the summer of 1956 considerable efforts were being made on the one hand to keep down the total wage bill, and on the other to repress tendencies toward "egalitarianism," which might remove the financial incentive from the factory and skilled workers.

The *People's Daily*, in publishing its reports and letters on the problem of wages and supply in October and November 1958, did not come out editorially in favor of any particular solution, but the general trend of opinion eventually seemed to favor the abolition of piece-wages and the adoption of a modified regular wage system. On October 16 the paper published a report of the state of affairs in Shanghai, where the sharp increase in production was said to have led to a disproportionate increase in piece-workers' wages and to a demand "by the masses" for the abolition of the piece-work system, which they regarded as an instance of "money taking command." According to the *People's Daily*, conditions allowed the transition to a supply or "semisupply" system, which should be carried out "as far as practicable." During the next week the Chinese press carried a number of reports (from Peking, Shanghai, and the Chishuyen locomotive works) on the abolition of piece-work wages within factories, and the consequent rise in morale, although some cadres in Shanghai "looked with infinite anxiety" on the prospect of its elimination.

Criticisms of the piece-wage system were extended to the wage system as a whole. It unfairly favored able-bodied couples with few or no children. It created in general too much inequality. It represented the remnants of a capitalist system. Workers had their pride and did not care for material benefits only. One correspondent even remarked that "young comrades consider wages as a dishonor." Anyhow, why should skilled workers receive more for the exercise of skills which they have learned at state expense? Eventually, however, the correspondents (and the *People's Daily* itself) seemed to settle for the continuance of the wage system. One of them (in the issue of November 22) exploded the romantic myth about the free-supply system in Yenan; this, he said, had soon developed into a low-wage system which was never a very important element in the economic life of the time. Mao himself had criticized the species of "rural socialism" which had sprung up ten years before, after land reform had been carried out in the "old revolutionary areas." At an earlier stage of the correspondence (October 17), it had already been urged that the commune system should not simply revert to the happy days of the past. The wartime system of free supply had been abolished after 1949, it was said, not because of an erroneous political attitude but because of its inferiority to the wage system in stimulating production. Certainly the goals of 1958 were to abolish the distinctions between town and country and those between manual and mental work; but such goals had nothing in common with the "absolute egalitarianism demanded by people under petty bourgeois illusions."

This countercriticism touched on the first essential point which must have determined the Chinese Communist Party eventually not to go too far in the direction of a free-supply system. Obviously, incentive was still needed in order to stimulate production. Again, for all the propaganda previously issued about the enthusiastic reception of the supply system, it evidently was not universally popular. An interesting and detailed report by the Party secretary of the Hsuanchuang commune in Hopei[71] describes the "half supply, half wage system" adopted there. The commune had tried to provide free clothing and soap as well as free grain, but had had to retreat from its position; it could not ensure sufficient supplies, and the money wage had provided insufficient stimulus. To popularize even a "half supply" system, much propaganda was needed. This article provides good evidence of the obvious fact, formally recognized in the Wuhan Resolution, that wage payments remained an essential condition of keeping up and increasing production. Another "negative aspect" of the supply system may have been exaggerated by Party officials in order to provide an excuse for food shortage. They said that it led to local overeating. Peasants were accused, for example, of having called in their relations to share in the free supplies.[72] It is likely enough that the free-supply system led to extravagant consumption on the spot; it is certain that a meal-ticket system was introduced in many communes.[73]

The system thus proved to be a poor incentive and an extravagance; it also encouraged excessive hopes of attaining speedy self-sufficiency in the communes and of a swift transition to the Communist society, in which payment would be made according to needs. It was therefore necessary in the Wuhan Resolution on communes to lay down the law very specifically about the limits of the free-supply system. It was accepted that any negation of the principle "to each according to his work" at this stage must dampen labor enthusiasm, and that the wage system must continue. In theoretical terms, this could be expressed as a caution to the enthusiasts of the Communist Party—conditions are "not yet ripe" for the transition from socialism to Communism. And this leads directly to the whole theoretical problem of transition.

6. *Some "good-hearted" but "overeager" comrades have thought that the process of building a socialist country with highly developed modern industry, agriculture, science, and*

culture in "fifteen, twenty or more years" is too slow (i.e., they have wished to hasten the transition to Communism). "Every Marxist must soberly realize that the transition to Communism is a fairly long and complicated process of development" (Document 36, section II).

This whole subject needed a lot of explaining to the good-hearted but overeager comrades and much of the explanation given is in highly theoretical terms, designed for scholars of Communism only; the question is usually discussed in terms of "collective ownership" (i.e., ownership by the commune) as opposed to "ownership by the people" (usually envisaged as ownership by the state on their behalf). The main texts are:

(a) The *Red Flag* article of September 1, 1958 (Document 29), of which the relevant passage runs:

> Of course, when the people's communes are established, it is not immediately necessary to transform collective ownership into ownership by the whole people and it is even less appropriate to strain to advance from socialism, i.e. the primary phase of communism, to its higher phase. The transition from collective ownership to ownership by the whole people is a process which may be fairly quick in one place and slow in another. After a period following the transition to ownership by the whole people, the productive forces of society will be expanded even more greatly;... the communist ideology, consciousness and moral character of the entire people will be raised immensely;...differences...between town and country...will gradually disappear;...the function of the state will only be to deal with aggression from external enemies...By that time our country will enter a new era, from the socialist era based on the principle of "from each according to his ability and to each according to his work" to the communist era based on the principle of "from each according to his ability and to each according to his needs."

(b) *The Wuhan Resolution itself* (Document 36). It will be recalled that this was adopted in December 1958. The main relevant points are that the gradual industrialization of rural areas is the way to the gradual transition from collective ownership to ownership of the whole people, and from the socialist to the Communist principle of "to each according to his needs." The process of building a socialist country with highly developed modern industries, agriculture, science, and culture will still take a long time—"fifteen, twenty or more years." Three interconnected but distinct stages are envisaged:

Transition from agricultural producers' cooperatives to communes.

Transition from "social collective ownership" to "social ownership by the people as a whole."

Transition from "socialism" to "Communism."

"Ownership by the people as a whole" is represented within the communes by the federation of communes (at the *hsien* or county level), which will take over the banks and other institutions formerly owned by the whole people (i.e., run by the state). The proportion of ownership by the federation of communes to ownership by the communes themselves should increase gradually.

There is a contrast between the time schedules stated or implied in the *Red Flag* article and the Wuhan Resolution. In September, it is said that the transition to ownership by the whole people may be fairly quick in some places, and the *People's Daily* editorial of September 3 (Document 30) talked of three to four, or five to six years as a reasonable pace. This ties in fairly closely with the statements in *Red Flag*, and by Liu Shao-ch'i and Ch'en Po-ta (Documents 25 and 27) about the coming of Communism; it does not correspond to the tone of the Wuhan Resolution, which argues for a much longer period of transition. An authoritative article appearing at the same time as the Wuhan Resolution makes the point clearly: productivity must be raised before proceeding to the Communist system of ownership by the whole people, and this process will take fifteen to twenty years.[74]

Even more bearish is an article in the technical journal *Financial and Economic Research* in January 1959 on the conditions for ownership by the whole people in people's communes.[75] These are specified as follows:

(1) The commodity production of the commune should far exceed its production for the purpose of supporting itself; but at present basically the production of the communes is still at the handicraft stage.

(2) The "accumulation" of the commune should be so large that it has to be put at the disposal of the state, if it is not to have disincentive effects on the spot. But at present "accumulation" is only just enough to cover the commune's own needs.

(3) There must be reasonable assurance of freedom from natural calamities before communes can pass to ownership by the whole people. Otherwise the state will be unduly burdened (this condition sheds an interesting light on the differences between a Communist and a welfare state).

(4) There must be approximate equality between communes in material conditions. Otherwise the equalization involved in the transition will discourage the more prosperous and harder working.

(5) There must be an awakening of "socialist consciousness" so that individual interests will not prevail over those of the people as a whole (in other words, when distribution takes place according to needs, people must be trained not to rate their own needs too high).

This last is a highly revealing document, and does much to translate the theoretical concept of transition to ownership by the whole people into concrete terms. The problems involved in such a transition are, it is seen, linked closely with those inherent in the introduction of the free-supply system, and in the discouragement of commodity exchange and currency. It was the "leftist" elements in the Communist Party which were pressing for more free supply, less commodity exchange, and in general, a quicker transition to ownership by the whole people and so to Communism. The process of discouraging them must have been a fairly painful one for the Party leaders.

Their decision to clamp down on speculation about the timetable of Communism was probably determined not only by theoretical considerations and shortages of supply but also by administrative problems. A number of the welfare functions formerly undertaken by the village administration (i.e., cultural, education, and health activities) now had to be performed by the commune administration which had replaced it, and eventually even by the "production brigade" administration corresponding to the old agricultural producers' cooperative. Muddle and inefficiency were likely to mark the period of transition of authority.

More serious were the financial problems. As the communes began to grow their own industries, and to supply the more primitive of their own industrial needs, the occasions for taxing products on their way from factory to end-user became less frequent. In one commune in Honan the last quarter of 1958 witnessed a drop of over 40 percent in revenue from industry and commerce taxes. There were further financial difficulties in launching the new organizational units. The business of checking production contracts with the communes was a tricky one. Either financial cadres contracted for a proportion of the commune's income, which meant that they could not be certain in advance of what state receipts would amount to, or they had to fix a figure in advance, and run the risk of being victims of "conservative" planning by the communes.[76]

The attitude of cadres toward the new system presented a curious and contradictory mixture of ideology and politics. They were reported to dislike it for the following reasons:

(1) It was a retreat from ownership by the whole people (i.e., state control) to collective ownership.

(2) They were suspicious of the competence of local Party leaders.

(3) They disliked being sent down to the communes and treated as peasants.

(4) They did not understand fully the significance of the free-grain-supply system, and hankered after the simplicities of the wage system.[77]

Curiously, left-wing purists of Communism and practical administrators found one aspect of the commune system that they could join in criticizing. This was a new brand of "localism" that had come in with the communes. In Communist language, the system contained a contradiction which had not been foreseen by the ideologists among its founders and was likely to prove most unwelcome to them. The communal administrations were likely, if given a free hand (and this was what, in the first instance, a "mass policy" involved), to grow their own local patriotism, and look after their own interests at the expense of those of their neighbors and of the state. Such localism had been sufficiently apparent in the agricultural cooperatives. It was increased by the encouragement of industrial self-sufficiency and the free-supply system in the communes. The Central Committee's "decisions on the improvement of financial and trade administration in rural areas" (December 20, 1958) did something to coordinate responsibilities and relations between the state and commune administrations;[78] but, though the attempt was made, it was not easy to represent the whole move as a step toward common ownership. The actual or threatened growth of localism explains some of the theoreticians' feeling in favor of passing on from the stage of collective ownership; and it explains very directly the changes of emphasis in the new year 1959 regarding coordination and countrywide planning ("the whole country a single chessboard").

One other very important point must be mentioned. This concerns Sino-Soviet relations and the extent to which they affected and were affected by the Chinese Communist Party's policy of advancing to Communism. The theme cannot be treated fully here, and it is in any case one for speculation rather than for historical narrative. Briefly, it seems that the Chinese leaders' decision to stabilize the communes may also have been determined in part by the Russian reaction to the more extravagant claims of August and September. The evidence on this point is mainly negative or indirect, including Khrushchev's remarks to Senator Hubert Humphrey in December 1959, the silence of the Soviet press about Chinese propaganda, the more obvious silence of the Soviet ambassador to Peking (particularly on the occasion of the anniversary of the October Revolution), and the propaganda about Khrushchev's economic theses for the Soviet Twenty-first Party Congress. Certainly the Chinese themselves, whether or not any diplomatic pressure was put upon them, by the end of the year were talking humbly of their own progress in socialist construction and of the Soviet Union's march toward Communism.

The period of consolidation from the end of 1958 until August 1959 also cannot be treated here in any detail. The general trends are plain. The administration and plans of the communes had to be consolidated. The development of local industries had to be rationalized and coordinated. Most of the methods proposed and individual goals set both for agriculture and industry seem to have been modest enough, at least by comparison with the propaganda of the summer of 1958. In addition, there was continuous propaganda for austerity, thrift, and invention to cut down production costs. At the same time, however, the Chinese People's Government was unwilling to admit that the Great Leap Forward had fallen short of expectations and announcements; the Government therefore stuck to its fantastic target figures for 1959, and was committed to a further leap forward—in the face, as it proved, of bad climatic conditions.

The first essential in the reorganization of communes which occupied the first four months of 1959 was adequate advance planning of output and allocation of resources. Another need was sensible administrative arrangements. Many defects of 1958 continued to be admitted in the process of reorganization—the sheer non-existence of plans in some communes, a neglect of accounting in the attempt to achieve maximum production at any cost, and so on. Incentives were more carefully studied, and there was less reliance on mass enthusiasm. In discussing agricultural production targets, for example, *Red Flag*[79] recommended that targets should be fixed in contracts at 15-20 percent below the highest level attainable, in order to give production brigades an extra incentive to work for bonus wages. Less than a year before, such advice would have led to a charge of rightist conservatism. It was still necessary to issue occasional warnings against attempts at self-sufficiency, which might endanger the cities' food supply, and the food shortage in the summer of 1959 led to earnest appeals to the communes to increase subsidiary food production, to devote more manpower to agriculture, and to give up the ideas previously inculcated about reducing sown acreage and relying on close planting to increase production.

Even before this time, however, there had been a shift of priorities from industry to agriculture. Chou En-lai, addressing the National People's Congress in April 1959 (Document 37) had insisted that agriculture must employ not less than 80 percent of China's total manpower and that factories and mines must stop recruiting from the countryside. This general line was later confirmed by various typical items of press evidence. Already in March 1959, manpower for the proposed leap in agriculture was becoming short and a first warning was issued not to draw away any more men from the country into factories.[80] In July, it was announced that in one county of Liaoning, 10,000 men were being transferred back to agriculture from communal industries.[81] Shortly afterward, communes were directed to take inventories of the items stored in their warehouses.[82] Much superfluous material had been bought in 1958, it was said, with which to start up local industries. This must now be transferred to factories which had the facilities for using it.

The same considerations of "thrift and economy" were being applied to industrial development. Chou En-lai in his speech of April 1959 (Document 37) laid strong emphasis on the need for coordinated planning (the single-chessboard policy), for adapting the plan to objective realities, and for ensuring that key projects had priority. He talked at length about the correctness of the 1958 "general line" and endorsed the fantastic targets set for a continuous leap forward (525 million tons for food grains, 18 million tons for iron and steel). But publicity during the following weeks dealt largely with the need for thrift and realism; there was, for example, the need for individual factory plans to take account of actual rather than potential capacity, and to get along with existing machinery.[83]

Economic Research in February [84] discusses the proper strategy for the "single chessboard" and emphasizes the priorities for communal industries as follows (they do not differ much from those given two months before in the Wuhan Resolution, Document 36):

(1) Industry serving agricultural production, especially mechanization and electrification.
(2) Processing of agricultural products.
(3) Supply of raw materials and semifinished products to larger industrial undertakings.

This is no more than common sense, but again it might well have been denounced as arrant conservatism in the summer of 1958.

All in all, those members of the Party who had been challenged by Liu Shao-ch'i in May 1958 to wait for the harvest must have felt largely justified in their skepticism by the beginning of 1959; and by the spring of 1959 they could have felt that the leaders of the Party had, so to speak, stolen a good many of the planks of the conservative platform. And, apart from one outburst by T'an Chen-lin in *Red Flag*, February 24, 1959, there was no major item of anti-rightist propaganda in the period between the issuing of the Wuhan Resolution and August 1959. As in 1956, the more radical elements of the Party had overplayed their hand, and the leaders had to adopt a number of the rightist policies. But one difference between the spring of 1959 and the fall of 1956 was that the Central Committee no longer considered itself to be balancing between two erroneous wings but rather identified itself with the right wing.

X. ANTI-RIGHTIST CAMPAIGN

The summer of 1959 in many respects resembled that of 1956, climatically and politically. Severe floods and droughts stretched the administrative machine to the utmost. At the same time the Party leaders were anxious to have as much as possible to show for the tenth anniversary of the establishment of the Chinese People's Republic on October 1. They therefore clung to production targets which would have been unattainable even under better climatic conditions, and tried to stimulate cadres, peasants, and workers to a second consecutive season of all-out effort. Throughout June and July numerous campaigns were in progress to encourage or stimulate various branches of production, and to demand decreased consumption. This applies particularly to the coal industry. The supply situation in fertilizers was pronounced acute, and drastic steps were urged to enable communes to produce more raw materials for light industry. But there were no public indications that industry or agriculture as a whole were falling down on the job, or that the projected second "Great Leap" was being sabotaged by political apathy or hostility.

Official charges of sabotage were reserved for the major political campaign which opened in August. In that month the Liaoning provincial committee of the Party, for example, revealed that "rightist ideas" had begun to be apparent in March, when the campaign for stepping up coal production was launched. And Po I-po in October 1959 spoke of a downward dip in industrial production figures during June and July, caused by "rightist-inclined opportunists." The Party was either content to let political grievances accumulate until they merited a major counter-campaign, or, more probably, attributed sincerely the cumulative failure of an impracticable economic policy to political rather than economic or normal human causes.

However this may be, in August a new and intense political campaign against "rightist-inclined opportunists" opened with a *People's Daily* editorial on August 6 (Document 38), which was required reading for all cadres. This was followed by openly advertised meetings of provincial Party committees to discuss the article, and to pledge activity against the Party rightists. The details of the publicity campaign which followed are briefly noted in the comments in Chapter X.

The timing and intensity of this campaign show that it was something very much more than a routine attempt to step up production after a summer of natural disasters. The immediate purpose was preparation for the communiqué of August 26, 1959 (Document 39), announcing revised figures for 1958 and revised targets for 1959 production. From a technical point of view, the figures registered, as the Party leaders tirelessly pointed out, a considerable leap forward over 1957, and a return to something like statistical common sense. It may thus far have been welcome to the more sophisticated section of the Chinese public. It amounted, however, to a major self-criticism and admission of irresponsibility (at least to those whose memories went back eighteen months) by the Central Committee.

Responsibility for inflated claims and for "tensions in the supply situation" could not in this case, as they were in the fall of 1956, be attributed primarily to the "blind optimism" of inexperienced rural cadres (though their inexperience in measuring bumper harvests was cited as an excuse). Moreover, the admissions of the Central Committee could not have come at a less convenient time. Numerous distinguished foreign delegations were soon to arrive for the October 1 celebration of the tenth anniversary of the assumption to power of the Chinese People's Government. The maximum appearance of prosperity and national unity was desirable.

The decision by the Central Committee to admit their past exaggerations must have been a difficult one. Presumably they felt that it involved lesser dangers than the alternative of letting their propaganda diverge more and more obviously from reality. It seems likely, for instance, that claims to have reached a 525-million-ton grain harvest (the 1959 target) would have induced expressions of obvious public cynicism, which could have affected the whole atmosphere of the October celebrations. It was therefore a reasonable and bold choice of risk by the Central Committee to announce, five weeks before October 1, a cutting back of target figures which brought them somewhere into line with reality, but still registered a very considerable "leap forward," and left public opinion time to recover.

This hypothesis accounts for the communiqué of August 26, with its call for a great production effort, and its discovery of a scapegoat more horrific than the "blindly optimistic cadres" of 1956. It was in line with the regular practice of the Party to attribute all failures to political causes, and it was thus natural for them to produce in a new context the specter of rightism. But one would be wrong to conclude that this was no more than a bogey resurrected for the particular occasion. It was probable, *a priori*, that rightist opposition within the Party, which had existed in May 1958 and been largely justified by the events of the next six months, would make itself heard in opposition to a repetition of the Great Leap Forward policy. Nor is it likely that the Central Committee would talk without very good cause of rightists within the Party—a Party which had been "rectified" on an unprecedented scale from the spring of 1957 to the spring of 1958. Mao had said in February 1957 that further "rectification campaigns" would be necessary, perhaps annually; but the general sense of propaganda by the leaders had been that, within the Party, rightism had been virtually eliminated. Some loss of face was therefore involved in admitting the reappearance of rightists within the Party. Again, this applies especially at this particular time. It is unlikely that a major attack on Party rightists, indicating lack of unity within the Party, would have been launched so near the October celebration if it had not been necessary—even urgently necessary.

To estimate the strength of rightist opposition within the Party, it is of interest to review the main themes of the Central Committee's counterattack. The main general criticisms aimed at "rightist opportunist ideas" (the list is taken principally from *Red Flag* of September 1, Document 43) are that they:

(1) neglect the efforts of the people;
(2) deny that "revolutionary undertakings are the tasks of the masses" (this charge is sometimes modified to the more plausible one that "the tasks of the revolutionary construction," as opposed to those of revolution itself, are said not to be suitable for the masses);
(3) criticize, without participating in, mass movements;

(4) discredit the achievements of the Great Leap Forward and magnify its shortcomings (the rightists were said to characterize it as a "petty-bourgeois fanatic movement" or more simply as "an awful mess," and this is reminiscent of the criticisms, quoted by Chou En-lai in 1957—Document 16—of the first Five-Year Plan and the policy of socialist construction as a whole);

(5) shirk tasks which are objectively possible. This shortcoming was elsewhere specifically linked with Mao's reproof—in Document 2—to rightist conservatives who failed to keep pace with the objective situation.

These general charges, and particularly the last, serve to show the historic continuity of the conservative line of thought within the Chinese Communist Party. Indeed this continuity was admitted in a *People's Daily* article on the "chronic disease of right deviation," which it said had been repeatedly analyzed by Mao since the latter half of 1955. "The characteristic symptom of this 'chronic disease' of right deviation is that after it has been overcome with respect to a certain new question, it always appears with regard to another new question."[85] More immediately interesting, however, are the specific lines of rightist criticism cited and countered by the Communist leaders. Much space was devoted in 1959 to the defense of the communes against the charges that they amounted simply to an unnecessary, overhasty, and insufficiently based advance toward Communist ideals.

Specifically, Chou En-lai (Document 41) dealt with the charges that the leaders' economic policy had led to unnecessary hardships; his defense amounted to little more than an admission that there were in fact small temporary shortages, particularly of meat, eggs, and fish, and that these were very largely a function of the public's increased purchasing power. Again the parallel with 1956 is striking.

Two specific points raised by Chou are worth noting incidentally. A grain shortage was admitted "for a very short period in the spring" and over an area amounting to less than 5 percent of the total area of China. This is of course a considerable admission, since the area specified might, and probably did, include all the big cities. Also (and this bears on Sino-Soviet relations) Chou En-lai felt bound to defend the regime against the charge that too much foodstuff had been exported. Again there is a reminiscence of 1956-57.[86] Chou's defense could have been much more categoric. Exports, he said, had been 17.8 percent higher than the previous year; but there had been only "a very small increase in the export of grain and subsidiary foodstuffs needed at home."

The other specific point is that much time and space was devoted to the rightist charges against the iron and steel campaign of 1958. It had evidently been described as extravagant or, at best, penny wise and pound foolish, involving forced labor, resulting in products of low quality, and representing again petty-bourgeois fanaticism. These charges were duly denied, but it was admitted then and in subsequent weeks that the smallest plants were being scrapped or regrouped into larger units, and that the quality of products needed much attention (especially if they were to be used in major industrial units). The need for improved quality in industry as a whole had been the subject of much propaganda in the spring and early summer of 1959.

Enough has been said here to illustrate the weight and seriousness as well as the continuity of rightist criticism within the Party. One footnote may be added to the history of the anti-rightist campaign in 1959. The barrage of propaganda ceased in October, but in the remaining months of the year some very important individual counterblasts appeared. Ch'en Po-ta in particular (who had played a prominent part in the summer of 1958 in the propaganda offensive against Yugoslav revisionism) added in *Red Flag* of November 16, 1959, a new dimension, so to speak, to the charges against the Party rightists. His explanation of their activity against the Great Leap Forward is that the class struggle by the bourgeoisie outside the Party inevitably influenced those within the Party who were "organizational but not ideological members." He implied that after the attacks by the non-Party rightists in 1957, and the international revisionists in 1958, a new danger had arisen:

> The demand for so-called equality at this moment is only a clamor of the exploiting class which is not willing to give up the exploitation system. The bourgeois rightists have voiced such a clamor in attacking socialism, while the right opportunist elements within the Party immediately have responded to this clamor. The revisionists,

or right opportunist elements, pay lip service to Marxism and also attack "doctrinairism." But the real targets of their attack are, actually, the most fundamental elements of Marxism... The current struggle against rightist opportunism... is a struggle of great significance which concerns the fate of our country and also the fate of socialism in our country.[87]

Taken at its face value, this suggests that the opposition within the Party, which had been mainly a technical one concentrating on economic issues and the means of attaining socialist construction, might—after successive disillusions with the policy of the leaders— have broadened into opposition to the Chinese leadership in general or even to some of the political principles of Communism.

It is of course hard to tell whether such polemics should be taken at their face value. They may be merely or partly intended to warn critics within the Party that technical criticism will be willfully misinterpreted as political high treason. That is perhaps the implication of a speech by Lu Ting-yi on October 31, 1959,[88] in which he says that the political line of demarcation is "to obey chairman Mao or not." One of the final anti-rightist blasts of 1959, however, delivered at the end of November,[89] uses the strongest language about "fantastic attempts to reform the Party according to the bourgeois outlook" and about a "handful of rightist-inclined opportunists in Hunan" (Mao's native province, and a famous nursery of rebellion) who "launched heinous attacks on the leadership of the party." The sober if not certain conclusion is that from the fall of 1958 until at least the end of 1959, rightist opposition within the Chinese Communist Party had been a considerable force, with growing grievances against the leadership.

XI. CELEBRATION OF THE TENTH ANNIVERSARY

The celebrations of the tenth anniversary (October 1, 1959) of the establishment of the Chinese People's Republic brought forth an outpouring of grandiose speeches and articles late in September and early in October congratulating the Party and the Chinese people on the achievements of the ten-year period. These statements were largely predictable, but there were also some reasoned comments on certain important problems of peripheral interest to this study, heretofore only incidentally mentioned in this General Introduction. One of these was the problem of regional autonomy. Another was the problem of the loyalty of the army.

The problem of regional autonomy, dealt with in Document 44, is one of great actual and potential importance to the Chinese People's Government. Soon after the establishment of the Communist regime in mainland China, there was speculation whether the Central Government could enforce its control over the whole mainland area, and whether there would be a resurgence of local warlords to exercise *de facto* authority in their own districts. There has in fact been little evidence of this kind of regionalism since 1949. Kao Kang was accused at the time of his elimination (1954) of trying to set up a "separate kingdom" in the Northeast, but it is hard to say how literally this should be taken. After his elimination and before the first Five-Year Plan came into effect, the administrative regions of China (a survival of civil war days) were abolished.

The vast size and the varied racial composition of China give rise to obvious administrative problems. There has been some feeling among Party leaders, even in the Han provinces of China, that the best local jobs should go, but often do not go, to local members (see part VI, above, and the commentary on Document 20, below). The Great Leap Forward and the process of communization have led to a natural increase in economic "localism"—the preference for local rather than national economic interests. It was to be expected even before the Great Leap Forward that economic localism, which was a problem in the Han provinces, would be reinforced by racial and religious considerations in the more distant provinces or autonomous regions, where the greater part of the population belonged to racial minorities. No doubt this is exactly what many of the Party leaders did expect; in consequence the official policy down to the end of 1957 consisted in damping down the zeal of the Han cadres sent to minority areas.

In the fall of 1957 the line was changed. The Central Committee may have argued that the "gentle" line had not led to any adequate results. It was officially claimed that the repercussions of the final "blooming period" in May and June 1957 had been felt in the distant provinces, and it may have been thought necessary to make a new show of authority there, even more than near Peking. Or the Central Committee may simply have been carried away by the faith that the Great Leap Forward could be pushed through there as elsewhere and that "politics should take command" evenly throughout China. For whatever reasons, the emphasis beginning in 1958 was on "socialist revolution" and the need to quell local nationalism. Wang Feng (in Document 44) says frankly that "only socialism can solve our nationalities problem." He further lays it down that "the nationalities problem is, in essence, though not in all its complexities, a class problem." In other words, the Party acted on the theory that anyone who resisted "socialist transformation" was a reactionary as much as a nationalist and that the "masses" even of racial minorities could successfully be mobilized against him.

There is some evidence of how the new policies worked out in 1958-59 in the remote Western and Northwestern provinces. The secretary of the Kansu provincial committee was among those who wrote in the *People's Daily* in May 1958 about local preparations for the Great Leap Forward. The implementation of the Great Leap was preceded by the expulsion from the Party of the "rightist anti-Party group" headed by the Vice-Governor. One of the slogans attributed to the rightists was that "Kansu is backward" (and presumably not ready for a leap). One-tenth of the Party cadres in Kansu were in fact said to be of the type that were anxious to settle accounts with the Party leadership after the fall.

Local papers of the same period give a lot more detail of controversies within the Kansu Communist Party. There was evidently much resentment among local cadres over the arrival of immigrant cadres, who stepped into the best posts. The provincial committee as a whole was accused of self-delusion about its achievements. From what was said in the local press about the aspirations of Party comrades to own farms themselves, and about resistance by independent peasants to the formation of cooperatives, it may be deduced that there were major troubles about agricultural policy from 1956 onward. These are likely to have been linked with problems arising from the continuing friction between Communist and Islamic interests. New China News Agency messages of October 1958 report the exposure of a leader of "rightist Islamic circles," Ma Chen-wu, in May. He was accused of supporting the revolt of the "bandit Ma Liang" and then accused of local opposition to the policy of collectivization. More important, he was said to have plotted to seize political leadership of the Ninghsia Hui autonomous region when it was formed in April 1958.[90]

There is scattered evidence of similar phenomena in other provinces of the West and Northwest, particularly from Sinkiang. Saifudin, the chief party official of the Sinkiang Uighur autonomous region, reporting to the National People's Congress in the spring of 1958,[91] made it clear that regionalism in Sinkiang had at certain points attained "separatist" proportions. He attributed the dangerous growth of local nationalism to the encouragement given by the rightist example in the spring of 1957. Rectification was now proceeding according to the decision of the Central Committee in the fall of 1957. Reports from local Sinkiang papers in July 1958 indicate that a "great debate" on the merits of socialism and capitalism was still necessary in the cooperatives there, nearly six months after this had been concluded in less remote parts of China. Even a year later, Chinese broadcasts from Urumchi (November 24, 1959), talked of reorganizing the communes in Sinkiang on the basis of a "struggle between the two roads" (socialism and capitalism). Opposition to the Great Leap Forward, the "general line," and communes existed among a small number of demobilized soldiers and commune members. A rectification campaign was also necessary among rural cadres.

Tsinghai was the scene in 1958 of racial and religious troubles, described in the local press of October 1958,[92] as "counterrevolutionary activities designed under the cloak of religion to split national unity" and resulting in death sentences against the chief offenders. The general propaganda picture in the local press is remarkably similar to that given of Tibet after the suppression of the rebellion in March 1959. Good-hearted peasants were reported to have overthrown reactionary herd owners and lamas. Local press reporters elicited from others much curious detail about the habits of reactionary Imams (this was presumably intended less to boost circulation than to discredit political opponents by an appeal to decent human sentiments).

Such evidence is of course typical and not exhaustive. All it shows, and the only conclusion that can be advanced here, is that in the more remote regions of China, racial and religious issues combine with economic localism, which is probably universal, to obstruct the Party's policy of collectivization. An interesting speculation, which cannot be pursued here, is how far fear of repercussions in the Western and Northwestern provinces determined the Government's ruthless policy toward the Tibetan revolt.

The second problem of peripheral interest that is illustrated in our final group of documents is that of the army. The essence of this problem can be briefly expressed. The great majority of the soldiers and officers are of peasant origin; and a number of the senior officers are keen professional soldiers. In either case they came into tacit or open opposition to Party policies toward the army. So much is clear from the criticisms met in some speeches by high officials, particularly that of the veteran military leader and new Defense Minister, Lin Piao (Document 46); but any attempt to dilate on the problems involved has to rest mainly on probabilities and speculation. It is likely, for example, that soldiers serving far away from home were upset by the news that their parents had had to abandon private holdings and join agricultural cooperatives or communes. Similarly it is probable that reports of the pace of agricultural work enforced in 1956 and 1958 disturbed them; and that, when forced to work on agricultural projects themselves, they would have preferred to do so at home. Expressions of discontent arising from these or other circumstances might, in the eyes of the Party, increase the need for political education in the army; and at this point the professionally-minded officers might begin to object.

Such officers were concerned by a number of other problems, in particular the division of work between defense and economic construction; they probably felt that military training was being neglected for things like water-conservation campaigns. Another grievance was the forced participation of the army, officers included, in all sorts of mass campaigns, such as political demonstrations and anti-pest exercises. Mao's decision to make all senior officers serve one month a year in the ranks is unlikely to have met with much enthusiasm, although some generals got good publicity from the change. Finally there was the feeling that the Government was unwilling to give the army the modern equipment necessary for its full efficiency. The air defeat over the Offshore Islands in September 1958 may have intensified this feeling.

It is possible (but no more can be said) that the resignations of the Chief of Staff, Su Yü, in October 1958 and of P'eng Teh-huai as Minister of Defense in September 1959 represented professional opposition to the theory of "politics in command" of the army. And professionalism in the army, no less than national feeling in the outer provinces, represents a possibly important brake on the Party's progress toward total control of mainland China.

SUMMARY AND CONCLUSION

No attempt will be made in this General Introduction to assess the successes and failures of the Chinese People's Government over its first ten years of existence. Instead, an appropriate conclusion may be to resume the account of political cross-currents within the Chinese Communist Party (as of October 1959) and to make some suggestions about the Party's efficiency as an instrument of government.

The preceding narrative may be summarized as follows. From 1955 through 1959 the Chinese Communist Party remained for the most part under the sway of its more radical, or leftist, wing. In order to launch the period of socialist construction, the Party combined at first a forward policy in agriculture and capital construction (opposed by the Party's conservatives) with a more liberal policy of encouragement to the intellectuals and with rectification of the Party's working style (opposed by the leftists). In the summer of 1957, this combined policy needed drastic revision. There was a crisis in the system of agricultural cooperatives, the rural cadres having failed to convert the masses of peasants to its virtues; and the extension of freedom of criticism to political affairs had revealed that the old bourgeois class too had not yet been sufficiently educated in socialism. It was plain that rectification as originally envisaged would not have the results expected of it by Mao early in 1957.

A much broader campaign of political education was now initiated, as preparation for a new economic policy. The leftists or ideologists were now dominant in the Party and were influenced by a very rosy picture of the Socialist Camp's prospects in the world; but their formulation of a really bold new leftist policy (the "general line," Great Leap Forward, and formation of communes)

SUMMARY AND CONCLUSION

took place only in the face of stubborn conservative opposition, probably on technical grounds, within the Party.

In the summer and fall of 1958 the new policy was accompanied by what came to be considered new and serious leftist deviations on the part of the overeager. It achieved considerable successes, but at the cost of much confusion, and obviously fell short of the leaders' extravagant claims. Many of the rightist criticisms had been justified, but face was for some time preserved. By the end of 1958 the main lines had been laid down for some adaptation to reality of the commune system and the general economic line, without any obvious recantation of previous policies.

The balance within the Party was then disturbed by the serious natural calamities of the summer of 1959, and a sharp recrudescence of rightist criticism within the Party against the continuance of radical economic policies. It became impossible to continue the pretense that a second major leap forward was in progress. The 1958 output figures and 1959 targets were revised. Partly but not entirely as a cover for this, a campaign of unprecedented sharpness was launched against "rightist-inclined opportunists" within the Party. Up to the end of 1959 there was occasional but very weighty Party propaganda against the rightists within Party ranks.

What conclusion may now be drawn about the state of the Chinese Communist Party as it completed ten years at the helm? In spite of its great successes during the 1950's and in the preceding decade, the Party continued to face the problem of assuring the complete loyalty of its membership. Teng Hsiao-p'ing, in his report of September 23, 1957, to the plenary session of the Eighth Central Committee of the Party (Document 19), stated the problem faced by the leaders in this respect. Of the working class, he said, 65 percent were "new workers," over half of whom were of "bourgeois" origin. As for the Chinese Communist Party itself, the majority of its members (then about 10.6 million) did not belong to the "working class." The majority of them, he said, had joined after victory in 1949, and lacked experience of class struggle and genuine class consciousness. The Party had grown too rapidly and had not paid enough attention to ideological training. Too much tenderness, he said, had been shown in the struggle against rightists in the Party. Too many young intellectuals were acting as leaders; more workers and peasants were needed. Too many cadres, newly settled in the provinces, were taking on a local color in their approach to the problems of government. There must be an appropriate number of local functionaries, Teng declared, but no "mistaken provincialism."

Theoretically, the rectification campaign of 1957-58 changed this state of affairs, strengthening the political consciousness of the Party and convincing the "broad masses" that the line of socialist construction was correct. Liu Shao-ch'i, in his speech of May 5, 1958, said that rightism within the Party had been eliminated, and that the Party together with the masses would work boundless miracles. His own speech suggested that the first conclusion was premature. Subsequent events were not such as to stimulate the more passive or to convert the more critical in the Party. *Red Flag* on October 1, 1959, celebrating the tenth anniversary of the Chinese Communist regime, carried an article with the title "Communist Party Members Should Be Marxist-Leninists, Not Fellow-Travelers of the Party," in which it quoted Mao Tse-tung to show that from 1942 there had always been people who were only organizational and not ideological members of the Party. Their passivity was now turned into "rightism."[93]

At the other extreme, "dogmatism," one of the principal objects of the rectification campaign of 1957 in its original phase, should have been eliminated by that campaign. But, as shown by the events of the late summer and autumn of 1958, there remained people who might be ideologically sound, but were also so obstinate or stupid as to pursue a radical line after the central directive had been changed. Leftist activity may have been somewhat exaggerated by the Party leaders. They may have found it convenient to cover their retreat, as symbolized in the Wuhan Resolution, by quoting and condemning the exaggerations in word and deed of certain leftists, dogmatists, or adventurists. But there is little doubt that there were in fact cadres in the fall of 1958 that went beyond the directives of the Central Committee. They could honestly claim to be doing no more than carrying out the spirit of the regime's instructions, or to be adhering, when in doubt, to a well-established Communist line (as in the controversy over the Hundred Flowers policy in 1956-57).

Of the two faults, then, excessive leftism is unlikely to be regarded as very dangerous by the Central Committee. Its leaders would indeed probably argue that the Party badly needs a leavening of "good-hearted but enthusiastic comrades," even if they sometimes overstep the mark. The "rightist-inclined opportunists" have constituted a divisive element of quite a different order within the Party. They represent in the first place a continuous and pragmatic, not a political opposition; their criticisms arise from, and have been to a considerable extent justified by, the course of events since 1957. They have been accused by the Party leadership (*Red Flag*, October 1, 1959) of judging things not by the standard of objective laws but by that of their subjective wishes, and of underestimating the need for class struggle. They could presumably retort, if they felt free to do so, that the leaders are overemphasizing the class struggle in order to avoid looking facts in the face; and that their forebodings, as recorded in Liu Shao-ch'i's speech of May 5, 1958, about the limited possibilities of the Great Leap Forward, were very largely justified. Their opposition to the leadership on partly technical grounds has been aggravated and made more effective by localism—the defense of communal or provincial economic interests against those of the Chinese Government—or by regionalism, in cases where racial issues combine to increase tension between the center and the periphery.

As an example of this process, and the lengths to which it may lead, the *People's Daily*, November 30, 1959, quotes the case of "some comrades wavering" in Hunan during the summer of 1959. The results were said to include (1) the resurgence of rightists within the Party, who ordered the disbanding of mess halls, and (2) open attacks upon the whole commune system by "landlords, rich and well-to-do peasants"—still identifiable as such, it seems, after at least three years of agricultural producers' cooperatives and one year of communes. This case may well have been exaggerated by the Party leaders for their own purposes, but taken at all literally it suggests that the internal organization of China was not at the time fully stabilized after the shakeup of 1957-58, and that the process of persuasion can be a two-way one. It is not only the cadres who convince the peasants; the peasants sometimes convinced the cadres during the second half of August 1959.

A year later, in August 1960, there were few overt signs of serious debate in the Chinese Communist Party, or of really serious administrative difficulties. The leaders claimed that the conservative opposition was effectively crushed in a rapid propaganda campaign.

Indeed, for many months after the end of 1959, little was heard of rightists within the Party. But this could not be taken as final evidence; for example, little was heard of conservative opposition between May 1958 and August 1959. The possibility of such opposition remains while there is still the possibility that the Central Committee will pursue extravagant and inefficient (though still perhaps effective) economic policies; and this possibility is of course always present. The Government is committed to a policy of "leap forward"—interrupted by pauses—a mixture of bold targets for heavy industry, light industry, and agriculture simultaneously; maximum investment in heavy industry; thrift and ingenuity in developing light industry; maximum work in the farm fields; "planned consumption" (i.e., the minimum necessary rations of food, clothes, and other necessities); and continual propaganda. The Central Committee would probably reckon that, if a maximum effort is exerted along these lines, total production can be raised soon enough to a level at which the needs of investment and of increased consumption can be met simultaneously; and that the Party can maintain adequate discipline until that time.

In this calculation, not only the morale of the people as a whole but also the morale and efficiency of the Party play an important and indeed a crucial part. It will not be easy for the Central Committee to escape the dilemmas which have hitherto confronted it. The Party must take command everywhere; but to do so, its own political education must be improved. "Sky-rocketing enthusiasm" must everywhere be displayed; but it must never degenerate into cynical ritual. Administration must be decentralized to check bureaucracy and encourage popular enthusiasm; but the cadres must not succumb to "parochialism." If the cadres at lower levels show, on a wide scale, signs of sympathizing with local as against central interests, encouraging popular demand (e.g., for more food and consumer goods at an earlier date), or merely lapsing into orthodox observance of routine, this may put the Central Committee's program out of gear. It is in this context that the continuance and efficacy of rightist opposition with the Party must be judged. This opposition is unlikely to act as more than an administrative brake. As such, how effective can it be? Some guess may be ventured on the basis of the historical record.

SUMMARY AND CONCLUSION 41

It cannot be expected that rightist opposition can force any great changes of policy on the Central Committee, until experience and experiment have proved the rightist point of view correct. But lack of enthusiasm among the local cadres could be an important factor in determining or hastening the failure of extravagant experiments, and might still act as a powerful brake in a country where administration has been considerably decentralized and communications are still not good.

The changes that such a process might bring about are unlikely to be large, sudden, or obvious. But, under a little-changed surface, they may be real. Many of the Party slogans are already flexible or self-contradictory and can be used, so to speak, in any direction. "Politics must take command," and the Party must be in control; but politics can order a Great Leap Forward or a period of consolidation with the subslogan, "The whole country a single chessboard." Cadres are ordered publicly to maintain "sky-rocketing enthusiasm" but to stick closely to "objective limits"; they may receive hints to concentrate on one or the other half of the order. The famous slogan of the Great Leap Forward—"More, faster, better, and more economically" may be similarly subdivided, with emphasis at one time on "faster" and at another on "better." The most that is likely to happen as the result of rightist activity within the Party is that emphasis will gradually be altered, the rightist clothes will be stolen piece by piece, and there will be a slow moderation of the Party's policy on the internal front.

Chapter I

THE FIRST FIVE-YEAR PLAN

(containing Document 1)

DOCUMENT 1

Report on the First Five-Year Plan for Development of the National Economy of the People's Republic of China in 1953-1957, delivered by Li Fu-ch'un, Vice-Premier of the State Council and Chairman of the State Planning Commission, July 5 and 6, 1955, at the Second Session of the First National People's Congress.

The English text is an official translation issued as a book with the above title by the Foreign Languages Press, Peking, October 1955. A translation of the Five-Year Plan itself was also issued by the Foreign Languages Press in 1956 under the title, *First Five-Year Plan for Development of the National Economy of the People's Republic of China in 1953-1957*. Section II of Li Fu-ch'un's speech is a full summary of the Plan. An official summary was also issued in August 1955 (CB 358).

Comment. The context in which Li Fu-ch'un made his report is discussed in our General Introduction, part I.

Official statistics of the period 1949–1959 are collected in *Ten Great Years*, published by the Foreign Languages Press, Peking, 1960.

Documents on economic organization are reproduced in Chao Kuo-chün, *Economic Planning and Organization in Mainland China: A Documentary Study (1949-1957)* (Cambridge, Mass.: Center for East Asian Studies, Harvard University), Vol. 1 (1959); Vol. 2 (1960).

The evolution of the first Five-Year Plan, its contents, and the extent of Soviet aid to China are discussed in: Choh-ming Li, *Economic Development of Communist China* (Berkeley: University of California Press, 1959); Choh-ming Li, "Economic Development: the First Decade," *China Quarterly*, January 1960; and T. J. Hughes and D. E. T. Luard, *The Economic Development of Communist China* (London: Oxford University Press, 1959).

A valuable article on recent economic history and prospects is that of Richard Moorsteen, "Economic Prospects for Communist China," *World Politics*, January 1959.

On Soviet aid, see also Allen S. Whiting, "Contradictions in the Moscow-Peking Axis," *World Politics*, February 1958.

On the political preparations for the 1955-56 "leap forward" (the anti-counterrevolutionary drive, and the campaigns against Hu Feng and Liang Sou-ming), see Theodore H. E. Chen, *Thought Reform and the Chinese Intellectuals* (Hong Kong: Hong Kong University Press, 1960), pp. 85-93. For more detail, see also CB 345, containing a speech by Lo Jui-ch'ing, Minister of Public Security, to the National People's Congress on July 27, 1955, on the suppression of counterrevolutionaries, and CB 350, containing speeches to the National People's Congress, July 1955, on Hu Feng and the need for ideological reform.

Salient points in the history of the Plan are as follows:

The "common program" adopted in September 1949 by the Chinese People's Political Consultative Conference called on the Chinese People's Government, in

TEXT OF DOCUMENT 1

Article 33, to draw up as soon as possible a "general plan for rehabilitating and developing the branches of public and private economy of the entire country." In the fall of 1952 it was announced that the period of rehabilitation would be completed at the end of the year; the transition to socialism would begin and the first Five-Year Plan would be inaugurated in 1953. A State Planning Committee was set up under the chairmanship of Kao Kang (this was changed in 1954, after his downfall, into the State Planning Commission with Li Fu-ch'un as chairman). In the meantime, the "general line" for the period of transition to socialism was evolved by the Central Committee of the Chinese Communist Party in the fall of 1952.

The main principles of the first Five-Year Plan were set out in a *People's Daily* editorial of September 16, 1953, but nothing else appeared in that year. The general line was extensively publicized by the Party from November 1953 on, and embodied in the preamble to the 1954 constitution, adopted by the first National People's Congress in September 1954. Work on the draft Plan, which, according to Li Fu-ch'un, was begun in 1951, was completed in February 1955. The draft was approved by the National Conference of the Party in March, adopted by the State Council on June 18, and submitted to and approved by the National People's Congress in July. The adoption of the national Five-Year Plan was followed by the drawing up of corresponding plans at the provincial level.

Many of Li Fu-ch'un's main themes, and the success of the first Five-Year Plan as a whole, are discussed further in subsequent documents (see especially Chapter IV). The following provide more detailed contemporary materials on incidental aspects of the Plan:

(a) Comparative analysis of Chinese and Soviet first Five-Year Plans: ECMM 10 (*Statistical Work Bulletin*, August 1955).

(b) Distribution of investment under the first Five-Year Plan: ECMM 14 (*Study*, Sept. 2, 1955).

(c) Geographical redistribution of industrial areas: ECMM 18 (*Current Events*, Sept. 10, 1955); ECMM 64 (*New Construction*, Nov. 3, 1956).

(d) Discussion of local plans at provincial level: URS, Vol. 1, No. 31 (Hunan papers, August-September 1955).

As always, the footnotes in the document which follows were in the text as we found it; and so was the editor's note on page 49.

──────────────TEXT OF DOCUMENT 1──────────────

Deputies to the National People's Congress:

The State Council of the People's Republic of China is submitting a bill on the First Five-Year Plan for Development of the National Economy to the second session of the First National People's Congress. On behalf of the State Council, I hereby submit this report on the plan to the current session of Congress.

The draft First Five-Year Plan for Development of the National Economy of the People's Republic of China was drawn up under the direct leadership of the Central Committee of the Communist Party of China and Chairman Mao Tse-tung. It was discussed and in the main approved by the National Conference of the Communist Party of China in March 1955. After revising the draft plan on the basis of opinions expressed in discussions at the Party's National Conference, the Central Committee of the Party submitted it to the State Council. The State Council in session has discussed and unanimously approved the draft plan, and now submits it to the second session of the First National People's Congress for examination and adoption.

It was on the basis of a restored national economy that we began to carry out our country's First Five-Year Plan. Before the liberation of our country, our national economy was ruthlessly plundered and seriously damaged by imperialism and the reactionary Kuomintang clique; the people lived a life of untold misery. The great revolution of the Chinese people overthrew the rule of imperialism and the Kuomintang reaction and established a people's democratic dictatorship led by the working class and based on the worker-peasant alliance. It turned key branches of the economy into the property of the entire people—these include the big banks, big industrial and commercial enterprises and railways originally monopolized by imperialism and the bureaucrat-comprador bourgeoisie—and it transformed landlord ownership of land into peasant ownership. This made it possible for the people of our country to build a new life for themselves at a rapid rate.

We successfully completed restoration of the national economy in the three years following the founding of the People's Republic of China. We did this by relying on the splendid initiative and creative spirit of the working class and the masses of the people in the front line of labour. We did this by relying on the victories of the whole nation on various fronts, such as in the reform of the agrarian system, the movement to resist American aggression and aid Korea, the suppression of counter-revolutionaries, and the *san fan* campaign (the movement against corruption, waste and bureaucratism) and *wu fan* campaign (the movement against bribery of government workers, tax evasion, theft of state property, cheating on government contracts, and stealing economic information for speculation). We did this by relying for guidance on the economic policy correctly laid down by the Communist Party of China and the Central People's Government which we carried out on the basis of the Common Programme. We did this with the support of the great Soviet Union and the People's Democracies.

In 1952, the year in which China completed the stage of economic recovery, the total value of output of industry and agriculture, including the value of output of industry, handicrafts, agriculture and subsidiary rural production (all values here and below being calculated in terms of constant prices of 1952), registered a 77.5 per cent increase compared with 1949. Modern industry showed an increase of 178.6 per cent, and agriculture (including subsidiary rural production) an increase of 48.5 per cent. With few exceptions the output of all major industrial and agricultural products surpassed peak pre-liberation levels. Because its restoration and development was relatively swift, the share of modern industry in the total value of output of industry and agriculture went up from 17 per cent in 1949 to 26.7 per cent in 1952. Transport and posts and telecommunications were restored and expanded together with industry and agriculture.

The tremendous achievements of the state in balancing revenue and expenditure and stabilizing commodity prices had a marked influence on the rapid rehabilitation of the national economy and improvement of the people's life.

We embarked on the transformation of our national economy while still in the period of rehabilitation. Step by step the socialist sector of the economy strengthened its leading role. In this period, while both state and private industry registered advances, the rate of advance of state industry far exceeded that of private industry, and in addition a section of private industry was converted into joint state-private enterprise. Hence, in the total value of industrial output (including that of modern industry and handicraft workshops but excluding that of handicraft co-operatives and individual handicraftsmen) the proportion represented by state, co-operative and joint state-private industrial enterprises rose from 36.7 per cent in 1949 to 61 per cent in 1952, while the proportion represented by private industry dropped from 63.3 per cent in 1949 to 39 per cent in 1952.

In this same period, the mutual-aid and co-operative movement in agriculture also made some initial advances. In 1952, trade handled by state concerns and co-operatives amounted to 63 per cent of the volume of wholesale trade on the domestic market and 34 per cent of the volume of retail sales. Foreign trade was brought under state control.

In general, during the period of rehabilitation, while our people's democratic dictatorship steadily consolidated itself, the socialist sector greatly strengthened its leading role and position in the national economy. This opened up possibilities for the introduction of a planned economy in our country, and set before us the task of drawing up a long-term plan for the development of the national economy.

The whole-hearted, unselfish and fraternal assistance of the Soviet Union is an important factor in enabling us to carry out our planned economic construction at a rapid rate. The assistance given us by the Soviet Government and people in designing new enterprises and supplying equipment essential for our construction, as well as a whole range of other items of aid, is an expression of the noblest and loftiest spirit of internationalism. As Stalin declared, "The point is not only that this assistance is the cheapest possible and technically superb. The chief point is that at the bottom of this co-operation lies a sincere desire to help one another and to promote the economic progress of all."

China's First Five-Year Plan covers the period from 1953 to 1957. The work of drawing up the draft plan had already begun in 1951, and, after being repeatedly supplemented and revised, was completed in February 1955, two years after the First Five-Year Plan had actually been put into operation. This was because our natural resources had been insufficiently studied, we had little statistical data on hand, we had to deal with many different forms of economy existing side by side, we lacked experience in drawing up long-term plans, and our experience in construction was very inadequate. Furthermore, taking the situation of our country as a whole, it was not until the end of July 1953 that an armistice was brought about in the war to resist American aggression and aid Korea which had begun in 1950. The second group of 91 projects constituting the main portion of the 156 industrial projects which the Soviet Union is helping us to build, was not finally decided upon until May 1953. All this attests to the fact that, in the past two years, the only course was to draw up a long-term plan while we were actually engaged in construction. Nevertheless, no time was lost in construction. This was because we had already completed the restoration of the national economy in 1952, and, starting from 1953, we were already able every year to draw up and execute yearly plans for the development of the national economy. In addition, as early as 1950, a decision was made and construction begun one after another on the first group of 50 projects which the Soviet Union was to help us build. China's First Five-Year Plan stands all the closer to reality and its successful completion is more assured precisely because we have done extensive preparatory work and acquired considerable experience in the course of carrying out the two yearly plans.

Now permit me to make the following explanatory remarks on our country's First Five-Year Plan for Development of the National Economy.

I. THE FUNDAMENTAL TASK OF THE STATE IN THE PERIOD OF TRANSITION

China's First Five-Year Plan for Development of the National Economy is based on the general line of the Communist Party of China in the period of transition, as put forward by the Central Committee of the Party in 1952, that is, on the basis of the fundamental task of the state in the period of transition.

The Chinese revolutionary movement led by the Chinese Communist Party falls into two stages, the new democratic revolution and the socialist revolution. The first stage of the Chinese revolution had as its task the overthrow of the rule of imperialism, feudalism and bureaucrat-capitalism in China by the broad masses of the people led by the working class, and the transformation of a semi-colonial and semi-feudal society into a new democratic society. This task has already been successfully accomplished. The founding of the People's Republic of China marked the basic completion of the first stage of the Chinese revolution and the beginning of its second stage. The task in the second stage of the Chinese revolution is to build a socialist society in China.

As Marxism-Leninism teaches, no state can build a socialist society at one stroke; there is a necessary period of transition from the time the proletariat overthrows the rule of reaction and the revolution is victorious, to the time a socialist society is attained. Lenin pointed out that after seizing state power the proletariat must use its ruling political position to carry out the economic tasks of socialism. In order to fulfil those tasks, it is essential not only to develop an industrial structure with heavy industry as its base, but also to bring forward the whole national economy, including agriculture, on to the technical basis of large-scale production and transform the many economic forms of which it is composed, into a single, socialist economy.

Proceeding from Lenin's theory concerning the transition period, the Central Committee of the Communist Party of China headed by Comrade Mao Tse-tung summed up the experience gained since the founding of the People's Republic of China and in 1952 put forward the general line of the Party for the period of transition. This general line was later adopted by the First National People's Congress in 1954 at its first session, and incorporated into our Constitution as the fundamental task of the state during the transition period.

The Preamble to the Constitution states: "From the founding of the People's Republic of China to the attainment of a socialist society is a period of transition. During the transition the fundamental task of the state is, step by step, to bring about the socialist industrialization of the country and, step by step, to accomplish the socialist transformation of agriculture, handicrafts and capitalist industry and commerce." Article 4 of the Constitution also provides: "The People's Republic of China, by relying on the organs of state and the social forces, and by means of socialist industrialization and socialist transformation, ensures the gradual abolition of systems of exploitation and the building of a socialist society."

Socialist industrialization is the keystone for building socialism in our country; the socialist transformation of agriculture and handicrafts and capitalist industry and commerce are two essential elements in this undertaking. The three are inseparable.

Large-scale industry provides the material basis for the building of a socialist society. Lenin always taught us: "The real and only basis upon which we could consolidate our resources for the creation of socialist society is large-scale industry." Without large-scale industry we shall not be able to pass on to socialism or transform agriculture and the whole national economy with modern technique.

As everyone knows, our country was a colonial, semi-colonial and semi-feudal state under the rule of imperialism; it had a backward economy. Before liberation, modern industry constituted only a very small fraction of our national economy; it consisted mainly of light industries, most of which were processing enterprises relying on imported raw materials. Our heavy industrial base was even weaker. What heavy industries there were mainly consisted of machine maintenance shops set up in China by the imperialist countries, or mines and factories which supplied the imperialist countries with raw materials and semi-processed goods. This very backward state of our national economy, occasioned by the absence of a heavy industrial base, caused our country and people for over a century to suffer weakness and poverty, and aggression and oppression by the imperialist powers. This backwardness was immeasurably worsened as a result of more than twenty years' rule of the reactionary Kuomintang clique headed by Chiang Kai-shek. All they were interested in was to pillage the people in a vicious and unrestrained way. They did not build up any industry worthy of the name. They boasted for a long time about building an iron and steel plant with an annual capacity of 100,000 tons. Years went by but even this small-scale project remained on paper though their families became astonishingly richer. Up to the eve of the War of Resistance to Japanese Aggression, the entire country, excluding the Northeast, turned out annually only about 40,000 tons of steel, and this was produced by plants erected towards the end of the Ching (Manchu) Dynasty or during the rule of the Northern Warlords. After occupying the Northeast and particularly in the period between 1939 and 1943, Japanese imperialism, aiming to plunder our resources and extend the war of aggression, expanded the iron and steel industry there. This, of course, was a purely colonial industry subordinated to the Japanese industrial system. Besides, many of these factories and mines were later seriously damaged by the reactionary Kuomintang clique. The situation was just as Chairman Mao Tse-tung stated in his book *On Coalition Government*, written in 1945: "China's industry cannot be developed unless the country is independent, free, democratic and united." Since the people took state power into their own hands after the liberation of their country, such an independent, free, democratic and united new China has emerged, and an industrialized new China is in sight. This new China was won as a result of a protracted and bloody struggle by the Chinese people led by the working class; that is why the industrialization of our country can only be socialist industrialization. Only socialist industrialization can resolve the contradiction between an advanced type of state power and a backward economy such as exists in our country, and turn an impoverished, weak China into a prosperous, mighty China.

Socialist industrialization is the central task of our country during the transition period, and the main link in socialist industrialization is to give priority to the development of heavy industry. Only by building a powerful heavy industry, that is, by establishing modern iron and steel, machine-building, power, fuel, non-ferrous metals and basic chemical industries, etc., can we produce various kinds of modern industrial equipment, and make possible the technical reconstruction of heavy industry itself as well as the light industries. Only thus can we supply agriculture with tractors and other modern farm machines and with sufficient quantities of fertilizers, and make possible the technical reconstruction of agriculture. Only thus can we provide up-to-date communication and transport facilities, such as locomotives, motor vehicles, steamships, aircraft, etc., and bring about the technical reconstruction of transport. And only so can we manufacture modern weapons to arm our fighters who defend the motherland, and consolidate our national defences. It is also only on the basis of the development of heavy industry that we will be able to achieve big advances in the technique of production and in labour productivity, that we will be able to bring about a steady increase in the output of agriculture and the consumer goods industries, and assure a constant rise in the living standards of the people.

Thus we can see that the policy of giving priority to the development of heavy industry is the only correct policy to make our country strong and prosperous and to create happiness for our people. By carrying out this policy, we will lay a strong material basis for socialism in our country.

Some people say that our international environment today is not like that of the Soviet Union after the victory of the October Revolution, and since we now have the Soviet Union and the People's Democracies to assist us, they ask, why should we be in a hurry to industrialize?

We believe such views to be wrong. At home, we are faced with a backward national economy, and abroad, with encirclement by vicious imperialism. If we did not carry out socialist industrialization, we would not be able to build a socialist society in our country, we would be in danger of being powerless in the face of imperialist aggression, of being unable to maintain our economic and political independence. To bring about the socialist industrialization of China and develop the national economy is clearly the proper duty of the Chinese people themselves. The assistance rendered us by the Soviet Union and the People's Democracies is a favourable factor in carrying out socialist industrialization in our country. Enjoying this advantage, it behooves us to work all the harder in construction and do our best to fulfil the task of socialist industrialization more rapidly.

To build socialism, we must solve the contradiction between small-peasant economy and socialist industrialization. Socialism cannot be built on the basis of a small-peasant economy; it must have a foundation of large-scale industry and large-scale collective farming. Socialist industrialization demands that the scattered and backward mode of production in agriculture be changed to a collective and advanced mode of production, that more grain and industrial crops be produced on the basis of collectivization and mechanization, and also that individual handicrafts take the path of co-operation. If they are to shake off poverty and suffering once and for all, the broad masses of peasants must give up the way of small-scale production which they followed for so long in the past, and take to the new way of collectivized and mechanized socialist agriculture. We must, therefore, bring about the socialist transformation of agriculture and handicrafts; that is, in accordance with the provisions of Articles 8 and 9 of the Constitution, encourage the individual peasants to organize producers', supply and marketing, and credit co-operatives on a voluntary basis, and encourage individual handicraftsmen and other non-agricultural individual working people to organize producers' co-operatives and supply and marketing co-operatives.

Some people take the view that since the Chinese peasants were given land in the course of the land reform and have been very enthusiastic in production, there is no reason why co-operation should be introduced. We consider this view wrong too. The reform of the feudal agrarian system was only a first step in the liberation of the peasants, because, since they were still farming small plots in a scattered manner and could not use modern farm machinery, they were not able to develop production further and protect themselves from natural calamities, nor were they able to fend off exploitation by urban and rural capitalists, not to mention, of course, major natural calamities or accidents which might happen to them. Only when agriculture and handicrafts turn gradually from individual to collective management, and on this basis equip themselves with modern technique, can the productive forces of agriculture be greatly developed, its capacity for reproduction increased and output raised to meet the demands of the nation's socialist industrialization. Only thus can the base for the development of capitalism be limited and finally eliminated, and the peasant masses and handicraftsmen finally free themselves from poverty and suffering and attain a life of abundance.

To build socialism, we must of course resolve the contradiction between capitalist and socialist economy. The capitalist system of private ownership of the means of production hinders the further development of the productive forces of our country. The anarchy of capitalist economy runs counter to the planned development of socialist economy. With the planned development of the national economy, the contradiction between capitalist and socialist economy becomes more clear-cut and acute. That is why we must carry through the socialist transformation of capitalist industry and commerce. This means, as laid down in Article 10 of the Constitution, that: "The policy of the state towards capitalist industry and commerce is to use, restrict and transform them. The state makes use of the positive sides of capitalist industry and commerce which are beneficial to national welfare and the people's livelihood, restricts their negative sides which are not beneficial to national welfare and the people's livelihood, encourages and guides their transformation into various forms of state-capitalist economy, gradually replacing capitalist ownership with ownership by the whole people; and this it does by means of control exercised by administrative organs of the state, the leadership given by the state sector of the economy, and supervision by the workers."

Some people harbour the hope that socialist and capitalist economy can go on existing side by side in the country over a protracted period, that socialist transformation of capitalist industry and commerce will not be carried out, or at least will not be carried out just at present. We also consider this way of thinking wrong. It is impossible for socialism and capitalism, whose systems of productive relations are anti-thetical, to develop alongside each other in a country without mutual interference. We can either take the path of socialism, or the path of capitalism; but the Chinese people will never allow the latter path to be taken. That we are taking the path to socialism is in accord with the natural law of historical development of our country. In the actual political and economic situation of China at the present time, it is not only necessary, but also possible, to transform capitalist industry and commerce through various forms of state-capitalism, and enable them to turn step by step into socialist enterprise. This has been proved by actual experience in the past five years.

It is clear from the foregoing that in order to build socialism, we must make a vigorous effort to bring about socialist industrialization, and simultaneously, the socialist transformation of agriculture, handicrafts and capitalist industry and commerce. But does this mean that we can complete the work of socialist industrialization and socialist transformation within the period of the First Five-Year Plan? No. According to Marxism-Leninism, the transition to socialism should be looked upon as a whole historical period. China is a big country with complex conditions; our national economy was originally very backward, with a small-peasant economy embracing over one hundred and ten million households and an enormous amount of handicraft production. Furthermore, capitalist industry and commerce occupy a fairly large proportion of the national economy. That is why the socialist industrialization and socialist transformation of our country is a Herculean task, requiring a comparatively long time. In the actual conditions of our country, it will take, not counting the three-year rehabilitation period, approximately 15 years, that is, about three five-year plans, to fulfil this fundamental task of the transition period. As Chairman Mao Tse-tung has said, we may, in the main, attain a socialist society in perhaps 15 years of intense work and arduous construction, but to build a powerful country with a high degree of socialist industrialization will require decades of effort, say, 40 or 50 years, or the whole second half of this century.

In building socialism, we must take practical steps based on existing realities in our country so as gradually to achieve socialist industrialization and socialist transformation. In industrial construction, it is necessary to proceed according to the availability of funds and technical forces and keep to the policy of concentrating our main efforts on priority projects. All thinking and action based on the assumption that every construction project must necessarily be large-scale and absolutely modern without regard to its degree of importance or urgency is harmful to the accomplishment of socialist industrialization. It usually takes about five years to build a modern heavy industrial enterprise, which calls for a whole series of laborious undertakings and well co-ordinated support from many quarters. Before we can achieve industrialization, we must build many such industrial enterprises equipped with up-to-date technique, so how can we expect to achieve success in a short time and without much effort?

Co-operation in agriculture and handicrafts is also no light task to be done in a short time. This is a major achievement which entails revolutionizing the mode of production and mode of life of hundreds of millions of peasants and tens of millions of handicraftsmen. For the labouring peasants and handicraftsmen to give up finally the way of the individual small producer and step out on to the new highroad of socialist development calls for a step-by-step process, a fairly long period of hard work and certain necessary transitional forms of organization. To bring about co-operation in agriculture and handicrafts demands not only that the economy as a whole must be placed in a position to give aid to agriculture and handicrafts, not only that the peasants and handicraftsmen should be literate and informed, but also that the peasants and handicraftsmen should personally experience the advantages of co-operation. All this needs time. Similarly, the transformation of capitalist industry and commerce should also be accomplished step by step as it passes through certain necessary transitional forms.

We have won a new China. We must redouble our efforts in economic construction to protect and consolidate this new China. This construction is, in the main, a task of socialist industrialization.

On the eve of the October Revolution Lenin said to the Russian people:

"Either it (humanity—Ed.) perishes, or it entrusts its fate to the most revolutionary class for the swiftest and most radical transition to a superior mode of production."

This is also true in China. Before the liberation Chairman Mao Tse-tung said: "Without industry, there can be no solid national defence, no people's welfare and no national prosperity and power." We cannot rely for a living solely on a backward small-peasant economy. We must repudiate the way of capitalism which drives the masses into bankruptcy. To avoid danger in their advance, the only way forward for the emancipated people of China is to work for the accomplishment of socialist industrialization, and on this basis to gradually transform the country's individual farming, individual handicrafts and capitalist industry and commerce, in line with the principles of socialism. Such are our tasks in the transition period. We will carry them out with a confidence founded on the successes we achieved during the rehabilitation period and in the initial two years of the First Five-Year Plan.

II. OUTLINE OF THE FIRST FIVE-YEAR PLAN

The general task set by China's First Five-Year Plan was determined in the light of the fundamental task of the state during the transition period.

It may be summarized as follows: We must centre our main efforts on industrial construction; this comprises 694 above-norm[1] construction projects, the core of which are the 156 projects which the Soviet Union is designing for us, and which will lay the preliminary groundwork for China's socialist industrialization; we must foster the growth of agricultural producers' co-operatives, whose system of ownership is partially collective, and handicraft producers' co-operatives, thus laying the preliminary groundwork for the socialist transformation of agriculture and handicrafts; and, in the main, we must incorporate capitalist industry and commerce into various forms of state-capitalism, laying the groundwork for the socialist transformation of private industry and commerce.

The implementation of our First Five-Year Plan is an important step in carrying out the fundamental task of the state during the transition period. The plan provides for construction on a considerable scale and a very rapid development of all branches of the national economy.

The total outlay for the country's economic construction and cultural and educational development during the five-year period will be 76,640 million yuan, or the equivalent in value of more than 700 million taels[2] of gold. Such an enormous investment in national construction would have been absolutely inconceivable in the past. This is possible only for a government led by the working class and working whole-heartedly in the interests of the people.

Investments in capital construction will amount to 42,740 million yuan, or 55.8 per cent of the total outlay for economic construction and cultural and educational development during the five-year

---

[1] To facilitate management and control of major capital construction projects, the state has, in the light of actual conditions in China, set an "investment norm" for every category of capital construction. Any construction project, whether it is new, rebuilt or restored, is classified as "above-norm" or "below-norm" according to whether its invested capital is above or below the "normal" figure. In industry, for example, the investment norm for the iron and steel, motor vehicle, tractor, shipbuilding, and locomotive and rolling stock manufacturing industries is ten million yuan. For the non-ferrous metals, chemical and cement industries it is six million yuan. For power stations, power transmission lines and sub-stations, the coal-mining, oil extracting, oil refining, machine-building (not including communications equipment) industries, motor vehicle and ship maintenance works, and textiles (including printing and dyeing) it is five million yuan. For the rubber, paper-manufacturing, sugar-refining, cigarette-making and pharmaceutical industries it is four million yuan. For the ceramics, food-processing (except for sugar-refining) and other light industries it is three million yuan.

[2] One tael = 1.1023 ounces.

period. Of the remaining 44.2 per cent, or 33,900 million yuan, part will be spent on work occasioned by the needs of capital construction, such as prospecting resources, engineering surveying and designing, stockpiling of equipment and materials, etc. Part will be spent to develop industrial production, transport, and posts and telecommunications, including such items as overhaul of equipment, technical and organizational improvements in production, trial manufacture of new products, purchase of miscellaneous fixed assets, etc.; another part will serve as circulating capital for the various economic departments; and still another part will go to funds allocated to all economic, cultural and educational departments for operating expenses and for the training of specialized personnel.

The sum of 42,740 million yuan for investments in the five-year capital construction programme is distributed as follows:

Industrial departments, 24,850 million yuan, or 58.2 per cent of the total amount to be invested;
Agriculture, water conservancy and forestry departments, 3,260 million yuan, or 7.6 per cent;
Transport, posts and telecommunications departments, 8,210 million yuan, or 19.2 per cent;
Trade, banking and stockpiling departments, 1,280 million yuan, or 3 per cent;
Cultural, educational and public health departments, 3,080 million yuan, or 7.2 per cent;
Development of urban public utilities, 1,600 million yuan, or 3.7 per cent;
Other items, 460 million yuan, or 1.1 per cent.

The foregoing percentages of distribution of capital investments show that the emphasis is on industry. They likewise show that in the distribution of investments the growing needs of departments other than industry have also been taken into account.

The proportion of state investments in agriculture is not large in our First Five-Year Plan, because agriculture cannot yet be extensively mechanized and it is not yet possible to undertake bigger projects in water conservancy and forestry on a large scale in this five-year period. Furthermore, capital investments in agriculture, water conservancy and forestry departments do not include relief funds for rural areas, agricultural loans and other items, nor do they include capital invested in production by the peasants themselves. If all these items are taken into account, the total amount of capital used to develop agriculture in the five-year period comes close to the total investment in industry.

Capital investment in transport in our First Five-Year Plan is also not large, but it can, in the main, satisfy the needs of the First Five-Year Plan period and the initial stage of the Second Five-Year Plan.

There are 694 above-norm projects, including those which the Soviet Union is helping China to build, among the new projects and reconstruction projects under our five-year programme of capital construction in industry. If we add to these the 252 projects in agriculture, water conservancy and forestry, the 220 projects in transport, posts and telecommunications, the 156 projects in culture, education and public health, the 118 projects in urban public utilities, and the 160 projects in other spheres, the total number of above-norm capital construction projects reaches 1,600. In addition to these, there are more than 6,000 below-norm construction projects, of which about 2,300 are in industry. In industry, 455 above-norm projects can be completed within the present five-year period, or a total of 1,271 if those in other spheres are included. The bulk of the below-norm projects can also be completed in this period. The completion of these projects will vastly increase the productive force of China's industry; it will assist the development of agriculture, increase transport capacity; and expand cultural and educational work.

In the sphere of industry, we list below figures showing the ultimate increases in annual production capacity of principal industrial items when all the above-norm and below-norm construction projects started in the First Five-Year Plan period are completed; and figures showing the increases in annual capacity by the end of the First Five-Year Plan period when part of them are completed:

Pig iron: ultimate increase in annual capacity, 5,750,000 tons; increase in annual capacity by the end of the five-year period, 2,800,000 tons.

Steel: ultimate increase in annual capacity, 6,100,000 tons; increase in annual capacity by the end of the five-year period, 2,530,000 tons.

Electric power: ultimate increase in annual capacity, 4,060,000 kilowatts; increase in annual capacity by the end of the five-year period, 2,050,000 kilowatts.

Coal: ultimate increase in annual capacity, 93,100,000 tons; increase in annual capacity by the end of the five-year period, 53,850,000 tons.

Metallurgical and mining machinery: ultimate increase in annual capacity, 190,000 tons; increase in annual capacity by the end of the five-year period, 70,000 tons.

Power-generating equipment: ultimate increase in annual capacity, 800,000 kilowatts. All projects will be completed within the five-year period.

Lorries: ultimate annual capacity, 90,000 vehicles; annual capacity by the end of the five-year period, 30,000 vehicles.

Tractors: ultimate annual capacity, 15,000, to be reached in 1959.

Chemical fertilizers; ultimate increase in annual capacity, 910,000 tons; increase in annual capacity by the end of the five-year period, 280,000 tons.

Cement: ultimate increase in annual capacity, 3,600,000 tons; increase in annual capacity by the end of the five-year period, 2,360,000 tons.

Cotton spindles: ultimate increase, 1,890,000 spindles; portion to be put into operation in the five-year period, 1,650,000 spindles.

Machine-made paper: ultimate increase in annual capacity, 186,000 tons; increase in annual capacity by the end of the five-year period, 95,000 tons.

Machine-processed sugar: ultimate increase in annual capacity, 560,000 tons; increase in annual capacity by the end of the five-year period, 428,000 tons.

In the sphere of transport, more than 4,000 kilometres of new trunk railways and branch lines will be built in the five-year period. If to this is added the mileage of railways to be restored, reconstructed, or double-tracked, extended station spurs, and industrial and other special lines, the total length of the railway network will be increased by some 10,000 kilometres. Upwards of 10,000 kilometres of highways will be built or rebuilt with capital provided by the Central People's Government in the five-year period and over 7,000 kilometres will be opened to traffic. Four hundred thousand tons deadweight of new steamships will be acquired in the five-year period.

In the sphere of agriculture and water conservancy, 91 mechanized state farms and 194 tractor stations (both above-norm and below-norm) will be set up in the five-year period. During this period, 13 big reservoirs will be built. In addition, dredging of waterways and repairing of dykes will involve 1,300 million cubic metres of earth and masonry work and we will begin the engineering project to harness the Yellow River.

Buildings with a total floor space of about 150 million square metres will be constructed in the five-year period, including factory buildings, housing for factory and office workers, schools and hospitals.

The industrial construction programme is the core of our First Five-Year Plan and the construction of the 156 industrial projects to be built with Soviet aid is in turn the core of the industrial construction programme. Within the period of the First Five-Year Plan, work will have begun on 145 of these 156 projects, while survey and designing work will have been carried out on the remaining 11 projects, which will go into construction in the period of the Second Five-Year Plan.

These industrial construction projects are large in scale and new in technique. Many of them are unprecedented in the history of Chinese industry. For example, in the eight-year period between 1953 and 1960, the integrated iron and steel works in Anshan, building on the basis of its original capacity, will complete, in the main, the construction or reconstruction of the following 48 major projects: 3 iron ore mines, 8 ore-dressing and sintering plants, 6 automatic blast furnaces, 3 modern steel-making plants, 16 rolling mills, 10 batteries of coke ovens, and 2 heat-resistant material shops. The latest achievements of Soviet technology will be utilized to the fullest possible extent in the building or reconstruction of these plants, mines and shops. When its reconstruction is completed, this integrated iron and steel works—the biggest of its kind in China—will increase its annual capacity to 2,500,000 tons of pig iron, 3,220,000 tons of steel and 2,480,000 tons of rolled steel. Its output of steel plates, sheets, tubes and other rolled steel of various specifications will, on the whole, be able to meet the country's requirements in the manufacture of locomotives, steamers, motor vehicles, tractors, etc. during the period of the First Five-Year Plan and the early years of the Second Five-Year Plan. Its annual output of rails of different specifications will be sufficient to lay more than 3,000 kilometres of railways.

Simultaneously with the reconstruction of the integrated iron and steel works in Anshan, construction will go ahead on two new integrated iron and steel works in Wuhan and Paotow. Fifteen thermal power stations each with a capacity of over 50,000 kilowatts are among the power plants to be built in the five-year period. After reconstruction the Fengman Hydro-electric Power Station will have a capacity of more than 560,000 kilowatts. Completion of these projects will vastly increase the supply of electric power in various regions.

Coal-mining enterprises to be built during the five-year period include 31 with a projected annual capacity (counting the original capacity) of more than one million tons of coal each. Among these, which include those designed in China, the annual capacity of the five biggest mining enterprises will reach the following levels by 1957: mines under the Fushun Mining Administration, 9,300,000 tons; mines under the Fuhsin Mining Administration, 8,450,000 tons; mines under the Kailan Mining Administration, 9,680,000 tons; mines under the Tatung Mining Administration, 6,450,000 tons; mines under the Huainan Mining Administration, 6,850,000 tons.

The First Motor Works will be completed in the present five-year period. When it reaches projected capacity, it will be able to provide transport with 30,000 lorries a year. The Second Motor Works, with double the capacity of the first, will also begin construction within the period of the First Five-Year Plan. These two plants will lay the foundation for China's motor car industry.

When the tractor plant, which will go into construction in the present five-year period, is completed in the period of the Second Five-Year Plan, China will be able to produce annually 15,000 54-h.p. tractors to meet the needs of agriculture.

When the two heavy machinery plants (one designed for us by the Soviet Union and the other by ourselves) which begin construction in the present five-year period are completed, they will be able, according to their projected capacities, to produce every year a complete set of iron smelting, steel-making, rolling mill and coke oven equipment for an integrated iron and steel works with an annual capacity of 1,600,000 tons of steel.

When all the plants making power-generating equipment to be started in the five-year period are completed, China will be able to manufacture 12,000, 25,000 and even 50,000-kilowatt power-generating units to meet the requirements of electric power development in all branches of the national economy.

Many of our light industrial plants were designed and built by ourselves, and many of these are of considerable size. The three cotton mills which have been or will be built in our capital Peking, for instance, will be equipped with 230,000 spindles and more than 7,000 looms. In all, 39 textile mills of considerable size will be built in the five-year period.

Many of these new industrial construction projects are large in scale and so are many railway, highway and water conservancy projects.

For example, the Lanchow-Sinkiang Railway which traverses Kansu and Sinkiang Provinces, the Paochi-Chengtu Railway connecting Northwest and Southwest China, the Yingtan-Amoy Railway linking Kiangsi and Fukien Provinces, and the Chining-Erhlien Railway linking China, the Mongolian People's Republic and the Soviet Union which are being built in the present five-year period, not only have a long over-all mileage, but also involve stupendous engineering feats in crossing deserts and towering mountain ranges.

The Sikang-Tibet and Chinghai-Tibet Highways, construction of which was carried on in the present five-year period, were opened to traffic in 1954, and have a total length of over 4,300 kilometres. They cut through mountain ranges rising several thousand metres above sea level where there is scarcely a trace of human habitation. The engineering work involved was particularly difficult and massive in scale.

The project for the complete harnessing of the Huai River, which has been going ahead in the present five-year period, provides for four big reservoirs at Nanwan, Poshan, Futseling and Meishan. These will be capable of storing more than 3,800 million cubic metres of water. At the same time, flood-control and measures to deal with waterlogging will be carried out on the main tributaries of the Huai—the Hungho, Juho, Suiho and Peifei Rivers. The Kuanting Reservoir completed in 1954, with a storage capacity of about 2,300 million cubic metres of water, will play an important role in preventing floods on the lower reaches of the Yungting.

The permanent control of the Yellow River and multiple-purpose development of its resources will begin in the present five-year period. The Yellow River flows for more than 4,800 kilometres through seven provinces, with a drainage area of 745,000 square kilometres. In the past, it has caused more damage than any other river in the country. According to the master plan for its multiple-purpose utilization, dozens of dams will be built on its middle and lower reaches and on its main tributaries. Huge reservoirs capable of regulating its flow and big hydro-electric power stations will be erected at the Sanmen Gorge and four other sites. The work of drawing up the master plan for the permanent control of the Yellow River and multiple-purpose development of its resources will be completed in the period of the First Five-Year Plan, and construction will begin on the river regulation and hydro-electric power installations at the Sanmen Gorge.

Three hundred and seventy-five thousand *mou*[3] of wasteland will be brought under cultivation at the Friendship State Farm built with direct Soviet assistance. This farm, equipped with large quantities of modern machinery and equipment presented by the Soviet Union, will play an important role as a model farm and pioneering venture in the mechanization of agriculture in China.

It is with direct Soviet aid that China will, in the present five-year period, begin construction for the peaceful utilization of atomic energy in the service of her national economy.

The examples listed so far are sufficient to show that we are now engaged in a great undertaking to build a happy life for the whole nation and generations yet to come. The fulfilment of the tasks of industrial and other construction laid down in our First Five-Year Plan will undoubtedly play a tremendous role in advancing China's socialist industrialization, and so remedy the economic backwardness of our country. This programme of socialist economic construction serves the long-term interests, the supreme interests, of the Chinese people as a whole.

During the period of the First Five-Year Plan, China's industrial productive force will be greatly enhanced by bringing into use the unused capacity of existing industrial enterprises as well as by putting new and reconstructed enterprises into operation. By 1957, the proportion of the output of modern industry in the total value of industrial and agricultural output will have risen from 26.7 per cent to 36 per cent.

The gross value of China's industrial output will increase by 98.3 per cent in 1957 compared with 1952, giving an average increase of 14.7 per cent a year as compared with the year before. The increase in value of modern industrial output will be 104.1 per cent, with an average annual increase of 15.3 per cent. Such a rate of industrial development is obviously fairly rapid. It has never been, nor could it be achieved in capitalist countries.

Markedly increased output of various industrial products will be achieved in the five-year period. The actual output of major items in 1952 and the planned output for 1957 compare as follows:

Steel: 1,350,000 tons to 4,120,000 tons (3.1 times).
Electricity: 7,260 million kilowatt-hours to 15,900 million kilowatt-hours (2.2 times).
Coal: 63,530,000 tons to 113 million tons (1.8 times).
Generators: 30,000 kilowatts to 227,000 kilowatts (7.7 times).
Electric motors: 640,000 kilowatts to 1,050,000 kilowatts (1.6 times).
Lorries: 4,000 (not yet produced in 1952).
Cement: 2,860,000 tons to 6,000,000 tons (2.1 times).
Machine-made paper: 370,000 tons to 650,000 tons (1.8 times).
Cotton piece-goods: 111,630,000 bolts to 163,720,000 bolts (1.5 times).
Machine-processed sugar: 249,000 tons to 686,000 tons (2.8 times).

Some people may complain: Does it befit China's position as a big country that even after completing her First Five-Year Plan, her steel production will be only around four million tons, lagging far behind the United States, Britain or even Japan?

We think that such people are looking only at one side of the question. The United States, Britain, Japan and other more industrialized countries all have nearly a century or more of industrial development behind them. We lag at least several decades and, in some cases, more than a century behind them in industrial development. It was only when the people took state power into their own hands that we were able to start planned construction.

It was only in 1907 that China built an iron and steel works at Hanyang. Steel production at that time was just a little over 8,500 tons. Even in 1933, steel production in China did not exceed 25,000 tons. Although this increased to over 400,000 tons in 1936, no less than 364,000 tons of this was

---

[3] One *mou* = one-fifteenth of a hectare or 0.1647 acre.

produced in the Northeast which was occupied by the Japanese imperialists. The year 1943 marked the peak of iron and steel production before liberation, with an output of over 1,800,000 tons of pig iron and over 900,000 tons of steel, by far the greater part of which was produced in the Japanese-occupied Northeast. Because of the destruction caused by the Chiang Kai-shek reactionary clique, pig iron production dropped to only 246,000 tons and steel to 158,000 tons in 1949, the year in which the People's Republic of China was founded. All this shows what a wretched legacy we inherited from old China.

It was not until the whole country was liberated that the Chinese Communist Party and the Chinese people assumed the difficult task of remedying China's economic and cultural backwardness. In the short space of three years, the national economy was restored and even developed somewhat, and now, industrial output is to be doubled within five years.

We have no magic formula for working miracles. How can we catch up with the industrialized capitalist countries in five years? Stalin said that "the high rate of industrial development... was not to be confused with the level of industrial development." Our rate of industrial development will be very rapid, but as regards the level of industrial development, we shall still, for a considerable period, lag behind some capitalist countries. Therefore, we must set our pace to catch up with them. We can state with absolute certainty that we do not need a hundred years to reach or surpass their industrial level. A few decades will be enough. It will take us only five years to surpass what it had taken decades to achieve under reactionary rule in China. Can such a pace of industrial development be considered slow?

The industrialization that our country is striving to achieve is socialist industrialization, modelled on Soviet experience and carried out with the direct assistance of the Soviet Union and the People's Democracies. It is not capitalist industrialization. Therefore, our industry, particularly those branches producing means of production, is capable of rapid development. As provided for in the First Five-Year Plan, investments in industries producing means of production account for 88.8 per cent of the total capital investment in industry, while investments in consumer goods industries make up 11.2 per cent. At the same time, according to the plan, the value of output of means of production will grow by 126.5 per cent within the five-year period, and that of consumer goods, 79.7 per cent. Accordingly, the proportion of the value of output of means of production to the total value of industrial output will rise from 39.7 per cent in 1952 to 45.4 per cent in 1957, and the proportion of the value of output of consumer goods will drop from 60.3 per cent in 1952 to 54.6 per cent in 1957.

Changes in the rates of growth of socialist and capitalist industrial production are also indicative of the socialist features of our industrial development. In the present five-year period, the value of output of state industry will increase by 130.1 per cent; co-operative industry will expand with great rapidity and so will joint state-private industrial enterprises which existed before the Five-Year Plan began. Within the five-year period, half of the capacity (measured in value of output) of private industrial enterprises will be incorporated into joint state-private industry. By 1957, therefore, the proportion of the value of output of the state, co-operative (including the processing plants of supply and marketing co-operatives and consumers' co-operatives but excluding handicraft producers' co-operatives) and joint state-private industries will rise to 87.8 per cent of the total value of the country's industrial output, while the proportion of the value of output of private industry will fall to 12.2 per cent. Furthermore, the major part of private industry will be engaged on government contracts for the manufacture and processing of goods and will thus be drawn into the orbit of state-capitalism.

The First Five-Year Plan sets suitable targets for increased agricultural output. In the five-year period, the total value of output of agriculture and subsidiary rural production is to increase by 23.3 per cent, an average rise of 4.3 per cent a year as compared to the year before.

According to the plan, the projected output of staple farm products for 1957 and the expected percentages of increase over 1952 are as follows:

Grain: 385,600 million catties,[4] an increase of 17.6 per cent.
Cotton: 32,700,000 *tan*,[5] an increase of 25.4 per cent.
Jute and ambary hemp: 7,300,000 *tan*, an increase of 19.7 per cent.

[4] One catty = 0.5 kilogramme or 1.1023 lb.
[5] One *tan* = 0.05 metric ton or 0.0492 long ton.

Cured tobacco: 7,800,000 *tan*, an increase of 76.6 per cent.

Sugar-cane: 26,300 million catties, an increase of 85.1 per cent.

Sugar-beet: 4,270 million catties, an increase of 346.4 per cent.

Oil-bearing crops: over 118 million *mou* will be sown, an increase of 37.8 per cent over the acreage in 1952.

One of the vital tasks of the Five-Year Plan is to overcome the excessive lag in the development of agriculture as compared with the development of industry. Under reactionary Kuomintang rule, China's agriculture not only made no headway but, on the contrary, suffered heavy damage. In 1936, grain output was 300,000 million catties. From that time on, it decreased almost every year until 1949 when it fell to only 226,000 million catties. Cotton output fell to 8,800,000 *tan*. After liberation, it took only three years for our country to reach a grain output of 327,800 million catties in 1952 and a cotton output of 26 million *tan*, thus exceeding the highest pre-liberation annual output in both crops.

The five-year plan for agriculture now provides for further increases over the 1952 base figures quoted above. In view of actual conditions in our country at the present time this growth in agriculture cannot be considered too slow, and we should strive our hardest to reach and surpass the targets set.

The agricultural producers' co-operative provides the basis for increasing agricultural output during the period of the First Five-Year Plan; it is also the only path along which the small-peasant economy can undergo socialist transformation. By 1957, about one-third of all the country's peasant households will have joined agricultural producers' co-operatives in their elementary form.

During the period of the First Five-Year Plan, transport and posts and telecommunications will be developed in proportion to keep pace with the expansion of industry and agriculture and the growing need for communications facilities. By 1957, railway freight mileage will reach 121,000 million ton-kilometres, or double the 1952 figure; railway passenger mileage will reach 32,000 million passenger-kilometres, or 59.5 per cent above the 1952 figure. Freight mileage of inland shipping will reach 15,300 million ton-kilometres, or 4.2 times that of 1952; passenger mileage of inland shipping will reach 3,400 million passenger-kilometres, a 78.7 per cent rise over 1952. Freight mileage of coastwise shipping will reach 5,750 million ton-nautical miles, or 2.9 times the 1952 figure. Passenger mileage of coastwise shipping will reach 240 million passenger-nautical miles, a rise of almost 140 per cent. Motor freight mileage will reach 3,200 million ton-kilometres, or 4.7 times as much as in 1952; motor bus passenger mileage will reach 5,700 million passenger-kilometres, or nearly treble the 1952 figure. Freight mileage of civil airlines will reach 8,050,000 ton-kilometres, or 3.3 times as much as in 1952. The total length of postal routes will reach 1.97 million kilometres, an increase of 45.2 per cent over the 1952 figure. There will be some expansion of other postal and telecommunication services.

On the basis of the growth and changes in the proportions of various branches of industry and agriculture indicated above, the total value of retail sales of commodities of all kinds will reach 49,800 million yuan in 1957, about 80 per cent more than in 1952. The breakdown figures show that the value of state retail trade will increase by 133.2 per cent while that of co-operative trade will increase by 239.5 per cent. As the process of socialist transformation develops during the five-year period, over half of the originally existing private business enterprises will be incorporated into various forms of state-capitalism and co-operative forms of small business organized by petty traders and pedlars. Taken together, the retail turnover of these two latter types of trade and of private commerce will still register a net increase during the five-year period. By 1957, state and co-operative trading operations will account for 54.9 per cent of the volume of all retail trade; various forms of state-capitalism and co-operative forms of small business, 24 per cent; and private commerce, 21.1 per cent.

There will be considerable progress in the fields of culture, education and scientific research during the five-year period. In 1957, higher educational institutions will enroll 434,000 students, a 127 per cent increase over 1952; senior middle schools will enroll 724,000 students, a 178 per cent increase over 1952; junior middle schools will enroll 3,983,000 students, a 78.6 per cent increase over 1952; primary schools will enroll 60,230,000 pupils, an 18 per cent increase over 1952. Over 70 per cent of the country's school-age children will be attending primary school in 1957.

There will be a considerable expansion of scientific research during the five-year period.

Twenty-three new research establishments will be added to the Academia Sinica alone, with 3,400 more research staff members. In the fields of publishing, broadcasting, literature and arts, the cinema, and popular cultural activities, comparatively rapid progress is also planned.

The Five-Year Plan makes appropriate provision for raising the people's material standards of living. In the five-year period, there will be an increase of 4.2 million in the number of employed; there will be a 33 per cent rise in average money-wages for factory and office workers; the funds disbursed by state enterprises and state organs for labour insurance, medical care, welfare services and cultural and educational facilities for their personnel will total over 5,000 million yuan; 46 million square metres of housing will be built by the state for factory and office workers.

Living standards of the rural population will also be gradually improved in the five years. With the expansion of agricultural output and the increased trend to commodity crop production, the purchasing power of the rural population will be nearly doubled. The state will allocate certain sums for the relief of peasants and other working people stricken by natural calamities, to tide them over difficulties in production or livelihood.

Considerable headway will be made in the field of public health during the five-year period. There will be 77 per cent more hospital beds and 74 per cent more doctors. The services of doctors of classical Chinese medicine will be more fully utilized.

It is clear that fulfilment of the First Five-Year Plan will bring about enormous changes in China's national economy. Swift development of the country's industry, particularly its heavy industry, during the five-year period, will begin to alter the face of our national economy and lay the preliminary groundwork for socialist industrialization. The rapid development of co-operative organization in agriculture and handicrafts in this period will lay a preliminary groundwork for the socialist transformation of agriculture and handicrafts. Again, in this five-year period, capitalist industry and commerce will gradually develop towards state-capitalism through such forms as incorporation into joint state-private enterprises, the placing of government contracts with private enterprise for the manufacture and processing of goods, the distribution of commodities on a commission basis by merchants acting as agents of the state, and the private retailing at fixed prices of commodities purchased from state wholesalers. A foundation will thus be laid for the socialist transformation of private industry and commerce. There is no doubt that these changes will result in the further strengthening of the people's democratic dictatorship in our country, the strengthening of our national defences and the creation of conditions for further improvement of the material and cultural well-being of the people of all nationalities.

The successful fulfilment of the First Five-Year Plan is a great undertaking. It will change the destiny of our country and enhance the well-being of our people. It can be said that the First Five-Year Plan is the first such long-term plan to make our country prosperous and strong and our people happy, a plan whose fulfilment will also increase the strength of the world camp of peace and democracy.

The completion of the First Five-Year Plan cannot mean, of course, the accomplishment of every task in every aspect of the nation's economic development. The construction of many important projects started in the First Five-Year Plan will have to be completed in the course of the Second Five-Year Plan; others will play an important role in production only in that latter period.

In the industrial field, even by the end of the First Five-Year Plan period, our machine-building industry will still not have reached a level and capacity able to satisfy the demands of technical reconstruction in every branch of the national economy. We shall still not be able to manufacture many types of heavy or precision machinery and equipment. It will also not be possible at that time to effect a radical improvement in the retarded state of certain branches of industry such as petroleum. As regards geographical distribution, although not a few new industrial enterprises will already have been built in the interior, we will still not have eradicated the irrational concentration of industrial enterprises in certain particular areas or in the coastal areas.

In agriculture, the socialist transformation of small-peasant economy will have been carried out only to the extent that about a third of the country's peasant households will have organized elementary forms of co-operatives; large-scale reconstruction of agriculture on a new technical basis will not have begun yet, and the lag of agriculture behind industry will not yet have been overcome completely. We will only have taken the first step in the socialist transformation of capitalist economy, a process which will take a long time to complete.

In the sphere of culture, the level of our science and technology will still fall short of requirements for the development of the national economy; the educational level of the broad masses of people will not yet be high; and there will still be large numbers of illiterates. It will still be impossible to completely eliminate unemployment, a legacy of old China, and to make full use of surplus labour power. The solution of all these problems requires continued effort in the periods of the Second and the Third Five-Year Plans.

III. SOME QUESTIONS ON THE FIRST FIVE-YEAR PLAN

1. Capital Construction in Industry and Transport

Now I would like to make some explanatory remarks on certain questions of capital construction in industry and transport. These concern the scale of capital construction, the ratio of investment between light and heavy industries, co-ordination between large, medium and small enterprises, geographical distribution of industry, the fixing of standards in capital construction, and the guaranteeing of the quality of engineering work.

A. The Scale of Capital Construction

In drawing up the Five-Year Plan, we repeatedly considered this question. We are of the opinion that, under present circumstances, the scale of construction already decided on is correct; it can and should be completed in the five-year period.

Some people express doubts as to whether such a scale of construction isn't too big. The reasons they advance are: China is still very backward and poor economically, the financial resources of the state are limited; our technical forces are insufficient, and we still lack a clear picture of our natural resources. So we are not up to the task of carrying out such large-scale capital construction within a period of five years. Therefore, these people feel that the scale of construction should be whittled down. They argue: "Let's not set such a stiff pace; let's cut the task down a little," or, "It's too tough on the peasants, let's ease up on the industrialization programme."

We don't hold with such opinions. Our reason, as we said before, is that if we are to raise ourselves out of our very backward economic situation, we have no alternative but to speed up industrial construction. In fact, we are engaged in industrial development precisely because this will make it possible for the peasants to shake off their poverty. All industrial projects laid down in the Five-Year Plan are essential. Reducing them would slow down our entire socialist construction plan and throw the state's construction programme out of gear.

Can the financial resources of our country meet the needs of construction on such a scale? Our answer is "yes." It is possible because our revolution has provided us with the following sources of accumulation of funds:

(1) The Chinese people have overthrown the rule of the imperialists in China, and it is already impossible for the imperialists to plunder vast amounts of our people's wealth as they did in the past. This has provided an important source of accumulation for our national construction.

(2) The Chinese people have overthrown feudalism and converted the system of landlord ownership of land into peasant ownership. The peasants no longer pay high rents to landlords. They use the fruits of their labour to improve their own livelihood, and can also use part of their gains to help national construction.

(3) The Chinese people have overthrown bureaucrat-capitalism and turned the property of bureaucrat-capitalists into the property of the whole people. Now the workers no longer produce for the profit of bureaucrat-capitalists but for the needs of the state and the people. This is another important source of accumulation for national construction.

(4) Although workers in private factories still have to give up part of the fruits of their labour in the form of profit for the capitalist owners, these capitalists can now get only what is laid down by law as their proper share of the profits. A considerable share of the profits of capitalist enterprises is either paid out as income taxes and reinvested in national construction, or is placed in reserve

funds to expand production in those enterprises. Under the conditions of our people's democratic dictatorship, this also benefits the state and the people.

All this shows that it has never been a question of China's lacking funds for construction, but rather that large sums used to flow into the pockets of the imperialists, landlords and capitalists. It is only since the victory of the people's revolution that the people of our land are able to use the funds earned by their labour for national construction, to build a happy future for themselves and posterity. It behooves us to make wise and timely use of these funds.

It is true that we have insufficient technical forces and that we do not have a clear knowledge of many of our natural resources. But can we not build and learn at the same time, with the help of the Soviet Union and the People's Democracies? Can we not in the course of construction gradually master the necessary skills and obtain a clear knowledge of our resources? In his *Strategic Problems of China's Revolutionary War* Chairman Mao Tse-tung wrote: "Reading books is learning, but application is also learning and the more important form of learning. ... As a revolutionary war is the concern of the masses of the people, it is often undertaken without previous mastery but is learnt through undertaking it—undertaking is itself learning." Chairman Mao was talking about revolutionary war, but to work for any cause of the people successfully one must learn in the course of actual work. This is a universal truth. Facts in the past few years prove that we have learnt many things in the midst of actual construction work and have become better acquainted with the situation as regards our natural resources. Obviously, marking time will not add to our skill and knowledge. We cannot accept the proposition that everything we do we must "undertake with previous knowledge" and that we should therefore reduce the scale of construction in the five-year period to lighten the responsibility which we should and can undertake. We cannot adopt such views.

The question then arises: can the scale of capital construction be enlarged?

In terms of demand, neither the capital construction programmes nor the production targets laid down in the draft Five-Year Plan for either heavy or light industry, whether it is the iron and steel, non-ferrous metals, chemical fertilizers, oil, machine-building or textile industries—none of these programmes and targets can satisfy the needs of the state. But whether or not the scale of construction can be expanded depends not only on the need but also on the possibility of achievement. We are Marxist-Leninists, not Utopians.

We hold that the scale of construction laid down in the Five-Year Plan is appropriate and should not be reduced, because a consideration of objective conditions existing in this country shows that it is possible to carry it out.

We hold, furthermore, that it is possible in the annual plans to expand in a suitable way certain essential units of construction such as in coal mining, oil production and railways, and we are prepared to do so. This is especially true with regard to our oil industry. In view of its low ouput which falls far short of our needs, we must make efforts to discover more oil resources and study means of developing synthetic oil production so as to expand the scale of construction in the oil industry.

But does this mean that we can expand construction projects arbitrarily and without limit, ignoring various objective conditions such as finance, technical forces and the supply of equipment?

Of course, we cannot proceed in such fashion. In regard to finance, our state expenditure for economic construction, cultural and educational development in the five-year period already amounts to 76,640 million yuan. As regards technical forces, all the huge and complex new enterprises called for by the Five-Year Plan are designed with the aid of the Soviet Union; our engineers and technicians are still unable to design such new enterprises independently. Regarding the supply of equipment, it is difficult for us to make great increases in this respect under present circumstances when China's machine-building industry cannot yet manufacture certain important items of equipment and complex machine parts. Because of these conditions, there are still certain limits to further expansion of construction in the five-year period. It is wrong to suppose that we can ignore objective conditions and expand the scale of construction without limit, or that we can neglect the most rational and most effective use of materials, manpower and financial resources and start things going haphazardly everywhere.

Oppose Right conservatism and oppose "Left" adventurism too—this is our conclusion regarding the question of the scale of capital construction.

TEXT OF DOCUMENT 1

B. The Ratio of Investment between Light and Heavy Industries

China's First Five-Year Plan allocates an especially large proportion of investment to heavy industry: It is even larger than the proportion of investment allocated to heavy industry in the First Five-Year Plan of the Soviet Union. It has been mentioned above that investment in industries manufacturing means of production accounts for 88.8 per cent of the total investment in industrial capital construction in the five-year period, while investment in the consumer goods industries accounts for 11.2 per cent. By the time the First Five-Year Plan of the Soviet Union was completed, however, investment in industries manufacturing means of production accounted for 85.9 per cent, and consumer goods industries 14.1 per cent of the total investment in industrial capital construction. Is it proper that our heavy industry should take up such a large, and light industry such a relatively small proportion of investments? Can we reduce the investment in heavy industry and increase that in light industry?

It is generally recognized that the ratio of investment between light and heavy industries must be determined on the principle that expansion of the means of production must have priority. The ratio in each period of development must, moreover, be fixed according to the actual situation in that period. At the present time the original foundations of heavy industry are extremely weak in our country; this calls for sustained effort to expand those foundations and promote the all-round development of the national economy. At the same time, there is still considerable unused capacity in both state and private light industrial enterprises and there are wide possibilities in handicraft production which can be called upon to serve as an important auxiliary to light industry. Because of lack of raw materials, on the one hand, light industry in our country cannot fully meet the daily growing demands of the people for many products and on the other hand, much light industrial equipment still does not operate to full capacity. The question of developing light industry in our country today is not, therefore, mainly a question of increasing investment but rather of increasing the supply of raw materials. Increased investments in light industry cannot be fruitful until there is a great increase in the production of certain raw materials for light industry, because without raw materials, factories cannot go into production even if they are built. However, if agriculture yields a rich harvest and the output of raw materials for light industry is greatly increased, and in the event of existing equipment being inadequate, we can consider an expansion in the yearly plans for building more light industrial plants. The progress of construction will not be delayed, because the building of light industrial plants is comparatively easy and they can be built in a comparatively short time.

For these reasons we consider that the First Five-Year Plan has set the proper ratio of investment between light and heavy industries.

C. Co-ordination between Large, Medium and Small Enterprises

If we stress concentration of efforts on the building of large priority projects, does it mean that we can pay less attention to or even ignore the construction of medium and small factories and mines?

Of course, there is no doubt that the big enterprises designed with the aid of the Soviet Union and supplied with Soviet equipment, such as integrated iron and steel works, motor vehicle, tractor and heavy machinery plants, etc., are indispensable to our country's industrialization. There can be no industrialization for our country without a number of such giant enterprises which form a sort of backbone for industry. However, this does not mean that we need only big enterprises, and can do without the medium and small ones. On the contrary, since medium and small enterprises can be built and put into operation in a comparatively short time, bringing quick returns on investment and adding to our productive capacity, they not only play an important role in increasing supplies of industrial products and supporting agricultural production but also constitute an indispensable factor in increasing accumulation of funds and in supporting and assisting construction of the big priority projects. This is why we should correct two mistaken tendencies. One is to fail to see the whole picture and to go ahead blindly with construction everywhere without regard to degree of importance or urgency, thereby interfering with the construction of priority projects. The other mistaken tendency is to devote all our attention to the construction of big enterprises at the expense of medium and small ones and concentrate an excessive proportion of state funds on construction of a few big enterprises, thereby making it impossible for investments to realize quick returns.

Our task is to arrive at a proper distribution of investments among big, medium and small enterprises in the course of industrial construction, and to effect co-ordination and mutual support in the construction of these various types of enterprises, so as to guarantee not only construction of the necessary priority projects but also quick returns from investments in many enterprises.

D. The Geographical Distribution of Industry

The old geographical distribution of our industry is highly irrational. According to 1952 statistics, industries producing more than 70 per cent of the total value of the country's industrial production were located in the coastal provinces. One of the important tasks of planned development of our national economy is gradually to correct this irrational distribution—a heritage of the old China—by adequately distributing our industrial productive forces over various parts of the country, locating industries in proximity to sources of raw materials and fuel and areas of consumption, distributing industries in accordance with the need to strengthen national defence, and developing step by step the economy of backward areas.

The five-year programme of capital construction provides for a more rational distribution of industrial areas. On the one hand, we must ensure a rational utilization of the industrial foundation already established in the Northeast and in Shanghai and other cities, by making full use of it. We must, in particular, carry out the necessary reconstruction of the industrial base in the Northeast centred on the integrated iron and steel works in Anshan so that it can quickly expand production to meet the requirements of the national economy and help create new industrial areas. On the other hand, we must make vigorous efforts to build up new industrial bases in North, Northwest and Central China, and make a start with a part of our industrial construction in Southwest China. In accordance with this policy, 472 of the 694 above-norm industrial enterprises to be built during the five-year period will be located in the interior and 222 in the coastal areas.

Railway-building in the five-year period has been planned so as to link up the old industrial bases with new ones, to meet the requirements of industrial construction and the development of the whole national economy. Following this principle of dispersal of industries, our task in municipal construction at present is not to develop big coastal cities but medium and small cities in the interior, at the same time duly restricting the development of big cities. The defect of headlong development in coastal cities should be corrected.

It is clear that the geographical distribution of capital construction for industries and railways mapped out in the draft Five-Year Plan conforms to the long-term interests of our country. As outlined by this programme, by the time the Second Five-Year Plan is fulfilled, our country will not only have strengthened its industrial base in the Northeast, but will have a number of new industrial bases in North, Northwest and Central China. This will considerably transform the economic life of a vast area of our country. As the geographical distribution of industry is based on the growth of heavy industry, it will eventually transform the whole nature of the original distribution of industry.

E. Fixing Standards in Capital Construction

In the construction or reconstruction of both enterprises and cities, we should draw a distinction between construction standards set for productive projects and those for non-productive projects. In the past few years, we neglected this distinction and as a result made mistakes by following incorrect principles in the building of many non-productive projects. The standards of many of these non-productive establishments are very much out of keeping with the present-day level of economic development in our country and the living standards of the people. In many places huge edifices have been erected that are quite inappropriate. Many enterprises have spent far too much money on auxiliary buildings, factory offices, living quarters, canteens, etc., which should have been put up economically. There have been some new factories and mines which, even before they went into production, were completely equipped with all such amenities as auditoriums and clubs and, what's more, the standards of these buildings are far too high. The standard of municipal construction in many new industrial areas is also too high: too much attention has been paid to premature modernization and civic "beautification." All this has resulted in waste of funds, manpower and material resources, violating the principle of priority in construction.

We are correcting these mistakes in accordance with the instructions of the Central Committee of the Communist Party of China and the National Conference of the Communist Party of China. In drawing a distinction between various standards of construction we should observe the following rules: many above-norm factories and mines, especially those with a high priority, should try their best to use the most up-to-date technique, and their factory buildings should, as far as possible, be adapted to the use of the most up-to-date equipment. As for non-productive projects, their standards of construction should be greatly lowered, and so should standards of city planning. By drawing this distinction between these two standards, we will be able to save unnecessary expenditure and devote the money saved to the building of more productive projects so as to speed up national construction. This is a momentous decision involving the long-term interests of national construction. Organs of the state, both central and local, and all enterprises should observe this decision: no violations of it should be permitted. I will say more on this question later on when I deal with the need to economize.

F. Guaranteeing the Quality of Engineering Work

So far, in speaking on capital construction in industry and transport, I have been dealing with questions of principle. But it is obviously not enough to have just correct principles. Given correct principles, the important thing is to do the work well. It is common knowledge that our present technical level is still very low. Furthermore, in order to save time, surveying, designing and building work on some of our construction projects have to be carried out concurrently; and much machinery and equipment has to be produced on an experimental basis in the course of construction. This accounts in certain cases for many serious shortcomings such as inferior quality, low rate of progress and much waste. Now the task confronting us is to overcome these defects, and the most important thing is to guarantee the quality of engineering work. We must realize that in the long run the quality of construction in new factories, mines and railways is of crucial importance. The Paochi-Tienshui Railway which was built during Kuomintang rule is of an extremely low engineering standard, and it can't be left in its present condition where it is unusable for days at a stretch; it must be rebuilt. In the past few years, we have restored many factories, mines and railways, but we must realize that to restore old factories, mines and railways is one thing; to build new ones is another. We should not think the latter as simple as the former. This is why in the future we should improve our work in the following respects in order to guarantee the quality of our engineering work:

(1) We must improve our designing; see to it that designers work according to correct principles and have a conscientious attitude towards their work; and that they avoid errors in designing.

(2) We must give more and better technical guidance to construction; build in strict accordance with design specifications; and, at the same time, actively spread the best experience of workers, engineers, technicians and administrative personnel and encourage rationalization proposals.

(3) The work of all concerned must be closely co-ordinated so that all equipment and material required in capital construction is up to the standard specified in designs and delivered in time.

(4) State organs and departments responsible for capital construction must make systematic and careful examinations of the quality of engineering work.

2. Industrial Production

The First Five-Year Plan of our country provides that the total value of industrial output will increase by 98.3 per cent, averaging a progressive increase of 14.7 per cent a year. Compared with the period of rehabilitation, this is a rather slow pace, but considering all the conditions of the First Five-Year Plan, it is rapid and forward-looking.

Conditions in the period of construction are different from those in the period of rehabilitation. It is quite natural that the rate of increase of industrial production during the period of construction should be slower than that during the period of rehabilitation, because it is easier to restore production in old enterprises than to build new enterprises and it is more difficult to utilize new techniques; furthermore, the base figures on which annual increases are computed rise from year to year as industrial output increases. Yet despite this, taking account of the productive potential of our present industrial equipment, we can achieve a still higher rate of increase of industrial production within the five-year period. If we work hard to find ways of overcoming difficulties, we shall not merely fulfil our plan but may even overfulfil it.

Fulfilment of the industrial production plan in the five-year period mainly depends on our old enterprises. A rough estimate of the total value of industrial output of the country shows that about 70 per cent of the rise in value of output from 1952 to 1957 will come from old enterprises, while about 30 per cent will come from newly built enterprises and those which underwent major reconstruction. In addition to supplying newly built enterprises with equipment and materials and the people with articles of daily use, the old enterprises also shoulder the important tasks of accumulating funds and training personnel. Therefore, we must work hard to start production in newly built and reconstructed enterprises at the earliest moment while guaranteeing the quality of engineering work. At the same time we must also pay attention to production in existing enterprises, and fully utilize their latent capacity in our efforts to overfulfil production plans.

In some departments and places, new factories and mines are built without much attention being given to utilization of old ones, and without finding ways and means of utilizing their unused capacity. This state of affairs is clearly wrong and should be corrected.

Local industry and handicrafts in our country play an important part in supplying the needs of production and of everyday life of the urban and rural population. During the past few years, because of defects in planning and other reasons, some branches of local industry made the mistake of expanding production blindly, thus adding difficulties to the organization of industrial production in the country as a whole. But in general it is right to actively promote local industries. In the future, too, in accordance with the requirements of the state plan and the policy of serving the needs of agricultural production, we should continue to make proper use of local industries and handicrafts. Some areas and certain departments underestimate the role of local industry and handicrafts in the national economy and therefore do not guide and help them actively or systematically. This is obviously wrong, and must be corrected.

The following three points are of decisive importance in fulfilling and overfulfilling industrial production targets set by the Five-Year Plan: increasing output and economizing in the use of industrial raw materials; trial manufacture of new types of products; improving management. I will now deal with these three points:

A. Increasing Output and Economizing in the Use of Industrial Raw Materials

One of the difficulties met in increasing the output of industrial goods during the five-year period is lack of industrial raw materials. I mentioned this before when I spoke on the question of the proportion of investment in light and heavy industries. This means first of all insufficient supplies of industrial crops. That is, for the time being, the increase in the production of raw materials such as cotton, jute, hemp, oil-bearing crops, tobacco, sugar-cane, etc., lags behind the demands of growing industrial production. Secondly, it means insufficient supplies of raw materials from heavy industry. The production of some of these raw materials is low, while others cannot at present be produced domestically. Of course, some raw materials could be imported, but because the increase in the output of home products is still insufficient or domestic consumption is too large, exports of home products are not as large as they should be; this reduces our foreign exchange income and therefore limits imports of industrial raw materials.

To overcome this difficulty we must increase production of such industrial crops as cotton, jute, ambary hemp, tobacco, sugar-cane, sugar-beet, peanuts, sesame seed, and rape-seed. We must fulfil and overfulfil the targets set in the Five-Year Plan for expansion of the sown areas of the above-mentioned industrial crops. At the same time, the yields of these industrial crops per unit area must be raised as high as possible. Take cotton, for example. It is possible within the five-year period to expand the sown area by more than 11 million *mou*. Because the main cotton areas are mostly in the old liberated areas, provided special attention is given to organizing agricultural producers' co-operatives in these areas, and as much state aid as possible is given to the cotton-growers, the per unit area yield in these regions can be raised still more. It is also possible to expand the sown area of tobacco and sugar-cane by more than one million *mou* each in the five-year period. While we must do everything possible to expand the areas sown to grain, we must at the same time increase the areas sown to certain industrial crops provided this does not affect the increase of grain production.

If we plant an additional 500,000 *mou* of tobacco, we can increase the output of cigarettes by 500,000 crates; if we plant an additional 400,000 *mou* of sugar-cane, we can increase the output of sugar by 100,000 tons. In the case of oil-bearing crops, it is not only possible to fulfil but also to overfulfil the plan of expanding the sown area by more than 32 million *mou* in the five-year period if the masses of peasants make full use of idle land to plant such crops.

We must increase the output of home products for export to obtain foreign exchange and to increase imports of necessary raw materials for industrial production. Provided local organs of the state and peasants throughout the country give special attention to this, we can definitely increase the output of home products for export.

Besides making vigorous efforts to increase the output of industrial raw materials, we must husband our supplies carefully and put an end to waste. If we can save an average of two catties of cotton in manufacturing each bale of cotton yarn, this alone will enable us to increase the output of cotton yarn by at least 20,000 bales annually. The latest data show that in the first quarter of 1955, the average amount of cotton used in producing a bale of cotton yarn in Shanghai's state and private textile mills was reduced to 386.1 catties, which is 7 catties below the specified standards set for the whole country in the first half of 1955. In achieving this result the average amount of cotton used for each bale of cotton yarn in state cotton mills was 384.98 catties; in joint state-private cotton mills, it was 386.65 catties; and in private cotton mills, 387.42 catties. These advanced methods of economizing cotton should be widely publicized.

To take another example, if a catty more oil can be extracted from every 100 catties of oil-bearing crops, the national production of edible oil can be raised by at least 100 million catties and more a year. The "soya bean oil extraction method" invented by Li Chuan-chiang in Szeping, Kirin Province raised the oil-extraction rate for every hundred catties of soya bean in 1954 to nearly 13.5 catties, about 2 catties over the average national extraction rate. In April 1955, the oil-extraction rate for every 100 catties of soya bean in the oil-extraction shop where Li Chuan-chiang works rose to over 14 catties. This advanced method of processing should be seriously studied and spread throughout the country.

In the case of all those industrial products which suffer from a shortage of raw materials, we should institute an energetic search for substitute materials and enlarge sources of raw materials so as to increase production.

There are considerable possibilities for raising the output of many products such as coal, phosphate fertilizer, salt, etc. We can definitely increase their output provided we organize production properly and make the necessary investments.

B. Trial Manufacture of New Types of Products

Another difficulty in increasing the output of industrial products in the five-year period is that certain enterprises, because of their low technical level, produce goods which do not suit current needs, while goods demanded by the market cannot yet be produced.

It is natural that in the course of our industrial progress certain urgently needed things cannot be produced for the time being. Improvements are being made in departments of the machine-building industry to remedy this state of affairs. But shortage of new products is not confined to departments of the machine-building industry. We should examine whether responsible departments at all levels have made reasonable efforts in the trial manufacture of new products, whether all those concerned throughout the country, and primarily the industrial departments, have considered this work as a common task and properly concerted their efforts. We do not think that we have tackled this task with sufficient energy. We must concentrate all available forces on the design and trial manufacture of new products, and give enthusiastic support to this work. In the case of some industrial products needed on the market such as certain metal products, machinery, chemicals and medical apparatus, we not only have the raw materials, but also the manufacturing ability; and it is only because we have not organized their production that these goods are not yet produced. Administrative departments guiding industrial enterprises should, therefore, always keep themselves informed of the needs of national construction and of the market, and produce goods to meet those needs.

It must be understood that the importance of trial manufacture of new products is not limited to raising present industrial output, but, what is more important, is a necessary means of raising the level of industrial technique in our country; and this in turn is a basic condition for fulfilling the task of socialist industrialization.

The economic departments of the state should set up agencies to guide research and trial manufacture of new products. These agencies should systematically study and collate data on the domestic and foreign manufacture of new products both of means of production and of consumer goods, improve planning, design, experiment and manufacture of new products, regularly sum up experience gained in the trial manufacture of new products, and examine plans for the trial manufacture of new products in order to ensure their fulfilment. The state should work out a system of awards to encourage manufacture of new products by state and private enterprises and handicraftsmen. It should reward inventions and innovations by scientists, technical personnel and the mass of workers, and encourage state and private enterprises to make good use of their inventions and innovations and organize trial manufacture of new products. It is the responsibility of government workers to watch for the emergence of new things and zealously nourish their growth. Those who attach no importance to new things or who do not respond to new things should be criticized.

A key method of increasing the range of new products and raising output is to strengthen co-ordinating and co-operative links within enterprises, between enterprises, and between various industrial departments. Industrial production is inter-linked and requires co-ordination. Only when there is co-operation and co-ordination can there be production and increased output. The scattered and unco-ordinated character of the old industrial equipment left to us makes it especially necessary for us to work together on an even broader scale, so that each enterprise can specialize, but at the same time co-ordinate its activities closely with production in other enterprises. We must give up thinking and acting on the assumption that an enterprise or industrial department can produce in isolation, without regard to others. Not only should the different parts of a single enterprise or enterprises of one industrial department co-operate among themselves, but various departments should co-operate in production. In order to make this co-operation effective, every workshop or section, every enterprise and every department should look at things from an over-all, not an isolated point of view.

All major items of work which call for close co-operation between enterprises or departments should be incorporated in the production plans of the state and the departments concerned; at the same time, the system of making contracts between enterprises and between the workshops of an enterprise should be introduced on a broad scale so that industrial departments and enterprises can effectively co-ordinate and dovetail their operations to improve the organization of industry.

C. Improving Management in Enterprises

During the past few years, considerable improvements have been made in the management of enterprises, and as a result, production plans were overfulfilled every year throughout the country. Not a few enterprises, however, failed to fulfil their plans; some failed to reach the targets for value of output; others reached the targets for value of output only, but not for types and quality of products; some reached the targets for types and quality of products, but not those for raising labour productivity and lowering production costs. Not a few enterprises showed a tendency in carrying out plans to work in spurts, alternating between slackness and rush work or starting at a leisurely pace and ending with a headlong rush. This uneven tempo of production is a source of confusion. Not a few enterprises still suffer losses from recurring accidents which cause injury or death, or damage to equipment. Because of shortcomings and low standards of management some industrial enterprises produce only restricted ranges of goods, of low quality and at high production costs. Therefore, in accordance with the provisions of Article 6, Section II, Chapter Three, of the draft Five-Year Plan on necessary measures for the realization of the plan of industrial production, all industrial enterprises must continually improve their management, take steps especially to improve technical management and business accounting, and strengthen political education among workers and staff, integrating political with economic work, raising the political awareness of the broad masses of workers and staff, bringing their initiative and creativeness into full play, and raising labour productivity.

We must recognize that we shall meet with certain difficulties in fulfilling our plans of industrial production; any complacent, over-optimistic attitude in regard to fulfilling industrial production plans is out of place. However, provided the working people throughout the country pull together to increase industrial output and raise the quality of industrial products, the fulfilment and overfulfilment of plans for the increase of industrial output by 98.3 per cent within five years is quite possible. Hence, there are no grounds for fear of difficulties and lack of confidence.

3. Increasing Agricultural Output

Agriculture supplies food for the whole nation. In addition, manufactured goods which use farm produce as raw material at present account for over half the total value of the country's industrial output. Furthermore, most of the foreign exchange needed for imports of equipment for industry and material for construction is obtained by exporting farm produce. The growth of agriculture is therefore a basic condition for ensuring the growth of industry and fulfilment of the whole economic plan.

We are now concentrating efforts on developing industry, but there must be no underestimation of the importance of developing agriculture. We cannot industrialize our country without an adequate development of agriculture. It is vital and urgent that we prevent or overcome any dislocation in the development of agriculture and industry during the course of socialist construction.

Under the First Five-Year Plan, the total value of output of agriculture and its subsidiary production will rise to 59,660 million yuan by 1957, an increase of 23.3 per cent in the five-year period. There will be 17.6 per cent more grain, making a total output of 385,600 million catties in 1957, an increase of 57,800 million catties. There will be 25.4 per cent more cotton, making a total output of 32,700,000 *tan* by 1957, an increase of over 6,600,000 *tan*.

These targets, though lower than those originally envisaged, are still very high considering the fact that they are based on the output of 1952, a year of record harvests. Furthermore, because the 1953 and 1954 plans for increasing agricultural output were not fulfilled in consequence of natural calamities, the targets set for increased production in the last three years of the Five-Year Plan period had to be raised. Intensive efforts will be needed to fulfil these targets.

Now I want to deal with three questions: co-operation in agriculture; measures for increasing agricultural output; and guidance in agricultural production.

First, the question of co-operation in agriculture.

During the period of the First Five-Year Plan, organizing agricultural producers' co-operatives must be actively and systematically carried out on a voluntary and mutually-beneficial basis, by relying on the poor peasants (including all new middle peasants who were formerly poor peasants) and firmly uniting with the middle peasants. The agricultural producers' co-operative is characterized by the pooling of land and unified management. That is to say, it is a type of agricultural producers' co-operative in which ownership of the means of production is only partially collective; it is semi-socialist in nature. However, this elementary form of co-operation, which turns scattered, small-peasant farm management into joint management uniting dozens of households, makes it possible to organize labour power and utilize land in a more rational way and also to accumulate funds for increased investment in farming, using improved tools, building irrigation works, improving farming technique and taking other measures for increasing production which are difficult for individual peasants. The considerable amount of information gathered from various parts of the country shows that an agricultural producers' co-operative can, if run successfully, raise output from 10 to 20 per cent during its first or second year. It is also able to increase output consistently year by year at an annual rate higher than that of the mutual-aid team and much higher than that of individual peasants. Under present conditions, the agricultural producers' co-operative is a means of increasing agricultural output that involves small investment and speedily yields good results. It is also a necessary step leading the peasants to socialism. The path to the uninterrupted growth of agricultural production in China lies through a gradual advance from this elementary form of co-operation with its initial technical improvements to a higher form of co-operation with mechanization of agriculture and other technical reforms.

Taking account of the experience gained in the movement for agricultural mutual aid and co-operation in the past few years and the successes already achieved in this field in various parts of the country, the First Five-Year Plan states that a third of all the peasant households in the country will have joined the present elementary form of agricultural producers' co-operatives within the period covered by the plan. In Northeast China and the provinces of Shansi, Hopei, Shantung and Honan and other older liberated areas, about half of all peasant households will have joined co-operative organizations. We should work for a more rapid pace of co-operation in areas growing industrial crops and on the outskirts of cities. This plan for co-operative farming is practicable. We must work hard to fulfil it. The state will give all possible financial and material support to the growth of agricultural producers' co-operatives.

Our movement for agricultural co-operation has achieved great success. Over 90 per cent of our agricultural producers' co-operatives organized in previous years are on a firm footing; most of them have markedly increased their output. There are also, however, a small number of agricultural producers' co-operatives in some places in which elements of coercion and commandism and other shortcomings exist because the work of organization was rather hurriedly and roughly done. Unless these shortcomings are rectified, not only will it be impossible to increase production, but a fall in output will likely result.

In regard to the agricultural producers' co-operative, we must therefore consistently follow the policy of giving active leadership to the peasants, maintaining a steady advance, and working hard to consolidate existing co-operatives while organizing new ones. We must hold firmly to the principle of voluntariness and mutual benefit on the part of the masses, prevent and correct cases of coercion and commandism and any actions which go against the interests of the middle peasants; we must satisfactorily solve the various problems which arise within the co-operative such as calculation of labour contributed, remuneration for land and other pooled means of production, finding funds for production and the determination of the ratio of reserve funds in relation to other items.

While we work to set up new agricultural producers' co-operatives, we must continue to set up and improve various forms of agricultural mutual-aid organizations in order to create conditions for the further development of agricultural producers' co-operatives. The enthusiasm which individual peasant households show for increasing production must be taken into consideration and vigorous assistance and leadership should be given to them to develop all their resources to the full and raise per unit area yields.

Secondly, since Chapter Four of the draft Five-Year Plan sets out measures for increasing agricultural output in great detail, I will speak only on the following points:

(1) Reclamation of arable wasteland.

Since our population is large while the area under cultivation is still limited, we must take energetic measures to open up arable land in a planned way so that we can finally solve the problem of shortages in agricultural produce. The expansion of China's cultivated area by over 38,680,000 *mou* as laid down in the Five-Year Plan is a minimum target, and every effort must be made and every means used to surpass it. One method is for state farms to reclaim land. Where local conditions permit, all state farms should expand their cultivated area by a reasonable amount. At the same time, wherever there are large tracts of reclaimable wasteland, efforts should be made to reclaim them and systematically build up new state farms. Another method is to use machines and other means to reclaim wasteland and to organize cultivation by pioneering emigrants. As this work is complex and has to be done on a considerable scale, the state, together with local authorities, should draw up a unified, practical scheme and give leadership to the work. Still another method is for the peasants themselves to open up wasteland locally. Since this is comparatively easy and small-scale work, it can be done under the leadership of local authorities.

Use should be made of all these methods of land reclamation in the next three years as an important means of increasing farm production.

A considerable part of the funds saved by the state by reducing expenditure on non-productive construction and appropriations to administrative organizations will be used in reclaiming wasteland.

An energetic investigation and survey of reclaimable wasteland will be conducted during the period of the First Five-Year Plan; we should complete the surveying of over 100 million *mou* of wasteland and have over-all plans ready for the opening up of from 40 million to 50 million *mou* of wasteland in preparation for the large-scale land reclamation work envisaged in the Second Five-Year Plan.

(2) Water conservancy works.

Water conservancy works can extend the irrigated area to increase agricultural output as well as preserve crops from the ravages of flood or drought. Increased agricultural output and other benefits brought about by the elimination or reduction of natural calamities through water conservancy works in many cases pay back within a few years the funds invested. Since the founding of the People's Republic of China, we have spared no efforts in building water conservancy works. Newly built large-scale works have played a tremendous role in fighting floods and drought in recent years, particularly in the battle against the heavy floods of 1954. During the First Five-Year Plan, we should, in addition to big projects financed by state investments, build many small irrigation works, benefiting from a few dozen *mou* to several hundred *mou* according to actual local needs and possibilities. Since these works are scattered and can be built with comparative ease, agricultural producers' co-operatives and individual peasants can be organized to build them. The state will give financial and material assistance where necessary.

(3) Full and effective use of land.

Because of the large size of our population, it is necessary and possible to make full use of our land. To extend land utilization, we should, in addition to reclaiming wasteland and enlarging the irrigated area, undertake soil improvement by changing alkaline or sandy soil into fertile fields, terracing land on slopes and turning arid land into irrigated fields. The number of times the land is cropped a year should be suitably increased where climate, rainfall, topography and other natural conditions and the supply of fertilizer, water conservancy, availability of man power, animal traction and other economic conditions permit. In upland areas a unified plan should be made wherever possible to co-ordinate the development of agriculture, animal husbandry, forestry and subsidiary rural occupations, and promote a diversified economy; at the same time, work on soil and water conservation should be intensified. The peasants should be encouraged to cultivate their land still more intensively, to put in more fertilizer and step by step adopt more advanced farming techniques suited to local conditions, such as enlarging the area under crops resistant to water-rot in low-lying areas, and enlarging the area under early-ripening crops and spring crops in areas where waterlogging from autumnal rains frequently occurs. Some provinces have already acquired initial experience in such activities, and this should be summed up and gradually spread to other areas in accordance with local conditions. Any other successful experience of the mass of the local peasants in raising output should also be publicized energetically and adopted on a widening scale.

Energetic and systematic measures should be taken to extend the area under industrial crops on slopes and uplands in suitable areas. Everything should be done to avoid enlarging the area under industrial crops at the expense of grain crops.

(4) Enlarging the acreage of rice, maize, potatoes, and other high-yield crops.

The yield of rice per unit area is nearly treble that of wheat; the yield of maize is estimated at 50 per cent above other coarse grains; while potato crops such as sweet potatoes and potatoes give yields per unit area which are five or six times more than coarse grains in general. (As food, two and a half catties of potatoes are equivalent to one catty of grain.) Without doubt, expansion of the area sown to these high-yield crops will certainly be a great help in reducing difficulties in the supply of food and fodder. If in coarse grain areas or other suitable areas we put another 10 million or 20 million *mou* of farmland under potato crops instead of grain, this will make it possible to raise the annual output of potato crops by 10,000 million to 20,000 million catties, though it will cut the annual output of grain by 2,000 million to 3,000 million catties. In coarse grain areas or other areas suitable for growing potato crops, local authorities should therefore study how to extend the area under potato crops and other high-yield crops, work out plans and energetically put them into practice. Agricultural departments and scientific research institutes should devote serious study to developing high-grade strains of potato crops and work out improved methods for preserving, storing and processing such crops.

(5) The use of improved animal-drawn ploughs, double-bladed two-wheeled and single-bladed two-wheeled ploughs, vigorous efforts to store and prepare manure, proper application of fertilizers, widespread promotion of the use of high-grade seed, elimination of plant diseases and insect pests—all these are effective ways of raising farm output and should be applied in accordance with local conditions. State authorities at all levels should improve their work of granting agricultural loans, increasing the supply of fertilizers and farm tools, providing services from agro-technical, tractor and water-pumping stations, and see to it that state farms set good examples in farm work. State authori-

ties at all levels should also conduct among the peasants experiments in the improvement of farming technique and seeds, and organize peasant training classes to carry out such experiments and publicize their results. By this means, aid given the broad masses of peasants will support their efforts to increase production.

Thirdly, on guidance for agricultural production.

In developing agricultural production, in addition to providing unified guidance throughout the country as regards principles, policies and practical steps to be taken, it is important to bring the initiative of the local people into full play, improve guidance given to agriculture by local Party and government bodies, and adopt effective measures for raising farm output, suited to actual local conditions. Every province must concentrate sufficient forces to guide efforts in raising farm output. All administrative regions, counties, districts and *hsiang*[6] must, without exception, lay special stress on giving guidance to agricultural production and the movement for mutual aid and co-operation in farming.

Local Party and government organs at all levels should map out five-year plans to increase agricultural output according to actual conditions in their localities and their practical experience. They should consistently carry out various policies concerning rural work and the raising of agricultural output which the Party and state have laid down, encourage the enthusiasm of the peasants for production and ensure the fulfilment of these plans. Local plans for raising farm output should be geared to meet the requirements of state plans. Local authorities, taking account of local possibilities, should set targets which are in excess of state assignments so that the state plan can be placed on a still firmer foundation. Such local plans for raising farm output should be made after careful consideration of the specific needs of the local population so that the produce of their farms will satisfy their varied demands and their enthusiasm for production can be stimulated and play its full part.

In some rural areas, local authorities and government workers have failed to concentrate their efforts on guiding agricultural production. They have not paid sufficient attention to working out effective methods of raising output and preventing natural calamities nor have they mobilized the masses to take steps to achieve these aims. This has left agriculture without proper guidance. In some places when modern experience and measures for raising farm output were applied, actual local conditions were not taken into account. Instead, regardless of effects, a stereotyped way of doing things was followed. In other places, patience was not exercised in educating and persuading the peasants to take up co-operative ways of farming, nor was the method adopted of demonstrating by concrete example. On the contrary, the principle of voluntariness on the part of the masses was violated and there was coercion and commandism. All such shortcomings in rural work must be corrected.

I wish to say a few words especially on the question of animal husbandry. The development of animal husbandry will increase the supply of draught animals and manure for agricultural production, of hides and hair for light industry, and of meat needed for the market. It will also raise the income of the peasants and herdsmen. Therefore, the various measures for the development of animal husbandry, laid down in Chapter Four of the Five-Year Plan, should be strictly carried out in all agricultural and stock-breeding areas so as to speed up the breeding of livestock and ensure the fulfilment and overfulfilment of the targets set out in the First Five-Year Plan for increases in the number of horses, cattle, mules, donkeys, sheep, pigs and other livestock. State authorities should do all they can, financially and technically, to assist the development of animal husbandry in areas inhabited by minority peoples and improve leadership of this work in livestock-breeding areas.

4. The Socialist Transformation of Capitalist Industry and Commerce

Now I would like to deal with certain questions arising out of the socialist transformation of capitalist industry and commerce by the state, namely: the question of the steps by which this transformation will be brought about, the question of arrangements for the transformation of capitalist industry, the question of arrangements for the transformation of capitalist commerce and the question of the duty of capitalists to abide by the laws of the state and accept the policy of transformation.

---

[6]*Hsiang* is an administrative unit of one or several villages.

TEXT OF DOCUMENT I

A. The Steps by Which Socialist Transformation Will Be Brought About

There are still a vast number of complex private industrial and commercial enterprises in our country. In 1953 more than two million people were engaged in private industry (not including individual handicraftsmen). There were more than 45,000 capitalist industrial enterprises each employing over ten workers and staff, a total of more than 1,500,000 workers and staff. In the field of commerce, in 1953 some 200,000 people were engaged in capitalist wholesale trade; 2,000,000 were engaged in capitalist retail trade, and there were several million small traders and pedlars. Quite a number of these people engaged in private industry and commerce were capitalists. It is no easy undertaking to bring about the socialist transformation of this tremendous number of complex private industrial and commercial enterprises.

In achieving the socialist transformation of private industry and commerce, a distinction should be made between those enterprises owned by capitalists and those owned by small proprietors working independently. We should adopt appropriate measures and flexible methods suited to these two groups.

The transformation of capitalist industry and commerce by the state is being realized in two steps: the first is to transform capitalism into state-capitalism, and the second is to transform state-capitalism into socialism.

State-capitalism is the transitional form through which the state carries out socialist transformation of capitalist industry and commerce. The Constitution of the People's Republic of China provides that capitalist industry and commerce should be encouraged and guided in the "transformation into various forms of state-capitalist economy, gradually replacing capitalist ownership with ownership by the whole people." That is to say, during the transition period, elimination of the system of capitalist exploitation is not to be carried out at one stroke, but step by step, through various forms of state-capitalist economy. We shall allow capitalists a necessary period of time to accept transformation gradually, through the transitional form of state-capitalism under the leadership of the state and the working class.

There are various forms of state-capitalist economy. The higher form is joint state-private enterprise; the intermediate and lower forms, in industry, are the accepting of government contracts for the manufacture and processing of goods by private firms, the purchasing and distribution by the state of the finished products of private enterprises; and in commerce, designation of certain merchants by the state to purchase specified goods for the state, designation of merchants working on a commission basis to sell goods on behalf of the state and the purchasing of goods from state stocks by merchants for retail at fixed prices.

In the past few years, the transformation of capitalist economy developed in general from the lower and intermediate forms to the higher form, from important trades to less important trades and from leading cities to medium and small cities. Experience has proved that this method of steady, systematic advance is quite suitable; we shall continue to use it.

Facts during the past few years prove that once capitalist economy is transformed into state-capitalist economy, it changes its character in varying degrees as the socialist element is infused into it. This restricts the anarchy of capitalist economy in production and management and the profit-grabbing activities of capitalists, and, in varying degrees, places this sector of the economy within the scope of the state plan. At the same time, since the status of the workers in production is changed, their enthusiasm for production is increased, and consequently labour productivity in the enterprises is raised and management improved; this makes it possible to deal suitably with labour-capital relations in such enterprises. This shows that in the actual conditions of our country it is both necessary and practicable to adopt the transitional form of state-capitalist economy to transform capitalist industry and commerce step by step, to overcome by degrees the contradiction between capitalist relations of production and the growth of the productive forces and thus facilitate the gradual replacement of capitalist ownership by ownership of the whole people.

The state transforms private manufacturing and commercial establishments run by independently working proprietors by organizing them step by step, according to the different conditions of different trades and the principle of voluntariness, into various forms of co-operation, guiding them, step by step, in the transition from various lower forms of co-operation to higher forms of co-operation so that they can effectively serve the needs of the country and society.

It is expected that under the First Five-Year Plan, the following advances will be made in transforming private industry and commerce: the greater part of private industrial enterprises will be transformed into various forms of state-capitalist economy, while the greater part of modern industrial enterprises owned by private interests will be transformed into the higher form of state-capitalist economy—joint state-private enterprises; over a half of all private commercial enterprises will be transformed into various forms of state-capitalist commercial enterprises or into small co-operative commercial concerns organized by small traders and pedlars.

B. Arrangements for the Transformation of Capitalist Industry

In regard to state, co-operative, joint state-private and private industries, the principle laid down by the state for unified planning with due consideration for all parties concerned should be observed in allocating production assignments, distributing raw materials and in the government purchasing programme. On the one hand, however, the state gives priority to the development of socialist industries while enterprises of the non-socialist economic sector do not have such priority; here lies a distinction. On the other hand, due consideration should be given to the role of private industry during the transition period in our country and, in some respects, especially regarding workers and staff, no distinction should be made between state and private enterprises.

In order to regulate private industry and commerce during the period of rehabilitation of the national economy, the state adopted the policy of giving contracts for the manufacture and processing of goods to some private factories (first of all the cotton mills). This policy has proved very effective in organizing the production of private industry. Since planned construction began in 1953, the state, in order to strengthen planned production, has carried out a policy of purchasing nearly the whole or the greater part of the supplies of many important raw materials and arranged unified allocation of raw materials thus purchased. By that time, the state had already brought the bulk of the output of private industrial concerns into the sphere of government contracts for the manufacture and processing of goods and the state purchasing and distribution programmes, thus turning these private industrial concerns into state-capitalist concerns of the lower and intermediate forms. There was an increase in the number of state contracts arranged for manufacture and processing of goods during the campaign to resist U.S. aggression and aid Korea and when large-scale construction work began in 1953; there was also some lack of planning in trade departments regarding such contracts and as a result, factories, both state and private, in some branches of industry rashly expanded capacity so when the volume of contracts for some types of goods showed a relative decrease in 1954, certain branches of industry found themselves working below capacity. In addition, allocation of raw materials and production assignments among state and private factories in those branches of industry which were operating below capacity, were not very well arranged for a time—joint state-private factories and private factories got smaller shares. The result was that private factories in certain branches of industry were faced with some difficulties. This state of affairs has now been remedied.

In accordance with the state's principle of unified planning with due consideration for all parties concerned, an over-all arrangement is being made to cover production in state and private industry. If necessary, state factories may be given more generous quotas with regard to allocation of raw materials and contracts. At the same time, however, due consideration must be given to joint state-private factories and private factories, so as to enable them to carry on production. This is because only by keeping private factories in operation can we help to strengthen the unity and solidarity of the working class, maintain the necessary economic alliance between the working class and the bourgeoisie during the transition period, and also smoothly carry out the transformation of capitalist industry and commerce.

In drawing up industrial production plans, the various industrial ministries of the Central People's Government should take account of the productive capacity of private industries, bring them into the plan and make good use of them. At the same time, special central and local agencies will be established which will, in collaboration with the industrial ministries concerned, share the work of looking after the joint state-private enterprises and private concerns.

In accordance with the principle of unified planning with due consideration for all parties concerned, and by means of an over-all arrangement within each branch of industry, the state is carrying through the transformation of private industries trade by trade. These arrangements involve not just a few factories, but all private factories in a given branch of industry. For instance, mergers of state and private capital are carried out in all enterprises which are ripe for it. Where conditions are not yet ripe for such mergers, the state, in so far as possible, negotiates contracts with enterprises for the manufacture and processing of goods, or purchases their products. Private owners of medium and small factories are encouraged, where conditions permit, to gradually arrange the joint operation of their factories or amalgamate them with the leading, bigger plants, thus creating conditions for future mergers of state and private capital. As for those factories which really lack conditions for transformation and must inevitably go out of existence, they are helped to make suitable arrangements for their workers and staff before closing down. Joint state-private enterprises are to be systematically increased in number and expanded by means of the measures listed above.

We should make energetic efforts to transform private industries into joint state-private enterprises, but we must proceed steadily and avoid rash steps. Preparatory work should be well done so that after such mergers, management will be improved, and there will be a clear system of responsibility and no drop in production.

Owners of private enterprises which are making profits should be allowed that portion of the profits due to them according to law. In joint state-private enterprises, private shareholders should also receive dividends according to law. At the same time, however, due punishment should be meted out to law-breaking capitalists who once more take to the "five evils" (bribery of government workers, tax evasion, theft of state property, cheating on government contracts, and stealing economic information for speculation) and also to those law-breaking capitalists who oppose the leadership of the state, undermine the unity of the working class and engage in sabotage.

C. *Arrangements for the Transformation of Capitalist Commerce*

There are two major categories of private trade: wholesale and retail. We should adopt the following measures towards merchants in these two categories:

The great majority of merchants engaged in wholesale business are capitalists with a relatively large capital and staff. If these wholesalers are allowed to control the market's sources of commodity supply, they will inevitably engage in unscrupulous profiteering and all sorts of speculation and hoarding to the detriment of the national welfare and the people's livelihood. Wholesale business in principal commodities must therefore be in the hands of state trading organizations. From 1950 to the first half of 1953, the turnover of wholesale dealers gradually declined as a result of the state buying up staple farm products, awarding contracts for manufacturing and processing goods and large-scale government purchasing of important industrial products. Since the second half of 1953, the state has carried out planned purchase and supply of grain, oil-bearing seeds, cotton and cloth, and in the case of the bulk of industrial products has excluded wholesale dealers, as a rule, from control over commodity supplies all the way from the factory to the retailer, thus making it impossible for them to speculate in or hoard those commodities the demand for which exceeds supply. Some wholesale dealers who have thus been deprived of their supply of commodities are permitted by the state to engage in wholesale trade by getting their supplies from the state; in other cases, the personnel of these private concerns are being given employment by state trading agencies.

Private wholesalers are allowed to carry on their business in some commodities in which state wholesale agencies do not trade or deal only with part of the market. The business of those private wholesalers who are still able to carry on will be transformed by the state gradually into state-capitalist enterprises.

Retailers form the overwhelming majority of merchants. Apart from the commercial capitalists, most retailers are shop employees, small traders and pedlars who do not employ shop assistants. The rest are handicraftsmen who sell their products themselves and those engaged in the food and drink and service trades. Compared with pre-liberation days, retail business has undergone a great change in recent years. Since the state began to give contracts for the manufacture and processing of goods and for state purchase and distribution of nearly all industrial products, and since the co-operatives began purchasing the principal agricultural products, most retailers, including shop-keepers and stallkeepers as well as pedlars, have had to depend for their supply of commodities on the wholesale agencies of state trading organizations and co-operatives. Consequently, their business largely consists in acting as distributors working on a commission basis on behalf of state trading organizations or co-operatives, or purchasing commodities from state and co-operative stores and retailing them at fixed prices.

With regard to the socialist transformation of commerce, after the winter of 1953 the volume of trade handled by private retailers was cut rather sharply as a result of the somewhat too rapid increase, in certain places, of the volume of retail trade handled by state trading organizations, and especially co-operatives. Readjustments have since been made. In order to enable private retailers, small traders and pedlars in urban and rural areas to maintain their business, the state has temporarily stopped the increase or suitably reduced retail sales of all state trading organizations and co-operatives in cities and towns where their volume of retail trade increased to an excessive degree. Co-operatives in towns have also appropriately reduced their retail trade in favour of wholesale trade; they have made arrangements whereby small traders and pedlars either work for them on a commission basis as distributors or purchase goods from them for retail at fixed prices. At the same time, all cities and towns should, taking local conditions into consideration, work out what should be the proportion between the volume of state and privately run retail sales in each trade, which will not only stabilize commodity market prices but also maintain the business of private retailers. We should also do our best to keep these proportions stable over a given period so as to enable the necessary arrangements to be made for those engaged in private trade, and carry out trade by trade the socialist transformation of private business.

D. The Duty of Capitalists to Abide by the Laws of the State and Accept the Policy of Transformation

In the course of socialist transformation, private industry and commerce can hardly avoid certain difficulties in carrying on production and doing business. Under the principle laid down by the state for unified planning with due consideration for all parties concerned, and for the over-all arrangement of private industry and commerce, industrial and commercial capitalists should do their best to overcome difficulties, place themselves under the leadership of the state economy, adhere to state plans, actively reorganize their enterprises and improve management so as to prepare the way for socialist transformation.

In the past few years, there has emerged a group of private industrialists and merchants who are patriotic and law-abiding, who adopt a positive attitude towards socialist transformation and set a good example for others. They receive approbation and due consideration from the state. On the other hand, there are still capitalists who adopt a negative attitude towards socialist transformation. Some of them still engage in illegal activities "which injure the public interest, disrupt the social-economic order, or undermine the economic plan of the state," activities prohibited by the Constitution, and they are again indulging in the "five evils," though in a more cunning way. Some of them have even resisted or sabotaged socialist transformation. Such people deserve public condemnation and punishment according to law.

The various complex forms that have been adopted for the socialist transformation of capitalist industry and commerce are products of the specific historical conditions of the transition period in which the working class forms an economic alliance with the bourgeoisie. At the same time, however, we must know that these also constitute a specific kind of class struggle. The view that transformation can be achieved without struggle does not conform either to the history of social development or to practical conditions, and so is entirely wrong. In accordance with the provisions of the Constitution, during the transition period we protect the right of capitalists to own means of production and other capital according to law, and permit law-abiding capitalists for a certain period to make profits as provided for by government regulations. At the same time, due punishment must be meted out to law-breaking capitalists. It is true that private retailers who hire no employees work themselves and so we should rally them together, but since they are working in the business of exchanging commodities, and, at the same time, are private owners, they can easily turn into speculators. This is why their socialist transformation also requires a certain degree and a certain form of struggle.

Experience in the past few years shows that the transformation of capitalist enterprises must be carried out in conjunction with the ideological remoulding of capitalists. We encourage capitalists to take steps to study the fundamental tasks and various policies of the state during the transition period, to remould themselves, abide by the laws of the state and actively support the cause of socialist transformation by the state.

5. Ensuring Stability of the Market

A stable market is a prerequisite for the carrying out of the First Five-Year Plan.

To ensure stability of the market, the draft First Five-Year Plan directs that we should:

(1) Continue to balance revenue and expenditure and increase reserves of financial and material resources;

(2) Increase the exchange of goods between town and countryside, between home and abroad, and expand the circulation of commodities in step with the growth of industrial and agricultural production;

(3) Implement step by step, on the basis of a vigorous effort to increase production, the policy of planned purchase and supply of certain principal industrial and agricultural products the supply of which lags behind demand.

The market was stabilized very soon after the founding of the People's Republic of China, that is, as early as the beginning of 1950. This was associated with such measures as balancing state revenue and expenditure, and state control of large reserves of material resources. By balancing state revenue and expenditure, it was possible to stabilize the value of the currency and commodity prices. By state control of large reserves of material resources, it was possible to supply the market with necessary materials and to fight the hoarding of goods and speculating by merchants. This stabilizing of the market was an important achievement of our country during the period of economic rehabilitation. It played a significant role in the rapid rehabilitation of the national economy and improvement of the people's livelihood. There can be no doubt that we must continue to consolidate this success during the period of planned economic construction.

Increasing the exchange of goods between town and countryside and between home and abroad, and expanding the circulation of commodities in order to facilitate the growth of production and economic prosperity and to consolidate the worker-peasant alliance—these are important aspects of our national economic policy. The First Five-Year Plan requires that we continue this policy by working energetically to increase production and the supply of goods.

Under the Five-Year Plan production of all major consumer goods sold by state and private trading concerns will increase in varying degrees. Here are several of the main items of mass consumption whose production will increase by the following amounts in 1957 as compared with 1952: grain, 13.3 per cent; pork, 57 per cent; edible vegetable oil, 65.9 per cent; aquatic products, 70.1 per cent; table salt, 34.3 per cent; sugar, 122.9 per cent; cotton piece-goods, 55.1 per cent; knit goods, 105.3 per cent; rubber shoes, 69.8 per cent; kerosene, 143.5 per cent; machine-made paper, 89.2 per cent; cigarettes, 87 per cent. Under ordinary conditions the rate of increase in the production of these main items of mass consumption is not low. Never before has China achieved such a high rate of increase in such a short time.

Nevertheless, over a fairly long period the situation will exist where the rate of growth of the people's purchasing power will be higher than that of the production of consumer goods, while the rate of growth of purchasing power will rise quicker in the countryside than in the city. This is because of the constant improvement of the people's livelihood, the rapid growth of the people's purchasing power, the fact that a large number of industrial enterprises established with state capital will only be able to make great increases in supplies of commodities after the lapse of a certain period of time, and because of the fact that the relatively slow increase in the production of industrial crops will for the time being unavoidably restrict production increases in a number of light industries. It is hardly possible to avoid, over a certain period of time, a situation in which supplies of many kinds of commodities fail to meet the demand.

At the first session of the First National People's Congress convened in 1954, Comrade Chen Yun explained in detail in his statement that the basic reason why supplies of such consumer goods as grain, edible oil, meat, piece-goods, etc., lagged behind rising demands was that the rate of growth of the people's purchasing power surpassed the rate of increase in the production of these consumer goods, and not, as some people supposed, that the production of consumer goods had been reduced in volume or that they had been exported in excessive amounts.

We are of the opinion that we should not allow a situation to develop in which supplies of certain consumer goods lag behind a rising demand; effective measures must be taken to solve this problem step by step.

An increase in the supply of consumer goods to the people can only be achieved gradually by developing industrial and agricultural production. Hence, the basic solution of the problem of certain consumer goods failing to meet rising demand lies in the development of industrial and agricultural production. This is the task of the whole people, particularly of the workers and peasants.

Apart from making efforts to increase production, for the purpose of continuing to maintain the stability of the market, the state must take into consideration the different circumstances in the production of major commodities and step by step carry out the policy of planned purchase and supply so that it will be possible to control sources of supply and organize the supply of commodities according to plan, and wage a serious fight against speculators and prevent merchants from manipulating the market.

The state started planned purchase and supply of grain in November 1953, and later followed this with planned purchase and supply of edible vegetable oil. In September 1954, planned purchase of cotton and planned purchase and supply of cotton cloth were also put into operation. In these two years, the state awarded contracts on a larger scale for manufacture and processing of industrial products by private firms and for state purchasing or distribution of goods manufactured by private firms. The state also increased its purchases of other principal agricultural products. The facts prove that these measures do not harm but benefit both the producers of commodities and the broad mass of consumers. They are disadvantageous only to speculators because they prevent speculation. There is no doubt that these measures are an important guarantee of fulfilment of the Five-Year Plan by the state and conform to the immediate and long-term interests of the people. The implementation of this policy will, of course, bring about a certain change in the way of life of hundreds of millions of people and a reorganization of supply and distribution. It is also very difficult to ensure that there are no shortcomings in the way this great reform works out during its first few years. But we must realize that our positive achievements are the main part of the picture.

In carrying out planned purchase and supply of grain, in the spring of 1955 the state began to apply a fixed quota system for producing, purchasing and marketing; it fixed the total amount which will be purchased under the plan throughout the country and this will not be changed during the next three years. Recently, because it was found that the supplying of grain to both town and countryside was not too well controlled or calculated, the state worked out practical measures to improve the supply of grain, took firm steps to reduce the amount of waste in consumption, so that the quota of grain purchased can be reduced to a suitable level and a certain quantity of grain held in reserve. These measures not only enable the state to bring the necessary amounts of grain under its control, thus ensuring a supply of grain to the people, but also to give further encouragement to the initiative of the peasants in increasing production and thus speed the growth of agricultural production. This is extremely important in improving relations between town and countryside, in strengthening the links between industry and agriculture, and consolidating unity between the working class and peasants. That is why we must persuade the working class, all others who are short of grain, and all grain consumers to economize grain as much as possible so as to reduce the amounts which the state must supply. This will enable the state to reduce the purchasing quota, and enhance the initiative of the peasants, particularly the middle peasants, in production.

There are some people who entertain doubts or even adopt an attitude of opposition to the policy of planned purchase and supply of grain. Some, seizing on certain defects in our work, deny the tremendous achievements made in carrying out this policy. They fail to see the fact that on the whole the situation is good. Such negative attitudes are of course quite wrong.

What are the advantages of planned purchase and supply of grain? The peasants themselves have given a very good answer to this question. On his return from a recent tour of inspection in the rural areas of Chekiang Province, Mr. Liang Hsi, deputy to the National People's Congress, related that the peasants in Hsinchien *hsiang*, Shaoshing County, enumerated twelve advantages: "It aids industry, helps prepare the liberation of Taiwan, helps the people in areas hit by natural calamities, stabilizes prices, promotes mutual aid and co-operation, increases and develops production, economizes grain and reduces waste, weakens capitalism, gives us bank savings on preferential terms, raises living standards, ensures fair shares for all and saves us time."

We can sum up these advantages in the following terms:

Firstly, it aids industrial construction and strengthens national defence.

This means to ensure that the grain they need goes to more than ninety million people in the cities, towns and industrial and mining areas and to several million more in national defence and public security units. Everyone knows that the peasants do not want the counter-revolution to stage a come-back and that they look forward to the liberation of Taiwan. But it is impossible to prevent a come-back of the counter-revolution and liberate Taiwan without industrial construction and the strengthening of national defences. So to support industrial construction and the strengthening of national defences is at the same time to safeguard the interests of the peasants themselves—and the peasants know this very well.

Secondly, it protects the purchase and sale of grain and other principal agricultural produce from manipulation by merchant speculators and protects both producers and consumers from exploitation by merchant speculators, who buy cheap and sell dear.

If planned purchase and supply were not enforced, merchants would manipulate the grain market and get rich on their ill-gotten gains, the stability of commodity prices throughout the domestic market would be disrupted, capitalism and the process of class differentiation in the rural areas would develop, thousands upon thousands of peasants would go bankrupt and the living standards of the masses of workers and the urban population would deteriorate. The peasants and the rest of the masses are clear on this point too.

Thirdly, it promotes the development of agriculture, animal husbandry, forestry, fishery, the salt industry and subsidiary rural production.

This means guaranteed supplies of grain to satisfy the needs of the poor peasants, rural handicraftsmen and other people who are short of grain, it means assured supplies of grain to peasants in areas under industrial crops, and non-agricultural labourers such as herdsmen, lumbermen, fishermen, salt producers and boat dwellers, so that they can get grain at reasonable prices and work productively free from worry.

Fourthly, the policy of planned purchase and supply of grain has played an important part in ensuring supplies of grain to people in areas hit by natural calamities.

In 1954, large areas of our country suffered damage by floods unprecedented in the past hundred years. If the state had not carried out this grain policy, there is no knowing how the people in the flood-stricken areas would have lived and restored production there. It is quite understandable that the people in the affected areas regard the People's Government as a good government, unexampled in Chinese history.

Fifthly, planned purchase and supply of grain has dealt a blow to merchant speculators and rich peasants, that is to say, to the rural capitalist economy; it has further weakened the influence of capitalism among the peasants and also weakened the tendency among them towards the spontaneous development of capitalism; thus, it has promoted the development of co-operation in agricultural production.

All this shows that planned purchase and supply of grain plays an important part in our country's socialist construction and the work of socialist transformation and serves the vital interests of the entire people. This is an important measure for fulfilling the fundamental task of the state in the period of transition. Facts prove that this policy is absolutely necessary and must be resolutely carried through. But the actual methods of purchase and supply should be constantly improved in order to overcome shortcomings and consolidate achievements.

We should supply the peasants, first of all and to the utmost extent, with necessary means of production and of life so that they can increase production and improve their living conditions with the money they get from the sale of grain. This will have an immediate effect on the smooth implementation of the grain purchasing plan; it will be a great help in relieving the pressure on the supply of grain exerted by the growing purchasing power in the countryside. This was why, in 1953, at the same time when planned purchase and supply of grain was introduced, the state decided that "in supplying manufactured goods which are necessary to both town and countryside, priority should be given to the countryside." During the past two years, state and co-operative trading concerns have carried out this policy with success, but not without shortcomings. The main defects were that supplies were not always timely nor did they always suit the need. The peasants' needs are practical and varied, and they differ from place to place. State and co-operative trading concerns must work conscientiously to improve supplies of manufactured goods to the countryside according to local differences, seasonal changes and the varying habits of the peasants.

6. Training Personnel for Construction

Shortage of scientific and technical personnel is obviously a serious obstacle in the way of our advance. One of the major political tasks that we have to fulfil in the periods of the First and Second Five-Year Plans is to train large numbers of engineers and technicians loyal to our motherland and the cause of socialism and equipped with up-to-date scientific knowledge; we must train skilled workers and specialists in all fields.

This work of training personnel for construction in the five-year period is being conducted along two lines: on the one hand, we are reorganizing, expanding and building institutions of higher education and secondary vocational schools; on the other hand, we are taking advantage of favourable conditions in enterprises and government bodies to open various kinds of spare-time schools and training classes.

Since the liberation of the country, the state has energetically reorganized and expanded institutions of higher education and secondary vocational schools; it has established new institutions and schools and rapidly increased the number of students. The main stress in higher education in the five-year period is on development of engineering colleges and natural science departments in universities. Colleges of agriculture and forestry, teachers' colleges, medical colleges, pharmacological institutes, and other types of schools are also being appropriately expanded. By 1957 China will have 208 institutions of higher education.

In secondary vocational education the emphasis is also on training technical and administrative personnel for industry and agriculture.

In training personnel for construction in institutions of higher education and secondary vocational schools, we must see to it that the standard of training is raised while we increase the number of students trained; we must find the correct balance between the need to raise the standard of training and the need to increase the number of students. The tendency to go after numbers only and ignore quality is clearly not in the interests of the state plan of construction. The higher engineering institutes have already begun to feel that the number of students has increased too rapidly while the standards of learning and skill of the students are not high enough. Factories and mines have universally put forward the proposal that higher professional standards must be demanded of technical personnel during training.

From now on we must pay keen attention to the standards demanded of students. Once we can guarantee such standards, we can then increase enrolments to a suitable level, seeing to it that the technical personnel trained are politically reliable, are competent, have an adequate knowledge of modern science and technology, and are at the same time in good health. The qualifications demanded of students can of course only be raised gradually, but we must take positive steps to raise them. We cannot expect too much too soon, nor mechanically demand the same from everybody. But there must be a minimum standard. For instance, conditions of enrolment of new students in institutions of higher education should require that they be at least politically reliable, physically capable of coping with the programme of studies and intellectually able to keep up with the class. It is impossible or very difficult to turn students who do not meet these minimum requirements into useful construction personnel.

In the light of this policy, the Ministry of Higher Education has revised the enrolment plan of higher educational institutions for the last three years of the First Five-Year Plan period. It has also decided to replace, by stages and within two to three years, the four-year system in engineering colleges with the five-year system and gradually abolish the two-year and three-year special courses. It has decided to take positive steps to reorganize secondary vocational schools, raise their standards and enlarge existing schools and build new ones as needed. At the same time, it has decided to look thoroughly into enrolment figures, studying the proportions of students in various specialized fields, so as to dovetail the training programmes of the various specialized institutes with the needs of operational departments.

In working out plans for the training of personnel for construction, special attention should be paid to spare-time education. The state should gradually open large numbers of correspondence schools and university night schools so that personnel who lack a systematic scientific and technical education can have a chance to increase their cultural, scientific and technical knowledge stage by stage. Regular workers' spare-time schools, ranging from primary and middle schools to universities, should also be gradually established on a large scale in the larger factories and mines or in industrial and mining areas, in order to bring about a steady rise in the workers' level of education and scientific and technical knowledge. In the past, our leading educational bodies and trade unions failed to give enough attention to workers' spare-time education, allowing it to go its own way. The standards of many spare-time schools could not be raised for lack of leadership, competent teachers and teaching materials. We must remedy this defect and give due attention to the training of factory and office workers on the job as a vital, organic part of the programme of training personnel for construction.

In order to meet the needs of nationwide economic construction, future plans of development should be designed to remedy gradually the over-concentration of institutions of higher education, especially engineering colleges, in the coastal cities. From now on, higher educational institutions, in general, should not be established or expanded on a large scale in the coastal cities, but should be set up gradually in the inland areas on a reasonable basis of distribution.

In order to meet the needs of the national minorities' economic and cultural development we must pay attention to training personnel from among them for industry, agriculture, transport, commerce and cultural work.

While a vigorous programme of training personnel for construction is being pushed ahead, state organs at all levels and all enterprises should pay the fullest attention to rational utilization of existing scientific and technical personnel. Many industrial enterprises, capital construction projects, economic agencies and leading economic organs have not yet rationally apportioned or utilized scientific and technical personnel, they have placed individuals in jobs unrelated to their specialized skills, or failed to bring their capacities and specialized skills into full play even though they were assigned to the right jobs. In general, an inordinate number of technical personnel are at present placed in high-level departments and administrative bodies. At the same time, some enterprises, factories and mines have not given sufficient backing to the inventions and rationalization proposals of such personnel. It should be recognized that the slightest waste of our technical forces is a loss to the national construction programme. We absolutely cannot allow a situation to continue in which, on one pretext or another, many people with specialized skills have been placed in unsuitable positions for prolonged periods, thus preventing them from making their full contribution to the country. On the other hand, we must also see that the political consciousness of our scientific and technical personnel is raised steadily in the course of their work, so that they will develop the outlook of men dedicated to working whole-heartedly for the people, serving the needs of the country's construction and unafraid of difficulties or hardships.

7. Improving the Material Well-Being and Cultural Standard of the People

The supreme aim of the people's revolution and socialist construction is to bring about a steady rise in the level of the people's standard of living and cultural well-being.

Since the liberation, there has been a progressive rise in the material well-being and cultural standard of the people of the various nationalities in China. In the three years of rehabilitation, along with the stabilization of commodity prices, the rise in the number of employed, wage increases and agrarian reform, the income of the urban and rural population has gone up and the people's material life has been improved to a marked degree, with a resultant invigoration of cultural life. The people of the national minorities are also to a certain extent living a better life as a result of the policy of the government in helping them to promote production and trade and stabilize social order, and the measures it has taken to improve cultural and public health work and so on. As I said in the second part of my report, the various production targets and measures laid down in the Five-Year Plan mean that the material and cultural level of the people of the entire country will be further raised.

The targets laid down in the Five-Year Plan for improving the material well-being and cultural standard of the people are the maximum that our country can achieve at the present stage. We do not deny that the present standard of living of our people is still relatively low. But the satisfaction of the people's needs is governed by the productive forces and material resources that society has at its disposal. Improvements in the people's standard of living must be based on development of production and a rise in labour productivity. Our industrial and agricultural output has grown year by year, but is still at a very low level. Labour productivity in industry and transport has risen year by year, but is still not high enough. If we want to develop production and maintain a high rate of development so as to create the material foundations for improving the people's life, we must expand construction in heavy industry and other branches of our economy. Therefore, we cannot use up all the fruits of increased production and labour productivity to better living standard; we must set aside a suitable portion as investment capital for the country's construction needs.

The question before us is: What is our choice—shall we set aside the necessary financial resources for the country's construction and thus lay the material basis for improving the people's life, or shall we raise wages to an unreasonable extent and spend carelessly, and thus pare down and delay the construction programme?

We are convinced that, taking into consideration the long-term interests of the entire people, we should first of all put aside whatever financial resources are needed for the country's construction and, at the same time, raise standard of living in accordance with the targets laid down in the Five-Year Plan.

The very purpose of construction is to raise future living standard. Unless we work hard at construction today, we cannot enjoy a happier life tomorrow. It is illusory and therefore wrong to think and act on the assumption that we can at one stroke bring about a sharp rise in the people's standard of living without having to do hard constructive work.

Of course, all personnel in state organs and enterprises should at all times concern themselves with the life of the masses and should gradually improve their well-being whenever conditions permit. It is wrong to adopt an attitude of unconcern with regard to the people's livelihood and not to try to solve those questions which must and can be solved. The correct thing to do is to integrate the people's immediate interests with their long-term interests, and in keeping with the prior needs of national construction, suitably raise the people's standard of living.

Everything possible must be done to ensure the attainment of the Five-Year Plan's targets and measures for improving the material well-being and cultural standard of the people. This will imbue our people of the various nationalities with a genuine feeling of the need for national construction and an understanding of the relation between this and the vital interests of everyone. This in turn will encourage them to take an active and creative part in the construction programme.

The question has been asked: Can we raise the production of consumer goods to levels above the targets laid down in the Five-Year Plan and so satisfy more of the people's needs?

We think that efforts should be made to raise production and to increase supplies. But it should be noted that for the time being the average increase of consumer goods which each person can actually get is limited. This is because the number of employed will continue to increase, the purchasing power of the peasants will continue to rise, those who took only a small share of these consumer goods in the past are probably going to increase their consumption of them, and, furthermore, China has a population of 600 million. We must, of course, continue our efforts to discover latent productive capacity, and it would be a mistake to ignore such efforts. But, as we have said earlier, there are for the time being certain limitations on supplies of industrial raw materials. Big increases in the output of agricultural produce or consumer goods made out of agricultural raw materials can be brought about only after large-scale mechanization of agriculture and large-scale mechanized reclamation of wasteland.

Another question which has been asked is: Can we expand the programme for cultural and educational development to meet the ever-increasing demands of the people?

We are of the opinion that more ways should be found in order to satisfy adequately the cultural and educational demands of the people. The various targets for development of cultural and educational undertakings in 1952 already exceeded peak pre-liberation levels, and it is on this basis that the Five-Year Plan has set targets for further development. However, some cultural and educational establishments are still unable to satisfy fully the people's growing demands for a richer cultural life. For example, the number of primary schools falls short of the needs of the children who have reached school age, that of the middle schools falls short of the needs of primary school graduates, and so on. To deal with this question, the state, while continuing the planned development of cultural and educational undertakings, encourages people to organize themselves certain cultural and educational services such as primary schools, peasants' spare-time schools, amateur theatrical groups, etc. The state will give guidance to the work of such establishments, and wherever possible, assistance in personnel, funds and materials. At the same time, state organs and enterprises everywhere should as far as possible open all types of special classes, night schools, correspondence schools, etc., in order to enable young people who cannot pursue their studies in schools to raise their educational level while continuing their work.

A rise in the people's standard of living can only be achieved by a steady advance; a happy life can be attained only by the hard work of the people themselves. We can be sure that, as a result of the industrious and painstaking labour of 600 million people and when China's productivity has been greatly raised in the course of several five-year plans, it will be possible to bring about an immense improvement in the people's material well-being and cultural standard. This is the only way to raise the standard of living of our people. There is no shortcut.

8. Practising Strict Economy

The First Five-Year Plan for Development of the National Economy centres on the vigorous development of heavy industry. Building up heavy industry requires large, long-term capital investments. These indispensable funds have to be accumulated internally. This makes necessary a regime of the strictest economy, which eliminates all unnecessary expenditure and all uncalled-for, non-productive expenditure, which permits no waste, not even the slightest, so that all possible funds can be accumulated for national construction and for building up necessary reserves for the state.

Summing up the First Five-Year Plan of the U.S.S.R., Stalin pointed out: "To exercise the strictest economy and to accumulate the resources necessary for financing the industrialization of our country—such was the road that had to be taken in order to secure the restoration of heavy industry and to carry out the Five-Year Plan." The road taken by the Soviet Union is the road which we must take now. Our national economy at the present time is more backward than that of the Soviet Union during its First Five-Year Plan. Consequently, the accumulation of funds for construction will be more difficult in this country than in the Soviet Union at that time. It is therefore all the more important and urgent for our country to practise strict economy in order to accumulate funds for construction. We must emulate the spirit of the Soviet people who in their time saved on food and clothing for the sake of national construction. We should also carry on our people's own fine traditions—of industriousness, frugality and perseverance.

In the past few years, with state organs continuing to increase their efficiency and state enterprises continuing to improve operation and management, we have succeeded each year in reducing costs of construction and installation of equipment, costs of production, transport, and posts and telecommunications and charges on circulation of commodities. By this means, we have accumulated more funds for national construction and cut down waste. These achievements should certainly be recognized, but it is also undeniable that serious waste still exists in certain spheres, departments, areas and enterprises. Quite a number of government workers have forgotten the Chinese Communist Party's revolutionary traditions of hard struggle. Not realizing that following the victory of the people's revolution, long, self-sacrificing efforts are still needed for socialist industrial construction, they frequently violate state regulations on practising economy and business accounting. Chairman Mao Tse-tung in his *Economic and Financial Problems During the Anti-Japanese War* wrote: "Economy deserves the attention of all our organizations, and particularly those engaged in economic and financial work." In building socialism, our present task is to follow these instructions of Chairman Mao Tse-tung still more earnestly, and effectively establish various regulations on practising economy, master the method of managing state organs and state-owned enterprises economically and wage a ruthless struggle against waste in all spheres.

First of all, we should drastically curtail building costs on non-productive projects. In the past few years, there has been widespread and serious extravagance and waste in the building of non-productive projects.

According to figures of the State Statistical Bureau, 21.6 per cent of the total investment of the six industrial ministries of the Central People's Government in 1953 and 1954 was non-productive investment. In the First Five-Year Plan of the Soviet Union, however, non-productive investment in the industrial departments comprised only 14.5 per cent of total investment. Non-productive investment formed 24.3 per cent of this country's capital construction investment in 1954. This unreasonable ratio must be changed.

In non-productive establishments, an astonishing amount of waste has been caused by blind adoption of a so-called "national style," undue emphasis on extravagant facades and decorations and the use of large quantities of costly or special materials in disregard of the principle of "suitability, economy and attractiveness as far as circumstances permit." Broad, towering roofs in the ancient palatial style, for example, caused a waste of 5,400,000 yuan on the 39 buildings erected by various state organs in the city of Peking. The building of the Changchun Institute of Geology, the so-called "Geological Palace," is a notorious example of extravagant building. It was built on the foundation of the unfinished imperial palace of the puppet "Manchukuo" state. But owing to much unnecessary decoration, the building cost comes to 220 yuan per square metre. If the cost of the original foundation is added, this soars to 300 yuan, which exceeds by 140 per cent the state-fixed ceiling cost of 125 yuan.

Building costs of some workers' housing projects are also excessive. The case of the workers' housing built in 1953 for the Anshan Iron and Steel Works may be cited as an example: here, housing with a floor space of 150,000 square metres was erected at a cost of 163 yuan per square metre.

Excessive ornamentation not only greatly increases building costs but greatly reduces the usable floor space of a building. The building cost of the main hall of a certain building in Peking is 293 yuan per square metre, but its usable floor space is only 44 per cent of the total floor space of the hall. The building cost of the general designing office of the Anshan Iron and Steel Works reached 240 yuan per square metre (this was 60 per cent above the budget, a waste of 1,380,000 yuan), but its usable floor space is less than 50 per cent of the total floor space of the building.

Such extravagant buildings which lay too much stress on form inevitably ignore the needs and interests of the people who use them. The cost of the laundry of a certain sanatorium, for example, reached 346 yuan per square metre, but, after the installation of the laundry machinery, the space left over was so small as to cause great inconvenience to the workers. The kitchen, which has a floor space of 450 square metres, costs 275 yuan per square metre but has no room for storing rice and flour.

Showy buildings naturally seem to require showy furniture and other interior appointments. Hence the growing fashion of buying such luxuries as rugs and sofas.

All this extravagant non-productive building is undesirable, because it does not conform to the principles of our socialist industrialization.

It is clear that by reducing needless expenditure in the building of such non-productive projects and eliminating other types of waste, we will be able to save very large amounts.

In the second place, we should drastically reduce construction costs of productive projects.

Personnel at some industrial construction projects do not follow the procedures prescribed for construction, nor do they try sufficiently hard to grasp what the real situation is and make systematic preparations for work. Sometimes they even purchase materials without making proper calculations and rush into construction before their plans are finalized. The result is widespread and serious waste of funds and idle dumps of material and equipment. The reconstruction of a certain iron and steel works affords a typical case of waste. Designs for its reconstruction went ahead even before it was decided to what extent the plant was to be reconstructed. Construction began even before the designs were finished. After construction began, major changes were constantly made in designs. The result was that blue prints could not be produced in time or were discarded after being produced. The drafting of some blue prints was not correctly timed to the order of construction and others were marked "For reference only." So none of these blue prints could be depended upon for construction purposes. Since designing and construction were going on at the same time, the plan of construction was constantly upset by the frequent change of designs. This resulted in the work going in fits and starts with intermediate periods of enforced idleness and rush work, and unnecessary stockpiling of equipment and materials. Under such conditions, haste often resulted in waste of time. Construction of this iron and steel works has barely begun and the amount of work done in 1954 was less than half that originally planned. Waste caused by enforced idleness of workers alone amounted to two million yuan, while materials worth more than seven million yuan were kept lying idle. This bitter lesson of beginning construction without adequate preparation and proper designing deserves the serious attention of all those in charge of capital construction projects.

The more important the construction project, the greater the possibility of waste. This is because such construction projects are supported by the whole nation and no expense is grudged. Since attention is mainly concentrated on finishing the project, people are apt to overlook or excuse the waste involved. In building the First Motor Works, up to the end of November 1954 materials worth 10,570,000 yuan were unnecessarily stockpiled, and 6,300,000 yuan were wasted as a result of materials made unsuitable or spoilt, equipment damaged, materials irrationally used, enforced idleness of workers, wrong designing and defective management.

Other causes of waste in construction include poor organization of labour, low rate of utilization of machinery and equipment and low quality of construction, all of which inevitably lead to low labour productivity and high construction costs.

It is obvious that the reduction of construction costs on productive projects will also save large sums.

Thirdly, we must greatly improve the system of business accounting in the various productive departments, and in transport, posts and telecommunications and commercial departments.

Products made in many of our enterprises are of poor quality and there are many rejects. Take some of the factories under the First Ministry of Machine-Building Industry for instance. Poor technique and low quality of products have resulted in a large number of rejects and articles which had to be made over again. The rate of rejects in iron castings in 1954 was 12.5 per cent and more than 20,000 tons of pig iron were spoilt. All this, plus rejects in processing, caused a year's loss of more than 20 million yuan.

In the first quarter of 1955, many products were of low quality. This is especially true of the products of enterprises under the Ministry of Heavy Industry and the First Ministry of Machine-Building Industry. Among the products of enterprises under the Ministry of Heavy Industry, 4,632 tons of pig iron produced in the first quarter of 1955 fell short of specifications due to excessive sulphur content. Thirty per cent of certain structural steels produced by the Anshan Iron and Steel Works was not up to specifications due to unsatisfactory chemical content. None of our glass-making enterprises fulfilled the target for production of Class A glass. Again, take for example the Dairen Factory and Mine Car Plant, one of the enterprises under the First Ministry of Machine-Building Industry: 90 per cent of the 322 50-ton open wagons produced by that plant in the first quarter of the year had to be done over again because they did not come up to design specifications. The Shenyang Second Machine Tool Plant is an extreme case. All the 380 drilling machines produced by the plant had to be done over again because violation of the regular procedure for trial manufacture resulted in failure of the finished products to meet design specifications. Rejected parts alone caused a loss of 1,200,000 yuan. Consequently, from September 1954 to the first quarter of this year, the plant failed to turn out any finished products. Forty per cent of the ploughshares produced were rejects because their curves did not follow specifications and their metal parts were not of the required hardness after heat treatment. In textile products, the Ministry of Textile Industry did not reach the planned rate of production of standard quality plain and printed cotton cloth during the first quarter of this year. The unevenness of quality and actual fall in the quality of certain products of light industry, such as rubber shoes and sugar, produced by enterprises under the Ministry of Light Industry, was more serious than before.

Mismanagement has caused waste of large sums and much material at many of our enterprises. Take the Harbin Foodstuffs Company for instance. In 1954 more than 50 cases of waste occurred in the company, amounting to an on-the-record loss of 570,000 yuan. In 1954, the animal products processing factory of this company showed a loss of more than 800,000 yuan. This is a mess and it is still not clear how much of this was due to waste in that factory.

In 1954 certain enterprises under the Ministry of Commerce incurred losses of eight million yuan in dead pigs and spoilt eggs alone due to inefficient management. This fact has been published in the press.

There are also many enterprises with an excess of non-productive personnel and many inflated departments and divisions. Take the Penhsi Iron and Steel Works for instance, which is far from being an isolated case. Workers form only 56 per cent of the total personnel of the company, while administrative personnel constitute one quarter. According to the findings of the Peking Municipal Committee of the Chinese Communist Party, the Shihchingshan Iron and Steel Works, the Shihchingshan Power Plant and the Chingho Woollen Textile Mill can reduce their staff by more than 3,600 men, which is one quarter of the total number of workers and staff of these three units.

It is obvious that considerable sums can be saved by improving business accounting in the various economic departments and thereby reducing waste and rejects, cutting the norm for materials consumed, lowering production costs and circulation charges and reducing personnel not directly engaged in production.

Fourthly, we must further reduce administrative expenses of state organs.

In the past few years, we have annually brought about a progressive reduction of the proportion of administrative expenses of state organs to total state expenditure. Nevertheless, up to the present, there are still many state organs which are over-staffed, and some of them are still blindly taking on new personnel. This has made it difficult to effect a further reduction in administrative expenses. In accordance with the principle of simplifying organization, reducing staff and reapportioning personnel, it has now been decided to start retrenchment in the central organizations by systematically transferring personnel from these organizations to productive departments at lower and intermediate levels. Local organizations at all levels should also carry out a systematic retrenchment. Facts prove that staff reduction in over-staffed organizations increases efficiency instead of reducing it. From now on, rigorous restrictions will be imposed on any increase of personnel in any state organ. Whenever an increase has to be made, we should, as far as possible, do it by shifting personnel from one department or organization to another. The state should decree that all government workers, including personnel in economic enterprises, should obey government orders to transfer to other work. Only in this way can we bring about a reasonable utilization of manpower and save the state's financial resources.

An immediate stop should be put to extravagance, which still exists in many state organs.

It is clear that a further considerable sum will be saved through retrenchment and elimination of extravagance in state organs.

In short, the state should, in the future, work out a series of regulations and arrangements for all-round economy, laying down what is permissible and what is impermissible. To do the impermissible will be a violation of law.

The State Council has decided that in the coming three years, the cost of construction and machine installation in productive enterprises should be brought at least 10 per cent below that set in the original plans, and that the building cost of various non-productive projects should be at least 15 per cent less than in the original plans. At the same time, with this as a basis, we should strive for a further annual reduction of 2 to 3 per cent or more in the costs of both productive and non-productive construction projects. In this way we can save at least 2,000 million yuan for the state. If invested in industrial construction, this sum is enough to build a metallurgical enterprise with an annual output of one and a half million tons of iron and steel, or 30 power plants of 50,000 kilowatts each, or five tractor plants, each with an annual output of 15,000 tractors. If invested in railway construction, this sum is enough to build more than 3,000 kilometres of railways. If applied to agricultural construction, it is enough to reclaim more than 40 million to 50 million *mou* of wasteland. This shows clearly how important strict economy is for the socialist construction of our country.

In order to practise strict, all-round economy, we should severely criticize all thinking which opposes economy and encourages waste.

(1) We should criticize the idea that we must do everything at once. This is because to do everything at once means no priority for construction. Furthermore, as a result of funds being thinly spread over an excessive number of projects, construction will be too long-drawn-out and we will not get quick returns on our investments.

(2) We should criticize the erroneous view that since we are building modern industrial enterprises, all non-productive buildings and amenities must also be modernized. This is because a modern living standard must be preceded by and based on a modern industry. To demand modern living standard without modernized industry as a foundation and without modernized agriculture means, in effect, to delay industrial modernization.

(3) We should criticize the idea of "budgeting liberally and spending sparingly," because a padded budget precludes the possibility of economizing. Liberal budgeting inevitably leads to liberal spending and waste.

(4) We must criticize the idea that a certain amount of waste is inevitable considering our lack of experience in construction work. If people responsible for work get this idea into their heads, then waste will truly become inevitable.

(5) We should criticize the idea that cases of waste are isolated and that waste is a "trifle." Such "trifles" exist in every factory, enterprise, government body and school. Once they are called "trifles," they are likely to be overlooked. But even a small case of waste will result in enormous waste if it is left unchecked. It is enormous if figured in terms of a whole department and still more the whole country for a year, five years, ten years or twenty years.

Only by viewing "trifles" in this light can we see the great need of rooting them out immediately, instead of heedlessly continuing to waste.

If we are to spread the movement for practising economy, we must overcome all the erroneous views mentioned above.

The state should improve financial control in order to ensure that regulations on practising economy are carried out. Not only financial departments should strengthen their financial control organizations. All enterprises and administrative and military departments should set up their own financial control organizations. All organizations and everyone concerned should observe the financial regulations and accept financial control. No organizations or individuals should excuse themselves or others where waste is concerned or substitute mutual forgiveness for mutual supervision and checking.

The movement for practising economy must embrace the entire population. People throughout the country, and first of all, factory and office workers, should mobilize to take an active part in the struggle in every enterprise and state organ to economize funds, eliminate waste and keep a strict check on financial matters.

9. The Soviet Union and the People's Democracies, and Our Construction

Now I wish to speak on the relation between the assistance which the Soviet Union and the People's Democracies are giving us and our construction programme.

Everyone knows that the fact that our country is able to push ahead so rapidly with the First Five-Year Plan for Development of the National Economy is inseparable from the assistance given to us by the Soviet Union and the People's Democracies, and particularly the assistance of the Soviet Union. The 156 industrial construction projects which the Soviet Union is helping us to design form the nucleus of industrial construction in our First Five-Year Plan.

The Soviet Union is giving systematic, all-round assistance to our country's construction. On the 156 industrial projects which the Soviet Union is helping us to build, she is helping us from start to finish of the whole process, beginning with geological surveys, selecting construction sites, collecting basic data for designing, designing itself, supplying equipment, directing the work of construction, installation, and getting into production, and supplying technical information on new types of products, and ending with directing manufacture of the new products. Designs provided by the Soviet Union make extensive use of the most up-to-date technical achievements, and all the equipment supplied to us by the Soviet Union is first-rate and of the latest type. The great Soviet working class, which is helping us with the greatest enthusiasm, is making every effort to produce the best equipment for us as quickly as possible. The great Soviet Government also gives us first priority in supplies of the best equipment.

The Soviet Government has also concluded a scientific and technical agreement with our government, on the basis of which the Soviet Union is giving a great deal of help to the economic construction of our country. The Soviet Government has also offered, on its own initiative, to give our country scientific, technical and industrial assistance in promoting research work in the use of atomic energy for peaceful purposes, and has also concluded an agreement with our country on the peaceful use of atomic energy.

In the midst of her own bustling construction for communism, the Soviet Union has sent large numbers of experts to our country to help us. They supply us with advanced experience gained in the socialist construction of the Soviet Union and give concrete help to us in all kinds of economic work. All of them possess not only a profound knowledge of science and technique and rich experience in practical work, but also a lofty spirit of internationalism and a selfless attitude to work. In industry, agriculture, water conservancy, forestry, railway, transport, posts and telecommunications, building construction, geology, education, public health and other departments, in scientific, technical and cultural co-operation, the Soviet experts faithfully and unreservedly contribute their experience, knowledge and skill. They regard the great cause of socialist construction of our country as their own. The communist working attitude of Soviet experts has set an example for the people of our country. It must be said that our great achievements in economic construction are inseparable from the help of the Soviet experts.

Tremendous efforts have been made by the Soviet Union to help our country train technical personnel. The Soviet Union has accepted a large number of students and trainees from our country and provided them with every convenience in their studies and practical training. This is an important aid to us in mastering modern industrial technique, guaranteeing that our new enterprises go into operation properly and that our scientific level is raised. The Soviet experts who have come to our country have also made big contributions in the training of our technical personnel.

The Soviet Union has extended a great deal of financial aid to our country both by a succession of loans granted us on the most favourable terms and by trade, selling us technical equipment and materials at low prices. Such benefits in loans and trade also help the speedy restoration and development of our country's economy, and particularly our industrial construction.

It is clear from the above that Soviet assistance plays an extremely important part in enabling us to carry on our present construction work on such a large scale, at such high speed, on such a high technical level and, at the same time, avoid many mistakes.

Besides Soviet aid, our work of national construction has also received economic and technical assistance from the People's Democracies such as Poland, Czechoslovakia, Hungary, Rumania and the German Democratic Republic. At the same time, such People's Democracies as Mongolia, Bulgaria and Albania also co-operate with us economically.

The struggle of the heroic Korean and Viet-Namese peoples for the independence and freedom of their countries plays an important part in the world movement for peace and democracy. Their struggle is also of enormous significance for the building of our country.

The Chinese Government and people express their heartfelt thanks for the aid of the Soviet Union and the People's Democracies, especially the great, long-term, all-round and unselfish assistance of the Soviet Union. In order to consolidate and advance the socialist industrialization of our country, we must further consolidate and develop our economic alliance and friendly co-operation with the Soviet Union and the People's Democracies, so as to promote the common economic advance of the socialist camp and strengthen the world forces of peace and democracy.

IV. STRIVE FOR THE FULFILMENT AND OVER FULFILMENT OF THE FIRST FIVE-YEAR PLAN

The First Five-Year Plan has been in operation for two years. It worked well as a whole in 1953 and 1954, although a number of mistakes and defects appeared in the course of planning and implementation.

The total value of output of industry and agriculture increased by 14.4 per cent in 1953 compared with 1952; and again by 9.4 per cent in 1954 compared with 1953. The average annual increase in the two years was 11.9 per cent, thus exceeding the average annual rate of increase of 8.6 per cent provided for by the Five-Year Plan.

Capital construction: In these two years, each annual plan for capital construction was nearly, though not fully, completed. The reasons were: delay in the work of collecting basic data needed for designing; the work of designing lagging behind schedule; blue prints, materials and equipment not supplied on time; lack of practical work schedules geared to the pace of construction; and a considerable amount of disorder at construction sites.

The actual amount of investment (i.e., the amount of work done) in the two years accounted for 32 per cent of the total investment for the five-year period. In the two years, 136 above-norm industrial enterprises went into production. Increases in production capacity of some principal industrial items are as follows: steel, 427,000 tons; electric power, 530,000 kilowatts; coal, 13 million tons; cement, 650,000 tons; cotton spindles, 700,000 spindles; machine-made paper, 40,000 tons; automobile tyres, 160,000; machine-processed sugar, 109,000 tons. During these two years, more than 1,400 kilometres of new railways were laid; track-laying on the Chining-Erhlien Railway and the Litang-Chanchiang Railway was completed. More than 6,600 kilometres of highways were built (including those built with capital provided by local authorities), among which the most important were the Sikang-Tibet and Chinghai-Tibet Highways. Several major water conservancy projects were completed in these two years, including the Sanho Dam and the Poshan Reservoir in the Huai River Basin, the Kuanting Reservoir on the Yungting River, and the cutting of a separate channel to the sea for the Taching and Tseya Rivers in Hopei Province. The main work on the Futseling Reservoir in the Huai River Basin was also completed. These projects later made a notable contribution in coping with the unusually heavy floods of 1954. In these two years, buildings of all kinds with a floor space of over 78 million square metres were erected by the state.

Industrial output: Both the 1953 and 1954 annual plans were overfulfilled. The total value of output of industry in 1954 was 53.7 per cent more than in 1952. There was a marked increase in the output of all principal products: pig iron production increased by 56 per cent; steel by 65 per cent; electric power by 51 per cent; coal by 26 per cent; cement by 61 per cent; timber by 111 per cent; cotton piece-goods by 37 per cent.

During these two years, labour productivity in state industry was raised by 29 per cent while costs of production dropped by 9.6 per cent.

In these first two years of industrial development, the changes brought about are:

First, in the total value of output of industry and agriculture, the proportion of the value of output of modern industry rose from 26.7 per cent in 1952 to 33 per cent in 1954;

Second, in the total value of output of industry, the proportion represented by state, co-operative and joint state-private industry rose from 61 per cent in 1952 to 75.1 per cent in 1954.

Agricultural production: As a result of the fact that in 1953 many areas suffered drought in spring and waterlogging in autumn and that in 1954 many areas experienced unusually heavy floods, plans for agricultural production in these two years were not fulfilled. However, taking the country as a whole, grain output in 1954 was still 3.4 per cent greater than in 1952, and during these first two years increases were registered in the yield of industrial crops including sugar-cane, sugar-beet, oil-bearing seeds and tobacco. Only cotton output declined.

There was great progress in the development of agricultural producers' co-operatives in these two years. By the end of 1954, there were nearly half a million such co-operatives, which provide favourable conditions for increasing agricultural output and furthering the growth of co-operation in farming.

Transport and posts and telecommunications: In these two years, railway freight mileage increased by 55 per cent; railway passenger mileage by 45 per cent; freight mileage of coastwise and inland shipping by 85 per cent; motor freight mileage by 175 per cent; there was also some expansion in civil air services and posts and telecommunications.

Trade: The total volume of retail trade in 1954 was approximately 41.7 per cent more than in 1952. The volume of state and co-operative trade rose from 63 per cent of the total volume of domestic wholesale trade in 1952 to 89 per cent in 1954. The volume of state and co-operative trade rose from some 34 per cent of the total volume of retail trade in 1952 to 58 per cent in 1954.

Culture, education and public health: In 1954, enrolment in institutions of higher education went up 33 per cent as compared with 1952; that of middle schools, 44 per cent; in primary schools, where attention in the past two years was focussed on improving educational standards, enrolment also increased. The number of hospital beds in 1954 was 34 per cent more than in 1952.

The total number of workers and staff in state, co-operative, joint state-private enterprises, cultural and educational establishments, and state organs rose by about three million during the two years. Excluding factory and office workers transferred from private enterprises to joint state-private enterprises and state enterprises, the actual increase was about two million. The total amount of wages paid throughout the country was increased by 56 per cent and the average money wages of factory and office workers rose by 14 per cent. During the two years, the peasants' income from agricultural production and subsidiary rural production rose by about 7 per cent.

The above figures show that the two annual plans for 1953 and 1954 were successfully fulfilled through the efforts of the whole people under the guidance of the Communist Party of China and the Central People's Government.

It is quite possible to fulfil and overfulfil the targets set by the Five-Year Plan. Imperialists and reactionaries have again and again spread shameless lies to the effect that industrialization is impossible in China, or that our Five-Year Plan has already failed. But the Chinese people, under the leadership of the Communist Party of China, have already shown and will continue to show to the world by convincing facts that we have the power not only to carry out the great task of the people's democratic revolution but also to fulfil the even greater task of socialist construction and socialist transformation.

It is true to say that all tasks set by the First Five-Year Plan of our country, no matter to what sphere they belong, are gigantic and arduous. The tasks of the last three years of the plan are even greater and more arduous than those of the first two. From 1955 to 1957, we must fulfil 68 per cent of the total investment programme in capital construction for the five-year period; many large-scale factory, mine, railway and water conservancy projects which have complex technical requirements are to be started simultaneously. The total value of output of industry is to be increased by 29 per cent compared with 1954; we will complete trial manufacture of many new types of technically complex products, and they will go into large-scale production.

Agriculture faces a very heavy task. Taking 1954 as a base, grain output is to be increased by 13.7 per cent, that is an increase of 46,600 million catties; cotton output is to be increased by 53.5 per cent, that is an increase of 11,400,000 *tan*. Railway freightage, in terms of ton-kilometres, will rise by 30 per cent over the 1954 figure. The tasks of highway and water transport are also very heavy. Compared with 1954, and as a result of the people's rising purchasing power, the volume of retail sales of commodities will increase by 27 per cent. Our tasks in the fields of culture, education, scientific research, health, etc., are also very heavy in the last three years.

Socialist transformation of agriculture, handicrafts, and capitalist industry and commerce demands more thorough and careful work; over-all arrangements should be made for private economy according to the policy of unified planning with due consideration for all parties concerned.

What has been said above makes it quite clear that the last three years are the most important period of the Five-Year Plan. Only by making a good job of the work assigned for these three years can we completely fulfil our Five-Year Plan.

Since our original productive forces were so weak, it is inevitable that difficulties should be met with in carrying out our large-scale construction plans in the First Five-Year Plan period. Our work is going ahead at a very intense pace. During the past two years and more, we dealt with many difficulties and accomplished many hard and complex tasks, but we must expect to meet all kinds of new difficulties in the future, and we will have to tackle even harder and more complex tasks.

We must be fully alive to difficulties caused by shortage of technical personnel and supplies of equipment lagging behind the requirements of construction, difficulties caused by the development of agriculture lagging behind the rapid development of industry, and difficulties which emerge in the process of bringing about over-all arrangements for all sectors of the economy in the course of socialist transformation. We must surmount these difficulties by using our manpower, material and financial resources in the most rational and effective way, improving our work in every field and adopting appropriate measures.

Our lack of experience in planning and the incompleteness of our statistical data are bound to affect the accuracy of our plans. In executing our plans, therefore, we must be constantly on the lookout to bring them into line with actual developments, iron out their imperfections and make them more accurate by learning from practical experience and the creative experience of the masses.

The First Five-Year Plan is of decisive significance as the programme of the Communist Party of China, leading the nation in the fight to realize the fundamental task of the transition period. Successful fulfilment of the First Five-Year Plan will be a decisive victory in the realization of this task. Under the leadership of the Communist Party of China and Chairman Mao Tse-tung, the people must close their ranks, mobilize their forces, make painstaking efforts to overcome all difficulties, increase production and practise strict economy, and work hard for the complete realization of the Five-Year Plan.

In the struggle to fulfil the Five-Year Plan, it is essential that the working class of the nation should bring their initiative and creativeness into full play and consistently raise labour productivity and lower production costs. To this end we must raise the level of the political consciousness and technical, educational and vocational levels of factory and office workers; labour emulation must be developed, labour discipline strengthened and the latest experience studied and publicized. In this way, the broad ranks of factory and office workers will be drawn into the active struggle for the complete fulfilment of the state plan.

As we all know, the Five-Year Plan for Development of the National Economy includes not only a plan for industry, but also plans for agriculture and all other branches of the economy. Therefore, the labour of all the personnel of various departments, the labour of factory and office workers in all state, co-operative, joint state-private, and private enterprises, of handicraftsmen and handicraft workshop employees, of workers and staff of all state farms, of members of agricultural producers' co-operatives and individual peasants, of herdsmen and fishermen, and of the working personnel of all economic departments of the state including industry, agriculture, water conservancy, forestry, railways, communications, posts and telecommunications, commerce, food, finance, banking, etc. are all indispensable and should be well co-ordinated in the struggle for fulfilment of the Five-Year Plan. All are engaged in a glorious task.

Workers and staff of state-owned enterprises, co-operative enterprises and state farms are not the only ones who must shoulder responsibility in reaching the targets set by the Five-Year Plan. Factory and office workers and all other personnel of joint state-private enterprises and private enterprises, members of agricultural producers' co-operatives and individual peasants, handicraftsmen and handicraft workshop employees, and the personnel of the state's economic departments, too, all have the responsibility of fulfilling the tasks assigned them under the Five-Year Plan. The First Five-Year Plan can be completely fulfilled only when the masses of the people throughout the country fulfil their production tasks.

Industry and agriculture are the two main parts of the national economy, and workers and peasants constitute the overwhelming majority of the working people of the country. The worker-peasant alliance was the basis on which the Chinese people's revolution won its great victory. The strengthening and consolidation of this alliance under the leadership of the working class will lay the basis for the fulfilment of the First Five-Year Plan and the future victory of socialism. We must, therefore, rely on the worker-peasant alliance as the basic social force which will bring into full play all the economic potentialities of our country, and, at the same time, prepare the necessary reserves to guarantee fulfilment of the First Five-Year Plan.

As is known, none of our economic activities in industry and agriculture and other economic departments are isolated operations; they must be supported by co-ordinated work in the fields of education, culture, health, judicial and supervisory work, public security, civil affairs, foreign affairs and national defence. The services of all personnel in these fields, including that of a section of people in the fields of culture and health who are working as individual professionals, are, therefore, also indispensable for fulfilment of the Five-Year Plan. All are doing honourable work. By doing their work at their respective posts conscientiously and well, they will in effect be fulfilling their responsibilities under the Five-Year Plan. Commanders and fighters of the Chinese People's Liberation Army are shouldering the great and glorious task of defending their motherland and the work of socialist construction.

During the past few years, many model workers and pioneer workers have appeared on the fronts of industry, agriculture, transport, communications and commerce; not a few have also appeared on the cultural and educational fronts. There are also many exemplary workers in the administrative departments. This redounds to the glory of our country. Such model workers and pioneer workers should display still greater initiative and creativeness and do their work still better. They must serve as pace-setters among the masses, as key personnel, and as links between the leadership and the masses, uniting them and guiding them forward in the struggle to overfulfil the Five-Year Plan.

Scientists and technical personnel have a weighty responsibility in the struggle to fulfil the Five-Year Plan. Science and technique are urgently needed for the work of socialist construction; without them socialism cannot be realized. So, no matter what their field of work, scientific research workers, engineers and technicians should continue to raise their ideological and scientific level, bring theory into ever closer relation to practice, and pay keen attention to the connection between their research work and production. They should develop to the full the role of science and technique in socialist construction, and contribute their knowledge to the state and people.

Young people and women should take an active part in the socialist construction of our motherland. Our young people should build up their bodies, acquire cultural and scientific knowledge, learn to love work, cultivate a fine moral character and do their jobs well so that they can help build and defend their country. Women, too, should raise their level of political consciousness, fit themselves better for work in production and take an active part in national construction.

The Five-Year Plan closely concerns the people of all nationalities and all sections of society. It demands that all the country's nationalities unite still more firmly and strengthen their mutual ties and co-operation in economic and cultural affairs. Under the leadership of the Chinese Communist Party and the Central People's Government, the people of all nationalities should actively participate in the political life and economic construction of the nation in a common effort to build up our motherland. At the same time, as laid down in the Constitution, regional autonomy for the national minorities must be realized; we must work hard to foster economic, cultural and educational developments in the areas where national minorities live; we must improve their medical and health services, and the Han people must give sincere assistance, both economic and cultural, to their brother nationalities, so that the living standard of the people of all national minorities may be gradually improved. Socialist transformation among the national minorities must take into account the special features in the development of the various nationalities; the will of the people must be respected.

Owing to the special historical conditions of our country, the working class has a sort of political and economic alliance with the national bourgeoisie. During the transition period, the national bourgeoisie still plays an important part in the national economy. The duty of private industrialists and businessmen during the implementation of the Five-Year Plan is to accept control by state administrative organs and the leadership of the state economy, accept supervision by the workers, operate in a manner beneficial to the national welfare and the people's livelihood, honestly adhere to the state plan, satisfactorily fulfil state assignments and accept socialist transformation. Thus, they will be able to perform their proper function correctly in carrying out the Five-Year Plan, and make definite contributions to its fulfilment.

Chinese resident abroad dearly love their motherland. They want it to prosper and grow in strength. The state must give attention to the protection of their proper rights and interests. At the same time, Chinese resident abroad should strengthen their unity, actively give their support to and participate in national construction.

To fulfil the Five-Year Plan smoothly, not only should there be unified national leadership as regards basic directions, policies and steps to be adopted, local state organs and Party organizations at all levels must also formulate concrete measures to attain assigned targets, particularly those having to do with agricultural production. Local state organs and Party organizations at all levels must not only shoulder responsibility for the direction of all kinds of local economic operations and cultural and educational work, they must also look after political and Party work in the factories and mines, at capital construction sites, and in economic enterprises and cultural establishments directly under the Central People's Government, which are located within the area of their jurisdiction. They must investigate the extent to which state assignments have been met by these enterprises and establishments and supervise and assist them in fulfilling state plans. Enterprises and establishments located in various parts of the country, which are directly under the Central People's Government, must follow the leadership of the local state organs and Party organizations. Any tendency to ignore local leadership must be resolutely fought and rectified. All ministries under the State Council must place full reliance on the initiative of local leading authorities in fulfilling the state plan.

TEXT OF DOCUMENT I
89

To advance our cause to victory, all Communist Party members, all personnel of state organs and enterprises should consistently improve their style of work and strive hard to overcome shortcomings and errors. There is no doubt that the overwhelming majority of our Communist Party members and personnel of state organs are serving the people industriously and devotedly. They work hard to accomplish the tasks entrusted them by the Party, the state and the people. They are able to keep close contact with the masses and conduct self-criticism. But it cannot be denied that there are certain members of the Communist Party and personnel in state organs who are resting on their laurels, and have developed very harmful attitudes of self-conceit; they are unwilling to expose and overcome shortcomings and errors in their work. They fail to go to the rank and file and give concrete leadership. Instead, they practise leadership in the abstract, working in the style of bureaucrats and paper work addicts, neglecting their responsibilities in regard to their work and to state property. There are even some such people who, for selfish ends, trumpet their own achievements, cover up errors and shortcomings in their work, and shield those who violate Party discipline and state laws. It is clear enough that if we do not wage an uncompromising struggle against these harmful tendencies, we will not be able to advance our cause, and our Five-Year Plan will not succeed. Therefore, the Party and state demand that all Party members and personnel of state organs, particularly those in leading positions, must faithfully perform their duties to the Party and state and set a good example for others. They must be diligent, frugal and hard-working. They must work hard to master their own specialities and deepen their political understanding, achieve a grasp of the situation at lower levels, and keep close touch with the masses. They must investigate and study conditions, solve the practical problems which crop up in their work, and bring to light and overcome shortcomings and errors. They must urge and help departments under their leadership to do still better in fulfilling state assignments.

We have already started construction on a gigantic scale. But we lack experience and our technical level is not high. If we do not work diligently to master our economic and other related tasks, we will not be able to carry out our Five-Year Plan smoothly. On the one hand, we should sum up our own experience, learn as we work and improve our skills. On the other hand, we should assimilate the world's latest knowledge and adapt it judiciously to our work and production. We should learn from all our brother countries, especially from the Soviet Union and Soviet experts. People often speak of their gratitude for the aid of the Soviet Union and our other brother countries, and this is quite natural in view of the magnanimous and disinterested help they have given us. But the best way to thank the Soviet Union and our other brother countries is to learn from their pioneering experience, to master the knowledge imparted to us by their experts in the course of construction, and use it well to fulfil our Five-Year Plan. We are working today under much more favourable conditions than those which the Soviet Union faced in its early years. The Soviet Union built socialism alone, in the face of capitalist encirclement, while we have the assistance of the Soviet Union and other brother countries with their rich experience and superb technique. We should take full advantage of these favourable conditions to learn, so that after a few five-year plans we will have accumulated a sufficient fund of experience in construction and raised our science and technique to an adequate level.

We must master the skills of economic work, and at the same time we must do our political work well. We must consistently disseminate the theories of Marxism-Leninism among the masses of the people, acquaint them with the policy of the Party at every stage, and publicize the Constitution of the People's Republic of China. All those who are in leading positions should seriously study the theories of Marxism-Leninism and the works of Chairman Mao Tse-tung, criticize and repudiate bourgeois ideology, and unceasingly raise their theoretical level so as to improve their work.

To carry out the Five-Year Plan under present circumstances means waging a special form of class struggle. Full implementation of the Five-Year Plan will bring about a tremendous upsurge in China's industry and the entire national economy; and it will weigh the scales of economic development sharply in favour of the socialist sector of the economy and against its non-socialist sector. In other words, the people's democratic dictatorship led by the working class and based on the worker-peasant alliance will be further consolidated. All this inspires and elates the nation and our friends all over the world.

The victory of the people means defeat for the enemies of the people, defeat for imperialism, defeat for the Chiang Kai-shek clique of traitors, and defeat for all anti-popular elements in their attempts to stage a come-back by counter-revolution. The enemies of the people will certainly not acquiesce in their own defeat. They will certainly use whatever means they can in attempts to wreck our Five-Year Plan. U.S. imperialism and the Chiang Kai-shek clique of traitors are stepping up their war threats against us; undercover remnants of the Chiang Kai-shek gang on the mainland are constantly engaged in all kinds of sabotage activities; some landlords and counter-revolutionaries are taking advantage of shortcomings in our work to incite trouble; and some law-breaking capitalists are resisting socialist transformation by every means. All this goes to show that the enemies of the people will adopt various methods to undermine the Five-Year Plan, and that implementation of the plan embodies a complex and acute class struggle. People throughout the country must maintain the highest political vigilance, wipe out all undercover counter-revolutionaries and defeat every kind of sabotage directed against the Five-Year Plan by the enemies and reactionaries at home and abroad. Quite a number of people working in state organs and enterprises have not been at all alert to sabotage activities by undercover enemies; they take a light attitude to various kinds of "accidents" caused by counter-revolutionaries. This is a very dangerous tendency which should be rectified immediately. In this respect, the recent exposure of the counter-revolutionary clique led by Hu Feng was an important victory of the whole people in their struggle against counter-revolutionary conspiracies.

The Communist Party of China is the pivotal force in the guidance of our work, and the unity of the Chinese Communist Party is the core of the unity of the entire Chinese people. Under the leadership of the Central Committee of the Party led by Comrade Mao Tse-tung, the Communist Party of China has always maintained a solid and unbreakable unity. The unity and solidarity in the Party has been still greater since the Fourth Plenary Session of the Seventh Central Committee of the Chinese Communist Party when the anti-Party bloc of Kao Kang and Jao Shu-shih was exposed and smashed. Kao Kang and Jao Shu-shih were agents of imperialism and the bourgeoisie in our Party, and the struggle against their anti-Party activities was a struggle in defence of the Communist Party, of socialist construction and communism. The smashing of the anti-Party bloc of Kao Kang and Jao Shu-shih was a great victory in the course of our socialist construction. It demonstrated the close unity of the Communist Party of China and showed that this unity would be further consolidated. The Communist Party of China will continue to heighten its vigilance to strengthen this unity; it will keep a sharp eye on and defeat the plots of the enemies at home and abroad; it will carry on a resolute struggle against all speech and action harmful to the unity of the Party; it will correct the conceit and complacency which infects certain of its members. It will rally its ranks still closer and give still more effective leadership to the nation in the struggle to fulfil the tasks of the First Five-Year Plan and the fundamental task of the state in the transition period.

Chairman Mao Tse-tung gave the following directive at the opening session of the First National People's Congress: "Our general task is to unite the people of the whole country, to win the support of our friends in all nations, to strive to build a great socialist state, and to bestir ourselves to defend peace between the nations and to further the cause of human progress."

In accordance with this directive, we must, under the leadership of the Chinese Communist Party, consolidate the unity among the people of all our various nationalities, the unity between the working class and peasantry and the people's democratic united front.

At the same time, on the basis of the solidarity of the whole Party and the entire people, we will strengthen our unity with our great ally, the Soviet Union, and the People's Democracies, adding our strength to the defence of world peace. We will also strengthen our friendly co-operation with all peace-loving countries in Asia and Africa. In accordance with the famous five principles of peaceful co-existence, our country has established relations of friendly co-operation with India, Burma and Indonesia. On the basis of these principles, we are ready to establish relations of peaceful co-operation with any country, and to expand economic and cultural ties with it so long as it has a similar desire and sincerity.

The principles of the foreign policy of the People's Republic of China are to safeguard the independence, freedom, sovereign rights and territorial integrity of our country, to uphold lasting peace among nations and friendly co-operation among the peoples of all lands, and to oppose the imperialist policies of aggression and war. We shall spare no effort in taking part in every struggle for the relaxation of international tension. The movement for peace, democracy and freedom carried on by the

TEXT OF DOCUMENT I

people in all countries in fact aids our national construction. All those who love peace, democracy and freedom should naturally help one another.

Deputies! The First Five-Year Plan of our country is a mighty plan; it will mean a first step away from our century-long history of economic backwardness; it will move our country one stage forward towards our goal of an industrialized, socialist society. As Chairman Mao Tse-tung has said: "We are now engaged in a great and most glorious task, never before attempted by our forefathers." Each one of us has a great responsibility. We lack experience, so we must work earnestly and industriously. Furthermore, we must summon up the same spirit that we had in the past when we strove for the victory of the revolution undaunted by difficulties or setbacks.

We have the leadership of the Chinese Communist Party and Chairman Mao Tse-tung; our home and foreign policies are correct. Given unity and hard work on the part of the people of all nationalities, democratic classes, democratic parties and all patriots throughout the country, the successful fulfilment and overfulfilment of our First Five-Year Plan for Development of the National Economy is assured.

Chapter II

THE SPEED-UP OF AGRICULTURAL COOPERATIVIZATION, 1955-56

(containing Documents 2, 3, 4, 5)

General comment. The crucial document of the four printed in this chapter is Mao Tse-tung's speech of July 31, 1955 (Document 2). This was not published, however, until the policy "suggested" by Mao had been ratified and formalized in the decisions of the Party's Central Committee in October 1955 (Document 3). The motives behind these decisions and the tensions within the Party to which they gave rise are discussed in our General Introduction, part II. The story of the various stages in the formation of cooperatives in China up to 1956, to which there are many allusions in Mao's speech, may be summarized as follows:

1. On December 15, 1951, the Central Committee of the Party circulated draft decisions on mutual aid and cooperativization, for experimental application. These decisions envisaged temporary and seasonal "mutual aid" teams at the lowest level, permanent "mutual aid" teams, and guided development of agricultural producers' cooperatives on a selective basis. In these cooperatives, peasants were paid dividends for the shares of land which they contributed; this form of cooperative was subsequently known as the "lower" or elementary form, in contrast to the "higher" form in which the peasants surrendered their land. It was emphasized in the draft decisions that cooperativization must proceed on a voluntary basis, and that incentive was all-important; "only under the call to produce more grain and increase their income can peasants be mobilized to organize themselves." After a period of experiment the draft was officially adopted by the Central Committee on February 15, 1953. An attempt was then made to establish cooperatives on a larger scale, but this came to grief and many cooperatives were dissolved. (Mao refers in Document 2 to "mass dissolution.")

2. On December 16, 1953, the Central Committee adopted further decisions on the development of agricultural producers' cooperatives, describing them as a "transitional form through which the peasants can be induced to advance naturally and willingly to socialism" (i.e., to collective farms). The cooperatives, it was said, had "fully revealed their superiority." According to Mao, it was decided to increase their numbers from 14,000 to 35,800 before the autumn harvest of 1954 (in fact, he said, the number rose to 100,000 in this period). At the same time there was continued emphasis on the principles that the development of cooperatives must be voluntary and that increased production and increased income for members were the basic criteria of their success.

3. In October 1954, the Central Committee decided, in Mao's words, to increase the number of cooperatives "six-fold, from one hundred thousand to six hundred thousand." (The text of this decision is not available.) The target was exceeded, but the pace proved too hot. In March 1955 the State Council ordered that the organization of more cooperatives be stopped. In April, there was, in Mao's words, "resolute contraction" of numbers, and the Party issued a warning that the mistakes of 1953 should not be repeated. However, even after the dissolution of some cooperatives, the number established in June 1955 was 650,000 (or, according to Mao's figures, 16.9 million out of a total of 110 million peasant households).

4. In the meantime there was criticism of "rightist" tendencies on this question at the Central Committee's Rural Work Conference in May 1955. In the spring of that year (presumably after March), according to Mao, the Central Committee had decided

that the figure of cooperatives could go up to a million by October 1956. Gradualness was nevertheless still the keynote of the agricultural section of Li Fu-ch'un's speech to the National People's Congress in July 1955 (Document 1). The target named by him was one million cooperatives by 1957 when, he said, the peasant households joining the present elementary form of cooperative would make up about one-third of all the country's peasant households.

5. Mao, in his speech of July 31, 1955 (Document 2), raised the target number to 1.3 million by October 1956 (i.e., a 100 percent increase in 14 months). In section X of the speech he envisaged that by the spring of 1958 about half the peasant population (55 million households) would be in cooperatives of the "semisocialist" (elementary) type. By 1960 the other half would have joined elementary cooperatives, and some of those already formed would have been transformed into higher-type "socialist" cooperatives.

6. In October 1955 the Central Committee adopted its decision (Document 3) calling for the basic completion of elementary cooperatives by the spring of 1958. Work was rushed forward, and Mao, in his preface of December 27, 1955, to the book *Socialist Upsurge in China's Countryside* (Document 4), said that his targets of July had already been far exceeded. He claimed an increase of 300 percent in the number of cooperatives in only four months.

7. The draft 12-Year Agricultural Program (Document 5) in January 1956 laid down that "all provinces...should, in the main, complete agricultural cooperation in its elementary form and set themselves the goal of getting about 85% of all peasant households into agricultural producers' co-operatives in 1956." Higher-stage cooperatives were to be formed by 1957 in "areas where co-operation is on better foundations," and by 1958 the "main work" of organizing them was to be completed throughout the country. Model regulations for "lower" and "higher" forms were adopted by the National People's Congress on March 17 and June 30, 1956 (CB 369, 399). Most important of all, the method of assessing and collecting grain tax was revised in measures promulgated by the State Council, August 25, 1955—known as the "Three Fixes." At the same time, a grain-rationing system, introduced for the cities in November 1953, was extended to country areas; see T. J. Hughes and D. E. T. Luard, *The Economic Development of Communist China* (London: Oxford University Press, 1959), p. 183.

A number of supplementary texts for the period 1949-1956, together with notes and bibliography, are given in Chao Kuo-chün, *Agrarian Policies of Mainland China: A Documentary Study, 1949-1956* (Cambridge, Mass.: Center for East Asian Studies, Harvard University, 1957). A short narrative of cooperativization in China, 1951-1955, with some interesting detailed quotations from Chinese press sources, is given in CB 373.

Other sources on points of detail are as follows.

CB 364, containing details of meeting of Central Committee, October 1955.

CB 362 and SCMP 1147 on the "Three Fix" policy. See especially the *People's Daily* editorial of Sept. 27, 1955, in SCMP 1147.

ECMM 20 (*Study*, Nov. 2, 1955) and ECMM 26 (*World Culture*, Dec. 5, 1955), containing some detailed articles on opposition within the Party to the new policy, and on the lessons to be learned from the experience of the U.S.S.R. in collectivization.

URS, Vol. 1, Nos. 14, 16, 27, and 28, containing material, mainly from the local Kwangtung press, on the problems set to provincial cadres by the new line on cooperatives. URS, Vol. 1, No. 11, has quotations from the Chekiang local press of May 1955, showing that dissolution of cooperatives took place with the encouragement of the local Party authorities (contrast Mao's speech—Document 2, section III).

DOCUMENT 2

The Question of Agricultural Cooperation, report by Mao Tse-tung, Chairman of the Chinese People's Republic and of the Central Committee, Chinese Communist Party, delivered at a meeting of secretaries of provincial, municipal, and autonomous region committees of the Party on July 31, 1955.

The English text is an official translation published as a pamphlet with the above title by the Foreign Languages Press, Peking, 1956. The translation, according to a publisher's note, was made from the Chinese text of the first edition published by the People's Publishing House, Peking, in October 1955.

_____TEXT OF DOCUMENT 2_____

I

Throughout the Chinese countryside a new upsurge in the socialist mass movement is in sight. But some of our comrades are tottering along like a woman with bound feet, always complaining that others are going too fast. They imagine that by picking on trifles, grumbling unnecessarily, worrying continuously and putting up countless taboos and commandments they are guiding the socialist mass movement in the rural areas on sound lines.

No, this is not the right way at all; it is wrong.

The tide of social reform in the countryside— in the shape of co-operation—has already reached some places. Soon it will sweep the whole country. This is a huge socialist revolutionary movement, which involves a rural population more than five hundred million strong, one which has very great world significance. We should guide this movement vigorously, warmly and systematically, and not act as a drag on it in various ways. In such a movement some deviations are inevitable. That stands to reason, but it is not difficult to straighten them out. Weaknesses or mistakes found among cadres and peasants can be done away with if we actively assist them. Guided by the Party the cadres and peasants are going forward; the movement is fundamentally healthy.

In some places they have made certain mistakes in the work, for example, barring poor peasants from the co-operatives and ignoring their difficulties, and at the same time forcing the well-to-do middle peasants into the co-operatives and interfering with their interests. But these errors have to be corrected by education, not just by reprimands. Mere reprimands solve no problems. We must guide the movement boldly, not act like one fearing the dragon in front and the tiger behind. Both cadres and peasants will change of themselves as they learn from their own experience in the struggle. Get them into action themselves: they will learn while doing, become more capable, and large numbers of excellent people will come forward. This "fearing the dragon in front and the tiger behind" attitude will not produce cadres. It is necessary to send large groups of cadres with short-term training into the countryside to guide and assist the agricultural co-operative movement; but the cadres sent down from above also have to learn how to work from the movement itself. Going in for training courses and hearing dozens of rules explained in lectures does not necessarily mean one knows how to work.

In short, leadership should never lag behind the mass movement. As things stand today, however, the mass movement is in advance of the leadership, which fails to keep pace with the movement. This state of affairs must be changed.

II

Now, at a time when the nation-wide co-operative movement is taking tremendous strides forward, we still have to argue such questions as: Can the co-operatives grow? Can they be consolidated? As far as some comrades are concerned, the crux of the matter seems to be that they are worried about whether the several hundred thousand existing semi-socialist co-operatives—mostly rather small, averaging twenty odd peasant households each—can be consolidated. Of course, unless they are, growth is out of the question. Some comrades are still unconvinced by the history of the growth of co-operation in the past few years and are still waiting to see how things go in 1955. They may even wait another year, till 1956, and only if still more co-operatives are firmly established by then will they be truly convinced that agricultural co-operation is a possibility and that the policy of the Central Committee of our Party is correct. That is why the work this year and next is so very important.

To show the possibilities of agricultural co-operation, to show that the policy of the Central Committee of our Party on agricultural co-operation is sound, it is perhaps not without value for us to discuss here the history of the agricultural co-operative movement in our country.

Even before the founding of the People's Republic of China, in the course of twenty-two years of revolutionary wars, our Party amassed experience, after land reform, in guiding the peasants to organize agricultural producers' mutual-aid groups of a rudimentary socialist character. At that time, there were mutual-aid working groups and ploughing teams in Kiangsi Province, work exchange teams in northern Shensi and mutual-aid teams in various places in north, east and northeast China. In isolated cases, agricultural producers' co-operatives of a semi-socialist or socialist character also came into being. During the war of resistance to Japanese aggression, for instance, there was an agricultural producers' co-operative of a socialist character in Ansai County in northern Shensi, but at that time such co-operatives were not recommended.

Only since the founding of the Chinese People's Republic has our Party led the peasants to organize agricultural producers' mutual-aid teams on a more extensive scale and begun organizing agricultural producers' co-operatives, based on the mutual-aid teams, in large numbers—that is, for about six years now.

On December 15, 1951, when the Central Committee of our Party issued to local Party organizations the first draft decisions on mutual-aid and co-operation in agricultural production to be tried out in various places, there were over three hundred agricultural producers' co-operatives. (This document was not published in the press in the form of Party decisions till March 1953.) Two years later, on December 16, 1953, our Party Central Committee issued its decisions on agricultural producers' co-operatives. By then the number of agricultural producers' co-operatives exceeded 14,000, forty-seven times as many as two years before.

That decision laid it down that, between the winter of 1953 and the autumn harvest of 1954, the number of agricultural producers' co-operatives would increase from this 14,000 odd to 35,800 odd, that is, only to two and a half times as many. But, as it turned out, during that year the number of co-operatives rose to 100,000, more than seven times as many.

In October 1954 the Central Committee of our Party took a decision to increase the number of co-operatives sixfold, from one hundred thousand to six hundred thousand. The result was 670,000 co-operatives. By June 1955, after preliminary weeding-out, the number was cut by twenty thousand, leaving 650,000—fifty thousand more than the planned target. The number of peasant households in co-operatives was 16,900,000—an average of twenty-six households to each.

These co-operatives are mainly in those northern provinces which were the first to be liberated. In most of the provinces liberated later, a number of agricultural producers' co-operatives have been set up. There are a fair number in Anhwei and Chekiang, but not very many in other provinces.

These co-operatives, generally speaking, are small, but among them are a few large ones, some embracing seventy or eighty households, some more than a hundred, and some whose membership runs into several hundred households.

Generally, too, the co-operatives are semi-socialist, but a few have passed into a higher stage and become socialist co-operatives.

While the co-operative movement in agricultural production among the peasants has been growing our country has already established a small number of socialist state farms. By 1957 there will be 3,038 state farms cultivating 16,870,000 *mou*[1] of land. They will include 141 mechanized farms (those existing in 1952 plus those set up in the course of the First Five-Year Plan) with 7,580,000 *mou* under cultivation. The number of non-mechanized state farms under local jurisdiction will be 2,897, with 9,290,000 *mou* under cultivation. During the period covered by the Second and Third Five-Year Plans there will be a great growth of state-operated agriculture.

In the spring of 1955 the Central Committee of our Party decided that the number of agricultual producers' co-operatives should go up to a million. This means a little more than a 50 per cent increase adding 350,000 to the original 650,000. Now I feel this increase is a bit too small. Possibly

---

[1] A *mou* is one sixth of an acre.— *Translator.*

the former figure of 650,000 should have been roughly doubled, i.e., the number of co-operatives ought to be increased to 1,300,000 so that in each of the country's 200,000 odd *hsiang*[2] except in some border areas, there might be at least one or several small agricultural producers' co-operatives of the semi-socialist type which would serve as an example for others. These new co-operatives would gain experience and in a year or two become "veterans," and others could learn from them. From now to the autumn harvest of October 1956 is fourteen months, and such a plan for the establishment of co-operatives ought to be feasible. I hope the responsible comrades in the various provinces and autonomous regions will go back and look into the question, work out a programme suited to actual conditions and report to the Central Committee within two months. We shall then hold a discussion and take a final decision.

The question is whether the co-operatives can be consolidated. Some people say that last year's plan to set up 500,000 was too big, too rash, and that this year's plan to set up 350,000 is too big, too rash, too. They doubt if that many co-operatives can be consolidated.

Is it really possible to consolidate them?

Needless to say, neither socialist industrialization nor socialist transformation is easy. A host of difficulties are bound to crop up as some 110 million peasant households turn from individual to collective management and go ahead with technical reforms in agriculture. But we should have confidence that our Party is capable of leading the masses to overcome such difficulties.

As far as agricultural co-operation is concerned, I think we should believe: first, that the poor peasants, and the lower middle peasants among both the new and old middle peasants,[3] are disposed to choose the socialist road and energetically respond to our Party's call for co-operation—the poor peasants because of their economic difficulties and the lower middle peasants because their economic conditions, though better than before liberation, are still not too good. Particularly active are those among them who have a deeper understanding.

Secondly, I think we should have confidence that our Party is capable of leading the people of the country to socialism. Our Party has led a great people's democratic revolution to victory and established a people's democratic dictatorship headed by the working class, and it can certainly lead our people to carry out, in the main, socialist industrialization and the socialist transformation of agriculture, handicrafts and capitalist industry and commerce, in the course of roughly three five-year plans. In agriculture, as in other fields, we have powerful and convincing proof of this—witness the first group of 300 co-operatives, the second of 13,700 and the third of 86,000—100,000 all told—all of which were established before the autumn of 1954 and all of which have been consolidated. Why, then, should not the fourth group of 550,000 co-operatives formed in 1954-55 and the fifth group of 350,000 (our provisional target) to be established in 1956-56 be consolidated too?

We must believe in the masses; we must believe in our Party: these are two cardinal principles. If we doubt these principles, we can do nothing.

III

To gradually achieve agricultural co-operation throughout China's rural areas, we must seriously give the existing co-operatives a check over.

Great emphasis must be placed on the quality of the co-operatives. We must oppose any tendency to neglect quality and concentrate solely on increasing their number or bringing a greater number of peasant households into them. That is why attention must be paid to checking over the co-operatives.

Co-operatives should be checked over not once, but two or three times a year. A certain number were checked over in the first half of this year (though in some places, apparently, this was done rather superficially, without taking enough trouble). I suggest a second checking in the autumn or winter of this year and a third in the spring or summer of next. Of the 650,000 existing

---

[2] *Hsiang* is an administrative unit of one or several villages.—*Translator*.

[3] Old middle peasants are those who were middle peasants before the land reform. New middle peasants are those who have risen to the status of middle peasants since land reform.—*Translator*.

co-operatives, 550,000 are new, set up last winter or this spring, and among these there are some "Class I" co-operatives, as they are called, which are pretty well consolidated. Adding the 100,000 old co-operatives already consolidated, the number already consolidated is not at all small. Cannot these co-operatives already consolidated gradually lead the others to consolidate? They certainly can.

We should treasure, not hinder, every bit of socialist initiative shown by peasants and cadres. It is our job to live with, breathe the same air as the members and cadres of the co-operatives and the county, district and *hsiang* cadres, not hamper their initiative.

Only where all, or nearly all the members of a co-operative have made up their minds not to carry on should a decision be taken to wind it up. If only some members have made up their minds not to carry on, they should be allowed to withdraw, while the majority continue. If the majority are determined not to carry on but a minority are willing, then let the majority withdraw and the minority continue. Even so, it is better than to wind it up. In one very small co-operative of only six households in Hopei Province, the three old middle-peasant households firmly refused to carry on and left. The three poor-peasant households decided to continue at all costs, stayed in, and the co-operative organization was preserved. The fact is, the road taken by these three poor-peasant households is the one which will be taken by five hundred million peasants throughout the country. All peasants working on their own will eventually take the road resolutely chosen by these three poor-peasant households.

With the adoption of a policy of what was called "drastic compression" in Chekiang Province—not by decision of the Chekiang Provincial Party Committee—out of 53,000 co-operatives in the province 15,000, comprising 400,000 peasant households, were dissolved at one fell swoop. This caused great dissatisfaction among the masses and the cadres, and it was altogether the wrong thing to do. A "drastic compression" policy of this kind was decided on in a state of terrified confusion. It was not right, too, to take such a major step without the consent of the Central Committee. As early as April 1955 the Central Committee gave this warning: "Do not commit the 1953 mistake of mass dissolution of co-operatives again, otherwise self-critical examination will again be called for." But certain comrades preferred not to listen.

In the face of success, there are, I think, two bad tendencies: one is that "dizziness with success" which makes for swelled-headedness and leads to "Leftist" mistakes. That, of course, is bad. The second is letting oneself be stunned by success, which leads to "drastic compression" and to Rightist mistakes. That is bad, too. At the present time, it is the latter that prevails. Some comrades are stunned by the hundreds of thousands of small co-operatives.

IV

Preparatory work before the co-operatives are set up must be done seriously and well.

Attention must be paid from the very start to the quality of the co-operatives; the tendency simply to increase their number must be opposed.

Fight no battle that is not well prepared, no battle whose outcome is uncertain: that was the well-known slogan of our Party during the past revolutionary wars. It applies equally well to the work of socialist construction. If you want to be sure of the outcome, there must be preparedness, full preparedness. A great deal of spade work must be done beforehand if you are going to set up a group of new agricultural producers' co-operatives in a province, administrative region or county. The main thing this work includes is (1) criticism of wrong ideas and summarization of experience gained in the work; (2) systematic and repeated publicity among the peasant masses of our Party's principles, policy and measures on agricultural co-operation; and explanation in the course of propaganda among the peasants not only of the benefits of co-operation but also of the difficulties that may be met with in expanding it, so that their minds are fully prepared; (3) taking into account the situation as it really is, drawing up a comprehensive plan for expanding agricultural co-operation for an entire province, administrative region, county, district or *hsiang*, and on the basis of this comprehensive plan working out an annual plan; (4) training cadres for co-operatives in short-term courses; (5) widespread expansion of agricultural producers' mutual-aid teams in large numbers and, whenever possible, getting such teams to join together and form combined groups of mutual-aid teams, so laying the foundations for further combination into co-operatives.

Given these conditions, it is possible, in developing co-operatives, to go a long way towards solving the problem of how to pay attention to both their number and quality. But still, once a group of co-operatives is set up, the work of checking them should be immediately undertaken.

Whether a group of co-operatives can be consolidated after it is established depends, first, on how well the preliminary spade work was done and, secondly, on how well the work of checking is carried out thereafter.

The work of both setting up and checking over co-operatives depends on the Party and Youth League branches in the *hsiang*. For that reason, both tasks must be closely linked with the work of building up and consolidating Party and Youth League organizations in the countryside.

The local cadres in the rural areas should be the mainstay both in establishing and checking over the co-operatives, and they should be backed up in their work and asked to shoulder responsibility. Cadres sent from above should be an auxiliary force; their function is to guide and help, not to take everything into their own hands.

V

Members of agricultural producers' co-operatives must obtain higher yields than individual peasants and those working in mutual-aid teams. Output certainly cannot be allowed to remain at the level reached by individual peasants or mutual-aid teams: that would mean failure. What would be the use of having co-operatives at all? Still less can yields be allowed to fall. Over 80 per cent of the 650,000 existing agricultural producers' co-operatives did increase their yields. That is a cheerful picture, showing that members of the co-operatives are taking greater initiative in production and that co-operatives are superior to mutual-aid teams, and far superior to individual farming.

Certain things are essential in order to increase yields: first, insistence on the principles of voluntariness and mutual benefit; secondly, improvement of management (planning and administration of production, organization of labour, etc.); thirdly, improvement of farming technique (deep ploughing and intensive cultivation, close planting, increasing the acreage of land which is cropped more than once a year, selection of seed, popularization of improved farm implements, the fight against plant diseases and pests, etc.); and fourthly, an increase in the means of production (including land, fertilizer, water conservancy works, draught animals, farm implements, etc.). These are necessary conditions for consolidating the co-operatives and ensuring increased production.

We must, while always insisting on the principles of voluntariness and mutual benefit, now pay attention to the following questions: (1) Is it better to leave the pooling of draught animals and large farm implements in the co-operatives for a year or two? Were fair prices for them agreed, and were repayments spread over too long a time? (2) Is the ratio between the dividend on land shares and payment for labour appropriate? (3) How should the co-operative acquire funds for investment? (4) Can members devote part of their labour to subsidiary rural production? (Because the agricultural producers' co-operatives we have now set up are generally semi-socialist in nature, attention must be paid to a proper settlement of these four questions, to avoid violating the principle of mutual benefit as between middle and poor peasants. Voluntariness can only be based on mutual benefit.) (5) How much land is it allowable to set aside for members of a co-operative to work on their own? (6) The question of the composition of the co-operative; and so on.

I shall now deal with the question of the composition of the co-operative membership. I think that, in the next year or two, in all areas where co-operatives are starting to grow or have only recently started to get going, that is, in most areas at present, we should first get the active elements of the following sections of the people organized: (1) the poor peasants, (2) the lower new middle peasants and (3) the lower old middle peasants. People in these sections who for the time being are not active must not be dragged in against their will. Wait till their understanding grows and they are interested in co-operatives, then draw them in group by group. These sections of people are fairly close to each other in their economic position. They either still have difficulties (in the case of the poor peasants who have been given land and are much better off than in pre-liberation days but still have difficulties owing to insufficient manpower, draught animals and farm implements), or are still not well off (in the case of the lower middle peasants). Therefore, they all have an active desire to organize co-operatives. Even so, for various reasons, the degree of their keenness varies:

some are very keen, some are, for the time being, not very keen, while others prefer to wait and see. So we should continue to educate for a while those who for the time being are reluctant to join co-operatives, even if they are poor or lower middle peasants, we should continue to educate for a time and wait patiently till their understanding grows; what we must not do is to go against the voluntary principle and drag them in against their will.

As for the upper middle peasants among the new and old middle peasants—that is, the middle peasants who are economically better off—except for those who have already become conscious that they must choose the socialist road and are really willing to join—who can be admitted—none of the rest are to be drawn in for the time being, certainly not dragged in reluctantly. This is because they have not yet become conscious that they must choose the socialist road, and they will make up their minds to join the co-operatives only after the majority of people in the rural areas have joined, or when the yield per *mou* of the co-operatives equals or surpasses that of the land of well-to-do middle peasants, and when they realize that they stand to gain nothing by going on working on their own, and that it is rather more profitable to join.

So the first thing to do is to divide those who are poor or still not well off (together they form about 60 to 70 per cent of the rural population) into groups according to their degree of understanding, and, in the next few years, to get them to organize themselves into co-operatives, and then go on to absorb the well-to-do middle peasants. In this way we can avoid running things just by issuing orders.

In the next few years we shall definitely not, in areas where the majority of the population have not joined in co-operation, take former landlords and rich peasants into the co-operatives. In areas where the majority of people have joined in co-operation, those co-operatives which are firmly established may, on conditions, at different times, take in group by group people who were formerly landlords and rich peasants but who have long given up exploitation, who are now engaged in labour and abide by law, letting them take part in collective labour and continue to reform themselves in the process.

VI

On the question of growth, the problem that calls for criticism at present is not rashness. It is wrong to say that the present pace of development of the agricultural producers' co-operatives has "gone beyond practical possibilities" or "gone beyond the consciousness of the masses." The situation in China is like this: its population is enormous, there is a shortage of cultivated land (only three *mou* of land per head taking the country as a whole; in many parts of the southern provinces the average is only one *mou* or less), natural calamities take place from time to time—every year large numbers of farms suffer more or less from flood, drought, gales, frost, hail or insect pests—and methods of farming are backward. As a result, many peasants are still having difficulties or are not well off. The well-off ones are comparatively few, although since land reform the standard of living of the peasants as a whole has improved to a greater or lesser extent. For all these reasons there is an active desire among most peasants to take the socialist road. Our country's socialist industrialization and its achievements are constantly intensifying it. For them socialism is the only solution. Such peasants amount to 60 to 70 per cent of the entire rural population. That is to say, most of the peasants, if they are to throw off poverty, improve their standard of living and withstand natural calamities, cannot but unite and go forward to socialism. This awareness is already taking an increasing hold on the masses of the poor and not so well-off peasants. The well-to-do or comparatively well-off peasants make up only 20 to 30 per cent of the rural population. They vacillate. Some try hard to take the road to capitalism. As I said before, a good many poor and not so well-off peasants whose level of understanding is low at the moment also mark time and waver. But compared with the well-to-do peasants, it is easy for them to accept socialism. That is how things stand now.

But some of our comrades ignore these facts and think that the several hundred thousand small semi-socialist agricultural producers' co-operatives that have sprung into being have "gone beyond practical possibilities" or "gone beyond the understanding of the masses." What this means is that all they see is the comparatively small number of well-to-do peasants, and forget about the majority—those who are poor or not well off. This is the first wrong-headed idea.

These comrades also underrate the leading role which the Communist Party plays in the countryside and the whole-hearted support which the peasant masses give it. They imagine our Party is already finding it difficult to consolidate the several hundred thousand small co-operatives, and that any great growth of co-operative farming is certainly inconceivable. They paint a pessimistic picture of the present situation in the Party's work in guiding agricultural co-operation and think that it "has gone beyond the level of the cadres' experience." It's quite true, the socialist revolution is a new revolution. In the past we only had experience of bourgeois-democratic revolution; we had no experience of socialist revolution. How can we get such experience: by sitting back and waiting for it, or by throwing ourselves into the struggle for the socialist revolution and learning in the process? How else can we get experience in industrialization if we do not carry out the Five-Year Plan, if we do not engage in the work of socialist industrialization? Co-operation in agriculture is one of the integral parts of the Five-Year Plan. If we do not guide the peasants in organizing one or several agricultural producers' co-operatives in every *hsiang* or village, where will the "cadres' experience" come from, how will the level of that experience be raised? Clearly the idea that the present state of development reached by the agricultural producers' co-operatives has "gone beyond the level of the cadres' experience" shows faulty thinking. This is the second wrong-headed idea.

The way these comrades look at things is wrong. They fail to grasp the essential, main aspects and instead exaggerate non-essential, minor aspects. I am not saying that these non-essential, minor aspects should be overlooked: they have to be dealt with properly one by one. But if we are to avoid confusion about the direction in which to proceed, we should not regard them as the essential, main aspects.

We must be convinced: first, that the peasant masses are willing, led by the Party, gradually to follow the socialist road; second, that the Party is able to guide the peasants to take this road. These two points are the essence, the crux of the matter. If we lack this conviction, it is impossible for us to virtually achieve socialism in the period of roughly three five-year plans.

VII

The Soviet Union's great historical experience in building socialism inspires our people and gives them full confidence that they can build socialism in their country. However there are different ways of looking at this question of international experience. Some comrades disapprove of the Party Central Committee's policy of keeping agricultural co-operation in step with socialist industrialization, the policy which proved correct in the Soviet Union. They consider that the prescribed rate of development for industrialization is all right, but that there is no need for agricultural co-operation to keep in step with industrialization, that it should develop very, very slowly. That is to disregard the Soviet Union's experience. These comrades do not understand that socialist industrialization is not something that can be carried out in isolation, separate from agricultural co-operation. In the first place, as everyone knows, the level of production of marketable grain and industrial raw materials in our country today is very low, whereas the state's demands for these items grow year by year. Therein lies a sharp contradiction. If, in a period of roughly three five-year plans, we cannot fundamentally solve the problem of agricultural co-operation, if we cannot jump from small-scale farming with animal-drawn farm implements to large-scale farming with machinery—which includes state-sponsored land reclamation carried out on a large scale by settlers using machinery (the plan being to bring under cultivation 400-500 million *mou* of virgin land in the course of three five-year plans), we shall fail to resolve the contradiction between the ever-increasing demand for marketable grain and industrial raw materials and the present generally poor yield of staple crops. In that case our socialist industrialization will run into formidable difficulties: we shall not be able to complete socialist industrialization. The Soviet Union once faced this problem in the course of building socialism. It solved it by systematically guiding and expanding agricultural co-operation. We too can solve this problem only by using the same method.

In the second place, some of our comrades do not think of linking up the following two factors: heavy industry which is the most important branch in the work of socialist industrialization and produces the tractors and other agricultural machinery, the chemical fertilizers, modern means of transport, oil, electric power for the needs of agriculture and so on, and the fact that all these can be found a use for or can be used on a big scale only on the basis of large-scale, co-operative farming. We are carrying out a revolution not only in the social system, changing from private ownership to common ownership, but also in technology, changing from handicraft production to mass production with up-to-date machinery. These two revolutions interlink. In agriculture, under the conditions prevailing in our country, co-operation must precede the use of big machinery. (In capitalist countries agriculture tends to develop along capitalist lines.) We can see, then, that industry and agriculture, socialist industrialization and the socialist transformation of agriculture, cannot on any account be separated, cannot be dealt with in isolation from each other. Moreover, there must be no attempt to over-estimate the one and underrate the other. Soviet experience in this matter, too, shows us the way to go, yet some of our comrades pay no attention and always look at things in isolation, as though they were not connected. What is more, there are two other things which some of our comrades do not think of linking up: the large funds which are needed to complete both national industrialization and the technical reconstruction of agriculture and the fact that a considerable part of these funds is derived from agriculture. Apart from the direct agricultural tax, accumulation of funds comes about by way of developing the production of light industry, which produces large quantities of consumer goods needed by the peasants. The peasants exchange their marketable grain and industrial raw materials for these goods. That satisfies the material demands of both the peasants and the state. It also accumulates funds for the state. But any large-scale expansion of light industry requires the development not only of heavy industry but of agriculture too. The reason for this is that you cannot bring about any great expansion of a light industry founded simply on small-peasant economy; but only one based on large-scale farming which, in the case of our country, means socialist co-operative agriculture. Only that type of agriculture can give the peasants much greater purchasing power than they have now. We again have the experience of the Soviet Union to draw on, but some of our comrades take no notice of it. They usually take the standpoint of the bourgeoisie and the rich peasants or that of the well-to-do middle peasants who have a spontaneous tendency to take the capitalist road. They think in terms of the few, rather than take the standpoint of the working class and think in terms of the whole country and people.

VIII

Some comrades have found grounds in the history of the Communist Party of the Soviet Union for criticizing what they call impatience and rashness in carrying out agricultural co-operation in our country at present. And does not the *History of the C.P.S.U. (B.) Short Course* tell us that many of their local Party organizations at one time did commit mistakes through impatience and rashness when it came to the question of the pace of co-operation? Should we not pay attention to this Soviet experience?

I think we certainly should pay attention to this Soviet experience. We must oppose any impatience and rashness, any step taken without preparation and without considering the level of understanding which the peasant masses have reached. What we should not do is to allow some of our comrades to cover up their dilatoriness by quoting the experience of the Soviet Union.

How did the Central Committee of our Party decide to carry out agricultural co-operation in China?

First, it prepared to accomplish the plan, in the main, in eighteen years. The little more than three years between the founding of the People's Republic of China in October 1949 and 1952 were spent in restoring the economy of our country. In this period, in the field of agriculture, besides completing land reform and bringing about the recovery of agricultural production, we made great efforts to promote the organization of agricultural mutual-aid teams and began to organize semi-socialist agricultural producers' co-operatives in all the old liberated areas. In this work some experience was gained. Then there followed the First Five-Year Plan, which began in 1953. It has now been running nearly three years and our agricultural co-operative movement has surged forward all over the country. We have been piling up experience. Eighteen years altogether will pass between the founding of the People's Republic of China and the completion of the Third Five-Year Plan. In this period, simultaneously with the virtual completion of socialist industrialization and socialist transformation of handicrafts and capitalist industry and commerce, we intend, in the main, to complete the socialist transformation of agriculture. Is this possible? Soviet experience tells us that it is. The Civil War in the Soviet Union ended in 1920. Agricultural co-operation was completed in the seventeen years between 1921 and 1937. The greater part of this work was done in the six years between 1929 and 1934. During this period, though some local Party organizations in the Soviet Union, just as the *History of the C.P.S.U. (B.) Short Course* records, made the mistake of getting "dizzy with success," the mistake was quickly rectified. Finally, by a great effort, the Soviet Union successfully completed the socialist transformation of its entire agriculture and at the same time revolutionized agriculture on the technical side. The Soviet Union's experience is our model.

Secondly, we have been taking steps to bring about a gradual advance in the socialist transformation of agriculture. The first step in the countryside is to call on the peasants, in accordance with the principles of voluntariness and mutual benefit, to organize agricultural producers' mutual-aid teams. Such teams contain only the rudiments of socialism. Each one draws in a few households, though some have ten or more. The second step is to call on the peasants, on the basis of these mutual-aid teams and still in accordance with the principles of voluntariness and mutual benefit, to organize small agricultural producers' co-operatives, semi-socialist in nature, characterized by the pooling of land as shares and by single management. Not until we take the third step will the peasants be called upon, on the basis of these small semi-socialist co-operatives and in accordance with the same principles of voluntariness and mutual benefit, to unite on a larger scale and organize large agricultural producers' co-operatives completely socialist in nature. These steps are designed to steadily raise the socialist consciousness of the peasants through their personal experience, to change their mode of life step by step and so minimize any feeling that their mode of life is being changed all of a sudden. Steps such as these can in the main avoid any drop in yields over a period of, say, the first year or two. More than that, these steps must ensure a year by year increase. And this can be done. Roughly 80 per cent of the existing 650,000 agricultural producers' co-operatives have increased output. Just over 10 per cent of them have shown neither an increase nor a decline. The output of the remainder has dropped. The state of affairs in both these latter categories is bad, and particularly so in the case of co-operatives where production has fallen. A great effort must be made to check over such co-operatives. Since about 80 per cent of all co-operatives increased output (by anything from 10 to 30 per cent), and since just over 10 per cent in their first year showed neither an increase nor a decline, it must be quite possible for them, in their second year, after checking, to show an increase; and, finally, since it is feasible for the remainder that have shown a decline in output to increase it in the second year, after checking, or at least to reach the stage of neither increasing nor reducing production, our progress in co-operation is on the whole healthy, and can in the main ensure that production does not fall, but rises. The taking of these steps is, moreover, a splendid school for training cadres. Through such steps administrative and technical personnel for the co-operatives are gradually trained in large numbers.

Thirdly, targets for the progress of agricultural co-operation are to be set once a year in the light of actual conditions, and a check on how the work of co-operation is being carried out made several times a year. In this way concrete measures for progress in the various provinces, counties and *hsiang* can be decided on every year according to changing conditions and their degree of success. In some places, progress may be held up for a while pending check over. In others, development and checking can proceed side by side. Part of the membership of some co-operatives may be allowed to withdraw. Individual co-operatives may, for the time being, be allowed to dissolve. In some places large numbers of new co-operatives may be set up, while in others only the number of peasant households in existing co-operatives may be increased. Whenever a number of co-operatives have been established in a province or county, there must be a time when we can stop for a check over before we go on to set up some more. The idea of never allowing any pause, any rest, is all wrong. As for supervising the movement, the Party Central Committee, and its provincial, area, municipal and autonomous region committees, must pay strict attention to it. Inspection is to be done not once but several times a year. Whenever a problem crops up, it should be solved right away. Problems should not be allowed to pile up till there is a whole batch of them to settle. Criticism should be made in good time; do not get into the habit of criticizing only after something has happened. For instance, in the first seven months of this year, the Central Committee itself has called three conferences of responsible comrades from various places, including the one now going on, to discuss the problems of co-operation in the countryside. This method of working out proper measures, suited to local conditions in different places and giving timely guidance, ensures that we shall commit fewer mistakes in our work and that, if mistakes are committed, they are quickly put right.

In view of what I have said, can we not say that the policy of our Party on the question of agricultural co-operation is the right one, one that can ensure the healthy development of the movement? I think we can and should say so. To characterize this policy as "rash" is utterly wrong.

IX

Some comrades, basing themselves on the viewpoint of the bourgeoisie, rich peasants or well-to-do middle peasants who have a spontaneous tendency to take the capitalist road, approach the problem of the worker-peasant alliance—a problem of the utmost importance—in the wrong way. They think that the present situation of the co-operative movement is critical. They advise us to "get off the horse" as we are riding along the road to co-operation. "If you don't," they warn us, "you're liable to break up the worker-peasant alliance." We think exactly the opposite is true. If we don't keep on our horse, we are liable to break up the worker-peasant alliance. They say "get off!" We say "get on!"—only one word different, but all the difference between one policy and another.

As everybody knows, we already have a worker-peasant alliance based on a bourgeois-democratic revolution against imperialism and feudalism, which took land from the landlords and distributed it to the peasants so as to free them from the bondage of feudal ownership. Now this revolution is a thing of the past and feudal ownership has been done away with. What still lingers in the countryside is capitalist ownership by the rich peasants and individual peasant ownership—an ocean of it. Everyone has noticed that in recent years there has been a spontaneous and constant growth of capitalist elements in the countryside and that new rich peasants have sprung up everywhere. Many well-to-do middle peasants are striving to become rich ones. Many poor peasants, lacking sufficient means of production, are still not free from the toils of poverty; some are in debt, others selling or renting their land. If this tendency goes unchecked, the separation into two extremes in the countryside will get worse day by day. Peasants who have lost their land and who are still having difficulties will complain that we do nothing to save them when we see they are up against it, nothing to help them overcome difficulties. And the well-to-do middle peasants who tend towards capitalism will also find fault with us, for they will never be satisfied because we have no intention of taking the capitalist path. If that is how circumstances stand, can the worker-peasant alliance stand fast? Obviously not. The problem is one that can be solved only on a new basis. That basis is, simultaneously, gradually, to bring about, on the one hand, socialist industrialization, the socialist transformation of handicraft industry and capitalist industry and commerce, and, on the other, the socialist transformation of agriculture as a whole through co-operation. In that way we shall put an end to the systems of rich-peasant economy and individual economy in the countryside and so let all people in the rural areas enjoy a common prosperity. Only in this way, we hold, can the worker-peasant alliance be consolidated. If we fail to act in this way, that alliance will really be in danger of breaking up. The comrades who advise us to "get off the horse" are completely wrong on this score.

X

We should realize, here and now, that an upsurge in socialist transformation will soon come about all over the country's rural areas. That is inevitable. By the end of the last year of the First Five-Year Plan and the beginning of the Second, that is, by the spring of 1958, there will be some 250 million people—about 55 million peasant households (averaging four and a half persons each)—in co-operatives of a semi-socialist type. That will mean half the whole rural population. By that time many counties and some provinces will have virtually completed the semi-socialist transformation of their agricultural economy; and in every part of the country a small number of semi-socialist co-operatives will have turned into fully socialist ones. During the first half of the Second Five-Year Plan (by 1960), we shall, by and large, accomplish this semi-socialist transformation among the remaining half of the rural population. By that time socialist co-operatives transformed from semi-socialist co-operatives will have grown in number.

During the First and Second Five-Year Plans, the main feature of reform in the countryside will still be social reform. Technical reform will take second place. The amount of sizable farm machinery will certainly have increased, but not to any great extent. During the Third Five-Year Plan, social and technical reform will advance side by side in the rural areas. More and more large farm machinery will be employed year by year. As for social reform, co-operatives after 1960 will gradually change, group by group and at different times from co-operatives of a semi-socialist nature to fully socialist ones. Only when socialist transformation of the social-economic system is complete and when, in the technical field, all branches of production and places wherein work can be done by machinery are using it, will the social and economic appearance of China be radically changed. The economic conditions of our country being what they are, technical reform will take longer than social reform. It is estimated that it will take roughly four or five five-year plans, that is, twenty to twenty-five years, to accomplish, in the main, the technical reform of agriculture on a national scale. The whole Party must work to carry out this great task.

XI

We must make comprehensive plans and give more active leadership.

There must be national, provincial, regional, county, district and *hsiang* plans to carry out co-operation in its separate stages. And as the work proceeds, these plans must be constantly revised in the light of actual conditions.

All Party and Youth League organizations, whether at provincial, regional, county, district or *hsiang* level, must pay serious attention to rural problems and earnestly work to improve the quality of their leadership in rural work. Leading comrades on local Party and Youth League committees at all levels should study the work of agricultural co-operation as fast as ever they can and make themselves experts. In short, what we have to do is to take the initiative, not remain passive; strengthen our leadership and not let it get slack.

XII

In August 1954 (this is, of course, no longer news), the report of the Heilungkiang Provincial Committee of the Communist Party of China said: "With the rise and spread of the tide of rural co-operation, all types of mutual-aid and co-operative organizations and all sections of the people in the rural areas have gone into action to a greater or lesser degree. Existing agricultural producers' co-operatives are planning and preparing to enlarge their membership; agricultural mutual-aid teams which intend to turn themselves into co-operatives are planning and preparing to draw in a larger number of households; the less qualified mutual-aid teams want to grow too and raise themselves to a higher level. Some people are busily preparing to join new co-operatives, others to join existing ones. Those who are not ready to join co-operatives this year are energetically preparing to join mutual-aid teams. The movement is very broad in its scope: it has become a mass movement. That is a new, striking thing about the great development of agricultural co-operation. But because some leading comrades in certain counties and districts cannot adjust themselves to this new phenomenon and do not give more active leadership when it is called for, in a number of villages and *tun* (the village in Heilungkiang Province is the administrative unit corresponding to the *hsiang* in the provinces south of the Great Wall; the *tun* in Heilungkiang is not an administrative unit, but is equivalent to the village in the provinces south of the Great Wall), when people start looking round for partners, certain unhealthy features have begun to appear. The strong seek out the strong and elbow the weak aside. There is a squabbling about who shall get capable cadres, poaching members and disunity. There is the thoughtless placing of capable cadres in one place. Rich and well-to-do peasants with a fairly strong capitalist outlook seize the chance to set up low-grade mutual-aid teams or 'rich peasants' co-operatives.' All this clearly shows that, with the rapid growth of agricultural co-operation, it is not enough, when thinking how to carry out Party policy and guide the movement, to think merely in terms of setting up new co-operatives. We must take into account the whole village (that is, the whole *hsiang*), and think in terms of the general advance of the agricultural co-operative movement, considering both enlarging old co-operatives and setting up new, both the development of the co-operatives and the improvement of the mutual-aid teams, this year, and next year, and even the year after. Only by so doing can the Party's policy be fully carried out and the agricultural co-operative movement grow healthily."

Is it really true only of Heilungkiang Province that "some leading comrades in certain counties and districts cannot adjust themselves to this new phenomenon and give more active leadership when it is called for"? Does such a state of affairs exist only in some counties and districts? I think it very likely that people of the same type with serious shortcomings, people whose leadership tails behind the movement, can be found in many leading organizations all over the country.

The report of the Heilungkiang Provincial Committee of the Party goes on to say: "Hsichin Village, Shwangcheng County, by combining leadership with the voluntary principle worked out a comprehensive plan for the whole village. This is a completely new way of guiding the big advance in co-operation. Its importance lies primarily in the fact that in working out such a comprehensive plan the Party's class line in the countryside was fully translated into life, the unity between poor and middle peasants strengthened, and a vigorous struggle waged against the rich-peasant tendency. Active cadres were also properly distributed in the interests of agricultural co-operation as a whole. Relations between the various co-operatives and between the co-operatives and mutual-aid teams were readjusted and strengthened, and thereby the agricultural co-operative movement was systematically carried forward along the whole front. Secondly, such planning set the task of expanding agricultural co-operation on a large scale squarely before the leading bodies at the basic level and before the masses. It brought home to the village branch of the Party how to lead. It showed the old co-operatives how to advance; it taught how new co-operatives should be set up; and it helped the mutual-aid teams see the true direction they had to take if they were to improve. The plan also gave full rein to the initiative and enthusiasm of the village branch of the Party and the masses, and proved in practice that the principle of relying on the Party branch and on the experience and wisdom of the masses was correct. Finally, it is precisely this planning that enabled us to obtain an even deeper knowledge of the situation in the village and enabled all aspects of Party policy to be concretely applied. Therefore, it was possible to avoid both impatience and rashness on the one hand, and conservatism and drifting on the other. As a result, the policy of the Central Committee of the Party—'active leadership, steady advance'—was correctly followed."

How were the "certain unhealthy features" mentioned in the report actually dealt with? The report itself did not provide a direct answer to that question. The report of the Shwangcheng County Committee of the Party, appended to the Heilungkiang Provincial Committee's report, did. It said: "As a result of carrying out a comprehensive plan based on a combination of leadership by the Party branch and voluntariness on the part of the masses, the unhealthy tendency to bar badly-off peasant households from the co-operatives was put right, the placing of too many capable cadres in one place was stopped, squabbling over capable cadres and new members disappeared, the links between the co-operatives and the mutual-aid teams became closer, attempts by the rich and well-to-do middle peasants to organize rich peasants' co-operatives or low-grade mutual-aid teams failed, and the plans of the Party branch were, by and large, carried into effect. The membership of two older co-operatives has gone up 40 per cent, skeleton organization for six new co-operatives is being set up, and two mutual-aid teams have been checked over. If everything goes well, next year (that is, in 1955) the whole village will be farming co-operatively. At present, the whole village is working energetically to fulfil this year's plan to develop agricultural co-operation, increase production and safeguard the crops. The general opinion among the village cadres is: 'If we had not done all this, everything would be in a mess. There would have been trouble not only this year but next year, too.'"

As I see it, this is the way we ought to do things.

Comprehensive planning, more active leadership—that is our policy.

DOCUMENT 3

Decisions on Agricultural Cooperation, adopted at the Sixth Plenary Session (Enlarged) of the Seventh Central Committee of the Chinese Communist Party, October 11, 1955.

The English text is an official translation published as a pamphlet with the above title by the Foreign Languages Press, Peking, 1956. In the same pamphlet, but not reprinted here, is a translation of "Explanatory Notes" by Ch'en Po-ta, member of the Rural Work Department of the Central Committee and an eminent theoretician; these notes were given in a speech to the Central Committee on October 4, 1955, a week before the draft of the decisions was adopted.

———————————TEXT OF DOCUMENT 3———————————

I

At the present moment, a profound movement of socialist transformation is taking place in the rural areas. Between the spring of 1954 and the summer of 1955 the number of agricultural producers' co-operatives rose from 100,000 to nearly 650,000. The number of peasant households in the agricultural producers' co-operatives rose from 1,800,000 to 16,900,000. That is about 15 per cent of all peasant households in China. The progress of the movement is, however, uneven. In many parts of the old liberated areas it has already assumed the form of a huge mass movement. This is because the peasants there have a richer experience of revolutionary struggle, and mutual-aid teams (which serve as a foundation for co-operation) have existed there for many years. For instance, in provinces in North China, like Shansi, 41 per cent of the peasant households have joined the co-operatives while in Hopei, 35 per cent have joined. Thirty-four per cent of all peasant households in the three northeastern provinces are in co-operatives. In some *hsiang*,[1] districts and even counties in these regions, 60, 70 or even 80 per cent of all peasant households have joined co-operatives. In the provinces in Southeast, Central-South, Southwest and Northwest China that were liberated later on, most *hsiang* already have their first groups of agricultural producers' co-operatives. This has paved the way for a great expansion of the agricultural co-operative movement.

The facts confirm the estimate of the Central Committee of the Party that the tide of social reform in the countryside—in the shape of co-operation—will soon sweep the entire country. It has already reached some places.

II

Faced with the daily growth of the agricultural co-operative movement, the Party's task is to lead the movement forward, boldly and according to plan, not timidly. It must be understood that in leading the peasants to overthrow imperialism and feudalism, our Party carried out a bourgeois-democratic revolution. But the aim of the working class is to continue the advance and follow up that revolution by leading the peasants to embark on a socialist revolution. In the earlier stage of the revolution the class struggle in the rural areas was chiefly a struggle between the peasants and the landlord class. The peasant question which had to be solved then was that of land. In this new stage of the revolution, however, the class struggle in the countryside is chiefly between the peasants on the one hand and rich peasants and other capitalist elements on the other. It is essentially a struggle over the choice between two roads—the development of socialism or of capitalism. The question to be solved is a new peasant question—the problem of agricultural co-operation. New relationships within the worker-peasant alliance and the leading role of the working class in this alliance must be established and strengthened on the basis of concerting the development of socialist industrialization and agricultural co-operation.

China's industry is growing rapidly. Facts show that if the development of agricultural co-operation fails to keep pace with it, if the increase in grain and industrial crops lags behind, China's

---

[1] An administrative unit of one or several villages.—*Translator.*

socialist industrialization will run into great difficulties. The situation has already changed fundamentally, but the attitude of some of our comrades to the peasant question still remains at the old stage. They fail to see the sharp struggle over the choice between the two roads which is now taking place in the rural areas. They fail to see the active desire of the majority of the peasants to take the road to socialism. They are satisfied that the peasants have obtained land from the landlords, and want to keep things as they are in the villages, or contend that the speed at which agricultural co-operation develops should be very slow. They fail to understand that this means abandoning the active leadership of the Party in the movement for agricultural co-operation and allowing capitalism to develop freely in the rural areas. This would result in undermining the worker-peasant alliance, losing working-class leadership of the peasantry and so heading the cause of socialism for defeat. Comrades with such misguided views are afraid to trust the masses. They are pessimistic about the policy on co-operation of the Central Committee of the Party and about the leadership of the local Party committees at various levels. They assume that our Party can hardly consolidate the several hundred thousand small co-operatives that already exist, and that any large-scale expansion is certainly inconceivable. They have put forward a Right-opportunist policy of "drastic compression," and in some places dissolved a large number of co-operatives by compulsion and "orders from above." Yet this pessimism is in practice shown to be unfounded by the growing consolidation of the several hundred thousand co-operatives which already exist, the increased output of the great majority of them, and the active desire of the peasant masses to join them. The bankruptcy of this Right opportunism is thus exposed and shown up for what it really is—a reflection of the demand of the bourgeoisie and the spontaneous growth of forces towards capitalism in the rural areas. The Sixth Plenary Session holds that the criticism made by the Political Bureau of the Central Committee against Right opportunism is absolutely correct and necessary. We can bring about a fundamental change in the Party's rural work and alter the situation in which leadership lags behind the mass movement only when this Right opportunism is thoroughly criticized and repudiated. This change is vital if progress in the agricultural co-operative movement is to continue till complete victory is won.

III

It is possible to develop agricultural co-operation primarily because we have established in our country a people's democratic dictatorship headed by the working class, and because this people's democratic dictatorship is now engaged in organizing our socialist construction. At the same time, it is possible because the majority of the peasants are willing to take the socialist road in order to get rid of exploitation and poverty. The majority here referred to are mainly the poor peasants who have not yet risen to a better economic position, the lower middle peasants among the new middle peasants who were formerly poor peasants, and the lower middle peasants among the old middle peasants.[2] Since the land reform the economic condition of these sections of the peasantry has improved to varying extents, but many peasant households still have their difficulties or are still not well-off, while some have again lost their share of land because of exploitation by rich peasants or speculative merchants, or because they were unable to withstand natural calamities. Therefore, if the Party fails to give the peasants active guidance along the socialist road, capitalism will inevitably grow in the rural areas and the separation of the rural population into two extremes will become serious. Actual experience has taught the peasants that they cannot go on living as they used to—farming scattered, tiny plots on their own—that the only way out is for a large number of people to come together, pool their labour and work under collective management. The advantages of this method were first shown by the numerous mutual-aid teams and, even more, later, by the large number of agricultural producers' co-operatives which were established. Agricultural producers' co-operatives can organize labour power rationally so that productivity can be raised more rapidly; they can systematically and effectively use land and extend the area under cultivation; they can resist or reduce the ravages of nature, and, with state help, gradually introduce technical reforms in agriculture. For these and other reasons, they are able to bring about a speedy development of the pro-

---

[2] Old middle peasants are those who were middle peasants before the land reform. New middle peasants are those who have risen to the status of middle peasants since the land reform.—*Translator*.

ductive forces in agriculture and give the peasants substantial benefits. That is what accounts for the growing popularity of agricultural producers' co-operatives among the peasants.

As the past few years' experience shows, the following procedure will enable the co-operative movement to develop on an even firmer foundation:

1. As the movement progresses, an acute struggle will be waged against the rich peasants and speculative merchants, and the peasants themselves will be educated in the midst of the struggle. The mass of the middle peasants in particular must be educated and convinced so that they can stop vacillating between the socialist and capitalist roads. Therefore, the movement must be given a firm core—a core formed of the active elements among the poor peasants who have not yet been elevated to a better economic position and those of the lower middle peasants among the new middle peasants who were formerly poor peasants. It should also include part of the active elements of the lower middle peasants among the old middle peasants. The first step to be taken by the Party in the co-operative movement should be to organize these people, so that they can set an example and convince other peasants.

2. Although these sections of the peasantry—the poor peasants and the lower middle peasants among both new and old middle peasants, stand fairly close to each other as far as their economic condition is concerned, their active desire to join the co-operatives will for a time differ in degree for various reasons. Therefore, every year we should carry out work among them so that they will, over the next few years, organize themselves group by group, according to the degree of their understanding, into new co-operatives, or be absorbed into existing ones. Patience must be exercised towards those who, for the time being, do not wish to join, even if they are poor or lower middle peasants. The principle of voluntariness should never be violated; they should not be dragged into co-operatives against their will. A peasant may put forward and withdraw his name for membership several times before he finally makes his mind up. He should be given plenty of time to consider the matter.

3. Well-to-do middle peasants (that is, the upper middle peasants among both the old and new middle peasants) have better farm tools and draught animals, their land is more intensively cultivated, its yield is higher, or they derive a bigger income from subsidiary occupations. As long as they still do not realize that the benefits derived from co-operative farming are greater than—or at least, for the time being, equal to—those obtained by working on their own, they will not readily join a co-operative. If they join reluctantly, frequent conflicts are bound to arise among the members over the practical question of benefits. That is why, when a co-operative is organized, it is not advisable at the start to accept well-to-do middle peasants unless they show a genuine willingness to join, still less to drag them in against their will. Efforts should be made to influence them by showing them the advantages of co-operative farming, letting them wait and see for a bit and not enrolling them till their understanding grows.

4. The middle peasants are the permanent allies of the working class and the poor peasants. Good relations should be maintained with them both inside and outside the co-operatives. Their interests should never be infringed nor their property taken from them. The backward ideas of the middle peasants, particularly the tendency towards capitalism of the well-to-do middle peasants, should be properly countered by convincing argument, not dealt with by arbitrary administrative methods. The purpose of criticism must be to achieve unity. It must never be used as a pretext for attacking the middle peasants.

5. Before setting up co-operatives it is essential that the masses should be mentally prepared and that Rightist tendencies in the Party should be censured and overcome. Our Party's principles, policy and measures on agricultural co-operation must be publicized, systematically and repeatedly, among the mass of the peasants. And not only should the advantages of co-operation be made known to them; they should also be made aware of the difficulties that may arise in the course of co-operation and how such difficulties can be overcome.

6. The masses should be prepared organizationally for the formation of co-operatives. Agricultural producers' mutual-aid teams must be promoted on a really widespread scale; wherever possible they should be combined into joint teams so as to lay the groundwork for turning them into co-operatives. Joint committees of mutual-aid teams and co-operatives may be established in villages where there are mutual-aid teams and co-operatives. These should hold regular meetings, to

which representatives of individual peasants should be invited so that experience can be exchanged and arrangements made for whatever mutual help is needed and possible. This will pave the way for the future merging of co-operatives, the gradual transformation of mutual-aid teams into co-operatives and the drawing of individual peasants step by step into the co-operatives.

7. Short-term training of cadres for running co-operatives is an important preparation for the setting up of co-operatives. Those to be trained should be carefully chosen.

IV

The growth of the co-operative movement should go hand in hand with the consolidation of existing co-operatives. It is one-sided and wrong to pay attention only to consolidation and disregard expansion, to deny that an increase in the number of co-operatives would help raise their quality. It is equally one-sided and wrong to pay attention only to expansion and to disregard consolidation, attaching importance only to the number of co-operatives and ignoring their quality. Therefore, once they are established, co-operatives should take steps to check over their work systematically. Checking over of the co-operatives should be carried out not just once, but twice or three times a year, so as to keep on improving their quality.

1. Each co-operative, in the light of its own special characteristics and current practical problems, should draw up a policy and measures for checking.

2. The work of checking should be carried out group by group, starting with those co-operatives which have the most problems. The varied experience gained in checking over different types of co-operatives should be made known to help push forward the entire movement.

3. Those carrying out the work of checking should have a warm and helpful attitude and approach this work with care. It should not be done in an oversimplified and arbitrary manner. It is utterly wrong to decide beforehand the number of co-operatives that must be cut down and then forcibly dissolve them.

It is also entirely wrong to be harsh towards those co-operatives which have been "spontaneously organized." They should be given warm help after careful consideration of their cases.

4. In checking over co-operatives, attention should be focussed on production, for that is the key issue. In the course of organizing production various problems should be unearthed and solved methodically; ideological work among co-operative members should be intensified; management improved; and the Party policy on the co-operative movement of voluntariness and mutual benefit thoroughly carried out.

5. During such checking, attention should also be paid to improving the make-up of the co-operatives, reshuffling their leading members as need arises, and training of new key personnel from among the poor peasants.

6. The *hsiang* Party and Youth League branches must be relied on both for establishing co-operatives and checking them over. The key to the successful running of co-operatives lies in the strengthening of the work of Party and Youth League branches. Therefore, the work of building and checking over co-operatives should be closely associated with the building and strengthening of the Party and Youth League branches in the countryside. In carrying out all such work the local cadres in the rural areas should be the mainstay, cadres sent from above should be an auxiliary force.

V

At the present stage agricultural producers' co-operatives in our country are generally of an elementary, semi-socialist type, characterized by the pooling of land and a single management. This kind of co-operative is a transitional form to the fully socialist type. Private ownership of land and some other important means of production is, in the main, or to a considerable extent, retained, and privately-owned means of production are not to be hastily turned into common property. That is to say, both during the period of establishing and of checking over co-operatives, the private property of the members should be dealt with in a reasonable way, in line with the principle of mutual benefit, so as to make it easier to expand the co-operatives and put them on a sound footing. This means that co-operatives pay a certain amount of compensation for the use of private land, draught animals and large farm tools, and reasonable prices for such private means of production as draught animals and farm tools when transferred to the co-operatives as common property.

The means of production owned by members of co-operatives differ in number and quality. Moreover, it is necessary for different co-operatives in different areas to take varying circumstances into account when they decide on how and when the means of production owned by members are to be hired or transferred to the co-operatives as common property. In view of this, suitable agreements must be reached between co-operative members, and chiefly between the poor and middle peasants, on all these questions, as well as on the question of subsidiary occupations.

1. As regards the land belonging to members of the co-operatives:

a. Methods of assessing the yield of land to be pooled in the co-operatives should be based on the quality of the land, giving due consideration to the economic interests of those members the yield of whose land is, owing to lack of means, relatively low but can be raised after being pooled in the co-operative. Likewise, due consideration should be given to the value of the labour and fertilizer previously applied to the land by its owner on the basis of its actual yield for a normal year. In this way, conflicts arising out of differences in the actual yield as well as in the latent productivity of the land can be solved amicably between the poor and middle peasants, and this will make for greater enthusiasm on the part of the members to raise the productivity of the land and to invest in it.

b. Different methods are used in different areas to decide what dividends will be paid on land pooled in co-operatives. Generally speaking, the method of giving a fixed dividend is good for encouraging the members' enthusiasm for work. The method of giving dividends on land and paying for labour according to a fixed ratio is suitable, however, in newly organized co-operatives or in areas where the yield tends to fluctuate. In certain places some methods supplementary to these have been adopted. Whatever method is used, attention should be paid to the following points:

The amount paid out in dividends on land should generally be lower than the amount paid out for labour. It is wrong to set the dividend on land too high. But at the same time consideration should be given to those co-operative member households which are short of labour power but have more land, especially those of the old, weak, orphaned or widowed, so that they can get a suitable income. It is just as wrong to fix the dividend on land too low.

The proportion of income decided on as dividend for land should not be arbitrarily standardized. Consideration should be given to the difference in conditions between areas which have relatively less land and more people, and those which have more land and fewer people, as well as to the specific circumstances of certain areas which grow industrial crops requiring more field work.

In view of the peasants' predilection for the private ownership of land, the amount of dividend which the co-operatives decide to pay on land should remain constant for a certain period, say two or three years after a co-operative is founded, and should not be lowered each year; still less should dividends on land be discontinued prematurely.

c. Co-operative members should be allowed to retain small plots of land of their own, amounting to about two to five per cent of the average individual land-holding in the village, for growing vegetables, or for subsidiary agricultural products and occupations. The produce of such plots may be kept for home use or sold on the market. Some co-operatives have refused to allow their members to retain any land for their own use. That is wrong.

2. As regards draught animals and farm tools belonging to members of the co-operatives:

a. Great care must be taken while deciding whether draught animals belonging to members shall be transferred to the co-operatives as common property. During the first year or two after they are formed, and while they are still economically weak or lack administrative experience, the co-operatives may retain the private ownership and rearing of draught animals, and hire them on a temporary or long-term basis so that the co-operatives may avoid incurring too many debts or losing animals through improper feeding. As productivity increases, the co-operatives may purchase the animals in such ways as circumstances permit. Those co-operatives which bought draught animals when they were established need not, however, reverse their decision, provided that they are organized on a sound basis and economically fairly well off and that the original owners of the animals or other members of the co-operative raise no objection.

In some places, there is no difficulty in getting fodder but the charge for the hire of draught animals is rather high. In cases like this, if it is beneficial to the production of the co-operatives to buy the animals somewhat earlier and if the owners consent, the co-operatives can do so provided local conditions permit. In other places, because of production needs or the local custom among the peasants of feeding their draught animals jointly, co-operatives may, in the period before the animals are purchased, adopt the method of individual ownership of animals and co-operative rearing (or co-operative rearing during busy seasons and private rearing during slack seasons). This is permissible if it is convenient for farm work and the draught animals can be fed properly.

b. Contracts for the hire or purchase of draught animals should be signed after the co-operatives have conducted thorough negotiations with members who own the beasts. Reasonable fees should be fixed for the hire of animals depending on their condition, and reasonable prices and terms of payment should be fixed for the purchase of animals by co-operatives. When payment is made by instalments, a certain amount of interest should be paid to owners before the final instalment is cleared. The length of time taken to pay off the instalments may vary according to economic conditions in various areas and co-operatives. In general, three years is reasonable; anyhow, it should not be longer than five. There are some co-operatives which set too low a price on draught animals and too long a period for payment; there are even cases where no definite date is set and no interest is paid at all. This has led to members neglecting their animals. It must be put right.

c. Co-operatives should make appropriate arrangements for the use of the big, medium and small draught animals which are hired, bought by the co-operatives or owned and used privately. In order to breed more draught animals, special care should be given to pedigree beasts and the protection of young animals.

d. In dealing with large and fairly large farm tools owned by members, too, co-operatives can, after renting for a certain period, buy them over one by one. Co-operatives should pay a reasonable sum for the hire of such tools and pay by instalments if they are bought. There are some co-operatives which use their members' farm tools for prolonged periods but pay nothing for their hire or upkeep, and no compensation when they are damaged. This must be corrected.

3. As regards means of production for subsidiary occupations such as groves of trees, fishponds, etc. belonging to members of the co-operatives:

a. A distinction should be made between those subsidiary occupations which are best run individually and those which are best run collectively. It is unsuitable to bring into the co-operatives means of production used in subsidiary occupations which can be made better use of under individual management, and it is even more unsuitable to make them the property of the co-operatives. Those which can be better used under collective management, which will help improve the economic status of all members to a greater extent, may be gradually brought under the management of the co-operatives after negotiations with the owners, either by hiring them or buying them on the instalment plan.

b. Members' small holdings of trees (including fruit trees, bamboos and other trees used for industrial purposes) may in general be left to the management of members themselves. Where members own groves or orchards and there is need for unified planning of agricultural and forestry production, they may be brought with the owners' consent under the single management of the co-operative, but the private ownership of them remains. The method of distributing income from such groves and orchards must be settled through thorough negotiations among members.

The question of fish-ponds owned by members may be dealt with according to circumstances in the same way as that of groves and orchards.

VI

In order to put their collective economy on a sound basis, agricultural producers' co-operatives should gradually build up common funds in two main forms, namely, a shares fund and a reserve fund.

The shares fund is built up in the following way. Every member makes a contribution towards the costs of production covering seed, fertilizer, fodder, etc., or towards the cost of draught animals and tools bought from members. The amount of the contribution is based on the amount of land pooled (or in some cases on an agreed ratio between the land and labour contributed, or in others, where land is plentiful and payment for it low, on labour only). The share each should pay should be properly worked out, and should be within the power of the majority of members to pay. Payments to the shares fund may be made in cash or kind. If the amount paid in kind is more than is needed, the balance should be credited to the member concerned as investment. Poor peasants who cannot afford to contribute to the shares fund may be helped by state loans.

The amount to be set aside each year as a reserve fund for increasing the co-operative's means of production must be decided according to the actual circumstances. Generally speaking, it is better in the first few years that it should not exceed five per cent of the total annual income from agriculture and subsidiary occupations (gross output less production costs). Later, as output grows, this proportion can be suitably raised. The fund set aside for the welfare of members should, in the first few years, generally speaking, not exceed one per cent of a co-operative's total annual income. Depending on local conditions, the relative amounts to be set aside for the reserve and welfare funds may be slightly higher in co-operatives in areas cultivating industrial crops.

When a member withdraws from a co-operative, he may take with him his share contribution but not any of the reserve fund or welfare fund. There must be a revision of the regulations given in the "Decisions on the Development of Mutual Aid and Co-operation in Agricultural Production" issued by the Central Committee of the Communist Party of China in March 1953, in as far as they specify "complete freedom for members to withdraw both their invested capital and their contributions to the reserve fund" when leaving the co-operatives.

Apart from the shares fund and the reserve fund, members should be encouraged to invest in the co-operatives, which should repay capital so invested, with interest, at regular intervals.

VII

Agricultural producers' co-operatives must adopt measures to ensure the growth of their productive powers and prove in practice that co-operatives are much superior to individual farming and mutual-aid teams.

1. They should draw up their annual production plans and long-term over-all production plans, make full use of all favourable factors in the co-operatives or in the locality, unearth the key factors which make for increased output, and develop the latent capacity in agricultural production.

a. They should improve farming skills and methods by such means as deep ploughing and intensive cultivation, planting rationally in close rows, increasing the number of crops harvested annually, using good seed, popularizing new farm tools and fighting plant diseases and pests.

They should pay attention to learning from veteran farmers and absorbing all that is valuable in their experience; they should take energetic measures to teach the young men and women members to improve their farming skills.

b. They should undertake capital construction where necessary and possible, for example, building small water conservancy projects, terracing fields, improving the soil, work on conservation of soil and water, buying draught animals and farm tools. They should use locally-produced natural fertilizer and make great efforts to accumulate and prepare fertilizer. Appropriate payment should be made to members who hand over their accumulated fertilizer to the co-operatives for public use.

c. They should expand the area under cultivation and plant high-yield crops. Wherever there are water-ways or other water sources, the acreage of rice should be extended as much as possible in order to further increase grain output.

d. A diversified economy should be developed in accordance with local conditions and with the plans of the local state organs, to include agriculture, handicrafts, livestock breeding, forestry, fruit growing, fishery and other subsidiary occupations.

To develop the economy of hilly, well-forested areas where livestock breeding prevails, producers' co-operatives may be organized to combine agriculture, forestry and livestock breeding.

2. The valuable experience of those co-operatives which have successfully built up a system of fixed responsibility for a specified job should be publicized, and labour power should be rationally organized. Where such a system of responsibility cannot be practised all the year round, it

may be adopted on a temporary or seasonal basis to prepare the ground for a year-round system of responsibility.

   a. Systems should be introduced to specify the responsibilities of production brigades and groups and their individual members as regards cultivation, livestock breeding and the care of farm tools. Labour discipline should be tightened up.

   b. A labour production quota (that is, a standard work-day) system covering both quantity and quality should be introduced on a piece-work basis, on the principle that "he who works more is paid more and he who works less gets less."

   c. A regular inspection system should be introduced whereby the work of the production brigades and groups and their individual members can be examined at all levels and any work that falls below standard improved in good time.

   d. A system of rewards for above-quota production should be adopted, tied to a seasonal or year-round system of responsibility. Those who overfulfil their production plans should be rewarded and those who fall behind because of slackness should have deductions made from their pay. In the event of natural calamities, production quotas should be revised taking into account the resultant difficulties. Those who work hard in combatting calamities and exceed their revised production quotas should be rewarded. Those who do little or nothing to combat natural calamities and so fail to reach the revised quotas should be penalized.

   3. An industrious and thrifty attitude should be encouraged in running co-operatives. Financial management and book-keeping should be improved. Financial work should be such as to supervise and ensure a growth in production and a proper distribution of income. Slack financial management should be cut out and waste and extravagance checked.

   a. A limit should be set to all expenditure. The simple and convenient system of "fixing a maximum expenditure for each item" should be widely adopted. Those who economize should be rewarded, and those guilty of corruption or waste penalized.

   b. Reliable book-keepers should be selected and a mutual-help network set up among book-keepers of co-operatives to exchange experience.

   4. Political, cultural and educational work should be improved to raise the level of socialist consciousness among co-operative members and develop their keenness and creativeness.

   a. Our country's socialist cause and the momentous significance of agriculture in the economic life of the nation should be widely publicized among co-operative members. The state plans for economic construction, particularly the agricultural production plan and the plan for the purchase of agricultural produce, should be publicized among co-operative members and they should be shown how to properly implement the policy of the state on rural work and the planned purchase of grain and other farm produce.

   b. The idea of collective concern for the co-operative and for common property should be instilled in members, and efforts should be made to gradually overcome individualist tendencies. Behaviour detrimental to labour discipline should be checked.

   c. Unity and mutual help should be promoted among production brigades and groups and individual members, and emulation in labour introduced. Unremitting research into and improvement of farming technique should be fostered. Care should be taken to bring the energies of the women and the younger members of the co-operatives into full play.

   d. Democracy should be promoted within the co-operatives and members encouraged to put forward rationalization proposals to improve the work.

   e. Plans should be drawn up to eliminate illiteracy over a period of years and to raise the cultural level of members, particularly of cadres.

   f. Co-operative members should be educated to raise their political vigilance so that they can wage an unrelenting struggle against all forms of counter-revolutionary sabotage.

VIII

Financial and economic departments concerned, and especially agricultural administrative departments, must treat financial and technical aid for the agricultural co-operative movement as one of their most important tasks.

1. Besides issuing loans to poor peasants to help them take up shares in agricultural producers' co-operatives, and thus facilitate co-operation between them and the middle peasants, the People's Bank and the Agricultural Bank should gradually increase the amounts loaned to agricultural producers' co-operatives for investment in capital construction, reduce interest rates where appropriate, and extend the period of repayment of loans which can be set at three to five years.

2. Departments concerned with agriculture should set up agro-technical stations in a planned way and make them centres for passing on technical aid by the state to agricultural producers' co-operatives (e.g., demonstrating the use of improved types of farm tools, the cultivation and use of better seed, methods of improving farming skills and eliminating insects and pests).

The work of state farms should be improved so that they give better assistance to the co-operatives and set an example to be followed.

3. Administrative departments concerned with the engineering industry, and with trade and handicraft production should make reasonable reductions in prices not only of farm tools but also of insecticides and insecticide spraying equipment. The quality of these products however must not be lowered when prices are reduced; on the contrary, efforts should be made to improve their quality.

To keep pace with the growth of the agricultural co-operative movement, all departments concerned with the engineering industry should pay special attention to research on the design, assembly and repair of improved types of farm tools. The first tractor plant should be completed as quickly as possible, and preparations begun at the earliest possible date for the second and third. They should also produce more machinery and equipment for water conservancy undertakings. Departments concerned with the chemical industry should increase the output of fertilizer.

4. Departments concerned with agricultural administration should pay attention to the training of a large number of book-keepers and gradually send a sufficient number of book-keeping instructors, who can travel from place to place to give guidance to co-operative farms in improving their book-keeping and accounting methods. Book-keepers in district or *hsiang* branches of the People's Bank, the Agricultural Bank and the supply and marketing co-operatives should do their best to help agricultural producers' co-operatives with their book-keeping and accounting.

IX

As the co-operative movement develops, many former landlords, rich peasants and counter-revolutionaries of various sorts will undoubtedly engage in all kinds of sabotage. We must be alert to the serious danger of such sabotage in the agricultural co-operative movement. Quite a number of landlords, rich peasants and counter-revolutionaries have already wormed their way in various guises into co-operatives. Some have even seized important positions in them, pushing their way into the leadership in an effort to turn them into their tools or destroy them by underhand means. They try to undermine the Party leadership in co-operatives, attack and victimize the active elements among the masses and the cadres of the co-operatives, slaughter livestock, destroy farm crops and even commit such crimes as arson and assassination. Some landlords, rich peasants and counter-revolutionaries have even organized sham co-operatives. It must therefore be laid down that:

1. In places where the great majority of peasants have not yet joined co-operatives, for the next few years landlords or rich peasants must be resolutely debarred from joining co-operatives. Only in those places where the great majority of peasants have joined co-operatives and the co-operatives are on a sound basis can former landlords or rich peasants be permitted to join in different groups at different time, and then only on condition that they are law-abiding and have for a long time ceased to exploit others and have themselves engaged in work. This may be done in order that their reform can be continued through collective work in production.

2. Landlords or rich peasants who have already joined the co-operatives should be dealt with individually according to how they have behaved since joining. Those who have engaged in sabotage must be resolutely expelled. Cases of serious misdemeanour should be handed over to the courts. Only those who work and are law-abiding may be permitted to remain and continue their reform in the co-operatives.

3. Measures appropriate to the circumstances must be taken to clean up and reorganize those co-operatives in which landlords, rich peasants or counter-revolutionaries have gained control of posts.

4. Sham co-operatives organized by landlords, rich peasants or counter-revolutionaries must be dissolved. Educational work suited to each individual case should be carried out among the poor and middle peasants who joined such co-operatives; they should be reorganized in a proper way.

In various provinces there are still backward villages where the agrarian reform was not carried out in a thorough-going way. Such villages total approximately 5 per cent of all villages. Feudal landlords, rowdies, counter-revolutionaries and other bad elements in these places are still exploiting and oppressing the peasants, either openly or in secret. In such villages, it is also possible to organize the active and reliable elements among the poverty-stricken peasants to form co-operatives. At the same time, it is essential to get the masses fully on the move as soon as possible, resolutely wipe out the feudal and counter-revolutionary forces, and so create the conditions necessary for smooth development of agricultural co-operation.

X

To give active, planned leadership to the movement for agricultural co-operation, national, provincial (or autonomous region), administrative region (or autonomous *chou*), county (or autonomous county), district, *hsiang* (or nationality *hsiang*) and village plans should be drawn up for the co-operative movement to be carried out in stages. In making such plans, attention should be paid to specific differences which the co-operative movement shows in different places, as well as to similarities.

Because different conditions obtain in different areas, the progress of agricultural co-operation may, generally speaking, differ in the following ways:

1. In places where the mutual-aid and co-operative movement is relatively well advanced, and where, by the summer of 1955, between 30 and 40 per cent of all peasant households had joined co-operatives, the movement can, generally speaking, be expanded by the spring of 1957 to embrace 70 or 80 per cent of the peasant households. That is to say, in such areas, the building of semi-socialist co-operatives can be basically completed by that time. Provinces in North and Northeast China and a larger or smaller area in certain other provinces will fall into this category.

2. Over a large part of the country, by the summer of 1955 approximately 10 to 20 per cent of all peasant households had joined co-operatives. In such areas the work of building semi-socialist co-operatives can be basically completed before the spring of 1958.

3. More time is needed to build co-operatives in areas where the foundations of the mutual-aid movement are relatively weak and where there are still only very few agricultural producers' co-operatives. These are for the most part border areas. There are some border areas where land reform has not yet been carried out and no mutual-aid teams or co-operatives have been organized at all. In such areas, it is necessary to advance fairly slowly, or even wait and see for a long time.

In drawing up plans for agricultural co-operation, the Communist Party committees in various provinces, municipalities and autonomous regions should select areas where conditions are ripe to try out the establishment of agricultural producers' co-operatives of an advanced (that is, entirely socialist) type. In some areas where the work of building semi-socialist co-operatives has been basically completed, plans may be drawn up to transform co-operatives of an elementary type into co-operatives of an advanced type, bearing in mind the need for increased production, the degree of the people's political consciousness and local economic conditions. Such a transformation should be carried out step by step—that is, by the trial establishment of a few co-operatives of an advanced type and a gradual, stage-by-stage increase in their number.

In areas where many nationalities live together co-operatives may be formed either by people of a single nationality or of several different nationalities.

In areas where livestock breeding is the only occupation of the people, experimental livestock breeding co-operatives may also be established if conditions permit.

Plans for agricultural co-operation in the various areas should include such branches of the economy as forestry, livestock breeding, fishing, salt production and other occupations. They should also include plans for supply and marketing co-operatives, credit co-operatives, handicraft producers' co-operatives, transport co-operatives, and plans for cultural and educational work and for the growth of the Party and the people's organizations.

In drawing up plans for agricultural co-operation, the Party committees at all levels, and first and foremost the *hsiang* Party branches and county Party committees, should simultaneously work out all-embracing, long-term production plans based on local conditions, all with the development of agriculture as their central aim.

XI

In planning agricultural co-operation, particular attention should be paid to the plans for *hsiang* and villages, because such plans are the foundation of the whole plan of agricultural co-operation. Party committees at all levels should give the Party organizations of a number of selected *hsiang* or villages guidance in the preparation of comprehensive plans for stage-by-stage development in the light of local conditions. This will build up experience that helps to guide the whole movement. Such plans should include the following measures:

1. The making of a concrete analysis of class relationships in the village and the way in which the mutual-aid and co-operative movement is being organized.

2. The making of arrangements for the establishment or expansion of mutual-aid teams and agricultural producers' co-operatives stage by stage and group by group. This should be done on a voluntary basis, taking into account the degree of understanding of various strata of the peasantry, their social relations and where they live and work.

3. The making of suitable arrangements to train and supply key personnel for the establishment of mutual-aid teams and agricultural producers' co-operatives, taking into account the interests of the whole movement for agricultural co-operation in the *hsiang* or village.

These plans should be carefully studied by the cadres and active elements among the peasants; they should be repeatedly discussed with the mass of the people. Running things by simply issuing orders must be avoided and necessary revisions made from time to time as the work goes ahead.

XII

The Party organizations of provinces (or autonomous regions), administrative regions (or autonomous *chou*), counties (or autonomous counties), districts and *hsiang* (or nationality *hsiang*) should pay close attention to rural questions and energetically improve the quality of their leadership in rural work. The leading responsible comrades of local Party committees at all levels should spare no pains in learning to become experts in agricultural co-operation. In short, what is needed is initiative, not passivity; active leadership, not its relinquishment.

Those in the leadership should base their work on the method of learning from the mass movement, familiarizing themselves with the actual situation, summing up experience and adopting a flexible approach in guiding the movement. Ignorance coupled with unwillingness to learn, the issuing of arbitrary orders and an irregular tempo of work—these are things which violate the principles on which the growth of the movement must be founded in actual practice. They represent subjectivism, not Marxism. There can be no correct leadership unless such subjectivism is opposed.

The leadership should respect and encourage initiative and creative ability among the masses; it should protect and foster these growing, developing forces. To impede or discourage the growth of new things emerging in society, instead of helping them wholeheartedly, or to try and force their growth artificially, in a rash and impetuous way, before conditions are ripe, instead of taking appropriate measures to foster their natural birth and development—are both methods which injure the tender shoots of the new. They are opportunist, not Marxist methods. There can be no leadership unless such opportunism is opposed.

The aim of the co-operative movement is to lead about 110 million peasant households from individual farming to collective farming and then go on to bring about technical reform in agriculture;

it is to eliminate the last vestiges of capitalist exploitation in the rural areas and establish socialism. This is a tremendous change affecting the livelihood of several hundred million people, and it is inconceivable that difficulties should not crop up. Opportunists and subjectivists lose the ability to exercise sober judgement and overcome the difficulties with which they are confronted, either because they do not realize that they need to rely on the masses and the Party, or because they have no confidence in them. However, ours is a well-tempered, well-steeled Party, a Marxist-Leninist Party closely linked with the people. Throughout the thirty years and more of its existence, our Party has weathered many storms in the revolution and faced many serious difficulties. But its close unity with the masses enabled it to overcome such difficulties one by one and lead the people's revolution to victory. The building of socialism is the cause of hundreds of millions of people. In the industrialization of our country, in the building up of agricultural co-operation and in every other aspect of our work, we should give full play to the creativeness and initiative of the masses, work in a realistic spirit and shun complacency and impetuosity. It is the conviction of the Sixth Plenary Session that if we do this we shall overcome all difficulties and go on to new and greater victories.

DOCUMENT 4

Preface by Mao Tse-tung to the book *Socialist Upsurge in China's Countryside*, December 27, 1955.

> The text of the preface used here is an official translation taken from the English-language edition of the book published by the Foreign Languages Press, Peking, in 1957.
>
> *Comment.* The preface is dated December 27, 1955. The *People's Daily* printed the preface on January 12, 1956, and on that same date the NCNA issued the first English version of it. The book itself, which is on the cooperative situation and which was compiled by the General Office of the Central Committee of the Party, was published in Chinese in the second half of January 1956. It consists of contributions from various hands; some of the items are introduced by Mao Tse-tung himself, as explained in his preface. English-language excerpts from the book are found in CB 388.

_____TEXT OF DOCUMENT 4_____

This book is a collection of material intended for people working in the countryside. The preface for it was originally written last September. Now, three months later, that preface is already out of date. The only thing to do is write another one.

This is the situation. The book has been edited twice, first in September and now again in December. The first time, 121 articles were selected, most of them reflecting conditions in the early half of 1955, a few covering the latter half of 1954. Advance copies of these articles were printed and distributed to responsible comrades from provincial, municipal, autonomous regional, and regional Party committees attending the sixth plenary session (enlarged) of the Seventh Central Committee of the Communist Party of China, held from October 4 to 11, 1955. Their comments were requested. Because they felt that additional material was needed, after the meeting supplementary material was sent in from most provinces, cities and autonomous regions. Since much of it reflected conditions in the latter half of 1955, it became necessary to edit the book again. We cut 30 articles from the original 121, and kept 91. To these we added 85 selected from the newly-received material, bringing the total in the present book to 176 articles—about 900,000 words. The comrades responsible for the editing have gone through all of the material, and have made some changes in phraseology, added notes to explain difficult terms and prepared a topical index. In addition, we have commented on some of the articles, criticizing certain erroneous ideas and making certain suggestions. To distinguish our comments from those of the editors of the periodicals in which the material originally appeared, ours have been signed "Editor." Because part of our comments were written in September and part in December, there is some difference between them in tone.

Much more than a mere question of material is involved, however. The point is that in the latter half of 1955 the situation in China underwent a fundamental change. At present (late December 1955), of China's 110 million peasant households, more than 70 million (over 60 per cent), in response to the call of the Central Committee of the Chinese Communist Party, have joined semi-socialist agricultural producers' co-operatives. In my report of July 31, 1955, on co-operation in agriculture I stated that 16,900,000 peasant households had joined co-operatives. But since then, in only a few months' time, over 50 million more have joined.

This is a tremendous event. It tells us that we need only one year—1956—to practically complete the change-over to semi-socialist co-operation in agriculture.* In another three or four years, that is, by 1959 or 1960, we can complete, in the main, the transformation from semi-socialist to fully socialist co-operatives. It tells us that if the needs of this expanding agriculture are to be met, the socialist transformation of China's handicrafts and capitalist industry and commerce should also be speeded up. It tells us that the scale and rate of China's industrialization, and the scale and rate of the development of science, culture, education, public health, and so on, can no longer be entirely the same as originally intended. All must be appropriately expanded and accelerated.

Is this rapid advance of co-operation in agriculture healthy? It certainly is. Every local Party organization is giving all-round leadership to the movement. The peasants are taking part in it with great enthusiasm and in a very orderly manner. Their keenness for production has reached unprecedented heights. For the first time the vast majority of the people see their future clearly. With the completion of three five-year plans, that is, by 1967, the production of grain and many other crops will probably double or treble the highest output prior to the founding of the People's Republic. Illiteracy will be wiped out in a relatively short time, say seven or eight years. Many of the diseases most harmful to man, such as schistosomiasis, diseases formerly considered incurable, we now are able to treat. In short, the people can see the great road open before them.

The problem facing the entire Party and all the people of the country is no longer one of combating rightist conservative ideas about the speed of socialist transformation of agriculture. That problem has already been solved. Nor is it a problem of the speed of transformation of capitalist industry and commerce, by entire trades, into state-private enterprises. That problem has also been solved. In the first half of 1956 we must discuss the speed of the socialist transformation of handicrafts. But that problem will easily be solved too.

The problem today is none of these, but concerns other fields. It affects agricultural production; industrial production (including state, joint state-private and co-operative industries); handicraft production; the scale and speed of capital construction in industry, communications and transportation; the co-ordination of commerce with other branches of the economy; and the co-ordination of the work in science, culture, education, public health, and so on, with our various economic enterprises. In all these fields there is an underestimation of the situation which must be criticized and corrected if the work in them is to keep pace with the development of the situation as a whole. People's thinking must adapt itself to the changed conditions. Of course no one should go off into wild flights of fancy, or make plans unwarranted by the objective situation, or insist on attempting the impossible. The problem today is that rightist conservatism is still causing trouble in many fields and preventing the work in these fields from keeping pace with the development of the objective situation. The present problem is that many people consider impossible things which could be done if they exerted themselves. It is entirely necessary, therefore, to keep criticizing these rightist conservative ideas, which still actually exist.

This book is intended for comrades working in the countryside. Can people in the cities read it too? They not only can, but should. It is all about new things. Just as every day, every hour, there

---

*Actually, by November 1956, over 96 per cent of all peasant households thoughout the country were in semi-socialist co-operatives and fully socialist advanced co-operatives. Eighty-three per cent of them had joined the advanced co-ops—*Translator.*

are new developments in the cities in the cause of socialism, so it is in the countryside. What are the peasants doing? What is the connection between what the peasants are doing and the activities of the working class, the intellectuals, of all who love their country? A look at this material about the rural areas will help supply the answers.

To enable more people to understand the situation in the countryside, we intend to select 44 of the 176 articles and publish them as an abridged edition of 270,000 words. In this way, those unable to read the entire collection will still be able to learn something of rural problems.

MAO TSE-TUNG

December 27, 1955

DOCUMENT 5

The Draft Program for Agricultural Development in the People's Republic of China, 1956-1967, submitted by the Political Bureau of the Party's Central Committee, January 23, 1956.

The English text is taken from a pamphlet, entitled as above, issued by the Foreign Languages Press, Peking, 1956. Also in the pamphlet, but not included here, is an explanation of the program by Liao Lu-yen.

Comment. Document 5 is the first draft of the 12-Year Agricultural Program. This draft was adopted by the Supreme State Conference on January 25, 1956. According to an editor's note in the source pamphlet, Mao Tse-tung made an address at the meeting in which he said that the country was at that moment "witnessing the flood tide of the great socialist revolution." Therefore the draft program set very ambitious targets. For some time after the summer of 1956, little was heard of the draft. A second and revised version was adopted in a very different political context on October 22, 1957; it may be found in Chao Kuo-chün, *Economic Planning and Organization in Mainland China: A Documentary Study (1949-1957)* (Cambridge, Mass.: Center for East Asian Studies, Harvard University), Vol. 1 (1959), pp. 157-178. A presumably final draft was approved by the Second Session of the Second National People's Congress, April 10, 1960; this may be found in CB 616, pp. 1-17.

Detailed comparison of the drafts reveals no very great differences (after the respective prefaces) between the 1956 and 1957 versions; the preface to the latter reflects more skepticism on the part of the government about the virtues of the peasant masses. On the whole, the 1956 version contains more specification than the corresponding paragraphs of the 1957 version. The two-wheel, two-share plow (paragraph 11) is dropped in the later version. The 1957 version is more emphatic about the care of draft animals and more flexible about the number of work-days to be expected from women (80-180) than the 1956 draft (at least 120).

The most important addition in the 1957 version is a sub-paragraph recommending that "Except in a few nationality areas, birth control and planned parenthood should be publicized and encouraged in order to avoid placing too heavy a burden on living expenses and in order to give the children a better education and good opportunities for employment" (paragraph 29, found in Chao Kuo-chün, just cited, p. 175). On birth control, see Document 15, below.

The 1960 version differs little from that of 1957—surprisingly little, in that references to agricultural producers' cooperatives are not altered, in spite of the institution of people's communes in the interval. In paragraph 27, in accordance with an announcement by T'an Chen-lin to the National People's Congress, the list of the "four evils" has been changed: "bed-bugs" have been substituted for "sparrows."

_____TEXT OF DOCUMENT 5_____

The great tide of agricultural co-operation that has swept China is bringing forth an immense, nation-wide growth of agricultural production, and this in turn is stimulating the development of the whole national economy and all branches of science, culture, education and public health.

To give the leading Party and government bodies at all levels and the people of China, particularly the peasants, a long-term programme of agricultural development, the Political Bureau of the Central Committee of the Chinese Communist Party, after consulting comrades holding responsible positions on Party committees in the provinces, municipalities and autonomous regions, has drawn up a draft national programme outlining the scale of agricultural development during the period 1956-1967 (the last year of the third Five-Year Plan). On a certain number of related questions this draft programme also touches upon work in the urban areas. It sets a number of important targets for agricultural production. Others will be specified in each of the five-year plans and in the annual plans.

This draft is now distributed so that it can be studied by the Party committees of all provinces (municipalities or autonomous regions), administrative regions (autonomous *chou*), counties (autonomous counties), districts and *hsiang* (nationality *hsiang*), as well as by all departments concerned, all of whom are asked to submit their views on it. At the same time workers, peasants, scientists and people from all walks of life who love their country should also be widely consulted. These views should be collected before April 1, 1956, so that the programme can be submitted for discussion and adoption by the seventh plenary session (enlarged) of the seventh Central Committee of the Communist Party of China which will be held some time after that date. It will then be presented to the state bodies and the people of the whole country, first and foremost the peasants, as a recommendation.

Except in some remote areas where democratic social reforms have not yet been introduced, every leading Party and government body of provinces (municipalities, autonomous regions), administrative regions (autonomous *chou*), counties (autonomous counties), districts and *hsiang* (nationality *hsiang*) should draw up specific plans, based on the present draft national programme and taking into account conditions peculiar to each locality. These plans should specify the successive stages of development of every aspect of their local work. At the same time all state departments concerned with economic affairs, with science, culture, education, public health, civic affairs or the judiciary should also review and revise their plans of work in accordance with the present national programme.

(1) Seeing that in 1955 more than 60 per cent of all peasant households were in agricultural producers' co-operatives, all provinces, municipalities and autonomous regions should, in the main, complete agricultural co-operation in its elementary form and set themselves the goal of getting about 85 per cent of all peasant households into agricultural producers' co-operatives in 1956.

(2) Areas where co-operation is on better foundations and where a number of co-operatives of advanced form are already functioning should, in the main, complete the change-over to co-operation of advanced form by 1957. Each district of the remaining areas should, in 1956, set up and run one or more large co-operatives of advanced form (each with a hundred or more peasant households) to serve as examples; and by 1958 they too should practically complete co-operation of advanced form.

In going forward to the advanced form of co-operation certain conditions must be observed: the change must be of the free will and choice of the members; the co-operative must have people capable of giving proper leadership; and it must be possible for over 90 per cent of the members to earn more after the change. When all such conditions in the elementary form of co-operatives are ripe, they should at different times, group by group, go over to the advanced form of co-operation, otherwise the growth of their productive forces will be hampered.

(3) Every agricultural producers' co-operative must make suitable arrangements to see that those of its members who lack manpower, are widows or widowers, who have no close relations to depend on, or who are disabled ex-service men, are given productive work and a livelihood, so that they have enough food, clothing and fuel, can bring up their children properly, and see

that the dead are decently buried, so that they are assured of help during their lifetime and decent burial thereafter.

(4) During 1956 attempts should be made to settle the question of admitting to the co-operatives former landlords and rich peasants who have given up exploitation and who have asked to join. This can be done on the following lines: (a) Those who have behaved well and worked well may be allowed to join co-operatives as members and change their status to that of peasants. (b) Those who have conducted themselves neither well nor badly, but have behaved fairly well, may be allowed to join as candidate members, with their status for the time being unchanged. (c) Those who have behaved badly the *Hsiang* People's Council should allow them to work in the co-operatives under supervision; those who have committed sabotage should be brought to trial as the law directs. (d) Whether they acquire the status of co-operative member or not, former landlords or rich peasants shall not, for a specified time after joining a co-operative, be allowed to hold any important post in it. (e) Co-operatives must work on the principle of equal pay for equal work, and pay former landlords or rich peasants in the co-operative the proper rate for the work they put in. (f) Sons and daughters of landlords or rich peasants who were under eighteen at the time of the land reform, or who were still at school, or who had taken part in work before the land reform and had been under the thumb of other members of the family, should not be treated as landlords or rich peasants, but should be allowed to join the co-operatives as members, be reckoned as of peasant status, and given work suited to their abilities.

(5) Counter-revolutionaries in the rural areas should be dealt with as follows: (a) Those who have committed sabotage or had committed other serious crimes in the past, and against whom there is great public feeling, should be put under arrest and dealt with in accordance with law. (b) Those who committed crimes which were commonplace in the past, but have not committed sabotage since liberation, and against whom public feeling is not great, should be allowed by the *Hsiang* People's Council to work in the co-operative under supervision, to be reformed by work. (c) Those who have committed minor crimes and since made amends, those who have served their sentence, been released and behaved well, and those who committed crimes but did deserving work in the campaign to suppress counter-revolutionaries, may be allowed to join the co-operative—some as members, no longer regarded as counter-revolutionaries but as peasants, and others for the time being as candidate members, not classified as peasants—depending on what they have done to make amends and what merit they have earned. In no case, however, whether they are admitted as members or not, must they be allowed to take on important posts in the co-operative for a specified time after joining. (d) Such counter-revolutionaries as have been allowed to work in the co-operatives under supervision should be paid for their work by the co-operative on the principle of equal pay for equal work. (e) Other members of the families of counter-revolutionaries should be allowed to join co-operatives, and enjoy the same treatment as anyone else without being discriminated against, provided they took no part in crimes committed by the counter-revolutionaries.

(6) In the twelve years starting with 1956, in areas north of the Yellow River, the Tsinling Mountains, the River Pailung, and the Yellow River in Chinghai Province, the average annual yield of grain should be raised from the 1955 figure of over 150 catties to the *mou* to 400 catties.[1] South of the Yellow River and north of the Huai the yield should be raised from the 1955 figure of 208 catties to 500 catties. South of the Huai, the Tsinling Mountains and the River Pailung it should rise from the 1955 figure of 400 catties to 800 catties per *mou*.

In the same twelve years the average annual yield of ginned cotton should be raised from the 1955 figure of 35 catties to the *mou* (the average for the whole of China) to 60, 80 or 100 catties depending on local conditions.

Everywhere vigorous steps should be taken to see that output targets set in state plans for grain, cotton, soya, peanuts, rape, sesame, hemp, cured tobacco, silk, tea, sugar-cane, sugar-beet, fruit, tea-oil and tung-oil trees, are reached. Besides this, all areas must take more energetic measures to develop all other marketable industrial crops. In large mountainous areas vigorous efforts should be made to grow all possible marketable industrial crops, provided that they not only produce enough food to make themselves self-sufficient, but also to build up a surplus against

---

[1] One catty = 1.1023 lb. One *mou* = 0.1647 acre.

times of natural calamities. In those parts of South China where conditions permit, vigorous efforts should be made to develop tropical crops.

Agricultural producers' co-operatives should encourage their members to grow vegetables on their own private plots by way of improving their standard of living. Peasants who live on the outskirts of cities or near industrial or mining districts should go in for market gardening in a planned way so that the supply of vegetables to these places can be ensured.

More medicinal herbs should be grown. Those which grow wild should be protected and, wherever possible, gradually brought under cultivation.

(7) All agricultural producers' co-operatives, besides producing enough food for their own consumption and to meet the requirements of the state, should, within 12 years starting from 1956, store enough grain for emergency use for a year, a year and a half or two years, according to local conditions. All provinces (municipalities or autonomous regions), administrative regions (autonomous *chou*), counties (autonomous counties), districts, *hsiang* (nationality *hsiang*) and all agricultural producers' co-operatives, should draw up detailed plans to meet this requirement. During the same period, the state too should store sufficient reserve grain for one to two years for use in any emergency.

(8) Live-stock breeding should be encouraged. Cattle, horses, donkeys, mules, camels, pigs, sheep and all kinds of poultry should be protected and bred. Special care should be taken to protect the females and young and improve breeds. State live-stock farms should be extended.

The prevention and cure of animal diseases is an important part of live-stock breeding. As far as possible, all areas should, within a period varying from 7 to 12 years, practically eliminate the most serious animal diseases such as rinderpest, hog cholera, Newcastle disease, pork measles (cysticercosis), contagious pleuro-pneumonia of cattle, foot and mouth disease, lamb dysentery, sheep mange, and glanders. For this purpose, within seven years starting from 1956, veterinary stations should be set up in all counties in agricultural areas and all districts in pasture areas. Veterinary work should be improved and extended. The co-operatives should have personnel with basic training in the prevention and cure of animal diseases.

Care should be taken to protect pastures, improve and grow grass for cattle fodder and encourage silage. Agricultural producers' co-operatives and live-stock breeding co-operatives should see that they have their own supplies of fodder and grass.

(9) There are two main ways of increasing the yield of crops: taking steps to increase production, and imparting better techniques.

(A) The chief steps to increase production are: (a) water conservancy projects and water and soil conservation; (b) use of improved farm tools, and gradual introduction of mechanized farming; (c) efforts to discover every possible source of manure and improve methods of fertilizing; (d) extension of the use of the best and most suitable strains; (e) soil improvement; (f) extension of multiple cropping areas; (g) planting more high-yielding crops; (h) improving farming methods; (i) wiping out insect pests and plant diseases; and (j) opening up virgin and idle land and extending cultivated areas.

(B) The chief steps to impart better techniques include the following: (a) provinces, municipalities and autonomous regions should collect data on the experience of the best co-operatives in their own areas in increasing yields, compile and publish at least one book a year, so as to spread this knowledge as widely and rapidly as possible; (b) agricultural exhibitions; (c) conferences of model peasants called at regular intervals by provinces (municipalities or autonomous regions), administrative regions (autonomous *chou*), counties (autonomous counties), districts, *hsiang* (nationality *hsiang*), with awards and citations to peasants who distinguish themselves in increasing production; (d) visits and emulation campaigns, the exchange of experience; and (e) imparting technical knowledge and encouraging peasants and cadres to take an active part in learning better techniques.

(10) Water conservancy projects and water and soil conservation. All small-scale water conservancy projects (for example, the digging of wells and ponds and the building of irrigation canals and dams), the harnessing of small rivers and water and soil conservation work should be carried out by local governments and agricultural producers' co-operatives systematically and on a large scale. This work and the large-scale water conservancy projects and the harnessing of the larger

rivers undertaken by the state should virtually eliminate all ordinary floods and droughts in 7 to 12 years, starting from 1956. The engineering industry, commercial undertakings and supply and marketing co-operatives should see that pumps, water-wheels, steam engines and other devices for raising water are made available.

Local governments and agricultural producers' co-operatives, basing their work on the unified plan for developing the economy of the mountainous areas, should wherever possible carry out the water and soil conservation work required by agricultural production, live-stock breeding and forestry, so that within 12 years striking results are achieved and soil erosion is, in the main, stopped.

Within twelve years starting from 1956 small hydro-electric power stations should be built where water power is available, each of them to serve one or several *hsiang*. This, alongside the great water conservancy and power projects undertaken by the state, will gradually bring electrification to the countryside.

(11) Promote new types of farm tools. Starting from 1956, within three to five years 6 million more ploughs with two wheels and two shares should be in use, together with a considerable number of sowers, cultivators, sprayers, dusters, harvesters, shellers and silage cutters. Good repair services should be maintained. Agriculture will be gradually mechanized as the industrial development of the country forges ahead.

(12) Within twelve years, starting from 1956, local governments and agricultural producers' co-operatives in most areas should have made themselves responsible for providing more than 90 per cent of all manure and other fertilizers needed—and in some places the whole of it. To work towards this position, peasants everywhere should be encouraged to do everything they possibly can to increase the amount of fertilizer, paying special attention to pig-breeding (and in some cases sheep-breeding), and providing adequate green manure crops. Local governments should take active steps to develop the manufacture of phosphate and potassium fertilizers, extend the use of bacterial fertilizer (including soya bean and peanut root nodule bacteria), and collect and utilize to the fullest extent urban waste and manure from other miscellaneous sources. At the same time the state will vigorously promote the chemical fertilizer industry.

(13) Energetic steps must be taken to breed and extend the use of improved strains suitable to local conditions and encourage work to improve seed. Within two or three years starting from 1956 picked seed should be in pretty general use for cotton growing, and within seven to twelve years the same should be true of such important crops as rice, wheat, maize, soya, millet, *kaoliang*, potatoes, rape, sesame, sugar-cane, tobacco and hemp. All agricultural producers' co-operatives should set aside land specially for growing seed as such. State farms should make themselves centres for increasing the amount of picked seed.

(14) Agricultural producers' co-operatives should take energetic steps to improve the soil and do everything they can to turn poor into fertile land.

(15) Extend the area of multiple crops. In twelve years starting with 1956 the average multiple crop index set for various areas will be raised to the following levels: (a) areas south of Wuling Mountains, 230 per cent; (b) areas north of Wuling Mountains and south of the Yangtse River, 200 per cent; (c) areas north of the Yangtse River and south of the Yellow River, Tsinling Mountains and River Pailung, 160 per cent; (d) areas north of the Yellow River, Tsinling Mountains and River Pailung and south of the Great Wall, 120 per cent; and (e) in areas north of the Great Wall, multiple crop areas should also be expanded as much as possible.

(16) More high-yield crops should be grown. First, the area under rice should be extended, and all available water resources used to grow more. In the twelve years starting 1956 the area under rice should be increased by 310 million *mou*, maize by 150 million *mou* and potatoes by 100 million *mou*.

(17) Methods of cultivation should be improved. Deep ploughing, careful cultivation, proper rotation of crops, intercropping and close planting, sowing in good time, thinning out and protecting young plants and improving field work—these things must be done to bring about good yields and good harvests.

(18) In seven or twelve years starting 1956, wherever possible, virtually wipe out insect pests and plant diseases that do most harm to crops. These include locusts, armyworms, rice borers, maize borers, aphides, red spiders, pink boll-worms, wheat smut, wheat nematode and black rot on

sweet potato. Local plans should include any other serious insect pests and plant diseases that can be wiped out. Greater attention should be paid to plant protection and quarantine measures to achieve this end.

(19) The state should reclaim waste land in a planned way and extend the area under cultivation. Wherever conditions permit, agricultural producers' co-operatives should be encouraged to organize branch co-operatives to carry out such reclamation. The work should be linked with the general plan of water and soil conservation so as to prevent any danger of water loss and soil erosion.

(20) Expansion of state farms. The area cultivated by state farms should be increased in the twelve years starting 1956 from the 1955 figure of 13,360,000 *mou* to 140 million *mou*. Vigorous work must be put in to improve the running of state farms, to raise their output, practise the strictest economy and cut down cost of production, so that state farms are the models of farming technique and management which they are expected to be.

(21) In the twelve years starting 1956 we must clothe every possible bit of denuded waste land and mountains with greenery. Wherever possible trees should be planted in a systematic way near houses, villages, along roads and rivers, as well as on waste land and mountains. To achieve that end, agricultural producers' co-operatives should set up decent-sized nurseries of their own to grow saplings, in addition to the nurseries started by the state.

We should plant and tend not only forests (including bamboo groves) for timber, but also other trees of economic value such as mulberry and oak (for feeding silkworms), and tea-trees, trees for varnish and fruit, and oil-yielding groves.

Afforestation plans should include the creation of wind-breaks, sand-breaks and shelter belts to protect farmland, the head-waters of rivers, sea coasts and cities.

Local agricultural producers' co-operatives should plant and look after trees along railways, roads and rivers, and the income derived from this source should accrue to the co-operatives. Afforestation work along railways and roads should tally with specifications made by the government departments concerned with railways and communications.

Firm steps should be taken to prevent insect pests and plant diseases in forests, and to improve measures to protect forests and combat forest fires.

(22) Energetic steps should be taken to raise the output of marine products and develop fresh-water fisheries. In the case of sea fishing, more safety measures should be adopted and more deep-sea fishing done. In the case of fresh-water fish farming more should be done to breed good stock and prevent fish diseases.

(23) If agriculture, forestry, live-stock breeding, subsidiary rural production, and fisheries are to develop to the full, if the national wealth and the income of the peasants are to grow, co-operatives must make fuller use of manpower and raise labour productivity. In the seven years beginning with 1956, every able-bodied man in the countryside ought to be able to put in at least 250 working days a year. Serious efforts should be made to draw women into the work of agricultural and subsidiary production. Within seven years, every able-bodied woman in the countryside should, besides the time she spends on household work, be able to give at least 120 working days a year to productive work. In addition, all those in the countryside who can contribute only "half manpower" or who are fitted only for light work should be encouraged to do well at whatever work they are fit for and suited to. At the same time energetic efforts should be made to improve technical skills, to improve labour organization and management, and so steadily raise the labour productivity of all members of co-operatives.

(24) Agricultural producers' co-operatives should work on the maxim "industry and thrift" in all they do. Industry means giving full encouragement to members to work conscientiously, to branch out into new fields of production, to develop a many-sided economy and to exercise minute care over everything. Thrift means being strictly economical, lowering the cost of production and opposing extravagance and waste. In all capital construction plans co-operatives should make the fullest use of their own manpower and the material and capital at their disposal.

(25) Improve housing conditions. As production by the co-operatives grows and the income of their members increases, agricultural producers' co-operatives should encourage and assist members to repair or build houses for their families and thus improve their housing conditions. This should

be done in a prepared, planned way, at different times and group by group, taking needs and possibilities into account, and on a voluntary and economical basis, for it will help them with their work, their political and cultural activity, and improve their health conditions.

(26) In seven or twelve years from 1956 determined efforts should be made to virtually wipe out wherever possible all diseases from which the people suffer most seriously, such as schistosomiasis, filariasis, hookworm, kala-azar, encephalitis, bubonic plague, malaria, smallpox and venereal diseases. Energetic steps should be taken to prevent and cure other diseases such as measles, dysentery, typhoid fever, diphtheria, trachoma, pulmonary tuberculosis, leprosy, goitre and Kaschin-Beck's disease.

To this end every effort should be made to train medical workers and gradually set up health and medical services in counties and districts, and clinics in villages.

(27) Wipe out the "four evils." In five, seven or twelve years beginning 1956 we should practically wipe out the "four evils"—rats, sparrows, flies and mosquitoes—wherever possible.

(28) We should improve our research in agricultural science, provide better technical guidance for agriculture and train in a planned way large numbers of people to handle the technical side of agriculture. A systematic effort is needed to start, improve and extend bodies undertaking research in agricultural science and those providing technical guidance. These bodies include colleges of agricultural science, regional and other specialized institutes of agricultural science, provincial agricultural experimental stations, model county breeding farms, and district agricultural instruction centres. In this way agricultural research and technical guidance will be of better service to developing agriculture. In the twelve years from 1956 agricultural departments at all levels should, to meet the needs of co-operative economy, between them be responsible for training five to six million experts of primary and intermediate grades for technical work in agriculture, forestry, water conservancy, live-stock breeding, veterinary work, farm management and accounting for agricultural producers' co-operatives.

(29) In five or seven years from 1956, dependent on the situation locally, we must virtually wipe out illiteracy. The minimum standard of literacy must be 1,500 characters. In every *hsiang* we should have spare-time schools to raise the educational standard of our cadres and the peasants. In the next seven or twelve years, again depending on the local situation, we should extend to all rural areas compulsory elementary education. Primary schools in the countryside should mostly be run by agricultural producers' co-operatives. In seven or twelve years, too, we should establish in the rural areas a wide network of film projection teams, clubs, institutes, libraries, amateur dramatic groups and other bodies for education and recreation. In the next seven to twelve years, every *hsiang* should have a sports field and sport should be a common sight in the countryside.

(30) Starting from 1956 we shall, in the next seven to twelve years, depending on local circumstances, extend the radio diffusion network to all rural areas. All *hsiang* and all large producers' co-operatives in agriculture, forestry, fishery, live-stock breeding, salt producing and handicrafts are called on to install either rediffusion loudspeakers or wireless sets proper.

(31) In seven to twelve years from 1956, varying with local circumstances, all *hsiang* and large co-operatives should have a telephone service. Radio telephone-telegraph equipment should be installed wherever it is needed. Inside seven years all villages are to be provided with a decent post and telegraphic service and a proper distribution of newspapers and periodicals.

(32) In a matter of five, seven or twelve years, starting from 1956, depending on differing local conditions, the whole countryside must be provided with networks of roads. All roads between one province (municipality or autonomous region) and another, between administrative regions (autonomous *chou*), counties (autonomous counties), districts and *hsiang* (nationality *hsiang*), must be built to specifications laid down by government departments concerned with communications. All roads must be constantly and carefully kept up.

In places served by water-ways, navigable channels should be dredged and kept in good order under whatever conditions are possible to improve communications.

(33) In seven to twelve years from 1956, depending on local circumstances, a network of hydrographical and meteorological stations and posts should be in the main completed so as to improve the work of providing agriculture with reliable weather and meteorological forecasts. All

areas should pay attention to such forecasts so that they can ward off such calamities as flood, drought, gale and frost.

(34) In the main, co-operation among handicraftsmen and salt producers, the fishing and waterside population, should be complete in 1957. Plans should be drawn up to extend co-operation in live-stock farming in the light of local conditions.

(35) Commercial bodies and supply and marketing co-operatives in rural areas should complete the reorganization of their buying and selling machinery in 1957, improve planning for the circulation of goods and ensure that all rural areas are given good service in the supply of goods and the purchase of agricultural produce.

(36) In 1957 there must be a rural credit co-operative in practically every *hsiang* to provide credit and encourage saving.

(37) Protection of women and children. The principle of equal pay for equal work must be rigidly adhered to wherever women do productive work. During busy times of the year on the farms agricultural producers' co-operatives should run crèches. When work is given out the health and physique of women members must be taken into consideration.

Organizations concerned with health should train midwives for the rural areas, do all they can to see that modern methods of delivering babies are used, provide post-natal care and take steps to cut down the incidence of maternal diseases and the infant mortality rate.

As co-operation in agriculture goes from strength to strength and as production rises and the peasants begin to live better, suitable regulations and restrictions should be made in regard to the employment of children in auxiliary work, with consideration to their age and strength.

(38) Young people in the country should be given every encouragement to show initiative in their work, to study and acquire scientific knowledge and skill. The young people in the rural areas should become the spearhead, the shock force in productive, scientific and cultural work in the countryside.

(39) Starting from 1956, in the next five to seven years steps should be taken in the light of local conditions to wipe out unemployment in the cities and provide work for all urban unemployed. The unemployed can find work not only in the cities but also on the outskirts of towns and cities, in the countryside proper, in areas where land reclamation is going on or in mountainous regions, in agriculture, forestry, live-stock breeding, subsidiary occupations, fishing, or in the fields of science, culture, education and health in the rural areas.

(40) Workers in the cities and peasants in the co-operatives must give each other every support. The workers must turn out more and better industrial goods which the peasants need, and the peasants must grow more and better grain and industrial raw materials which industry and town-dwellers need. Besides this, workers in the cities and peasants in the co-operatives should arrange get-togethers, visit one another, and write to each other. They should keep in constant touch, give each other encouragement and swap experience so as to promote the development of industry and agriculture and help consolidate the alliance between the workers and the peasantry led by the working class.

Chapter III

FLOWERS AND SCHOOLS

(containing Documents 6, 7, 8)

General comment. The link between the first Five-Year Plan, representing the effort toward "socialist construction," and the attempt to mobilize and simultaneously recondition the non-Communist intellectuals of China is discussed in our General Introduction, part III. So also is the Chinese Communists' use of Khrushchev's denunciation of Stalin at the Soviet Twentieth Party Congress (February 1956) in order to correct the "working style" of their own cadres.

The preliminaries of the Hundred Flowers campaign began in the fall of 1955. At this time deputies of the National People's Congress and members of the National Committee of the Chinese People's Political Consultative Conference wrote a report embodying the results of an "inspection of conditions relating to intellectuals." Meetings were held in Peking by the "Democratic" parties in December 1955 to discuss the "unity and reform" of the intellectuals. Their main emphasis was on the correctness of the Communist Party's policy and on the duties of the intellectuals and "Democratic" parties themselves (including a requirement to conduct a "comprehensive investigation and study" of intellectuals with whom they were in contact).

The Communist Party itself seems to have forced the pace in trying to get active cooperation. The Central Committee held a special meeting from January 14 to 20, 1956, attended by representatives of Party committees at provincial and lower levels, and of the relevant ministries, institutes of learning, and mass organizations. It was this audience which was addressed by Mao Tse-tung (who called on them to unite with intellectuals outside the Party) and by Chou En-lai (Document 6). The Party meeting was followed by a plenary session of the Chinese People's Political Consultative Conference to which Chou En-lai made a political report, identical in substance with his previous speech.

The 12-year plan for scientific development mentioned by Chou En-lai toward the end of his speech to the Party meeting had been the subject of separate discussion. After the approval of the first Five-Year Plan the Chinese Academy of Sciences had issued a directive (September 15, 1955) on the drawing up of a 15-year long-range plan for the advancement of science. At a meeting of the Supreme State Council on January 25, 1956, Mao Tse-tung laid down that "our people must have a long-range plan aiming to rectify, within a few decades, our backwardness in economic, cultural and scientific development" (quoted at page 115 of Chen work cited below, from *People's Daily*, Jan. 26, 1956). Liu Shao-ch'i, in his report to the Eighth Party Congress in September 1956 (Document 9), stated that a "preliminary overall plan" had already been drawn up. It is evident from subsequent references that scientific work was proceeding on the basis of a draft plan, which was never published.

The early stages of the Hundred Flowers campaign are discussed in Theodore H. E. Chen, *Thought Reform of the Chinese Intellectuals* (Hong Kong: Hong Kong University Press, 1960), Chapters XI–XIII, with copious references to the contemporary Chinese press; and incidentally in Roderick MacFarquhar, *The Hundred Flowers Campaign and the Chinese Intellectuals* (New York: Praeger, 1960), which concentrates almost exclusively on the period May–July 1957.

DOCUMENT 6

On the Question of Intellectuals, by Chou En-lai, Prime Minister and Secretary of the Party Central Committee, a report delivered January 14, 1956, to a special conference convened by the Central Committee.

The English text is taken from CB 376. It is a translation from an NCNA release of January 29, 1956. Most of the translating was done by the U.S. Consulate General, Hong Kong; but an official NCNA translation was used for certain passages (indicated in the CB) which had comprised an English-language release.

Comment. The question of "de-Stalinization" as it affected the Chinese Communist Party is briefly discussed in the comment on Document 7. The first phase of the Hundred Flowers policy is discussed in the comment on Document 8.

Supplementary material may be found as follows:

(a) The general Party campaign to mobilize intellectuals: CB 374-376 and 402; ECMM 32 (*New Construction,* Feb. 3, 1956).

(b) The genesis and development of the 12-year scientific plan: Theodore H. E. Chen, *op. cit.,* pp. 115-116; SCMP 1061 and 1062; CB 343 (reorganization of Chinese Academy of Science; ECMM 20 (*Science Journal,* November 1955); and URS, Vol. 2, No. 25 (*People's Daily,* June 12, 1955).

──────────────── TEXT OF DOCUMENT 6 ────────────────

Comrades:

In order to strengthen leadership of the Party over intellectuals, to strengthen the leadership of the Party over work in the scientific and cultural fields as a whole, the Central Committee has decided to convene a session to discuss the question of intellectuals.

The decision of the Central Committee is a part of the entire struggle of the whole Party, led by the Central Committee, for the opposition to conservative ideology and the exertion of efforts for the fulfillment of the general task during the transition period.

As we all know, during 1955, on the basis of the advocacy of Comrade Mao Tse-tung, the Central Committee of the Party carried out a series of struggles against rightist conservative ideology. The most important results of this series of struggles have been:

(1) The steady and thorough development of the movement in both government organs and in society for the wiping out of counter-revolutionaries with the anticipated basic realization of the movement on a nation-wide scope within the next two years;

(2) The phenomenal advances made in the movement for the cooperativization of agriculture, on the foundation of the rapid growth of the consciousness of the masses, with the anticipated basic realization on a nation-wide scope of semi-Socialist cooperativization within the current year, and with the pushing forward of the movement toward complete Socialist cooperativization;

(3) The rapid development of the changeover of capitalist industry and commerce by whole trades to public-private joint ownership, with the possibility of the basic fulfillment of the task on a nation-wide scope within the current year; and

(4) The advanced fulfillment and the overfulfillment of the first Five Year Plan for the Development of National Economy as a whole, with the anticipated fulfillment by certain production departments in 1956 of the production plans originally scheduled for fulfillment in 1957, and with the possibility of the advanced fulfillment and overfulfillment of the plan by other departments.

All these gigantic and moving achievements could not have been imagined one year ago. Had there not been developed the struggle against rightist conservative ideology, then these achievements would not have been made even today. It may thus be seen that conservative ideology presents a most serious threat to our Party.

The basic demands of the struggle against rightist conservative ideology should be the greater consolidation and development of the people's democratic dictatorship, the advanced fulfillment of Socialist transformation, the overfulfillment of the State's industrial development plans, and the accelerated technical reform of our national economy. This struggle is of great world significance. In our great country with its 600 million population, the advanced fulfillment and the accelerated progress of these tasks, their fulfillment on the biggest possible scale, quickly, effectively and economically, will all the more rapidly and greatly augment the forces of the Socialist camp as a whole, all the more facilitate our task in the prevention of the outbreak of a new war, and, should the mad aggressors dare to precipitate a new war, will place us in a much more favorable position. For this reason, the Central Committee of the Party has decided to make opposition to rightist conservative ideology the central question for the 8th National Congress of the Party, and has demanded of all work departments in the whole Party to develop this struggle.

The question of intellectuals has been brought up on this foundation.

What relationships, exactly, are there between the question of intellectuals and our current task of the acceleration of Socialist construction?

We are building up a Socialist economy, in a word, in order to satisfy to the maximum extent the constantly growing needs, material and cultural, of the whole society. To achieve this end, we must continually develop our social productive power, continually raise labor productivity, and continually register improvement on the foundation of high technique and in accordance with the continual increase of social production. For this reason, in this age of Socialism as compared with any previous age, there is the greater need for the fullest elevation of production technique, the greater need for the fullest development of science and utilization of scientific knowledge.

We want to develop our Socialist construction on the biggest possible scale—quickly, effectively and economically. It is essential that we rely on the energetic labor not only of the working class and the broad masses of the peasants, but also of the intellectuals. For this it is essential for us to rely on the close cooperation of physical and mental labor, on the fraternal alliance of the workers, peasants and intellectuals. The different forms of construction we are now engaged in need the participation of intellectuals in ever growing numbers.

As an example, if we want to discover mineral deposits, we must have a number of geological experts, taking with them a large number of university and middle school graduates to the waste mountains and desolate areas for surveys, investigations, check-ups, and drilling experiments. And if we want to develop mines, build factories, construct railways and undertake water conservancy projects, we must have a large number of engineers and technicians for surveys, designs, construction and installation. A factory has to produce, and every link in the process of production, from the designing of products to the examination of the finished articles, there is need for technical forces of a definite quantity and a definite level. The management of industry and commerce more and more calls for various kinds of technical knowledge. To build up a modern national defense system, there is need for scientific experts of all kinds. Without teachers and doctors, we cannot have schools and hospitals. Without cultural workers and artists, we cannot have our cultural life. In the rural areas, with the realization of the mechanization and electrification of agriculture, there will naturally be the need for large numbers of engineers for the agricultural machinery, engineers for the power stations, agronomists and accountants. Even today, for the realization of the many items which must receive immediate attention in the provisions of the 1956-1967 national program for agricultural development (draft), such as the production of modern animal-powered farm implements, chemical fertilizers, and pumping machines, the extermination of the major pests, the elimination of human diseases and animal epidemics, we must also rely on the active services of scientific and technical workers, vegetation protection experts, medical workers and veterinary surgeons.

The intellectuals have already become an important factor in every aspect of the life of our state. To deal with the question of the intellectuals correctly, in a way that will stimulate their activity and enable them to apply their energies more fully to serve our great work of Socialist construction, has therefore become an important factor in our efforts to fulfill the fundamental task of the period of transition.

What is the fundamental question of intellectuals at the present moment? The fundamental question now is that the forces of our intelligentsia are insufficient in number, professional skills and political consciousness to meet the requirements of our rapid Socialist construction. Certain unreasonable features in our present employment and treatment of intellectuals and, in particular, certain sectarian attitudes among some of our comrades towards intellectuals outside the Party, have to some extent handicapped us in bringing the existing powers of the intelligentsia into full play. It is imperative that we give better leadership, overcome the weaknesses and take a series of effective measures to mobilise and fully apply the powers of the intellectuals by ceaselessly raising their political consciousness, training up new forces on a large scale to add to their ranks and raising their professional skills as much as possible so as to meet the growing demands raised by the state on the intellectuals. This is now the fundamental task for our Party as on the question on the intellectuals.

I

To discuss the Party's task on the question of intellectuals, we must first make an observation of the present conditions of intellectuals.

Our Party has always attached great importance to the question of the intellectuals. Back in 1939, the Central Committee of the Party passed the decision draft by Comrade Mao Tse-tung on the large scale absorption of intellectuals and this decision was being effectively carried out in the various anti-Japanese bases. Since the liberation of the mainland, the Party has applied the policy of uniting, training and reeducating them on a nation-wide scale.

The Central Committee of the Party considers that the revolution has need for the absorption of the intellectuals, while construction all the more has need for the absorption of the intellectuals. Especially since our country before the liberation was culturally backward and scientifically backward, we must all the more be adept in the utilization of the historical legacy of old society in the form of the group of intellectuals so that they may serve our Socialist national construction. The Central Committee of the Party further considers that the intellectuals of the past age in China, though under the various influences of imperialism and the Kuomintang, so that a portion of them joined the revolution, another portion sympathized with the revolution, the majority adopted a neutral attitude of waiting and seeing toward the revolution, and only a very small number opposed the revolution. Facts are growingly proving to China's intellectuals that apart from joining the lot of the working class and the Communist Party, there is no other outlet for them. Accordingly, unity with the intellectuals is necessary and completely possible.

Starting from such a recognition, the Central Committee of the Party has adopted the policy of "taking them over en masse" in dealing with the intellectuals of the past age, continuing to give appropriate jobs to the overwhelming majority of them, with some of them assigned posts of responsibility. The originally unemployed intellectuals have been placed in employment, or otherwise provided for. Politically, the Party has given many representative figures of the intelligentsia high positions. The Central Committee of the Party considers that the intellectuals of the past age must be aided in self reform so that they may abandon the ideology of the landlord class and the bourgeois class, and accept the ideology of the working class.

To achieve this end the Party has adopted a series of measures. The Party has organized them to participate in land reform, in the suppression of counter revolutionaries, in the campaign of resisting the United States and aiding Korea, in the "3-anti" and "5-anti" movements, in visits to factories and rural areas, in visits to the Soviet Union, in taking part in various international movements. The Party has also led them in the study of the basic knowledge of Marxism-Leninism, the criticism of the idealist viewpoint of the bourgeois class, in opposition to the Hu Feng counter revolutionary clique and other counter revolutionaries, and on the foundation of such studies in the development of criticism and self criticism. In the professional field the Party has also adopted many measures to assist them to grasp the principle of combining theory with practices, to study the advanced experiences of the Soviet Union, to improve work methods and to advance their professional skill.

The overwhelming majority of the intellectuals have become government workers in the service of Socialism and are already part of the working class. While uniting, training and reeducating the old intellectuals, the Party has made a very great effort to foster the growth of new intellectuals in large numbers, and there is already a considerable number of laboring class origin. Because of this, a fundamental change has taken place among Chinese intellectuals in the past six years.

In regard to the current political conditions of intellectuals, statistical data have been compiled in many units. These statistics show that among the higher intellectuals, about 45 percent are progressive elements who actively support the Communist Party and the People's Government, actively support Socialism, actively serve the people. Another 40 percent are the middle-of-the-road elements who support the Communist Party and the People's Government, and generally can fulfill the tasks assigned them, but politically not sufficiently progressive. Together the above two groups constitute 80 percent of all. Apart from them, a little over 10 percent are backward elements who lack political consciousness or ideologically oppose Socialism. Only a few percent are included among the counter revolutionaries and other bad elements.

Compared with the first stage of the revolution, the change has been rapid. According to statistical data on 141 teachers in 4 higher institutions of Peking, Tientsin and Tsingtao, for example, in the past six years, the progressive elements increased from 18 percent to 41 percent, while the backward elements were reduced from 28 percent to 15 percent. It is inevitable that a large proportion of the intellectuals have been strongly and increasingly influenced by our great cause of Socialist transformation and Socialist construction. From the new life of China they see, too, the close link between the future for the nation and their own future.

Attention must be given here to the fact that the ideological situation of the intellectuals is not fully in keeping with the changes in their political and social status. Many progressive elements still have to varying degrees the idealism of the bourgeois class and the ideology and work style of individualism, not to speak of the middle-of-the-road elements. In addition, the intellectuals in many units, particularly the more backward ones among them, have been slow in making changes. This also reflects the fact that we have done very little work among them.

In the past six years, there has been a very rapid growth in the number of intellectuals. At the moment, it is estimated that there are about 100,000 higher intellectuals in the whole country engaged in scientific research, education, engineering, public health work, education and the arts. According to statistical data available for some of them, one third of the figures represents post-liberation increases. In some departments the increase has been specially rapid. For instance, in the first stage of the liberation, there were hardly 200 geological workers, but in 1955, according to statistical returns from the Ministry of Geology, Ministry of Heavy Industry, Ministry of Petroleum Industry, and Ministry of Coal Industry, the number of geological engineers alone had been increased to 497, while technicians graduating from higher institutions reached 3,400.

In the six years after the liberation, 217,900 students have graduated from higher institutions in the country. Though not all of them have reached the standards of higher intellectuals referred to by us, they nevertheless constitute a new force in the intellectual world, and the reserve force for our experts. It must be pointed out that many youths, though not yet reaching the status of experts, are already shouldering the tasks of experts, and are doing well. Of the teaching staff of 42,000 in the higher institutions, only 17.8 percent are professors and associate professors, 24 percent are lecturers, and 58.2 percent are assistants. Some of the assistants have already taken up teaching work. The same situation is to be found in the engineering world. There are in all some 31,000 engineers of all grades in the whole country, while technicians who have graduated from higher institutions number 63,600, and among them many are actually performing the duties of engineers, some of whom should have been promoted engineers. In addition, as reserves for higher intellectuals, there are also a large army of other intellectuals who in the course of field work and spare-time study are continually raising their knowledge levels.

There is really no definite boundary line between the so-called higher intellectuals and general intellectuals. According to available statistics, there are now, in all, 3,840,000 intellectuals engaged in scientific research, education, engineering, public health work, education and the arts. They represent a great force in our Socialist construction. It is an extremely important task of the Party and the state correctly to appraise and employ these intellectuals and help them, in a planned way, to go ahead steadily, both politically and professionally. Though in the present report I am laying emphasis on the questions affecting higher intellectuals, but the greater part of the principles discussed are likewise applicable to intellectuals in general.

As stated above, the intellectuals of our army have already become a large force. In view of the size of our country, however, and the rapid pace of our construction—and the fact that the pace is becoming still faster—we have to extend the ranks of the intellectuals still faster, in particular the ranks of the highly trained intellectuals, so as to meet the urgent needs of Socialist construction. It must be admitted that there are still many defects in our work in the fostering and promotion of the new born forces, defects which obstruct the even more rapid expansion of the ranks of the intellectuals.

A marked rise has taken place in the level of professional skill of Chinese intellectuals in the past six years. Pedagogical reform has been carried out in the higher institutions throughout the country, many new departments and specialization courses never conducted in the past have been added, large quantities of textbooks have been newly compiled and translated, and pedagogical quality has been raised. Marked achievements have also been registered by the scientific and technical circles of the country in geological surveys, designing and carrying out of capital construction, designing and trial manufacturing of new products, in all of which fields great efforts have been exerted. As the result of painstaking efforts in studying from the Soviet Union, China's engineers have learned many modernized designing and work enforcement methods in the building of factories, mines, bridges, and conservancy projects. They have greatly raised their capacity in the designing of large sized machinery, locomotives, and ships. During the period from 1952 to 1955, about 3,500 kinds of new machine products have been successfully produced, and a small number of these have reached world standards. In the field of metallurgy, China is now in the position to produce more than 240 kinds of high quality steel and alloys, and the utilization rate of blast furnaces and open case furnaces in China has reached the levels of the Soviet Union of 1952. In the field of scientific theory, some of our achievements in mathematics, physics, organic chemistry and biology have roused the attention of the scientific world, and in some departments contributions have been made to practical production.

But as a whole, the state of China's science and technique is still very backward. We are still unable to acquire and put into use very many of the latest scientific achievements of the world. We are also still unable to solve independently of the Soviet experts, many of the complex technical questions now arising in our work of construction. Yet till recently, we have failed to draw up comprehensive plans for raising our scientific and technical levels. We have even failed to make the fullest and most effective use of our existing forces. Our backwardness in technical science is inseparable from our weak foundations in scientific theory. It is precisely in scientific research that our strength is the less.

From the above simple description we can see that our achievements have been very great, but there are many defects.

What policy, then, are we to adopt on the question of the intellectuals? What tendencies are to be prevented and corrected?

The chief existing tendency as regards the intellectuals is sectarianism. But at the same time there is also the tendency of passivity and an inclination towards compromise. The first tendency underestimates the colossal political and professional advances made by the intellectuals, underestimates their great positive role in our Socialist cause, fails to recognize them as a part of the working class. It upholds the view that production is dependent on the workers and technique is dependent on the Soviet experts. And so there has not been earnestly implemented the Party's policy for intellectuals, and no serious study and solution is made of the questions affecting intellectuals. No interest is paid to the full mobilization of the intellectuals and the promotion of their positive role, the further reform of intellectuals, the expansion of the ranks of the intellectuals, and the raising of the professional skill of the intellectuals—all pressing problems.

The second tendency only takes into account the progress of the intellectuals and fails to see their defects. They are overestimated and blindly trusted, and there is even a lack of vigilance against the bad elements. And so no effort is made to educate and reform them, or else though their defects are noticed, due to various anxieties which should not have been entertained, education and reform measures are withheld.

The two tendencies are opposite to each other in form, but both of them in practice lead to a kind of rightist conservatism. Both lead to the abandonment of leadership, lack the spirit for active struggle, and obstruct our correct solution of the question of intellectuals and questions affecting scientific and cultural work. Both obstruct the development of our Socialist cause.

We must oppose both of these two wrong tendencies together. We cannot overlook the existing forces of the intellectuals, nor can we feel satisfied over them. We cannot indefinitely rely on the Soviet experts, nor can we relax our efforts in the most effective study of the advanced scientific techniques of the Soviet Union and other countries. The only correct principle is to stimulate and bring into full play the existing forces of the intelligentsia so as to carry out the Socialist construction of our country on a large scale, quickly, effectively and economically; and at the same time to spare no effort to reeducate them still further, add to their numbers and raise their level as rapidly as possible, at a speed and scale as really keeps up with the huge pace of development of our state in all its aspects.

II

The fullest mobilization of the intellectuals and the bringing into full play their strength is not only necessary for the intensive construction program in our country today, but is also the prerequisite to the further reform, expansion and elevation of the ranks of the intellectuals.

Generally speaking, intellectuals have been mobilized in large numbers under the leadership of our Party. Otherwise, the great progress and the great contributions to the State made by them referred to above, would have been unthinkable. We must first affirm this point. This is the major phase of the situation.

But there exist actually many defects in our work, including some serious defects. In the current high tide of Socialist construction and transformation, there is need for us to strengthen leadership, to rapidly overcome our defects, if we are to more fully mobilize the intellectuals and promote their positive role.

The first thing to be done in order to stimulate and bringing into full play the strength of the intelligentsia is to improve the manner of employing and placing them, so that they can develop their specialized skills to the benefit of the state.

In the employment and placing of intellectuals, we have under general conditions done a good job, and many intellectuals have shouldered many heavy tasks in national construction, and their capacity is being continually raised in the midst of practical work.

But still we cannot say that we have done everything in the employment of and arrangements for the intellectuals, and that none of them have been overlooked. As an example, in many organs, because of the inappropriate distribution of work, or because of the defects in the organization of work, there are still a few intellectuals who are idle to the point of having no work to do, and very often these very intellectuals had been assigned to the organs concerned precisely because of their possession of certain technical knowledge. This state of the waste of the most valuable assets of the State must be eliminated. Again, in the higher institutions in the country, there are still a few teachers who have not been assigned classes. Among them there are some who are not incompetent to take charge of classes, or who only need a short term of study before they will be fully capable of taking charge of classes. These teachers must be given classes to teach. And where the teachers are really not capable of being placed in charge of classes, other work for which they are qualified should be assigned them, such as editing and translation work, publishing work, and library work, so that they may not remain idle. And in society, there are also a very small number of unemployed intellectuals who possess certain labor power. The local authorities or the Central Government should look into their situation and allot them definite work.

In some areas, there still exists the situation of the failure to assign proper tasks to intellectuals in their employment and in making arrangements for them. Some scientists wish to undertake scientific research, and it is to the best advantage of the State that they engage in scientific research. But they are assigned administrative work in government organs and schools. Some experts, as the result of wrong assignments given them, are doing jobs for which they have not been prepared. Some are assigned to one task today, and another task the next, but never sent to the job for which they are qualified. According to statistics from four units of the Ministry of Light Industry, prepared by the 4th General Office of the State Council, about 10 percent of higher intellectuals are employed in posts for which they are not qualified. This is a very serious loss. We must adopt resolute measures to correct this state of affairs resulting from bureaucratism, sectarianism and departmentalism, so that specialists are placed in places where they are most needed.

Secondly, we must understand the intellectuals thoroughly and give them due confidence and support so that they can work with real initiative.

Intellectuals are generally satisfied with the confidence and support we are giving them. But we still must see our defects in this work. In the matter of giving intellectuals confidence and support, as stated above, one tendency is to indiscriminately give them excessive confidence and support politically and professionally, to the extent of revealing some state secrets to people not concerned with them altogether, or even to certain unreliable elements, or to assign tasks of great responsibility to ally incompetent hands so that damage is brought to the work. This situation exists and must be corrected. Another tendency is the failure to give them due confidence, such as the refusal to despatch to factories those who should have been allowed there, or to refuse them access to data which may be revealed to them. Such a situation also exists and must be corrected.

State secrets must be unconditionally preserved, and any relaxation is not permitted. The problem, however, is the correct demarcation of the boundaries of secrecy, and there should be no extension at random of its scope, to prevent damage to work and difficulties for the workers. At the same time, there must be a correct estimation and understanding of the past history of the intellectuals, so that some of them may not, due to their "complex historical record," be subjected over a long period to unnecessary suspicion. Among the higher intellectuals today, many have a complex past history, and this is not to be wondered at. But only a small number of them have political problems, and an overwhelming minority of them still have political problems at present. And many intellectuals who still have their political problems unsolved are in the position because the leadership comrades did not assume full responsibility to deal with their problems, so that their solution has been delayed. Stronger forces must therefore be centralized, and outstanding cases affecting the past of these intellectuals dealt with according to the degree of urgency so that their positions will be clarified and they may be placed on proper employment.

Intellectuals outside the Party must not only enjoy our confidence, but also enjoy our support. That is to say, they must be given jobs and authority, their views must be respected, the results of their professional research and work must be valued. There must be promoted and extended academic discussions of Socialist construction. Their creations and inventions must be given opportunities for experiment and extension. A small number of Party members and League members do not respect the leadership of intellectuals who are non-members of the Party but occupy higher positions above them. This situation must be corrected.

The failure to give due confidence and support to some intellectuals is the major manifestation of sectarianism in some of our comrades in dealing with the question of intellectuals. Not a few comrades are still not used to the practice of consulting intellectuals outside the Party on matters, or to give them timely guidance and assistance. Some comrades easily get themselves estranged from intellectuals outside the Party, and even adopt the attitude of respecting them but keeping them at a distance. In this way, there is a lack of mutual understanding, and estrangement becomes the easier. However, they are important workers of our State, the quality of their work will directly affect national construction, and so we have the responsibility to learn to use the attitude of dealing with our own comrades in our approach to them, in correctly understanding them, and to give them guidance and assistance so that they may promote their active role in work.

The third thing to do is to provide the intellectuals with the necessary working conditions and appropriate treatment.

The work conditions and treatment of intellectuals today have been greatly improved compared with the days before the liberation. But as stated above, there are also problems calling for urgent solution in this connection.

With reference to the working conditions of the intellectuals, an important problem today is the fact that many among them cannot most effectively distribute their own working time. Many intellectuals deeply feel that they are spending too much time on meetings of a non-professional nature and on administrative work. These meetings and many other tasks may not need their participation. It seems that the better known a scientist, a writer or an artist, the more of his time will be occupied for meetings, administrative work, and social activities. This is a serious situation on our cultural front. The Central committee considers it essential to ensure that they have at least five-sixths of the working day (or 40 hours a week) available for their professional work. The remaining time can be used for political study, attending necessary meetings and taking part in social activity. This demand should be resolutely and thoroughly implemented. It is beneficial for intellectuals to participate in social activities. The defect today is that such activities are concentrated in a few persons. The situation must be adjusted, and as many persons as possible should be made to participate in such activities so that they will not become an undue burden for a small number of persons. Some experts hold too many concurrent jobs and this situation must also be adjusted.

Some intellectuals in their work feel the lack of needed books and reference materials and equipment, or the lack of suitable assistants, so that their efficiency has been affected. This situation actually exists. As an example, many units with large quantities of reference materials have not paid adequate attention to this valuable asset, and no cadres have been assigned to put the materials in order, so that some experts cannot make use of the materials for their research. The main reason leading to this is our lack of familiarity of their needs, or though their requests for materials have been made several times, we have failed to solve their problem. Some workers do not wish to take trouble over these "minor matters," and this is a mistake. This is not a "minor matter," we must rapidly and earnestly solve this problem.

As to the treatment of intellectuals, generally speaking there has been an improvement compared with the days before the liberation. But in order to enable the higher intellectuals to devote greater energy to their work, their treatment should be appropriately raised. Some higher intellectuals have to spend unnecessarily much time over trifling matters in their living, and this must be considered a loss of the state's labor power. Some higher intellectuals have very inferior living quarters. In Peking and other cities where the increase of population has been rapid, there is often the situation in which several families are crowded into one very small house. Their rest and entertainment facilities are also not well organized. All these problems must be earnestly solved by the competent departments.

In solving the questions of the living conditions and treatment of the intellectuals better, we should take chiefly in the following three ways. First, we should tell the administrative personnel of all the departments concerned to regard the living conditions of the intellectuals as a matter of importance. Second, we should educate the trade union organisations in all the departments concerned and the consumers' cooperatives to strive to expand their services for the benefit of the intellectuals. Third, we should make suitable adjustment in the salaries of intellectuals on the principle of remuneration according to work, so that their earnings are commensurate with their contribution to the state. The tendency of equalitarianism in the systems of remuneration and other irrational features should be eliminated. In addition, a small number of intellectuals who are not within the scope of state workers, such as some actors, painters and practitioners of traditional medicine, at present derive comparatively small incomes. The problem should also be solved separately by competent departments.

Another important problem connected with the treatment of intellectuals is the system of promotion. In our promotion system today, there are many irrational provisions. There are too many grades and the differences between grades are small. A graduate of a higher institution is placed at a too low grade. There are no definite measures and standards for grade promotions. In many units, for several years there has not been undertaken the work of classification, and some people have not had the chance for promotion. This irrational system of promotion greatly obstructs the ambition for advancement on the part of the intellectuals, and obstructs especially the fostering of new forces and the selection of intellectuals generally for better positions. This system must be rapidly revised. In addition, an important measure for the encouragement of intellectuals' ambition for advancement and the stimulation of scientific and cultural progress is to be found in the conferment on intellectuals of degrees and titles, and the enforcement of systems for the encouragement of inventions, creations and excellent writings. The competent departments are now engaged in the formulation of these various systems and they should be decided and published as soon as possible.

In some respects, the political treatment of intellectuals also needs to be improved. The major problem here is to eliminate the situation of the lack of concern for the political life of intellectuals as found in many units. Some intellectuals take us to task for making them listen to long reports several times a year, but more intellectuals take us to task for not letting them listen to a single report a whole year. Similarly, in regard to social activities, some feel that they have to participate too often, but more people consider that if they are given just one opportunity to participate, they will feel greatly stimulated. In this respect, there is need for us to make appropriate adjustments. In addition, we must carry out education among the workers, and let them understand how to correctly deal with intellectuals, so that their proper sense of self respect may not be unwittingly impaired, since all righteous laborers should have such self respect.

What I have said so far are some of the necessary conditions for the mobilization of intellectuals and the bringing into full play their strength. Naturally, to realize this goal, there is need for them to be educated and reformed, to be given political and professional leadership. We shall deal with this later. At any rate, the conditions discussed above are all indispensable. With these conditions, we shall more fully mobilize the intellectuals to bring into full play their strength in the construction of the great motherland, and the more better promote their own political and professional advancement.

III

One of the important political tasks of the Party during the period of transition is to continue to help the intellectuals to carry out self reeducation.

Our Country is now in the stage of transition, a stage of the most penetrating transformation of society. The system of private ownership of the means of production in existence for several thousand years is to be changed into the system of Socialist public ownership. The system of exploitation in existence for several thousand years is to be permanently wiped out. All men are to be changed into laborers of various types. This heaven-rending change cannot but draw forth fierce reaction in the various regions of our social life and ideological domain. Accordingly, all social problems of this period, among them the question of the intellectuals, cannot be observed apart from the class struggle. The various divisions and changes of intellectuals politically are reflections of the development of the class struggle within the ranks of the intellectuals. We have seen that among the intellectuals today, there are a few percent who are counter revolutionaries and other bad elements (such as swindlers and gangsters). These people have to be weeded out of the ranks of the intellectuals. In addition, there is also a small number who ideologically oppose Socialism or who do not fully understand Socialism. In dealing with these, we must criticize their mistaken ideology, and as far as possible strive to win them over to the Socialist side.

The wiping out of counter revolutionaries hidden in the ranks of the intellectuals has been attended with great success during the past year. We are continuing efforts to strive for the basic elimination of counter revolutionaries within the next two years.

In the struggle against counter revolutionaries, do not involve those people who only had normal social relationships with counter revolutionaries. This is an important point, for there are many such people among intellectuals. If in the past they were incorrectly confused with the counter revolutionaries, the situation must now be clearly explained to them. As to those who had only historical relationships with counter revolutionary organizations, and who since the liberation have actually changed their stand, after they have fully accounted for their past, they should be treated as ordinary people.

We have stated earlier that between some intellectuals and our Party, there still exists a certain state of estrangement. We must take the initiative in removing this estrangement. But it often comes from both sides: on the one hand our comrades have failed to approach them, failed to understand them, while on the other hand, some of the intellectuals have adopted an attitude of reservation toward Socialism, or even an attitude of opposition. In our enterprises, schools and organs, in society, there are still such intellectuals. They make no distinction between the Communist Party and the Kuomintang, no distinction between the Chinese people and the imperialists. They are not satisfied with the policies and measures of the Party and the People's Government, linger over capitalism and even linger over feudalism. They oppose the Soviet Union and are not willing to learn from the Soviet Union. They refuse to study Marxism-Leninism, and even slander Marxism-Leninism. They belittle labor, belittle the laboring people, belittle the cadres who grew from the ranks of laborers, and are not willing to be together with workers, peasants, and worker and peasant cadres. They do not like to see the growth of the new forces, and consider the progressive elements speculators. They do not only constantly create disputes and a state of antithesis between the intellectuals and the Party, but also create disputes and a state of antithesis between the intellectuals themselves. They are vainglorious, and look upon themselves as the best in the world, and will not accept the leadership and criticism of any other. They reject the interests of the people, the interests of society, and deal with all problems from the viewpoint of their own individual interests, supporting whatever is in keeping with their own interests and opposing whatever is at variance with their own interests.

Of course, among the intellectuals today there are but very few who have all the faults mentioned above. Nevertheless, there are quite a few who have one or more kinds of the faults listed. Not only the backward elements, but also some of the middle-of-the-road elements are guilty of some of the mistakes mentioned. And quite a few among the progressive elements are guilty of narrow-mindedness, self conceit, and looking at problems from the viewpoint of individual interests. If such intellectuals do not change their stand, then even if we exert efforts to establish closer contact with them, there will still remain a state of estrangement between them and us.

For this reason, we must not only reform the backward elements, but also do our best to educate the middle-of-the-road elements to make them leave their present situation and change into progressive elements, while the present progressive elements must be further aided to make even greater progress, to study Marxism-Leninism, to rid themselves of the influences of capitalism, individualism and idealism. We must foster among the higher intellectuals large numbers of "red experts" who will resolutely struggle for the Socialist cause. Today some higher intellectuals have already been converted into red experts, while many others hold this aspiration. We must enthusiastically help them to carry out self reform, to realize their aspiration. Mistaken are all attitudes that tend to boycott and discriminate against them.

Generally speaking, our program in the struggle to carry further the reeducation of the intellectuals is as follows in the present stage: to root out completely the counter revolutionary elements still hidden in the ranks of the intellectuals, to reduce to the minimum the number of backward elements, to lead as many of the middle-of-the-road elements as possible to become progressives and change the progressives into full Socialist intellectuals.

We already have rich experience and made tremendous achievements in the reeducation of the intellectuals. Our present task is to sum up this experience, overcome certain shortcomings in our past work, and to carry this work forward in a more planned way. Since we know the various political divisions of the intellectuals, we must decide, according to these general conditions, on plans for the education of the progressive elements, the middle-of-the-road elements and the backward elements separately, and apply various measures which have been proved effective.

Generally speaking there are three ways along which the reeducation of the intellectuals proceeds. One is through observation and taking part in social life; the other is through the work in their professions; and the third is through general theoretical study. All three are connected with each other. A person's thinking usually changes under the influence of all these three factors. But generally the broadest and most direct education is that received in social life. As we all know, many intellectuals began their ideological changes with their participation in land reform and the campaign for resistance against the United States and for aid to Korea. During the past few years, visits to factories and rural areas have also effectively assisted the intellectuals in gaining confidence in Socialism. But we have not yet systematically organized this work, and especially have we failed to include in our plans many middle-of-the-road elements and backward elements. Henceforth, the organization of intellectuals for visits to Socialist construction projects must be considered an important task, and overall arrangements made for them. Those who have so far never participated in these visits should be given an opportunity to do so.

Practical work in their respective professions is also of great effect in the ideological reform of intellectuals. During the past few years, the reform of teaching methods and the adoption of Soviet textbooks have changed the understanding of many teachers who in the past had no confidence in the Soviet Union and did not believe in Marxism-Leninism. Similarly, the creations in production techniques by the masses of our workers and peasants, the extension of Soviet scientific techniques, and the exemplary work carried out by Soviet experts have also converted many scientific and technical personnel into accepting the superiority of the Socialist system. Henceforth, the experiences in these lines must be further developed. On the question of the study of the Soviet Union, however, in the past there had also been such defects as undue haste, arbitrary learning, and mechanical application. Some comrades even arbitrarily rejected the achievements of the capitalist countries in science and technique. These defects should henceforth be avoided.

The study of Marxism-Leninism is of decisive significance for the firm establishment among intellectuals of the revolutionary concept of life and the scientific concept of the world. In some areas today, such studies have not been well organized, the levels of the directors of study are too low, or the plans and methods of study do not meet with the needs of higher intellectuals. These defects must be overcome. On the principles of voluntariness and linking up with professional duties, there must be provided certain essential basic courses in Marxism-Leninism. The intellectuals must be aided in the study of theory through the adoption of such media as self-study, night universities, correspondence schools, and scientific discussion groups.

Since the reeducation of the intellectuals reflects the class struggle, the process itself cannot possibly be free from certain struggle. First and foremost we must require of all intellectuals love of country, adherence to the constitution and a clear distinction between ourselves and the enemy. Next, there is bound to be a sharp struggle between Socialist and capitalist ideology and between the ideologies of materialism and idealism. The process of changing the intellectuals ideologically is inseparable from the development of ideological struggle among them.

Since the liberation, the ideological reform movement led by the Party and the criticism of idealist ideology have produced great effects on the promotion of the progress of the intellectuals. In this ideological struggle, attention must be given to the fact that change in a person's thinking proceeds by way of his or her own consciousness. It is impossible to solve the problem crudely. There are people who persist in their own wrong thinking. If they do not turn against the people in speech and action and, even more, if they are prepared to devote their knowledge and energies to serving the people, we must be able to wait for the gradual awakening of their consciousness and help them patiently, while at the same time criticising their wrong ideology.

To assist intellectuals to seek progress, it is of important significance for the leadership personnel of the Party to have direct contacts with them. Many intellectuals hope that we can give them aid and criticism ideologically and politically, and feel that we have given them too little aid in this respect. Not a few intellectuals not only find it very difficult to contact members of local Party committees and leadership comrades, but also find it difficult to have opportunities for talks with the members of the Party committees in their own work units, with whom they are together. These intellectuals say that we "use more, and aid less" in dealing with them, or even "only use, but do not aid" them. Still others of them say that we only look them up on three occasions: (1) when making a transfer of post; (2) when asking for their past history; and (3) when they have committed a mistake. These criticisms are pointed, and should rouse our attention. We must include in the plans for the reform of intellectuals talks with them on ideological and political matters, and criticism as that to fellow comrades. Forums have been organized for exchanges of views with them, a thing which they welcome, and these should be regularly held. In accordance with concrete conditions, some intellectuals outside the Party may be invited as observers to certain meetings of Party organs and Party branches, to enable them to better understand the desires of the Party, and to receive more education from the Party.

To assist intellectuals to make greater progress, in addition to placing reliance on members of the Communist Party, the progressives who now constitute about 40 percent of all intellectuals should also be organized to take part in the task. The Youth League, the trade unions, and the various democratic parties and groups in the past few years have done a lot in this respect, and their resources should further be utilized in a planned manner.

Since we have accumulated many experiences in the reform of intellectuals and have the support of the progressive forces, and since intellectuals generally have received growingly penetrative education in Socialism in the midst of the phenomenal development of the construction of the motherland, their future progress must be more rapid than that of the past years. Plans for the reeducation of the intellectuals should be drawn up, to include a 7-year plan covering 1956 to 1962 and annual plans. We should certainly be able to increase the number of progressives among the higher intellectuals, people who will fight energetically for Socialism and accept the basic Marxist-Leninist viewpoints, to over three-fourths and reduce the proportion of backward elements to about five percent by the end of the second Five Year Plan.

Plans should also be drawn up regarding the admission of intellectuals into the Party. Already progressive intellectuals have requested for admission into the Party. As an example, of the 1,920 engineering and technical personnel in the Non-Ferrous Metals Designing Board of the Ministry of Heavy Industry, 605, or 31.7 percent, have applied for membership in the Party. In the six higher institutions in Tientsin, of the 291 teachers of the rank of lecturer and above, 106, or 36.4 percent, have applied for membership in the Party. Of the 131 research workers in the North China Agricultural Science Research Institute, 53 or 40 percent have applied for membership in the Party. But in the past few years we have seldom admitted into the Party members of their ranks, and this was a tendency to isolationism. This tendency must be corrected. Naturally we must rigidly abide by the qualifications of Party members in admitting new members. But we believe that among these various applicants, many have the requisite qualifications for membership. We plan to admit one-third of all the higher intellectuals into the Party by 1962. We consider this feasible as the ranks of the higher intellectuals are growing and the number of progressives among them is increasing.

In fulfilling these plans, a further fundamental change will be made in the ideological and political situation of the Chinese intellectuals. It will be possible for us on the whole to complete this special historical task of reeducating intellectuals during the period of transition. After this, like all other people, the intellectuals will still have to go on with their self-education, through study and in practice, and advance to still higher standards on the new levels. But this will have become a regular task by them.

IV

To meet the requirements of the rapid development of national construction, the ranks of our intellectuals must be expanded numerically and their professional skills raised.

China's present scientific and cultural forces are far smaller than that of the Soviet Union and the other world powers, and their quality is far inferior. This is very much out of balance with the needs of our great Socialist country which has 600 million people. We must move forward quickly and mend our pace, we must try in every possible way to expand speedily and raise our country's scientific and cultural strength to catch up with the most advanced international levels before very long. This is a great fighting task for the Communist Party, the intellectuals and all the people of our country.

We always say that our science and culture are backward, but we do not always look into the places where backwardness is apparent. Comrades! I wish here to speak a little more on the scientific situation, not only because science is a decisive factor in our national defense, economic and cultural enterprises, but also because in the world of science as a whole, during the past two or three decades, specially colossal and rapid progress has been registered, progress which has thrown us far behind in the field of scientific development.

Modern science and technique are advancing by leaps and bounds. The process of production is being gradually completely mechanized, completely automatized and controlled at long distances, so that labor productivity is being raised to unprecedentedly high levels. Different kinds of machinery for high temperature, high pressure, and high speed operation as well as for super high temperature, super high pressure and super high speed operation are being designed and produced. Transport machines on land, on water and in the air are having their speeds daily increased, and the super speed plane has exceeded the speed of sound. These technical advances demand the use of materials possessing special qualities, and various kinds of new metals and alloys, as well as materials produced with chemical and artifical methods, are being continually added to meet the new needs. The production techniques and specifications of various production departments are undergoing daily changes to guarantee the further acceleration and betterment of the process of production. The useful components of material resources are utilized to the greatest extent. The greater economy is practiced in raw materials. The quality of products is continually raised.

The peak of the latest developments is the application of atomic energy. Atomic energy has provided mankind with a new source of incomparably powerful energy. It has opened up great prospects for all scientific departments. At the same time, with the progress in electronics and other branches of science, automatic electronic controllers have been produced (such as electronic computer which can do 15,000 mathematic computations per second). They have begun to replace certain mental labor under specific conditions, just as other machines have replaced physical labor. This has greatly raised the level of automation technique. These fresh achievements have brought mankind to the threshold of a new revolution in science, technique and industry. This revolution, as Comrade Bulganin has said, "is far exceeding for its significance the industrial revolution associated with steam and electricity."

We must keep pace with this advanced scientific level of the world. We must bear in mind that while we are making headway, others are also advancing rapidly. Therefore, we must apply our energies in this direction on the most intensified scale. Only by mastering the most advanced sciences can we make our national defences impregnable, make our economy powerful and up-to-date and provide ourselves with adequate conditions for joining the Soviet Union and the people's democracies in defeating the imperialist powers, either in peaceful competition or in any aggressive war which the enemy may unleash.

It is very hard at present to estimate accurately how long will be needed for our scientific achievements to catch up with the most advanced world levels. Yet we must chart our task now—and that is to bring our country's most vital scientific departments near to the most advanced world levels by the end of the third Five Year Plan so that we shall be able, by our own efforts, to achieve speedily whatever other countries may do in the way of up-to-date achievements. Having laid such a foundation, we should be able to deal more thoroughly with the question of catching up world levels.

To fulfill this great task, we must first discard all servile thinking, which is a sign of lack of national self-confidence. "Since we cannot immediately change the backwardness of the scientific situation in China, we shall at any rate have to rely on Soviet assistance." It is true we need to rely on Soviet assistance to do away with our backwardness. But how are we to utilise this assistance? One way is the absence of overall planning and without distinguishing between what is essential and what is non-essential, is to seek a solution from the Soviet Union to every question, great and small, that crops up, and to send mostly middle school graduates, rather than scientists, to study in the Soviet Union. The result would be to remain forever in a state of dependence and imitation, increase the burden on Soviet scientific circles indefinitely, impede the systematic, rapid development of our science, and affect the speed of strengthening the scientific, economic and defence forces of the entire Socialist camp. The other way is to make an overall plan that distinguishes between what is essential and urgent and what is not so essential and urgent and to systematically utilize the latest achievements of Soviet science so as to bring ourselves abreast of Soviet levels as quickly as possible. This means that Soviet help should be sought only on pressing tasks and efforts should be made to learn technique in the process. At the same time, all our scientific departments that need to learn from the Soviet Union, should systematically send more mature scientists to study there or invite Soviet experts to this country to help us set up bases for scientific research, so as to be able, from the levels already reached by the Soviet Union, to launch further studies and train personnel in China within the shortest possible time. We can thus make the most effective and reasonable use of Soviet assistance and promote the planned development of our science so that it will be possible to hasten establishing relations of mutual help between the scientific groups of our two countries. This will promote the strengthening of the scientific, economic and defence forces of the entire Socialist camp. The latter way is one repeatedly suggested by Chinese and Soviet scientists and is the only correct way we should follow.

In order to raise the scientific level of our country in a systemic way, it is also necessary to eliminate the tendency to short-sightedness. Appropriate ratios should be maintained and a correct division of labor and cooperation made between theoretical and technical work, and between long-term and immediate requirements, so as to avoid a lack of balance. In the past few years, all kinds of work in our country were at their beginning, and we for the moment needed to throw in greater strength in technical operations, so that less attention was paid to long range needs and theoretical work. This was unavoidable and readily understandable. But if we still do not pay attention in good time to greater work to meet long term needs and to theoretical work, there we shall be committing a very grave mistake. Without a definite amount of theoretical scientific research as the foundation, we shall not be able to register progress and transformation of a basic nature in our technique. But the growth of the forces for theoretical study must be slower than the growth of the forces of technical application, while the results of the theoretical work are generally indirect and cannot be readily recognized all at once.

Precisely because of this, a tendency to short-sightedness still exists among many comrades who are not willing to employ the forces necessary for scientific research and constantly ask scientists to solve comparatively simple questions for them regarding technical application and production procedures. It is certainly unquestionable that theory must not be divorced from practice and we must fight against any theoretical study which is dissociated from practice. But the main tendency at present is the neglect of theoretical study.

This condition is reflected not only in the field of natural sciences, but also reflected in the field of the social sciences. At the present moment we have allotted to the field of the social sciences forces much weaker than those allotted to the field of natural sciences, viewed from the needs of the State. Take the case of the members of the Academic Departments of the Chinese Academy of Sciences. There are 192 members in the departments for the natural sciences, and more than half of them are at present in the position to devote a large share of their time in scientific work. In the field of the social sciences, there are 51 members, and at the moment only a few of them are in the position to devote the greater part of their time in scientific research.

The two tendencies described above react on each other, and are combined with each other. We must thoroughly correct these incorrect tendencies, and change the situation that is not conducive to the development of science.

The State Council has entrusted the State Planning Commission with the task of mapping out, in the course of three months and in conjunction with all departments concerned, a long-term plan for the development of science from 1956 to 1967. In mapping out this plan, it is necessary to proceed from the possibilities and need to introduce in the shortest possible time the most advanced scientific achievements in the world to the Chinese departments of sciences, national defence, production and education and, as soon as possible, to make up the branches of science in China that we most lack and most urgently need for national construction. Thus the scientific and technical level of these branches in China will be raised in 12 years almost to those of the Soviet Union and other big world powers.

What is the most rapid and most effective course for the realization of our object?

Such a road is as follows:

First, we must send a number of groups of experts, outstanding scientific workers and university graduates, in the shortest possible time, to the Soviet Union and other countries to study experimental knowledge or to study as post graduate students for one to two years for the branches which we most urgently need. On their return to the country they will immediately establish the foundations for the development of these branches in the Academy of Sciences and the various departments of the Government. New cadres will thus be fostered in great numbers. At the same time, in accordance with needs, students will continue to be despatched annually for experimental studies and research.

Second, for some of the branches of science, we should ask a number of groups of experts from the Soviet Union and other countries to assist us in the shortest time to set up scientific research bodies in the Academy of Sciences and other departments concerned, train personnel or engage in overall cooperation with Chinese scientific circles.

Third, we should organize in a planned way large numbers of scientific workers and technical personnel to learn from the Soviet experts now in China, using them as teachers, or not using them as ordinary workers. In the process of the construction and production of the 156 industrial projects which the Soviet Union is helping us build, there should be systematically organized large numbers of technical personnel to study and grasp the new technical principles connected with the projects, and these should be rapidly taught other workers.

Fourth, we should concentrate the best scientific forces and the best university graduates in the field of scientific research. The largest forces should be employed to strengthen the Chinese Academy of Sciences to make it the locomotive for leading the work in the whole country in the raising of scientific level and fostering new scientific forces.

Fifth, scientific forces in all the institutes of higher learning should be directed to develop scientific research energetically under the guidance of the plan to develop science throughout the country, and there should be fostered in large quantities scientific and technical new forces attaining the levels of modern science and technique.

Sixth, government departments, in particular those in the fields of geology, industry, agriculture, water conservancy, transportation, national defense and health, should initiate and strengthen necessary research bodies with dispatch. Responsibility should be taken to introduce the most modern achievements in the world of science, in a planned manner and systematically, to practical application, so that as rapidly as possible the world's most modern techniques will be installed in the different departments of our country.

For the earnest, and not merely nominal, launching of the march on science, we must grasp the time element. A year can easily pass away and be wasted in empty talk and procrastination. The Party's Central Committee calls for decision before the end of April this year on the long-term plan for the development of science, specific plans for this year and next co-ordinated with the long-term plan, and the first group of scientists to carry out immediately the long-term plan and the plans for this and next years (this includes the names of those to be sent abroad, the number of Soviet experts to be engaged and the number of people and the names of those most important who are to be shifted to scientific research from other posts). All possible efforts must be made to strive to carry out the plan to dispatch people and shift work by the end of June. As to the plans for the expansion of scientific research work in the higher institutions throughout the country and the expanded fostering of scientific forces, they must be attended to after the summer vacation this year.

For the realization of the plan for the march on science, we must prepare all the necessary conditions for the development of scientific research. We must make it possible for the scientists to obtain the necessary books, publications, archives, technical data and other facilities for work. Funds for the procurement of books and publications for the various research organizations and institutions of higher learning must be increased and they should make full use of them. We must strengthen the work in libraries, archives and museums, improve considerably the importation of foreign books and publications and make a rational distribution of books and publications now in stock. It is necessary to expand the teaching of foreign languages and increase the translation of important foreign works.

The principles discussed above generally are also applicable to other cultural and educational departments. All cultural and educational departments must draw up overall plans for the period from 1956 to 1967, and adopt the most effective measures for their realization.

Our plan to develop scientific and cultural forces must be one that can improve quality and increase the number. Ours is a big country and to meet the needs in all fields there must be a sufficiency in quantity for only on the basis of a sufficiency in quantity can quality be required in general.

For the expansion of our scientific and cultural forces, we must first increase the enrollment in the higher institutions according to plan, and at the same time pay attention to the fostering of the existing intellectuals of the general level, continually raising their professional levels. They are not only the most important reserve force and cooperators of the higher intellectuals as stated above, but quantitatively they are much greater than the higher intellectuals. They are distributed all over the country and in different work departments, and shoulder a heavy responsibility in national construction. The different departments of the Central Committee and the various provincial and municipal authorities must draw up special plans to assist them in improvement, in the rapid raising of their professional levels, and in promoting the elite members among them to the ranks of the higher intellectuals.

Our Party is successfully settling the question of agricultural cooperation and handicraft cooperation and successfully settling the question of the transformation of capitalist industry and commerce. The entire Party and working people throughout the country are striving to fulfill the Five Year Plan ahead of schedule and overfulfill it. All the people are imbued with confidence in success and enthusiasm in the struggle. Following the upsurging tide of Socialist economic construction, there will be a swelling tide of cultural work. To reach an overall settlement of the series of questions relating to intellectuals is undoubtedly most essential at such a time to our cause of Socialist transformation and Socialist construction.

In the tasks brought up in connection with intellectuals, we cannot say there are no difficulties. But these difficulties will not be greater than those of the transformation of our 500 million peasants and the transformation of the country's capitalist industry and commerce, cannot be greater than those of the realization of the first Five Year Plan. In the past six years, our Party has already registered colossal achievements in the leadership of intellectuals and the leadership of scientific and cultural enterprises. Today we have more experience and greater facilities compared with the past. On the foundation of the past experiences, our Party will certainly achieve greater victories in its leadership of the intellectuals in the scientific and cultural fields. Baseless are those views which hold that the Party is not capable of leading intellectuals in scientific and cultural construction.

The question lies in adeptness at study. Both the departments in the Central Committee and the various local authorities must learn to better lead the intellectuals and to better lead scientific and cultural enterprises. We must not think that since we are members of the Communist Party, it is natural for us to be able to lead intellectuals in scientific and cultural construction and will never commit mistakes. Such is a most dangerous way of thinking. In some areas, some of our comrades are precisely holding such an attitude, so loss has been brought on the work of the Party. In dealing with any question, we must persist in the attitude of frankness, "saying what we know, and admitting our ignorance." What we do not know we must not pretend we know. But we must change ignorance into knowledge. Our Party must train a large number of cadres well versed in scientific and cultural knowledge in all their fields. If only we will earnestly take up the job, we shall surely acquire the knowledge aimed at.

Many of the tasks mentioned in the present report will have to be solved in a unified manner by the Central Committee. We propose to effect the following division of labor in dealing with these questions:

With reference to questions of an administrative nature on the treatment of intellectuals, because these require unified provisions and control, the State Council is preparing to create a Chinese Experts Bureau to assume responsibility for this task. Prior to the inauguration of this machinery, all relevant departments must immediately take steps, on the basis of the directive of the Central Committee, to solve the various questions affecting intellectuals now. After the inauguration of the new Bureau, the various relevant departments will still not be spared their responsibility for directly dealing with problems which come within their jurisdiction, for the Experts Bureau will only be responsible for the solution of problems which is not conveniently handled by a department independently. The Experts Bureau has the responsibility of undertaking unified plans, making unified adjustments, carrying out unified inspection and supervision in respect of various problems of an administrative nature affecting intellectuals. Where the actions taken by various departments on the question of intellectuals are found improper, the Experts Bureau has authority to correct them in accordance with established procedure.

With reference to problems of a political nature affecting intellectuals, the continued ideological reform of intellectuals and the disposal of counter revolutionaries among intellectuals, the various relevant departments will also assume direct responsibility, with the Department of Propaganda of the Central Committee carrying out unified supervision. The Department of Propaganda of the Central Committee will regularly inspect the conditions relating to the implementation of the Central Committee's policy for intellectuals in different departments and in different areas, overcome the defects in their work, disseminate advanced experiences acquired by them, and make timely recommendations on the subject to the Central Committee.

The admission of intellectuals to the Party shall be taken care of by the Department of Organization of the Central Committee. Work connected with the different democratic parties and groups among the intellectuals shall be taken care of by the United Front Work Department of the Central Committee. Trade Union work among the intellectuals shall be taken care of by the All China Federation of Trade Unions. However, in the solution of the more important problems in these fields, contact should be made with the Department of Propaganda of the Central Committee.

In order to strengthen leadership, and disposal and inspection of problems affecting intellectuals, Party committees of all levels and all work departments must separately assign different appropriate organs regular responsibility for various issues. There must be regularly convened technical meetings, regularly exchanged experiences, and continually realized improvement in work carried out.

Comrades! We are convinced that through our work the intellectuals will rally still more closely around the Party and contribute their efforts more enthusiastically to the great cause of Socialism. The alliance formed by workers, peasants and intellectuals all over the country will have new signs of consolidation daily and it will become more powerful with the development of our work. Relying on this alliance, we can build our country, in not too long a time, into a great industrialized Socialist country that is entirely modern, prosperous and powerful. In not too long time, we will certainly be able to realize the great declaration of Comrade Mao Tse-tung: "We shall emerge in the world as a highly cultured nation."

DOCUMENT 7

On the Historical Experience of the Dictatorship of the Proletariat, editorial in the *People's Daily*, April 5, 1956.

The English text used here was published in a booklet entitled *The Historical Experience of the Dictatorship of the Proletariat* by the Foreign Languages Press, Peking, in 1959. An editor's note in the booklet says the article was written on the basis of a discussion at an enlarged meeting of the Political Bureau of the Party's Central Committee. The booklet also contains a second editorial which appears as Document 13 in this collection.

Comment. The Party in 1954 had attacked excessive individualism and supported the principle of "collective leadership" in connection with the Kao Kang case. A resolution of the fourth plenary session of the Seventh Party Congress (February 10, 1954), adopted at about the time when Kao Kang was said to have committed suicide, criticized those leaders who "exaggerated the role of the individual" and ran their departments as "separate kingdoms." For about two years after this, little was publicly said about the subject. Then on March 30, 1956, the *People's Daily* published a translation of the *Pravda* editorial of March 28, "Why Is the Cult of the Individual Alien to Marxism-Leninism?" In that editorial Stalin was specifically attacked. Its publication in the *People's Daily* was the first open Chinese reaction to Khrushchev's revelations in his speech to the Twentieth Party Congress in February. This reaction was followed within a week by the authoritative pronouncement reprinted here. Then on July 16, 1956, was published a "Collection of Criticisms on the Stalin Issue" made by foreign Communist parties (SCMP 1332).

Further background material may be found as follows:

(a) The effect of Khrushchev's revelations on the Communist bloc as a whole: Zbigniew K. Brzezinski, *The Soviet Bloc: Unity and Conflict* (Cambridge: Harvard University Press, 1960).

(b) The "crude application" to Chinese conditions, 1927–1936, of Stalin's doctrine "isolate the middle-of-the-roader": Conrad Brandt, Benjamin Schwartz, and John K. Fairbank, *A Documentary History of Chinese Communism* (Cambridge: Harvard University Press, 1952), especially pp. 97 ff., 123 ff., 165 ff., 217 ff.

(c) The Kao Kang case: Peter S. H. Tang, *Communist China Today* (New York: Praeger, 1957), pp. 81-92.

(d) The Chinese treatment of the idea of "collective leadership" as expounded by the Russians beginning in 1953: CB 384. Also, in ECMM 38 and 45 (*Outlook*, April 21, 1956, and *Political Study*, May 13 and June 13, 1956) are some routine elucidations of the *People's Daily* text. In ECMM 76 (*Political Study*, Feb. 13, 1957), it is pointed out that jettisoning the cult of the individual does not involve any diminution of proper respect for the leadership.

---------------------TEXT OF DOCUMENT 7---------------------

The 20th Congress of the Communist Party of the Soviet Union summed up the fresh experience gained both in international relations and domestic construction. It took a series of momentous decisions on the steadfast implementation of Lenin's policy in regard to the possibility of peaceful co-existence between countries with different social systems, on the development of Soviet democracy, on the thorough observance of the Party's principle of collective leadership, on the criticism of shortcomings within the Party, and on the sixth Five-Year Plan for development of the national economy.

The question of combating the cult of the individual occupied an important place in the discussions of the 20th Congress. The Congress very sharply exposed the prevalence of the cult of the individual which, for a long time in Soviet life, had given rise to many errors in work and had led to ill consequences. This courageous self-criticism of its past errors by the Communist Party of the Soviet Union demonstrated the high level of principle in inner-Party life and the great vitality of Marxism-Leninism.

In history and in all the capitalist countries of today, no governing political party or bloc in the service of the exploiting classes has ever dared to expose its serious errors conscientiously before the mass of its own members and the people. With the parties of the working class things are entirely different. The parties of the working class serve the broad masses of the people; by self-criticism such parties lose nothing except their errors, they gain the support of the broad masses of the people.

For more than a month now, reactionaries throughout the world have been crowing happily over self-criticism by the Communist Party of the Soviet Union with regard to this cult of the individual. They say: Fine! The Communist Party of the Soviet Union, the first to establish a socialist order, made appalling mistakes, and, what is more, it was Stalin himself, that widely renowned and honoured leader, who made them! The reactionaries think they have got hold of something with which to discredit the Communist Parties of the Soviet Union and other countries. But they will get nothing for all their pains. Has any leading Marxist ever written that we could never commit mistakes or that it is absolutely impossible for a given Communist to commit mistakes? Isn't it precisely because we Marxist-Leninists deny the existence of a "demigod" who never makes big or small mistakes that we Communists use criticism and self-criticism in our inner-Party life? Moreover, how could it be conceivable that a socialist state which was the first in the world to put the dictatorship of the proletariat into practice, which did not have the benefit of any precedent, should make no mistakes of one kind or another?

Lenin said in October 1921:

> Let the curs and swine of the moribund bourgeoisie and the petty-bourgeois democrats who trail behind it heap imprecations, abuse and derision upon our heads for our reverses and mistakes in the work of building up our Soviet system. We do not forget for a moment that we have committed and are committing numerous mistakes and are suffering numerous reverses. How can reverses and mistakes be avoided in a matter so new in the history of the world as the erection of a state edifice of an unprecedented type! We shall struggle unremittingly to set our reverses and mistakes right and to improve our practical application of Soviet principles, which is still very, very far from perfect.[1]

It is also inconceivable that certain mistakes made earlier should for ever preclude the possibility of making other mistakes later or of repeating past mistakes to a greater or lesser degree. Since its division into classes with conflicting interests, human society has passed through several thousand years of dictatorships—of slave-owners, of feudal lords and of the bourgeoisie; but it was not until the victory of the October Revolution that mankind began to see the dictatorship of the proletariat in action. The first three kinds of dictatorship are all dictatorships of the exploiting classes, though the dictatorship of feudal lords was more progressive than that of slave-owners, and that of the bourgeoisie more progressive than that of feudal lords. These exploiting classes, which once played a certain progressive role in the history of social development, invariably accumulated experience in their rule through making innumerable mistakes of historic import over long periods of time and through repeating these mistakes again and again. Nevertheless, with the sharpening of the contradiction between the relations of production which they represented and the productive forces of society, still they inevitably committed mistakes, bigger and more, precipitating a massive revolt of the oppressed classes and disintegration within their own ranks, and thus eventually bringing about their destruction. The dictatorship of the proletariat is fundamentally different in its nature from any of the previous kinds of dictatorship, which were dictatorships by the exploiting classes. It is a dictator-

---

[1] V. I. Lenin, *Collected Works*, Vol. II, Part 2, Moscow, 1952, p. 597.

ship of the exploited classes, a dictatorship of the majority over the minority, a dictatorship for the purpose of creating a socialist society in which there is no exploitation and poverty, and it is the most progressive and the last dictatorship in the history of mankind. But, since this dictatorship undertakes the greatest and the most difficult tasks and is confronted with a struggle which is the most complicated and tortuous in history, therefore, many mistakes, as Lenin has said, are bound to be made in its operation. If some Communists indulge in self-exaltation and self-complacency and develop a rigid way of thinking, they may even repeat their own mistakes or those of others. We Communists must take full account of this. To defeat powerful enemies, the dictatorship of the proletariat requires a high degree of centralization of power. This highly centralized power must be combined with a high level of democracy. When there is an undue emphasis on centralization, many mistakes are bound to occur. This is quite understandable. But whatever the mistakes, the dictatorship of the proletariat is, for the popular masses, always far superior to all dictatorships of the exploiting classes, to the dictatorship of the bourgeoisie. Lenin was right when he said:

> If our enemies reproach us and say that Lenin himself admits that the Bolsheviks have done a host of foolish things, I want to reply by saying: yes, but do you know that the foolish things we have done are entirely different from those you have done?

The exploiting classes, out for plunder, have all hoped to perpetuate their dictatorship generation after generation, and have therefore resorted to every possible means to grind down the people. Their mistakes are irremediable. On the other hand, the proletariat, which strives for the material and spiritual emancipation of the people, uses its dictatorship to bring about communism, to bring about harmony and equality among mankind, and lets its dictatorship gradually wither away. That is why it does its utmost to bring into full play the initiative and the positive role of the masses. The fact that, under the dictatorship of the proletariat, it is possible to bring into play without limit the initiative and the positive role of the masses also makes it possible to correct any mistakes committed during the dictatorship of the proletariat.

Leaders of Communist Parties and socialist states in various fields are duty bound to do their utmost to reduce mistakes, avoid serious ones, endeavour to learn lessons from isolated, local and temporary mistakes and make every effort to prevent them from developing into mistakes of a nationwide or prolonged nature. To do this, every leader must be most prudent and modest, keep close to the masses, consult them on all matters, investigate and study the actual situation again and again and constantly engage in criticism and self-criticism appropriate to the situation and well measured. It was precisely because of his failure to do this that Stalin, as the chief leader of the Party and the state, made certain serious mistakes in the later years of his work. He became conceited and imprudent. Subjectivism and one-sidedness developed in his thinking and he made erroneous decisions on certain important questions, which led to serious consequences.

With the victory of the Great October Socialist Revolution, the people and the Communist Party of the Soviet Union, under the leadership of Lenin, established the first socialist state on one-sixth of the earth. The Soviet Union speedily carried out socialist industrialization and collectivization of agriculture, developed socialist science and culture, established a solid union of many nationalities in the form of a union of the Soviets, and the formerly backward nationalities in the Soviet Union became socialist nationalities. During the Second World War, the Soviet Union was the main force in defeating fascism and saving European civilization. It also helped the peoples in the East to defeat Japanese militarism. All these glorious achievements pointed out to all mankind its bright future— socialism and communism, seriously shook the rule of imperialism and made the Soviet Union the first and strong bulwark in the world struggle for lasting peace. The Soviet Union has encouraged and supported all other socialist countries in their construction, and it has been an inspiration to the world socialist movement, the anti-colonialist movement and every other movement for the progress of mankind. These are the great achievements made by the people and the Communist Party of the Soviet Union in the history of mankind. The man who showed the Soviet people and Communist Party the way to these great achievements was Lenin. In the struggle to carry out Lenin's principles, the Central Committee of the Communist Party of the Soviet Union, for its vigorous leadership, earned its credit, in which Stalin had an ineffaceable share.

After Lenin's death Stalin, as the chief leader of the Party and the state, creatively applied and developed Marxism-Leninism. In the struggle to defend the legacy of Leninism and against its enemies—the Trotskyites, Zinovievites and other bourgeois agents—Stalin expressed the will and wishes of the people and proved himself to be an outstanding Marxist-Leninist fighter. The reason why Stalin won the support of the Soviet people and played an important role in history was primarily because he, together with the other leaders of the Communist Party of the Soviet Union, defended Lenin's line on the industrialization of the Soviet state and the collectivization of agriculture. By pursuing this line, the Communist Party of the Soviet Union brought about the triumph of socialism in the Soviet Union and created the conditions for the victory of the Soviet Union in the war against Hitler; these victories of the Soviet People conformed to the interests of the working class of the world and all progressive mankind. It was therefore quite natural for the name of Stalin to be greatly honoured throughout the world. But, having won such high honour among the people, both at home and abroad, by his correct application of the Leninist line, Stalin erroneously exaggerated his own role and counterposed his individual authority to the collective leadership, and as a result certain of his actions were opposed to certain fundamental Marxist-Leninist concepts which he himself had propagated. On the one hand, he recognized that the masses were the makers of history, that the Party must keep in constant touch with the people and that inner-Party democracy and self-criticism and criticism from below must be developed. On the other hand, he accepted and fostered the cult of the individual, and indulged in arbitrary individual actions. Thus Stalin found himself in a contradiction on this question during the latter part of his life, with a discrepancy between his theory and practice.

Marxist-Leninists hold that leaders play a big role in history. The people and their parties need forerunners who are able to represent the interests and will of the people, stand in the forefront of their historic struggles and serve as their leaders. It is utterly wrong to deny the role of the individual, the role of forerunners and leaders. But when any leader of the Party or the state places himself over and above the Party and the masses instead of in their midst, when he alienates himself from the masses, he ceases to have an all-round, penetrating insight into the affairs of the state. As long as this was the case, even so outstanding a personality as Stalin could not avoid making unrealistic and erroneous decisions on certain important matters. Stalin failed to draw lessons from isolated, local and temporary mistakes on certain issues and so failed to prevent them from becoming serious mistakes of a nation-wide or prolonged nature. During the latter part of his life, Stalin took more and more pleasure in this cult of the individual, and violated the Party's system of democratic centralism and the principle of combining collective leadership with individual responsibility. As a result he made some serious mistakes such as the following: he broadened the scope of the suppression of counter-revolution; he lacked the necessary vigilance on the eve of the anti-fascist war; he failed to pay proper attention to the further development of agriculture and the material welfare of the peasantry; he gave certain wrong advice on the international communist movement, and, in particular, made a wrong decision on the question of Yugoslavia. On these issues, Stalin fell victim to subjectivism and one-sidedness, and divorced himself from objective reality and from the masses.

The cult of the individual is a foul carry-over from the long history of mankind. The cult of the individual is rooted not only in the exploiting classes but also in the small producers. As is well known, patriarchism is a product of small-producer economy. After the establishment of the dictatorship of the proletariat, even when the exploiting classes are eliminated, when small-producer economy has been replaced by a collective economy and a socialist society has been founded, certain rotten, poisonous ideological survivals of the old society may still remain in people's minds for a very long time. "The force of habit of millions and tens of millions is a most terrible force" (Lenin). The cult of the individual is just one such force of habit of millions and tens of millions. Since this force of habit still exists in society, it can influence many government functionaries, and even such a leader as Stalin was also affected by it. The cult of the individual is a reflection in man's mind of a social phenomenon, and when leaders of the Party and state, such as Stalin, succumb to the influence of this backward ideology, they will in turn influence society, bringing losses to the cause and hampering the initiative and creativeness of the masses of the people.

The socialist productive forces, the economic and political system of socialism and the Party life, as they develop, are increasingly coming into contradiction and conflict with such a state of mind as the cult of the individual. The struggle against the cult of the individual which was launched by the 20th Congress is a great and courageous fight by the Communists and the people of the Soviet Union to clear away the ideological obstacles in the way of their advance.

Some naive ideas seem to suggest that contradictions no longer exist in a socialist society. To deny the existence of contradictions is to deny dialectics. The contradictions in various societies differ in character as do the forms of their solution, but society at all times develops through continual contradictions. Socialist society also develops through contradictions between the productive forces and the relations of production. In a socialist or communist society, technical innovations and improvement in the social system inevitably continue to take place; otherwise the development of society would come to a standstill and society could no longer advance. Humanity is still in its youth. The road it has yet to traverse will be no one knows how many times longer than the road it has already travelled. Contradictions, as between progress and conservatism, between the advanced and the backward, between the positive and the negative, will constantly occur under varying conditions and different circumstances. Things will keep on like this: one contradiction will lead to another; and when old contradictions are solved new ones will arise. It is obviously incorrect to maintain, as some people do, that the contradiction between idealism and materialism can be eliminated in a socialist or communist society. As long as contradictions exist between the subjective and the objective, between the advanced and the backward, and between the productive forces and the relations of production, the contradiction between materialism and idealism will continue in a socialist or communist society, and will manifest itself in various forms. Since man lives in society, he reflects, in different circumstances and to varying degrees, the contradictions existing in each form of society. Therefore, not everybody will be perfect, even when a communist society is established. By then there will still be contradictions among people, and there will still be good people and bad, people whose thinking is relatively correct and others whose thinking is relatively incorrect. Hence there will still be struggle between people, though its nature and form will be different from those in class societies. Viewed in this light, the existence of contradictions between the individual and the collective in a socialist society is nothing strange. And if any leader of the Party or state isolates himself from collective leadership, from the masses of the people and from real life, he will inevitably fall into rigid ways of thinking and consequently make grave mistakes. What we must guard against is that some people, because the Party and the state have achieved many successes in work and won the great trust of the masses, may take advantage of this trust to abuse their authority and so commit some mistakes.

The Chinese Communist Party congratulates the Communist Party of the Soviet Union on its great achievements in this historic struggle against the cult of the individual. The experience of the Chinese revolution, too, testifies that it is only by relying on the wisdom of the masses of the people, on democratic centralism and on the system of combining collective leadership with individual responsibility that our Party can score great victories and do great things in times of revolution and in times of national construction. The Chinese Communist Party, in its revolutionary ranks, has incessantly fought against elevation of oneself and against individualist heroism, both of which mean isolation from the masses. Undoubtedly, such things will exist for a long time to come. Even when overcome, they re-emerge. They are found sometimes in one person, sometimes in another. When attention is paid to the role of the individual, the role of the masses and the collective is often ignored. That is why some people easily fall into the mistake of self-conceit or blind faith in themselves or blind worship of others. We must therefore give unremitting attention to opposing elevation of oneself, individualist heroism and the cult of the individual.

To counter subjectivist methods of leadership, the Central Committee of the Communist Party of China adopted a resolution in June 1943 on methods of leadership. In discussing now the question of collective leadership in the Party, it is still worthwhile for all members of the Chinese Communist Party and all its leading personnel to refer to this resolution, which declared:

> In all practical work of our Party, correct leadership can only be developed on the principle of "from the masses, to the masses." This means summing up (i.e. co-ordinating and systematizing after careful study) the views of the masses (i.e. views scattered and unsystematic), then taking the resulting ideas back to the masses, explaining and popularizing them until the masses embrace the ideas as their own, stand up for them and translate them into action by way of testing their correctness. Then it is necessary once more to sum up the views of the masses, and once again take the resulting ideas back to the masses so that the masses give them their whole-hearted support... and so on, over and over again, so that each

time these ideas emerge with greater correctness and become more vital and meaningful. This is what the Marxist theory of knowledge teaches us.

For a long time, this method of leadership has been described in our Party by the popular term "the mass line." The whole history of our work teaches us that whenever this line is followed, the work is always good, or relatively good, and even if there are mistakes they are easy to rectify; but whenever this line is departed from, the work is always marred by setbacks. This is the Marxist-Leninist method of leadership, the Marxist-Leninist line of work. After the victory of the revolution, when the working class and the Communist Party have become the leading class and party in the state, the leading personnel of the Party and state, beset by bureaucratism from many sides, face the great danger of using the machinery of state to take arbitrary action, alienating themselves from the masses and collective leadership, resorting to commandism, and violating Party and state democracy. Therefore, if we want to avoid falling into such a quagmire, we must pay fuller attention to the use of the mass line method of leadership, not permitting the slightest negligence. To this end, it is necessary for us to establish certain systems, so as to ensure the thorough implementation of the mass line and collective leadership, to avoid elevation of oneself and individualist heroism, both of which mean divorce from the masses, and to reduce to a minimum subjectivism and one-sidedness in our work which represent a departure from objective reality.

We must also learn from the struggle of the Communist Party of the Soviet Union against the cult of the individual and continue our fight against doctrinairism.

The working class and the masses of the people, guided by Marxism-Leninism, won the revolution and took state power into their hands, while the victory of the revolution and the establishment of the revolutionary regime opened up boundless vistas for the development of Marxism-Leninism. Yet because Marxism, since the victory of the revolution, has been generally recognized as the guiding ideology in the whole country, it often happens that not a few of our propagandists rely only on administrative power and the prestige of the Party to instil into the minds of the masses Marxism-Leninism in the form of dogma, instead of working hard, marshalling a wealth of data, employing Marxist-Leninist methods of analysis and using the people's own language to explain convincingly the integration of the universal truths of Marxism-Leninism with the actual situation in China. We have, over the years, made some advances in research in philosophy, economics, history and literary criticism, but, on a whole, many unhealthy elements still exist. Not a few of our research workers still retain their doctrinaire habit, put their minds in a noose, lack the ability to think independently, lack the creative spirit, and in certain respects are influenced by the cult of Stalin. In this connection it must be pointed out that Stalin's works should, as before, still be seriously studied and that we should accept, as an important historical legacy, all that is of value in them, especially those many works in which he defended Leninism and correctly summarized the experience of building up the Soviet Union. Not to do so would be a mistake. But there are two ways of studying them—the Marxist way and the doctrinaire way. Some people treat Stalin's writings in a doctrinaire manner, with the result that they cannot analyse and see what is correct and what is not correct—and even what is correct they treat as a panacea and apply indiscriminately; inevitably they make mistakes. For instance, Stalin put forward a formula that in different revolutionary periods, the main blow should be so directed as to isolate the middle-of-the-road social and political forces of the time. This formula of Stalin's should be treated according to circumstances and from a critical, Marxist point of view. In certain circumstances it may be correct to isolate the middle forces, but it is not correct to isolate them under all circumstances. Our experience teaches us that the main blow of the revolution should be directed at the chief enemy to isolate him, while as for the middle forces, a policy of both uniting with them and struggling against them should be adopted, so that they are at least neutralized; and, as circumstances permit, efforts should be made to shift them from their position of neutrality to one of alliance with us, for the purpose of facilitating the development of the revolution. But there was a time—the ten years of civil war from 1927 to 1936—when some of our comrades crudely applied this formula of Stalin's to China's revolution by turning their main attack on the middle forces, singling them out as the most dangerous enemy; the result was that, instead of isolating the real enemy, we isolated ourselves, and suffered losses to the advantage of the real enemy. In the light of this doctrinaire error, the Central Committee of the Communist Party of China, during the period of the anti-Japanese war, formulated a policy of "developing the progressive forces, winning over the middle-of-the-roaders, and isolating the die-hards" for the purpose of defeating the Japanese aggressors. The progressive forces in question consisted of the workers, peasants and revolutionary intellectuals led by, or open to the influence of, the Communist Party. The middle forces in question consisted of the national bourgeoisie, the democratic parties and groups, and democrats without party affiliation. The die-hards referred to were the comprador-feudal forces headed by Chiang Kai-shek, who were passive in resisting the Japanese and active in fighting the Communists. Experience, gained through practice, proved that this policy of the Communist Party suited the circumstances of China's revolution and was correct.

The invariable fact is: doctrinairism is appreciated only by the mentally lazy; it brings nothing but harm to the revolution, to the people, and to Marxism-Leninism. To enhance the initiative of the masses, to stimulate their dynamic creative spirit, and to promote rapid development of practical and theoretical work, it is still necessary, right now, to destroy blind faith in dogma.

The dictatorship of the proletariat (in China it is a people's democratic dictatorship led by the working class) has won great victories in countries inhabited by nine hundred million people. Each of them, whether it is the Soviet Union, or China or any other People's Democracy, has its own experience of success as well as its own experience of mistakes. We must keep on summing up such experience. We must be alive to the possibility that we may still commit mistakes in the future. The important lesson to learn is that the leading organs of our Party should limit errors to those of an isolated, local, temporary nature, and permit no isolated, local, initial mistakes to develop into mistakes of a nation-wide or prolonged nature.

The history of the Communist Party of China records the making of serious mistakes on several occasions. In the revolutionary period from 1924 to 1927, there appeared in our Party the wrong line represented by Chen Tu-hsiu, a line of Right opportunism. Then, during the revolutionary period from 1927 to 1936, the erroneous line of "Left" opportunism appeared in our Party on three occasions. The lines pursued by Li Li-san in 1930 and by Wang Ming in 1931-1934 were particularly serious, while the Wang Ming line was the most damaging to the revolution. In this same period the erroneous, anti-Party Chang Kuo-tao line of Right opportunism in opposition to the Party's Central Committee, appeared in a key revolutionary base, doing serious damage to a vital section of the revolutionary forces. The errors committed in these two periods were nation-wide, except for that caused by Chang Kuo-tao's line which was confined to one important revolutionary base. Once again there emerged in our Party during the war of resistance to Japanese aggression a wrong line, represented by Comrade Wang Ming, which was of Right opportunist nature. However, since our Party had drawn lessons from what happened during the previous two periods of the revolution, this wrong line was not allowed to develop, but was corrected by the Central Committee of our Party in a comparatively short time. After the founding of the People's Republic of China, there appeared in our Party in 1953 the anti-Party bloc of Kao Kang and Jao Shu-shih. This anti-Party bloc represented the forces of reaction at home and abroad, and its aim was to undermine the revolution. Had the Central Committee not discovered it quickly and smashed it in time, incalculable damage would have been done to the Party and to the revolution.

From this it will be seen that the historical experience of our Party testifies that our Party too has been tempered through struggles against various wrong lines of policy, thus winning great victories in the revolution and in construction. As to local and isolated mistakes, they often occurred in our work, and it was only by relying on the collective wisdom of the Party and the wisdom of the masses of the people, and by exposing and correcting these mistakes in time, that they were nipped in the bud before they became mistakes of a nation-wide or prolonged nature, doing harm to the people.

Communists must adopt an analytical attitude to errors made in the communist movement. Some people consider that Stalin was wrong in everything; this is a grave misconception. Stalin was a great Marxist-Leninist, yet at the same time a Marxist-Leninist who committed several gross errors without realizing that they were errors. We should view Stalin from an historical standpoint, make a proper and all-round analysis to see where he was right and where he was wrong, and draw useful lessons therefrom. Both the things he did right and the things he did wrong were phenomena of the international communist movement and bore the imprint of the times. Taken as a whole, the international communist movement is only a little over a hundred years old and it is only 39 years since the victory of the October Revolution; experience in many fields of revolutionary work is still inadequate. Great achievements have been made, but there are still shortcomings and mistakes. Just as one achievement is followed by another, so one defect or mistake, once overcome, may be followed by another which in turn must be overcome. However, the achievements always exceed the defects, the things which are right always outnumber those which are wrong, and the defects and mistakes are always overcome in the end.

The mark of a good leader is not so much that he makes no mistakes, but that he takes his mistakes seriously. There has never been a man in the world completely free from mistakes. Lenin said:

> Frankly admitting a mistake, ascertaining the reasons for it, analysing the conditions which led to it, and thoroughly discussing the means of correcting it—that is the earmark of a serious party; that is the way it should perform its duties, that is the way it should educate and train the *class*, and then the *masses*.

True to the behest of Lenin, the Communist Party of the Soviet Union is dealing in a serious way both with certain mistakes of a grave nature committed by Stalin in directing the work of building socialism and with the surviving effects of such mistakes. Because of the seriousness of the effects, it is necessary for the Communist Party of the Soviet Union, while affirming the great contributions of Stalin, to sharply expose the essence of his mistakes, to call upon the whole Party to take them as a warning, and to work resolutely to remove their ill consequences.

We Chinese Communists are firmly convinced that as a result of the sharp criticisms made at the 20th Congress of the Communist Party of the Soviet Union, all those positive factors which were seriously suppressed in the past as a result of certain mistaken policies will inevitably spring everywhere into life, and the Party and the people of the Soviet Union will become still more firmly united in the struggle to build a great communist society, such as mankind has never yet seen, and win a lasting world peace.

Reactionary forces the world over are pouring ridicule on this event; they jeer at the fact that we are overcoming mistakes in our camp. But what will come of all this ridicule? There is not the slightest doubt that these scoffers will find themselves facing a still more powerful, for ever invincible, great camp of peace and socialism, headed by the Soviet Union, while the murderous, blood-sucking enterprises of these scoffers will be in a pretty fix.

DOCUMENT 8

Let a Hundred Flowers Blossom, a Hundred Schools of Thought Contend! address by Lu Ting-yi, Director of the Propaganda Department of the Central Committee of the Party, May 26, 1956, to a gathering of scientists, social scientists, doctors, writers, and others in Peking, revised by the author and published in the *People's Daily* on June 13, 1956.

> The English text is taken from a pamphlet of the same title issued by the Foreign Languages Press, Peking, 1958. A postcript and an appendix appearing at the end of the pamphlet are omitted here. The six numbered notes at the end of the document are reprinted as they appeared in the booklet.

> *Comment.* The speech by Mao Tse-tung to the Supreme State Conference on May 2, 1956, in which he is thought to have resurrected the slogan about "blooming and contending," is not available.

> For data on Hu Feng, Hu Shih, Liang Sou-ming, and Yü P'ing-po, see Peter S. H. Tang, *Communist China Today* (New York: Praeger, 1957), pp. 374 ff.

> For discussion of the Flowers-and-Schools doctrine at the session of the National People's Congress in June 1956, see CB 400 and 402.

───────────────TEXT OF DOCUMENT 8───────────────

Mr. Kuo Mo-jo, President of the Chinese Academy of Sciences and Chairman of the All-China Federation of Literary and Art Circles, has asked me to speak on the policy of the Chinese Communist Party on the work of artists, writers and scientists.

To artists and writers, we say, "Let a hundred flowers blossom." To scientists, we say, "Let a hundred schools of thought contend." This is the policy of the Chinese Communist Party. It was announced by Chairman Mao Tse-tung at the Supreme State Conference.

In applying this policy we have gained some experience, but it is still far too scanty. Furthermore, what I am saying today is merely my own personal understanding of this policy. You here are scientists specializing in the natural and social sciences, doctors, writers and artists; some of you are members of the Communist Party, some friends from democratic parties, and others non-party friends. You will readily see how immensely important this policy is in the development of Chinese art, literature and scientific research—the work you yourselves are engaged in—so if you think I am mistaken on any point, please don't hesitate to correct me. Then we can all do our bit to promote the common cause.

I. WHY THIS POLICY, AND WHY THIS EMPHASIS ON IT NOW?

If we want our country to be prosperous and strong, we must, besides consolidating the people's state power, developing our economy and education and strengthening our national defence, have a flourishing art, literature and science. That is essential.

If we want art, literature and science to flourish, we must apply a policy of letting a hundred flowers blossom, letting a hundred schools of thought contend.

Literature and art can never really flourish if only one flower blooms alone, no matter how beautiful that flower may be. Take the theatre, an example which readily comes to mind these days. Some years back there were still people who set their face against Peking opera. Then the Party decided to apply the policy summed up in the words "let a hundred flowers blossom side by side, weed through the old to let the new emerge" to the theatre. Everybody can see now how right it was to do so, and the notable results it led to. Thanks to free competition and the fact that the various kinds of drama now all learn from one another, our theatre has made rapid progress.

In the field of science, we have historical experience to draw on. During the period of the Spring and Autumn Annals (770-475 B.C.) and of the Warring States (475-221 B.C.) more than two thousand years ago, many schools of thought vied with each other for supremacy. That was a golden age in the intellectual development of China. History shows that unless independent thinking and free discussion are encouraged, academic life stagnates. And conversely, when they are encouraged, academic growth speeds up. But, of course, the state of affairs existing in those ancient times was very different from what it is in present-day China. At that time, society was in turmoil. The various schools of thought did vied with each other, spreading their ideas; but they did so spontaneously, with no sort of conscious, organized leadership. Now the people have won a world of freedom for themselves. The people's democratic dictatorship has been set up and consolidated. There is a popular demand that nothing should be allowed to impede the onward march of science. That is why we consciously map out an all-embracing plan for scientific development and adopt a policy of letting a hundred schools of thought contend to give vigour to academic growth.

One cannot fail to see that in class societies art, literature and science are, in the last analysis, weapons in the class struggle.

This is quite clear in the case of art and literature. Here we can see things that are obviously pernicious. The stuff written by Hu Feng is one such example. Pornographic and gutter literature that debauches people and turns them into gangsters is another. Still another example is the so-called literature summed up in phrases like "let's play mah-jong and to hell with state affairs," "the moon in America is rounder than the moon in China," etc. It is perfectly right and proper for us to look on literature of this pernicious kind as on a par with flies, mosquitoes, rodents and grain-eating sparrows and rid ourselves of it all.[1] This can only benefit, not harm our literature. Thus we say there is art and literature, for instance, that serves the workers, peasants and soldiers, and art and literature that serves the imperialists, landlords and bourgeoisie. What we need is art and literature that serves the workers, peasants and soldiers—art and literature that serves the people.

The existence of class struggle is also fairly clear in philosophy and the social sciences. Hu Shih's views on philosophy, history, education and politics have been held up to public odium.[2] The repudiation of his views is a reflection of class struggle in the field of the social sciences. We are perfectly justified in denouncing them. We are also justified in denouncing Mr. Liang Sou-ming's ideas.[3] We are also right in criticizing other philosophical schools of bourgeois idealism and bourgeois sociology.

Now let us see how things stand in the field of natural science. Every scientist has his own political viewpoint, although natural science itself has no class character. Formerly some who specialized in the natural sciences blindly worshipped the United States, while others tended to be "nonpolitical." It is right and proper to criticize all such things as undesirable—and such criticism is a reflection of class struggle.

We cannot fail to notice too that although art, literature and scientific research have a close bearing on the class struggle, they are not, after all, the same thing as politics. Political struggle is a direct form of class struggle. Art, literature and the social sciences give expression to the class struggle sometimes in a direct, and sometimes in a roundabout way. It is a one-sided, rightist way of looking at things to assume that art, literature and science have nothing to do with politics and that "art for art's sake," or "science for science's sake" is a justified standpoint. To look at things in that way is certainly wrong. On the other hand, it is one-sided and "leftist" to oversimplify things and equate art, literature and science with politics. This view is equally wrong.

"Letting a hundred flowers blossom, a hundred schools of thought contend" means that we stand for freedom of independent thinking, of debate, of creative work; freedom to criticize and freedom to express, maintain and reserve one's opinions on questions of art, literature or scientific research.

The freedom we uphold is not the same as that based on the type of democracy advocated by the bourgeoisie. The freedom advocated by the bourgeoisie really means freedom for only a minority, with little or no freedom for the working people. The bourgeoisie exercises a dictatorship over the working people. Jingoes in the United States bellow about the "free world"—a free world in which jingoes and reactionaries have all the freedom and every freedom, while the Rosenbergs are put to death because they stand for peace. We, on the contrary, hold that there must be democratic liberties among the people, but that no freedom should be extended to counter-revolutionaries: for them we have only dictatorship. This is a question of drawing a political demarcation line. A clear political line must be drawn between friend and foe.

"Let a hundred flowers blossom, a hundred schools of thought contend": that means freedom among the people. And we urge that, as the people's political power becomes progressively consolidated, such freedom should be given ever fuller scope.

Among the people there are points of agreement and points of difference. Our country has a constitution and it is a public duty to abide by it—this is an agreement among the people. That is to say, the people agree among themselves that they should love their country and support socialism. But there are other matters on which they do not agree with one another. In ideology there is the difference between materialism and idealism. This difference in outlook exists not only while there are classes—it will go on existing even when there are no classes, when we live in a communist society. While classes exist, the contradiction between materialism and idealism takes the form of contradiction between classes. After the disappearance of classes, as long as there are contradictions between the subjective and the objective, between the progressive and the backward, between the forces of production and production relations in society, contradiction between materialism and idealism will go on existing, even in socialist and communist societies. The struggle between materialism and idealism will be a protracted one.

Members of the Communist Party are dialectical materialists. We Communists of course stand for materialism and against idealism—nothing can change that. But, precisely because we are dialectical materialists and understand the laws governing the development of society, we hold that a strict distinction must be made between the battle of ideas among the people and the struggle against counter-revolutionaries. Among the people themselves there is freedom not only to spread materialism but also to propagate idealism. Provided he is not a counter-revolutionary, everyone is free to expound materialism or idealism. There is also freedom of debate between the two. This is a struggle between conflicting ideas among the people, but that is quite different from the struggle against counter-revolutionaries. We must suppress and put an end to the activities of counter-revolutionaries. We also have to wage a struggle against backward, idealist ways of thinking among the people. The latter struggle can be quite sharp, too; but we embark on it with the intention of strengthening unity, ending backwardness and creating an ever closer unity among the people. When it comes to questions of ideas, administrative measures will get us nowhere. Only through open debate can materialism gradually conquer idealism.

There will be diverse opinions, too, on matters of a purely artistic, academic or technological nature. This is, of course, quite all right. In matters of this sort, there is freedom to voice different opinions, to criticize, counter-criticize and debate.

In short, we hold that while it is necessary to draw a clear political line between friend and foe, we must have freedom among the people. To "let a hundred flowers blossom, a hundred schools of thought contend" is the expression of that freedom among the people in art, literature and science.

Conditions are ripe for this policy. So let us see how things stand now.

First of all, in key parts of the country we have won a decisive victory in every aspect of the work of socialist transformation. In these areas in the next few years the system of exploitation of man by man will be ended. All the former exploiters will be transformed into working people living by their own honest toil. Our country will become a socialist state without exploiting classes.

Secondly, the political outlook of Chinese intellectuals has undergone a fundamental change, and a still more fundamental change is taking place. Comrade Chou En-lai dwelt on this at some length in his "Report on the Question of Intellectuals." In this connection let us briefly review the latest struggle we have been engaged in.

This is an ideological struggle against bourgeois idealism; and it must be said that in the course of it most intellectuals have given a very good account of themselves and made remarkable progress.

In this struggle academic circles concentrated their main fire on Hu Shih and Hu Feng, two counter-revolutionaries. These men are not simply idealist in their outlook. They are politically counter-revolutionary. We also criticized the philosophical, socio-political views of Mr. Liang Sou-ming and bourgeois individualist ideas in artistic and literary circles. As everybody can see now, it was right to wage this struggle because it was necessary in advancing the cause of socialist transformation.

During this struggle the Central Committee of the Chinese Communist Party pointed out that we needed to strive resolutely against all ideas that hampered academic criticism and discussion. Such harmful ideas expressed themselves in many different ways. There was idolatry of the "leading lights" of the bourgeoisie, who were held up as "authorities" immune from criticism. There was an overbearing, supercilious attitude characteristic of the bourgeoisie towards young Marxists, who were kept in the background. Some Party members, setting themselves up as "authorities," were intolerant of criticism and never went in for self-criticism. Other Party members, afraid of "wrecking the united front," or "doing harm to unity," dared not criticize others. Still others, for reasons of personal friendship or for "face-saving" reasons, failed to criticize others' mistakes, and even covered them up.

The Central Committee of the Party has made it clear that in academic criticism and discussion the principle that should be observed is that no one should have any special privileges. It is wrong to set oneself up as an "authority" and suppress criticism, or turn a blind eye to wrong, bourgeois ideas, to let things drift or even capitulate to such wrong ideas.

The Central Committee also pointed out that academic criticism and discussion ought to be based on persuasion, reasoning and honest consideration of the facts. That is to say, we should encourage earnest discussion, but discussion on a scientific basis. Criticism and discussion should be the result of careful study; there is no place for crude oversimplification or high-handed proceedings. We should proceed by free discussion, not have recourse to administrative measures. Anyone criticized should be allowed to answer back, and such counter-criticism should not be muzzled. A minority who hold a different opinion should be allowed to keep it: this is not a case where the principle of the minority obeying the majority applies. Those who make mistakes over questions of scholarship and are still loath, even after criticism and discussion, to publish articles to correct their views, need not be asked to do so. In the academic world, even when a conclusion on any given question has been reached, discussion is still permissible if fresh differences of opinion arise.

The Central Committee also said that while we are criticizing wrong, bourgeois ideas and conducting criticism and discussion on questions of scholarship, we must stick to the policies mapped out by the Party—the policy of maintaining the united front and the policy of uniting and remoulding intellectuals. We must make a distinction between people who stick to wrong, bourgeois ideas and those who, while holding such wrong ideas, lean towards materialism, and we should approach them in different ways. A clear distinction must be made between those who are counter-revolutionaries politically and those who merely make mistakes in the academic field. Scholars who hold seriously mistaken, bourgeois ideas in the academic field should still be given suitable jobs as long as they are not engaged in counter-revolutionary activity. It is our job to see that they can go on doing research work for the benefit of society. We should respect any special knowledge they have which is beneficial to society, see to it that it is made full use of and passed on to our young people. We should also encourage them to take an active part in academic criticism and discussion so that they can remould themselves in the process.

All these instructions helped us combat bourgeois idealism and conduct criticism in academic circles without going too far wrong. Now, as we look back on our past activity, we find that we did, in the main, do the right thing in the course of this struggle, and made no bad mistakes either way. But some defects and mistakes there still were—in the way Mr. Yu Ping-po was criticized for instance.[4] In the matter of politics, Mr. Yu is blameless. The mistakes he committed were only in the field of literature, and it was necessary for us to criticize him from an academic and ideological point of view. Many articles on Mr. Yu did that and did it very well. But some were not so well written; they were not very persuasive and were couched in too virulent a tone. As to the allegation that Mr. Yu "monopolized the use of rare, ancient Chinese books," that was without foundation. I feel I ought to clear up this point.

So far we have been talking about the past. Now let us see how things are at present.

The situation now is vastly different. If a year or two back bourgeois idealism still had wide currency, if the Hu Fengs did not hesitate to launch furious attacks on the ideological front, if many intellectuals could not tell idealism from materialism or understand the harm idealism could do to the cause of socialism, now tremendous progress has been made in intellectual circles.

In some organizations the campaign against the reactionary ideas of Hu Feng and Hu Shih has not been carried to a proper conclusion; and the work of ferreting out hidden counter-revolutionaries has not been completed. In all such organizations we should carry on, not stopping half way, because only by carrying through the campaign can we create conditions favourable to the many things that need to be done in the future. It should be emphasized over and over again that well over 90 per cent of the people in these organizations are ordinary, decent people (including those who are a bit backward), who should be brought into the common struggle against counter-revolutionaries.

Thirdly, we still have enemies, and the class struggle is still going on inside the country. But our enemies, and our enemies inside the country in particular, have had their teeth drawn.

Who are these enemies? Abroad, we face aggressive imperialist forces with the jingoes of the United States at their head; at home, we face the Chiang Kai-shek clique entrenched on Taiwan and some other stray left-overs of the counter-revolution. These are our enemies. We must keep up a relentless struggle against them; we must not relax our efforts.

Fourthly, the political and ideological unity of the people has been greatly strengthened and is growing stronger day by day.

It is because of all this that the Central Committee of the Chinese Communist Party is now emphasizing the policy of letting a hundred flowers blossom, a hundred schools of thought contend. By this policy we shall bring into full play all that is good and useful in society in order to give better service to the people, and pool our efforts to create a flourishing art and literature and put our scientific work on a level with the best in the world.

Under the guidance of the government, many scientists are engaged in drawing up a twelve-year plan of work in the natural sciences. Twelve-year plans for philosophy and the social sciences are also being worked out. The making and realization of such plans is a magnificent task for our scientists. The implementation of the policy of letting a hundred schools of thought contend is an important guarantee of success of this task.

II. STRENGTHEN UNITY

Let a hundred flowers blossom, a hundred schools of thought contend: that is a policy to mobilize all the positive elements. It is also, therefore, a policy that will in the end strengthen unity.

On what basis are we to unite? On the basis of patriotism and socialism.

What do we unite for? To build a new, socialist China and combat our enemies both at home and abroad.

There are two kinds of unity: one is built on mechanical obedience and the other on our own conscious, free will. What we want is the latter.

Are those engaged in art, literature and science united? Yes, they are. Compare the situation in the days when the Chinese People's Republic was just founded with what we have now and you find we now have a far closer unity among artists, writers and scientists. This has come about as a result of our work for social reforms and changes in our ways of thought. It would be wrong to deny or ignore this. But even so, we cannot say that our unity is all it should be: there is still room for improvement.

In what respect? Well, first and foremost, some Communist Party members have forgotten Comrade Mao Tse-tung's warning about the evils of sectarianism. Success turns some people's heads and they get swelled-headed and sectarian.

In his "Rectify the Party's Style of Work"—a speech he made in 1942—Comrade Mao Tse-tung had this to say:

"Many of our comrades are much given to swaggering before non-Party people, despising and belittling them, and are unwilling to show them respect or appreciate their good qualities. This is precisely a sectarian tendency. Having read a few Marxist books, these comrades become arrogant rather than modest and habitually dismiss others as no good without knowing that they themselves are really tyros and smatterers. Our comrades must realize the truth that the Party members are always a minority as compared with non-Party people. Suppose there were one Communist in a hundred Chinese, then among China's population of 450,000,000 there would be 4,500,000 Communists. Yet, even if our membership reached such a colossal figure, the Communists would still form only one per cent of the whole population, while 99 per cent of our countrymen would remain outside the Party. On what grounds, then, can we refuse to co-operate with non-Party people? As to all those who are willing to, or in all probability can, co-operate with us, we have not only the duty to co-operate with them but absolutely no right to exclude them. But, failing to realize this, some of our Party members despise or even exclude those who are willing to co-operate with us. There are no grounds whatsoever for doing so. Have Marx, Engels, Lenin and Stalin given us any grounds for that? No. On the contrary, they have always earnestly urged us to link ourselves closely with the masses and not isolate ourselves from them. Has the Central Committee of the Chinese Communist Party given us any grounds? No. There is not a single one among all its decisions that says that we can isolate ourselves from the masses and stand alone. On the contrary, the Central Committee has always told us to link ourselves closely with the masses and not to isolate ourselves from them. Thus any practice that isolates us from the masses has no sanction at all, and it is simply a mischief done by the sectarian ideas of some comrades' own invention. As the error of sectarianism is still very serious in a section of our Party members and hinders the implementation of the Party line, we should start a great educational campaign within the Party to deal with it. First of all, we should make our cadres thoroughly understand how serious the problem is and how utterly impossible it is to overthrow our enemy and attain the goal of revolution unless the Communists are united with non-Party cadres and people." (*Selected Works of Mao Tse-tung*, English edition, Vol. IV, pp. 42-43, Lawrence & Wishart, London, 1956.)

As everyone knows, in the past few years we have fought a series of battles in the Party against sectarianism in artistic, literary and scientific circles. We have waged this struggle in organizations dealing with public health and research in the natural sciences, in literature and art, and in the social sciences. We shall go on waging this struggle and we call on all Party members working in these fields to make an end of this sectarianism.

In the course of these struggles we have gained some experience, and I should like to say something about this.

(1) As everyone knows, the natural sciences, including medicine, have no class character. They have their own laws of development. The only way they tie up with social institutions is that under a bad social system they make rather slow progress, and under a better one they progress fairly rapidly. The theoretical side of this question was settled long ago. It is, therefore, wrong to label a particular theory in medicine, biology or any other branch of natural science "feudal," "capitalist," "social-

ist," "proletarian" or "bourgeois." It is wrong, for instance, to say that "traditional Chinese doctors are feudal doctors," that "doctors of the Western school are capitalist doctors," that "Pavlov's theory is socialist" or "Michurin's theory is socialist," or that "Mendel's and Morgan's principles of heredity are capitalist" and so on. We must not believe such stuff. Some people make this sort of mistake because they are sectarian. Others do it unconsciously by trying to emphasize, but not in the proper way, that one ought to learn from the latest scientific achievements in the Soviet Union. These mistakes stem from different causes, so we must not lump them under one head, but deal with them in the light of specific circumstances.

While pointing out such mistakes, we must also point out one of another kind: for instance, denial of the fact that Pavlov's or Michurin's theories are important. The jumping-off point of those who make this mistake is, again, not always the same. Some of them are politically opposed to the Soviet Union, and for that reason inclined to deny even the scientific achievements of the Soviet Union. Others, because they do not belong to the same school of thought, simply won't yield an inch. In the case of the former it is a question of political viewpoint. With the latter it is a question of academic thinking. So these mistakes too must be dealt with in the light of specific circumstances and not lumped together.

(2) With regard to works of art and literature, the Party has only one point to make, that is, that they should "serve the workers, peasants and soldiers," or, in terms of today, serve the working people as a whole, intellectuals included. Socialist realism, in our view, is the most fruitful creative method, but it is not the only method. Provided he sets out to meet the needs of the workers, peasants and soldiers, the writer can choose whatever method he thinks will best enable him to write well, and he can vie with others. As to subject-matter, the Party has never set limits to this. It is not right to lay down such dicta as: write only about workers, peasants and soldiers; write only about the new society; or write only about new types of people. If literature and art are to serve the workers, peasants and soldiers, it stands to reason that we must praise the new society and positive people. But at the same time we must also criticize the old society and negative elements; we must praise what is progressive and criticize what is backward. So the choice of subject-matter in literature is extremely wide. Creative writing deals not only with things that really exist, or that once existed, but also with things that never existed—the gods in the heavens, animals and birds who talk, and so on. One can write about positive people and the new society, and also about negative elements and the old. Furthermore, it is difficult to show the new society to advantage if we fail to describe the old, hard to show the positive to advantage if we leave out what is negative. Taboos and commandments about choice of subject-matter can only hamstring art and literature, and result in writing to formula and bad taste. They can only do harm. As for questions relating to the specific characteristics of art and literature, the creation of the typical, and so on, they must be the subject of free discussion among writers and artists, letting them freely hammer out differences of opinion till they gradually reach agreement.

In the theatre we have already had experience of applying the principle, "let a hundred flowers blossom side by side, weed through the old to let the new emerge." That has been most valuable. What we must do now is to apply the same principle to all other branches of art and literature.

(3) In the field of philosophy and social sciences our achievements have been great. But for that very reason, there is a great danger of sectarianism. If we do not pay prompt attention to this, there is a serious danger of mental stagnation. Since the founding of the People's Republic, the teaching of Marxism-Leninism has spread among the intellectuals. There have been campaigns to remould our thinking, struggles against bourgeois idealism and a drive to weed out hidden counter-revolutionaries. All this activity is right and necessary, and has borne good fruit. We must, however, consider the seamy side of things as well. Some Party members have a tendency to monopolize academic studies in philosophy and the social sciences. They claim to be always right, fail to see the merits of others, or even forget that others have any merits. They fail to see the progress made by others. They take offence at the critical opinions of others. They always see themselves as the erudite teachers and others as their puny pupils—mere idealists or bourgeois scholars—now and for ever after. This is extremely dangerous. If things go on like this, they themselves are likely to degenerate, and philosophy and social sciences in our country will cease to progress and lose their vitality. These comrades had better stop this self-glorification right away; they had better be modest, listen more often to

others' criticism, work harder at their studies, make a point of learning what they can from people outside the Party, and really co-operate with them so as to avoid setbacks to our work in philosophy and the social sciences.

Our People's Republic is nearly seven years old now. Although there are still some people who cling to idealist ways of thinking and bourgeois ideas, many have made great progress. In research and educational work in philosophy and social sciences, we must consider redeploying our forces, bit by bit, as the situation demands, revising methods and measures which were wrong from the start, or which were right at one time but are now out of date. This is something we must do so that we can mobilize all the positive elements for promoting our work in these spheres. Both philosophy and the social sciences are important branches of knowledge, so we must do good work in these fields.

Here, in passing, I should like to mention the question of modern history. Modern history is an extremely important branch of social science, but we have not achieved much in the past few years in this field. I hear that people are expecting the Central Committee of the Chinese Communist Party to compile a textbook on the history of the Party, after which they propose to write books on modern history based on it. Please don't wait any more. The Central Committee is not going to compile any such textbook. All it is going to do is to publish a chronicle of events of the Party and collections of documents. Our scholars who specialize in modern history should, therefore, get down to independent study of the various problems of modern history. And in research in modern history, too, the policy of letting a hundred schools of thought contend must apply; no other will do.

Finish with sectarianism and unite with all who are ready to co-operate, all who possibly can co-operate with us. Put aside the desire to monopolize things. Get rid of unreasonable rules and commandments, and apply the policy of letting a hundred flowers blossom, letting a hundred schools of thought contend. Do not think only of the interests of your own department; try to give more help to others and to other departments. Don't be self-conceited and cocksure. Be modest and discreet and respect others. That is how to rid ourselves of the shortcomings which have marred our work in building up unity; that is how to strengthen our unity to the utmost.

We hope, too, that writers, artists and scientists who are not Party members will also pay attention to the question of securing closer unity. And here I would like to repeat part of what Comrade Chou En-lai said in his "Report on the Question of Intellectuals."

"We have already pointed out that there is still a certain distance between some intellectuals and our Party. We must take the initiative to remove this. For this distance, both sides usually bear responsibility. On the one hand, our comrades do not approach or try to understand the intellectuals; on the other, certain intellectuals still have reservations regarding socialism or even oppose it. There are such intellectuals in our enterprises, schools, government offices and society as a whole. Failing to differentiate between friend and foe, between the Communist Party and the Kuomintang, between the Chinese people and imperialism, they are dissatisfied with the policies and measures of the Party and the People's Government and hanker after capitalism or even feudalism. They are hostile to the Soviet Union and unwilling to learn from her. They refuse to study Marxism-Leninism, and sneer at it. Despising labour, the labouring people and government workers who come from families of working people, they refuse to mix with workers and peasants or government cadres of worker or peasant origin. Unwilling to see the growth of new forces, they consider progressives as opportunists, and often stir up trouble and hostility between intellectuals and the Party as well as among intellectuals themselves. They have enormous conceit, thinking themselves Number One in the world, and refusing to accept anyone's leadership or criticism. Denying the interests of the people or of society as a whole, they view everything only from their personal interests. What is to their personal advantage they accept, what is not to their personal advantage they oppose. Of course, there are very few intellectuals today who have all these faults; but not a small number have one fault or another. Even some of the middle group often hold some of the wrong views mentioned above, let alone the backward intellectuals. And not a few progressives are still guilty of such faults as narrow-mindedness, arrogance, and the tendency to view everything from their personal interests. Unless such intellectuals change their stand, however hard we may try to approach them, there will still be a distance between us and them."

That is to say, we must call on Party members and, equally, on people outside the Party to make a great effort, to strengthen our unity.

Individualism and parochial prejudice can also be found in artistic, literary and scientific circles. There is also a lack of mutual understanding between scientific workers of long standing and the newcomers. These things are bad. We ought to—and I am sure we can—get rid of them. If only Party members try to set a good example and work hard with people outside the Party, there should be no difficulty in solving this problem.

III. CRITICISM AND STUDY

In regard to criticism, our policy of letting a hundred flowers blossom, a hundred schools of thought contend means freedom to criticize and freedom to counter-criticize.

Some of the criticism we have today is of the thunderbolt variety; some of it is milk and water. How do we tackle this question?

There are two kinds of criticism. One is criticism directed against the enemy—what people call criticism that "kills at a blow," criticism with no holds barred. The other is criticism directed against the honestly mistaken—well-meant, comradely criticism, made in the cause of unity, intended to achieve unity through struggle. In making this kind of criticism, one must always bear the whole situation in mind. The critic should rely on reasoning, and his aim should be to help others. One should never adopt an attitude of "the Revolution is none of your business!" like the "Imitation Foreign Devil" in Lu Hsun's *The True Story of Ah Q*.[5]

But, in either case, criticism must be the outcome of careful study. One must not dash into print with a criticism the moment one spots something. It should be written only after thorough study and after a good deal of thinking.

The idea that criticism necessarily implies invective is wrong. When we were in Yenan, there was a counter-revolutionary called Wang Shih-wei. Later we had that other counter-revolutionary, Hu Feng. Both of them, in their "essays" or in other ways, attacked the Party and the people's regime. It stands to reason that we should give such counter-revolutionaries blow for blow. But it would be wrong to use the same method among ourselves—the people.

Concerning criticism directed against the honestly mistaken, I should like to recommend four articles: 1. "Reform Our Study" (Mao Tse-tung), 2. "Rectify the Party's Style of Work" (Mao Tse-tung), 3. "Oppose Party Jargon" (Mao Tse-tung), and 4. "On the Historical Experience of the Dictatorship of the Proletariat" (the *People's Daily*). The first three articles are criticisms of two comrades, Wang Ming and Po Ku,[6] who had made serious mistakes; the fourth is a criticism of Comrade Stalin, a comrade known for his outstanding services, who also made very serious mistakes—a comrade whose achievements outweighed his mistakes. When one reads these articles, one realizes that there can be criticism couched neither in excessive nor lukewarm terms—criticism which is a help to many. It can be seen with what great care the authors of these articles studied things before they wrote. And this is precisely the type of criticism we must encourage.

It is a very difficult job to reach the heights in science or art. It is difficult because only those who get to grips with reality make the grade, because there is no room for the smart aleck. We should give every support to our scientists, writers and artists. In our social system, scientists and artists who do honest work merit support, not blows. When one is engaged in independent thinking, in complicated and creative labour, it is impossible never to make mistakes. In the first place, people make wrong judgements simply because of gaps in their knowledge. In the second place, one can go wrong by exaggerating what is correct and treating it as absolute truth. Lenin said: "... it is enough to take one little step further—a step that might seem to be in the same direction—and truth becomes error." (*"Left-wing" Communism, An Infantile Disorder*, Lenin, *Selected Works*, Vol. II, p. 433, Foreign Languages Publishing House, Moscow, 1952.) There are people who are genuine advocates of all that is progressive, but who still make mistakes simply because they are a bit over-hasty, and often make mistakes of this kind. And thirdly, some people make mistakes because of their idealist outlook, and there is nothing strange about that, because "human cognition is not (... does not go in) a straight line, but a curve, endlessly approaching a series of circles, spirals. Any segment, fragment or part of this curve can be turned (turned in a one-sided way) into a self-contained, finite straight line which (if you don't see the wood for the trees) will then lead you into a morass, into quasi-religious obscurantism (where it fortifies the class interest of the ruling classes)!" (Lenin: *Philosophical Notebooks*,

p. 330, State Political Publishing House, Leningrad, 1947.) In the process of human cognition, mental sluggishness, the error of seeing things as if they had no connection with anything else (what we call "going into the ox horn") and viewing things one-sidedly are all things that lead to idealistic mistakes.

It is quite common for people to make mistakes in all innocence. There is no such person as a man who never makes mistakes. We must make a sharp distinction between mistakes like this and statements consciously directed against the revolution. Criticism of such mistakes must only be made for the good of others; it must be cool-headed criticism, well reasoned. In making it, we must bear the whole situation in mind and act in a spirit of unity, with the intention of achieving unity. We must do all we can to help those who have made mistakes correct them, and those criticized should have no apprehensions about being criticized.

It is easy to make mistakes. But mistakes should be rectified immediately, the sooner the better. It is sticking to one's mistakes that does the harm. As far as being criticized is concerned, one should stick to what is right, and dissent if others are wrong in their criticism. But if the other party is right you must rectify your mistakes and humbly accept others' criticism. To admit a mistake frankly, to root out the causes of it, to analyse the situation in which it was made and thoroughly discuss how to correct it is, as far as a political party is concerned, the hallmark of a mature party. As far as the individual is concerned, it is the hallmark of a realist. To accept criticism when one has made a mistake is to accept the help of others. Besides helping the person concerned, that also helps the progress of science, art and literature in our country; and there is certainly nothing wrong with that!

As regards study in general, we must continue to see to it that the study of Marxism-Leninism is organized on a voluntary basis. At the same time, we must acquire a broad range of general knowledge; we must critically study things both past and present, things at home and from abroad, and critically learn from both friends and foes.

Marxism-Leninism is being enthusiastically studied by most of our intellectuals. That is a good thing. The scientific theories of Marx and Lenin are the cream of human knowledge, truth that is everywhere applicable. Once there were people who thought that Marxism-Leninism was not applicable in China; but such ideas have been proved sheer nonsense. Without scientific Marxist-Leninist theory to guide us, it is unthinkable that the revolution could have been victorious in China. It is also unthinkable that we could have achieved the tremendous successes and made the rapid progress that we have in construction and in scientific and cultural work.

There are still, however, many shortcomings and mistakes in our study of Marxism-Leninism, and the main defect is a tendency to doctrinairism.

Fifteen years ago, in May 1941, Comrade Mao Tse-tung wrote his article "Reform Our Study." Later, in February 1942, he wrote "Rectify the Party's Style of Work" and "Oppose Party Jargon." These three articles were the main documents used in the campaign in Yenan to improve Party work. That was an ideological campaign directed against subjectivism, and mainly against doctrinairism. It was the greatest Marxist-Leninist movement in the intellectual life of our country since the May the Fourth Movement of 1919. During the period of the bourgeois-democratic revolution in our country, the Chinese revolution nearly foundered on doctrinairism. It was, and is, a bitter enemy of Marxism-Leninism. We must not forget that painful experience. We must also be fully alive to the fact that if academic studies are conducted in a doctrinaire way, and if artistic and literary work and scientific research are led by people who take up a doctrinaire attitude, things are bound to go wrong. That is because such an attitude runs directly counter to the Marxist-Leninist attitude of looking at things as they are.

I should like to avail myself of this opportunity, in speaking to you writers, artists and scientists, of seriously recommending to you those three articles of Comrade Mao Tse-tung's—"Reform Our Study," "Rectify the Party's Style of Work" and "Oppose Party Jargon"— and the "Resolution on Some Questions in the History of Our Party" adopted by the Sixth Central Committee of the Chinese Communist Party at its seventh plenary session, on April 20, 1945. I hope that every worker in these fields will read and re-read these documents till he really knows the difference between doctrinairism and Marxism-Leninism, till he discovers why the former is the bitter enemy of the latter and why it is necessary to wage a resolute struggle against doctrinairism.

We must have a broad range of general knowledge.

In medical science, agronomy, philosophy, history, literature, drama, painting and music, etc., China has a rich heritage. This heritage must be studied seriously and accepted critically. The point is not that we have done so much in these fields, but that we have done too little, and have not been serious enough in our approach. There is still this attitude of belittling our national heritage, and in some spheres it is still a really serious problem.

What kind of heritage are we to accept and how?

If we were to accept only what is perfect by present-day standards, there would be nothing left for us to take over. On the other hand, if we were to accept our cultural heritage uncritically, we should simply be taking the attitude summed up in the phrase "everything Chinese is best."

We suggest that in dealing with our cultural heritage the principle should be: Carefully select, cherish and foster all that is good in it while criticizing its faults and shortcomings in a serious way. At present our work suffers because we do neither well. There is a tendency to reject offhand even what is good in our cultural heritage. At present that is the main trend. The recent performance of the Kunshan opera *Fifteen Strings of Cash* shows how wrong it was to say there was nothing good in Kunshan opera. And if there is such a tendency in the theatre, what about other branches of art, literature and scientific research? We must admit that there are similar tendencies in them too, and we must do something about it. At the same time, we can also see a tendency not to criticize, or even to gloss over shortcomings in and blots on our cultural heritage. This attitude is neither honest nor sincere, and that we must alter, too.

Workers in art, literature and science need to learn from the people. The wisdom of the people is inexhaustible. There are still many treasures among the people that have not yet been discovered or, though discovered, not made good use of. Take medical science for instance. In the past, needling and cautery and special curative breathing exercises were scorned; only now are they being taken notice of. But other "popular" healing methods such as osteopathy, massage and herbal medicines have even now not received the attention due to them.

Then take music and painting. Not enough attention has been paid to our national heritage in these two spheres of creative activity. Wherever there are such tendencies they must be corrected.

As they come from the people things are often not systematically developed or are crude or lack theoretical explanation. Some of them have more than a bit of the "quack" about them, or a taint of the superstitious. There is nothing surprising about that. It is the duty of our scientists, artists and writers not to despise these things but to make a careful study of them, to select, cherish and foster the good in them, and, where necessary, put them on a scientific basis.

We must have our national pride, but we must not become national nihilists. We oppose that misguided attitude known as "wholesale Westernization." But that does not mean that we can afford to be arrogant and refuse to learn good things from abroad. Our country is still a very backward one; we can make it prosperous and strong only by doing our best to learn all we can from foreign countries. Under no circumstances is national arrogance justified.

We must learn from the Soviet Union, from the People's Democracies, and from the peoples of all lands.

To learn from the Soviet Union—that is a correct watchword. We have already learned a little, but much remains to be learned. The Soviet Union is the world's first socialist state, the leader of the world camp of peace and democracy. It has the highest rate of industrial development. It has a rich experience in socialist construction. In not a few important branches of science it has caught up with and surpassed the most advanced capitalist countries. It stands to reason that it is worth our while to learn from such a country and such a people. It is utterly wrong not to learn from the Soviet Union.

Nevertheless, in learning from the Soviet Union we must not mechanically copy everything in the Soviet Union in a doctrinaire way. We must make what we have learned fit our actual conditions. That is a point we must pay attention to. Otherwise, we shall run into trouble.

Besides learning from the Soviet Union, we must also learn from the People's Democracies. Every People's Democracy has its own special merits. Some of them have advanced further than China in industry and scientific technique, others are more advanced in other fields. To learn from them all is well worth-while. Arrogance in this connection is entirely out of place.

People in countries other than the Soviet Union and the People's Democracies have different social institutions and political systems. Social institutions and political systems may come and go, but the people will live on and continue to progress. It is not without good reason that this is so. We must therefore critically study all their good points—in art and literature, in science, in their customs and habits, in every sphere. Here too a feeling of superiority is quite out of place.

Apart from learning from our friends, we must see what we can learn from our enemies—not to learn what is reactionary in their systems but to study what is good in their methods of management or in their scientific techniques. Our aim in this is to speed the progress of our socialist construction, so as to build up our strength to ward off aggression and safeguard peace in Asia and throughout the world.

I also want to say something about Party members learning from people outside the Party.

The knowledge possessed by not a few of our Party members is less than it should be. Non-Party people usually lack a fundamental knowledge of Marxism-Leninism, but for many of our non-Party friends who are keen on studying Marxism-Leninism, this is really a thing of the past, or soon will be. Anyhow, plenty of them have bridged, or are bridging this gap, so this question will soon solve itself. The point I want to make is that it is time for Party members to take note of their own inadequacies and remedy them. There is only one way to do so: to seek advice and learn honestly and modestly from those who know. The great majority of those intellectuals who are not Communist Party members study very hard. Members of the Communist Party must not be behind-hand in learning from them. This is an important point as regards our studies.

Now that this policy—"let a hundred flowers blossom, a hundred schools of thought contend"—has been put forward, many problems will crop up one after the other and demand solutions. I hope all of you will do some hard thinking on such questions. Today I have only touched upon some matters of principle, and anything I say is open to correction.

Translators' Notes

1. Flies, mosquitoes, rodents and grain-eating sparrows are considered "four evils" in China as carriers of diseases or pests which destroy crops and food.

2. In 1917, Hu Shih (b. 1891) joined the movement for a new culture as an advocate of subsituting the vernacular for the classical literary language. Later, when the cultural movement associated with the May the Fourth Movement of 1919 advanced and the ideas of Marxism-Leninism spread among the people, he withdrew to the side of the imperialists and comprador-bourgeoisie as an opponent of socialism and revolutionary action. He was a rabid advocate of pragmatism in its most reactionary, subjective idealist form. This led him to support the Kuomintang's demagogic theories of piecemeal reform—and the whole philosophy of bourgeois individualism. Politically, he supported the rule of the warlords and opposed the revolutionaries led by Sun Yat-sen. Then after Chiang Kai-shek betrayed the revolution in 1927, he came out as a supporter of Chiang's dictatorial rule at home and capitulation to the imperialists. From then on, he was, and remains today, an enemy of the Communist Party and the people's revolution and a faithful hanger-on of the American imperialists and Chiang Kai-shek. For this reason he is repudiated by the whole nation.

Hu Shih held several important posts in old China's universities and academic institutions, and was thus able to spread his reactionary ideas there. Some of his pernicious influence has persisted in such circles, and that is why since liberation, in the course of the general criticism of obscurantism, his ideas have come under heavy fire.

3. At the time of the May the Fourth Movement of 1919, Liang Sou-ming opposed the campaign for a new culture. He advocated preservation of the old feudal culture with some slight reforms. Later he promoted a "rural construction movement" the aim of which was, as Liang himself said, to resist the peasant movement led by the Communist Party. He denied that there were any exploiting classes in China and advocated co-operation between peasants and landlords, the formation of armed forces by the landlords themselves to protect the old order, and the setting-up of schools for peasant-farmers to indoctrinate them with feudal ideas. Playing into the hands of the imperialists, he opposed industrialization and wanted China to remain an agricultural country. After liberation he gave his support to the People's Government, and became a member of the National Committee of the Chinese People's Political Consultative Conference. Liang's ideas have naturally come in for much criticism.

4. Yu Ping-po is a veteran writer who became well known during the time of the May the Fourth Movement. He has specialized in Chinese classical literature, and for many years made an intensive study of the famous classical novel *The Dream of the Red Chamber*. He was deeply influenced by Hu Shih's mistaken views on the study of the classics. After the Japanese surrender, Yu joined the Chiu San Society, one of China's many democratic parties. He supported the students' patriotic movement and opposed the corrupt rule of the Kuomintang. He is now a research fellow of the Institute of Literary Studies of the Chinese Academy of Sciences, and a deputy to the National People's Congress.

5. Ah Q is the hero of the famous novel *The True Story of Ah Q* by Lu Hsun (1881-1936). Ah Q is a poor odd-job man in a village and lives from hand to mouth. During the Revolution of 1911, he is fired with a desire to join the Revolution and goes for advice to the son of Chien, the local squire, a pseudo-revolutionary, called "Imitation Foreign Devil" by Ah Q because he dresses like a foreigner and apes foreign ways, who tells him that the Revolution is none of his business.

6. Comrades Wang Ming (Chen Shao-yu) and Po Ku (Chin Pang-hsien) fell into doctrinaire ways and made serious "leftist" mistakes as Communist Party leaders in the years 1931-1935. The interested reader will find the main facts of these events in the "Resolution on Some Questions in the History of Our Party," in Vol. IV of the *Selected Works of Mao Tse-tung*, Lawrence & Wishart, London, 1956. Comrade Po Ku was killed in a plane accident on his way from Chungking to Yenan in February 1946.

Chapter IV

THE EIGHTH PARTY CONGRESS

(containing Documents 9, 10, 11, 12)

General comment. The problems of the Eighth Party Congress, which had to approve a second Five-Year Plan at a time when the first all-out effort at "socialist construction" had run into or caused great difficulties, are discussed in our General Introduction, part IV. This Party Congress met from September 15 to 27, 1956. It produced the following six important documents, of which (a), (e), and (f) are reprinted here as Documents 9, 10, and 11.

(a) Liu Shao-ch'i's political report (Document 9).

(b) Resolution of the Congress on the political report. This resolution is to a great extent implicit in Document 9, and is summarized in our comment on that document.

(c) Revised constitution of the Party, summarized in Document 9.

(d) Teng Hsiao-p'ing's report on the revised constitution. Some parts of this are repeated in the same man's report of September 1957 on rectification (Document 19), which contains a full statement of the Party's tasks and problems.

(e) Proposals of the Congress for the second Five-Year Plan (Document 10).

(f) Chou En-lai's report on these proposals (Document 11).

These six items, together with some introductory remarks by Mao Tse-tung, comprise the first of three volumes of records of the Party Congress issued in English translation by the Foreign Languages Press, Peking, 1956, under the title, *Eighth National Congress of the Communist Party of China*. The texts of Documents 9, 10, and 11 are taken from that volume.

From another source we also reprint in this chapter, as Document 12, a Party directive on agricultural cooperatives issued shortly before the Party Congress began.

DOCUMENT 9

Political Report of the Central Committee of the Communist Party of China, delivered by Liu Shao-ch'i, September 15, 1956, to the Eighth Party Congress.

The English text is from *Eighth National Congress of the Communist Party of China*, Foreign Languages Press, Peking, 1956, Vol. I, pp. 13–111.

Comment. For background on sections I and II of Liu's report (the "general line" and "socialist transformation"), see the comments on Document 1 and Documents 2–5 above. Fuller accounts of the economic history of the years 1949–1955 are given in Peter S. H. Tang, *Communist China Today* (New York: Praeger, 1957), and Choh-ming Li, *Economic Development of Communist China* (Berkeley: University of California Press, 1959). For the historical background to Liu's section VI, which is on rightist and leftist opportunists, see Conrad Brandt, Benjamin Schwartz, and John K. Fairbank, *A Documentary History of Chinese Communism* (Cambridge: Harvard University Press, 1952).

Section III of Liu's report covers in detail the problems of "socialist construction" to which the bulk of the Congress' resolution is devoted. The resolution, approving and following the main lines of the report (with minor differences of order and formulation), defines the principal task as being to resolve the contradiction between the advanced socialist system and the backward productive forces of society. The resolution also contains sections on the development of cultural, educational, and health work by means of the Hundred Flowers policy; on the strengthening of the people's democratic dictatorship by means of combatting bureaucracy and uniting with intellectuals and the Democratic parties; on Party leadership ("anti-subjectivism" and the "mass line"); and on the international socialist front.

Section VI of Liu's report briefly describes the changes in the Party constitution. The main objects of these changes are to increase the initiative of Party members at the lower levels, and to enforce the mass line—i.e., to keep the Party as a whole in touch with the masses. These points are elaborated in Teng Hsiao-p'ing's report on the revision of the Party constitution, and he adds the following practical measures:

1. The mass line must be vigorously expanded on the Party's educational network.

2. Leading personnel must be given ample time to go deep into the midst of the masses, instead of spending most of their time in offices.

3. Lower organizations of the Party must have the assurance of being able freely to criticize the upper levels.

4. Supervision of bureaucratic practices by the Party and the state must be strengthened.

5. Party organizations at all levels must check up regularly on the "working style" of all members.

6. Finally the Party must strengthen cooperation with non-Party people and carry out thoroughly a united-front policy.

For a full discussion of the revisions in the Party constitution and a comparison between the Communist Parties in China and the U.S.S.R., see H. F. Schurmann, "Organizational Principles of the Chinese Communists," *China Quarterly*, April-June 1960, pp. 47–58.

───────────────TEXT OF DOCUMENT 9───────────────

Comrades!

Eleven years have passed since the Seventh National Congress of our Party. In these eleven years two great historical changes of world-wide significance have taken place in our motherland. In 1949, our Party led the people in overthrowing the reactionary rule of imperialism, feudalism, and bureaucrat-capitalism, and establishing the People's Republic of China. In the second half of last year and the first half of this, our Party led the people on to win a total and decisive victory in the socialist transformation of agriculture, handicrafts and capitalist industry and commerce. These two victories have brought about a series of fundamental changes in our country's internal and external relations.

Except in Taiwan, which is still occupied by the U.S. aggressors, all the forces of foreign imperialism, which sat on the backs of the Chinese people for the last hundred years, have been driven out. China has become a great independent and sovereign country.

That tool of foreign imperialism—the bureaucrat-comprador bourgeoisie—has been eliminated as a class on the mainland of China.

Except in a few localities, the feudal landlords have also been eliminated as a class. The rich peasants are also being eliminated as a class. Landlords and rich peasants who used to exploit the peasants are being reformed; they are making a fresh start in life and becoming people who live by their own work.

The national bourgeois elements are in the process of being transformed from exploiters into working people.

The broad masses of the peasantry and other individual working people have become socialist working people engaged in collective labour.

The working class has become the leading class of the state. Its ranks have increased; it has a very much deeper class consciousness and its cultural and technical levels have been greatly raised.

The intellectuals, who have changed their outlook, are now organized as a force in the service of socialism.

All the nationalities in our country have come together to form one great family of united fraternal nationalities.

The people's democratic united front, led by the Communist Party, has been further broadened and consolidated.

Our country has taken her place in the socialist camp, headed by the Soviet Union, which is striving for a lasting peace and for the progress of mankind; she has forged unbreakable ties of friendship and co-operation with the great Soviet Union and the People's Democracies. In the victorious war to resist U.S. aggression and aid Korea, our people put a check to the rage and ferocity of the imperialist aggressors. In international relations our country stands resolutely for the five principles of peaceful coexistence. The international position of our country has been elevated.

These changes have not only aroused unprecedented revolutionary enthusiasm among the six hundred million people of our country, it was inevitable that they should exert a great power of attraction in international life, particularly among all the oppressed nations and exploited peoples.

The task confronting the Party now is to build China into a great socialist country as quickly as possible by relying on the hundreds of millions of working people who have been liberated and are now organized, by uniting with all the forces at home and abroad that can be united, and by turning to full account all conditions that are favourable to us.

In order to fulfil this gigantic task, we should correctly sum up the experience of past struggles, complete the socialist transformation of our country, strengthen our socialist construction, improve and perfect the political life of our country, correctly handle international affairs, and further consolidate our Party. Discussion of all these questions and the decisions reached thereon at our Congress will give impetus to our Party and the people of our country to achieve new and still greater victories on the basis of victories already won.

I. THE PARTY'S GENERAL LINE IN THE PERIOD OF TRANSITION

Eleven years ago, the Party's Seventh Congress placed before the Party the task of "boldly rousing the masses to action, expanding the people's strength, and uniting all forces in the country that can be united, in order to defeat the aggressors and build a new China." That task was fulfilled in 1949.

The reactionaries themselves often choose the road to ruin. The policy of the Seventh Congress of our Party was to call on the Kuomintang to form a coalition government with the democratic forces of the country. As early as the first years of the War of Resistance to Japanese Aggression, our Party reached agreement with the Kuomintang on united action against Japan. After that, and especially following the conclusion of the War of Resistance, our Party time and again conducted peace negotiations with the Kuomintang, in an effort to avert civil war and to bring about social and political reforms in China by peaceful means. In 1946, together with several other democratic parties, we reached an agreement with the Kuomintang concerning peace and the reconstruction of the country. But, subsequently, the Kuomintang reactionaries, supported by U.S. imperialism, launched a major civil war throughout the country in an attempt to wipe out the forces that represented the Chinese people, that is, the Chinese Communist Party and all other progressive democratic forces. They miscalculated. While our Party was working for peaceful reform, it did not allow itself to be put off its guard or to give up the people's arms. Our policy was as follows: if the Kuomintang wanted peace and was willing to carry out reforms in conditions of peace, then that was beneficial to the people and we would strive for it with all our might. At the same time, we knew that whether or not the desire for peace would be fulfilled depended not on us but on the ruling class at the time. If the Kuomintang reactionaries should insist on forcing war on the people, we had made sufficient preparations; we would mobilize the people's forces to defeat them and compel the instigators of war to reap what they had sown. And that was precisely the verdict of history: those who had wanted to wipe out the people's forces were themselves wiped out by the people's forces.

Unlike the reactionaries, the people are not warlike. Even during the war, wherever it was possible to achieve liberation peacefully, as in the case of Peking, Suiyuan, Changsha, Kunming, western Szechuan, Sinkiang, and Tibet, we strove, made approaches and conducted negotiations to this end, and we did achieve peaceful liberation. But when the people were compelled to take up arms, they were completely justified in doing so. To have opposed the people taking up arms and demanded that they submit to the attacking enemy would have been to follow an opportunist line. Here, the question of following a revolutionary line or an opportunist line became a major issue involving the question whether our six hundred million people should or should not capture political power when conditions were ripe. Our Party followed the revolutionary line and today we have the People's Republic of China.

Since the establishment of the People's Republic of China, the working class has won the power to rule throughout the country in conditions of a firm alliance with several hundred millions of peasants; the party of the working class—the Chinese Communist Party—has become the party that leads the state power of the whole country; therefore, the people's democratic dictatorship has in essence become a form of the dictatorship of the proletariat. Thus, it has become possible for the bourgeois-democratic revolution in our country to be directly transformed, by peaceful means, into a proletarian-socialist revolution. The establishment of the People's Republic of China signifies the virtual completion of the stage of bourgeois-democratic revolution in our country and the beginning of the stage of proletarian-socialist revolution: the beginning of the period of transition from capitalism to socialism.

What are the basic characteristics of the period of transition in our country?

First, our country is industrially backward. In order to build a socialist society, we must develop socialist industry, above all, heavy industry, so as to transform China from a backward agricultural country into an advanced industrial country. This, however, will take a considerable time.

Second, in our country the allies of the working class consist not only of the peasantry and the urban petty-bourgeoisie, but also of the national bourgeoisie. For this reason, in order to transform our old economy, we must use peaceful means of transformation not only in the case of agriculture and handicrafts, but also in the case of capitalist industry and commerce. This needs to be done step by step; this too needs time.

On the basis of the actual conditions of our country, the Central Committee has thus defined the Party's general line in the period of transition: to bring about, step by step, socialist industrialization and to accomplish, step by step, the socialist transformation of agriculture, handicrafts and capitalist industry and commerce over a fairly long period. This general line of the Party was first put forward in 1952, when the period of the rehabilitation of the national economy had come to an end. It was accepted by the National People's Congress in 1954, and written into the Constitution of the People's Republic of China as the fundamental task of the state in the transition period.

The Party's general line in the transition period is a beacon that guides our work in every field. Any work that deviates from the general line, immediately lands itself in mistakes, either Rightist or "Leftist." In the last few years the tendency of deviating from the Party's general line to the Right has manifested itself mainly in being satisfied merely with what has been achieved in the bourgeois-democratic revolution, in wanting to call a halt to the revolution, in not admitting the need for our revolution to pass on into socialism, in being unwilling to adopt a suitable policy to restrict capitalism in both town and countryside, in not believing that the Party could lead the peasantry along the road to socialism, and in not believing that the Party could lead the people of the whole country to build socialism in China. The tendency of deviating from the Party's general line to the "Left" has manifested itself mainly in demanding that socialism be achieved overnight, in demanding that some method of expropriation be used in our country to eliminate the national bourgeoisie as a class, or some method be used to squeeze out and bankrupt capitalist industry and commerce, in not admitting that we should adopt measures for advancing, step by step, to socialism, and in not believing that we could attain the goal of socialist revolution by peaceful means. Our Party resolutely repudiated as well as criticized these two deviations. It is quite obvious that had our Party accepted any of these views, we would not be able to build socialism, and would not be successfully building socialism as we are doing today.

In 1953, in accordance with the general line of the transition period, our country began to carry out its First Five-Year Plan for development of the national economy. The original estimate made by the Party's Central Committee was that fulfilment of the fundamental task of the transition period would require the time needed to carry out three five-year plans. Our experience in implementing the First Five-Year Plan has confirmed that the industrialization of the country will require the time needed to carry out three five-year plans or even a little longer. However, the task of socialist transformation will be basically fulfilled in the First Five-Year Plan period and, except in a few localities, it will be completely fulfilled in the Second Five-Year Plan period.

II. SOCIALIST TRANSFORMATION

We have achieved a decisive victory in the socialist transformation of agriculture, handicrafts and capitalist industry and commerce in our country.

According to statistics ending June this year, 110 million, or 91.7 per cent of the 120 million peasant households, in China have joined agricultural producers' co-operatives; 35 million households are in elementary co-operatives while 75 million, or the great majority of them, are in co-operatives of the advanced type. Mutual aid and co-operation in animal husbandry has also made progress.

Individual handicraftsmen throughout the country have joined producers' co-operatives of various forms; 90 per cent of individual handicraftsmen are in industrial producers' co-operatives, producers' groups or supply and marketing co-operatives. Individual fishermen, individual salt producers and labourers working on their own in the transport services have, in the main, been drawn into co-operative organizations.

The great bulk of capitalist industry and commerce in the country has come under joint state-private operation by whole trades. Individual tradesmen have also generally formed themselves into co-operative organizations, which purchase for the state or co-operative trading networks, or act as their commission agents.

All these achievements have been made mainly during the upsurge of socialist transformation in agriculture, handicrafts and capitalist industry and commerce which began in our country in the latter part of 1955.

This upsurge in socialist transformation is not a fortuitous phenomenon; it is the logical outcome of the development and maturing of various social conditions in our country since 1949.

After the establishment of the People's Republic of China, the People's Government confiscated all enterprises operated by bureaucrat-capital which had had a stronghold on all the economic arteries of our country. These enterprises, including the Japanese, German and Italian concerns in China taken over by the Kuomintang government following the victory in the War of Resistance to Japanese Aggression, were turned into socialist, state-owned enterprises; the state came into possession of the largest banks, practically all the railway lines, most of the iron and steel industries and other key sections of heavy industry and certain essential departments of light industry. This laid the foundation for the socialist sector to hold the economic heights in our country.

Subsequently the People's Government made a major effort to develop state-owned industries, state-owned transport services and other state-owned enterprises. In 1949 the value of production of state-owned industries only amounted to 26.3 per cent of the total value of industrial production; in 1952 it had climbed to 41.5 per cent, and by 1955 it was up 51.3 per cent.

The People's Government transformed all private banks and banking houses into unified, joint state-private banks under the leadership of state banks. All bank credit and insurance businesses and all transactions in bullion and foreign currency are now concentrated in the hands of the state. The People's Government has introduced a system of control over foreign trade and foreign exchange. It has also established a nation-wide, uniform and powerful network of state trade and trade through the supply and marketing co-operatives, gained control of the principal industrial raw materials and the supply of principal commodities, gradually brought about the nationalization of wholesale trade, and consolidated the leading position of socialist trade in the country's market.

The development of a strong socialist economy in our country has laid the material basis for the socialist transformation of agriculture, handicrafts and capitalist industry and commerce. But, in order to accomplish the tasks of socialist transformation, we must also adopt policies and measures suited to conditions in China so that the broad masses of our peasants and handicraftsmen will gladly take to collective economy, and the national bourgeoisie accept socialist transformation without much reluctance.

What policies and measures have we adopted? I shall now briefly discuss the movement for the transformation of agriculture, handicrafts and capitalist industry and commerce.

First of all, let us take up the socialist transformation of agriculture.

We launched the movement for agricultural co-operation on the basis of a thoroughly completed land reform. In carrying out the land reform, our Party did not take the simple and easy way of merely relying on administrative decrees and of "bestowing" land on the peasants. For three solid years after the establishment of the People's Republic of China, we applied ourselves to awakening the class consciousness of the peasants, and particularly of the poor peasants, to the fullest possible extent by following the mass line in fully arousing the peasant masses; we accomplished the task of land reform through the efforts of the peasants themselves. Was it necessary for us to spend so much time on it? We consider that the time spent was absolutely necessary. Because we had used such a method, the peasant masses stood up on their own feet, got themselves organized, closely followed the lead of the Communist Party and the People's Government, and took the reins of government and armed forces in the villages firmly into their hands. Thus, the land reform succeeded not only in eliminating the landlords as a class and weakening to a great extent the rich peasants in the economic realm but also, politically, in overthrowing the landlord class and isolating the rich peasants. The broad masses of the awakened peasants held that exploitation whether by landlords or by rich peasants was a shameful thing. Conditions were thus created which were favourable to the subsequent socialist transformation of agriculture and helped shorten to a great extent the time needed to bring about agricultural co-operation.

In the old China, 60 to 70 per cent of the rural population were poor peasants and farm labourers. They were, respectively, the semi-proletarians and proletarians of the countryside, who found it very easy to accept the leadership of the working-class party. They have shown great enthusiasm not only in the bourgeois-democratic revolution but also in the socialist revolution. Improvements in the economic position of the peasant masses took place after the land reform, and not a few of the poor peasants and farm labourers have since moved up to become middle peasants. However, 60 to 70 per cent of the rural population remained poor peasants or lower middle peasants, owing to the fact that in China's rural districts there is a large population while there is little land, the average arable area per head in the country being only three *mou* (approximately one-fifth of a hectare), and in many places in the southern part of the country only one *mou*, or even less. There was no guarantee for these peasants that they could achieve a life of prosperity by continuing with individual farming. Such being the case, the poor peasants and the not so well-off peasants, who constituted the great majority of the rural population, actively responded to the Party's call and showed themselves willing to take the path of agricultural co-operation.

Following the land reform we immediately and on a wide scale set about establishing among the peasants mutual-aid organizations for agricultural production which contain rudiments of socialism—organizations in which the peasants engage in collective labour. Inasmuch as the mutual-aid teams achieve better results than individual peasants "working on their own," 40 per cent of the country's peasant households joined the mutual-aid organizations in 1952, and the number rose to nearly 58 per cent in 1954. In 1952, on the basis of these mutual-aid organizations, the Central Committee of the Party began to promote in a systematic way the semi-socialist agricultural producers' co-operatives—an elementary type of co-operative characterized by the pooling of land as shares and a single management but with land and other principal means of production still privately owned by the members. There were only some three hundred of this type of co-operative at the end of 1951, but having shown their advantage compared to the mutual-aid organizations, their numbers increased by the first half of 1955 to 670,000, with approximately 17 million peasant households. In the latter part of 1955 the agricultural producers' co-operatives began to go forward by leaps and bounds. This, as we all know, followed on the correction by the Party's Central Committee and Comrade Mao Tse-tung of the Rightist conservative ideas within the Party which had tended to stifle the peasant masses' enthusiasm for agricultural co-operation. The co-operatives of an elementary type were subsequently reorganized, group after immense group, into the advanced type, which is socialist in character and capable of organizing production in a more effective way. In these advanced co-operatives, the land and other principal means of production are changed from private into collective ownership.

Facts have proved that such a step-by-step measure taken by our Party was appropriate. For it enabled the peasants to benefit continuously from the movement for agricultural co-operation, to gradually accustom themselves to the ways of collective production, to forsake more naturally and smoothly the system of private ownership of land and other principal means of production and accept in its stead the system of collective ownership. In this way losses which might have resulted from sudden changes could be averted, or greatly reduced.

In the movement for agricultural co-operation the class policy of the Party has been to establish the poor peasants and those lower middle peasants who have moved up since the land reform from the status of poor peasants in favourable positions to exercise leadership in the co-operatives, and firmly unite with the middle peasants. The well-to-do, or comparatively well-to-do, middle peasants constitute a minority in the rural districts, but the fact remains that they can still exert a considerable influence on the lower middle peasants, and even on the poor peasants. Generally speaking, these well-to-do middle peasants in our country give their support to the Communist Party and the People's Government, and a great number of them had "stood up" in the land reform. But when it comes to taking the path of agricultural co-operation they inevitably waver. In consolidating the alliance with the middle peasants, the key lies in steadfastly adhering to the policy of voluntariness and mutual benefit in the movement for agricultural co-operation. This policy of voluntariness and mutual benefit holds good for everyone without exception, and for the middle peasants it is of still greater significance. The Party not only forbids dragging reluctant middle peasants into the co-operatives; it further lays it down that in the early stages of their development the co-operatives are to admit the poor peasants and the lower middle peasants first of all, and are generally not to take in the comparatively well-to-do middle peasants as members. Furthermore, the Party lays it down that both before and after the middle peasants join the co-operatives, their interests must not be infringed, and they must not be taken advantage of, particularly when it comes to dealing with the means of production which they pool in the co-operatives. It goes without saying that the middle peasants are also not allowed to infringe the interests, or take advantage of the poor peasants. The state's correct policy on food has also had a salutary effect on the middle peasants. By introducing in 1953 a system of planned purchase and supply of grain and other principal farm products and by fixing reasonable prices for such purchases and supplies, the state has, in the main, put an end to capitalist profiteering in these commodities in the market. Again, in 1955, the state fixed the amount of grain to be purchased and corrected the mistake of purchasing 7,000 million catties[1] of grain in excess of need the year before, thus relieving the peasants of their misgivings that the state might go in for excessive purchases. Because the Party unswervingly adopted the policy of uniting with the middle peasants and because the middle peasants realized the futility of taking the path of capitalism and saw the superiority of the co-operatives, made more and more obvious by the rise in production, the broad masses of the middle peasants at last stopped wavering in the high tide of the co-operative movement and eagerly applied for co-operative membership.

With regard to former landlords and rich peasants, the Party has consistently paid attention over the last few years to leading the peasants to forestall and combat their wrecking activities in the co-operative movement. In the initial stage of agricultural co-operation they were barred from the co-operatives. It was only after the movement had been crowned with success that the Party decided to permit them to work in the co-operatives on the basis of equal pay for equal work but with different status, depending on the conditions of each case. The purpose of this was to reform them, so that they could make a fresh start in life.

By virtue of the policies mentioned above, we have been able to accomplish in the main the socialist transformation of agriculture less than four years after land reform was completed throughout the country, organizing 110 million peasant households all over the country into approximately one million agricultural producers' co-operatives, of varying sizes and of both elementary and advanced types.

---

[1] A catty is approximately 1-1/3 lbs or 1/2 kilogramme.

Next, let us take up the socialist transformation of the handicrafts and other sections of individual economy.

Barring the very limited field in which they can market their own products, the individual handicraft working people in our country have to rely on state trading departments and the supply and marketing co-operatives and capitalist enterprises for raw materials, for the marketing of their goods, and for loans of capital. Most of them have found things difficult and have nothing to fall back on in the event of illness, injuries or death. Their production techniques are mostly backward and there is a possibility of their being ousted by modern machinery. So they hope to organize themselves together and overcome their difficulties under the leadership of the state sector of the economy. Viewed from the interests of the national economy as a whole, much of our handicraft production must needs be preserved and developed, mainly for the sake of satisfying the immense needs of the home market and also partly for the sake of meeting export requirements. There are in China a considerable number of individual fishermen, salt producers, small merchants and pedlars and labourers working on their own in the transport services, and their conditions are very much the same as those of the handicraftsmen.

The socialist transformation of handicrafts, fisheries, salt production and transport services generally takes the form of co-operation. Over the last few years the co-operative movement in these fields has achieved some success. By 1955 the number of handicraftsmen in handicraft producers' co-operatives had reached 29 per cent of all these handicrafts, but it was not until the first half of this year that the movement for co-operation in the handicrafts and other sections of individual economy began to surge forward. Of the newly formed co-operatives, some came into being through the transitional stage of producers' groups, but most were set up during the high tide of the co-operative movement earlier in the year. Apart from this a small section of the handicrafts as well as a small section of sailing junks and animal-drawn carts operated along capitalist lines have been turned into joint state-private concerns along with the rest of capitalist industry and commerce.

Small merchants and pedlars are individual working people in the realm of commerce. In the socialist transformation, they have generally taken the road of co-operation, forming themselves into co-operative stores or groups, while a small section of them have been drawn into joint state-private management along with the rest of capitalist commerce. The co-operative groups formed by the small merchants and pedlars act as commission agents and make purchases for state trading departments and the supply and marketing co-operatives. Their way of management will follow the old practice of dispersed and mobile operations to suit the consumers' convenience, and features peculiar to their management which conform to social needs will be preserved as of old.

Lastly, we come to the question of the socialist transformation of capitalist industry and commerce.

The big bourgeoisie who held a dominant position in our country were chiefly the bureaucrat-comprador bourgeoisie. As has been said before, they have long since been eliminated as a class by the revolution. In the old China, there were contradictions between the national bourgeoisie on the one hand and imperialism, the feudal forces and bureaucrat-capital on the other. During the bourgeois-democratic revolution, the national bourgeoisie had a dual character: on the one hand they were willing, under certain conditions, to take part in the struggle against imperialism and the reactionary rule of the Kuomintang, and on the other they often tended to vacillate and compromise in the struggle. After the founding of the People's Republic of China, they have given support to the people's democratic dictatorship, the Common Programme and the Constitution, expressed their willingness to continue to oppose imperialism, and stood for the land reform; but they also have a strong desire to develop capitalism. Therefore our policy towards the national bourgeoisie is, as in the past, still one of simultaneously uniting with them and waging struggles against them, of attaining unity with them through struggle. That is to say, the working class maintains its political alliance with the national bourgeoisie on the basis of the worker-peasant alliance. Economically, there are two sides to capitalist industry and commerce: a positive side which is beneficial to national welfare and the people's livelihood, and a negative side which is not beneficial to national welfare and the people's livelihood. Because of this, the state has adopted a policy of using, restricting and transforming capitalist industry and commerce. In accordance with this policy, the working class has, moreover, established an economic alliance with the national bourgeoisie, in which the state sector of the national economy exercises its leadership over the capitalist sector, thus, through various forms of state capitalism, transforming step by step the capitalist system of private ownership into the system of socialist ownership by the whole people.

The state must adopt the policy of using capitalist industry and commerce not only because it is possible for the national bourgeoisie to accept this policy, but also because it is necessary to make use of them in the economic sphere during the transition period. In the early days after liberation of our country, we were confronted with the tremendous task of restoring our national economy which had been seriously damaged by imperialism and the reactionary rule of the Kuomintang. At the same time, because of a very backward economy and the preponderance of small production, it was necessary for us to make use of all available economic forces, so as to facilitate the work of rehabilitating and building up our national economy. While giving priority to the development of the state sector of the economy over the past few years we have carried out a policy of "taking into account both public and private interests and benefiting both labour and capital," and given equal treatment, by and large, to the private sector in the allocation of raw materials and certain other matters. In this way, workers in privately-owned factories were saved from unemployment, and the capitalists were able to make some profits. Thanks to this policy, those industrial and commercial enterprises owned by capitalists that were beneficial to the national welfare and the people's livelihood were able to keep going and even expand to some extent. Facts prove that, during the period of restoring and building up our national economy, capitalist industry and commerce have in many respects served as an auxiliary to the state sector of the national economy. The implementation of the policy of using capitalist industry and commerce enabled the state to obtain more industrial products which were used to exchange for grain, industrial raw materials and other agricultural products with the peasants and to have a constant and fairly adequate supply of goods and materials on the market; this facilitated stabilization of prices. Of course this policy is not, by any means, a policy that allows capitalism to develop unchecked. With regard to the negative side of capitalist industry and commerce which is not beneficial to the national welfare and the people's livelihood, the state must carry out a policy of restriction. Such a policy of restriction is inseparably linked with the policy of utilization.

As restrictions placed by the state on capitalist industry and commerce clash with the narrow class interests of the bourgeoisie, it is inevitable that many of the capitalists should show opposition to or violate these restrictions. The struggle between restriction and counter-restriction has been the chief form of class struggle inside our country for the past few years, reflecting the chief class contradiction in our country—the contradiction between the working class and the bourgeoisie. Since the founding of the People's Republic, constant and repeated struggles between restriction and counter-restriction have been waged between the state and the capitalist sector of the economy concerning the scope of activity; taxation; market prices; terms for the state placing orders with private enterprises to process and manufacture goods, for state purchasing and marketing of the products of private enterprises, and for using private enterprises as retail distributors or commission agents of the state; and working conditions for the workers. The chief struggles in this respect were the campaign in the spring of 1950 against profiteering in order to stabilize commodity prices and the *wu fan* movement in 1952—a movement against the bribery of government workers, tax evasion, theft of state property, cheating on government contracts and stealing economic information from government sources. These struggles were waged because many capitalist elements were engaged in unlawful activities detrimental to the national welfare and the people's livelihood, and resolute measures had to be taken to stop them. In the course of these struggles, attention was paid to avoiding and correcting the mistake of imposing on capitalist economy too rigid or too many restrictions. The basic policy of the Party and the state has been to completely isolate, through these struggles, those few capitalist elements who persist in their illegal activities from the masses of people as well as from the other members of the bourgeoisie, and to rally together the great majority of the capitalist elements willing to abide by the laws and decrees of the state.

The aim of carrying out the policy of utilization and restriction by the state is to bring about the socialist transformation of capitalist industry and commerce. This transformation consists of two steps: the first is to transform capitalism into state capitalism, and the second is to transform state capitalism into socialism. What is state capitalism under the leadership of a state where the proletariat holds power? "State capitalism," said Lenin, "is capitalism which we shall be able to restrict, the limits of which we shall be able to fix." Through the transitional form of state capitalism we allow the national bourgeoisie a necessary period of time to gradually accept transformation, under the leadership of the state and the working class. In industry, as the state controlled most of the industrial raw materials, the method was introduced in 1950 whereby private industrial enterprises were supplied with raw materials, orders were placed with them for processing and manufacturing goods, and their goods were exclusively purchased and marketed by state enterprises. Thus, as an initial step, private industry was brought into the orbit of state capitalism. By 1954, further steps were taken to transform capitalist industry in a planned way through the form of joint state-private operation of enterprises, and most of the important, large-scale privately-owned industrial enterprises were converted into joint state-private management. In commerce, as the state controlled the sources of all the important agricultural and industrial products through state and co-operative commerce, it has been possible to wholesale goods to private commercial enterprises according to terms laid down by the state, and get them to act as retail distributors or commission agents for the state. By 1954, the number of commercial enterprises assuming this elementary form of state capitalism—enterprises serving as retail distributors or commission agents for the state—had already increased considerably. With the ground thus laid, when, in the period between the autumn and winter of 1955, the high tide of agricultural co-operation blocked the way for the development of capitalism in the countryside once for all and so effected a basic change in the alignment of class forces in our country, conditions were ripe for converting capitalist industry and commerce by whole trades into joint state-private management. Such joint state-private management of whole trades is the highest form of state capitalism in our country and constitutes a major step of decisive importance in turning capitalist ownership into socialist public ownership.

In order to achieve socialism through state capitalism, which is a peaceful means of transition, we have adopted a policy of redemption by steps in nationalizing means of production privately owned by the bourgeoisie. Before the bringing of private enterprises into joint state-private management by whole trades, redemption took the form of distribution of profits, viz., portioning out to the capitalists part of the profit (say, one-fourth) according to the net earnings of the enterprises. After the conversion of private enterprises into joint state-private management by whole trades, redemption has taken the form of payment of a fixed rate of interest, i.e., for a certain period the state pays, through the special companies for whole trades, a fixed rate of interest on their investments to the capitalists. Furthermore, with regard to the capitalists and their representatives, work has been found by the government departments concerned for those who are able to work, and proper arrangements have been made or relief provided for those who cannot, so as to ensure their livelihood. This is also a necessary measure of redemption. Both Marx and Lenin pointed out that, under certain historical conditions, the adoption of the policy of redemption by the proletariat towards the bourgeoisie is permissible and advantageous. This has already been borne out by practice in our revolution.

In the course of bringing about the socialist transformation of capitalist industry and commerce, we have carried out the transformation of enterprises in conjunction with the remoulding of individuals. That is to say, while the enterprises are being transformed, educational measures are adopted to remould the capitalists gradually, enabling them to be transformed from exploiters into working people earning their own living. The chief aim of our policy of simultaneously uniting with the national bourgeoisie and waging struggles against them, of attaining unity with them through struggle, is to re-educate them. Restrictions imposed on the capitalist sector of the economy and struggles against the unlawful activities of the bourgeoisie were a kind of important practical education. Readjustments and overall arrangements of private enterprises, and unified planning with due consideration for all parties concerned, enabling the capitalists to play their respective parts, were yet another kind of important practical education. We welcomed those who adopted a positive attitude in the course of socialist transformation. As for those who remained sceptical, we educated them and indicated our willingness to give them time. In the case of those who put up resistance, we waged such struggles as were necessary, the aim still being to remould them. Such a policy of using different measures in different cases was also a kind of important practical education. Moreover, we have used such means as giving talks, holding discussion meetings and conducting classes among capitalists, organizing the capitalists and the members of their families to study, inducing the capitalists to practise criticism and self-criticism among themselves and so forth, to educate them and help them solve their ideological problems. This is aimed at raising the ideological level of the progressives among them—that is, those who support socialist transformation—and making the middle groups and backward elements gradually change their attitude and follow the example of the progressives, thereby disintegrating the die-hards. In a word, our aim is to rally together the majority and weaken resistance, so as to facilitate socialist transformation.

The policy of utilization, restriction and transformation of capitalist industry and commerce by the state and every single measure taken on the basis of it, are not the result of wishful thinking or arbitrary decision, but proceed from a study of actual conditions and situations and consideration of what the national welfare and the people's livelihood demand. This policy and the measures taken for its implementation enjoy the support of the broad masses of people, and the capitalists have not a leg to stand on to reject or oppose them. It can now be stated with conviction that with the exception of a very few die-hards who still attempt to put up resistance, it is possible, in the economic sphere, for the overwhelming majority of the national bourgeoisie to accept socialist transformation and gradually change into real working people.

Our work of bringing about the socialist transformation of agriculture, handicrafts and capitalist industry and commerce has not been free from shortcomings and mistakes; our policy was not mature from the very beginning and partial deviations occurred in carrying it out. Nevertheless, the extremely complex and arduous historical task of converting the system of private ownership of means of production into the system of socialist public ownership has now been basically accomplished in our country. The question of who will win in the struggle between socialism and capitalism in our country has now been decided.

This does not mean to say, however, that our task in socialist transformation is entirely completed. Many urgent and important problems remain for us to tackle. What are our tasks from now on?

In agricultural co-operation, we have to win over, on the basis of the policy of voluntariness and mutual benefit, a small number of peasant households still outside co-operatives to join the co-operatives, and give guidance to the transformation of elementary co-operatives into co-operatives of the advanced type. But we have to be patient and give them time; coercion or commands in any form will not be allowed. The most urgent problem awaiting solution now is that all possible efforts must be made to ensure an increase in the output of about a million co-operatives now existing and in the income of their members. Some of the co-operatives which were rather hastily set up have either to solve many problems which have been left unsolved or to readjust their present form of organization. Most of the co-operatives still do not have enough experience to lead scores or hundreds of peasant households in collective production; the Party must help the cadres in these co-operatives to gain such experience in the quickest way possible. Many co-operatives lay far too much emphasis on collective interests and collective management, mistakenly ignore the personal interests and freedom of the members and overlook domestic subsidiary occupations. Such mistakes must be quickly corrected. In order to bring into play the enthusiasm for production on the part of the members in an effective way and to consolidate the co-operatives, the principle of running the co-operatives industriously, economically and democratically must be adhered to, and ideological education among the members in socialism and collectivism must be unceasingly strengthened. Peasants who until a short time ago had been working on their own have now become members of co-operatives; this is indeed a tremendous change in the life of hundreds of millions of peasants. Co-operative cadres must fully realize the significance of this change, assume with a proper sense of responsibility the important task of giving leadership which co-operative members have entrusted to them, and whole-heartedly serve the interests of the members. They should realize that co-operatives can be consolidated only when the members themselves really feel that they are the masters of the co-operatives and when their income will increase every year.

In the transformation of handicrafts and what used to make up other sections of individual economy, actual problems arising in the course of development of various kinds of co-operative organizations must be tackled on the merits of each case, taking account of the characteristics of the different trades and using various forms. Here, it would be wrong to ignore different concrete conditions and use a set form for all cases. A number of co-operative organizations will, under suitable conditions, develop and become state enterprises or be amalgamated into state enterprises; others will for a long time to come maintain the collective ownership of means of production; and still others will, under the administration of socialist enterprises, keep their original form of management in which the co-operatives will enjoy the profit or bear the loss themselves. All kinds of co-operatives must pay attention to keeping and developing whatever fine traditions the original individual economy had in production and in management. After co-operation the quality of handicraft products must by all means be improved, and not deteriorate, while the range of their variety must be extended and not reduced.

In the transformation of capitalist industry and commerce, the problems arising in the course of development should likewise be solved on the merits of each case, taking into consideration, as before, the characteristics of the different trades and the needs of various aspects of the social economy. Reckless application of a set method to different cases must also be avoided to prevent losses. Systematic educational and organizational work should be continued among the workers and staff in the enterprises, so that they will fully understand and carry out their tasks in the transformation of enterprises, in production, and in uniting with and educating the capitalists and their representatives. Outstanding workers and employees should be chosen to take part in the management of enterprises. With regard to the capitalists and their representatives, arrangements should be made for their work and livelihood; amicable working relations should be established between them and state representatives; and further efforts should be made to strengthen the political education of the capitalists and their representatives. As many of them have rich experience in management and technical knowledge, understand the actual needs of the consumers, are well acquainted with market conditions and are proficient in making careful and detailed calculations, our personnel working in the enterprises must, apart from helping to re-educate them, learn earnestly from them and take over their useful experience and knowledge as part of our social heritage. While the transformation of capitalist industry and commerce has now only reached the stage in which private enterprises have been converted into joint state-private management by whole trades, we must make preparations to transform these enterprises into state enterprises of a fully socialist character at some opportune moment in the future.

Only when we have accomplished the various tasks mentioned above can the question of socialist transformation in our country be thoroughly solved. We are convinced that our Party, working as ever in unity with the people of the whole country, will be able to accomplish these tasks successfully in the not distant future, so that the socialist construction of our country will enjoy the most favourable conditions for development.

III. SOCIALIST CONSTRUCTION
Implementation of the First Five-Year Plan and
Preparation for the Second Five-Year Plan

Three years and eight and a half months have elapsed since we embarked on our First Five-Year Plan for development of our national economy. By next year, we shall have fulfilled this plan and drawn up the Second Five-Year Plan covering the period from 1958 to 1962. The central task that now confronts our Party and the whole people is to strive to overfulfil the First Five-Year Plan and to make vigorous preparations for the Second Five-Year Plan.

Tremendous successes have been achieved in implementing the First Five-Year Plan. Even our enemies cannot deny them.

We have made big advances in industrial capital construction. In the past few years, we have expanded our iron and steel base in the Northeast; started building two new iron and steel bases in Inner Mongolia and Central China respectively; built and expanded a number of power stations, coal-mines, oil wells, non-ferrous metallurgical works and mines, chemical works, factories producing building materials, machine-building works, and light industrial plants. The First Five-Year Plan has provided that construction should start on 694 above-norm projects in the field of industrial construction and that 455 of these are to be completed in the five-year period. Actually, some 800 projects can be started, and nearly 500 completed in this period. Investments in capital construction in the first three years of the plan plus the sum planned for this year already amount to 35,500 million yuan, or 83 per cent of the total investment of 42,700 million yuan which the plan sets aside for capital construction in the five-year period.

The First Five-Year Plan has provided for a 90.3 per cent increase in the total value of industrial production in the five-year period. This target will be exceeded. The total value of industrial output provided for in this year's annual plan has already reached the figure set for 1957 in the Five-Year Plan. Furthermore, this year's planned production figures for steel, steel products, metal-cutting machine tools, cement, motor-car tires, cotton yarn, cotton piece-goods, paper, etc. have all surpassed the targets set for 1957. Thanks to the rapid development of her heavy industry, China has begun producing lorries, jet planes, and power generating equipment with a capacity of 6,000-12,000 KW, etc. By 1957, we shall be producing for ourselves above 60 per cent of all the machinery and equipment needed for the economic construction of our country.

In agriculture, it is also possible to surpass the targets set by the First Five-Year Plan for total value of agricultural production and output of staple food and industrial crops. The plan provides for a 23.3 per cent increase in the total output value of agriculture and agricultural subsidiary occupations in 1957, compared with 1952. Owing to severe natural calamities, the increase in 1953 and 1954 was rather slight. But in 1955, a 14.8 per cent increase was registered as compared with 1952. Despite the fact that relatively severe floods, drought and wind-storms have again occurred this year, grain output can, on the basis of agricultural co-operation, still reach the level set for 1957.

In water conservancy, a series of projects have been undertaken in the past three years in the Huai River valley, along the middle reaches of the Yangtse, and along many other rivers. As regards the Sanmen Gorge multi-purpose water conservancy project on the Yellow River, preparations for actual construction have been made. Many minor water conservancy projects have also been completed in various rural areas.

In transport, the targets set by the First Five-Year Plan to build more than 4,000 kilometres of new railways and 10,000 kilometres of main highways will be surpassed this year.

Rapid strides have also been made in domestic and foreign trade, in education and culture, and in public health.

Initial improvements have been made in the living standards of workers and employees. It is estimated that, compared with 1952, the average wages of workers and employees throughout the country will increase this year by 33.5 per cent. The actual sum paid yearly by the state and individual enterprises for labour insurance, and for medical services, culture and education, and welfare facilities for workers and employees, amounts to approximately 13 per cent of their total annual wages, or about 4,400 million yuan in four years. The floor space in living quarters built by the state for workers and employees in the past three years plus that planned for the current year amounts to more than 50 million square metres.

It should be pointed out that, owing to objective limitations, it will not be possible to reach the targets set by the First Five-Year Plan for a few items of products such as crude oil, edible vegetable oils and cigarettes, but the First Five-Year Plan as a whole will be overfulfilled.

Though there is the possibility that we will overfulfil the First Five-Year Plan both in our total investment on capital construction and in construction projects, we must suitably mobilize the necessary financial and material resources and make energetic efforts to complete construction plans for part of certain important construction projects. As for other above-norm projects, we must also make every effort to fulfil the plan as far as possible.

Although the various heavy industrial departments have surpassed their production plans, we must continue our efforts to ensure the better fulfilment of the country's capital construction plan by producing more iron and steel, machinery, equipment and building materials, and by correspondingly increasing the output of coal, electricity, petroleum, non-ferrous metals, chemicals, etc. At the same time, related questions of transport and urban construction must also be solved.

We must also make serious efforts in the field of agriculture. We must make further efforts to increase the output of grain and cotton. We must see to it that agricultural and commercial departments take effective measures to bring about as quickly as possible an increase in the yield of oil-bearing crops, and in the number of pigs and other domestic animals, and the output of certain agricultural subsidiary occupations, which have not increased fast enough in the past few years and, on one occasion, even showed a drop in some cases.

As soon as we have fulfilled the First Five-Year Plan, we shall immediately start on the second. Therefore, it is necessary that the present Congress discuss and adopt the proposals of the Party concerning this second plan. With regard to these proposals, Comrade Chou En-lai will make a special report on behalf of the Central Committee of the Party.

What is the basic task of the Second Five-Year Plan?

The Central Committee of the Party holds that, in order to satisfy the needs of socialist expanded reproduction in our country, fulfil the task of socialist industrialization, strengthen international cooperation between the countries of the socialist camp, and help to promote a common economic upsurge in all the socialist countries, we should build, in the main, an integrated industrial system within the period of three five-year plans on the basis of our large population and rich resources. Working along this line, the basic task of the Second Five-Year Plan, briefly speaking, is as follows: (1) to continue industrial construction centred on heavy industry, promote the technical reconstruction of our national economy and lay a firm foundation for the socialist industrialization of our country; (2) to continue our efforts in socialist transformation and to consolidate and extend the system of collective ownership and ownership by the whole people; (3) to develop the production of our industry, agriculture and handicrafts, and correspondingly develop our transport and commerce, on the basis of developing capital construction and completing socialist transformation; (4) to make energetic efforts to train personnel for construction and strengthen scientific research so as to meet the needs of socialist economic and cultural development; and (5) to strengthen the national defences and raise the level of material and cultural well-being of the people on the basis of the growth of industrial and agricultural production.

During the period of the First Five-Year Plan, generally speaking, we have not been able to make heavy and precision machinery ourselves and, therefore, cannot ourselves supply many major projects with the main equipment they need. In the case of home-made steel products, we have not been able to keep up with demands, in terms of either quantity or variety; there are many kinds of high-grade alloy steel which we cannot yet produce; the non-ferrous metals industry has only a limited range of products; our radio-engineering industry is still very weak; and we have practically no organic synthetic chemical industry to speak of. In the second five-year period, we should make efforts to build up those branches of industry which, as mentioned above, are weak or which we lack. We should redouble our efforts so that, by 1962, we shall ourselves be able to produce approximately 70 per cent of the machinery and equipment needed for our economic construction, including some heavy and precision machinery. With regard to fuels, the output of petroleum falls far short of demand. We must gradually improve this situation.

During the Second Five-Year Plan period, we must carry on geological prospecting on a larger scale so as to unearth a greater variety and greater quantities of hidden resources; the work of capital construction too must be pressed ahead on a larger scale. During the second five-year period, investments in capital construction will approximately be double what they were in the first five-year period. Besides continuing the construction of bases for the iron and steel industry in Northeast and Central China, and in Inner Mongolia, new industrial bases will be established in the area of the Sanmen Gorge, in the Kansu-Chinghai area, in Sinkiang, and in Southwest China. When the capital construction plan for the second five-year period is completed, many of our machine-building and metallurgical works, power stations, coal-mines, petroleum enterprises, chemical works, and factories manufacturing building materials will have modern, advanced technical equipment.

Production should be greatly increased in the various branches of heavy industry. By 1962, production of steel must be raised from the 4.12 million tons planned for 1957 to 10.5-12 million tons; coal, from 113 million tons to 190-210 million tons; and electricity, from 15,900 million KWH to 40,000-43,000 million KWH.

There must, likewise, be a relatively high rate of development of light industry. By 1962, the output of cotton yarn should be increased from the 5 million bales planned for 1957 to 8-9 million bales; edible vegetable oils, from 1.79 million tons to 3.1-3.2 million tons; sugar, from 1.1 million tons to 2.4-2.5 million tons; and machine-made paper, from 650,000 tons to 1.5-1.6 million tons.

In order to meet the requirements of the national economy as a whole, the Second Five-Year Plan should raise agricultural production to a higher level along the line laid down in the Draft National Programme for Agricultural Development (1956-1967). In 1962, the output of grain should be about 500,000 million catties; of cotton, about 48 million *tan*[2] furthermore, efforts should be made to surpass these two targets. Energetic steps should be taken to increase the output of soya beans, oil crops, sugar crops, and other industrial crops and agricultural subsidiary occupations. Among subsidiary occupations special efforts should be made to develop pig-breeding.

It is necessary to continue to expand rail, road, water transport and tele-communications facilities. Existing lines of communication should, step by step, undergo necessary technical reconstruction. We must continue to rationalize the transport system, make full use of the potentialities of the existing facilities. At present there is a heavy strain on railway traffic on certain lines. We must pay attention to improving this situation. During the second five-year period, 8,000-9,000 kilometres of new railways will be built; the Lanchow-Sinkiang Railway will be extended to the Chinese-Soviet border, and trunk lines will link the provinces of the Northwest and the Southwest.

In order to increase the variety of available materials and equipment, we must make full use of all our own technical personnel, make efforts to improve research and the designing of products, and manufacture new products. It is wrong to neglect our own technical personnel and not make the best use of them and train them.

According to preliminary estimates, our national income at the end of the Second Five-Year Plan should be about 50 per cent bigger than it will be at the end of the First Five-Year Plan. In addition to bigger capital accumulations for the state, the people's livelihood will also be improved to a fair extent. Within the five-year period, there will be an increase of about six to seven million in the number of workers and employees. The average wages of workers and employees will be increased by 25-30 per cent, while the total income of the peasants will also be increased by 25-30 per cent. Supplies of grain, cotton piece-goods and other important consumer goods, such as edible oils, sugar, kerosene and coal, will also show an increase.

The brief outline given above shows that the proposals of the Party for the Second Five-Year Plan envisage a tremendous and rapid development of our national economy. According to these proposals, fulfilment of the Second Five-Year Plan will provide the necessary conditions for fulfilling in the main in the Third Five-Year Plan the general task in the transition period.

The rate of development in the Second Five-Year Plan as proposed by the Central Committee of the Party is both forward-looking and feasible. It must be forward-looking, or else we shall let slip the good opportunities that we have today and fall into the error of conservatism. But it must also be feasible, or else it will not enable the economy to develop in the correct ratio, and will put too great a burden on the people, or result in divergencies among the different branches of the national economy, making it impossible to fulfil the plan, and causing waste. This would be an error of adventurism.

It is obvious that the Second Five-Year Plan calls for a bigger investment than does the first. Our national economy has developed, and our financial situation, along with it, has improved. But we must realize that our funds are still limited, and we must use them as effectively and economically as we can. One important way of increasing our fund for construction is to economize more on military and administrative expenses. The Central Committee of the Party had already decided on this policy in 1950. But it was not carried out earlier because of the outbreak of the war to resist U.S. aggression and aid Korea. Though in recent years we have made great efforts to economize on military and administrative expenses, the estimated expenditure on national defence and for administrative purposes will still account for 32 per cent of all state expenditure in the first five-year period; appropriations for economic construction and cultural development will amount to approximately 56 per cent. During the second five-year period, the proportion going to military and administrative expenses must be reduced to about 20 per cent so that the proportion of expenditure on economic construction and cultural development can be raised to 60-70 per cent. In economic construction and cultural development, it is, nevertheless, imperative that funds be spent rationally and with due emphasis on certain key fields. Thus, in the second five-year period, the technical reconstruction of our national economy must be centred, first and foremost, on heavy industry, particularly the machine-building and metallur-

---

[2] One *tan* equals 50 kilogrammes.

gical industries. In the meantime in all enterprises, all state organs, and in social life as a whole, we must continue to practise economy and eliminate waste. Waste, under all circumstances, is a hindrance to the development of production and the improvement of our living standards. We have just begun our national construction so it behoves us to strive all the harder to save every bit of money we can for construction and to use it to the best advantage. We will have to export part of our consumer goods in exchange for machinery and equipment needed by our industrial construction. We will have to bear with certain temporary difficulties in our daily life for the sake of our future happiness. It is our Party's long-term policy in building socialism to carry on national construction, to run enterprises and co-operatives, and handle all other affairs in an industrious and economical way. This is also the principle that must be followed in drafting and implementing the Second Five-Year Plan.

Now, we shall explain in general terms some of the experience we have gained in the past few years in industry, agriculture, commerce, and education and culture as well as some problems which we must now try to solve.

Industry

In regard to industry, we shall deal here only with a few relatively important questions, namely, the relationship between heavy and light industries, the geographical distribution of industries, the quality of products and construction work, the livelihood of workers and employees, and leadership in enterprises.

The industrialization of our country is based upon the development of heavy industrial production, that is, production of industries manufacturing means of production. In old China, the value of production of industries manufacturing means of production made up a very small proportion in the total value of industrial production, and in 1949, it only amounted to 26.6 per cent. This is an indication of the backwardness of China's productive forces. The policy of socialist industrialization followed by our Party calls for a fundamental change in this situation and ensures that priority will go to development of industries manufacturing means of production. In 1952, the value of production of industries manufacturing means of production was about 35.6 per cent of the total value of production of our industries; by the end of the First Five-Year Plan, the proportion will probably rise to more than 40 per cent.

In order to develop our national economy according to plan, we must carry through the policy of giving priority to the development of heavy industry. Some comrades want to lower the rate of development of heavy industry. This line of thinking is wrong. We put this question to them: If we do not very quickly establish our own indispensable machine-building industry, metallurgical industry and other related branches of heavy industry, how are we going to equip our light industry, transport, building industry and agriculture? Unless we do this we shall not be able to get various kinds of machines, steel products and cement, electric power and fuel, all of which are essential, and our national economy will remain in a backward state for a long time. It is obvious that we cannot afford to let this happen.

But there are also other comrades who one-sidedly stress the importance of developing heavy industry. They want to lower the rate of development of light industry and other branches of the national economy. This line of thinking is also wrong. They do not realize, firstly, that with the people's demands for consumer goods growing day by day, a shortage of commodities may result if there is no adequate development of light industry, and this, in turn, will affect the stability of commodity prices and of the market. In the countryside in particular, if there is not a sufficient supply of industrial products to exchange at stable and reasonable prices for agricultural produce, the consolidation of the worker-peasant alliance as well as the development of agricultural production may be adversely affected. Secondly, light industry needs comparatively small investments, and enterprises in this field can be established in a relatively short time. So the turnover of capital is relatively quick, and funds can be accumulated relatively rapidly. Furthermore we can use the funds accumulated by light industry precisely to help develop heavy industry. This shows that, funds, raw materials and market permitting, appropriate attention to the development of light industry will not hamper but, on the contrary, will benefit the building up of heavy industry.

As to the geographical distribution of industries, attention must be paid at present to co-ordination between the coastal regions and the interior, between large enterprises on the one hand and medium and small on the other, and between state enterprises run by the central authority and those run by local authorities.

During the period of the First Five-Year Plan, we have gradually shifted the emphasis of our industrial development to the interior in order to achieve a rational distribution of our productive forces, give industrial enterprises better access to natural resources and secure a balanced development of our industry and the national economy as a whole. This is changing the abnormal state of affairs left over from pre-liberation days when more than 70 per cent of China's industries were concentrated in the coastal provinces. But this does not mean that we can deny or at all ignore the part played by the industries in the coastal provinces. We must make full use of the favourable conditions existing in the coastal provinces, develop the industries there in a suitable way and use them to support the development of industries in the interior, and so accelerate the industrialization of the country. Liaoning, Shanghai, Tientsin and other industrial areas have made an outstanding contribution in this respect in the period of the First Five-Year Plan. In the second five-year period, in addition to making maximum use of the industrial bases in Northeast and East China, we must also appropriately bring the facilities of Hopei, Shantung and South China into full play in developing industry.

In the second five-year period, we must build and renovate small and medium enterprises in a planned way while building our large enterprises, in order to co-ordinate them with the building and operation of these large enterprises, accelerate industrial development, strengthen co-operation between industries, enlarge the variety of products, and facilitate full utilization of our resources and existing enterprises, particularly the large number of joint state-private enterprises.

We must take care to properly co-ordinate the initiative displayed by the various economic departments under the central authority with that of the local economic organizations. In the past, some central departments did not pay enough attention to the development and overall arrangement of local industries, and thus made it impossible for them to tap their potentialities. On the other hand, some local authorities went blindly ahead building and expanding certain industries, regardless of whether there was enough equipment in the country to spare for them, and without reference to the resources and other economic conditions in the localities concerned. This has also caused loss to the state. Both these deviations must be corrected.

To fulfil the state production plan, efforts must be made to improve the quality of products, both in light and heavy industry, in state enterprises run by the central authority and those under the charge of local authorities. In the same way, to fulfil the state construction plan, capital construction departments in industry and transport and in every other field must strive to improve the quality of engineering work. This is one of the most urgent questions in our socialist construction.

The superiority of socialism should reveal itself not only in the quantity and speed, but also in the quality, of our economic achievements. We have turned out quite a number of heavy and light industrial products of fine quality and have completed quite a number of engineering projects of fine quality too. However, owing to the backward equipment and low technical level of some enterprises, the absence in others of proper standards for finished products or of proper technological regulations, the failure in other cases to introduce a strict system of checks for quality and technical supervision, and particularly the fact that the leading bodies of some enterprises have not paid sufficient attention to guaranteeing the quality of their products and the quality of construction projects but placed one-sided emphasis on quantity of products and speed of construction, the quality of quite a number of products and engineering projects is not as good as it should be. Certain products fail to measure up to the required specifications and had to be classified as low quality goods. The indirect effects of the system of exclusive purchase and marketing by the state of the products of the private enterprises in the commercial sphere, and the defects which arose in the process of its operation, as well as a certain amount of confusion in the transformation of private industry and commerce, all served to dull the sense of responsibility in a number of light industrial enterprises in regard to the quality of their products and even led to serious cases where the quality of many products fell off. All this has caused loss to the state and the people, and we must put an end to this sort of thing without delay. All enterprises whose technical level is not as high as it should be and whose equipment is backward must take effective measures so as to master their respective techniques in a short time and gradually bring about a change in the backward state of their equipment. All enterprises should set up reasonable standards for finished products and adequate technological regulations. All factories, mines and construction sites which do not have a strict system of inspection should without delay set up departments and a system to check quality and provide technical supervision, and work out appropriate measures for dealing with products which do not come up to the required standards and engineering work which falls short of specifications. Vigorous measures should be taken to improve the quality of raw materials and other materials as well as the supply of them. As regards light industrial products, the policy of grading products and fixing prices according to quality should be strictly carried out and, in the case of a certain number of products, the system of selective purchasing should step by step be put into practice. What is even more important, educational work should be carried on among all workers and employees concerned, regarding the need to guarantee and raise quality, so that those who lack a sense of responsibility for quality can rid themselves completely of this wrong attitude.

To gradually improve the livelihood of workers and employees on the basis of increased production plays an important part in elevating the enthusiasm of the broad masses of workers and employees. What problems call for solution with regard to improving the livelihood of workers and employees? First and foremost, we must see to it that their wages are gradually increased on the basis of the development of production; we must thoroughly carry out the principle of "to each according to his work," to improve the wage system and the system of incentive payments. Secondly, we must make conscientious efforts to improve safety measures in production and intensify labour protection. Thirdly, we must ensure and improve the supply of non-staple foods. Fourthly, we must gradually increase welfare facilities for workers and employees and make energetic efforts to solve their housing and other urgent problems. Fifthly, we must ensure that workers and employees have time to look after their domestic affairs and take proper rest.

Many problems which confront the workers and employees cannot be solved in a short time until we make greater advances in socialist construction. We must work hard. We should not concentrate on individual and immediate interests at the expense of national, long-term interests. This must be made clear to the workers and employees. But, on the other hand, it is wrong to place a one-sided stress on the national, long-term interests and neglect the individual and immediate interests of the workers and employees. Some problems relating to the livelihood of workers and employees at present must and can be solved. They remain unsolved only because leaders of enterprises, trade union organizations and the departments concerned have not made serious efforts to solve them. We must resolutely oppose such bureaucratic attitude of indifference to the welfare of the masses.

The principles mentioned above with regard to questions of the livelihood of the workers and employees apply to workers and employees in all enterprises as well as to all state employees.

Whether the initiative of the workers and employees can be given full play depends largely on whether the system and work of leadership in enterprises is sound. What do we mean by sound leadership in enterprises?

A system of leadership which combines collective leadership with personal responsibility, with the Party as the nucleus should be set up in all enterprises. All major problems should be brought up for collective discussion and decisions arrived at as a result of joint effort; all day-to-day affairs should be handled according to the principle of division of labour and fixed responsibility. The leaders of enterprises, Party organizations, administrative departments, and the trade union and Youth League organizations in enterprises should know how to explain to the masses clearly the immediate tasks confronting their enterprises; they should learn to be good at rousing the masses to start socialist emulation and advanced workers campaigns, to put forward rationalization proposals, and constantly improve the work. The leading personnel of the various organizations in the enterprises should know how to keep in close touch with the masses, how to identify themselves with the rank and file, understand their feelings and demands, and actively help them solve their problems.

Improvement of the leadership in enterprises is not the concern only of the enterprises themselves; it also concerns the higher state organs. Here it should be pointed out that the higher state organs have often been too strait-laced and too rigid in controlling enterprises, thereby hampering the initiative and flexibility of the enterprises and causing losses to our work which might have been avoided. We must make sure that, under the unified leadership and plan of the state, the enterprises have appropriate powers to make their own decisions in the management of plans, finance and personnel, in the allotment of workers and employees, in regard to welfare facilities, etc. But this does not mean that the higher state organs should slacken their leadership. Just the contrary. Quite a number of the higher state organs did not really keep in close touch with their enterprises, and their leadership of these enterprises was often ill-timed and not specific enough. The leading organs of our economic departments should make a serious effort to do a good job of what they are charged with; they should not meddle with what is none of their business and what they can afford to ignore. Only by combining strong leadership at the higher state organs with initiative exercised by the enterprises themselves can we forge ahead rapidly with our work.

Agriculture

The proposals for the Second Five-Year Plan have set immense tasks for increasing agricultural production and the peasants' income. How are we to fulfil these tasks?

We are carrying out agricultural co-operation without farming machinery. The mechanization of agriculture in our country can only be brought about in a proper and gradual way, after the country is industrialized and in accordance with different farming conditions in different localities. It is estimated that by the end of the Second Five-Year Plan the acreage of land cultivated by machines will be only one-tenth of the land under cultivation in this country. As in the first five-year period, the amount of new land to be brought under cultivation will only amount to some tens of millions of *mou*, that is, approximately one-twentieth of the area of land already under cultivation. By 1962 the amount of chemical fertilizer produced in China will be only enough to provide, on an average, each *mou* of crop area with less than three catties. Under these circumstances, the main method of increasing agricultural production in the second five-year period will still be to rely on the agricultural producers' co-operatives and the peasants to raise per *mou* yields by such means as building water conservancy works, applying more manure to the land, ameliorating the soil, improving seeds, introducing the use of new-type farm tools on a wider scale, increasing the area sown to more than one crop a year, improving methods of cultivation, and preventing plant diseases and insect pests.

We should take note of the fact that such measures open up tremendous possibilities for increasing farm output. In regard to water conservancy, for instance, the present irrigated area only amounts to one-third of all the cultivated land in the country, but water sources can be found in many parts of the remaining two-thirds of the land and these can be used for irrigation purposes. With regard to fertilizer, there is an abundant supply of such natural fertilizer as night soil, animal manure and green manure, all of which are of great value in increasing yields. But in quite a number of places, these sources of manure have not yet been fully utilized. China's countryside, furthermore, has tremendous reserves of manpower organized on the basis of agricultural co-operation. If we press ahead persistently with these measures in a proper way, there is every possibility of reaching the targets for increased output envisaged in the proposals for the Second Five-Year Plan.

It is still a very important task to ensure increases in the output of grain and cotton in the second five-year period. Meanwhile, it is also an important task to ensure increases in the yields of other industrial crops and in the output of animal husbandry and subsidiary occupations. According to statistics, even excluding the output produced by the peasants in subsidiary occupations for their own consumption, the value of output of various industrial crops, animal husbandry and subsidiary occupations amounts to some 50 per cent of the total value of agricultural products in the country, which approximates to and even exceeds the percentage accounted for by grain, and is therefore of great importance to the peasants' income. These industrial crops, and products of animal husbandry and subsidiary occupations are furthermore of tremendous importance to light industry, to the supply of non-staple foods for the people and of products for export. Take pig-breeding as an example. In the second five-year period, we expect to increase the number of pigs from 138 million head as planned for 1957 to some 250 million in 1962. This is because pig-breeding is of importance to the supply of meat both in towns and villages throughout the country, manure for farm crops, as well as meat and bristles for export. We must do all we can to promote pig-breeding. All local Party organizations, local governments and departments in charge of agriculture, therefore, must effectively improve the guidance they give to the cultivation of industrial crops and promotion of animal husbandry and subsidiary occupations. In the light of local and state needs and guided by the plans of the central and local authorities, they should help agricultural producers' co-operatives to map out comprehensive plans, suited to their own conditions, to increase the production of grain, industrial crops, animal husbandry and subsidiary occupations. In promoting subsidiary occupations, we should take account of the necessary division of labour between the collective management of the co-operative and the domestic arrangements of its individual members, so that the enthusiasm and initiative of both sides can be given proper scope. At present, many co-operatives tend to neglect or even unreasonably restrict their members in managing their own subsidiary cottage occupations. This deviation should be corrected.

A correct price policy has to be implemented to increase the production of industrial crops and promote development of animal husbandry and subsidiary occupations. Our price policy since the founding of the People's Republic has, in general, been correct and mindful of the interests of the peasants. But some mistakes have nevertheless been committed in implementing this policy. During the past few years, production of certain kinds of industrial crops, pig-breeding, and other subsidiary occupations did not increase fast enough or even decreased. This was partly due to the fact that purchasing prices for these products were fixed at a rather low level. Those prices which were set too low should be properly readjusted after investigation and study.

To ensure development of agricultural production, it is important to make sure that, alongside that development, the income of the peasants is increased. The Central Committee of the Party requires that co-operatives throughout the country in the first few years after they are set up should, under normal harvest conditions, strive to increase the income of 90 per cent of their members; afterwards, on the basis of developing production, the members in general should be able to increase their income every year. To this end, it is not only necessary for the state to have correct tax and price policies, it is also necessary for the co-operatives to fix a correct ratio between the co-operative's reserve fund and the personal income of members. The co-operatives should therefore refrain from making arbitrary increases in expenditure for production or management, or in the amounts going to reserve or welfare funds; at the same time state taxes should be held at an appropriate rate. We should firmly maintain a policy of distribution which takes proper account of the interests of the state, of the collective and of the individual members.

Commerce

In keeping with industrial and agricultural development, our country has also achieved remarkable successes in home and foreign trade during the period of the First Five-Year Plan. In home trade, the volume of domestic retail sales, according to this year's plan, will be 66.3 per cent more than in 1952. During the last few years, we have stabilized commodity prices, increased the exchange of goods between city and countryside and met the needs of the people. In foreign trade, the total value of our import and export trade this year will be 65 per cent greater than in 1952. Before the liberation of the country, China mainly imported consumer goods. Since 1950, over 90 per cent of our imports have been means of production. Our foreign trade has ensured the needs of national construction for equipment and materials and has developed our country's economic co-operation and bonds of friendship with the Soviet Union, the People's Democracies and other countries.

According to preliminary estimates for the Second Five-Year Plan, the volume of domestic retail sales in our country in 1962 will, on the basis of further development of the national economy, be about 50 per cent more than in 1957, while the total value of import and export trade will also be greatly increased.

The socialist transformation of private commerce having, in the main, been completed, a unified socialist market has come into existence, and socialist commerce is now playing an extremely important role in the national economy. It is through the medium of socialist commerce that consumer goods and a part of the means of production coming from industry, and the marketable portion of agricultural products are distributed to departments of industrial production, the agricultural producers' co-operatives and the broad masses of consumers. Our country's commercial work will be still heavier in the future owing to the growing purchasing power of the people, their increasing needs for consumer goods, especially for non-staple foods, the rapid development of agricultural co-operation and industrial construction, and the daily increasing demands of foreign trade on export products. Commercial departments must, in accordance with the needs of the people and export requirements, do all they can by means of price policy and purchasing measures to help improve the quality and quantity of industrial and agricultural products. They must continue to develop the commercial network, increase the circulation of commodities, improve the purchasing and supply of industrial and agricultural products, and see to it that the commercial network is so arranged as to facilitate procurement of commodities as well as sales of goods to the people.

The further development of commerce demands in particular that earnest efforts be made to improve co-ordination between purchasing and marketing, correctly implement the price policy and properly readjust the prices of certain commodities.

Many measures concerning purchasing and marketing which were taken during the period when capitalist enterprises were utilized, restricted and transformed must now be changed and replaced by measures which suit existing economic conditions in our country. Before the changeover of capitalist industry and commerce into joint state-private management by whole trades took place, in the case of industrial products produced by capitalist concerns, our state trading organizations placed orders with private enterprises for processing and manufacturing goods, and purchased and marketed all their products. In regard to agricultural products, apart from the planned purchase by the state of grain, cotton, and oil-bearing crops, the supply and marketing co-operatives were entrusted with making unified purchases, or the state trading organizations themselves made direct purchases, of the greater part of the remaining products. Strict control was enforced on the market of cities and towns, uniform prices were fixed for commodities, and restrictions were placed on the scope of certain commercial activities of private enterprises for processing and manufacturing goods, and purchased and marketed all their prodtion also resulted in some undesirable effects as mentioned above: the quality of some industrial products fell off and there was less variety to choose from; the output of some agricultural products and products of subsidiary occupations decreased; the exchange of some commodities was hampered. We must overcome these defects. We should improve the present system of market control and abolish restrictions that are too strict and inflexible. Within the limits of the unified socialist market, we should permit a free market, subject to the guidance of the state, to exist and develop to a certain extent, and to supplement the state market.

For twelve years before the liberation our country was in the grip of severe inflation and commodity prices constantly fluctuated. In view of this, the Party's basic policy after the liberation was to stabilize commodity prices. That is to say, regardless of whether certain commodity prices were reasonable or not, the first thing to do was to stabilize the prices of various commodities at the levels then prevailing. After this had been done, readjustments were then made in regard to certain very unreasonable commodity prices. This basic policy of our Party was correct, and its implementation was crowned with success. It played a beneficial role in promoting the growth of the country's industrial and agricultural production. Nevertheless, there have been many mistakes and shortcomings in implementing our price policy. Commercial departments must sum up their past experience and, acting under the principle of continuing to stabilize commodity prices, work out a more comprehensive policy and price structure suited to present concrete conditions and beneficial to industrial and agricultural production. An important principle governing our price policy is to fix purchasing prices so that they help to increase production. In order to improve the quality of industrial and agricultural products, the policy of grading products and fixing prices according to quality must be carried out both in purchasing and marketing. If the difference between buying and selling prices of goods bought and sold locally is too big, it should be suitably reduced. The difference between wholesale and retail prices of low-priced petty commodities should be suitably increased. All attempts to extract excessive commercial profits in violation of the state's price policy must be strictly prohibited.

The importance of commercial work demands that all personnel engaged in it throughout the country must learn how to do business better. We must make a careful study of all the useful experience accumulated in the commercial field, and train the necessary cadres and experts according to plan, so as to raise socialist commerce in our country to a still higher level.

Culture and Education

Cultural and educational work occupies an important place in socialist construction as a whole. During the past few years, it has made great headway in our country. The enrolment in institutions of higher learning has increased from 116,000 in 1949 to 380,000, as planned, in 1956; in middle schools, from 1,268,000 to 5,860,000; and in primary schools, from 24,390,000 to some 57,700,000. The number of books printed has risen from over 100 million copies in the early period of liberation to 1,600 million this year; during the same period, the number of hospital and sanatorium beds has risen from 106,000 to 339,000.

The Second Five-Year Plan provides that the enrolment in institutions of higher learning should increase by about 100 per cent; the enrolment in secondary vocational schools, senior middle schools and junior middle schools should increase correspondingly. The Second Five-Year Plan requires that special efforts be made to step up the training of specialists and the development of scientific research, so that we may speedily master the latest scientific achievements of the world. Our scientists have already drawn up a preliminary overall plan for the development of science in 1956–1967. This plan lays it down that in those urgently-needed branches of science and technology we should approach the advanced levels in the world in about twelve years' time. We should firmly support all scientific research bodies and institutions of higher learning in their concerted effort to realize this aim.

To enable our science and art to flourish and serve the cause of socialist construction, the Central Committee of the Party has put forward the policy "Let flowers of many kinds blossom, let diverse schools of thought contend!" Scientific truth is such that the more it is subjected to argument, the clearer it becomes; while in art there must be room for diversity of styles. On questions of an academic or artistic nature, the Party should not rely on administrative orders to exercise its leadership; it should promote free discussion and free emulation to foster the development of science and art.

To bring our cultural revolution to fruition, we must do our best, step by step, to wipe out illiteracy. Furthermore, financial resources permitting, we must gradually expand our primary education, with a view to introducing in different areas and by stages universal, compulsory primary education within twelve years. At the same time, we must continue to strengthen general and technical education for workers and employees, and general education for that section of government workers whose educational level is rather low. We should help those national minorities who are without a written language to create one.

We should arm our intelligentsia and all our people with socialist, Marxist-Leninist ideology, and criticize feudal and bourgeois ideologies. We have done extensive work along these lines during the past few years, and this has contributed greatly to the success of socialist transformation in our country. But we all know that it is more difficult and it will take more time to change old ideologies than to transform old relations of production. We must continue to intensify our work on the ideological front. While criticizing feudal and bourgeois systems of thought, we must exercise great care in taking over what is of use to the people from the cultural heritage of the past.

In order to accomplish the various tasks set in culture and education, we must further expand and strengthen the ranks of our intellectuals. We must train an enormous number of new intellectuals, especially intellectuals of labouring-class origin, in the schools and by means of spare-time education for cadres. At the same time, we must enlist the services of bourgeois and petty-bourgeois intellectuals in building socialism and learn from them. However, we must not allow the bourgeois and petty-bourgeois ideas which they bring with them to corrupt the ranks of the proletariat. On the contrary, we must make every effort to help them become new intellectuals closely linked with the working people. Thanks to the systematic work our Party has done over a long period of time, the great bulk of our intellectuals have already formed a close alliance with the workers and peasants; a considerable number of the intellectuals have become believers in communism and have joined our Party. Our task from now on should be to carry through the policy of uniting, educating and remoulding the intellectuals, and make better use of them, so that they will render still more effective service to the great cause of building up our motherland.

IV. THE POLITICAL LIFE OF THE STATE

The fundamental question of the revolution is the question of state power. Why is it that we have been able to bring about a fundamental change in the face of our country and score such tremendous achievements in socialist transformation and socialist construction within the short space of seven years? Is it not because we have succeeded in leading the working class and the broad masses of people to seize political power throughout the country? Is it not because ours is an entirely new type of state power—the state power of the people's democratic dictatorship?

In order to develop on a large scale our socialist construction, which has already started, and to bring the socialist transformation in our country to completion, we must continue to consolidate the people's democratic dictatorship, and improve the work of the state.

The state founded by us, like that in other socialist countries, is the most democratic, the most efficient, and the most consolidated in the history of mankind. The founding of the People's Republic of China has lifted several hundred million people, hitherto insulted and injured, suffering from cold and hunger, from the position of slaves to the position of masters. Consequently, their life and liberty are now guaranteed, their labour is honoured, and women enjoy equal status with men. Large numbers of outstanding workers, peasants, women and youth participate in the administration of the state, thus turning our state organs into organs serving the people industriously and honestly. Our country is now united as never before. As a result of thorough democratic reform, and the victory in the suppression of counter-revolutionaries; of the achievements we have made in socialist transformation, and of the development in our socialist construction; and also because of other measures taken by the people's government, our society has reached an unprecedented state of stability.

All states in the world are, in essence, class dictatorships. The question is which classes exercise dictatorship over the other classes. All landlord-bourgeois states are the tools with which a minority rules over the majority, the exploiters rule over the labouring people. The great achievement of the Russian October Revolution is that it reversed this situation for the first time, turning the state into an instrument with which the majority rules over the minority, the labouring people rule over the exploiters. Despite the fact that the revolution in our country has many characteristics of its own, Chinese Communists regard the cause for which they work as the continuation of the great October Revolution. Our people's democratic dictatorship is the dictatorship of the masses of people, headed by the working class, over the reactionary classes, reactionary cliques and the exploiters who oppose the socialist revolution. Ours is a democracy that belongs not to a minority but to the overwhelming majority—to the workers, peasants and all other labouring people, as well as all those who support socialism and love their country.

The people's democratic dictatorship in our country has gone through the period of bourgeois-democratic revolution and is passing through the period of the socialist revolution. Before the nation-wide victory of the bourgeois-democratic revolution, the people's democratic dictatorship had already been established in the revolutionary bases. This dictatorship was meant to fulfil the task of the bourgeois-democratic revolution because it only brought about reforms in the feudal land system. It did not change the ownership of means of production by the national bourgeoisie, or individual ownership by the peasants. After the founding of the People's Republic of China, the people's democratic dictatorship began to shoulder the task of bringing about the transition from capitalism to socialism. That is to say, it was to change the private ownership of means of production by the bourgeoisie and the small producers into socialist, public ownership; and to eliminate in a thorough way the exploitation of man by man. Such state power, in its essence, can only be the dictatorship of the proletariat. Only when the proletariat, through its vanguard, the Chinese Communist Party, has employed this weapon of state power without the slightest hindrance and closely rallied around itself all the working people and all other forces that are ready to accept socialism, jointly to implement the line of policy of the proletariat and, on the one hand, build the economic and cultural life along the road to socialism and, on the other, suppress the resistance of reactionary classes and cliques and guard against the intervention of foreign imperialism, will it be able to fulfil this serious and complex task.

It is quite obvious: If without the leadership of the proletariat, our peasants and national bourgeoisie were not able to gain victory even in the stage of bourgeois-democratic revolution, then what social force other than the proletariat can take up the responsibility of such leadership in the stage of socialist revolution? Without the firm, far-sighted, impartial and selfless leadership of the proletariat, even the poverty-stricken peasants cannot really move towards socialism, much less the bourgeoisie, which, by nature, is utterly alien to socialism. The fact that our bourgeoisie has heralded its acceptance of socialist transformation with a fanfare of gongs and drums is something of a miracle. What this miracle shows is precisely the great strength of the correct leadership of the proletariat and the absolute need for the dictatorship of the proletariat.

Some people may ask: Since our people's democratic dictatorship at the present stage is in essence a form of the dictatorship of the proletariat, how is it that other classes, other parties and democratic personalities having no party affiliations participate in exercising state power? Why is it necessary that the people's democratic united front in our country should continue to exist?

We must realize that the dictatorship of the proletariat requires not only that the proletariat should exercise strong leadership over the state organs, but also that the broadest masses of the people should participate actively in the state organs. Neither of these can be dispensed with. The proletariat can establish the dictatorship of the great majority over the reactionary classes, and achieve socialism only by entering into an alliance with the broad masses of people who are capable of embracing socialism. Is this not perfectly clear? "The dictatorship of the proletariat," said Lenin, "is a special form of class alliance between the proletariat, the vanguard of the working people, and the numerous non-proletarian strata of working people (the petty-bourgeoisie, the small proprietors, the peasantry, the intelligentsia, etc.), or the majority of these; it is...an alliance aiming at the final establishment and consolidation of socialism." The scope of the class alliance spoken of by Lenin may vary with varying historical conditions, but there should be no doubt whatever that the dictatorship of the proletariat is always a definite form of alliance between classes.

The worker-peasant alliance is the basis of the people's democratic dictatorship and of the people's democratic united front in our country. Over 80 per cent of our whole population are peasants. It would be out of the question to realize socialism without an alliance with the peasantry. In the course of protracted revolutionary struggles, our Party entered into flesh-and-blood relations with the peasantry. Since the founding of the People's Republic we have paid attention to the further strengthening of these relations: in the land reform, in the movement for mutual aid and co-operation, in the guidance of agricultural production and economic and cultural affairs in the villages, in the formulation and implementation of tax, food and price policies. The peasantry has taken the important position due to it in the political life of our country. Practically all the working personnel in the numerous organs of state in the rural districts throughout the country are peasants. However, we must admit that the defect of not paying enough attention to the concrete interests of the peasantry is still by no means infrequent in our work. Since the realization of agricultural co-operation, the worker-peasant alliance has entered a new and more advanced stage. But at the same time, overestimation of the present economic capacity of the agricultural co-operatives by many Party organizations and organs of state and their abuse of the "conveniences" resulting from co-operation have given rise once more to a tendency towards bossiness in village work. In order to further consolidate the worker-peasant alliance, we must resolutely overcome these defects.

This policy towards the peasants likewise applies to handicraftsmen, small shopkeepers and pedlars, and other individual working people, who have recently joined various kinds of co-operatives. They too form an important social stratum in our country. Because they live and pursue their economic activities in scattered localities, our work among them has been rather inadequate. They have now organized themselves, and many urgent problems which they face have to be solved. We must take effective measures to strengthen our relations with them, so that proper attention may be given to their economic and political interests.

The national bourgeoisie occupies a special position in our people's democratic dictatorship and in our people's democratic united front. During the War of Resistance to Japanese Aggression, certain representative individuals from among the national bourgeoisie had already been brought into the government organs in the revolutionary bases. Since this was done during the period of bourgeois-democratic revolution, it was easy to understand. Since the founding of the People's Republic, even more representatives of the national bourgeoisie and its parties have been taking part in the organs of our state, which is a dictatorship of the proletariat in its character. Furthermore, they have continued to maintain the political alliance with the working class and the Communist Party in the building of socialism. How has this come about? What can be the meaning of such an alliance today, when socialist transformation has already been achieved in the main? Isn't it something of a burden?

True, our national bourgeoisie, including big, middle, and small capitalists and bourgeois intellectuals, constitutes a class which, next to the bureaucrat-bourgeoisie, has been the smallest in our society. Furthermore this class is very feeble both politically and economically. However, both now and in the past, it has always had a considerable influence and played an important role in our society. On the one hand, this is because, historically, it developed modern industry, and led the old democratic revolution; because it participated in the new-democratic revolution to a certain degree; and because, under the particular conditions obtaining after the founding of the Chinese People's Republic, it took the attitude of accepting the leadership of the working class and the Communist Party, and later gradually took the attitude of accepting socialist transformation. On the other hand, this is because, at a comparatively early date, this class became acquainted with modern knowledge, and some knowledge of technology and management of modern enterprises. Even today, it is a class which is comparatively rich in modern knowledge, and includes a comparatively large number of intellectuals and specialists. During the past few years, the national bourgeoisie has taken part in the rehabilitation of the national economy. It has participated in, or given support to, such struggles as the land reform, the suppression of counter-revolutionaries, and the Movement to Resist U.S. Aggression and Aid Korea. It has thus helped us to isolate the enemy to the greatest possible extent and has added to the strength of the revolution. In the course of socialist transformation, the alliance of the working class with the national bourgeoisie has played a positive role in educating and remoulding the bourgeois elements. In the future we can continue our work of uniting, educating and remoulding them through this alliance so that they may place their knowledge in the service of socialist construction. Thus, it can be readily seen that it is wrong to regard this alliance as a futile encumbrance.

In recent years, most of the national bourgeoisie have experienced the profound change of socialist transformation. Our task is to continue and to improve our co-operation with them, with a view to giving full play to their abilities and expert knowledge, and helping them to further remould themselves. Such co-operation should, as in the past, be at once uniting with them and waging struggles against them. Class struggle will go on until socialist transformation is completed. Even after that, there will still be struggles between socialist and capitalist stands, viewpoints and methods over a long period of time. Our principal ways of conducting such struggles are education and persuasion. It is only for the few individuals who adopt a hostile attitude towards socialism and violate laws of the state that necessary compulsory methods of reform are adopted in accordance with the circumstances in each case.

The democratic parties in our country were organized mainly during the War of Resistance to Japanese Aggression, and their relationship with our Party has long been one of co-operation. When the People's Republic of China was founded, they took part in the people's government. Thereafter, they came gradually to support the cause of socialism. It is our view that, from now on, a policy of long-term co-existence of the Communist Party and the democratic parties and of mutual supervision between them should be adopted. The social basis of China's democratic parties is the national bourgeoisie, the upper strata of the petty-bourgeoisie and intellectuals of these classes. After the completion of socialist transformation, members of the national bourgeoisie and the upper strata of the petty-bourgeoisie will become a section of the socialist working people; and the democratic parties will become parties of this section of the working people. Since survivals of bourgeois ideology will linger on for a long time in the minds of this part of working people, there will be need for the democratic parties, over a long period, to keep in touch with them, represent them, and help them to remould themselves. At the same time, as the democratic parties and the Communist Party will co-exist for a long time, the parties will be able to supervise each other. Our Party is not one that works for self-interest, it is one that places itself whole-heartedly in the service of the people. We still have shortcomings. It is certain that we shall have shortcomings even in the future; nor is it likely that we shall make no mistakes. Of course, to overcome these shortcomings and mistakes, we must, first of all, encourage more vigorous self-criticism within our Party, and rely on supervision by the masses of the working people as a whole. But at the same time, we should be adept in benefiting from supervision and criticism by members of all democratic parties, and by democrats without party affiliations.

Representatives of the democratic parties and democrats without party affiliations occupy important posts in many of our state organs. There are also a large number of non-Party personnel working in our government organs, schools, enterprises and armed forces. This situation requires that members of our Party establish good relations and work in co-operation with them. The reason why we must raise this question is that there are still some members of our Party who hold that everything should absolutely be "of one colour"; who are unwilling to see non-Party people work in state organs; who do not consult with them when circumstances require, and do not respect the authority that goes with their posts. This is a kind of sectarian viewpoint. The Communists, at any given time, constitute a minority of the people. Therefore they have the obligation to co-operate with non-Party people under all circumstances. The Party must teach its members who are not good at co-operating with non-Party people to speedily overcome such shortcomings. This, at present, is one of the important tasks in consolidating the people's democratic united front.

With the triumphant advance of the socialist cause in our country, the scope of our people's democratic united front will become ever broader. We must persist in uniting with individuals from the upper strata of the national minorities, patriotic people in religious circles, and other patriotic personalities who are influential in society in one way or another. We must continue to unite with patriotic Chinese living in various places abroad; they too are a component part of the united front. In short, our task is to mobilize all positive factors to contribute to the building of socialism.

It can be seen from this that the broadest united front and the broadest patriotic unity, instead of impairing our proletarian dictatorship, are conducive to its consolidation and development.

Our state system combines a high degree of democracy with a high degree of centralism. This system has shown its superiority during the last few years. Of course this does not mean that the work of the state is perfect and flawless. Many of our organs of state, and their functionaries, often depart, in their way of work, from the correct principles of our state system; they obstruct the vigour and strength of our state system instead of turning it to full account. Nor do we mean that our state system has perfected itself in every respect. It will still take a fairly long time for it to mature and perfect itself step by step.

What major tasks now confront us in improving our state administration?

In keeping with the new situation in socialist transformation and socialist construction, an important task in the work of the state today is to extend democracy and to carry on the struggle against bureaucracy.

There is bureaucracy in many of our state organs characterized by arm-chair leadership which does not understand and which suppresses the opinions of subordinates and the masses, and pays little attention to the life of the masses. Such bureaucracy takes the form of isolation from the masses and a break with reality, seriously hinders the growth of democracy in national life, hampers the unfolding of popular initiative, and holds back the advance of the cause of socialism. We must make earnest, systematic efforts to improve the work of state organs, trim and simplify their organizations, clearly define the responsibility of every government worker, and help functionaries to change such ways of work as busying themselves exclusively with holding meetings and signing documents without contacting the people or studying the relevant policies and the actual situation. We must work out concrete measures to ensure that responsible personnel of all departments of the Central People's Government, and of the provincial and municipal governments frequently visit subordinate organizations, acquaint themselves with their conditions, check upon the work done and listen to opinions. We must see to it that they strictly put these things into practice.

The struggle against bureaucracy will be a long one. But we are fully confident that, under our people's democracy, we shall gradually eliminate the bureaucratic vices. This is because our state is poles apart from the exploiters' states, in which a minority of the people oppress the majority, and because our system, instead of protecting bureaucracy, is opposed to it. In order to combat bureaucracy effectively, we must strengthen supervision of the work of the state through several channels at the same time.

Firstly, we must strengthen the leadership of state organs, and supervision over them, by the Party. Party committees at all levels must, from time to time, check up on the work of Party organizations within the government organs at all levels. Apart from this, all departments under Party committees should be responsible for constant supervision over Party organizations and Party members in the government departments concerned.

Secondly, we must reinforce supervision by the National People's Congress and its Standing Committee over the departments of the Central People's Government; and supervision by all local people's congresses over all local government organs. To achieve this end, the practice of inspection by the people's deputies must be strengthened, so that they can collect the opinions of the masses of the people in an extensive way. The people's congresses at all levels must do their utmost to examine, criticize and discuss the work done by the governments.

Thirdly, we must reinforce supervision over subordinates by superiors, and vice versa within government organs at all levels. In the struggle against bureaucracy, the supervisory organs of the state should fully carry out the role assigned to them.

Fourthly, we must strengthen supervision by the masses of the people, and by the low-ranking government workers, over the organs of state. Criticisms and exposures from below must be encouraged and supported. Those who suppress people making criticism or avenge themselves on the critics must be duly punished.

Another important problem in state administration today is the need to properly readjust the administrative powers and functions of the central and local authorities. This also accords with the needs of extending democratic life and overcoming bureaucracy.

With the founding of the People's Republic of China, in order to establish and consolidate the unity of the country, we opposed departmentalism; we concentrated in the hands of the central authority a large number of affairs which should come within the province of the central authority. This was absolutely necessary, but during the past few years, some departments under the central authority have taken on too many jobs and imposed too many or too rigid restrictions on local departments and ignored special circumstances and conditions in the localities. Even when they should have consulted with the local authorities they did not do so. Some departments issued too many formalistic documents and forms, imposing too much of a burden on the local authorities. This not only did not facilitate the work of the local authorities, but dissipated the energies of the central authority and fostered the growth of bureaucracy. It is unthinkable that, in such a big country as ours, the central authority could take on itself all the various jobs of the state and do them well. It is absolutely necessary for the central authority to devolve some of its administrative powers and functions onto the local authorities. As regards a good deal of the work of the state, such as agriculture, small and medium industries, local transport, local commerce, primary and secondary education, local health services, local finance, and so forth, the central authority should only put forward general principles and policies and map out general plans, while the actual work should be referred to the local authorities for them to make arrangements for carrying it out in a manner suitable to a particular place and a particular time. Some of the cadres working in the central organs should also be sent to work in the localities. The provinces, municipalities, counties and townships should be given a definite range of administrative powers and functions. On the basis of such a principle, the central authority, in conjunction with the local authorities, is now making a study of the problem, drawing up a concrete plan and preparing to put it step by step into practice. In this way, the initiative of both the central organs and the local organs will be brought into full play, and both the central and local authorities will have the necessary flexibility; and it will also be more convenient for them to carry out mutual supervision. This is of great importance in pushing forward socialist construction on every front in our country.

It is an important task in the conduct of state affairs to deal correctly with questions concerning the national minorities. We must put still greater efforts into helping the national minorities make economic and cultural progress so that they can fully play a positive part in the socialist construction of our country.

Very great changes have taken place in the conditions of the national minorities in the past few years. In most areas a decisive victory has been won in democratic reform and socialist transformation within the national minorities. Of the more than 35 million people of the national minorities in China, 28 million inhabit areas where socialist transformation has been basically completed; 2.2 million inhabit areas where socialist transformation is being carried out; and nearly 2 million inhabit areas which are undertaking democratic reforms; thus only some 3 million still inhabit areas which have not yet carried out democratic reforms. In the future, in regions which still await democratic reform and socialist transformation, we must continue to pursue the prudent policy we have been pursuing all along. That is to say, all reforms must be deliberated in an unhurried manner and settled through consultation by the people and the public leaders of the nationality concerned, the settlement being in accord with the wishes of the nationality itself. In carrying out reform, peaceful means must be persisted in, and no violent struggle should be resorted to. In regard to the members of the upper strata of the national minorities, after they have given up exploiting and oppressing the working people, the state will take appropriate measures to see that they do not suffer as regards political treatment or in their standards of living, and will convince the people of the need for co-operation with them for a long time to come. In regard to religious beliefs in the areas of the national minorities, we must continuously and persistently adhere to the policy of freedom of religious belief and must never interfere in that connection during social reform. We should help those who live by religion as a profession to find a proper solution of any difficulties of livelihood with which they are faced.

In order that the national minorities may grow into modern nationalities, the most fundamental thing, the key, besides carrying out social reforms, is to develop modern industries in the areas they inhabit. During the First Five-Year Plan period, the state has established a number of new industrial bases in some national minority areas and started a number of large-scale modern industries and transport services. It will continue to do so in the period of the Second Five-Year Plan. This is in accord with the common and fundamental interests of the people of all nationalities in the country. The people of Han nationality and all minority nationalities should work hard together for the complete realization of this state plan. At the same time, to meet the special needs of the minority peoples, central ministries and departments and provincial governments and governments of the autonomous areas should step by step start up a number of local industries in areas inhabited by the national minorities, observing the principle of keeping within the objective possibilities and not going beyond what is economically justified. In all industries in these areas, whether they are state-owned under the central authority or are run by local authorities, attention must be paid to helping the national minorities to form their own working class and create their own scientific-technical and administrative personnel. Only thus can the national minorities achieve modern levels in their development in all fields at a relatively rapid rate.

Owing to actual conditions created by history, the national minorities stand in need of large-scale aid by the people of Han nationality in carrying out social reform and in economic and cultural construction. Hence the continued improvement of relations between the Han and minority peoples and between the Han and minority cadres assumes particular importance. At present, in order to improve these relations, the main thing is to overcome great-Hanism.

In the past few years, a great many Han cadres have been working in areas inhabited by the national minorities. Most of them correctly followed the Party's policy towards nationalities, fulfilled the tasks assigned them by the Party, and earned the appreciation of the national minorities. But there have also been a section of Han cadres who did not respect the authority that goes with the posts of the minority cadres and their opinions and, instead of patiently helping the national minorities run their own house, simply took everything into their own hands. These shortcomings and mistakes are attributable to the tendency of great-Hanism existing in the minds of some comrades, a tendency to look down upon the national minorities.

As all the nationalities in China have worked side by side to give the country her history and her culture, so too in future they will certainly work side by side to build our great socialist motherland. While the levels attained by China's national minorities in their development vary, it is absolutely not true that all of them are backward in all aspects. Some of them have attained the same or roughly the same level as the Han nationality, others have attained a higher level in one or another respect, and it is worthwhile for the Han people to learn from them. Each nationality has its own strong points. The idea that the national minorities are good at nothing and are inferior to the Han nationality in everything is a viewpoint characteristic of great-Hanism.

To overlook the important part played by the national minorities in the socialist construction of our country is another manifestation of great-Hanism. Although the minority peoples constitute only 6 per cent of the country's total population, the areas inhabited by them roughly amount to 60 per cent of the country's total area. Many of these areas are rich in various kinds of industrial resources. It is clearly wrong to think that our country can be built into a great socialist country through the efforts of the Han people alone, without the concerted efforts and active participation of the national minorities.

All such great-Hanist tendencies and viewpoints as mentioned above must be effectively corrected. Only by overcoming even the slightest manifestation of great-Hanism will it be possible to successfully overcome the sentiments of local nationalism among the national minorities and to enable all the fraternal nationalities to unite all the more closely in our big family of the people's democracy.

In order to consolidate our people's democratic dictatorship, to preserve order for socialist construction and safeguard the people's democratic rights, and to punish counter-revolutionaries and other criminals, one of the urgent tasks facing our state at present is to begin the systematic codification of a fairly complete set of laws and to put the legal system of the country on a sound footing.

During the period of revolutionary war and in the early days after the liberation of the country, in order to weed out the remnants of our enemies, to suppress the resistance of all counter-revolutionaries, to destroy the reactionary order and to establish revolutionary order, the only expedient thing to do was to draw up some temporary laws in the nature of general principles in accordance with the policy of the Party and the people's government. During this period, the chief aim of the struggle was to liberate the people from reactionary rule and to free the productive forces of society from the bondage of old relations of production. The principal method of struggle was to lead the masses in direct action. Such laws in the nature of general principles were thus suited to the needs of the time. Now, however, the period of revolutionary storm and stress is past, new relations of production have been set up, and the aim of our struggle is changed into one of safeguarding the successful development of the productive forces of society, a corresponding change in the methods of struggle will consequently have to follow, and a complete legal system becomes an absolute necessity. It is necessary, in order to maintain a normal social life and to foster social production, that everyone in the country should understand and be convinced that as long as he does not violate the laws, his civil rights are guaranteed and will suffer no encroachment by any organization or any individual. Should his civil rights be unlawfully encroached upon, the state will certainly intervene. All state organs must strictly observe the law, and our security departments, procurator's offices and courts must conscientiously carry out the system of division of function and mutual supervision in legal affairs.

The counter-revolutionaries are bent on undermining our state and our construction and endangering the security of the people, so it is the duty of our state organs to suppress and weed out counter-revolutionaries. In 1950, we led a nation-wide struggle for the suppression of counter-revolutionaries and dealt their activities a severe blow. In 1955, we carried out another struggle against counter-revolutionaries in the country at large and we ferreted out counter-revolutionaries hidden in public organizations throughout the country. As a result of these large-scale mass campaigns, social order has been greatly improved and national security strengthened.

In dealing with counter-revolutionaries and other criminals, we have all along followed the policy of combining punishment with leniency. All those who make honest confessions, repent of their crimes and make some amends by doing something to their credit, receive lenient treatment. As everyone knows, this policy has achieved great results. Since the second half of last year, because of the effect of this policy of combining punishment with leniency, because of the upsurge of socialist transformation, and because the masses of the people have a higher level of political consciousness and are better organized, counter-revolutionaries have met with increasing difficulties in their activities. As a result, a sharp split has taken place among the counter-revolutionaries. Whole batches of counter-revolutionaries have given themselves up to the government. This fact proves on the one hand that there are counter-revolutionaries still at large and it is absolutely wrong to think that we can relax our vigilance; and on the other hand, that so long as our policy is correct, counter-revolutionaries can be wiped out, and there are no grounds for the belief that counter-revolutionary activities are getting more serious.

Our public security organs, our procurator's offices and our courts must continue to wage a determined struggle against counter-revolutionaries and other criminals. But, as has been mentioned above, this struggle must be conducted with strict observance of the law, and, in accordance with the new situation which obtains today, further steps must be taken to put the policy of leniency into practice. The Central Committee of the Party holds that, with the exception of a handful of criminals who have to be condemned to death in response to public indignation caused by their atrocious crimes, no offenders should be given the death penalty, and, while serving their terms of imprisonment, they should be accorded absolutely humane treatment. All cases involving the death penalty should be decided upon or sanctioned by the Supreme People's Court. In this way step by step we shall be able to achieve our aim of completely abolishing the death penalty, and this is all to the good of our socialist construction.

Furthermore, in order to defend our country, we must continue to strengthen our national defence, we must continue to strengthen our national defence army—the glorious Chinese People's Liberation Army. The People's Liberation Army must strive to raise its fighting capacity to a higher level, guard our frontiers and coast lines vigilantly and defend our territorial integrity.

Our motherland's territory Taiwan is still under the occupation of the U.S. imperialists. This is a most serious threat to the security of our country. The liberation of Taiwan is entirely China's internal affair. We are willing to bring Taiwan back to the embrace of the motherland through the peaceful means of negotiation, and avoid the use of force. If force has to be used, it would only be when all possibilities for peaceful negotiation have been exhausted or when peaceful negotiations have failed. Whatever means we adopt, we shall win the ultimate victory in the just cause of liberating Taiwan.

V. INTERNATIONAL RELATIONS

In order to build our country into a great socialist state, we must not only unite with all the forces at home that can be united with, we must also strive to bring about all favourable international conditions and unite with all forces throughout the world that can be united with.

What is the international situation in which our country now finds itself?

Generally speaking, the present international situation is favourable to our socialist construction. This is because since the Second World War the forces of socialism, national independence, democracy and peace have grown to an unprecedented extent, whereas the policy pursued by the imperialist aggressive bloc for active expansion, for opposing peaceful co-existence and for preparing a new world war, has become increasingly unpopular. In these conditions, the world situation cannot but lead to a relaxation of tension; lasting world peace is beginning to become a possibility.

There was no other socialist country in the world when the people of the Soviet Union embarked upon their socialist construction after the October Revolution, but the conditions are fundamentally different now when the people of our country are carrying on socialist construction. After the Second World War, not only has the Soviet Union become more powerful, but many new socialist countries have come into being in Europe and Asia. The socialist countries, including China, have a combined population of over nine hundred million—one-third of the world's total population and are geographically linked together as one vast expanse of land, forming a big family of fraternal, socialist countries headed by the Soviet Union. The fraternal friendship, mutual assistance and co-operation that exist among us are being constantly developed and consolidated. The Soviet Union and other socialist countries have re-established friendly relations with the Federal People's Republic of Yugoslavia. Our country has also established diplomatic relations and developed friendly intercourse with the Federal People's Republic of Yugoslavia.

At the present time, the socialist countries are mobilizing all the efforts of their peoples at home in the service of peaceful socialist construction; their industrial and agricultural production is forging ahead at a rate which the capitalist countries can hardly equal. In our foreign relations, we consistently follow a fixed policy of peace and advocate peaceful co-existence and friendly co-operation among all nations. We believe in the superiority of the socialist system and we are not afraid to engage in peaceful competition with capitalist countries. Our policy accords with the interests of all the peoples of the world. All forces that love peace, demand national independence and strive for social progress will have our sympathy and support. The socialist countries enjoy ever increasing prestige among the peoples throughout the world and are exerting an ever greater influence on the development of the international situation. The socialist countries headed by the Soviet Union have become a stout bulwark in the struggle for lasting world peace.

The Twentieth Congress of the Communist Party of the Soviet Union, held last February, was an important political event of world significance. It not only drew up the Sixth Five-Year Plan of gigantic proportions, decided on many important policies and principles for further development of the cause of socialism and repudiated the cult of the individual which had had grave consequences inside the Party. It also advocated further promotion of peaceful co-existence and international co-operation, making an outstanding contribution to the easing of international tension.

The strength and monolithic solidarity of the socialist countries constitute a most favourable international condition for the socialist construction of our country.

Another development of great historic significance after the Second World War is the extensive victories gained in the movement for national independence. Besides the Democratic Republic of Viet-Nam, the Democratic People's Republic of Korea and the People's Republic of China which have already taken the road to socialism, there are a number of countries in Asia and Africa which have shaken off the colonial bondage and achieved national independence. These nationally independent countries, our great neighbour India included, have a total population of more than 600 million, or one-fourth of the human race. The overwhelming majority of these countries are all pursuing a peaceful, neutral foreign policy. They are playing a growing role in world affairs. The success of the Asian and African Conference at Bandung, and the new developments in the national independence movements in many Asian and African countries, especially the recent world-shaking event—the nationalization of the Suez Canal Company by Egypt—prove that the movement for national independence has become a formidable world force. In the past, most of the countries in Asia and Africa were colonies or semi-colonies of imperialism and were converted by the imperialists into their rear in preparing and waging wars. But now these countries have become forces opposing colonialism and war, and upholding peaceful co-existence. In the meantime, the struggle against colonialism is also spreading in the Latin American countries. The imperialists are doing their utmost to hold back the rising tide of the national independence movement. But this tide cannot be held back. It will, in the end, sweep over the whole of Asia, Africa and Latin America, and thus put an end to the rule of colonialism once and for all.

There can be no doubt that the existence of the socialist countries and their sympathy and support for the national independence movement have greatly facilitated the development and victory of this movement. At the same time, the upsurge of the national independence movement has likewise weakened the imperialist forces of aggression. This is favourable to the cause of world peace, and therefore favourable to the peaceful construction of the socialist countries. That is why the friendship and co-operation between the socialist countries and the nationally independent countries conform not only to their common interests but to the interests of world peace as well.

These great historical changes run counter to the desires of imperialism, especially U.S. imperialism. U.S. monopoly capital, taking advantage of the favourable position it gained as a result of the wealth amassed by it during the Second World War, has engaged in frantic expansionist activities after the war, first and foremost, to gain control over the vanquished countries—Germany, Japan, etc., to seize the spheres of influence of Britain, France and other countries in Asia and Africa, and has done its utmost to dominate the world. It has organized military blocs, established military bases, created international tension, and prepared for a new war. U.S. imperialism describes all these activities as "defence against communist aggression." But, after all, lies cannot cover up facts. Aggression is utterly incompatible with socialism. In socialist countries, the class depending upon aggression, colonies and foreign markets for their fortunes has been eliminated, and the social roots of aggression against foreign countries have, therefore, been completely destroyed. In imperialist countries, on the other hand, those groups which depend upon aggression to make their fortunes will never, of their own accord, desist from aggression. The facts are very clear to the people of the world. The Soviet Union, China, and the other socialist countries actively champion the principle of peaceful co-existence, and the development of economic and cultural relations between East and West, and these countries have taken the lead in reducing their armed forces and military expenditures. U.S. imperialism is doing just the opposite; it continues with its arms drive, opposes the development of East-West relations, and fears peaceful co-existence as it does doomsday. At this very moment, U.S. armed forces are still occupying China's Taiwan and overrunning the territories of Japan, South Korea, the Philippines and the countries of Western Europe, all of which are thousands of kilometres away from the borders of the United States.

The use of the slogan of "defence against communism" and "fighting communism" as a smoke screen to cover up the attempt of a country to dominate the world was already prevalent even before the Second World War. Naturally the imperialists nurse extreme hatred for the socialist countries. But they too know that the socialist countries, strong and united as one, cannot be shaken. Therefore, the main activities of U.S. imperialism at present are actually, under the pretext of "fighting communism," to suppress its own people, and, as far as possible, to control and interfere in the vast areas lying between the socialist countries and the United States.

These activities of the U.S. imperialists have met with increasing opposition from all quarters, and have further intensified the inherent contradictions within the capitalist system itself. The countries and peoples which once suffered, or are suffering, from colonialism are becoming increasingly aware that U.S. imperialists are today the biggest colonialists, and the most predatory. In Asia and in Africa, an ever growing number of nationally independent countries have adopted the policy of peace and neutrality, refusing to join the aggressive military blocs of the United States. This has put a powerful check on the colonial expansion of U.S. imperialism. Among the Western nations, too, an ever larger number have gradually come to realize the real damage done to them by the expansionist policy of the United States. Neutralist tendencies on the part of these nations are also growing with each passing day. They refuse to let themselves be tied to the American war-chariot and they favour, instead, peaceful co-existence with socialist countries. Britain and France, the two major allies of the United States, once hoped to maintain their vested interests by relying upon the power of the United States. But in fact, trailing after the U.S. policy of arms drive and war preparations has only exposed them to penetration by American influence, while the heavy burden of military expenditure has an increasingly harmful effect on the development of their national economies. This has in turn intensified the dissatisfaction with and opposition to American monopoly and American domination on the part of the major allies of the United States, and has particularly intensified the contradictions between Britain and the United States. At the same time, among the broad masses of the people in various Western countries, the movements for peace and democracy, in opposition to the U.S. policy of arms drive and war preparations, are expanding on an ever wider scale. The American people themselves have gradually come to realize what back-breaking burdens this policy has imposed on them, and the peril of war it has brought. Even inside the ruling circles of the United States, there is a section of more sober-minded people who are becoming more and more aware that the policy of war may not, after all, be to America's advantage.

The foreign policy of the ruling circles of Britain and France has now bogged down in a morass of contradictions and confusion. Under the impact of the existing international situation as a whole, Britain and France have to some extent expressed their desire for peaceful co-existence, but still attempting to cling to the privileges of colonialism. They are unwilling to abandon the policy of resorting to force and the threat of force against the national independence movements. This has been particularly clearly shown by developments since the government of Egypt took back the Suez Canal Company. The British and French governments plan to resort to military intervention to violate the sacred sovereignty of Egypt and seize the Suez Canal again. The United States supports the aggressive actions of Britain and France on the one hand while on the other, it attempts to take advantage of the situation to seize their interests in the Middle East. The struggle between the aggressive policy of imperialism and the anti-aggression movement of nationally independent states is being intensified in the Middle East. Egypt has the widespread sympathy all over the world. Public opinion throughout the world demands a peaceful settlement of the dispute over the Suez Canal. If, instead of following the road of peaceful settlement, Britain and France choose to carry out armed intervention, they will not only meet with the heroic resistance of the Egyptian people and the people of the Arab countries but inevitably they will arouse the resolute opposition of the broad masses of the people of the whole camp of socialism, the people of Asia and Africa and Latin America and the people of the Western countries as well as the resolute opposition of the broad masses of the people of Britain and France themselves. The world is heading for peace. The policy of armed intervention on the question of the Suez Canal, and indeed on all other questions relating to the national independence movements can only result in utter failure.

There can be no doubt that the imperialists will continue to create tense situations, that they will continue to oppress all peoples whom it is within their power to oppress, and that the danger of war still exists. We shall be making a mistake if we slacken our vigilance on this point. In its struggle for peace and progress, mankind has still to traverse a most tortuous and devious path. But the overall outlook for the world is a bright one. Given the solidarity and the concerted efforts of the forces of the socialist countries and the forces for peace and democracy the world over, lasting peace for the world and the cause of human progress will eventually triumph.

Our firm and steadfast policy in international affairs is to strive for world peace and human progress. During the past few years, our efforts in this respect have been fruitful.

During their revolutionary struggle, the Chinese people had the support of the camp of peace, democracy and socialism, headed by the Soviet Union. Shortly after the founding of the People's Republic of China, we concluded a Treaty of Friendship, Alliance and Mutual Assistance with the great Soviet Union. Events over the past few years have shown that the great alliance between China and the Soviet Union is a main pillar of peace in the Far East and the world. The Soviet Union has given great assistance to socialist construction in our country; and the People's Democracies in Europe and Asia have also given us help in various ways. The Chinese people will never forget this comradely assistance from fraternal countries. Such assistance has been and will always be indispensable to us. The unity and friendship between China, the great Soviet Union and the other socialist countries, built upon the basis of a community of objectives and mutual assistance, is unbreakable and eternal. To further consolidate and strengthen this unity and friendship is our supreme international duty, and is the basis of our foreign policy.

China has herself suffered from the scourge of colonialism. China's territory, Taiwan, is even now under the control of the United States. The Chinese people deeply sympathize with and actively support the struggle which all oppressed peoples and all countries that are suffering from aggression are waging against colonialism and for national independence. Every victory won in this struggle, whether in Asia, Africa or in Latin America, will further strengthen the forces of peace.

China has much in common in past experience, in present circumstances, and in cherished hopes, with the other countries of Asia and Africa which have just freed themselves from the rule of colonialism. In international relations in general, and in our mutual relations in particular, we all share the desire for mutual respect for territorial integrity and sovereignty, non-aggression, non-interference in each other's internal affairs, equality and mutual benefit, and peaceful co-existence. These common desires are embodied in the five principles initiated by China and India. Acting on these principles, we have already established ties of friendship and co-operation with many Asian and African countries, thereby promoting peace in this area.

On the basis of the five principles we are striving, in the first place, to establish good neighbourly relations with all neighbouring countries. We have profound and traditional friendships with these countries and there is no dispute between us that cannot be settled. There exist between our country and some neighbouring countries certain questions left over from the past. The imperialists are doing their utmost to take advantage of this situation to undermine and disrupt our efforts to develop or establish friendly relations with neighbouring countries. But this attempt is doomed to failure. All questions between China and her neighbouring countries can be settled by peaceful negotiation in accordance with the five principles. The development or establishment of friendly relations between China and her neighbouring countries is in our interests as well as theirs.

Our country has already established normal relations with a number of Western countries in Europe.

Our country is prepared to establish normal diplomatic relations with all of those countries which have not yet established diplomatic relations with our country. We believe that the establishment of such relations is beneficial to both sides.

Our policy of peaceful co-existence based on the five principles does not exclude any country. We have the same desire for peaceful co-existence with the United States. But the United States has been consistently hostile to our country. It has occupied our territory Taiwan, sent spies into our country to engage in subversive activities, imposed an embargo on our country, done its utmost to bar us from international affairs, and insolently deprived us of our country's rightful place in the United Nations. Despite all this, our government has made efforts to settle our disputes with the United States by peaceful negotiation. We have repeatedly proposed a conference between the foreign ministers of China and the United States to settle the question of easing as well as eliminating the tension in the Taiwan area. Our efforts in this connection are made solely for the purpose of easing international tension, and by no means signify acquiescence in aggression. As the whole world knows, the Chinese people will not hesitate to make sacrifices to safeguard the independence and security of their motherland. But even now, the attitude of the United States government towards us is far from realistic or reasonable. And what is the result? Despite the fact that the U.S. imperialists have resorted to all kinds of vicious means to disrupt our country and attempted to isolate us, the great New China stands firm on its feet in this world. Justice is on our side; world-wide sympathy is with us. It is not we that stand isolated in the world, but precisely the U.S. imperialists themselves. If the U.S. imperialists do not want to suffer further setbacks, their only way out is to adopt a realistic, reasonable attitude towards our country. This fact is no longer a secret even to the Americans themselves.

The Chinese people and all the peoples of the world need peace. They all want to promote economic and cultural relations and friendly contacts with one another. In the past few years the Chinese people have participated actively in all kinds of international activities beneficial to world peace. We have actively developed economic and cultural exchanges with the peoples of various countries. We have also increased our contacts with the people's organizations and personages of every walk of life in various countries. Though we have come up against many man-made obstacles in all these activities, every day we are winning more friends all over the world. Facts prove that the iron curtain is not on our side; our doors are wide open to all.

Such is the basic policy which we have followed in dealing with international affairs. We shall continue to carry out this policy.

VI. THE LEADERSHIP OF THE PARTY

During the period from the Seventh to the Eighth National Congress of the Party, along with the victory of the revolution and the changes that have taken place in the situation of our country, there have also been great changes in the Party itself. It is now a party that leads the state power over the whole country and it enjoys very high prestige among the masses of the people. The Party organization has grown; it has a membership of 10,730,000, of whom 14 per cent come from the ranks of the workers, 69 per cent from the peasantry and 12 per cent from the intellectuals. Party organizations are spread throughout the country, and among the various nationalities as well. The overwhelming majority of Party members have been tempered in great revolutionary struggles. Even the new members who joined the Party after 1949—and who constitute more than 60 per cent of the membership—are, in the main, outstanding and active elements who have come forward in the mass revolutionary struggles and in socialist labour over the last few years. On the whole, the Party is more closely bound to the masses of the people; it has gained richer and more comprehensive experience in its work; and never before has its unity been as strong as it is today.

As we have said before, the cause of socialism in our country cannot do without the dictatorship of the proletariat which is realized through the leadership of the party of the proletariat—the Communist Party. The strength of leadership of the Chinese Communist Party lies in the fact that it is armed ideologically with Marxism-Leninism, is correct in its political and organizational lines, rich in experience in struggle and in work, skilled in crystallizing the wisdom of the people of the whole country and turning that wisdom into a united will and disciplined action. And not only in the past, but in the future too, the leadership of such a party is essential in order to ensure that our country can deal effectively with complex domestic and international affairs. This view is shared by all sections of the people and democratic parties in our country as a result of their experience in life.

Nevertheless, in the work of our socialist construction there are comrades, though very few, who have tried to weaken the leading role of the Party. They confuse the question of the Party giving leadership in various spheres of state affairs in regard to principles and policies with the question of purely technical matters; they think that since the Party is still a layman in the technical side of these things, it should not exercise leadership over such work, while they themselves can go on taking arbitrary action. We have criticized this wrong viewpoint. In all work the Party should and can play a leading role ideologically, politically and in matters of principle and policy. Of course, that does not mean that the Party should take everything into its own hands, or interfere in everything. Neither does it mean that it should be content with being a layman in things it does not understand. The Party calls on its cadres and members to study painstakingly in order to master the things they do not understand in their work. For the more we study, the better will we be able to lead.

As we have said before, the line followed by the Party since its Seventh Congress has been correct and this has been proved by facts. But it must be admitted that in shouldering the increasingly heavy tasks of today the Party is not without difficulties, nor will it make no mistakes. In the sphere of socialist transformation and socialist construction and in the political life of the country, we have had shortcomings and made mistakes of a temporary nature and of limited scope. In handling international affairs we have also not been entirely free from shortcomings and mistakes. Therefore, one of the tasks confronting the Party leadership is to study and analyse past mistakes, draw lessons from them, so as to be able to make fewer mistakes in our future work, and, as far as possible, avoid repeating past mistakes, and prevent small mistakes from developing into big ones.

To enable our Party to continue to maintain its correct and sound leadership in the future, the main thing is to see to it that Party organizations and Party members make fewer ideological mistakes. There are struggles in our Party between correct ideology and wrong ideology and between the correct line and the wrong line. These struggles are the reflection of the class struggle and various social phenomena. Since the petty-bourgeoisie originally constituted the majority of the population of our country, the feelings and sentiments of this class often influence us, and constantly exert pressure on us. The bourgeoisie likewise influences us in various ways. The Party must constantly carry on inner-Party education so as to prevent the bourgeois and petty-bourgeois ideologies from impairing its political purity. Our mistakes have not only social roots, but also ideological roots. If a person does not understand that a correct understanding of things can only be based on an objective and all-round reflection of reality, but insists on acting according to his own subjective and one-sided approach to things, then he will go on making mistakes, great or small, even though his intentions are good. In order to prevent mistakes, therefore, the basic thing is to acquire an accurate knowledge of objective reality, and correctly differentiate between right and wrong.

In view of the fact that at present nine out of ten of our members joined the Party after the Seventh Congress, we think it will not be without practical value to review briefly the basic experience in the history of the Party showing how the correct line effectively overcame the wrong one.

During the thirty-five years of its existence, our Party has four times made serious mistakes in its line: namely, the mistakes of Chen Tu-hsiu's Rightist-opportunist line in the first half of 1927 and the mistakes of the "Leftist"-opportunist line on three occasions in the following seven years. But during the twenty-one years since the Tsunyi Conference of January 1935, our Party, under the leadership of the Central Committee headed by Comrade Mao Tse-tung, has not made any mistake in its line. How can this historical change be explained? Quite obviously, it cannot be explained merely by the length of the Party's existence, or the amount of experience gained by the Party, for the mistakes committed by the Party between 1931 and 1934 were even more serious than the "Leftist" mistakes twice committed before. Neither can it be explained merely by the personal qualities of the leading personnel of the Party in a certain period, for the majority of the leading personnel who had previously made mistakes later did good work for the Party. The history of the Party leads us to this conclusion: the amount of experience gained by the Party and the choice of leaders do have an important bearing on whether the Party makes mistakes, but what is more important is whether the rank-and-file Party members, and primarily the high-ranking cadres, can, in the various periods, apply the Marxist-Leninist stand, viewpoint and method to sum up experience in the struggle, hold fast to the truth and correct mistakes. This is the primary criterion by which the level of Marxist-Leninist understanding of Party cadres is judged. The higher the level of Marxist-Leninist understanding of Party cadres, the greater will be their ability to distinguish between correct and wrong opinions, between good and bad leading personnel, and the greater will be their ability in work.

Before 1934, the Party had accumulated rich experience, but its leading organs at the time did not make a serious study of it. Although the Party on several occasions repudiated the wrong lines, in practice it confined itself to taking disciplinary measures against the leading personnel who had made mistakes; it did not make a correct analysis of these mistakes nor point out how these mistakes had stemmed from their ideological understanding, and thus it failed to help the Party cadres to raise the level of their understanding. Particularly during the years 1931-1934 when the "Leftist" opportunists headed by Wang Ming and Po Ku and other comrades held sway in the Party, they failed to learn lessons from the mistaken lines followed on several occasions in the past; moreover, their dogmatic way of thinking and their high-handed arbitrary way of doing things increased the mistakes of subjectivism and sectarianism to proportions unheard of in the history of our Party. They adopted extremely adventurist policies both in political and in military affairs, completely disregarding the actual conditions of the various classes of our country at that time and ignoring the relative strength of our side compared with that of the enemy. In inner-Party life, too, they completely wrecked the democratic system within the Party and waged unbridled inner-Party struggles. Their mistaken leadership caused serious defeats in the revolutionary struggle, and resulted in the loss of 90 per cent of the revolutionary bases and of the Workers' and Peasants' Red Army, and of practically all the Party organizations and revolutionary organizations led by the Party in Kuomintang-controlled areas.

But things have been different since 1935. This change which the Party underwent in 1935 comes about chiefly from the fact that the majority of the high-ranking Party cadres had raised their level of political understanding by learning from the experience of their failures. After that, instead of meting out severe punishment to comrades who had made mistakes, the Central Committee of the Party still assigned them to suitable leading posts. The Party patiently waited for and helped these comrades to recognize their mistakes ideologically. Furthermore, the Central Committee of the Party systematically helped all Party cadres to gradually grasp the principle of integrating Marxist-Leninist theory with practice and to understand the principle that our subjective knowledge must conform to objective reality. Thanks to the great improvement in the Party's ideological and organizational work, the cause of the Party had a speedy development. In order to help all Party cadres, including comrades who had made mistakes, make an earnest study of the historical experience of the Party and master the correct method of thinking and of work so as to make fewer mistakes, the Central Committee of the Party, seven years after the Tsunyi Conference, launched throughout the Party the famous "Rectification Campaign" to combat subjectivism, sectarianism and Party jargon. In the course of the campaign, all Party cadres carefully checked up on their own ideology and work, checked up on the Party's leadership on the ideological, political and organizational planes and conducted sharp criticism and self-criticism—all in accordance with the Marxist-Leninst stand, viewpoint and method. This raised the level of Marxist understanding of large numbers of Party cadres and improved their ability to distinguish between right and wrong within the Party. Large numbers of cadres began to understand the mistakes caused by doctrinairism which represents a divorce from reality, and the mistakes of empiricism which represents a divorce from theory. They adopted the style of work based on maintaining a close contact with the masses, conducting investigations and studies, and seeking the truth from a study of facts. They were thus able to do their work both within and without the Party more in conformity with reality and fewer major mistakes were made.

The above-mentioned historical experience gained by our Party fully demonstrates that, in order to ensure the smooth advance of the Party's work and to avoid major mistakes, the key lies in overcoming subjectivism ideologically.

At the present time serious mistakes of subjectivism are found in the thought and work of many cadres; they have caused losses to our work which could have been avoided. We are now confronted with new conditions and new tasks, and we must solve many problems which are more complicated than those of the past, and with which we are unfamiliar. Under such circumstances, subjectivist mistakes will inevitably grow if we do not endeavour to raise the level of our Marxist-Leninist understanding, do not strive to acquire new knowledge, do not diligently learn new ways of work, but instead rest content with praise for our past victories. At the same time, the great multitude of new members who have joined our Party have not yet received adequate training in Marxism-Leninism. It is also very easy for them to fall under the influence of subjectivism and doctrinairism.

In order to effectively combat subjectivism, it is necessary to make systematic efforts to raise the Marxist-Leninist level of our Party. Firstly, we must make serious effort to intensify the systematic study of Marxism-Leninism by our cadres, primarily our high-ranking cadres. This will enable them to become adept at applying the Marxist-Leninist stand, viewpoint and method, in observing and solving problems in actual life; increase their ability to keep their bearings and distinguish between right and wrong in complex situations; and know how to study and sum up their own working experience with the aid of Marxist-Leninist theory and derive from experience a knowledge of the laws governing the development of things. Secondly, it is necessary to step up the teaching of integration of theory with practice among the masses of new Party members, so as to enable them to understand step by step the Marxist-Leninist stand, viewpoint and method, acquire a basic knowledge of the general principles of Marxism-Leninism, the Party's history and the present state of our socialist construction, and realize what damage may result from subjectivism, including doctrinairism and empiricism. Among new Party members who are intellectuals, particular stress must be laid on recognizing the danger of doctrinairism. Thirdly, it is necessary to strengthen the theoretical work of the Party. We should quickly rally, both inside and outside the Party, the necessary forces for carrying on Marxist-Leninist scientific studies—the study of major problems and basic experience in the socialist transformation and socialist construction of our country, of current international problems, of basic Marxist-Leninist theory and other branches of science closely connected with Marxism-Leninism. This series of studies should be brought into line with the pressing needs of the practical work of the Party, and also with the pressing need to carry on Marxist-Leninist teaching of the integration of theory with practice, among the broad masses of Party members and young people.

In order to effectively combat subjectivism, the Party's leading organs at all levels should all considerably strengthen the work of investigation and research into actual conditions. The mistakes of Rightist conservatism, of impetuosity and rashness, of trying to do things by coercion and commands, that have occurred in the Party's work in the past few years, have all stemmed from a lack of earnest effort to analyse correctly the actual conditions of things and to sum up the experience of the masses. Like certain working personnel in the state organs referred to above, not a small number of Party functionaries have begun to get conceited and complacent. Ensconced in their offices, they substitute empty talk for investigation, and formulate policies on the basis of their impressions, rather than go into the midst of their subordinates and listen to their opinions, check up on how Party decisions are being carried out and see whether or not these decisions have proved correct in the course of practice, and take pains to study new things and correctly further their development. The Party must educate them to keenly realize what damage has been done the work by subjectivist methods of work as described above; must help them learn how to carry out matter-of-fact investigations and studies of conditions among the masses; must help them to learn the method of work—"from the masses and back to the masses"; and make them realize that this is indispensable if they are to continue to hold leading posts in the Party.

In order to bring the Party's role of leadership as much in line as possible with objective realities, to facilitate the summing up of the experience and opinions of the masses and reduce the possibility of making mistakes, Party organizations at all levels must without exception adhere to the Party's principle of collective leadership and broaden democratic life within the Party. All important questions must be thoroughly discussed by the proper collective bodies before decisions are taken, and argument and debate on diverse viewpoints must be allowed without any restraint, in order that various opinions from the masses, both inside and outside the Party, may be more or less fully reflected; in other words, in order that the various aspects present in the course of development of objective realities will be more or less fully reflected. Every leader must be good at listening patiently to and taking into careful consideration opinions contrary to his own, and resolutely approve opposite views if reasonable, or whatever is reasonable in them; he must continue to work amicably with and never turn his back on any comrade who, prompted by the correct motives and following normal procedure, may have put forward an opinion contrary to his own. Only in this way can we achieve collective leadership and Party unity in deed, and not in name only, and assure that its organization will improve and its cause prosper.

The question of thorough application of the Party's principle of collective leadership and the extension of inner-Party democracy is given full attention in the new draft of the Constitution of the Communist Party of China put forward by the Central Committee. As Comrade Teng Hsiao-ping is going to give a detailed explanation of the draft Constitution, there is no need for me to dwell on it here. The draft Constitution makes some new provisions in respect of the rights of Party members and of Party organizations at lower levels. It is provided in the draft Constitution that Party members have the right to give full play to their creative ability in work, and, while unconditionally carrying out Party decisions, have the right to reserve and submit their own views to a leading body of the Party, in case they should disagree. The draft Constitution provides that all questions of a local character or questions that need to be decided locally should be handled by local organizations so as to find solutions appropriate to local conditions, and that should a lower Party organization find that a decision made by a higher organization does not suit the actual conditions in its locality or department, it should request the higher organization to modify the said decision. The draft Constitution further provides that Party congresses at and above the county level will have a fixed term, and will meet once a year. These provisions will certainly give a powerful impetus to the initiative of Party organizations of all levels and of the entire membership.

Naturally, the extension of democratic life in our Party will not in any way weaken our Party's centralism, but, on the contrary, strengthen it; the full play of the initiative of our Party members will not in any way weaken Party discipline, but, on the contrary, strengthen it. Similarly, our Party's principle of collective leadership does not in any way negate the need for personal responsibility or the important role of leader; on the contrary, it is the guarantee that a leader can play his personal role in a correct and most effective way. As everyone knows, the reason why the leader of our Party, Comrade Mao Tse-tung, has played the great role of helmsman in our revolution and enjoys a high prestige in the whole Party and among all the people of the country is not only that he knows how to integrate the universal truth of Marxism-Leninism with the actual practice of the Chinese revolution, but also that he firmly believes in the strength and wisdom of the masses, initiates and advocates the mass line in Party work, and steadfastly upholds the Party's principles of democracy and collective leadership.

A correct attitude towards comrades who have committed mistakes is one of the necessary conditions of correct Party leadership.

It is very easy to take severe disciplinary measures against comrades who have committed mistakes even to the point of expelling them from the Party. But if the ideological cause of those mistakes is not removed, severe disciplinary measures not only cannot ensure that the Party will not again make the same mistakes, but may lead to making even greater mistakes. When the "Leftist"-opportunist line held sway in our Party, the practice of "ruthless struggle and merciless blows" in inner-Party struggle only resulted in obscuring the line between right and wrong and the loss of vitality within the Party; it sapped the effective strength of the Party, and brought great losses to its cause.

Having corrected the mistakes resulting from the opportunist lines of Wang Ming and Po Ku and other comrades, the Party's Central Committee headed by Comrade Mao Tse-tung also radically altered the wrong forms of inner-Party struggle.

In inner-Party struggle the Party first of all draws a strict line between the question of right and wrong within the Party and the question of the counter-revolutionaries, the degenerate elements and other bad elements who have sneaked into the Party.

The Party adopts a firm attitude and weeds out the counter-revolutionaries who have sneaked into the Party, alien class elements who persistently engaged in splitting and disruptive activities inside the Party, and other incorrigibly corrupt and degenerate elements. It is true that some counter-revolutionaries and other bad elements have sneaked into our ranks. We have weeded out some of them, and we will continue to keep a close watch on them and weed them out. But facts prove that there are only a very small number of such people. Since our Party came to power, however, the tendency to corruption and degeneration, violation of laws and discipline and moral degeneration has developed to a certain extent. We must resolutely put an end to this grave state of affairs. In the past we conducted a mass struggle against corruption, waste and violation of laws and discipline, and later on, smashed the anti-Party bloc of Kao Kang and Jao Shu-shih who tried to seize the leadership of the state and Party by conspiratorial means. In the future too we must wage a constant struggle, ideological and organizational, against corruption and degeneration and constantly expel the incorrigibly corrupt and degenerate elements from the Party.

But the Party steadfastly adheres to the following principles in dealing with any comrade who has made mistakes in his work owing to a faulty ideology: "Take warning from the past in order to be more careful in the future; treat the illness in order to save the patient," and "not only clear up a man's ideological problem but also unite with him as a comrade." Emphasis is placed on ideological education; disciplinary action is not to be resorted to rashly. It is necessary to criticize these comrades' mistaken ideas in a practical manner and analyse the causes of their mistakes. This is the way to help them and continue to unite with them so that we can carry on our work together. Although, when necessary, appropriate disciplinary action may be taken against comrades who have made serious mistakes in work or they may be transferred to other suitable posts, it is essential to help them patiently and in a comradely manner to see and correct their mistakes so that we can achieve unity with them. In a word, a comrade who has made a mistake, provided the mistake is one that permits of correction within the Party, and that he himself is ready to make the effort, must be allowed to stay in the Party and correct his mistake; there should be no abuse of organizational powers by taking inappropriate disciplinary measures against him. On the other hand, if rough and crude methods are used to rectify mistakes of an ideological nature, not only will these mistakes remain uncorrected, and be liable to be repeated, but the feeling of harmony which should exist in the Party is bound to be impaired, and ordinary differences of opinion may even develop into an organizational split.

The Party has raised the level of Marxist-Leninist understanding among its members, strengthened the investigation and study of the actual situation, broadened democracy within the Party, and adopted a correct policy regarding mistakes in work. As a result, the unity and solidarity of the Party are bound to grow stronger day by day. And this, of course, is to the advantage not only of the Party, but of the entire working class and the people of the whole country since the Party is the leading core of the entire working class and the masses of people of the whole country.

We must firmly rally the entire Party, and this we do precisely for the purpose of building the solidarity of the entire working class and the people of the whole country on a firm basis. The source of our strength lies in our ability to rely closely on the working class and on the masses of the people. In order to build China into a great socialist country, we must do our utmost to continue to strengthen solidarity between the Party and the masses.

The overwhelming majority of the people of our country have already got themselves organized. The various people's organizations are the essential ties with which our Party links itself with the masses. In addition to the co-operatives organized by the peasants which I have dealt with previously, the most important people's organizations are the trade union organizations, the Youth League organizations and the women's organizations.

Our trade union organizations now have 12,000,000 members and play an important part in national construction. The Party should improve its leadership over the work of the trade unions, and through them, foster our working class so that it will become an organized and politically conscious class possessed of culture and technique, and rally the masses of workers closely round the Party. In socialist construction, trade union organizations should, on the one hand, rally the workers, by means of education and persuasion, to strive for a constant rise in labour productivity through socialist emulation drives and campaigns for outstanding workers, and on the other hand, they should intimately concern themselves with the livelihood of the masses, develop their function of supervision and carry on a valiant struggle against bureaucracy in all enterprises which manifests itself in violation of laws and discipline, and in infringement of the interests of the masses, and in showing no regard for the livelihood of the masses. The tendency to neglect either side of this twofold task is wrong and should be corrected.

The China New Democratic Youth League with a membership of 20,000,000, will soon be renamed the Chinese Communist Youth League. Thanks to the fruitful efforts made by the Youth League over the past few years, shock forces for socialist construction are constantly emerging from among our energetic young workers and employees, young peasants, young scientific and technical personnel and all other young intellectuals. They form a vast reserve of new recruits for the Party. Led by the Party, the Youth League should carry on ideological and organizational work in a more vigorous way among Youth League members and the broad masses of the young people, and overcome the defects of certain of its organizations which paid no heed to adopting a style of work suited to the characteristics of the youth, refusing to give full play to the activity and initiative of the broad masses of young people through education and persuasion.

Our Party has all along concerned itself with and supported the women's emancipation movement; it has made the complete emancipation of women one of the important objectives of the cause it works for. The women of our country now occupy a more and more important position in industrial and agricultural work and in many professions. Women cadres at various posts are rapidly becoming an impressive force. The Party should continue to give them every encouragement in their desire to advance, help women overcome certain special difficulties in taking up work, and assist them in improving their skills. The Party should also correct any mistaken ideas of discrimination against women which exist either inside or outside the Party, and pay attention to the introduction of a new spirit of ethics in social and family life based on the equality of men and women and the protection of women and children. The Democratic Women's Federation with branch organizations throughout the country is a popular women's organization. The Party should concern itself with these organizations and help them in their work, and through them strengthen the ties between the Party and the broad masses of women.

In order to make the close ties between our Party and the masses of the people still firmer, we must continue to intensify our work in every field among the masses. Constant education in wholehearted service to the people must especially be given to all cadres and Party members. An important hallmark of a good Party member and a good leader is that he is familiar with the living and working conditions of the people, concerns himself with their welfare and knows what lies uppermost in their hearts. He sticks to hard-working and plain-living, and shares the people's joys, sorrows and hardships. He can accept their criticism and supervision and does not put on airs in front of them. He takes his problems to the masses to consult with them, and the masses willingly tell him what they have to say. As long as our Party is made up of such Party members, our strength will be for ever inexhaustible and unconquerable.

Just as at home, our Party relies on the support of the people, so, internationally, we rely on the support of the international proletariat and the peoples of all countries. Without the great international solidarity of the proletariat of the various countries, without the support of the world's revolutionary forces our socialist cause cannot advance to victory, nor can that victory be consolidated even when it is won.

We must continue to strengthen our fraternal solidarity with the Communist Parties and the Workers' Parties of all countries; we must continue to learn from the experience of the Communist Party of the Soviet Union and the Communist Parties of all other countries in regard to revolution and construction. In our relations with all fraternal parties, we must show the warmth of our feelings and take a modest attitude. We must resolutely oppose any dangerous inclination towards great-nation chauvinism or bourgeois nationalism.

The Chinese revolution is part of the world's proletarian revolution. In our achievements are the fruits of the struggle of the working class and working people of all countries. The Central Committee of the Communist Party of China avails itself of this opportunity to extend heartfelt thanks and pay its respects to the fraternal parties of all countries and, through them, to the working class and working people of their countries, and assure them of our lasting solidarity with them.

Let all comrades of our Party be for ever united! Let us be for ever united with the masses of the people of our country, with the working class of all countries and with the peoples of the whole world! Our great cause of socialism will definitely triumph! No force in the world can stop us from winning victory!

DOCUMENT 10

Proposals of the Eighth National Congress of the Communist Party of China for the Second Five-Year Plan for Development of the National Economy (1958-1962), adopted September 27, 1956.

The English text is from *Eighth National Congress of the Communist Party of China*, Foreign Languages Press, Peking, 1956, Vol. I, pp. 229-259.

Comment. The proposals were submitted for discussion to the State Council, which approved them in February 1957 and passed them on to the State Planning Commission, which was charged with preparing from them a full plan for presentation to the National People's Congress. Actually the proposals of the Eighth Party Congress represent all that was publicly known of the second Five-Year Plan during the 1950's. For general discussions, see T. J. Hughes and D. E. T. Luard, *The Economic Development of Communist China* (London: Oxford University Press, 1959); Choh-ming Li, *Economic Development of Communist China* (Berkeley: University of California Press, 1959); Choh-ming Li, "Economic Development: the First Decade," *China Quarterly*, January 1960; and Richard Moorsteen, "Economic Prospects for Communist China," *World Politics*, January 1959. All of those sources were also given in our comment on Document 1 relating to the first Five-Year Plan. Other supplementary reading material is listed in the comment on Document 11, below.

_____ TEXT OF DOCUMENT 10 _____

During the period of China's First Five-Year Plan, the people of the whole country have demonstrated unprecedented socialist enthusiasm and launched a great movement for socialist construction and socialist transformation. A decisive victory has been gained in socialist transformation and socialist construction is going ahead successfully.

At present, the international situation has definitely tended towards relaxation; the work of construction in the great Soviet Union and the People's Democracies is expanding daily; unity and co-operation among the socialist countries is growing ever closer. The people's democratic dictatorship is more consolidated than ever and there is still greater unity among all the nationalities, democratic parties and patriots of our country. All these factors have created very favourable conditions for the successful completion of our First Five-Year Plan. In view of our achievements in national construction during the past three years and more, it is estimated that most of the targets set by our First Five-Year Plan will be overfulfilled, and socialist transformation, in particular, will be accomplished ahead of schedule. In bringing our First Five-Year Plan to a successful conclusion in 1957, we shall have laid the preliminary groundwork for socialist industrialization; at the same time, with the exception of a few areas, we shall have put agriculture and handicrafts, in the main, on a co-operative basis and transformed all capitalist industrial and commerical concerns into joint state-private enterprises.

As the First Five-Year Plan will soon be brought to a successful conclusion, it is necessary now, in good time, to draw up the Second Five-Year Plan for development of the national economy (1958-1962). The Eighth National Congress of the Communist Party of China, therefore, makes the following proposals concerning this plan to be submitted to the State Council of the People's Republic of China for discussion. We suggest that the State Council prepare a draft plan as soon as possible and submit it to the National People's Congress for consideration and decision, so that the efforts of the whole nation can be mobilized to carry out the tasks to be set by the Second Five-Year Plan.

The Second Five-Year Plan is of vital importance in carrying out the fundamental task of our country during the transition period. The Second Five-Year Plan must promote our socialist construction by forward-looking and really sound measures, and complete socialist transformation on the basis of the successful fulfilment of the First Five-Year Plan, so as to ensure that, in approximately three five-year plans, we can, in the main, build up a comprehensive industrial system and transform our backward agricultural country into an advanced socialist industrial country. Hence the principal tasks of the Second Five-Year Plan should be: (1) to continue industrial construction with heavy industry as its core and promote technical reconstruction of the national economy, and build a solid foundation for socialist industrialization; (2) to carry through socialist transformation, and consolidate and expand the system of collective ownership and the system of ownership by the whole people; (3) to further increase the production of industry, agriculture and handicrafts and correspondingly develop transport and commerce on the basis of developing capital construction and carrying through socialist transformation; (4) to make vigorous efforts to train personnel for construction work and strengthen scientific research to meet the needs of the development of socialist economy and culture; and (5) to reinforce the national defences and raise the level of the people's material and cultural life on the basis of increased industrial and agricultural production.

In order to guarantee fulfilment of these principal tasks, it is proposed that in drawing up the Second Five-Year Plan the following principles and measures be adopted in regard to development and transformation of the national economy.

(1) In view of the domestic and international situation and the general trend of current events, it is necessary as well as possible to continue to maintain a fairly rapid rate in the development of our national economy during the Second Five-Year Plan period. As provided for in the First Five-Year Plan, 1957 will see an increase of 51.1 per cent in the total value of industrial and agricultural output (here and below, including that of modern industries, handicrafts and agriculture), as compared with 1952, but this increase, it is estimated, may in actual practice be more than 60 per cent. In the Second Five-Year Plan period, as newly-built enterprises and enterprises undergoing reconstruction are brought successively into operation, as the productive potentialities of existing enterprises are further developed, as the productive potentialities of the equipment of private industrial enterprises are brought into play after they have come under joint state-private management or state ownership, and as the productive forces of agriculture and handicrafts are further developed after being organized into co-operatives, it is required that the total value of industrial and agricultural output in 1962 show an increase of about 75 per cent as compared with 1957 (here and below, this refers to the targets of the annual plan for 1957 set by the First Five-Year Plan). The value of industrial output (here and below, including modern industry and handicrafts) will be about double the planned figure for 1957 and that of agricultural output will increase by about 35 per cent. The rates of growth of industrial and agricultural output stated above appear to be somewhat high because they are compared with the planned targets set by the First Five-Year Plan, and no account is taken of the possibility that those targets will be overfulfilled. If comparison is made with the actual achievements of the First Five-Year Plan, then the rates of growth laid down in the Second Five-Year Plan will, as stated above, be relatively lower.

Our First Five-Year Plan provides that in 1957, capital goods industry will account for 38 per cent of the value of industrial output while consumer goods industry will account for 62 per cent; but it is expected that the share of capital goods industry may actually exceed 40 per cent. In the Second Five-Year Plan period, the rate of increase in the value of industrial output will still be faster in capital goods industry than in consumer goods industry. It is required that by 1962 capital goods industry and consumer goods industry will each represent about 50 per cent.

(2) Because of the growth of industrial and agricultural output, the increase in labour productivity and the practice of strict economy in various branches of the national economy, it is possible to increase the national income in 1962 by about 50 per cent as compared with 1957. During the Second Five-Year Plan period, we should maintain in the distribution of the national income a correct proportion between consumption and accumulation, and the part which goes to accumulation may slightly exceed that of the first five-year period so as to speed up socialist construction and ensure gradual improvement of the people's livelihood.

With the increase of national income and the growth in the proportion of state-owned economy in the national income, state revenue will show a considerable increase during the Second Five-Year Plan period, as compared with the First. Expenditure must correspond to revenue so that a balance is maintained, while certain reserves are set aside to meet any unforeseen difficulties. At the same time, funds for extending credits should be suitably increased to ensure a balance between credit receipts and payments.

During the Second Five-Year Plan period, while strengthening our national defences and increasing administrative efficiency, we should as far as possible reduce national defence and administrative expenditures, and increase expenditure on economic construction and cultural development so as to ensure the rapid advance of socialist construction. Under the First Five-Year Plan about 56 per cent of total expenditure goes to economic construction and cultural development. This figure should be raised to between 60 and 70 per cent under the Second Five-Year Plan, while expenditure on national defences and administration should be reduced from about 32 per cent of total expenditure under the First Five-Year Plan to about 20 per cent under the Second. The rest of expenditure will be allocated for the state's material reserves, for credit funds, repayments of domestic and foreign debts and general reserve funds.

On the basis of a bigger revenue, the proportion of state investments in capital construction during the Second Five-Year Plan period can be raised from about 35 per cent of all state expenditure in the first five-year period to about 40 per cent so as to speed up socialist construction. Thus, state investments in capital construction in the second five-year period may be about double what they are in the first. In order to ensure a rapid development of industry and agriculture—the two principal branches of the national economy—the proportion of capital construction investments in industry by the state should be raised from 58.2 per cent under the First Five-Year Plan to about 60 per cent under the Second; the share going to agriculture, forestry and water conservancy should increase from 7.6 per cent to about 10 per cent.

(3) The central task of our Second Five-Year Plan is still to give priority to the development of heavy industry. This is the chief index of our country's socialist industrialization, because heavy industry provides the basis for a strong economy and national defence, as well as the basis for the technical reconstruction of our national economy.

It is required that the output of the main products of heavy industry reach approximately the following levels in 1962:

Product	Unit	Target for 1962	Target for 1957	Actual output in 1952	Peak annual output before liberation	
					Year	Output
Electricity	100,000,000 KWH	400–430	159.0	72.6	1941	59.6
Coal	10,000 tons	19,000–21,000	11,298.5	6,352.8	1942	6,187.5
Crude oil	10,000 tons	500–600	201.2	43.6	1943	32.0
Steel	10,000 tons	1,050–1,200	412.0	135.0	1943	92.3
Aluminium ingots	10,000 tons	10–12	2.0	—	—	—
Chemical fertilizers	10,000 tons	300–320	57.8	19.4	1941	22.7
Metallurgical equipment	10,000 tons	3–4	0.8	—	—	—
Power-generating equipment	10,000 kw.	140–150	16.4	0.67	—	—
Metal-cutting machine tools	10,000 units	6–6.5	1.3	1.4	1941	0.5
Timber	10,000 cubic metres	3,100–3,400	2,000.0	1,002.0	—	—
Cement	10,000 tons	1,250–1,450	600.0	286.0	1942	229.3

In the Second Five-Year Plan period, we must make vigorous efforts to expand the machine-building industry, particularly that making industrial equipment, and continue to expand the metallurgical industry to meet the needs of national construction. At the same time, we should also energetically develop the electric power, coal mining and building material industries, and strengthen the backward branches of industry—the oil, chemical and radio equipment industries. We should press ahead vigorously with the establishment of industries utilizing atomic energy for peaceful purposes.

No effort should be spared in this five-year period in strengthening the weak links in our industry and in opening up new fields, such as the manufacture of various kinds of heavy equipment, machine tools for special purposes, precision machine tools and instruments, the production of high-grade alloy steels, the cold working of steel products, the mining and refining of rare metals and the setting up of an organic synthetic chemical industry, etc. At the same time, we should also pay attention to multiple-purpose utilization of resources, particularly the over-all use of the associated non-ferrous metals.

(4) While giving priority to the development of heavy industry, we should suitably speed up the growth of light industry on the basis of a higher level of agricultural development, so as to meet the growing needs of the broad mass of the people for consumer goods and contribute to the state's accumulation of funds.

It is required that output of the main light industrial products reach approximately the following levels in 1962:

Product	Unit	Target for 1962	Target for 1957	Actual output in 1952	Peak annual output before liberation	
					Year	Output
Cotton yarn	10,000 bales	800–900	500.0	361.8	1933	244.7
Cotton piece-goods	10,000 bolts	23,500–26,000	16,372.1	11,163.4	—	—
Salt	10,000 tons	1,000–1,100	755.4	494.5	1943	391.8
Edible vegetable oils	10,000 tons	310–320	179.4	98.3	—	—
Sugar (including hand-made sugar)	10,000 tons	240–250	110.0	45.1	1936	41.4
Machine-made paper	10,000 tons	150–160	65.5	37.2	1943	16.5

In the Second Five-Year Plan period, in all those branches of light industry which are needed by society and which have an adequate supply of raw materials, the productive potentialities of the existing equipment should be brought into full play; the proportion of investments in light industry should be suitably increased; and new construction should be undertaken according to needs and possibilities, so as to further increase the production of light industrial goods. Efforts should be made to produce a greater variety of light industrial goods, improve quality and reduce costs, so as to produce low priced, high quality goods.

In order to increase the output of light industrial products, efforts should be made by industrial enterprises under local authorities to make greater use of local resources and waste materials to produce more consumer goods of all kinds suited to the needs of the local population; the various areas, furthermore, should organize mutual exchange of products. We should continue to develop the handicraft industries on the basis of the co-operative system so as to satisfy the many-sided needs of the people.

(5) During the Second Five-Year Plan period, we must continue to establish, or energetically prepare to establish, new industrial bases in the interior taking into account local resources as well as the principle of rationally distributing our productive forces in order gradually to achieve a balanced development of our economy throughout the country. In carrying on large-scale industrial construction in the interior, we must, however, at the same time, make vigorous efforts to make full use of and suitably develop the existing industries in the coastal areas. This is not only to meet the growing needs of the state and the people, but also to support construction work in the interior. In capital construction in industry, attention should be paid to co-ordination between large, medium and small-sized enterprises and to their proper dispersion geographically.

In these five years, we should continue the construction of the industrial bases in Northeast China, Central China and in Inner Monogolia with the iron and steel industry as their core; start the construction of new industrial bases in Southwest China, Northwest China, and the area around the Sanmen Gorge, with iron and steel industry and hydroelectric power stations as their core; carry on with the building of oil and non-ferrous metal industries in Sinkiang; make energetic efforts to utilize the existing industrial bases in East China; bring into full play the role in industry of North and South China; and intensify geological prospecting in Tibet in order to prepare the way for its industrial development.

To ensure the completion of the above-mentioned construction projects, we must further expand and improve our geological work so as to collect all the data which economic construction needs concerning mineral deposits and geological conditions; speed up the training of designers and reinforce the ranks of builders and installation workers. At the same time, we should improve urban construction in accordance with the needs of industrial development.

(6) We must make vigorous efforts to promote agricultural production so that agriculture and industry are developed in a co-ordinated way and that the needs of the state and the people are satisfied.

During the Second Five-Year Plan period, increase in the output of grain should be ensured in the first place so as to propel the development of agriculture as a whole. At the same time, increased production of major industrial crops, especially cotton and soya beans, should be ensured so as to propel the development of light industry. In developing agriculture, we should encourage a diversified rural economy and bring about a considerable expansion of stock-breeding, forestry, fisheries and subsidiary cottage occupations so as to ensure an increase in the peasants' income and raise the living standards of the people.

It is required that the output of staple agricultural products reach approximately the following levels in 1962:

Product	Unit	Target for 1962 (approx.)	Total output in 2nd five years (approx.)	Target for 1957	Actual output in 1952	Peak annual output before liberation	
						Year	Output
Grain	100,000,000 catties	5,000	22,000	3,631.8	3,087.9	1936	2,773.9
Cotton	10,000 *tan*	4,800	21,000	3,270.0	2,607.4	1936	1,697.6
Soya beans	100,000,000 catties	250	1,100	224.4	190.4	1936	226.1

We must try our best to overfulfil the targets for the staple farm products listed above, and take effective measures to ensure increased output of other oil-bearing crops and sugar crops. We must make efforts to increase the output of natural silk, tea, tobacco, jute and ambary hemp, fruits and medicinal herbs. In the vicinity of cities and industrial and mining districts, the growing of more vegetables and increased production of other non-staple foods to supply their needs should be regarded as an important task.

It is required that the number of main kinds of livestock reach approximately the following targets in 1962:

Item	Unit	Target for 1962 (approx.)	Target for 1957	Actual number in 1952	Peak number before liberation	
					Year	Number
Cattle	10,000 head	9,000	7,361	5,660	1935	4,826.8
Horses	”	1,100	834	613	1935	648.5
Sheep and goats	”	17,000	11,304	6,178	1937	6,252.0
Pigs	”	25,000	13,834	8,977	1934	7,853.0

Attention should be paid to promoting pig-breeding so as to increase supplies of meat and manure. In addition, extensive breeding of chickens, ducks, geese, rabbits and other poultry and domestic animals should be undertaken.

As the targets for the production of soya beans, oil-bearing crops and the breeding of livestock were not fulfilled in the first few years of the First Five-Year Plan, effective measures must be adopted in the Second Five-Year Plan period to remedy this state of affairs. In conformity with the needs of the state and the people, and taking into account natural conditions in different areas, we should arrange the proportions of grains and various industrial crops as suited to the various localities, and appropriately organize livestock-breeding and subsidiary agricultural occupations in order to ensure a well co-ordinated development of the various branches of agriculture.

Agricultural producers' co-operatives should, in conformity with the Model Regulations for Advanced Agricultural Producers' Co-operatives and the principle that co-operatives must be run industriously, thriftily and democratically, check over and consolidate their organizations, train and promote various types of cadres, and strengthen management and the organization of production. On the principle of taking care of both the needs of the state and the welfare of the peasants, reasonable proportions should be worked out for distributing income as between the collective and the individual members. Where the collective work of the co-operatives is not affected, appropriate arrangements should be made to allow members the necessary time off to work in their own individual interests; they should be allowed to engage in various subsidiary agricultural occupations which are best undertaken by the peasants individually so as to further encourage their initiative in production and promote the development of agricultural and subsidiary production. In order to prevent difficulties arising in management and the organization of production which may adversely affect agricultural production, care should be taken to see that, as agricultural producers' co-operatives develop, they are not recklessly merged into large units.

To develop agricultural production during these five years, we must energetically popularize all feasible measures for increasing production on the basis of co-operative farming in order to get still higher yields of grain and industrial crops per unit area. The principal measures for increasing production are: expanding the irrigated area; developing sources of manure and fertilizers and improving their use; popularizing step by step new-type farm tools suited to local needs; popularizing high-grade seeds of agricultural crops suited to local conditions, and promoting the work of seed-rejuvenation; improving techniques and methods of cultivation; suitably enlarging the area of land planted to several crops a year and reclaiming waste land in the vicinity of villages; suitably increasing the area planted to high-yield crops; improving soil, with special attention to improvement of red soils and alkaline soils; vigorously preventing and eliminating plant diseases and insect pests. In order to prevent loss from indiscriminate popularization, the latest experience gained in increasing production should first be tried out experimentally and then, after the method has been mastered, popularized step by step in areas with more or less the same conditions.

During the Second Five-Year Plan period, we should do our utmost to build water conservancy projects; take more effective measures to prevent flood and drain water-logged areas; extend the work of water and soil conservation; strive to reduce damage caused by heavy floods and drought and step by step end damage caused by less serious floods and drought. Alongside the large-scale water conservancy projects undertaken by the state, the agricultural producers' co-operatives and the people in general should be mobilized to take vigorous and well-planned action in building medium and small-sized water conservancy projects; and attention should be paid to the utilization and improvement of existing water conservancy facilities.

We should, so far as conditions permit, reclaim waste lands in Northeast, Northwest and South China, expand the cultivated area, and suitably develop state farms in order to increase the production of grain and industrial crops for the state.

During the Second Five-Year Plan period, we should actively develop forestry, mobilize the masses to plant trees and grow forests, do all we can to conduct reafforestation of denuded areas owned by the state and improve the work of nursing saplings, raise the survival rate, prevent forest fires and guard against insect pests, and step by step extend afforestation. We should make vigorous efforts to promote the cultivation of marine products and fisheries both in fresh-waters and shallow seas, and improve and extend our surveying and protection of aquatic resources. We should set up weather stations and weather posts according to plan, and improve our work in weather forecasting and our warning system to guard against natural calamities.

Industry, commerce and transport must improve co-ordination and co-operation with agriculture so as to promote its growth. Attention should be paid to strengthening the work of extending rural credits, in order to give more vigorous support to agricultural production.

(7) In the Second Five-Year Plan period, in order to cope with the needs of industrial and agricultural production and of national defences, we should suitably expand transport, postal and tele-communication services, and build more new railways and highways, postal and tele-communication lines, and water and air transport lines. At the same time, we should, according to plan, add to and

improve existing transport and postal and tele-communication equipment, make full use of and suitably expand traditional transport facilities, improve our organization of transport services, and do our utmost to increase the efficiency of transport and communications services.

Both freight and passenger mileages of railways, highways, shipping and civil aviation should show a corresponding increase in these five years.

It is required that 8,000–9,000 kilometres of new railways be built in these five years. The trunk railway lines from Lanchow to our border in Sinkiang, from Paotow to Lanchow, from Neichiang to Kunming, from Chungking to Kweiyang and from Lanchow to Tsaidam will be completed. In addition, a number of railway junctions and branch lines serving factories, mines and forestry will also be constructed.

It is required that 15,000–18,000 kilometres of trunk highways be constructed or reconstructed in these five years. In accordance with local needs and resources, rough roads, cart tracks and other kinds of roads, too, will be built in various localities of the country to gradually expand local road networks.

We should increase our fleets of river, coastal and sea-going vessels as needed by transport; press ahead with harbour construction and establish new navigational aids. Inland shipping lines should be extended and the organization of transport services on rivers and their tributaries improved.

Equipment and facilities of air transport for civil and special purposes should also be suitably increased.

We should step by step expand and reconstruct the national postal and tele-communication networks in line with the needs of developing the economy and culture of the whole country.

(8) In the Second Five-Year Plan period, in order to stimulate the growth of industrial and agricultural production and meet the growing needs of national construction and the people's livelihood, we should continue to improve and readjust our network of trading establishments, further increase the circulation of commodities and improve our work in the purchase and supply of industrial and agricultural products. At the same time, we should continue to maintain stable commodity prices and gradually readjust unfair prices. In regard to the purchase of industrial products, the method of fixing prices according to the quality of goods will be introduced, while in the case of some products the method of selective purchasing will be employed; this will spur backward factories to improve their work and the quality of their products, and increase their variety.

With the increase of the people's purchasing power in these five years, it is required that the volume of retail trade in 1962 be about 50 per cent greater than in 1957. There should be a corresponding increase in sales by state trading concerns and co-operatives of daily necessities, such as grain, meat, aquatic products, edible vegetable oils, sugar, cotton piece-goods, knit goods, coal and kerosene, to the people in towns and villages, and of means of production to agricultural and handicraft producers' co-operatives.

We should continue to carry out the policy of planned purchase and sale of grain, edible oil and cotton piece-goods and the policy of planned purchase of cotton to ensure proper distribution. Free purchase and sale under the unified direction of the state should be guaranteed so far as concerns commodities which the peasants retain after planned purchases by the state and those which are not covered by the plan. This will expedite commodity circulation and satisfy the people's needs. Besides the state markets, some free markets under the guidance of the state should be maintained or suitably developed according to plan to promote a brisk commodity exchange between town and countryside and to supplement the state markets.

We should improve our work in purchasing and supplying materials for export so as to ensure a balance between imports and exports.

We should improve our work in supplying materials that come under the distribution plan of the state, maintain a balance between supply and demand, perfect our supply and marketing organizations, improve the allocation and delivery of goods and materials, and strengthen our work in accumulating important material reserves, so as to ensure the even and systematic progress of national construction.

(9) In carrying the socialist transformation of private industry and commerce to completion, we must, step by step and in a planned way, effect the necessary economic reorganization and make ap-

propriate personnel arrangements in joint state-private enterprises, and bring about step by step nationalization of these enterprises when the conditions for doing so are ripe. At the same time, we must preserve and develop the strong points of these enterprises and continuously increase the variety and improve the quality of their products.

Outstanding workers and staff of joint state-private enterprises should be promoted to take part in the management of these enterprises. Attention should also be paid to forging unity with and educating those who represent the interests of private capital in such enterprises. We should make full use of their knowledge of production techniques and useful experience in management and help them turn into working people in the full sense of the term.

As economic reorganization is carried out, care should be taken not to amalgamate more than is necessary small factories and shops which are operationally fairly flexible and can easily be adapted to serve the many-sided needs of society. Small industrial enterprises needed by society and properly operated should be kept as they are. They should not be merged without careful consideration lest co-ordination and co-operation among the enterprises concerned be weakened. In the commercial field, it is even more necessary to operate in various ways. Trading establishments should be scattered in a reasonable way over a given locality and managed separately while being placed under the guidance of state concerns and co-operatives. To meet the daily needs of the local population, an appropriate number of small traders and pedlars should be allowed to carry on their business in the residential areas of towns and in villages.

Handicraft producers' co-operatives should direct attention to checking over and consolidating their organization, manage production efficiently, organize the supplies of raw materials and the marketing of their products. They should observe the principle of "to each according to his work" and ensure that the income of their members in general be increased. Their scope of operation should be suitably defined and their leadership and co-ordination with other parties concerned be strengthened. It is also necessary to maintain and develop the strong points of these handicraft trades, and to increase the variety and raise the quality of their products. Where necessary and possible, some handicraft trades can be gradually mechanized or partially mechanized to expand production.

It is also not desirable to over-concentrate handicraft producers' co-operatives. Decentralization should be effected to a suitable extent in certain handicraft trades. Some handicraftsmen, particularly those who make special artistic products, should be allowed to continue working on their own. Subsidiary handicraft occupations of the peasants, with their own local markets, may, as conditions demand, be managed by the peasants individually or brought under the management of the agricultural producers' co-operatives, to meet local needs.

(10) We should press ahead with the technical reconstruction of our national economy and, first of all, technical reconstruction in heavy industry, so as to swiftly raise the technical level of our industry. In the Second Five-Year Plan period, we should, so far as conditions permit, install up-to-date technical equipment, make use of the latest scientific achievements and master the new techniques involved in the important industrial and mining enterprises concerned with machine-building, metallurgy, chemicals, power, oil, coal and radio equipment, which are being newly built or are undergoing major reconstruction, so as to bring our industry onto the road of modern technique. In existing enterprises all latent productive capacity should be made full use of, and, in accordance with the demands of the actual situation, some of their out-of-date equipment should be renovated systematically and step by step so as to raise their technical level. To get a rapid increase in output the best experience and methods of production, whether foreign or domestic, should be spread effectively and systematically to all newly built, reconstructed, and other existing enterprises, with due regard to actual conditions in each enterprise.

Technical reconstruction of our national economy must be based mainly on our heavy industry, and the machine-building industry in particular, and furthermore, it should be commensurate with our strength in technical personnel, financial and natural resources, and labour power, and proceed gradually and with proper emphasis where needed. In certain most labour-consuming branches of economy, important work processes and major projects and projects that cannot be tackled without machines should be gradually mechanized, and to an ever increasing extent; in other places, our tremendous reserves of labour power should continue to be used. The technical renovation of transport, and postal and tele-communication services should also be carried out step by step, commensurate with our level of industrial development, the possibilities of our economic and other resources, and the needs of transport and communications.

In the Second Five-Year Plan period, so far as technical improvements in agriculture are concerned, emphasis should be put on extension of irrigation and strengthening measures of flood prevention and drainage of water-logged areas, trial manufacture and popularization of improved farm tools suited to local needs, increased production of fertilizers, improvements in cultivation techniques, the growing of high-grade seeds and the breeding of better strains of livestock. At the same time, we should, in the light of specific conditions, make suitable use of tractors on state farms, in reclaimed areas, and in areas raising industrial crops.

(11) We should energetically develop scientific research with emphasis on particular subjects in accordance with the needs of national construction. During the Second Five-Year Plan period, we should continue to learn from the latest scientific and technical achievements in the Soviet Union and other countries, and start building up in our country the most advanced branches of science and techniques known to the world, such as the science of atomic energy, electronics, and the techniques of automation and remote control; we should also achieve marked results in other important fields of scientific and technological research so that within the period of the Third Five-Year Plan we can, in many important fields of science and technology, approach the most advanced levels attained in the world.

In this five-year period, giving proper emphasis to particular fields, we should gradually strengthen research work in the Chinese Academy of Sciences, in the research institutes of the various government departments and enterprises concerned, and in universities and colleges, and effectively bring about division of work and co-operation among them. We should gradually build up a national network of scientific research institutes.

We should carry through the Party's policy of uniting with, educating and remoulding the intellectuals and the principle of "letting diverse schools of thought contend," and encourage them to cultivate independent thinking and engage in free discussion. We should make more suitable use of the services of intellectuals, and pay attention to improving their working conditions and give full play to their enthusiasm and creative ability so as to meet the needs of development of scientific research and economic and cultural development.

During the Second Five-Year Plan period, we should do all we can to train personnel for construction work, to develop higher education and secondary vocational education; continue to send graduates from universities and colleges and teachers abroad to study subjects which are still lacking in China; systematically and step by step develop spare-time higher education and secondary vocational education, so as to train more specialists in various fields we need for national construction. At the same time, attention should be paid to the development of workers' technical schools, and efforts should be made to train skilled workers in various ways.

In developing higher education, we should lay stress on engineering and the natural sciences; make vigorous efforts to promote the study of pedagogy, agriculture and forestry, and give due attention to other subjects. In this five-year period, the number of university and college graduates is expected to reach approximately 500,000, which is roughly 80 per cent more than the number aimed at in the First Five-Year Plan. In 1962 the total enrolment in universities and colleges is expected to reach approximately 850,000, which is roughly double the number aimed at in 1957.

We should vigorously increase the number of senior and junior middle schools and enlarge the existing ones to provide adequate enrolment for the universities, colleges and secondary vocational schools, and to satisfy properly the needs of government departments, factories and mining enterprises for specialized personnel and skilled workers. At the same time, we should step by step extend primary education to ever larger sections of the population, and do all we can to help agriculture producers' co-operatives organize literacy classes for children in order to make up for the shortage of primary schools.

We should make efforts to wipe out illiteracy throughout the country; carry out the reform of written Chinese step by step according to plan; and step by step establish spare-time primary and secondary schools for workers and peasants so as to ensure a constant rise in the cultural level of the mass of workers and peasants.

We should continue to adhere to the principle of "letting flowers of many kinds blossom," foster art and literature on an extensive scale, encourage in every way creative work in art and literature, promote art and literary criticism, actively carry on the work of editing, revaluing and popularizing the best part of the heritage of our national culture so as to make the various types of folk art and literature dearly loved by the masses still more perfect in form and varied in content.

We should energetically foster the growth of the cinema, and step by step and according to plan, improve our work in publication and radio broadcasting.

(12) Relations between the central and local authorities should be properly readjusted. Under the unified leadership of the central government and in accordance with the state plan, local authorities, departments and basic-level units should bring their initiative in economic and cultural development into full play and mobilize the forces of the people on an extensive scale to speed up socialist construction as much as possible.

Guided by the principles of unified leadership, level-by-level administration, and suiting our actions to the place and matter in hand, we should improve the state administrative system; define the scope of administration in enterprises, institutions, planning and finance; properly extend the administrative powers of the provincial and autonomous regional authorities and municipal authorities of cities directly under the central authority; and pay attention to improving and strengthening the work of the various departments of the central government. Extension of the administrative powers of local authorities will, on the one hand, enable the local authorities to shoulder more responsibilities and give fuller play to the positive factors and productive potentialities of the localities concerned, and on the other hand, enable the various departments of the central government to concentrate their efforts, devote greater attention to over-all planning and to the study of principles and policies, grasp the central links in their work, improve the check-up of work, and organize exchanges of experience, thereby reinforcing the leadership of the central government.

In accordance with the requirements of the state plan and the specific conditions of their area, local authorities should draw up local economic development plans. They should first of all give firmer leadership to agricultural production. At the same time, while co-ordinating a balanced development on a local scale with that on a national scale, they should also undertake industrial construction as needed, and give firmer leadership to local industries and handicrafts. Local industries and handicrafts should be developed mainly for the needs of the local population, especially the peasants. They should also turn out products needed for export and by consumers in other parts of the country, produce various kinds of building materials, process goods for the state industrial enterprises under the central authorities and co-operate with them in production.

Local authorities must pay attention to improving their work in purchasing industrial goods, farm products and the special products of their own districts and increase the supply of consumer goods and means of production needed by agriculture and handicrafts, so as to encourage production and satisfy the needs of the people. At the same time, local authorities must, according to needs and possibilities, improve local transport and communications and promote educational, cultural and public health work.

(13) To promote economic and cultural development in the national minority areas, we must improve the work of construction there and by degrees bring about a change in the backward state of these areas.

In our national minority areas we should develop industry in a planned and well-prepared way and according to the actual needs and possibilities. We should pay attention to helping expand agriculture, forestry and stock-breeding in these areas, and gradually build water conservancy projects and introduce technical improvements in agriculture, forestry and stock-breeding. We should help improve their transport, postal, tele-communication, trading, banking and credit facilities step by step. At the same time, we should also devote attention to development of their cultural and educational work; make vigorous efforts to train cadres and scientific and technological workers from among them; help them to create or reform their own written languages, set up public health organizations, organize mobile cinema teams; and improve and extend the distribution of publications in national minority languages.

Social reforms in the national minority areas should, in accordance with the wishes of the people and leading public personages of the different nationalities and the specific conditions of the time in each area, be carried out gradually and in a well-prepared way so as to meet the requirements of economic and cultural development in the areas concerned.

(14) The living standards of the people should be raised step by step on the basis of increased production. A correct proportion should be maintained between the rise in labour productivity and the increase in wages of workers and employees; a correct distribution should be made of the income of the agricultural producers' co-operatives. A rational use should be made of labour power and unemployment in cities should be reduced step by step and brought to an end.

During the Second Five-Year Plan period, we should make great efforts to raise labour productivity, requiring industrial and building departments to raise it by 50 per cent in these five years. During the five-year period, the number of workers and employees in the various branches of the national economy will increase by six to seven millions.

Wages should be gradually increased on the basis of ensuring an increase in labour productivity. The average wages of workers and employees will go up by 25 to 30 per cent in these five years. The working hours of workers and employees working under conditions harmful to health should be suitably reduced.

We should continue to improve housing conditions of workers and employees, and, as conditions permit, build more houses; gradually improve transport facilities for city residents and public services in cities; gradually improve and set up more nurseries and kindergartens; and improve the work of canteens in enterprises, public institutions and government organizations. We should take practical measures to improve labour protection, sanitation and safety devices in factories and mines, to protect workers in production. Vigorous steps should be taken to reduce or eliminate those occupational diseases which cause serious harm to the workers. Special attention should be paid to improving the working conditions of those people who work in pits, in high temperatures, at high altitudes and are engaged in field work and the working conditions of women. The scope of labour insurance should be extended, and the system of labour insurance should be improved.

During the Second Five-Year Plan period, in order to stimulate the peasants' initiative in production, we should, except when extraordinary natural calamities intervene, see to it that co-operative members in general increase their income on the basis of increased agricultural production. In these five years, as agricultural production grows, the total income of the peasants will probably go up by about 25 to 30 per cent.

The welfare funds of agricultural producers' co-operatives should be suitably used so that the whole amount is spent on labour protection and on improving the material well-being of their members.

In these five years, with the development of handicraft production, the income of members of handicraft producers' co-operatives should also show a suitable increase.

Public health work should be further expanded in the Second Five-Year Plan period. The number of beds in hospitals and sanatoria and that of public health organizations should be suitably increased. Simple beds for the sick should be extensively provided in rural areas step by step. Preventive measures against disease and medical services in the countryside should be improved. Medical personnel should be trained according to plan. Doctors of traditional Chinese medicine and those trained in Western medicine should be encouraged to learn from each other. Serious efforts should be made to study and systematize Chinese medicine and Chinese pharmacy. The utmost efforts should be devoted to the prevention and cure of those diseases which cause the most harm to the people.

The mass sports movement should be widely extended step by step to make our people more physically fit. Due regard should be given to the physical condition of people participating lest there be adverse effects due to overstrain.

(15) In the Second Five-Year Plan period, in order to increase accumulation and speed up socialist construction, we should continue to adhere to the principle of increasing production and practising economy and enforce a system of practising strict economy.

In these five years, as a result of the rapid growth of production and the expansion of capital construction, there will be a steadily rising demand for materials, funds and cadres in all branches of the national economy. At the same time, the steady rise in the level of the people's material life will result in a growing demand for consumer goods. Therefore, it is necessary for us to strive to increase production and carry on our fine tradition of working hard and living thriftily, economizing in the use of manpower, material and financial resources and making the increase in production and the practice of economy a regular, long-term task in socialist construction.

In the Second Five-Year Plan period, departments charged with industry, transport and commerce should make further efforts to lower costs of production and transport and costs of distribution of commodities. In their building activities, capital construction departments should continue to strictly follow the principle of providing buildings that suit their purpose, that are economical and as beautiful as circumstances permit, lower building costs and raise the quality of construction. Cultural, educational and public health departments and state administrative organs should also observe the principle of reducing staff but increasing efficiency and practising economy; they should cut expenditure and combat extravagance and waste.

(16) Aid from the Soviet Union and the People's Democracies is an important condition for building socialism in our country. In the course of developing our national economy and building a comprehensive industrial system, we must, therefore, strengthen co-operation with the Soviet Union and the People's Democracies, and expand our economic and cultural exchanges and trade with them so that mutual support and help among these fraternal countries can be promoted. Given this relationship based on division of labour and co-operation in the economic and technical spheres and in scientific research, it is possible to make the fullest, mutually beneficial use of the material resources, latent productive capacity and scientific and technological achievements of these countries, thus accelerating the growth of their national economies and bringing about a common upsurge in the economies and cultures of all the socialist countries with the Soviet Union at their head.

Economic co-operation, trade relations, and cultural and technical exchanges with countries with different social systems, particularly with those in Asia and Africa, should be developed on the principle of equality and mutual benefit to promote the peaceful co-existence and the economic development of the peoples of all lands.

* * *

The Eighth National Congress of the Communist Party of China holds that the Second Five-Year Plan for development of the national economy of our country will be a plan to bring about a further all-round upsurge in our economy and culture. Fulfilment of this plan will make it possible for our country to further strengthen her economy and national defences, to raise the level of our science and technology, improve the material well-being and cultural standards of our people; and eliminate, in the main, the capitalist system, thereby laying a solid foundation for the accomplishment of the fundamental task of the state in the period of transition.

In order that the work of drawing up the Second Five-Year Plan may be well done, the departments of the State Council and the local authorities must, in the course of drafting the Plan, put all the targets on a forward-looking and completely sound basis. They must, on the one hand, take full account of all favourable conditions and combat the Rightist, conservative tendency to ignore the latent forces and underestimate the socialist enthusiasm of the masses. On the other hand, they must take full account of all unfavourable conditions and difficulties that are liable to occur, and combat the impetuous and adventurist tendency to depart from actual realities, give no consideration to possibilities, and overlook the planned and well-proportioned development of the various branches of the national economy.

Judging from the implementation of the First Five-Year Plan, it is difficult to anticipate at an early date many of the factors to be encountered in carrying out a long-term plan. This is particularly so in carrying out a plan for agricultural production at the present time and for a fairly long period to come, when it is still very difficult to prevent losses from natural calamities. Yet success or failure in fulfilling the plan for agricultural production has a profound influence on the execution of the whole plan for the national economy of our country. That is why in drawing up a long-term plan the targets should be put on a pretty sound basis. In drawing up each annual plan, however, so far as conditions permit, we should actively bring into play all our potentialities so as to ensure fulfilment and overfulfilment of the long-term plan.

The drawing up of the Second Five-Year Plan is a strenuous, difficult and complicated task and one of great significance. Organizations of the Communist Party of China at all levels should, therefore, take an active and practical part, together with government organs, in completing this task successfully, organize the masses for extensive discussion of the Plan, and combat subjectivism and bureaucracy in this work, so as to ensure that this plan conforms with reality and the fundamental task of the state in the period of transition and thus serves as a guide to successful development of our country's socialist construction.

The Eighth National Congress of the Communist Party of China calls on all comrades of the Party, under the leadership of the Central Committee and Comrade Mao Tse-tung, to continue their efforts to further unite with the people of all nationalities, all the democratic parties, people's organizations, Chinese nationals resident abroad and all patriots, and continue to consolidate and expand the people's democratic united front to strive for the overfulfilment of the First Five-Year Plan and make vigorous preparations for the Second Five-Year Plan.

DOCUMENT 11

Report on the Proposals for the Second Five-Year Plan for Development of the National Economy, delivered by Chou En-lai, September 16, 1956, to the Eighth Party Congress.

The English text is from *Eighth National Congress of the Communist Party of China*, Foreign Languages Press, Peking, 1956, Vol. I, pp. 261-328.

Comment. This is one of the most factual, frank, and interesting of Chinese official documents. For further general criticism by a Chinese official of the first Five-Year Plan, see ECMM 81 (*New Construction*, February 1957). Supplementary material on some of Chou's important points may be listed as follows.

(a) Excessive expansion of capital construction work (Chou's section I):

—speech by Po I-po, Chairman of the State Economic Commission, in *Eighth National Congress of the Communist Party of China*, Foreign Languages Press, Peking, 1956, Vol. II, pp. 45-62.

—Party directive on waste and extravagance in agricultural producers' cooperatives, April 4, 1956 (SCMP 1268).

—speech on the same subject to the National People's Congress by Teng Tzu-hui, Vice-Premier and frequent official spokesman on agricultural affairs, in June 1956 (CB 393).

—speech to the National People's Congress by Li Hsien-nien, Minister of Finance, in June 1957 (CB 464).

—speech to the National People's Congress by Po I-po, in June 1957 (CB 465).

Further incidental material from Chinese press sources on the fall in quality, rise in accident rates, and slackening of labor discipline resulting from the expansion of industry in 1956 may be found in URS, Vol. 2, No. 17; Vol. 3, Nos. 9, 24; Vol. 7, No. 13.

(b) The case of the two-wheel, two-share plow (Chou's section I): ECMM 56 (*Planned Economy*, Sept. 23, 1956).

(c) Free markets (Chou's section III, 6). The introduction of "free markets" in 1956, particularly as an incentive to the peasants, and their virtual abolition in 1957, is discussed in T. J. Hughes and D. E. T. Luard, *The Economic Development of Communist China* (London: Oxford University Press, 1959), pp. 185-189. See also, among extensive press discussion, ECMM 64 (*Current Events*, Nov. 10, 1956; *Study*, Nov. 2, 1956), and ECMM 136 (*New Construction*, March 13, 1958).

(d) Local initiative in administration (Chou's section III, 8). Chou had spoken on this subject to the National People's Congress in June 1956 (CB 398). In the present document he reported that the State Council (perhaps inspired by a pronouncement by Mao on the "ten sets of relationships"—see comment on Document 25) had called a number of national meetings from May to August 1956, to discuss overcentralization. Views were being sought, he said, on a draft resolution introduced by the State Council. As it turned out, various measures devolving more responsibility, organizational and financial, on local authorities were passed from the fall of 1957 through the spring of 1958. These essentially formed an administrative prelude to the Great Leap Forward and the formation of communes, and are discussed in our comments in Chapter VII.

─────────────────────TEXT OF DOCUMENT 11─────────────────────

Comrades,

Our First Five-Year Plan for Development of the National Economy will be successfully fulfilled a little more than a year from now. In order that we may smoothly begin construction under the Second Five-Year Plan as soon as the First is fulfilled, the Central Committee of the Party deems it necessary to make an early start on drawing up the Second Five-Year Plan. Now, the Central Committee submits its Proposals for the Second Five-Year Plan for examination by the Eighth National Congress of the Party. After being discussed and adopted by the Congress, they will be presented to the State Council for discussion.

The fundamental principles and policies concerning our Second Five-Year Plan for Development of the National Economy have already been expounded in the Political Report delivered by Comrade Liu Shao-chi on behalf of the Central Committee. Now, I am entrusted by the Central Committee with the task of delivering to the Congress this Report on the Proposals for the Second Five-Year Plan.

I. IMPLEMENTATION OF THE FIRST FIVE-YEAR PLAN

Before speaking on the Proposals for the Second Five-Year Plan, I shall first talk about the basic conditions of the implementation of the First Five-Year Plan.

In the course of implementing the First Five-Year Plan, thanks to the efforts of the people, and above all to the efforts of the working people of the whole country, victories which are quicker and greater than expected have been gained in both our work of socialist construction and of socialist transformation. Our achievements are tremendous, but there have also been some defects and errors in our work which we must strive to correct.

In regard to capital construction: It is estimated that, by the end of 1957, our investments in capital construction will probably exceed the planned total by more than 10 per cent; and that the programme for the above-norm construction projects included in the Plan, with a few exceptions, will be completed on or ahead of schedule and, furthermore, a number of new construction projects which are to be started in this period are added in each year. It is estimated that, by the end of 1957, some 500 newly built or reconstructed above-norm industrial enterprises will have been completed. This will increase the productive capacity of our industry, and help to establish new branches of industry and renovate to a certain degree some older ones, thereby beginning to alter the hitherto extremely backward state of China's industry. Through construction work under the First Five-Year Plan, our industrial base in the Northeast, with the Anshan Integrated Iron and Steel Works as its core, will be greatly reinforced. In Inner Mongolia, Northwest China and North China, many new industrial cities will take shape. The length of railways newly built or restored within these five years will reach some five thousand and five hundred kilometres. Important trunk lines such as the Chining-Erhlien and the Paochi-Chengtu lines are already finished. The Yingtan-Amoy Railway is nearing completion. The Lanchow-Sinkiang Railway has already been extended to the west of Yumen. Important highways such as the Sikang-Tibet and Chinghai-Tibet roads have been completed and opened to traffic. Completion of these railways and highways has strengthened the links between the vast areas of our Northwest and Southwest and other parts of the country. In the field of water conservancy, the work to bring the Huai River under permanent control is continued; the construction of the pivotal water conservancy and hydroelectric engineering project at Sanmen Gorge on the Yellow River has started; a number of large water conservancy projects and many small and medium ones have likewise been started. The many completed water conservancy projects have already begun to play a definite part in preventing floods and irrigating farmland. In the past few years, great achievements have also been made in geological work to meet the needs of our capital construction. As stated above, in terms of investments and progress in building most of the major projects, capital construction under the First Five-Year Plan will probably reach our original goals. But it should also be pointed out that some branches of our economy will possibly fail to fulfil their original investment plans; part of the construction work of a few major projects will possibly fall behind the original schedule. These branches and construction projects, in the period of more than a year from now, should step up their work and strive for the fulfilment of the original plans as far as possible. It should likewise be pointed out that some construction units concerned themselves only with speed, and overlooked quality and safety, thus resulting in poor quality, many accidents, and waste in construction work. This should be a lesson to us.

In regard to industrial production: The total value of industrial output (here and below, this includes the value of output of modern industries and handicrafts, being calculated in terms of constant prices of 1952) has every year exceeded the value set in the annual plan. In 1956 it will reach the level set for 1957 in the Plan. By 1957 it will possibly exceed by about 15 per cent the target originally set in the Plan. As to the output of major industrial products, in 1957 the overwhelming majority of them will surpass the planned targets. For instance, steel will reach 5,500,000 tons; electricity, 18,000 million kilowatt-hours; coal, 120 million tons; metal-cutting machine-tools, 30,000 units; power-generating equipment, 340,000 kilowatts; timber, 24 million cubic metres; cotton yarn, 5,600,000 bales; machine-processed sugar, 800,000 tons; and machine-made paper, 800,000 tons. As to important new industrial products, we are now able to manufacture power-generating, metallurgical and mining equipment and new types of metal-cutting machine-tools, which our country could not make in the past. We are also able to produce motor-vehicles and jet planes, which we were unable to make in the past. We have begun producing a certain amount of large-type steel products and high-grade alloy steels which we were unable to produce before. But owing to the shortage of raw materials, a slack market, or technical reasons, the original output plan for several kinds of products may not be fulfilled—for instance, oil, sulphur black, edible vegetable oils, cigarettes and matches.

In regard to agricultural production: In 1953 and 1954, many areas of our country suffered rather severe natural calamities. Consequently the agricultural production plans for these two years were not fulfilled. Nevertheless, the food crop surpassed that of 1952, which was a year of bumper harvests. The year 1955 was again one of good harvests. The output of grain (here and below not including soya beans) reached 349,600 million catties, that of cotton reached 30,360,000 *tan*, and the output of other agricultural products also increased. In 1956 many areas have suffered severely from floods, water-logging, typhoons and drought, resulting in a measure of damage to certain crops, especially cotton. But, because the whole countryside is in the high tide of the co-operative movement, production will be increased in those areas untouched by natural calamities, and the 1956 total output of grain the whole country will still be able to reach the level to be attained in 1957 as set down in the First Five-Year Plan. Provided that there are no particularly severe natural calamities in the coming year and more, it will be possible in 1957 for the main grain and certain industrial crops to exceed the targets set in the original Plan. But soya beans, peanuts, rape-seed, jute, ambary, and certain kinds of livestock will probably not be able to reach the original targets. We must take effective measures to strengthen these weak links.

In regard to transport, posts and tele-communications: Alongside the development of industrial and agricultural production and the expanding scale of capital construction, there has been an annual increase in the volume of traffic and of business handled by our posts and tele-communications. It is estimated that, in 1957, the target for freight mileage handled by all major transport departments will possibly be overfulfilled. But, because the plan for the technical reconstruction of certain existing lines and equipment has not been fulfilled, certain lines and transportation centres are at present overburdened and congested with traffic. Endeavours are being made to alter this situation.

In regard to commerce: With the constant growth of socialist commerce, a well-planned and well-organized domestic market has already taken shape, and the leading position of socialist commerce is being consolidated. In 1956 the volume of retail trade will increase by 66.3 per cent as compared with 1952, and the total value of imports and exports, by 65 per cent. It is estimated that, by 1957, all plans for retail sales and for the sales of most commodities in the home market, and plans for exports and imports, will be fulfilled, and some even overfulfilled. In the past few years, the volume of commodity circulation in the country has been expanded on the basis of increased production, and, as a result of carrying out the policy of planned purchase and distribution in regard to several kinds of the most essential daily necessaries, supplies of the people's daily necessaries have been ensured. This has secured, in the main, stability of prices and promoted industrial and agricultural production and the improvement of the people's life. At present, the chief defect in commerical work is that the supply of commodities is not well-organized, and business management is unsatisfactory. This has created overstocking of some goods at one time and shortage at another.

In regard to culture, education, scientific research and public health: Considerable advances have been made in all these fields in the past few years. It is estimated that by 1957, except for a few branches, we shall be able to overfulfil all the targets, including those for higher, secondary and primary education, scientific research, journalism, publications, broadcasting, literature, arts, cinema, physical culture and medical service. For instance, the 1957 enrolment in institutions of higher learning will reach about 470,000, surpassing the original target by about 9 per cent, and there will be 68 research institutes under the Chinese Academy of Sciences, 17 more than in the original plan.

In regard to co-operation in agriculture and handicrafts: By the end of June 1956, a total of 992,000 agricultural producers' co-operatives had been organized throughout the country. Their members made up 91.7 per cent of the country's peasant households; those belonging to co-operatives of the advanced type constituted 62.6 per cent of all peasant households. Approximately 90 per cent of all the handicraftsmen had been organized. It is our estimate that by the end of 1957, after we have worked for another year and more, co-operation in agriculture and handicrafts will be virtually universal throughout the country, except for a few border areas.

In regard to socialist transformation of private industry and commerce: By the end of June 1956, 99 per cent of capitalist industrial enterprises, in terms of output value, and 98 per cent in terms of number of workers and employees, had come under joint state-private operation. Of the private commercial and catering establishments, 68 per cent in terms of number of shops, and 74 per cent in terms of number of personnel, had been transformed into joint state-private shops, co-operative shops or co-operative groups. The conversion of capitalist industry and commerce into joint state-private enterprises by whole trades and the introduction of the system of a fixed rate of interest on shares have prepared the way for the nationalization of capitalist means of production.

Here I wish to speak briefly about the improvement of the people's material well-being.

Taken as a whole, the rate of increase of the wages of the workers and employees in the past few years was in the main compatible with that of labour productivity. However, in a certain period of time, the rate of increase in wages lagged far behind that of labour productivity. For instance, labour productivity in industry (excluding private industry) in 1955 was about 10 per cent higher than in 1954, while the average wages of the workers and employees increased only 0.6 per cent. A similar situation was found in other branches of the national economy. Immediately after we discovered this mistake in our work at the end of 1955 we set about correcting it. Beginning from April 1956, we implemented a nation-wide reform of the wages system, fixing the average wages of the workers and employees for 1956 at about 13 per cent above that of 1955. Thus the average wages of the workers and employees in 1956 will be 33.5 per cent higher than in 1952, surpassing the 33 per cent increase in five years laid down in the First Five-Year Plan. The increase of labour productivity will also exceed the original target. In state-owned industrial enterprises, for instance, labour productivity, according to the 1956 target, will be 70.4 per cent higher than in 1952, surpassing the 64 per cent increase in five years stipulated in the First Five-Year Plan.

During the past few years, we stabilized the agricultural taxes for the benefit of the peasants, and appropriately raised the price of grain purchased by the state, thus gradually improving the life of the peasants on the basis of expanded production. But we also made some mistakes. In 1954, because we did not completely grasp the situation of grain production in the whole country, and purchased a little more grain from the peasants than we should have, discontent arose among a section of the peasants. In 1955, we carried out the policy of fixed quotas for the production, purchase and marketing of grain, which set the minds of the peasants at ease and raised their enthusiasm in production. It is now estimated that the total income of the peasants can be increased by about 30 per cent in these five years.

From the situation described above, it can be seen that our First Five-Year Plan can definitely be fulfilled successfully. Most of the targets can be surpassed, if we make strenuous efforts and if no particularly serious natural calamities or unexpected accidents occur. The execution of the First Five-Year Plan has brought about, and its overfulfilment will further bring about, profound changes in our national economy. This expresses itself mainly in the following: Industrial and agricultural production has been raised greatly, with the total output value of industry and agriculture (including the output value of modern industries, handicrafts and agriculture) in 1957 estimated to increase by more than 60 per cent compared with 1952; the share contributed by the value of industrial output (including output of handicrafts) to the total value of industrial and agricultural output will be approximately 50 per cent, with industry producing capital goods accounting for over 40 per cent of total industrial output—a fact that will strengthen the leading role of industry in the national economy. Furthermore, as a decisive victory has been scored in socialist transformation, the socialist sector has assumed the predominant position in all fields—industry, agriculture, transport and commerce. Now, all branches of our national economy are prospering, and culture, education, and scientific research are entering a flourishing period. This has created conditions for the continued raising of the people's standard of living.

It should be pointed out that the unity of our people of all nationalities, all democratic parties and all patriots under the leadership of the Communist Party of China, and the initiative and enthusiasm they have shown in the task of socialist transformation and socialist construction are the foundation and guarantee for the great achievements enumerated above.

We must also point out that the great Soviet Union and the People's Democracies have given us tremendous assistance in the carrying out of our First Five-Year Plan. During this period, the Soviet Union has granted us loans on favourable terms, helped us to design 205 industrial enterprises and supplied the bulk of the equipment for them, sent large numbers of outstanding experts to China and rendered us much technical aid in other ways. The People's Democracies, too, have given us much assistance in equipment, materials, technical forces and so on. Experts from the Soviet Union and the People's Democracies who are working in China have been making outstanding contributions to the cause of socialist construction in our country. We wish to take this opportunity to express our deep gratitude for the sincere, fraternal assistance given us by the Soviet Union and the People's Democracies.

In carrying out the First Five-Year Plan, we have acquired considerable experience and learnt not a few lessons. By drawing on these, we shall be able to work still better in socialist construction. Here I only wish to put forward some views on certain questions which we consider to be fairly important in guiding economic work during the past few years.

First, we should, in accordance with needs and possibilities, set a reasonable rate for the growth of the national economy and place the Plan on a forward-looking and completely sound basis, to ensure a fairly balanced development of the national economy. Since it is difficult for us, while drawing up the long-term plan, to fully envisage the various new circumstances and questions that may arise in the course of its implementation, we should set the long-term targets in a comparatively realistic way and leave it for the annual plans to make the necessary adjustments. The targets set in the First Five-Year Plan are, in the main, correct. The arrangements of the annual plans of the past four years were, by and large, suited to the specific conditions of the time, and were therefore capable of ensuring an overfulfilment of our First Five-Year Plan. But it should be pointed out that in certain parts of our annual plans for 1955 and 1956, we erred on the side of setting the targets too high or too low, which gave rise to certain difficulties in our work.

In drawing up the 1955 plan, because of the crop failures in the previous two years, we narrowed down the scale of capital construction a bit too much, and in the campaign to practise economy in that year, we made inappropriate cuts in investments for certain non-productive capital construction projects. And as the plans for capital construction were changed frequently and issued to the departments concerned very late, they were not quite satisfactorily fulfilled. As a result, not only was there an excessive financial surplus, but also a temporary false surplus of important building materials like steel products, cement and timber. If we had, at an earlier date, prepared a number of reserve projects and enlarged the scale of construction in time or if we had increased our state reserves of certain materials in a planned way, this temporary laying-up of materials could have been resolved. However, since we underestimated the developments ahead and regarded temporary surpluses of materials as a relatively permanent phenomenon, we resorted to export to resolve our difficulties with temporary surpluses of steel products and cement. This was clearly not the right thing to do.

At the time when we drew up the plan for 1956, owing to the bumper harvest of the previous year and to the great victories won in socialist transformation, it was necessary as well as possible to set a fairly high tempo for development of the national economy. But we failed to strike a proper balance between the scale of capital construction and the capacity for supplying materials, and therefore we set the scale of capital construction somewhat larger than it should be. At the same time, there appeared in certain branches of the national economy a tendency to do many things at once and to have them done in a hurry. As a result, not only were our national finances somewhat strained, but there occurred a serious shortage of building materials, such as steel products, cement and timber. The state reserve of materials was too heavily drawn upon, and quite a strained situation was brought about in various spheres of the national economy.

Experience shows that, in drawing up the long-term plan, we should set the targets realistically in accordance with the basic requirements of socialist industrialization and with the possibilities of the material and financial resources and manpower of the country. At the same time, a certain amount of reserves should be built up so that the plan can be put on a sounder basis. But while drawing up annual plans, we should bring whatever potentialities we have into play according to the conditions which will possibly develop in the current year and subsequent years, so as to ensure fulfilment and overfulfilment of the long-term plan. Experience further shows that we should guard against two different tendencies in drawing up the annual plans: when conditions are favourable, we must discern the unfavourable factors confronting and ahead of us and guard against impatience and rashness; when conditions are unfavourable, we must see that there also exist many favourable factors confronting and ahead of us and guard against timidity and hesitance. That is to say, we should make an over-all analysis of the objective conditions, and at the same time try as best as we can to make a unified plan for the main targets of the current year and the next year, so that each of the annual plans may dovetail with the next and advance at a fairly even pace.

Secondly, we should co-ordinate key projects with over-all arrangements, so that the various branches of the national economy can develop proportionately. During the past few years, while giving priority to the development of heavy industry, we adopted the policy of speeding up agricultural co-operation to push forward the development of agricultural production, and correspondingly developed light industry, thus making it possible to avoid the danger of dislocation between the several major branches of the national economy.

In dealing with this relationship between key projects and over-all arrangements, we have, however, also made mistakes in some cases. For instance, in 1953, in the construction work of some departments and localities there appeared the tendency to do everything at once and do it everywhere, taking no account of actual conditions, and recklessly running ahead. As a result, this affected the priority construction projects of the state, gave rise to difficulties in finance and waste of manpower and material resources. Such a tendency recurred in the beginning of 1956, following the publication of the Draft National Programme for Agricultural Development (1956–1967). Some departments and localities, impatient for success, attempted to accomplish within three or five years, or even one or two years, tasks that required seven or twelve years to complete. These tendencies were all discovered and corrected by the Central Committee in good time.

In the same period, there appeared another tendency—the tendency to give certain important tasks too much emphasis so that they fell out of step with other related tasks. For example, in the beginning of 1956, in order to speed up agricultural development, we overestimated the needs in that year for the two-wheeled, double-shared plough and the small-size steam engine, and drew up production plans for too high an output of them. Although plans for the two products were repeatedly revised to reduce output, the planned figures were still too high. As a result, too much steel was consumed, thus creating more tension in the supply of steel in 1956. Also, some machine-building factories were made to rush up production at one time and reduce it at another. To take another example, in the course of our construction, certain industrial enterprises advanced too rapidly so that the raw materials needed were not all available. The result was that it was impossible for those enterprises to give full play to their productive capacity. At the start of our industrial construction, things like these might not be entirely avoidable. But it was not impossible to foresee them and make more judicious preparations against them.

In our construction work during the past few years, we have made arrangements that are on the whole appropriate with regard to the relationship between the central and the local authorities, and between the coastal areas and the interior. But there were still shortcomings in this respect. For some time, we laid emphasis on the construction work undertaken by the central authorities, but paid inadequate attention to the development of local construction work; we laid emphasis on construction work in the interior, but paid inadequate attention to that in the coastal areas. Hereafter, we should constantly pay attention to readjusting the above-mentioned relationships, so as to avoid one-sidedness.

The foregoing shows that while we lay emphasis on key projects, it does not mean that they can be developed in isolation, independent of an over-all arrangement; and while we require an over-all arrangement, it does not mean that we may lay equal emphasis on all things without giving assurance to the key projects. In drawing up plans and arranging our work, we must neatly co-ordinate key projects with over-all arrangement.

Thirdly, we should build up our reserves and perfect our system of stockpiling materials. Loss of balance is bound to occur frequently as our national economy develops. Hence we must lay aside the necessary reserves of materials, financial resources, mineral resources, productive capacity, etc., and in particular, we must increase state-held stocks of materials, so that an even growth of our national economy and the smooth execution of annual plans may be ensured, and that any unexpected difficulties that may arise can be coped with. In the next few years, our agricultural production is still very much subject to the influence of natural calamities. To meet possible crop failures, we must have stocks of grain and of major industrial crops. In order to meet the needs of the daily expansion of the scale of our construction and production, we must also have stocks of equipment and raw materials. Furthermore, we still lack experience in planning, and our plans are often incomplete and inaccurate. Even if they are fairly accurate at the moment when they are drawn up, they may be thrown out of balance by unforeseeable factors. For instance, in 1956, when the utilization rate of the open-hearth and blast furnaces was raised as a result of the introduction of new technique, the supply of ores and coke failed to catch up. In order to eliminate or mitigate the unbalanced conditions which may occur in carrying out the plan, we must also hold the necessary reserves.

Although the state's stocks of materials were not very large in the past few years, they played a part in meeting the demands of our production and capital construction, and made a contribution towards easing the tense material shortages of 1956. It should be pointed out, however, that in the past we did not grasp the full importance of keeping reserves of materials. As I have said before, in 1955, when there was a small surplus of certain materials, we injudiciously exported part of them. So when the scale of capital construction was expanded in 1956, an acute shortage of these materials was felt.

We must understand that in a country like ours where the economy is backward and the population is large, shortage of materials will occur frequently for a long time to come, whereas any surplus will be transient. Therefore we need to pay still more attention to augmenting our reserves and instituting a storage system, for the state to store necessary materials, and especially important materials the supplies of which are not so abundant. All state enterprises should also keep proper material reserves. Of course, the storage of materials, whether made by the state or by state enterprises, should be carried out in a well-planned way, and the quantities of materials should be fixed within reasonable limits and increased gradually. We cannot expect to make big increases at once because this would harm our current production and construction. Furthermore, we must also combat the wrong view of regarding the overstocking of products caused by blind production as storage of materials by the state, because this would inevitably cause state funds to run to waste or lie unused, which is also harmful to our production and construction.

Fourthly, the relationship between economy and finance should be correctly handled. Years of experience tell us that our financial revenue must be based on our economic development, and our financial expenditure must also, and above all, ensure the development of our economy. Thus, we should first of all consider the economic development plan, particularly the plan for industrial and agricultural production. Then, basing ourselves on it, we should draw up the financial plan, with which to ensure the successful carrying out of the economic plan. If, instead of enlarging our financial resources in accordance with the conditions of our economic development, we set our targets for financial revenue too low, or, if we only worry about cutting financial expenditure and keep too much in reserve, we will tend to hold back the full development of economic construction. This would be wrong.

In drawing up our financial revenue plan, we must take into account the prospects of economic development and the correct ratio between accumulation and consumption, and avoid placing the figures so high as to put a great strain on our efforts. In drawing up our financial expenditure plan, apart from making a correct distribution in line with the demands of ensuring the construction of key projects and the proportionate development of the national economy, we should also give consideration to the balance between the scale of construction and the supply of materials and keep in hand a definite amount of reserve funds to meet unexpected needs, and avoid placing the figures so high as to put a great strain on our efforts. It would be obviously wrong, too, to take only the demands of construction into account and ignore the financial possibilities, or without considering whether there are adequate supplies of equipment, materials and technical personnel, put forward indices which are too high and excessively big plans for investments.

Comrades often like to argue whether or not there should be "financial limitations." In our view, it is of course wrong to ignore the demands of economic development, and subjectively set up limitations which hamper economic development. We should oppose such limitations. But, if financial plans conform to the actual condition of economic development, and embody the correct relations between accumulation and consumption, between priority construction projects and overall arrangements, then such financial plans must undoubtedly be strictly carried out, and should by no means be branded as "financial limitations" and blindly challenged.

It should also be pointed out here that many of the shortcomings and mistakes in our work are inseparable from subjectivism and bureaucracy among the leadership. Some leading comrades sit up on high, do not approach the masses, are ignorant of the actual conditions, and are subjective in dealing with questions and making arrangements for work. Consequently one can hardly expect their decisions to be correct; in fact, they may be wrong. Bureaucracy at higher levels, moreover, fosters commandism at lower levels.

At present the various departments of the State Council are overstaffed and divided into too many levels, causing the lower organizations to be inundated with official documents, telegrams and forms. There are leading cadres in certain departments who are not even aware what directives have been issued from and what regulations have been made in their departments. A quick end must be put to such manifestations of bureaucracy.

Although we have made great achievements in our governmental work, we must never allow ourselves to have the slightest feeling of self-complacency and conceit. It should also be observed that our national economy is developing at high speed, and that the situation changes often and rapidly. New problems can appear anywhere at any moment, and many of these problems are interlinked and crisscrossed with complications. Therefore, we must constantly maintain close contact with the masses, get down to reality, strengthen the work of investigation and study, take changes in the situation in hand, make concrete analyses of conditions, both favourable and unfavourable, and estimate both advantages and difficulties correctly so that decisions can be made in time to regulate the activities of all departments and aspects of our national economy in order to avoid dislocation and clashes. In this vast country of ours, where situations are complicated and sweeping changes in the economy are taking place, any sort of negligence may result in big mistakes and great losses. Consequently, the overcoming of subjectivism and bureaucracy is of especially great importance.

II. FUNDAMENTAL TASKS OF THE SECOND FIVE-YEAR PLAN

The Central Committee of the Party considers that in drawing up the Second Five-Year Plan for Development of the National Economy we should start from the anticipated achievements of the First Five-Year Plan, bear in mind the basic requirement that by about the end of the Third Five-Year Plan period we must fulfil the fundamental task of the state in the transition period, and make a practical appraisal of the various conditions inside and outside the country during the Second Five-Year Plan period, so that the planning may be all-embracing. Only in this way can the plan be both forward-looking and sound.

The Central Committee of the Party suggests that the fundamental tasks of the Second Five-Year Plan for Development of the National Economy should be: (1) to continue industrial construction with heavy industry as its core and promote technical reconstruction of the national economy, and build a solid foundation for socialist industrialization; (2) to carry through socialist transformation, and consolidate and expand the system of collective ownership and the system of ownership by the whole people; (3) to further increase the production of industry, agriculture and handicrafts and correspondingly develop transport and commerce on the basis of developing capital construction and carrying through socialist transformation; (4) to make vigorous efforts to train personnel for construction work and strengthen scientific research to meet the needs of the development of socialist economy and culture; and (5) to reinforce the national defences and raise the level of the people's material and cultural life on the basis of increased industrial and agricultural production.

The main purpose of the socialist industrialization of our country is to build up, in the main, a comprehensive industrial system approximately within a period of three Five-Year Plans. Such an industrial system will be able to produce the principal machinery, equipment and materials to meet in the main the needs of our expanded reproduction and of the technical reconstruction of our national economy. It will also be able to produce various types of consumer goods to satisfy suitably the needs born of the ever-rising living standards of the people.

Some may ask: Given the continuous development of the economies of the socialist countries headed by the Soviet Union, and given the possibilities of economic and technical co-operation among the socialist countries, is it still necessary for our country to set up a comprehensive industrial system? We think that even though our country's situation today is quite different from that of the Soviet Union in the early years of its establishment when it was economically isolated and could not get assistance from other countries and that the existence and development of the Soviet Union and People's Democracies is a very favourable condition for our socialist construction, yet a populous country like ours, which has rich resources and great demands, still needs to build its own comprehensive industrial system. This is because, in accordance with our internal requirements, we must quickly alter the long-term backwardness of our national economy; and in accordance with international requirements, the establishment of a powerful industry in our country can promote a common economic upsurge in the socialist countries and add to the forces in defence of world peace. The parasitic view that we need not build our own comprehensive industrial system, and can rely wholly on international assistance, is therefore wrong.

Another view, that we can close our doors and carry on construction on our own, is wrong too. Needless to say, the establishment of a comprehensive industrial system in our country requires assistance from the Soviet Union and the People's Democracies for a long time to come. At the same time it is also necessary for us to develop and expand economic, technical and cultural exchanges with other countries. Even when we have built up a socialist industrial state, it will still be inconceivable that we should close our doors and have nothing to ask from others. Facts show that, not only will economic and technical co-operation among the socialist countries expand continuously, but, with the daily growth of the forces of the peoples of various countries in the struggle for peace, democracy and national independence, and the international situation tending more and more towards relaxation, economic, technical and cultural relations between us and various other countries of the world will certainly expand from day to day. Therefore, the isolationist view of socialist construction is also wrong.

In order to lay a solid foundation for the socialist industrialization of our country, it is necessary, during the Second Five-Year Plan, to continue to expand our metallurgical industry, to make vigorous efforts to speed the construction of our machine-building industry to strengthen our electric power, coal-mining and building material industries, and to energetically develop the backward branches of our industry—the oil, chemical, and radio equipment industries. At the same time, we should also press ahead with the technical reconstruction of our national economy and, first of all, technical reconstruction of industry, so as to raise the technical level of our industry.

As attested by experience, industrial construction, with heavy industry as its core, cannot and should not be carried on in isolation, but must be co-ordinated with other branches of the national economy, especially agriculture. Agriculture is a necessary condition for industrial development, and for the development of the entire national economy. To retard the development of agriculture would not only have a direct adverse effect on the development of light industry and the betterment of the people's livelihood, but greatly affect the development of heavy industry as well as of the national economy as a whole; it would also adversely affect the consolidation of the worker-peasant alliance. Therefore, in the Second Five-Year Plan period we should continue to make great efforts to develop agriculture so that its development may be co-ordinated with that of industry. To ensure a well-proportioned, mutually co-ordinated development of all branches and aspects of the national economy, we should arrange proper relations between heavy industry and light industry, between industrial and agricultural production on the one hand and transport and the circulation of commodities on the other, between economic construction and cultural development, between national construction and the livelihood of the people. At the same time, we should make further adjustments in the relations between the central and the local authorities, between the areas close to the coast and the interior, and between the various nationalities. All this is intended to harness all positive factors and useful forces to the great cause of building socialism.

In the Second Five-Year Plan period, it will be possible for our capital construction, and industrial and agricultural production, to keep up their expansion at a relatively high speed. The Central Committee holds that in this period, on the basis of increased state revenue, state investments in capital construction can be increased from the figure of about 35 per cent of the total state revenue in the first five-year period, to about 40 per cent. Hence investments in capital construction in the second five-year period will be about double those in the first. As regards industrial and agricultural production, according to preliminary calculations, the total value of industrial output in 1962 will be about 100 per cent more than in 1957. Within this total, the value of output of both capital goods and consumer goods will increase considerably, but the rate of increase in capital goods will be still greater. The total value of agricultural output will increase by about 35 per cent. By 1962, the total value of industrial and agricultural output will be about 75 per cent above the figure set for 1957 by the First Five-Year Plan.

It should be explained here that the increased percentages as enumerated in the Proposals for the Second Five-Year Plan are calculated with the planned targets set in the First Five-Year Plan as the basis, and no account is taken of the possibility that these targets may be surpassed. They thus appear to be relatively high. After the conclusion of the First Five-Year Plan, if the figures actually achieved in 1957 are used as the basis, then the percentage increases in the Proposals may turn out to be relatively lower. For instance, China's steel output for 1962 as suggested in the Proposals is 10,500,000-12,000,000 tons. This represents an increase of 150-190 per cent, as compared with the 1957 target set in the First Five-Year Plan—which is 4,120,000 tons. But compared with the 1957 output of steel as now envisaged, which is 5,500,000 tons, the increase will be about 100-120 per cent.

We consider that the rates of expansion of capital construction and industrial and agricultural production, mentioned above, are suitable, being put on a forward-looking and perfectly sound basis. We are convinced that if only we rely on the masses and bring their initiative and creative ability into play, we can mobilize great strength, overcome all difficulties in the path of our advance and successfully accomplish the tasks set by the Second Five-Year Plan just as we have done in the First.

III. SOME MAJOR QUESTIONS CONCERNING THE PROPOSALS FOR THE SECOND FIVE-YEAR PLAN

I have explained above the fundamental tasks of the Second Five-Year Plan. The specific principles and targets with regard to the Second Five-Year Plan have been dealt with in the Proposals put forward by the Central Committee. Here, I shall only speak briefly on a number of major questions concerning the Proposals for the Second Five-Year Plan.

1. Reasonable Accumulation And Distribution Of Funds

The scale of our national construction will depend on the amount of funds we can accumulate and how we distribute them. If we amass more funds and distribute them properly, the rate of expanded reproduction in society will be faster, and we shall be able to bring about a well-proportioned development of the various branches of the national economy. Therefore, a reasonable solution of the questions of accumulation and distribution of funds is of great importance.

National income is the material wealth newly created in production by the working people of the whole country. In socialist countries, the entire national income belongs to the working people themselves. They use a part of it for the maintenance and improvement of their own living standards and the other part for expanded reproduction of society, i.e., on accumulation. In the distribution and redistribution of national income, a suitable proportion must be maintained between the part for consumption and the part for accumulation. If the proportion of consumption is too small, the improvement of the life of the people will be impeded. If the proportion of accumulation is too small, expanded reproduction of society will be slowed down. Both would be detrimental to the people.

In the Second Five-Year Plan period, our national income will probably rise by approximately 50 per cent as compared with the first five years. Because our national economy is still very backward, with agriculture still occupying a relatively large part, and because the standard of living of our people is still relatively low, the portion of national income going to accumulation cannot and should not be increased too much and too fast, but may be slightly bigger than that in the first five-year period. Thus, in the Second Five-Year Plan period, the amount of accumulation will still show a great increase along with the rise in the national income.

After the problem of the accumulation of funds is solved, we must also solve the problem of distributing such funds. Taking into account the present internal and international conditions, the Central Committee considers that, for the Second Five-Year Plan period, it is necessary and possible for us to cut down appropriately in our state budget the proportion of expenditure going to national defence and administration, and to raise that going to economic, cultural and educational undertakings. In the first five-year period, expenditure for national defence and administration constitutes approximately 32 per cent of all state expenditure. In the second five-year period, we should endeavour to cut it down to approximately 20 per cent. In this way, expenditure for economic, cultural and educational undertakings can be raised from approximately 56 per cent in the first five-year period to 60-70 per cent in the second, thereby ensuring a rapid progress in the economic, cultural and educational spheres.

In distributing state investments in capital construction, a relatively high rate of development should be ensured for industry and agriculture. In the total amount of investments, investments in industry may be raised from 58.2 per cent in the first five-year period, to approximately 60 per cent in the second; and investments in agriculture, water conservancy and forestry may be raised from 7.6 per cent to around 10 per cent. In addition, attention should be paid to proper allocation of investments for transport, posts and tele-communications, for cultural, educational, scientific and public health departments, for urban construction departments and commerce, so that each may retain an appropriate proportion.

In distributing industrial investments, suitable proportions should be kept between light and heavy industries. In the first five years, as there are still considerable potentialities in our light industry, the Plan stipulates that investments in light industry should constitute 11.2 per cent of the total industrial investment (this has been raised a little in the course of implementation)—a percentage which is appropriate. Considering the gradual rise in consumption by the people in the second five years, and that our productive capacity in certain products of light industry will be inadequate, we deem it necessary to suitably increase the percentage of investments in light industry. However, some of the light industrial enterprises have not fully tapped their potentialities, large numbers of joint state-private enterprises, in particular once reorganized, will be able to further increase their output, and the handicrafts, being put on the co-operative basis, will also further increase the production of consumer goods. In allocating investments to light industries, we should also take these factors into account.

2. Correct Arrangement Of The Capital Construction Programme

Apart from the reasonable distribution of investments necessary in capital construction, which we have just dealt with, attention should also be paid to the following questions related to capital construction:

(1) Question Of Strengthening The Machine-Building And Metallurgical Industries

In our industrial construction, which has heavy industry as its core, special attention should be paid to building up the machine-building and metallurgical industries.

The development of the machine-building industry is one of the principal links in the establishment of a comprehensive industrial system in our country. During the First Five-Year Plan period, we are still unable to make many heavy machines, precision machines and complete sets of equipment for many types of factories. We are therefore compelled to import about 40 per cent of the machines and equipment needed for our construction. Hence a crucial question in our industrial construction from now on will be the vigorous development of the machine-building industry—particularly the manufacture of various types of heavy equipment, special-duty machine-tools, precision machine-tools, and instruments which we need but of which we are short. Through our construction under the Second Five-Year Plan, we should strive to raise the percentage of machines and equipment produced at home to about 70 per cent of our needs.

Metallurgy is the foundation of heavy industry; unless we have a powerful metallurgical industry, it will be difficult for us to develop machine-building. In the First Five-Year Plan period, we supplied only about 80 per cent of the nation's steel needs from domestic production while we imported all, or nearly all, our supplies of many special types of steel products. Hence, another crucial question in our industrial construction from now on will be the vigorous development of metallurgy. We should strive to ensure that as a result of construction in the Second Five-Year Plan, the quantities and types of steel products and major non-ferrous metals produced will meet, in the main, the needs of the various branches of the national economy, and in particular, of machine-building.

Among the various branches of heavy industry, we must not only strive to develop the machine-building and metallurgical industries, but also strengthen many other weak links and fill up many blanks. For instance, the mining and refining of rare metals, the establishment and expansion of an organic synthetic chemical industry, the peaceful utilization of atomic energy, etc. should all be taken as important aspects of our construction and given sufficient attention.

To develop heavy industry, it is necessary to continue to improve and expand geological work and correctly link general reconnaissance with priority prospecting work. Efforts should be made to explore more mines and more kinds of ores, and collect more data on mineral deposits so as to satisfy the long-term as well as immediate needs of industrial construction.

(2) Question Of Geographical Distribution Of Productive Forces

In order to achieve a rational distribution of productive forces in our country, to promote the economic development of all areas, and to adapt the geographical disposition of our industries to the situation of our resources and national defence, it is necessary to build new industrial bases in the interior in a planned way. We must firmly adhere to this policy. The building up of new industrial projects in the interior will also promote the economic and cultural development of the national minority areas. During the Second Five-Year Plan period we must continue the construction of the industrial bases in Central China and Inner Mongolia with the iron and steel industry as their core; actively proceed with the construction of new industrial bases in Southwest China, Northwest China and the area around the Sanmen Gorge, with iron and steel industry and large-type hydro-electric power stations as their core; carry on with the building of oil and non-ferrous metal industries in Sinkiang; and intensify geological work in Tibet in order to prepare the way for its industrial development.

At the same time, we must make full use of the existing industrial bases in areas near the coast. Many of the materials, equipment, funds and technical personnel needed for industrial construction in the interior have to be supplied and supported by the existing industries in the cities near the coast. We may say that the existing industrial bases in the areas near the coast are the starting-point of the industrialization of our country. And it is not only to meet the daily-increasing needs of our state and people but also to build up more powerful industrial bases in the interior that we make full use of and strengthen the industrial bases in the areas near the coast. In the Second Five-Year Plan period, we should continue to strengthen the industrial base in Northeast China, make full use of and strengthen to a proper extent the industries of the cities near the coast in East, North and South China, so that they may play a more active role in national construction.

To be sure, in making full use of the existing industrial bases in the cities near the coast, we must proceed rationally and avoid thoughtlessness in our work. To proceed rationally is to reconstruct those enterprises which it is necessary as well as possible to reconstruct, but not to reconstruct all existing enterprises. It is to set up, as a rule, fewer new enterprises in those cities in which there are already a fairly large number of industrial enterprises. It also requires that, before building new enterprises and reconstructing existing ones, we should take into account sources of raw materials, market conditions, techniques of production, and transport facilities, and pay attention to a rational division of work with other areas.

As to the distribution of industrial enterprises, whether in the interior or along the coast, our policy is to achieve both proper dispersion and mutual co-ordination, and to combat both the tendency towards over-concentration and towards neglect of correlation.

In carrying out the rational distribution of industrial productive forces, we shall build up many new cities and enlarge many existing ones. To achieve this, we should strengthen the work of city planning and urban construction, so as to co-ordinate them with industrial construction.

(3) Question Of Co-ordination Between Large Enterprises On The One Hand And Small And Medium Enterprises On The Other

The many large-scale industrial enterprises which we began to build during the First Five-Year Plan period and those which we shall begin to build in the Second Five-Year Plan period constitute the backbone of a self-reliant and comprehensive industrial system in our country. But while we are building large-scale enterprises, it is also necessary to build up a good number of small and medium ones. We need these so that, in a relatively short period of time, we can turn out more industrial products to satisfy the needs of both national construction and of consumption by the people.

Some hold that we should establish more large enterprises and fewer small or medium enterprises, because to set up large enterprises is more rational economically and technically. Some other people, however, think we should set up more small and medium enterprises and fewer large enterprises, because to set up the former requires less time, and the investments yield a quicker return. We think that neither is true in all cases. In certain industries or under given conditions, it is reasonable to establish large enterprises, while in others or under different conditions, it might be more reasonable to establish small or medium ones. For each branch, generally speaking, there should be some large enterprises to serve as the backbone, and there should also be many small and medium enterprises to support the large ones.

In order that the enterprises may be built in a more rational way, we may, whenever this is necessary and feasible, establish a large enterprise stage by stage. As regards small and medium enterprises, wherever resources are plentiful and other conditions are available, we may draw up a comprehensive plan to pave the way for future development. Further, when planning the co-ordination of small and medium enterprises with large ones, we should first utilize the existing small and medium enterprises and handicrafts under state ownership or joint state-private ownership so as to exploit their productive potentialities.

3. Development Of Industrial Production

It is provided in our First Five-Year Plan that in 1957 the total value of industrial output (including the value of output of the handicrafts) will increase by 90.3 per cent as compared with 1952. The Central Committee proposes that the total value of industrial output in 1962 should approximately double that set originally in the plan for 1957. The reasons why, in the Second Five-Year Plan period, the increase of the total value of industrial output can be maintained at a rather high speed, are that in this period the number of newly-built and reconstructed enterprises going into operation will increase; most of the existing enterprises will take technical measures to increase production or undertake technical reconstruction; the joint state-private enterprises will have accomplished their economic reorganization, and will have, in the main, been nationalized; all the handicrafts, with a few exceptions, will have been organized into co-operatives; and agricultural development will also possibly proceed at a rather high speed.

Regarding the development of industrial production, I should like to speak here only about the following questions:

(1) Question Of Turning To Account The Productive Potentialities Of Industrial Enterprises

According to a rough calculation, by 1957, the output value of newly-built and reconstructed enterprises will account for about 15 per cent of the total value of industrial output; whereas by 1962, that of the newly-built and reconstructed enterprises to be completed in the first and second five-year periods will account for about 50 per cent. Therefore, it is of great significance for the development of industrial production to strengthen our organizational work and turn these enterprises to the fullest account.

In the newly-built industrial enterprises and those which have undergone major reconstruction, especially those of heavy industry, a period of time should be allowed from their entering into operation to the full attainment of the designed productive capacity, during which the technical personnel and workers will get acquainted with the properties and capacity of the machinery and equipment and the technological processes. But this period can be shortened if the labour enthusiasm and wisdom of the technical personnel, workers and employees are given full play. Moreover, some of the productive capacities set down in the designing data can be exceeded. As shown by the statistics of April 1956, of the 141 above-norm industrial construction projects successively put into operation in the period from 1953 to 1955, 30 have reached ahead of schedule and surpassed their designed capacity, 33 will be able to reach their designed capacity ahead of schedule, 71 will be able to reach their designed capacity on time, and only 7 will fail to do so. That is to say, nearly half of the enterprises will be able to shorten the period allotted and attain their designed capacity ahead of schedule. An instance in this respect is the reconstructed Shenyang Pneumatic Tools Plant, which attained the designed capacity in the second year of its reconstruction, as against the four years which it was estimated to take, and is expected to more than double its designed output capacity in 1957. Another instance is the newly-built Fushun Aluminium Works, which was put into operation in the beginning of 1955, and at the end of the same year, its output already reached about 110 per cent of its designed capacity. From this it is evident that newly-built and reconstructed enterprises have very great potentialities for production. In order to turn these potentialities to the fullest account, the primary thing to do is to strengthen the preparatory work for production, especially training of personnel, preparation in technique, organization of co-operation, and the supply of materials. The departments concerned should study, summarize and popularize the concrete experience gained in these matters.

But it can by no means be said that, given the newly-built and reconstructed enterprises, we need no longer pay attention to production in the older enterprises. In the Second Five-Year Plan period the output value of the older enterprises will still make up a fairly large part of the total value of industrial output, and many of the newly-built and reconstructed enterprises will still have to rely on their co-operation and support. We must take different measures in accordance with actual conditions. We should systematically reconstruct or carry out the technical renovation of certain enterprises. In the case of others, we should readjust their equipment and provide them with some new equipment. With the rest, we should continue to improve their operation and management so as to give full play to their potentialities.

(2) *Question Of Promoting Specialization And Co-operation In Industrial Production*

Labour productivity can be raised, production costs reduced and technical development advanced by specialization and co-operation in industry, especially in heavy industry. But specialization and co-operation in industry are rather complicated problems which can only be settled severally and step by step over a fairly long period as our country's industrial level rises and in accordance with concrete conditions and possibilities. We must not do this work blindly and crudely.

In the First Five-Year Plan period, we have been bringing into full play the possibilities of existing multiple-product factories and seeing to it that their production meets the manifold needs of national construction and the people's life. On the other hand, in the machine-building industry, we have begun to set up some specialized plants according to types of products and have reorganized some machine-building plants whose products used to be too varied, turning them in the direction of specialization. All this is entirely necessary. In the Second Five-Year Plan period, apart from setting up a few specialized factories, we should make rational adjustments of the planned list of products which the various types of newly-built and reconstructed enterprises will produce so as to avoid both the defect resulting from too great a variety of products and the tendency towards undue specialization. With respect to existing enterprises, we should on the one hand suitably readjust the planned list of products in certain enterprises so as to rationalize their production, and on the other hand retain some of the multiple-product factories. In the case of most of the joint state-private enterprises, we should allow them to continue to turn out the kinds of products which they have been manufacturing, to meet the manifold needs of society and the requirements of state enterprises for co-operative support. In an industrial area or an industrial city, we may make an over-all arrangement, in accordance with the needs and possibilities, to organize specialized production of certain forgings, castings and standard products. In promoting specialization in industrial production, we should guard against the tendency to produce fewer types of products.

With the gradual development of industrial production towards specialization, the task of co-operation becomes heavier and more complicated. Thus it is necessary to take further corrective action against the inclination to work in isolation and reluctance to co-operate. Enterprises which must and can co-operate should lay down concrete tasks of co-operation in their annual plans, and enter into co-operation contracts.

(3) Question Of Raising The Quality And Increasing The Variety Of Products

Inferior quality and lack of variety of many industrial products, particularly certain products of light industry, have become an outstanding problem in current industrial development and adversely affected national construction and the people's life. There is no doubt that the quality of many products of our heavy and light industries is being steadily improved and their types constantly increased. But this is not the case for all industrial products. The quality of certain industrial products even continues to deteriorate while fewer are produced. A big effort must be made to remedy this.

Although the low quality and limited range of industrial products can to a large extent be attributed to our low technical level and out-of-date equipment, this does not mean that it is impossible for us to raise the quality of our industrial products and increase the number of types produced, still less can this be used as an excuse for lowering quality and producing fewer types. Some industrial departments have failed to pay due attention to the quality and variety of their products and lack long-term plans and effective measures to deal with this question. In examining the execution of plans, these departments are very often too much concerned about whether the output target is reached, but not whether the targets for quality and the production of new types of products are achieved. Prizes are awarded to those who have overfulfilled the output plan in quantity but not to those who have raised the quality and increased the types of products. All these are important reasons for the present low quality and limited variety of industrial products. Besides, in regard to products of light industry, they were, in the past, purchased and distributed *in toto* by the commercial departments. Products of higher and lower quality and of new and old types were bought and sold at the same prices or with only a slight difference in prices. These systems and measures also fostered the tendency of enterprises to overlook the quality and variety of products. Therefore, right now as well as in the Second Five-Year Plan period, the various industrial departments should work out long-term development plans in regard to industrial technique, energetically mobilize personnel for the designing of new products and strengthen leadership over the designing and trial manufacture of new products, strengthen the technical management of the enterprises, improve the supply of raw materials, and introduce a system of awarding prizes for good quality products. They should, in particular, encourage the broad mass of workers and employees to strive for improved quality and a greater variety of products. At the same time, the commercial departments should gradually introduce the system of selective purchase of certain commodities and the method of grading commodities and fixing prices according to quality.

4. Development Of Agricultural Production

In the Proposals for the Second Five-Year Plan, the Central Committee proposes that grain output in the five years will total about 2,200,000 million catties, with the 1962 output amounting to about 500,000 million catties; while the output of cotton in the five years will total about 210 million *tan*, with the 1962 output amounting to approximately 48 million *tan*. Compared with the original target for 1957, the total value of agricultural output in 1962 will show an increase of approximately 35 per cent. These targets have been advanced on the basis of the following considerations: On the one hand, with the exception of a few areas, the advanced form of co-operation will have been reached in agriculture and thus we will be able to further implement the provisions of the Draft National Programme for Agricultural Development (1956–1967), extensively adopt various measures for increasing production and spread all the experience gained in this respect; at the same time the irrigated area and the area under cultivation will be expanded, the supply of chemical fertilizers will be increased, and the means of production and farming techniques will be improved. All this will promote the further development of agricultural production. On the other hand, losses due to various kinds of natural calamities are still unavoidable, many rivers which cause serious damage still cannot be completely harnessed, land reclamation still cannot be carried out on a larger scale, and conditions for agricultural mechanization are not yet all ready. All this places a limit on the extent to which we can increase the rate of development of agricultural production. But of course, we should make full use of the favourable conditions mentioned above, in an effort to achieve a greater growth of agricultural production during the period of the Second Five-Year Plan.

As regards the development of agricultural production, special attention should be paid to the following two questions:

(1) Question Of Increasing Yields

The chief way to increase agricultural production in the Second Five-Year Plan period is, on the basis of co-operation, and relying on the labour enthusiasm of the peasants, to gradually improve the technique of agricultural production, build irrigation works, increase the use of manure and fertilizers, and popularize advanced experience, so as to increase yields. In implementing these measures to increase production, we must follow the principle of co-ordinating the work of the state with that of the co-operatives.

As regards the construction of irrigation works: On the one hand, the central and the local authorities should undertake a certain number of large and medium water conservancy projects, such as the projects for the permanent control of the Yellow River, the Huai River and the Haiho River, and flood and water-logging prevention projects in various places. On the other hand, the co-operatives should build small-scale irrigation works in large numbers, improve the existing irrigation installations, and strengthen the work for the conservation of soil and water. In low lands subject to water-logging, they should devise and put into effect various measures for its prevention and drainage, and change the farming system so as to reduce the damage caused by it.

As regards increasing the use of manure and fertilizers: On the one hand, the state should energetically develop the fertilizer industry, and try to import more chemical fertilizers, in order to increase their supply. On the other hand, and principally, the co-operatives and their members should accumulate manure by extensively raising pigs (or sheep in some places), make green manure and collect other natural fertilizers.

As regards popularizing various technical measures and advanced experience in increasing production: We should actively promote the work of technical guidance. On the one hand, we should draw on the advanced experience of other places in increasing production and popularize it in a way suitable to local conditions, and based on scientific experiment and study. On the other hand, we should pay close attention to summing up and popularizing advanced experience acquired locally in increasing production.

Here we should especially point out that we must be both active and prudent in carrying out new technical measures and popularizing advanced experience. In the past few years we have achieved great results in this work, but in some places there have been mistakes of mechanical application and enforcement by coercion, resulting in ill consequences. Hereafter, measures for increasing production and advanced experience should be popularized step by step only after they have been proved effective through experiments; and, furthermore, in the course of popularization, appropriate steps should be mapped out in conformity with the specific local conditions of the time. Meanwhile, the local peasants, especially the old and experienced peasants, should be consulted; one should never seek to spread any measure or experience by coercion. Nor should local habits in farming be rashly rejected.

(2) Question Of Developing A Diversified Agricultural Economy

We must pay adequate attention to grain which ensures the livelihood of the people and is the basis for developing agricultural economy as a whole. During the past few years, all localities have attached importance to the increase of grain and cotton yields. This is quite necessary. But some localities have consequently not given adequate attention to increasing production in other branches of agricultural economy—industrial crops (except cotton), livestock-breeding, forestry, fisheries, sericulture, and subsidiary cottage occupations. In addition, some agricultural products and local and special products have been affected by the low prices fixed for purchase by the state. As a result of all this, our agricultural economy has been unable to achieve an all-round, full development, which in turn has adversely affected the development of our national economy as a whole and the income of the peasants. Therefore, the local authorities, down to every agricultural producers' co-operative, in planning for their production, should work out an over-all plan of agricultural development, taking into account the historical and present conditions of the locality, the natural environment and economic and technical conditions, and the peasants' ways of production and life, so as to avoid any tendency towards uniformity and one-sidedness. In pastoral areas, forest areas and fishing areas, plans should be worked out centring on livestock-breeding, forestry and fishery respectively, and at the same time providing for the development of agriculture and other subsidiary occupations according to existing possibilities.

We should adopt many concrete measures to promote the all-round development of agricultural economy. The various kinds of production which the peasants are in the habit of engaging in and which are needed by society should continue to be carried on and further developed. We should encourage the co-operatives as well as enterprises and plantations managed by the central or local authorities to undertake, under the technical guidance of the state, the production of things that are urgently needed by society, and especially those of great economic value, such as sub-tropical and tropical crops, and those agricultural and subsidiary occupation products which are needed for export. We should encourage the members of co-operatives to undertake separately the subsidiary cottage occupations where unified management by the co-operatives is unnecessary. The commercial departments should set reasonable purchasing prices for such agricultural products and subsidiary occupation products and improve purchasing systems. At the same time, the departments concerned should give suitable help to the co-operatives in restoring trades for the processing of agricultural products in rural districts.

5. Development Of Transport And Posts And Tele-Communications

In the Second Five-Year Plan period, with the development of industrial and agricultural production, the expanding of the scale of capital construction, and the development and construction in the interior and the border areas, there is need for a great increase in transport and communication facilities. This requires us to give priority to railway building projects, and build a corresponding nation-wide transport and communication network. Thus the transport, postal and tele-communication departments are faced with the following gigantic tasks: on the one hand, we should proceed with the necessary reconstruction and technical renovation of existing lines and facilities; on the other hand, we should continue to build new lines, mainly railways and highways in the Northwest and Southwest, and ports on the coast and the Yangtse River, and also increase necessary transport and communication facilities. The transport and postal and tele-communication departments should work out an over-all plan according to the above-mentioned twofold task and in order of importance and urgency, so as to ensure fulfilment of the tasks in the spheres of transport and posts and tele-communications put forward in the Proposals for the Second Five-Year Plan.

Some transport and communication lines are already somewhat strained at the present time. This is mainly due to insufficient capacity of facilities. However, it should also be noted that there are still certain potentialities in some transport and communication lines and facilities which have not yet been exploited. Therefore, the transport and postal and tele-communication departments should vigorously take effective technical measures, and strengthen the organizational work in transport and communications.

Our country lacks modern transport facilities and lines, and those we have are not evenly distributed; furthermore there are immense numbers of such traditional means of transportation as junks and animal-drawn vehicles in our country; they are widely distributed and will remain for a long time to come an important auxiliary force of transport and are, in some areas, at present even the main force of transport. In view of this, we should make full use of these means of transport, and properly develop and carry out technical improvement on them step by step. We should make combined use of modern and traditional means of transport wherever possible, so as to meet the ever increasing needs of transportation.

6. Strengthen Work In Commerce

To better the life of the people, not only must we increase their money income, but also see to it that a definite amount of commodities suiting their needs is made available to them. According to a rough estimate, the volume of various consumer goods for everyday use and part of the means of production to be sold to the people of town and countryside, that is, the total volume of retail trade in 1962, will increase by about 50 per cent as compared with the targets originally planned for 1957. This is an arduous task for the commercial departments. They must keep strengthening their work in purchasing and marketing; continue to carry through the policy of planned purchase and distribution in regard to major daily necessaries; build up commercial networks in a rational way; and organize according to plan a number of free markets under the guidance of the state to meet the growing needs of the people. In the field of foreign trade, we should organize export of suitable materials according to plan so as to ensure imports of equipment and materials needed for national construction.

As a link between production and consumption, and between industrial and agricultural production, commerce is not only entrusted with the task of meeting the needs of the people's everyday life and the needs of part of our production as well as that of accumulating funds for the state, but is also entrusted with the task of stimulating the growth of industrial and agricultural production. As the law of value still plays a certain role in our economic life, and an important role in certain fields, its correct application and the correct handling of our price policy will stimulate the growth of our industrial and agricultural production.

In the First Five-Year Plan period, commodity prices in our country have been, by and large, stable and the price relations between industrial and farm products have on the whole been reasonable. This indicates that our price policy has been correct. It has promoted the development of our industrial and agricultural production and national construction and contributed to guaranteeing the smooth progress of our socialist transformation. But there were still some defects and mistakes in the execution of our price policy. They found expression mainly in the following: the prices for the purchase of some farm produce and special and local products were fixed too low, or fluctuated between high and low, which adversely affected increases in their production, or even led to reduced production in some cases; the difference between the prices of some products of light industry of different qualities and types was too small, which adversely affected the work of improving the quality and increasing the variety of these products. These defects have been detected and put right step by step, but they are not yet wholly eradicated. In the future, we need to make further study and readjustment in regard to commodity prices.

Correct handling of the price policy is a very complicated matter. In a country like ours where the population is very large and the economic conditions varied, we must take a very prudent attitude towards price readjustment, and must not go about it in a rash manner. For instance, to unduly raise the price of farm produce purchased by the state will do harm to our industrial production, to our workers' life, and to the maintenance of a correctly proportioned development of different kinds of farm produce. To unduly cut the selling price of industrial products may result in deficient supplies of commodities. Therefore, both undue rises and undue cuts in prices will be unfavourable to the growth of industrial and agricultural production and improvement of the people's livelihood. In the Second Five-Year Plan period, we shall keep to the policy of stabilizing our prices, but make suitable adjustments as needed in the case of certain unreasonable prices.

As a result of the victory in socialist transformation, socialist economy has assumed a predominant position in our country. This enables us to make better use of the law of value, within proper limits, to stimulate production of those industrial and farm products which are small in output value but great in variety, and that need not be purchased and marketed exclusively by the state, so as to meet the many-sided needs of the life of the people. In order to meet the situation described above and prevent a lowering of quality and reduction in the variety of products resulting from over-rigid and excessive control, we shall, now and in the Second Five-Year Plan period, adopt many important measures in the field of commerce. For instance, a number of free markets will be organized in a planned way under the leadership of the unified state market; producers will be allowed, within certain limits, to market their own products; the method of selective purchase by the state will be adopted in regard to certain industrial products of daily use; and the method of grading and fixing prices according to quality will be adopted in regard to all commodities. Far from disrupting the unified state market, these measures will supplement it in a helpful way.

7. Reorganization Of Enterprises And Arrangements For Personnel During The Socialist Transformation

In regard to the work of socialist transformation, I shall only deal with the following two questions:

(1) Question Of Reorganization Of Small And Medium Joint State-Private Enterprises, And Of Handicraftsmen And Small Traders' Co-operatives

As the large joint state-private enterprises came under joint operation at an earlier date, their production and management have already been brought into the orbit of state planning step by step, and their systems of operation and management have also, on the whole, undergone preliminary reform. But the large numbers of scattered small and medium joint state-private enterprises that recently came into being remain to be properly reorganized and arranged. Many individual handicraftsmen and small traders and pedlars having been brought into co-operatives, these co-operatives also need reorganization and arrangement. Only by so doing can we enable their members to carry on their production and operation under more rational conditions, so as to gradually adapt themselves to the planned management of the state. In conducting reorganization, we must pay attention to preventing and rectifying the tendency towards over-concentration.

In the field of industry, small-sized factories certainly have their shortcomings, but they are more mobile and flexible in production and management, and find it easier to adapt themselves to varied, ever-changing needs. Therefore, all small factories that are rationally operated and able to meet the needs of society should be preserved and not merged or eliminated thoughtlessly. As regards handicraft co-operative organizations, we should refrain, as a rule, from making them over-concentrated. We should follow the principles of developing production, meeting the needs of society and increasing the income of their members and allow big co-operatives, small co-operatives and groups to exist side by side. Certain manufacturing trades and especially many repairing trades and personal service establishments should be allowed to operate on a scattered basis and retain their original features of management, so that they can serve the inhabitants directly and can draw upon the family for auxiliary labour for production. Some of the handicrafts may be allowed to carry on their production individually under the leadership of the handicraft co-operative organizations. They may also be allowed to produce and market all by themselves, without being organized.

In regard to commerce, trading establishments should be so distributed as to suit the convenience of the people to the greatest extent. Therefore, it is all the more improper to get them over-concentrated. They should rather be duly dispersed and operated in a great variety of ways to serve the population. Our leading commercial organizations have usually given more thought to their own convenience in administration, and less to the convenience of the inhabitants, thus giving rise to the tendency towards over-concentration—undue concentration and elimination of a number of small shops and traders and pedlars. This tendency must be quickly corrected. From now on, both in the residential quarters of cities and in the wide countryside, we should preserve a considerable number of small traders and pedlars to serve the people better in such forms as co-operative shops, co-operative groups, distributors for the state on a commission basis or even buying and marketing all by themselves.

(2) Question Of Making Arrangements For And Re-educating Industrial And Merchant Capitalists And Small Proprietors

As capitalist industry and commerce comes under joint state-private operation, we should train outstanding workers and employees and promote them to take part in the management of the enterprises. At the same time we should draw in the former industrial and merchant capitalists and small proprietors to take part in operational and managerial work or assume some leading positions. With the institution of joint operation and the system of paying fixed rates of interest on shares to the capitalists, the bourgeois elements in the enterprises take on a dual nature—they are at once capitalists and staff members. Therefore, the representatives of the state shares should co-operate well with all those representing the interests of the capitalists and give free scope to their special knowledge and their initiative and, in the process of working with them, make efforts to re-educate them, help them overcome their bourgeois ideas and style of work, help them score achievements in work and gradually turn them into working people in the real sense of the term; we should not assume a discriminatory attitude towards them. By so doing, we shall do good to the enterprises as well as to the state and the working class. In order to do this work satisfactorily, we should see to it that workers and employees of the enterprises understand the matter and regard the work of uniting with and re-educating the capitalists and their agents as an important task.

The overwhelming majority of the hundreds of thousands of capitalists and their agents in the joint state-private enterprises have certain production skills or management experience, and some of them are highly skilled or have rich experience. We must make full use of their production skill and what is useful in their management experience. In these respects the state's representatives should endeavour to learn from them.

8. Improving The State Administrative System And Bringing Local Initiative Into Full Play

In the Second Five-Year Plan period, an increasing number of construction projects in the country will be undertaken by the local authorities or completed through the concerted efforts of the central and local authorities. Therefore, to afford local authorities free scope for their initiative is an essential condition for the accomplishment of our socialist construction.

Now that decisive victory has been won in the socialist transformation of our country and our people's democratic dictatorship has been further consolidated, we must and can, in keeping with the principles of unified leadership, level-to-level administration, devising what is appropriate in each locality and in each case, define more clearly the respective sphere of jurisdiction of the central and the local authorities, and improve the state administrative system, so that local initiative can have free scope. In the period from May to August this year, the State Council called a series of national meetings on questions concerning the state administrative system. At these meetings the existing situation of excessive centralization was examined, the question of improving the state administrative system was discussed, and a draft resolution for improving the system was introduced. The State Council is now extensively soliciting views from different circles on this draft resolution.

In defining the respective spheres of jurisdiction of the central and the local authorities, we deem it necessary to observe the following principles: (1) Explicit stipulations should be made so that the provinces, autonomous regions, and municipalities directly under the central authority will have a definite degree of jurisdiction over planning, finance, enterprises, public institutions, materials and personnel. (2) All enterprises and public institutions which are vital to the national economy as a whole and which are concentrated, of an over-all nature and of key importance and should be administered by the central authorities, while the rest should, as far as possible, be administered by the local authorities. When enterprises and public institutions are handed over by the central to the local authorities, their planning and financial and personnel administration should in general be handed over as well. (3) The administration of enterprises and public institutions should be effectively improved, and dual leadership in which in some cases the central authorities play the main role while the local authorities a subsidiary one and in other cases vice versa, should be promoted, so as to strengthen effectively our leadership over enterprises and public institutions. (4) Important plans and financial targets under the administration of the central authorities should be issued to the local authorities in a unified way by the State Council, and the method hitherto employed of having many important targets issued separately by various departments should be changed. (5) The local authorities must be allowed a certain latitude for flexible readjustment regarding certain important targets of the plan and quotas of personnel. (6) Specific arrangements should be made with regard to the various autonomous rights in the national autonomous regions and attention be paid to helping the national minority regions in their political, economic and cultural development. (7) The state administrative system should be improved step by step. Certain important changes should be carried out steadily and in orderly progression, i.e., to make preparations for them this year, to give them a try-out next year and to carry them through in the Second Five-Year Plan period.

In order to carry out effectively the above-mentioned principles, the essential point in our opinion is to duly extend the jurisdiction of the local authorities under the unified leadership of the central authorities. As the local authorities are in closer contact with the primary units of enterprises and public institutions and with the masses and enjoy greater facilities to understand the actual conditions they will, as their jurisdiction is extended, be able to organize more effectively all local forces and positive factors for socialist construction.

In order to bring into fuller play the initiative of the localities and strengthen further the unity among all nationalities of the country, we should, at present and in the Second Five-Year Plan period, pay more attention to the work among national minorities. In all areas where national minorities live in compact communities and where autonomous administrations should be, but have not yet been, set up, we should according to the provisions of the Constitution energetically help them to set up such administrations. We should strictly respect the autonomous rights of the national autonomous regions. We should train and promote large numbers of cadres from among the national minorities, unceasingly raise their political understanding and their ability in tackling various kinds of problems so that they may prove equal to their responsibilities, and exercise the functions and powers that go with their posts. In areas where national minorities live in compact communities, or where a number of national minorities live together, or where they are scattered among other nationalities, the equal rights of nationalities, freedom of religious belief, and the habits and customs and language of each national minority should be respected. As for those national minorities who have still no written languages or whose written languages are not yet fully developed, we should energetically help them create or reform them.

9. Training Personnel For Construction Work And Promoting Scientific Research

In the Second Five-Year Plan period, in order to build a firm basis for socialist industrialization, proceed with national construction, and push ahead the technical reconstruction of our national economy, we must make great efforts to train personnel for construction work and promote scientific research.

(1) Question Of Training And Distribution Of Personnel For Construction

It is the foremost task of education to train for the state personnel for the work of construction, especially industrial technicians and personnel for scientific research. In the past few years, our work of training such personnel has made marked progress, but from the point of view of national construction, the personnel trained in our universities, colleges and secondary vocational schools are still inadequate to meet actual needs, especially with regard to quality and types of qualifications. Therefore, in the Second Five-Year Plan period, we should further develop our higher education and secondary vocational education, and draw up comprehensive plans according to the principles of "giving priority to the most important aspects and due consideration to the rest" and of co-ordinating needs with possibilities.

In order to improve the work of training personnel for construction, we must pay due consideration to the relation between numbers and quality. In the past few years, we have put undue emphasis on numbers and neglected quality; this is a tendency which must be corrected. Educational institutions should do their utmost to increase the number of students as far as possible on condition that their quality is ensured to a certain extent. Government and other organs which need cadres should, however, take into consideration actual needs and practical possibilities, and should not make a big demand which outruns what the educational institutions can supply, so that the number of students will not be recklessly increased to the detriment of quality.

In both higher education and secondary vocational education, practical measures, measures which are not subjectively designed, should be taken to readjust their faculties and departments and set up special fields of study, to improve the educational plan, teaching programmes, textbooks and teaching methods, so that the trainees will be better able to meet actual needs of various branches of the national economy. At present, the greatest difficulties in developing and raising the levels of higher education and secondary vocational education are the shortage of teachers and the low standard of the students. It is therefore necessary to select a suitable number of fine graduates from universities and colleges and train them as research students, and to send some university and college graduates as well as faculty members to study abroad certain select subjects which are absent from our own curricula, so as to increase the number of teachers. At the same time, senior and junior middle schools must be appropriately developed and run well, and the standard of middle-school students raised. Our universities and colleges and secondary vocational schools are in general not well-off in books and laboratory apparatus. This inadequacy should be gradually remedied; and buildings necessary for the development of these institutions should also be provided.

To train personnel for construction, we must also develop spare-time education, that is, help those workers and employees qualified for advanced education to enter evening schools or correspondence schools where they will be trained into specialized personnel of intermediate and higher levels. Those who attend these schools must do so of their own free will, and they should carry on their study at different times and in groups. The institutions concerned should guarantee the time needed by those workers and employees who take up spare-time studies. Such time should not be too long, nor should the studies be too intense, lest their work or health be affected.

In view of the shortage of scientific and technical personnel, a rational distribution of personnel for construction becomes all the more important. In the distribution of such personnel to meet the needs of production and construction and of scientific research and teaching, we should give priority to what is most important and at the same time have due regard to the rest. Also we should continue to rectify the cases of improper allocation of scientific and technical personnel, and those in which cadres have not been given work suited to their abilities.

(2) *Question Of Strengthening Scientific Research*

Recently, under the direct leadership of the Central Committee of the Party and the State Council, several hundred outstanding scientists from all parts of the country got together and drafted a comprehensive twelve-year plan for the nation-wide development of science and technology, and another for the development of philosophy and the social sciences, putting forward respectively the most important research tasks in the natural and social sciences. This is a very important step for raising the level of our scientific research, and for ensuring that many important branches of science and technology in our country will within twelve years approach the advanced levels of development in the world. It is necessary to complete these two plans at an early date under the leadership of the Central Committee of the Party and the State Council and organize all the forces devoted to scientific research in the country to fulfil step by step the tasks laid down by these two plans. Since the tasks to be undertaken in this regard are very arduous and we still have an insufficient number of experts in scientific research while modern science and technology are developing at a tremendous pace, and since, in addition, those branches of science to which we now give priority in our research work are our weak points or even form gaps in our work, we should concentrate our forces on first dealing with important problems and avoid the tendency to do everything at once and so disperse our forces indiscriminately in various fields.

In order to promote scientific research, we must step by step build up the institutes of scientific research in the Chinese Academy of Sciences, government departments and enterprises and put them on a sound basis, strengthen scientific research in the universities and colleges, and see to it that a division of labour and close co-operation and co-ordination are achieved. Scientific research institutes should be rationally distributed in various localities. Scientific research should be closely co-ordinated with the various kinds of national construction work, especially economic construction. In scientific research, the principle of "letting diverse schools of thought contend" must be strictly followed and free discussion of academic questions encouraged, so as to give full play to the initiative and creative ability of those engaged in scientific research.

In order to promote our scientific research, it is also necessary to solve in time the problem of providing the requisite literature, material, instruments and laboratories; to make vigorous efforts to improve the working conditions of those engaged in scientific research; and to further enhance inter-

10. Further Improvement Of The People's Life

In the Second Five-Year Plan period, it will be possible for us to further improve the life of the people on the basis of expanded production and increased national income.

Fundamentally, all our construction work is undertaken in the interests of the people. In the course of our work, however, it is often not easy to co-ordinate satisfactorily the long-term interests of the people with their immediate interests, and the interests of the collective with those of the individual. Therefore, it is necessary for us to maintain a suitable proportion in the use of national income between accumulation and consumption, and to see that the life of the people is improved step by step while a gradual expansion of the scale of national construction is ensured.

Here, I shall deal with the following questions in particular:

(1) Question Of Improving The Material Well-Being Of Workers And Employees

In the Second Five-Year Plan period, the average wages of workers and employees will be raised by 25 to 30 per cent. Such a rate of increase will be in keeping with the level of economic growth and the rate of increase of labour productivity in our country. In view of the experience mentioned above, we must, in the annual plans, constantly maintain a suitable proportion between the increase of wages and that of labour productivity, so that the wages of workers and employees may be raised comparatively evenly along with the rise in labour productivity. Moreover, in making annual plans for the increase of the wages of workers and employees, we should pay attention to the possibilities of production and supply of daily necessaries, so as to avoid dislocation between the increase of wages and the supply of commodities. In readjusting the wages of workers and employees, the principle of "to each according to his work" must be adhered to, so as to further improve the wages system.

To improve the material well-being of the workers and employees, we should, apart from further raising their wages, adopt both now and in the Second Five-Year Plan period practical measures wherever possible to improve step by step their housing, safety, medical and health services and duly provide additional welfare amenities. In this connection, the State Council has worked out some specific measures which will be announced and put into effect in the near future.

We should continue to fight against the bureaucratic attitude of indifference to the life of the workers and employees. In fact, it is not entirely owing to the lack of financial or material resources that much of what might have been done for the welfare of the workers and employees has not yet been done. It is mainly because the leading personnel of some of the departments concerned have adopted a bureaucratic attitude towards improvement of the life of the workers and employees. It should be pointed out that some of the welfare amenities can be provided without any increase in state expenditure. If only we rectify our bureaucratic style of work, concern ourselves more about the life of the masses and conscientiously carry out the plan and the various regulations of the state in this regard, we shall be able to do better the important work of improving the material well-being of the workers and employees.

(2) Question Of Improving The Material Well-Being Of The Peasants

To improve the material well-being of the peasants, we should, on the one hand, pay attention to readjusting the proportion between the state's accumulation and the income of the co-operatives to provide a correct solution for the question of the peasants' contribution to the state's revenue, and, on the other hand, pay attention to readjusting the proportion between the common accumulation of the agricultural producers' co-operatives and the income of the individual members to provide a correct solution for the question of distribution of the total income of co-operatives. In the Second Five-Year Plan period, the agricultural tax should be kept in proper relation to the state revenue, and the agricultural tax proper and additional taxes should be combined so as to simplify the tax system. At the same time, all co-operatives are required to adhere to the provisions of the "Model Regulations for Advanced Agricultural Producers' Co-operatives," so that their reserve and welfare funds and administrative expenses will in general not exceed the proportions prescribed in the regulations. If this is done and if the plan for increased agricultural output is fulfilled in the Second Five-Year

Plan period, it will be possible for the peasants to increase their total income by 25 to 30 per cent in the five years.

In the Second Five-Year Plan period, the state will continue in every way to help the agricultural producers' co-operatives expand production; state investments in water conservancy projects and agriculture will be greatly increased as compared with those under the First Five-Year Plan; agricultural loans will also be increased. At the same time, the state will again allocate special relief funds for rural areas affected by natural calamities. With regard to many hilly areas and old revolutionary base areas where natural conditions are unfavourable, the state should from now on pay particular attention to helping the local people develop production and improve their living.

(3) Question Of Raising The Cultural Standards Of The People

In the Second Five-Year Plan period, along with the progress of economic construction and the increase of the people's cultural demands, we should, in accordance with the provisions of the Proposals, continue to make efforts to wipe out illiteracy, develop primary school education, promote spare-time education for workers and peasants, and push ahead step by step with the reform of written Chinese. At the same time, we should take further steps to promote cultural work for the masses and expand our work in journalism, publications, broadcasting, literature, art and the cinema. In undertaking work in these fields, special attention should be paid to improving quality.

Energetic but steady steps should be taken in our cultural and educational work among the broad masses. In wiping out illiteracy and developing primary school education, social, cultural, and publication work during the past few years, we made the mistake of being either conservative or rash, thereby causing damage to our work, which should not have occurred. We should learn a lesson from this and promote our cultural and educational work in future in a practical way, according to actual needs and possibilities.

In promoting cultural and educational work among the masses, we must rely fully on the masses and follow the mass line. The mistake of taking everything into one's own hands and imposing one's will upon the masses occurred quite often in educational and cultural work in the past. Henceforward, these mistakes must be rectified. We should insist that the voluntary principle is observed, and that the masses are constantly consulted. In regard to the undertakings which really meet the needs of the masses and which can and will be undertaken by the masses of their own accord, such as village schools, literacy classes, clubs, and spare-time theatrical troupes, we should give them support and help and strengthen our leadership of them. Of course, in making use of the strength of the masses, we must always try to save the people's time and energy, and must not arbitrarily increase the people's burdens.

(4) Question Of Improving The Health Of The People

In the Second Five-Year Plan period, we must continue to develop public health and medical services, take further steps for the development of physical culture and athletics, and appropriately promote birth control.

In the past few years, the patriotic movement for better sanitation has played an important part in the improvement of environmental sanitation and reduction of diseases. In the last year or two, however, we have somewhat relaxed our leadership over this movement. Henceforward, we must make further efforts to carry on this movement more thoroughly and regularly, so as to further improve environmental sanitation in town and countryside and reduce the incidence of contagious and occupational diseases. At the same time, we should also actively popularize our experience in combating schistosomiasis, and eliminate, by periods, by districts, and in a planned way, the most harmful local diseases. The basic units of health organizations throughout the country have played an important part in the prevention and cure of diseases. The public health departments should henceforward strengthen their leadership of them.

There still exist many defects in health and medical services. For instance, because of bad administration and high fees charged in the hospitals, full use has not been made of the beds which are now still limited in number, and some people cannot afford to see doctors and be hospitalized. Beds in the sanatoria have not been brought under unified management, thus resulting in great waste. Besides, there are also defects in the system of free medical services and in the system of medical work. In order to eliminate these defects, the public health departments should make investigations and study conscientiously to devise practicable methods for improvement.

We should further popularize physical training among the masses, effectively improve the physique of the people and raise our level in sports. In doing so, we must see that the training is conducted step by step and with due regard for the specific conditions of people engaged in production, studies and other kinds of work, as well as their physical fitness. The standards fixed for them should not be too high and no immediate achievements should be expected from them. Generalization should also be avoided.

To protect women and children and bring up and educate our younger generation in a way conducive to the health and prosperity of the nation, we agree that a due measure of birth control is desirable. Health departments should, in co-operation with other institutions concerned, carry out intelligent propaganda and adopt effective measures towards this end.

11. Continuing To Practise Strict Economy

Industriousness and thrift are fine traditions of our people. All state organs, state enterprises, public institutions and co-operatives should practise strict economy in order to make full use of manpower, materials and money, thereby stepping up the socialist construction of our country.

A year ago, the Central Committee of the Party and the State Council called upon all government workers and the people of the whole country to practise economy and eliminate waste. They were asked to put an end to such undesirable things as carrying on too many non-productive projects, high construction costs of productive projects, low quality of engineering work and industrial products, heavy damage to and loss of materials, over-expansion and over-staffing of organizations. Considerable improvements have been made after more than a year's effort. However, it should be pointed out that not all departments have strictly practised economy and cases of waste still exist. Furthermore, in the course of practising economy and opposing Rightist conservative ideas, there arose a one-sided emphasis on economy and the tendency towards stressing quantity and speed at the expense of quality and economy, and as a result quite a few engineering projects and industrial products were found to be defective in quality. Some had to be done over again, and others were of less use than they should have been or even became useless. Thus not only was the goal of practising economy not attained, but waste was caused.

In the Second Five-Year Plan period, because of the enlarged scale of national construction, we will still come up against many difficulties in regard to material supplies, funds and technical personnel. The practice of strict economy and rational utilization of materials, money and manpower are important methods of overcoming these difficulties. It should be recognized that economy or waste depends much on whether the planning is good or not. Economy ensuing from good planning is the greatest economy, while waste caused by bad planning is the greatest waste. Therefore, state organs at all levels and enterprises should first of all do their work in drawing up plans well. All enterprises should improve supervision of technical-economic norms and extend the introduction of various kinds of reasonable, advanced norms. They should strengthen technical control, improve the quality of industrial products and engineering projects, and reduce the number of rejects, products of inferior quality and waste and accidents resulting from engineering defects. They should enforce the system of personal responsibility and put an end to the state of affairs in which responsibility for work is not specified. All this is intended to prevent waste and tap all potentialities conducive to economy. All public institutions should curtail unnecessary expenditure and personnel, strengthen financial management and auditing, so as to lower the proportion of expenditure for public institutions in the budget. All co-operatives should continue to carry through the principle of "industry and thrift" in their operation.

The state administrative organs should continue to cut down overlapping organizations and reduce superfluous staff. Generally speaking, the state administrative organizations at different levels are at present still inflated and over-staffed. This is more true of the organizations at higher levels than those at lower levels, more true of big organizations than small ones. We must take effective measures to continue the readjustment of organizations at all levels and re-apportionment of government cadres. The structure of administrative organizations is to be simplified. An appropriate number of people working in organizations at the higher levels is to be transferred to lower organizations, and part of the personnel in non-productive departments is to be transferred to productive departments. These are effective measures of practising economy in state organs at the present time.

12. Strengthening Our Unity And Co-operation With The Soviet Union And The People's Democracies, And Expanding Economic, Technical And Cultural Co-operation And Contacts Among Nations

In order to accomplish socialist construction, we must, in addition to mobilizing all positive factors at home, unite with all international forces that can be united with and make use of all international conditions favourable to us. We have made consistent efforts to strengthen our unity with the great Soviet Union and the People's Democracies and carry out all-round co-operation with them and give each other support. We have also been endeavouring to develop economic co-operation, trade relations and cultural and technical contact with countries having different social systems, especially with those in Asia and Africa.

The mutual help and co-operation between China and the Soviet Union and the People's Democracies is based on an unbreakable fraternal friendship, and aims at promoting the common economic advance of all socialist countries and continuously improving the material well-being and cultural standards of their peoples.

As stated above, both in the period of rehabilitation of our national economy and in the period of carrying out the First Five-Year Plan for Development of the National Economy, we have received enormous all-round and sincere aid from the Soviet Union as well as important aid from other fraternal countries. This aid has enabled us to tide over many difficulties and made it possible for our cause of socialist construction to forge ahead at a fairly high speed. In the Second Five-Year Plan period, the Soviet Union and the People's Democracies will continue to give us large-scale, fraternal help. Particularly noteworthy are the big enterprises to be designed and equipped with this help; such enterprises will form yet another stone in laying the foundation for the socialist industrialization of our country. In the past, we have benefited very much by learning from the advanced experience of the Soviet Union and the People's Democracies in construction and in the spheres of science and technology. In future, we will go on earnestly learning from them.

As a member of the socialist camp, China, too, has its duty. We must acquit ourselves well of this duty. It is our duty to provide our brother countries with a large amount of farm produce, animal products, minerals and certain kinds of machinery and industrial products which they need in construction. We must make efforts to increase production or, to an appropriate extent, economize in home consumption to ensure the supply of these goods. We also need to have a sound plan for production and consumption at home in order to guarantee the necessary export goods for trading with other countries on the principle of equality and mutual benefit, each supplying what the other needs.

In the past few years, our co-operation and contacts with many Asian and African countries in the economic, technical and cultural fields have become increasingly closer. Such co-operation and contacts have been developed on an even wider scale especially since the Asian-African Conference. The overwhelming majority of the Asian and African countries urgently desire to overcome their economic and cultural backwardness caused by protracted colonial rule, and are therefore deeply aware of the necessity of economic and cultural co-operation among themselves. Our country has always advocated co-operation in these fields with other countries in Asia and Africa on the principle of equality and mutual benefit and with no conditions attached, in order to help promote each other's independent development economically and technically and, in the cultural field, to help each other develop its outstanding good features and learn from each other. This co-operation contributes to the safeguarding of the national independence of the Asian and African countries and the expansion of the area of peace. It is, therefore, beneficial to our peaceful construction. At present, the scope of this co-operation is still not very large. But the important thing is that countries in Asia and Africa have begun to co-operate with each other and are increasing their contacts with the Latin American countries. There is undoubtedly a great future for such co-operation and contacts.

We are also willing to develop economic, technical and cultural contacts with other countries of the world on the principle of equality and mutual benefit. We have consistently endeavoured to extend our trade with the Western countries and are ready to take in all that is useful in their science, technology and methods of management to serve our work of construction. Although the United States has been carrying out an embargo against us and has forced many other countries to follow suit, this policy which totally contradicts the interests of the people of all countries has, however, met with increasingly strong opposition from all quarters. Sooner or later, this unreasonable, artificial barrier will be swept aside.

We advocate the expansion of co-operation and contacts among nations in the economic, technical and cultural fields not only because this will speed up the completion of our socialist construction, but also because it will provide a reliable basis for peaceful co-existence between nations. Therefore, it conforms in every way to the interests of the people throughout the world and to the interests of the cause of peace.

* * *

Comrades! The day is not far off when the First Five-Year Plan will be successfully completed and the Second Five-Year Plan will begin. In the coming year or so, all the comrades of the Party, under the leadership of the Central Committee and Comrade Mao Tse-tung, should redouble their efforts and, together with the workers, peasants and intellectuals, and together with the various nationalities, political parties and all the patriotic people of the country, fight for the overfulfilment of the First Five-Year Plan and make active preparations for the Second Five-Year Plan. Provided we remain modest and prudent, guard against self-conceit and rashness, and correct subjectivist ideas and bureaucratic styles of work among us, we shall be able to mobilize all our forces and overcome all difficulties, and march forward in triumph in our struggle to build China into a great socialist industrial power.

DOCUMENT 12

On Strengthening Production Leadership and Organizational Construction of Agricultural Producer Cooperatives, directive of the Party's Central Committee and the State Council, September 12, 1956.

The English text is the NCNA translation of September 12, and includes some NCNA notes published at the time. It was reproduced in SCMP 1382, which is the immediate source used here.

Comment. This directive of the Party's Central Committee and the State Council is included with the documents of the Eighth Party Congress because it represents the same comparatively sober and factual line of thought found in Chou En-lai's report (Document 11). The target date for the completion of the higher form of cooperative remains as before, but a number of problems are admitted and discussed much more realistically than in Documents 2-5 above, particularly:

the importance of industrial crops;
the proper care of draft animals;
individual "sideline" production (no attempt should be made by the authorities in the cooperatives to take this over);
the need for realistic local production targets and plans;
the avoidance of "commandism" by the cadres in carrying out such things as irrigation works;
the proper distribution of income between "accumulation" and payment of members;
the payment of proper compensation for assets surrendered by individual peasants;
the importance of fixing compulsory deliveries and prices of compulsory sales at an appropriate level;
the institution of a free market for some produce;
the appropriate size (not too large) for cooperatives;

the importance of concentrating the food-processing industries into the cooperatives and away from the cities.

The awareness and discussion of these problems by the Party indicates a much less "anticonservative" mood in September 1956 than had prevailed in 1955. Supplementary reading on the state of the agricultural producers' cooperatives, the task of the cadres, and discontent and sabotage by peasants, may be found in a mass of press material, including:

CB 393, Teng Tzu-hui to the National People's Congress, June 1956, on some weaknesses of the cooperatives.

CB 447, Ch'en Cheng-jen to the Chinese People's Political Consultative Conference, March 1957, on some defects and errors of the cooperatives.

ECMM 74 (*Grain*, Jan. 25, 1957); ECMM 76 (*China Youth*, Feb. 1, 1957); ECMM 80 (*Planned Economy*, Feb. 9, 1957); ECMM 83 (*Chinese Agriculture*, March 10, 1957); ECMM 88 (*Grain*, April 25, 1957); ECMM 100 (*Finance*, August 1957).

URS, Vol. 2, No. 12; Vol. 3, Nos. 5, 6, 26; Vol. 5, Nos. 10, 15, 16.

Of these ECMM 88 (*Grain*, April 25, 1957) is typical, and the most important example. From this article it becomes evident that there was much misreporting of grain yields in order to avoid the grain tax, and that the cadres had also erred in (a) "blind optimism" about the increase of grain output to be expected as the result of collectivization; (b) underestimating the urban consumption of grain; (c) overestimating the "political awareness" of peasants; (d) allowing too much grain to be sold on the free market.

_____TEXT OF DOCUMENT 12_____

Thanks to the increasingly great superiority of agricultural cooperativization in the past several years, the achievements in socialist industrialization, the rising enthusiasm of the majority of people in following the path of socialism, and especially the correction of some cadres' rightist conservative thinking as a result of the resolution of the seventh plenary session of the Sixth Central Committee and Comrade Mao Tse-tung's report on the question of agricultural cooperativization, an upsurge of agricultural cooperativization has begun throughout the country, its scope and intensity both being unprecedented. The development of the agricultural cooperativization movement has been rapid and healthy. By the spring of this year, agricultural cooperativization had been basically completed in most areas of China.

The upsurge of agricultural cooperativization has stimulated an upsurge in agricultural production. Besides, the Central Committee of the Party presented at the right time the draft 12-year program for developing agriculture in China, thereby pointing out the target of long-range struggle in agricultural development and further heightening the enthusiasm of the broad masses of peasants for cooperativization and production. Unprecedentedly gigantic tasks have been carried out with regard to farmland irrigation, accumulation of fertilizers, improvement of farming techniques, improvement of the farming system, propagation of advanced experiences, and afforestation. The wheat and early rice this year both had a high yield. Although the autumn crops in many provinces have been affected by serious calamities, the total output of food crops this year may still reach the 1957 target stipulated in the First Five Year Plan.

The calamity-stricken areas this year are about the same as compared with 1954, but the food output will exceed that of 1955, which was a bumper year. This illustrates the superiority of socialist cooperative economy. The great historical victory which we have gained in agricultural cooperativization will undoubtedly speed up our country's socialist industrialization and modernization of agriculture.

However, after the materialization of agricultural cooperativization and as a result of a basic change in the production relations in rural areas, a series of new questions and conflicts have appeared in the new production relations. Meanwhile, insufficiency of experience and the impatience of some comrades in the face of the upsurge of revolution have resulted in certain shortcomings in our work.

The above-mentioned questions and shortcomings have appeared because of new and changed circumstances in the rapid development of agricultural cooperativization. Some of the questions and shortcomings are inevitable and cannot be avoided completely. We should affirm our achievements, overcome shortcomings, consolidate our success, continue to advance, and strive to accomplish the basic completion of high-level agricultural cooperativization throughout the country in 1957 (with the exception of some order areas – NCNA). Meanwhile, we should endeavor to further consolidate and improve the existing agricultural producer cooperatives and make use of all advantageous factors to achieve overall development in agricultural production.

In view of the above, Party committees and people's councils at all levels must adopt concrete measures to solve the following questions, with reference to local conditions:

I. TO INSURE THE OUTPUT OF FOOD CROPS AND COTTON, INCREASE THE PRODUCTION OF OTHER ECONOMIC CROPS, DEVELOP ANIMAL HUSBANDRY, AND ENGAGE IN DIVERSE PRODUCTION ACTIVITIES, SO AS TO ACHIEVE OVERALL DEVELOPMENT IN PRODUCTION.

Food crops and cotton are the basis for developing farm economy. Cotton is the most important economic crop. The increase in the output of food crops and cotton is of foremost importance in insuring the people's livelihood and developing the national economy. Therefore, in agricultural production, the central policy of increasing food crops and the cotton output must be continued, and cannot be changed in the least. In the past several years, it has been perfectly correct for all localities to adhere to the policy of increasing food crops and the cotton output.

However, while insuring the increased output of food crops and cotton, steps must be taken to also increase the output of other economic crops and develop animal husbandry, forestry, fishery, and diverse sideline produce so as to achieve overall development.

The different economic crops, animal husbandry, and the various sideline produce occupy a large proportion of the income of the rural areas—as much as 40 to 50 percent of the total income from agriculture in many provinces, and if neglected, the income of the cooperative members will be undoubtedly affected and so will the balanced development of the national economy and the people's livelihood.

Meanwhile, farming, forestry, fishery, animal husbandry, different kinds of sideline production, the transportation business, and handicraft production are all integral parts of the farm economy and supplement one another. Only by engaging in diverse production activities can we increase the output of food crops and cotton more effectively, use the land more rationally, distribute the labor hours of the whole year more efficiently, and increase labor efficiency and productivity more fully. Therefore, the backward situation in the production of certain economic crops, animal husbandry, and in sideline production during the past several years caused by diverse reasons must be speedily rectified, as follows:

(1) In accordance with prevalent local conditions and based on needs (including the needs of the State, the cooperatives, and cooperative members) and feasibility, we should help the cooperatives to map out plans for the overall development of production centering around the development of food crops and cotton production (centering around food crops in ordinary areas and around cotton in cotton-producing areas) and to make overall arrangements with regard to farmland, labor power, draft animals, money, and farming techniques.

While mapping out such plans, the habit of the local peasants in cultivating certain particular economic crops or engaging in certain particular types of sideline production should be continued. Those which have been discontinued should be resumed and those capable of being developed should be energetically developed.

In the factory and mining areas and the suburbs, efforts should be made to develop vegetable, fruit, livestock, and poultry farming so as to meet the needs of the cities.

(2) For a considerably long time to come, draft animals will be still the chief source of power in agricultural production.

Positive measures must be taken to help the cooperatives establish and improve the system of caring for and using draft animals. Generally speaking, draft animals are to be separately put under the care of specially assigned personnel. The cooperatives should make overall arrangements to solve fodder problems while the State, in the course of making collective purchases, should also allow for enough feed in accordance with the measures of the "three fixed quotas." Overexertion of draft animals should be avoided.

Special care should be taken to protect the studs, female animals, pregnant animals, and young animals. The mating, prenatal, and epidemic prevention work should be also properly executed. In the eagerness to cut down production expenditures some agricultural producer cooperatives have exploited the draft animals to the utmost or have sold or slaughtered some animals which were declared, but were not actually, surplus. If such practices are not checked, future production activities will be endangered.

The State commerce departments should be responsible for solving the question of the supply of draft animals. In the pastoral areas, plans should be mapped out to develop animal husbandry and animal husbandry products. In order to facilitate the development of animal husbandry, steps should be taken also to develop agricultural production wherever possible, so as to solve the problem of food for the people and animals of the pastoral areas.

Hog raising has a great deal to do with solving the question of fertilizer, increasing the income of the cooperatives and cooperative members, and meeting the people's need for meat as well as the country's export needs. All localities are urged to conscientiously implement the directive of the State Council of July 1 of this year.

(3) In the hilly regions, overall production plans coordinating agriculture, forestry, animal husbandry, and other sideline production should be drawn up, with emphasis on forestry, agriculture, or animal husbandry as the case may be, depending upon the prevalent local conditions.

In reclaiming uncultivated hills, the regulations governing water and soil conservation must be observed. Reclamation of slopes by wantonly destroying the trees is not allowed.

(4) The agricultural producer cooperatives should actively develop sideline production. With the exception of the sideline production which must be collectively run by the cooperatives, the families of members should be encouraged and helped to engage in all other types of sideline production either by themselves or with the cooperatives to which they belong.

In the first few years after their establishment, the cooperatives should concentrate on agriculture, animal husbandry, and the principal sideline production. All other types of sideline production suitable for individual management should be run by the cooperative members.

The practices of indiscriminately putting sideline production all under the collective management of the cooperatives or of restricting the activities of cooperative members to engage in sideline production must be rectified. Naturally, the practice of cooperative members devoting themselves solely to family sideline production to the detriment of collective production should also be avoided.

II. TO MAINTAIN THE INDEPENDENCE OF THE COOPERATIVES IN PRODUCTION AND MANAGEMENT, UNDER THE DIRECTION OF THE STATE PLAN.

Planned management is one of the basic characteristics of the socialist economy. The development of our national economy follows a definite plan. The production activities of the cooperative must be carried out according to plan, in conformity with the State Economic Plan. This is an established principle.

In the early part of this year, some cooperatives set their food production targets too high, not in conformity with reality. This deviation has been corrected. On the other hand, the plans of the high-level authorities on the proportions of acreages of different crops were too rigid and often not in conformity with actual conditions. Since the low-level authorities were required to implement such plans, commandism on their part resulted. This shortcoming must also be rectified.

Agricultural production differs from industrial production. A greater portion of agricultural production is self-supporting in nature and is at the same time dependent on natural and geographical conditions. Agricultural producer cooperatives are not State enterprises, but are managed under a collective system or partial collective system. Therefore, we cannot draw up agricultural production plans as we draw up industrial production plans. The method of coordination from the high to low levels and from low to high levels must be adopted in mapping out agricultural production plans, and such plans are to be made respectively by the Central and local authorities. The Central authorities should gradually pass from the transitional period of mapping out production plans to the drawing up of purchasing and distribution plans for farm products.

The Central Government's agricultural production and purchase plan only affects Government organs at the provincial level. The Government organs at the provincial level can make their own practical arrangements for agricultural production and purchase plans in accordance with the plan mapped out by the Central Government and with their own local conditions. The local Government organs and other basic-level organs are allowed to make certain adjustments in production targets fixed by the Central Government and other upper-level government organs.

Different planning methods for various kinds of crops may be adopted. As for the food crops, the State can only stipulate the total output target of food crops, the distribution target, and the purchase target of various kinds of food crops. As regards animal products and other economic crops which are fairly important commercially, the State can stipulate a somewhat detailed purchase target according to the varieties of products. As for the miscellaneous crops, agricultural subsidiary products and other native and special products, it is unnecessary to include them in the State plan. However, some of these products may be listed in the production plans of Government organs at provincial and *hsien* levels. The purchase departments and commercial departments may sign direct contracts with the agricultural cooperatives and encourage the latter systematically to produce these products.

In fulfilling the agricultural taxation and collective purchase plans to the State and in fulfilling the contracts signed with other economic departments, agricultural producer cooperatives may map out their own production plans according to their own requirements. Agricultural cooperatives may use the plans mapped out by the Central Government and local government organs as a guiding principle or as reference material. However, direct orders cannot be issued to the cooperatives to carry out their work in accordance with the afore-mentioned plans. Only by following the above procedure can the production and management of agricultural cooperatives be maintained under the economic plan of the State and the production enthusiasm of agricultural cooperatives be increased.

III. ACTIVELY AND FIRMLY CARRY OUT TECHNICAL REFORM AND DISSEMINATE ADVANCED EXPERIENCES ACCORDING TO LOCAL CONDITIONS.

Given the actual condition that the agricultural mechanization has not yet been realized in China, and because it is still impossible to launch large-scale reclamation of wasteland (according to actual conditions, each locality must endeavor to launch a small-scale reclamation movement and do its best to increase the acreage of farmland), our fundamental method of developing agricultural production at the present stage is on the basis of agricultural cooperativization, to rely on the laboring enthusiasm of the peasants to gradually carry out technical reform and to raise the yield per unit area (including the construction of water conservancy works, land grading, soil improvement, farm tool improvement, distribution of seedlings of excellent strain, accumulation and production of fertilizer, insect control, improvement of farming techniques, and changing of farm practices).

During the past several years, particularly since last winter, each locality has fully utilized the favorable conditions resulting from the agricultural cooperativization movement and adopted effective measures to carry out technical reform and disseminate advanced experiences, such as the construction of small-scale irrigation projects, the conversion of dry land into irrigated land, the changing from single-crop to double-crop harvest, the promotion of modern farm tools, the selection of seedlings of excellent strain, and the development of fertilizer sources.

The volume of work was unprecedented and the results achieved were tremendous. However, owing to unrealistic production plans, insufficient technical guidance, impetuous steps taken by some cooperatives, and the aimless promotion of advanced experiences owing to a poor knowledge of agricultural production, the practice of commandism was reported in certain localities, causing losses in agricultural production and adversely affecting the enthusiasm of the peasants. The current task is not only to sum up the successful experiences acquired in various places for active dissemination, but also to analyze the causes of failures for immediate correction.

The CCP Central Committee held that the principle of carrying out technical reform and the dissemination of advanced experiences should be active, not conservative. However, the method must be suitable to local conditions and the steps taken must be careful. The work cannot be conducted impetuously. Advanced experiences from all localities must be absorbed including those from foreign countries. Special attention must be paid to the nature of the soil and no advanced experience should be disseminated in any locality before experimental work is conducted.

Two steps must be taken in the dissemination of the advanced experiences which we have already mastered: Trial promotion should be launched in selected areas, and then this should be disseminated in large areas. Meanwhile, three steps must be taken in disseminating advanced experiences which have not yet been mastered: first, trial promotion should be launched in selected areas, second, experimental areas should be increased, third, they should be disseminated in large areas.

The dissemination of advanced experiences must be carried out in accordance with the principle of willingness. If cooperative cadres and members refuse to accept some advanced experiences which are important for increasing production, they can only be convinced by seeing actual examples. They should not be forced to accept these advanced experiences. However, it is also incorrect to allow the peasants to carry out technical reform according to their free will.

Henceforth, it is necessary to consolidate the exemplary role of the State-owned farms and ranches, the work of agrotechnical stations, and scientific research work in agriculture so as to adequately combine scientific techniques with the actual experiences of the peasants.

It is not only necessary to disseminate foreign advanced experiences among the broad masses of the people, but also necessary to sum up the experiences in increasing production gained by the peasants, especially by the older peasants. Progressive scientific methods of foreign countries should be promoted in those areas where conditions are similar to those of the foreign countries. Only by following these principles in carrying out technical reform and disseminating advanced experiences can mistakes be avoided and the goal of increasing production be achieved.

IV. STRENGTHEN LABOR MANAGEMENT AND RAISE LABOR PRODUCTIVITY.

The raising of labor productivity is a most important way of increasing the production of agricultural cooperatives and of insuring in cooperative members' incomes. The rational mobilization of collective labor is another important way of increasing the labor productivity of agricultural cooperatives. In this work many localities have had certain favorable experiences.

However, owing to insufficient experience and lack of attention to implement work regulations, certain shortcomings in labor management still exist, labor productivity has not yet been satisfactorily increased, and slackness and waste have been reported in many localities. In order to raise labor productivity gradually, attention must be given to the several problems concerning labor management.

(1) In accordance with production requirements, constant attention must be paid to maintaining an even progress in the fulfillment of the labor production plan.

In formulating and revising the work plan, it is not only necessary to insure evenness in production in a general way for the whole year, but also necessary to guarantee it for each season. It must be done in such a way as to insure that there will be enough labor for the busy season and a way to utilize the surplus labor during the slack season. In this way, the requirements of labor for agricultural production, subsidiary production, and agricultural basic construction will be met properly.

Attention must also be given to the equitable distribution of manpower among production teams and groups, so that they may be able to carry out their work in an even manner. As for male labor, female labor, full labor, and half labor (full labor refers to a full man-day and half labor to a half man-day - Ed.), attention must be paid to the rational, coordinated utilization of manpower, so as to gain full productivity from every working member.

(2) Rational adjustment of work groups.

At present, some production teams and groups are too large. These teams and groups should be readjusted according to current technical conditions and farm work requirements. According to the experiences gained from various localities, the small-scale team (those comprising an average of 20 to 40 farming households - NCNA) and small-scale group (those comprising an average of seven to eight farming households - NCNA) are very suitable for most of the localities in China under current conditions.

(3) Consolidation of quota system management.

The consolidation of quota system management is a very delicate and practical task, and we should not be satisfied with the general quota. There is a difference between the industry and agriculture quotas. In agricultural production geographical factors are involved and production is constantly affected by changes in natural conditions. Therefore, the targets fixed by Government organs at the provincial and *hsien* levels can only be used as a guide for the agricultural cooperatives.

It is either impossible or unnecessary to emphasize a unified quota for all agricultural cooperatives. When necessary, the production quota fixed by each cooperative should also be adjusted. At the same time, production teams can make their own necessary adjustments so long as they do not change their total (wage?) points. Attention must be paid to summing up experiences and to adopting certain methods nor promoting the quota system during the transitional period so as to improve quota system management.

(4) The raising of labor productivity should be carried out in connection with the rational improvement of labor organizations, rational utilization of labor, consolidation of labor protection, improvement of farm tools, and improvement of and increase in production techniques. Improper practices contrary to the above-mentioned principle should be avoided such as the improper expansion of work hours, increase in work, and arbitrary assignment of work without considering the health of cooperative members. Labor protection must be given to all women cooperative members, particularly to pregnant women.

(5) Under the condition of observing collective labor leadership, certain measures must be taken to provide cooperative members with enough time to take care of their family sideline work and family affairs. In this connection, many cooperatives have been too strict. From now on, the regulations for cooperatives should be so implemented that every cooperative member can freely utilize his own time after fulfilling the labor quota assigned to him by the cooperative.

V. *PROPERLY CARRY OUT INCOME DISTRIBUTION WORK IN COOPERATIVES.*

Income distribution work is one of the important tasks in consolidating the cooperatives. It is an important aspect of socialist production. If consideration is given to both general interests and the individual interests of cooperative members, the broad masses of cooperative members will be able to fully understand the superiority of the socialist economy. Every cooperative member must understand that although production is the foundation of distribution, yet production development may be affected if distribution is not made properly.

Collective interest is the foundation for the individual's interest. However, if collective interest is overemphasized and the individual's interest is not properly recognized, collective interest will be hampered. Therefore, production and distribution, State, collective, and individual interests should be appropriately linked.

The Central Government proposed to allocate 60–70 percent of cooperative incomes for distribution to members, and to strive for an increase in income for 90 percent of all cooperative members. This is the implementation of this link.

A large number of agricultural cooperatives are still in the primary stage, their foundations are fragile, and in addition some cooperatives last spring wasted money in unnecessary arrangements, made more payments on basic expenditures and reduced incomes from subsidiary products. It is really difficult to guarantee income increases for 90 percent of the members. Thus the various agricultural cooperatives are urged to pay much attention to increasing agricultural and subsidiary production and to successfully carrying out distribution work.

First, the principle of strict economy and hard work should be adhered to. Production expenditures should be minimized in considering production increases. Nonproductive expenditures should be avoided or held to a minimum. Accounts of cooperatives should be open to inspection by members monthly or quarterly so as to practice democracy in the economy. Every effort should be made to avoid extravagance and to prevent embezzlement.

Second, after guaranteeing delivery of agricultural taxes to the State and reserving a certain amount for productive expenditures, the public reserve funds and public welfare funds of cooperatives this year in general should not be over 5 percent of the total income of cooperatives. The principal agricultural taxes should be maintained at last year's level and local levies should not be increased too much. Cooperatives should distribute 60-70 percent of their incomes to members.

Cooperatives in normal, favorable areas should strive to increase the incomes of 90 percent of their members. Generally speaking, the financial work of cooperatives in various localities is backward; the local Party and government units should consolidate their leadership in the direction.

Third, in distribution, cooperatives should stick to the principle of each according to his work —the more work the more pay—and equal pay for men and women members for equal work. It is wrong to distribute according to classes or to the number of dependents of members.

Appropriate care should be given to those members who are unable to do full amount of work and to those suffering from accidents through the use of public welfare funds or through productive arrangements. As regards the distribution of grain crops, appropriate attention should be given to those able-bodied and hard-working members who may need more food supplies.

Fourth, the system of distribution in advance for labor should be established, especially during the interval between the first and second crops. This is important for insuring the daily livelihood of poor members and for encouraging positiveness in work. The sources of advance distribution are cooperative incomes from subsidiary products and income from selling agricultural products.

Fifth, households entitled to the benefits of the "five guarantees" should be treated by the cooperative accordingly and in accordance with its production conditions. In addition, arrangements should be made for them to participate in production if conditions permit. Compensation for land or aid from the Government relief or public welfare funds should be given to them to settle their livelihood difficulties so that their standard of living will not be lower than that prior to their joining cooperatives.

VI. THOROUGH IMPLEMENTATION OF MUTUAL BENEFIT POLICY.

The mutual benefit policy is one of the reasons for the success of our agricultural cooperativization. It has not only been significant during the setting up of cooperatives, but also in consolidating the cooperatives. The policy should be followed in disposing of the means of production of the poor and middle farmers when they join cooperatives, and in settling questions involving economic relations among members.

In order to continuously carry out the mutual benefit policy, the following problems should be settled:

First, in many places the valuation of groves is too low; at times no price has been fixed for a certain number of trees or saplings. In other places, small holdings of trees, which should not be placed under collective ownership, are compulsorily transferred to cooperative property. In the protection of trees, development of forestry production, and consolidation of internal unity of cooperatives, the opinions of the masses should be considered and the regulations governing agricultural cooperatives should be followed.

Those means of production which have not yet been placed under common ownership should be properly transferred. In cases where production has been underestimated a reevaluation should be made. This would enhance internal unity in the cooperatives, benefit agricultural production, and insure success in the struggle to increase the incomes of 90 percent of the cooperative members. Due consideration should be given to this work. However in cases where transfers have been made properly, with no complaints from cooperative members, it is not always necessary to make readjustment.

Second, in certain places, draft animals, farm tools, and tools for subsidiary production which have not been transferred or transferred at a low valuation should be disposed of according to the above-mentioned policy. Certain large or costly tools or equipment for subsidiary production which have been pooled into the cooperative at a given price may not be paid for in 4 or 5 years. Members who formerly owned such means of production may be consulted and the period of payment prolonged.

Third, in order to increase the members' trust, cooperatives should pay without fail the dividends for members' investments, returns from their groves and refund the amount left over after from their investment of draft animals and farm tools in the cooperative.

Fourth, members' investments should be on a voluntary basis. Compulsory allotments or deductions should be avoided. In addition, credit cooperatives should absorb members' savings, help to settle their production or livelihood difficulties, and to finance agricultural cooperatives. However, credit cooperatives must follow the principle of freedom of deposit and withdrawal and maintain secrecy in their dealings with depositors. Agricultural cooperatives should not be permitted to freeze members' deposits in credit cooperatives. A proper value should be placed on the fertilizers produced by cooperative members so as to encourage them to accumulate and to produce more fertilizer.

Fifth, in some places, the plots of land kept for the members' own use are inadequate or even not permitted. Cooperative regulations should be observed to let members keep certain plots of land for their own use, in order to satisfy their livelihood requirements or to permit cattle raising. But there must not be kept excessive plots.

VII. CONSOLIDATION OF COOPERATIVE ORGANIZATION AND CONSTRUCTION.

The organization and construction of cooperatives should be in accordance with the principles of the socialist economic system and existing basic conditions with respect to the administrative level, the technical level, and production plans.

First, the scale of an agricultural cooperative is of importance in its organization and construction. At present, the scale of the majority of cooperatives is reasonable. However, cooperatives in certain districts have been overly ambitious in mapping out projects, creating difficulties in the administration and internal unity of cooperatives. The Central Government and the CCP Central Committee hold that the scale of an agricultural cooperative should be fixed so as to benefit production and internal unity, to fit the existing administrative level, and to strengthen friendly relations among members.

Under present conditions, it is suitable for the cooperatives to confine their sizes to approximately 100 households for each cooperative in mountainous areas, 200 households in rough hillside areas, and 300 households in the plain areas. In the case of big villages containing more than 300 households, a cooperative may be established to embrace the whole village. This rule should be followed in establishing new or amalgamating old cooperatives in the future.

In regard to existing large cooperatives, all those that can be operated properly should be maintained. Those which are inefficient in production, causing a majority of the cooperative members to demand a division of the cooperative, should be so divided in a suitable manner. In both cases, however, the change must be made with the voluntary consent of all the cadres and members of the cooperative concerned through consultation. It should by no means be dictated by higher authorities for the cooperatives to reorganize accordingly.

With the exception of those that must be divided or amalgamated, the cooperatives in general should refrain from reorganizing during the few years after establishment. This is of great importance in the consolidation of the new production relationship.

Second, according to current experience, villages in which there is a great difference in the distribution of land, in the levels of income, and in the nature of production and management should not be incorporated into one cooperative under present circumstances, because this will be detrimental to both production and the consolidation of the cooperative concerned. Attention should be paid to this experience, and efforts should be made to suitably settle existing disputes within cooperatives of this type arising from such differences.

In regard to individual households scattered in remote mountainous areas, smaller cooperatives or mutual-aid teams may be organized by themselves, or large cooperatives in adjacent areas should be asked to accommodate them. In the latter case, these households should be permitted to engage in production individually, to keep their own accounts, and to shoulder their own responsibilities in production.

In the case of some cooperatives consisting of several villages which are carrying out production smoothly, consolidated properly, and are able to operate successfully, an effort should be made to continue them in that way without disorganization.

Third, to maintain the rational division of labor in society in the past in the interests of production, all non-peasant personnel, such as full-time petty merchants, transportation workers, physicians, teachers, and others, may be permitted not to join agricultural producer cooperatives. Those who have already joined may retain or withdraw their membership according to their own wishes.

Rural full-time petty merchants and transportation workers should be treated according to measures governing the socialist transformation of industry, commerce, and transport. This will be beneficial to the normal circulation of commodities between urban and rural areas. Part-time petty merchants and transportation workers and the dependents of such full-time merchants and workers, however, should still be absorbed into the cooperatives according to the principle of willingness.

Fourth, the leadership of the cooperative is a major issue in the organization and construction of cooperatives. In this regard, we must pay primary attention to the work of making members of poor peasant status in the leadership constitute a majority and of strengthening their solidarity with the middle peasants. In the meantime, we must not only select outstanding members from the young and strong to join the leadership but also those from the old. In this way good coordination will exist among the young, strong, and old. They will respect and learn from one another and develop to the full their respective talents. All deviations of looking down upon the young or the old should be corrected.

Fifth, responsible organizations of various provinces, special administrative areas, and *hsien* should establish schools and short-term training class for training agricultural producer cooperative cadres (including administrative and technical cadres) in a planned manner. Similar attention should be paid to the training of women cadres. Leadership in this work should be intensified and strengthened so that noticeable results may be obtained in a short time.

Cadres assigned by higher authorities to the cooperatives should try their best to assist local cadres, respect their views, and train them to work independently. The local cadres must be consulted before the issuance of any decisions or technical measures. All practices of coercion, commandism, dictating work, and issuing instructions outside one's authority should be prevented and remedied.

Sixth, the democratic administration of the cooperatives should be strengthened. Production plans, work plans, financial plans, and income distribution plans of the cooperative must be discussed and formulated in a democratic manner. General meetings and representative meetings should be convened regularly for the election and reelection of the administrative and supervisory committees and for the delivery of business reports to the cooperative members. The cooperative members should be encouraged to assume constant supervision over the leadership for the improvement of relations between cadres and members of the cooperative.

Seventh, former landlords, rich peasants, and rural counterrevolutionary elements no longer engaged in counterrevolutionary activities should be allowed with due discretion to join agricultural producer cooperatives for production. This measure has proved beneficial to the reform of these elements and, therefore, should be continued in order to assist in their reform. In the meantime, however, vigilance should be exercised to guard against subversive activities which might be carried out by these elements.

VIII. THE PRICES OF A NUMBER OF AGRICULTURAL PRODUCTS SHOULD BE READJUSTED SO AS TO IMPROVE THE PROCUREMENT AND SUPPLY WORK IN RURAL AREAS.

Agricultural production is closely related to commerce. The production of economic crops, animal byproducts, and subsidiary products, in particular, is principally for marketing purposes. For this reason, commercial work in general and the prices fixed for these products in particular have a great influence upon agricultural production. We must try to improve our commercial work and formulate our price policy in such a way as to stimulate production and the all-round development of agricultural and subsidiary operations.

First, the purchasing prices of a number of agricultural products should be worked out in consultation with the peasants. All the prices which have been too low for the development of production should be suitably raised. In cases where the difference between the buying and selling prices of the same product is too great, measures should be adopted to reduce the difference for the benefit of the cooperatives and peasants and the development of their enthusiasm in production.

In the meantime, to make the readjustment of prices more practical the central authority and local authorities governing the division of responsibility in the readjustment of prices issued by the Central People's Government, the prices of all products which are produced and sold in the same locality should be readjusted by the local authorities concerned.

In readjusting the price of a product, however, attention should be paid to the work of maintaining a reasonable rate of exchange between this product and other products so as to head off a chain reaction involving a wide variety of products. To maintain a reasonable rate of exchange between products of different localities and products of different varieties, the extent of the readjustment of prices should be decided by responsible organs of the Central People's Government.

Second, the work of assigning the "three fixed quotas" in the unified procurement and supply of grain in rural areas should be continuously perfected to correct the deviation of fixing the quotas either too high or too low. In addition, the policy of not increasing the quota of grain procurement according to the increase in production should be resolutely observed. The total quantity of grain purchased by the State this year should be maintained at the same level as that of last year.

The practice of making advance purchases of principal agricultural products should be perfected. Deposits for such products should be increased to the maximum, and be paid promptly in order to assist the agricultural producer cooperatives in establishing their system of advancing wages to their members for the contribution of labor.

Third, the quantity of products assigned to peasants for procurement by the State, such as live hogs, should be fixed according to the actual production of the peasants concerned with due consideration to the needs for such products of peasants themselves.

Fourth, the administration and management of commercial enterprises should be improved in such a way as to reduce the number of links in the chain of commodity circulation, simplify the organization of the enterprises, reduce administrative expenses, and simplify procedures in procurement and supply. In the meantime, attention should be paid to the work of strengthening the political education program among commercial personnel in order to improve their working spirit. The practice of giving unreasonably low rations and offering unreasonably low prices for products to be procured by these personnel should be corrected inasmuch as such practice will alienate them from the masses.

Fifth, free markets under the leadership of the socialist economy should be established one by one. These markets should be open to all agricultural and subsidiary products not included among the number of those products to be procured in a unified manner by the State either directly or through the supply and marketing cooperatives, and to all products owned by the peasants after having fulfilled their tasks of selling them to the State.

In case a buying spree breaks out or the prices quoted in the market are out of line with the official prices, local authorities of the Party and the Government may hold conferences with related organizations to make adjustments.

Sixth, the rates and levying measures of agricultural taxes and subsidiary production taxes should be adjusted and rearranged according to the new conditions after the completion of cooperativization in the interests of production.

Seventh, the agricultural products processing industry should not be centered in cities, because it will be unable to conveniently supply the peasants with sufficient fodder and fertilizer. This has also caused the work of subsidiary production in rural areas to dwindle. For this reason, the cities should not be allowed to have too many rice mills, cotton-gin mills, and oil mills. Generally speaking, excepting the raw materials needed by existing processing factories, all agricultural products for processing should be supplied to local *hsiang* and *chen* factories or to factories established by individual agricultural producer cooperatives. (The State may supply the peasants with coarse grain for processing by the peasants themselves.) With regard to the products that must be processed in cities, the prices of byproducts (such as bean and oil cakes) should be readjusted to suit the purchasing power of the peasants and arrangements should be made for a certain portion of the byproducts to be returned to the locality from whence the products were supplied.

IX. ADJUSTMENT OF RELATIONS BETWEEN THE HANDICRAFT PRODUCER COOPERATIVES AND AGRICULTURAL PRODUCER COOPERATIVES.

In the main, cooperativization of handicrafts has been completed throughout the country. Because of the quick development of this work and also because of the lack of coordination between handicraft producer cooperatives and agricultural producer cooperatives in the matter of handicraft production an abnormal state of affairs has come about.

On the one hand, there has been a struggle for members and markets between handicraft producer cooperatives in cities and in rural areas and between those in different localities. This has destroyed the former harmony in the division of markets in the handicraft industry and caused confusion in the supply and marketing of handicraft products.

On the other hand, a number of handicraft producer cooperatives have restricted some agricultural producer cooperatives from engaging in certain handicraft production tasks, while a number of agricultural producer cooperatives have seen fit to employ handicraft workers from cities, to establish their own handicraft products selling centers, to deliberately increase the production of handicraft products, or to restrict the supply of raw materials to urban handicraft producer cooperatives in discrimination against specialized handicraft industry.

To solve this problem, overall arrangements must be made in the spirit of giving due consideration to both urban and rural areas.

First, urban and rural handicraft workers should be organized differently. Handicraft workers in rural areas should generally be incorporated in agricultural producer cooperatives according to the principle of willingness. Handicraft workers in cities and *chen* should join handicraft producer cooperatives. Handicraft producer cooperatives in cities and *chen* should not restrict agricultural producer cooperatives from engaging in handicraft industrial production, nor should agricultural producer cooperatives try to employ handicraft workers from cities and to establish handicraft products selling centers. On the other hand, agricultural producer cooperatives should try to absorb the rural dependents of urban handicraft workers into their organization according to the principle of willingness.

Second, high-level specialized rural handicraft workers may establish specialized teams within agricultural producer cooperatives in rural areas. These teams may establish their own remuneration system and shoulder their own responsibilities in business. When necessary each member of the handicraft production team may work individually and be responsible for his own operation either within or outside of the cooperative. The cooperative should not restrict their activities.

With regard to the question of providing guidance to these handicraft workers and the question of securing markets for them, assistance should be given them by local handicraft industry administrative organs of the Party and the People's Government and local supply and marketing cooperatives. An effort should be made to eliminate discrimination of one locality against another. An agricultural producer cooperative may request its own handicraft production teams to carry out certain jobs for it at remunerations fixed according to a reasonable standard.

Third, handicraft production should be carried out in a more planned manner and the shortcoming of blindness in production should also be surmounted. As for commodities which are in great demand by the people, utmost efforts should be exerted to promote the supply and marketing of these commodities in all areas.

If new enterprises of different trades are to be established in certain localities, it is necessary to consider the marketing of goods turned out by these enterprises. At the same time, close attention should be paid to insure that the newly established enterprises will not hamper the division of labor between sideline production in rural areas and handicraft production in cities and towns and the relation between supply and marketing of handicraft products between cities and towns as well as between regions, so as to avoid confusion.

Fourth, there are still conflicts between handicraft industry engaged in auxiliary production in rural areas and the handicraft industry of cities and towns. Local Party and Government organs should negotiate with leading departments concerned and assist the handicraft industry in solving its questions in connection with marketing and the supply of raw materials.

X. CONSOLIDATE GUIDANCE OVER AGRICULTURAL PRODUCER COOPERATIVES IN NATIONAL MINORITY AREAS.

There are, in general, many differences in the economic conditions between national minority areas and other inland localities. All have their own production and livelihood characteristics. Therefore, in carrying out the agricultural cooperativization movement and the work of establishing cooperatives, this work should be arranged in such a way that it will be in line with the principle of self-willingness and will also take into consideration the characteristics of different nationalities. If this is not done, it will affect production and solidarity among nationalities.

In areas where many nationalities reside, every different nationality should establish its own cooperative, so as to eliminate differences in production, in modes of living, and in the religions of different nationalities. Only when cooperative members of a nationality are incapable of establishing their own cooperatives or when it is absolutely necessary, will the formation of joint cooperatives of different nationalities be permitted.

Among the joint cooperatives of different nationalities, close attention must be paid to the further expansion of the special abilities of various kinds of production which they have mastered. Particularly should attention be paid to safeguarding the interests of cooperative members in national minority areas, so as to insure a greater income for national minority cooperative members.

In cases where national minorities are unable to render mutual assistance due to certain difficulties, the abrupt merging of cooperatives so as to form joint cooperatives is not permissible.

Attention should also be paid to the training of leading cadres in national minority areas. Joint cooperatives of different nationalities should be established on the basis of the stipulations prescribed in the program of cooperatives and absorb more outstanding persons from among different national minorities to take part in guiding the cooperatives. Respect must also be paid to the customs and practices of different national minorities.

In order further to develop animal husbandry cooperatives in pastoral areas, it is necessary to adopt a much more rigid and effective guiding principle. Under the principle of further developing the animal husbandry industry and other favorable conditions, leading organs at various levels of different national minorities should conscientiously establish animal husbandry cooperatives on a trial basis, so as to draw experiences from this experiment, and gradually disseminate these experiences among the peasants of various national minorities. Any haste in carrying this out should be completely eliminated.

XI. STRENGTHEN THE WORK OF BASIC-LEVEL ORGANIZATIONS IN RURAL AREAS.

Basic-level organizations in rural areas have played a very important role in our Socialist revolution and production and in heightening the standards of cadres. However, it is necessary to point out that since the launching of the agricultural cooperativization movement and the abolition of *chu* and the combination of *hsiang*, basic-level organizations in rural areas have not only neglected to strengthen their work in coping with the demand of the new environment, but have also shown signs of developing certain weaknesses.

During the abolition of *chu* and the combination of *hsiang*, many localities transferred large numbers of *chu* cadres to other areas and failed to keep some of these cadres to form the backbone of *hsiang* organizations. This negligence has weakened the leadership of basic-level organizations.

On the other hand, some comrades were of the opinion that following the agricultural cooperativization movement, things would be improved. However, they underestimated the new troubles arising from the new environment and failed to recognize the necessity of further developing democracy under the new environment. As a result, commandism and the practice of treating matters in an oversimplified manner developed, and practical work in rural areas has become very weak.

Party organizations at various levels should pay close attention to this phenomenon, and effective measures should be adopted as quickly as possible to remedy the situation.

First, it is necessary for Communist organs at various levels to realize the significance of the work of basic-level organizations from the ideological point of view and effectively strengthen the Party's leadership in rural areas.

It is also necessary for them to realize that the successful implementation of all guiding principles and policies of the Party relies to a great extent upon the basic-level organizations. This is especially true now that agricultural cooperativization has just materialized and many new problems have arisen, and while we still lack experience in solving these problems.

Therefore, any move which might weaken the role of the Party and government basic-level organizations in rural areas or any negligence in recognizing the importance of the role of these organizations will cause damage to the undertakings of the Party as well as the people.

Second, the abolition of *chu* and the combination of *hsiang* should be carried out with great conscientiousness; this should not be carried out simultaneously with the merging of cooperatives or the advancement of cooperatives to the higher stage. While carrying out abolition and combination, it is important to leave behind a certain number of vital *chu* and *hsiang* cadres. The transfer of all cadres to other localities will greatly reduce the leading force in *hsiang* and cooperatives.

Third, the working spirit of the mass line should be rigidly implemented. Branch organs and members of the Chinese Communist Party should conduct investigations and studies by penetrating deep into the broad masses of the people, so as to achieve a thorough understanding of the thoughts and the degree of enthusiasm of the broad masses, and to improve their leadership over the cooperatives.

Inside the cooperatives, branches and members of the CCP should implement the policy of operating cooperatives in a democratic way: this means consultation with cooperative members on matters of great importance, rigid observation of the working style giving back to the masses what was brought from the masses. This will enable them to establish collective leadership on a truly democratic foundation; and this collective leadership will not become dictatorship by a few.

Fourth, it is necessary to clarify the distribution of work among the Party, Government, and cooperative and to eliminate confusion between the Party and cooperative, and between the cooperative and the government. In its leadership over cooperatives, the Party Branch must not interfere in everything, and monopolize matters. Administrative matters originally handled by the people's government should continue to be so handled, and the cooperative should not take them over. The erroneous tendency for Party, Government, and cooperative cadres to hold too many jobs concurrently, should be corrected.

Aside from the above problems, the Party organs and government of various localities should pay attention to the strengthening or production and to relief work in calamity-stricken areas, particularly in areas where calamities caused severe damage. Party organs and governments of various localities should, in accordance with actual conditions, adopt and seriously implement effective measures to promote production and relief work. All the above-mentioned constitute questions which should be solved in order to successfully fulfill the tasks of cooperativization, to consolidate the great victories of cooperativization, and to cope with the needs of the upsurge in production.

When these questions are solved, all positive factors will be applied to promote further the cooperatives and the upsurge of agricultural production. At this time and during the next 2 or 3 years, leading organs of the Party and Government at all levels should continue to devote their efforts to strengthening their leadership over rural work; and, particularly, responsible members of Party committees should make all efforts to implement the resolutions of the Sixth Plenary Session of the Seventh CCP Congress, personally attending to their duties, promptly summarizing all experiences, fully controlling the rural areas, and familiarizing themselves with their undertakings so as to meet the needs of the new situation following cooperativization.

To successfully implement the above directive, it is hoped that leading organs of the Party and Government at all levels, and the State organs concerned will, in accordance with the actual conditions of the locality and the work of various departments, seriously study this directive and devise effective measures for its implementation. They shall also report to the CCP Central Committee and the State Council on their progress.

Chapter V

CHINA AND THE SOCIALIST CAMP, 1956-57

(containing Document 13)

General comment. Though China's foreign policy falls outside the scope of this volume, the attitude of the Chinese People's Government toward events in Eastern Europe during the fall and winter of 1956-57 bears very closely on its domestic policy toward "doctrinaires" and "revisionists." For reasons briefly sketched in our General Introduction, the voice of the Chinese People's Government commanded at this time unusual and disproportionate weight within the "Socialist Camp" as a whole. The Chinese did not miss the opportunity of making their views widely heard, and the doctrines evolved by them to cover the internal affairs of the Camp proved later to be of considerable importance in dealing with heresies within China.

The first crucial date was October 30, 1956, when the Soviet government issued a declaration "On Friendship and Cooperation between the Soviet Union and other Socialist States." In this declaration, designed to prevent Hungary's defection from the Camp, it was asserted that "the countries of the great commonwealth of socialist nations can build their relations only on the principle of full equality, respect for territorial integrity, state independence and sovereignty, and non-interference in the domestic affairs of one another." The declaration was immediately endorsed by the Chinese People's Government, which reasserted its own "five principles of peaceful coexistence" (first enunciated in the Sino-Indian agreement of April 1954 over Tibet); backed Polish and Hungarian demands for the withdrawal of Russian troops; and condemned "great-nation chauvinism."

Then occurred the second Russian intervention in Hungary. On November 11, Marshal Tito gave his full exposition of the Yugoslav position; he pleaded for greater freedom for all countries in the Camp to follow their own paths to socialism; condemned Stalinism and the first Russian intervention in Hungary; but justified the second intervention. By the end of the year the Chinese People's Government seems to have made up its mind that, whatever might be the dangers of further Stalinist behavior by the U.S.S.R. within the Camp, they were outweighed by the dangers of disintegration in the Camp that might arise if Tito and other comparative independents were allowed to operate freely and attract people like Gomulka to his doctrines.

This is the background of the *People's Daily* editorial of December 29, 1956, printed below as Document 13. As in the editorial of April 5, 1956 (Document 7, above), the basic features of the socialist system emphasized are the dictatorship of the proletariat and the leading role of the U.S.S.R.—though "great-nation chauvinism" is still condemned. The justification of the dictatorship of the proletariat is the continued struggle against "imperialism"; this is reflected in remnants of the "class struggle" within countries of the Socialist Camp (a concept which was shortly to prove important for China itself). Chou En-lai visited Eastern Europe on short notice in January 1957, in order to mend fences, particularly between the U.S.S.R. and Poland, on the basis of this position.

Further background material may be found as follows:

(a) Chinese relations with the Soviet-bloc countries: Zbigniew K. Brzezinski,

The Soviet Bloc: Unity and Conflict (Cambridge: Harvard University Press, 1960), especially pp. 276-282.

(b) Chinese interpretations of the Hungarian crisis: Documents 16 and 25 below; also ECMM 64 (*China Youth*, Dec. 1, 1956), justifying the Soviet interventions.

(c) Contradictions within the Socialist Camp: ECMM 72 (*China Youth*, Dec. 16, 1956).

(d) "Revisionism": ECMM 73, 74, 82, 87 (*Political Study*, Feb. 13, 1957; *Study*, Jan. 18, 1957; *Study*, March 3, 1957; *Theoretical Study*, Feb. 16, 1957).

It was made clear from the first that the editorial printed below as Document 13 was regarded as of exceptional importance. The editorial was accompanied by a note saying that it had been prepared by the *People's Daily* editorial staff on the basis of a discussion at an enlarged meeting of the Political Bureau (Politburo) of the Party Central Committee. ECMM 88 (*Study*, April 3, 1957) shows that the text remained a subject for very special attention by the cadres.

DOCUMENT 13

More on the Historical Experience of the Dictatorship of the Proletariat, editorial in *People's Daily*, December 29, 1956.

The English text is taken from a booklet entitled *The Historical Experience of the Dictatorship of the Proletariat*, Foreign Languages Press, Peking, 1959, pp. 21-64. As usual the notes in the document were inserted by the Chinese Communists themselves.

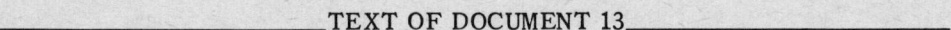
TEXT OF DOCUMENT 13

In April 1956, we discussed the historical experience of the dictatorship of the proletariat in connection with the question of Stalin. Since then, a further train of events in the international communist movement has caused concern to the people of our country. The publication in Chinese newspapers of Comrade Tito's speech of November 11, and the comments on that speech by various Communist Parties, have led people again to raise many questions which call for an answer. In the present article we shall centre our discussion on the following questions: first, an appraisal of the fundamental course taken by the Soviet Union in its revolution and construction; second, an appraisal of Stalin's merits and faults; third, the struggle against doctrinairism and revisionism; and fourth, the international solidarity of the proletariat of all countries.

In examining modern international questions, we must proceed first of all from the most fundamental fact, the antagonism between the imperialist bloc of aggression and the popular forces in the world. The Chinese people, who have suffered enough from imperialist aggression, can never forget that imperialism has always opposed the liberation of all peoples and the independence of all oppressed nations, that it has always regarded the communist movement, which stands most resolutely for the people's interests, as a thorn in its flesh. Since the birth of the first socialist state, the Soviet Union, imperialism has tried by every means to wreck it. Following the establishment of a whole group of socialist states, the hostility of the imperialist camp to the socialist camp, and its flagrant acts of sabotage against the latter, have become a still more pronounced feature of world politics. The leader of the imperialist camp, the United States, has been especially vicious and shameless in its interference in the domestic affairs of socialist countries; for many years it has been obstructing China's liberation of its own territory Taiwan, and for many years it has openly adopted as its official policy the subversion of the East European countries.

The activities of the imperialists in the Hungarian affair of October 1956 marked the gravest attack launched by them against the socialist camp since the war of aggression they had carried on in Korea. Just as the resolution adopted by the meeting of the Provisional Central Committee of the Hungarian Socialist Workers' Party pointed out, the Hungarian affair was the result of various causes, both internal and external; and while any one-sided explanation is incorrect, among the causes international imperialism "played the main and decisive part." Following the defeat of their plot for a counter-revolutionary come-back in Hungary, the imperialist powers headed by the United States have manoeuvred the United Nations into adopting resolutions directed against the Soviet Union and interfering in Hungary's internal affairs. At the same time, they stirred up a hysterical anti-communist wave throughout the Western world. Although U.S. imperialism is taking advantage of the fiasco of the Anglo-French war of aggression against Egypt to grab British and French interests in the Middle East and North Africa in every way possible, it has pledged itself to eliminate its "misunderstandings" with Britain and France and to seek "closer and more intimate understanding" with them to repair their united front against communism, against the Asian and African peoples and against the peace-loving people of the world. To oppose communism, the people and peace, the imperialist countries should unite—this is the gist of Dulles' statement at the NATO council meeting on the so-called "need for a philosophy for living and acting at this critical point in world history." Somewhat intoxicated by his own illusions, Dulles asserted: "The Soviet communist structure is in a deteriorating condition (?), with the power of the rulers disintegrating (?).... Facing this situation, the free nations must maintain moral pressures which are helping to undermine the Soviet-Chinese communist system and maintain military strength and resolution." He called on the NATO countries "to disrupt the powerful Soviet despotism (?) based upon militaristic (?) and atheistic concepts." He also expressed the view that "a change of character of that [communist] world now seems to be within the realm of possibility (!)."

We have always considered our enemies our best teachers, and now Dulles is letting us have another lesson. He may slander us a thousand times and curse us ten thousand times, there is nothing new in this at all. But when Dulles, putting the matter on a "philosophic" plane, urges the imperialist countries to place their contradiction with communism above all other contradictions, to bend all their efforts towards bringing about "a change of character of that [communist] world" and towards "undermining" and "disrupting" the socialist system headed by the Soviet Union, this is a lesson that is extremely helpful to us, though such efforts will certainly come to naught. Although we have consistently held and still hold that the socialist and capitalist countries should co-exist in peace and carry out peaceful competition, the imperialists are always bent on destroying us. We must therefore never forget the stern struggle with the enemy, i.e. the class struggle on a world scale.

There are before us two types of contradiction which are different in nature. The first type consists of contradictions between our enemy and ourselves (contradictions between the camp of imperialism and that of socialism, contradictions between imperialism and the people and oppressed nations of the whole world, contradictions between the bourgeoisie and the proletariat in the imperialist countries, etc.). This is the fundamental type of contradiction, based on the clash of interests between antagonistic classes. The second type consists of contradictions within the ranks of the people (contradictions between different sections of the people, between comrades within the Communist Party, contradictions between the government and the people in socialist countries, contradictions between socialist countries, contradictions between Communist Parties, etc.). This type of contradiction is not basic; it is not the result of a fundamental clash of interests between classes, but of conflicts between right and wrong opinions or of a partial contradiction of interests. It is a type of contradiction whose solution must, first and foremost, be subordinated to the over-all interests of the struggle against the enemy. Contradictions among the people themselves can and ought to be resolved, proceeding from the desire for solidarity, through criticism or struggle, thus achieving a new solidarity under new conditions. Of course, real life is complicated. Sometimes, it is possible that classes whose interests are in fundamental conflict unite to cope with their main common enemy. On the other hand, under specific conditions, a certain contradiction among the people may be gradually transformed into an antagonistic contradiction when one side of it gradually goes over to the enemy. Finally, the nature of such a contradiction may change completely so that it no longer belongs to the category of contradictions among the people themselves but becomes a component part of the contradiction between ourselves and the enemy. Such a phenomenon did come about in the history of the Communist Party of the Soviet Union and of the Communist Party of China. In a word, anyone who adopts the standpoint of the people should not equate the contradictions among the people with contradictions between the enemy and ourselves, or confuse these two types of contradiction, let alone place the contradictions among the people above the contradictions between the enemy and ourselves. Those who deny the class struggle and do not distinguish between the enemy and ourselves are definitely not Communists or Marxist-Leninists.

We think it necessary to settle this question of fundamental standpoint first, before proceeding to the questions to be discussed. Otherwise, we are bound to lose our bearings, and will be unable to explain correctly international events.

I

The attacks by the imperialists on the international communist movement have long been concentrated mainly on the Soviet Union. Recent controversies in the international communist movement, for the most part, have also involved the question of one's understanding of the Soviet Union. Therefore, the problem of correctly assessing the fundamental course taken by the Soviet Union in its revolution and construction is an important one which Marxist-Leninists must solve.

The Marxist theory of proletarian revolution and the dictatorship of the proletariat is a scientific summing-up of the experience of the working-class movement. However, with the exception of the Paris Commune which lasted only 72 days, Marx and Engels did not live to see for themselves the realization of the proletarian revolution and the dictatorship of the proletariat for which they had striven throughout their lives. In 1917, led by Lenin and the Communist Party of the Soviet Union, the Russian proletariat carried the proletarian revolution to victory and established the dictatorship of the proletariat; it then successfully built up a socialist society. From this time on, scientific socialism was transformed from a theory and ideal into a living reality. And so, the Russian October Revolution of 1917 ushered in a new era, not only in the history of the communist movement but also in the history of mankind.

The Soviet Union has achieved tremendous successes in the 39 years since the revolution. Having eliminated the system of exploitation, the Soviet Union put an end to anarchy, crisis and unemployment in its economic life. Soviet economy and culture have advanced at a pace beyond the reach of capitalist countries. Soviet industrial output in 1956 is 30 times what it was in 1913, the peak year before the revolution. A country which before the revolution was industrially backward and had a high rate of illiteracy has now become the world's second greatest industrial power, possessing scientific and technical forces which are advanced by any standards, and a highly developed socialist culture. The working people of the Soviet Union, who were oppressed before the revolution, have become masters of their own country and society; they have displayed great enthusiasm and creativeness in revolutionary struggle and in construction and a fundamental change has taken place in their material and cultural life. While before the October Revolution Russia was a prison of nations, after the October Revolution these nations achieved equality in the Soviet Union and developed rapidly into advanced socialist nations.

The development of the Soviet Union has not been plain sailing. During 1918-1920, the country was attacked by 14 capitalist powers. In its early years, the Soviet Union went through severe ordeals such as civil war, famine, economic difficulties, and factional splitting activities within the Party. In a decisive period of the Second World War, before the Western countries opened the second front, the Soviet Union, single-handed, met and defeated the attacks of millions of troops of Hitler and his partners. These stern trials failed to crush the Soviet Union or stop its progress.

The existence of the Soviet Union has shaken imperialist rule to its very foundations and brought unbounded hope, confidence and courage to all revolutionary movements of the workers and liberation movements of the oppressed nations. The working people of all countries have helped the Soviet Union, and the Soviet Union has also helped them. It has carried on a foreign policy that guards world peace, recognizes the equality of all nations, and opposes imperialist aggression. The Soviet Union was the main force in defeating fascist aggression throughout the world. The heroic armies of the Soviet Union liberated the East European countries, part of Central Europe, north-east China and the northern part of Korea in co-operation with the popular forces of these countries. The Soviet Union has established friendly relations with the People's Democracies, aided them in economic construction and, together with them, formed a mighty bulwark of world peace—the camp of socialism. The Soviet Union has also given powerful support to the independence movements of the oppressed nations, to the peace movement of the people of the world and to the many peaceable new states in Asia and Africa established since the Second World War.

These are incontrovertible facts that people have known for a long time. Why is it necessary then to bring them up again? It is because, while the enemies of communism have naturally always denied all this, certain Communists at the present time, in examining Soviet experience, often focus their attention on the secondary aspects of the matter and neglect the main aspects.

There are different aspects to Soviet experience in revolution and construction as far as its international significance is concerned. Of the successful experience of the Soviet Union, one part is fundamental and of universal significance at the present stage of human history. This is the most important and fundamental phase of Soviet experience. The other part is not of universal significance. In addition, the Soviet Union has also had its mistakes and failures. No country can ever avoid these entirely, though they may vary in form and degree. And it was even more difficult for the Soviet Union to avoid them, because it was the first socialist country and had no successful experience of others to go by. Such mistakes and failures, however, provide extremely useful lessons for all Communists. That is why all Soviet experience, including certain mistakes and failures, deserves careful study while the fundamental part of the successful Soviet experience is of particular importance. The very fact of the advance of the Soviet Union is proof that the fundamental experience of the Soviet Union in revolution and construction is a great accomplishment, the first paean of victory of Marxism-Leninism in the history of mankind.

What is the fundamental experience of the Soviet Union in revolution and construction? In our opinion, the following, at the very least, should be considered fundamental:

(1) The advanced members of the proletariat organize themselves into a Communist Party which takes Marxism-Leninism as its guide to action, builds itself up along the lines of democratic centralism, establishes close links with the masses, strives to become the core of the labouring masses and educates its Party members and the masses of people in Marxism-Leninism.

(2) The proletariat, under the leadership of the Communist Party, rallying all the labouring people, takes state power from the bourgeoisie by means of revolutionary struggle.

(3) After the victory of the revolution, the proletariat, under the leadership of the Communist Party, rallying the broad mass of the people on the basis of a worker-peasant alliance, establishes a dictatorship of the proletariat over the landlord and capitalist classes, crushes the resistance of the counter-revolutionaries, and carries out the nationalization of industry and the step-by-step collectivization of agriculture, thereby eliminating the system of exploitation, private ownership of the means of production and classes.

(4) The state, led by the proletariat and the Communist Party, leads the people in the planned development of socialist economy and culture, and on this basis gradually raises the people's living standards and actively prepares and works for the transition to communist society.

(5) The state, led by the proletariat and the Communist Party, resolutely opposes imperialist aggression, recognizes the equality of all nations and defends world peace; firmly adheres to the principles of proletarian internationalism, strives to win the help of the labouring people of all countries, and at the same time strives to help them and all oppressed nations.

What we commonly refer to as the path of the October Revolution means precisely these basic things, leaving aside the specific form it took at that particular time and place. These basic things are all universally applicable truths of Marxism-Leninism.

In the course of revolution and construction in different countries there are, besides aspects common to all, aspects which are different. In this sense, each country has its own specific path of development. We shall discuss this question further on. But as far as basic theory is concerned, the road of the October Revolution reflects the general laws of revolution and construction at a particular stage in the long course of the development of human society. It is not only the broad road for the proletariat of the Soviet Union, but also the broad road which the proletariat of all countries must travel to gain victory. Precisely for this reason the Central Committee of the Communist Party of China stated in its Political Report to the Party's Eighth National Congress: "Despite the fact that the revolution in our country has many characteristics of its own, Chinese Communists regard the cause for which they work as a continuation of the Great October Revolution."

In the present international situation, it is of particularly great significance to defend this Marxist-Leninist path opened by the October Revolution. When the imperialists proclaim that they want to bring about "a change of character of the communist world," it is precisely this revolutionary path which they want to change. For decades, the views put forward by all the revisionists to revise Marxism-Leninism, and the Right-opportunist ideas which they spread, have been aimed precisely at evading this road, the road which the proletariat must take for its liberation. It is the task of all Communists to unite the proletariat and the masses of the people to beat back resolutely the savage onslaught of the imperialists against the socialist world, and to march forward resolutely along the path blazed by the October Revolution.

II

People ask: Since the basic path of the Soviet Union in revolution and construction was correct, how did Stalin's mistakes happen?

We discussed this question in our article published in April this year. But as a result of recent events in Eastern Europe and other related developments, the question of correctly understanding and dealing with Stalin's mistakes has become a matter of importance affecting developments within the Communist Parties of many countries, unity between Communist Parties, and the common struggle of the communist forces of the world against imperialism. So it is necessary to further expound our views on this question.

Stalin made a great contribution to the progress of the Soviet Union and to the development of the international communist movement. In "On the Historical Experience of the Dictatorship of the Proletariat" we wrote:

> After Lenin's death Stalin, as the chief leader of the Party and the state, creatively applied and developed Marxism-Leninism. In the struggle to defend the legacy of Leninism against its enemies—the Trotskyites, Zinovievites and other bourgeois agents—Stalin expressed the will and wishes of the people and proved himself to be an outstanding Marxist-Leninist fighter. The reason why Stalin won the support of the Soviet people and played an important role in history was primarily because he, together with the other leaders of the Communist Party of the Soviet Union, defended Lenin's line on the industrialization of the Soviet state and the collectivization of agriculture. By pursuing this line, the Communist Party of the Soviet Union brought about the triumph of socialism in the Soviet Union and created the conditions for the victory of the Soviet Union in the war against Hitler; these victories of the Soviet people conformed to the interests of the working class of the world and all progressive mankind. It was therefore quite natural for the name of Stalin to be greatly honoured throughout the world.

But Stalin made some serious mistakes in regard to the domestic and foreign policies of the Soviet Union. His arbitrary method of work impaired to a certain extent the principle of democratic centralism both in the life of the Party and in the state system of the Soviet Union, and led to a partial disruption of socialist legality. Because in many fields of work Stalin estranged himself from the masses to a serious extent, and made personal, arbitrary decisions concerning many important policies, it was inevitable that he should have made grave mistakes. These mistakes stood out most conspicuously in the suppression of counter-revolution and in relations with certain foreign countries. In suppressing counter-revolutionaries, Stalin, on the one hand, punished many counter-revolutionaries whom it was necessary to punish and, in the main, accomplished the tasks on this front; but, on the other hand, he wronged many loyal Communists and honest citizens, and this caused serious losses. On the whole, in relations with brother countries and parties, Stalin took an internationalist stand and helped the struggles of other peoples and the growth of the socialist camp; but in tackling certain concrete questions, he showed a tendency towards great-nation chauvinism and himself lacked a spirit of equality, let alone educating the mass of cadres to be modest. Sometimes he even intervened mistakenly, with many grave consequences, in the internal affairs of certain brother countries and parties.

How are these serious mistakes of Stalin's to be explained? What is the connection between these mistakes and the socialist system of the Soviet Union?

The science of Marxist-Leninist dialectics teaches us that all types of relations of production, as well as the superstructures built up on their basis, have their own course of emergence, development, and extinction. When the old relations of production on the whole no longer correspond to the productive forces, the latter having reached a certain stage of development, and when the old superstructure on the whole no longer corresponds to the economic basis, the latter having reached a certain stage of development, then changes of a fundamental nature must inevitably occur; whoever tries to resist such changes is discarded by history. This law is applicable through different forms to all types of society. That is to say, it also applies to socialist society of today and communist society of tomorrow.

Were Stalin's mistakes due to the fact that the socialist economic and political system of the Soviet Union had become outmoded and no longer suited the needs of the development of the Soviet Union? Certainly not. Soviet socialist society is still young; it is not even 40 years old. The fact that the Soviet Union has made rapid progress economically proves that its economic system is, in the main, suited to the development of its productive forces; and that its political system is also, in the main, suited to the needs of its economic basis. Stalin's mistakes did not originate in the socialist system; it therefore follows that it is not necessary to "correct" the socialist system in order to correct these mistakes. The bourgeoisie of the West has not a leg to stand on when it tries to use Stalin's errors to prove that the socialist system is a "mistake." Unconvincing too are the arguments of others who trace Stalin's mistakes to the administration of economic affairs by the socialist state power, and assert that once the government takes charge of economic affairs it is bound to become a "bureaucratic machine" hindering the development of the socialist forces. No one can deny that the tremendous upsurge of Soviet economy is the result precisely of the planned administration of economic affairs by the state of the working people, while the main mistakes committed by Stalin had very little to do with shortcomings of the state organs administering economic affairs.

But even where the basic system corresponds to the need, there are still certain contradictions between the relations of production and the productive forces, between the superstructure and the economic basis. These contradictions find expression in defects in certain links of the economic and political systems. Though it is not necessary to effect fundamental changes in order to solve these contradictions, readjustments must be made in good time.

Can we guarantee that mistakes will not happen once we have a basic system which corresponds to the need and have adjusted ordinary contradictions in the system (to use the language of dialectics, contradictions at the stage of "quantitative change")? The matter is not that simple. Systems are of decisive importance, but systems themselves are not all-powerful. No system, however excellent, is in itself a guarantee against serious mistakes in our work. Once we have the right system, the main question is whether we can make the right use of it; whether we have the right policies, and right methods and style of work. Without all this, even under a good system it is still possible for people to commit serious mistakes and to use a good state apparatus to do evil things.

To solve the problems mentioned above, we must rely on the accumulation of experience and the test of practice; we cannot expect results overnight. What is more, with conditions constantly changing, new problems arise as old ones are solved, and there is no solution which holds good for all times. Viewed from this angle, it is not surprising to find that even in socialist countries which have been established on a firm basis there are still defects in certain links of their relations of production and superstructure, and deviations of one kind or another in the policies and methods and style of work of the Party and the state.

In the socialist countries, the task of the Party and the state is, by relying on the strength of the masses and the collective, to make timely readjustments in the various links of the economic and political systems, and to discover and correct mistakes in their work in good time. Naturally, it is not possible for the subjective views of the leading personnel of the Party and the state to conform completely to objective reality. Isolated, local and temporary mistakes in their work are therefore unavoidable. But so long as the principles of the dialectical materialist science of Marxism-Leninism are strictly observed and efforts are made to develop them, so long as the principles of democratic centralism of the Party and the state is thoroughly observed, and so long as we really rely on the masses, persistent and serious mistakes affecting the whole country can be avoided.

The reason why some of the mistakes made by Stalin during the later years of his life became serious, nationwide and persistent, and were not corrected in time, was precisely that in certain fields and to a certain degree, he became isolated from the masses and the collective and violated the principle of democratic centralism of the Party and the state. The reason for certain infractions of democratic centralism lay in certain social and historical conditions: the Party lacked experience in leading the state; the new system was not sufficiently consolidated to be able to resist every encroachment of the influence of the old era (the consolidation of a new system and the dying away of the old influences do not operate in a straightforward fashion but often assume the form of an undulating movement at turning points in history); there was the constricting effect which acute internal and external struggles had on certain aspects of the development of democracy, etc. Nevertheless, these objective conditions alone would not have been enough to transform the possibility of making mistakes into their actual commission. Lenin, working under conditions which were much more complicated and difficult than those encountered by Stalin, did not make the mistakes that Stalin made. Here, the decisive factor is man's ideological condition. A series of victories and the eulogies which Stalin received in the latter part of his life turned his head. He deviated partly, but grossly, from the dialectical materialist way of thinking and fell into subjectivism. He began to put blind faith in personal wisdom and authority; he would not investigate and study complicated conditions seriously or listen carefully to the opinions of his comrades and the voice of the masses. As a result, some of the policies and measures he adopted were often at variance with objective reality. He often stubbornly persisted in carrying out these mistaken measures over long periods and was unable to correct his mistakes in time.

The Communist Party of the Soviet Union has already taken measures to correct Stalin's mistakes and eliminate their consequences. These measures are beginning to bear fruit. The 20th Congress of the Communist Party of the Soviet Union showed great determination and courage in doing away with blind faith in Stalin, in exposing the gravity of Stalin's mistakes and in eliminating their effects. Marxist-Leninists throughout the world, and all those who sympathize with the communist cause, support the efforts of the Communist Party of the Soviet Union to correct mistakes, and hope that the efforts of the Soviet comrades will meet with complete success. It is obvious that since Stalin's mistakes were not of short duration, their thorough correction cannot be achieved overnight, but demands fairly protracted efforts and thoroughgoing ideological education. We believe that the great Communist Party of the Soviet Union, which has already overcome countless difficulties, will triumph over these difficulties and achieve its purpose.

It was not to be expected, of course, that this effort of the Communist Party of the Soviet Union to correct mistakes would get any support from the bourgeoisie and the Right-wing Social-Democrats of the West. Eager to take advantage of the opportunity to erase what was correct in Stalin's work as well as the past immense achievements of the Soviet Union and the whole socialist camp, and to create confusion and division in the communist ranks, the Western bourgeoisie and Right-wing Social-Democrats have deliberately labelled the correction of Stalin's mistakes "de-Stalinization" and described it as a struggle waged by "anti-Stalinist elements" against "Stalinist elements." Their vicious intent is evident enough. Unfortunately, similar views of this kind have also gained ground among some Communists. We consider it extremely harmful for Communists to hold such views.

As is well known, although Stalin committed some grave mistakes in his later years, his was nevertheless the life of a great Marxist-Leninist revolutionary. In his youth, Stalin fought against the tsarist system and for the spread of Marxism-Leninism. After he joined the central leading organ of the Party, he took part in the struggle to pave the way for the revolution of 1917. After the October Revolution, he fought to defend its fruits. In the nearly 30 years after Lenin's death, he worked to build socialism, defend the socialist fatherland and advance the world communist movement. All in all, Stalin always stood at the head of historical developments and guided the struggle; he was an implacable foe of imperialism. His tragedy was that even when he made the mistakes he believed what he did was necessary for the defence of the interests of the working people against encroachments by the enemy. Stalin's mistakes did harm to the Soviet Union, which could have been avoided. Nonetheless, the Socialist Soviet Union made tremendous progress during the period of Stalin's leadership. This undeniable fact not only testifies to the strength of the socialist system but also shows that Stalin was after all a staunch Communist. Therefore, in summing up Stalin's thoughts and activities, we must consider both his positive and negative sides, both his achievements and his mistakes. As long as we examine the matter in an all-round way, then, even if people must speak of "Stalinism," this can only mean, in the first place, communism and Marxism-Leninism, which is the main aspect; and secondarily it contains certain extremely serious mistakes which go against Marxism-Leninism and must be thoroughly corrected. Even though at times it is necessary to stress these mistakes in order to correct them, it is also necessary to set them in their proper place so as to make a correct appraisal and avoid misleading people. In our opinion Stalin's mistakes take second place to his achievements.

Only by adopting an objective and analytical attitude can we correctly appraise Stalin and all those comrades who made similar mistakes under his influence, and only so can we correctly deal with their mistakes. Since these mistakes were made by Communists in the course of their work, what is involved is a question of right versus wrong within communist ranks, not an issue of ourselves versus the enemy in the class struggle. We should therefore adopt a comradely attitude towards these people and not treat them as enemies. We should defend what is correct in their work while criticizing their mistakes, and not blankly denounce everything they did. Their mistakes have a social and historical background and can be attributed especially to their ideology and understanding. In just the same way, such mistakes may also occur in the work of other comrades. That is why, having recognized the mistakes and undertaken their correction, it is necessary that we regard them as a grave lesson, as an asset that can be used for heightening the political consciousness of all Communists, thus preventing the recurrence of such mistakes and advancing the cause of communism. If, on the contrary, one takes a completely negative attitude towards those who made mistakes, treats them with hostility and discriminates against them by labelling them this or that kind of element, it will not help our comrades learn the lesson they should learn. Moreover, since this means confusing the two entirely different types of contradiction—that of right versus wrong within our own ranks and that of ourselves versus the enemy—it will only help the enemy in his attacks on the communist ranks and in his attempts at disintegrating the communist position.

The attitude taken by Comrade Tito and other leading comrades of the Yugoslav League of Communists towards Stalin's mistakes and other related questions, as their recently stated views indicate, cannot be regarded by us as well-balanced or objective. It is understandable that the Yugoslav comrades bear a particular resentment against Stalin's mistakes. In the past, they made worthy efforts to stick to socialism under difficult conditions. Their experiments in the democratic management of economic enterprises and other social organizations have also attracted attention. The Chinese people welcome the reconciliation between the Soviet Union and other socialist countries on the one hand, and Yugoslavia on the other, as well as the establishment and development of friendly relations between China and Yugoslavia. Like the Yugoslav people, the Chinese people hope that Yugoslavia will become ever more prosperous and powerful on the way to socialism. We also agree with some of the points in Comrade Tito's speech, for instance, his condemnation of the Hungarian counter-revolutionaries, his support for the Worker-Peasant Revolutionary Government of Hungary, his condemnation of Britain, France and Israel for their aggression against Egypt, and his condemnation of the French Socialist Party for adopting a policy of aggression. But we are amazed that, in his speech, he attacked almost all the socialist countries and many of the Communist Parties. Comrade Tito made assertions about "those hard-bitten Stalinist elements who in various Parties have managed still to maintain themselves in their posts and who would again wish to consolidate their rule and impose those Stalinist tendencies upon their people, and even others." Therefore, he declared, "Together with the Polish comrades we shall have to fight such tendencies which crop up in various other Parties, whether in the Eastern countries or in the West." We have not come across any statement put forward by leading comrades of the Polish United Workers' Party saying that it was necessary to adopt such a hostile attitude towards brother parties. We feel it necessary to say in connection with these views of Comrade Tito's that he took up a wrong attitude when he set up the so-called "Stalinism," "Stalinist elements," etc., as objects of attack and maintained that the question now was whether the course "begun in Yugoslavia" or the so-called "Stalinist course" would win out. This can only lead to a split in the communist movement.

Comrade Tito correctly pointed out that "viewing the current development in Hungary from the perspective—socialism or counter-revolution—we must defend Kadar's present government, we must help it." But help to and defence of the Hungarian Government can hardly be said to be the sense of the long speech on the Hungarian question made before the National Assembly of the Federal People's Republic of Yugoslavia by Comrade Kardelj, Vice-President of the Federal Executive Council of Yugoslavia. In the interpretation of the Hungarian incident he gave in his speech, Comrade Kardelj not only made no distinction whatsoever between ourselves and the enemy, but also told the Hungarian comrades that "a thorough change is necessary in the (Hungarian—Ed.) political system." He also called on them to turn over state power wholly to the Budapest and other regional workers' councils, "no matter what the workers' councils have become," and declared that they "need not waste their efforts on trying to restore the Communist Party." "The reason," he said, "was because to the masses the Party was the personification of bureaucratic despotism." Such is the blue-print of the "anti-Stalinist course" which Comrade Kardelj has designed for brother countries. The comrades in Hungary rejected this proposal of Comrade Kardelj's. They dissolved the Budapest and other regional workers' councils which were controlled by counter-revolutionaries and persisted in building up the Socialist Workers' Party. We consider that it was entirely right for the Hungarian comrades to act in this way, because otherwise Hungary's future would belong not to socialism but to counter-revolution.

Clearly, the Yugoslav comrades are going too far. Even if some part of their criticism of brother parties is reasonable, the basic stand and the method they have adopted infringed the principles of comradely discussion. We have no wish to interfere in the internal affairs of Yugoslavia, but the matters mentioned above are by no means internal. For the sake of consolidating the unity of the international communist ranks and avoiding the creation of conditions which the enemy can use to cause confusion and division in our own ranks, we cannot but offer our brotherly advice to the Yugoslav comrades.

III

One of the grave consequences of Stalin's mistakes was the growth of doctrinairism. While criticizing Stalin's mistakes, the Communist Parties of various countries have been waging a struggle against doctrinairism among their ranks. This struggle is entirely necessary. But by adopting a negative attitude towards everything connected with Stalin, and by putting up the erroneous slogan of "de-Stalinization," some Communists have helped to foster a revisionist trend against Marxism-Leninism. This revisionist trend is undoubtedly of help to the imperialist attack against the communist movement, and the imperialists are in fact making active use of it. While resolutely opposing doctrinairism, we must at the same time resolutely oppose revisionism.

Marxism-Leninism holds that there are common, fundamental laws in the development of human society, but that in various nations there are strongly differentiated features. Thus all nations pass through the class struggle, and will eventually arrive at communism, by roads that are the same in essence but different in specific form. The cause of the proletariat in a given country will triumph only if the universal truth of Marxism-Leninism is properly applied in the light of its special national features. And so long as this is done, the proletariat will accumulate new experience, thus making its contribution to the cause of other nations and to the general treasury of Marxism-Leninism. Doctrinaires do not understand that the universal truth of Marxism-Leninism manifests itself concretely and becomes operative in real life only through the medium of specific national characteristics. They are not willing to make a careful study of the social and historical features of their own countries and nations or to apply in a practical way the universal truth of Marxism-Leninism in the light of these features. Consequently they cannot lead the proletarian cause to victory.

Since Marxism-Leninism is the scientific summing-up of the experience of the working-class movement of various countries, it follows that it must attach importance to the question of applying the experience of advanced countries. Lenin wrote in his book *What Is To Be Done?*:

> The Social-Democratic movement is in its very essence an international movement. This means not only that we must combat national chauvinism, but also that a movement that is starting in a young country can be successful only if it implements the experience of other countries.[1]

What Lenin meant here was that it was necessary for the Russian working-class movement, which was just beginning, to utilize the experience of the working-class movement in Western Europe. His view applies, likewise, to the use of Soviet experience by younger socialist countries.

But there must be a proper method of learning. All the experience of the Soviet Union, including its fundamental experience, is bound up with definite national characteristics, and no other country should copy it mechanically. Moreover, as has been pointed out above, part of Soviet experience is that derived from mistakes and failures. For those who know how best to learn from others this whole body of experience, both of success and failure, is an invaluable asset, because it can help them

---

[1] V. I. Lenin, *Selected Works*, Vol. I, Part 1, Moscow, 1952, p. 227.

avoid roundabout ways in their progress and reduce their losses. On the other hand, indiscriminate and mechanical copying of experience that has been successful in the Soviet Union—let alone that which was unsuccessful there—may lead to failures in another country. Lenin wrote in the passage immediately following the one quoted above:

> And in order to implement this experience, it is not enough merely to be acquainted with it, or simply to transcribe the latest resolutions. What it requires is the ability to treat this experience critically and to test it independently. Anybody who realizes how enormously the modern working-class movement has grown and branched out will understand what a reserve of theoretical forces and political (as well as revolutionary) experience is required to fulfil this task.[2]

Obviously, in countries where the proletariat has gained power, the problem is many times more complex than that referred to by Lenin here.

In the history of the Communist Party of China between 1931 and 1934, there were doctrinaires who refused to recognize China's specific characteristics, mechanically copied certain experiences of the Soviet Union, and caused serious reverses to the revolutionary forces of our country. These reverses were a profound lesson to our Party. In the period between the Tsunyi Conference of 1935 and the Party's Seventh National Congress held in 1945, our Party thoroughly examined and repudiated this extremely harmful doctrinaire line, united all its members, including those who had made mistakes, developed the people's forces and thus won victory for the revolution. If this had not been done, victory would have been impossible. It is only because we discarded the doctrinaire line that it has become possible for our Party to make fewer mistakes in learning from the experience of the Soviet Union and other brother countries. It is because of this too that we are able to understand fully how necessary and arduous it is for our Polish and Hungarian comrades to correct today the doctrinaire errors of the past.

Errors of doctrinairism, whenever and wherever they occur, must be set right. We shall continue our efforts to correct and prevent such errors in our work. But opposition to doctrinairism has nothing in common with tolerance of revisionism. Marxism-Leninism recognizes that the communist movements of various countries necessarily have their own national characteristics. But this does not mean that they do not share certain basic features in common, or that they can depart from the universal truth of Marxism-Leninism. In the present anti-doctrinaire tide, there are people both in our country and abroad who, on the pretext of opposing the mechanical copying of Soviet experience, try to deny the international significance of the fundamental experience of the Soviet Union and, on the plea of creatively developing Marxism-Leninism, try to deny the significance of the universal truth of Marxism-Leninism.

Because Stalin and the former leaders in some other socialist countries committed the serious mistake of violating socialist democracy, some unstable people in the communist ranks, on the pretext of developing socialist democracy, attempt to weaken or renounce the dictatorship of the proletariat, the principles of democratic centralism of the socialist state, and the leading role of the Party.

There can be no doubt that in a proletarian dictatorship the dictatorship over the counter-revolutionary forces must be closely combined with the broadest scope of people's, that is, socialist, democracy. The dictatorship of the proletariat is mighty and can defeat powerful enemies within the country and outside it and undertake the majestic historic task of building socialism precisely because it is a dictatorship of the working masses over the exploiters, a dictatorship of the majority over the minority, because it gives the broad working masses a democracy which is unattainable under any bourgeois democracy. Failure to forge close links with the mass of the working people and to gain their enthusiastic support makes it impossible to establish the dictatorship of the proletariat, or at any rate impossible to consolidate it. The more acute the class struggle becomes, the more necessary it is for the proletariat to rely, most resolutely and completely, on the broad masses of the people and to bring into full play their revolutionary enthusiasm to defeat the counter-revolutionary forces. The experience of the stirring and seething mass struggles in the Soviet Union during the October Revolution and the ensuing civil war proved this truth to the full. It is from Soviet experience in that period that the

---

[2] V. I. Lenin, *op. cit.*, Vol. I, Part 1, pp. 227-28.

"mass line" our Party so often talks about was derived. The acute struggles in the Soviet Union then depended mainly on direct action by the mass of the people, and naturally there was little possibility for perfect democratic procedures to develop. After the elimination of the exploiting classes and the wiping out in the main of the counter-revolutionary forces, it was still necessary for the dictatorship of the proletariat to deal with counter-revolutionary remnants—these could not be wiped out completely so long as imperialism existed—but by then its edge should have been mainly directed against the aggressive forces of foreign imperialism. In these circumstances, democratic procedures in the political life of the country should have been gradually developed and perfected; the socialist legal system perfected; supervision by the people over the state organs strengthened; democratic methods of administering the state and managing enterprises developed; links between the state organs and the bodies administering various enterprises on the one hand, and the broad masses on the other, made closer; hindrances impairing any of these links done away with and a firmer check put on bureaucratic tendencies. After the elimination of classes, the class struggle should not continue to be stressed as though it was being intensified, as was done by Stalin with the result that the healthy development of socialist democracy was hampered. The Communist Party of the Soviet Union is completely right in firmly correcting Stalin's mistakes in this respect.

Socialist democracy should in no way be pitted against the dictatorship of the proletariat; nor should it be confused with bourgeois democracy. The sole aim of socialist democracy in the political, economic and cultural fields alike, is to strengthen the socialist cause of the proletariat and all the working people, to give scope to their energy in the building of socialism and in the fight against all anti-socialist forces. If there is a kind of democracy that can be used for anti-socialist purposes and for weakening the cause of socialism, it certainly cannot be called socialist democracy.

Some people, however, do not see things that way. Their reaction to events in Hungary has revealed this most clearly. In the past the democratic rights and revolutionary enthusiasm of the Hungarian working people were impaired, while the counter-revolutionaries were not dealt the blow they deserved, with the result that it was fairly easy for the counter-revolutionaries, in October 1956, to take advantage of the discontent of the masses to organize an armed revolt. This shows that Hungary had not yet made a serious enough effort to build up its dictatorship of the proletariat. Nevertheless, when Hungary was facing its crisis, when it lay between revolution and counter-revolution, between socialism and fascism, between peace and war, how did communist intellectuals in some countries see the problem? They not only did not raise the question of realizing a dictatorship of the proletariat but came out against the righteous action taken by the Soviet Union in aiding the socialist forces in Hungary. They came out with declarations that the counter-revolution in Hungary was a "revolution" and with demands that the Worker-Peasant Revolutionary Government extend "democracy" to the counter-revolutionaries! In certain socialist countries some newspapers, even to this day, are wantonly discrediting the revolutionary measures taken by the Hungarian Communists who are fighting heroically under difficult conditions, while they have said hardly a word about the campaign launched by reactionaries all over the world against communism, against the people and against peace. What is the meaning of these strange facts? They mean that those "Socialists" who depart from the dictatorship of the proletariat to prate about "democracy" actually stand with the bourgeoisie in opposition to the proletariat; that they are, in effect, asking for capitalism and opposing socialism, though many among them may themselves be unaware of that fact. Lenin pointed out time and again that the theory of the dictatorship of the proletariat is the most essential part of Marxism; that acceptance or rejection of the dictatorship of the proletariat is "what constitutes the most profound difference between the Marxist and the ordinary petty (as well as big) bourgeois."[3] Lenin asked the Hungarian proletarian regime of 1919 to use "mercilessly rigorous, swift and resolute force" to suppress the counter-revolutionaries. "Whoever does not understand this," he said, "is not a revolutionary, and must be removed from the post of leader or adviser of the proletariat."[4] So if people reject the fundamental Marxist-Leninist principles regarding the dictatorship of the proletariat, if they slanderously dub these

---

[3] V. I. Lenin, op. cit., Vol. II, Part 1, p. 233.
[4] Ibid., Vol. II, Part 2, p. 209.

principles "Stalinism" and "doctrinairism" simply because they have perceived the mistakes committed by Stalin in the latter part of his life and those made by the former Hungarian leaders, they will be taking the path that leads to betrayal of Marxism-Leninism and away from the cause of proletarian revolution.

Those who reject the dictatorship of the proletariat also deny the need for centralism in socialist democracy and the leading role played by the proletarian party in socialist countries. To Marxist-Leninists, of course, such ideas are nothing new. Engels pointed out long ago, when struggling against the anarchists, that as long as there is concerted action in any social organization there must be a certain degree of authority and subordination. The relation between authority and autonomy is relative and the scope of their application changes with different stages of the development of society. Engels said that "it is absurd to speak of the principle of authority as being absolutely evil, and of the principle of autonomy as being absolutely good,"[5] and that for anyone to insist on such an absurdity was in fact to "serve the reaction."[6] In the struggle against the Mensheviks, Lenin brought out most clearly the decisive significance of the organized leadership of the Party for the proletarian cause. When criticizing "Left-wing" communism in Germany in 1920, Lenin stressed that to deny the leading role of the Party, to deny the part played by leaders and to reject discipline, "is tantamount to completely disarming the proletariat *in the interest of the bourgeoisie*. It is tantamount to that petty-bourgeois diffuseness, instability, incapacity for sustained effort, unity and organized action, which, if indulged in, must inevitably destroy every proletarian revolutionary movement."[7] Have these principles become obsolete? Are they inapplicable to the specific conditions in certain countries? Will their application lead to the repetition of Stalin's mistakes? The answer is obviously "no." These principles of Marxism-Leninism have stood the test of history in the development of the international communist movement and of the socialist countries, and not a single case that can be called an exception to them has been found so far. Stalin's mistakes did not lie in the practice of democratic centralism in state affairs, nor in putting leadership by the Party into effect; it lay precisely in the fact that, in certain fields and to a certain degree, he undermined democratic centralism and leadership by the Party. The correct practice of democratic centralism in state affairs and the proper strengthening of leadership by the Party in the socialist cause are the basic guarantees that the countries in the socialist camp will be able to unite their people, defeat their enemies, overcome their difficulties and grow vigorously. It is precisely for this reason that the imperialists and all counter-revolutionaries, bent on attacking our cause, have always demanded that we "liberalize," that they have always concentrated their forces on wrecking the leading bodies of our cause, and on destroying the Communist Party, the core of the proletariat. They have expressed great satisfaction at the current "instability" in certain socialist countries, which has resulted from the impairment of discipline in the Party and the state organs, and are taking advantage of this to intensify their acts of sabotage. These facts show of what great importance it is, in the basic interests of the masses of the people, to uphold the authority of democratic centralism and the leading role of the Party. There is no doubt that the centralism in the system of democratic centralism must rest on a broad basis of democracy, and that the Party leadership must maintain close ties with the masses. Any shortcomings in this respect must be firmly criticized and overcome. But such criticism should be made only for the purpose of consolidating democratic centralism and of strengthening the leadership of the Party. It should in no circumstances bring about disorganization and confusion in the ranks of the proletariat, as our enemies desire.

Among those who are trying to revise Marxism-Leninism on the pretext of combating doctrinairism, some simply deny that there is a demarcation line between the proletarian and the bourgeois dictatorships, between the socialist and the capitalist systems and between the socialist and the imperialist camps. According to them, it is possible for certain bourgeois countries to build socialism without going through a proletarian revolution led by the party of the proletariat and without setting up a state led by the party; they think that the state capitalism in those countries is in fact

---

[5] K. Marx and F. Engels, *Selected Works*, Vol. I, Moscow, 1955, p. 637.
[6] *Ibid.*, Vol. I, p. 638.
[7] V. I. Lenin, *Selected Works*, Vol. II, Part 2, p. 366.

socialism, and that even human society as a whole is "growing" into socialism. But while these people are publicizing such ideas, the imperialists are mobilizing all available military, economic, diplomatic, espionage and "moral" forces, actively preparing to "undermine" and "disrupt" socialist countries which have been established for many years. The bourgeois counter-revolutionaries of these countries, whether hiding at home or living in exile, are still making every effort to stage a come-back. While the revisionist trend serves the interest of the imperialists, the actions of the imperialists do not benefit revisionism but point to its bankruptcy.

IV

It is one of the most urgent tasks of the proletariat of all countries in its fight against imperialist onslaughts to strengthen its international solidarity. The imperialists and reactionaries in various countries are trying in a thousand and one ways to make use of narrow nationalist sentiments and of certain national estrangements among the peoples to wreck this solidarity, thereby destroying the communist cause. Staunch proletarian revolutionaries firmly uphold this solidarity, which they regard as being in the common interest of the working class of all countries. Wavering elements have taken no firm, clear-cut stand on this question.

The communist movement has been an international movement from its very inception, because the workers of various countries can throw off joint oppression by the bourgeoisie of various countries and attain their common aim only by joint effort. This international solidarity of the communist movement has been of great help to the proletariat of various countries in developing their revolutionary cause.

The triumph of the Russian October Revolution gave enormous impetus to the fresh advances of the international proletarian revolutionary movement. In the 39 years since the October Revolution, the achievements of the international communist movement have been immense, and it has become a powerful, world-wide political force. The world proletariat and all who long for emancipation place all their hopes for a bright future for mankind on the victory of this movement.

During the past 39 years the Soviet Union has been the centre of the international communist movement, owing to the fact that it is the first country where socialism triumphed, while after the appearance of the camp of socialism—the most powerful country in the camp, having the richest experience and the means to render the greatest assistance to other socialist countries and to the peoples of various countries in the capitalist world. This is not the result of anyone's arbitrary decision, but the natural outcome of historical conditions. In the interests of the common cause of the proletariat of different countries, of joint resistance to the attack on the socialist cause by the imperialist camp headed by the United States, and of the economic and cultural upsurge common to all socialist countries, we must continue to strengthen international proletarian solidarity with the Soviet Union as its centre.

The international solidarity of the Communist Parties is a type of relationship entirely new to human history. It is natural that its development cannot be free from difficulties. The Communist Parties of all countries must seek unity with each other as well as maintain their respective independence. Historical experience proves that mistakes are bound to occur if there is no proper integration of these two aspects, and one or the other is neglected. If the Communist Parties maintain relations of equality among themselves and reach common understanding and take concerted action through genuine, and not nominal, exchange of views, their unity will be strengthened. Conversely, if, in their mutual relations, one Party imposes its views upon others, or if the Parties use the method of interference in each other's internal affairs instead of comradely suggestions and criticism, their unity will be impaired.

In the socialist countries, the Communist Parties have assumed the responsibility of leadership in the affairs of the state, and relations between them often involve directly the relations between their respective countries and peoples, so the proper handling of such relations has become a problem demanding even greater care.

Marxism-Leninism has always insisted upon combining proletarian internationalism with the patriotism of the people of each country. Each Communist Party must educate its members and the people in a spirit of internationalism, because the true national interests of all peoples call for friendly co-operation among nations. On the other hand, each Communist Party must represent the legitimate national interests and sentiments of its own people. Communists have always been true patriots, and they understand that it is only when they correctly represent the interests and sentiments of their nation can they really enjoy the trust and love of the broad mass of their own people, effectively educate them in internationalism and harmonize the national sentiments and interests of the peoples of different countries.

To strengthen the international solidarity of the socialist countries, the Communist Parties of these countries must respect the national interests and sentiments of other countries. This is of special importance for the Communist Party of a larger country in its relations with that of a smaller one. To avoid any resentment on the part of the smaller country, the Party of a larger country must constantly take care to maintain an attitude of equality. As Lenin rightly said, "It is...the duty of the class-conscious communist proletariat of all countries to treat with particular caution and attention the survivals of national sentiments among countries and nationalities which have been longest oppressed."[8]

As we have already said, Stalin displayed certain great-nation chauvinist tendencies in relations with brother parties and countries. The essence of such tendencies lies in being unmindful of the independent and equal status of the Communist Parties of various lands and that of the socialist countries within the framework of international bond of union. There are certain historical reasons for such tendencies. The time-worn habits of big countries in their relations with small countries continue to make their influence felt in certain ways, while a series of victories achieved by a Party or a country in its revolutionary cause is apt to give rise to a sense of superiority.

For these reasons, systematic efforts are needed to overcome great-nation chauvinist tendencies. Great-nation chauvinism is not peculiar to any one country. For instance, country B may be small and backward compared to country A, but big and advanced compared to country C. Thus country B, while complaining of great-nation chauvinism on the part of country A, may often assume the airs of a great nation in relation to country C. What we Chinese especially must bear in mind is that China too was a big empire during the Han, Tang, Ming and Ching dynasties. Although it is true that in the hundred years after the middle of the 19th century, China became a victim of aggression and a semi-colony and although she is still economically and culturally backward today, nevertheless, under changed conditions, great-nation chauvinist tendencies will certainly become a serious danger if we do not take every precaution to guard against them. It should, furthermore, be pointed out that some signs of this danger have already begun to appear among some of our personnel. That was why emphasis on fighting the tendency towards great-nation chauvinism was laid both in the resolution of the Eighth National Congress of the Communist Party of China and the statement of the Government of the People's Republic of China issued on November 1, 1956.

But it is not great-nation chauvinism alone that hinders international proletarian unity. In the course of history, big countries have shown disrespect for small countries and even oppressed them; and small countries have distrusted big ones and even become hostile to them. Both tendencies still exist to a greater or lesser extent among the peoples and even in the ranks of the proletariat of various countries. That is why, in order to strengthen the international solidarity of the proletariat apart from the primary task of overcoming great-nation chauvinist tendencies in bigger countries, it is also necessary to overcome nationalist tendencies in smaller countries. No matter whether their country is big or small, if Communists counterpose the interests of their own country and nation to the general interest of the international proletarian movement, and if they make national interests a pretext for opposing the general interest, and not really upholding international proletarian solidarity in actual practice but on the contrary damaging it, they will be committing a serious mistake of violating the principles of internationalism and Marxism-Leninism.

Stalin's mistakes aroused grave dissatisfaction among people in certain East European countries. But then neither is the attitude of some people in these countries towards the Soviet Union justified. Bourgeois nationalists try their best to exaggerate shortcomings of the Soviet Union and

---

[8] V. I. Lenin, *op. cit.*, Vol. II, Part 2, pp. 469-470.

overlook the contributions it has made. They attempt to prevent the people from thinking how the imperialists would treat their countries and their peoples if the Soviet Union did not exist. We Chinese Communists are very glad to see that the Communist Parties of Poland and Hungary are already putting a firm check on the activities of evil elements that fabricate anti-Soviet rumours and stir up national antagonisms in relations with brother countries, and also that these Parties have set to work to dispel nationalist prejudices existing among some sections of the masses and even among some Party members. This is clearly one of the steps urgently needed to consolidate friendly relations among the socialist countries.

As we pointed out above, the foreign policy of the Soviet Union has, in the main, conformed to the interests of the international proletariat, the oppressed nations and the peoples of the world. In the past 39 years, the Soviet people have made tremendous efforts and heroic sacrifices in aiding the cause of the peoples of the various countries. Mistakes committed by Stalin certainly cannot detract from these historic achievements of the great Soviet people.

The Soviet Government's efforts to improve relations with Yugoslavia, its declaration of October 30, 1956, and its talks with Poland in November 1956 all manifest the determination of the Communist Party of the Soviet Union and the Soviet Government to thoroughly eliminate past mistakes in foreign relations. These steps by the Soviet Union are an important contribution to the strengthening of the international solidarity of the proletariat.

Obviously, at the present moment, when the imperialists are launching frenzied attacks on the communist ranks in the various countries, it is necessary for the proletariat of all nations to strive to strengthen its solidarity. Faced as we are with powerful enemies, no word or deed which harms the solidarity of the international communist ranks, no matter what name it goes by, can hope to receive any sympathy from the Communists and working people of the various countries.

The strengthening of the international solidarity of the proletariat, with the Soviet Union as its core, is not only in the interests of world proletariat but also in the interests of the independence movement of all oppressed nations and of world peace. Through their own experience, the broad masses of the people in Asia, Africa and Latin America find it easy to understand who are their enemies and who their friends. That is why the imperialist-instigated campaign against communism, against the people and against peace has evoked such a faint response, and that from only a handful among the more than one thousand million people who inhabit these continents. Facts prove that the Soviet Union, China, the other socialist countries and the revolutionary proletariat in the imperialist countries are all staunch supporters of Egypt's struggle against aggression, and of the independence movement in the countries of Asia, Africa and Latin America.

The socialist countries, the proletariat in the imperialist countries, and the countries striving for national independence—these three forces have bonds of common interest in their struggle against imperialism and their mutual support and assistance is of the greatest significance to the future of mankind and world peace. Recently the imperialist forces of aggression have again created a certain degree of tension in the international situation. But by the joint struggle of the three forces we have mentioned, plus the concerted efforts of all other peace-loving forces in the world, a new lessening of such tension can be achieved. The imperialist forces of aggression failed to gain anything from their invasion of Egypt; instead, they were dealt a telling blow. Furthermore, thanks to the help given by the Soviet troops to the Hungarian people, the imperialists were frustrated in their plan to build an outpost of war in Eastern Europe and to disrupt the solidarity of the socialist camp. The socialist countries are persisting in their efforts for peaceful co-existence with the capitalist countries, to develop diplomatic, economic and cultural relations with them, to settle international disputes through peaceful negotiations, to oppose preparations for a new world war, to expand the peace area in the world, and to broaden the scope of application of the five principles of peaceful co-existence. All these efforts will certainly win ever more sympathy from the oppressed nations and the peace-loving people throughout the world. The strengthening of the international solidarity of the proletariat will make the warlike imperialists think twice before embarking upon new adventures. Therefore, despite the fact that the imperialists are still trying to resist the efforts described above, the forces for peace will eventually triumph over the forces for war.

* * *

The international communist movement has a history of only 92 years, reckoning from the establishment of the First International in 1864. Despite many ups and downs, the progress of the movement as a whole has been very rapid. During the First World War, there appeared the Soviet Union, covering one-sixth of the earth. After the Second World War, there appeared the camp of socialism, which now has a third of the world's population. When the socialist states commit errors of one kind or another, our enemies are elated while some of our comrades and friends become dejected; a number of them even waver in their confidence as to the future of the communist cause. However, there is little ground for our enemies to rejoice or for our comrades and friends to feel dejected or to waver. The proletariat has begun to rule the state for the first time in history: in some countries this occurred only a few years ago, and in the oldest only a few decades ago. So how could anyone expect that no failures would be encountered? Temporary and partial failures have occurred, are still occurring, and may also occur in the future. But a person with foresight will not feel dejected and pessimistic because of them. Failure is the mother of success. It is precisely the recent temporary, partial failures that have enriched the political experience of the international proletariat and will help to pave the way for great successes in the years to come. Compared with the history of the bourgeois revolutions in Britain and France, the failures in our cause are virtually of no account. The bourgeois revolution in Britain started in 1640. The defeat of the king was followed by Cromwell's dictatorship. Then came the restoration of the old royal house in 1660. It was not until 1688 when the bourgeois party staged a coup d'etat inviting to England a king who brought along with him troops and naval forces from the Netherlands that the British bourgeois dictatorship was consolidated. During the 86 years from the outbreak of the French revolution in 1789 to 1875, when the Third Republic was established, the bourgeois revolution in France went through a particularly stormy period, swinging in rapid succession between progress and reaction, republicanism and monarchy, revolutionary terror and counter-revolutionary terror, civil war and foreign war, the conquest of foreign lands and capitulation to foreign states. Although the socialist revolution faces the concerted opposition of the reactionaries throughout the world, its course as a whole is smooth and remarkably steady. This is a true reflection of the unparalleled vitality of the socialist system. Though the international communist movement met with some setbacks recently, we have learned many useful lessons from them. We have corrected, or are correcting, the mistakes in our own ranks which need to be rectified. When these errors are righted, we shall be stronger and more firmly united than ever before. Contrary to the expectation of our enemies, the cause of the proletariat will not be thrown back but will make ever more progress.

But the fate of imperialism is quite different. There, in the imperialist world, fundamental clashes of interest exist between imperialism and the oppressed nations, among the imperialist countries themselves, and between the government and the people of these imperialist countries. These clashes will grow more and more acute and there is no cure for them.

Of course, in many respects, the new-born system of proletarian dictatorship still faces many difficulties, and has many weaknesses. But, compared with the time when the Soviet Union was struggling alone, the situation is a good deal better. And what new birth is not attended with difficulties and weaknesses? The issue is the future. However many twists and turns may await us on our forward journey, humanity will eventually reach its bright destiny—communism. There is no force that can stop it.

Chapter VI

"CONTRADICTIONS" AND "RECTIFICATION"

(containing Documents 14, 15, 16, 17, 18, 19, 20)

General comment. The background of Mao Tse-tung's speech of February 27, 1957, on "contradictions" (Document 14) is discussed in our General Introduction. So are the main themes of this chapter—the initiation of the campaign to "rectify the working style" of the Chinese Communist Party, the transformation of free criticism within understood limits into fundamental attacks on Communist policy, the subsequent tightening of Party control, and the change of the original "rectification campaign" for the Party into an educational campaign for the whole nation.

The first stages at least of rectification occurred at a time of considerable economic shortage and tension resulting from the attempted leap forward in 1956, and extending well into 1957. References to the economic background down to the spring of 1957 are contained in our comments on Documents 11 and 12 above.

Two recent books deal in considerable detail with the period of free criticism in May–June 1957. Theodore H. E. Chen, in *Thought Reform of the Chinese Intellectuals* (Hong Kong: Hong Kong University Press, 1960), treats it as part of the general campaign to convert intellectuals or render them harmless, from 1949 on. The book contains many references to press material of those months. Roderick MacFarquhar's *The Hundred Flowers Campaign and the Chinese Intellectuals* (New York: Praeger, 1960), is devoted, despite the title, entirely to the spring months of 1957. The bulk of it consists of quotations from the criticism voiced at the political or intellectual forums of May 1957, arranged according to professions (journalists, scholars, and so on). In view of the copious material and references available in these books, the comments in this chapter have not been burdened with long lists of source material.

DOCUMENT 14

On the Correct Handling of Contradictions among the People, speech by Mao Tse-tung to the Eleventh Session (enlarged) of the Supreme State Conference, February 27, 1957.

The text used here is from the third printing (1959) of an official translation issued in pamphlet form (with the above title) by the Foreign Languages Press, Peking, 1957. The translation was made from the first published Chinese text, that of the People's Publishing House, Peking, June 1957. Other translations in English may be found in the *New York Times* of June 19, 1957; in CB 458, June 20, 1957; and in *Supplement to People's China,* July 1, 1957.

Comment. Mao's famous speech on "contradictions" represents a fairly late stage in the preparation for the 1957 campaign to rectify the Party's working style. At a plenary session of the Party's Central Committee on November 15, 1956, Mao had called on all government workers, economic personnel, etc., to "struggle, through rectification of work style, against the tendencies towards subjectivism, sectarianism, and bureaucratism." An article in *China Youth,* January 16, 1957 (ECMM 70), says that the Party "recently decided that as from 1958 our working style will be rectified throughout the Party." It also says that during 1957 all Party and government organs should start to study six documents, which were listed.

The first was Mao's report of 1941, entitled "Reform Our Study," which may be found in Mao Tse-tung, *Selected Works* (London: Lawrence & Wishart, 1954), Vol. IV, pp. 12-20.

The next two were speeches delivered by Mao in 1942, "Rectify the Party's Style in Work" and "Oppose the Party's 8-legged Essay." They may be found, though not under those titles, in Conrad Brandt, Benjamin Schwartz, and John K. Fairbank, *A Documentary History of Chinese Communism* (Cambridge: Harvard University Press, 1952), pp. 375-392 and pp. 392-407.

The fourth was "Resolutions on Some Questions in the History of Our Party," adopted at the Sixth Party Congress in 1945. This is reprinted in Mao's *Selected Works*, cited above, Vol. IV, pp. 171-224.

The fifth and sixth documents named by *China Youth* were two very recent editorials in the *People's Daily* on the historical experience of the dictatorship of the proletariat, which are reprinted in the present volume as Documents 7 and 13 above.

The *China Youth* article of January 16, 1957, suggests that the rectification campaign may have been started sooner than originally intended.

Mao's speech of February 27, printed here, was followed by another on March 12 to a "National Propaganda Work Conference"; the text is not available. This too, it appears, was designed to encourage the intellectuals to express themselves more freely. There is evidence, in the accusations later made against Chang Po-chün (cited in URS, Vol. 8, No. 18), of a third speech by Mao, made to a meeting of the Supreme State Conference on April 30, in which he is said to have proposed that the Party Committee system be abolished in schools.

The rectification campaign itself was formally initiated by a Central Committee directive on April 27, 1957 (but see comment on Document 16, below). Mao's speech of February 27 was not published until June 18, after the Party's counterattack on criticism from the Democratic parties was well under way, and shortly after some passages from the alleged original version of the speech had been transmitted from Warsaw by an American newspaper correspondent (Sidney Gruson, *New York Times*, June 13, 1957). The speech as originally delivered was not officially published. The title page of the pamphlet issued by the Foreign Languages Press, Peking, says, "The author has gone over the text based on the verbatim record and made certain additions." The New China News Agency said the same thing in issuing the document in June. It seems likely that the revisions and additions in the published version were substantial and that among the additions were the six criteria (section 8) to distinguish "flowers" from "poisonous weeds"; these criteria could hardly have been regarded as a stimulant to free discussion unless they had been accompanied by some very liberal glosses. There are also passages, especially that in section 2 promising a "comprehensive review of the work of suppressing counter-revolution," which seem to refer to specific criticisms made against the Party's policies in May. (On this see also CB 466, speech by Tung Pi-wu, President of the Supreme People's Court, to the National People's Congress in July 1957.)

Supplementary material may be found as follows:

(a) The theory of contradictions: CB 202 (the reissue in 1953 of Mao's 1937 article on "Contradictions"). Also ECMM 72 illustrates the maximum width and vagueness of the term "contradiction" with an article (*Political Study*, Dec. 13, 1956) on the major contradiction between backward conditions and the desire to become a modern industrialized state. ECMM 86 and 95 (*Study*, April 18 and May 18, 1957) contain evidence of misunderstanding within the Party of the theory of contradictions.

(b) Rectification: Brandt, Schwartz, and Fairbank, *op. cit.*, pp. 372 ff. (material from Mao's 1942 speeches on this subject).

(c) Development of the rectification campaign: ECMM 97 (*Study*, June 3, 1957), and ECMM 72 (*Political Study*, Jan. 13, 1957). For speculation on Mao's individual part in launching the campaign, see URS, supplement to Vol. 8, No. 18, which quotes extensively from the "confessions" of "rightists" in July 1957, e.g., *People's Daily*, July 17, 1957.

Developments, particularly in agriculture, during the summer and fall of 1957 are discussed in the comment on Document 19, below. Two points, however, may be specially noted here:

First, in section 3 of Mao's February 27 speech, in the course of his discussion of agricultural contradictions, and in order to meet the charges that the peasants' life was too hard, he said that "we are prepared to stabilize over a number of years the total amount of the grain tax and the amount of grain purchased by the state at approximately something over 80,000 million catties a year [40 million tons]." This promise was not kept, for reasons explained by Li Hsien-nien to the National People's Congress in February 1958 (CB 493). But Li promised that agricultural taxation would be stabilized at a new and slightly higher level. For fuller comparative figures, see ECMM 135 (*Current Events*, April 6, 1958).

Second, in his section 9, Mao mentions that a few workers and students went on strike in 1956 for material benefits. For further instances and discussion, see ECMM 97 (*Current Events*, June 6, 1957); MacFarquhar, cited above, pp. 233-234 (Kwangtung) and 241-242; and URS, Vol. 9, No. 20 (quoting local papers on strikes in Kweilin and Chungking, summer of 1957).

―――――――――――――――TEXT OF DOCUMENT 14―――――――――――――――

Our general subject is the correct handling of contradictions among the people. For convenience' sake, let us discuss it under twelve sub-headings. Although reference will be made to contradictions between ourselves and our enemies, this discussion will centre mainly on contradictions among the people.

1. TWO DIFFERENT TYPES OF CONTRADICTIONS

Never has our country been as united as it is today. The victories of the bourgeois-democratic revolution and the socialist revolution, coupled with our achievements in socialist construction, have rapidly changed the face of old China. Now we see before us an even brighter future. The days of national disunity and turmoil which the people detested have gone for ever. Led by the working class and the Communist Party, and united as one, our six hundred million people are engaged in the great work of building socialism. Unification of the country, unity of the people and unity among our various nationalities—these are the basic guarantees for the sure triumph of our cause. However, this does not mean that there are no longer any contradictions in our society. It would be naïve to imagine that there are no more contradictions. To do so would be to fly in the face of objective reality. We are confronted by two types of social contradictions—contradictions between ourselves and the enemy and contradictions among the people. These two types of contradictions are totally different in nature.

If we are to have a correct understanding of these two different types of contradictions, we must, first of all, make clear what is meant by "the people" and what is meant by "the enemy."

The term "the people" has different meanings in different countries, and in different historical periods in each country. Take our country for example. During the War of Resistance to Japanese Aggression, all those classes, strata and social groups which opposed Japanese aggression belonged to the category of the people, while the Japanese imperialists, Chinese traitors and the pro-Japanese elements belonged to the category of enemies of the people. During the War of Liberation, the United States imperialists and their henchmen—the bureaucrat-capitalists and landlord class—and the Kuomintang reactionaries, who represented these two classes, were the enemies of the people, while all other classes, strata and social groups which opposed these enemies, belonged to the category of the people. At this stage of building socialism, all classes, strata and social groups which approve, support and work for the cause of socialist construction belong to the category of the people, while those social forces and groups which resist the socialist revolution, and are hostile to and try to wreck socialist construction, are enemies of the people.

The contradictions between ourselves and our enemies are antagonistic ones. Within the ranks of the people, contradictions among the working people are non-antagonistic, while those between the exploiters and the exploited classes have, apart from their antagonistic aspect, a non-antagonistic aspect. Contradictions among the people have always existed. But their content differs in each period of the revolution and during the building of socialism. In the conditions existing in China today what we call contradictions among the people include the following: contradictions within the working class, contradictions within the peasantry, contradictions within the intelligentsia, contradictions between the working class and the peasantry, contradictions between the working class and peasantry on the one hand and the intelligentsia on the other, contradictions between the working class and other sections of the working people on the one hand and the national bourgeoisie on the other, contradictions within the national bourgeoisie, and so forth. Our people's government is a government that truly represents the interests of the people and serves the people, yet certain contradictions do exist between the government and the masses. These include contradictions between the interests of the state, collective interests and individual interests; between democracy and centralism; between those in positions of leadership and the led, and contradictions arising from the bureaucratic practices of certain state functionaries in their relations with the masses. All these are contradictions among the people. Generally speaking, underlying the contradictions among the people is the basic identity of the interests of the people.

In our country, the contradiction between the working class and the national bourgeoisie is a contradiction among the people. The class struggle waged between the two is, by and large, a class struggle within the ranks of the people. This is because of the dual character of the national bourgeoisie in our country. In the years of the bourgeois-democratic revolution, there was a revolutionary side to their character; there was also a tendency to compromise with the enemy, this was the other side. In the period of the socialist revolution, exploitation of the working class to make profits is one side, while support of the Constitution and willingness to accept socialist transformation is the other. The national bourgeoisie differs from the imperialists, the landlords and the bureaucrat-capitalists. The contradiction between exploiter and exploited, which exists between the national bourgeoisie and the working class, is an antagonistic one. But, in the concrete conditions existing in China, such an antagonistic contradiction, if properly handled, can be transformed into a non-antagonistic one and resolved in a peaceful way. But if it is not properly handled, if, say, we do not follow a policy of uniting, criticizing and educating the national bourgeoisie, or if the national bourgeoisie does not accept this policy, then the contradiction between the working class and the national bourgeoisie can turn into an antagonistic contradiction as between ourselves and the enemy.

Since the contradictions between ourselves and the enemy and those among the people differ in nature, they must be solved in different ways. To put it briefly, the former is a matter of drawing a line between us and our enemies, while the latter is a matter of distinguishing between right and wrong. It is, of course, true that drawing a line between ourselves and our enemies is also a question of distinguishing between right and wrong. For example, the question as to who is right, we or the reactionaries at home and abroad—that is, the imperialists, the feudalists and bureaucrat-capitalists— is also a question of distinguishing between right and wrong, but it is different in nature from questions of right and wrong among the people.

Ours is a people's democratic dictatorship, led by the working class and based on the worker-peasant alliance. What is this dictatorship for? Its first function is to suppress the reactionary classes and elements and those exploiters in the country who range themselves against the socialist revolution, to suppress all those who try to wreck our socialist construction; that is to say, to solve the contradictions between ourselves and the enemy within the country. For instance, to arrest, try and sentence certain counter-revolutionaries, and for a specified period of time to deprive landlords and bureaucrat-capitalists of their right to vote and freedom of speech—all this comes within the scope of our dictatorship. To maintain law and order and safeguard the interests of the people, it is likewise necessary to exercise dictatorship over robbers, swindlers, murderers, arsonists, hooligans and other scoundrels who seriously disrupt social order.

The second function of this dictatorship is to protect our country from subversive activities and possible aggression by the external enemy. Should that happen, it is the task of this dictatorship to solve the external contradiction between ourselves and the enemy. The aim of this dictatorship is to protect all our people so that they can work in peace and build China into a socialist country with a modern industry, agriculture, science and culture.

Who is to exercise this dictatorship? Naturally it must be the working class and the entire people led by it. Dictatorship does not apply in the ranks of the people. The people cannot possibly exercise dictatorship over themselves; nor should one section of them oppress another section. Law-breaking elements among the people will be dealt with according to law, but this is different in principle from using the dictatorship to suppress enemies of the people. What applies among the people is democratic centralism. Our Constitution lays it down that citizens of the People's Republic of China enjoy freedom of speech, of the press, of assembly, of association, of procession, of demonstration, of religious belief and so on. Our Constitution also provides that organs of state must practise democratic centralism and must rely on the masses; that the personnel of organs of state must serve the people. Our socialist democracy is democracy in the widest sense, such as is not to be found in any capitalist country. Our dictatorship is known as the people's democratic dictatorship, led by the working class and based on the worker-peasant alliance. That is to say, democracy operates within the ranks of the people, while the working class, uniting with all those enjoying civil rights, the peasantry in the first place, enforces dictatorship over the reactionary classes and elements and all those who resist socialist transformation and oppose socialist construction. By civil rights, we mean, politically, freedom and democratic rights.

But this freedom is freedom with leadership and this democracy is democracy under centralized guidance, not anarchy. Anarchy does not conform to the interests or wishes of the people.

Certain people in our country were delighted when the Hungarian events took place. They hoped that something similar would happen in China, that thousands upon thousands of people would demonstrate in the streets against the People's Government. Such hopes ran counter to the interests of the masses and therefore could not possibly get their support. In Hungary, a section of the people, deceived by domestic and foreign counter-revolutionaries, made the mistake of resorting to acts of violence against the people's government, with the result that both the state and the people suffered for it. The damage done to the country's economy in a few weeks of rioting will take a long time to repair. There were other people in our country who took a wavering attitude towards the Hungarian events because they were ignorant about the actual world situation. They felt that there was too little freedom under our people's democracy and that there was more freedom under Western parliamentary democracy. They ask for the adoption of the two-party system of the West, where one party is in office and the other out of office. But this so-called two-party system is nothing but a means of maintaining the dictatorship of the bourgeoisie; under no circumstances can it safeguard the freedom of the working people. As a matter of fact, freedom and democracy cannot exist in the abstract, they only exist in the concrete. In a society where there is class struggle, when the exploiting classes are free to exploit the working people the working people will have no freedom from being exploited; when there is democracy for the bourgeoisie there can be no democracy for the proletariat and other working people. In some capitalist countries the Communist Parties are allowed to exist legally but only to the extent that they do not endanger the fundamental interests of the bourgeoisie; beyond that they are not permitted legal existence. Those who demand freedom and democracy in the abstract regard democracy as an end and not a means. Democracy sometimes seems to be an end, but it is in fact only a means. Marxism teaches us that democracy is part of the superstructure and belongs to the category of politics. That is to say, in the last analysis, it serves the economic base. The same is true of freedom. Both democracy and freedom are relative, not absolute, and they come into being and develop under specific historical circumstances. Within the ranks of our people, democracy stands in relation to centralism, and freedom to discipline. They are two conflicting aspects of a single entity, contradictory as well as united, and we should not one-sidedly emphasize one to the denial of the other. Within the ranks of the people, we cannot do without freedom, nor can we do without discipline; we cannot do without democracy, nor can we do without centralism. Our democratic centralism means the unity of democracy and centralism and the unity of freedom and discipline. Under this system, the people enjoy a wide measure of democracy and freedom, but at the same time they have to keep themselves within the bounds of socialist discipline. All this is well understood by the people.

While we stand for freedom with leadership and democracy under centralized guidance, in no sense do we mean that coercive measures should be taken to settle ideological matters and questions involving the distinction between right and wrong among the people. Any attempt to deal with ideological matters or questions involving right and wrong by administrative orders or coercive measures will not only be ineffective but harmful. We cannot abolish religion by administrative orders; nor can we force people not to believe in it. We cannot compel people to give up idealism, any more than we can force them to believe in Marxism. In settling matters of an ideological nature or controversial issues among the people, we can only use democratic methods, methods of discussion, of criticism, of persuasion and education, not coercive, high-handed methods. In order to carry on their production and studies effectively and to order their lives properly, the people want their government, the leaders of productive work and of educational and cultural bodies to issue suitable orders of an obligatory nature. It is common sense that the maintenance of law and order would be impossible without administrative orders. Administrative orders and the method of persuasion and education complement each other in solving contradictions among the people. Administrative orders issued for the maintenance of social order must be accompanied by persuasion and education, for in many cases administrative orders alone will not work.

In 1942 we worked out the formula "unity—criticism—unity" to describe this democratic method of resolving contradictions among the people. To elaborate, this means to start off with a desire for unity and resolve contradictions through criticism or struggle so as to achieve a new unity on a new basis. Our experience shows that this is a proper method of resolving contradictions among the people. In 1942 we used this method to resolve contradictions inside the Communist Party, namely, contradictions between the doctrinaires and the rank-and-file membership, between doctrinairism and Marxism. At one time in waging inner-Party struggle, the "left" doctrinaires used the method of "ruthless struggle and merciless blows." This method was wrong. In place of it, in criticizing "left" doctrinairism, we used a new one: to start from a desire for unity, and thrash out questions of right and wrong through criticism or argument, and so achieve a new unity on a new basis. This was the method used in the "rectification campaign" of 1942. A few years later in 1945 when the Chinese Communist Party held its Seventh National Congress, unity was thus achieved throughout the Party and the great victory of the people's revolution was assured. The essential thing is to start with a desire for unity. Without this subjective desire for unity, once the struggle starts it is liable to get out of hand. Wouldn't this then be the same as "ruthless struggle and merciless blows"? Would there be any Party unity left to speak of? It was this experience that led us to the formula: "unity—criticism—unity." Or, in other words, "take warning from the past in order to be more careful in the future," and to "treat the illness in order to save the patient." We extended this method beyond our Party. During the war it was used very successfully in the anti-Japanese bases to deal with relations between those in positions of leadership and the masses, between the army and the civilian population, between officers and men, between different units of the army, and between various groups of cadres. The use of this method can be traced back to still earlier times in the history of our Party. We began to build our revolutionary armed forces and bases in the south in 1927 and ever since then we have used this method to deal with relations between the Party and the masses, between the army and the civilian population, between officers and men, and in general with relations among the people. The only difference is that during the Anti-Japanese War, this method was used much more purposefully. After the liberation of the country, we used this same method—"unity—criticism—unity"—in our relations with other democratic parties and industrial and commercial circles. Now our task is to continue to extend and make still better use of this method throughout the ranks of the people; we want all our factories, co-operatives, business establishments, schools, government offices, public bodies, in a word, all the six hundred million of our people, to use it in resolving contradictions among themselves.

TEXT OF DOCUMENT 14

Under ordinary circumstances, contradictions among the people are not antagonistic. But if they are not dealt with properly, or if we relax vigilance and lower our guard, antagonism may arise. In a socialist country, such a development is usually only of a localized and temporary nature. This is because there the exploitation of man by man has been abolished and the interests of the people are basically the same. Such antagonistic actions on a fairly wide scale as took place during the Hungarian events are accounted for by the fact that domestic and foreign counter-revolutionary elements were at work. These actions were also of a temporary, though special, nature. In a case like this, the reactionaries in a socialist country, in league with the imperialists, take advantage of contradictions among the people to foment disunity and dissension and fan the flames of disorder in an attempt to achieve their conspiratorial aims. This lesson of the Hungarian events deserves our attention.

Many people seem to think that the proposal to use democratic methods to resolve contradictions among the people raises a new question. But actually that is not so. Marxists have always held that the cause of the proletariat can only be promoted by relying on the masses of the people; that Communists must use democratic methods of persuasion and education when working among the working people and must on no account resort to commandism or coercion. The Chinese Communist Party faithfully adheres to this Marxist-Leninist principle. We have always maintained that, under the people's democratic dictatorship, two different methods—dictatorial and democratic—should be used to resolve the two different kinds of contradictions—those between ourselves and the enemy and those among the people. This idea has been explained again and again in our Party documents and in speeches by many responsible Party leaders. In my article "On the People's Democratic Dictatorship" written in 1949, I said: "These two aspects, democracy for the people and dictatorship over the reactionaries, when combined, constitute the people's democratic dictatorship." I also pointed out that, in order to settle questions within the ranks of the people, "the methods we use are democratic, that is, methods of persuasion and not of compulsion." In addressing the Second Session of the National Committee of the People's Political Consultative Conference in June 1950, I said further: "The people's democratic dictatorship uses two methods. In regard to the enemy, it uses the method of dictatorship, that is: it forbids them to take part in political activities for as long a period of time as is necessary; it compels them to obey the laws of the People's Government, compels them to work and to transform themselves into new people through work. In regard to the people, on the contrary, it does not use compulsion, it uses democratic methods, that is: it must allow the people to take part in political activities, and, far from compelling them to do this or that, use the democratic methods of education and persuasion. This education is self-education among the people, and criticism and self-criticism is the fundamental method of self-education." We have spoken on this question of using democratic methods to resolve contradictions among the people on many occasions in the past, and, furthermore, we have in the main acted on this principle, a principle of which many cadres and many people have a practical understanding. Why then do some people now feel that this is a new issue? The reason is that, in the past, an acute struggle raged between ourselves and our enemies both within and without, and contradictions among the people did not attract as much attention as they do today.

Quite a few people fail to make a clear distinction between these two different types of contradictions—those between ourselves and the enemy and those among the people—and are prone to confuse the two. It must be admitted that it is sometimes easy to confuse them. We had instances of such confusion in our past work. In the suppression of counter-revolution, good people were sometimes mistaken for bad. Such things have happened before, and still happen today. We have been able to keep our mistakes within bounds because it has been our policy to draw a sharp line between our own people and our enemies and where mistakes have been made, to take suitable measures of rehabilitation.

Marxist philosophy holds that the law of the unity of opposites is a fundamental law of the universe. This law operates everywhere, in the natural world, in human society, and in man's thinking. Opposites in contradiction unite as well as struggle with each other, and thus impel all things to move and change. Contradictions exist everywhere, but as things differ in nature, so do contradictions. In any given phenomenon or thing, the unity of opposites is conditional, temporary and transitory, and hence relative; whereas struggle between opposites is absolute. Lenin gave a very clear exposition of this law. In our country, a growing number of people have come to understand it. For many people, however, acceptance of this law is one thing, and its application in examining and dealing with problems is quite another. Many dare not acknowledge openly that there still exist contradictions among the people, which are the very forces that move our society forward. Many people refuse to admit that contradictions still exist in a socialist society, with the result that when confronted with social contradictions they become timid and helpless. They do not understand that socialist society grows more united and consolidated precisely through the ceaseless process of correctly dealing with and resolving contradictions. For this reason, we need to explain things to our people, our cadres in the first place, to help them understand contradictions in a socialist society and learn how to deal with such contradictions in a correct way.

Contradictions in a socialist society are fundamentally different from contradictions in old societies, such as capitalist society. Contradictions in capitalist society find expression in acute antagonisms and conflicts, in sharp class struggle, which cannot be resolved by the capitalist system itself and can only be resolved by socialist revolution. Contradictions in socialist society are, on the contrary, not antagonistic and can be resolved one after the other by the socialist system itself.

The basic contradictions in socialist society are still those between the relations of production and the productive forces, and between the superstructure and the economic base. These contradictions, however, are fundamentally different in character and have different features from contradictions between the relations of production and the productive forces and between the superstructure and the economic base in the old societies. The present social system of our country is far superior to that of the old days. If this were not so, the old system would not have been overthrown and the new system could not have been set up. When we say that socialist relations of production are better suited than the old relations of production to the development of the productive forces, we mean that the former permits the productive forces to develop at a speed unparalleled in the old society, so that production can expand steadily and the constantly growing needs of the people can be met step by step. Under the rule of imperialism, feudalism and bureaucrat-capitalism, production in old China developed very slowly. For more than fifty years before liberation, China produced only a few score thousand tons of steel a year, not counting the output of the north-eastern provinces. If we include these provinces, the peak annual output of steel of our country was only something over nine hundred thousand tons. In 1949, the country's output of steel was only something over one hundred thousand tons. Now, only seven years after liberation of the country, our steel output already exceeds four million tons. In old China, there was hardly any engineering industry to speak of; motor-car and aircraft industries were non-existent; now, we have them. When the rule of imperialism, feudalism and bureaucrat-capitalism was overthrown by the people, many were not clear as to where China was headed—to capitalism or socialism. Facts give the answer: Only socialism can save China. The socialist system has promoted the rapid development of the productive forces of our country—this is a fact that even our enemies abroad have had to acknowledge.

But our socialist system has just been set up; it is not yet fully established, nor yet fully consolidated. In joint state-private industrial and commercial enterprises, capitalists still receive a fixed rate of interest on their capital, that is to say, exploitation still exists. So far as ownership is concerned, these enterprises are not yet completely socialist in character. Some of our agricultural and handicraft producers' co-operatives are still semi-socialist, while even in the fully socialist co-operatives certain problems about ownership remain to be solved. Relationships in production and exchange are still being gradually established along socialist lines in various sectors of our economy and more and more appropriate forms are being sought. It is a complicated problem to settle on a proper ratio between accumulation and consumption within that sector of socialist economy in which the means of production are owned by the whole people and that sector in which the means of production are collectively owned, as well as between these two sectors. It is not easy to work out a perfectly rational solution to this problem all at once.

To sum up, socialist relations of production have been established; they are suited to the development of the productive forces, but they are still far from perfect, and their imperfect aspects stand in contradiction to the development of the productive forces. There is conformity as well as contradiction between the relations of production and the development of the productive forces; similarly, there is conformity as well as contradiction between the superstructure and the economic base. The superstructure—our state institutions of people's democratic dictatorship and its laws, and socialist ideology under the guidance of Marxism-Leninism—has played a positive role in facilitating the victory of socialist transformation and establishment of a socialist organization of labour; it is suited to the socialist economic base, that is, socialist relations of production. But survivals of bourgeois ideology, bureaucratic ways of doing things in our state organs, and flaws in certain links of our state institutions stand in contradiction to the economic base of socialism. We must continue to resolve such contradictions in the light of specific conditions. Of course, as these contradictions are resolved, new problems and new contradictions will emerge and call for solution. For instance, a constant process of readjustment through state planning is needed to deal with the contradiction between production and the needs of society, which will long remain as an objective reality. Every year our country draws up an economic plan in an effort to establish a proper ratio between accumulation and consumption and achieve a balance between production and the needs of society. By "balance" we mean a temporary, relative unity of opposites. By the end of each year, such a balance, taken as a whole, is upset by the struggle of opposites, the unity achieved undergoes a change, balance becomes imbalance, unity becomes disunity, and once again it is necessary to work out a balance and unity for the next year. This is the superior quality of our planned economy. As a matter of fact, this balance and unity is partially upset every month and every quarter, and partial readjustments are called for. Sometimes, because our arrangements do not correspond to objective reality, contradictions arise and the balance is upset; this is what we call making a mistake. Contradictions arise continually and are continually resolved; this is the dialectical law of the development of things.

This is how things stand today: The turbulent class struggles waged by the masses on a large scale characteristic of the revolutionary periods have, in the main, concluded, but class struggle is not entirely over. While the broad masses of the people welcome the new system, they are not yet quite accustomed to it. Government workers are not sufficiently experienced, and should continue to examine and explore ways of dealing with questions relating to specific policies.

In other words, time is needed for our socialist system to grow and consolidate itself, for the masses to get accustomed to the new system, and for government workers to study and acquire experience. It is imperative that at this juncture we raise the question of distinguishing contradictions among the people from contradictions between ourselves and the enemy, as well as the question of the proper handling of contradictions among the people, so as to rally the people of all nationalities in our country to wage a new battle—the battle against nature—to develop our economy and culture, enable all our people to go through this transition period in a fairly smooth way, make our new system secure, and build up our new state.

2. THE SUPPRESSION OF COUNTER-REVOLUTION

The question of suppressing counter-revolutionaries is a question of the struggle of opposites in the contradiction between ourselves and the enemy. Within the ranks of the people, there are some who hold somewhat different views on this question. There are two kinds of persons whose views differ from ours. Those with a rightist way of thinking make no distinction between ourselves and the enemy and mistake our enemies for our own people. They regard as friends the very people the broad masses regard as enemies. Those with a "leftist" way of thinking so magnify contradictions between ourselves and the enemy that they mistake certain contradictions among the people for contradictions between ourselves and the enemy, and regard as counter-revolutionaries persons who really aren't. Both these views are wrong. Neither of them will enable us to handle properly the question of suppressing counter-revolution, or to correctly assess the results in this work.

If we want to correctly evaluate the results of our efforts to suppress counter-revolution here, let us see what effect the Hungarian events had in our country. These events caused some of our intellectuals to lose their balance a bit but there were no squalls in our country. Why? One reason, it must be said, was that we had succeeded in suppressing counter-revolution quite thoroughly.

Of course, the consolidation of our state is not primarily due to the suppression of counter-revolution. It is due primarily to the fact that we have a Communist Party and a Liberation Army steeled in decades of revolutionary struggle, as well as a working people which has been similarly steeled. Our Party and our armed forces are rooted in the masses; they have been tempered in the flames of a protracted revolution; they are strong and they can fight. Our People's Republic wasn't built overnight. It developed step by step out of the revolutionary bases. Some leading democrats have also been tempered in one degree or another in the struggle, and they went through troubled times together with us. Some intellectuals were tempered in the struggles against imperialism and reaction; since liberation many of them have gone through a process of ideological remoulding which was aimed at making a clear distinction between ourselves and the enemy.

In addition, the consolidation of our state is due to the fact that our economic measures are basically sound, that the people's livelihood is secure and is steadily being improved, that our policies towards the national bourgeoisie and other classes are also correct, and so on. Nevertheless, our success in suppressing counter-revolution is undoubtedly an important reason for the consolidation of our state. Because of all this, although many of our college students come from families other than those of the working people, all of them, with few exceptions, are patriotic and support socialism; they didn't give way to unrest during the Hungarian events. The same was true of the national bourgeoisie, to say nothing of the basic masses—the workers and peasants.

After liberation, we rooted out a number of counter-revolutionaries. Some were sentenced to death because they had committed serious crimes. This was absolutely necessary; it was the demand of the people; it was done to free the masses from long years of oppression by counter-revolutionaries and all kinds of local tyrants; in other words, to set free the productive forces. If we had not done so, the masses would not have been able to lift their heads.

Since 1956, however, there has been a radical change in the situation. Taking the country as a whole, the main force of counter-revolution has been rooted out. Our basic task is no longer to set free the productive forces but to protect and expand them in the context of the new relations of production. Some people do not understand that our present policy fits the present situation and our past policy fitted the past situation; they want to make use of the present policy to reverse decisions on past cases and to deny the great success we achieved in suppressing counter-revolution. This is quite wrong, and the people will not permit it.

As regards the suppression of counter-revolution, the main thing is that we have achieved successes, but mistakes have also been made. There were excesses in some cases and in other cases counter-revolutionaries were overlooked. Our policy is: "Counter-revolutionaries must be suppressed whenever they are found, mistakes must be corrected whenever they are discovered." The line we adopted in this work was the mass line, that is, the suppression of counter-revolution by the people themselves. Of course, even with the adoption of this line, mistakes will still occur in our work, but they will be fewer and easier to correct. The masses have gained experience through this struggle. From what was done correctly they learned how things should be done. From what was done wrong they learned useful lessons as to why mistakes were made.

Steps have been or are being taken to correct mistakes which have already been discovered in the work of suppressing counter-revolutionaries. Those not yet discovered will be corrected as soon as they come to light. Decisions on exoneration and rehabilitation should receive the same measure of publicity as the original mistaken decisions. I propose that a comprehensive review of the work of suppressing counter-revolution be made this year or next to sum up experience, foster a spirit of righteousness and combat unhealthy tendencies. Nationally, this task should be handled by the Standing Committee of the National People's Congress and the Standing Committee of the People's Political Consultative Conference; and locally, by the provincial and municipal people's councils and committees of the People's Political Consultative Conference. In this review, we must help and not pour cold water on the large numbers of functionaries and activists who took part in the work. It is not right to dampen their spirits. Nonetheless, wrongs must be righted when they are discovered. This must be the attitude of all the public security organs, the procuracies and the judicial departments, prisons or agencies charged with the reform of criminals through labour. We hope that wherever possible members of the Standing Committee of the National People's Congress and of the People's Political Consultative Conference and the people's deputies will all take part in this review. This will be of help in perfecting our legal system and also in dealing correctly with counter-revolutionaries and other criminals.

The present situation with regard to counter-revolutionaries can be stated in these words: There still are counter-revolutionaries, but not many. In the first place, there still are counter-revolutionaries. Some people say that there aren't any and that all is at peace; that we can pile up our pillows and just go to sleep. But this is not the way things are. The fact is that there still are counter-revolutionaries (this, of course, is not to say you'll find them everywhere and in every organization), and we must continue to fight them. It must be understood that the hidden counter-revolutionaries still at large will not take it lying down, but will certainly seize every opportunity to make trouble, and that the United States imperialists and the Chiang Kai-shek clique are constantly sending in secret agents to carry on wrecking activities. Even when all the counter-revolutionaries in existence have been rooted out, new ones may emerge. If we drop our guard we shall be badly fooled and suffer for it severely. Wherever counter-revolutionaries are found making trouble, they should be rooted out with a firm hand. But, of course, taking the country as a whole, there are certainly not many counter-revolutionaries. It would be wrong to say that there are still large numbers of counter-revolutionaries at large. Acceptance of that view will also breed confusion.

3. AGRICULTURAL CO-OPERATION

We have a farm population of over five hundred million, so the situation of our peasants has a very important bearing on the development of our economy and the consolidation of our state power. In my view, the situation is basically sound. The organization of agricultural co-operatives has been successfully completed and this has solved a major contradiction in our country—that between socialist industrialization and individual farm economy. The organization of co-operatives was completed swiftly, and so some people were worried that something untoward might occur. Some things did go wrong but, fortunately, they were not so serious. The movement on the whole is healthy. The peasants are working with a will and last year, despite the worst floods, droughts and typhoons in years, they were still able to increase the output of food crops. Yet some people have stirred up a miniature typhoon: they are grousing that co-operative farming won't do, that it has no superior qualities. Does agricultural co-operation possess superior qualities or does it not? Among the documents distributed at today's meeting is one concerning the Wang Kuo-fan Co-operative in Tsunhua County, Hopei Province, which I suggest you read. This co-operative is situated in a hilly region which was very poor in the past and depended on relief grain sent there every year by the People's Government. When the co-operative was first set up in 1953, people called it the "paupers' co-op." But as a result of four years of hard struggle, it has become better off year by year, and now most of its households have reserves of grain. What this co-operative could do, other co-operatives should also be able to do under normal conditions, even if it may take a bit longer. It is clear then that there are no grounds for the view that something has gone wrong with the co-operative movement.

It is also clear that it takes a hard struggle to build up co-operatives. New things always have difficulties and ups and downs to get over as they grow. It would be sheer fancy to imagine that building socialism is all plain sailing and easy success, that one won't meet difficulties or setbacks or need not make tremendous efforts.

Who are the staunch supporters of the co-operatives? They are the overwhelming majority of the poor peasants and lower middle peasants. These together account for more than seventy per cent of the rural population. Most of the rest also cherish hopes for the future of the co-operatives. Only a very small minority are really dissatisfied. But quite a number of persons have failed to analyse this situation. They have not made a comprehensive study of the achievements and shortcomings of the co-operatives and the causes of these shortcomings; they take part of the picture for the whole. And so, among some people a miniature typhoon has whirled up around what they call the co-operatives having no superior qualities.

How long will it take to consolidate the co-operatives and end these arguments about their not having any superior qualities? Judging from the actual experience of many co-operatives, this will probably take five years or a bit longer. As most of our co-operatives are only a little over a year old, it would be unreasonable to expect too much from them so soon. In my view, we'll be doing well enough if we succeed in establishing the co-operatives during the period of the First Five-Year Plan and consolidating them during the Second.

The co-operatives are steadily being consolidated. Certain contradictions remain to be resolved, such as those between the state and the co-operatives, and those within and between the co-operatives themselves.

In resolving these contradictions we must keep problems of production and distribution constantly in mind. Take the question of production. On the one hand, the co-operative economy must be subject to the unified economic planning of the state but at the same time it should be allowed to retain a certain leeway and independence of action without prejudice to unified state planning or the policies and laws and regulations of the state. On the other hand, every household in a co-operative can make its own plans in regard to land reserved for private use and other economic undertakings left to private management, but it must comply with the overall plans of the co-operative or production team to which it belongs.

On the question of distribution, we must take into account the interests of the state, the co-operative, and the individual. We must find the correct way to handle the three-way relationship between the tax revenue of the state, accumulation of funds in the co-operative and the personal income of the peasant, and pay constant attention to making readjustments so as to resolve contradictions as they arise. Accumulation is essential for both the state and the co-operative, but in neither case should this be overdone. We should do everything possible to enable the peasants in normal years to raise their personal incomes year by year on the basis of increased production.

Many people say that the peasants lead a hard life. Is this true? In one sense, it is. That is to say, because the imperialists and their agents oppressed, exploited and impoverished our country for over a century, the standard of living not only of our peasants but of our workers and intellectuals as well is still low. We will need several decades of intensive efforts to raise the standard of living of our entire people step by step. In this sense, "hard" is the right word. But from another point of view, it is not right to say "hard." We refer to the allegation that, in the seven years since liberation, the life of the workers has improved but not that of the peasants. As a matter of fact, with very few exceptions, both the workers and the peasants are better off than before. Since liberation, the peasants have rid themselves of landlord exploitation, and their production has increased year by year. Take the case of food crops. In 1949, the country's output was only something over 210,000 million catties. By 1956, it had risen to something over 360,000 million catties, an increase of nearly 150,000 million catties. The state agricultural tax is not heavy, amounting only to some 30,000 million catties a year. Grain bought from the peasants at normal prices only amounts to something over 50,000 million catties a year. These two items together total over 80,000 million catties. More than one half of this grain, furthermore, is sold in the villages and nearby towns. Obviously one cannot say that there has been no improvement in the life of the peasants. We are prepared to stabilize over a number of years the total amount of the grain tax and the amount of grain purchased by the state at approximately something over 80,000 million catties a year. This will help promote the development of agriculture, and consolidate the co-operatives; the small number of grain-short households still found in the countryside will no longer go short; so that with the exception of certain peasants who grow industrial crops, all peasant households will then have reserves of food grain or at least become self-sufficient; in this way there will be no more poor peasants and the standard of living of all the peasants will reach or surpass the level of that of the middle peasants. It's not right to make a superficial comparison between the average annual income of a peasant and that of a worker and draw the conclusion that the one is too low and the other too high. The productivity of the workers is much higher than that of the peasants, while the cost of living for the peasants is much lower than that for workers in the cities; so it cannot be said that the workers receive special favours from the state. However, the wages of a small number of workers and some government personnel are rather too high, the peasants have reason to be dissatisfied with this, so it is necessary to make certain appropriate readjustments in the light of specific circumstances.

4. THE QUESTION OF INDUSTRIALISTS AND BUSINESS MEN

The year 1956 saw the transformation of privately owned industrial and commercial enterprises into joint state-private enterprises as well as the organization of co-operatives in agriculture and handicrafts as part of the transformation of our social system. The speed and smoothness with which this was carried out are closely related to the fact that we treated the contradiction between the working class and the national bourgeoisie as a contradiction among the people. Has this class contradiction been resolved completely? No, not yet. A considerable period of time is still required to do so. However, some people say that the capitalists have been so remoulded that they are now not much different from the workers, and that further remoulding is unnecessary. Others go so far as to say that the capitalists are even a bit better than the workers. Still others ask, if remoulding is necessary, why doesn't the working class undergo remoulding? Are these opinions correct? Of course not.

In building a socialist society, all need remoulding, the exploiters as well as the working people. Who says the working class doesn't need it? Of course, remoulding of the exploiters and that of the working people are two different types of remoulding. The two must not be confused. In the class struggle and the struggle against nature, the working class remoulds the whole of society, and at the same time remoulds itself. It must continue to learn in the process of its work and step by step overcome its shortcomings. It must never stop doing so. Take us who are present here for example. Many of us make some progress each year; that is to say, we are being remoulded each year. I myself had all sorts of non-Marxist ideas before. It was only later that I embraced Marxism. I learned a little Marxism from books and so made an initial remoulding of my ideas, but it was mainly through taking part in the class struggle over the years that I came to be remoulded. And I must continue to study if I am to make further progress, otherwise I shall lag behind. Can the capitalists be so clever as to need no more remoulding?

Some contend that the Chinese bourgeoisie no longer has two sides to its character, but only one side. Is this true? No. On the one hand, members of the bourgeoisie have already become managerial personnel in joint state-private enterprises and are being transformed from exploiters into working people living by their own labour. On the other hand, they still receive a fixed rate of interest on their investments in the joint enterprises, that is, they have not yet cut themselves loose from the roots of exploitation. Between them and the working class there is still a considerable gap in ideology, sentiments and habits of life. How can it be said that they no longer have two sides to their character? Even when they stop receiving their fixed interest payments and rid themselves of the label "bourgeoisie," they will still need ideological remoulding for quite some time. If it were held that the bourgeoisie no longer has a dual character, then such study and remoulding for the capitalists would no longer be needed.

But it must be said that such a view doesn't tally with the actual circumstances of our industrialists and business men, nor with what most of them want. During the past few years, most of them have been willing to study and have made marked progress. Our industrialists and business men can be thoroughly remoulded only in the course of work; they should work together with the staff and workers in the enterprises, and make the enterprises the chief centres for remoulding themselves. It is also important for them to change certain of their old views through study. Study for them should be optional. After they have attended study groups for some weeks, many industrialists and business men, on returning to their enterprises, find they speak more of a common language with the workers and the representatives of state shareholdings, and so work better together. They know from personal experience that it is good for them to keep on studying and remoulding themselves. The idea just referred to that study and remoulding are not necessary does not reflect the views of the majority of industrialists and business men. Only a small number of them think that way.

5. THE QUESTION OF INTELLECTUALS

Contradictions within the ranks of the people in our country also find expression among our intellectuals. Several million intellectuals who worked for the old society have come to serve the new society. The question that now arises is how they can best meet the needs of the new society and how we can help them do so. This is also a contradiction among the people.

Most of our intellectuals have made marked progress during the past seven years. They express themselves in favour of the socialist system. Many of them are diligently studying Marxism, and some have become Communists. Their number, though small, is growing steadily. There are, of course, still some intellectuals who are sceptical of socialism or who do not approve of it, but they are in a minority.

China needs as many intellectuals as she can get to carry through the colossal task of socialist construction. We should trust intellectuals who are really willing to serve the cause of socialism, radically improve our relations with them and help them solve whatever problems that have to be solved, so that they can give full play to their talents. Many of our comrades are not good at getting along with intellectuals. They are stiff with them, lack respect for their work, and interfere in scientific and cultural matters in a way that is uncalled for. We must do away with all such shortcomings.

Our intellectuals have made some progress, but they should not be complacent. They must continue to remould themselves, gradually shed their bourgeois world outlook and acquire a proletarian, communist world outlook so that they can fully meet the needs of the new society and closely unite with the workers and peasants. This change in world outlook is a fundamental one, and up till now it cannot yet be said that most of our intellectuals have accomplished it. We hope that they will continue making progress, and, in the course of work and study, gradually acquire a communist world outlook, get a better grasp of Marxism-Leninism, and identify themselves with the workers and peasants. We hope they will not stop halfway, or, what is worse, slip back; for if they do they will find themselves in a blind alley.

Since the social system of our country has changed and the economic basis of bourgeois ideology has in the main been destroyed, it is not only necessary but also possible for large numbers of our intellectuals to change their world outlook. But a thorough change in world outlook takes quite a long time, and we should go about it patiently and not be impetuous. Actually there are bound to be some who are all along reluctant, ideologically, to accept Marxism-Leninism and communism. We should not be too exacting in what we expect of them; as long as they comply with the requirements of the state and engage in legitimate pursuits, we should give them opportunities for suitable work.

There has been a falling off recently in ideological and political work among students and intellectuals, and some unhealthy tendencies have appeared. Some people apparently think that there is no longer any need to concern themselves about politics, the future of their motherland and the ideals of mankind. It seems as if Marxism that was once all the rage is not so much in fashion now. This being the case, we must improve our ideological and political work. Both students and intellectuals should study hard. In addition to specialized subjects, they should study Marxism-Leninism, current events and political affairs in order to progress both ideologically and politically. Not to have a correct political point of view is like having no soul. Ideological remoulding in the past was necessary and has yielded positive results. But it was carried on in a somewhat rough and ready way and the feelings of some people were hurt—this was not good. We must avoid such shortcomings in future. All departments and organizations concerned should take up their responsibilities with regard to ideological and political work. This applies to the Communist Party, the Youth League, government departments responsible for this work, and especially heads of educational institutions and teachers. Our educational policy must enable everyone who gets an education, to develop morally, intellectually and physically and become a cultured, socialist-minded worker. We must spread the idea of building our country through hard work and thrift. We must see to it that all our young people understand that ours is still a very poor country, that we can't change this situation radically in a short time, and that only through the united efforts of our younger generation and all our people working with their own hands can our country be made strong and prosperous within a period of several decades. It is true that the establishment of our socialist system has opened the road leading to the ideal state of the future, but we must work hard, very hard indeed, if we are to make that ideal a reality. Some of our young people think that everything ought to be perfect once a socialist society is established and that they should be able to enjoy a happy life, ready-made, without working for it. This is unrealistic.

6. THE QUESTION OF NATIONAL MINORITIES

The people of the national minorities in our country number more than thirty million. Although they constitute only six per cent of China's total population, they inhabit regions which altogether comprise fifty to sixty per cent of the country's total area. It is therefore imperative to foster good relations between the Han people and the national minorities. The key to the solution of this question lies in overcoming great-Han chauvinism. At the same time, where local nationalism exists among national minorities, measures should be taken to overcome it. Neither great-Han chauvinism nor local nationalism can do any good to unity among the nationalities, and they should both be overcome as contradictions among the people. We have already done some work in this sphere. In most areas inhabited by national minorities, there has been a big improvement in relations among the nationalities, but a number of problems remain to be solved. In certain places, both great-Han chauvinism and local nationalism still exist in a serious degree, and this calls for our close attention. As a result of the efforts of the people of all the nationalities over the past few years, democratic reforms and socialist transformation have in the main been completed in most of the national minority areas. Because conditions in Tibet are not ripe, democratic reforms have not yet been carried out there. According to the seventeen-point agreement reached between the Central People's Government and the local government of Tibet, reform of the social system must eventually be carried out. But we should not be impatient; when this will be done can only be decided when the great majority of the people of Tibet and their leading public figures consider it practicable. It has now been decided not to proceed with democratic reform in Tibet during the period of the Second Five-Year Plan, and we can only decide whether it will be done in the period of the Third Five-Year Plan in the light of the situation obtaining at that time.

7. OVERALL PLANNING, ALL-ROUND CONSIDERATION AND PROPER ARRANGEMENTS

The "overall planning and all-round consideration" mentioned here refers to overall planning and all-round consideration for the interests of the six hundred million people of our country. In drawing up plans, handling affairs or thinking over problems, we must proceed from the fact that China has a population of six hundred million people. This must never be forgotten.

Now, why should we make a point of this? Could it be that there are people who still do not know that we have a population of six hundred million? Of course, everyone knows this, but in actual practice some are apt to forget it and act as if they thought that the fewer people and the smaller their world the better. Those who have this "exclusive-club" mentality resist the idea of bringing all positive factors into play, of rallying everyone that can be rallied, and of doing everything possible to turn negative factors into positive ones serving the great cause of building a socialist society. I hope these people will take a wider view and really recognize the fact that we have a population of six hundred million, that this is an objective fact, and that this is our asset.

We have this large population. It is a good thing, but of course it also has its difficulties. Construction is going ahead vigorously on all fronts; we have achieved much, but in the present transitional period of tremendous social change we are still beset by many difficult problems. Progress and difficulties—this is a contradiction. However, all contradictions not only should, but can be resolved. Our guiding principle is overall planning and all-round consideration, and proper arrangements. No matter whether it is the question of food, natural calamities, employment, education, the intellectuals, the united front of all patriotic forces, the national minorities, or any other question— we must always proceed from the standpoint of overall planning and all-round consideration for the whole people; we must make whatever arrangements are suitable and possible at the particular time and place and after consultation with all those concerned. On no account should we throw matters out the back door, go around grumbling that there are too many people, that people are backward, and that things are troublesome and hard to handle.

Does that mean that everyone and everything should be taken care of by the government alone? Of course not. Social organizations and the masses themselves can work out ways and means to take care of many matters involving people and things. They are quite capable of devising many good ways of doing so. This also comes within the scope of the principle of "overall planning, all-round consideration and proper arrangements." We should give guidance to social organizations and the masses of the people everywhere in taking such action.

8. ON "LETTING A HUNDRED FLOWERS BLOSSOM," AND "LETTING A HUNDRED SCHOOLS OF THOUGHT CONTEND,"* AND "LONG-TERM CO-EXISTENCE AND MUTUAL SUPERVISION"

"Let a hundred flowers blossom," and "let a hundred schools of thought contend," "long-term co-existence and mutual supervision"—how did these slogans come to be put forward?

They were put forward in the light of the specific conditions existing in China, on the basis of the recognition that various kinds of contradictions still exist in a socialist society, and in response to the country's urgent need to speed up its economic and cultural development.

The policy of letting a hundred flowers blossom and a hundred schools of thought contend is designed to promote the flourishing of the arts and the progress of science; it is designed to enable a socialist culture to thrive in our land. Different forms and styles in art can develop freely and different schools in science can contend freely. We think that is harmful to the growth of art and science if administrative measures are used to impose one particular style of art or school of thought and to ban another. Questions of right and wrong in the arts and sciences should be settled through free discussion in artistic and scientific circles and in the course of practical work in the arts and sciences. They should not be settled in summary fashion. A period of trial is often needed to determine whether something is right or wrong. In the past, new and correct things often failed at the outset to win recognition from the majority of people and had to develop by twists and turns in struggle. Correct and good things have often at first been looked upon not as fragrant flowers but as poisonous weeds. Copernicus' theory of the solar system and Darwin's theory of evolution were once dismissed as erroneous and had to win through over bitter opposition. Chinese history offers many similar examples. In socialist society, conditions for the growth of new things are radically different from and far superior to those in the old society. Nevertheless, it still often happens that new, rising forces are held back and reasonable suggestions smothered.

The growth of new things can also be hindered, not because of deliberate suppression, but because of lack of discernment. That is why we should take a cautious attitude in regard to questions of right and wrong in the arts and sciences, encourage free discussion, and avoid hasty conclusions. We believe that this attitude will facilitate the growth of the arts and sciences.

Marxism has also developed through struggle. At the beginning, Marxism was subjected to all kinds of attack and regarded as a poisonous weed. It is still being attacked and regarded as a poisonous weed in many parts of the world. However, it enjoys a different position in the socialist countries. But even in these countries, there are non-Marxist as well as anti-Marxist ideologies. It is true that in China, socialist transformation, in so far as a change in the system of ownership is concerned, has in the main been completed, and the turbulent, large-scale, mass class struggles characteristic of the revolutionary periods have in the main concluded. But remnants of the overthrown landlord and comprador classes still exist, the bourgeoisie still exists, and the petty bourgeoisie has only just begun to remould itself. Class struggle is not yet over. The class struggle between the proletariat and the bourgeoisie, the class struggle between various political forces, and the class struggle in the ideological field between the proletariat and the bourgeoisie will still be long and devious and at times may even become very acute. The proletariat seeks to transform the world according to its own world outlook, so does the bourgeoisie. In this respect, the question whether socialism or capitalism will win is still not really settled. Marxists are still a minority of the entire population as well as of the intellectuals. Marxism therefore must still develop through struggle. Marxism can only develop through struggle—this is true not only in the past and present, it is necessarily true in the future also. What is correct always develops in the course of struggle with what is wrong. The true, the good and the beautiful always exist in comparison with the false, the evil and the ugly, and grow in struggle with the latter. As mankind in general rejects an untruth and accepts a truth, a new truth will begin struggling with new erroneous ideas. Such struggles will never end. This is the law of development of truth and it is certainly also the law of development of Marxism.

*"Let a hundred flowers blossom," and "let a hundred schools of thought contend" are two old Chinese sayings. The word "hundred" does not mean literally the number as such, but simply "numerous."—*Translator.*

TEXT OF DOCUMENT 14

It will take a considerable time to decide the issue in the ideological struggle between socialism and capitalism in our country. This is because the influence of the bourgeoisie and of the intellectuals who come from the old society will remain in our country as the ideology of a class for a long time to come. Failure to grasp this, or still worse, failure to understand it at all, can lead to the gravest mistakes—to ignoring the necessity of waging the struggle in the ideological field. Ideological struggle is not like other forms of struggle. Crude, coercive methods should not be used in this struggle, but only the method of painstaking reasoning. Today, socialism enjoys favourable conditions in the ideological struggle. The main power of the state is in the hands of the working people led by the proletariat. The Communist Party is strong and its prestige stands high. Although there are defects and mistakes in our work, every fair-minded person can see that we are loyal to the people, that we are both determined and able to build up our country together with the people, and that we have achieved great successes and will achieve still greater ones. The vast majority of the bourgeoisie and intellectuals who come from the old society are patriotic; they are willing to serve their flourishing socialist motherland, and they know that if they turn away from the socialist cause and the working people led by the Communist Party, they will have no one to rely on and no bright future to look forward to.

People may ask: Since Marxism is accepted by the majority of the people in our country as the guiding ideology, can it be criticized? Certainly it can. As a scientific truth, Marxism fears no criticism. If it did, and could be defeated in argument, it would be worthless. In fact, aren't the idealists criticizing Marxism every day and in all sorts of ways? As for those who harbour bourgeois and petty bourgeois ideas and do not wish to change, aren't they also criticizing Marxism in all sorts of ways? Marxists should not be afraid of criticism from any quarter. Quite the contrary, they need to steel and improve themselves and win new positions in the teeth of criticism and the storm and stress of struggle. Fighting against wrong ideas is like being vaccinated—a man develops greater immunity from disease after the vaccine takes effect. Plants raised in hot-houses are not likely to be robust. Carrying out the policy of letting a hundred flowers blossom and a hundred schools of thought contend will not weaken but strengthen the leading position of Marxism in the ideological field.

What should our policy be towards non-Marxist ideas? As far as unmistakable counter-revolutionaries and wreckers of the socialist cause are concerned, the matter is easy: we simply deprive them of their freedom of speech. But it is quite a different matter when we are faced with incorrect ideas among the people. Will it do to ban such ideas and give them no opportunity to express themselves? Certainly not. It is not only futile but very harmful to use crude and summary methods to deal with ideological questions among the people, with questions relating to the spiritual life of man. You may ban the expression of wrong ideas, but the ideas will still be there. On the other hand, correct ideas, if pampered in hot-houses without being exposed to the elements or immunized from disease, will not win out against wrong ones. That is why it is only by employing methods of discussion, criticism and reasoning that we can really foster correct ideas, overcome wrong ideas, and really settle issues.

The bourgeoisie and petty bourgeoisie are bound to give expression to their ideologies. It is inevitable that they should stubbornly persist in expressing themselves in every way possible on political and ideological questions. You can't expect them not to do so. We should not use methods of suppression to prevent them from expressing themselves, but should allow them to do so and at the same time argue with them and direct well-considered criticism at them.

There can be no doubt that we should criticize all kinds of wrong ideas. It certainly would not do to refrain from criticism and look on while wrong ideas spread unchecked and acquire their market. Mistakes should be criticized and poisonous weeds fought against wherever they crop up. But such criticism should not be doctrinaire. We should not use the metaphysical method, but strive to employ the dialectical method. What is needed is scientific analysis and fully convincing arguments. Doctrinaire criticism settles nothing. We don't want any kind of poisonous weeds, but we should carefully distinguish between what is really a poisonous weed and what is really a fragrant flower. We must learn together with the masses of the people how to make this careful distinction, and use the correct methods to fight poisonous weeds.

While criticizing doctrinairism, we should at the same time direct our attention to criticizing revisionism. Revisionism, or rightist opportunism, is a bourgeois trend of thought which is even more dangerous than doctrinairism. The revisionists, or right opportunists, pay lip-service to Marxism and also attack "doctrinairism." But the real target of their attack is actually the most fundamental elements of Marxism. They oppose or distort materialism and dialectics, oppose or try to weaken the people's democratic dictatorship and the leading role of the Communist Party, oppose or try to weaken socialist transformation and socialist construction. Even after the basic victory of the socialist revolution in our country, there are still a number of people who vainly hope for a restoration of the capitalist system. They wage a struggle against the working class on every front, including the ideological front. In this struggle, their right-hand men are the revisionists.

On the surface, these two slogans—let a hundred flowers blossom and a hundred schools of thought contend—have no class character: the proletariat can turn them to account, so can the bourgeoisie and other people. But different classes, strata and social groups each have their own views on what are fragrant flowers and what are poisonous weeds. So what, from the point of view of the broad masses of the people, should be the criteria today for distinguishing between fragrant flowers and poisonous weeds?

In the political life of our country, how are our people to determine what is right and what is wrong in our words and actions? Basing ourselves on the principles of our Constitution, the will of the overwhelming majority of our people and the political programmes jointly proclaimed on various occasions by our political parties and groups, we believe that, broadly speaking, words and actions can be judged right if they:

(1) Help to unite the people of our various nationalities, and do not divide them;

(2) Are beneficial, not harmful, to socialist transformation and socialist construction;

(3) Help to consolidate, not undermine or weaken, the people's democratic dictatorship;

(4) Help to consolidate, not undermine or weaken, democratic centralism;

(5) Tend to strengthen, not to cast off or weaken, the leadership of the Communist Party;

(6) Are beneficial, not harmful, to international socialist solidarity and the solidarity of the peace-loving peoples of the world.

Of these six criteria, the most important are the socialist path and the leadership of the Party. These criteria are put forward in order to foster, and not hinder, the free discussion of various questions among the people. Those who do not approve of these criteria can still put forward their own views and argue their case. When the majority of the people have clear-cut criteria to go by, criticism and self-criticism can be conducted along proper lines, and these criteria can be applied to people's words and actions to determine whether they are fragrant flowers or poisonous weeds. These are political criteria. Naturally, in judging the truthfulness of scientific theories or assessing the aesthetic value of works of art, other pertinent criteria are needed, but these six political criteria are also applicable to all activities in the arts or sciences. In a socialist country like ours, can there possibly be any useful scientific or artistic activity which runs counter to these political criteria?

All that is set out above stems from the specific historical conditions in our country. Since conditions vary in different socialist countries and with different Communist Parties, we do not think that other countries and Parties must or need to follow the Chinese way.

The slogan "long-term co-existence and mutual supervision" is also a product of specific historical conditions in our country. It wasn't put forward all of a sudden, but had been in the making for several years. The idea of long-term co-existence had been in existence for a long time, but last year when the socialist system was basically established, the slogan was set out in clear terms.

Why should the democratic parties of the bourgeoisie and petty bourgeoisie be allowed to exist side by side with the party of the working class over a long period of time? Because we have no reason not to adopt the policy of long-term co-existence with all other democratic parties which are truly devoted to the task of uniting the people for the cause of socialism and which enjoy the trust of the people.

As early as at the Second Session of the National Committee of the People's Political Consultative Conference in June 1950, I put the matter in this way:

"The people and the People's Government have no reason to reject or deny the opportunity to anyone to make a living and give their services to the country, so long as he is really willing to serve the people, really helped the people when they were still in difficulties, did good things and continues to do them consistently without giving up halfway."

What I defined here was the political basis for the long-term co-existence of the various parties. It is the desire of the Communist Party, also its policy, to exist side by side with the other democratic parties for a long time to come. Whether these democratic parties can long exist depends not merely on what the Communist Party itself desires but also on the part played by these democratic parties themselves and on whether they enjoy the confidence of the people.

Mutual supervision among the various parties has also been a long-established fact, in the sense that they advise and criticize each other. Mutual supervision, which is obviously not a one-sided matter, means that the Communist Party should exercise supervision over the other democratic parties, and the other democratic parties should exercise supervision over the Communist Party. Why should the other democratic parties be allowed to exercise supervision over the Communist Party? This is because for a party as much as for an individual there is great need to hear opinions different from its own. We all know that supervision over the Communist Party is mainly exercised by the working people and Party membership. But we will benefit even more if the other democratic parties do this as well. Of course, advice and criticism exchanged between the Communist Party and the other democratic parties will play a positive role in mutual supervision only when they conform to the six political criteria given above. That is why we hope that the other democratic parties will all pay attention to ideological remoulding, and strive for long-term co-existence and mutual supervision with the Communist Party so as to meet the needs of the new society.

9. CONCERNING DISTURBANCES CREATED BY SMALL NUMBERS OF PEOPLE

In 1956, small numbers of workers and students in certain places went on strike. The immediate cause of these disturbances was the failure to satisfy certain of their demands for material benefits, of which some should and could be met, while others were out of place or excessive and therefore could not be met for the time being. But a more important cause was bureaucracy on the part of those in positions of leadership. In some cases, responsibility for such bureaucratic mistakes should be placed on the higher authorities, and those at lower levels should not be made to bear all the blame. Another cause for these disturbances was that the ideological and political educational work done among the workers and students was inadequate. In the same year, members of a small number of agricultural co-operatives also created disturbances, and the main causes were also bureaucracy on the part of the leadership and lack of educational work among the masses.

It should be admitted that all too often some people are prone to concentrate on immediate, partial and personal interests, they do not understand or do not sufficiently understand long-range, nationwide and collective interests. Because of their lack of experience in political and social life, quite a number of young people can't make a proper comparison between the old and new China; it is not easy for them to thoroughly comprehend what hardships the people of our country went through in the struggle to free themselves from oppression by the imperialists and Kuomintang reactionaries, or what a long period of painstaking work is needed before a happy socialist society can be established. That is why political educational work should be kept going among the masses in an interesting and effective way. We should always tell them the facts about the difficulties that have cropped up and discuss with them how to solve these difficulties.

We do not approve of disturbances, because contradictions among the people can be resolved in accordance with the formula "unity—criticism—unity," while disturbances inevitably cause losses and are detrimental to the advance of socialism. We believe that our people stand for socialism, that they uphold discipline and are reasonable, and will not create disturbances without reason. But this does not mean that in our country there is no possibility of the masses creating disturbances. With regard to this question, we should pay attention to the following:

(1) In order to get rid of the root cause of disturbances, we must stamp out bureaucracy, greatly improve ideological and political education, and deal with all contradictions in a proper way. If this is done, there won't usually be any disturbances.

(2) If disturbances should occur as a result of bad work on our part, then we should guide those involved in such disturbances on to the correct path, make use of these disturbances as a special means of improving our work and educating the cadres and the masses, and work out solutions to those questions which have been neglected in the past. In handling any disturbances, we should work painstakingly, and should not use over-simplified methods, nor declare the matter closed before it is thoroughly settled. The guiding spirits in disturbances should not be removed from their jobs or expelled without good reason, except for those who have committed criminal offences or active counter-revolutionaries who should be dealt with according to law. In a big country like ours, it is nothing to get alarmed about if small numbers of people should create disturbances; rather we should turn such things to advantage to help us get rid of bureaucracy.

In our society, there is also a small number of people who are unmindful of public interests, refuse to listen to reason, commit crimes and break the law. They may take advantage of our policies and distort them, deliberately put forward unreasonable demands in order to stir up the masses, or deliberately spread rumours to create trouble and disrupt social order. We do not propose to let these people have their way. On the contrary, proper legal action must be taken against them. The masses demand that these persons be punished. Not to do so will run counter to popular will.

10. CAN BAD THINGS BE TURNED INTO GOOD THINGS?

As I have said, in our society, it is bad when groups of people make disturbances, and we do not approve of it. But when disturbances do occur, they force us to learn lessons from them, to overcome bureaucracy and educate the cadres and the people. In this sense, bad things can be turned into good things. Disturbances thus have a dual character. All kinds of disturbances can be looked at in this way.

It is clear to everybody that the Hungarian events were not a good thing. But they too had a dual character. Because our Hungarian comrades took proper action in the course of these events, what was a bad thing turned ultimately into a good thing. The Hungarian state is now more firmly established than ever, and all other countries in the socialist camp have also learned a lesson.

Similarly, the world-wide anti-Communist and anti-popular campaign launched in the latter half of 1956 was of course a bad thing. But it educated and steeled the Communist Parties and the working class in all countries, and thus turned out to be a good thing. In the storm and stress of this period, a number of people resigned from the Communist Parties in many countries. Resignations from the Party reduce Party membership and are, of course, a bad thing, but there is a good side to this also. Since the vacillating elements unwilling to carry on have withdrawn, the great majority of staunch Party members are more firmly united for the struggle. Isn't this a good thing?

In short, we must learn to take an all-round view of things, seeing not only the positive side of things but also the negative side. Under specific conditions, a bad thing can lead to good results and a good thing to bad results. More than two thousand years ago Lao Tzu said: "It is upon bad fortune that good fortune leans, upon good fortune that bad fortune rests." When the Japanese struck into China, they called this a victory. Huge areas of China's territory were seized, and the Chinese called this a defeat. But China's defeat carried within it the seeds of victory, and Japan's victory carried within it the seeds of defeat. Hasn't this been proved by history?

People all over the world are now discussing whether or not a third world war will break out. In regard to this question, we must be psychologically prepared, and at the same time take an analytical view. We stand resolutely for peace and oppose war. But if the imperialists insist on unleashing another war, we should not be afraid of it. Our attitude on this question is the same as our attitude towards all disturbances: firstly, we are against it; secondly, we are not afraid of it.

The First World War was followed by the birth of the Soviet Union with a population of 200 million. The Second World War was followed by the emergence of the socialist camp with a combined population of 900 million. If the imperialists should insist on launching a third world war, it is certain that several hundred million more will turn to socialism; then there will not be much room left in the world for the imperialists, while it is quite likely that the whole structure of imperialism will utterly collapse.

Given specific conditions, the two aspects of a contradiction invariably turn into their respective opposites as a result of the struggle between them. Here, the conditions are important. Without specific conditions, neither of the two contradictory aspects can transform itself into its opposite. Of all the classes in the world the proletariat is the most eager to change its position; next comes the semi-proletariat, for the former possesses nothing at all, while the latter is not much better off. The present situation in which the United States controls a majority in the United Nations and dominates many parts of the world is a transient one, which will eventually be changed. China's situation as a poor country denied her rights in international affairs will also be changed—a poor country will be changed into a rich country, a country denied her rights into a country enjoying her rights—a transformation of things into their opposites. Here, the decisive conditions are the socialist system and the concerted efforts of a united people.

11. THE PRACTICE OF ECONOMY

Here I wish to speak briefly on practising economy. We want to carry on large-scale construction, but our country is still very poor—herein lies a contradiction. One way of resolving this contradiction is to make a sustained effort to practise strict economy in every field.

During the *san fan* movement in 1952, we fought against corruption, waste and bureaucracy, and the emphasis was on combating corruption. In 1955 we advocated the practice of economy with considerable success; our emphasis then was on combating unduly high standards for non-productive projects in capital construction, and economy in the use of raw materials in industrial production. But at that time economy as a guiding principle was not conscientiously carried out in all branches of the national economy, nor in government offices, army units, schools and people's organizations in general. This year we have called for economy and elimination of waste in every respect throughout the country.

We still lack experience in construction. During the past few years great successes have been achieved, but there has also been waste. We must gradually build a number of large-scale modern enterprises as the mainstay of our industries; without these we shall not be able to turn our country into a modern industrial power in several decades. But the majority of our enterprises should not be built in this way; we should set up a far greater number of small and medium enterprises and make full use of the industries inherited from the old society, so as to effect the greatest economy and do more things with less money. Since the principle of practising strict economy and combating waste was put forward in more emphatic terms than before by the Second Plenary Session of the Central Committee of the Communist Party of China in November 1956, good results have been obtained. This economy drive must be carried out in a thorough, sustained way. Just as it is with criticism of our other faults and mistakes, combating waste is like washing our face. Don't people wash their faces every day? The Chinese Communist Party, the other democratic parties, democrats not affiliated to any party, intellectuals, industrialists and business men, workers, peasants and handicraftsmen—in short, all the 600 million people of our country—must increase production, practise economy, and combat extravagance and waste. This is of first importance both economically and politically. A dangerous tendency has shown itself of late among many of our personnel—an unwillingness to share the joys and hardships of the masses, a concern for personal position and gain. This is very bad. One way of overcoming this dangerous tendency is, in our campaign, to increase production and practise economy, to streamline our organizations and transfer cadres to lower levels so that a considerable number of them will return to productive work. We must see to it that all our cadres and all our people constantly bear in mind that, while ours is a big socialist country, it is an economically backward and poor country, and that this is a very great contradiction. If we want to see China rich and strong, we must be prepared for several decades of intensive effort which will include, among other things, carrying out a policy of building our country through hard work and thrift—of practising strict economy and combating waste.

12. CHINA'S PATH TO INDUSTRIALIZATION

In discussing our path to industrialization, I am here concerned principally with the relationship between the growth of heavy industry, light industry and agriculture. Heavy industry is the core of

China's economic construction. This must be affirmed. But, at the same time, full attention must be paid to the development of agriculture and light industry.

As China is a great agricultural country, with over eighty per cent of its population in the villages, its industry and agriculture must be developed simultaneously. Only then will industry have raw materials and a market, and only so will it be possible to accumulate fairly large funds for the building up of a powerful heavy industry. Everyone knows that light industry is closely related to agriculture. Without agriculture there can be no light industry. But it is not so clearly understood that agriculture provides heavy industry with an important market. This fact, however, will be more readily appreciated as the gradual progress of technological improvement and modernization of agriculture calls for more and more machinery, fertilizers, water conservancy and electric power projects and transport facilities for the farms, as well as fuel and building materials for the rural consumers. The entire national economy will benefit if we can achieve an even greater growth in our agriculture and thus induce a correspondingly greater development of light industry during the period of the Second and Third Five-Year Plans. With the development of agriculture and light industry, heavy industry will be assured of its market and funds, and thus grow faster. Hence what may seem to be a slower pace of industrialization is actually not so, and indeed the tempo may even be speeded up. In three five-year plans or perhaps a little longer, China's annual steel output can be raised to 20,000,000 tons or more from the peak pre-liberation output of something over 900,000 tons in 1943. This will gladden people both in town and countryside.

I do not propose to talk at length on economic questions today. With barely seven years of economic construction behind us, we still lack experience and need to get more. We had no experience to start with in revolutionary work either, and it was only after we had taken a number of tumbles and learned our lesson that we won nation-wide victory. What we must do now is to cut the time we take to gain experience in economic construction to less than it took us to get experience in revolutionary work and not pay such a high price for it. We'll have to pay some sort of price, but we hope that it will not be as high as that paid during the revolutionary period. We must realize that a contradiction is involved in this question between the objective laws of development of socialist economy and our subjective understanding, a contradiction which needs to be resolved in practice. This contradiction will also manifest itself as a contradiction between different persons, that is, a contradiction between those who have a relatively accurate understanding of objective laws and those whose understanding of them is relatively inaccurate; and so this is also a contradiction among the people. Every contradiction is an objective reality, and it is our task to understand it and resolve it as correctly as we can.

In order to turn our country into an industrial power, we must learn conscientiously from the advanced experience of the Soviet Union. The Soviet Union has been building socialism for forty years, and we treasure its experience.

Let us consider who designed and equipped so many important factories for us. Was it the United States? or Britain? No, neither of them. Only the Soviet Union was willing to do so because it is a socialist country and our ally. In addition to the Soviet Union, some brother countries of Eastern Europe also gave us assistance. It is perfectly true that we should learn from the good experience of all countries, socialist or capitalist, but the main thing is still to learn from the Soviet Union.

Now, there are two different attitudes in learning from others. One is a doctrinaire attitude: transplanting everything, whether suited or not to the conditions of our country. This is not a good attitude. Another attitude is to use our heads and learn those things which suit conditions in our country, that is, to absorb whatever experience is useful to us. This is the attitude we should adopt.

To strengthen our solidarity with the Soviet Union, to strengthen our solidarity with all socialist countries—this is our fundamental policy, herein lies our basic interest. Then, there are the Asian and African countries, and all the peace-loving countries and peoples—we must strengthen and develop our solidarity with them. United with these two forces, we will not stand alone. As for the imperialist countries, we should also unite with their peoples and strive to co-exist in peace with those countries, do business with them and prevent any possible war, but under no circumstances should we harbour any unrealistic notions about those countries.

DOCUMENT 15

Birth Control and Planned Families, speech by Madame Li Teh-ch'üan, Minister of Health, to the Third Session of the National Committee of the Second Chinese People's Political Consultative Conference, March 7, 1957.

The text is taken from CB 445. It is a translation made by the U.S. Consulate General, Hong Kong, from the *People's Daily* of March 8, 1957.

Comment. This subject does not fit in obviously with the theme of contradictions and rectification; but the "contradiction" between China's population and China's resources (or between their rates of growth) was and is a key problem for any Chinese Government. And the freer discussion of it was important as evidence that the Party was encouraging a more factual attitude toward such vital issues. The subject never gained a prominent place in the official pronouncements of the Chinese Communist leaders. The question of birth control had nevertheless been the theme of much argument and official propaganda at a lower level.

The turning point in Chinese official policy on the subject was the census of 1953-54, the results of which—including a population estimate of 583.6 million—were published in November 1954. Already in July 1954, the Minister of Health had submitted measures on birth control to the Government for its approval. The deputy Shao Li-tzu was active at the National People's Congress sessions of 1954 and 1955 in advocating intensification of birth control propaganda. In August 1956 the Minister of Health issued directives to all branches of the Chinese health services about the intensification of propaganda and the distribution of contraceptives.

Shortly afterward Chou En-lai, in his speech on the second Five-Year Plan (Document 11), remarked: "To protect women and children and bring up and educate our younger generation in a way conducive to the health and prosperity of the nation, we agree that a due measure of birth control is desirable"—section III, 10(4). The general line of subsequent discussion in Chinese periodicals was that birth control involved no concession to "Malthusianism," but simply a better planning and spacing of families, thus conserving the mother's strength without in the long run diminishing the population.

This is the background of Madame Li Teh-ch'üan's speech. In the words of *China Youth*, May 1, 1957 (ECMM 95), birth control, "once regarded as a noxious weed," should now take its place as "a sweet-smelling flower." From the spring of 1957, for about a year, there were well-publicized and detailed exhibitions on birth control, at least in the major towns of China. These seemed to cease in the summer of 1958, and the general tone of major official pronouncements at the time of the Great Leap Forward (Document 25, below) was that "man is a producer more than a consumer"; there is a labor shortage in China, and therefore, at least by implication, the more Chinese in the world the better. In fact, however, it seems that it was only *public* discussion of the problems of birth control that was damped down and the major public exhibitions that were closed. The final version of the 12-Year Agricultural Plan, for example, as approved by the National People's Congress in April 1960 (see comment on Document 5, above), still recommended birth control in crowded areas, and other references to a continuing but muted campaign of the subject can be found in the Chinese press.

Supplementary material may be found as follows:

(a) General: S. Chandrasekhar, *China's Population: Census and Vital Statistics* (Hong Kong: Hong Kong University Press, 1959); Leon Triviere's May 1957 essay in *Contemporary China*, Vol. II (1958); Leo A. Orleans, "Birth Control, Reversal or Postponement," in *China Quarterly*, July-September 1960. Also, Shao Li-tzu's 1956 speech to the National People's Congress, together with much more material about propaganda for birth control at this time, is given in URS, Vol. 4, No. 12, one of the principal sources being *People's Daily*, July 26, 1956. CB 445 includes further speeches on birth control at the meetings of the National Committee of the Chinese People's Political Consultative Conference, March 1957. CB 469 includes the submission by Ma Yin-ch'u, then Rector of Peking University, to the National People's Congress in July 1957, justifying birth control on a remarkable number of economic grounds. ECMM 128 (*Financial and Economic Research*, February 1957) has a denunciation of Wu Ching-ch'ao for "Malthusianism" and a reference to Chou En-lai's treatment of birth control in his speech to the Eighth Party Congress.

(b) Opening of birth control clinics: ECMM 72 (*Current Events*, December 1956).

(c) Birth control exhibitions in February and March 1957. References in local press are collected in URS, Vol. 7, No. 3.

(d) Propaganda of the Great Leap Forward period. ECMM 142 (*Planned Economy*, June 1, 1958) contains an attack on Ma Yin-ch'u's thesis, but an admission that planned parenthood is needed. ECMM 184 (*Women of China*, July 1959) suggests that birth control propaganda was being conducted down to the end of the period covered by the present volume.

────────────────────TEXT OF DOCUMENT 15────────────────────

At the second conference of the second National Committee of the Chinese People's Political Consultative Conference held in February, 1956, I reported to you that we should actively and energetically accomplish the great and glorious task of improving public health in strict accordance with the 40 articles of the Program for Agricultural Development (Draft), put forward by the Central Committee of the Chinese Communist Party, so that industrial, agricultural and all other workers and their descendents may live in better health and greater happiness. Now a year has passed. Following the decisive victory of Socialist transformation, with the concern and under the leadership of Party and government organizations at various levels, through the efforts of the public health officers and with the support of the broad masses of the people, public health work has won solid achievements and definite progress. Public health departments have not only formulated long-range plans for eliminating disease, but have also mobilized the people to fight against the diseases which are to be eliminated in the plans. Great achievements have been obtained in the fight to prevent diseases including schistosomiasis, filariasis, hookworm, kala-azar, encephalitis, bubonic plague and malaria as provided in Article 26 of the Program for Agricultural Development (Draft). This is especially true of the fight to eliminate schistosomiasis. Under the leadership of the nine-member group of the Central Party Committee for the prevention of schistosomiasis, we have still greater achievements to record. In 1956, 400,000 people were cured of this disease, and there emerged villages and village-groups which had completely eliminated certain species of snails. We have obtained a wealth of experience in prevention of the disease and have increased our confidence that it can be wiped out within a definite period of time.

In regard to the work of herbalists, we should further change our ideas about them and stop despising and ostracizing them. In order satisfactorily to bring to light the fatherland's medical inheritance and to develop the role of herbalists, we have organized more than 5,000 western-style doctors to study Chinese medicine (4,845 of them attended classes during their spare time and 303 in six big cities attended as full-time students), encouraged and organized the engagement of apprentices by herbalists, founded four herbalist colleges, and established 67 herbalist hospitals and more than 1,200 herbalist outpatient clinics.

We have also done much work in regard to our march toward science, scientific research, and public health services including sanitation and prevention of epidemics, medical treatment, women's and children's health, distribution of medicines and medical education. But it should also be stated that the speed of the progress with many of our tasks still lags far behind national construction and the development of objective requirements. Very great problems still exist in the implementation of the policy of emphasizing preventive work and of the policy toward Chinese medicine, in medical treatment, in public health services, in birth control and contraception, and in the training and employment of cadres. Some problems are still very serious. Even in our own organizations, work on public health has not been satisfactorily carried out. As time will not allow me to discuss all these problems, I will just report to you on the problem of contraception, for which all of you have shown special concern.

During the last year, with the interest of various circles in contraception and under their guidance and encouragement, we have laid great attention to this problem and have done a great deal of work. We have actively and extensively developed propaganda on contraception, published popular pamphlets on the subject, printed many pictures for propaganda purposes in various places, given many speeches, held forums and exhibitions and shown projection slides, thus enabling many people to understand more about contraception.

The Ministry of Public Health, in its "directive on contraception" issued in August, 1956, clearly demanded that medical and public health organizations at various levels should all assume the responsibility for giving technical guidance about contraception, and that provincial and municipal leading departments of public health should train cadres for giving such guidance. It also said that outpatient clinics might, according to requirements, be established in big or industrial cities to give contraceptive guidance and to take full charge of developing this work. Many local authorities have carried out a great deal of work in accordance with this directive. Formerly, medicine sales departments could not openly sell contraceptive medicines and instruments, nor even could hospital dispensaries and public health centers, to the inconvenience of the masses. Now such conditions have been changed. The supply of contraceptive medicines and instruments is generally enough to meet the demand. We have amended the provisions governing surgical operations for purposes of induced abortion or sterilization, abolishing the old prohibition of induced abortion except when there was serious danger to health. Thus the provision has been made further to conform to the requirements of the masses of people under changing circumstances.

However, if we look at the matter more closely, these remedies are still very inadequate to the requirements of really planned childbirth. Many people still do not understand the great significance of contraception to national construction and prosperity and to the future happiness of individuals, families and the younger generation. They even believe that contraception is unnatural, or say that to promote contraception is to deal a blow to the new method of delivering babies. These comrades fail to see that our country is a big over-populated country, and that in the course of our Socialist construction various undertakings are being developed in a planned manner. If our population growth is not in accordance with planned childbirth, it will prevent our country from quickly ridding itself of poverty and becoming prosperous and powerful. For instance, taking the rate of our population growth as 2.5 percent, there will be an increase of 15 million people every year and our population will reach over 700 million in the period of the second five-year plan [1958-1962]. Actually, owing to the development of medical and public health work and to the improvement of living conditions, the rate of natural increase will be more than 2.5 percent. As reported in the *Jen Min Jih Pao*, the number of babies born to the 7,000 employees and workers of the Shenhsin No. 9 Cotton Weaving Factory in Shanghai during the last seven years has been more than 7,000. The 180 employees and workers of the Research Institute of Skin and Venereal Diseases directly under the Ministry of Public Health have given birth to 70 babies during the last three years. In these two cases the rate of increase is more than ten percent. With such a high rate of population growth, the increase of our industrial and agricultural production, however rapid, will certainly fail to satisfy adequately the requirements of the increased population. Due to the great increase in the number of children in particular, the number of nurseries, kindergartens and primary schools must also be greatly increased; this will inevitably affect the speed of development of the State industrialization program. The problem has a more serious bearing on the happiness, health, work and training of individuals, families and the younger generation.

Our birth-rate is really very high. As reported in the *Jen Min Jih Pao*, an investigation of 19 State cotton mills in Shanghai, made by Shanghai public health departments, showed that, of the 609 pregnant women workers, 17 percent conceive twice a year, 53 percent once a year on an average, and 22 percent twice in three years. Such frequent childbirth not only imposes a heavy burden upon one's family and affects one's own health, work and studies, but also makes it difficult to look after and bring up the children satisfactorily. Of the 3,213 families in Tungwench'angko and Anfu Hutung investigated by the comrades of a health center in Peking, 643, or 20 percent, each have more than four children. The average monthly income of each of these families is about ¥80, which means, on an average, about ¥13 for each person's living expenses (including adults). The average living expenses for each person will be ¥10 in a family with five children and less than ¥5 in a family with many children. Illness caused by malnutrition is serious. For example, Chao, a worker in the Post Office, who lives in Shunch'eng Street, has a monthly income of ¥70. His wife is 28 and has given birth to six children, some of whom are suffering from rickets while one daughter will become an invalid. Now this woman is pregnant again. Sun, a worker in a joint State-private meat store, who lives in Chinglou Hutung, has a monthly income of ¥40. His wife, afflicted with mental disease, has given birth to nine children (one of whom has been given to another family) and had a miscarriage this year. Although the State, under the present circumstances, can give some relief to such families, they remain in great want and are unable to look after and bring up their children satisfactorily.

Although the living conditions in rural areas are different, the average annual income of an able-bodied worker is only ¥40-¥50, and the problem of frequent childbirth must also be serious. Our 500 million peasants each could have, on an average, three *mow* [half an acre] of land. Now, owing to the growth of population, each can have, on an average, only a little over two *mow*. Thus, it can be seen that birth control, contraception, proper adjustment of the frequency of childbirth, and planned childbirth are not only not immoral, but actually indispensable to morality and the State's responsibility to the people.

Some people hold that contraception is only women's business. There are husbands who do not understand their wives' points of view in desiring birth control. They not only fail to co-operate with their wives, but also quarrel and fight with them; this makes matters even worse.

People who oppose contraception on the ground that we now have new methods of delivering babies, are obviously wrong. Contraception is intended to achieve planned pregnancy and childbirth, while the new method of delivery means that babies are delivered by scientific methods to keep the mother and the baby healthy. We must satisfactorily protect and bring up new-born babies according to the Constitution's provision that "mothers and children shall be protected by the State." If we fail to do so, then we are really immoral and violating the fundamental function of public health work.

Henceforth, in order further to make a success of this task, we must develop propaganda on contraception more intensively, so that everyone fully understands the great significance of planned childbirth to the State, the families, the individuals and the young generation. We must make this propaganda achieve the objective of enabling every family, every man and woman to understand contraception, breaking down all obstacles caused by misunderstandings about it.

We have still not done enough in regard to contraceptive guidance. On the one hand, some people regard childbirth after marriage as a "mystery," which cannot be talked about and is shameful. On the other hand, some public health and medical personnel hold that contraceptive guidance does not belong to the scope of medical treatment and public health services, and that they cannot take the initiative to give this guidance energetically. Henceforth we have to abandon these viewpoints. We should understand that childbirth is a natural physiological phenomenon of marriage and that there is nothing "mysterious" or shameful about it. Proper birth control and planned childbirth are legitimate demands. Public health personnel must break away from the narrow scope of merely curing disease and providing health services and come to regard the giving of guidance in planned childbirth, and the satisfying of this demand of the masses, as their duty. As to the performance of operations for purposes of induced abortion and sterilization, all personnel concerned with women's and children's health services and midwives' work should henceforth make the decision whether to perform the operation mainly on the basis of the wish of the individuals, and limitations on its discretion should be abolished. But this does not signify the promotion of induced abortion, which we are compelled to carry out in certain circumstances. Induced abortion is not only harmful to a woman's health, work and studies, but also cannot achieve the purpose of birth control. In future, we must try to solve such problems as the improvement of the quality of contraceptive medicines and instruments, the increase of their quantities, and the lowering of their prices, so as to enable us to achieve a close co-ordination between this supply on the one hand and our propaganda and guidance on the other to satisfy the requirements of planned childbirth.

COMMENT ON DOCUMENT 16   299

Now I would like to tell you about the decrease of the population of minority nationalities before liberation. As our nationalities areas had been under reactionary rule and imperialist oppression for several hundred years, minority peoples generally had little knowledge of hygiene, many of them were afflicted with venereal diseases, and their birth-rate was low and death-rate was high. Therefore, their population decreased year by year. Take Inner Mongolia as an example. In the early years of the Ch'ing dynasty, the Ikechao League had a population of over 400,000; by 1936 only 8,400 people were left. Before liberation, on an average 87 babies were born every year in Ch'enpa-erhhu Banner in Hulunpoi-erh League, but 113 persons died. According to statistics for 1922, the whole Banner had over 7,000 people, and in 1950 there were little over 4,000.

Since liberation, owing to the energetic development of work to eliminate syphilis and improve women's and children's health, the birth-rate has been gradually raised and population has been increasing markedly. From 1950 to 1953, the population of Ch'enpa-erhhu Banner was increased by 310; this reversed the tendency to population decrease for many years past. Therefore, not only should we refrain from promoting contraception for many minority nationalities, but we should also encourage and help them to increase population.

I should point out here that although contraceptive guidance seems to be a concrete task, it is also a difficult and complicated task, according to our experience gained during the last few years. This is specially true at present when this task is still at the stage of propaganda by issuing general calls and by giving directions and has not yet reached the stage of having strong organization and leadership. Apart from asking public health personnel to make every endeavour, we must also strengthen the concerted efforts of the various social circles. Trade unions, women's federations, Red Cross societies and Youth League organizations all have the responsibility for organizing and promoting this work. The Ministry of Commerce, the Ministry of Foreign Trade, and the Ministries of Industries concerned, must regard the satisfactory supply of contraceptive medicines and instruments as one of their duties. Here I also hope that Party and government organizations at various levels will strengthen their leadership in this work so as to achieve these vital results.

DOCUMENT 16

Report on the Work of the Government by Chou En-lai, June 26, 1957, to the Fourth Session of the First National People's Congress.

The English text is the NCNA translation of June 26 as transcribed in CB 463. The mimeographed text in CB 463 contains many typographical errors. As usual, when it is obvious that an error is only typographical and when its remedy also is obvious, we are correcting it. But when a passage is so garbled that we cannot be sure of the precise language of the translator, we are leaving it alone, as on page 320, thirteen lines from bottom, and page 328, twelve lines from bottom.

Comment. This speech contains interesting comments on "ideological remolding," mentioned by Chou as the fifth major campaign since 1949. It provides an "initial" answer to the question: "whom should the intellectuals serve?" It also contains some further significant admissions about criticism of the Party line in 1955-56, and the state of the Chinese economy. For these, see General Introduction, part IV.

The most important passages, however, deal with the outbreak of anti-Party criticism in May-June 1957 which emerged from the rectification campaign (see the general comment at the outset of the present chapter). Here is the sequence of salient events:

Even before the Party directive on rectification was issued on April 27 (SCMP 1523) the campaign was under way within Party branches and government organizations. Bulletins were issued by the Party's Committee for Central Organs and by the State Council, describing progress in organizing the rectification campaign among Party branches. From about April 20 to May 10, meetings were organized by ministries, provincial governments, and so on, to discuss "internal" contradictions—e.g., between town and country, between collective and individual interests, and between the desire of students to remain at school and of the government to have them engage in manual labor. A particularly thorough report was produced by the Kwangtung Party Committee, which referred, among other "negative phenomena," to thirteen outbreaks of strikes in 1956 (cf. last paragraph of comment on Document 14 above).

In early May, meetings of intellectuals were sponsored by local Communist Party branches to discuss similar questions. In particular, on May 8, at the request of the United Front Work Department of the Party, the "Democratic" parties held a special forum to express views on interparty relations and to criticize the Communist Party.

It was from this meeting, and similar ones within the Democratic parties, that emanated the first major public criticisms of the Communist Party from outside its own ranks. These were reinforced early in June by similar and sometimes violent criticism of the Party from academic and student circles.

Beginning June 8 the *People's Daily* began to hit back in its editorials, accusing "right wingers" of challenging the Party to a class struggle. Meetings of indignant workers throughout the country were reported, and the resolutions of these meetings formed the standard ammunition of the Party's counterattack. By mid-June, the "rightist" spokesmen of the Democratic parties were "confessing" their errors and crimes, and this process continued through and beyond the sessions of the National People's Congress from June 26 to July 15 (Documents 17 and 18 below).

The rectification campaign, which in its original form had applied to the Chinese Communist Party alone, was now transformed into a general campaign of education in the basic principles of "socialism" and a "great debate" on a mass level. From July 26 to at least August 20 a minor terror campaign was conducted by the Party. There were in this period continual announcements of the arrest of counterrevolutionaries plotting to conduct sabotage or overthrow the government; some of these persons were sentenced to death.

Although Chou still spoke about the evils of "sectarianism" and bureaucracy (section IV of his text below), there was from now on an end of any concessions to intellectuals. They became the object of special supervision and suspicion (see comment on Document 20 below). Nevertheless, some of their criticism had struck home and needed to be countered at the highest level. It is, for example, clear from section IV of Chou En-lai's speech that there had been criticism about the absence of any codes of civil or criminal law in Communist China. Chou took this charge seriously enough to defend the government by saying that such things take time and must be preceded by provisional regulations and a trial period.

Supplementary material on the criticism of the Chinese Communist Party voiced by the Democratic parties, intellectuals in various professions, and students is listed in the comment on Documents 17 and 18. On the general economic background, see CB 464, 465, and 468 (reports by Li Hsien-nien, Po I-po, and Foreign Trade Minister Yeh Chi-chuang to the National People's Congress in June–July 1957); CB 469 (Ma Yin-ch'u's memorandum to the National People's Congress); and CB 483 (Li Fu-ch'un's address to the December 1957 meeting of the All China Congress of Trade Unions).

──────────────────TEXT OF DOCUMENT 16──────────────────

Fellow deputies:

It is exactly a year since the third session of the First National People's Congress closed. It has been a year of great changes. During this period, we have won a fundamental victory in our socialist revolution; this has brought about historic and deep-going changes in our social life. There have been tremendous achievements too in the field of socialist construction, and this has made it possible for us this year to fulfill and even overfulfill the First Five-Year Plan for Development of the National Economy. In the course of our socialist revolution and construction, we have gained much valuable experience and learned some useful lessons. All this will ensure the further advance of our socialist cause. Such, in brief, are the great achievements of the past year that will be gloriously recorded in our history.

The State Council has decided that I should make a report on the work of the government during the past year to the fourth session of the First National People's Congress. My report will review the work of the government over the past year and answer opinions expressed concerning government work in the light of the principles put forward in the speech "On the Correct Handling of Contradictions among the People" delivered by Chairman Mao Tse-tung at the 11th enlarged session of the Supreme State Conference. My report will be divided into five parts: 1. The socialist revolution. 2. Socialist construction. 3. The people's livelihood. 4. The basic state system. 5. National and international unity.

I. THE SOCIALIST REVOLUTION

The year 1956 saw virtual completion of the socialist transformation of private ownership of the means of production in our agriculture, handicrafts and capitalist industry and commerce. Peasant households numbering 120 million and handicraftsmen numbering over 5 million went over from individual economy to collective economy. Some 70,000 private industrial enterprises have come under joint state-private management. Nearly two million big, medium-sized and small commercial establishments have been turned into state-private stores, cooperative stores and cooperative groups or transformed into state stores. This is a great socialist revolution, changing the old system of private ownership of the means of production which has lasted several thousand years into a system of public ownership.

Because conditions were ripe and thanks to the correct leadership of the Communist Party and the People's Government and to the efforts of the people in every part of the country, there was no damage to social property, law and order was maintained, and social production suffered no falling off in the course of this great revolution. On the contrary, we achieved enormous successes in various fields of work in the year following the basic victory won in this great revolution.

The natural calamities that struck us in 1956 were not only the worst since liberation, but also the worst in the last few decades. About 230 million *mow* of land was affected and about 70 million people suffered from these calamities. It was indeed a severe test as we were in the first year of launching agricultural cooperation on a national scale. But with the vigorous leadership and support given by the Party and the government, peasants throughout the country turned the advantages of cooperative farming to good account and succeeded in pushing up farm output. The total output value of farm produce in 1956 was some 58,300 million yuan, showing an increase of 2,740 million yuan over 1955 and approaching the target set for the final year of the First Five-Year Plan. Staple food crops (soya beans excluded) totalled 365,000 million catties, showing an increase of 15,400 million catties over 1955 and exceeding the target set for the final year of the First Five-Year Plan. Then came the high tide of agricultural cooperation. We were busy with the organization of cooperatives and what with collecting manure, composting; building water conservancy and other capital construction projects and with our main attention centered on increasing grain output, the growth of some of our auxiliary farm occupations was adversely affected for a time in certain places.

In 1956, cotton and rape-seed were the most severely hit crops and output fell below the level of 1955. But in our first year of agricultural cooperation, except in areas seriously hit by natural calamities, 75% of our peasant households increased their income in varying degrees; only about 10 percent of them suffered a drop in income. Last year the government spent 860 million yuan on precautionary measures against flood, filling breaches in the dykes, restoring dykes, extending relief, and granting loans to those affected by the calamities so that they could begin production anew to help themselves and to tide over the difficulties. From July last year to the present, the government has made an additional allocation of 7,000 million catties of food grain to help people in the stricken areas. Collective efforts and mutual-aid in production among the agricultural producers' cooperatives themselves have also played a very important role in bringing relief to the affected areas.

In 1956, owing to a simultaneous growth in urban and rural capital construction and in production and a sudden increase in the demand for means of production, there was a run on supplies of various materials and equipment, particularly building materials and metal products. In spite of this, handicrafts and joint state-private enterprises increased production and business in 1956. The total output value of handicrafts in 1956 amounted to 11,700 million yuan, an increase of 16 percent over 1955, while the total industrial output value of joint state-private enterprises amounted to 19,100 million yuan, showing an increase of approximately 32 percent over 1955. In 1956, commercial concerns under joint state-private operation, cooperative stores and groups handled 11,100 million yuan of the nation's total volume of retail trade. This was an increase of more than 15 percent over 1955. Within less than 12 months after capitalist industry and commerce had gone over to joint state-private management by the whole trades, the government had already completed the work of assessing the value of the shares held by private owners and fixing the interest rates to be carried by these shares; arrangements were also made as regards the work to be done by private owners and their agents.

As everyone knows, once small-scale production is changed into collective socialist economy, capitalism loses its basis of existence and development. It is clear therefore what the situation would have been like if the government had not followed a policy of non-discrimination and made proper arrangements for private industry and commerce and for their transformation, or if the private industrialists and merchants did not choose to come into the jointly-operated state-private enterprises and so refused transformation during the high tide of agricultural cooperation and handicraft cooperation, and the rapid expansion of socialist economy. There would have been no room for those two million-odd private industrial and commercial establishments to produce, do business and develop. They were sure to be seriously weakened or even squeezed out of business, while the members of their staffs, the workers and numbers of their employees would have been confronted with unemployment and the hardships of finding jobs elsewhere.

Such a situation would have been bad for the people and the state, and worse still for the industrialists and businessmen. That is why ever since the founding of the People's Republic, the Party and the government have brought private industry and commerce into the over-all arrangements of the state, and adopted a policy of utilizing, restricting and transforming private industry and commerce. Since the private industrialists and businessmen realized in what direction the wind was blowing and what the people desired, socialist transformation was in the main completed in 1956 so far as concerns the change in the private ownership of the means of production with private industry and commerce switching over to joint state-private management by the whole trades. It was no mere accident, it was the result of the historical development of our country that the three big socialist transformations of agriculture, handicrafts and capitalist industry and commerce were, in the main, achieved at one and the same time.

With the nation-wide triumph of the bourgeois-democratic revolution in 1949, the revolution in our country entered the stage of socialist revolution. Subsequently we launched five major movements— land reform, resistance to American aggression and aid to Korea, suppression and weeding out counter-revolutionaries, the San Fan (3 anti) and Wu Fan (5 anti), and ideological remolding.

Land reform completely destroyed the foundation of feudalism. The movement to resist American aggression and aid Korea defeated the provocation launched against New China by the American imperialists and smashed the pro-American feelings and worship and fear of the United States that infected a section of our people, especially many of our intellectuals. The suppression of counter-revolution dealt a telling blow to counter-revolutionaries of all kinds, and thereby consolidated the people's democratic dictatorship. The San Fan and Wu Fan movement succeeded in beating back the ferocious attacks of the bourgeoisie, and created favorable conditions for the socialist transformation of private industry and commerce. The ideological remolding campaign provided the opportunity to examine and to criticize many reactionary ideas and gave an initial answer to the question—whom should the intellectuals serve?

It was obvious that without the victories gained in these campaigns, it would have been impossible for us to gain a basic victory in the socialist revolution in so short a time after the birth of New China. These movements were waged in the form of mass struggle under the leadership of the Party. If these struggles did not take such a form, it would have been impossible for us to mobilize the broad masses of our people, to win victories and to steel the masses in these movements, and raise their political understanding, so as to pave the way for the three big socialist transformations. It follows that we should not cast doubts either on the achievements or methods of the five major movements. The victories of the five major movements ensured the smooth and step-by-step development of three big transformations, which in themselves were also carried out in a gradual, planned way.

In the socialist transformation of agriculture, the process of development was from mutual-aid teams to cooperatives of a semi-socialist type and then on to cooperatives of socialist type. In the socialist transformation of handicrafts, the process of development was from supply and marketing groups, the lower form of handicraft cooperatives characterized by scattered production and joint management to the higher form of handicraft cooperatives—from small-scale cooperatives to large-scale ones. The socialist transformation of capitalist industry and commerce went through the process of development from government contracts placed with private enterprises for processing and manufacturing goods, state bulk purchase and marketing of their products, transformation into joint state-private enterprises in individual cases and then to transformation into joint state-private enterprises by whole trades. At the same time, these three socialist transformations were carried out in coordination with each other. Once we understand this process of historical development of the five major movements and the three big transformations and their interrelationship as described above, we shall understand the basic reason why we succeeded not only in carrying on normal industrial and agricultural production but also in developing industry and agriculture during the very first year of these great historic changes that affect the lives of 600 million people.

In the huge mass movements mentioned above, there were deviations and mistakes in the practical work. Some of these mistakes and deviations have already been investigated and dealt with by the government, others are now under investigation. We welcome more criticisms and suggestions from the people of the whole country. Of course in examining deviations and mistakes, we must analyse the subjective and objective causes, determine which of these deviations and mistakes were avoidable at the time and which were not entirely avoidable, or were even impossible to avoid. Only by doing so can we determine clearly their character, extent and scope. We must resolutely correct those deviations and mistakes which were really avoidable at the time and guard against them in future; we should apologize publicly to those people who suffered unnecessarily in the movement. Problems left over from the movements should be speedily handled by the departments concerned.

However, the deviations and mistakes in the movements cannot overshadow the objective need at the time for launching these movements or the main achievements attained. Take for instance the movement for ideological remolding, because it took the form of a mass movement, certain problems were handled in a crude way and, as a result, it hurt the self-respect of certain bourgeois intellectuals from the old society. But this movement really helped the great majority of the intellectuals to pass, in the main, the tests of the socialist revolution. This is proved by the fact that, during the present rectification campaign, the overwhelming majority of the intellectuals support socialism.

Now let us take the suppression of counter-revolution for another example. In the cases dealt with by the government over the past years, the counter-revolutionaries fell under the following four categories:

(1) 16.8% of the counter-revolutionaries dealt with were sentenced to death, because they had committed heinous crimes and public wrath was extremely strong against them. The overwhelming majority of these counter-revolutionaries were sentenced to death between the time of liberation and 1952. These sentences were absolutely necessary at the time;

(2) 42.3% were sentenced to reform through labor; 25.6% of these, having served out their terms, have been released or placed in production jobs, while 16.7% are in custody and being reformed through labor;

(3) 32% were put under surveillance; 22.9% of these have regained freedom of action, and only 9.1% are still under surveillance;

(4) 8.9% were given clemency after arrest and they were set free after some re-education.

From these figures we see that 57.4% of these counter-revolutionaries have been released or are no longer under public surveillance after undergoing reform through labor or after being shown clemency. Thus they have been given the opportunity to lead a new life. As for the remaining ones, they are still undergoing reform through labor or are still under public surveillance. They too will be given the opportunity to lead a new life if they atone for their crimes, abide by the law and honestly go through the process of reform. According to preliminary investigations made by the government, only in a very small number of cases had there been deviations in dealing with counter-revolutionaries, while the overwhelming majority were correctly dealt with. Some persons are of the opinion that over 90% of the cases against counter-revolutionaries had been mishandled. This is sheer nonsense. Chairman Mao Tse-tung has proposed that a review of the work in this movement be made. We believe that the results of the investigations will further prove this point.

The five major movements of the past were either the thorough completion of the democratic revolution, or were an integral part of the socialist revolution. Therefore, one certainly cannot use individual or partial mistakes made in these revolutionary movements to undermine the movements' achievements. Even though mistakes made by some units or in some places may be fairly serious, the achievements of these movements cannot be denied. Whenever our Party and government advocated a certain movement, they always did so to meet some pressing, objective need and only after a careful study had been made and experiments carried out in certain places to gain experience. Furthermore, every movement mobilized broad masses of people to take part and obtained their support.

This guaranteed that the achievements of the movement were the main thing and deviations and mistakes only occurred in individual cases. Some people contend that to say the achievements were the main thing in these movements while there were only individual cases of deviations and mistakes is "doctrinaire," a "ready-made formula" or a "new type of jargon." The fact is that these people put forward their slogans against "doctrinairism," "formulas" and "new jargon" for the purpose of exaggerating the mistakes and denying the achievements so that certain people who lack a firm stand or are unable to distinguish right from wrong would take these deviations and mistakes of an isolated and partial character to mean that they were mistakes of a fundamental and all-pervading character of these movements. In this way, they hoped to achieve their aim of undermining the achievements of our revolutionary movements and opposing our socialist revolution.

When we say that the socialist revolution has triumphed in the main and that the turbulent class struggle waged by the masses on a large scale has, in the main, been concluded, we do not mean to say that class struggle has ended. When we now bring to the fore the question of correctly handling contradictions among the people, we do not mean to say that there are no longer contradictions between ourselves and the enemy. It should be pointed out that at present classes still exist in our country. Although the landlord class and the bureaucrat-bourgeoisie were eliminated long ago, the persons who once comprised these classes are still in the course of remolding themselves through labor and in life itself, and their inherent class ideology and class sentiments have not yet been completely changed. Although the overwhelming majority of private industrialists and businessmen have taken part in joint state-private enterprises, the dual character of the bourgeoisie is still there. This is because they still draw a fixed rate of interest from the joint enterprises, and exploitation still exists in their relationship with the working class. For instance, some people advocate or support a 20-year extension of interest payments on private capital invested in joint state-private enterprises. Others want the 20 years' interest to be paid in one lump sum. Some say that drawing interest on investment is not exploitation but only "income obtained without working for it;" that there is no longer any essential difference between members of the bourgeoisie and members of the working class; and even that "bureaucracy is a more dangerous enemy than capitalism." All this absurd reasoning comes from the profit-seeking greedy exploiter-minded side of the bourgeoisie. It is a smoke-screen for attempts at the restoration of capitalism. The fact that a handful of capitalists have come out with a proposal that state representatives withdraw from the joint state-private enterprises is a particularly glaring sign of their refusal to accept socialist transformation. Does this not show clearly that the bourgeoisie still has a dual character? And does this not show clearly that it is still necessary for the bourgeois elements to continue to remold themselves? The socialist transformation of the bourgeois elements means that we want them to go through a process of self-criticism and gradually change their bourgeois class stand, ideas and sentiments, that is to say, we want them to "cast off their old selves and take on new selves"—to make a change inside out.

This is something that cannot be attained without long years of efforts at remolding. What's bad about this for the great bulk of the industrialists and businessmen who are willing to accept socialist transformation? Is it not a fact that more and more of them are now coming to realize this point? It may be seen from what we have said above that within the contradictions among the people, the antagonistic aspect of the contradiction between the bourgeoisie and the working class still exists at present and we still have a severe class struggle, let alone the contradictions between ourselves and the enemy—that is, contradictions between the people on the one hand and the domestic counter-revolution and foreign imperialism on the other. As everybody has seen with his own eyes, in the present rectification campaign there is both ideological and political struggle. Therefore, while we are correctly handling the contradictions among the people, we absolutely cannot afford to ignore either the presence of class struggle or the contradictions between ourselves and the enemy. It is one of our important tasks to see that the fruits of the socialist revolution are made secure and that socialist transformation is carried forward to completion.

II. SOCIALIST CONSTRUCTION

Socialist construction and socialist revolution in our country are being carried on at the same time. In our First Five-Year Plan for Development of National Economy, we have correctly worked out programs in which construction and transformation are coordinated. And in 1956, along with the upsurge of socialist transformation, socialist construction advanced by leaps and bounds. Both in scale and speed, the economic, educational and cultural development made in 1956 greatly exceeded that in each of the first three years of the five-year plan; in certain branches it even exceeded the sum total of growth made in the three previous years.

To illustrate, let me cite some figures.

While the total value of our industrial output (exclusive of the output value of handicraft industry, same for below) increased by 17,700 million yuan in the first three years of the five-year plan, the increase in 1956 alone amounted to 13,900 million yuan. Because of this rapid development, the total value of industrial output for 1956 reached 58,600 million yuan, exceeding the target set for 1957 by the First Five-Year Plan.

As regards the principal industrial products, while the output of steel increased by a total of 1,500,000 tons in the first three years of the five-year plan, in 1956 alone it registered an increase of 1,610,000 tons. The output of metal-cutting machine tools did not show any marked increase in the first three years over the 1952 figure because of the redistribution of installations and the change of models. But much progress was made by the addition of new varieties and improvement of quality. On this new basis, there was an increase in 1956 of more than 12,200 machine tools over the 1955 figure. Besides, output of electricity, coal, petroleum, chemical fertilizers, cement, and other heavy industrial products also made considerable progress in 1956 as compared with the annual output of the three years. Such important new products as jet planes, trucks, heavy-type power-generating equipment and single-spindle automatic lathes were also successfully turned out in 1956. Because of the favorable conditions afforded by the bumper harvests in 1955, the output of light industry made rapid headway. For instance, while the output of cotton yarn in the first three years of the First Five-Year Plan increased by a total of 350,000 bales, in 1956 it increased by 1,270,000 bales. In the first three years, the output of cotton piece goods increased by a total of approximately 20,500,000 bolts, in 1956 alone the increase was close to 43 million bolts. The output of sugar in the first three years increased by 160,000 tons, in 1956 alone it increased by approximately 110,000 tons.

In spite of grave natural calamities, the total value of agricultural output in 1956, as we said before, increased by 2,740 million yuan, which compared favorably with the average annual increase of 2,380 million yuan of the first three years. With the active collaboration between the state and the agricultural cooperatives, agricultural construction made great headway in 1956. While 36 million *mow* of waste land was reclaimed in the first three years of the First Five-Year Plan, in 1956 alone 29 million *mow* was reclaimed. In the first three years irrigated land was expanded by something over 41 million *mow*; in 1956 alone the figure exceeded 100 million *mow*.

In 1956 about 14,000 million yuan was spent on capital construction, amounting to one-third of the total investment provided for in the First Five-Year Plan, thus changing the state of things when only slightly over one half of the total investment quota for the five-year plan had been fulfilled in the first three years, and bringing the fulfillment ratio up to 86% by the end of the first four years. This ensures the overfulfillment of the capital construction plan for the first five years. In 1956 the newly-added productive capacity of steel in 1956 was 1,420,000 tons; the newly built and rebuilt railways reached 3,108 kilometers.

In line with the rapid development of production and construction, great progress was made in transport and trade in 1956. While the volume of freight carried by modern means of transport throughout the country in the first three years increased by 112 million tons, in 1956 alone the increase was 93 million tons. In the first three years the total retail sale of commercial establishments increased by 11,300 million yuan, in 1956 alone it registered an increase of 6,200 million yuan.

Our cultural and educational work also made great headway in 1956.

It is evident the achievements made in 1956 were tremendous. This equipped the state with fairly adequate power to render assistance to the newly-born cooperative economy and the joint state-private economy thus strengthening the positions of socialist economy and consolidating the success of socialist revolution. This also made it possible for the targets of the First Five-Year Plan to be fulfilled and overfulfilled in a smoother way and prepared favorable conditions for the launching of the second Five-Year Plan.

The 1956 national construction work was, on the whole, properly arranged by the government. There were, however, not a few shortcomings and mistakes, which will be set forth in detail in the reports on the state budget and on the national economic plan to be delivered on behalf of the State Council by vice-premiers Li Hsien-nien and Po I-po respectively. Certain expenditure items in the 1956 state budget and certain targets set in the national economic plan for 1956 were larger than they ought to be. From the financial point of view, expenditure exceeded revenue by 1,800 million yuan in the state budget, 1,620 million yuan was paid out of the surplus accumulated in previous years and contingency funds in local budgets, 180 million yuan was overdrawn from the banks, and there was a slight excess in the issue of bank notes, with the result that about 2,000 million yuan's worth of stock-piled materials was made use of.

In the economic, cultural and educational field, 1,500 million to 2,000 million yuan too much was spent on capital construction, and the increase in the number of workers and employees, in the enrollment of new college and middle school students, and in the wages for a number of workers and employees was too big. As a result, although 1956 recorded a 41% increase in capital goods output and a 22% increase in consumer goods output, there was tension in the supply of both these types of goods, and the national reserve of materials was cut down. The main cause of the tension in the supply of materials was that investments in capital construction were a little too big, the range of projects too wide, which resulted in the increase in financial expenditures, in the total number of workers and employees and their wages, as well as in the consumption of capital goods and consumer goods.

We should make a concrete analysis of our capital construction in 1956. There were a lot of projects the building work of which had been completed in the three years before 1956, and which needed to be equipped with machinery in 1956. There were also a lot of other projects the blue-prints of which had already been drawn up and the preparation for building completed, and whose construction should start in 1956. In addition, a number of new items of capital construction needed to be arranged in 1956 because there was an increase in designing and building personnel and because more and more of equipment could be produced in China. That being the case, the number of items of capital construction was greatly expanded. So far as the projects were concerned, the great majority of them were well planned, although some of them were launched too soon or the building work was carried on too fast. There were also certain items which were not well planned and obviously a mistake. Those items which were begun too soon or advanced too fast indeed caused some losses in 1956, but they are necessary as part of the long-range program of national construction. Some of the items, chiefly non-productive ones, wasted a lot of money, because the standards of quality were set too high. We should take all these as lessons and do our best to avoid them in the future.

TEXT OF DOCUMENT 16

307

It was in the second and third quarters of 1956 that we began to discover the tense situation in the supply of certain materials resulting from excessive investments in capital construction. We adopted certain remedial measures and prevented continued development of the tension in supply. Then we profited by past experience, and in drawing up the drafts of the national economic plan and the state budget for 1957, we reduced the amount of investments in capital construction and suitably increased the state reserve.

The figures in the 1957 draft state budget and draft plan for development of the national economy now submitted to the congress for consideration show that our socialist construction is advancing on a forward-looking and fully sound basis. Compared with the state budget of 1956, the 1957 budget registers an increase of nearly 2% in revenue and a decrease of 4% in expenditure in order to avoid a deficit such as the one incurred last year. The total value of industrial output will increase by 4.5% over that of 1956, amounting to 60,300 million yuan, and that of agricultural production by 4.9%, amounting to 61,100 million yuan. Investment in capital construction will be reduced to 11,100 million yuan, which is 20% less than that for 1956—but is still 1,400 million yuan more than the amount originally fixed for 1957 in the five-year plan, and the total investment for the five years will still exceed that originally provided in the five-year plan by approximately 5,000 million.

For the past five-odd months of this year, the budget and the plan have in general been well implemented. If the people of the whole country will carry out the campaign for increasing production and practicing economy, pursue the policy of building up the country by hard work and thrift and strive to reap a good harvest under conditions when there will be no great natural calamities, we shall successfully reach our various targets set for 1957 and ensure the fulfillment and overfulfillment of our First Five-Year Plan, thus laying the groundwork for our socialist industrialization. A proposal for the second five-year plan for the development of our national economy was put forth by the Chinese Communist Party at its Eighth National Congress. The proposal has been accepted by the State Council and the concrete plan is being worked out by the departments concerned.

It should be pointed out that the great achievements already made and yet to be made in our construction under the First Five-Year Plan are inseparable from the assistance given us by the people and the Government of the Soviet Union. In the First Five-Year Plan period, the Soviet Union designs and equips for us 156 projects, gives our country long-term credits of a large amount on favorable terms, and sends over large numbers of technicians and experts to help with our construction work. Such sincere assistance calls for a renewal of our heartfelt thanks to the Soviet Government and people. There are now still people who attempt to deny the tremendous significance of the Soviet Union's sincere assistance to our country. They are obviously bent on breaking the friendship between China and the Soviet Union, undermining our international solidarity, and so to wreck our socialist construction.

Recently, some people take a different view of the achievements in socialist construction in our country.

Some think that we advanced too hastily all along the line in 1956 in our plan for developing the national economy and that in 1957 we retreated too hastily all along the line. Obviously such a view is incorrect. Our 1956 plan was drawn up in the upsurge of socialist transformation and construction. The basic victory of the socialist revolution fired the enthusiasm of the working people in building socialism. They vied with one another in demanding an increase in production and raising their work quota. The bumper harvest in 1955 provided material conditions for the development of the national economy. At the same time, capital construction, which had been carried forward to the fourth year of the five-year plan, required an expansion in scope. All these explain that the acceleration of the rate of construction was not only necessary but also possible. It was in conformity with these conditions that the 1956 plan took a leap forward and achieved successes in all fields as we have described. It is true that some targets were set too high. But this was a shortcoming rather limited in scope. Take capital construction for example. Even though it exceeded the planned figure by 1,500 million to 2,000 million yuan, the amount made up only 5 percent or 6 percent of the whole year's expenditure, and so it was a shortcoming of limited scope. Consequently, it can by no means be said that construction in 1956 advanced too hastily all along the line.

In 1957, because the crop yield in the previous year was not so good and because the state's financial and material reserves were somewhat reduced, it was wholly necessary that we should slow down to a suitable extent the tempo of construction and build up our reserve so as to make better progress in the future. This was by no means beating a hasty retreat all along the line. We ought to know that nothing develops in a straight line. With the changes in objective conditions, the tempo of development must vary, and quite often disequilibrium will occur. The same is true of the progress of socialist construction. Particularly in our country, which is poor and with a large population, where agriculture is predominant and natural calamities occur frequently, it is unrealistic to expect the national economy to develop at a uniform and even pace every year.

Some people think that our First Five-Year Plan has been completely bungled. They are entirely wrong. Whether viewed from the angle of industrial production, agricultural production, capital construction, cultural and educational work, or finance, our First Five-Year Plan has been a success; it has worked well; it has not been bungled.

If we compare the planned figures for 1957 with the actual figures for 1952, there is to be an increase of 120 percent in the value of our total industrial output, that is, an increase of 33,300 million yuan.

Take the case of steel. The total output for the First Five-Year Plan period will reach 16,300,000 tons. By comparison, in old China (including the northeastern provinces when they were under Japanese occupation) the aggregate steel output for the 49 years between 1900 and 1948 was only 7,600,000 tons. Of course, compared with the industrially developed countries, our present steel production is still very low. Hence, we must continue to adhere to our policy of priority development for heavy industry with sufficient attention to the development of agriculture and light industry.

The total value of output of China's agriculture in 1957, if the plan is fulfilled, is estimated at 26 percent higher than that of 1952, that is, an increase of 12,760 million yuan. Take the cases of grain and cotton. Actual output for the five years between 1952 and 1956 was 1,658,000 million catties of grain and 130 million piculs of cotton. By comparison, the five-year output for the relatively good years of 1932 to 1936 in China before liberation was only 1,300,000 million catties of grain and 60,500,000 piculs of cotton. And don't forget that the 1952 to 1956 period included two bad years of natural calamities.

In the First Five-Year Plan period, we started work on more than 800 big, above-norm industrial enterprises, numerous water conservancy and railway-building projects, the Yangtse River Bridge, and so on. These projects are all on a pretty big scale, involving relatively up-to-date techniques, and among them, the 156 construction projects designed and equipped for us by the Soviet Union are of first-rate quality technically. These projects have already played an enormous role in our socialist industrialisation and agricultural development program during the First Five-Year Plan, and they are bound to play an even bigger role in future.

The building of most of these projects would be unthinkable in old China. Over 8,500 kilometers of railways will have been newly built by the end of the First Five-Year Plan. By contrast, only something over 2,600 kilometers of railways was built by the Kuomintang government in all the 22 years of its rule.

There are also tremendous advances in our cultural and educational work in the First Five-Year Plan period. For example, 280,000 men and women will have graduated from Chinese institutions of higher learning in the course of the plan, providing large numbers of trained personnel for the building of the New China. In old China, only 210,000 graduates were turned out in the 36 years between 1912 and 1947.

Again, take the case of finances. During the First Five-Year Plan period, the government has balanced the budget at the figure of 136,914 million yuan for both revenue and expenditure. Of this, China obtained 3,100 million yuan of foreign loans, the equivalent of only 2.3 percent of the budgetary revenue. This fully demonstrates that our country relies mainly on internal accumulation to finance our huge construction program. Over 60 percent of the budget expenditures in this five-year period is spent on the construction program of the state. The proportion of outlays on economic development and on social, cultural and educational undertakings has increased from year to year, while the proportion spent on administration and national defense has steadily decreased. These facts fully show that our First Five-Year Plan is a plan of peaceful economic up-building and cultural development.

In the course of our large-scale construction work, there has been an improvement in the people's living conditions as a result of increased production. This is a point which I shall speak about later on.

The splendid results accomplished under our First Five-Year Plan are indisputable realities. Those who allege that our First Five-Year Plan has been bungled take a hostile attitude to socialism and deliberately seek to negate the achievements won by the hard labors of our entire people. Such individuals have the greatest dislike for planned socialist economy and a longing for capitalist economy. But their difficulty is that the wide masses of people are not for capitalism but are firmly for socialism.

Some people say that planned purchase and marketing has been a pretty mess. This is a direct attack on the socialist economic system. Socialist planned economy cares for the livelihood of all the 600 million people in China and is fundamentally different from capitalist free enterprise which only permits a small minority to wax rich and live in luxury, while leaving the majority to the dogs. China has a big population and our economy is still very backward, so the supply of consumer goods cannot be plentiful. In agriculture, the harvests may be good this year and bad the next, and often good here and bad there. To make up for this unbalance, in a good year or in bumper crop areas, provision has to be made against the bad years and for less fortunate areas, and also against serious natural calamities or other unforeseen circumstances. In industry and transportation, large-scale construction is proceeding. The urban population is steadily growing.

These are reasons why, in a country like ours, if we do not introduce planned purchase and marketing and reasonable distribution of food grain and other principal consumer goods, we shall be unable to ensure the livelihood of the great masses of the working people, or to carry on socialist construction successfully. The planned purchase and marketing of grain and other principal consumer goods is, therefore, an important policy of distribution in our socialist economy. Four years' practical experience proves that this policy has guaranteed to the people in city and country the supply of necessary consumer goods at fair prices, free from exploitation by private merchants. This has been true even in the years when natural calamities or crop failures happened and in areas seriously hit by them. This policy has bolstered the industrial construction program and ensured market stability, thus helping the successful advance of our socialist cause. How can it be said that planned purchase and marketing has been a pretty mess?

Those who hold such a view are a small minority who only crave for their own ease and comfort or stick fondly to capitalist free enterprise as a means of making a fortune. In criticizing this erroneous view, however, we do not deny certain shortcomings in the carry out of planned purchase and marketing. For instance, in the planned purchase and marketing of grain, for a time, allocation was too liberal, and as a result we had purchased far too much in some areas, and left not enough reserves for the peasants. Another case is the planned marketing of cotton cloth. Since there was an increase in the production of cotton cloth last year, supply to consumers was rather generous. This year as production decreased, we had to reduce the supply a little bit. All these shortcomings in our work are due to our failure to take a long-range view and to plan on the basis of over-all needs. The government will continue to check up on all such mistakes and shortcomings and strive to overcome them.

Some people are against learning from the experience of the Soviet Union, and even say that the mistakes and shortcomings in our construction work are also the result of learning from the Soviet Union. This is a very harmful point of view. We believe that learning from the Soviet Union has been absolutely necessary. The question lies in how we ourselves do the learning. If we do not learn well, the responsibility lies wholly with us. The Soviet Union is the first country in the world to have established socialism and has a rich fund of advanced experience. If we who are engaged in building socialism do not learn from the Soviet Union, are we then to learn from the experience of the United States in building capitalism? In fact, it is exactly because we have conscientiously studied the advanced experience of the Soviet Union that we have been able to avoid taking many unnecessary detours and so gained great achievements in our construction work.

Of course, we should not mechanically copy the experience of other countries; even successful experience must be used with discretion, and in applying such experience care must be taken to see that it is adapted to the actual conditions in our own country. We are now doing what our forbears never did. Before we have had practical experience ourselves, it is not at all easy to select the right kind of experience from other countries, and still harder to adapt such experience to the actual conditions in our country. To sharpen our ability to choose and to apply good experience will take time and perhaps also mean paying a price. If we do our learning well, we can shorten the time required and pay a smaller price. That is why we must continue our efforts and criticize and overcome doctrinaire methods of learning. At the same time, we must also refute the revisionist view that the universal truths of Marxism and the advanced experience of the Soviet Union should all be repudiated as mere dogma. At present, when the rightists are opposing socialism with revisionism, it is of even greater importance that we combat revisionism. It should be positively stated that in the future we must still learn earnestly from the Soviet Union and from all other socialist countries. Of course, wherever possible, we should also learn from the experience of other countries which is useful to the people.

Now I should like to say something about educational reform and the question of "storming the fortress of science."

On the question of educational reform. Any given culture is the reflection in the ideological sphere of a given political and economic system and serves that system. Education in old China was mainly feudal and bourgeois and meant to facilitate the enslavement of the people; it served the small number of people who constituted the ruling class and was a tool of imperialism. Education in New China is basically different from education in old China; it must reflect the new economy and politics of socialism, serve the masses of working people, and meet the requirements of our country in socialist transformation and socialist construction. Therefore, it has been necessary for us to carry out a fundamental reform of the educational system inherited from the old society. In the past few years we undertook such reforms and achieved very good results. This must be affirmed.

In the future, along with the victory of the socialist revolution and the progress of socialist construction, we should continue to carry out certain necessary reforms. In implementing educational reforms, the educational departments have in the past made certain blunders, mainly in rejecting certain factors that were rational in the old educational system, failing to systematically sum up and carry forward the experience of revolutionary education in the liberated areas, and in failing in the course of studying Soviet experience, to adapt it sufficiently to China's actual conditions. These shortcomings must be corrected. But if there are people who, because of these flaws, deny that the achievements in educational reforms are the main thing, or even deny that there was any need for such reforms at all and so attempt to turn the educational system of today back onto the old path of education in pre-liberation China, they will be all wrong.

A rather outstanding question in the reform of education has been the reorganisation of the various colleges and faculties in institutions of higher learning and the reform of teaching methods. In old China, institutions of higher learning, which had to suit the requirements of the imperialists and the reactionary rulers at home, were abnormally concentrated in the big coastal cities; most of them had inflated and overlapping faculties, and their educational aims were too general and vague. The proportion of engineering faculties in the universities and colleges was small and most of the materials used were copied from the capitalist countries. This kind of education could not possibly meet our requirements in building socialism. Furthermore, the international situation in the first few years after liberation and the building of new industrial bases in inland areas both required that some of our universities and colleges be moved into the interior.

That was the background against which the educational departments and the various institutions carried out, during the past years, the gigantic task of reorganising colleges and faculties and of reforming teaching methods. This led to a fundamental change in the features of our higher education and made it possible for our universities and colleges to meet, in the main, the requirement of training personnel for the building of socialism. But shortcomings arose in the process of reorganization and reform. For example, inappropriate arrangements were made for some colleges and universities, the opinions and experience of veteran teachers were not sufficiently heeded. We should carefully assess our experience in this regard, affirm our achievements and overcome our shortcomings. For the future, we should do our utmost to stabilize the situation in our higher educational institutions to facilitate improvement in standards of teaching. We should also steadily improve the present facilities for specialized studies, teaching program and teaching materials, in the light of the actual conditions in our country.

From the things that have come to light recently during the rectification campaign, it can be seen that there is need for special attention to strengthening political and ideological education in the schools. First and foremost, school teachers, who are engineers of the human soul, responsible for training up the next generation should continue their own voluntary self-education and self-remolding on the basis of the ideological remolding they underwent in the past. Much has been achieved in ideological remolding among school teachers in the past, but the rectification campaign has proved that it is not an easy matter for them to arm themselves with the proletarian ideology, for them to be able to take a firm stand amidst tempestuous class struggles, to distinguish clearly between right and wrong and guide the students along the right way. Therefore, they should continue their efforts gradually learning Marxism-Leninism in order to acquire a correct political outlook, and improving their attitude toward labor, gradually making themselves one with the workers and peasants.

Next, educational departments at all levels and school teachers should intensify political and ideological education of the students in accordance with the ideological situation among the students. They should train up the students as personnel for building up the country, loyal to the socialist cause, plain-living and hard-working, combining mental and manual labor. In the past the teaching materials and methods of political education were defective in that they tended to be diverged from reality. We should sum up our experience in this respect and make improvements in the future. Political instructors have done quite a lot of work in the schools over the past few years. They should continue their efforts, raise their own level and play a still greater part.

Let me turn now to the subject of students joining in labor after graduation. Our growing national economy requires that the cultural level of the workers and peasants be constantly raised, with large numbers of cultured and educated youth joining the ranks of the laborers. Since the liberation, the number of primary and secondary schools and higher educational institutions has greatly increased. To meet the pressing national need for the upper and medium categories of construction personnel, the higher education institutions and secondary technical schools took in an especially large number of new students. So in the past few years there arose a situation in which all graduates of senior secondary schools entered the higher educational institutions and most graduates of junior secondary schools continued their studies in the senior secondary schools, with only a small portion of them taking part in industrial and agricultural production. In 1956 in particular, the enrollments in the higher educational institutions and secondary technical schools were a bit too large; the percentage of graduates of junior and senior secondary schools enjoying the opportunity of further education also rose.

It must be pointed out however that this situation was temporary and abnormal. As the state makes proper arrangements in this matter, the situation will gradually normalize. In 1957, both higher educational institutions and secondary schools will enroll fewer students, according to plan. From now on our educational establishments at all levels will be developed steadily on the basis of the development of the national economy. So, on the one hand, more and more graduates of primary and secondary schools will enter schools at a higher level year by year, and on the other hand, an increasing number of them will go into productive labor. This is the only way for our country to have an increasing number of educated manual workers, while the ranks of the intellectuals expand. This situation is a normal and healthy one and will remain so for a long period of time.

Education in old China was monopolized by the landlords and bourgeoisie. Very few working people had an opportunity to enter primary schools, not to mention secondary schools and higher educational institutions, and still less of an opportunity to go abroad to study. Things are fundamentally different in New China. Education in New China is open to the working people. In recent years with the improvement in the living standards of the working people, their desire to send their sons and daughters to school has become more urgent. So, although our educational work has developed in recent years on a scale and at a speed unknown at any time in Chinese history, yet it still cannot meet the ever-increasing needs of the people. Our educational work can gradually expand only on the basis of the development of production; it is impossible to do all good things overnight.

Our educational policy in future should be to train up socialist-minded, cultured and healthy working people. This policy was not sufficiently clear in the past. Graduates of the primary and secondary schools, except for a small number of them who will go on studying in higher schools, should take part in industrial and agricultural production. The higher educational establishments should also improve labor education, and their graduates in general should take part in some kind of manual work; certain systems should be drawn up for this purpose and put into practice gradually. In the past, the educational departments have not paid enough attention to labor education, nor have they adopted any effective measures in this matter. At the same time, hang-overs of the mentality of the exploiting classes, as expressed in the old saying "Every vocation is inferior, only scholars are superior" or "Distinguished scholars are entitled to high government posts," still linger on among the general public and particularly among a number of government functionaries. As a result, an unhealthy situation arises in which quite a number of young persons and students look down on manual work, look down on workers and peasants and are not willing to participate in industrial and agricultural production after graduation.

We must explain very clearly to all students that our country has a bright future only because the working people have become the masters, that labor is the most glorious thing in our country and it is the workers and peasants who have the best future. Young persons and students should regard participation in industrial and agricultural production as the greatest of honors; they should understand at the same time that this task is beset with difficulties. The youth of New China must not allow themselves to be frightened by any hardships they may have to face; they should make up their minds to overcome them and carry on honest labor. Parents of students all over the country and public opinion in general should encourage the students to participate in productive work, particularly in agricultural production. They should continue to criticize the thinking and actions of those parents and government functionaries who look down on manual labor and interfere with the students participating in industrial and agricultural production. The educational departments should thoroughly and yet steadily improve the present educational system, curriculum and teaching methods in accordance with the educational policy just mentioned and on the basis of the educational reform effected in the past few years.

Furthermore, I would like to say a few words on the question of sending students to study abroad. During the last seven years we have sent more than 7,000 students abroad. The general criteria by which students are chosen to be sent abroad are political, scholastic and physical qualifications. This is as it should be. In order to train higher intellectuals loyal to the cause of socialism, we used to stress the importance of examining one's political qualifications when sending students abroad before the basic victory of the socialist revolution—this was absolutely necessary. But at the same time there was formalism in the examination of the students' political qualifications, and there were a few cases where the political character of the student sent abroad proved to be bad. We must draw a lesson from this shortcoming in our work.

Then, too, inadequate attention was sometimes paid to examining the students' scholastic and physical qualifications. We have now decided generally not to send senior secondary school graduates but to send university undergraduates and postgraduate research students abroad to study special courses that are not available at home. In selecting students to be sent abroad, sufficient importance must at all times be attached to examining one's political qualifications, and the shortcomings mentioned above must be overcome. Some people have complained that among the students sent abroad too large a proportion was taken up by the sons and daughters of revolutionary cadres. What are the facts? According to figures available for the 1952-1956 period, of the 6,435 persons who were sent abroad to study, only less than 3.5 percent were sons and daughters of revolutionary cadres. Thus, it can be seen that the complaint mentioned above does not accord with the facts.

The call to storm the fortress of science: in the past year following this call, important headway has been made in the field of science. The long-term program for scientific development, 1956-1967 has been drawn up and a tentative plan put into practice on a trial basis. A plan for the natural sciences has been tentatively drawn up for the year 1957. The State Council's Planning Committee for Scientific Development has become a permanent body. Marked advances have been made in the organization of various scientific research institutions, and the ranks of scientific workers are expanding. The guiding principles have been established for the organizational structure of scientific work. A system of coordination among different branches of scientific work has begun to operate. Some plans have been mapped out while others are being made, for gradually solving the problems of supplying books, journals, apparatus and providing other facilities for scientific work. Equipment for carrying out certain important scientific experiments is also being prepared. An atomic reactor of the heavy water type, with a power output of 7,000 kilowatts and a cyclotron producing alpha particles with 25 million electronic volts energy is being rapidly built in our country with Soviet help. Scientific research has also achieved much during the year. All this has stirred the enthusiasm of our numerous scientific workers to storm the fortress of science. Meanwhile, various departments and local organizations are taking an active interest in the development of science in our country.

While the broad ranks of our patriotic intellectuals are moving on in a surging tide toward science, some people allege that scientific work in China after liberation lags behind what it was in the Kuomintang days. There are even people who say that in the next 12 years the question is not how to attain to the international level, but how to make up what we missed during the last 12 years, as if we were slipping back and as if nothing had been achieved in science since liberation. Can we agree to such a statement? Let us look at the facts:

First, the volume of our scientific work—whether in research personnel, institutions, funds or equipment—is infinitely greater then during the Kuomintang days, though, of course, the present scale is still far from what we need for building our country.

Second, the scientific and technological level nowadays is likewise incomparably higher than in the Kuomintang days. Outstanding is the fact that fresh advances have been made in the research work of many old scientific institutions. A number of new branches of science are being studied, notably some sciences and now technologies that have a direct bearing on industrial construction and the building up of our national defences. New courses have been opened, too, in the schools of higher learning.

Third, scientific work in New China is characterized, among other things, by the close link between science and production. Production serves as a basic motive force in the development of science. During the years of Kuomintang rule, because of the decline in industrial and agricultural production, the scientists had no chance to play their role in production even though they did some research work. In the eight years since liberation, however, the departments in charge of production have sent to the departments of scientific research a great number of problems needing solution in consequence of the expansion of production. In this respect, our scientists have every opportunity to give full play to their ability and have made enormous achievements. But our forces of scientific research are still far from able to satisfy all needs of production.

Fourth, with Marxism providing proper guidance, the social sciences in our country have also made new advances in the struggle to criticize and repudiate bourgeois social sciences. Such advances would be inconceivable in Kuomintang days. Social sciences have a strong class character, and the critical attitude we took toward bourgeois social sciences after the victory of the revolution was absolutely necessary.

Fifth, the ranks of scientific workers are growing fast. Older generations of our scientists, having gone through ideological remolding and done much practical work, have generally raised both their political awareness and their professional ability. With students coming back from abroad, we are strengthening various branches of scientific research. The number of students who graduate from schools of higher learning is a great source of recruits to carry forward science in our country.

In the light of these facts, how can one say that scientific work in New China lags even behind what it was in Kuomintang days? And how can one say that we must make up for what was missed in the past 12 years? Of course, we by no means intend to deny the efforts made and achievements attained by Chinese scientists under extremely difficult conditions in Kuomintang days. We have always regarded the hard-won achievements of these scientists as a component part of China's treasure-house of science. Those who say that science in New China lags behind Kuomintang days are simply denying all that our scientists have achieved during the last eight years and are trying to deny the advantages inherent in our socialist system.

Some people are sceptical about the planning of scientific work. They hold that it is impossible to draw up a long-term national plan for scientific work; and that our scientists must be allowed to work separately and of their own free will. After the basic victory in socialist revolution and during our intellectuals' enthusiastic march on the fortress of science, it was quite necessary to invite hundreds of scientists to put their heads together and work out a blueprint for the development of science in our country charting the general outlines and path for the advance of our scientific work to help the cause of socialist construction. The fundamental task of scientific and technical research is to develop production and conquer nature. Unless we have our existing scientific forces properly organized and geared to the needs of socialist construction and work out a relatively comprehensive, long-term plan, our scientific work would be unguided and we should not be able to achieve the desired results. Such a plan, however, must be subjected to constant supplement and revision, or even to major changes in the light of various new circumstances which may occur. Nevertheless, we should not deny the need for this plan, for if the first blueprints are not made today, we cannot possibly have a more and more comprehensive plan for scientific work in the future. Socialist economy is a planned economy, and our scientific work must be well planned if it is to be geared to the needs of socialist construction. Apart from the work laid down in the state plan, scientists should undoubtedly be allowed to pursue other research work for which they are specially qualified so as to give full scope to the scientists' energies and abilities. But any attempt to oppose planned guidance of scientific research and reduce our scientific work to a state of anarchy is bad both for socialism and for science.

The principles of cooperation must be carried out for the effective development of scientific research in our country. All departments concerned must work in cooperation with each other. The government has formulated and partly put into operation this year rather good coordination programs in the fields of medical science, agronomy and machinery. The result is that large quantities of manpower and materials have been saved for the state and the advance of our scientific work has been speeded up. This method should be widely spread about. Some people support the development of scientific work of their own department, but do not support or ever restrict the development of scientific work in other departments. Often they express their opposition to cooperation in work even to the extent of rejecting the state's national disposition of manpower and resources. This is a serious departmentalist style of work and should be criticized. Unified arrangements should be made concerning the scientific research forces available in our country. On the one hand, there must be an appropriate division of work, and on the other hand, what is even more important, close cooperation. On the one hand, we must "let a hundred schools of thought contend," and, on the other, we must combat factionalism which hinders cooperation. Our scientific research setup should comprise four elements: the Chinese Academy of Sciences, universities and colleges, research bodies under the various central industrial departments and local research bodies. Under this system the Academy of Sciences becomes our leading academic organ and the center of research work on key subjects, with universities and colleges, research bodies under the central industrial departments (including factories, mines and laboratories) and those under the local authorities as a broad base for our research work. This is a question of principle in the organization of our scientific workers. We call on the responsible cadres of all departments concerned to make serious efforts to cultivate a spirit of cooperation and popularize the coordination program, to speedily rectify bad, departmentalist styles of work.

The progress of scientific work in New China is a result of the efforts of Chinese scientists, under the leadership of the Chinese Communist Party and the People's Government. Some people hold that the Chinese Communist Party and the People's Government are not able to direct scientific work. They say that, at present, many of the leaders are not scientists, and that "laymen" are not qualified to lead the "experts". Others even hold that the existence of the State Council's Planning Committee for the Development of Science is a manifestation of distrust of our scientists. The Chinese Communist Party and the People's Government have at all times taught their cadres to learn all the time what they do not understand in the course of their work, gradually raising their vocational level to do a good job. There are two aspects of leadership over scientific work: leadership in science and leadership in political ideology and administration. In dealing with academic questions, we have never approved of intervention by administrative orders. Our policy is "let a hundred schools of thought contend", that is, solving academic questions through free discussion among scientists and through objective practice. Leadership by the Party and government over scientific work is more necessary in the spheres of political ideology, guiding principles, policies, plans, etc. The facts of the last eight years prove this. The State Council's Planning Committee for the Development of Science is the very institution responsible for the guiding principles, policies, plans and important measures for scientific work as well as for unified planning of the work to be undertaken by the Academy of Sciences, universities and colleges, and research institutes under central and local authorities. The 12-year plan for development of science was the result of the collective efforts of hundreds of Chinese scientists, while most of the members of the Planning Committee are themselves scientists. How can the existence of the committee be described as manifestation of distrust of our scientists? If the idea that the "laymen" are not qualified to lead the "Experts" implies that only specialists are qualified to lead in their own field, this not only negates political leadership over science but is tantamount to ruling out the possibility of any unified leadership in scientific research. Because scientific pursuits are highly specialized, and there could not be a leader of scientific workers who was himself a master of all branches of science. Such an idea can only show the seeds of disintegration in the ranks of scientific workers and is therefore harmful to the development of scientific work.

III. THE PEOPLE'S LIVELIHOOD

Since the liberation, along with the rapid restoration and development of industrial and agricultural production in our country, there has been a marked improvement in the living standards of the broad masses of the people. First let us look at the living conditions of the peasants who make up over 80 percent of our population. Since the liberation the total value of our agricultural production has risen from year to year. In 1949 it was 32,600 million yuan. By 1956 this had risen to 58,300 million yuan, a 79 percent increase. The increase in the total value of agricultural production has been accompanied by increased purchasing power on the part of the peasants. In 1950 their purchasing power was 8,100 million yuan. By 1956 it had risen to 19,100 million yuan—an increase of 136 percent. The consumer goods supplied to the peasants by the state also increased correspondingly. Between 1950 and 1956, the state supplied three times as much cloth, 2.9 times as much rubber shoes, and nearly twice as much salt, 3.3 times as much sugar, 12 times as much kerosene, and 2.4 times as much cigarettes. Such a great increase in the output and consumption of our over 500 million peasants was never seen in old China.

Next, let us examine the living conditions of the workers and employees who form the second largest group in our population. At the end of 1949 there were about 8 million workers and employees in our state organizations, state and private enterprises and public services. By the end of 1956 their number had increased to 24 million, including about 3 million comprising those formerly in private enterprises who are now in state or joint state-private enterprises as well as cadres working in rural areas. Thus in seven years we have found jobs for about 13 million people, something unheard of in China in the past. In 1952 the average wage for all workers and employees was 446 yuan a year, but in 1956 this had risen to 610 yuan, an increase of nearly 37 percent in four years. Such a rate of increase was also unknown in China in the past. Some people close their eyes to such marked change in the people's living standards in New China, and say that our living standards have gone down since the liberation. But as workers and peasants constitute the vast majority of our people, and their living standards have improved, how can we say our people's livelihood has deteriorated? It should be admitted that in the case of a small number of highly qualified intellectuals and a small number of workers and employees, although their livelihood now is better than during the years just before liberation, their standards of living have not yet regained the level before the outbreak of the War against Japanese Aggression. But, considering the living standards of the masses of workers and peasants are still rather low, it is not possible to raise the living standards of the intellectuals too much or too rapidly. As for the exploiters in the old society who constitute only a small minority of the population, it is quite proper that their living standards should be lower than their pre-liberation level. In a society ruled over by exploiting classes, a minority of exploiters lead a life of unbridled luxury, while the masses of the working people who create the wealth of society are poor and half starved. Only in our new socialist China do we consider the interests of the people as a whole, first ensuring the needs of the working people who constitute the vast majority while at the same time taking into account the legitimate needs of the other sections. Those who say our people's living standards have dropped since liberation either take exceptional cases as typical of the whole and pass uncritical judgement accordingly, or are thinking only of a minority of exploiters and not of the working people.

China is an agricultural country, a poor country, economically and culturally backward, with a large population and a small area of arable land. This being so, our living standards are very low compared with those of highly industrialized countries. Though our industry and agriculture have been rapidly rehabilitated and developed since the liberation, the increase in output per capita is still rather slow. Increased production and national wealth are the material base for improving the people's livelihood. The rate of improvement of living standards depends on the rate of development of production, among which the rate of increase of the production of consumer goods, in the present conditions of our country, depends to a fairly great extent on the rate of increase of agricultural output. Ours is a country of 600 million people. If everyone's purchasing power increases by one yuan per year, that means an increase of 600 million yuan for the country, and the state must provide an additional 600 million yuan worth of consumer goods. If people spend this money on food, that means supplying an additional 6,000,000,000 catties of grain. If they spent it on clothes, that means supplying an additional 20 million bolts of cloth—or increasing the production of cotton by 2 million piculs. Between 1952 and 1956 our output of consumer goods increased on the average each year by about 3,000 million yuan. If we deduct the small amount to be kept in reserve and the part consumed by the increased population each year, only four yuan per head per year could be used to improve the people's livelihood. These figures indicate that the improvement in living standards each year is limited. If this limit is exceeded, we shall have a shortage of consumer goods and a disparity between our purchasing power and the supply of goods, which will make prices unstable. This being so, the living standards of our 600 million people can only be improved gradually on the basis of increased production, and we must not demand too rapid an improvement. Some people do not consider these factors, however, but think once we enter socialism our living standards should immediately rise instead of realizing that this can only be achieved gradually after a long period of hard work and arduous construction. In the past we did not make this sufficiently clear to the people, and that was a mistake. But there are other people who keep complaining because China's living standards are so low and keep praising the American way of life. They are dreaming of pulling China back to the old semi-colonial road, so that they can once more lead the life of an exploiting minority.

Some people say there is too great a discrepancy between the living standards of our workers and peasants. Is this in accordance with the facts? We should admit that there is a difference between their living standards; but when we compare their living conditions we must take into account their different historical background and the differences between town and country life. In the old Chinese countryside, the majority of our peasants were ragged and were half famished, feeding on husks for six months out of the year. Since the liberation, as a result of land reform and the cooperative movement, 20 percent–30 percent of our peasants today have a little more than enough, about 60 percent make an adequate living, and 10 percent–15 percent are short of food and clothes and need aid from the state or the agricultural producers' cooperatives. The average peasant's net income from agricultural production for the country as a whole is about 70 yuan a year, so that each peasant household gets about 300 yuan. The net income from agricultural production referred to here includes not only the income distributed to the peasant by his producers' cooperative, but also the income derived from his private-run agricultural productive work.

Of course, the income of peasants varies in different parts of the country, that of a peasant in arid areas is less than 70 yuan, and that of a peasant in fertile areas is more than 70 yuan. In 1956 the average yearly wage of workers and employees was 610 yuan, more than twice the income of a peasant household. If we simply compare these figures, there does appear to be too great a discrepancy. But if we take into consideration the different conditions in villages and towns, that puts a different complexion on the matter. To keep yourself clothed and fed in the country you need on the average only five yuan a month, while to live at a comparable standard in the city costs 10 yuan. So we believe although there is a difference between the living standards of workers and peasants it is not too great. Moreover, as the labor productivity of the workers is much higher than that of peasants, it is proper that there should be a reasonable difference in income. During the wage adjustments in the past, we set too high a rate of pay for porterage, odd jobs, apprentices and certain part-time work. This was a serious mistake and we should correct it. The peasants were justified in complaining that the wages of such workers were too high; but this has nothing in common with the malicious attack of those who deliberately exaggerate the disparity between the living standards of workers and peasants in order to sow discord between them and weaken the worker-peasant alliance. In future, in fixing the wages of the categories of workers mentioned above, due consideration must be paid to the conditions of the peasants in that area, and adjustments must be made so that their living standards are proportionate. We should also educate the workers so that they understand that industry cannot develop in isolation. For the raw materials and market for our industry and the articles they need in their daily life, they must rely to a large extent on increased agricultural output and the support of the peasants. While the peasants' living standards cannot rise too fast, the workers should not demand unduly rapid improvement in their livelihood.

Some people say that there is also a great discrepancy between the life of high-ranking and low-ranking employees. This is correct if it means that our country is very poor, the living standards of workers and peasants are still very low, and therefore there should not be too great a difference between the pay of high-ranking and low-ranking employees. The criticism is wrong, however, if it aims at denying that there should be a reasonable difference in pay for different types of work. Under the socialist system, the principle suited to the productive forces is that of "to each according to his work". In a socialist society there should still be differences between the payments given by the state for simple and complex work, as well as between labor by the hand and by the brain. It would have a bad effect on the raising of productivity and the improvement of vocational and technical skill if we were to abolish such differences. So on the one hand we should oppose undue discrepancies in wages, and on the other hand oppose equalitarianism. Last year, during and after the wage reform, in order to suitably reduce the discrepancy in wages between high-ranking and low-ranking employees, the state took steps to control or lower the salaries of heads of enterprises and high-ranking personnel of state organizations. In future, we shall continue to adopt measures to readjust and solve step by step the irrational features in salary, housing and medical service enjoyed by the high-ranking personnel as well as other irrational features left over from the "supply system". As for those who deliberately exaggerate the differences in the treatment of higher and lower employees, or go so far as to describe the leading personnel as "exploiters," they are either extremely childish and ignorant or malicious.

I wish now to express some views on labor employment, the wage system, the apprentice system and the people's cultural life.

Let us first take labor employment. As I have said above, as a result of the efforts made during the years since the liberation, there has been an increase of 13 million in the ranks of the country's workers and employees and the unemployed left over from the old society has been basically taken care of; as to the higher intellectuals, we have undertaken a registration of the unemployed and from now on we shall year by year find them work suited to their special qualifications and living conditions. Since the liberation, our people have had a secure livelihood, public medical and sanitary services have improved, and social relief and welfare work have expanded; thus there has been a very great increase in the population. But because our industry is still very backward, and we have already increased the number of workers in the state organizations and industrial enterprises unwarrantedly, in future we can only take on new workers each year when they are absolutely needed to develop the work and increase production. For a long time to come, therefore, the main field for labor will still be on the land. The handicraft industries and service trades also play an auxiliary part in labor employment. Recently local labor offices in Shanghai, Kiangsu and Kwangtung have taken active steps appropriate to the local conditions to find employment for some 10,000 persons in handicraft industries, service trades and other auxiliary public services. This is a good example for all to follow. In future we should continue to encourage the people themselves and various social organizations to devise means to broaden the scope of employment, and help the government solve the unemployment problem. In social welfare work, we should also make full use of the resources of the people and popular organizations, to encourage mutual aid among them, and to set afoot various forms of welfare work. The methods of mutual help and mutual relief publicized recently by the All-China Conference of Workers' Dependents have proved efficacious, and these should be popularized.

Next we come to the problem of the wage system. This is a very complicated problem involving production and distribution. It expresses the relationship between different sections of the working class, different enterprises, different localities and different professions. It also expresses the relationship between the industrial workers and the peasants, between accumulation and consumption, between collective and individual interests, immediate and long-range interests. We should properly adjust these different relationships, but even after we have solved the old inequalities and contradictions, there will be new inequalities and contradictions; so we shall have to readjust and solve these problems incessantly.

Just after the liberation, the wage system in our country was most chaotic. The wage system left over from the old regime was extremely irrational, with great gaps between high and low grades, and between what was considered important and unimportant. It reflected the abnormal development of the semi-colonial economy and the competition between different economic groupings and the ruling clique in old China. At the same time, many old cadres and workers were still provided for by the supply system of the old liberated areas. This confusion in the wage system was quite unsuited for state organizations and state-owned enterprises under unified control. After several reforms in the wage system in 1950, 1952 and 1956, we have begun to establish a wage system which is on the whole suitable for our conditions. However, it is still far from perfect. There are still unrealistic and unfair practices in the grading of wages, in the system of piece work wages, in the apprentice system, the system of subsidies and rewards, as well as in the regulations governing the workers' welfare, as labor insurance, free medical service, welfare funds and so forth. We should continue to make readjustments here. There were also many shortcomings in the work of wage reform. While learning from the advanced experience of other socialist countries in this respect, we did not combine it enough with the actual condition in our country. We did not carefully study what was useful in our former wage system, and even simply ignored them. We should learn a lesson from this.

As regards the apprentice system, it was right to do away with the bad feudal rules of pre-liberation days in our apprentice system, but there was much good in it, such as the term of apprenticeship, the techniques to be learnt, the pay for apprentices, and the rewards for their masters. We should make a careful study of these things, and adopt some of them. Our present method of short-term training classes for technicians and short-term training of apprentices should be reconsidered and amended. As experience shows, the technicians trained in short-term courses usually have a very limited technical knowledge, and lack the ability to work independently or do different types of work. At the same time, because the apprentices' wages are unduly high, they are promoted so fast after their apprenticeship, and the examinations for promotion are not sufficiently fair, it is easy for young workers to look down on practical experience, and some of them have become conceited. They consider it very easy to master technical knowledge, and have not enough respect for the technical experience acquired by old workers through hard study and practice. They are often too proud to ask for the old workers' advice or learn from them. This tendency has hampered the unity between young and old workers and damaged the relationship between masters and apprentices. We must patiently educate these young workers, and make them realize that all-round technical experience cannot possibly be acquired in a few months or even in a few years: one can only master it gradually through long practice, continuous hard work and diligent study. Our old workers are among the treasures of our country, they have a wealth of technical skill as well as of political and social experience. After undergoing long years of exploitation and oppression in the old society, they now know happiness and equality in our new society; so they understand most keenly how to value and safeguard the fruits of our revolution. Young workers are their successors in our socialist construction, and the creators of a wonderful life in future. But being young they lack political and social experience, so their best way to raise their class consciousness and technical skill is to learn from the old workers and to steel themselves in the course of work. In the villages, too, we should teach the young peasants to respect the old peasants, and learn humbly from their experience both in farming and political life. Among the intellectuals, we should teach the young to respect old scientists, educationists, engineers, physicians, writers and artists, and humbly study the knowledge and experience which they have accumulated through years of hard study.

We come now to the question of cultural life. China is culturally backward. More than 70 percent of our total population is illiterate. Directly after the liberation, we actively campaigned against illiteracy and popularized education. Primary school pupils have increased from 24 million-odd in 1949 to more than 63 million in 1956. From 1949 to 1956 more than 22 million illiterates in various parts of the country have learned to read and write. The money spent by the government on popular education between 1951 and 1957 amounts to nearly 4,900 million yuan, more than 24 percent of the total allocations for culture and education, and more than 54 percent of the money spent on education in general. This development is fairly rapid. Still we cannot yet satisfy the demand for all children of school age to enter school. Apart from state-run schools, we should take energetic measures to encourage schools run by the community or by private individuals, and make full use of the resources of public bodies and of the people to supplement the efforts of the state. In the past our campaign against illiteracy suffered from fluctuations, while in our primary and kindergarten education there were cases where mistakes were made in giving them excessive advantages. We are now correcting these mistakes. There has been a great improvement too in the cultural life of our people, and in future we must, under the guidance of the principle of "letting a hundred flowers blossom" and "learning from the old to create the new," do even more to bring the initiative and creative genius of the cultural and artistic workers and of the people into full play. The state can only run a few experimental artistic, cultural or athletic organizations, which should eventually become self-supporting. Most of the cultural and artistic organizations of various kinds should be encouraged to become undertakings run by the cultural and artistic workers themselves. Our experience shows that complete reliance on the state as in the past, is inappropriate. More important still is the development of spare-time cultural and athletic activities among the people. Those who take part in such activities, whether state-run, community-run, or organized by the people in their spare time, should learn from past experience and from one another, so as to raise their standard and gradually meet the cultural needs of the people.

We have not done too little either in the past few years to improve our medical and health services, as well as our preventive medicine. The ranks of our medical workers have rapidly grown, and great improvements have been made in sanitary work in our cities and countryside, as well as in individual hygiene. Some of the most dangerous infectious diseases, such as the plague, cholera and smallpox, are virtually under control. However, in leading health campaigns of a mass character, our medical departments still sometimes blow hot, blow cold. And the medical services still embody many irrational features or practices which inconvenience the people. Among our medical and sanitary workers, we still find cases of lack of unity and mutual respect. From now on, these shortcomings should be resolutely overcome; we should firmly adhere to the mass line, thoroughly reform our medical work, give full play to the doctors of traditional medicine, and strengthen the unity of medical and sanitary workers, so as to ensure the further development of our national health.

The aim of the socialist revolution and socialist construction is to increase production and raise the people's living standards, so that all workers in our socialist society may enjoy a prosperous, cultured, happy life. This has been the great ideal the working people of our country have looked forward to for decades. Our country is still very poor, however. We are still culturally backward and confronted with many difficulties, and we lack experience. If we want to shake off poverty and backwardness for good, and build China into a socialist country with a modernized industry and modernized agriculture in which our people will enjoy a happy life, we shall have to battle long and hard. Victory in this battle is not a question of a few years but of tens of years. From the leadership downward we must encourage a hardworking thrifty and simple way of life, and maintain and improve upon our fine revolutionary tradition of struggling arduously and perseveringly. And we of the elder generation must teach the young folk, so that they understand that a good life can be achieved only by our own tireless labor.

IV. THE BASIC STATE SYSTEM

Ours is a people's democratic dictatorship, led by the working class and based on the worker-peasant alliance. In our country, all power belongs to the people. The people exercise state power through the National People's Congress and local people's congresses of all levels. Democratic centralism operates in these and other state bodies. The Constitution expressly lays it down that these constitute the basic system of our state. Our state system is the superstructure which rests on the socialist economic relations of our country. It is by virtue of this state system that we have secured a fundamental victory in the socialist revolution and ensured great triumphs in socialist construction. We must continue to rely on this state system to ensure success in building a socialist society in China. It therefore stands to reason that we will allow no wavering on this question of the basic state system of our country.

But, of course, this does not mean that there is no room for perfecting, improving or developing various aspects of our state system. On the contrary, improvement and development is often necessary. Social institutions under socialism in our country are still in their infancy and survivals of old relations of production are bound to find expression in some parts of our state apparatus. But there can be no doubt that as the days pass remnants of these old relations of production will go out of existence, while socialist relations of production will fully establish themselves and make still greater advances. Therefore, certain forms of organization and methods of work in our basic state system must be constantly improved as our economy advances and changes take place in the political situation. But it is only a short time since we embarked on the building of socialism in China and our experience is very limited, so the perfecting of the basic state system of our country can come about only as a result of practical work in socialist construction and through a gradual building up of experience.

All the more, then, do the various institutions and forms of organization in political, economic, cultural and other fields devised according to our basic state system, need constantly improving as conditions change. For instance, in the sphere of relations between the central and local authorities, in the early days of the liberation, military and political commissions (or administrative committees) were set up for the greater administrative areas for the sake of better administration. But by 1954 we abolished these organizations to meet the need to strengthen centralized management as called for by a planned economy. Then in the last two years, as regards certain matters, the central authorities were found to have taken too much into their own hands; there were shortcomings resulting from rigidity in administration. To get rid of these shortcomings we began an examination of the government structure. The government has now decided to make suitable readjustments expanding the powers of local authorities, so that their creative initiative may be fully developed under the coordinating leadership of the central authorities, and thus advance the cause of socialist construction. All these changes are obviously necessary and appropriate. This example is enough to explain why we must constantly improve our institutions and forms of organization as objective conditions require, otherwise they will not fit in with the economic base, fail to serve its needs, and even hinder economic development.

As things are at present, there is still much to be desired, and, as far as various aspects of our institutions are concerned, here and there one can find shortcomings. This may be due, on the one hand, to the fact that timely changes have not been made when called for by the situation in certain institutions which at the time of their establishment were found to be needed an suitably organized. On the other hand, this may be due to the fact that a thorough study of the problems on hand was not made at the time, and as a result the institutions established were not entirely in keeping with objective requirements, or even wrongly established. Again, certain flaws in our institutions have arisen because insufficient consideration was given to the practical conditions of our country when we were learning to adapt the up-to-date experience of other socialist countries. Wherever shortcomings and mistakes are found in our institutions, the departments concerned under the State Council must consider useful suggestions from any quarter and work out ways to improve and perfect our institutions, or abolish such as are no longer suitable.

I should like to make a few observations on the question of the legal system in which many people have taken an interest. It must be said that while the legal system in our country today is not all it should be, neither is it a question of "there is no law to go by," as some people make it out to be. After the establishment of the Chinese People's Republic, and in the years immediately preceding and following the proclamation of our Constitution we have drawn up and put into force many important laws, such as the Trade Union Law, Labor Insurance Regulations, Land Reform Law, Regulations Governing National Regional Autonomy, Electoral Law, Marriage Law, National Service Law, Model Regulations for Agricultural Producers' Cooperatives, Regulations Governing Punishment for Corruption, Regulations Governing Arrest and Custody, etc. Moreover, the government has, as the need arose, devised rules and regulations for separate localities and issued many decisions and directives. All these, in fact, have for the time being served the purpose of law.

In the early days of the foundation of our state, and throughout the period of transition, political and economic conditions changed rapidly, and it was, and continues to be difficult to draw up laws of a fundamental character suited to long-term periods. For instance, it is difficult to draft the civil and criminal codes before the completion, in the main, of the socialist transformation of the private ownership of the means of production and the full establishment of socialist ownership of the means of production. Under these circumstances, it is necessary and proper for the state to issue provisional regulations, decisions and directives as terms of reference for general observance. It is only when these regulations, decisions and directives have proved effective that we can go ahead to sum up experience on which to draw up long-term laws. The laws of capitalist countries were not complete either in their early stages, and it was years before they were drawn up. Socialist transformation of the private ownership of the means of production has now been completed in our country and socialist ownership of the means of production has been established. We have also acquired experience in various fields of work. So it is now possible for us to draw up various socialist laws in the light of this experience and after a review of existing laws and regulations. For example, a draft criminal code is now ready and a civil code and regulations governing public security are in process of being drafted by the departments concerned.

Certain right-wing elements have come out with quite a number of utterances of a destructive nature, on the pretence of helping the Communist Party with its rectification campaign. Not a few such views are aimed directly against the basic state system of our country. The right-wing elements have taken their stand on bourgeois democracy to attack our state system. They slandered the people's democratic dictatorship, describing it as the root of all mistakes and shortcomings. They tried to negate our achievements and magnify such shortcomings as occurred in our work for the purpose of defaming our state system. They attempted to set up apart from the National People's Congress,—the supreme organ of state power in our country—certain other organs of state power, such as what they called a "political planning council," a "rehabilitation committee," and such like. What they are really trying to do is to get our state power away from the vanguard of the working class—away from the leadership of the Communist Party. They dressed up these destructive views of theirs in all sorts of ways, in an attempt to deceive those who have not been able to see through their disguises. Of course, these anti-socialist views must not be confused with criticisms made in good faith. We welcome criticisms of shortcomings and mistakes offered with the purpose of perfecting and developing our socialist system. But what the right-wing elements are in fact trying to do is to drive our country from the path of socialism to the path of capitalism. This will not be permitted by the broad masses of the people.

Our state system has two functions: democracy and dictatorship. Some people believe that with a basic victory in our socialist revolution dictatorship no longer has a function to play. This is wrong. It is wrong because there are remnants of counter-revolutionaries in our country who are still trying to engage in wrecking activities at every opportunity. And among those who come from the exploiting classes there are still persons who engage in activities to undermine the cause of socialism. Furthermore, there are still robbers, swindlers, murderers, arsonists, gangs of hooligans and all sorts of bad characters who attempt serious violations of law and order. In particular, there is the fact which we must not for a moment forget: American imperialism and the Chiang Kai-shek clique are constantly trying to organize armed provocations against us and sending agents and spies to carry out wrecking and subversive activities in our mainland. In these circumstances, we must not weaken the functioning of the dictatorship in our state system; we must improve the way of the dictatorship functions and, continue to consolidate our defences and safeguard the cause of socialism.

As laid down in the provisions of our Constitution, citizens of our country enjoy a wide measure of democracy and freedom. With socialist construction striding forward, these civil rights will be further extended and still more adequate safeguards will be provided. In capitalist countries, only the exploiting class, which constitutes a very small section of the population, enjoys freedom but not the broad mass of the working people who have no real freedom to speak of. It is entirely different with the socialist states; guarantees are devised to see that the broad masses do enjoy the freedoms laid down in the Constitution, while the counter-revolutionaries, constituting only a small part of the population, are deprived of their freedom. The right-wing elements say there is far too little freedom in our country, and speak as if there is freedom only when facilities are granted and guarantees are provided by the state for those who want to oppose the basic state system laid down in the Constitution, and to oppose socialism in words and deeds. It is quite clear that the people will not agree to give them this sort of freedom.

The right-wing elements have also chosen to attack our electoral system. They say that only direct elections of the kind held in capitalist countries can be described as the most democratic. As a matter of fact, although some capitalist countries have so-called universal, direct suffrage the bourgeoisie in power has always tried to manipulate things by every means, especially by using its purse and administrative measures to control elections in order to preserve their rule.

In our country, the opposite is the case. Here the electoral system safeguards first of all the democratic rights of the workers, peasants and other working people; then it gives consideration to members of the bourgeoisie, which accounts for only a small part of the population, and other individuals who are patriotic. This is so that they too can have a certain number of representatives in our organs of state power.

At present, direct elections are the rule at the lower level while indirect elections are held from the county level upward. This way of conducting elections is judged a better form of democracy suited to conditions in our country today. But this does not exclude the gradual adoption, when conditions are ripe, of the method of direct elections also to levels above the county. During elections, it has been found suitable to draw up a joint list of candidates as a result of consultations between the Communist Party, other political parties and people's organizations. On this question of candidates the fact that the number of candidates is the same as the number to be elected is a result of joint consultations. Future practical steps in this matter will, as in the past, be decided by joint consultations between all interested parties. In a word, the electoral system of our country is such that it really serves to protect the democratic rights of the greatest number of people, it unites all forces that can be united for the cause of socialism; it is not a travesty of elections designed to defraud the people and protect the interests of the few.

The suffrage is only one of the democratic rights enjoyed by our people. The democratic life of our country has a much richer content than this. The Constitution provides: "All organs of state must rely on the masses of the people, constantly maintain close contact with them, heed their opinions and accept their supervision." It is precisely this mass line that our state organs follow in their work. Many important laws are fully deliberated upon and discussed by the masses while they are being drawn up. The state economic plans were finalised only after control figures or draft plans put forward by the departments concerned had been discussed by the rank and file members of production units at the basic levels. To encourage the masses of workers and staff to take an active part in managing enterprises and in exercising supervision over administrative work, we are promoting a system of workers' councils in the enterprises. In agricultural cooperatives, we are instituting a system of general meetings of members and management committees in accordance with the policy of democratic management of cooperatives.

Citizens of our country are constantly putting forward criticisms and suggestions regarding various aspects of government work through their deputies, through the supervisory organs, people's organisations and through newspapers and magazines. They also often make known their views to the leading organs at various levels by direct correspondence or by personal calls. It is through these methods that government organs are kept informed at all times of the opinions of the people and improve their work accordingly. Leading government organizations, however, are not doing very satisfactory work in dealing with the people's criticisms, suggestions, calls and correspondence. We must bring about a rapid change in this situation and demand that government organizations at all levels attach great importance to this work. The current rectification campaign is another vivid manifestation of the democratic life of our country. To get the masses to publicly expose and criticise the shortcomings and mistakes of our state organs and government personnel in order to overcome these shortcomings and mistakes—this is something which none of the so-called free and democratic capitalist countries can or dare do.

However, it should be pointed out that bureaucratic ways still exist—indeed, even to a serious degree—in our administrative organizations at various levels. The socialist system has only just been established in our country. The personnel of our government offices are still constantly infected by influences of the old society, especially by bourgeois ideology. The people's level of literacy and culture is still not a high one and this inevitably limits in one degree or another their exercise of the right to take part in the management and supervision of state affairs. For these reasons, it is possible for bureaucracy to develop in our government offices. At the same time, the growth of bureaucracy is aided by certain shortcomings in our state administrative apparatus, for instance, over-inflated organizations, too many rungs in the administrative ladder, over-centralisation of powers in certain fields, etc. Bureaucratic practices impair relations between our state organs and the people and greatly harm our work. We must continue to expand the scope of democracy, rely on the supervision by the masses, and so wage a relentless fight against bureaucracy.

Democratic centralism operates in our state organs by combining widespread democracy with a high degree of centralism. We are not practising democracy for its own sake. We need widespread democracy because we want to rally all the forces that can be rallied to build socialism and develop the social forces of production. If we had only democracy without centralism, it would be impossible to get the whole of our people to make a well-organized, concerted effort directed to a common aim and according to a unified plan. It would therefore be impossible to achieve the great aim of building a socialist society in our country. The practical operation of democratic centralism varies with changes in the objective situation. We all know that in the past, during the revolutionary wars and the socialist revolution, we put more emphasis on centralism than on democracy. But even in war-time and during the period of revolution, centralism was still based on a wide measure of democracy. All this was because otherwise we should not have been able to meet war-time exigencies or ensure the victory of the socialist revolution. After the socialist revolution was basically accomplished, it became possible for us to further extend the scope of our democracy. In the past two years, the extension of democracy has been very marked both in relations between the central and local authorities and in the sphere of economic management. But under no circumstances should we completely repudiate centralised leadership merely because we have extended democracy. Because of their natural bent toward anarchism the petty bourgeoisie often take a fancy to so-called "absolute democracy," in other words, democracy without centralised leadership. Such "absolute democracy" would only turn the people into a scattered and disorganized mass, unable to safeguard their interests by collective power. That is why the rightist elements who oppose socialism have a particular liking for this concept of "absolute democracy." They want to use this concept to weaken the will of the laboring people and shatter their sense of organization and their fighting spirit. In order to defeat the conspiracies of the rightist elements, we must firmly safeguard our system of democratic centralism so that the idea of so-called "absolute democracy" cannot penetrate into our ranks.

The leading role of the Chinese Communist Party in the political life of the state is set forth in clear terms in our Constitution. The Communist Party is the vanguard of the working class, and the leadership of the Communist Party shows the leadership of the working class. Led by the Communist Party, the Chinese people have achieved two great victories—in the democratic revolution, and in the socialist revolution. The leadership of the Communist Party is also necessary in the building of socialism, because to build socialism calls for transforming society according to the world outlook of the working class. It is the unshakable purpose of the Communist Party to lead the entire Chinese people to build a prosperous and happy Communist society—a society without exploitation or classes, in other words, the world of universal harmony the Chinese people have always dreamed of. Can there be any party other than the Communist Party that is able to lead the Chinese people in achieving this lofty purpose? Certain rightist elements describe this leading position of the Communist Party in the political life of the state as a "monopoly of the state by the Party." This is malicious slander. As a matter of fact, it is precisely under the leadership of the Communist Party that the Chinese people have really become masters of their own country, that they have been able to give full play to their talents and energies to build a new life. The workers of Peking said recently: "China under the leadership of the Communist Party is a country where the working class 'monopolizes' the state, where the people 'monopolize' the state." This is the best reply to the hue and cry about the Communist Party "monopoly of the state." This talk about the so-called "monopoly of the state by the Party" aimed to represent the Communist Party as a sect divorced from and opposed to the masses. That is why some rightist elements have further declared that the Communist Party is the root cause of sectarianism. This is sheer slander entirely contradicted by the facts. As a matter of fact, the Chinese Communist Party has at all times opposed sectarianism. During both the democratic and socialist revolutions, the Communist Party insisted on rallying all the forces that could be rallied, thus bringing about the great revolutionary unity of the people of the entire country. After the basic victory in the socialist revolution, the Chinese Communist Party further took the initiative in putting forward the policy of long-term co-existence with the democratic parties and mutual supervision. Furthermore, the ultimate aim of the Chinese Communist Party is to bring about a Communist society in which all classes will be abolished, and all political parties, including the Communist Party, will die out. There is absolutely no place in such a party for sectarianism. The Communist Party has always taught its members to pay constant attention to strengthening its ties with the masses and strictly forbids its members to adopt a sectarian attitude towards people outside the Party. The reason why the Chinese people trust the leadership of the Communist Party is precisely because they see clearly from the facts that the Chinese Communist Party is a working class party which serves the people wholeheartedly.

In building a socialist society, the worker-peasant alliance is the basic force, but it is also necessary to rally all other classes and strata which support socialism and are willing to accept socialist transformation. The people's democratic united front based on the worker-peasant alliance and led by the Communist Party is the concrete manifestation of the great revolutionary unity of the people of the whole country. Such a united front better enables us to keep contact and unite with the broad masses of the people and to give expression to the views and demands of all sections of the people so that the state can take timely and appropriate steps to bring their interests into harmony and correctly handle contradictions among them. Also, through the various democratic parties and groups and people's organizations brought together in the united front, it is possible to do better education in socialist ideology, more effectively carry through socialist transformation and advance the cause of socialist construction. This is the function and purpose of the policy put forward by the Communist Party for long-term co-existence with the democratic parties and mutual supervision. What the people expect of the democratic parties is that they should firmly adhere to the socialist stand and pay attention to ideological remolding so that they can play a positive role in state affairs to the fullest extent of their capabilities. The people's democratic united front will inevitably be further consolidated and developed as it keeps pace with the progress of socialist construction. It is wrong to doubt the significance of the united front policy, to underestimate its role, or to slight the importance of united front work.

At the same time, it must be affirmed that the Communist Party is the guiding force and the core of the united front, and that socialism is the political basis of the united front and the common goal of struggle for the people of the entire country. These unshakable principles mark out the path which all democratic parties and groups within the united front must keep to, and any party or group which departs from this path excludes itself from the united front.

The organs of state power in our country are made up of representatives of the various nationalities, classes, parties and groups, and people's organizations, under the leadership of the Communist Party. All major policies of the state are discussed and drawn up by the state organs concerned only after exchange of views and various ways of consultation between those concerned have been exhausted, while representatives of the various democratic parties and democrats without party affiliations also take part in executing these policies in the organizations concerned. This method, in which the various democratic parties and groups and non-party democrats participate in the state administration under the leadership of the Communist Party, can better unite the people of the whole country and mobilize all positive forces for the building of socialism. This precisely shows the advantages of our state system. The much-vaunted two-party or multi-party systems of capitalist countries under which different political parties get in and out of office are nothing but travesties of democracy which the various cliques in the bourgeoisie use to hoodwink the working people. What some rightist elements are now dreaming of is to transplant to China this bourgeois system of multi-party politics and alternation in office-holding by various parties, to replace our system of people's democracy.

When I was entrusted by the first session of the National People's Congress in 1954 to form a government, I drew up the composition of the State Council in accordance with the principle of the people's democratic united front led by the Communist Party as stipulated in the Constitution. At that time, members of the democratic parties and groups other than the Communist Party and non-party democrats made up something over one-fourth of the total membership of the government. This ratio was also largely maintained when the government membership was later enlarged. These arrangements were made in the light of the situation obtaining at that time and as we look back today we still think they were appropriate.

The firm and strong core of leadership by the Communist Party in all government institutions, schools, enterprises and popular organizations is essential in order to ensure the correct execution of government policies in all fields. The principle of the overall leadership of the Communist Party is to be understood mainly in a political sense; it does not imply that all practical work must be directly managed by the Communist Party. Indeed, work in many specialised fields should be in the hands of experts. By experts I include here of course experts who are also Communist Party members. As for the specific organisational forms and working methods adopted to put Communist Party leadership into practice, these can and should take various shapes according to the time and the task in hand, to bring into fuller play the leading role of the Party and to give full scope to the initiative of both the leaders and the led, Communist Party members and people who are not Communist Party members and to enable them to cooperate better. Well-intentioned criticisms and suggestions made by many people in regard to this deserve careful study. But the rightist elements have put forward frenzied demands like "Let Communist Party organizations quit government institutions and schools!", "No recruitment of new members by the Communist Party among intellectuals!". "There must be no Party system outside the state apparatus!", "Let the Communist Party go out of office!" etc. These are all of a piece and supplement the above-mentioned fallacies about "bureaucracy being a more dangerous enemy than capitalism" or "a political planning council," or "a rehabilitation committee", the talk about the "Communist Party's monopoly of the state", "alternation in office-holding by various parties," etc. These are all aimed at drawing the people's political power away from the leadership of the party of the working class so that these people can change the nature of our state along capitalist lines.

Some people have criticized the lack of a clear division of function between the Party and the government. This question needs a bit of analysis. In directly issuing political calls and announcing policy-making decisions to the masses, the Party, far from hampering the work of the government, renders it great help. Party and government organizations of the same level have jointly published a number of decisions in the nature of political calls or policy directives and certain instructions whose implementation took on the character of a mass movement and which called for joint work by the Party and the government. Inspections in certain fields of work were made jointly by the Party and government organizations concerned. Sometimes, members of the Communist Party and other democratic parties in responsible positions have been invited to attend government meetings. These methods have been found helpful in improving work and should continue to be used in the future. But, in some departments, there have indeed been cases where Communist Party organizations have monopolized the work and taken over administrative control; on some specific questions, they have bypassed the administration and directly interfered with the work. This sort of thing befits neither the work of the government nor the work of the Party and should be corrected.

Some people have raised the issue that non-Communist leading members in state organizations, schools, or enterprises do not have the authority that should go with their posts. There were, indeed, a number of facts to support what they said. But a detailed analysis of the question will show that several different cases are involved. The first case, is where Communists and non-Communists cooperate closely and are not divided by "walls" or "moats". The second case is where some Communist Party organizations and officials do not have sufficient respect for the functions and powers of non-Communists and even adopt an attitude which is discriminative or keep them at arms length. This is a grave mistake of a sectarian character. The third case is where some non-Communists fail to devote enough effort to the duties that go with their posts. They stand aloof from and look askance at Communist Party organizations and members; but in these cases, on the other hand, the Communist Party organizations and leading officials concerned have often made inadequate efforts to approach and help them. The two latter cases deserve our serious attention. We must make energetic efforts to correct them.

In settling this question the key lies first of all in education of their members by Communist Party organizations so that they wholeheartedly carry out the united front policy of the Party, overcome sectarianism, and learn to respect, unite with and help non-Communists in their work, listen humbly to their opinions and criticisms, and learn from their professional skills and experience so as to improve both themselves and their work.

Systems of work that adversely affect unity and aggravate misunderstandings should be changed. At the same time, people outside the Communist Party should, on their part, courageously perform their functions and duties, rid themselves of any feelings of antipathy they may have with regard to cadres coming from the working class or peasantry and any feelings of suspicion and disunity as regards Communist Party members, and be sincere and open-minded in working with Communist Party members. They should criticise defects in the work whenever they occur and put forward their proposals. They must also study harder to raise their ideological level and understanding of things so that Communist Party members and non-Communists will work together in close cooperation and harmony. Some non-Communists who are still inclined to opposing socialism should particularly make greater efforts to remold themselves and rid themselves of such sentiments.

The rectification campaign that is going on in the Communist Party is also a rectification campaign in state organizations. Its aim is to effectively overcome bureaucracy, sectarianism and subjectivism. We should welcome and consider all constructive criticisms directed against these erroneous ideas and styles of work even when the critic is prejudiced and, without taking everything into consideration, goes to extremes in his attitude, or when the criticism is not fully based on fact. We should accept whatever there is in it that is beneficial and proceed to improve our work. Some rightist elements have alleged that proletarian dictatorship is the root cause of bureaucracy, sectarianism and subjectivism or, in reproaching our state organs with shortcomings and defects, compare them with the state organs of the exploiting classes. Such preposterous assertions must be repudiated. In countries of bourgeois dictatorship, state organs are means by which the bourgeoisie oppress and exploit the masses. They are fundamentally opposed to the interests of the people. In these state organs, bureaucracy, sectarianism and subjectivism are not only unavoidable, but also ineradicable. The case with our state organs is entirely different. Socialism is the common cause of the whole people with the working class in the lead. A socialist country must and can mobilize the broadest masses of the people to take part in the management and supervision of state affairs. That is why, fundamentally speaking, there is no place in a socialist society for bureaucracy, sectarianism and subjectivism. We must and certainly can wipe out these germs, and the guarantee of this is the intrinsic vitality of our basic state system.

V. NATIONAL AND INTERNATIONAL UNITY

Fellow deputies! We can all see that the people of our country have made very great achievements in a very short period. Our socialist revolution has gained a basic victory. The socialist construction is being carried on steadily and on a large scale. The people's livelihood is gradually improved. A basic system of state that corresponds to the socialist economic base of our country has been established and is instrumental in consolidating and pushing forward the cause of socialism in our country. On what forces have we relied to ensure ourselves one victory after another in succession? At home, we have relied upon the great unity of our people of different nationalities under the leadership of the Communist Party. Internationally, we have relied upon the unity between our country and other countries in the socialist camp headed by the Soviet Union, and the unity between our country and all other peace-loving countries and peoples of the world. At present, we are confronted with a task that is even more difficult and greater than before. To carry out this task successfully, we must make further efforts to strengthen the great unity of the people on the basis of socialism, criticize and repudiate all ideas that are opposed to socialism and continue to weed out the overt and covert remnants of counter-revolutionaries. Internationally, we should further strengthen the great unity of the socialist camp and the great unity among all the peace-loving countries and peoples of the world. Isolate the imperialist aggressive blocs and fight for a lasting world peace and the peaceful co-existence among nations of different social systems.

On the question of the great unity of the people throughout the country, we must first of all make clear the definition of the people. At the present stage, the world "people" refers to the various nationalities, democratic classes, democratic parties, people's organizations and patriots of all walks of life that support socialism and take part in socialist construction, i.e. all those who enjoy the rights of citizens under the constitution. The counter-revolutionary elements, reactionary forces and groups and those who are still under surveillance or being reformed through labor are our enemies who stand in hostility to socialism and in opposition to the people. After the basic victory in the socialist revolution, while the contradictions between ourselves and the enemy still exist, the number of our enemies in the country has greatly reduced, and this fact has brought the contradictions among the people to the fore. This is the reason why Chairman Mao Tse-tung, in his speech on February 27, 1957 at the 11th session (enlarged) of the Supreme State Conference, specially told us that we must learn to be good at distinguishing between the two types of contradictions different in nature—the contradictions between ourselves and the enemy and the contradictions among the people—and pointed out the principles and ways of correctly handling the contradictions among the people. But it is not impossible for one of the two types of contradictions to turn into the other. Those who are still under surveillance, when they become new men after being reformed through labor, can enjoy the rights of citizens and become part of the people. On the other hand, some individuals or groups who are now part of the people may become the enemy of the people if they persist in their anti-socialist position, resist socialist reform and seek to undermine the socialist construction.

In the present stage of great social changes in China, some within the ranks of the people, for the time being, are not accustomed to the new socialist system, others would even feel repulsive to it. In the course of social development, people often fall into three categories—the progressive, the intermediate and the backward—in their thinking and standpoint and often divide themselves into leftists, those in the middle and rightists. This is determined by the objective law of social development and the objective law of development of man's thinking and is not an artificial classification. The working class wants to reform the society in accordance with their world outlook. This implies that it must also remold the standpoint and ideologies of the people of other classes so that they can meet the demand of social development.

The bourgeois rightists, though they are within the ranks of the people, stand in opposition to socialism and even take actions that are not in the interests of the socialist cause. We must, therefore, draw a sharp line between ourselves and the rightists politically and ideologically and wage a necessary determined struggle against them so that the overwhelming majority of the genuine patriots will see why the standpoints and actions of the rightists are wrong. As soon as the rightists are wholly isolated, changes will take place among them. We hope that the rightists, helped by outside prodding, and profiting by their own experiences and increased awareness, will repent and accept the opportunities of remolding themselves. For them the door of socialist transformation still remains open. But it is quite possible that a very small number of rightists will persist in their reactionary stand, refuse to remold themselves and even take actions to sabotage the socialist construction. In that case they will cut themselves away from the people.

To build a firm unity of all our people on the basis of socialism is the aim of a long-term struggle and, to attain this aim we must wage a consistent battle on two fronts. On the one hand we must handle contradictions among the people correctly and make serious efforts to overcome subjectivism, bureaucracy and sectarianism in our ways of thinking and of doing things; on the other hand we must thoroughly criticize and repudiate the rightists' utterances against socialism, against the basic system of our state, against the leading role of the Communist Party, and against national and international unity, so that the distinction between right and wrong in regard to these fundamental questions is made crystal clear. We believe that the overwhelming majority of the people of our country are truly patriotic and take the side of socialism. Both the rectification campaign being carried out by the Communist Party and the review of its work done by the government will ensure that contradictions among the people be resolved consistently as they crop up and that mistakes be corrected. Those who try to take advantage of contradictions among the people and the rectification campaign of the Communist Party to sow discord within the ranks of our people and to sabotage our cause of socialism will not succeed. On the contrary, the exposure of their plots will serve to teach the people of the whole country to rally more closely round the Communist Party.

With our own country united, we can better consolidate unity between ourselves and all other countries in the socialist camp and unity between ourselves and all other peace-loving countries and peoples in the world.

During the past year, world peace has been constantly threatened by the policy of arms expansion and war preparation of the imperialist bloc of aggression headed by the United States. But the ever-growing forces of peace have succeeded in making the general international situation develop in a direction favorable to the people throughout the world in their struggle for a lasting peace and against war.

The imperialist bloc of aggression attempted to make a breach in Hungary and then smite the other socialist countries one by one. But the Hungarian people beat back this imperialist attack, and all the countries in the socialist camp have learnt a deep and useful lesson from the events in Hungary. The result has been not the weakening, but the strengthening of the unity of the entire socialist camp. The visits of Comrade Voroshilov, President of the Presidium of the Supreme Soviet of the USSR, and of the premiers of Czechoslovakia and Poland to our country not long ago, as well as the exchange of visits between leaders of the socialist countries during recent months, have played an important part in strengthening the unity of the socialist camp. The facts have proved that, despite all attempts at sowing discord and dissension, international socialist solidarity built on the basis of proletarian internationalism and the principle of equality among nations is unbreakable.

During the past year, the Soviet Union has put forward a series of reasonable proposals on such major international questions as disarmament, prohibition of the use of weapons of mass destruction, cessation of nuclear weapons tests, abolition of military bases in foreign countries, the withdrawal of armed forces from foreign countries, and the holding of a "summit" conference among the big powers. All this has helped ease the international situation. In order to safeguard peace in the Near and Middle East, the Soviet Union has proposed that the big powers pledge to respect the sovereignty and independence of the countries in that area, and refrain from interfering in their internal affairs. These proposals by the Soviet Union are what all the countries in the socialist camp advocate. This fully proves that we socialist croachment on our rights by other countries, and that we stand resolutely for peaceful co-existence among all nations.

The great victory which the heroic Egyptian people won in defeating the British and French aggression and safeguarding Egypt's sovereignty over the Suez Canal, marked a new upsurge in the struggle against colonialism. Their struggle was also in defense of world peace. During the past year, such nationalist countries in Asia and Africa as India, Burma, Indonesia, Ceylon, Egypt and Syria have played a more and more important role in defending world peace. The Japanese people's struggles against US military occupation, to win independence and freedom and to defend world peace have also made great progress. All these are important factors in bringing about a relaxation in the international situation.

The United States, however, took advantage of the weakened positions of Britain and France, did its best to seize their colonies and spheres of influence in the Near and Middle East, in North Africa and other parts of the world, and intensified its enslavement and oppression of the people in those places. This is the new colonial policy of the United States. Because this policy is more cleverly camouflaged and because the people of some countries still lack experience in the struggle, it is quite possible that the designs of the United States colonialists will succeed for a time in certain countries, such as Jordan, and put a temporary check on the struggle of their people for national independence. But like every other movement of the people, the movement for national independence and against colonialism cannot be suppressed. The increasingly brazen intervention and ruthless enslavement and oppression by the United States will surely serve to rouse the people of these countries more thoroughly and make them see more clearly the true colors of the US colonialists. This is proved by the fact that, with each passing day, in almost all the countries dominated by the United States, there is a louder and more insistent demand for putting an end to US control, for the adoption of a policy of peace and neutrality and in opposition to aggressive military blocs. The struggle for national independence and against colonialism is a long-term and complex struggle advancing in a seesaw fashion, a struggle that will win ultimate victory. Every setback, every difficulty met in this struggle teaches the people of the various countries to raise their level of political consciousness and helps them in the long run to find the right way leading their struggle to victory.

It is of special importance to note that even in China's territory of Taiwan which is under the tight grip of the US aggressors, the people have launched a large-scale movement against the United States, a movement, moreover, which occurred directly after the United States had established its guided missile base in Taiwan. The United States has now delcared the unilateral annulment of subparagraph 13 (D) of the Korean Armistice Agreement in order that it may bring modern weapons into South Korea. In so doing, the United States attempts, on the one hand, to continue to obstruct the peaceful unification of Korea, menace the Korean Democratic People's Republic and aggravate tension in the Far East, while on the other hand it is also to strengthen its colonial rule in South Korea and suppress the people there. This shows that the United States, treading the footprints of the old colonialists, cannot but ever more depend on bayonets to maintain its new colonial rule. It can be definitely stated that the new colonialism of the United States will end up no better than the old colonialism. The Chinese Government fully agrees with the proposal put forward by the Government of the Korean Democratic People's Republic for the holding of an international conference with wide participation of countries concerned, and strongly condemns the United States for its unilateral action in disrupting the Korean Armistice Agreement.

Attempts made by the United States to seize the colonial interests of its allies and to encroach on their sovereignty have resulted in an increasingly clear tendency on the part of these countries to move further away from it. Among the principal allies of the United States there is a growing tendency to shake off US economic and political control, and an increasing willingness to come to terms and carry on mutually beneficial dealings with the socialist countries. At the same time, the people of all countries in the world, including the American people, are conducting a peace movement which daily grows in scale. This is clear evidence that more and more people are condemning the policy of arms expansion and war preparation of the US aggressive clique.

The danger of war still exists. We must not for a moment relax our vigilance toward the US aggressive clique. But because the socialist camp has become more powerful and more united, because the ranks of the peace-loving countries and peoples are constantly expanding, because the demand of the American people for peace is growing and because the US aggressive clique is finding itself more and more isolated, provided we can unite with all the international forces that can be united with and persist in our struggles, it is possible for us to bring about a further relaxation in the international situation and force the imperialist war bloc to accept the principle of peaceful co-existence.

Fellow deputies! The international situation is favorable for our socialist construction. Basing ourselves on the brilliant directives of Chairman Mao Tse-tung on the correct handling of contradictions among the people, we Chinese people are forging an even stronger unity through our rectification campaign against bureaucracy, sectarianism and subjectivism and through our victorious struggles of exposing and repudiating the anti-socialist rightists. So long as we continue to exert efforts to strengthen national and international unity and carry through the policy of increasing production and practising economy and building our country by hard work and thrift, no force on earth can block the victorious advance of our great socialist cause.

DOCUMENTS 17 and 18

My Preliminary Examination, written statement by Lo Lung-chi, Minister of the Timber Industry, and *I Bow My Head and Admit My Guilt before the People*, written statement by Chang Po-chün, Vice-Chairman of the Democratic League and Minister of Communications. Both statements were presented to the National People's Congress on July 15, 1957.

The English texts are from CB 470 and are translations made by the U.S. Consulate General, Hong Kong, from the *People's Daily*, July 16, 1957.

Comment. Lo and Chang, with particularly hostile emphasis on Chang, were the main targets of the Communist Party's counterattacks against the "Democratic" parties' spokesmen in June and July 1957. The general accusation against the so-called "Chang-Lo Alliance" was that the two men had organized an "invisible conspiracy" against Communist rule, spreading chiefly among Western-trained intellectuals.

Of the two, there is more mention of Lo in the Chinese press before May 1957. He had been a spokesman for the intellectuals at the National People's Congress in June 1956 (CB 402). At the sessions of the Second National Committee of the Chinese People's Political Consultative Conference in March 1957 (CB 444) he had blamed the slow progress of the Hundred Flowers campaign on the Party cadres who were overeager in defending the faith. (Chang by contrast was more restrained.) At the forum of the Democratic parties in May 1957, Lo Lung-chi gave a frank account of the role played both by the technical ministries and by the Democratic parties ("neither eye nor nose," but only expendable tail) vis-a-vis the Communist Party. That part of his recorded remarks which aroused most resentment in the Party was the suggestion that the National People's Congress and the Chinese People's Political Consultative Conference should jointly establish a commission to investigate the injustices committed in the course of the Three Antis, Five Antis and anti-counterrevolutionary campaigns of 1952, 1953, and 1955.

Chang Po-chün at the same forum complained of discrimination in ministries and academic life against non-Communists and made another of the suggestions which were later most violently condemned, viz., that all major political questions should be discussed by joint meetings of political planning commissions from the National People's Congress, the Chinese People's Political Consultative Conference, the Democratic parties, and the mass organizations.

There is no record of discussion in the forum of the student question, which is one of the main subjects of Chang's subsequent confession and hence, it may be deduced, of Party anxiety. The Party wanted urgently to impose or to reimpose strict control on educational and intellectual life.

This was the object of another of the Party's principal charges against Chang and Lo—that the two of them had systematically misdirected the Peking daily *Kwang Ming Jih Pao* (of which Chang was the owner) and the Shanghai cultural periodical *Wen Hui Pao*. Ch'u An-p'ing, editor of the Peking paper, was another principal target of Party criticism in June and July (at the May forum he had coined a wounding phrase about the "Communist dynasty"). Association with the *Wen Hui Pao* was one of the main counts against the famous authoress Ting Ling when she was accused in August of anti-Party activity.

Chang's statement of July 15 was not his first retraction. This had taken place on June 14 and had been pronounced insufficient. The last of his confessions to be noted took place as late as May 4, 1959, when he spoke to the Third National Committee of the Chinese People's Political Consultative Conference on the infinite wisdom of the masses and his own successful remolding (CB 583).

Meantime, Lo had to make a further confession on August 27, 1957, at a series of rectification meetings held by the Central Committee of the Democratic League.

Theodore H. E. Chen, in his *Thought Reform of the Chinese Intellectuals* (Hong

Kong: Hong Kong University Press, 1960), and Roderick MacFarquhar, in his *The Hundred Flowers Campaign and the Chinese Intellectuals* (New York: Praeger, 1960), provide a much fuller narrative of events, and a mass of supplementary material and references. Little more is necessary here.

Supplementary material may be found as follows.

(a) The main collections of relevant material in the CB series are: CB 452, containing correspondence in *People's Daily*, January and April 1957, on the proper limits of literary blooming; CB 459, containing the text of, and correspondence about, a story which attracted much attention for its implicit criticism of the Party, "A Young Man in the Organization Department"; CB 470, further confessions of rightists; CB 472 (p. 14), an account of Party Provincial Committees' propaganda work conferences to discuss Mao's speech of February 27; CB 481, chronology of events, May-August 1957.

(b) On long-term coexistence and mutual supervision between the Chinese Communist Party and the Democratic parties, see also SCMP 1333 (criticism by the "Peasants and Workers" Party of the United Front, July 1956); ECMM 60 (*China Youth*, Oct. 1, 1956); and ECMM 69, 78, 105, 124 (*Study*, Dec. 2, 1956; Feb. 3, 1957; Feb. 18 and Aug. 3, 1958).

(c) On the exposure of prominent rightists, see SCMP 1679, 1687, 1691, containing cases in the Ministry of Supervision and Supreme Court in December 1957.

──────────────────TEXT OF DOCUMENT 17──────────────────

My Preliminary Examination
by
Lo Lung-chi

I am a guilty creature of the Chinese People's Republic. I have spoken and acted against the Communist Party and socialism. With a twinge of conscience, I stand on the solemn rostrum and bow before the deputies. I plead guilty before the people of the country.

The Party and the people have treated me well since the liberation. I have been given a fairly high position in the State organization and a fairly important post in people's groups. Here with my feet on this post and position, I have spoken and acted against the Party and socialism.

The baleful influence I have thus exercised is great and my guilt grave.

Following the struggle against rightists, I feel the greatest compunction for my wrongdoings and repentance for my guilt. I am prepared to use the person as I am today to struggle against the person as I was yesterday and to lay bare my own guilt.

I am to be held culpable for egging on and adding fuel to the subversive acts of rightists and even reactionary and counter-revolutionary elements against the Party through the speech I made on May 22 at the conference of the United Front Work Department. I suggested then the organization in the Standing Committees of the National People's Congress and the Political Consultative Conference of a committee comprising members of the Communist Party, the democratic parties and the various quarters concerned to "encouraged wronged persons to appeal" and to right the wrongs done in the "Three-anti's, five-anti's" and the "liquidation of counter-revolutionaries campaigns." In the light of the current political system of our country and the Communist leadership we have accepted, this suggestion was gravely erroneous. I did not urge the original wrong-doing organ to right the wrongs but attempted to organize an additional committee for the purpose. Here I trespassed upon the functionary powers of the State's examination, procuration, judicial and public security organs and did harm to the political system. I did not ask the original Party organs to reverse the wrongs done in the "three anti's, five anti's" and the "liquidation of counter-revolutionaries" movements but worked for the establishment of a new organ to do it. Here I attempted to negate the leadership of the basic level of the Party. My speech was tantamount to an utterance of grievances on behalf of the counter-revolutionary and reactionary elements and a show of encouragement that they continue to work against the law. After I made this speech, papers and broadcasting stations in Hongkong and Taiwan played it up as an aid to propaganda and this indicated that I had lost in my speech the stand of the Chinese people and had become a spokesman for the enemy. At the same time, I received more than 170 letters supporting my erroneous assertions. Without bothering to ask what were the motives behind these letters, I told my secretary to answer them with the request that the writers endeavor to build up a public opinion for advice to the Political Consultative Conference and the United Front Work Department. Though I had replied to only five of the letters, I must admit that my motive was bad; it was to stimulate the criminal acts of reactionary elements. This was an action unfavorable to the Party and socialism. I bow before you and confess my guilt.

Secondly, the assertion which I made at the conference of the United Front Work Department concerning the contradiction in the Party and democratic parties' development of membership among intellectuals was in fact an expression of the hope that the Communist Party draws no membership from the intellectuals, thereby enabling the democratic parties to enlarge their organizations and strengthen their power in opposition. Though I said in the speech that I did not object to intellectuals joining the Party and that Party membership was itself a glory, the import was that the Party wash its hands from intellectuals so as to give democratic parties opportunities to expand in this direction. This was meant to get rid of Communist leadership and socialism. I had thought that young Communist members in cultural and educational organs were not competent to lead old higher intellectuals. At a conference of the Democratic League, I said:

"Proletarian petit intellectuals and petit bourgeois higher intellectuals are a contradiction."

In this tone I had treated the question of intellectuals on the basis of the levels of knowledge and the numbers of these intellectuals. I did not view the question in the light of the nature of such knowledge; whether it was that of Marxism-Leninism or otherwise. And I also failed to look at the matter from the class stand. I did not realize that in a socialist society, the bourgeois class should be led by the proletarian class. For more than a year, I had issued a series of erroneous statements at conferences of the National People's Congress and the People's Political Consultative Conference speaking on behalf of the bourgeois class. In such statements, I laid no emphasis on ideological remoulding of old intellectuals but attempted to put the responsibility for the lack of close liaison between Communist members and old intellectuals squarely on the shoulders of the Communist Party. I laid no emphasis on the transformation of the old intellectuals but stressed the faults of Communist members. All this aggravated the intellectuals' opposition to the Party and socialism. In my statement at the Political Consultative Conference, I even went to the length of interpreting the Chinese saying "Intellectuals are prepared to die for friends whom they love" as a desire of the intellectuals for the Party's condescension to the point of humbleness. Here, I completely negated the Party's policies on uniting, educating and transforming intellectuals. This was a great mistake of mine. As regards my objection to young communist members leading higher intellectuals, I hopelessly misunderstood the significance of the Party's leadership. Because I personally had great respect for Chairman Mao, Chairman Liu and Premier Chou, I had the secret satisfaction that I had in this way accepted the Communist Party's leadership. I was blind to the fact that Communist leadership was meant to be leadership by the whole Party. I did not understand that objection to leadership by the lower level of the Party was equal to an opposition to leadership by the Party as a whole. Thus, my statements tended to lower the prestige of the Party and were anti-Party and anti-socialist. This is the second point for which I must humbly confess my guilt.

Thirdly, as vice-Chairman of the China Democratic League, I had for over a year endeavored, in collaboration with Chang Po-chun, to divert the League to the rightist course, depriving it of its role as assistant to the Party and throwing into confusion backward members of the League in the face of rampant attacks by rightist elements. This was unfavorable to the Party's leadership and the socialist cause. The rightist course which the League had pursued gave a mighty fillip to the subversive activities of the rightists. There was nothing accidental in this matter. The League was a political organization of middle and higher intellectuals, having a membership of 30,000. Among these, the majority were progressive. Since the second session of the League's congress in 1956, it had laid too much emphasis on the absorption of middle-of-the-road and backward elements as members, causing a sharp rise in the number of such elements in the league. In the past year, the League had not seriously undertaken the education and transformation of its members and this gave rise to some rightist elements deviating from rally around the Party and socialism. In the past year, I had, in collaboration with Chang Po-chun, made misinterpretations of the "Let All Flowers Bloom and Let All Schools Of Thought Contend" policy, turning the slogan into an instrument of rightists against the Party and socialism. The policy was originally intended to encourage renovations and free competition. It was a policy to nurture up independent thinking and free discussion. It was a good policy for China's artistic and scientific development. Through the Chang Po-chun and Lo Lung-chi alliance, I had manipulated the slogan into a political weapon, advocating unconditional "great contention and great blooming" and had, under the cloak of the slogan, maliciously attacked the Party and opposed its leadership. "Long-term co-existence and mutual supervision" was originally intended to encourage ideological transformation of the classes to which the democratic parties belonged, to promote mutual criticisms and expostulations and to encourage such parties to be firm on the socialist stand as efficient assistants to the leading Party. But the alliance had distorted it into a stratagem for expansion in organization, strengthening of power and elevation of positions of the democratic parties, to stand up against the Party. In spring this year, organs of the League in the various areas reported that such a deviation had already appeared. Despite these reports, Chang Po-chun and I made no amends and I even supported Chang's suggestion relative to the central work of the contention and blooming. In May, Chang and I spoke at the forum of the United Front Work Department. Chang suggested the establishment of a "political planning board" and I put forward the idea for a "committee for the righting of wrongs done". These absurd ideas served to step up the vociferous clamors of the rightists.

The League had now some 30,000 members and about 100 units scattered over the country. It had basic organizations in middle and higher cultural and educational organs. As a political organization, it exercised a great influence on educational and cultural work. Chang Po-chun and I were the first and second vice-Chairman of the League and were responsible for its administration. When we made the absurd statements on the contention and blooming and long-term co-existence and mutual supervision, others followed and the influence was bad and far-reaching. It was not without reason, therefore that rightists launched rampant attacks in cultural and educational organizations and that rightist elements of the League started activities against the Party and socialism in May this year. The Chang-Lo alliance, having its hands on the reins of the League, had sown the seeds. This is the third point for which I must confess my guilt.

Fourthly, since 1949, sectarianism and invisible organization had prevailed in the Central Committee of the League, clogging upon its unity and obstructing the leading Party's implementation of the policy for education and transformation of intellectuals. Components of this invisible organization were basically victims of English and American education and intellectuals of bourgeois ideology. This organization was not only entrenched in Peking but scattered over provinces in the eastern, central-south and southwestern parts of the country. Its aim was to usurp the leadership of the League for personal gains and prominence. It was an aim wicked and shameful. This invisible organization ceased its activities in 1952 and was felt to be no longer existing. But the spiritual connection and ideological communion that had taken hold of its components were not eradicated. Such components were generally friends, schoolmates and colleagues wedded in ideology. When one of them made an absurd statement or started an erroneous activity, especially when I myself made such a statement, others joined in chorus. On the commencement of the rectification campaign, in May this year, we found groups of these components in Peking and elsewhere almost unanimous in speaking and acting against the Party and socialism and even collusive with rightist elements in a plot against the Party and socialism. Though I had never issued any secret directive nor sent any men to the areas for contact, my ideological communion with these components goaded me on to join the chorus. In the struggle today against rightists, such components had all been found seriously guilty and were objects of counter attacks. I ruminated and concluded that I had not only led myself but others astray. This is the fourth point for which I confess my guilt.

Fifthly, I had no understanding of the international situation and never made a careful analysis of it. In my private conversations, I gave some erroneous assertions which shook the people's faith in the force of the peace camp. In the past years, I had often read British and American newspapers and magazines and as I had no full mastery of Marxist-Leninist theories, I fell easy victim to the poisonous Anglo-American insinuations. Also, I had no thorough understanding of the de-Stalin event in the 20th Soviet congress and the Polish and Hungarian incidents. So, on the outbreak of the

Polish and Hungarian incidents with which came vacillations of the socalled progressive elements in Britain, the United States and other capitalist countries, I jumped to the conclusion that they were signs of a split in the peace camp and not indications of a strengthened peace force. I did not appraise the world situation in the light of the increasingly strengthened peace force and I did not estimate the peace force in view of the accelerating tempo of anti-aggression and anti-colonial movements in the world. Thus, I concluded that the international situation was getting worse rather than better. I expressed these erroneous views in a small group of the Political Consultative Conference when it met to discuss Premier Chou's report on his visits to the 11 countries as well as my private conversations with Pu Hsi-hsiu, Pan Ta-kuei and Wang Tsao-shih. I liberally disseminated pessimistic reports detrimental to unity among socialist nations and unity among peace-loving people of the world. This is the fifth point for which I must confess my guilt.

Sixthly, I had allowed myself to be partial in my help to certain social enterprises and to let my backward ideology influence them. My connection with the *Wen Hui Pao* was a typical example. None could deny that I had been very much concerned with the establishment and resumption of the paper. On the one hand, I had wanted Pu Hsi-hsiu to do her job well for the friendship I had with her and, on the other, I had been under the erroneous impression that in China today, there should be a folk mouthpiece. For this reason, I had encouraged whenever opportunities offered, the *Wen Hui Pao* to differentiate from the way the *Jen Min Jih Pao* operated. As Hsu Chu-cheng had often complained to me about the Party group in the paper, I had directly and indirectly told responsible personnel of the *Wen Hui Pao* that they should not be too superstitious about the Party group's leadership and that they could contact Peking in case of matters they could not decide on. Pu Hsi-hsiu and I saw each other every day, and she often consulted me on the management of the paper. Through her, I had infused unhealthy and unprogressive ideas into the paper, and dragged her to the rightist course, causing the paper to commit errors. In March and April this year, the *Wen Hui Pao* was a paper of which the public had a high opinion. Today, it was an object of struggle owing mainly to the mistakes it committed in the course of the rectification campaign. This happened in May and June this year and in May Pu Hsi-hsiu went to the Northeast on a tour of inspection. As she came back, I went abroad on June 3. Even if I did have the intention of utilizing the *Wen Hui Pao* to intensify rightist propaganda, the fact remained that I could not have conceivably made use of this periodical. I am only telling the truth and I have no intention of shirking responsibilities. Rightists Hsu Chu-cheng and Pu Hsi-hsiu on the paper have acknowledged responsibilities for rightist views and I am to blame for the encouragement I gave to the paper not to rely too much on the Party group's leadership and for the infusion through Pu Hsi-hsiu of rightist ideas. I am to be held responsible for failure to have genuine love for this social enterprise and for the conversion, through my influence, of the beloved paper before the liberation into the present anti-Party and anti-socialist mouthpiece. This is the sixth point for which I must confess my guilt.

Seventhly, it was a serious mistake of mine to have been inactive in my government work and to have had no genuine love for my fellow workers. In the past years, I had not been enthusiastic enough about the people's cause, had been contented with my official position and had turned myself into a big bureaucrat. Since I assumed the post of Minister of Timber Industry, I had not seriously studied my work nor fulfilled my responsibilities. I had often thought to myself that the industry was for me and for this reason I had often procrastinated. This obstructed the work of the Ministry. Because I was self-conceited and arrogant, I was not frank with my fellow workers and did not get along well with them. I was short-tempered and had often looked down upon my colleagues and castigated them harshly. For example, my attitude toward my two secretaries, particularly, to my confidential secretary, Shao Tze-yun, was none that manifested love and help. Because she refused to comply with my wish that she join the China Democratic League, I was cold to her and even prevented her from participating in the Communist Party. These were the concrete examples of my endeavors to expand the organization of the League and to prevent intellectuals from joining the Communist Party. I was not serious with my government job, was not honest toward my fellow workers, obstructed the national construction and acted against the Communist Party's leadership. This is the seventh point for which I must confess my guilt.

Eighthly, I had been proud and self-conceited for the past years and had stayed at the backward status. I had not studied hard and I had not tried to transform myself. Whenever I glanced over Marxist-Leninist writings, I had secret pleasure in myself that I had grasped the essence applicable to all others which I did not have to learn. Whenever I learned a thing or two in Marxist-Leninist writings, I used them liberally as a whitewashing implement. I never condescended to the progressive elements of the League and had often labelled them as dogmatists. This arrogant and self-conceited attitude had not only ruined myself but had impeded the desire for advance on the part of the persons whom I was in daily contact. Satisfaction at a backward status, thus ruining myself and my associates, is the eighth point for which I must confess my guilt.

Of course, I have more mistakes and sins than the eight points I have listed above. I am making today a preliminary explanation for those mistakes which I have committed over the year. As regards the statements and activities which I made and understood before the liberation, I can find many more mistakes in them. My political background is dirty. Thirty years ago, I edited the "New Moon" magazine and wrote articles criticizing communism. I had participated into Chang Chun-mai's National Socialist Party. When I started the China Democratic League, I actually had in mind a third road. I had always spread political thoughts of the British-American bourgeois democracy. I had also maintained secret contact with American George Marshall and John Leighton Stuart. Since this is a fact known to all, I shall omit a repetition here. Let me now proceed with a confession of my personal way of thinking.

I am a combination of feudal and bourgeois thoughts. From the time when I was five or six years old to my matriculation into Tsinghua University, I stayed with the family of my father and brothers. This was the type of big family of the old society. In the period till I came back from Britain and the United States, I received the bourgeois type of education. As I returned to the country, I spoke and acted in vivid reflection of Anglo-American bourgeois thought. Politically, I was in favor of a third road. On the liberation in 1949, Chang Lan, formerly Chairman of the Democratic League, and I came to Peking. Because I had strong bourgeois thought and individualism, I was quite particular about position and name. I was thus responsible for sectarianism in the League and I must admit meanwhile that I had then sentiments contrary to those of the Communist Party. When Chang Tung-sun was found in collusion with American spies, members of the League and the public seriously suspected me. Director Li Wei-han of the United Front Work Department took the responsibility to explain that I had nothing to do with the spy case and suggested that I be elected member to the Political Consultative Conference. I came to realize that the Party was fair and clairvoyant. I was very grateful to the Party. I had increasing faith in the Party. Since then, I had read some Marxist-Leninist writings and Chairman Mao's articles. Though I did not know well dialectic materialism and historical materialism and though I did not accept Communist world outlook, I began, nevertheless, to appreciate good points about communism. In the face of the great achievements accomplished in our national construction, I had often told myself that such achievements would not have been possible without the Communist Party's leadership. This I had often told my foreign guests. Over the years, my political position had been raised and my livelihood had become steady and remain untransformed as might my bourgeois ideology, I dared to say that I had neither plot nor ambition to overthrow the Party or to uproot the socialist cause. Even if I were a very selfish man, what good could I expect from overthrowing the Party and socialism. Following the convention of the 20th Soviet Congress and the outbreak of the Polish and Hungarian incidents, I had for a while doubts about communism. But I did feel that the advocacy by the Chinese Communist Party under Chairman Mao's leadership for "coordination of the practices of the Chinese revolution" was, after all, different from the situations in Poland and Hungary. China, under the leadership of the Communist Party, had a bright future. Of this I was deeply convinced. It was true that when the question of intellectuals was brought up in 1955, I was sympathetic with the intellectuals and I had always wanted to speak a couple of good words for them to make them happy. This was the root of the mistakes which I had made over the two years. I had not been firm on my stand but had spoken on the stand of the bourgeois class for the intelligentsia. I had not appreciated the true significance of the Party's leadership and I had made too low an estimate of the progressiveness of our intellectuals. I had attempted to ingratiate myself into the favor of the intellectuals, especially old intellectuals, counting on this to expand the organization and raise the position of the China Democratic League, thereby acquiring a relatively big voice in decisions on national affairs. This was where my dream stopped. I do not have and have never had any scheme for the overthrow of the Party and socialism or for reinstitution of capitalism in the country.

But you may ask why I have spoken and acted against the Party and socialism. I can only say today that the sub-consciousness of my bourgeois thought was at work. Chairman Mao has said that bourgeois and petit bourgeois will definitely show their thought and conception and will definitely reflect their thought and conception on political matters and they will use all possible means to show their true selves. This penetrates into the hearts of all persons with bourgeois thought. I, of course, acknowledge that I am a full-fledged bourgeois. With my political position gradually raised over the years, I have become increasingly arrogant and self-conceited and I have completely lost myself. With this thought in my brain, I will sooner or later give myself away. If I do not make any mistake today, I certainly will some later days. Here, I attempt to establish that though I have had no intention to oppose the Party and socialism, I have committed the guilt of speaking and acting against the Party and socialism. This attests to the necessity of ideological transformation and the importance of the struggle against rightists. Otherwise, intellectuals who speak and act as I do and I myself would have unconsciously gone into a blind alley.

I have now made a preliminary explanation for my mistaken assertions and acts. Mistakes that I have committed should not be put on the shoulders of Chang Po-chun and those that he has made should not be hurled on me. As regards the alliance which Chang and I formed, we should also make a clear explanation.

Here I must point out that I am an ideologically backward element as is Chang Po-chun and that though we were together at Peitaiho last year, we have never been alone together nor have we had any secret talks since then. When we spoke at the conference of the United Front Work Department, we had not exchanged notes. But as there was ideological connection between us, we found ourselves much in common in absurd speeches and acts.

On the strength of my alliance with Chang Po-chun, I had always supported his opinions on important matters relating to the League with the result that the League had committed many blunders in its policies. For example: In the work conference of the League in March this year, Chang Po-chun suggested the contention and blooming as the central work of the League for 1957. I endorsed and supported this suggestion. When he emphasized the expansion of the League in view of the program for the development of membership of democratic parties to several millions, I immediately felt that the League should further develop from the mark of two millions in 1956 and for this reason, I joined in the emphasis for its expansion. Most important of all was the establishment in May of four committees, namely, the party member committee, the scientific committee, the position and power committee and long-term coexistence and mutual supervision committee. Chang Po-chun called me up to advise that he was going to invite the propaganda, school, and educational and cultural committees to discuss the great contention and blooming. I expressed my agreement over the phone. The four committees came into existence by a decision of the League's Central Committee but I must confess that I had consulted neither Chairman Shen nor vice-Chairmen Shih Liang and Kao Chung-ming nor its standing committee on the matter. The aims and designs of the four committees are clear today. The Party Member Committee is to work for the abolition of Party groups in institutes of higher learning, the Position and Power Committee and the long-term co-existence and mutual supervision Committee to expand the organization of the League and to increase its power, thereby climbing to the position of deciding on national affairs and holding reins of government jointly with the Communist Party and to stand up against the Party in case of differences in opinion. And the Scientific Committee has already worked out a series of scientific systems against the Party and socialism. Following the establishment of the Committees, Chang Po-chun told me that he was going to have the League send men to promote work in the diverse fields and to collect materials for submission to the Central People's Government. To this suggestion, I agreed. After I left the country on June 3, he took over the leadership and undertook the necessary arrangements of which I was not informed. As regards the utilization of the legal organization for illegal activities and for the realization of a scheme against the Party and socialism, I did subscribe and I am to be held responsible for this.

I can only explain this much in connection with my alliance with Chang Po-chun. He is manager of the *Kuang Ming Jih Pao* and for three to four years, I have not inquired about the affairs of the paper. Since he is Chairman of the China Peasants and Workers' Democratic Party, I am not able to poke my nose into the affairs of that party. If he has any political ambition or any ambition with intellectuals, he has told me none. As regards his opinions and suggestions on a bicameral system and on the development of members of the democratic parties to several millions, I did not agree and in fact criticized them before Kao Chung-ming and other members of the League but I have never told Chang this straight in the face. If I have any political ambition and wishes, I have told him none. This is the true status of my connection with Chang Po-chun in the past. I do not conceal nor fabricate any.

In the explanations made by many persons in the press, the term "Chang-Lo alliance" has been freely used and it is believed that this alliance is the supreme directing organ for the rampant offensive against the Party and that it is the well-planned central organization of the plot. I wish to offer no explanation. I have given the truth about the guilt resulting from my alliance with Chang Po-chun. I suggest that the leadership Party and the people make thorough investigations. If any thing is found that tends to show my deliberate concealment of certain schemes and plots in the Chang-Lo alliance, I am prepared to receive the due punishment.

Dear Deputies! I am standing on the rostrum, bowing to you in repentance of my guilt. I have not come to explain it away. The press already has laid bare my words and acts and has exposed my past guilts and current schemes. I am not disposed to make any explanation. The question now is not whether I have said this or that, whether I have done this and that, whether I have conspired with this or that group of persons or which group of the rightist clique I have instigated. I do believe that the Communist Party is fair and unbiased and will not wrong the innocent. The truth will come out. I also request that the deputies grant me a further opportunity to make a thorough explanation. As regards those questions relating to the League, I will explain them at the League. I am always ready to acknowledge mistakes I have made and I hope that things that are not true will be so established.

Dear Deputies! My mistakes are grave as are my guilts. With contrition, I own that I have failed to live up to the expectations of Chairman Mao, the leadership Party and the scores of thousands of the League members. I have failed to live up to the expectations of the people and the nation.

Mere acknowledgement of my guilts is not sufficient. I am called upon to decide whether I should repent and rectify my mistakes or persist in wrong-doings thereby cutting myself off from the nation and the people.

I am grateful to the leadership Party and the Government for the "door of socialist transformation that is open to me." So goes the Chinese proverb, "there is nothing greater than the immediate rectification of mistakes." Before the deputies today, I pledge that I will be determined and brave in any march toward the door of transformation. I want to transform myself radically. And I want to work honestly for the socialist cause and the Chinese people.

TEXT OF DOCUMENT 18

I Bow My Head and Admit My Guilt Before the People
by
Chang Po-chün

I am an offender guilty of serious political mistakes. With your leniency I am permitted to stand before you and to use a few minutes to admit my mistakes and guilt and express my greatest determination to reform myself. Premier Chou said in his report on government work: "If the rightists, with external prodding and benefitting by their experience and awareness, repent and accept transformation, the door of socialist transformation still remains open to them." With all my heart I accept and thank for the denunciation and exposure by deputies in the last few days who brought to light my ugly and absurd words and actions. Since the whole nation brought to light my erroneous speeches and actions, the enemies of our state like the imperialists, Chiang's men in Taiwan and a handful of counter-revolutionaries hidden in our country have been exploiting, with great rejoicings, our reactionary speeches and actions as an instrument of propaganda in their attempt to damage the prestige of our great fatherland. This makes me extremely sad and I feel my crime becomes more serious. "It grieves the friend and gladdens the heart of the enemy". I have a deep feeling that in reprimanding and criticizing me the people of our country and the deputies are rescuing me from getting perished and are giving me a chance of rebirth. I wish to express my heartfelt thanks once again to the whole nation and all the deputies.

My erroneous thinking and crime have their historical root, bear the nature of a reactionary class and are consistent in character. I came from the landlord class and for a long time received feudal and bourgeois education. After betraying the glorious Communist Party of China in 1927, I degenerated into a leading element following the middle-of-the-road course and "being 30 per cent against the Communists and 70 per cent against Chiang". I organized the so-called Third Party—predecessor of the China Peasants' and Workers' Democratic Party. The Third Party devoted itself to political and military speculation, becoming active when there was an opportunity and stopping its activities when there was no opportunity. This rightist opportunism had been reserved right after the great victory in the Chinese people's revolution. Although on the occasion of the 30th anniversary of the birth of the great and glorious Communist Party of China on July 1, 1951, I published my self-criticism headed "The Communist Party Has Saved Me" showing my repentance, I did not pull out the root of my bad thoughts. Consequently, my stand was not firm, vacillating between the "left" and the "right" and frequently showing myself to be a double dealer. I hankered after the old things; outwardly I accepted new things but actually I kept myself away from them. This latent bad thought reasserted itself after the 20th congress of the Soviet Communist Party criticized Stalin's cult of individuality. I went too far to subject Stalin to vicious criticism. As to the great socialist construction in the Soviet Union, I sometimes under-rated its achievements and sometimes emphasized its drawbacks. In opposing doctrinairism, I even belittled the basic theories of Marxism-Leninism and I never gave them a serious study. This gave rise to the so-called revisionist thinking opposed to Marxism-Leninism. This new bad thought was a continuation of my old rightist opportunism.

The danger of my new bad thought was that it served the bourgeoisie. As pointed out by Chairman Mao, it "stands against or tries to weaken the people's democratic dictatorship and the Communist Party leadership, stands against or tries to weaken socialist transformation". Nor was that all. My bad thought went so far that I took from Malenkov's report to the 19th congress of the Soviet Communist Party words to the purport that "the banner of democracy and freedom can no longer be held by the bourgeoisie and will have to be held by the working class". That was why I said these two sentences in my speech at the CPPCC session this year: "I love socialism but I also love democracy". I obviously took the erroneous view that socialism and democracy are opposed to each other. This erroneous thinking was precisely what was disproved by the "More on the Historical Experience of the Dictatorship of the Proletariat".

Apart from this, I absurdly regarded the science and technology of capitalist countries and their "democratic way of life" as the strength of their life. I took the erroneous view that, if our socialism is added to science and technology and "democracy", our national life will be more perfect. Since last year, I often preached in many private conversations and at meetings such thought of the bourgeois rightists under the signboard of revisionism. This poison did much harm to others. Not only did it find favor with the rightists of the China Democratic League and the China Peasants' and Workers' Democratic Party but also the mind of some progressive elements was unconsciously poisoned. This was an offense committed by me.

I can hardly be pardoned for my erroneous speeches and actions that I, guided by such vicious anti-socialist and anti-popular rightist thinking, have committed during the past year, particularly during the period of the Party's rectification campaign.

In 1956 I proposed that the CPPCC should be regarded as the "senate", a disguised form of bourgeois democratic parliament. The aim was to expand the "democracy" advocated by me so that under such conditions I myself could bring my part into full play and non-Party democrats could bring their part into full play. At a forum called by the CCP United Front Work Department this year, I erroneously proposed establishment of a "political planning council" and advocated more study of the state policies and guiding principles and strengthening of the rights of democratic parties. I placed the CPPCC, democratic parties and people's organizations in the same position as the NPC. It was a pure attempt to substitute bourgeois democracy for proletarian dictatorship and for the system of the people's congress. It was a violation of the Constitution. Such an advocacy was bound to lead to restoration of capitalism.

Nor was that all. According to my subjective desire I distorted the "long-term co-existence and mutual supervision" and "let all flowers blossom and all schools of thought contend" policies and Chairman Mao's speech "On Correct Handling of the Contradictions Among the People". I stressed the supervisory role of democratic parties and took the erroneous view that the socialist revolution has basically been completed and class struggle has basically been concluded. I took the erroneous view that all strata, particularly the upper and middle intellectuals, have made progress and may be given a free room of development. When the Party Center proposed rectification of working style and asked democratic parties to help the Party in its rectification campaign, I laid more stress on the development of organizations. I expected each democratic party to recruit several hundred thousand members and several democratic parties to recruit one or two million members. I also stood for expansion of the organizations of democratic parties to the *hsien* level and suggested that democratic parties hold consultations over recruitment of members in different *hsien* areas. I said once: "After basic completion of the socialist revolution, the character and task of democratic parties should be re-evaluated and should be placed on a higher plane". This absurd advocacy was an attempt to enlarge the political influence of democratic parties and increase political capital so as to meet the political desire of individuals. It was an attempt to weaken the Party leadership and bring about a situation in which democratic parties "stand on equal terms" with the Party. It would jeopardize the interests of the Party to the most.

The question of Chang-Lo alliance. Prior to 1956 I and Lo Lung-chi struggled for personal power. After 1956, because of the same mind we embarked upon the dangerous path of Chang-Lo alliance. The basic reason for our alliance was that both of us took the bourgeois stand and my political opinion corresponded to his demand. As a result of the alliance, some higher intellectuals who were for him and against me in the past changed their attitude and agreed with me. Lo Lung-chi told me time and again: "Where you go I will go." He proposed that Shen Chun-ju of the China Democratic League be made honorary chairman, I be the chairman and he be the first vice chairman. I did not agree. Since last year, he backed me in the work of the Democratic League, and on the personnel matters of the League like the appointment of Fei Hsiao-tung, Fan Pu-chai, Pan Kuang-tan, Tseng Chao-lun and Wu Ching-chao I met the desire of Lo. The work of the China Democratic League was divided in such a way that he took charge of propaganda and I took charge of culture and education. I agreed to let him take charge of the *Chengming* (Contention) monthly without my interference. I backed him over the question of intellectuals in the Democratic League and the CPPCC. I even backed him over his insistent demand for control of the cultural club.

Why did I compromise with Lo Lung-chi? I wanted to acquire a certain political influence among the higher intellectuals within the China Democratic League. I wanted to make a good job through Lo among the intellectuals. Higher intellectuals within the League like Fei Hsiao-tung, Pan Ta-kui, Tseng Chao-lun, Wu Ching-chao, Pan Kuang-tan, Hua Lo-keng, Chien Tuan-sheng and Ma Che-min had personal relations with Lo. Thus I needed Lo's support in order to expand my influence among the higher intellectuals. In this respect, it can be said that our ideological affinity led to a political alliance. We utilized each other and were adapted to each other.

Early May this year when the Communist Party started its rectification campaign, I arbitrarily arranged with Lo a meeting of some responsible comrades of propaganda, culture-education and organization departments to discuss the question of setting up four teams. Vice Chairmen Shih and Kao were not consulted beforehand on this matter.

The four teams were:
(1) The team for "long-term co-existence and mutual supervision" and "letting all flowers blossom and all schools of thought contend".
(2) The team for scientific planning.
(3) The team for performing duties.
(4) The team for Party committees in institutes of higher learning.

These four teams were organized for the purpose of preaching bourgeois democracy and science and confusing the people's view that socialism is superior and Party leadership is unshakable. The objective was to be achieved by disseminating the bourgeois views of the higher intellectuals. In consequence, ideological confusions were brought about and a few higher intellectuals were enabled to step up their conspiratorial activities and launch ferocious attacks on the Party. For instance, the suggestions put forward by the team for scientific planning concerning the system of sciences in our country jeopardized Party leadership over scientific work and disturbed the planning and unification of scientific research to such a serious extent as pointed out by vice chairman Kuo Mo-jo and deputy Pan Tze-nien. The other three teams did not call meetings or do any work but their political impact was equally serious and evil.

Professors Tseng Chao-lun, Chien Wei-chang and Fei Hsiao-tung and Secretary General Hu Yu-chih of the China Democratic League came to see me in the afternoon of June 5. Referring to the rectification campaign in the institutes of higher learning, the three professors were unanimously of the opinion that the situation was serious and demonstrations might take place any moment and that if the situation was not properly handled and if the students were united with the city dwellers, an incident like the Hungary incident was possible. They added that, while the situation was serious, they knew how to handle it and could "develop it or control it" but the Party committees could do nothing. I shared their view and decided to call a meeting the next day, also with the participation of professors Huang Yao-mien, Tao Ta-jung and Wu Ching-chao. Vice chairman Shih, Standing Committee member Min Kang-hou and director Yeh Tu-yi were also invited to the meeting. We had a talk on the things we talked the first day. I subscribed to their opinions at the time. This shows that taking the stand of the bourgeois rightists I backed an anti-Party plot to substitute the China Democratic League for the Party in the leading position in the institutes of higher learning.

Chu An-p'ing joined the *Kuang Ming Jih Pao* as editor-in-chief on April 1 this year. I had a very high opinion of him and felt that he was capable. And his journalistic view and thinking corresponded to mine in some respects. This identical view found its expressions in the following editing policy pursued by the *Kuang Ming Jih Pao* during the period in question:

(1) Publish more accounts of the activities of democratic parties and activities of individuals of democratic parties.
(2) Publish more accounts of the scientific and technical inventions in capitalist countries.
(3) Publish more accounts of the activities of socialist parties in nationalist countries.

This policy tallied with my bourgeois idea. The editing policy of the *Kuang Ming Jih Pao* was thus changed and the paper was made a mouth-piece preaching bourgeois democracy. What was more hateful, I agreed to the action of Chu An-p'ing to despatch correspondents to organize forums in nine major cities and to stir up disturbances everywhere so as to undermine the Party rectification campaign. Meanwhile, Lo maintained closer relations with Chu and gave directives to Chu on the policy of the *Kuang Ming Jih Pao* which was under Chu's charge. In consequence, the rightist thinking on the part of Chang, Lo and Chu had its common effect on the *Kuang Ming Jih Pao*.

In the first half of this year, I encouraged Li Po-chiu of the China Peasants' and Workers' Democratic Party to recruit members in Peking. When the rectification campaign was started, I told him to organize forums. The Peking Municipal Committee of the China Peasants' and Workers' Democratic Party organized in May twenty-one forums attended by some 500 persons from the circles of medicine, health, engineering, agriculture, education, arts and Peking opera. Further, I despatched Wang Yi-fan to the Northeast region, Yang Yi-tang to Shantung and Chang Yun-chuan to Honan to recruit members. My plan for recruiting large numbers of members was designed to influence the scientific, technical, medical and health personnel through the China Peasants' and Workers' Democratic Party in the same way as I tried to influence the university professors through the China Democratic League. In both cases, my objective was to acquire political capital and expand my political influence.

With a view to expanding my political influence inside and outside the China Peasants' and Workers' Democratic Party, I reorganized the *Hsueh Hsi Tung Hsun* into the *Chien Chin Pao* last year, changed the past practice of publishing more accounts of reports on Party affairs, and added some new features like old poetry and paintings. This was a demonstration of survival of feudalism in my mind. In the second half last year, I also contemplated restoration of the *Chung Hua Lun Tan* (China Tribune)—published during the period of anti-Japanese war—as a comprehensive publication to expand free academic debates. I intended to invite some famous men of letters, scientists and historians to organize an editing committee for the purpose of "making literary acquaintance and talking politics". This has so far not materialized, but my attempt to play my part in cultural-educational and scientific-technical circles is clearly revealed. These ideas and methods obviously accorded with my political schemes.

I was accustomed to a patriarchal way of leadership within the China Peasants' and Workers' Democratic Party. For instance, Huang Chi-hsiang was elected vice chairman in undemocratic ways at the 3rd plenary session of the China Peasants' and Workers' Democratic Party in March this year. This caused dissatisfaction among the comrades within the party. This shows that I regarded the China Peasants' and Workers' Democratic Party as a private organization, forgetting that it is a component of the people's democratic united front. Often I did not show respect to Communist Party leadership. I jeopardized the organizations of the leading party. My mistake was serious. I must completely change my direction from now on, return the China Peasants' and Workers' Democratic Party to its components, sincerely accept the leadership of the Communist Party, and guide the China Peasants' and Workers' Democratic Party to become a political organization for building socialism and effecting socialist transformation.

The above mistakes show that my political and ideological degeneration has reached such a shameful, detestable and dreadful state in the past year. I forgot myself in my elation. I was blinded by the lust for gain. My political ambition was ever growing. I attempted to expand the influence of my reactionary political program, spread the poisons and translate it into reality, taking advantage of my position and utilizing conferences, forums, private conversations, as well as two democratic parties and the propaganda agency of the *Kuang Ming Jih Pao*. All these erroneous speeches and actions show that, taking reactionary stand of bourgeois rightists, I negated the most fundamental system of our state, negated the dictatorship of the proletariat, negated democratic centralism and negated Party leadership. My speeches and actions were completely anti-Party, anti-popular and anti-socialist in character. I cannot shirk the responsibility for this serious crime. I am willing to ask punishment from the whole nation, from the Party and the government.

The whole nation is demanding stern punishment of me, a rightist. This is what should be done and I am prepared to accept it. I hate my wickedness. I want to kill the old and reactionary self so that he will not return to life. I will join the whole nation in the stern struggle against the rightists, including myself. The great Chinese Communist Party once saved me, it saved me once more today. I hope to gain a new life under the leadership and teaching of the Party and Chairman Mao and to return to the stand of loving the Party and socialism. I will mend my way and whole-heartedly serve socialism.

Deputies! This self-examination is merely one showing that I bow my head and admit my guilt; it is not comprehensive, nor penetrating. All explanations that must be made will be made to the units concerned. Finally, I hope that deputies will continue to subject my erroneous words and actions to stern exposure and criticism.

DOCUMENT 19

Report on the Rectification Campaign, by Teng Hsiao-p'ing, General Secretary of the Party's Central Committee, September 23, 1957, to the Third Plenary Session (enlarged) of the Eighth Central Committee.

> The English text is taken from CB 477. Most of it was reprinted from the English-language release issued by NCNA on October 19, 1957. Certain passages in the original Chinese text were not included in the NCNA English release, and these were translated and inserted by the U.S. Consulate General, Hong Kong. They are indicated by sidelining in the CB. The editor's note on page 346 was in the NCNA release.

Comment. The importance of this Central Committee meeting for the charting of a new "general line" for 1958 is discussed in our General Introduction, parts VI and VII. A few points may be underlined here.

    1. *Dissatisfaction with old-style intellectuals.* Section II of Teng's speech gives strong expression to this, saying, "The whole Party must gear its attention to training revolutionary experts. All members of the Party, if they are in a position to do so, must... turn themselves into experts who are both 'red' and expert" (three-fourths

through section II). Practical measures to this end are sketched in his section VII. Material on the need for a new type of political education may be found in ECMM 106 (*Study*, Aug. 3, 1957, on stepping up political courses at institutes of higher learning); ECMM 108 and 116 (*New Construction*, Sept. 3, 1957, on opposing the revival of "bourgeois economics" and "bourgeois sociology"); ECMM 115 (*Study*, Nov. 18, 1957, on compulsory reading courses for Party school and institutes of higher learning).

2. *Free markets and peasant discontent*. The "free markets," opened in September 1956 in order to ease the grain supply situation (General Introduction, part IV) were later blamed for the re-emergence of capitalism among the peasants. They were closed again for grain and other important products in September 1957 (SCMP 1599). There is a mass of press material on peasant discontent from the summer of 1957 to the end of the year. The object of the Party was to prove that the general burden was not great; that complaints resulted from occasional cases of incorrect thinking; and that the incorrect thoughts were inspired by rightist saboteurs. Articles of particular interest may be found in ECMM 85 and 88 (*Grain*, Jan. 1 and April 25, 1957, on the disruptive effects of the free markets); ECMM 102-104 (*Current Events*, Aug. 21, *Political Study*, Aug. 13, and *Study*, Aug. 18, 1957, on the question of the peasants' burden and rightist propaganda); ECMM 106, 112 (*Grain*, Aug. 25, and *Political Study*, Sept. 13, 1957, on the rural cadres' lack of ability or will to control the situation). URS, Vol. 9, No. 1, contains articles from the Kwangtung press illustrating special difficulties in that province.

Shortly after Teng Hsiao-p'ing's report, the Central Committee issued a directive on the management of agricultural producers' cooperatives (Sept. 27, 1957), designed to limit their size, make the management system more flexible, and improve relations between cadres and peasants (URS, Vol. 8, No. 26).

3. *Numbers and social make-up of the Party*. On these and related questions, see also Teng Hsiao-p'ing's report on the revision of the Party constitution, September 1956 (discussed in the general comment in Chapter IV, above, and the comment on Document 9); the article by Liu Lan-t'ao in the *People's Daily*, Sept. 28, 1959 (Document 45 below); and a report by Lo Jui-ch'ing, Minister of Public Security, on investigations into the Party carried out between June 1955 and October 1957—text in ECMM 118 (*Study*, Jan. 3, 1958). In the course of these investigations, said Lo Jui-ch'ing, 5,000 counterrevolutionaries were discovered within the Chinese Communist Party, 260 of them leading cadres at *hsien* (county) level or higher. The proportion is small in comparison with the purges of 1936-37 in the Communist Party of the Soviet Union.

Further material on the class provenance of Party members and new factory workers may be found in ECMM 82 (*Political Study*, Feb. 13, 1957); ECMM 83 (*Study*, March 18, 1957); and ECMM 90 (*Trumpet*, March 28, 1957). The last makes it clear that in order to consolidate the Party there was to be no further recruitment in 1957.

Other articles indicating troubles at grass-root level are in ECMM 90 (*Political Study*, April 13, 1957, saying the duties of cadres should be stabilized and the rush for transfers and promotions stopped); and ECMM 119 (*Study*, Oct. 18, 1957, denying tension between new and old cadres). On "localism" among the Party cadres, see comments on Documents 20 and 25 below.

Lesser points of interest are as follows:

(a) Teng says in his section III that in the interest of "people's justice" there is a provision for agricultural producers' cooperatives or *hsiang* authorities to exercise restrictive powers of an indefinite nature, without invoking court procedure, on "certain bad elements who 'do not commit serious crimes but always commit small crimes.'"

(b) Teng remarks, also in section III, on peasants wanting to go to the cities. There had been a series of directives by provincial and municipal committees in April 1957, urging them to return to the country (SCMP 1513, 1534). A directive limiting movement from the countryside was issued by the State Council on December 13, 1957.

(c) The "wall papers" (Ta Tse Pao) to which Teng refers in his report were large-character sheets, stuck or hung on the walls of factories. They were extensively used during the more general stage of the rectification campaign as a means of eliciting mass opinion or of mobilizing mass support for the Party line.

(d) The "workers' congresses" under the leadership of the local Party Committee, mentioned in Teng's section IV, seem to have been a very faint echo of the Yugoslav practice of industrial democracy. They were introduced by the Central Committee, as a check on Party bureaucracy, in March 1957. Little was heard of them in the years following.

(e) The exact nature of the three documents submitted by the Politburo to the Central Committee on the shift of power to lower levels is not clear. These are mentioned in Teng's section VIII. The reference is probably to directives which ultimately resulted in the decrees on decentralization of administration and financial authority (see our comments on Documents 16 and 25, also part VII of our General Introduction).

―――――――――――――――TEXT OF DOCUMENT 19―――――――――――――――

I. THE GENERAL SITUATION OF THE CAMPAIGN

The rectification campaign and the anti-rightist struggle which began in May this year had, up to August, been carried out in organizations of the Party and the government, institutions of higher learning, democratic parties, and news and publishing, scientific and technical, literary and art and medical circles at the municipal and provincial levels and higher. Since then, the movement has gradually been spread to the workers, peasants, industrial and commercial circles and faculty members of primary and middle schools. At the same time, the armed forces have also launched the rectification campaign. Now this is being broadened into a nation-wide rectification campaign.

At a meeting attended by the secretaries of some of the provincial and municipal Party committees held in Tsingtao last July, Comrade Mao Tse-tung made an over-all estimation of the nature and status of the rectification campaign and the anti-rightist struggle, and put forward a clear policy for the further development of the movement. Now the nation-wide movement is developing smoothly along the lines mapped out by the Party's Central leadership.

The significance of the current criticism of the bourgeois rightists must not be underestimated. This is a socialist revolution on the political and ideological fronts. The socialist revolution on the economic front alone in 1956 (in the ownership of the means of production) was not enough, and it is not consolidated. The great national debate now going on has solved or is solving such important questions as whether the revolution and the work of construction have been correct (or whether the achievements in the revolution and construction are the main aspect of the picture), whether the road of socialism should be taken, whether the leadership of the Communist Party is wanted or not, whether the proletarian dictatorship is wanted or not, whether democratic centralism is wanted or not and whether the foreign policy of our country has been correct, etc. If we fail to win complete victory in this debate, we will not be able to continue our advance. If we win this debate, the socialist transformation and socialist construction in our country will be greatly advanced.

The aim of this movement is to solve contradictions of two different characters, namely contradictions between ourselves and the enemy and those among the people themselves. In the period of socialist revolution in our country, the contradictions between the reactionary bourgeois rightists and the people are contradictions between ourselves and the enemy, are antagonistic, irreconcilable and life and death contradictions. The contradictions between the people and the counter-revolutionaries in city and countryside, landlord and rich peasant elements who are still engaged in sabotage in the villages, and rogues, hoodlums, robbers, murderers, rapers, criminals guilty of corruption and embezzlement, of seriously undermining social order and of gravely violating the law, and those whom the public regard as bad elements—all these are also contradictions between ourselves and the enemy. All contradictions other than these are contradictions among the people themselves.

The rectification of working style among the people themselves also consists of questions of two social categories different in nature. The question with the bourgeoisie and bourgeois intellectuals is one of enabling them to accept socialist remolding; the question with the petty bourgeoisie (peasants and self-employed workers in city and countryside), particularly with the rich middle peasants, is also one of enabling them to accept socialist remolding. As for the fundamental forces of the working class and the Communist Party, the question is one of rectifying their style of work.

The purpose of the rectification campaign is to direct the struggle along the line of correcting political orientation, raising the ideological level, correcting shortcomings in work, uniting the masses, and isolating and breaking up the bourgeois rightists and all other anti-socialist elements.

Resolute struggle must be waged against the enemy and methods of exposing, isolating and breaking up—and in certain cases punishing and suppressing—must be used. Within the ranks of the people themselves, the principal method is education, the method of "unity-criticism-unity". Those among the people who break the law will also be punished according to law, and such punishment is also educative.

The development of the movement in the past four months and more has conformed entirely to the analysis by the Central Committee and Comrade Mao Tse-tung, and fully proves the correctness of the Central Committee's policy.

The movement shows that it is necessary to wage a resolute struggle against the bourgeois rightists and other anti-socialist elements in the urban and rural areas. The attacks started by them against the socialist road and the leadership by the Communist Party were hectic and vicious. They had their programs, organizations and plans, and their aim was to restore capitalism and rule by the reactionaries.

The movement shows that it is necessary to continue the socialist remolding of the bourgeoisie and the bourgeois intellectuals, the petty bourgeoisie and especially, the well-to-do middle peasants. Not a few of them still hanker for capitalism and dislike socialism, and as the leadership of the proletariat and the Communist Party over them is not yet consolidated they provide a market for the activities of the rightists. But the overwhelming majority of them can accept socialism, by means of criticism and education. We must make great efforts to unite with and educate the middle elements so to isolate the rightists and swell the ranks of the left.

The movement shows that it is also necessary to conduct a large-scale movement of socialist education in the working class and the poor and lower middle peasants in the countryside. These are the most determined forces in defense of socialism. Educating them in socialism will enable them to carry on the struggle with better weapons. Furthermore, the small fraction of them who still have petty bourgeois ideology may succumb to bourgeois influences. If earnest efforts are made to bring out the facts and reason with them, they can easily understand.

The movement shows that it is essential to conduct a large-scale rectification campaign among the rank-and-file of the Communist Party, in the leading organizations and among leading functionaries of the Party, Government and people's organizations at all levels and in the enterprises. The Party is in the main healthy and most Party functionaries are sound. Full and frank discussions by the masses have exposed a large number of shortcomings in our work and our working style. Some of the shortcomings are serious and it would be very dangerous not to correct them. Moreover, among the Party and Youth League members there are a few rightists and some who are strongly influenced by rightist ideas.

The movement shows that in the struggle unswerving trust should be placed in the majority of masses and the mass line should be carried out fully. Full and frank expression of opinions, bringing out the facts and using reasoning, putting up wall papers and holding discussions and debates, this is the socialist democracy enjoyed by the overwhelming majority of the people and something unimaginable in a bourgeois democracy. This is the way to handle contradictions correctly in the ranks of the people and also the way to educate and unite the masses to struggle against the enemy. Allow all opinions to be expressed fully and frankly, as if lighting a fire to smoke out the enemy as well as purify ourselves of our shortcomings. We need to do both.

Facts show that fear of the full and frank expression of opinions, fear that there might be trouble, and lack of confidence in the degree of the class consciousness of the majority of the people and in the wisdom and strength of the masses—such right deviationist viewpoints are very harmful and have already been discredited by the facts.

The development of the movement has been healthy and remarkable results have been achieved. The results are even more remarkable in the units in which frank expression of opinions has been fully solicited and where attention has been paid to correcting the shortcomings in work. The development of the movement on the whole is that the rightists have been isolated and broken up, the middle elements have turned to the left and the left group has been growing in strength.

But the movement should be carried on to a still further stage and on a still broader scale. It should not be wound up hastily, and should not be started strong and end weak. We must strive for complete victory. In organs of the central, provincial (municipal), administrative district and *hsien* levels, the campaign must pass through four stages, namely, the stage of full and frank discussions (at the same time undertaking rectification and improvement), the stage of counter-attacking the rightists (at the same time undertaking rectification and improvement), the stage of emphasis on rectification and improvement (at the same time continuing full and frank discussions), and the stage when each person must study documents, undertake criticism and self review, and raise his own level. In all units where the anti-rightist struggle has achieved a decisive victory, there must be carried out the timely entry into the third stage with rectification and improvement as the main contents, at the same time developing a systematic criticism of bourgeois ideology.

Naturally, in some units conditions are different from those in the government organs, and the stages of the development of the campaign are not completely identical. For example, in the countryside, there are places where full and frank discussions are being developed, and there are places where struggle has been developed against the bad elements and criticism levelled against well-to-do middle peasants, but these activities are different from the anti-rightist struggle in the government organs. In dealing with peasants and workers, it is necessary to carry out education in socialism, but only a small portion of such people have to be subjected to criticism and self criticism, and it is also not possible here to follow the example in dealing with functionaries of government organs every one of whom will be required to study documents and to carry out criticism and self review.

For workers, peasants and students, during the stage when emphasis is laid on rectification and improvement, they must continue to engage in full and open discussions, supervise and help leading functionaries to rectify and improve, but they themselves are not required to lay emphasis on rectification and improvement, these matters being intended for the leading functionaries.

Furthermore, during the third and fourth stages, if rightists continue to be discovered, or if the original rightists have not yet bowed their heads, the anti-rightist struggle must of course be continued.

Accordingly the four stages mentioned cannot be made too watertight. Generally speaking, for the leading functionaries, all the four stages must be gone through, and must be thoroughly disposed of. The complete success of the campaign is not merely decided at the stage of the anti-rightist struggle, but more than ever decided at the third stage where emphasis is laid on rectification and improvement, and the fourth stage where each person is required to study documents, criticize and make self review, and raise his own level.

II. ON BOURGEOISIE AND INTELLECTUALS

The present struggle against the rightists is primarily being carried out among the bourgeoisie and intellectuals. Among them are the industrialists and merchants, the democratic parties and groups, and such circles as those in education, journalism, publishing, literature, the arts, science and technology and medicine as well as many employees in government institutions and university students. Intellectuals are not a class, but separately belong to different classes. However, in the present situation of our country most of the intellectuals come from bourgeois and petty bourgeois families, and their education has been bourgeois in nature. So, for the sake of convenience they are mentioned together with the bourgeoisie.

The elimination of the bourgeoisie is a fundamental question for the socialist revolution. The bourgeoisie, and especially its intellectuals, now constitute the main force that can challenge the proletariat. Politically they still have status, capital and influence, and the proletariat needs their knowledge. But unless they firmly undertake socialist remolding, clashes between them and the proletariat would be inevitable. The only way out for the bourgeois intellectuals is to remold themselves and serve the socialist economic base. Otherwise there is the danger of one becoming a "gentleman hanging from a beam", neither reaching heaven above, nor standing on the earth below.

The policies of the Communist Party toward the bourgeois elements and the intellectuals are consistent. It carries out the buying out policy regarding the bourgeois industrialists and businessmen, and strives to win them over to serve socialism. The Party's policy towards the various democratic parties and groups is one of long-time co-existence and mutual supervision. In the fields of learning and culture, the Party maintains that all schools of thought should contend and all flowers bloom. The premise of all these policies is socialism. The Communist Party has always firmly maintained the view that the bourgeois elements and bourgeois intellectuals must be thoroughly remolded and gradually integrated into the working class. The leadership of the Communist Party, the proletarian dictatorship and the system of democratic centralism are inviolable. The basic policies of the Party, such as those of suppressing counter-revolutionaries, of cooperation, and of the state purchase and marketing of the chief agricultural productions, are inviolable. Marxist-Leninist propaganda and political education must be strengthened, erroneous thinking must be criticized, "poisonous weeds" must be rooted out. Permitting the growth of "poisonous weeds" is intended to educate the masses through negative examples, to uproot them and use them as fertilizer, and to temper the proletariat and the masses in struggle. The Party has also pointed out that to deal with the contradictions between the proletariat and the bourgeoisie as contradictions among the people, one of the conditions is the acceptance by the bourgeoisie of our policies of socialist transformation and of the leadership of the Communist Party; otherwise they would turn into contradictions between the people and the enemy.

In general the bourgeoisie put up no resistance to the socialist transformation in 1956. This was because: (1) economically they no longer had any other way-out; (2) through "3-anti" and "5-anti" movements (Editor's note: the movement against corruption, waste and bureaucracy; and the movement against the capitalists' abuses of bribery, tax evasion, theft of state property, cheating and stealing economic information), the majority of them came to realize that there would be no way out by opposing the proletariat; (3) after joint state-private management, the government made appropriate arrangements for them economically and politically. But the change of ownership does not mean the completion of the socialist revolution, nor does it mean the extinction of the class struggle. The political and ideological struggle between the bourgeoisie and the proletariat is not ended, and, under certain conditions, it can become acute again. The recent frantic attacks launched by the rightists against the Communist Party and socialism serve to illustrate this point.

In the course of the socialist revolution the bourgeoisie and its intellectuals fall into three categories—the left, middle, and right. Those on the left support socialism and the leadership of the Communist Party. The rightists stubbornly oppose socialism and the leadership of the Communist Party. The minority of the bourgeoisie and its intellectuals fall into the left or right groups, and majority being in the middle. The right wants to contend with the left for control of the middle. The right always wants to attack the Communist Party and socialism but must wait for an opportunity. The right considers its opportunity to have arrived with the Hungarian incident, the bringing forward of the policy of a hundred schools of thought contending and the policy of long-term co-existence, the propagation of the correct handling of the contradictions among the people and the rectification campaign of the Party.

Mostly the rightists come from the exploiting classes. In their past, many of them joined reactionary parties and groups and were rightists during the period of democratic revolution. But history develops and men change. Many of those who were rightists in the period of the democratic revolution have shown change while others who were then part of the middle even of the left have become rightists now. This demonstrates that new political break-ups will inevitably occur during the socialist revolution.

The rightists mainly carried out their activities in places where intellectuals are concentrated, such as universities and colleges, certain government institutions, the press and publishing houses, literary and art organizations, and the fields of political science, law, the sciences, technology, medicine and health work. In the past the intellectuals have been through several movements, and most of them have made progress in varying degree while a few have joined the left. Most of them either can now accept or are not opposed to socialism. But many of them are imbued with the bourgeois world-outlook and it requires a considerable period for them really to become intellectuals of the working class. Because the ranks of the working class intellectuals are still relatively weak and under certain conditions the middle elements may still follow the rightists, the rightist intellectuals were particularly frantic in their recent attacks.

The rightists in the various democratic parties and groups functioned as the core of the rightist attacks, because the people have granted them a certain political status and they could make use of their legal positions to issue orders and enlist followers. The democratic parties are the products of the period of democratic revolution and although a number of their members have moved to the left during the socialist revolution, most of them have not yet changed their bourgeois stand-point for that of the proletariat. Therefore, the rightists at one time got the upper hand in many organizations of the democratic parties.

The essence of the various reactionary programs put forward by the bourgeois rightists during their attacks against the Party is opposition to socialism and opposition to the Communist Party's leadership. Their main arguments politically are: (1) Praising the bourgeois and opposing the socialist economic and political systems and culture. (2) Opposing the country's basic policies such as its foreign policy, policy of state purchase and distribution, policy concerning intellectuals and the five great movements. (3) Denying the achievements of the people's democratic revolution, of the socialist revolution and socialist construction, and denying the ability of the Party and the proletariat to lead national construction. (4) Opposing the Party's leadership in state work, opposing the Party's leadership in all departments (particularly in cultural, educational, scientific and technical departments), and demanding that the Communist Party leadership in certain basic organizations (particularly in institutions of higher education, the press and publishing houses) be removed.

The main arguments of the rightists in academic and cultural fields are: laymen cannot lead experts; Marxism is dogmatism; socialist countries have neither science nor culture, and are inferior to capitalist countries. They demand that bourgeois sociology, economics, history, and idealist philosophy be restored. They demand from the Party and the People's Government so-called "independence" and "freedom": so-called "freedom of the press", "freedom of publication" and "freedom for literature and arts" etc.

The rightist offensive showed that most of the bourgeoisie and bourgeois intellectuals were unwilling to accept the leadership by the proletariat and the Communist Party. The Communist Party naturally cannot exercise leadership over a portion of those in the democratic parties and among the intelligentsia and the industrial and commercial circles—the rightists—because they are enemies of the people. Its leadership is also not very consolidated among the majority (the middle elements), and the Party's leadership has not yet been established in some cultural and educational organizations. The rightists went in for a trial of strength with us. They tried and failed and then they came to the realization that their day was gone and they had no hope. Only then did the majority of the bourgeoisie and bourgeois intellectuals (the middle elements and part of the rightists) gradually give way, gradually discard their bourgeois standpoint, come over to the side of the proletariat and make up their minds to accept the leadership of the proletariat.

After more than three months' struggle, in general there has been decisive victory in the struggles in the democratic parties, in the universities and colleges, among other intellectuals and in organizations at and above provincial and municipal levels.

The task of the moment is to carry the anti-rightist struggle thoroughly to its end. For this reason we must continue to oppose the rightist trend, but we must also prevent the spreading of the scope of attack over too wide an area and the danger of employing simple and crude methods. We must pay attention to the rigid division of the boundaries between the extreme rightists, the rightists and the middle rightists, consistently pay attention to the examination of the lists of rightists in relevant units, and correct from time to time demarcations which are not appropriate. We must attach the greatest importance to the work of uniting with the middle group, and the promotion of the breaking up of the rightists, assisting those of them who have shown signs of repentance to gradually reform. We must realize that some rightists can be reformed, and after their reform they will still be useful to the people.

Those organizations in which the stage of anti-rightist struggle has ended should resolutely and in time move over to the stage of rectifying the style of work and making improvements and of ideological education. At present there are not a few units which lack the determination to enter the stage of rectification and improvement, and this situation must be corrected. When we say that the anti-rightist struggle has reached a certain stage, we mean that all the rightists have been exposed, criticized and isolated, and the majority of the rightists have been made to bow before the masses and admit their crimes. We do not say that the review of, and admissions by all the rightists have been carried to a state of thorough completion. There must be a portion of the rightists who will not repent, and they must bring their reactionary viewpoints with them to their graves. The majority of the rightists will also not really change themselves within a short time. But as long as they are isolated from the masses, our struggle has been successful.

Apart from the rightist views among a small number of people, bourgeois intellectuals have other serious erroneous points of view, particularly individualism, liberalism, anarchy, equalitarianism and nationalism. In the stage of ideological education, criticism and self-examination, emphasis must be concentrated on the systematic criticism of such erroneous viewpoints. This is one of the most important tasks that must be carried out during this rectification campaign.

The ideological transformation of the intellectuals is a long-term task, likely to take another ten or more years to complete. But in the current campaign, efforts should be made to give wide-spread socialist education to bourgeois intellectuals and members of the industrial and commercial circles in general; to wipe out the positions of bourgeois ideology; to change the political features of many cultural and educational departments and democratic parties fundamentally; and to establish firm leadership over the middle elements and to consolidate this leadership as soon as possible.

Great efforts must be made to strengthen the leading cadre on the cultural and educational fronts and thoroughly overhaul many cultural and educational organizations. In order to build socialism, the working class must have its own forces of technicians, its own professors, teachers, scientists, journalists, writers, artists and Marxist theorists. This must be a vast force and cannot be composed of only a few people. The whole Party must gear its attention to training revolutionary experts. All members of the Party, if they are in a position to do so, must make serious and tenacious efforts in theoretical and vocational study and turn themselves into experts who are both "red" and expert. In order to achieve this goal, central and local authorities should, as early as possible, draw up specific and concrete plans and carry them out with every effort.

In order to cultivate a working class intelligentsia, the new intellectuals must be educated in the revolutionary spirit, the ideological and political education and education through labor in schools must be revolutionized and strengthened. The work of training intellectuals from among workers and peasants must be strengthened, and outstanding revolutionary intellectuals systematically recruited into the Party.

Although most of the several million existing intellectuals are still middle elements, the great majority of them are willing to advance. They must be included in the plan of the working class to train its own intellectuals. They are an important asset of the country, and their efforts are needed in socialist construction in the fields of economy and culture and in training new forces. Great efforts need, therefore, to be made to unite with them, win them over, and educate them, correcting their erroneous points of view, helping them to reform themselves and, using appropriate and not crude methods, to enable them gradually to abandon a middle position and come over to the working class.

Through the rectification campaign and the study of Marxism-Leninism, we shall help them to penetrate the ranks of the masses, to approach realities. We must have more conversations with them, make friends with more of them, listen to their recommendations on work, assist them in the solution of difficulties in work. Our past defects in this field must be overcome. The absolute majority of the views brought forward by the intellectuals during the period of full and open discussions are correct, and they should be earnestly studied and dealt with.

A series of concrete measures should be adopted to carry through the policy of letting a hundred schools contend and letting a hundred flowers bloom in academic and cultural work. Of course, this is a socialist policy, and the policy must be executed in conformity with the six standards listed by Comrade Mao Tse-tung, to encourage socialist and not capitalist science and culture to flourish.

The principle of dealing with the rightists is one of combining a serious attitude with leniency. The political and ideological struggle must be thoroughly waged but the cases ought not to be handled too heavily, in order to continue to break up the ranks of the rightists and reform them. But leniency should not be so unlimited as to confuse the demarcation between the people and the enemy and between right and wrong. Such questions must be handled appropriately.

A new united front which serves socialism is needed during the period of socialist revolution. The policy of long-term co-existence and mutual supervision among the parties should be carried out on the basis of the six standards. The opinion that the democratic parties and groups no longer have a role is erroneous.

The central organs of the various democratic parties and groups recently held national conferences on rectification work, and we should assist them, simultaneous with the continued penetration of their struggle at the central and provincial and municipal levels, to bring their struggle actively and step by step to all their basic level organizations deeply, so that they may change to the stage of general rectification, break down their capitalist stand, and establish their socialist stand.

The measures for rectification among the hardcore elements in industrial and commercial circles are generally the same as those for the democratic parties and groups. For bourgeois elements in general, on the basis of their different conditions, some may participate in the rectification campaign among hardcore elements in industrial and commercial circles, and others may participate in the rectification campaign for separately organized groups. There must be exposed and criticized the activists of rightist among the capitalists who resist socialist transformation, and their encroachment upon the ideology of the masses of workers. There must be struggle against their activities which seriously violate the law, so as to educate the majority and to consolidate the socialist front. Clandestine factories must be banned, and they must be made to come into the open, so that they may be placed under control, supervision and transformation. For small scale industrialists and merchants, the emphasis is on socialist education, and when possible they may also be organized for debates, somewhat similar to the rectification measures for workers and peasants. Those among them guilty of serious violations of the law must also be exposed and struggled against. Generally, all industrialists and merchants must be made to receive education, and there must be no repetition of what happened in certain past movements when a portion of the people (principally small sized industrialists and merchants) were forgotten.

III. CONCERNING THE COUNTRYSIDE

The situation in the rural areas on the whole is sound: the cooperatives are, in the main, stable; grain output has increased, and the working style of the functionaries has improved. But because of the short period since the founding of the cooperatives, limited experience and serious natural calamities, there are still difficulties and shortcomings.

Agricultural cooperation has been carried out and the question of the ownership of the means of production has in the main been solved. But this does not mean that there is no problem in the countryside.

There is a part of the peasantry which still do not clearly grasp the relationship between the state, the cooperative and the individual's household. There exists among such people individualism and group exclusiveness, which disregard the national and collective interests.

On the question of the state purchase and sale, the contradictions between the well-to-do peasants and the state are comparatively more prominent. Not a few among them resort to various measures to sell less of their surplus grain and other major agricultural products, and certain people even carry out speculative activities. Especially after the opening of the free markets, the spontaneous trend toward capitalism on the part of some peasants has re-emerged.

The great majority of the well-to-do middle peasants joined the cooperatives under the influence of the course of the developments. But most of them are wavering ideologically. A few of them who clung to the capitalist road either took the lead in creating disturbances to withdraw their membership after joining the cooperatives unwillingly or carried out sabotage against the cooperatives from outside. They generally want to compete with the cooperatives. In addition, they also constitute the major force in the countryside which resists the policy of state purchase and sale, and engages in speculation in food-grain.

Counter-revolutionaries, bad elements and some of the landlords and rich peasants also took the chance to carry out sabotage. They fabricated reactionary views, spread rumors, took to superstitious beliefs, indulged in gambling, incited counter reckonings, instigated trouble, and even organized counter revolutionary organizations to stage riots.

In the recent period, there has existed within the Party a serious rightist deviationist ideology, namely the view that the struggle in the countryside between the two roads has come to an end, that there is no longer any need to stress the class line and that efforts can be exclusively devoted to production and relaxing socialist education among the peasants. There was lack of vigilance against sabotage by the reactionaries and powerful counter-blows were not given them in time. Among functionaries in the countryside, there are also a minority who, due to changes in their domestic economy, have developed the capitalist ideology. These people in effect take the stand of the well-to-do middle peasants on such basic questions as cooperation and state purchase and sale, and express doubt and dissatisfaction over the policy of the Party and the state.

It can be seen from this that as in the cities, there is still in the countryside the struggle between the two roads—the socialist road versus the capitalist road. A considerably long period is needed before this struggle can be resolved in our thorough victory. This is the task for the entire period of transition.

The purpose of the movement of socialist education now going on in the countryside throughout China is: (1) to distinguish right from wrong in the general debate and to hold fast to our confidence and determination to take the socialist road; (2) to analyse and criticize the bourgeois and individualist ideology of the well-to-do middle peasants and overcome the capitalist influence in the countryside; (3) to expose and deal blows to the acts of sabotage by the landlords, rich peasants, counter-revolutionaries and other bad elements; (4) on the basis of mass criticism and self-criticism, to put the cooperatives on a sound basis, rectify the working style of the members of the Communist Party and Young Communist League, improve the working style of the functionaries, overcome shortcomings in work in order to improve relations between the Communist Party members and the masses and between the functionaries and the masses, ensure purity in the ranks of the Communist Party, consolidate the cooperatives, stabilize the policy of state purchase and marketing and raise agricultural production.

The method of launching the movement of socialist education in the countryside must also necessarily be that of full and frank expression of opinions and general debate. It must be done by having faith in the majority of the masses.

Several different methods have now been adopted in the country but they are more or less the same. There is no need to insist on identical methods in view of the different conditions in different localities. Notwithstanding the methods taken, they should in no way restrict full and frank expression of opinions. Present experience shows that only by full and frank expression of opinions can there be a general debate and that only through the debate can the statements and actions of the anti-socialist elements be exposed, the distinction between right and wrong be made and class consciousness be raised. What is of particular importance is that only through the full and frank expression of opinions can the masses say what they wish, criticize the shortcomings and mistakes of the functionaries, expose the shortcomings in work and clarify the functionaries about the real state of affairs so as to help improve the work, raise the ideological level of the functionaries and their ability to work. At the same time, the principle of "using words, not hands" should be resolutely observed in the movement and any crude and rough method should be guarded against and corrected.

As a rule, the slogan of an anti-rightist struggle will not be raised among the peasants and other working people. No bourgeois rightist "label" should be used.

Facts gathered from different areas prove that among functionaries of the *hsien, ch'ü* and *hsiang* levels, there are small numbers of class dissidents, elements who seriously violate the law and Party discipline, and elements who have developed the capitalist trend to a serious extent. To strengthen the leadership of the countryside, to struggle against the above mentioned elements, and to criticize various rightist ideological trends, we must make a good job of the holding of conferences of functionaries of these levels in each *hsien*. Such conferences of functionaries of the three levels must adopt the measure of full and frank discussion.

Firm blows should be dealt to the counter-revolutionaries and bad elements in the countryside. Only by so doing can righteousness be upheld and evil eliminated. Counter revolutionaries and bad elements who have been sentenced and who return to crime after their release on expiry of their sentences must be rearrested and sentenced again. Criminals who seriously violate the law and discipline and those acknowledged by the public as bad elements must be resolutely punished severely. Illegal organizations and Taoist sects must be resolutely banned. Gambling must be prohibited. Some workers in political and judicial departments today abandon their duties in dealing with people who should be arrested and punished, and fail to arrest and sentence them. This is not right. It is wrong to inflict heavy punishment for a light crime, but it is equally wrong to inflict a light penalty for a serious offense. The present danger is more of the latter category. This deviation must be corrected under the leadership of Party committees of different levels.

The above principles also apply in the cities.

In various parts of the countryside there are generally certain bad elements who "do not commit serious crimes but always commit small crimes." In dealing with such elements, it will be too troublesome if the court has to attend to their every single act. But if they are left alone, great injury will be done to the production order and the social order. Consideration may be given to the practice of the drawing up of a practical common pact by the congress of members of a cooperative or the people's congress of a *hsiang* with the ratification of the higher level government, to place restraint on such people. A mediation committee may be provided to assume responsibility for the enforcement of such a pact. One who violates the pact may be suitably punished by the cooperative or the *hsiang* government. This is a mass measure for self education, self supervision and self restraint. It is an important method by which socialism may restrict individualism, change old customs and habits, and evolve new customs and habits. Not only in the countryside, but also in the cities, in factories and mines, in government organs and schools, the method may be put on trial. Certain roguish elements in the cities who undermine the socialist order may be despatched to the countryside of the local province, with the government entrusting them to the care of cooperatives with the necessary conditions for production under surveillance. Questions relating to this matter may be brought to the attention of the State Council for the study of appropriate measures for submission to the Standing Committee of the National People's Congress for decision.

Those whose "class label" of landlord or rich peasant was removed, but who have now been found engaging in disruptive activities should be "re-labelled."

It is necessary to conduct a struggle by means of reasoning and argument against those well-to-do middle peasants with deep-rooted capitalist ideology who are engaged in capitalist activities. However, they should not be treated the same as the landlords, rich peasants and counter-revolutionaries and bad elements. For the well-to-do middle peasants, the question remains one persisting in uniting with them, educating them and reforming them.

For peasants working on their own, we must not discriminate against them or be specially strict with them. We must endeavor to educate them into joining the cooperatives one after another of their free will. However, they should not be accorded conditions more favorable than that of the cooperatives. They, like the cooperative members, must undertake the various obligations to the state.

For well-to-do middle peasants and peasants working on their own, in addition to giving them political education, we must adopt certain economic measures to restrict their spontaneous tendency toward capitalism. Well-to-do middle peasants who demand to withdraw from a cooperative will only be allowed to do so after a great debate, and after appropriate arrangements economically have been provided for certain peasants with reduced incomes (with adequate concessions made by the withdrawing party) so as to realize the goal of making the majority of the peasants remain in the cooperative and only a minority leave it. For a small number of members who are resolute in their demand for withdrawal, they should be dismissed from the cooperative after their mistaken words and deeds have been criticized and their political influence has been taken away from them.

To restrict the development toward capitalism on the part of members of cooperatives, appropriate limitations must be imposed on land retained for self cultivation, reclamation of wasteland by individual effort, operation of side-line production individually, and the activities of the free markets in the countryside.

For peasants working on their own, they must be placed under proper control by the *hsiang* government or by a cooperative entrusted by the *hsiang* government, and they must not be given the "freedom" to carry out capitalist activities and acts which undermine the interests of the cooperatives (such as influencing the members of cooperatives, hiring farm hands for exploitation, buying saplings, issuing usurous loans, engaging in speculative trading, evasion of tax payments, and renting out of land). Such acts must be restricted or stopped. Enterprises and organs in cities wishing to enroll workers or temporary work hands in the countryside must go through the cooperatives, or enter into contracts with the cooperatives, and they must not be allowed to freely recruit cooperative members and peasants working on their own. The State Council will provide measures on this point.

I do not intend to go far on the question of how to integrate the debate on the two roads, socialist or capitalist, with the work of putting the agricultural productive cooperatives on a sounder basis, improving their management and carrying through the policy of mutual benefit, since the Central Committee of the Party has already issued three special directives on this. I want only to emphasize here that the class line in the countryside is still of decisive significance. It would be incorrect to forget class analysis and the class line in the countryside. It is imperative to ensure the supremacy of the poor and poor middle peasants while putting the cooperatives on a sounder basis. Generally speaking, the principal functionaries of the cooperatives should be poor or poor middle peasants.

Functionaries of cooperatives must resolutely participate in production labor. Today many functionaries have already done so and they have exerted a good influence. But there are still not a few functionaries who have not actively and fully carried out this provision, and some even refuse to do so. It is necessary for us to continue supervising them into implementing the measure earnestly, and to persist in it regularly.

The consolidation of the cooperative system depends fundamentally on the growth in agricultural production. Only by increasing production and consequently, the income of the peasants, thus showing the great superiority of cooperation, is there a reliable guarantee for the triumph of the socialist road over the capitalist road.

Only when the per-hectare yield of the cooperatives comes up to or exceeds the average per-hectare yield of the local well-to-do middle peasants, can the vacillation of the well-to-do peasants be ended and can they be persuaded to take the socialist road.

China is a big country with a population of over 600 million. Of this more than 80% is rural population. If we do not develop agricultural production, not only will the lives of the great majority of the population, the worker-peasant alliance and the unity of the people be affected, but also industry cannot be developed rapidly.

The Draft National Program for Agriculture from 1956-1967 formulated in January, 1956, had inspired the peasants and played a good role. Now, the Central Committee of the Party has, on the basis of the experience gained in the past year and more, made some amendments to the draft program and recommend that this plenary session approve in general this program, so that wide publicity and discussion may be started throughout the country.

Following the general debate in the countryside on the socialist and capitalist roads, another general debate on agricultural production centering on this program should be organized so as to bring about an upsurge this Winter in agricultural production and construction and to give impetus to the cooperatives in working out their long-range plans for agricultural development with the active participation of the cooperative members.

After discussion throughout the country, the Central Committee will make another revision and have it discussed at the congress of the Party toward the end of the year, and then forward it to the State Council for discussion and adoption, to be finally forwarded to the National People's Congress for discussion and adoption, and then formally promulgated, to provide the criterion for the formulation of agricultural plans and the development of agricultural production during the next ten years.

It will be impossible to realize this 40-article Program if we do not possess the required stamina, to regularly struggle against the trend of conservatism. The gigantic achievements of the high tide of production in 1956 must be affirmed. These achievements exceed those of any single year after liberation, and in some cases even exceed the sum of achievements for several years. Naturally there are also defects. We must make a good job of summing up experiences, but we must not underestimate the great achievements because there are defects. In agricultural production in 1957, the good side is that work is being carried out on firmer ground, but the phenomenon in some areas of a lack of stamina must be corrected.

Agriculture holds a very important place in the socialist construction of our country. The goal of our efforts is to build our country into a modernized industrial country and a modernized agricultural country. Simultaneous with the prior development of heavy industry, we must exert all out effort in the development of agriculture. In the past few years we have been conducting greater propaganda on industry and despatched a large group of functionaries to work in industry, and this was necessary and produced positive effects. But we have not given sufficient efforts to propaganda on agriculture. Today we must stress propaganda on the important significance of the development of agriculture, and change the undesirable atmosphere which has emerged during the past two years, when agricultural production is not held in high esteem, the peasants want to go to the cities, the urban dwellers are not willing to go to the countryside, and the people living in the lowlands are not willing to go up the hills.

Whether the national program for agriculture can be carried out depends on the second five-year plan. Therefore, the whole Party must strengthen its leadership over agriculture. In our future national construction work, we should increase our investments in the capital construction of agriculture (including water conservancy) and make every effort to expand the chemical fertilizer industry and other industries which can promote the development of agriculture.

The production level of the great majority of cooperatives in the country should in five years reach or surpass that of the well-to-do middle peasants, so that the average per capita income of the collective economy of the cooperatives plus that of the household side-occupations of the cooperative members will reach or surpass the level of the local well-to-do middle peasants. At present, around 80% of the peasant households in the countryside have reached the level of ordinary middle peasants before cooperation. Of this, 20%-30% have reached the level of the well-to-do middle peasants, and generally only some 15% are still poor. It is therefore entirely possible to reach such a level in five years.

When there are increases in the income of the cooperative members, every effort should be made to increase the common funds of the cooperatives. Gradual expansion of the capital construction of the cooperatives by their own resources is not only a reliable way to develop production and increase income, but also constitutes the material basis for the consolidation of the socialist system (cooperatives). Only if the cooperatives acquire more common property can they become rock-firm; otherwise, they will be as easily dispersed as mounds of sand.

Where the peasants earn more and live better, the practice of economy and the management of households by industry and frugality should be advocated. The money which is saved may be invested in the agricultural cooperatives or deposited in the banks or credit cooperatives. Grain, too, has to be consumed frugally. In addition to fulfilling and overfulfilling state purchases, the agricultural cooperatives and individual peasant households should set grain aside against famine.

A campaign should be launched this Winter and next Spring to accumulate fertilizer and build irrigation projects, as it was done in the Winter of 1955-1956. Other appropriate capital construction work should also be carried on. The Central Committee and the State Council have issued a special directive on this task. Different areas should take into account different conditions and separately bring forward local concrete targets and concrete plans.

All production-increase measures of cooperatives must fully employ the mass line, and thoroughly implement the principle of the democratic management of cooperatives. There must be adeptness in the method of persuasion to rouse the activism of the masses for undertaking various enterprises conducive to the development of production and the solution of the various problems of the cooperatives. It must be borne in mind that even if all the enterprises we promote are fully correct and greatly successful, if they have not been decided after earnest discussion by the masses, there will still be dissatisfaction. And in fact there must be portions of our work which fail or do not produce the desired effects, and if they had not been discussed by the masses, the latter must blame us. But if everything is done through the decision of the masses, even losses will be borne by all, and all will learn the lesson and unity and correction will be easier. Functionaries of the basic level must be educated to pay regular attention to this point.

IV. ON THE WORKING CLASS

The rectification campaign in the ranks of the working class is a question of raising the ideological level and class consciousness and improving working style. It is different in principle from the question of the acceptance of the socialist remolding by the bourgeoisie, the bourgeois intellectuals and the petty bourgeoisie. Therefore, stress should be laid on improving work and conducting socialist education among the masses. The general masses of workers must not be handled with the same methods used in government organs and schools in dealing with bourgeois intellectuals.

At present, the situation in the ranks of the working class organizationally and ideologically is generally good. Of the over 11 million industrial workers, about 85% come from worker, peasant and other working people origin. About 35% of them were workers before liberation, and 13% are Communist Party members (plus Young Communists, the percentage comes to 29).

But a concrete analysis should be made of the situation in the working class, past movements proved that all veteran workers were the basic support for the Party and the cause of socialism. Of the new workers who constitute 65% of the total number, over one half come from peasant, student and city poor origin. Petty bourgeois ideology and style of work are rather strong in them. There are in addition about 3% (in some cases more than 5%) of the new workers who were landlords, rich peasants, capitalists, members of the reactionary armed forces and police or former idlers and their exploiting class ideology and bad habits have not been adequately reformed.

Therefore, it is necessary to launch a widespread thorough-going movement of socialist education among the workers during the rectification campaign. It is necessary to improve the cultivation and training of the backbone and core of the working class through the campaign. It is necessary to conduct further investigation and purge the ranks of the working class of undesirable elements. Through the rectification campaign and the movement of socialist education, the working class will be tempered as a conscious, organized and disciplined militant force.

The main contents of this education are questions concerning the leading position and responsibility of the working class in the socialist revolution and construction, and questions concerning the political tasks of the workers in the dictatorship of the proletariat. The workers should be helped to recognize that they must, under the leadership of the Communist Party, constantly raise their own consciousness, strengthen their sense of organization and discipline, and increase their class unity; they must develop the excellent tradition of working hard, maintain the noble character of being just and selfless, work hard in production, save and economize, and lead the people throughout the country by their own good examples in working to complete the building of socialism.

In those factories where the majority of workers are new ones, stress should be laid on solving the question of changing their standpoint. It is absolutely necessary to lay down the clearcut task of ideological remolding among the new workers.

Subjects for discussion should be formulated on the basis of the workers' personal experience and the questions they raise and in conjunction with the political and economic life of the country and the concrete situation in their own enterprises. In general, such subjects as these can be discussed: (1) How should the working class discharge its responsibilities as the leading class; (2) What is the relationship between the individual and the collective and between the individual and the state; (3) What is the relationship between improvement in living standards and the growth of production; (4) What is the relationship between freedom and discipline, and between democracy and centralism; (5) What is the relationship between the workers and peasants (mainly that the workers' living standards should not be much higher than those of the peasants).

The wall-papers should be used fully for the full and frank expression of opinions among the workers. Such papers are simple in form, lively in style, attract attention easily and they are convenient in mobilizing the masses. They are sharp and clear, vivid and colorful in criticizing the shortcomings of the leading personnel and the workers and in raising rationalization proposals. The wall-papers can gradually be turned into an important form for constantly developing criticism and self-criticism in the factories, offices or schools.

In the factories, the rectification campaign, socialist education and the remolding of the ideology of the new workers will have to rely on the veteran workers and those with longer working years and more political education. We must fully promote the active role of the veteran workers and use their rich production and living experiences, their class awakening, their organizational nature, their sense of discipline to unite with and educate the new workers, especially young workers. During the past few years not a few functionaries have somewhat neglected the role of the veteran workers and in certain policies and measures, such as grade promotion, piece wages, work arrangements, labor insurance, and employment of children, they have not given sufficient concern for the veteran workers. This must be improved.

The leadership must conscientiously rectify its working style, improve the work and from start to finish thoroughly carry out the policy of making improvements in the course of the rectification campaign.

It is necessary to investigate and overcome bureaucracy, subjectivism and sectarianism. It is necessary to make it a regular system that the leading functionaries (including those of the Communist Party, the administration, the trade unions and the Young Communist League) do physical labor. It is necessary for them to utilise every possible opportunity to master technique and work and strive, step by step, to transform themselves from laymen into experts. It is necessary for them to be well-versed in the conditions of production, maintain close relations with the workers and concern themselves with the welfare of the masses. They should be one with the workers in their daily life and resolutely abolish the privileges that separate them from the masses. They should assist and guide functionaries at the level of foremen to overcome commandism so that they can boldly undertake responsibility and at the same time take the mass line.

It is necessary to make great efforts to carry out retrenchment and reduce staff in the Communist Party, the administration, the trade unions and the Young Communist League as well as surplus staff engaged in non-productive work in enterprises. Attention must be paid to training functionaries from the ranks of the workers and fully utilize the activists and functionaries who are completely or partially engaged in production. Stress should be laid on bringing the technicians and staff together with the workers and they should be organized to engage in actual production work so that large numbers of excellent functionaries can be trained who have both actual production experience and maintain close ties with the masses.

Those regulations and systems that affect production and unity and restrict the initiative of the workers should be resolutely revised or abolished. At the same time, appropriate and necessary new systems of management and the system of political education should be established so that the achievements of the rectification campaign can be consolidated by systems.

The workers' congress under the leadership of the Communist Party Committee is a good form to broaden democracy in the enterprises, recruit the masses of workers to take part in the management of the enterprises and overcome bureaucracy. It is one of the effective methods to handle correctly the contradictions within the ranks of the people. It should be fully exercised in the present rectification campaign and should be popularized throughout the country after experience with it on a trial basis has been summed up.

According to the provisions of the Central Committee of the Communist Party, the functions of the workers' congress are: (1) to hear and discuss the work report submitted by the factory manager, examine and discuss the production, financial, technical and wage plans of the enterprise and the major measures to put these plans into effect, periodically to review the carrying out of these plans and put forward proposals; (2) to examine and discuss the use of the premium funds, amenity funds, medical funds, labor protection funds, trade union funds as well as other expenditures for the workers' welfare. Decisions can be made on these matters and submitted to the administration of the enterprise or to other quarters concerned to act upon, provided these decisions are not contrary to the instructions and directives of the higher level organizations; (3) in case of necessity, to recommend to the higher level administrative body the dismissal of certain leading functionaries of the enterprise; (4) to submit proposals to the higher level administrative body in case there is disagreement with its decisions. But if that administrative body still adheres to its original decision after studying these proposals, the decision should be carried out.

Technical personnel and staff members of enterprises are still mostly within the scope of bourgeois intellectuals. The rectification campaign is mainly intended to make them accept socialist transformation, and in general the methods used in rectification in the government organs may be followed. But because these people directly participate in production and construction, and are more closely connected with the workers, there is a difference between them and the higher intellectuals in organs and schools. Accordingly, different persons and concrete conditions must be taken into account, and separate treatment given them, and there should not be adopted simplified methods.

As to the absolute minority of anti-socialist elements among the workers, as well as rogues, hoodlums and bad elements who seriously violate the law and discipline, they should be criticized and suitably struggled against. Where conditions are particularly serious or where the persons concerned refuse to reform after repeated education, they should be dismissed from the factory on the conclusion of the campaign, and dealt with suitably. But there must be no indiscriminate consideration as politically anti-socialist elements and no struggle launched against the following categories:

(1) Those who are ideologically backward, given to strange ways of speech, lax in labor discipline, or expressing dissatisfaction with the leadership over work or living questions;

(2) Those who have provincial conceptions, the ideology of departmentalism, and sectarian feelings; and

(3) Trouble makers generally.

Special attention must be given to the prevention of dealing people blows and retaliation, the prevention of the emergence of sectarian struggles.

Special care must be taken in the handling of problems among veteran workers and demobilized servicemen transferred to production posts.

The rectification campaign in the handicraft and transport cooperatives must be combined with the overhauling of the cooperatives. There must be fully promoted the activism of the workers and the poor independent laborers for taking to the road of socialism, paying attention to unity with members comparatively more well-off and possessing techniques, exposing and criticizing the capitalist tendency of original small owners and a portion of the well off independent laborers, stopping those of them who attempt sabotage. The cooperatives must be consolidated on the foundation of the big debate of victory and the rectification of the functionaries.

Dependents of workers and employees in the cities and other laboring people must also universally develop the socialist education government under the unified leadership of the local Party committee, and as far as possible organized full and open discussions, carry out debates and distinguish clearly between big right and big wrong.

V. ON MINORITY NATIONALITIES

In all national minority areas and among all the national minority populations where the socialist transformation of the ownership of means of production has basically been completed, socialist education should also be carried out and an appropriate struggle waged against the rightists.

Socialist education and anti-rightist struggles among the national minorities have the same content as in the Han areas, but stress should also be laid on opposition to nationalist tendencies. Among the mass of the people, the method is to compare the new society and the old to bring out the benefits and necessity of national solidarity and unity within the big family of nationalities under the leadership of the Chinese Communist Party and the Central People's Government, and to expose the subversive activities of bad elements against national unity. It should be pointed out to the officials and members of the upper strata of the national minorities that the tendencies of local nationalism and Han chauvinism are both bourgeois, anti-socialist tendencies and a danger to the solidarity and unity of the various nationalities of the socialist motherland. We laid absolutely necessary emphasis in the past on opposition to Han chauvinism among officials of Han nationality and we will continue to stand firmly opposed to it. But it is now similarly necessary to emphasise opposition to local nationalism among officials of minority nationalities.

It should be clearly recognised that all those who make use of narrow nationalist sentiments and the estrangement between nationalities left over from the past in order to divide national unity and undermine the unification of the motherland act contrary to China's constitution and jeopardize the socialist cause of our country. They are all anti-socialist rightists. As regards those extremely bad elements who openly instigate national divisions, they should be resolutely exposed and repudiated in order to keep them completely isolated, to educate the masses and the functionaries.

In carrying out socialist education against nationalism among the national minorities, the key lies with the Party organisations in the national minority areas. Bourgeois nationalism among the people of a nationality can be overcome and solidarity and unity among various nationalities can be consolidated only when a really proletarian-minded Communist nucleus is formed in each of them.

Party members of all nationalities must understand that nationalism is an important aspect of bourgeois ideology which is fundamentally irreconcilable with the world outlook of the proletariat; that it is an ideology opposed to Marxism-Leninism and Communism and that such a bourgeois ideology cannot be tolerated within the Communist Party.

Therefore, the Communist Party organisations in the national minority areas must work out plans to carry out education against bourgeois nationalism and, in accordance with specific conditions, make necessary criticism of the nationalist tendencies conspicuous among some Party members of the nationality.

In the schools training national minority officials, the policy for political education there should be changed. In the future, stress should be put on class education and education in the Marxist-Leninist position on the nation, so that the students can acquire a Communist outlook regarding the world and man.

It takes a long time to reach a complete settlement of the national question. Therefore criticism of nationalist tendencies must not be made too hastily, but should be conducted carefully from the top to the bottom under leadership. Such criticism must have the support of the majority of the Party functionaries and non-Party activists of the nationality. Functionaries of Han nationality should continue to pay attention to examining into and criticising the tendency of Han chauvinism, while local functionaries of the nationality should lay stress on examining into and criticising local nationalism. Only when constant attention is paid to opposing bourgeois nationalism (including great-nation chauvinism and local nationalism) will it be possible steadily to raise the ideological level of the Communist Party members and the masses of people of various nationalities and consolidate and strengthen the solidarity and unity of the nationalities.

In the national minority areas where democratic reforms have been completed but socialist transformation is not yet carried out, the struggle against rightists must not be waged among the general public. But socialist education can be conducted within certain sections and in appropriate way.

VI. CONCERNING THE ARMED FORCES

In the armed forces, a few rightists were also uncovered in the anti-rightist struggle. This is of great significance to the consolidation of the armed forces. But the composition of the armed forces in general is comparatively pure. Therefore, after the conclusion of the anti-rightist struggle, efforts should be concentrated on rectifying the style of work within the forces with emphasis on rectifying the working style of the officers.

In the midst of the great social changes in the past few years, the political and ideological situation among officers in the armed forces is basically healthy. But because we are in a peaceful environment and large number of new elements have joined the armed forces, and certain workers have inappropriately stressed specialization to the neglect of ideological and political work, during the past few years among officers individualism and the trend toward a lack of organization and a lack of discipline have had some development. Some officers consider that the great task of the revolution has been consummated, and since they had contributed meritorious service, they must be awarded according to their merits. They no longer attend to their tasks with vigor but seek fame, status and good treatment, become taken up with considerations of personal gain or loss, and are not willing to work in places where there are hardships. In relations between officers and the rank and file, relations between the higher and lower levels and relations between the army and civilians, there are also certain defects which must be overcome. The links between the armed forces and the local Party and government organs are not close enough, and there is a constant lack of study and education in policies relating to socialist transformation and socialist construction. A small number of officers and men still have some incorrect views on many questions connected with rural work today.

The above questions must be earnestly solved through rectification and socialist education.

The rectification campaign in the administrative units of the armed forces of various levels and military academies can be carried out by way of wall newspapers, debate meetings and criticism and self-criticism. In the ranks of the armed forces, the main thing is to carry out socialist education and organize debates under leadership.

The armed forces shoulder the heavy tasks of national defense and military training, and during the period of the rectification campaign attention must be paid to the need for not relaxing combat preparedness and training work. This is especially so for the armed forces on the first line. The goal of the rectification campaign is to raise socialist awakening, promote unity in the armed forces, strengthen discipline and reinforce combat strength and not the opposite of these.

VII. ON THE COMMUNIST PARTY AND THE YOUNG COMMUNIST LEAGUE

At present our Party has 12,712,000 members (including 2,800,000 probationary members). Among them are more than 1,740,000 workers, more than 8,500,000 peasants, more than 1,880,000 intellectuals and more than 600,000 members with other backgrounds.

During the rectification campaign and the struggle against the rightists, the majority of the Party members behaved well. However, many problems have also been exposed.

Large volumes of matter relating to bureaucracy, sectarianism and subjectivism have been exposed during the campaign. One section of the Party members possess bourgeois individualism to a serious degree, zealously craving for personal enjoyment and keeping their minds on honor and position. There are also a very small number of Party members who have lost their revolutionary spirit or have even degenerated, become corrupt, and offended against the law and against discipline.

In the course of the campaign, the rightists within the Party have come into the open. The discovery of these spokesmen of the bourgeois class is of great significance for the consolidation and purification of our Party. In addition, there are still some Party members who have serious rightist ideology and are extremely discontented with the Party. Their views diverge from those of the Party over some important policy questions and they have shown political vacillation in the current struggle.

The rise of these serious problems within the Party has social and ideological origins: (1) The majority of the Party members are not from the working class; (2) The Party has grown rapidly without adequate attention having been paid to quality and the ideological and political work has lagged behind; (3) What is more important is that the majority of Party members joined the Party in the days after victory. At the time when they joined, they lacked genuine socialist consciousness. After joining the Party, they have been in an environment of cooperation with the bourgeoisie for a long time without experiencing direct and acute class struggle against the bourgeoisie. The majority of the 1,880,000 intellectuals among the Party members have not experienced training in productive labor, nor have they gone through serious tests of the class struggle.

In the struggle against the rightists, the rightists within the Party must be treated equally and as seriously as the non-Party rightists. However, there are now some comrades who, in the struggle against inner-Party rightists, have exhibited to a more serious extent the trend of sentimentalism, and this is especially noticeable in the expressions of regret, the show of weakness, and the reluctance to take action in dealing with some veteran Party members who should be demarcated as rightists.

When the campaign proceeds into the third and fourth stages, it is more necessary to tackle carefully the task of rectification within the Party than outside. Apart from the errors of bureaucracy, subjectivism and sectarianism (including sectionalism and group exclusiveness) among leading functionaries which must be corrected in all seriousness, the rightist ideas among rank and file Party members must also be criticised. All kinds of bourgeois and petty-bourgeois ideology must be criticised.

The work of ideological and political education must be strengthened. During the current rectification campaign, a comprehensive ideological and political survey of every Party member must be made. The weaknesses of inadequate attention to ideological and political education, unhealthy organisational life and loose discipline must be seriously corrected.

During the rectification campaign, except for renegades and those who have gravely offended against the law and disciplinary rules, consideration should be shown to all Party members and Young Communist League members. Great efforts must be made to help them correct their errors and overcome their shortcomings, improve their working methods, and raise their working ability, their ideological and political level. The Party members and cadres must be educated to be vigorous, to have revolutionary will and to have the attitude of serving the people selflessly and whole-heartedly.

It is necessary to have a conscientious check-up of all the basic organisations of the Communist Party in conjunction with the rectification campaign. Through the rectification campaign, the purity of the ranks of the Communist Party and the consolidation of the Party organisation must be achieved.

Rightists inside the Party should be dismissed from the Party. If their cases are less serious and they make a showing in changing for the better, and are not dismissed from the Party, their rightist "label" may be taken away.

All kinds of bad elements who have infiltrated into the ranks of the Party, elements who have seriously violated the law and Party discipline, those who have degenerated to the point beyond salvation, and those with serious bourgeois individualist thinking and acts who fail to repent after repeated education must be purged from the Party.

People who have lost their revolutionary will and cannot play the role of a Communist Party member and fail to reform after criticism and education, should be persuaded to resign from the Party or else purged from the Party.

In deciding on the expulsion of a member of the Party, his mistakes must be verified, the prescribed procedure must be followed, and after his dismissal, concern should continue to be given him politically and ideologically, special personnel assigned to maintain contact with him, to place him under observation and to educate him.

We must strengthen the education of probationary Party members, and carry out a rigid examination to prevent those who do not possess the full qualifications for Party membership from becoming into full members of the Party.

To ensure a constant readjustment of the composition of the Party membership and to infuse fresh blood into the Party, people who are really qualified for membership, particularly veteran workers and outstanding higher intellectuals, may be accepted into the Party in a selective manner on the basis of the rectification campaign and the anti-rightist struggle and on the condition that the quality of the membership is assured.

The rectification campaign and the anti-rightist struggle place each Party member, and particularly each functionary, to a test. It is necessary here to say something about the work of the Party relating to its functionaries.

Our Party has paid consistent attention to selecting outstanding workers, peasants and intellectuals closely linked with the masses of workers and peasants for various leading positions. This is the line of the Party's work regarding functionaries.

During a certain period in the past, we had assigned to leadership organs of various levels too large a number of young intellectuals who had not been steeled in production labor or tested in actual struggles. This was a defect.

Hereafter, we should continue to choose functionaries from among the excellent elements of the workers and peasants but these should be workers and peasants with a certain cultural level. We should likewise select functionaries from among the better elements of intellectuals, but they should be intellectuals who have been steeled in production work and struggle and maintain close connection with the workers and peasants. Those intellectual functionaries who have not been tempered in practical struggle and have no experience of working in an organisation at the lowest level should systematically be sent to do production work in villages and factories for a few years, or to do practical work in an organisation at the lowest level for a few years. All leading personnel in the Party, government and the mass organisations at various levels should be tempered in practical struggle and equipped with the experience of working at the lowest level. Those who are not should make up for it. This is also true of those working in the fields of literature, the arts, press, theoretical work and in other fields of propaganda.

An appropriate scheme should be worked out to enable graduates from universities and colleges and technical schools first to do manual work in organisations of production which are suited to their specialities. Only after one or more years of work, can they be assigned to jobs according to their specialities and their record in manual work.

Serious efforts should be made to create conditions to enable manual workers in production work to have opportunities to raise their cultural and technical knowledge and to enable part of them who can proceed to advanced education to enter universities and colleges.

Only by seriously carrying through this working line regarding functionaries can the Party and the state do the work of selecting functionaries on a reliable basis, and establish a force of functionaries dedicated to the cause of Communism and capable of weathering storms.

The question of the "localization" of functionaries is one which must be correctly solved in connection with the Party's work relating to its functionaries. On this question there are certain confused viewpoints which must be clarified.

In the early stage of the liberation, the Central Committee brought forward the policy of reliance on the functionaries in the old liberated areas for the development of work in the new liberated areas, and this was entirely correct. Today, the absolute majority of these functionaries are doing good work, and have established ties with the local masses. In other words they have been "localized", and should continue to work in these areas. A small number of people face difficulties in continuing their work, or reveal improper attitudes, and these must be mobilized for return to their home districts or to the place where they previously worked to participate in production, or other appropriate arrangements must be made for them.

All areas must promote an appropriate number of local functionaries for work, and while this point has already received attention, it should continue to receive attention. At present, in most areas, harmonious and normal relations exist between functionaries from the outside and local functionaries. But there are also some comrades who lack a correct understanding of the "localization" of functionaries, and some people even entertain the attitude of boycotting functionaries from the outside. This is the manifestation of a kind of mistaken provincialism, and should be corrected during this rectification campaign.

It must be pointed out that the "localization" of functionaries is not the highest principle of the Party's policy relating to functionaries. The highest principle of the Party's functionaries policy is primarily "communization". All functionaries, whether coming from outside areas or are local inhabitants must first be communized, and provincialism is incompatible with communism. The promotion of local functionaries must still be subservient to the principle of the possession of both character and talent, and within certain scopes there should be appropriate regulation. For example, at the *hsien* level, it may not be at all desirable to have a hundred percent local functionaries, much less at levels above the *hsien*.

The Young Communist League is a powerful assistant to the Party. Party organisations at various levels should pay close attention to the consolidation of the League and to raising the quality of the membership. Tremendous achievements have been made in the work of the League. But during the full and frank expression of opinions and the anti-rightist struggle, many problems have come to the fore among members of the League, particularly in regard to the League's policy of appointing functionaries and its ideological and political education. A serious check-up of the organisation and work of the League must be carried out in connection with the rectification campaign.

Members of the Young Communist League who have committed various serious mistakes, when subjected to the handling of the organization, may be dealt with basically in accordance with the various principles applying to the handling of Party members committing the various mistakes, but they must be treated more leniently compared with Party members, and greater stress must be laid on education.

VIII. IMPROVING THE WORK AND STRIVING FOR COMPLETE VICTORY

The improvement of the work and the struggle against the rightists are of equal importance and neither must be neglected.

The consolidation and strengthening of Party leadership depends on the Party itself, on the correctness of its leadership and on whether the shortcomings and mistakes in the work are really corrected. The anti-rightist struggle in itself cannot eliminate our shortcomings and mistakes.

In the course of the campaign, many criticisms and views have been brought forward both inside the Party and outside it. The absolute majority of these criticisms and views are correct, and though some of them are more radical, they are still beneficial.

In our work, a defect which has been more prominently revealed is as follows: many of the regulations and systems are irrational and impractical, and contradict one another. This affects relations between the higher and lower levels, between different units of the same level, between different departments, between different portions of the masses, and the development of production is affected. Some of these things have been incorrect when first provided, but others were originally correct, but because of the changes in conditions, they should have been revised but have not been revised in time. Some provisions should have been made by local authorities according to local expediences and should not have been laid down by the Central Committee in a unified manner. Some have been produced by different departments of the Central Committee under the situation of each looking after its own needs with proper co-ordination. Some were unavoidable because of lack of experience but others could have been avoided. Here there are instances of excessive centralization and also instances of dispersionism. Similar conditions also are to be found in certain provisions made by the local authorities.

Many leadership organs and leadership functionaries are seriously divorced from realities, seriously divorced from the masses. Comrades with responsibility are busy in routine matters and have too little contact with the masses, not understanding well the questions among the masses. Many irrational living systems have abetted the tendency of functionaries to get themselves divorced from the masses. Not a few functionaries are conceited and self complacent, thinking that they are always right and refusing to take to the massline, never consulting the masses on matters which come up for attention. Not a few functionaries are unwilling to have contacts with non-Party masses and non-Party elements.

These conditions cannot be allowed to remain unchanged, and they must be resolutely changed.

Ours is a big country with a population of 600 million. It is a great and arduous task to rally 600 million people to the work of building socialism with one mind and purpose. To carry out this task, it is necessary to persist in the mass line, correctly handle the contradictions among the people and create a vigorous political situation which combines centralism with democracy, discipline with freedom and united will with personal ease of mind. In such a political situation, the Party and the state will become consolidated to a greater extent and more able to weather storms and more able to overcome difficulties. This is of advantage to the advance of the socialist revolution and socialist construction and to China's industrialisation and the modernisation of its agriculture in a shorter period.

To create such a political situation, it is necessary on the one hand to carry the anti-rightist struggle through to the end, strengthen the dictatorship over the counter-revolutionaries and consolidate the discipline of the Party and the state; and, on the other hand, to overcome sectarianism, bureaucracy and subjectivism.

In order to rectify working style and improve the quality of work, efforts should now be concentrated on the following three points:

(1) Overcoming sectarianism and the tendency toward special privilege. Members of the Communist Party must be just and selfless, become one with the masses and share the lot of the people. They should keep in close contact with non-Party people and make friends with many of them. There should not be a great difference between the living standards of the functionaries and the masses. Regulations or systems that tend to give the functionaries special privileges over the masses should be abolished and a plain, simple living should be advocated. Leading officials must keep in close contact with their subordinates and the masses and functionaries must take part in physical labor. There should be no great difference in the living standards of workers and peasants and between urban and rural areas. In improving living standards, consideration must be given to the conditions of the great majority of the people in the country. Therefore, at present, we should persist in a rational low-wage system and do our best to ensure everyone a livelihood.

(2) Altering irrational regulations in the working systems and organisation and making appropriate readjustment in the relations between the Party and the government and between higher and lower levels concerning centralisation and unification on the one hand and division of work and responsibility on the other. What should be centralised, divided or shifted to lower levels must be. Both over-centralisation and excessive decentralisation must be corrected.

The Political Bureau of the Central Committee of the Party has submitted to this plenary session three documents concerning industrial, commercial and financial systems. The spirit underlying these documents is to shift part of the power to lower levels so as to release local initiative, strengthen the leadership of various enterprises and public institutions and overcome subjectivism and bureaucracy. At the same time, it will not impair unified leadership and major construction projects. This change definitely means an improvement upon the present system. But the new regulations, too, will not be perfect. They need to be supplemented and improved in the course of being carried out. It should be noted that when some authority is shifted to lower levels, new contradictions may emerge and therefore greater attention to strengthening planning and coordination is required. Both central and local authorities should take note of this.

The excessive number of functionaries in the Party and government organs and non-productive personnel in enterprises and public institutions, and the inflated and overstaffed organisations have contributed to the growth of subjectivism and bureaucracy. There must be vigorous retrenchment. This retrenchment and reduction of non-productive personnel has a great significance for present national construction in three ways: First, it will overcome the subjectivism and bureaucracy which cause a departure from reality and alienation from the masses. Secondly, it will create a whole army of steeled functionaries who are devoted to the cause of Communism and can weather storms. Thirdly, it will save considerable manpower and money, strengthen the labor force and the lower levels and speed up construction work.

Accordingly, all units should rapidly formulate plans for retrenchment and mobilize large numbers of personnel to production posts, to basic level units which need reinforcement, or make other provisions for the reduced personnel. Many unnecessary and duplicated machineries should be abolished, merged or have their levels reduced. For the retrenchment of organizations, apart from young intellectuals among the functionaries who must participate in production labor or work at the basic level as much as possible, other functionaries must also in part return to production posts or the basic level units. In our country we must promote the excellent tradition in which functionaries can serve in both the higher and lower levels, can be divorced from production and can also return to production.

(3) Broadening democracy among the people and continuing to strengthen the democratic system. It is essential to persist in using methods as gentle as rain and as mild as a breeze, the method of "unity-criticism-unity", in dealing with contradictions among the people. Leading functionaries at all levels must respect fully the democratic rights of the people, constantly listen to their voice and demands, give serious consideration to reasonable, different and opposing views of all kinds, wholeheartedly accept the criticism and supervision of the masses and resolutely overcome their shortcomings and mistakes. "In settling controversial issues among the people, we can only use democratic methods, methods of discussion, of criticisms, of persuasion and education, not coercive, high-handed methods." Only by carrying out this directive of Comrade Mao Tse-tung, can the enthusiasm of the masses be aroused and their class consciousness enhanced. Only by doing so, will the masses in the future boldly express their criticism and opinions on political matters and argue and persist in the truth.

The anti-rightist struggle is to pave the way for the correct handling of contradictions within the ranks of the people. We definitely will not allow anyone to make use of the anti-rightist struggle to obstruct the expression of opinions by the people and to settle controversial issues among the people by coercive and high-handed methods. In order to educate the widest masses, especially to dispel the misgivings of the middle elements, the anti-rightist struggle must continue, with special attention to the principle of bringing out the facts, presenting the arguments and convincing by reason, guarding against over-simplified and crude methods and avoiding exaggeration and one-sidedness. In dealing with the wrong viewpoints of the middle elements and the workers and peasants, it is necessary to use the method of patient persuasion and education. In dealing with academic controversies, it is particularly important to fight against arbitrariness and lack of mature consideration. We must see to it that the outcome of the anti-rightist struggle is favorable for carrying out the policy of "let a hundred schools of thought contend, a hundred flowers blossom," and not contrariwise; that it is favorable for the cultivation of an atmosphere in which the people do not hesitate to speak up, and not contrariwise.

We must work to achieve complete success in the current campaign. By complete success, we mean both success in the anti-rightist struggle and success in improving our work and reforming our ideology; and what is more, we must see to it that the outcome of the struggle leads to a political situation as described above.

Today the anti-rightist struggle must still be penetratingly and extensively developed. We have already scored a decisive victory in this field, but our task in the improvement of work has just begun. This calls for special attention.

In the improvement of work, some areas and some units have done a better job. The experience of these units prove that the views brought forward by the masses may in the main be immediately accepted and realised by the relevant units, and only a small portion of the questions have to be solved by the higher level or by the Central Committee in a unified manner.

In order to earnestly improve our work, we must continue to give a free hand in the mobilization of the masses for free contention and free blooming, so that the views of the masses may be reviewed without reservation. The different departments and units of the Central Committee and the local organisations must organize special sub-committees under responsible members to extensively collect the views of the masses on work improvement, and after their careful study, plans and programs for work improvement should be drawn up and gradually enforced. All departments and all units must from time to time report conditions relating to work improvement to the higher level and the Central Committee.

In many units in the whole country, the rectification campaign has entered the high tide of work improvement. In these units there has emerged a new situation characterized by great vitality. Many defects which had not previously been overcome after years of procrastination have now been overcome very rapidly. Problems which in the past took a long time to solve are now being solved very quickly. The activism of the masses has been greatly raised, the ties between the Party and the masses, and those between the functionaries and the masses have been greatly strengthened. But there are still leadership comrades in many units who do not attach importance, or do not attach sufficient importance to the improvement of work. Some are afraid that defects will be exposed, and from the very start of the campaign, would not allow the masses to contend and bloom. Some, after blooming and contention, have utilized the anti-rightist struggle to cover up their own mistakes in the attempt to avoid rectification and improvement, and get through the present test under cover. There are individual cases of dealing blows on and retaliating against people who brought up opinions. All these cannot be permitted.

In the course of improving the work, our slogans to the masses should be: express your opinions resolutely, boldly and thoroughly; our slogans to the leading functionaries should be: improve the work resolutely, boldly and thoroughly. The Communist Party committees at all levels should conscientiously strengthen their leadership in the third and fourth stages of the rectification campaign so as to make the campaign a complete success.

DOCUMENT 20

Adhere to the Correct Line of the Party and Win Victory of the Rectification Campaign on Every Front, work report by Chiang Hua, First Secretary of the Chekiang Provincial Committee of the Chinese Communist Party, to the Second Session of the Second Chekiang Provincial Congress, December 9, 1957.

The text is taken from CB 487 and is a translation by the U.S. Consulate General, Hong Kong, from the *People's Daily* of December 28, 1957.

Comment. The Second Session of the Second Chekiang Provincial Congress was from December 9 to 13. According to the NCNA of December 26, 1957 (CB 487) the session "transmitted and studied the spirit" of the third plenum of the Eighth Central Committee of the Chinese Communist Party in the previous September (see Document 19) and developed debates on many important problems. The news agency reported: "The delegates unanimously agreed that it was a rectification meeting of the socialist revolution, a mobilization meeting for socialist construction, and a meeting of victory and unity with historical significance." The meeting's most important business was "the exposure of the rightist anti-Party...activities" and the expulsion from the Party of Sha Wen-han, Governor of Chekiang; Yang Ssu-yi, Vice-Governor; P'eng Jui-lin, Chief Procurator of the Chekiang People's Procuratorate; and Sun Chang-lu. All these had been members of the Party's provincial committee. On December 30, Sha Wen-han and Yang Ssu-yi were dismissed as Governor and Vice-Governor, and also as deputies to the National People's Congress. The charges against the four men are expanded, but not in detail, in section IX of Chiang Hua's report printed here. The principal assertion is that they "consistently and viciously attacked the provincial committee."

After adopting Chiang Hua's report, the delegates, according to the NCNA release of December 26, recorded the achievements of the past year, and, looking to the future of their province's agricultural development, held that "as long as the leadership would ...adopt the mass line...and encourage the backward to emulate and catch up with the advanced, it would be entirely possible to reach the target of a 800-*catty* [per mou] yield in the next five years" (i.e., to reach in seven years the targets of the 12-Year Agricultural Plan).

Here is an anticipation of the Great Leap Forward along the lines probably decided by the Party's Central Committee in September, and under the slogans launched by Mao Tse-tung and Liu Shao-ch'i in November (Documents 21 and 22). The main interest of Chiang Hua's report, however, is historical, not prophetic. It illustrates the working out at provincial level of the rectification policy as laid down by the Central Committee meeting of September, and incidentally illustrates a number of the "contradictions" which arose at grass-root level in working out policy lines. In a prefatory note to the report of Chiang Hua's speech, the *People's Daily* of December 28 recommended that it should be studied carefully. "Long as it is, the article is worthy of being read through with patience."

Particular points of interest are:

1. Chiang Hua discusses in his section I the failure by Party members to grasp Mao's doctrine about contradictions and the right way to solve them. See our General Introduction, part VI.

2. He discusses in his section II the disintegration of cooperatives. This process had happened also on a large scale in 1955. See our general comments in our Chapters II, IV, and VI.

3. His section II also deals with the difficulty of collecting food-grains, given the "ideological backwardness" of the peasants, and the sympathies of many Party members with those who want to surrender less grain. See our General Introduction, and our comment on Document 19, above.

4. In his section IX, Chiang Hua mentions skepticism and "dispersionism" among Party members. Some simply disregarded directives from above; others in their zeal "accused the Provincial Committee of consistent rightist tendency and rightist opportunism." Some light is here thrown on the intellectual ancestry of those "good-hearted but overenthusiastic" comrades who pursued an extreme policy at the time of the formation of people's communes.

For further details of the Chekiang Provincial Congress, see CB 487. For the function of provincial Party congresses in purging the Chinese Communist Party and preparing the way for the more radical policies of 1958, see our General Introduction, part VII, and CB 509.

On the question of localism among Party cadres, see Document 19 above (section VII); and comments on Document 25 below. Typical illustrations of how local patriotism worked out on the practical level are provided in ECMM 106 (*Grain*, Aug. 25, 1957) and ECMM 107 (*Political Study*, Sept. 13, 1957). In addition, URS, Vol. 10, No. 7, contains interesting material of this time on the campaign against localism in Kwangtung (*People's Daily*, Dec. 14, 1957). Here resentment against Peking policies was closely linked with personal feeling against "south-bound" cadres, and a "great debate" had to be launched on "historical questions." On this, see also ECMM 129 (*Study*, March 3, 1958) for a call to "oppose parochialism" by the director of the Propaganda Department of the Kwangtung Provincial Committee of the Party.

———————————TEXT OF DOCUMENT 20———————————

Comrades:

I am directed by the Provincial Committee to deliver a work report to the 2nd session of the 2nd Party congress.

It has been one year and four months since the 1st session of the 2nd Party congress was held. During the period under review, the Party organizations in Chekiang, having completed socialist transformation of the ownership of the means of production, carried on a great socialist revolution on the political and ideological fronts and achieved a decisive victory under the correct leadership of the

Party Center and Chairman Mao. Simultaneous with this, a momentous victory has been won in Socialist construction. The ranks of the Party, having been tempered in the struggle, were further strengthened politically, ideologically and organizationally. Our task ahead is to carry through the socialist revolution to the end and to win a complete victory of the rectification campaign on the political and ideological fronts; at the same time, we should undertake socialist construction as much, as quickly, as good and as economically as possible and reinforce the material basis of the Socialist system. The rectification campaign will bring out the leading theme of all kinds of work. The victory of the rectification campaign will call forth the socialist activity and creativeness of all Party organizations and people and stimulate them to further efforts to carry out the principle of developing industry and agriculture simultaneously based on priority development of heavy industry, to fulfill and overfulfill the 1958 national economic plan and the Second Five-Year Plan and to realize early the revised draft of the national program for agricultural development.

I. THE RECTIFICATION CAMPAIGN AND THE ANTI-RIGHTIST STRUGGLE

The main characteristic of the situation in 1957 is that, based on the socialist transformation of the ownership in the means of production, socialist revolution is carried on on the political and ideological fronts. Practice has proved that socialist revolution completed in 1956 on the economic front alone (as regards ownership of the means of production) was not enough and stable. It is only through the rectification campaign and the anti-rightist struggle in 1957 that socialist revolution has won a decisive victory.

The campaign has taken the following course of development in the past year. Beginning from March this year, we organized all cadres inside and outside the Party to study Chairman Mao's report, "On the Correct Handling of Contradictions Among the People"; as from May, a rectification campaign and anti-rightist struggle were started among the organs at *hsien* and municipal levels and above and in the educational circle, journalistic circle, literary and art circles, scientific and technical circles and the health circle; beginning from August, a rectification campaign and socialist education campaign were gradually launched in the countryside and in the primary organizations of cities. The rectification campaign is now spreading far and wide throughout the province.

The socialist consciousness of the cadres and masses was considerably enhanced during the rectification campaign and the anti-rightist struggle. A group of rightists were ferreted out from the leading organs of *hsien* and municipal levels and above. Bourgeois rightists inside and outside the Party for a time stood against socialism and Party leadership on each front; now, their schemes have completely failed and they are isolated among the people.

The all-people rectification campaign has been launched throughout the province, and most of the leading organs at *hsien* and municipal level and above have acquired preliminary experience in contending, blossoming and debate. Contending, blossoming and debate begin to become regular methods of work. These new forms of socialist democracy appropriate to the new historical period are now gradually grasped by cadres. The working style and working methods on the part of the cadres are undergoing a change: this is a progress of important significance.

In the countryside, the rectification campaign strengthened the conviction and determination of the majority of the peasants to follow the road to cooperation. The campaign criticized the capitalist thinking and individualism represented by the well-to-do middle peasants. It dealt blows to the subversive activities of landlords, rich peasants, counter-revolutionaries and other depraved elements, thereby strengthening the socialist position in the countryside and raising a new high tide of agricultural production.

In factories and mines, the rectification campaign enhanced the political awareness of the worker masses, strengthened labor discipline, raised the rate of attendance and cemented the relations between the Party and the masses. Social habit of industry and thrift began to be formed and an impetus was given to the new high tide of production.

Practice in the past year has borne out the correctness of the directives of the Party Center and Chairman Mao. As long as the rectification campaign is grasped, all kinds of work are improved and a new atmosphere of activity is created. But it should be noted that, so far as we are concerned, the socialist revolution in the political and ideological spheres is merely a process of study, practice, experience accumulation and gradual advance. In the process of this radical change, it is evident that there are differences and controversies over some questions. On the basis of the directives of the Party Center and Chairman Mao, I make the following critical analysis of these questions:

1. Looking back over the situation in the past year, in particular the first half of this year—both rightist and 'leftist' tendencies showed themselves. The rightist tendency is to overlook the continued existence of contradiction between ourselves and our enemies, while the 'leftist' tendency is to exaggerate this contradiction and, in tackling contradictions among the people, to try and use methods appropriate to contradiction between ourselves and our enemies.

Class struggle has not altogether come to an end following the basic completion of the socialist revolution in the ownership of the means of production. The struggle between the bourgeoisie and the proletariat and the struggle between the capitalist road and the socialist road remain the chief contradictions in the period of transition to socialism, only this contradiction finds its expression for the most part not, as between the productive forces and the relation of production but as between the economic base and the superstructure.

In the struggle against the rightists, some people with rightist tendencies inside the Party failed to see that the struggle between the capitalist and socialist roads remains sharp and complex and the contradiction between the bourgeois rightists and the working people is between ourselves and our enemies. They failed to understand that the anti-rightist struggle is one of life and death, as between socialism and capitalism, involving basic questions of right and wrong and that failure to pursue this struggle relentlessly contains the danger of the Party and the country perishing. Consequently, they showed serious political wavering and sentimentality in face of the vicious attacks of the rightists on the Party and on socialism. Only when their rightist thinking is thoroughly repudiated is it possible for the campaign to go deeper.

Inside the Party there is also a section of people who, exaggerating the contradiction between ourselves and the enemy, thought that the struggle between the two roads invariably manifested itself in contradiction between ourselves and the enemy. They held that the Provincial Committee showed a rightist tendency when it stressed correct handling of contradictions among the people in the first half of this year. The outlook of these comrades was also wrong. The struggle between the socialist and capitalist roads, it should be understood, can manifest itself in contradictions either of the enemy-versus-the people kind or within the ranks of the people. But in our country in present conditions the former are relatively few and the latter many. Judging by the problems revealed during contending and blossoming and in the troubles that were stirred up, the overwhelming majority belonged to the category of contradictions among the people themselves. Some were due to the wavering and the discontent of the bourgeoisie, the bourgeois intellectuals and the rich middle peasants in regard to the socialist system, reflecting the struggle between the two roads. Some were due to lack of experience on the part of the leadership at various levels on how to consolidate the socialist system, or to shortcomings and errors in their work and their working style which were not few, and the fact that the masses were still unaccustomed and not adjusted to the new system; these are not, or not entirely, in the category of struggle between the two roads. Taking advantage of the opportunity created during our correct handling of the internal contradictions among the people, the rightists, counter-revolutionaries and other anti-socialist elements stirred things up and launched frenzied attacks on the Party and socialism, thus creating confusions. But when things go too far there is always a back-lash. When they were exposed in their true reactionary colors, the masses rightly became angry and those sections of the people who had been misled for the moment sobered up. So the mass anti-rightist struggle came into being. The results of the struggle show that the great majority of the masses are reliable and the rightists are indeed very few. We must therefore have firm confidence in the great majority of the masses. While it is wrong to overlook the contradictions between ourselves and the enemy, we must never exaggerate the strength of the masses. We must not regard the wavering and discontent over socialism on the part of the bourgeois elements and bourgeois intellectuals, who are not in the category of rightists, and that of the rich middle peasants, as contradictions between ourselves and the enemy and, in handling them, wrongly use methods appropriate to contradictions between ourselves and the enemy.

2. Many comrades fail to recognise clearly that the situation is sometimes tense and sometimes

relaxed and is not moving in a straight line. Before and after the upsurge in the three major transformations the bourgeois elements beat gongs and drums accepting the socialist transformation and the well-to-do middle peasants in the countryside, seeing the general trend, joined the cooperatives. At that time, too great a stress on class struggle would have been out of line with the objective conditions prevailing then. It was perfectly correct for us to put timely emphasis on the correct handling of contradictions among the people and on the rectification campaign. But when the rightists and the other anti-socialist elements took advantage of the rectification campaign to attack the Party and showed themselves in their full reactionary colors, we suggested that a struggle be waged against them and that socialist revolution be completed on the political and ideological fronts. We were given immediate and energetic support by the masses while the rightists fell back into complete isolation. It is clear from this that the circumstances attending class struggle fluctuate. Since the present struggle has achieved a decisive victory, the mass enemy has been compelled to retreat and the situation in the class struggle may be relaxed for a certain time. But the bourgeois rightists and other anti-socialist elements are never reconciled to their doom and in certain conditions are liable to launch new attacks on socialism. Such fluctuations in the struggle will occur repeatedly for a number of years to come. As the socialist revolution takes deeper root and the building of socialism grows, the internal class struggle in the course of these fluctuations will gradually diminish in strength until it finally disappears. Some comrades do not see the operation of these laws in the changing situation and set the anti-rightist struggle against the correct handling of contradictions among the people. This is obviously wrong.

3. As regards disturbances, some comrades see only their negative side. They do not see that, human initiative can be applied to turn bad things into good.

For instance, it is bad that many agricultural cooperatives collapsed in the course of the disturbances in Hsienchu County in the first half of this year.

But the rightist tendencies, bureaucracy and commandism among the cadres were effectively corrected when the provincial and regional committees of the Party sent in cadres to strengthen the leadership and draw conclusions from the experience and the lessons. The destructive activities of the enemy were thwarted. A campaign of socialist education was launched in the countryside. Many poor and lower middle peasants learned from their personal experience that the collapse of the cooperative brought them great difficulties in production and livelihood. They themselves demanded that the cooperatives be restored. Now over 70% of the peasant households are in the cooperatives and a conspicuous improvement has taken place in all kinds of work. So the bad has been turned into its opposite and become good.

We must realise that though disturbances cause some damage, they can serve to expose both shortcomings and errors in our work and show us the destructive activities of the enemy. They can train our cadres and teach the masses. They can also stimulate the leadership to overcome subjectivism and bureaucracy. As long as we are able to learn from the disturbances and conscientiously improve our work, we shall be able to convert negative into positive factors.

4. Many comrades still do not fully appreciate the new forms of mass line—the great airing of views, the general debate and the putting up of wall papers. Some showed little determination or confidence during the great airing of views and general debate, fearing trouble, or that they might not be able to win the debate, or that the fires unleashed might burn them themselves. This sort of wrong thinking shows lack of faith in the great majority of the masses and in the wisdom and strength of the masses. We should be confident that the great majority of the basic masses of workers and peasants support socialism and also that in China's circumstances the great majority of the bourgeois elements, the bourgeois intellectuals and the upper petty bourgeoisie (or the well-to-do middle peasants in the countryside) can accept the socialist transformation. It is therefore fully possible for us to carry the rectification campaign through in combination with the masses. Experience proved the great airing of views and general debate to be the only way to solve questions thoroughly as they needed to be. This method, while it provides the possibility of correctly handling internal contradictions among the people, overcoming shortcomings and errors in the leadership and certain wrong viewpoints among the masses, also exposes the enemy and rallies and educates the masses in struggle against the enemy.

Here it is worth stressing the question of convincing others by means of persuasion and pressure.

Some comrades doubt the need and correctness of handling the internal contradictions by means of persuasion and education. They fail to understand that the method of persuasion, that is working closely with the masses and linking up with them, winning them for the correct ideas, consulting them in all matters and respecting the views of the great majority is our Party's consistent working method by following the mass line which has long proved effective in practice. During the revolutionary wars, when the situation was tense, it was impossible to take time to develop general debate. During the five major campaigns and three great socialist transformations, when the primary task was to change the old relations of production and the chief form was the storm and stress of mass class struggle, it was also impossible to take time to develop general debate. Now, in the socialist revolution on the political and ideological fronts, when the question to be solved is the remolding of human thinking and the improvement of work, the great airing of views and general debate provide the best forms of completing this task. These forms are a new development of our Party's working method by following the mass line. We must consciously learn to apply them in all fields of work and make them regular practice and a tradition.

Against all the enemies opposed to socialism, we must adopt the method of dictatorship, that is, the method of prevailing upon them by pressure and dealing them serious blows. Failure to do means that rightist errors will be committed. But in handling contradictions between the working people and the bourgeois rightists—contradictions between the enemy and ourselves—we should in general continue using the method of the great airing of views, general debate, putting the facts on the table, reasoning and convincing others by logical argument. This is because contradictions between the enemy and ourselves are often mixed up with contradictions within the ranks of the people. If these methods are not adopted, it will be difficult to win over the middle masses and isolate the rightists. Only by such methods can the middle masses be helped to heighten their socialist consciousness, draw a clear line between the major questions of right and wrong and completely expose, isolate and break up the rightists. At the same time, as the people are very powerful, it is not necessary to adopt a policy of extremes against the rightists.

It appears from the above that a number of comrades in our Party have not grasped the directives of the Party Center and Chairman Mao and hold many wrong views of the new situation, new task and new method. All Party organizations in the province must lead Party members to study the directives of the Party Center and Chairman Mao seriously and learn how to apply them in practical work. On no account may they take an old view of the new situation and solve the new problem in old ways.

Our present task is to win a complete victory in the rectification campaign. On each front and in all kinds of work we should, through the rectification campaign, resolve the question of whether to follow the socialist road or the capitalist and the question of whether the principle and policy on all kinds of work are correct, thereby to raise the ideological level of the masses, correct the shortcomings and mistakes in work, unite with the masses, and isolate all the rightists and anti-socialist elements. Therefore, public debate should be extensively deepened and extended, centering on the important questions of present work, so that right and wrong can be distinguished, the majority of the people can be educated and united, the present work can be pushed forward and a high tide of agricultural production and construction can be raised.

The all-people rectification campaign should be intensified throughout the province this winter and the next spring. Leading organs at *hsien* level and above must pass through four stages of the rectification campaign: contending and blossoming (linked up with administrative improvement); hitting back at the rightists (linked up with administrative improvement); stressing administrative improvement (while continuing contending and blossoming); studying documents, examining and improving oneself. All those units which have achieved victory in the struggle against the rightists may pass over to the third stage with administrative improvement as the main feature. Only socialist education campaign should be launched while no anti-rightist struggle will be waged among the workers, peasants, handicraftsmen, and small traders. Following contending and blossoming the second stage should generally shift to administrative improvement. If there appear any conspicuously wrong utterances, debate should be held and right and wrong distinguished in combination with administrative improvement.

Administrative improvement and anti-rightist struggle are of first rate importance. At the moment, the administrative improvement is only at its start, and all the leading organs must attach importance to this link, strengthen their leadership over administrative improvement and win victory in the struggle against the rightists, victory in administrative improvement and victory in ideological re-education.

II. RURAL WORK

The rural situation as a whole was good. Agricultural producer cooperatives were further strengthened, agricultural production was constantly developed, food-grain work was gradually normalized and the relations were markedly improved between cadres and the masses.

With the exception of silkworm cocoons, output of food-grains, cotton, hemp and oil-bearing materials (including tea-oil trees) as well as domestic livestock and poultry, forestry and fishery showed an increase during 1957. Output of food-grains in the suburban areas of Wenchwo and in Huangyen and Wenling averaged more than 800 catties per *mow*; output of cotton in Tzuhsi *hsien* averaged more than 100 catties, fulfilling the target of the national program for agricultural development ahead of schedule. There appeared many 1,000-catty teams and 1,000-catty cooperatives and even 1,000-catty *hsiang* areas.

Food-grain work also achieved great success. Despite natural disasters last year, the target of grain taxation and collection was in the main fulfilled. Delivery of grains into state granaries took place at a greater rate than last year, and the target of grain deliveries can be fulfilled provided we firmly grasp the work.

In overhauling the agricultural producer cooperatives, we carried out the class line of the Party and the guiding principle of running the cooperatives by industry and thrift and in democratic ways. We improved the administration and management of cooperatives, distribution measures and the relations between cooperative functionaries and the masses.

All these facts show that the results of rural work were great and fundamental. Nevertheless, there were also some drawbacks. For instance, a small number of people stirred up disturbances in some areas in the spring this year; a few cooperatives were disintegrated, man-made tightness was experienced in the supply of food-grains in some localities; there was some production cut back in some areas. But these phenomena were partial ones and the errors and defects could hardly be avoided in the course of advance. We must not, on this account, under-estimate the results or neglect the main current and the essential aspect of our work.

What are the rural tasks ahead?

1. Carry on the socialist education campaign in the rural areas.

The all-people rectification campaign and the socialist education campaign are the key to all problems in the countryside. We should through this movement strengthen the conviction and determination of the peasant masses to follow the socialist road; criticize capitalist and individualist thinking represented by some well-to-do middle peasants; overcome vacillation on the part of some well-to-do middle peasants; expose and fight against the subversive activities on the part of landlords, rich peasants, counter-revolutionaries and other depraved elements. At the same time, we must overhaul the cooperatives, the Party and the League, improve the working style of cadres, overcome bureaucracy, subjectivism and sectarianism, purify the Party and League organizations, consolidate the cooperatives, strengthen unified purchase and marketing, and raise a high tide of agricultural production.

As a result of the recent debate on the two different roads, centering on food-grain work and agricultural cooperation, a profound change has taken place in the countryside. The socialist consciousness of the peasants was heightened. Capitalist thinking represented by well-to-do middle peasants was subjected to criticism. Subversive activities on the part of landlords, rich peasants and counter-revolutionaries were dealt blows. A high tide of agricultural production took shape. In such a favorable situation, we must launch the socialist education campaign to aid the high tide of agricultural production. In order to achieve this, it is necessary to direct the rectification campaign at the primary level to the drawbacks and mistakes in our work—to 'kindle fire to burn oneself'—to burn all the negative factors that hinder the consolidation of cooperatives and development of production. In this way, the activity of the masses can be directed to raise a high tide of production and to deepen the rectification campaign at the high tide of production. At the same time, where the debate has not been thoroughly held, the masses should still be aroused to air their views and the necessary debate should still be organized centering on production and the draft program for agricultural development. Following the contending and blossoming at the lower level, we should energetically improve the administration without pressing for debate. The important thing to do in connection with administrative improvement is to enlighten cadres on the advantage of administrative improvement and the advantage of simultaneous administration and debate. Further, cadres should be assisted in classifying the suggestions put forward by the masses. The suggestions should be divided into those that are correct and should be adopted at once; those for which the higher bodies should be held responsible; those for which cadres concerned should be held responsible; those that are due to misunderstanding and should be explained to the masses; those that are wrong and should be subjected to criticism at opportune moment. In this way, cadres will have their confidence increased and are not likely to be frightened by a mass of suggestions. At the same time, right and wrong can be distinguished and their consciousness and activity can be heightened.

To hold debate linked up with administrative improvement is another indispensable step. During the public debate, some questions concerning both practice and principle should be brought up in the light of actual conditions. During the debate, we must place facts on the table and reason and guard against such wrong methods as applying pressure, making exaggerated charges, beating etc. We must see to it that debate is held penetratingly and thoroughly to solve ideological problems.

The Party Center has issued concrete directives on how to overhaul the cooperatives in coordination with the rectification campaign. In this connection, the Provincial Committee in July put forward nine measures which should be firmly implemented. In overhauling the cooperatives from now on, the Party secretaries must take the lead and the rank-and-file of the Party must run the cooperatives. Further, we must grasp the following links:

(1) Carry out the class line of the Party and see that the former poor peasants and lower middle peasants (mainly the lower middle peasants who are between the poor peasants and new middle peasants of the present) predominate in the leadership of the cooperatives and the upper middle peasants are properly represented in the leadership. During the rectification campaign, secretaries of Party sub-branches, cooperative directors and deputy directors, supervision heads, chief bookkeepers and production team heads should be examined; well-to-do middle peasants guilty of serious capitalist thinking and elements showing very bad behavior must be removed from offices; activists among the impartial and capable poor peasants and lower middle peasants should be elected to perform the leading duties of the cooperatives.

(2) Carry out the guiding principle of running the agricultural producer cooperatives by industry and thrift and in democratic ways. This guiding principle must be emphasized at the same time of carrying out the principle of running household affairs by industry and thrift. All cooperative members, men and women, should be taught to run their cooperatives and households by industry and thrift and to oppose waste and loafing. A democratic system should be instituted and perfected through the discussion and revision of cooperative regulations and on the basis of the rectification campaign. The cooperative functionaries must perform physical labor and the question of their remuneration must be properly solved.

(3) Make a good job of distribution in cooperatives. Before a good job can be made of distribution, members must be taught to state their actual output. Further, the relations between the State, the cooperatives, and members' families must be properly handled. In particular, care should be taken to increase accumulation and storage of food-grains to meet emergency needs. After autumn distribution, final accounts must be made public at an early date.

(4) Those cooperatives owning forests must settle, this winter and the next spring, the question of bringing forests under the cooperative ownership. This question is one of socialist transformation of the means of production; without solving this question, it is impossible to strengthen the cooperatives and develop the mountainous areas.

(5) Questions like the side occupations, private plots, rural market control and individual peasants etc. should be properly handled in accordance with relevant regulations.

2. We must firmly combat rightist conservatism and facilitate the arrival of a production high tide.

Agricultural production in 1957 had its good aspects: the 1956 lesson was learned, work was done on a business-like basis and subjectivism and commandism were less pronounced. The main defect was lack of vigor. In some cases, the results of last year's work were under-estimated and a mass of correct things were not affirmed. Drawbacks and mistakes were exaggerated and individual examples of failure were cited to negate many successful production-increase measures. There were even cases where vigor was regarded as a sign of 'going too far'. This dampened the activity of cadres and the masses to a certain and lent itself to the growth of conservative ideas.

Conservative ideas have all along, as borne out by facts in the past years, been obstacles in the way of agricultural production. The first expression of conservative ideas was under-estimation of the production potentiality. Some comrades tried to justify their conservative ideas by the fact that production of food-grains did not increase at a great rate during the period of the First Five-Year Plan. It is true that during the period of the First Five-Year Plan agricultural production either showed no increase or declined in some *hsien* areas like Lungyu, Chuhsien, Tientai and Lishui etc, but these concrete conditions could not be taken as indication that the latent power of agricultural production was not large. For during the same period, production was up by more than 40% in many *hsien* areas like Huangyen, Linan and Haining. A number of low-yield areas were transformed into high-yield areas. The preponderant difference in output also pointed to a considerable potentiality of production. For instance, output of corn per *mow* amounted to only 100 catties in general, 400-500 catties in some cases and more than 1,000 catties in special cases. Output of cotton averaged only 78 catties per *mow* and some land yielded more than 200 catties per *mow*. Output of potatoes and sweet potatoes averaged only 1,000 catties per *mow*, but the highest yield reached 20,000 catties. Average output of soya beans amounted to scores of catties per *mow* but some high-yield land yielded 500 catties and more. It follows the rate of production increase depends on leadership, on whether the work is good or bad. The second expression of conservative ideas is to stress the particularity of local conditions and to be insensible to advanced things. It is held that output cannot reach 800 catties in mountainous areas or in areas with poor facilities of water conservancy. The natural conditions indeed have a great bearing on production but the effect is not absolute. Pingyang *hsien*, for instance, has the same natural conditions as existing in Huangyen *hsien*; and the climate in Pingyang *hsien* is even better. But the average output per *mow* in Huangyen *hsien* is 200 catties higher than in Pingyang *hsien*. Besides, natural conditions are not unchangeable and we can by no means wait for the bounty of the nature. Typical examples of high yield are found everywhere, whether in mountainous areas, along the coast, in the North or in the South. All these facts show that, if vigor is displayed and production-increase measures suited to local conditions are taken, production can be increased to a considerable extent in all areas. The third expression of conservative ideas is to demand more loans from the State and more supply of commercial fertilizer, fodder and food rations. It is held that production cannot be increased without these conditions. They do not understand that in order to overcome difficulties in production they must rely on the masses. There are numerous facts to show that these difficulties can be overcome if only the masses are set in motion. There are also some comrades who displayed vigor at the start but became passive as soon as they suffered some setbacks. The result was that the 40-article program was set aside and advanced experiences were not popularized.

It is a long-term and fundamental task to realize the national program for agricultural development in the rural areas. The basic spirit that permeates the national program for agricultural development is to take a leap in agricultural production by utilizing all kinds of positive factors and adopting all kinds of successful production-increase measures. Our province should strive to achieve the target of 800 catties per *mow* during the period of the Second Five-Year Plan or a little longer. At the same time, we should strive to develop other production and step up the output of other crops in general and cotton, silkworm cocoon, hemp and tea in particular. We should also develop forestry, fishery, livestock-breeding and side occupations. Simultaneous with the development of production, rigid economy must be practiced. In particular, food-grains must be built up in a year of ordinary crop or plenty so that no shortage of grains will be felt in a year of crop failure. We must exert our efforts in two ways —increasing production and practicing economy—so that in five years or less we may raise the production and income level of the cooperatives to that of local well-to-do middle peasants, thereby to lay a strong material basis for the cooperatives. On this basis we should step by step undertake economic and cultural construction, change the backwardness of the rural areas and build a new countryside of socialism.

There will be more favorable conditions for the development of production from now on. Socialist transformation of agriculture has in the main been accomplished; experience in high yield has been acquired in the past two years; side by side with the industrialization industry will give more aid to agriculture. Therefore, if we set the masses in motion, show a determined spirit and make up our mind to learn and do the job, we shall certainly be able to take a leap in agricultural production. All the Party organizations and cadres should with full conviction strive to achieve this target. Of course, there will be difficulties. But as pointed out in the introduction to the national program for agricultural development, man is the determining factor in doing things. So far as we the emancipated people are concerned, there are no difficulties that cannot be overcome. Being fearless of difficulties—such is the character of our working people.

The Party organizations of Chekiang must now do the following work:

(1) Preach the importance of developing agriculture and overcome the ideas of not settling down in agricultural production and not aiding agricultural production. The masses should be widely aroused to study and discuss the program for agricultural development and to open a public debate on the program. This public debate should aim at changing the undesirable attitude of the peasants who want to go to the cities, of the urban people who do not want to go to the farms, and of the primary and middle school graduates who do not want to take part in agricultural production. The debate should be held to rally all the rural cadres and peasants to devote themselves to agricultural production and to rally its aides to give wholehearted aid to agricultural production.

(2) Strengthen the guiding principle of leadership and draw up long-range production plans for provincial, district, *hsien*, *ch'ü*, *hsiang* and cooperative levels before May of the next year. The process of drawing up the plans is the process of learning and popularizing the advanced experience and overcoming the conservative ideas. Production state should be analysed at all levels, from province down to the cooperatives. The key to increase of production should be found out by comparing the output and tracing the reasons. Those backward units should be helped to find why they remain backward. Ways and means must be devised to catch up with the advanced. All those backward units should make up their mind to catch up with the advanced after exerting arduous efforts. They should constantly ask themselves: "If others can do it, why can't I?" The process of implementing the program for agricultural development is a test for every Party member and cadre. Those cadres who are full of vitality and are willing to learn should be commended while those who lack vitality and refuse to learn should be subjected to criticism. Those who refuse to mend their ways despite education must be removed from the leading posts.

All the five measures to popularize the advanced experiences laid down in the national program for agricultural development are successful ones and must be taken on a large scale. Agro-technical exhibitions should be held in each *hsien* area for the purpose of introducing the advanced experiences. Mass visits and competition should be organized to learn advanced experiences and create conditions for catching up with the advanced. At the same time, each advanced cooperative ought to be appointed to help one or several cooperatives. Through learning from each other and competing with each other, common development is to be achieved, the backward is to catch up with the advanced, and the advanced is to make further progress. Such study and help should be organized on a number of occasions each year and should be carried through to the end. There are about 3,000,000 *mow* capable of yielding 800 catties of food-grains each in the province; if this method of help and study is carried on, it is possible for all the 31,500,000 *mow* in Chekiang to reach 800 catties per *mow* during the period of the Second Five-Year Plan or a little longer. Care should be taken to carry out the program of agro-technical training. All the cadres transferred to the farms must learn agro-technology. A system should be widely instituted whereby cadres build experimental farms.

(3) Launch a grand winter production drive with the building of water conservancy projects, accumulation of manure and development of side occupations as the main features. To raise a high tide of winter production, the targets of conservancy projects, accumulation of manure and cultivation of spring crops should be set with the aim of achieving 800 catties (or 1,000 catties) per *mow*. Cadres

and cooperatives must be urged to fulfill these targets. Small conservancy works should be taken as the main measure and medium and large works as the supplementary measure in building water conservancy works, and these projects should be mainly built by the masses themselves. All the agricultural producer cooperatives are required to work out plans for eliminating ordinary flood and drought and to carry them out step by step. Water conservancy projects should be geared to the improvement of soil and transformation of the backward land. Manure is to be accumulated mainly by stepping up the per hectare yield of green manure crop, by raising more hogs and sheep to increase stable manure, and by utilizing all kinds of natural manure. Care should be taken to improve the method of fertilization and raise the fertilizing effect and rate of utilization. Special care must be taken to apply fertilizer to spring crops in order to ensure a good harvest of spring crops. This question was not given adequate attention in the past and must be given serious attention this year. Unified arrangements must be made for agriculture and side occupations during the winter. It is wrong to slacken side occupations.

(4) Develop agricultural production in mountainous areas and seas. Ideas of belittling the mountainous areas and seas must be overcome, and production in mountainous areas and seas must be grasped. To cover mountainous areas with green, to plant trees and to take good care of existing forests—such are important features of winter production in mountainous areas. Plans should be worked out for covering barren hills with green. Water and soil conservation, road-building, river dredging—such are important measures to develop production in mountainous areas, measures that should be carried out to the full. The key to the development of fishery lies in gradual increase of accumulation, increase of tools, improvement of technique and raising of unit production. At the same time, agriculture and production of sea-weeds should be developed along the sea lanes. All the Party committees in areas of fishery production should strengthen leadership over fishery. All the departments concerned should extend energetic aid to fishery production.

(5) Close coordination between agriculture and economic and cultural undertakings. All the economic and cultural undertakings in the countryside—such as the business of supply and marketing, credit and handicraft cooperatives, the anti-illiteracy campaign, the elimination of liver fluke and other diseases, the elimination of four evils, the building of rediffusion network and tele-communications network, the building of roads etc.—must serve agricultural production and must expand in the course of developing agricultural production. All the leading organs of industry, handicrafts, communications and transport, commerce, finance, culture and education should draw up and carry out plans for serving agricultural production.

Once the vigor is gained, we must not forget the mass line. There are two kinds of leadership over agricultural development. One is to go into the thick of reality, sum up and popularize advanced experiences, combine vigor with the mass line and combine vigor with business-like activities. The other is merely to raise the targets without studying concrete measures, to call general meetings and issue calls without exercising concrete guidance, to monopolize things and commit commandism. We should encourage the former working style and combat the latter working style.

All the leading bodies are required to make unified arrangements and introduce proper division of labor in order to fulfill the targets of winter production and other tasks. The cooperatives are required to make unified arrangements for labor power. The 1955 experience in completing several kinds of work simultaneously should be fully applied, unified leadership exercised, responsibility divided and keypoints established in *hsiang* areas. All kinds of work should be closely coordinated and done at separate stages, centering on the central task.

3. Fulfill the target of grain collection and procurement.

The contradiction between production of and demand for food-grains will continue to exist for a long time to come. In view of this, we must impress upon the peasants the necessity for industry and thrift in running their households and for economizing food grains so as to aid the national construction. We must teach them to change their habit of consuming food-grains without plans. Once this fundamental ideological problem is solved, other concrete problems can be solved right away.

The question of food-grains is an important aspect of the struggle between two different roads in the countryside. Without overcoming the capitalist tendency on this question, the development of production and consolidation of cooperatives will encounter considerable difficulties. Some comrades of our Party take the one-sided view that, if more food-grains are supplied to the peasants, their work can be done easily. These comrades, instead of relying on the poor peasants and lower middle peasants for making a good job of their work, merely demand more food-grains from the State. This is manifestation of departmentalism. There are also a few people within the Party who are dissatisfied with the policy of planned purchase and sale of food-grains and who sympathize with and support those families which do not sell surplus food-grains and which make illegal purchase of food-grains. These persons should be subjected to stern criticism and disciplinary measure. There are also some people within the Party who, on various excuses, demand lowering of the fixed amount of output and raising of the grain ratio, that is, they demand less purchase and more sale. Their arguments are that the fixed levels of production, supply and sale are not reasonable and the quantity of grains kept for self-use is inadequate. According to surveys, the fixed levels of production, supply and sale are basically reasonable; it is true the levels are not even in some cases but, generally speaking, the fixed level of production is lower than the actual production. In the majority of cases of complaints about too high level of fixed production, actual output is under-stated. Only in isolated cases is the fixed level of production set too high. The amount of food-grains kept for self-use is adequate; the peasants now consume more food-grains than in the past and their living standard has been raised. It is not right not to compare with the past, not to eat coarse and sundry grains. It is not right to expect to ascend to heaven by one step.

This year's targets of grain collection and procurement and the tasks of making additional purchase from increased output must be fulfilled, and the target of sales must not be exceeded. This makes it necessary to inculcate over-all idea in the mind of all cadres and people. Through the public debate we should overcome departmentalism and individualism. We should impress upon them why they must take a long-range view and make up shortage by plenty. We should overcome the idea of relying on the State in a year of crop failure while making no provisions in a year of plenty. Further, it is necessary to verify the output. Output is to be verified in the following ways: all members are persuaded to state their actual output with the help of Party and League members, poor peasants and lower middle peasants. Don't sit in offices arguing about output because this way of doing things will get nowhere. On the basis of verification of output and collection and purchase, a good job must be made of account settlement, and supply certificates should be issued to the households so as to make a good job of unified marketing of food-grains. To give importance to collection and purchase and to belittle unified sale—such has been the main drawback in food-grain work in the past year; we must not repeat this drawback this year.

To ensure fulfillment of the food-grain tasks, the Party committees should make a good job of food-grain collection, purchase and sale within a certain period and in the light of different conditions. The work cannot be done well if Party leadership is slackened and if it is simply left in the hands of the business departments.

III. INDUSTRIAL PRODUCTION AND THE WORKING CLASS

The total value of industrial and handicraft production in 1957 is expected to top the First Five-Year Plan target by 10.12%. Capital construction projects like the hydro-electric power stations at Hsinanchiang River and Huangtankou, the Chekiang Iron and Steel Works, the Silk and Satin Factory, the meat processing plants etc. are being built. The No. 1 blast furnace in the Shaohsing plant of the Chekiang Iron and Steel Works has gone into operation.

The total value of production in 1957, in the case of state-private enterprises, is expected to be 13.7% higher than 1956. This proves the unrivaled superiority of the socialist system over capitalist system.

When this year's industrial plan was first drawn up, production was expected to be 22,000,000 yuan less than last year; now the total value of production is expected to be 140,000,000 yuan above 1956. This is the result of the popular increase-production and practice-economy drive in factories and mines and of the socialist education campaign, which heighten the political consciousness of the worker masses, implement the guiding principle of industry and thrift, overcome the difficulties arising from shortage of raw materials, and raise the technical level.

TEXT OF DOCUMENT 20

The problem of industrial production will be as follows from now on:

1. Implement the guiding principle of developing industry and agriculture simultaneously based on priority development of heavy industry. The efforts of the peasants, and the aid of industry and all sides, must be relied upon for translating the program for agricultural development into reality. With agriculture developed, industry will gain a more rapid growth. To give effective aid to agriculture, chemical fertilizer industry must be strenuously developed in the first place. Preparations for building the Chekiang chemical fertilizer plant should be pressed forward and the Party organizations of all levels should aid the construction of the plant. Chemical fertilizer industry producing bone powder, lime and grass cakes as well as chemical industry producing insecticides and veterinary drugs should also be actively developed. Secondly, agricultural machinery industry should be developed. Seedling transplanting machines and grinders urgently needed by agriculture must be turned out within a short time, and the problem of repair to agricultural machinery must be actively solved. Thirdly, hydroelectric power industry must be developed. In addition to building large hydroelectric power plants, industry should actively aid the countryside in building small hydroelectric power plants, produce cheap-priced and good-quality hydro-electric power equipment, and accelerate the rate of electrification of the countryside. Fourthly, iron, steel, fuel and cement industries must be developed. Where conditions are present, small coal pits, iron mines, non-ferrous metal mines, non-metallic mines and small salt yards should be built provided resources are not destroyed and water and soil conservation is not adversely affected.

2. Systematically and actively develop light industry by exploiting local resources. Light industry should face agriculture and meet the growth of the national economy.

Our province is rich in natural resources and, provided there is a strong will to develop production, all things—grass, trees, earth, stones, sea water, air, scraps etc.—can be used for developing industrial production. Concerning construction capital, we should make use of local financial surplus, absorb floating capital, encourage investments by overseas Chinese, utilize social relief funds for organizing production, organize demobilized servicemen and people to undertake production, and utilize huts, temples and halls as living quarters and factory premises. Factories should grow from smallness to bigness, from nothing to something and develop from manual labor to machinery. Care should be taken to develop the role of existing technical personnel in fostering the technical forces. A group of young cadres with the standard of senior middle schools should be selected to work in factories and to learn technology in the course of their work. Men should be sent to advanced areas and factories and mines to learn advanced technology. The role of old workmen should be brought into full play.

We must continue to carry out the policy of combining large, medium and small enterprises and fully utilizing small industry and handicrafts. Special importance should be given to developing medium and small enterprises, mainly agriculture, forestry, fishery, livestock-breeding and processing industry. The merits of medium and small enterprises and handicrafts are that they call for small amount of investments, can go into operation quickly and can easily change the variety of products. They are therefore able to make full use of the scattered local resources, meet the needs of the local people in a better way and relieve the pressure of long-distance transportation on the trunk communication lines. Construction capital should be distributed in such a way as to successfully overcome the weak links in the economy of this province and also to take care of the needs of medium and small enterprises. A number of industries have to be developed gradually on the basis of the existing foundation of handicrafts, but the ownership of the handicraft cooperatives need not be changed in a great hurry. The policy of combining large, medium and small enterprises, combining industry and agriculture and combining heavy industry and light industry will facilitate more rapid growth of the industry in this province.

Exploiting the potentiality of the existing enterprises, improving quality, reducing the production cost, stepping up the output and increasing the variety of new products—such are important questions that must be given constant attention. It is not right to neglect full utilization of the existing enterprises. The experiences of advanced areas and advanced enterprises should be summed up and popularized, technical measures strengthened and technical reform gradually carried out if necessary and possible.

As regards handicrafts, we must make overall plans and unified arrangements and strengthen leadership. Through the rectification campaign we must criticize capitalism, departmentalism, and individualism, follow a correct political trend and overcome one-sided chase after high profits, blind raising of commodity prices, raising of wages, neglect of accumulations and sub-standard work. Through the rectification campaign and overhaul of cooperatives we should establish the hegemony of the handicraftsmen and the poor, independent laborers in the handicraft cooperatives, improve the working style of cadres and raise the level of administration and management. Proper arrangements must be made for the cooperative accumulations and for the relationship between wages and State collection of taxes so that the communal property of cooperatives will continue to increase and production will keep on developing. Except in the case of individual trades, the leadership of handicrafts should be maintained in its present state.

3. Intensify the rectification campaign and the socialist education drive among the organizations of industry and communications.

The organizational state and ideological state of the working class on the whole are good. But large numbers of new elements have found their way into the ranks of the working class along with the development of economic and construction work. Of the 215,000 workers and office employees in the departments of industry, about half are old workers who had worked before liberation and half are new workers who have joined the departments of industry since liberation. Of the latter, over half were recruited following the democratic reform of factories and mines. The number of new workers recruited in 1956 alone make up 20.9% of the total industrial workers employed in Kwangtung. The family and personal backgrounds of the new workers are complicated; they include peasants, free occupationists, small pedlers and merchants, urban poor people, housewives and students. The majority of them are enthusiastic in their work but they have also brought with them views of economism and egalitarianism and the bad habits of liberalism; besides, generally speaking, they have not undergone class struggle. About 9% of the new workers come from families of landlords and bourgeoisie or else they themselves were elements of the exploiting class. The class consciousness and bad habits of these persons have not been transformed. In addition, a small number of counter-revolutionaries and bad elements have also found their way into the ranks of the working class over the past years.

The rectification campaign of the working class is mainly designed to rectify their thinking and working style and heighten their socialist awakening. But so far as the new workers are concerned the first thing to do is to transform their standpoint. Through the rectification campaign the hardcore elements of the working class will be fostered, bad elements will be ferreted out and the ranks of the working class will be purified. During the rectification campaign and in all kinds of work in factories and mines, we must rely on the aged workers and those workers whose length of service is long and whose political consciousness is high, and must bring the active role of old workers into full play.

There are still some comrades and workers who consider that the living standard of the workers has not improved or has not improved much. This view is a reflex of individualism, egalitarianism and economism within the Party and among the workers following increase of large numbers of new workers. In 1957, the workers of industrial organizations in our province got an average wage increase of 42% and the number of workers enjoying the benefits of labor insurance increased from some 20,000 to 148,000. Through the wage reform there has been instituted a wage system which basically corresponds to the socialist principle of payment according to work. The wage increase as a whole is not slow. During the rectification campaign, we should enable cadres and workers to understand that the living standard of the workers has been raised to a considerable extent and that from now on we should take as our point of departure the six hundred million people, the development of production and the consolidation of the worker-peasant alliance. We should impress upon them that one-sided stress of better living standard will defeat our socialist cause and run counter to the long-term interests of the working class and the whole nation. It goes without saying that certain difficulties faced by the workers in their life, that should be overcome and can be overcome, must be overcome step by step by the masses. Workers' safety in production must be given serious attention.

Party leadership over the trade union activities must be strengthened. In trade union activities we must combat both the syndicalism that rejects Party leadership and the economism that does not center on production.

We must seriously enforce the mass supervision system under Party leadership and periodically call workers' congress so as to develop the socialist activity of the worker masses and strengthen the supervision over the leadership of the enterprises from below.

Administration must be improved through contending and blossoming. Taking the province as a whole, the following problems must be tackled:

Implement the State Council regulations on improvement of the industrial management. With the exception of a few technically complicated and large-scale enterprises and those enterprises whose business must be placed under the direct management of the provincial level, all industrial enterprises should be placed under the management of the municipal and *hsien* levels. The administrative authority of the personnel in charge of enterprises should be appropriately enlarged; profits should be divided between the State and enterprises; the financial and personnel systems of enterprises should be improved.

Industry, agriculture, commerce, communications and transport should strengthen cooperation and coordination. Outstanding problems of cooperation and coordination should be solved on the basis of self-criticism and mutual understanding. In order to develop industry, industrial raw materials must be developed provided the area of food-crop land is not reduced; the per hectare yield of industrial crops must be raised and the variety and quality of raw materials must be improved. In developing handicrafts in the countryside, urban handicrafts must be taken into consideration. Industry is required to supply the departments of commerce with goods and to accept raw materials supplied by the commercial departments. The departments of commerce should facilitate industrial and agricultural production through procurement of farm produce and marketing of manufactured goods. The development of communications and transport should cater to the industrial and agricultural production and capital construction and, in particular, should aid the exploitation of mountainous areas.

Implement the guiding principle of industry and thrift in building the country, running enterprises and doing all kinds of work. We must prevent unnecessary spending of money, cut all kinds of nonproductive expenditure and accumulate the State funds bit by bit for the purpose of developing production. Concerning the building of new factories and mines from now on, the standard of design should be lowered in a revolutionary way provided the production requirements are met. Moreover, the existing buildings should be utilized as far as possible and no new building projects should be undertaken where possible. Dormitories and office buildings will not be built in general.

Administrative machinery and personnel must be retrenched in a revolutionary way. We must try to reduce all the administrative and service personnel to 10% of the total number of workers and office employees in the province. Personnel retrenched should be mainly transferred to the production posts and a few may be assigned to the basic levels to strengthen the weak links.

Strengthen further the leadership of the Party over enterprises and institute and perfect a system of leadership whereby the collective leadership with the Party committees as the core is combined with personal responsibility. The leadership of the Party organizations over basic-level enterprises may be strengthened through the rectification campaign and by transferring cadres to the lower levels. At the same time, the role of trade unions and Young Communist League must be brought into full play under the single leadership of the Party committees.

Two high tides now appear in factories and mines: the high tide of socialist education and the high tide of production. We should see that these two high tides give impetus to each other and that the campaign for increasing production and practicing economy and the campaign of outstanding workers are intensified so that we can achieve still greater victory on the political, economic and ideological fronts during 1958.

IV. FINANCE AND TRADE

With industrial and agricultural production developed, the market has risen in increasing prosperity over the past year. The total value of industrial and agricultural products purchased will be 16.86% higher than last year and retail sales will be 7.7% higher. Market supply can in the main satisfy the demand. The budgetary financial revenue is expected to top the target and budgetary expenditure will leave a little surplus. The volume of money in circulation basically corresponds to the market demand. All this plays an important part in ensuring socialist construction and meeting the people's living needs.

The general problem of financial and trade work from now on is to facilitate the development of industrial and agricultural production and appropriately to meet the living needs of the people. Concrete tasks will be as follows:

1. Launch a rectification campaign. The departments of finance and trade have huge organizations and their personnel are in a complicated state of mind. During the rectification campaign, ideas of subordinating to the single leadership of the Party committees, aiding the development of industrial and agricultural production, serving the masses in a better way and strengthening the cooperation and coordination with other departments must be clearly established so as to heighten the socialist consciousness of all cadres and employees. The system in which the collective leadership with the Party committees as the core is combined with personal responsibility must be instituted in enterprises. Also a mass supervision system under the single leadership of the Party committees must be introduced. Workers' congress or workers' council should also be instituted and perfected. At the same time, the campaign for increasing production and practicing economy must be deepened, the guiding principle of industry and thrift must be implemented, and overlapping agencies must be reduced or merged while administrative staff and superfluous staff must be cut.

2. Aid agricultural and industrial production, translate the program for agricultural development into reality and develop local industry. Financial work should aim at increasing the revenue and increasing the State accumulation; expenditure should be used primarily for the purpose of meeting the needs of economic growth. Administrative expenditure must be firmly slashed while corruption and embezzlement of funds must be prohibited and unnecessary spending of money combated. Credit and loans should guarantee provision of funds for developing industrial and agricultural production and procuring commodities. The departments concerned should expand savings deposits and organize idle funds to aid production. Commercial work must be such as to strengthen procurement of farm produce, enlarge timely supply of capital goods and consumer goods, ensure supply of raw materials for local industry and aid the marketing of local manufactured goods. The departments of finance and trade must strengthen their cooperation with the departments of industry, handicrafts and agriculture and guard against departmentalism.

3. Improve the financial and commercial systems and transfer part of the power of financial and commercial administration to the *hsien* and municipal levels. All systems must be improved at the same time of improving the administrative system. The commercial administrative machinery and the administrative machinery of enterprises should be merged in principle. The relation between commerce and industry should be changed from one of processing raw materials and fulfilling orders to that of purchase and marketing. The ratio of profits should be adjusted between industry and commerce. A system of linking contract should gradually be introduced in respect to farm produce. A pro-rata system of agricultural tax should be introduced on the basis of adjustment of output. The industrial and commercial tax must also be reformed. Such reforms constitute important steps towards development of the national construction. The reforms must be effected actively and steadily.

4. Tighten up market control. The Party committees and people's councils must strengthen single leadership and control over the departments of commerce and guard against the 'each for his own' practice. Commodities subject to State control must be barred from the free market. Close cooperation should be maintained with neighboring areas. Control over the free market must be tightened up so as to develop its positive role and restrict its negative role.

V. THE WORK AMONG INTELLECTUALS AND CULTURAL AND EDUCATIONAL WORK

Since last year, we have firmly implemented the Party directive on the policy concerning intellectuals and the 'let all flowers blossom and all teachings contend' guiding principle. The year 1957 saw a rectification campaign and anti-rightist struggle waged among the intellectuals. This series of work has strengthened the relations between the Party and the intellectuals and heightened the socialist awakening of the intellectuals. At the same time, a group of Party members have been recruited from among the intellectuals and the ranks of the leftists have been strengthened, thereby creating favorable conditions for effecting further reform of the intellectuals.

Relying on the leadership of the Party and the strength of the masses, the departments of culture, education and health have achieved further progress in their work during the past year. The tasks of culture and education outlined in the program for agricultural development have been fulfilled in some cases. For instance, the Anhsia *tsun* in Lungchuan *hsien* has been transformed from a village of illiterates into one free of illiterate young people. Liver fluke has in the main been eliminated in many rural areas of Shaohsing municipality, Tehching *hsien* and Chuchi *hsien*. Mosquitoes and flies have in the main been wiped out in Nanhsun *chen* of Wuhsing *hsien* and Paisha *ch'ü* of Ningpo municipality. Mosquitoes, flies and epidemics have in the main been eliminated at Hsingpajan *tsun* of Chinhua *hsien*.

The cultural and educational tasks become heavy with the development of socialist economy and construction. We must go a step further to strengthen the Party leadership over the work among the intellectuals and the cultural and educational work so that the work among the intellectuals and the cultural and educational work can serve the socialist construction in a better way.

To build socialism, the working class must have their own intellectuals professors, teachers, scientists, journalists, artists and Marxist theoreticians. All those Communist Party members who are qualified to do so must make serious and diligent studies of theories and trades and rapidly become red experts. A number of comrades still do not fully grasp the importance of raising the level of political theories, science, and culture. They lack consciousness in studies and even refuse to make progress. Such a tendency should be subjected to strict criticism. All Party members whose cultural standard is below that of middle schools must learn culture and make up their mind to become experts in one line in three, five, eight or ten years.

With a view to fostering the intellectuals of the working class, we must keep the door open to workers and peasants in our educational work. From now on, the institutes of higher learning, intermediate specialization schools and other schools must give priority of enrolment to worker and peasant cadres, workers' and peasants' children and intellectual youths who have been tempered in physical labor. At the same time, efforts must be made to develop spare-time cultural education, run middle schools for workers and peasants and appropriately develop spare-time middle schools. The political and ideological education in schools must be intensified and the socialist awakening of the students heightened so that they can become intellectuals of the working class.

In order to foster the intellectuals of the working class, it is also necessary to reform the bourgeois intellectuals. Apart from a small number of leftists, the greater part of the intellectuals are middle-of-the-roaders and a few are the rightists. The middle-of-the-roaders should be helped in proper ways to effect self-reform so that they can pass over to the standpoint of the working class. It is therefore necessary to carry through to the end the rectification campaign and the anti-rightist struggle among the intellectuals. The rightists must be bared and criticized, intellectuals in general educated and their socialist awakening heightened. In addition, it is necessary to guide and help them study Marxist-Leninist theories and current policies and to organize them to perform physical labor so that they can get acquainted with the worker and peasant masses. At the same time, it is necessary to admit into the Party those intellectuals who have stood the test in the anti-rightist struggle and who are qualified for Party membership.

We must go a step further to implement the Party principle concerning cultural and educational work. In literature and arts, we must criticize the literary and art thinking of the bourgeoisie and adhere to the guiding principle of serving politics and serving workers, peasants and soldiers. In press work we must criticize the journalist view of the bourgeoisie and see that the press work can serve the socialist revolution and socialist construction in a better way. In political and ideological education, we must criticize the reactionary revisionist view and preach Marxism-Leninism. In school education, we must criticize the bourgeois view on education and adhere to the guiding principle of opening the door to workers and peasants and fostering the socialist laborers. In scientific research, we must criticize the academic view of research that separates theory from practice, and persist in the guiding principle of serving the national construction. In health work, we must criticize the belittlement of prevention and politics and the mutual exclusion of the western and traditional medicines, and persist in the guiding principles of taking prevention as the main measure, combining technology with the mass movement and uniting the western and traditional medicines. In all kinds of cultural and educational work, we must stick to the 'let all flowers blossom and all teachings contend' guiding principle, and open free and practical debates so as to facilitate the development of science and culture, provided the debate does not run counter to the six political standards set by Chairman Mao.

In cultural and educational work, we must stick to the guiding principle of industry and thrift and overcome extravagance and waste. We must combat the idea of letting the State monopolize everything. Cultural and educational work should be done as much, as fast, as good and as economically as possible. Efforts must be made to improve the quality of cultural and educational work. In order to reconcile the contradiction in which the cultural and educational work cannot meet the needs of the people, it is necessary from now on for the masses to undertake cultural and educational work. The masses should be encouraged and helped to run primary and middle schools, kindergartens, clinics and literary and art undertakings. Liver fluke and other endemics that endanger the health of the people must be wiped out through the efforts of the masses. The four evils must be wiped out and illiteracy eliminated. At the same time, birth control should be encouraged and successful methods of birth control must be propagated.

VI. THE BOURGEOISIE AND DEMOCRATIC PARTIES

Following the socialist transformation of capitalist industry and commerce, an anti-rightist struggle has been waged since May this year among the bourgeoisie and the democratic parties. This struggle has scored a decisive victory.

In view of bourgeois attack on the Party, some comrades are sceptical of the Party policy on the bourgeoisie and the democratic parties and are sceptical of the correctness of handling the contradictions between the proletariat and the bourgeoisie as contradictions among the people. These comrades are wrong. Practice bears out the correctness of the policy of peaceful transformation. The means of production was not destroyed during the transformation while productive forces were raised. After the industrial and commercial establishments came under state-private ownership, 60% of the bourgeois elements have joined productive labor and some of them have achieved good records in the socialist emulations. Under the historical conditions peculiar to our country, to handle the contradictions between the proletariat and the bourgeoisie as the internal contradictions among the people will help to win over the majority of bourgeois elements to accept transformation and help the struggle against the bourgeois rightists as evidenced by the victory of the anti-rightist struggle.

In view of the rightists who have appeared among the leading components of the democratic parties, some comrades doubt the necessity for the existence of the democratic parties. This view is also wrong. Practice proves that the democratic parties play an active part in uniting with, educating and transforming the national bourgeoisie, the upper strata of the petty bourgeoisie and their intellectuals. The suggestions put forward by most of the components of the democratic parties during the period of contending and blossoming were well-intentioned and helpful to us. From now on, we should continue to carry out the correct guiding principle of 'long-term co-existence and mutual supervision', taking as our basis the six political standards set by Chairman Mao.

The rectification campaign and the anti-rightist struggle must be intensified and carried through to the end. In the first place, the anti-rightist struggle must be carried through to the end through contending, blossoming and debate. Those units which have concluded their struggle against the rightists must enter the stage of administrative improvement and ideological re-education.

The following work must be done seriously in order to consolidate the results of the rectification campaign and the anti-rightist struggle and to reform further the bourgeois elements:

1. Continue to reform the bourgeois elements in enterprises. To take part in productive labor—such is a necessary measure to effect radical reform of the bourgeois elements. Thus, personnel of the capitalist side who are in charge of administrative work and are capable of performing physical labor should be systematically and discriminatively required to perform physical labor. For the present, typical experiments may be carried out in all municipalities and the experience acquired may be gradually popularized later on. At the high tide of transformation a small part of small proprietors also came under state-private ownership. These small proprietors practiced slight exploitation in the past and now take part in physical labor. Many of them want to give up the fixed interest payment and want to have the capitalist "label" removed. These questions may be resolved following conclusion of the rectification campaign.

2. Continue to organize studies of political theories on a voluntary basis among the democratic parties and industrialists and merchants. This is one of the important ways of ideological re-education for them. The main document to be studied is Chairman Mao's article 'Correct Handling of Con-

traditions Among the People'; other documents should also be studied together with this article. Public debate should be organized in the light of the political and ideological state of the democratic parties, industrialists and merchants and on the basis of the six political standards set by Chairman Mao. The propaganda department and the united front work department of the Provincial Committee should work out plans for the whole province. Leadership over this work must be strengthened in all areas.

3. Take effective measures to strengthen, raise and enlarge the leftist forces and strengthen the ties between the leftists and the middle-of-the-roaders. Responsible comrades of the Party committees are required to maintain regular contact with the non-Party people and to strengthen the ties between the Party people and non-Party people.

4. Strengthen the party leadership over the CPPCC, the democratic parties and industrial and commercial federations and bring the role of these organizations into full play.

VII. THE QUESTION OF ROUNDING UP COUNTER-REVOLUTIONARIES

The two large-scale campaigns for rounding up counter-revolutionaries and the struggle against the enemies in the past years have dealt telling blows to the counter-revolutionaries, bad elements and the criminal elements in Kwangtung. The public campaign for suppressing counter-revolutionary and the internal campaign for rounding up hidden counter-revolutionaries have achieved great results.

In May and June this year when the bourgeois rightists launched a ferocious attack, remnant counter-revolutionaries and other bad elements as well as some landlords and rich peasants in the countryside became active. In view of this, we organized counter-attack and dealt blows to the subversive activities of the enemy. We arrested a group of counter-revolutionaries, bad elements and landlords and rich peasants guilty of unlawful activities. We dealt blows to the evil influence and developed the good influence. During the period under review, some comrades of the political and legal departments one-sidedly stressed check-up of mistakes and deviations and did not maintain adequate vigilance against the subversive activities of the enemy. Some persons who should be arrested were not placed under arrest and some serious crimes were lightly punished. It was a rightist deviation. The Provincial Committee did not rectify such rightist thinking on the part of certain comrades of the political and legal departments.

Since the counter-revolutionary activities are spasmodic, our struggle against the enemy should be intensified at one time and slackened at another. Leniency must be tempered with severity. In stressing severity we must not forget leniency; in stressing leniency we must not forget severity. That is to say, when the enemies become so unlawful as to call for severe blows, we should adopt a policy of leniency towards the wavering elements among them so as to facilitate their disintegration; when the enemies are disintegrated and the policy of leniency is stressed, we should still deal with the inveterate enemies severely in order to crush their subversive activities. All is designed to round up the remnant counter-revolution. The dividing line between leniency and severity should be like this: severity to the culprits who are caught in the act and who put up resistence and to those who commit the crime again; leniency towards those guilty of past crimes, to those who confess to their crimes and to those accomplices. The Provincial Committee in the past years has followed this law and correctly carried out the policy of combining leniency with severity in leading the campaign for rounding up counter-revolutionaries. This is one of the important reasons for the victory of the campaign. Some comrades, not understanding why the campaign should be intensified or slackened according to the circumstances and why severity should be tempered with leniency, advocate either one-sided severity or boundless leniency. These comrades are wrong.

The campaign for rounding up counter-revolutionaries has won a great victory but not yet a complete victory. Chairman Mao said: "There are still counter-revolutionaries but their number is not large." That is to say, we must neither exaggerate the strength of the enemy nor show lethargy. We must carry on with the guiding principle of 'rounding up all counter-revolutionaries'.

The main tasks ahead in the struggle against counter-revolutionaries are as follows:

1. Arouse further the masses to round up remnant counter-revolutionaries and carry on with the campaign within their ranks. Counter-revolutionaries and bad elements already ferreted out must be dealt with as early as possible.

2. Stern measures must be taken to deal with the counter-revolutionaries who are caught in the act of subversive activities, landlords and rich peasants who settle accounts with the peasants, leaders of the reactionary societies who carry on restoration activities and counter-revolutionaries of the past who refuse to confess to their serious crimes. Persons who commit crimes again after being released should be placed under arrest and punished again. Hoodlums, thieves and criminals guilty of murder, rape, corruption and breach of public order and law must be punished according to law. Criminals who carry on black market activities and speculation, refuse to pay tax and undermine the policy of unified purchase and marketing as well as persons who are undesirable characters in the eyes of the public must also be punished according to law. Reactionary societies must be banned and gambling prohibited.

3. Carry out the State Council decision on labor custody. Those elements of government organs, schools and in the society who should be placed under labor custody should be turned over to the labor custody organs so as to purify the organizations and strengthen social security.

4. During the debate on two different roads, landlords, rich peasants, remnant counter-revolutionaries and other bad elements should be examined and judged by the masses. Elements who carry on subversive activities again after removal of their 'labels' should be either punished according to law or labelled once more or demoted to candidate members.

To round up all counter-revolutionaries and strengthen the people's democratic dictatorship, the Party committees must strengthen their leadership over the political and legal departments, pay attention to examining and appointing cadres of the political and legal departments, and maintain the purity of these departments. The political and legal departments must accept the leadership of the Party committees. Insubordination of certain personnel to the leadership of the Party committees is not to be condoned. Organizational measure should be taken against those who refuse to mend their ways despite education.

VIII. MILITARY WORK

Chekiang is located along the coast, and the regular task there is to strengthen the sea and frontier defense and prevent enemy raids and penetration. The Party committees always attach importance to the frontier and sea defense. The frontier defense is strengthened by the frontier military units and the masses, particularly the militia. Much has been accomplished in military service work, the military-building and resettlement of demobilized servicemen. The military work also has its drawbacks which must be corrected. Idea of relying on the masses for strengthening the frontier defense is not clearly established; militia work is not given due importance in some cases; demobilized servicemen are not properly educated and some of them are not properly resettled; some Party committees exercise weak ideological leadership over military service cadres; some military service cadres do not take an active part in the central tasks; some military service organs are not efficient.

One important aspect of national defense consists in building of the reserves for national defense, that is, military service work and militia work. Concerning this province's task of recruitment, the Party committees should make proper arrangements and organize forces to ensure their fulfillment.

The rectification campaign of the army is now in progress. Comrade Teng Hsiao-ping pointed out in his report on the rectification campaign: "In the midst of the great social changes in the past few years the political and ideological situation among officers in the armed forces is basically healthy. But because we are in a peaceful environment and certain number of new elements have joined the armed forces, and certain workers have inappropriately stressed specialization to the neglect of ideological and political work, during the past few years among officers individualism and the trend toward a lack of organization and a lack of discipline have had some development." Such is the situation among the armed forces in the military district. As a whole, the armed forces have satisfactorily handled the relations between the army and the government and between the army and the people. They have assisted the government and people in doing many useful things such as battling flood, harvesting, sowing and donating farming implements. But a few comrades of the armed forces are self-complacent and some even breach law and discipline. This to a certain extent hinders the improvement of relations between the army and the government and between the army and the people. Some drawbacks exist in the relations between officers and men and between the upper and lower levels. Some drawbacks also exist in the policy education concerning socialist transformation and socialist construction. For this reason, the armed forces should, upon conclusion of the anti-rightist struggle, concentrate on improvement of work and intensify socialist education. Further, they should overcome subjectivism and bureaucracy on the part of cadres, improve further the relations between officers and men and between the upper and the lower levels, intensify education in supporting the government and loving the people and improve the relations between the army and the government and between the army and the people. Hereafter the Party committees should strengthen their leadership over the armed forces and the armed forces should firmly accept the Party leadership and supervision. In addition, during the period of the rectification campaign, the armed forces should tighten up discipline and must not slacken combat preparations and training.

IX. PARTY WORK

The political consciousness of Party members has generally been heightened during the great rectification campaign and anti-rightist struggle. Party organizations have been further purified and strengthened.

One of the important results achieved by this Party congress is the thorough exposure of the anti-Party and anti-socialist activities on the part of rightists Sha Wen-han, Yang Ssu-yi, Peng Jui-lin and Sun Chang-lu hidden within the provincial Party committee. It would appear from what has been brought to light at the congress that politically and ideologically they are completely the same as the non-Party rightists. When the non-Party rightists launched attack on the Party, they gave active support to these rightists and, during the struggle against the rightists, they did everything to protect the rightists. Within the Party they spread the bourgeois ideas of parochialism, sectarianism and individualism and attempted to transform the Party. They went to the length of defying the guiding principle of the Central Committee, refused to carry out the directives of the provincial committee and consistently and viciously attacked the provincial committee. They destroyed the principle of democratic centralism and carried on activities to split the Party. Their criminal activities are concentrated expressions of the interests and aspirations of the bourgeoisie and are fundamentally incompatible with the interests of the Party, the interests of socialism and the interests of the people. That is to say, they have completely degenerated into agents of the bourgeoisie within our Party.

These anti-Party and anti-socialist activities on the part of the Party rightists, as pointed out by many comrades at the congress, have several years' history behind them. Their criminal activities caused serious damage to the Party cause, damaged the Party prestige, weakened the Party unity and hampered the unified and centralized leadership of the Party. What must be particularly noted here is that the political and ideological tendencies represented by them have become negative factors to corrode the Party. These tendencies must be thoroughly brought to light and criticized.

It appears from the rectification campaign that a certain tendency towards dispersion exists in our Party organizations. The provincial and local Party committees, it must be noted, have actively carried out the directives of the Party Center and achieved great results. But certain important directives of the Party Center and certain important measures formulated by the provincial committee are not firmly carried out in some areas and by some departments. This state of affairs is due, so-far-as the provincial committee is concerned, to failure to exercise concrete guidance, carry out strict check-up and take a serious action. It also shows that a few members of the provincial committee and the responsible persons of certain areas and certain departments failed to take a correct attitude towards the directives of the Central and provincial committees, and failed to observe strictly the democratic centralism. Particularly since the provincial committee committed the mistake of 'firmly retreating' over the question of agricultural cooperation in 1955, some comrades became sceptical of the leadership of the provincial committee. Some even had this to say at the Party congress last year: "the greater the distance from the provincial committee the better". At the cadres' conference this year some accused the provincial committee of "consistent rightist tendency" and "rightist opportunism". Holding these completely erroneous views, these comrades took their own course in practical work, seriously weakening the united will and fighting capacity of the Party. The present congress has subjected these erroneous tendencies to serious criticism. Some comrades have examined their errors. This is quite necessary if the Party unity is to be strengthened and the fighting capacity of the Party is to be increased.

It also appears from the rectification campaign that amidst the socialist revolution and socialist construction the overwhelming majority of Party members loyally worked for the Party. But a sort of very dangerous tendency has developed among part of the Party members. Some comrades strive for their personal reputation, position and pay. They even openly bargain with the Party and, in doing so, regard it as a matter of honor instead of shame. They would be dissatisfied with the Party when they did not have their way. Some comrades, proceeding from individualism, often show themselves to be unprincipled in the struggle within the Party. Instead of drawing a dividing line over major questions of right and wrong, they take into primary consideration their personal interests. Or else, they hypocritically appear as the impartial, denouncing both parties to the struggle in equal terms and losing sight of the serious danger the anti-Party elements can do to the Party. They are sentimental and compromising with those guilty of serious errors. It must be realized that such individualism, liberalism and conceit are very dangerous and, if they are allowed to take their own course, will cause Party disunion and disagreements and provide ideal soil and climate for the anti-Party activities. The present congress session is of tremendous significance in that the overwhelming majority of our comrades have consciously realized that individualism, liberalism and conceit are precisely what must be combated in the social revolution going on at present in the political and ideological fields. All have realized that only by thoroughly criticizing these extremely harmful tendencies during the rectification campaign can we strengthen the unified will, action and discipline of the Party and can we increase the fighting capacity of the Party and arouse all the Party members to pull themselves up and wage a self-less struggle for socialist revolution and construction.

The struggle at the present congress session is a struggle of principle over the major questions of right and wrong. The struggle has fundamentally solved problems that had long existed within the Party organizations of Chekiang. This is a great victory. The present problem is to enlighten all Party members of our province, taking the lessons of this struggle as teaching materials. This is to be done in order to transform the negative factors into positive factors and to enlarge upon the results of this struggle.

What are the important lessons and experiences we should learn in the inner-Party struggle over the past years?

We now find ourselves in a great historical period of socialist revolution and socialist construction. For the sake of the victory of socialism, we must wage a determined struggle against the rightists within our Party. Unless we win in this battle, socialism will be hopeless. The representatives of the Party rightists are Sha Wen-han, Yang Ssu-yi, Peng Jui-lin and Sun Chang-lu. They are our enemies hidden in our Party. We all know that a fortress can easily be taken from within. If we do not wage a determined struggle against them and if we are sentimental about them, the Party will be unable to weather the storm at the crucial moment.

The political degeneration of the Party rightists, it should be noted, is not fortuitous. Ideologically, they are extremely selfish bourgeois individualists. Individualism is their common road to the rightist quagmire.

The inner-Party struggle, as borne out by the historical experience of our Party, is a reflex of the social class struggle. The revolutionaries must also transform themselves if they want to transform the society and Nature. They must overcome capitulationism within the Party during the anti-Japanese war; they must carry out the rectification campaign and overcome the thinking of landlords and rich peasants during the agrarian reform; during the struggle against the five evils of the bourgeoisie, they must carry out the 3-anti campaign to overcome the bourgeois thinking. That is to say, in each different historical period of revolution they must wage a determined struggle against the ideological tendencies that represent the interests of the reactionary class. They must wage this determined struggle before the purity and unity of the Party can be ensured and before the revolutionary tasks can be fulfilled. It should be realized that a number of our Party members have joined the Party for personal considerations. If they do not undergo radical transformation and do not establish the communist world outlook and if they stick to their standpoint of bourgeois individualism, they will be unable to pass the test of socialism. To struggle for socialism or for personal fame, position and remuneration, to wage a selfless struggle for the great cause of the Party or for personal interests—such is a struggle between the standpoint of the proletariat and the standpoint of the bourgeoisie. Without solving this problem there cannot be strong revolutionary will, vitality and vigor in the socialist revolution and socialist construction and there cannot be any spirit of wholeheartedly serving the people.

"The tree wants to be quiet but the wind does not stop". Struggle is unavoidable. Persons in our Party who are imbued with serious individualism of the bourgeoisie will always stubbornly demonstrate themselves and try to transform the Party according to the bourgeois features and change the Party cause into an instrument to meet personal desires. When they cannot have their way they will incite inner-Party struggle at all opportunities. The main purpose of inner-Party struggle is to persist in the correct principle and line and combat the erroneous principle and line. For instance, the 5th Party conference in 1955 combated the erroneous principle of 'firm retreat' in agricultural cooperation; the victory of the struggle brought about a high tide of agricultural cooperation accompanied by a high tide of production. But the inner-Party struggle incited by Sha Wen-han, Yang Ssu-yi, Peng Jui-lin and Sun Chang-lu was a struggle of the bourgeois standpoint against the proletarian standpoint. Cherishing despicable personal aims they tried to seize the political leadership and persisted in their mistakes over long period of time until they degenerated into anti-Party elements. Thus the struggle against them this time is nothing but a struggle between socialism and capitalism over the major questions of right and wrong, i.e. a struggle between communism and collectivism on the one hand and the bourgeois individualism on the other. Having learned this lesson, all Party organizations must intensify the ideological work of the Party a hundred-fold, persist in communist education for all Party members, maintain the organizational life of the Party, constantly guard against bourgeois corrosion of the Party ranks and, in a preventive spirit, expose and criticize individualist thinking within the Party so as to maintain the ideological purity of the Party.

All persons imbued with serious bourgeois individualism are always not firm politically. They are likely to accept the bourgeois influence and degenerate into revisionists. Their characteristic consists in consistently negating the success of work, negating the Party leadership and negating the advantage of socialism. They negate the Party nature and class nature of the press work and mix up the fundamental distinction between the press work of the proletariat and the press work of the bourgeoisie. They negate the fundamental direction of literary and art work to serve workers, peasants, soldiers and politics. They negate the Party leadership over the state power and promote the bourgeois view of the state and political power. Frequently, distorting facts they present a gloomy picture of the Party and spread evil effect of suspicion over Party leadership. In inner-Party life, they one-sidedly stress democracy and combat centralism and one-sidedly stress freedom and combat discipline. The democracy they advocate is unguided democracy which encourages slander against the Party. Their so-called freedom means freedom to oppose the Party and freedom from Party discipline. Instead of upholding the Party unity and Party unification and centralization, they criticize the so-called 'vulgar upholding of the Party unity'. Facts of the past years have proved that these persons have done serious harm to the cause of the Party. Since they are 'Communist Party members' and 'veteran cadres' with more political capital to mislead others, they have done more serious harm to the Party than the non-Party rightists have done. And this tells us one thing: in the ideological struggle of the Party from now on, we must combat both doctrinairism and revisionism and for the present we should lay emphasis on the struggle against revisionism which is the main danger at the moment.

All persons imbued with serious individualism of the bourgeoisie are often characterized by serious sectarianism and parochialism. This is because they need such tendencies to fulfill their personal ambitions and carry on their anti-Party activities. They carry on the sectarianian or parochialist activities, looking at things from the standpoint of personal interests or sectarian interests. They are in favor of things which are to their advantage and are against things which are not to their advantage. In order to build their personal prestige in ordinary time, they build connections with other people, taking advantage of their relations with the old comrades, old subordinates and local cadres. When they attack the Party, they carry on small clique activities, find their support inside and outside the Party and make trouble for the Party. Parochialism, one of the expressions of sectarianism, jeopardizes the Party to the same extent. In the past, the Party raised the 'localization' slogan, the main spirit of which is aimed at building close ties between cadres and the local people. Local cadres are in a favorable position to build close ties with the local people, but cadres from other areas will become local after they have worked for a certain period of time and built close ties with the local people. The 'localization' slogan must not be used as excuse for developing parochialism. On no account are those with ulterior motives allowed to exploit this slogan for sowing dissension between outside cadres and local cadres or carry on sectarian activities. Some people err in acting as 'representatives of local cadres' or in stressing employment of local people as secretaries of the Party committees. As pointed out by Comrade Teng Hsiao-ping, "the 'localization' of cadres is not the highest principle of the Party's policy relating to cadres. The highest principle of the Party's cadres policy is primarily 'communization', and provincialism is incompatible with communism."

With a view to consolidating the results of the anti-rightist struggle, all the Party organizations in Chekiang should organize discussion of the main experience and lessons of this struggle among Party cadres so that they can receive a profound ideological education.

With the rightists inside and outside the Party exposed and defeated, it will be possible for the leading organs of our Party to devote themselves to correcting their shortcomings and mistakes in their work. Upon conclusion of the anti-rightist struggle, the Party committees at *hsien* level and above must direct the edge of the struggle against the drawbacks and mistakes in our work. Bureaucracy, sectarianism and subjectivism exist in our work to a considerable extent. Failure to rectify these drawbacks and mistakes will hinder the smooth progress of the socialist revolution and socialist construction and will dampen the activity of the masses. All leading cadres must therefore 'kindle fire to burn themselves' and must make up their mind to rectify their shortcomings and mistakes resolutely, boldly and thoroughly.

In addition to the administrative improvement mentioned above, we must tackle the following problems in our Party work:

1. The Party committees must organize and urge all organs, enterprises and business units to make up their mind to retrench their machinery in revolutionary ways and mobilize large numbers of leading cadres and Party members and cadres (with a certain degree of political awakening and cultural knowledge) to the production posts and the primary units, primarily to the primary units in the countryside. This will have many advantages: Firstly, the leaders can form a compact whole with the masses instead of sitting in their office issuing administrative orders. It will ensure timely reflection of the situation to the higher and lower levels and will overcome bureaucracy and subjectivism on the part of the leading organs. Secondly, Party members and cadres who have never performed labor and worked at the primary level before can form a compact whole with the workers and peasants, can know their feelings and can remold their thoughts, thereby to create conditions for building ranks of cadres who are able to stand the test and the storm and stress. Thirdly, the activity of the working people can be stimulated and a social habit of honoring the labor can be established. At the same time, these Party members and cadres can impart to the peasants their cultural and scientific knowledge and help them sum up their practical production experience. Fourthly, State expenditure can be cut and social wealth can be increased. Therefore, all the leading organs must, in the light of the actual conditions and tasks, strenuously retrench, merge their organizations and cut their staff. All the enterprises and business organs should work out a proper ratio of non-productive staff to the total number of personnel, cut the non-productive staff, raise the work efficiency and change the irrational systems and division of labor. This is a revolution in thinking, organization and working style; it can be achieved only by relying on the masses and following the mass line. To this end, all the personnel and members of staff must be aroused to air their views and open debate for the purpose of criticizing ideas of departmentalism, ideas of belittling physical labor and working people, ideas of seeking life enjoyment and avoiding hard life, ideas of separating oneself from production. A public opinion should be formed to honor labor and encourage the building of socialism. The debate is aimed at ideologically guaranteeing the transfer of cadres to the lower level. In addition, personnel of the leading organs should institute a system of regularly performing physical labor.

2. Overhaul the primary organizations of the Party in the light of the actual conditions exposed during the rectification campaign and the anti-rightist struggle. The primary organizations of the Party were generally built and developed in the course of various movements. They have been tempered and tested during the movements. As a whole, conditions are satisfactory. But the problems brought to light during the rectification campaign are serious. Some withdrew from their cooperatives and followed the way of the rich peasants after their living standard had risen. Some took the lead in

undermining the system of united purchase and marketing. Some breached law and discipline. Some are undesirable elements having wormed their way into the Party. In addition, some have lost their revolutionary will and cannot play the role of Communist Party members. In the circumstances, all the primary organizations of the Party must be overhauled during the rectification campaign so that they can really become fortress of solidarity with the masses. Party rightists, undesirable elements who have wormed their way into the Party, elements guilty of breach of law and discipline, incorrigible elements, elements who are imbued with serious bourgeois individualism and guilty of serious individualist acts and who refuse to mend their ways despite education must be expelled from the Party upon verification of the facts. Those who have lost their revolutionary will and cannot play the part of the Communist Party members should be advised to quit the Party or purged from the Party. The above organizational measures should be taken at the latter stage of the rectification campaign.

The leadership should be strengthened in connection with the recruitment of Party members. Only the best elements among the veteran workers and higher intellectuals who have proved themselves qualified for Party membership during the movements may be admitted as Party members. Generally speaking, pending the next Party congress no Party members should be recruited, so that our forces may be concentrated to consolidate the organizations. In respect to candidate members, education must be intensified and strict observation and fulfillment of the procedures of approval of membership must be carried out in order to prevent disqualified persons from joining the Party.

Simultaneous with the rectification and Party over-haul, the organizations and work of the Young Communist League must also be seriously overhauled. The League has achieved great success in recent years. But many problems remain to be solved in connection with the political and ideological education for League members and in connection with the cadres policy. All the Party committees should strengthen their leadership over the League and develop the role of the League organizations as subsidiary to the Party during the rectification campaign. Moreover, the League organizations must be strengthened and purified during the rectification campaign.

3. Strengthen the ideological work of the Party. The struggle of socialist thinking against the capitalist thinking will exist for a long time to come. If the socialist thinking does not expand itself and does not weaken the effect of the capitalist thinking, then capitalist thinking will prevail within a certain time and in a certain sphere. The struggle against all sorts of capitalist thinking should be taken as the fundamental and long-term aim of the ideological work of the Party. The Party committees must take their leadership over the ideological work as their regular and primary task. The cultural and educational work is an indispensable part of the socialist construction and is an extremely important line of the ideological work of the Party. All the Party committees must place the cultural and educational work under their control in accordance with the directives of the Central Committee. The first secretaries of the Party committees should personally take charge of this work and periodically discuss and check up this work. The propaganda departments and the cultural and educational departments of the Party committees should organize special forces to take charge of the work among the intellectuals and the cultural and educational work. In the next half to one year, each comrade in charge of this work is required to investigate one or two primary units so that experience can be gradually accumulated.

Upon conclusion of the campaign for rounding up counter-revolutionaries and the anti-rightist struggle, the counter-revolutionaries, bad elements and the rightists brought to light must be sternly dealt with according to the Party policy in order to purify the cultural and educational ranks. At the same time, we must, with the greatest determination, transfer a group of Party cadres (who have undergone political struggle, have a certain cultural level and are suitable to do the work among the intellectuals) from the Party organizations, government organizations and other units to lead the cultural and educational organs in general and the primary units in particular. Through the rectification campaign we must raise the ideological level and improve the ability of the existing cadres doing the cultural and educational work. Cadres unfit for this type of work must be removed.

The press and publications are the most powerful weapons used by the Party on the ideological front. Prior to the anti-rightist struggle, the rightists inside and outside the Party launched attack on the press and publications led by the Party. This attack was by no means fortuitous. Learning this lesson, the Party committees should resolutely strengthen their leadership over the press work, remove the rightists and politically unreliable elements from the editorial departments and appoint a group of politically tested cadres to run the press and publications. The broadcasting stations and rediffusion stations should also be overhauled. The press and broadcasting work is a political work, in connection with which the Party committees must show their maximum interests and exercise supervision. All the secretaries of the Party committees who are in charge of press work should regularly read the papers published by the central and local levels in May to July this year, and compare them so that they can constantly improve their own press work. The Party committees must also intensify ideological education for cadres. They should encourage serious reading of books and papers and criticize the bad habits of those cadres who idle away their time and seek no progress. Serious study and discussion of the important documents of the Party must be organized by the Party committees among the leading cadres. Upon conclusion of the rectification campaign and the anti-rightist struggle, the Party schools and cadres' schools should restore enrollment of students. The organization department and propaganda department of the provincial committee should work out a plan for training cadres in rotation and for fostering in five years a group of politically tested and experienced theoreticians so as to provide each *hsien* committee with one or two cadres versed in the basic theories (primarily the writings by Chairman Mao). The Party committees should seriously interest themselves in the creative works of literature and arts and politically help the literary and art workers to create heroic inspiring images of heroes through artistic forms of novels, plays, songs, fine arts and music. This is a powerful weapon to educate the masses. Those politically reliable cadres who are successful in creative work should be given concrete guidance and help so that they can gradually become the best writers of the working class. Through this debate on socialism and the propagation of the national program for agriculture, the Party system of political work should gradually be made a regular in all factories and the countryside. Where conditions are present, the socialist system of patriotic days should gradually be instituted. It behooves the *hsien*, *ch'ü* and *hsiang* organizations to sum up experience in this work and gradually develop the political work into a system. On all festival days, socialism should be preached among the masses in all factories and rural areas.

Comrades: This congress session and the cadres' conference have lasted nearly two months. The time has been long but the problems tackled are many and important. It is anticipated that as a result of this congress session the Party unity and unification will certainly be strengthened under the correct leadership of the Party Center and Chairman Mao, the fighting capacity of the Party will certainly be increased considerably and the socialist vigor of the Party cadres inside and outside the Party will be heightened in building socialism. "Conquer difficulties where they are" and "Overcome the backwardness and build modern industry and agriculture with bare hands"—let these watchwords arm all the Party cadres and people! Let them work hard, overcome difficulties and achieve a new leap on all fronts!

Chapter VII

THE "GREAT LEAP FORWARD"

(containing Documents 21, 22, 23, 24, 25, 26)

General comment. The Great Leap Forward dates from the spring of 1958 and primarily affected the development of China's internal economy. It may therefore appear incongruous to put under this heading documents dating from the fall of 1957 (Documents 21 and 22), or documents dealing with foreign policy (Documents 21 and 23). The reasons for this arrangement are first, that the Great Leap Forward policy was conceived in the fall of 1957 and put into execution only after endorsement by the National People's Congress and much discussion at provincial and lower levels of the Party, and second, that it was determined in part by the Chinese leaders' view of the general position of the Socialist Camp. On these themes, see our General Introduction.

DOCUMENT 21

Speech at Moscow Celebration Meeting, by Mao Tse-tung, November 6, 1957, to a joint meeting of two soviets of the Supreme Soviet of the U.S.S.R. (namely the Soviet of the Union and the Soviet of Nationalities) in celebration of the 40th anniversary of the October Revolution.

The text is taken from the English-language Peking magazine *People's China,* Dec-1, 1957.

Comment. Mao's speech is mainly remarkable for his support of Soviet leadership within the Socialist Camp and his implication that it is the "Imperialist Camp" only which will suffer significant losses in a war. Mao himself obtained, or could at least claim to have obtained, at the Moscow meeting something like Socialist Camp endorsement for his own internal policies. He emphasized in his speech those aspects of Russian internal policy which had obvious counterparts in China: "developing agriculture, reorganizing the administration of industry and construction, extending the power of the union republics and local organizations, opposing the anti-Party group, consolidating unity within the Party and improving the Party and political work in the Soviet army and navy." The declaration of the Communist Parties contained some texts important for the final stages of the Chinese rectification campaign and for the ideological foundations of the Great Leap Forward. Thus: "In condemning dogmatism, the Communist Parties believe that the main danger at present is revisionism." The declaration also said the "general laws" of the construction of socialism include "the creation of a numerous intelligentsia devoted to the working class, the working people and the cause of socialism."

On the Chinese role at the Moscow Conference, particularly vis-a-vis Poland, see Zbigniew K. Brzezinski, *The Soviet Bloc: Unity and Conflict* (Cambridge: Harvard University Press, 1960), Chapter 12.

———————————TEXT OF DOCUMENT 21———————————

Dear Comrades:

On the occasion of the fortieth anniversary of the Great October Socialist Revolution, I myself and the other members of the Chinese delegation, representing the National People's Congress and the

State Council of the People's Republic of China, the Central Committee of the Chinese Communist Party, and all the people and Communist Party members of China, have the honour to offer warm fraternal congratulations to the people, government and Communist Party of the great Soviet Union (*enthusiastic applause*), and to all the comrades and friends present here. (*Enthusiastic applause.*)

As our revolutionary teacher Lenin pointed out time and again, the great revolution carried out by the Soviet people forty years ago initiated a new epoch in world history.

Historically there have been revolutions of many kinds, but none to compare with the October Socialist Revolution.

For thousands of years the working people of the world and all progressive humanity have dreamed of building a society in which there would be no exploitation of man by man. This dream was realized on one-sixth of the earth's land surface for the first time in history by the October Revolution. This revolution proves that, without the landlords and the bourgeoisie, the people are completely capable of building a free and happy new life in a planned way. It also proves that different nations of the world are completely capable of living together amicably once there is no imperialist oppression.

In the past forty years the Soviet people have travelled a hard road. The imperialists tried by every means to destroy the world's first socialist republic. The enemies of the Soviet Union appeared for a time to be stronger than the Soviet Union and twice launched armed attacks against it. But the courageous Soviet people, led by their glorious Communist Party, thoroughly smashed the attacks of the aggressors. (*Applause.*)

The Soviet Union has been invincible because it is a country in which the socialist system has replaced the capitalist system and the dictatorship of the proletariat has replaced the dictatorship of the exploiting classes—a country which develops its social productive forces at a speed of which the capitalist countries are incapable—and a country which truly practises proletarian internationalism, genuinely opposes national oppression and helps oppressed nations to emancipate themselves. Such a country enjoys the enthusiastic support of all its own people and of the peoples of all other countries in the world. The Soviet Union enjoys these two kinds of support to a degree without parallel in the history of nations.

The face of the Soviet Union has changed completely in the past forty years. Before the revolution Russia was relatively backward economically and technically. Now the Soviet Union has become one of the world's first-class industrial powers. The living standards of the Soviet people have been steadily rising. The scale of development of educational, scientific and cultural establishments in the Soviet Union far surpasses that of the capitalist countries. The Soviet Union set up the world's first atomic power station, made the world's first batch of passenger jet planes and intercontinental ballistic rockets and launched the world's first and second man-made earth satellites. The whole world acknowledges that the success of the Soviet Union in launching the man-made earth satellites on two occasions has opened up a new era in the conquest of nature by man. Not only the Soviet people, but also the world proletariat and all mankind can take pride in all this. (*Applause.*) Only a few reactionaries are unhappy about it.

The creative application of Marxism-Leninism by the Communist Party of the Soviet Union in tackling practical tasks has ensured unbroken success in the Soviet people's construction work. The fighting programme for communist construction in the Soviet Union put forward by the Twentieth Congress of the Communist Party of the Soviet Union is a good example. The wise measures taken by the Central Committee of the Communist Party of the Soviet Union on the questions of overcoming the cult of the individual, developing agriculture, reorganizing the administration of industry and construction, extending the power of the union republics and local organizations, opposing the anti-Party group, consolidating unity within the Party and improving the Party and political work in the Soviet army and navy, will undoubtedly promote still further the consolidation and development of all undertakings in the Soviet Union.

Throughout the world the people have begun to see their own future ever more clearly in the successes gained by the Soviet people. Essentially, the path of the Soviet Union, the path of the October Revolution, is the bright common way for the progress of all mankind. (*Enthusiastic applause.*) The masses of the people throughout the world celebrate the fortieth anniversary of the October Revolution warmly, because the history of the past forty years has convinced them that the proletariat is certain to defeat the bourgeoisie, socialism is certain to defeat capitalism, and the oppressed nations are certain to defeat the imperialists. Of course, difficulties, twists and turns still face the people. But it was well said by Lenin thirty-six years ago: "The important thing is that the ice has been broken, the road is open and the path has been blazed." (*Enthusiastic applause.*)

The people's revolution led by the Chinese Communist Party has always been a part of the world socialist revolution of the proletariat initiated by the October Revolution. The Chinese revolution has its own national characteristics and it is entirely necessary to take these into consideration. But in our own revolution and socialist construction we have made full use of the rich experience of the Communist Party and the people of the Soviet Union. The Chinese people are fortunate in having the experience of the October Revolution and of the socialist construction in the Soviet Union, which enables them to make fewer mistakes, to avoid many others and to pursue their cause fairly smoothly, although they still face many difficulties.

It is clear that, after the October Revolution, if a proletarian revolutionary of any country should overlook or not seriously study the experience of the Russian revolution, of the proletarian dictatorship and of socialist construction of the Soviet Union, and should fail to use these experiences analytically and in a creative way in the light of the specific conditions in his own country, he would not be able to master Leninism, which represents a new stage in the development of Marxism, and he would not be able to solve the problems of revolution and construction in his own country correctly. He would either commit doctrinaire or revisionist mistakes. We must oppose both these deviations simultaneously, but at present, to oppose revisionist deviation is a particularly urgent task.

It is equally clear that, since the October Revolution, any government that refuses to be on friendly terms with the Soviet Union only harms the real interests of its own people. (*Prolonged, enthusiastic applause.*)

In the world today a series of European and Asian countries with an aggregate population of over nine hundred million people have victoriously taken the path of the October Revolution and form a powerful world system of socialism. Capitalism has for some time lost its superiority, and socialism has become invincible.

In the end the socialist system will replace the capitalist system. This is an objective law independent of human will. No matter how hard the reactionaries try to prevent the advance of the wheel of history, revolution will take place sooner or later and will surely triumph. (*Prolonged, enthusiastic applause.*) "To lift a rock, merely to crush one's own foot" is a Chinese saying to describe the action of fools. The reactionaries of every country are just such fools. Their persecution of the revolutionary people will only end in rousing the people to broader and fiercer revolution. (*Enthusiastic applause.*) Did not persecution by the Russian tsar and Chiang Kai-shek of the revolutionary people serve precisely to stimulate the great Russian and Chinese revolutions?

As well as staking their fate on the oppression of the peoples at home and in the colonial and semi-colonial countries, the imperialists put their hope in war. But what can they expect out of war? In the past half century, we have experienced two world wars. After the First World War, the Great October Socialist Revolution took place in Russia. And after the Second World War, more revolutions took place in East Europe and in the East. If the imperialist warriors are determined to start a third world war, they will bring about no other result than the end of the world capitalist system. (*Enthusiastic applause.*)

The governments and peoples of the socialist countries are the builders of a new peaceful life. We absolutely do not want war, and are firmly opposed to a new world war. The Soviet Union, China and the other socialist countries have been consistently working for the relaxation of international tension. The proposals made again and again by the Soviet Union for disarmament and the prohibition of the manufacture, use and testing of weapons of mass destruction, represent the common stand of the socialist countries, and accord at the same time with the interests of all peoples. We firmly stand for peaceful competition between the socialist and the capitalist countries, and for the settlement of the internal affairs of each country by its own people in accordance with their own desires. We firmly maintain that all nations should practise the well-known Five Principles of mutual respect for sovereignty and territorial integrity, non-aggression, non-interference in each other's internal affairs, equality and mutual benefit, and peaceful co-existence.

The U.S. imperialists obstinately try to interfere in the internal affairs of other countries, including those of the socialist countries. For example, they are interfering with the liberation of Taiwan by China and they engineered the counter-revolutionary riots in Hungary. They are particularly rabid in interfering in the internal affairs of those countries situated in the area between the U.S. and the socialist camp. The U.S. is still planning to invade independent Syria through Turkey or Israel, it is still conspiring to subvert the anti-colonialist Egyptian Government. This maniac aggressive policy of the U.S. has not only precipitated a crisis in the Middle East, but has also created the danger of a new world war. All people in the world who love peace and freedom stand by Syria and oppose the U.S. and Turkish aggressors, just as they stood by Egypt and opposed the British, French and Israeli aggressors in October last year. The Soviet Government has served warning on the U.S. and Turkey to give up their aggressive plan immediately. The Chinese Government and people resolutely support Syria in its struggle to defend itself and firmly endorse the just position of the Soviet Union. (*Prolonged, enthusiastic applause.*)

The imperialist wolves should remember that the days when they could manipulate the fate of humanity and carve up the Asian and African countries as they liked have gone for ever.

The U.S. imperialists have tried and are still trying hard to undermine the liberation of the Chinese people. But in the end they could not prevent the six hundred million Chinese people from bravely taking the path of socialism. (*Applause.*) In the short period of eight years, China has already achieved such results in various fields of construction as it was not able to achieve in the past hundred years. In China, a handful of bourgeois rightists try to oppose taking the path of socialism and oppose the leading position of the Communist Party in national life, and the close alliance between China and the Soviet Union and the other socialist countries. Their vain efforts have been utterly defeated by the counter-attack of the people throughout our country. (*Applause.*)

The Chinese people, under the leadership of the Communist Party, are carrying out a vigorous rectification campaign in order to develop socialism in China rapidly and on a firmer basis. It is a campaign to resolve correctly the contradictions which actually exist among the people and which have to be resolved immediately, by means of a nation-wide debate which is both guided and free, carried out in the urban and rural areas on such questions as the socialist road and the capitalist road, the basic systems and major policies of the state, the working style of the Communist Party and government functionaries, and the welfare of the people—a debate conducted by bringing out the facts and by argument. This is a socialist campaign of self-education and self-remoulding by the people and great successes have already been recorded in it. The socialist consciousness of the people has been rapidly raised, false ideas clarified, shortcomings in work overcome, unity within the ranks of the people strengthened, and labour discipline and productivity increased, wherever the campaign has been carried out. (*Applause.*) We are now carrying forward this people's self-education campaign among our six hundred million people stage by stage and section by section and it is probable that in another few months nation-wide success will have been achieved. In future we intend to conduct a rectification campaign every year or every other year—the time it takes can be greatly shortened—as one of the main methods of resolving various social contradictions in our country during the whole period of transition. The basic starting point in practising this method is the firm confidence that the majority of the masses are after all on our side and that they will listen to reason. This point has been proved by all our experience in the campaign.

In many years of revolutionary practice we have developed the method of the rectification campaign in accordance with the Leninist principles of keeping in close contact with the masses, recognizing the initiative of the masses, and practising criticism and self-criticism. The correctness of this method has once again been proved by the present socialist self-education movement.

China has received brotherly assistance towards its socialist construction in many fields from the Soviet Union. In celebrating the fortieth anniversary of the October Socialist Revolution, please allow us to express our heartfelt gratitude to the Communist Party, the government and the people of the Soviet Union, for giving China such friendly help. (*Enthusiastic, prolonged applause.*)

Soon after it was founded, the People's Republic of China concluded a Treaty of Friendship, Alliance and Mutual Assistance with the Soviet Union. This is a great alliance of two great socialist countries. We share the same destiny and the same life-spring with the Soviet Union and the entire socialist camp. (*Enthusiastic applause.*) We regard it as the sacred international obligation of all socialist countries to strengthen the solidarity of the socialist countries headed by the Soviet Union. (*Applause.*)

All possible means of sowing discord are used by the imperialist powers headed by the U.S. in their efforts to disrupt the friendship and solidarity of the socialist countries headed by the Soviet Union. But reality is sure to disappoint the imperialists. The socialist countries headed by the Soviet Union are more closely united than ever. Since the dawn of history, it was not possible for relations between nations to be based on such identity of interests, such mutual respect and confidence, and such mutual assistance and inspiration as between the socialist countries. This is because the socialist countries are of an entirely new type in which the exploiting classes are overthrown and the working people are in power. The principle of integrating internationalism with patriotism has been practised in the relations between these countries. We are closely bound by common interests and ideals. Marx said in his inaugural address to the Workingmen's International Association: "Past experience has shown how disregard of that bond of brotherhood which ought to exist between the workmen of different countries, and incite them to stand firmly by each other in all their struggles for emancipation, will be chastised by the common discomfiture of their incoherent efforts." This teaching of Marx more than ninety years ago will never be out-of-date for us. (*Applause.*)

Dear comrades, the fact that representatives of the working class and masses of the people of various countries of the world are here today to attend this grand meeting of the Supreme Soviet of the Soviet Union held to celebrate the fortieth anniversary of the October Revolution demonstrates in itself the great solidarity of the people's forces of the world and symbolizes the flourishing condition of the international socialist movement. Let us continue our efforts to strengthen the solidarity of the socialist countries, and of the working people and oppressed nations of the world, in order to attain new and greater victories. (*Prolonged, enthusiastic applause.*)

Long live the Great October Socialist Revolution! (*Prolonged, enthusiastic applause.*)

Long live the solidarity and friendship of the socialist countries headed by the Soviet Union! (*Prolonged, enthusiastic applause.*)

Long live the great banner of Marxist-Leninist internationalism! (*Prolonged, enthusiastic applause.*)

The proletariat and peace-loving people of the whole world, unite! (*Prolonged, enthusiastic applause.*)

DOCUMENT 22

The Significance of the October Revolution, speech by Liu Shao-ch'i, November 6, 1957, to a mass rally in Peking in celebration of the 40th anniversary of the Russian October Revolution.

> The English text is taken from CB 480, which reprinted an NCNA translation originally issued November 6, 1957.

> *Comment.* Liu's is the first major Chinese pronouncement of this period in which economic depression in the "Imperialist Camp" is listed among the factors favoring the Socialist Camp. This claim was subsequently treated as a major asset (see Document 25). Liu devotes a considerable amount of space to exposing the ideas of "bourgeois rightists" (a stage of the rectification campaign, which, according to the official program, should have been already completed). This suggests that such ideas were still thought to be prevalent within the Party itself (see Document 25). The principal interest of his speech, however, lies in the last part, where he discusses the disjunction between doing things "quicker and better" and doing them "slower and aim[ing] at lower standards." Thus, assuming that the more cautious policy is simply a lazy one, he assures his audience that by relying on mass initiative "we will certainly be able to carry out correctly the policy of achieving quantity, speed, quality and economy." In Document 25, the same speaker makes it clear that this line was agreed upon by the Central Committee in September 1957. Combined with the slogans of

"thrift and economy" and "red and expert" it represents the essence of the Great Leap Forward.

---------------------- TEXT OF DOCUMENT 22 ----------------------

Comrades, friends,

We are gathered here today to celebrate the 40th anniversary of the great October Socialist Revolution. This is not only a festival of the people of the Soviet Union, but also a common festival of the working class, the laboring people, the oppressed nations and all progressive mankind throughout the world.

Although the October Revolution triumphed in Russia only, it opened up a new era in the whole of human history. Since then, all peoples throughout the world are progressing step by step along the basic path opened up by the October Revolution and will enter at different times a new historic epoch, the epoch of socialism and Communism.

Human life dates back hundreds of thousands of years, but the recorded history of human society is only a few thousand years old. The history of these thousands of years has been the history of the class society and class struggles of mankind. The majority of mankind are leading a life of suffering under exploitation and oppression, they are not yet able to master the laws of social development in a conscious way. Only after entering the socialist and communist society, can man get rid of anarchy in production, carry on planned production and distribution, and be relieved from the distress of exploitation and oppression of man by man. It is only from this point, as Engels said, "that men with full consciousness will fashion their own history," and realize "humanity's leap from the realm of necessity into the realm of freedom." The historic epoch of man being master of his own destiny dates from the October Socialist Revolution. Previous human history was only the pre-history of human society. Therefore, the great day of November 7, 1917 is worthy to be observed and celebrated by the laboring people and all progressive mankind throughout the world. The Chinese people feel particularly happy in celebrating this festival at a time when we, advancing along the path of the October Revolution, have won victory in our socialist revolution and have begun our new life in history.

The great significance of the October Socialist Revolution in the entire human history has become increasingly clear with the passing of time. Now that we are 40 years away from that revolution, we can see what a tremendous change the world has undergone in these 40 years.

The development of the Soviet Union in the past 40 years proves the absolute superiority of the socialist system over the capitalist system, and the much greater speed of development of socialist production than that of capitalist production. The total industrial output of the Soviet Union in 1957 is 33 times that in 1913, the peak year before the revolution. In the corresponding period, production in the United States only increases 4.1 times, and in Britain and France only 1.8 times. As everybody knows, the United States suffered no damage but made a lot of money in the two world wars, while the Soviet Union had to carry on construction in extremely difficult conditions, sustained serious damage in several wars, at home and with foreign countries, and was for long encircled by world capitalism. Notwithstanding this, the Soviet people, under the leadership of the Communist Party of the Soviet Union, were able in a very short period to build their economically backward country into a first-rate world power with modern industry and agriculture. This fact fully demonstrates the superiority of the socialist system. Culture and sciences have also been developing in the Soviet Union at a very high speed. The legion of scientific and technical personnel in the Soviet Union is of a greater magnitude than that in any other country. The Soviet scientists have set up the first atomic power station in the world, established the biggest charged particle accelerator, made the inter-continental ballistic rocket and its launcher and, after successfully launching the first man-made earth satellite, launched a few days ago a second one, which is heavier and farther away from the earth and contains a living creature and various scientific apparatus and instruments, thus paving the way for man's conquest of the interplanetary space. At the call of the 20th Congress of the Communist Party of the Soviet Union, the productive enterprises of the Soviet Union plan to catch up with and surpass the most developed capitalist country in production per capita in a relatively short period of history. The Soviet people are now marching forward along the path of Communist construction, and the mighty Soviet Union has become the strongest bulwark in defense of world peace.

TEXT OF DOCUMENT 22

In the 40 years since the October Revolution, socialism has triumphed in a series of countries in Europe and in Asia following the Soviet Union. Socialism has become a world system. The socialist countries comprising over one-third of the world population have formed a socialist camp headed by the Soviet Union. All the socialist countries are marching victoriously forward with full confidence along the path blazed by the October Revolution. Their productive forces are all developing with a speed unattainable by the capitalist countries. The firm unity and the growing strength of the socialist camp has become a decisive factor in the world situation.

In the 40 years since the October Revolution, the national independence and liberation movements in Asia, Africa and Latin America have developed to an unprecedented extensive scope, and a number of nationally independent states have been founded. They are a great world force. The demand of all oppressed peoples for independence has enjoyed and will continue to enjoy the sympathy and support of the socialist countries. Mutual friendly relations in line with the five principles of peaceful co-existence have been established and developed between many nationally independent countries and the socialist countries, which together form a broad zone of peace.

In the 40 years since the October Revolution, the working class movements in the capitalist world have, under the leadership of the Communist parties of the respective countries, made great development. They are also an important force in the world for peace, national liberation and human progress.

The above-mentioned tremendous changes of a fundamental character are all directly connected with the victory of the October Socialist Revolution. Owing to these changes, the imperialist rule over the world is beset with a deep crisis and the various contradictions within the imperialist system are growing sharper with each passing day. The imperialist countries headed by the United States are now faced with the threat of an economic crisis. Since the Second World War, the United States has been carrying out frantic expansionist activities, establishing military bases, organizing military blocs, creating tensions, preparing for a new war, practising colonial rule, bolstering systems of national oppression and enslavement everywhere, and backing reactionary rules and force everywhere. The United States imperialists are now again carrying out aggressive plots in the Near and Middle East and instigating armed aggression against Syria, and they once more encounter the opposition of the broad masses of the world. The Soviet Union, China and other socialist countries sympathize with and support Syria in its struggle. If the US imperialists and their henchmen should dare to unleash a war in this area, they would meet with the same ignominious failure which Britain, France and Israel did last year in their adventure in Egypt.

Peoples throughout the world are against war and for peace. The foreign policy of peace pursued by the Soviet Union, China and the other socialist countries is welcomed everywhere. In celebrating the 40th anniversary of the October Revolution, we can see that the peace movement has become the broadest movement in the world and there is already hope for the realization of a lasting peace among mankind.

To sum up, the 40 years since the October Revolution has been 40 years of decline of capitalism and imperialism, and 40 years of rise of socialism, of upsurge of the proletarian revolutionary movement and national independence and liberation movements, 40 years of extensive growth of world peace movement, 40 years which is a source of joy, inspiration and confidence to progressive mankind.

From these tremendous changes taking place in the world in the past 40 years, we can see the great role played by the October Socialist Revolution in the history of mankind. From them we can also foretell along what course human history will move forward. Infinitely great and bright is the future of human history opened up by the October Socialist Revolution.

The Chinese revolution is a continuation of the great October Revolution. The aim of our revolution, like that of the October Revolution, is to build up a socialist society, and after that to build up a communist society.

Only socialism can save China—this is a truth conclusively proved by the Chinese people's revolutionary practice. In the past, some people still wavered on the question whether our country should follow the path of capitalism or of socialism. But the truth proved by the facts of the past several years and made clear especially through the nation-wide debate on the two roads and the education in socialist ideology carried out this year, has become the steadfast faith of the broad masses of the people.

The socialist revolution in our country in the ownership of the means of production was in the main completed in 1956. This represents a great change. But a mere change in the economic system is insufficient. The class struggle between the bourgeoisie and the working class is not yet at an end. The reactionary bourgeois rightists would not reconcile themselves to the death of the capitalist system and, hostile to socialism, they seek opportunity to have a trial of strength with the people. The struggle between the two roads of socialism and capitalism is still a longterm one. Hence, in addition to bringing the socialist revolution on the economic front to its completion, we should carry out a thorough-going socialist revolution on the political and ideological fronts too. Only when complete victory is gained in the struggles on the political and ideological fronts, and when the material base of socialism is greatly strengthened through economic construction work, will the socialist system be consolidated and an all-round victory be won in the socialist revolution. This is our historic task in the entire transition period.

Some bourgeois rightists do not oppose socialism in words, but in actuality they concentrate their energy on opposing leadership by the Communist Party and the proletarian dictatorship. According to them, it seems that socialism can be built without Party leadership and without the proletarian dictatorship. This is a sheer hoax. The socialist revolution is the most profound and broadest revolution in history; it is the most thorough-going revolution in politics, economy and ideology. It not only seeks to replace ownership by the capitalists and various petty private owners with socialist ownership by the entire people and collective ownership by the working people, and to thoroughly eliminate the system of exploitation and its sources, but also to reorganize social life as a whole on the basis of public ownership and along socialist lines, and to develop economy and culture as fast as possible and in planned way so that the socialist system may be provided with adequate economic base and cultural conditions. To carry out these tasks smoothly, it is necessary to put down firmly any designs of the elements of the exploiting classes which are already overthrown to restore their rule; it is necessary at the same time to reeducate the peasantry and other petty bourgeois elements in a socialist spirit, to educate those bourgeois elements and bourgeois intellectuals who are willing to remould themselves, and to overcome their ideas, traditions and habits which are incompatible with socialist transformation and planned economy. It is clear that no other class besides the proletariat is able to lead the fulfillment of such complicated and serious tasks. The 40 years' history of the Soviet Union, the practical experience of the Chinese revolution and the experience of other socialist countries prove that the basic path of the October Revolution is the only correct path. The socialist revolution can be thoroughly completed only under the proletarian dictatorship and only when the proletariat, through its vanguard the Communist Party, exercises leadership over the state power and the wide masses of the people. In opposing the Communist Party and the proletarian dictatorship, the rightists oppose socialism and the basic interests of the Chinese people. In the present conditions in China, if we did not have the leadership of the proletariat, we would have that of the bourgeoisie; if we did not have the proletarian dictatorship, we would have the dictatorship of the bourgeoisie and the landlords, which would actually drag China back to the old state of a semi-colonial and semi-feudal country. There is no middle way.

The bourgeois rightists say that the proletarian dictatorship and leadership by the Communist Party give rise to sectarianism. This is a totally erroneous assertion. In human history, the proletariat is the most unselfish class which is most capable of fighting unswervingly for the interests of humanity as a whole. The proletariat must liberate the whole humanity in order to liberate themselves. The interests of the Chinese proletariat are identical with the fundamental interests of all Chinese people. Only the proletariat really proceed from the interests of the 600 million people instead of those of any group of people in doing work, drawing up plans and considering matters. Certain Communists also commit sectarian errors. This is because they do not have pure Party spirit, but still have certain non-proletarian ideas. Only by practising the proletarian dictatorship and leadership by the Communist Party can we overcome sectarian mistakes and eliminate step by step through education various sectarian sentiments among Party members and the people. If we should not practise the proletarian dictatorship and leadership by the Communist Party, then whose dictatorship and leadership would we have? With the dictatorship and leadership of any class other than the proletariat, the question would not be one of committing sectarian mistakes, but of no end of jostling between fractions and sharp and complicated class conflicts and leading once again to foreign imperialists' penetration of our country. Politics and leadership which transcend the classes are non-existent. Either one way, or the other. The rightists do not really want to eliminate sectarianism, but want to establish their own leadership and the bourgeois dictatorship.

The bourgeois rightists also attack Marxism-Leninism which is the philosophy guiding all our work. They say that socialism can be built without the guidance of Marxism-Leninism and that it is doctrinairism to follow the Marxist-Leninist theories. This is also a totally erroneous assertion. Marxism-Leninism is the world outlook of the proletariat; it is the science about the laws of development of nature and society, the science of the socialist revolution and the building of socialism and Communism. The socialist cause cannot triumph without the guidance of Marxism-Leninism and Marxist-Leninist ideological education among the people. That is why those who oppose socialism invariably oppose Marxism-Leninism. The Marxist-Leninist general truths about the proletarian revolution are a summary of the revolutionary experience of all mankind, and they must also be enriched and developed by new experience. The doctrinaire tendency which alienates the Marxist-Leninist general truths from revolutionary practice is what we oppose. But the rightists, in opposing doctrinairism, actually oppose Marxism-Leninism itself. They are trying to supplant Marxism-Leninism by bourgeois ideology as guidance to our state life so as to facilitate the restoration of capitalism. There are also certain persons within the revolutionary ranks who are using the capitalist viewpoints to "revise" the general truths of Marxism-Leninism under the disguise of opposing doctrinairism. This revisionist tendency is the main danger at the present time. We must resolutely oppose the tendency of revisionism while striving to overcome doctrinairism.

The bourgeois rightists oppose the Communist Party by all means, but like all other anti-Communists in history they cannot but end up in failure. This is because the basic propositions of the Communist Party are no fancy but are based on the inevitable objective laws of social development. When conditions are ripe for a socialist revolution, and the broad masses of the people eagerly demand the realization of socialism, the socialist revolution waged by the masses led by the Communist Party is not to be resisted by anyone. When this occurs, all people, whether pro or con, must willy-nilly take the road of socialism sooner or later, because it is the inevitable course of historical development. The proletariat, the broad masses of working people and other progressives and those who are willing to accept socialist transformation take this road consciously and willingly under the leadership of the Communist Party; the exploiters, however reluctant to give up their life based on exploitation, if they do not wish to destroy themselves, will also be compelled to take this road. The general trend is that this road must be taken, the only difference being that the majority are going ahead of their own accord, while a minority do so under compulsion. There may be a difference in precedence, but no freedom of standing still. There are also some whose political consciousness is inadequate and though they are taking the road of socialism, do so somewhat reluctantly and are constantly wavering, they are not taking this road happily. Those people on the one hand admit the merits of socialism, but on the other hand feel restricted by the socialist system, which narrow their freedom, and feel that their will is not respected by others, which makes them unhappy. They take the road of socialism with insufficient consciouness. This is because they fail to recognize and respect the objective laws and fail to act consciously in accordance with the objective laws independent of human will. When they get to know and pay enough respect to the objective laws independent of human will, follow the socialist road whole-heartedly, and consciously change their ideas, traditions and habits which are incompatible with socialism, they will then be really free and happy citizens in a socialist society. One of the important functions of the nation-wide rectification campaign now going on in our country is exactly to enable people to see that the overwhelming majority of the people will be able to advance on the road of socialism consciously and happily.

Following the October Revolution, the Soviet Union set up the Soviet state system which is the most extensive socialist democracy in history. The system of the people's congress in our country is a state system of the same pattern as the Soviet, and is also the most extensive socialist democracy in history.

The nation-wide rectification campaign now going on in our country takes the form of full and frank expression of opinions, general debates, wall papers, discussions, forums, etc. This is a very good form for the life of socialist democracy in our country, and an important development of it.

The bourgeois rightists loudly complained that socialism is not democratic, and asked for democracy, and even for unlimited democracy. But when the thousands upon thousands of masses launched the extensive democratic movement to counter them, the rightists become afraid of democracy and do not want it any more, but turn against it. The truth is that democracy is always of a class nature. No democracy in history ever stood separate from a class dictatorship. Bourgeois democracy is democracy for a minority and at the same time dictatorship over the majority, that is, over the working people. The people's democracy under the leadership of the proletariat is democracy for the majority and at the same time dictatorship over a minority, that is, over the exploiters who are opposed to revolution. The so-called "democracy" demanded by the bourgeois rightists is in actuality bourgeois democracy which is a democracy to wreck the proletarian dictatorship and Party leadership in our country, a democracy to undermine socialism and restore capitalism, in a word, a reactionary "democracy." Our people's democracy under the leadership in our country, a democracy to build socialism and eliminate capitalism, a democracy to combat the bourgeois rightists and all reactionary forces which resist the socialist revolution and seek to wreck socialist construction, and at the same time a democracy to overcome bureaucracy, sectarianism and subjectivism on the part of the leading organs, and to educate the masses of the people, raise their socialist consciousness, and reinforce their discipline. This is revolutionary democracy, a democracy of an unprecedentedly extensive scope.

The bourgeois rightists also loudly complained that there is only centralism but no democracy in our country. They oppose centralism and unity, and demand an anarchic democracy. Their aim is to restore capitalist free competition, wreck the socialist principle of planned economy, and disrupt the socialist social order and discipline. Our people's democracy under the leadership of the working class is a democracy under centralized guidance. Without a high degree of centralism, we would not be able to defeat the enemies of socialism in our country, nor would we be able to build up a socialist society in which production and distribution are carried on in a planned way. Of course, this high degree of centralism must be based on an extensive democracy. Experience shows that a most extensive democracy practised among the working people, which encourages them to give full and frank expression to all their opinions through general debates, will not hinder but on the contrary will help bring about a high degree of centralism.

The form of full and frank expression of opinions through general debate and wall papers is a means which can most effectively rouse the initiative and sense of responsibility of the broad masses of the people, and is also a very good means of their self-education and self-remoulding. This means can be used to expose the enemy and mobilize and educate the masses to struggle against them, and also used to handle correctly contradictions among the people, to overcome in a better way all shortcomings and mistakes in the work of the leading organs, and to facilitate the overcoming of some erroneous views among the masses. The discovery in our country of this form of socialist democracy has made it easier for us to handle our affairs. The great significance and role of this form, however, is not yet well understood by every cadre. There are still some people who are afraid that this might lead to a "national turmoil," or that criticism might be directed against themselves. This is thinking in the wrong way. We should believe in the majority of the masses, because the majority of the masses uphold socialism and wish to accomplish the socialist construction. They talk reason and are reasonable. Although the rightists attempted to take advantage of the opportunity of the full and frank expression of opinions to cause disturbance in the people's order, they ended up in being set upon by the people from all sides. The full and frank expression of opinions by the masses and general debates are in the final analysis favorable to the proletariat and socialism, and unfavorable to the enemy of socialism. Of course, the flames of the full and frank criticism will not only burn out the enemy but our own short-comings and mistakes as well. Far from being dreadful, this is a matter to rejoice at. All cadres loyal to the socialist cause should welcome the exposure and criticism of their own shortcomings and mistakes by the masses and should not be afraid of "being licked by the fire." When the initiative of the masses is brought into full play, and when there is correct leadership, the masses will be able to take a suitable account of our various shortcomings and mistakes and help us find the means to overcome and correct them. We proceed from a firm belief in the masses, in the majority of the masses. The policy to which we should firmly adhere is: "resolutely, boldly and thoroughly to let the masses air their views, and to rectify our ways and improve our work resolutely, boldly and thoroughly," so as to overcome bureaucracy, sectarianism and subjectivism, to improve our work in various fields, to educate the masses and to combat the enemy of socialism. Our aim is to create a vigorous political situation which combines centralism with democracy, discipline with freedom, and united will with personal ease of mind so as to facilitate the socialist revolution and construction in our country.

This is the last year of China's First Five-Year Plan. The basic tasks and main targets set in the First Five-Year Plan will be fulfilled or over-fulfilled. We have already laid a preliminary basis for our industrialization, but the material base of China's socialist system is still far from adequate. Therefore, it is possible and also necessary for us, in the course of our second and third five-year plans or in a longer period, to carry out a policy of developing industry and agriculture simultaneously with continued priority emphasis on heavy industry so as to build our country into a great socialist power with modern industry, modern agriculture and modern science and culture.

There are two ways to accomplish this task: one way is to do things quicker and better, and the other to do things slower and aim at lower standards. Which way should we adopt? The Central Committee of the Party considers that the former way should be adopted and the latter rejected. That was why the Central Committee put forth in the winter of 1955 the slogan of accomplishing more in socialist construction at a greater speed and achieving better quality at the lowest costs. Some people expressed doubt at the correctness of this slogan. They were opposed to doing more at a greater speed under the pretext of seeking better quality and greater economy, and proposed to do less and go slower. Of course, this slogan must be carried out in a practical way in the light of the actual conditions, but not in a subjectivist way neglecting the realities. We should oppose those who seek to do more at a greater speed out of wishful thinking and departing from actual conditions, but we should certainly not oppose but actively support those who seek to do so in a practical way and taking the actual conditions into account. We must carry out the slogan as a comprehensive and unified whole, but not partially and one-sidedly. The requirements of quantity, speed, quality and economy restrict each other. It is naturally wrong to seek quantity and speed at the expense of quality and economy, it is also wrong to seek the latter at the expense of the former, and even worse to seek quality at the expense of economy. We should strive to achieve quantity and speed in various fields under the condition of ensuring quality and economy. We are bound to commit mistakes if we doubt and reject totally without making analysis the slogan of achieving quantity, speed, quality and economy. The facts in the last two years have proved that vague doubt and rejection harbored by some people hinder the advance of our cause, damage the socialist initiative of the masses, and prevent the mobilization of potentialities, and result not in the achievement of quantity and speed, nor in quality and economy, but in greater waste of manpower, money and resources. All Communist Party members and Communist Youth League members, all advanced elements and all working people should seek to advance our cause and take an active attitude in bringing into full play the potentialities in all sections of our national economy. By relying on the initiative of the masses, we will certainly be able to carry out correctly the policy of achieving quantity, speed, quality and economy, to push forward the socialist construction of our country.

In order to build socialism while achieving quantity, speed, quality and economy, we should advocate industry, frugality and hard working in every field of work, whether in running factories, cooperatives, enterprises, schools or any other undertakings. Industry and thrift should also be practised in housekeeping, so that the same principles may prevail in building the country and keeping the house, and become a social convention. The state and the cooperatives should increase their accumulation, and the individuals and households should also increase their savings so far as possible instead of spending all their income. Many young workers and functionaries have now a fairly big income but little or no family burden. They should save up their surplus money against future needs. The Chinese people must have noble aspirations and high spirits, persist in the merits of industry and frugality so as to build China into one of the richest and strongest nations in the world within the next decades. Heavy eating and drinking, luxury and waste are ways detrimental to the realization of the present historic tasks of the Chinese people, and a sign of lack of noble aspirations.

To build up socialism, the working class must have its own force of scientific and technical personnel, its own professors, teachers, scientists, journalists, writers, artists, jurists and Marxist-Leninist theorists. This force also includes all those intellectuals who, though coming from the old society, have been really remoulded and firmly take the working class stand. China is a big country and to build socialism is an arduous and complicated task; therefore the working class must have a vast force of intellectuals, a small number will not do. It is the common historic task of our Party and all our people to cultivate and expand this force. Our Party members, League members and revolutionary intellectuals must make serious and tenacious efforts in their vocational studies so as to master various special techniques and scientific knowledge. All those who are in a position to do so should work hard to turn themselves into experts who are both "red" and expert. The work can not be done well if we are "red" but not "expert." Our government functionaries and experts in various fields should make up their minds to remould themselves so as to serve the workers and peasants and work for socialism whole-heartedly; they should incorporate their individual interests in the collective interests of the masses, but not place the former above the latter. Such should be the red experts. The slogan of "first expert then red" is a call for alienation from politics designed to induce the intellectuals to refuse to remould themselves and reject the working class stand. This is in reality a slogan to lead people to the old way of the bourgeois intellectuals. Our intellectuals must understand that it is impossible to keep away from politics. Alienation from revolutionary politics might lead to reactionary politics. Lack of a correct political stand might lead to a reactionary one. Such people can never work for our socialist cause sincerely and reliably, nor serve the workers and peasants wholeheartedly, even if they succeed in attaining some knowledge and technique.

In our construction we must persist in learning from the Soviet Union, from its advanced experiences and advanced scientific knowledge and technology. The Soviet Union has accumulated rich experience in revolution and construction in the past 40 years. Up to now no other socialist country has such comprehensive experience as the Soviet Union. This is a priceless asset which the Soviet people have offered to mankind. Neglect of this asset would be harmful to our people and also to the cause of socialist revolution and socialist construction. To value truly this asset requires that we adopt a correct attitude in learning from it in connection with the actual conditions in China.

The Soviet Union was always the most faithful friend of the Chinese people throughout the latter's protracted and arduous struggles against imperialism and feudalism. Soon after the victory of the Chinese revolution, the Soviet Union concluded with our country a treaty of friendship, alliance and mutual assistance. Our country has received immense assistance from the Soviet Union in its socialist construction. On behalf of the Chinese Communist Party, the Chinese Government and the Chinese people, I express heartfelt thanks to the Communist Party of the Soviet Union, the Soviet Government and the Soviet people. Comrade Mao Tse-tung said in Moscow in 1950 upon the conclusion of the Sino-Soviet Treaty: "Everybody can see that the unity of the great Chinese and Soviet peoples sealed by the treaty will be lasting, inviolable and unswerving. This unity will inevitably influence not only the florescence of the great powers—China and the Soviet Union—but also the future of all humanity and the victory of peace and justice the world over." The Chinese people will firmly stand together with the Soviet people for ever in the noble cause of safe-guarding world peace and promoting human progress.

The banner of the October Revolution is one of proletarian internationalism. We must educate our people in the spirit of integrating internationalism with patriotism, and must combine the interests of our nation with the common interests of the people of the world. Bourgeois nationalism is incompatible with the fundamental interests of our people and the interests of socialism. We must continuously strengthen the solidarity of the socialist camp headed by the Soviet Union and promote a common economic and cultural upsurge in the socialist countries. We must unite with the proletariat, the oppressed nations and all peace-loving people of the world to work jointly for the triumph of the just cause of peace, democracy and socialism.

Let us march forward bravely holding even higher the banner of the October Revolution.
Long live the great October Socialist Revolution!
Long live the great Soviet Union and its Communist Party and people!
Long live the unbreakable fraternal alliance between China and the Soviet Union!
Long live the socialist camp headed by the Soviet Union!
Long live the great solidarity of the proletariat of the whole world!
Long live the great solidarity of the people of the whole world!
Long live Marxism-Leninism!
Long live the just cause of peace, democracy and socialism!

DOCUMENT 23

The Present International Situation and China's Foreign Policy, report by Chou En-lai, February 10, 1958, to the Fifth Session of the First National People's Congress.

> The English text is taken from CB 492, which reprinted an NCNA translation originally issued February 11, 1958. (In the first sentence of Chou's second paragraph, the omission before the word "marked" may be "people," but indications are that more than one word was omitted from the sentence.)
>
> *Comment.* Chou En-lai's speech gives a picture of the world situation that is very optimistic from the "socialist" point of view. It seems probable that this sort of appraisal did something to determine the domestic as well as the foreign policy of the Chinese People's Government during the next months. Particularly interesting is the link suggested by Chou En-lai between the 1956 events in Hungary and the outspoken criticism of the Chinese Communist Party by the "Democratic" parties in China, and the implication that in its present domestic policies the Party had the backing of the socialist countries as a whole. On the "series of bilateral and multilateral talks" (Chou's paragraph 5), see Zbigniew K. Brzezinski, *The Soviet Bloc: Unity and Conflict* (Cambridge: Harvard University Press, 1960), pp. 279-281. The call to "surpass Britain in the output of steel, iron... in 15 years or slightly more" was first issued on December 12, 1957, at the National Economic Planning Conference in Peking. It was the counterpart of the declared intention of the U.S.S.R. to catch up with the U.S.A., and provided a suitably concrete and stimulative long-term target for the Chinese people.

―――――――――――――――TEXT OF DOCUMENT 23―――――――――――――――

Deputies:

It is only something over half a year since the conclusion of the fourth session of the First National People's Congress. However, in this fairly brief period, profound and momentous changes have taken place in both the domestic and international situations.

In the latter half of 1957 the Chinese people, led by the Chinese Communist Party and Chairman Mao Tse-tung, repulsed the frenzied attacks of the bourgeois rightists and, in accordance with Chairman Mao's brilliant directives on the correct handling of contradictions among the marked by its vigour and vitality. In 1957, the people of our country fulfilled and overfulfilled our First Five-Year Plan for socialist construction, and laid a preliminary basis for the industrialization of our country. At the present time, the rectification campaign which continues with growing intensity is enabling our people to take great forward leaps in construction, filling them with enthusiasm and fresh ardour and infusing an unprecedented new spirit into our work in various fields. Compared with the situation in the first half of 1957, we can all see that the thriving noble spirit of socialism has now prevailed over the noxious spirit of capitalism that for a time ran riot in our country. Our nation rides the rising tide; it is driving full-steam ahead in the work of socialist construction.

In this same period of half a year and more, a decisive change has taken place in the international situation that favors our socialist construction, the socialist camp, the cause of world peace and the progress of mankind. As all the world knows, in October and November 1957 the Soviet Union launched two artificial earth-satellites, while on the occasion of celebrating the 40th anniversary of the great October Socialist Revolution, representatives of the Communist and Workers' parties of the socialist and other countries met in Moscow and issued two statements of great historic significance demonstrating the unity of the Communist and Workers' parties of various countries. This has brought about a new change in the long-standing superiority of the forces of socialism over those of imperialism, and of the forces of peace over those of war, a new turning point in the world situation. As Chairman Mao Tse-tung has said, in the present international situation it is not the west wind which prevails over the east wind, but the east wind which prevails over the west wind.

In 1956, taking advantage of the opportunity when we of the socialist countries were rectifying certain mistakes in our work and overcoming certain difficulties encountered in our progress, the aggressive imperialist bloc stirred up an hysterical anti-Soviet, anti-Communist and anti-popular back current throughout the world. They engineered armed counter-revolutionary riots in Hungary in an attempt to make a breach through Hungary and then proceed to smite the other socialist countries one by one. They fanned up chauvinism and encouraged revisionism in various forms in an endeavor to undermine the foundation of the socialist countries and the solidarity among them. Losing their heads, they screeched that the critical moment of the collapse of the socialist countries had arrived and that the socialist countries were faced with insurmountable difficulties. This anti-Soviet, anti-Communist and anti-popular back current stirred up by the imperialists led the bourgeois rightists in our country to think that their chance had come; at the same time it caused some muddle-headed people in the ranks of the Communist movement to suffer a temporary loss of confidence in the future of Communism.

But the dark clouds did not hover long over the socialist countries. The Hungarian people, with the internationalist help of the Soviet Union, repulsed the attack of the imperialists. The other countries in the socialist camp drew a profound and instructive lesson from the Hungarian events. Through a series of bilateral and multilateral talks, the socialist countries steadily strengthened and improved their mutual relations. The Moscow Conference of the Communist and Workers' parties of the socialist and other countries carried these developments to a new level. The Declaration of the Communist and Workers' Parties of the Socialist Countries summarises the experience of the international Communist movement over the last century, and especially over the last 40 years. It points out the way to strengthen the solidarity of the socialist countries on the basis of Marxism-Leninism and proletarian internationalism; it also points out the way to greater unity with all the forces that can be united with in the cause of world peace and the progress of mankind. The Moscow Conference marks the commencement of a new stage in the solidarity of the socialist countries and the international solidarity of the Communist movement.

The imperialist camp is accustomed to brag about its supremacy in the fields of science, technology and industrial production. But the fact that the Soviet Union is the first country to launch successfully far superior man-made earth satellites shows that the Soviet Union has already definitely outstripped the United States in many important fields in science and technology. The Soviet Union has set with full confidence to catch up with and surpass the United States in the output of the most important industrial products in 15 years. The Chinese people is striving to catch up with and surpass Britain in the output of steel, iron and other major industrial products in a period of 15 years or slightly more. In a corresponding period, the other socialist countries will undoubtedly make great progress too in industrial and agricultural production. Thus, in a short historical period, it can be seen that the socialist camp will leave the imperialist camp far behind not only in the rate of industrial and agricultural development, but also in volume of output. This is the inevitable result of the superiority of the socialist system.

We of the Socialist countries have always stood for peaceful coexistence and peaceful competition among nations with different social systems. We have never taken, nor will we ever take advantage of our supremacy to bully others. On the contrary, we are working all the more actively for peace and we are all the more confident that we will be the victor in peaceful competition precisely because we have attained supremacy. Since December 1957, the Government of the Soviet Union has made many important peace proposals one after the other fully testifying to the Soviet Union's consistent stand of upholding peace and also giving expression to the sincere desire for peace of all the socialist countries. The Government of the Soviet Union has proposed the following: to hold a summit conference with the participation of the Eastern and Western countries and a number of countries which are not members of military blocs and pursue a policy of peace, such as India, Afghanistan, Egypt, Yugoslavia, Sweden and Austria; to put an immediate stop to tests of atomic and hydrogen weapons; to implement the proposal for the establishment of a Central European zone free of atomic armaments put forward by Poland and endorsed by Czechoslovakia and the German Democratic Republic; to conclude a non-aggression treaty between the countries party to the Warsaw Treaty and those party to the North Atlantic Treaty; to ensure the independence and peace of the countries in the Near and Middle East, etc. The Chinese Government fully endorses these proposals. These peace proposals have become increasingly popular, and have served to raise greatly both the political and moral prestige of the socialist countries.

Everybody can see now that, compared with the imperialist camp, our socialist camp has definitely gained supremacy in population and popular support, in the rate of industrial and agricultural development and in a number of important fields in science and technology. Even the imperialist aggressors cannot but admit that they stand before an invincible socialist camp headed by the Soviet Union, stronger and more united than ever before.

The existence of this mighty socialist camp and its powerful support to national independence movements has inspired all those peoples striving to win or preserve their freedom and independence, and provides increasingly favorable conditions for them to wage successfully their heroic struggle against imperialism and colonialism.

Taking advantage of the failure of Britain, France and Israel in their war of aggression against Egypt, the United States put out the Eisenhower doctrine which purports to fill the "vacuum" in the Near and Middle East and Africa, and is an attempt to grab the colonial positions of Britain and France and suppress the people's national independence movements in that area. The deceptive nature of the Eisenhower doctrine got the upper hand temporarily in their intrigues in Jordan, and then undertook subversive activities in Syria. When those activities were suppressed by the Syrian people, the United States instigated Turkey to pose an armed threat to Syria, thus again creating acute tension in the Near and Middle East. But just as the British and French aggressors underestimated the resistance of the Egyptian people, the aggressive circles of the United States underestimated the solidarity of the heroic Syrian people and other Arab peoples, and misjudged their determination to safeguard their national independence. Also, they obviously failed to take sufficient account of the firm support which the Soviet Union and other peace-loving countries and peoples give to the Arab peoples. As is well known, vehemently opposed by the peoples throughout the world, the aggressive United States designs on Syria ended in ignominious failure. We hail this as another great victory for the Arab peoples.

Recently, a united Arab republic was proclaimed by Egypt and Syria. We warmly greet the founding of this new state and sincerely hope that the United Arab Republic will rely on the patriotic and democratic forces in Egypt and Syria to greatly encourage the Arab countries to strengthen their solidarity, smash all schemes designed to split the Arab peoples and win even greater victories in their common struggle to safeguard national independence and oppose colonialism.

Facts prove that the general trend to vigorous development of the national independence movements is not to be checked. In the past six months, the peoples of the countries in the Near and Middle East and in Africa, especially those of the Yemen, Algeria, Ifni of Morocco, and Oman, have waged unremitting and heroic struggles against colonialism, in which they have won the sympathy and support of all peace-loving peoples.

Meanwhile, the national independence movement has made great progress in Southeast Asia. The Federation of Malaya was proclaimed, although this was only Malaya's first step towards complete independence. Singapore is also striving to attain independence in the shortest time possible. In our friendly neighbor Indonesia a struggle has been waged to recover West Irian, shake off colonialist economic control completely and safeguard national sovereignty and independence. The imperialists hope to subdue Indonesia by means of splitting and subversive activities and by creating economic difficulties within the country. The United States imperialists pose as neutrals, but actually they have played the leading role in these plots. It is very clear that the United States aims at supplanting the Netherlands. The plots of the imperialists are many and varied, and the Indonesian people face a long and tortuous struggle. However, we are convinced that so long as all patriotic and democratic forces in Indonesia unite together, and persist in their struggle for the cause of defending their country's sovereignty and independence, as President Sukarno has again and again called on them to do, the plots of the imperialists will surely suffer defeat, and the struggle of the Indonesian people will assuredly be victorious. The Chinese people and Government will unswervingly support the Indonesian people in this just struggle to the utmost of their ability.

It was under these conditions of the victorious advance of the national independence movements in Asia and Africa that an Asian-African people's solidarity conference was held in Cairo with nearly 50 countries participating. The Asian socialist countries took an active part in this conference, at which countries with different social systems cooperated very well. Most of the countries taking part in the conference were African, which shows that the masses of the African people have entered the arena of international politics. These delegates of the Asian and African peoples came from widely different social strata, a proof that the movement for national independence and for the defense of world peace has more and more taken on a mass character in the countries of Asia and Africa. The Cairo Conference adopted important resolutions on questions of vital interest to the Asian and African people as well as on major international issues. The conference reaffirmed the resolute support of the Asian and African peoples for the five principles of peaceful co-existence and the ten principles of the Bandung Conference, and advocated extensive cooperation among Asian and African countries in the economic, cultural and other fields. The conference called for the immediate cessation of nuclear weapon tests and held that Asia and Africa should be a peace zone in which no foreign country should deploy nuclear and rocket weapons. The conference strongly condemned the sinister activities of the imperialists as a source of human woe, and particularly pointed to the Baghdad pact and the Eisenhower doctrine as infringing on the independence of the Arab countries, impairing their sovereignty, and endangering their security. The conference maintained that all peoples are entitled to the sacred rights of freedom, self-determination, sovereignty and independence. These resolutions without doubt voiced the common will of the hundreds of millions of people in Asia and Africa. There is still a long struggle ahead in the national independence movements in Asia and Africa, and there will inevitably be more twists and turns in their future development, but the Asian and African peoples have already stood up and will never again be crushed.

It is only a year since the Eisenhower doctrine was put forward by the United States, but, its aggressive substance thoroughly exposed, it has already suffered ignominious defeat. It has become odious to the people of Asia and Africa. US aggressive circles are still trying to push forward their plots of war and aggression by means of the Baghdad Pact and Manila Treaty. But, faced with the resolute opposition of the powerful socialist camp and the awakened peoples of Asia and Africa, the new plots of the United States imperialists will fail just as the old ones did.

In contrast to the increasing prosperity and monolithic solidarity of the socialist countries, the imperialist camp is faced with serious economic recessions and political crises.

Since the latter half of 1957, a general decline in production and increase of unemployment has appeared in the United States, Britain, France and some other Western countries. With these signs of economic recession growing more and more pronounced, the struggle for markets is becoming ever more acute. Just as it was in all previous capitalist economic recessions, each capitalist country is trying hard to shift the burden of the recession onto other countries. This further sharpens and intensifies the contradictions within the imperialist camp.

Faced with an ever more serious economic recession, the United States is trying hard to use its dominant position in the imperialist camp to tighten its control over its allies, increase its interference in their affairs and step up its plunder of them. This cannot but provoke increasing resistance among the allies of the United States and strengthen their tendency to move away from it. In order to blackmail and control its allies, the United States used to fabricate so-called threats from the socialist countries and boast of its strength and advantageous position immune from attack, as if only the United States is able to "protect" its allies who need "protection." But the allies of the United States have come to see more and more clearly that the real danger lies in the economic results of their following the United States in expanding armament and preparing for war and in the encroachment on their sovereignty and interests by the United States under the name of "protection." When the Soviet Union outstripped the United States in some important fields in science and technology and came into possession of intercontinental guided missiles, the United States bluff for blackmailing its allies went bankrupt, as did the myth about its "strength" and "advantageous position." The United States has now put forward the slogan of "interdependence" and tried to retain and tighten its control on its allies. But the latter cannot but give serious thought to the fact that the United States is not a reliable stay to fall back on, that a continued arms drive when various types of weapons are being invented and improved daily will only land them in economic bankruptcy, and that allowing their territories to be converted into United States bases for guided missiles will only bring destruction upon themselves first of all in case a war is set going by the United States. The broad masses in the allied countries of the United States are opposing with growing vehemence their heavy burden of military expenses, the deployment of guided missiles in their countries, and the flight of United States airplanes carrying nuclear weapons over their heads. This fact too compels the governments of those countries to grow more sober on the question of war or peace.

The socialist countries consistently pursue a policy of peaceful co-existence. The important peace proposals put forth recently by the Soviet Union, in particular, have further exploded the lie of the United States aggressive circles about so-called threats from the socialist countries. More and more capitalist countries have begun to realize more sharply that, under the existing international situation, peaceful co-existence with the socialist countries is not only possible but also necessary. But the United States aggressive circles and a very few of their followers still persist in the policy of armament expansion and war preparations, refuse to ease international tension, and endeavor to obstruct the holding of East-West negotiations on the most pressing current international questions. This is further widening the differences between the United States and its allies.

At the last NATO conference in Paris, contradictions among the Western countries developed to such an extent that it was no longer possible to cover them up. The United States originally hoped, through the Paris conference, to step up armament expansion and war preparations by the Western countries and set up bases for nuclear and rocket weapons on the soil of the members of the North Atlantic Treaty Organization. But developments at the conference went directly contrary to the expectations of the United States. At the conference Norway and Denmark openly refused to allow the establishment of United States guided missile bases on their territory, and many other countries were hesitant on this question owing to the pressure of the people at home. The peace proposals of the Soviet Government caused great interest and gave rise to long discussions at the conference. The communique after the conference, while advocating armament expansion and war preparations in an attempt to aggravate international tension, had to leave room for the holding of East-West talks to parry pressures at home and abroad. After the conference, even Britain expressed its approval in principle of a non-aggression treaty between the countries concerned, although it remains to be seen whether it will stick to this proposition.

The problem before the US aggressive circles and their followers is now quite clear. If they should obstinately reject peaceful co-existence and persist in their policy of armament expansion and war preparations, they will become even more isolated in the world than they are and bring upon themselves even more serious political and economic crises. If they should grow so reckless as to attempt to find a way out through war, they will only be digging their own graves and seeking their own destruction. The time has come for them to do some sober thinking and make a wise choice.

The people of the whole world eagerly desire peace. The favorable international situation and the peace proposals put forward by the Soviet Government have enhanced the confidence of all peace-loving countries and people in striving for peace. The Chinese Government and the governments of other brother countries have successively expressed their support for the proposals of the Soviet Government. China is prepared, together with other countries, to make positive efforts to realize these proposals and to undertake corresponding obligations. Our great neighbor India which is always concerned for world peace and international security has given active support to the proposal of the Soviet Union for an East-West summit conference. In line with his basic idea of expanding the area of peace, Prime Minister Nehru has expressed himself against the setting-up of bases for guided missiles in Europe and Asia and for the establishment and expansion of an area free from weapons of mass destruction. These propositions are what the Chinese people have all along supported. Egypt has also clearly said it welcomes the proposal of the Soviet Union for a summit conference with the participation of Egypt. A movement for the immediate holding of an East-West summit conference is now surging up rapidly all over the world and the Soviet peace proposals have become a great force for easing the international situation and promoting peaceful co-existence among nations. Although the United States aggressive circles and their followers are still unwilling to discard their policy of armament expansion and war preparations, and are still creating all sorts of excuses to obstruct East-West talks, the days when they could do as they liked and order others about at will in international politics have long since passed. The world forces for peace are stronger today than ever before and the conditions for securing a lasting world peace are unprecedentedly favorable. So long as all the peace-loving countries and peoples maintain their solidarity and persevere in the struggle, as they have up till now, they will be able to cause the international situation to continue to develop in a direction favorable to peace and compel the imperialist aggressive forces to accept peaceful co-existence.

Since the day of its founding, our country has looked upon the defense of peace as its sacred duty. Our country is a member of the socialist camp headed by the Soviet Union. To enhance the strength and solidarity of this camp is our primary international obligation in the defense of peace. In our relations with the other socialist countries during the past half year, we should first of all mention the visit to Moscow of the Delegation of the People's Republic of China headed by Chairman Mao Tse-tung to take part in the celebrations of the 40th anniversary of the great October Socialist Revolution. This is another major event in Sino-Soviet relations following the visit to China of Chairman Voroshilov of the Presidium of the Supreme Soviet of the Soviet Union. In this same period, we also received the Hungarian Government Delegation headed by Premier Kadar, the Bulgarian Government Delegation headed by Premier Yugov, and Vice-President Vukmanovic of the Executive Council of the Federal People's Republic of Yugoslavia. In return for the visits of the delegation of our National People's Congress, the Soviet Union, Czechoslovakia and Yugoslavia all sent parliamentary delegations to visit our country. When the Chinese people were enthusiastically celebrating the 40th anniversary of the October Revolution, a Soviet delegation representing all walks of life headed by Comrade Andreyev, President of the Soviet-Chinese Friendship Association, came to our country to take part in the celebrations. We and our brother countries also exchanged various professional delegations to learn from one another and strengthen our cooperation. We should particularly mention here the Sino-Soviet Agreement on Scientific Cooperation signed in January 1958, under which the Soviet Union will give us tremendous assistance in the development of our science and technology. The development of our relations with the other socialist countries during the past year is a typical embodiment of the spirit of solidarity, cooperation and mutual assistance prevailing in our big family of socialist countries.

Together with India and Burma, our country initiated the five principles of peaceful co-existence. And during the past half year, the tremendous development in the relations between our country and the nationalist countries of Asia and Africa has provided further living examples of the five principles in action. Through visits to our country of leaders and eminent individuals of many countries, we have had many opportunities to make contacts with them and to increase our mutual understanding and friendship. During this period, we received Vice-President Dr. Radhakrishnan of India, Prime Minister Daud of Afghanistan, former Vice-President Dr. Hatta and Speaker of Parliament Sartono of Indonesia, Chief Justice U Myint Thein, Deputy Prime Ministers U Ba Swe and U Kyaw Nyein and a parliamentary delegation of Burma, and Deputy Prime Minister Crown Prince Mohammed El-Badr of the Yemen. His Royal Highness Mohammed El-Badr was the first leader of an Arab state to visit our country. During his visit, China and the Yemen signed a treaty of friendship, a treaty of commerce and an agreement on scientific, technical and cultural cooperation. This is of great significance both to the strengthening of Sino-Yemeni relations and to the further development of relations between China and all the Arab states. Besides our mutual friendly visits with the other Asian and African countries, our mutual study and cooperation in various specialized fields have also been further developed. This is particularly important for us Asian and African countries which are relatively backward in the economic, cultural, scientific and technical fields.

During the past half year, the present Japanese Government adopted an unfriendly attitude towards New China in many ways and a fourth nonofficial Sino-Japanese trade agreement failed to be signed owing to the unreasonable restrictions and insulting regulations which the Japanese Government tried to impose on the Chinese side. Nevertheless, contacts and trade relations between the Chinese and Japanese peoples still developed to a great extent, showing the common desire of our two peoples for peace and friendship. During this period, the number of Japanese friends visiting China was again greater than that from any other Asian or African country, and China also sent many important delegations to visit Japan. The Chinese people are thankful to the Japanese people and organizations who received and helped the various Chinese delegations so well. The Chinese people are glad to see the opening in Canton of the Exhibition of Japanese Commodities and wish it success.

We have always advocated the settlement of questions between nations by means of negotiation. A good example in this regard is the treaty on the question of dual nationality concluded between our country and Indonesia. This treaty has been ratified recently by the Indonesian Parliament and the Standing Committee of our National People's Congress respectively, and will come into effect soon. Our government has, in accordance with the principles approved by the fourth session of the First National People's Congress, continued friendly talks with the Government of Burma on the boundary question. We have no doubt whatever that Burma and China will settle this question together in a spirit of mutual respect and mutual understanding.

During the past six months, the relations between our country and the North European countries have been satisfactory. A delegation of our National People's Congress paid a return visit to Finland and was accorded a warm reception. Our country has concluded trade agreements with Finland, Sweden and Denmark, and also made contacts with Norway on the question of trade.

During this period, a number of major West European countries showed keen interest in developing trade and technical cooperation with China. Visits to China were paid by a parliamentary secretary of the British Board of Trade, a non-official economic delegation from France and another from West Germany. We welcome this desire for cooperation, and on our part have sent delegations to Britain, France, Austria and Belgium to explore the possibilities of developing trade and technical cooperation with these countries. But it must be pointed out that with the continued embargo on China, these possibilities are of course subjected to much restriction. A noteworthy happening in the past half year was the visit to China of American youth delegates in defiance of obstruction and threats by the State Department of the United States. The American youth delegates had an opportunity of comparing what they saw with the slanderous propaganda of the State Department. They also discovered through their contacts with Chinese people that a great deal of common ground exists between the Chinese and American peoples in respect to peace and friendship.

Since the armistice in Korea, China and the Korean Democratic People's Republic have continuously taken active steps in an effort to convert the armistice into a lasting peace and bring about the peaceful unification of Korea. The United States, however, has taken a diametrically opposed attitude. It has not only tried hard to obstruct a peaceful settlement of the Korean question, but openly violated the Korean Armistice Agreement. In June last year, the United States unilaterally announced the abrogation of the provisions in the Korean Armistice Agreement forbidding the introduction into Korea of reinforcing weapons. Since then the United States, disregarding the protests of the Korean and Chinese side, has introduced into South Korea atomic guns, guided missiles and other weapons of new types; recently it even held a so-called "atomic attack" exercise near the military demarcation line. In so doing, the United States aimed at both further obstructing a peaceful settlement of the Korean question and aggravating tension in the Far East, so that it can strengthen its colonial rule over the South Korean people, and further convert South Korea into its atomic base. This proves that the continued stay of US forces in South Korea constitutes a threat both to the Korean people and to peace in the Far East. The Korean and Chinese peoples cannot allow this state of affairs to continue.

With a view to realizing the peaceful unification of Korea, the Government of the Korean Democratic People's Republic has just proposed the following: to withdraw all foreign forces from North and South Korea simultaneously; to hold nation-wide free elections under the supervision of a neutral nations' organization within a definite period following the withdrawal of all foreign forces; to conduct consultations between North and South Korea on an equal footing on economic and cultural intercourse between them, the holding of nation-wide elections and other problems; and to reduce the armed forces of North and South Korea to the minimum within a short period of time. These important proposals of the Government of the Korean Democratic People's Republic are not only in full accord with the eager desires of all the Korean people, but also provide a new practicable way of gradually easing tension in the Far East. The Chinese Government fully supports the proposals of the Korean Government, and holds that all foreign forces should be withdrawn from Korea within a set period; it has already stated that it is prepared to open discussions with the Government of the Korean Democratic People's Republic on the question of withdrawal of the Chinese People's Volunteers from Korea. The Chinese Government asks the governments of the United States and of other countries participating in the United Nations forces also to take measures to withdraw United States and all other foreign forces from South Korea.

The Chinese Government has always maintained that the Korean question should be settled by the Korean people themselves, and that foreign interference is impermissible. Everybody knows that it was only when US forces had invaded the Korean Democratic People's Republic and at the same time time occupied our territory of Taiwan and seriously jeopardized the security of our country that the Chinese people organized their Volunteers to proceed to Korea to resist American aggression and aid Korea. The Chinese People's Volunteers are a righteous force, a force against aggression, diametrically opposed in nature to the US aggressive forces. Since the armistice in Korea, China together with the Korean Democratic People's Republic has repeatedly proposed to the United States that all foreign forces be withdrawn simultaneously from North and South Korea. Realization of this proposal is a prerequisite for the holding of free elections throughout Korea and the peaceful unification of Korea. But the United States has continued to reject the proposals of the Korean and Chinese side, thus causing the present deadlock in Korea. With a view to breaking this deadlock and promoting peace in the Far East, the Chinese Government now responds to the proposal put forward once more by the Korean Government for the withdrawal of all foreign forces from Korea, and is prepared to take the initiative in order to promote its realization. We consider that the time has come for all parties concerned to take positive steps and to work together for a peaceful settlement of the Korean question.

As one of the parties to the Geneva agreements and a close neighbor of the Indo-Chinese countries, China is at all times concerned with the consolidation of peace in Indo-China and the over-all implementation of the Geneva agreements. The Chinese Government fully supports the Government of the Vietnam Democratic Republic in its unremitting efforts to promote the peaceful unification of Vietnam, and is of the opinion that the present situation in which implementation of the Geneva agreements in Vietnam is being obstructed and disrupted should not continue. The establishment of a coalition government in the Kingdom of Laos and the settlement of the question of the provinces of Samneua and Phongsaly were signs that great progress has been made in the implementation of the Geneva agreements in Laos. The Chinese Government welcomes the peaceful unification of the Kingdom of Laos on the basis of the Geneva agreements, which provides a more favorable condition for the independent development of Laos. Although the United States has not given up its attempt to drag Laos into the Manila treaty bloc, Laos, like Cambodia, adheres to a policy of peace and neutrality. During the past few years, relations between China and Cambodia have developed well. The Chinese Government will also strive to develop good-neighborly relations between China and Laos in accordance with the five principles of peaceful co-existence affirmed in the joint statement issued in 1956 by the Chinese and Laotian premiers.

Now let me speak about relations between China and the United States.

It is now two and a half years since the Sino-American ambassadorial talks started in August 1955. Although China put forward a series of positive proposals on the question of easing tension in the Taiwan area, the United States persistently demanded that China recognize the status quo of United States occupation of Taiwan, and tension in the Taiwan area continues. This has prevented any progress in the talks on the main questions in relations between China and the United States. Meanwhile, the Chinese side has made many efforts in seeking a gradual improvement of Sino-American relations starting with the settlement of those questions which are comparatively easy to settle and which would create a favorable condition for settling major issues between China and the United States. In the past half year the Chinese side successively proposed that the Chinese and United States governments admit correspondents of the other side to their respective countries for news coverage on an equal and reciprocal basis, and that the two governments open negotiations on judicial assistance between the two countries. Everybody can see that these are proposals to settle practical matters and that they are fair and reasonable, and beneficial to both parties. Given a sincere desire to improve relations, there should not be any difficulty in reaching agreement on these matters. But these proposals were rejected by the United States Government practically out of hand. The question of news coverage and judicial assistance were first raised with China by American journalists and United States judicial authorities. The Chinese Government is willing to see the wishes of the parties concerned in the United States realized. But efforts on the part of the Chinese Government alone will be in vain until the United States Government changes its rigid and hostile attitude.

United States persistence in the Sino-American talks in asking China to accept the present state of United States occupation of Taiwan is inseparable from its scheme to create "two Chinas."

The United States openly occupied Taiwan at the same time as it unleashed its war of aggression in Korea and stepped up its intervention in Indo-China. Not reconciled to their defeat on the Chinese mainland, the United States ruling circles at that time attempted to throttle the young People's Republic of China by a three-pronged drive from Korea, Indo-China and Taiwan. However, after several years of serious trials of strength, the Korean war was terminated, peace was restored in Indo-China, and with New China developing and growing day by day the possibility of the liberation of Taiwan by the Chinese people has also increased. The policy of the United States of being hostile to the Chinese people, refusing to recognize New China and shutting out New China from international life has not only failed to prejudice in the least the existence and development of New China, but, on the contrary, has more and more isolated the United States itself. In order to extricate itself from this awkward situation and yet continue its occupation of Taiwan, the United States has been trying to create "two Chinas."

The United States holds ambassadorial talks with China, and yet at these talks demands that China accept the status quo of its occupation of Taiwan. This is in substance an attempt to create "two Chinas," which is of course absolutely unacceptable to the Chinese side. In the United Nations, the United States has met with growing opposition in obstructing the restoration to China of its legitimate rights, and it has come to see that it is impossible to bar China from the United Nations forever. That is why the method now used by the United States is first to create wherever possible a state of "two Chinas" in certain international conferences and organizations so as to establish gradually a fait accompli of "two Chinas" in international affairs. As early as in November 1956 at the 16th international Olympic games and in June 1957 at the Special Committee of the International Geophysical Year, the United States already tried to carry out its scheme through the instrumentality of its followers. But by October 1957 at the 19th International Red Cross Conference held in New Delhi with 80 countries participating, the United States itself came out to carry out its scheme. At this conference, the United States delegate insisted on inviting the Chiang Kai-shek clique in Taiwan to send a delegation of the so-called Republic of China to attend the conference alongside the delegation of the People's Republic of China. Although the United States proposal was carried by a majority of 62 votes for to 44 votes against, out of the total number of 135 votes it was only a minority that seconded the United States proposal, while the majority in various ways supported China's just stand against the creation of "two Chinas." This dirty trick of the United States aroused general indignation at the conference, and the delegations of all the socialist countries and many Asian and African countries as well as the North European countries, siding with the Chinese delegation, withdrew from the conference in a strong protest. Some other delegations stayed on in the conference to continue the struggle against the United States proposal. The United States was thus placed in an extremely isolated position, both politically and morally.

However, it should also be pointed out that the United States is not without followers in its plot to create "two Chinas." There are some who attempt to invite representatives of the People's Republic of China to participate in certain international organizations and conferences while retaining the representatives of the Chiang Kai-shek clique, thus creating a situation of "two Chinas." Of course, among these there are also people who are truly friendly to China but who naively think that they are introducing New China into international organizations and activities, not knowing that they are in fact duped by the US scheme to create "two Chinas." There are also some who deliberately spread the absurd contentions that the status of Taiwan is as yet undetermined and that the people in Taiwan, autonomy for Taiwan, or putting Taiwan under trusteeship, all of which are methods to pave the way for the United States plot of creating "two Chinas." Taiwan is Chinese territory. Both the Cairo and Potsdam declarations affirmed that Taiwan should be restored to China. And Taiwan was indeed returned to China after the Japanese surrender. The Chiang Kai-shek clique itself cannot deny these facts. Even the United States Government which is now bent on creating "two Chinas" acknowledged these facts on more than one occasion. The great majority of the people in Taiwan are of Han nationality, while the national minorities there, like other national minorities on the mainland, are also members of the big family of nationalities making up China. The absurdities concerning the status of Taiwan and the nationality of Taiwan are completely groundless. No schemes to separate Taiwan from the motherland through the fabrication of these absurdities can ever be realized.

The British Government, while recognizing the People's Republic of China, has been helping the United States to keep the Chiang Kai-shek clique in the seat of China usurped by it in the United Nations. Britain is also the propaganda center of the absurd contention about the undetermined status of "Taiwan." Recently, flirtation between the British Government and the Chiang Kai-shek clique has markedly increased. China is willing to see its relations with Britain improved, but it will never acquiesce in or tolerate the British practice of following the United States in creating "two Chinas." If Britain does not change its double-faced attitude towards China, Sino-British relations will inevitably be adversely affected.

The movement of the Japanese people for the restoration of Japan-China diplomatic relations has become an increasingly powerful force that is not to be ignored in Japanese political life. However, Japanese Prime Minister Nobusuke Kishi attempted to make use of this for ulterior purposes. On November 12, 1957 he stated before the Foreign Affairs Committee of the Japanese House of Councillors that the tension in the Taiwan Straits "is the result of the Nationalists and Communists claiming sovereignty over mainland China, and until their contentions are adjusted, there can be no allaying of tension." This is not only an attempt to shield the United States in occupying Taiwan, but also to justify the United States plot of creating "two Chinas." This attempt has long been seen through by the Japanese people. For example, the Goodwill Delegation of the Japanese Social-Democratic Party, the Delegation of the Japanese National Council for the Restoration of Japan-China Diplomatic Relations and the Delegation of the Japan-China Friendship Association, which visited China in succession during 1957, all expressed a warm desire to promote normalization of relations between China and Japan, were of the opinion that the liberation of Taiwan is China's domestic affair and opposed the creation of "two Chinas." This shows that it is impossible to hoodwink the Japanese people by confusing right with wrong through false arguments about "two Chinas," nor is it possible to make the Japanese people's widespread movement for the restoration of Japan-China diplomatic relations serve the plot of creating "two Chinas."

The Chinese Government and people are firmly opposed to the scheme to create "two Chinas." We absolutely will not allow this scheme to materialize in any form or on any occasion. There is only one China—the People's Republic of China. The crucial issue in Sino-American relations today is not that China wants American recognition but that the United States antagonizes the Chinese people, occupies Chinese territory and even wants China to accept this occupation as lawful. This is a great issue between right and wrong which is not to be obscured. Taiwan is an inalienable part of Chinese territory. The Chinese people are determined to liberate Taiwan. All the Chinese people are opposed to the American scheme to create "two Chinas." Even members of the Chiang Kai-shek clique in Taiwan provided they are patriotic, would not like to see a situation with "two Chinas." Of course, the United States would not scruple to rear a more pliant puppet regime in Taiwan in order to realize its schemes. But our great nation has never yielded to foreign oppression and our compatriots in Taiwan have also a glorious revolutionary tradition. So long as all patriotic Chinese persist in their struggle for the complete unification of their motherland and will not permit American occupation of Taiwan to be legalized, Taiwan will certainly return to the bosom of the motherland. Recognition or no recognition by the United States, China will exist and go on developing. Exclusion of China with its 600 million population from the United Nations only hurts the United Nations itself. We will never allow a state of "two Chinas" to arise in any international organization, conference or occasion. Such is our firm and unshakable stand.

Fellow deputies! The past year was no ordinary year. In the past year tremendous changes very favorable to us took place both in the international and domestic situations. Never before have the causes of socialism and of peace flourished as they do today. An immensely bright future is before us. The time is propitious for us to do great deeds. Let us further strengthen the unity of our people, the solidarity of the socialist countries and that of the people of the whole world, and rouse our revolutionary spirits to win even greater and more brilliant victories in the cause of the socialist construction of our motherland and the cause of world peace and the progress of mankind.

DOCUMENT 24

Resolution on the Moscow Meetings of Representatives of the Communist and Workers' Parties (which were held November 14-19, 1957), adopted May 23, 1958, by the Second Session of the Eighth Party Congress of the Chinese Communist Party.

> The English text is an official translation published by the Foreign Languages Press, Peking, 1958, as the first 13 pages of a 92-page pamphlet entitled *In Refutation of Modern Revisionism*.
>
> *Comment.* The most interesting problem raised by the Chinese Communist Party's attack on the Yugoslav League of Communists is how far it can be taken at its face

value. The resolution has been included in this collection on the assumption that it was intended partly to serve domestic ends. On this, see our General Introduction, part VII, also Zbigniew K. Brzezinski, *The Soviet Bloc: Unity and Conflict* (Cambridge: Harvard University Press, 1960), Chapter 13, and R. Lowenthal, "Shifts and Rifts in the Moscow-Peking Axis," in *Problems of Communism*, January 1959.

The international background may be summarized as follows. The Yugoslavs sent a delegation (not headed by Marshal Tito) to the Moscow meetings in November 1957, and signed the Peace Manifesto proposal put forward by Gomulka. They refused, however, to sign the Declaration of the Communist Parties, which acknowledged the leadership of the U.S.S.R. and which laid down general lines for socialist construction in the various countries of the Socialist Camp.

On March 13, 1958, the Yugoslav League of Communists published the draft program for its congress to be held in April. In this document, it condemned not the "Imperialist Camp" alone, but also Stalin, for the division of the world into blocs. The League proclaimed the view that socialism was developing already, by means of nationalization, in capitalist countries, and that its further development would not necessarily require violent revolution. The Yugoslavs rejected any attempt to dictate the way to socialism, and (implicitly anticipating the charges against them) said that they rejected not only "bourgeois revisionism" but also "revisionism springing from bureaucratism and Statism." Such views showed that the Yugoslavs were sticking to the theoretical formulation which had been evolved during the period of their break with Moscow (1948-1955). This would allow neither that the "dictatorship of the proletariat" was justified by the external threat of imperialism, nor that there was any necessity for a uniform type of leadership in countries of the Socialist Camp along general lines laid down with Russian and Chinese advice.

After publication of the Yugoslav draft, the other Communist parties criticized it confidentially to the Yugoslavs with no apparent effect. On April 5, 1958, the Yugoslavs were confidentially informed that no Soviet delegation would attend their congress due to open on April 22. On April 17, the Yugoslavs published some minor revisions of their program, but the press campaign against them opened with the issuance on April 19 of a critique in the Russian theoretical journal *Kommunist* (probably written and set up before the Yugoslav amendment came to hand).

The campaign continued to be fairly restrained, at least on the part of the major Communist powers, until the Chinese joined in with a scathing editorial in the *People's Daily* of May 5. Thereafter the violence of Chinese criticism exceeded that of the Russians. The main documents are the editorials in *People's Daily* on June 4 and 6 (the former suggests that within the Chinese Communist Party there were critics of the extreme anti-Yugoslav line), and articles in *Red Flag*, June 1 and 16 (the former is a very thorough critique by the authoritative Ch'en Po-ta).

The report on the Moscow meetings by Teng Hsiao-p'ing to the Second Session of the Eighth Party Congress (mentioned at the outset of Document 24) is not available. "Opposing revisionism," however, had been a constant Party slogan since June 1957. The *People's Daily* editorial of December 29, 1956 (Document 13) had criticized firmly but in moderate terms the Yugoslav attitude on the Hungarian question. Articles quoted in ECMM 73 and 74 (*Political Study*, Feb. 13, 1957, and *Study*, Jan. 18, 1957) imply that from November 1956 on, the Chinese Communist Party had taken a severe view of Yugoslav revisionist tendencies and had thought it worthwhile to warn cadres against them.

———————————TEXT OF DOCUMENT 24———————————

The Eighth National Congress of the Communist Party of China, at its Second Session, having heard the report delivered by Comrade Teng Hsiao-ping on the meeting of representatives of the Communist and Workers' Parties of the socialist countries held in Moscow from November 14 to 16, 1957, and the meeting of representatives of 64 Communist and Workers' Parties held from November 16 to 19, unanimously endorses the Declarations adopted by the two meetings and expresses satisfaction with the work of the delegation of the Communist Party of China headed by Comrade Mao Tse-tung during the two meetings.

The Moscow meetings of the Communist and Workers' Parties of various countries and the two Declarations they adopted ushered in a new stage in the international communist movement of our time and were a very great inspiration to the labouring people and all forces for peace, democracy and progress throughout the world. The Communist Parties throughout the world have welcomed and given their support to the two Declarations. The Communist Party of the United States of America, after clearing out the revisionist John Gates, has also endorsed the stand taken by these Declarations. Only the League of Communists of Yugoslavia has not only openly assumed an attitude of opposition to the Declaration of the meeting of representatives of the Communist and Workers' Parties of the socialist countries, but has also adopted an anti-Marxist-Leninist and out-and-out revisionist programme at its Seventh Congress, and set it against the Declaration of the Moscow meeting. At their Congress, in an effort to defend their anti-Marxist-Leninist and out-and-out revisionist programme, Tito and other leaders of the League of Communists of Yugoslavia made a series of vicious attacks against the international communist movement and the socialist camp with the Soviet Union as its centre, whereas in regard to U.S. imperialism, that most ferocious enemy of the people in every part of the world, they were sycophantic and deeply grateful.

At present, the international communist movement has the important responsibility to adhere firmly to the viewpoints expressed in the Declaration of the meeting of representatives of the Communist and Workers' Parties of the socialist countries, to defend the fundamental principles of Marxism-Leninism and oppose modern revisionism.

The Declaration of the meeting of representatives of the Communist and Workers' Parties of the socialist countries sums up the experience of the international communist movement in the past century, especially in the past forty years; expounds the common principles which the Communist Parties of all countries must abide by in the socialist revolution and socialist construction; puts forward the basic policy of the Communist Parties in rallying the broad masses of the people to the struggle for the cause of peace, democracy and socialism; it lays the ideological and political foundation for solidarity among the Communist Parties and strengthens the unity of the socialist camp headed by the Soviet Union. It is an epoch-making document which is in the nature of a programme for the international communist movement.

Analysing the current international situation, the Declaration points out that "world development is determined by the course and results of the competition between two diametrically opposed social systems," that "while socialism is on the upgrade, imperialism is heading towards decline," that the colonial system is crumbling and that "capitalist economy is bound to encounter new deep slumps and crises." It points out that the question of war or peaceful co-existence has become the basic issue in world politics, while the existence of imperialism is the source of aggressive wars. It points out that the aggressive imperialist circles of the United States have become the centre of world reaction, the most deadly enemy of the peoples. It says: "By this policy these anti-popular, aggressive imperialist forces are courting their own ruin, creating their own grave-diggers." At the same time, the Declaration points out that the forces of peace have so grown that there is a real possibility of averting wars and that at the forefront of the forces of peace is the indestructible socialist camp headed by the Soviet Union. The Declaration says: "An alliance of these mighty forces can prevent war, but should the bellicose imperialist maniacs venture, regardless of anything, to unleash a war, imperialism will doom itself to destruction, for the peoples will not tolerate a system that brings them so much suffering and exacts so many sacrifices."

The Peace Manifesto adopted at the meeting of representatives of 64 Communist and Workers' Parties points out that the threat to peace and the security of the people comes from "the capitalist monopolies which have amassed unprecedented riches from the two world wars and the current arms drive." It appeals to people of goodwill throughout the world: Organize and fight for peace!

The correctness of the appraisal of the international situation made in the Declaration of the meeting of representatives of the Communist and Workers' Parties of the socialist countries is confirmed by the development of events. In the past six months, in the socialist camp, economic and cultural construction in the Soviet Union, China and many other brother countries has shown a continuous upward trend. In Asia, Africa and Latin America, there has been a fresh advance in the national liberation movement waged against the imperialists and their lackeys, and in some countries fierce struggle is going on. Meanwhile, the imperialist countries have landed in a new, grave and deep economic crisis. This began first in the United States, where capitalism is most developed, and the economic crisis of the United States is now hitting the whole capitalist world. On the issue of peace or war, the Soviet Union, Poland, the German Democratic Republic, Rumania and other brother countries have put forward a series of peace proposals. The Soviet Union has stopped the testing of nuclear weapons before others; the governments of the Korean Democratic People's Republic and of our own country jointly decided to withdraw the Chinese People's Volunteers from Korea. These facts demonstrate to the people throughout the world the determination of the countries in the socialist camp to do all in their power to secure peace. Despite the desire for peace of the people of all countries, the aggressive bloc headed by the U.S. imperialists persists up to now in its refusal to stop nuclear tests, to end the cold war, to reduce armaments and to withdraw its troops from Korea, and it is doing all it can to delay the convening of a summit conference. The U.S. imperialists have been occupying our Taiwan. They have gone so far as to interfere openly in the internal affairs of Indonesia, aiding and abetting and supplying the rebel clique in that country with materials and now they are interfering in the internal affairs of the Lebanon. We must be awake to the fact that U.S. imperialism and the imperialist bloc headed by it are still actively threatening war, preparing for new wars, stepping up their political, economic and cultural aggression against many countries in Asia, Africa and Latin America, undermining the internal unity of these countries and even resorting to armed force to suppress national liberation movements. It is our task to rally the peace-loving forces of the whole world to safeguard peace and smash the war schemes of the aggressive imperialist bloc headed by the United States.

The Declaration of the meeting of representatives of the Communist and Workers' Parties of the socialist countries points out that in adhering to the principle of combining the universal truths of Marxism-Leninism with the concrete practice of revolution and construction in various countries, attention must be paid to overcoming revisionism and doctrinairism. The Declaration lays stress on the theoretical foundation of Marxism-Leninism—dialectical materialism—refutes metaphysics and idealism, and holds that "the application of dialectical materialism in practical work and the education of Party functionaries and the broad masses in Marxism-Leninism are urgent tasks of the Communist and Workers' Parties." To the question of what is the main danger now facing the international communist movement, the Declaration gives this clear-cut answer: "The main danger at present is revisionism, or, in other words, right-wing opportunism, which, as a manifestation of bourgeois ideology, paralyses the revolutionary energy of the working class and demands the preservation or restoration of capitalism." The Declaration points out: "The existence of bourgeois influence is an internal source of revisionism, while surrender to imperialist pressure is its external source." Making a special note of the emergence of modern revisionism, the Declaration points out: "Modern revisionism seeks to smear the great teaching of Marxism-Leninism, declares that it is 'outmoded' and alleges that it has lost its significance for social progress. The revisionists try to exorcize the revolutionary spirit of Marxism, to undermine faith in socialism among the working class and the working people in general. They deny the historical necessity for a proletarian revolution and the dictatorship of the proletariat during the period of transition from capitalism to socialism, deny the leading role of the Marxist-Leninist party, reject the principle of proletarian internationalism and call for rejection of the basic Leninist principles of Party organization and, above all, of democratic centralism and for transforming the Communist Party from a militant revolutionary organization into some kind of debating society."

We Chinese Communists, like the Communists of other countries, note with pleasure that since the publication of the Declaration, fresh achievements have been made by the fraternal Parties in the countries of the socialist camp in socialist revolution and socialist construction, in ideological and political work and in unity and co-operation. New progress has also been made by the fraternal Parties in the capitalist countries in the struggle against revisionism and right-wing renegades, in the work of consolidating their own ranks, defending the Marxist-Leninist unity of the Party and increasing its militant strength, and in the work of establishing close ties with the workers, peasants and the rest of the broad masses of the labouring people.

It is clear that, to wage a joint struggle against imperialism for the common cause of the proletariat of the whole world, the unity and solidarity of the Communist Parties in all countries on the basis of Marxism-Leninism is of special importance. Brother Parties should strengthen their mutual contacts. All talk and action that go against this unity and solidarity are harmful, they must be resolutely opposed.

The truth of the judgment made in the Declaration that the main danger at present is revisionism, that is, right-wing opportunism, has also been confirmed by the facts. On a series of fundamental questions, the Programme of the League of Communists of Yugoslavia recently approved by its Seventh Congress betrays the principles of Marxism-Leninism, sets itself against the Declaration of the meeting of representatives of the Communist and Workers' Parties of the socialist countries, and turns against the Peace Manifesto adopted by the meeting of representatives of 64 Communist and Workers' Parties, which bears the signature of the representative of the League of Communists of Yugoslavia. Just as the Congress of the League of Communists of Yugoslavia has the right to adopt its programme, so the Communist Parties of other countries have the right, as well as the obligation, to criticize and repudiate this revisionist programme in their effort to preserve the purity of Marxism-Leninism.

This programme of the League of Communists of Yugoslavia asserts, on the one hand, that "the swelling wave of state-capitalist tendencies in the capitalist world is the most obvious proof that mankind is indomitably moving into the era of socialism through a wide variety of different roads," and that the state apparatus in the capitalist world is "a regulator in the sphere of labour and property relationships, of social rights and social services and other social relations," which tends increasingly "to restrict the role of private capital" and "deprive the owners of private capital of certain independent functions in the economy and in the society." On the other hand, the Programme of the League of Communists of Yugoslavia describes ownership by the whole people, that is, ownership by the state, in the socialist countries as "state capitalism," and they hold that it is directly from the foundation of this so-called "state capitalism" that "bureaucracy and bureaucratic-statist deformities" are produced. In this way the Programme smears socialism and glorifies capitalism, smears the proletarian dictatorship and glorifies the bourgeois dictatorship.

The Programme of the League of Communists of Yugoslavia holds that "factors of socialism" are taking shape in the capitalist countries and that provided the working class "exercises incessant pressure" on the bourgeois state apparatus and strives to "win a decisive influence" in it, it will be possible to "secure the development of socialism." Here, in an attempt to sap the revolutionary energy of the working class in capitalist countries, the Programme spreads the erroneous view that there is no need to carry out the proletarian revolution, no need to smash the capitalist state machine, no need to set up a proletarian dictatorship.

The leading group of the League of Communists of Yugoslavia claim to be standing outside the socialist camp and the imperialist camp. In fact this is not so; they have always directed the spearhead of their attack against the socialist camp headed by the Soviet Union, but have not dared to touch U.S. imperialism in the least. They describe the two fundamentally different world economic-political systems, the socialist camp and the imperialist camp, as a "division of the world into two antagonist military-political blocs" and do their utmost to smear the socialist camp and glorify the imperialist camp. It should be pointed out that quite a number of countries, though they are not socialist countries, have adopted the policy of neutrality which opposes war and supports peace. This is of positive significance to the maintenance of world peace; it is opposed by the aggressive imperialist forces, but has the sympathy of the peace-loving peoples of all countries. On the other hand, the so-called position outside the blocs advocated by the leading group of the League of Communists of Yugoslavia, which aims at disrupting the solidarity of the socialist countries, caters to the policy of the imperialists headed by the United States against communism, against the Soviet Union and the socialist camp. That is why it is applauded and rewarded by the U.S. imperialists.

The Programme of the League of Communists of Yugoslavia quotes some phrases of Marxism-Leninism just to disguise itself with a cloak of Marxism-Leninism and thus make it easier to deceive others. In method of thinking, the Programme substitutes for revolutionary materialistic dialectics a sophistry which turns the facts upside down and confuses right with wrong; politically, it substitutes the reactionary theory of the state standing above classes for the Marxist-Leninist theory of the state, and reactionary bourgeois nationalism for revolutionary proletarian internationalism; in political economy, it defends monopoly capital and obscures the fundamental differences between capitalism and socialism. The Yugoslav revisionists betray the Marxist-Leninist theories concerning the class struggle of the proletariat, the proletarian revolution and the proletarian dictatorship, and thus completely forsake the Marxist-Leninist doctrine about the political party of the proletariat. In a wild attempt to undermine and disintegrate the Communist Parties of various countries, they propagate a series of absurdities which deny the leading role of the Communist Party in socialist revolution and socialist construction, attack the Communist and Workers' Parties in the socialist countries, and slander the Communist Parties in the capitalist countries as "ceasing to act as a revolutionary creative factor and motive power of social development in their respective countries."

This out-and-out revisionist programme is put forward for the purpose of splitting the international communist movement. It is propounded at the very time when the general crisis of capitalism is deepening and when the revisionist harangues of the right-wing socialists are daily losing their paralysing effect on the working class and the labouring masses. That is why the service rendered by this Programme to imperialism, especially U.S. imperialism, is tantamount to "sending it a present of firewood in cold weather."

The Eighth National Congress of the Chinese Communist Party at its Second Session considers as basically correct and necessary the criticism made in 1948 by the Information Bureau of the Communist and Workers' Parties in its resolution "Concerning the Situation in the Communist Party of Yugoslavia" in regard to the fact that the Yugoslav Communist Party departed from the principles of Marxism-Leninism and took the wrong road of bourgeois nationalism, although there were defects and mistakes in the methods adopted at that time in dealing with this issue. Our Party agreed with and supported that criticism. The second resolution concerning the Yugoslav Communist Party adopted by the Information Bureau of the Communist and Workers' Parties in 1949, however, was incorrect and it was later withdrawn by the Communist Parties which took part in the Information Bureau meeting. Since 1954, the Central Committee of the Communist Party of the Soviet Union headed by Comrade N. S. Khrushchev initiated improvement of relations with Yugoslavia and has adopted a series of measures to this end. This was entirely necessary and correct. This initiative of the Communist Party of the Soviet Union had the approval of all socialist countries and the Communist Parties of various countries. We also took similar steps to those of the Soviet Union and established relations between China and Yugoslavia and between the Chinese and Yugoslav Parties. Starting from the desire for unity, the Communist Party of the Soviet Union and some other Communist Parties concerned made necessary self-criticism of past defects in their relations with Yugoslavia. In order to improve relations with the League of Communists of Yugoslavia, the Communist Parties of various countries have since then made their best efforts, waiting patiently for the leaders of the League of Communists of Yugoslavia to return to the stand of Marxism-Leninism. But the leaders of the League of Communists of Yugoslavia have completely ignored the well-intentioned efforts of the Communist Parties of various countries; they have failed to realize their own mistakes and have not made any self-criticism. Furthermore, they have continuously attacked and slandered the socialist countries and the Communist Parties of various countries, and have gone so far as to echo the attacks of the imperialists against the socialist camp and the international communist movement. They played the inglorious role of provocateur and interventionist in the counter-revolutionary uprising in Hungary. Their schemes failed only because the leading comrades of the Hungarian Socialist Workers' Party consistently maintained a principled and correct attitude during and after suppressing the counter-revolutionary uprising. And now, when the Moscow meetings have strengthened the solidarity of the Communist Parties of various countries, they display a stubborn anti-Marxist-Leninist standpoint in their Programme and intensive hostility towards the socialist countries and the Communist Parties of various countries. There is no doubt that by this stand and conduct, the Yugoslav leaders have alienated themselves from the ranks of the international communist movement. This is in no way in the interests of the true Communists of Yugoslavia and of the Yugoslav people.

The Eighth National Congress of the Chinese Communist Party at its Second Session fully endorses the decision of the Party's Central Committee not to send a delegation, but only an observer to be present at the Seventh Congress of the League of Communists of Yugoslavia. It is the unanimous opinion of the Congress that a resolute struggle must be waged against the modern revisionism which has emerged in the international communist movement. It is the sacred duty of our Party towards the international working class to work, together with the fraternal Parties, for the complete defeat of modern revisionism politically and theoretically, and for the safeguarding of Marxism-Leninism and the unity of the international communist movement on the basis of Marxist-Leninist ideology.

The Eighth National Congress of the Chinese Communist Party, at its Second Session, expresses full confidence that the cause of peace, democracy and socialism will win through all obstacles to score fresh and still greater victories throughout the world.

DOCUMENT 25

The Present Situation, the Party's General Line for Socialist Construction and Its Future Tasks, by Liu Shao-ch'i, May 5, 1958. This "title" is taken from Liu's opening paragraph; the title in the source pamphlet is given merely as "Report on the Work of the Central Committee of the Communist Party of China to the Second Session of the Eighth National Congress."

> The English text is taken from a pamphlet entitled *Second Session of the Eighth National Congress of the Communist Party of China*, Foreign Languages Press, Peking, 1958, pp. 16–66.
>
> *Comment.* Liu Shao-ch'i's report is the keynote speech of the Great Leap Forward. Its contents are discussed at some length in our General Introduction, part VII. The general line seems to have been laid down in broad terms at the meetings of the Central Committee in September 1957, and sloganized by Liu Shao-ch'i himself on November 6 (Document 22 above). The policy was probably discussed in more detail in Party committees at provincial level and below. Here it seems to have encountered opposition, the strength of which is indicated by the detailed arguments with which Liu tried to counter it. The link between the political debate within the Party and the successive raising of industrial and agricultural targets is discussed in our General Introduction, part VII.
>
> Further material may be found as follows:
>
> (a) *Decentralization.* The theoretical foundation for this development had been laid, according to Liu, by Mao's pronouncement of April 1956 on the "ten sets of relationships." See the summaries in Liu's report printed here (section II) and in ECMM 141 (*Study*, June 18, 1958).
>
> Chou En-lai, speaking to the National People's Congress in June 1956 (CB 398), and apparently in answer to criticisms, promised "more concrete definition of the division of power between central and local authorities, as provided in the Constitution of 1954." He further said that a preliminary draft on the division of powers had already been circulated to all provinces for discussion, and that a new plan could be put into practice in 1957. In the meantime, meetings of the State Council were held in the summer of 1956 to discuss decentralization (see paragraph d of our comment on Document 11).
>
> Little seems to have been done until, on November 15, 1957, the State Council promulgated a resolution on the improvement of the industrial, commercial, and financial management systems, designed to come into force in 1958, and to give "full play to the initiative of localities and enterprises." See ECMM 146 (*New Construction*, August 1958).
>
> Li Hsien-nien then explained the policy of decentralization to the National People's Congress on February 1, 1958 (CB 493), saying that it would allow agricultural

TEXT OF DOCUMENT 25

producers' cooperatives and other enterprises more control over their own surpluses. The process was hastened—again according to Liu—by decisions of the Central Committee, reached in the spring of 1958; and new agricultural tax laws of June 1958 gave further power to the local authorities (SCMP 1786 and 1792).

(b) *General economic policy of the Great Leap Forward.* On this, see T. J. Hughes and D. E. T. Luard, *The Economic Development of Communist China* (London: Oxford University Press, 1959), Chapter VI; CB 493 and 494 (speeches by Li Hsien-nien and Po I-po to the National People's Congress in February 1958); and CB 508 (speech by Vice-Premier T'an Chen-lin, on agriculture, to the Eighth Party Congress in May 1958). See also ECMM 131, containing an article by T'an Chen-lin (*Study*, March 18, 1958), on "Factors Bringing Agricultural Production to a High Tide." Of the four listed, two are political (Party leadership and "socialist education"). The other two concern the experience of cooperatives in increasing yields, and in irrigation and water conservancy projects. On this, see ECMM 111 and 119 (*China Water Conservancy*, Sept. 14, 1957, and *Water Conservancy Journal*, Dec. 29, 1957).

(c) *The industrial drive in the provinces, February-May 1958.* Details are given in ECMM 137 (*Economic Research*, May 17, 1958—covering Hunan), and in various local papers quoted in URS, Vol. 11, No. 21; Vol. 12, Nos. 10, 17; Vol. 13, No. 3. The cutting down of purchasing power and safety measures to fulfill the requirements of "thrift and economy" are illustrated in ECMM 132 (*Financial and Economic Research*, April 15, 1958); ECMM 136 (*Study*, March 3, 1958); and ECMM 139 (*Political Study*, May 13, 1958).

(d) Material on the specific aspects of Liu's report mentioned at the end of part VII of the General Introduction may be found as follows:

U.S. recession: ECMM 129, 131, 137 (*World Culture*, March 5, April 20, and May 10, 1958).

The "mass line": ECMM 132 and 136 (*Study*, April 18 and March 3, 1958—the latter by Po I-po); ECMM 138 and 146 (*Red Flag*, July 16 and Oct. 1, 1958—on rightist criticism of the mass line).

Local Party opposition: The bulk of the relevant material is conveniently assembled in CB 509. See also the following references, mainly to local papers (some of which describe opposition after Liu's report):

Anhwei: Party purge, January-March. SCMP 1736.
Honan: Party purge, June-July. CB 515 (a very interesting account).
Kwangtung: Party purge, February. URS, Vol. 13, Nos. 14, 22, 26.
Liaoning: Party purge, June-October. SCMP 1901 and 1925.
Shantung: Party purge, October-November. SCMP 1924, ECMM 169.

Opposition in the national-minorities areas of China is discussed in our Chapter XI, notes to Document 44.

(As usual, the footnotes in the document that follows were in the source pamphlet and are reprinted here as part of the document.)

_____ TEXT OF DOCUMENT 25 _____

Comrades!

On behalf of the Central Committee I now report to the Second Session of the Party's Eighth National Congress on its work. My report deals with the present situation, the Party's general line for socialist construction and its future tasks.

I

Over a year has passed since the First Session of the Eighth National Congress. During this time, the Party has correctly carried out and developed the policies laid down at the First Session, and achieved great successes in every field of work.

In the past year or so, many changes of great historic significance have taken place, internationally and at home.

Internationally, all of us know the now famous conclusion drawn by Comrade Mao Tse-tung that the world situation has recently reached a new turning point in its development. In extent of popular support, size of populations and rate of development of production, the socialist camp headed by the Soviet Union has long since surpassed the imperialist camp. For a time in 1956, however, the sky was overcast. The imperialist camp and reactionaries in various countries on more than one occasion launched violent campaigns against communism, against the people and against national independence. The imperialists incited and aided the counter-revolutionary uprising in Hungary, and at the same time carried out armed aggression against Egypt. At that time we pointed out that the dark clouds would soon disperse. As it turned out, the revolutionary proletariat of Hungary, with the help of the Soviet Union and the support of the revolutionary forces of the world, quickly stamped out the uprising. The struggles of Egypt and Syria against aggression also triumphed with the support of the Soviet Union and the forces of peace throughout the world. In October and November last year, the Soviet Union launched two artificial earth satellites. This made the whole world acknowledge that in science and technology too the Soviet Union has surpassed the United States, the most developed of the capitalist countries. In November last year, a meeting of the Communist and Workers' Parties of the socialist countries was held in Moscow, followed by a meeting of sixty-four Communist Parties. These meetings issued two declarations of historic significance, greatly strengthened the solidarity of the ranks of the international working class and the socialist camp, and promoted the development of the world peace movement. All this shows that the east wind has prevailed over the west wind, and will continue to do so in the future.

The Moscow Meetings of Communist and Workers' Parties marked the beginning of a new stage in the present-day international communist movement. Comrade Teng Hsiao-ping will give a special report on the Moscow meetings and the declarations adopted at these meetings. All I wish to say here is that the development of the international situation over the past six months has proved that the appraisal and analysis made in the Moscow declarations are wholly correct. The United States, leader of the imperialist camp, is now in the throes of another serious economic crisis; its production has fallen off drastically and the number of unemployed increased enormously. This crisis is hitting the entire capitalist world, and has thoroughly exploded the deceptive propaganda spread since the war by bourgeois politicians and scholars, reformists and revisionists that capitalist economy can avoid crises. The contradictions within the imperialist countries have deepened, and the workers' and people's movements in these countries have made much headway. The contradictions among the imperialist countries, first of all those between the United States, Britain and France, have sharpened, though at present they are still mutually linked up in the NATO, the Bagdad Treaty Organization and the SEATO for the objective of opposing communism, the people and the national independence movements. The tendency to neutralism continues to grow in many capitalist countries. In Asia, Africa and Latin America, national independence movements are forging ahead. Though the imperialists are trying to undermine these movements by underhand means and by force, and though certain sections of the bourgeoisie in those nations are trying to restrict the growth of the people's forces which are most resolutely opposed to imperialism, facts have proved that they cannot hold back the historical advance of the people's national and democratic struggles. The struggle of the Indonesian Government and people in defence of their national sovereignty and unity is pushing ahead triumphantly. The Algerian people are waging heroic struggles against the colonial rule of the French imperialists. The people of the whole world strongly demand peace. They demand that the proposals made by the Soviet Union for a summit conference, for the easing of international tension, for the reduction of armaments and the banning of the use and testing of nuclear weapons, be put into effect and that colonial rule and interference in the internal affairs of other countries be ended. But the imperialist bloc headed by the United States is stubbornly opposed to all this. Thus U.S. imperialism is becoming increasingly discredited in the eyes of the world. The U.S. imperialists still continue their war threats and preparations for a new war. We must be keenly vigilant against this. But, as the Moscow Declaration says: "Should the bellicose imperialist maniacs, regardless of everything, venture to unleash war, imperialism will doom itself to destruction, for the peoples will not tolerate a system that brings them so much suffering and exacts so many sacrifices."

In contrast to the situation in the imperialist camp, the socialist camp is growing stronger and more prosperous day by day. The economies of the Soviet Union, China and many other socialist countries are developing much faster than before; the living standards of their peoples are steadily improving. The unity of the socialist camp is becoming more firmly consolidated and its relations of mutual aid are being further extended. The peace proposals of the Soviet Union and our other fraternal countries of Eastern Europe, and the withdrawal of the Chinese People's Volunteers from Korea have greatly enhanced the prestige of the socialist camp among the peace-loving peoples and countries the world over. The fact that the economies of the countries in the socialist camp are making rapid progress and are free from crisis, is bringing more and more people in the capitalist countries to a clear realization that socialism is the only bright road before them.

Faced with acute contemporary struggles between the socialist system and the capitalist system and between the working class and the bourgeoisie, the imperialists, in an attempt to save themselves from destruction, have not only resorted to threats of war, war preparations, armed aggression and intensified exploitation and suppression of the people in their own countries and in the colonies and semi-colonies, but have tried hard to find new tools among the ranks of the working class so as to undermine from within the socialist countries and the international communist movement. Recently at its Seventh Congress, the League of Communists of Yugoslavia adopted an anti-Marxist-Leninist and out-and-out revisionist programme in opposition to the Declaration of the Moscow Meetings of Communist and Workers' Parties. This programme runs diametrically counter to the interests of the international communist movement and only suits the needs of the imperialists and particularly the U.S. imperialists. Therefore, we must wage a resolute struggle against modern revisionism. This is one of the major tasks facing us internationally at the present time. Only by thoroughly crushing modern revisionism and resolutely defending Marxism-Leninism can the unity of the international communist movement and the socialist countries be strengthened. By basing ourselves on this unity we can further rally the working people throughout the world and all those who oppose imperialism, war and national enslavement in a common struggle to win greater victories for the cause of world peace, national independence, democracy, freedom and socialism.

The present international situation is undoubtedly favourable to the peoples striving for peace, democracy, national independence and socialism and those engaged in peaceful socialist construction in various countries. It is unfavourable only to the aggressive imperialist bloc and the revisionists who persist in defending imperialist policies and betraying the interests of socialism.

In China, as everyone can see, the rectification campaign led by the Chinese Communist Party and conducted in accordance with the guiding principles laid down by Comrade Mao Tse-tung for the correct handling of contradictions among the people, has achieved great results on the political, economic, ideological and cultural fronts. It is the purpose of the rectification campaign, by means of criticism and self-criticism, to raise the level of communist consciousness of the masses and to adjust relationships among the people in a systematic way so that they may meet the needs of consolidating the socialist system and further expanding the productive forces of society. Serving as a lever, the rectification campaign has pushed forward the work of the Party and the state in every field. The rectification campaign of the Communist Party and the struggle against the rightists have developed into a rectification campaign among every section of the people, and the upsurge in this nation-wide rectification campaign has in turn brought about a new upsurge in production and construction throughout the country.

The rectification campaign and the anti-rightist struggle are the socialist revolution carried out on the ideological and political fronts in our country. They are a decisive struggle between the socialist road and the capitalist road. Thanks to the victory in this struggle, a communist ideological emancipation movement is taking place among the broadest masses of the people. This is bringing about profound changes in the alignment of class forces in our country.

There are two exploiting classes and two labouring classes in China today. One of the exploiting classes comprises the bourgeois rightists who oppose socialism, the landlord and compradore classes whose rule had been overthrown, and other reactionaries. The bourgeois rightists are to all intents and purposes agents of the imperialists, the remnant feudal and compradore forces, and Chiang Kai-shek's Kuomintang. The other exploiting class comprises the national bourgeoisie and their intellectuals who are accepting socialist transformation step by step. Most of them are in a state of transition, wavering between the socialist road and the capitalist road. One of the labouring classes comprises the peasants and other labourers who formerly worked on their own. The overwhelming majority of these have joined co-operatives and are becoming increasingly enthusiastic supporters of socialism. The other is the working class, the most advanced contingent of the whole people and the leading force in our state power and the cause of socialism. All these four categories of people have undergone tremendous changes in the course of the rectification campaign and the anti-rightist struggle.

As a result of the anti-rightist struggle, the anti-communist, anti-popular and anti-socialist bourgeois rightists have been thoroughly isolated by the masses and their ranks have begun to disintegrate. With victory won in this struggle, further heavy blows have also been dealt against the remnant counter-revolutionaries and all sorts of bad elements who tried to undermine socialism. Socialist public order has been greatly strengthened.

The anti-rightist struggle has also been of profound significance within our Party. We expelled a number of rightists from the Party. They were alien class elements who had sneaked into the Party and renegades to the cause of socialism. They developed individualism, sectarianism, localism and nationalism to an extreme degree within the Party and carried out revisionist and other anti-socialist and anti-communist activities. In league with the rightists outside the Party, they attacked the Party and the socialist system. To rid the Party of these alien class elements and renegades is a great victory for its cause.

The national bourgeoisie, the bourgeois intellectuals and the members of the various democratic parties, who stand in the middle of the road and are half-hearted about socialism, have changed, or are changing, to a greater or lesser degree, their old political outlooks in the course of the struggle against the rightists, in the subsequent drive against waste and conservative ideas and practices, and in the great leaps forward in production and other fields of socialist construction. Most of these people, sensing "the compelling force of circumstances," now feel that they must make further progress and must not remain in their middle-of-the-road position as before. They have begun to admit their dual character in relation to the socialist revolution and the need to correct their many wrong views. They have expressed their determination to remould themselves, "give their hearts" to the Communist Party and strive to become left-wingers. Many intellectuals have taken an active part in the rectification campaign and indicated their resolve to become socialist-minded and professionally expert so as to turn themselves into thoroughly red specialists. Some of them have gone among the working people, taking part in manual labour, so as to build sincere contacts with the broad masses of the working people.

In many regions inhabited by national minorities, in the course of the rectification campaign and the struggle against the rightists, local nationalism has been seriously criticized, certain separatists and bourgeois rightists among the national minorities who impair the unity of the motherland have been exposed, and, at the same time, the tendency towards Han chauvinism among certain Han cadres has been further overcome. In this way, the socialist consciousness of the masses among the national minorities has been raised and there is a new look to the brotherhood and unity of the various nationalities.

The experience of the rectification campaign and the anti-rightist struggle once again shows that throughout the transition period, that is, before completion of the building of a socialist society, the main contradiction inside our country is and remains that between the proletariat and the bourgeoisie, between the socialist road and the capitalist road. In certain fields this contradiction manifests itself as a fierce life-and-death struggle between the enemy and ourselves; that was the case in the attack launched by the bourgeois rightists in 1957. This attack was repelled, but in the future they will try again to make trouble whenever opportunity arises. We must, therefore, be prepared to wage prolonged and repeated struggles against the bourgeois rightists before their contradictions with the people can be fully resolved. We must also continue to suppress other remnant counter-revolutionaries and all sorts of criminals breaking law and order. In the actual conditions existing in our country, however, the contradictions between the two classes and the two roads in most cases manifest themselves as contradictions within the ranks of the people. As to the contradictions among the people— be they contradictions between the national bourgeoisie and petty bourgeoisie on the one hand and the proletariat on the other, or contradictions within the proletariat arising from bourgeois and petty bourgeois influences upon sections of the proletariat—they should, as a rule, be resolved through the rectification campaign. As to contradictions among the working people arising from differences in their conceptions of right and wrong, or between the advanced and the backward elements among them, since some are connected with bourgeois and petty bourgeois influences, and most of them do not fall into the category of contradictions between classes at all, it is all the more obvious that such contradictions should be resolved by means of the rectification campaign.

The political atmosphere among the working people has also undergone a deep change following the rectification campaign and the anti-rightist struggle. The political consciousness and socialist initiative of the masses, whether workers or peasants, have been greatly enhanced, as a result of the socialist revolution on the ideological and political fronts and the great debates on the capitalist road and the socialist road, which have been carried out on the broadest scale among the masses, and as a result of the development to the fullest extent of criticism and self-criticism in regard to mistakes and shortcomings in our work, by encouraging a full and frank airing of views, great debates and the posting of *tatsepao*.* Leading cadres in many units have made sincere self-criticisms before the masses and earnest efforts to improve their work and ways. This has moved the masses and strengthened their faith in the leading role of the Party; at the same time it led them on their own initiative, to criticize their own shortcomings, rectify the wrong ideas and backward habits which they carried over from the old society, and to improve their own work. This, in all places where the rectification campaign has been carried out thoroughly, has put both the masses and the cadres at ease; any estrangement that existed between them in the past has been eliminated. Feeling that the Party has given its heart to them, the masses too give their hearts to the Party. As a result, all sorts of negative trends reflecting surviving bourgeois ideas in these places have been greatly reduced and the just spirit of communism is in the ascendant. Many who were formerly backward are now ideologically emancipated and, becoming communist-minded, they are rapidly catching up with the more advanced. This is an important sign of the great victory we have won in the socialist revolution on the ideological and political fronts.

In the greater part of the country today, in the cities and countryside, in offices, enterprises, schools and army units, *tatsepao* are being put up, debates are being held, criticism and self-criticism are being vigorously conducted. Throughout the nation a new custom, a new habit is taking shape—to handle all contradictions among the people correctly by way of the rectification campaign, namely, by "starting from the desire for unity, to solve contradictions through criticism or struggle and thus to achieve a new unity on a new basis." Criticism and self-criticism among the masses and cadres all aim at overcoming bureaucracy, sectarianism and subjectivism, doing away with the "five bad airs": bureaucratic airs, apathetic airs, extravagant airs, arrogant airs and finicky airs, doing away with every kind of waste and conservative practices in construction, correcting what is irrational in the organization and management of labour and changing those regulations and institutions that restrain development of the forces of production and the initiative of the masses. By relying on the exposures, criticisms, and proposals made by the masses and their supervision and practical work, many problems long unresolved have been solved rapidly. The masses openly criticize leading personnel by name and also openly criticize each other by name without mincing words and without the slightest hesitation. The aim of such criticism and self-criticism is to serve the interests of the state and the collective, to do better work in the common cause of socialism. Towards those being criticized their attitude is that of a real comrade; they don't aim to "deal them a fatal blow," but acknowledge their achievements and help them to correct their shortcomings and make progress. This is the noble, communist way of doing things.

Radical changes in human relations have taken place in our country with the development of criticism and self-criticism. Cadres in industrial and mining enterprises and agricultural co-operatives have begun to devote regularly part of their time to participation in manual labour alongside the rank and file of workers and peasants. Many leaders of rural work are working on "experimental plots" alongside the peasants. Large numbers of office workers and intellectuals have gone to the countryside and the mountain areas or to work in the basic units of enterprises. The example set by the masses has inspired the cadres and that set by the cadres has also inspired the masses. Managerial personnel now directly participate in some manual labour; and the workers in some managerial work. The relationship of mutual aid and co-operation, of learning from each other and of emulation, between those in the upper and the lower grades, between the managerial personnel and those who directly take part in production, between brain and manual workers, between city and countryside, has greatly de-

---

*Opinions and criticisms written out in bold Chinese characters on large sheets of paper and posted freely for everybody to see.

veloped. Many who were prone to bossiness have changed a great deal in this rectification campaign. So long as we continue to make use of the *tatsepao* and the debates, and constantly practise criticism and self-criticism, we shall certainly be able to get rid of the bossy style of work effectively and thoroughly, and gradually eliminate the evil bureaucratic habits carried over from thousands of years of history.

Such universal criticism and self-criticism as was unfolded in the course of the rectification campaign, such sharp attacks against bureaucracy and the subsequent achievement of such equality in human relations, are unthinkable in any capitalist country. Never before has there been a political party like our Party of the proletariat that regards the interests of the people as its only interest, that firmly trusts the majority of the masses and is bold enough to practise democracy on such an extensive scale. The bourgeois rightists and the revisionists allege that bureaucracy is a product of the proletarian dictatorship. The fact is just the opposite. Only the socialist state can, under the leadership of the Communist Party, gradually eliminate bureaucracy by relying on the revolutionary initiative of the working people. In order to develop the people's democracy and eliminate bureaucracy, it is necessary to strengthen the leading role of the Party and the dictatorship of the proletariat, not to weaken them.

Our principle is democratic centralism. Our democracy is democracy under centralized guidance and our centralism is centralism based on democracy. The facts prove that the practice of the most broadly-based democracy among the people, instead of hampering centralism, facilitates the realization of a high degree of centralization. Instead of weakening socialist discipline, it facilitates the consolidation of socialist discipline based on conscious acceptance by the masses. When cadres shed their bureaucratic airs and haughty attitude and mix with the masses, the prestige of the leadership waxes instead of waning. Thanks to the rectification campaign, a vigorous and lively political situation is developing throughout our public life in which there are both centralism and democracy, both discipline and freedom, both unity of will and personal ease of mind.

The broad masses of the working people have realized more fully that individual and immediate interests depend on and are bound up with collective and long-term interests and that the happiness of the individual lies in the realization of the lofty socialist ideals of all the people. That is why they have displayed an heroic communist spirit of self-sacrifice in the work. Their slogan is: "Hard work for a few years, happiness for a thousand." This mighty torrent of communist ideas has swept away many stumbling blocks—individualism, departmentalism, localism and nationalism. In city and countryside, people vie with each other in joining in all kinds of voluntary labour. In building irrigation works, the peasants in many places have thrown aside the age-old narrow-minded idea of only looking after their native places. In the nation-wide emulation drive, many advanced units and individuals have enthusiastically passed on their technical experience, inventions and creations to the backward units and individuals so that the latter can catch up with them. Many enterprises, organizations, schools, army units and individuals have taken the initiative in co-ordinating their activities with those of others so as to promote the progress of all concerned. All this is, as Lenin said, "the actual beginning of communism," "the beginning of a change which is of world historic significance."

All the factors mentioned above have combined to form the great revolutionary drive for socialist construction. Comrade Mao Tse-tung has put forward the slogans "catch up with and outstrip Britain in 15 years," "build socialism by exerting our utmost efforts and pressing ahead consistently to achieve greater, faster, better and more economical results," "to be promoters of progress not of retrogression," "build our country and run our households industriously and with frugality" and "battle hard for three years to bring about a basic change in the features of most areas"—all these calls have quickly gripped the imagination of the huge army of hundreds of millions of working people and have been transformed into an immense material force. There has emerged in physical labour and other work a high degree of socialist initiative, a surging, militant spirit, a keenness in learning and studying that will not rest short of its aims, a fearless creative spirit. An emulation drive in which the backward learn from and catch up and compete with the advanced has been launched between individuals, production teams, enterprises, co-operatives, counties and cities. Set norms are being constantly surpassed and new techniques invented. Time after time the masses outstrip the targets set by enterprises and administrative organs.

The spring of 1958 witnessed the beginning of a leap forward on every front in our socialist construction. Industry, agriculture and all other fields of activity are registering greater and more rapid growth.

To begin with industry. The total value of industrial output for the first four months of this year was 26 per cent higher than in the same period last year; the April increase was 42 per cent. According to estimates made on the basis of the present situation, China's steel output this year will be over 7.1 million tons, coal output will reach 180 million tons; 60,000 machine-tools will be produced and irrigation machinery with more than 3.5 million horse-power; the output of chemical fertilizers will amount to 1.35 million tons. In view of this, the rate of growth of China's industrial production this year will be much higher than that set in the original plan and will surpass that of any year in the First Five-Year Plan period.

The revolutionary energy of the masses of workers has also found expression in the trial manufacture of new products, in technical renovation, in the improvement of quality and lowering of production costs. In the first four months of the year, many kinds of small-sized tractors were successfully produced on a trial basis. Several of them can be used equally well for the cultivation of paddy fields, dry fields, mountain areas and terraced fields or for transport, for operating irrigation machinery or generating power for the processing of agricultural products and other purposes. In the first four months of the year, Shanghai successfully produced more than one thousand kinds of new products on a trial basis. By adopting the new technique of three-tapping troughs, the Taiyuan Steel Plant has raised productivity by nearly 50 per cent. As labour productivity is being raised and raw materials are saved, it will be possible to reduce production costs in industry this year by about 10 per cent compared with last year. This will save the state about 1,400 million yuan.

An upsurge is shaping up in capital construction in industry this year. Nearly one thousand above-norm* projects will be under construction this year; this is more than the total number of such projects under construction in the First Five-Year Plan period. In addition, construction work has already started on thousands of medium and small-sized coal mines, power stations, oil refineries, iron and steel plants, non-ferrous mines, chemical fertilizer plants, cement plants, engineering works and agricultural and animal products processing plants.

The output of local industry this year will show a considerable increase as a result of widespread industrial capital construction undertaken by local authorities. Take iron and steel for example. The amount of iron to be produced by local enterprises this year will reach 1,730,000 tons (as against the 593,000 tons produced last year) and that of steel will reach 1,410,000 tons (as against the 790,000 tons of last year). The rapid growth of the local industries is one of the outstanding features of this year's industrial upswing.

As a result of the intensive drive against waste and conservatism, the costs of capital construction in industry this year will be greatly reduced. In many cases, the same amount of funds needed to build one factory in the past now suffices to build two. For example, in terms of the planned costs, where it would previously have cost about 1,000 million yuan to build an iron and steel plant with an annual capacity of one million tons, such a plant can now be built for little more than 400 million yuan; for 60 million yuan we can now build a nitrogenous fertilizer plant with an annual capacity of 50,000 tons of synthetic ammonium, in the past such a plant would have cost 130 million yuan. The time needed for building a capital construction project, too, is much shorter now than in the past.

The upsurge in agriculture last winter and this spring gave a vigorous push to the new industrial upsurge of this year. The rapid development of industry in turn has prompted an even swifter growth of agriculture.

In agriculture, the most striking leap took place in the campaign of the co-operative farmers to build irrigation works. From last October to April this year, the irrigated acreage throughout the country increased by 350 million *mou*, that is, 80 million *mou* more than the total added during the eight years since liberation and 110 million *mou* more than the total acreage brought under irrigation in the thousands of years before liberation. At the same time, more than 200 million *mou* of low-lying and easily waterlogged farmland was transformed and irrigation facilities were improved on another 140

---

*The "norm" of investment in capital construction for heavy industry ranges between five and ten million yuan and that for light industry, between three and five million yuan.

million *mou* of land. The loss of water and soil was brought under control over an area of 160,000 square kilometres. This gives proof of the power to conquer nature which the masses of the people have demonstrated in the field of agriculture following the great socialist revolution on the economic, political and ideological fronts and the release on a tremendous scale of our social productive forces.

In the same period, the peasants all over the country accumulated about 310,000 million *tan* of fertilizers (including all kinds of fertilizers, mostly clay and mud fertilizers). This averages over 18,000 catties to a *mou*, which, calculated according to the amount of plant nutrients, is more than three times the amount accumulated in 1956, one of the best of recent years. In many places, work was undertaken on a large scale to improve the soil and level the ground.

In the first four months of this year, over 290 million *mou* of land was afforested in the country, one and a half times the total acreage afforested in the past eight years. Big advance was also registered in the development of mountain areas, land reclamation, utilization of wild plants, etc.

The labour organization of our agricultural co-operatives has made further improvement. In most co-operatives, attendance by able-bodied members (men and women) in collective work was over 90 per cent in last winter and this spring.

A mass movement to improve farm tools is now spreading throughout the countryside. Tens of millions of peasants have made all sorts of improved and semi-mechanized farm implements, water lifts, means of transportation and equipment for processing farm produce. Thus the centuries-old tradition of primitive manual labour has begun to change and labour productivity has increased enormously. At the same time, the peasants in various places have made energetic efforts to improve systems and methods of cultivation in accordance with local conditions. This is the budding of a great technical revolution in the rural areas.

Work is also going ahead by leaps and bounds in transport and communications, commerce and other branches of the national economy. New records and inventions are being made continuously.

Rapid developments are also taking place in the fields of culture, education and public health. Energetic efforts are being made in many villages throughout the country to eliminate illiteracy and establish large numbers of primary and secondary schools financed by the people. Cultural and artistic activities among the masses are advancing quickly. The public health campaign centred on the elimination of the four pests* has already spread to every urban and rural district and achieved notable results.

The fact is that the growth of the social productive forces calls for a socialist revolution and the spiritual emancipation of the people; the victory of this revolution and emancipation in turn spurs a forward leap in the social productive forces; and this in turn impels a progressive change in the socialist relations of production and an advance in man's ideology. In their ceaseless struggle to transform nature, the people are continuously transforming society and themselves.

Karl Marx prophesied that the proletarian revolution would usher us into a great epoch when "twenty years are concentrated in a day." If in past revolutionary struggles we experienced such great times, then is not our present socialist construction another great time again? Here one can see how the courageous and hard-working Chinese people, under the leadership of the great Chinese Communist Party and its leader Comrade Mao Tse-tung, have poured forth their history-making strength and wisdom in endless measure.

II

The current mighty leap forward in socialist construction is the product not only of the successful development of the anti-rightist struggle and the rectification campaign but also of a correct implementation of the Party's general line—to build socialism by exerting our utmost efforts, and pressing ahead consistently to achieve greater, faster, better and more economical results.

Comrade Mao Tse-tung has often said that there are two methods of carrying on socialist transformation and construction: One will result in doing the work faster and better; the other slowly and not so well. Which method shall we adopt? This has been an issue. In his work *On the Question of Agricultural Co-operation* published in 1955, Comrade Mao Tse-tung provided a theoretical solution to the

---

*Rats, flies, mosquitoes and grain-destroying sparrows.

struggle between these two methods regarding the socialist revolution in the ownership of the means of production. Furthermore, this struggle was decided in practice by the upsurge in socialist transformation which took place between the autumn of 1955 and the spring of 1956. There was also a conflict between the two methods in connection with the socialist revolution on the political and ideological fronts, and this too was worked out theoretically by Comrade Mao Tse-tung in his article *On the Correct Handling of Contradictions Among the People* published last year, and was resolved in practice by the rectification campaign and anti-rightist struggle which began last year. In connection with socialist construction too, the Central Committee of the Party and Comrade Mao Tse-tung have always taken a clear-cut stand, insisting that the method of working faster and better be adopted and the other method, of working slowly and not so well, be rejected. However, on this question some comrades still clung to such outmoded ideas as "keeping to the right is better than keeping to the left," "it's better to go slower than faster" or "it's better to take small steps than to go striding forward." The struggle between the two methods in dealing with this question was not fully decided until the launching of the rectification campaign and the anti-rightist struggle.

As early as March 1949, the Seventh Central Committee of the Party pointed out in its resolution adopted at its Second Plenary Session: "China's economic heritage is backward but the Chinese people are brave and industrious, and with the victory of the Chinese people's revolution, the establishment of the Chinese People's Republic, the leadership of the Chinese Communist Party, and the help of the proletariat in other countries throughout the world, and primarily the help of the Soviet Union, economic construction in China will be carried on not slowly but probably at a considerable speed. We can already count the days when China will attain prosperity. There are no grounds whatsoever for being pessimistic about China's economic revival." In mapping out the First Five-Year Plan for Development of the National Economy, the Central Committee of the Party refuted all fallacious views favouring the slowing down of economic construction. The rate of development of the national economy envisaged in the First Five-Year Plan was unprecedented in China's history. Nevertheless, the Central Committee of the Party believed that the Plan not only could be fulfilled, but could probably be fulfilled ahead of schedule and overfulfilled. As a matter of fact, in the winter of 1955 when it was apparent that a decisive victory of the socialist revolution in the ownership of the means of production was to be won very shortly and when a mass upsurge in production and construction was beginning to take place, the "norms" set in the First Five-Year Plan should have been revised upward. Comrade Mao Tse-tung issued a timely call for a speedier tempo than that envisaged in the First Five-Year Plan. In December 1955, he wrote in the preface to the book *Socialist Upsurge in China's Countryside*:

> The problem facing the entire Party and the nation is no longer one of combating rightist conservative ideas about the speed of the socialist transformation of agriculture. That problem has already been solved. Nor is it a problem of the speed of transformation of capitalist industry and commerce, by entire trades, into state-private enterprises. That problem too has been solved. In the first half of 1956 we must discuss the speed of the socialist transformation of handicrafts. But that problem will easily be solved too. The problem today is none of these, but concerns other fields. It affects agricultural production; industrial production (including state, joint state-private and co-operative industries); handicraft production; the scale and speed of capital construction in industry, communications and transport; the co-ordination of commerce with other branches of the economy; and the co-ordination of activities in science, culture, education, public health, and so on, with various economic undertakings. In all these fields there is an underestimation of the situation which must be criticized and corrected if these activities are to keep pace with the development of the situation as a whole. People's thinking must adapt itself to changed conditions. Of course no one should go off into wild flights of fancy, or make plans unwarranted by the objective situation, or insist on attempting the impossible. The problem today is that rightist conservatism is still causing trouble in many fields and preventing work in these fields from keeping pace with the development of the objective situation. The present problem is that many people consider impossible things which could be done if they exerted themselves. It is absolutely necessary, therefore, to keep on criticizing rightist conservative ideas which actually exist.

Comrade Mao Tse-tung subsequently summed up the ideas expounded in this preface in the slogan of building socialism by achieving "greater, faster, better and more economical results." He pointed out that the urgent task confronting the entire Party was to overcome rightist conservative ideas which actually existed. He called on all members of the Party to be promoters of progress and not of retrogression in construction, in order to push forward vigorously the country's industrial and agricultural production and construction.

On the proposal of Comrade Mao Tse-tung, the Party in January 1956 put before the people a "Draft National Programme for Agricultural Development, 1956 to 1967." This is a programme for developing socialist agriculture by achieving "greater, faster, better and more economical results." Not only did it set great goals for rural work throughout the country but it gave a correct orientation for development of the entire work of socialist construction.

In April of the same year, at an enlarged meeting of the Political Bureau of the Central Committee of the Party, Comrade Mao Tse-tung made a report on "Ten Sets of Relationships" in which he called the whole Party's attention to the correct handling of the relationships:

1 — between industry and agriculture and between heavy and light industries;
2 — between coastal industries and inland industries;
3 — between economic construction and national defence;
4 — between the state, the co-operatives and the individual;
5 — between the central and local authorities;
6 — between the Han people and the national minorities;
7 — between the Party and non-Party people;
8 — between revolution and counter-revolution;
9 — between right and wrong inside and outside the Party, and
10 — international relations.

In this report, Comrade Mao Tse-tung outlined a series of important policies in amplification of the general line of building socialism by achieving "greater, faster, better and more economical results." Under items 1 and 5, he set forth the principle of developing industry and agriculture simultaneously while giving priority to heavy industry, and the principle of combining centralization of powers with decentralization. Under items 2 and 3, he pointed to the necessity of making full use of the industrial bases in the coastal areas and amassing ample funds for economic construction. He pointed out under item 4 the necessity of handling correctly the relations between the individual and the collective, between the part and the whole, and between consumption and accumulation. The remaining items centred mainly around the view of correctly handling contradictions among the people, a view which was later elaborated. The general idea of the report was to mobilize all positive factors and available forces for building China into a modern, prosperous and mighty socialist state in the shortest possible time. It was on the basis of the guiding lines and policies laid down by Comrade Mao Tse-tung on handling the ten sets of relationships that the Central Committee of the Party drew up its political report for the First Session of the Eighth National Congress.

These guiding lines and policies formulated by Comrade Mao Tse-tung have played a tremendous role in our work. In 1956, every phase of China's economy and culture made a mighty leap forward. In that year, industrial output shot up 31 per cent, capital construction 62 per cent, and agricultural output 4.9 per cent despite severe natural calamities. Thus, within a space of four years, we reached ahead of schedule the targets set in the First Five-Year Plan for total value of industrial output, and total output of food crops and communications and transport; in capital construction, we also created favourable conditions for the overfulfilment of the First Five-Year Plan.

There were individual defects in our work during the leap forward in 1956. These consisted mainly in a certain strain in supplying the market due to the taking on of an excessive number of new workers and staff and excessive increases in certain categories of wages. These defects paled before the tremendous achievements made at the time and the problems arising from these defects were solved after a few months of efforts by the people throughout the country in a campaign launched at the call of the Party to increase production and practise economy. However, some comrades at the time magnified these defects and underestimated the great achievements attained, and hence regarded the leap forward of 1956 as a "reckless advance." In a flurry of opposition to this so-called "reckless advance," some people even had misgivings about the principle of "achieving greater, faster, better, and more economical results" and the 40-article Programme for Agricultural Development. This dampened the initiative of the masses and hampered progress on the production front in 1957, and particularly on the agricultural front. But the Party soon corrected this error. The Third Plenary Session of the Central Committee of the Party held in September last year reaffirmed the need to adhere to the principle of achieving "greater, faster, better and more economical results" in building socialism. Following that, the Central Committee made public a revised version of the Draft Programme for Agricultural Development, and Comrade Mao Tse-tung issued a militant call to overtake and surpass Britain in the output of iron and steel and other major industrial products in 15 years. Such correct guidance by the Central Committee, combined with the initiative of the masses evoked by the rectification campaign and the anti-rightist struggle, gave rise to the all-round forward leap which is currently developing on an even larger scale in our socialist construction. Many of those comrades who expressed misgivings about the principle of building socialism by achieving "greater, faster, better and more economical results," have learned a lesson from all this. But some of them have not yet learned anything. They say: "We'll settle accounts with you after the autumn harvest." Well, let them wait to settle accounts. They will lose out in the end!

The development is U-shaped, i.e., high at the beginning and the end, but low in the middle. Didn't we see very clearly how things developed on the production front in 1956—1957—1958 in the form of an upsurge, then an ebb, and then an even bigger upsurge or, in other words, a leap forward, then a conservative phase and then another big leap forward?

The Party and the masses have learned a lesson from this U-shaped development.

Now the people everywhere are full of confidence in the forward leap in production; they are determined to further speed up socialist construction. They are eager to remove the obstacles placed in their way by technical and cultural backwardness. In view of basic victory of the socialist revolution already achieved on the economic, political and ideological fronts, the Central Committee of the Party and Comrade Mao Tse-tung consider that the time is ripe to set new revolutionary tasks before the Party and the people, that now is the time to call for a technical revolution and, along with it, a cultural revolution.

Marx, Engels and Lenin often pointed out that the watchword of the working class should be "uninterrupted revolution." In putting forward new revolutionary tasks in good time, so that there is no halfway halt in the revolutionary advance of the people, the revolutionary fervour of the masses will not subside with interruptions of the revolution, and Party and state functionaries will not rest content with the success won and grow arrogant or apathetic, the Central Committee of the Communist Party and Comrade Mao Tse-tung have always guided the Chinese revolution by this Marxist-Leninist theory of uninterrupted revolution. Already on the eve of the victory of the democratic revolution, the Seventh Central Committee of the Party, in a resolution adopted in March 1949 at its Second Plenary Session, clearly put forward the task of "transforming the new-democratic state into a socialist state." After the founding of the People's Republic of China and immediately following the completion of land reform, the Central Committee, in December 1951, pointed out the road to collective farming through the mutual-aid and co-operative movement, and in 1953 carried out extensive publicity and education among the people for the socialist transformation of agriculture, handicrafts and private industry and commerce. After the socialist revolution in the ownership of the means of production had been basically won, the Central Committee launched the socialist revolution on the ideological and political fronts. All this has enabled the revolution to advance at the opportune moment from one stage to another, scoring one victory after another.

The issuance of the call for the technical and cultural revolution means that our constantly developing revolution must now advance to a new stage. The broad masses of workers, peasants and intellectuals have given an immediate and enthusiastic response to this timely call of the Party. In fact, the masses have already swung into action. In many places, the great march to overcome our technical and cultural backwardness has already started with vigour and vitality.

As we have noted above, the Party's general line for socialist construction, which has gradually taken shape during the past eight years of construction, has proved its correctness at every step in the course of practical work. While this line still needs to be tested further in future practice, to be developed and perfected, we believe that the correctness of its basic orientation and its major principles should and can be regarded as established.

In the light of the practical experience gained in the people's struggle and of the development of Comrade Mao Tse-tung's thinking in the past few years, the Central Committee of the Party is of the opinion that the following are the basic points of our general line, which is to build socialism by exerting our utmost efforts, and pressing ahead consistently to achieve greater, faster, better and more economical results:

To mobilize all positive factors and correctly handle contradictions among the people;

To consolidate and develop socialist ownership, i.e., ownership by the whole people and collective ownership, and consolidate the proletarian dictatorship and proletarian international solidarity;

To carry out the technical revolution and cultural revolution step by step, while completing the socialist revolution on the economic, political and ideological fronts;

To develop industry and agriculture simultaneously while giving priority to heavy industry;

With centralized leadership, over-all planning, proper division of labour and co-ordination, to develop national and local industries, and large, small and medium-sized enterprises simultaneously; and

By means of all this to build our country, in the shortest possible time, into a great socialist country with a modern industry, modern agriculture and modern science and culture.

Based on the requirements of this general line, what are the main tasks facing the Party and the people in the technical and cultural revolutions?

The main tasks of the technical revolution are as follows:

To put the national economy, including agriculture and handicrafts, systematically and in a planned way on a new technological basis, i.e., the technological basis of modern, large-scale production, so that machinery can be used wherever feasible and electrification is brought to all the cities and villages of the country;

To turn all big and medium-sized cities throughout the country into industrial cities; and to build up new industrial bases in those places where the necessary conditions exist, to enable all the county towns and many townships to have their own industries, and to increase the value of industrial output of all the provinces and autonomous regions and even most of the special administrative regions and counties so that it exceeds the value of their agricultural output;

To set up a transport network and post and telecommunications services equipped mainly with modern facilities, reaching every part of the country; and

While introducing as far as possible the world's up-to-date techniques, to launch a widespread mass movement in the cities and villages throughout the country to improve tools and introduce technical innovations so that semi-mechanized or fully mechanized operations can be properly combined with the necessary hand work.

To meet the requirements of the technical revolution, we must at the same time carry through a cultural revolution, promoting culture, education and public health in the interest of economic construction. The main tasks in this are as follows:

To wipe out illiteracy, to institute compulsory primary education and step by step to bring secondary schools to the townships in general, and higher educational institutions and scientific research bodies to the special administrative regions in general and to many counties;

To complete the work of devising written languages for the national minorities or improving those already in existence and to make energetic efforts to reform the written languages used by the Han people;

To wipe out the "four pests," improve sanitary conditions, promote sports, eliminate the principal diseases, break down superstitions, reform customs and change habits, and invigorate the national spirit;

To promote cultural and recreational activities among the masses and develop socialist literature and arts;

To train new intellectuals and remould the old intellectuals in order to establish a gigantic force of tens of millions of working-class intellectuals, consisting of technicians, who will account for the greatest number, professors, teachers, scientists, journalists, writers, artists and Marxist theoreticians.

By vigorously carrying out the Party's general line for socialist construction and bringing about a technical revolution and a cultural revolution, we shall achieve an enormous development of our social productive forces and a great increase in our labour productivity. This will enable our industry to catch up with and surpass Britain within 15 years or less in the output of iron and steel and other major industrial products, enable our agriculture, on the basis of carrying out the National Programme for Agricultural Development ahead of schedule, to surpass quickly the agricultural achievements of the capitalist countries, and our science and technology, on the basis of carrying out the twelve-year Programme for the Development of Science, to catch up with the world's most advanced levels in the shortest possible time.

The speed of construction has been the most important question confronting us since the victory of the socialist revolution. The aim of our revolution is to expand the social productive forces as quickly as possible. Our country's economy has been very backward, and there are imperialist countries abroad; only by speeding up construction to the utmost can we, within the shortest possible period, consolidate our socialist state and raise the people's standards of living. The speedy building of socialism in a big country like ours, with a population of more than 600 million, will greatly enhance the supremacy already possessed by the socialist camp headed by the Soviet Union, promote mutual aid and co-operation between the countries in the socialist camp and between all the forces of peace throughout the world, and help to defend world peace.

Some people do not recognize the importance of increasing the speed of construction; they do not approve of the policy of consistently achieving greater, faster, better and more economical results, and they have raised various objections.

Some say that speeding up construction makes people feel "tense," and so it's better to slow down the tempo. But are things not going to get tense if the speed of construction is slowed down? Surely one should be able to see that a really terribly tense situation would exist if more than 600 million people had to live in poverty and cultural backwardness for a prolonged period, had to exert their utmost efforts just to eke out a bare living, and were unable to resist natural calamities effectively, unable to put a quick stop to possible foreign aggression and utterly unable to master their own fate. It was to pull themselves out of such a situation, that the hundreds of millions of our people summoned up their energies to throw themselves, full of confidence, into the heat of work and struggle. This is simply normal revolutionary activity to which we should give our heartiest approval. This kind of "tension" is nothing to be afraid of.

It goes without saying that we should guide the workers and peasants to direct their efforts to improve their technique, tools, methods of work and labour organization so as to bring about a forward leap in production. We should see to it that the masses enjoy necessary rest periods as production surges ahead, so as to alternate hard battles with necessary rest and enable production and construction to advance in a rhythmic manner; in addition, we should pay attention to safety measures.

During this great movement in which hundreds of millions of people have been mobilized, it is inevitable that there should be some defects in our work even while great successes are being scored, and that, as we advance, we should meet with some difficulties—even great, unforeseeable difficulties. We should make provision for all this. The broad masses of our people who have forged a solid unity among themselves will certainly not be frightened by these defects and difficulties, and they will surely be able to overcome them in good time. Some people criticize us for "craving greatness and success," for seeking "quick success and instant benefits." What they say about us is right! And shouldn't we crave greatness for our 600 million people and the success of socialism? Should we rather crave smallness and court failure, reject success and benefits, and rest content with lagging behind and doing nothing?

Some people wonder whether the implementation of the policy of consistently achieving greater, faster, better and more economical results won't lead to waste. Of course, if this policy is followed out piecemeal and if we merely go in for quantity and speed and neglect quality and economy, or vice versa, then of course there will be waste. "Greater" and "faster" results are concerned with quantity and speed; "better" and "more economical" with quality and cost. They supplement and condition each other. Facts have proved that by implementing the policy of achieving greater, faster, better and more economical results in a comprehensive way, the initiative and potentialities of the people can be brought into fullest play, and the greatest economies can be effected in developing production and construction. Conversely, opposition to this policy and restriction of the initiative and potentialities of the people will certainly result in great wastes of manpower, money, materials and precious time.

Others are worried that implementation of this policy will throw the various branches of production off balance as well as financial revenue and expenditure. There is bound to be imbalance. Even if we do not carry out this policy, there will always be imbalance, because any balance is temporary and conditional, and hence relative. There is no absolute balance. Of course, in order to conform to the objective law of the proportionate development of socialist economy, a balance should be maintained between the various branches of our national economy over a certain period of time and to a certain extent. This is precisely the purpose of planning in a socialist state. The question is how that balance should be brought about: by getting the backward to catch up with the advanced, or by forcing the advanced to fall back in line with the backward? To overcome the imbalance between financial revenue and expenditure, the positive approach is to expand production and better exploit financial resources; the negative approach is to view things purely from the financial angle, and put a curb on the development of construction. Back in 1942 in his work *Economic and Financial Questions During the Period of the Anti-Japanese War,* Comrade Mao Tse-tung pointed out why the negative approach is wrong. "While a good or bad financial policy may affect the economy," he wrote, "it is the economy as a whole that determines the financial situation. We will never overcome our financial difficulties unless we have a sound economy, or achieve an abundance of financial resources without developing the economy." He wrote: "The conservative view which overlooks the development of the economy or fails to exploit financial resources better, but wants to overcome financial difficulties by cutting down on essential expenditures, cannot solve any questions at all." Since the time of the Anti-Japanese War, our financial difficulties have all been solved successfully on the basis of this principle put forward by Comrade Mao Tse-tung. It is clear, therefore, that what we should guard against is not the occurrence of imbalance, but alarm when imbalance appears, and proneness to get the advance to fall back in line with the backward—a desire "to trim the toes to fit the shoe," or "to give up food for fear of choking."

Thus, none of the criticisms directed against the policy of increasing the speed of construction and of achieving greater, faster, better and more economical results, can hold water.

Why is it that, to increase the speed of construction, industry and agriculture must be developed simultaneously? This is because ours is a large agricultural country, and of our over 600 million people, more than 500 million are peasants who constitute a most powerful force both in the revolutionary struggle and construction. Only by relying on this powerful ally and giving full play to the peasants' initiative and creativeness can the working class of our country achieve victory. The paramount importance of the peasantry as an ally is just the same in the period of construction as it was in the period of revolution. Whenever political mistakes were made they invariably had something to do with this question. While giving priority to the growth of heavy industry, we must make great efforts to develop agriculture, which means to get the greatest domestic market in the world to place immense orders for heavy and light industrial products, including farm machinery, chemical fertilizers, building materials, fuels, electrical power and transport facilities; and to mobilize the biggest labour force in the world to increase the production of foodstuffs, meat, vegetables, etc., and the output of cotton and other industrial crops, to contribute its astonishing labour power to produce enormous wealth, accumulate large amounts of funds for national industrial construction, and itself to build small industrial enterprises in the villages. The energetic development of agriculture, therefore, will certainly speed up the industrialization of our nation and growth of the entire national economy; it will help greatly to improve the livelihood of the people throughout the country and consolidate the worker-peasant alliance. Without the rapid development of agriculture, there can be no rapid development of light and heavy industries, or of the national economy as a whole. The facts in the past eight years, and in this year in particular, have fully proved this.

Some comrades are worried that, though the development of agriculture can accumulate funds for industrialization, it will for the present at least divert some funds which could be used by the state for industrialization. The upsurges in agriculture in 1956 and 1958 have proved such worries unnecessary. So long as we know how to rely on this great force of our 500 million peasants, we can greatly expand the scope of agricultural construction even if there is no increase in state investments in agriculture. The state has invested 1,450 million yuan to harness the Huai River, and completed over 1,600 million cubic metres of masonry and earth work in the past eight years. But by depending mainly on the labour, money and material resources of the peasants themselves, in six months of the winter of 1957 and spring of 1958, more than 12,000 million cubic metres of masonry and earth work were completed in Honan and Anhwei Provinces alone.

Some people doubted whether agricultural production could expand very rapidly. They quoted authoritative works, chapter and verse, to prove that agriculture could only advance slowly and that, what is more, its growth could in no way be guaranteed. Some scholars even asserted that the rate of agricultural growth could not keep pace with the growth of population. They argued that as the population grows, consumption will increase and there won't be much of an increase in accumulation. From this they draw their pessimistic conclusions on the rate of growth of agriculture in our country, and, indeed, of the national economy as a whole. Underlying such ideas is an underestimation of the organized revolutionary peasants of our country, and the facts inevitably gave them the lie. The great forward leap in agricultural production and construction this year has not only completely knocked the bottom out of their contention that agriculture cannot make quick progress but also blown sky high their argument that a big population impedes accumulation. All they see is that men are consumers and that the greater the population, the bigger the consumption. They fail to see that men are first of all producers and that when there is a large population there is also the possibility of greater production and more accumulation. Their views obviously run counter to Marxism-Leninism.

Why is it necessary to undertake the simultaneous development of national and local industries, and of large, small and medium-sized enterprises to increase the speed of construction? Since the development of industrial production is the universal demand of the whole population, it is necessary to follow the principle of building industries by the efforts of the whole Party and population, and completely explode the myth that industry can be run only by the few. "The fire burns high when everybody adds wood to it"—it is only when all central and local authorities at every level down to the co-operatives get going at it, only when there is a division of labour and co-operation between big, small and medium-sized enterprises, that we can achieve greater, faster, better and more economical results. It is necessary for the central, provincial, municipal and autonomous region authorities to build a certain number of big enterprises. Big enterprises which have a big output and a high technical level can solve key problems having a decisive bearing on the national economy. They form the backbone of the force that pushes forward the industrial development of the country. But small and medium-sized enterprises have the advantages which big enterprises do not have: they require less investments and can more easily absorb funds from scattered sources; they require less time to build and produce quicker results; they can be designed and equipped locally; they can make do with various simple types of equipment which are readily available in the localities. They can be set up over a wide area so as to facilitate industrialization of the country as a whole, promote the training of technical personnel throughout the country and a balanced development of the economies of the various regions. They can produce a great variety of goods and can be flexibly adapted to produce new types of goods. Close to the sources of raw materials and markets, they can reduce transport costs and make flexible use of available resources, making it easier to bring about a satisfactory relation between supply, production and sales. It is easier for them to make flexible use of the labour power available in the countryside and of casual labour, depending on the amount of work to be done, and thus help reduce the differences between city and countryside, between workers and peasants.

In the period of the First Five-Year Plan, we paid attention first of all to the development of industries run by the Central Government, to giant enterprises; this was absolutely necessary. But not enough attention was paid to the development of local industries and small and medium-sized industries; this was a shortcoming. In the past two years or more, the Central Committee has repeatedly pointed out that this shortcoming must be remedied. With the improvements made in the system of industrial management and the encouragement to develop small and medium-sized industries, there is a growing initiative in various regions to develop their own industries. In quite a short space of time, industrial plants will dot every part of the country like stars in the sky provided the twenty-odd provinces, municipalities under the central authority and autonomous regions, over 180 special administrative regions and autonomous *chou*, over 2,000 counties and autonomous counties, over 80,000 towns and townships, over 100,000 handicrafts co-operatives and over 700,000 agricultural co-operatives in the country display full initiative in a proper way in developing industry. In that case, industrial development in our country will naturally be much faster than if it depended solely on a number of big enterprises run by the Central Government. This will inevitably result in: 1. quickening the pace of the nation's industrialization; 2. quickening the pace of mechanization of agriculture; and 3. quickening the speed at which differences between city and countryside are reduced.

A big development of local industries, and of small and medium-sized enterprises, will give rise to many new problems which it is difficult for us to foresee at the moment. But here it must be especially emphasized that this growth of local industries and small and medium-sized enterprises which we encourage must be placed under centralized leadership and over-all planning, with a proper division of labour and co-ordination of efforts; there must be no blind development nor development through free competition. To prevent or reduce any possible waste in resources and funds and idle stocks of products, the Central Government and local authorities at all levels must seriously improve the work of co-ordination and balance, firmly oppose capitalist ideas in management, and any tendency to localism or departmentalism. At the same time, whether in national or local industries, in giant enterprises or small and medium-sized enterprises, it is necessary to oppose resolutely any tendency to chase only after the latest technical equipment, while failing to make full use of all that is on hand; oppose any tendency to overemphasize the role of experts to the disparagement of the great role that can be played by the workers and peasants in developing new production techniques. All such tendencies which lead away from reality and from the masses, no less than the tendency to resign oneself to backwardness and make no attempts to advance, are detrimental to the nation's progress in construction.

The Party's general line for socialist construction is the application and development of its mass line in socialist construction. We must fully combine centralized leadership with decentralized management and co-ordinate, the resources of the Central Government with those of the local authorities, the resources of the state with those of the masses, the giant undertakings with small and medium-sized plants, the striving to raise the quality of work with popularization—all this is applicable not only to industry but also to other economic and cultural undertakings, and to the technical and cultural revolutions as a whole. .All Party and state functionaries must acquire a deep and comprehensive understanding of the Party's general line for socialist construction and follow this line in their work. As for scientific, technical, cultural and educational workers, they must be specially taught to adhere firmly to the principle of keeping in close contact with reality, production and the masses so that they can effectively serve the socialist cause of the proletariat and promote the growth of the social productive forces.

III

The tasks of the Party at present are, on the basis of the rectification campaign, to continue to handle contradictions among the people, systematically improve the work of the state, strengthen the work of Party organizations at all levels, and work unswervingly for the implementation of the general line for socialist construction.

As mentioned above, the rectification campaign which started in May 1957 has achieved great results. But, we would be making a big mistake to become dizzy with the successes already won and think that now everything is all right. We must not overlook the fact that the development of the campaign is not even. In some units, some places and among some people, it has not been carried out thoroughly enough, it has not got down to the roots of things. In some units, styles of work marked by bureaucracy, commandism, sectarianism and subjectivism have not been shaken; there are even cases where leading positions are still occupied by bourgeois rightists and rotten elements; and the initiative of the masses is still being hampered. Even in places where the campaign has been carried out fairly thoroughly, not all the problems brought up by the masses that must be solved have received satisfactory solutions. The leading organizations must undertake a thorough check-up, make energetic efforts to strengthen weaker units, give serious consideration to the suggestions of the masses, and persist in carrying through the rectification campaign to complete victory.

The central task of the rectification campaign is to handle correctly the contradictions among the people and improve human relations in socialist labour and all other group activities. We have in the main accomplished the socialist transformation of the means of production, which is the prerequisite for changing the relationships between men. In a society where exploitation of man by man exists, such as in economic organizations under Kuomintang rule, there is antagonism between the exploiters and the exploited, and class antagonisms are also reflected in the relations between the ordinary administrative personnel and actual producers, between the ordinary brain workers and manual workers. With the carrying out of socialist transformation of the ownership of the means of production, these antagonisms have been transformed in the main and a comradely relationship of mutual aid and co-operation is shaping up between the administrative personnel and brain workers on the one hand and the rank and file on the other. However, many of the administrative personnel and brain workers have not yet learned to treat the masses on a footing of complete equality; they have not yet done away with some survivals of the working style of the Kuomintang and still have certain bureaucratic airs. This makes it difficult for them to gain the full confidence of the masses. This has also prevented part of the workers and peasants from taking the sort of attitude to socialist labour that befits the masters of the state and the enterprises. This state of affairs has been radically changed as a result of the rectification campaign. In many state enterprises and co-operatives, genuine comradely mutual aid and co-operation develops successfully between the administrative personnel and brain workers and the masses, the advantages of socialist production relations are given full play, and thereby the productive forces of society are further released.

The present task is to effect a thorough and systematic readjustment in the relationships between people, rooting out the capitalist and feudal survivals of bygone days and building completely new socialist relations, not only in all our enterprises and co-operatives, but in all government and popular organizations, schools, and in every walk of life. All functionaries (and first of all those who are members of the Communist Party) must, irrespective of their position or seniority, get rid of their bureaucratic airs, behave like ordinary labouring people, treat their subordinates and the rank and file as real equals, and make them feel that you are one of them and that you have given your hearts to them, in a word, be at one with the masses. The leading personnel at all levels must go down to the lower levels of administration and out among the masses. The system under which leading personnel at the national, provincial, municipal and autonomous region levels spend one-third of their time each year at the lower levels of administration and among the masses must be carried through.

The rectification campaign must also be carried through to the end in the People's Liberation Army. The People's Liberation Army is the defender as well as builder of the cause of socialism. It has a glorious tradition of industry, bravery, hard work and plain living, and of forging close ties with the masses. Thanks to the rectification campaign, this glorious tradition has been further developed. The relations between the higher and lower ranks in the army, between officers and men and between the army and the people have become still closer and the leadership of Party committees of various levels over army units has been strengthened. Earnest efforts must be made to consolidate all these achievements of the rectification campaign. The Central Committee of the Party and the local Party committees must further strengthen their leadership over military work, pay attention to political work in the army, military training, and the work of the militia. They should look into these things several times a year. This will greatly help raise the political and military qualities of the army, thereby helping to strengthen our national defence, and the cause of liberating Taiwan and defending peace.

In those enterprises, offices, organizations, schools and army units where reforms have been carried out, the rectification campaign will soon enter the fourth stage when each individual studies documents, and undertakes self-criticism and self-examination so as to raise his own ideological level. During this stage, all cadres, and those who are Party members in particular, must seriously study the Party's policies and its style of work, sum up the gains derived from the rectification campaign, examine the shortcomings in their thinking and work, undertake criticism and self-criticism so as to raise their own level of political understanding, and further strengthen unity within the Party and unity between the Party and the masses. Leading cadres at the county level and above and those at the battalion level and above should pay special attention to studying the Party's general line for socialist construction and the Marxist-Leninist ways of thinking and doing things.

A positive attitude must be taken towards the rectification campaign among the national bourgeoisie, the bourgeois intelligentsia and the various democratic parties and groups; they must be given help in educating and remoulding themselves. A thoroughgoing rectification campaign among these people will result in the further consolidation of the people's democratic united front, which is led by the Communist Party, on the new basis of serving socialism. It will enable the people's democratic united front to continue to play its part in the life of the state, and the democratic parties to co-exist for a long period of time with the Communist Party and exercise mutual supervision in meeting the needs of the new society.

Of course, it is impossible to resolve all contradictions through one single rectification campaign. To build a socialist and communist society, we must not only wipe out all the old systems of exploitation and oppression of man by man, but also utterly eliminate obsolete ideas and habits which are derived from and served these old systems; we must eliminate bourgeois ideology and foster proletarian ideology, that is to say, eventually eliminate all vestiges of the exploiting classes and exploiting systems from the minds of the people. This is a much more difficult task than that of eliminating the exploiting classes economically. It can be accomplished only through a long and complicated process of education and struggle. As to other contradictions among the working people outside this scope, such as those between the right and the wrong, between the advanced and the backward, they will always exist and must be resolved continually as they arise. Progress will be made in the process of resolving them. Therefore it is undoubtedly wrong to imagine that a single rectification campaign can settle all questions at a single stroke and that there will be no more twists and turns or ups and downs in the struggle. That is why from now on the method of the rectification campaign, the method of criticism and self-criticism through full and frank airing of views, great debates and posting *tatsepao* must be made the regular method of reforming ideology and improving work. All-round rectification campaigns should be launched at set intervals to handle systematically the contradictions among the people and other contradictions that may have come to light at that time.

Under all circumstances, a strict distinction must be drawn between the methods used to handle contradictions among the people and those used to handle contradictions between the enemy and ourselves. So far as ideological problems among the people are concerned, no matter whether it is a case of a few against the many, or of the many against a few, they must be tackled by means of persuasion and education, not by means of force and coercion. In the fields of culture and academic studies we must continue to carry out the policy of "letting a hundred flowers blossom and a hundred schools of thought contend." This is a method, a scientific Marxist method, of promoting constant progress and advance in the sciences and arts. It is also a method of resolving contradictions among the people. As to the utterances and activities of those who aim to undermine socialism and restore capitalism, we have never sanctioned such utterances and activities, because they are not permitted under the socialist system. But we allow the anti-socialist poisonous weeds to grow and confront the people with contrasts, so that by way of comparison, the people can see clearly what they really are, and roused to indignation, rally together to uproot them. In this way, the fighting ability of the masses will be tempered and it will open up bright prospects for the socialist blossoming of a hundred flowers. This policy has been publicly announced. It was followed in the past and will be followed in the future. The existence of poisonous weeds is an objective phenomena. They will keep cropping up ten thousand years hence. But the poisonous weeds which will emerge in the far distant future will not wear the stamp of class struggle as they do now. Since poisonous weeds exist objectively, if we did not allow them to grow as they are, they would have appeared in disguise, and poisoned the people in secret. We had better tell them openly: "Poisonous weeds are illegal, they've got to be uprooted when they grow. But we do not stop you from sprouting if you want to. Whoever wants to come out and fight, let them do so!" This policy has proved very effective. Large numbers of poisonous weeds furiously attacked the people, and were uprooted by them. Those which have not been uprooted have learned nothing from those which have been eradicated; they still come out and fight. They will certainly come out if they are given the chance, and we shall have to uproot them again. To uproot poisonous weeds is a question between the enemy and ourselves. To let a hundred flowers blossom is a question among the people. These are two different kinds of contradictions and there are two different methods of handling them. The reactionary rightists of the bourgeoisie claimed to be one of the hundred socialist flowers. But that was simply a fraud. They can't be recognized as such.

In improving the work of the state, the most important task at the moment is to find quick and correct solutions to the problem of combining centralization with decentralization. As I said before, this is at present a key problem in carrying out the Party's general line for socialist construction. Local authorities should be allowed greater scope so that construction in all fields throughout the country can develop along the line of achieving greater, faster, better and more economical results, and the central government departments can concentrate upon the things they should assume responsibility for. This principle was put forward by Comrade Mao Tse-tung back in April 1956 in his report on "Ten Sets of Relationships." In actual work, we commenced to carry out this principle, but until quite recently it was being carried out very slowly and not at all thoroughly. In accordance with the discussions at the Nanning and Chengtu conferences convoked by the Central Committee of the Party in the spring of this year, from now on, with the exception of some special, key enterprises or enterprises of an experimental nature, all enterprises formerly run and managed by the various ministries under the State Council will, as a rule, be handed over to the local authorities and placed under their management. Light industries will be handed over to the local authorities first; later, heavy industries will gradually be handed over. Authority to run other economic undertakings, as well as cultural, educational, political and judicial affairs will also be handed over to the local authorities. The central authorities must see to it that the initiative of the provinces, municipalities and autonomous regions is brought into full play; on their part, the latter must see to it that the initiative of the special administrative regions, autonomous *chou*, counties, autonomous counties and townships is brought into full play.

With the improvement in the managerial system, the forward leap in production and construction and the raising of the political consciousness of the masses, existing rules and regulations governing economic and other work must be improved thoroughly and systematically. The experience of the rectification campaign shows that many of these rules and regulations are necessary and suitable, but that there are also quite a few which are wholly superfluous or even breed waste and conservatism, hamper the initiative of the local authorities and the masses and hinder the carrying out of the general line for socialist construction. Our task is thus to mobilize the masses to make an over-all examination of all existing rules and regulations in the light of the policy of building socialism by achieving greater, faster, better and more economical results, by means of full and frank airing of views and great debates so that things may be dealt with in a discerning way after a serious study has been made of the opinions voiced by the masses. Those parts of existing rules and regulations which are necessary and justifiable should be preserved; the rest should be revoked or revised, or replaced by new ones suited to local conditions and current needs, which should be introduced to other places after an experimental phase. Improvement of rules and regulations is a work of great importance; the various regions and departments must devote a certain amount of time and manpower to it and, while doing so, concretely solve urgent problems so as to keep the high tide of production and construction rolling.

One of the important questions of the day which must claim our attention is the continued streamlining of state organs, enterprises and undertakings, improvement of organization and management of labour and the reform of irrational rules and regulations in these fields. Since being streamlined last year, many state-owned and joint state and private enterprises, building, transport and commercial enterprises, and other undertakings and state organs have overcome in great measure the overlapping and overstaffing which resulted from previous defects in the allocation of labour power and management of labour. But this problem has not yet been completely settled. There are even cases where workers and employees who have not done any work at all over long periods are still kept on the payroll. Such cases of waste of manpower and funds, which amount to expropriation of the fruits of other people's labour, are impermissible. We must, while improving the managerial system and rules and regulations, further streamline our organizations and use every possible rational means to raise the rate of utilization of labour power and labour productivity. We must promptly transfer redundant workers and employees to other jobs, so that not a single working day is wasted, and everyone who has some ability can be properly engaged in production or other useful work.

On condition that production is expanded and the living standards of the people are steadily improved, the proportion of funds in the national income going to accumulation should be suitably increased both in state and collective economies so that we can build socialism with greater and faster results. State policies in regard to wages, subsidies, welfare, bonuses, prices, taxes and profits must take state, collective and individual interests into account. Certain reasonable differentials between the living standards of workers and peasants, between living standards in city and countryside, and between the wages for various trades, technical grades and localities are necessary, but unreasonable and excessive differences must be avoided. Measures suited to conditions in the rural and semi-rural regions must be worked out in regard to wages, labour insurance and welfare in enterprises run by the counties and administrative units below the county level; the measures now in force in big enterprises in big cities should not be mechanically applied here.

Both the rectification campaign and improvements in the work of the state are aimed at making the superstructure meet the needs of the economic base, and the relations of production meet the needs of the development of productive forces. Therefore, these efforts must, directly or indirectly, result in the development of production and construction and, first of all, in the successes of great forward leaps in production and construction this year. This year is the first year of the Second Five-Year Plan, the first of three years of hard struggle; it is also the first of the fifteen years in which we are to catch up with Britain. Our achievements this year will be an important gauge of the success of the rectification campaign and the general line for socialist construction, and everybody is watching. So, we must pay great attention to the work of this year and try to do it well. The important thing here is that the leadership must really be in the van of the masses, in the van of the movement, and not lag behind them. The masses are now very enthusiastic; this is the main thing we must rely on if we are to make all our undertakings advance rapidly. We must set great store by this enthusiasm, and never throw cold water on it. Leaders, however, must combine revolutionary enthusiasm with business-like sense. They must be able not only to put forward advanced targets but also to adopt effective measures in time to ensure the realization of the targets. They must not indulge in empty talk and bluff. The targets we put forward should be those that can be reached with hard work. Do not lightly publicize as plan that which is not really attainable, lest failure dampen the enthusiasm of the masses and delight the conservatives. Allowance should be made for difficulties and shortcomings and care should always be taken in the course of the work to uncover difficulties and shortcomings and, without exaggerating or minimizing them, and by working together with the masses overcome them, by every possible means and in a realistic manner. If this is done, we shall surely achieve very great things in our work, unless exceptionally severe natural calamities or other accidents intervene.

The guarantee of success in all our work of socialist construction is the Party's correct leadership. The Central Committee of the Party and local Party committees at all levels must be the leading core of the government at all levels. In the past few years, the leadership of the Party concentrated its efforts mainly on the socialist revolution. While we shall continue to pay attention to this work, we now can and must concentrate greater efforts on socialist construction. Party committees at all levels must give the same resolute leadership to socialist construction and the technical and cultural revolutions as they have been giving the democratic and socialist revolutions. The mistaken tendency among some people both inside and outside the Party to think that the Party cannot lead construction work, or work in the fields of science and technology, culture and education must be thoroughly corrected.

In the period of socialist construction, the period of technical and cultural revolutions, the Party cadres must have a real understanding of their jobs and the necessary knowledge in science and technology to guide the work properly. All Party cadres must put themselves to work on "experimental plots," since this is a good method of combining political work with professional activities and enabling the cadres to keep in close touch with the masses. Naturally, while paying attention to technique and one's own speciality, one must never ignore politics. We must neither become shallow "politicians" who know nothing about their jobs, nor "practical men of business" who have lost their bearings. To be both "red" and "expert"—this is the way of progress for intellectuals and technicians throughout the country; this is also the way of progress for all Party cadres at all levels.

Ideological and political work is always the soul and guide of every kind of work. In every case, abandonment or neglect of ideological and political work by the Party will divorce us from the masses and lead us astray. In the past few years, among leading cadres in the field of construction, we have seen, on the one hand, the shortcomings of not being well versed in their jobs or not trying to learn about them, while, on the other hand, there has also been a tendency to ignore ideological and political work although they have learned their jobs. It should be realized that machines are made and operated by men, and materials are produced only through the efforts of men. It is man that counts; the subjective initiative of the masses is a mighty driving force. To ignore this great driving force will run counter to Marxism-Leninism. Some people say that ideological and political work can produce neither grain nor coal or iron. This is like failing to see the wood for the trees. One may ask: have we not produced more grain, coal and iron by formulating and carrying out correct political lines, by correctly handling contradictions among the people, and by raising the socialist consciousness of the workers and arousing the enthusiasm of the masses, and are we not going to produce more and more by so doing?

Party committees at all levels must pay attention to ideological trends inside and outside the Party, strengthen ideological and political work, pay attention to theoretical problems, seriously study the line and policies of the Party and put a firm stop to the vulgar habit which has prevailed hitherto in many places and departments, of talking about professional matters only and ignoring ideological problems. Party committees at all levels must pay attention to work in connection with the press, the school education and culture, and must regard as a major political task the fostering and training of an army of working-class intellectuals and Marxist-Leninist theoreticians.

Marxism-Leninism is the theoretical foundation on which all the work of our Party is based. The whole Party must learn to apply Marxism-Leninism and dialectical materialism to practical work, and thoroughly oppose any tendency to doctrinairism and empiricism. Doctrinairism and empiricism are forms of subjectivism and metaphysics which are divorced from practice and from the masses; they hinder people from acquiring the ability to analyse and sum up experience, to distinguish between the essence and the outward appearance of things, between the main trend and side issues and thus make them prone to commit political mistakes. We must free ourselves completely from the shackles of doctrinairism and empiricism, and foster a lively and active growth of our minds and our work. We must respect the practical deeds of the masses, their revolutionary drive and creative spirit; and this means respect for materialism and dialectics. We must learn from Comrade Mao Tse-tung and from many other comrades who keep in close contact with the masses (including the many leaders of the Party at the central, provincial, special administrative regional, county and township levels and among the masses). We must follow their examples in invariably applying Marxism-Leninism, dialectics, and materialism to practical work, in combining the universal truths of Marxism-Leninism with the actual practice of the Chinese revolution, and combining a serious and principled stand with a lively, creative spirit, in identifying themselves with the millions, seeing the correct direction, grasping the truth, and throwing themselves into the struggle for that truth, dauntlessly braving all difficulties.

We are now in a great period in the history of our country, the period of development by leaps and bounds. Our Party and our country now need a host of people who think, speak and act with courage and daring, who dare to topple the old idols, to make innovations and create new things, who dare to uphold the truth, conquer ever new positions for the truth and raise the banner of progress and revolution. Only by relying on such people can we lead the people of the whole country in making one forward leap after another and complete the great work of socialist construction by achieving greater, faster, better and more economical results.

For more than a hundred years our country suffered from the oppression of foreign aggressors which made us backward in many respects. Although China has been liberated and has made rapid advances in every field, the mentality of quite a few of our people still bears the imprint of the oppressed, their minds are still filled with all kinds of shibboleths, fears and feelings of inferiority. Instead of exerting their utmost efforts, they are apathetic, and instead of pressing ahead consistently, they are resigned to backwardness. The proletariat and the people's militants must rid themselves lock, stock and barrel of such states of mind; they should cultivate the noble way of firmly believing in the truth, resolutely relying on the masses and being fearless of any authority. We must remember that modesty helps one to make progress whereas conceit makes one lag behind. But the practical modesty we advocate has nothing to do with any sense of inferiority. We have a population of more than 600 million and our Party has ties of flesh and blood with this vast population. By relying on this great force we can, or soon can, do anything within the realms of human possibility. It is true that for the time being this population of 600 million and more is economically poor and culturally is like a clean sheet of white paper. But what does this matter to Marxist-Leninist revolutionaries? Comrade Mao Tse-tung has put it well: "In addition to other characteristics, our more than 600 million people are characterized by poverty and 'whiteness.' This appears to be a bad thing, but in fact it is a good thing. Poor people want to change, to work hard and make a revolution. A clean sheet of white paper has nothing written on it and is therefore well suited for writing the newest and most beautiful words on and for drawing the newest and most beautiful pictures." Isn't this a fact? Our 600 million and more people have already far surpassed the most advanced capitalist countries in the West in the speed of the upsurge of their revolutionary consciousness and of the victories of their revolutionary struggles and will definitely far surpass them too in the speed of economic and cultural growth. In history, it is always the newcomers who outstrip the old, always the new-born things, which for a time appear weak and small but represent what is progressive, that defeat the moribund things, which appear powerful but represent what is conservative. Within a very short historical period we shall certainly leave every capitalist country in the world far behind us. And so, shouldn't we have confidence in ourselves and discard everything that smacks of superstition, fear and feelings of inferiority?

The inevitable victory of our cause is also grounded in the fraternal aid of the countries in the socialist camp headed by the great Soviet Union—which is internationally the most important factor in our favour. We shall continue to draw on the advanced experience of the Soviet Union and other countries, continue to strengthen mutual assistance and co-operation with the other countries in the socialist camp and, shoulder to shoulder with our fraternal parties in all countries, raise still higher the banner of Marxism-Leninism and reinforce the militant solidarity of the international communist movement. We resolutely support the peace proposals of the Soviet Union, the efforts of the peoples of all lands to safeguard peace, and all national movements which oppose aggression, defend their sovereign rights and seek independence. The struggles of the people of all countries support our cause and through our work we in turn support the people of all countries.

Comrades! Let us, on the basis of the Party's general line for socialist construction, strengthen ceaselessly the unity of the entire Party and unity between the Party and all the people. Let us strengthen ceaselessly our solidarity with the Soviet Union and other countries in the socialist camp and with all the peoples of the world in the common cause of peace, democracy and socialism. Victory will surely be ours!

DOCUMENT 26

Education Must Be Combined with Productive Labor, article by Lu Ting-yi, alternate member of the Politburo, in *Red Flag*, July 1, 1958.

The English text is taken from a booklet with the above title, published by the Foreign Languages Press, Peking, 1958. The article was written, according to a publisher's note, "on the basis of the conclusion drawn at a conference of educational work convened by the Central Committee of the Party." The six numbered notes on Chinese classical authors, etc., at the end of this document are reprinted as they appeared in the booklet.

Comment. For a discussion of the mixture of economic and ideological motives behind the movement for combining education with productive labor, see our General Introduction, part VII. There is a marked contrast in tone between Lu Ting-yi's Flowers-and-Schools speech of May 1956 (Document 8) and this 1958 article with its insistence on mass initiative and political guidance ("all the social sciences must be guided by politics, and education is no exception"). Another interesting general point about the article is the spate of Marxist quotations, unique in pronouncements by Chinese leaders at this period. The system of people's communes and the propaganda about the advance to Communism (Document 27) are foreshadowed in references in the latter part of Lu's article (p. 447 below).

Lu Ting-yi says that the principle of combining work with study was applied in all schools as the result of a measure adopted at the end of 1957. He also mentions the agricultural middle schools established by a measure in early 1958. There are numerous other references to such measures or policies, but it is difficult to deduce their exact timing. The most informative statements are to be found in *People's Education*, April 1, 1958 ("Two Major Reforms in General Education"—the two reforms being the combination of labor and production and the strengthening of political and ideological education). It is clear only that directives on study and labor and agricultural middle schools had been issued by the Central Committee by March 1958. Political and ideological reform in schools had been carried out in the fall of 1957. See also ECMM 138 (*Red Flag*, July 16, 1958—Ch'en Po-ta on part study, part work): ECMM 139 (*People's Education*, May 16, 1958—agricultural middle schools in Kiangsu), and ECMM 151 (*Current Events*, Oct. 27, 1958—Central Committee's program on half study, half labor).

Material on other themes may be found as follows:

On the dispatch of cadres to the country, from 1956 on, see CB 453 (report to and resolution of the Congress of the National Democratic Youth League, May 1957); ECMM 85, 114, 120 (*China Youth*, April 1, Oct. 1, and Dec. 16, 1957); ECMM 117 (*Political Study*, Nov. 13, 1957); and ECMM 133 (*Planned Economy*, April 9, 1958). The SCMP series contains much quotation from the local press, e.g., 1442 (Heilungkiang, Hunan, Szechuan), 1462 (Kiangsu), 1464 (Anhwei, Shansi) and 1470 (Kwangtung). Also, SCMP 1618 and 1869 contain texts of decrees enforcing manual and physical labor for cadres, September 1958. Finally, URS, Vol. 10, No. 1, and Vol. 11, Nos. 16, 24, contain further useful material, especially from *China Youth*, April 7, and *Theoretical Study*, April 1 and 28, 1958.

On the notion of red and/or expert, see Documents 19 and 22, above; also ECMM 121 (*China Youth*, Dec. 1, 1957); ECMM 126 (*Study*, Jan. 3, 1958); and ECMM 133 (*Teaching and Research*, Feb. 4, 1958). An article in *People's Daily*, Oct. 1, 1959 (CB 600) shows that the issues, whether one can be "expert" without being "red" or whether it is possible to become "expert" first and "red" afterward, were still alive at that time.

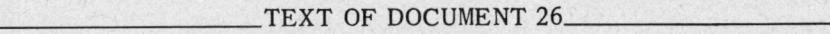

TEXT OF DOCUMENT 26

Education in our country has developed very rapidly since early this year. Figures compiled by the State Statistical Bureau up to the end of June, as yet incomplete, report 1,240 counties with universal primary school education, 68,000 middle schools[1] run by the people themselves, more than 400 institutions of higher learning newly established by the local authorities, approximately 90 million or more people attending literacy courses, and 444 counties in which illiteracy has been wiped out in the main. The victory in the rectification campaign and the struggle against the bourgeois rightists has given rise to the great leap forward in the industry and agriculture of our country. The leap forward, in turn, has precipitated an upsurge in the technical and cultural revolutions. The great advance in education is one of the signs of the high tide of the cultural revolution.

Two measures adopted at the end of last year and early this year pushed forward the advance in education. One was the application in all schools of the principle of combining work with study. The other was the establishment of agricultural middle schools. The practice of working while studying begins to combine the ordinary schooling with productive labour. It breaks the age-old tradition in the schools of looking down on physical labour, changes the atmosphere in the schools and has a very good influence on the social atmosphere. The agricultural middle schools are vocational (technical) schools set up by the people themselves, on a part-work and part-study basis. Schools of this kind meet the pupils' desire to continue their studies and also prepare agricultural technicians. They are comparatively simple to set up and meet the practical needs of today. Without state financing, they still lighten the economic burden on students' families. Therefore, from the moment they were encouraged, they have been springing up like bamboo shoots, numbering tens of thousands in a few months. With primary school graduates freed from worry about lack of opportunity for further study, the number of primary schools run by the people themselves has also increased greatly and primary school education has rapidly become universal in many provinces, autonomous regions and cities.

To meet the growing needs of production, adult education has also developed, the literacy campaign is in full swing and all sorts of spare-time general and technical schools have sprung up in great numbers. This high tide of the cultural revolution has spread from the countryside to the cities, where another stream is evident—the establishment of factories by schools and the setting up of schools by factories.

Now this combination of schooling and productive labour has given rise to the campaign to reform school curricula and the efforts to change school systems, as well as to change the composition of the teaching staffs, etc. Our educational work is like a hundred flowers in bloom, like "ten thousand horses galloping ahead." Education is now breaking the bounds of exclusive control by the experts and of doctrinairism to become the work of the whole Communist Party and the people as a whole, to become socialist education suited to the situation in our country. This transformation has been taking place under the leadership of the Communist Party. Such absurdities as "more, faster, better and more economical results cannot obtain in education," "laymen cannot lead experts," "Communist Party committees do not understand education," "the masses do not understand education," etc. are being smashed to smithereens.

Our state is a proletarian dictatorship, a socialist state. Our education is not bourgeois but socialist education. Socialist education is inconceivable without Communist Party leadership. Socialist education is one of the powerful weapons for transforming the old and building the new society. The purpose of the socialist revolution and socialist construction is to do away with all exploiting classes and all systems of exploitation including their remnants and to bring into being a communist society in which the principle "from each according to his ability and to each according to his needs" is carried out, and the difference between town and country and between mental and manual labour eliminated. This is precisely the purpose of socialist education. Such education can be led only by the political party of the working class, the Communist Party; the bourgeoisie is not qualified to lead education of this type. Only under the leadership of the Communist Party can educational work assume the new countenance that we see it has today.

During the past few years, prolonged debates on educational policy have taken place. Many theoretical and practical problems were settled at the conferences on educational work convened by the Central Committee of the Chinese Communist Party in April and June of this year.

The educational policy of the Chinese Communist Party has always been that education should serve the politics of the working class and be combined with productive labour; and to apply this policy, education must be led by the Communist Party. This is the direct opposite of the educational policy of the bourgeoisie. Bourgeois education is led by bourgeois politicians; it serves the politics of the bourgeoisie, that is, it serves the dictatorship of the bourgeoisie; it is incompatible with proletarian dictatorship. Under the socialist system, the bourgeoisie dare not advocate directly and openly that education should be led by bourgeois politicians and be a weapon against the proletarian dictatorship; it can only put forward the hypocritical, deceptive propositions that "education should be led by experts" and "education for education's sake," with the aim of preventing education from serving the proletarian dictatorship. In our socialist country, therefore, the educational policy advocated by the bourgeoisie is embodied in the propositions "education for education's sake," "mental and manual work are separate" and "education should be led by experts."

Education is, first and foremost, the transmission and acquisition of knowledge. But what is knowledge? What is the purpose of transmitting and acquiring knowledge? We Communists interpret these questions differently from the bourgeoisie. Most bourgeois pedagogues hold that only book knowledge is knowledge and that practical experience cannot be regarded as knowledge. They therefore take the view that education means reading books; the more a man reads the more knowledge he has and those possessing book knowledge are of a higher order. As for productive labour, particularly manual labour and manual workers, they think all this is humiliating and leading one to nowhere. There are other bourgeois pedagogues who maintain that education is life and vice versa. They do not understand life as the practice of class struggle and struggle for production, nor do they stress the importance of theory. So in the end they write off education in effect. These two sets of bourgeois views, though they appear to be diametrically opposed to each other, stem from the same root. They imply that there is no class differentiation among human beings and that pedagogy is a branch of learning that stands above classes.

We Communists view the question differently. We believe that pedagogy is a branch of social sciences. All the social sciences must be guided by politics, and education is no exception. People require education to wage the class struggle and the struggle for production. We believe there are only two kinds of knowledge in the world. One is knowledge of the class struggle. The class struggle is the struggle between groups of men of different economic status and this has already existed for several thousand years. In the present period of transition in our country, there is still class struggle. In the future, when classes no longer exist, even though there will be no class struggle, there will still be contradictions among the people; therefore, for ten thousand years to come there will still be poisonous weeds, that is, there will be struggle between truth and falsehood, between the advanced and the backward, between those who promote and those who impede the development of the productive forces.

The other kind of knowledge is the knowledge of the struggle for production, that is, the knowledge men gain in their struggle against nature. Philosophy is the summing up and generalization of the two kinds of knowledge. The importance of philosophy consists in the fact that the philosophy of dialectical materialism provides men with a correct way of thinking. The essential distinction between men lies not in differences of "disposition" or personality, but, first of all, in their different class standpoints and, in addition, their ways of thinking. Class standpoints and ways of thinking are interrelated and at the same time are distinct from each other. Errors often emanate from two sources—class origin and the way of thinking. To avoid making great errors or to commit fewer errors, people must study politics and philosophy.

We Communists also maintain that there are two kinds of one-sided, fragmentary knowledge. One is book knowledge completely divorced from practical activity. Comrade Mao Tse-tung says: "What sort of knowledge is the bookish information of the students? Granted that their information is entirely true knowledge, it is still not knowledge acquired through their own personal experience but only a matter of theories written down by their forefathers to sum up the experiences of the struggle for production and of the struggle between classes. It is entirely necessary that they should inherit this kind of knowledge, but it must be understood that in a certain sense such knowledge is to them still something one-sided, something which has been verified by others but not yet by themselves. The most important thing is that they should be well versed in applying such knowledge in life and practice. Therefore, I should advise those who have only bookish knowledge but little or no practical experience that they should be aware of their own shortcomings and be modest."

Experience without theory, which is usually perceptual or partial, is also a kind of one-sided, fragmentary knowledge. Comrade Mao Tse-tung says: "Those comrades who are engaged in practical work will also come to grief if they misuse their experience. True, these comrades are often rich in experience which is certainly valuable, but it would be a great danger if they should rest content with such experience. They ought to realize that their knowledge is usually perceptual and partial, and that they lack rational and comprehensive knowledge; in other words, they are not equipped with theory, and their knowledge is thus comparatively incomplete. Without comparatively complete knowledge it is impossible to do revolutionary work well." What is then comparatively complete knowledge? Comrade Mao Tse-tung says: "There is only one kind of true theory in the world, the theory that is drawn from objective reality and then in turn verified by it; nothing else can be called theory in our sense." "All comparatively complete knowledge is acquired through two stages, first the stage of perceptual knowledge and secondly the stage of rational knowledge, the latter being the development of the former to a higher plane." "There are two kinds of incomplete knowledge: one is knowledge already contained in books and the other is knowledge which is usually perceptual and partial, and both are one-sided. Only through an integration of the two can excellent and comparatively complete knowledge emerge." ("Rectify the Party's Style in Work," *Selected Works of Mao Tse-tung*, Vol. IV)

The purpose of education is to enable students to acquire comparatively complete knowledge and not one-sided, incomplete knowledge. It follows that teachers are required to have comparatively complete knowledge.

Our educational workers always say that "education is the people's business." This is good, because in our country this is true. But as the experience of the past nine years shows, there are two different interpretations of this phrase. The bourgeois pedagogues maintain that the masses of the people are entitled to receive education; but as to running education, that is only for the experts, not for the masses of the people. Their slogans are: "the professors must run the schools"; "laymen cannot lead experts"; "the Party does not understand education"; "the masses do not understand education"; "students must not criticize teachers"; etc.

These myths advanced by the bourgeois pedagogues were even accepted as true by some of our comrades, who forgot that our Party on hundreds and thousands of occasions had been called "laymen," yet, as it ultimately turned out, proved in fact rather more expert than any experts.

Some of our comrades advocated this sort of proposition: (1) only the state may run schools and (2) only one kind of school—general, full-time schools—may be set up. Past experience shows that the bourgeois pedagogues are keenly interested in this proposition because it ties the hands of the masses and does not permit them to set up schools. The bourgeois pedagogues know that if education were run along these lines, our country would find it very difficult to institute universal primary and secondary education and have no hope at all of instituting universal higher education, because the state has no way of carrying the huge burden of expenditures involved without heavy damage to production.

We Communists do not agree with the bourgeois pedagogues. We think that it is for the socialist revolution and socialist construction that the masses of the people need education. As the masses of the people are able to conduct revolution and construction, they are, of course, capable not only of receiving education but also of running education. In running education, it is necessary to rely on a corps of specialists, for without a powerful specialized corps things will not go well, and at present, this corps of specialists still needs to be greatly strengthened by transferring cadres and establishing teachers' training schools. But the corps of specialists in education must integrate with the masses, and reliance on the masses in running education is the more important. Only by linking the specialized educational workers with the masses, adhering to the mass line of "from the masses and back to the masses," and carrying out the policy of setting up schools by the whole people under the leadership of the Party, is it possible, in fact certain, for our country's educational work to achieve greater, faster, better and more economical results. And only by fully applying the policy of setting up schools by the whole people under the leadership of the Party is it possible to do all-round planning, duly considering and co-ordinating all aspects, so that not only does the educational work grow, but grows in a way that helps, and does not impede the development of production.

Our educational workers always say, too, that "educational work must receive leadership from the Party." This is undoubtedly correct. Socialist education must be led by the Communist Party and educational work in the socialist People's Republic of China must be led by the Communist Party of China. But there are also different interpretations of what leadership is and what kind of leadership is needed. What the bourgeois pedagogues call "Party leadership" is "Party leadership in political matters and our leadership in vocational matters." On questions unrelated to education they may listen to the Party; but if the Party has something to say about educational principles, policies, systems, methods and so on, they regard it as unacceptable. In words they want Party leadership, but in practice they do not want it; on minor questions they may listen to the Party, but, on major questions they want to have their own way in defiance of the Party. Some of our comrades in the Party who work in the educational field put themselves up as experts in relation to Party committees and fail to respect their leadership. This is an expression of bourgeois influence in our Party.

In the past few years, the "theory" that the principal laws governing educational work are to be drawn from the study of the history of education, was spread widely in educational circles in our country. From this it would follow that to run socialist education it is just necessary to study the history of education, while recognizing Party leadership in the abstract; as for specific Party leadership, this is not needed.

Study of the history of education, provided it proceeds from the viewpoint of Marxist historical materialism, is indeed useful and helps towards an understanding of the laws which governed education for thousands of years in the era of class society. However, it must be understood that the laws governing education in the history of class society are not the same as the laws governing socialist education, much less the laws governing socialist education in China. For the past thousands of years, education was in the hands of the slave-owners, the landlord class and the bourgeoisie. The principal laws to be derived from this history are those governing exploiting-class education. They are certainly a far cry from the laws of socialist education. Mistakes would be inevitable if these laws were copied as the laws of socialist education.

What the facts show is that the so-called theory that "the principal laws governing educational work are to be drawn from the study of the history of education" is in reality a pretence by which the study of the history of education is used to keep bourgeois educational ideas, policies, systems, methods and so on intact under the socialist system and to palm these off as socialist.

In China's history of education there is one aspect which is of the people. There was the Confucian idea that "in the matter of instruction, no distinction should be made between men of all sorts and conditions"; Mencius' idea that "the people are more important than the king"; the idea of Hsun Tzu that "man will overcome nature"; Chu Yuan's criticism of the vices of royalty; Szema Chien's eulogy of resistance to evil; the ancient materialism of Wang Chung, Fan Chen, Liu Tsung-yuan, Chang Tsai and Wang Fu-chih; the democratic literature of Kuan Han-ching, Shih Nai-an, Wu Cheng-en and Tsao Hsueh-chin[2] and the democratic revolution of Sun Yat-sen. The conditions in which these people lived varied. Many of them did not write specifically on education. But what has just been referred to could not but have its impact on the education of the people. All this must be mentioned in talking about the history of Chinese education.

But taking the major aspects, education over the past thousands of years was certainly an instrument in the hands of the exploiting classes, while socialist education is an instrument in the hands of the working class. This change, from an instrument of the exploiting classes to an instrument of the working class, is a qualitative leap in education and a great revolution in education itself. To study the history of education without seeing this qualitative leap is to depart from dialectics; it is metaphysical. We advocate the study of the history of education but we oppose the view that the principal laws of socialist education can be found through such study because it would lead us to right deviationist mistakes.

Moreover, even the laws of socialist education, though they are of the same character in different countries, differ in their specific features. Doctrinaire mistakes would be made if the specific features of one's own country are not studied. What are the specific features of our country? First, ours is a socialist country; second, it has a huge population and covers a vast area; third, its economy and culture are backward; fourth, it is led by the Communist Party and its industry and agriculture are leaping forward rapidly; and fifth and most important, our country has carried out a serious rectification campaign and anti-rightist struggle, the people are encouraged to air their views, contend, debate to the fullest extent and publicize their views in *tatsepao*.[3] We must define our educational principles, policies, systems, methods and so on in accordance with these characteristics of our own, combining the universal truths of Marxism with the specific conditions of our country.

It is clear, therefore, that the so-called theory that "the principal laws governing educational work are to be drawn from the study of the history of education" is a most pernicious "theory" which divorces education from reality and leads it to right deviationist and doctrinaire mistakes. Not to proceed from the objective realities of one's own country is subjective, anti-Marxist thinking. If we err in our way of thinking, we cannot find out the major laws governing the development of things. If we do not proceed from reality and if we go against the universal truths of Marxism, we will surely make mistakes, either right deviationist or doctrinaire mistakes, or both. This is the important lesson we should draw from the educational work of our country.

We are Marxists and so we maintain that it is necessary to proceed from objective reality. Therefore we must first study our own conditions seriously and take to it with enthusiasm. We also study the experiences of our fraternal countries seriously, and we study history seriously, but our purpose is not to copy or transplant but to understand history, understand historical materialism in the field of education, so as to have examples for study with the aid of which we can do our work satisfactorily in accordance with our own conditions. Whatever work we do, we must rely closely on the leadership of the Party because it is none but the Communist Party that understands our conditions best and knows Marxism best. The Communist Party is the highest form of organization of the working class; it must and can give leadership in everything. From the Central Committee down to the basic organizations, the Communist Party is the organized, disciplined vanguard of the working class. We have relied on this vanguard for victory in the revolutionary war and for success in the socialist revolution on the economic, political and ideological fronts and we must rely on it for victory in the technical and cultural revolutions. Our educational workers should accept Party leadership not only in politics but also in the sphere of educational ideas, policy and work. Only in this way will it be possible to keep up with the times and avoid mistakes or make fewer mistakes.

In the final analysis, the debate on education that has been going on in recent years boils down to the question of "what is all-round development." Marxists believe in "producing fully developed human beings" and in achieving this through education. It is well that our educationalists often talk about all-round development. Yet there are differences of principle in the interpretation of "all-round development." Judging by our country's experience in education in the past nine years, although the bourgeois pedagogues do not directly and openly oppose all-round development and even appear to "support the principle actively," yet they interpret it one-sidedly as meaning education through learning of extensive book knowledge. They do not hold with students studying politics and participating in productive labour. In fact they vulgarize the idea of all-round development and equate it with the bourgeois educational line which rears "know-alls."

We Communists interpret all-round development in an entirely different way. The essence of all-round development is that the students should acquire comparatively broader knowledge, become versatile people capable of "going over in sequence from one branch of production to another, depending on the requirements of society or their own inclinations." (F. Engels: *Principles of Communism*) We maintain that workers should be versatile in industrial production and peasants should be versatile in agricultural production; moreover that workers should at the same time be peasants and peasants should be workers. We maintain that civilians should take up military service and retired military men go back to production. We maintain that cadres should participate in physical labour and productive workers in administration. All these propositions are already being put into practice gradually. Measures such as these which involve both the division of labour and change of work conform to the needs of society. They are more reasonable than the division of labour under the capitalist system. They not only increase production but enable the state to carry out reasonable readjustment of the productive forces when this becomes socially necessary, without causing social upheaval.

Our leap forward in industry and agriculture is already giving rise to the problem of the partial transfer of producers to other branches of production when what they are making grows in output to the point where it meets the current maximum demands of the people and there is even a surplus. Without such transfer there would be failure to meet the demands of the people, to develop the productive forces of society continuously and raise the people's living standards continuously. Our educational and other relevant spheres of work must prepare the ground for such transfers. Education should enable the students to acquire broad knowledge. But how broad depends on concrete objective and subjective conditions. In the future, when communist society is fully consolidated, developed and mature, men will be trained in many kinds of work and be able to undertake many professions while specializing in selected fields. This is what we aim at. We must march to this goal.

In our country's present conditions, we can train people to do many kinds of work, but cannot yet train "people to be capable of undertaking any profession." The essence of all-round development is also that the knowledge imparted to the students must be not one-sided and fragmentary, but comparatively complete knowledge. This requires that education should serve politics and be combined with productive labour. Speaking of his ideal of education in the future, Karl Marx referred to "an education that will, in the case of every child over a given age, combine productive labour with instruction and gymnastics, not only as one of the methods of adding to the efficiency of production, but as the only method of producing fully developed human beings." (*Capital*, Vol. I) That is, he urged that students acquire comparatively complete knowledge and be able to engage not only in mental labour but manual labour as well. Book knowledge alone, however broad, is still partial and incomplete. People with extensive book knowledge alone and without experience of practical work are only what the bourgeoisie calls "know-alls." They are not what we regard as people of all-round development. Physical development is necessary in childhood and this development must be sound. In addition, a communist spirit and style and collective heroism should be inculcated in childhood. This is the moral education of our day. Both are linked with the development of intellectual education. Both are related to manual work and therefore the principle of combining education with labour is unshakable.

In brief, the all-round development we stand for is this: students should be enabled to acquire comparatively complete, broader knowledge, grow up physically fit and acquire communist morals. In his *On the Correct Handling of Contradictions Among the People,* Comrade Mao Tse-tung said: "Our educational policy must enable everyone who gets an education to develop morally, intellectually and physically and become a cultured, socialist-minded worker." This is our educational principle of all-round development. "A cultured, socialist-minded worker" is a man who is both politically conscious and educated. He is able to undertake both mental and manual work. He is what we regard as developed in an all-round way, both politically and professionally qualified. He is a worker-intellectual and an intellectual-worker.

We insist on the educational principle of all-round development. We consider that the only method to train human beings in all-round development is to educate them to serve working-class politics and combine education with productive labour. We say the only method, because there is no other way to achieve this aim. Bourgeois pedagogues do not agree. They consider the only method to train people to have what they call "all-round development" is to read books and learn by rote. They are absolutely against students learning politics and, in particular, students becoming labourers. According to our educational principle of all-round development, we can and must rely on the masses to run education. According to the bourgeois educational principle of so-called "all-round development," they can rely only on experts to run education; they cannot rely on the masses. According to our educational principle of all-round development, education must be under the leadership of the Communist Party. According to the bourgeois educational principle of so-called "all-round development," education can only be led by the experts; it does not need the leadership of the Communist Party as the Communist Party is "a layman." From this we see that different interpretations of all-round development lead to different and even opposite conclusions. That is why we say that the debate on education in recent years ultimately boils down to the question of "what is all-round development." This is essentially a struggle between proletarian and bourgeois educational ideas.

If we followed our bourgeois pedagogues' attitude towards knowledge, towards education as the business of the people, towards leadership by the Communist Party and towards all-round development, our educational work would be dragged back to the old bourgeois road. Precisely because of this, it is necessary to give a clear explanation of our communist interpretation of these questions.

Great achievements have been made in our educational work, under the leadership of the Chinese Communist Party, in the past nine years since the founding of the People's Republic of China. These are—the recovery of the right to run education, a right formerly usurped by the imperialists; the satisfactory taking over of the schools all over the country; the abolition of the fascist system of school management practised by the Kuomintang reactionary clique, the abolition of its fascist education and domination of the students by its special agents; the setting up of a socialist educational system; and the wiping out, in the main, of the counter-revolutionaries and other bad elements hidden in educational circles. In addition, courses in Marxism-Leninism have been opened in the schools; ideological remoulding has been conducted among the teachers and students; the universities and departments have been reorganized and teaching systems reformed; and struggles have been waged against the bourgeois rightists. The number of students in institutions of higher learning, middle schools and primary schools has in all cases increased several fold; big advances have been made in the campaign against illiteracy and in spare-time cultural and technical education; the policy of working while studying has begun to be applied in all schools; organizations of the Chinese Communist Party have been established among the educational workers; and large numbers of people have been trained as cadres for socialist construction.

But the struggle between working-class and bourgeois ideas proceeds continuously on the educational front. This is in the nature of a struggle between the socialist and the capitalist roads. Bourgeois thinking has hampered the development of education. When the bourgeois rightists made their ferocious attacks, they even attempted to use the students as a stepping stone for the restoration of capitalism. This was at one time the dream of Chang Po-chun, Lo Lung-chi, Tseng Chao-lun, Chien Wei-chang and others of their ilk. Our victory in the anti-rightist struggle and the great leap forward in industry and agriculture have turned bad things to good account and enabled people to understand better the danger and baneful consequences of bourgeois thinking in educational work. The work in the past nine years has given us experience and enabled us to explain our Party's policy of educational work more clearly and systematically.

The chief mistake or defect in our educational work has been the divorce of education from productive labour. The policy of combining education with productive labour was put forward by our Party early in 1934. Comrade Mao Tse-tung already then said: "What is the general policy for the Soviet[4] culture and education? It is to educate the broad masses of the toiling people in the spirit of communism, to make culture and education serve the revolutionary war and the class struggle, to combine education with labour and to enable the broad masses of the Chinese people to enjoy civilization and happiness." In 1954 when the period of economic rehabilitation was over and the First Five-Year Plan already in operation, the Central Committee of the Party raised the question of adding productive labour to the curricula of the schools. But the proposal encountered obstruction and was not carried through at that time. The Central Committee of the Party repeatedly stressed its policy that education must be combined with productive labour—at the national conference on propaganda work in March 1957, in the editorial of *Renmin Ribao* (*People's Daily*) on April 8 of the same year and at the Nanning meeting in January 1958. It is only now that this policy of the Party has been carried out on a nation-wide scale. Education must serve politics, must be combined with productive labour and must be led by the Party—these three things are interrelated. Education divorced from productive labour is bound to lead, to a degree, to the neglect of politics and of Party leadership in educational work, thus divorcing education from the realities of our country and eventually causing right deviationist and doctrinaire mistakes.

The combination of education with productive labour is required by our country's socialist revolution and socialist construction, by the great goal of building a communist society and by the need to develop our education with greater, faster, better and more economical results.

The aim of our socialist revolution is to wipe out all exploiting classes, all systems of exploitation, including their remnants. Basic victory has now been won in the socialist revolution on the economic front. On the political and ideological fronts, too, the socialist revolution has achieved decisive victory. As the Second Session of the Eighth National Congress of the Communist Party of China has pointed out in its resolution, our task is "to actively carry out the technical and cultural revolutions while continuing with the socialist revolution on the economic, political and ideological fronts."

The cultural revolution is to enable all 600 million Chinese people, except for those who are incapable, to do productive work and to study. This means to make the masses of our workers and peasants intellectuals as well and our intellectuals labourers too. Only when the masses of the workers and peasants and the intellectuals alike develop along the line of making up what they lack, is it possible to change thoroughly the irrational legacy of the old society and eradicate the backwardness of each, i.e., eliminate the cultural deficiency of the masses of workers and peasants and eliminate the bourgeois thinking of the intellectuals. This is, therefore, a very far-reaching revolution which demands that education must serve working-class politics, that it be combined with productive labour.

Marx said: "An early combination of productive labour with education is one of the most potent means for the transformation of present-day society." (Karl Marx: *Critique of the Gotha Programme*) It is impossible to carry through the cultural revolution without combining education with productive labour. Cultural revolution is beneficial to the country, to the masses of workers and peasants as well as the intellectuals. Only those who stick to the bourgeois standpoint do not want such a revolution. The bourgeois policy of education for education's sake, and divorcing mental from physical labour, is incompatible with the socialist revolution.

Our socialist construction demands the utmost effort and consistent pressing ahead; it demands building the country industriously and thriftily; it also demands technique and culture and the training of large numbers of socialist-minded and professionally proficient technicians in conformity with the principle of achieving greater, faster, better and more economical results. These needs of socialist construction also demand the combination of education with productive labour. Lenin said: "It is impossible to visualize the ideal of future society without combining the training and education of the young generation with productive labour. Neither training and education without productive labour, nor productive labour without parallel training and education could have been raised to the height demanded by present-day technique and the state of scientific knowledge" (*Pearls of Narodniks' Hare-brained Schemes*). The policy of combining education with productive labour will certainly raise the quality of education. This holds true for intellectual and for moral and physical education. The educational policy of divorcing mental and manual labour cannot meet the needs of socialist construction.

The future communist society will be one of "from each according to his ability and to each according to his needs," a society in which the differences between town and country and between mental and manual labour are eliminated. Our big leap forward in industry and agriculture has made the attainment of communism no longer a far distant prospect. One hundred and ten years ago Marx and Engels in the Communist Manifesto formulated ten measures to establish a communist society, which "will be pretty generally applicable... in the most advanced countries." Of these, the first eight have already been carried out in China, through the adoption of methods suitable to the actual conditions of our country; and the last two, namely "the combination of agriculture with manufacturing industries; the gradual abolition of the distinction between town and country" and "the combination of education with industrial production," are beginning to be carried out.

It is clear to everyone that because of the application, in the course of industrial development, of the policy "to develop industry and agriculture simultaneously while giving priority to heavy industry; and, with centralized leadership, over-all planning, proper division of labour and co-ordination to develop national and local industries, and large, small and medium-sized enterprises simultaneously," industry has appeared in the rural areas and, with it, the phenomenon of workers who are simultaneously peasants and peasants who are simultaneously workers. This phenomenon has the embryo of communist society.

Because the principle of combining education with productive labour is beginning to go into operation, with schools setting up their own factories and farms, and factories and agricultural co-operatives establishing their own schools on a large scale, the phenomenon of students who are at the same time workers and peasants and of workers and peasants who are students at the same time is beginning to appear. This, too, has the embryo of communist society. It can be imagined that when China enters into communism, our basic social organizations will be many communist communes. With few exceptions, each basic unit will have workers, peasants, traders, students and militia. In the field of education, each basic unit will have its own primary and secondary schools and institutions of higher learning; at the same time everybody will have the time to acquire education as both labourer and intellectual. In *The Housing Question* Engels anticipated this situation when he said: "And it is precisely this industrial revolution which has raised the productive power of human labour to such a high level that—for the first time in the history of humanity—the possibility exists, given a rational division of labour among all, of producing not only enough for the plentiful consumption of all members of society and for an abundant reserve fund, but also of leaving each individual sufficient leisure so that what is really worth preserving in historically inherited culture—science, art, forms of intercourse—may not only be preserved but converted from a monopoly of the ruling class into the common property of the whole of society, and may be further developed." To attain this prospect, our educational work must not go in the direction of divorcing mental and manual labour but in the direction of combining mental with manual labour and education with productive labour.

To the bourgeois educationalists it seems impossible to get greater, faster, better and more economical results in education. But the tremendous growth in educational work since the beginning of this year has proved that the application of the mass line in educational work can make it develop with greater, faster, better and more economical results. The combination of education with labour, making education an activity that is warmly welcomed by the workers and peasants, is an important way of arousing mass initiative in the setting up of schools. The principles of running schools by applying the mass line under Communist Party leadership are: First, to combine unity with diversity. The purpose of the training is unified, that is, to train socialist-minded, educated workers; but the schools can be run by the central or local authorities, factories and mines, enterprises and agricultural co-operatives, and the forms the schools can take are varied. They may be full-time, or part-work part-study, or spare-time schools; they may collect fees or be free of charge. As production grows further and working hours can be shortened, the present spare-time schools will be similar to part-work part-study schools. When production develops considerably and public accumulation rises greatly, the schools that now charge fees will similarly become free.

Second, to combine the spreading of education widely with the raising of educational levels. The level of education must be raised on the basis of popularization and popularization must be so guided as to raise the level of education. Some of the full-time, the part-work part-study and the spare-time schools undertake the task of raising educational levels at the same time as education is being spread extensively through part-work part-study and spare-time courses. Since the schools that popularize education are part-work part-study or spare-time schools, they can meet the whole or the greater part of their expenditures themselves, and can find teachers locally in accordance with the principle that "every capable person can teach." They can develop gradually by perfecting their curricula, equipment and teaching staff with aid from the government. In schools where courses in labour are lacking, the stress should be on introducing them and in schools where the deficiency is in the basic courses the stress should be on introducing these, so that both kinds of schools go forward to fill in what they lack and apply the principle of combining theory with practice more effectively.

Third, to combine over-all planning with decentralization, to bring into play the initiative of both the various central government departments and the local authorities and the masses so as to develop education with greater, faster, better and more economical results. In planning educational work, the central and the local authorities, guided by the Party committees, can develop education as fast as possible and enable this development to benefit, not hamper, the growth of production.

Fourth, to apply the mass line in the political, administrative, pedagogic and research work in the schools. In all such work, it is necessary, guided by the Party committees, to adopt the method of open and free airing of views, and *tatsepao* and the method of the "three combinations" (for instance, in working out teaching plans and programmes, the method can be adopted of combining the efforts of the teachers and the students under the leadership of the Party committee and in teaching, the method of inviting people with practical experience to give lectures, in co-ordination with the teachers in special fields, under the leadership of the Party committee, and so on), and to establish democratic relations of equality—changing the old irrational relations—between the leadership and the rank and file and between the teachers and the students. Experience shows that remarkable achievements have been made where these methods have been adopted.

A struggle has to be waged before the combination of education with labour is effected, and this struggle will be a protracted one. Why? Because this is a revolution upsetting old traditions in educational work that have persisted for thousands of years. The principle of divorcing mental from manual labour has dominated educational work for thousands of years. All the exploiting classes in history have adhered firmly to this principle. More than two thousand years ago, Confucius took a stand against combining education with productive labour. He condemned Fan Chih[5] who "requested to be taught husbandry" and "requested to be taught gardening" as a "small man." Mencius opposed Hsu Hsing,[6] saying: "Those who labour with their minds govern others; those who labour with their strength are governed by others. Those who are governed by others support them; those who govern others are supported by them. This is a principle universally recognized." On this point, bourgeois pedagogues are in full accord with Confucius and Mencius. Originally, education was linked with productive labour, but was separated in class society; now the link will be reforged.

Fourier and Owen, the Utopian socialists of the eighteenth century, were the first to put forward the idea of combining education with productive labour. Marx, Engels and Lenin all endorsed this idea. In Volume I of *Capital* Marx expressed the view that a part-work part-study system of schooling was more suitable for children than full-time study. In "The Directives to the Delegates of the Provisional Central Council on Some Questions" he suggested: "In a reasonable social order every child must become a productive worker starting at the age of nine."

He maintained that children from the age of nine to twelve should do two hours' work every day in a workshop or at home, children from thirteen to fifteen years of age four hours and from sixteen to seventeen years of age six hours. He believed that "the combination of remunerative productive labour, mental education, physical exercise and polytechnical training elevates the working class considerably above the level of the higher and middle classes." Marx once foretold that "there can be no doubt that when the working class comes into power, as inevitably it must, technical instruction, both theoretical and practical, will take its proper place in the working-class schools." (*Capital*, Volume I) Only in a socialist country led by the working class and the Communist Party can the principle of combining education with productive labour be carried into effect and play a great role in revolution and construction. Marx's prophecy will come true in our country.

We must realize that to carry the combination of education with productive labour into effect means a fight with the old traditions that have persisted for thousands of years. Without the communist style of toppling down the old idols, burying doctrinairism, and daring to think, speak and do, without the creative spirit of combining the universal truths of Marxism with the concrete realities of our country, we cannot succeed. Today, in our educational work, vigorous efforts are being made to pull down the out-dated and set up the new. Bourgeois and doctrinaire ideas are being broken down and new, Marxist educational theories, systems and methods, curricula and school systems suited to our country are being created. This educational revolution has solid economic foundations. The Marxist doctrine of historical materialism teaches that the superstructure must conform to the economic base. The political system is superstructure, the concentrated expression of economic life. Education comes into the category of ideology and is also superstructure; it serves politics. Class society which has existed for thousands of years has had ownership by slave-owners, landlords or capitalists as its economic base. The political systems that conform to these types of ownership are the dictatorships of the slave-owners, the landlords and the bourgeoisie. The types of education that serve these dictatorships are those of the slave-owners, the landlords and the bourgeoisie. These types of education differ from each other, but all have this in common that education is divorced from productive labour, mental from manual labour, and manual labour and manual labourers are despised. The divorce of mental from manual labour is needed by all the exploiting classes, including the bourgeoisie.

Our society has socialist ownership as its economic base. The political system suited to socialist ownership is proletarian dictatorship. Our education serves the proletarian dictatorship. Therefore, contrary to the old traditions that persisted for thousands of years, it must apply the principle of combining education with productive labour so as to eliminate the difference between mental and manual labour; and this also means wiping out the survivals of all the systems of exploitation that have existed in history, so that humanity may enter into communist society.

The principle of combining education with productive labour is needed by the working class and all other working people. This principle, which conforms to the people's desires, will certainly prevail. On the other hand, the principle of divorcing mental from manual labour, since it does not conform to the socialist economic base and the people's requirements, will sooner or later be discarded by the people even though it has a tradition of thousands of years. With politics in command, with leadership by the Communist Party, and the rallying of the entire Party and all educational workers who can be rallied to fight against bourgeois educational policy and for the application of the Party's educational policy, we can so carry through our cultural revolution that all of our 600 million people are able to do productive work and all are able to study, changing them into new men who are both labourers and intellectuals.

NOTES

[1]In China the primary schools cover the first six years of schooling. Middle schools account for the years after primary school, up to college.

[2]Confucius (551–479 B.C.), great philosopher and educationalist of ancient China.

Mencius (c. 390–305 B.C.), famous philosopher of the Warring States period and a follower of Confucius. In his book *Meng Tzu*, a collection of his sayings preserved by his disciples, he said: "The people are most important; next comes the government; the king is the least important."

Hsun Tzu (c. 340–245 B.C.), a materialist thinker of the Warring States period. In the chapter "On Heaven" in his book *Hsun Tzu* he expounded the theory that man will overcome Heaven.

Chu Yuan (c. 340–278), a great patriotic poet and statesman of the Warring States period. In his poetical work *Li Sao* he severely criticized the rulers of his state because they listened to the words of treacherous ministers and persecuted the loyal ones.

Szema Chien (c. 145–90 B.C.), a great historian, outstanding thinker and literary writer of the Han dynasty. In his work *Shih Chi* (*Historical Records*) he paid tribute to the heroic leaders of peasants in their revolt against tyrants, and exposed the vices and crimes of the rulers of different historical periods.

Wang Chung (27–107), a materialist and atheist of the Eastern Han dynasty. He wrote a book called *Lun Heng* (*Impartial Discussion*) in which he attacked the various kinds of religious doctrines and superstitions spread by the feudal rulers. He carried materialism and atheism to a further stage of development.

Fan Chen (c. 450–515), famous materialist of the Southern and Northern Dynasties. He wrote the book *Shen Mieh Lun* (*Extinction of Spirit*) in which he expounded the doctrine of atheism. He explained the relation between spirit and matter from the materialist standpoint of view, holding that spirit is a function of matter. He mercilessly attacked Buddhism to which the feudal rulers were greatly devoted.

Liu Tsung-yuan (773–819), a famous literary writer and materialist of the Tang dynasty. In his writings he attacked theism, religion, and superstitions. In an essay on feudalism he held that emperors do not rule by the Mandate of Heaven.

Chang Tsai (1020–1077), philosopher of the Sung dynasty. In his book *Cheng Meng* (*Right Teaching for Youth*) he explained his view of Nature from the materialist standpoint, sometimes with a dialectical approach in its crude form.

Wang Fu-chih (1619–1692), materialist thinker and patriot of the period between the Ming and Ching dynasties. In his commentaries on *Yi Ching* (*Book of Change*) and *Shu Ching* (*Book of History*) he held the theory that practice comes before knowledge.

Kuan Han-ching (c. 1227–1297), playwright of the Yuan dynasty. He was the author of *Midsummer Snow*, *Butterfly Dream*, and other plays.

Shih Nai-an (1296–1370), great literary writer of the Yuan dynasty. He was the author of *Shui Hu* (*Water Margin*).

Wu Cheng-en (c. 1500–1582), literary writer of the Ming dynasty and author of *Hsi Yu Chi* (*Pilgrimage to the West*).

Tsao Hsueh-chin (c. 1722–1763), great literary writer of the Ching dynasty and author of *Hung Lou Meng* (*Dream of the Red Chamber*).

[3]Opinions and criticisms written out in bold Chinese characters on large sheets of paper and posted for everybody to see.

[4]This refers to the Soviet areas in China which existed at that time under the leadership of the Chinese Communist Party.

[5]Fan Chih, disciple of Confucius. The *Analects* record a conversation between Fan Chih and Confucius. Fan said that he wanted to learn farming; Confucius said that he was not so good a teacher as the peasant. Fan Chih said that he wanted to learn how to plant vegetables; Confucius said that he was not so good a teacher as the kitchen-garden keeper. After Fan Chih had left Confucius told his other disciples that Fan was a man with no great ambition. This conversation shows that Confucius had a contempt for productive labour and that he was against the combination of education with production.

[6]Hsu Hsing, a thinker of the Warring States period. He held the theory that all men, be they kings or common people, should till the land and weave cloth themselves. Mencius did not agree with Hsu Hsing. He held that those who work with their brain govern while those who engage in manual labour are governed. Those who are governed must support those who govern. From this we can see that Mencius was against the combination of brain work and manual labour.

Chapter VIII

PEOPLE'S COMMUNES: THE PHASE OF ENTHUSIASM

(containing Documents 27, 28, 29, 30, 31, 32)

General comment. The official history of the formation of the communes is given in a *People's Daily* editorial of August 29, 1959 (Document 42 below). A discussion of the economic and ideological and other motives behind the move is contained in our General Introduction. There is a great deal of literature on this subject. A good general account is in T. J. Hughes and D. E. T. Luard, *The Economic Development of Communist China* (London: Oxford University Press, 1959), Chapter XIII. See also the very informative essay by A. V. Sherman, entitled "The People's Commune," in *The Chinese Communes*, a booklet published by *Soviet Survey*, London [1959].

Translations of Chinese sources are listed, as appropriate, in the comments on Documents 27-36. The CB and ECMM series, however, contain a mass of further material which should be consulted by anyone who wishes to study the subject in detail. On a number of important themes which gave rise to subsequent discussion within the Party (the militia system, the wage and supply system, the question of "collective ownership"), comments are included in our Chapter IX.

Material on certain other themes, which belong to the first period of the formation of communes but are not illustrated by the documents in this chapter, may be found as follows:

(a) *Collective schools*: CB 540 (*Kuang Ming Jih Pao*, Oct. 24, 1958—Liu Shao-ch'i on boarding schools; primary boarding schools set up in Paoting); ECMM 155 (report from Honan in *Education Fortnightly*, Nov. 11, 1958—collectivization of schools realized in Hsingchuang district); URS, Vol. 13, No. 21 (*China Youth*, Oct. 16 and 31, 1958, quoting Liu Shao-ch'i on boarding schools).

(b) *Reduction of family life*: ECMM 155 (*China Youth*, Nov. 16, 1958), for a conventional account of how far the old family system needs to be changed; ECMM 162 (*Architectural Journal*, November 1958) and JPRS 564D (*Architectural Journal*, October 1958), for plans of new buildings in communes; URS, Vol. 14, No. 14 (report from Canton in *Industrial and Commercial Circles*, Dec. 9, 1958), for an address on the trend away from the family and toward collective life, by the Director of the Propaganda Department of the Kwangtung Provincial Committee of the Party.

DOCUMENT 27

New Society, New People, article by Ch'en Po-ta in *Red Flag*, July 1, 1958.

The English text is taken from CB 517, and is a translation by the U.S. Consulate General, Hong Kong, from the *Red Flag* article.

Comment. The author is one of the senior Chinese theoreticians. He was in 1942 secretary to Mao Tse-tung. Other important contributions from his pen appeared in February 1956, on the leap forward in cooperativization, and in June 1958, on Yugoslav revisionism (see general comment in our Chapter II and comment on Document 24). For indications that something like communes was taking shape, in some cases

long before August 1958, see Documents 31 and 32 below: also NCNA, Jan. 22 and
Feb. 2, 1956 (the latter a speech by Ch'en Po-ta to the Chinese People's Political
Consultative Conference); CB 509 (organization of Shansi); CB 517, especially quotations from *People's Daily*, Aug. 11, 1958 ("labor armies" in Shansi) and from *Red Flag*, Aug. 16, 1958 (mess halls organized in 1957); ECMM 100 (*Planned Economy*, Aug. 9, 1957—how to organize rural labor power); ECMM 147 (*Red Flag*, Sept. 16, 1958—new organization during the 1956 leap forward); and ECMM 155 (*New China*, Nov. 10, 1958—regulations of the Shansi labor army).

———————————————TEXT OF DOCUMENT 27———————————————

To carry out gradually the technological revolution and cultural revolution simultaneously with the socialist revolution on the political and ideological fronts, to develop industry and agriculture simultaneously with priority development of heavy industry, to develop central and local industries simultaneously under centralized leadership, over-all planning and in coordination and to develop large, medium-sized and small enterprises simultaneously are the main points of the general line laid down by the 2nd session of the 8th National Congress of the Party on the basis of Chairman Mao's recommendations for socialist construction—to build more, faster, better and more economically by exerting efforts to the utmost and pressing ahead consistently. It is proved ever more clearly that these main points are of great revolutionary significance for accelerating the socialist development of our country, particularly for stimulating the creativeness of localities and the people.

The high degree of creativeness of localities and the people has been demonstrated in the irrigation movement and accumulate-manure campaign since last winter and autumn. The present movement for developing medium and small industrial enterprises once again demonstrates the might of such a high-degree creativeness.

According to data released by the State Bureau of Statistics, the local units and agricultural producers cooperatives have started construction work this year on more than 800,000 small and medium-sized factories and mines. It is remarkable that before June this year 12,680 small blast furnaces will have been built capable of increasing the iron-smelting capacity by 20,000,000 tons, that before June next year more than 200 small converters will have been built capable of increasing the iron-refining capacity by 10,000,000 tons, three times the existing capacity of the Anshan Steel Works, and that after completing more than 1,400 small and medium-sized nonferrous metals mining enterprises, output of copper and aluminum will top the 1957 national level.

Thus, in a little more than one year a number of departments will catch up or surpass the national scope of the First Five-Year Plan as regards development of medium and small industrial enterprises. Thanks to the massive development of local medium and small industrial enterprises, some departments of industry are expected to reach this year the output targets which they originally planned to achieve by 1962 i.e. the end of the Second Five-Year Plan period.

In agriculture, it can also be seen generally that barring extraordinary natural disasters, output of some main crops this year will also reach or approach the output envisaged for the last year of the Second Five-Year Plan.

Such is the outlook of leap forward achieved in the productive force of society through the full display of local creativeness and mass creativeness.

True, possibility does not amount to reality. But when we think of the heroic spirit of the millions shown in working miracles and when we think of the inexhaustible potentialities of localities, we shall be convinced that the above possibility will certainly be translated into reality.

The main points of the general line thoroughly solved the problems arising from the general revival of our national economy and its high rate of growth, thereby constantly reforming the society as a whole.

The first issue of *Hung Chi* carried two news letters from the Och'eng *hsien* committee in Hupeh—"Hsukuang No. 1 cooperative sets up small factories in traditional ways" and "How does the Hsukuang No. 1 cooperative direct and manage small factories". Both news letters related new things developed in a cooperative. The first news letter dwelt on how a cooperative set up a series of "small factories" which pressed forward the development of agriculture. The second news letter dwelt on how to unite the agricultural administration and industrial administration. This cooperative is a brilliant example showing the high-degree display of local creativeness and mass creativeness and is actually a miniature of the general revival of our national economy. It said that "these small factories are marked by fast construction, fast production and great results": this shows the part the local and mass creativeness will play in the industrialization of our country. From these two news letters we see China leaping forward and new society and new people emerging. Here the people are almost all heroes with great vigor and strong will. They dare to think, say and act; and when they act they are able to listen to the opinions of all, take a firm footing and keep good order. In a word, they have ideal and methods. In Chairman Mao's word, they are "writing the newest and most beautiful characters" and "painting the newest and most beautiful pictures" on a clean sheet of paper.

The methods adopted by this cooperative consist generally of the following:

(1) To transform a cooperative into a basic-level organization of both agricultural cooperation and industrial cooperation, actually a people's commune in which agriculture and industry are combined.

(2) To develop industry for the purpose of meeting the needs of the cooperative and serving agricultural production and not for the purpose of profit-making.

(3) To make do with available things. Small factories to be built first and then gradually expanded.

(4) To launch an "all-round men" campaign. Members are to master the farming technique as well as techniques of industry. "Peasants in the field and workmen in factories".

(5) To learn while working and acquire experience everywhere. To acquire some ordinary knowledge of science and technology first and then gradually raise their knowledge. Technological revolution is integrated with cultural revolution.

(6) Administrative personnel are to learn both the art of administration and the industrial technique. They are to be both functionaries and workmen.

(7) Except in individual and special cases, work points are to be recorded for industry as is done for agriculture. In general, work points applicable to factories may not be higher or lower than those applicable to agriculture but should be flexible in certain ways. They should vary with different types of work.

(8) Working hours are the same for industry and agriculture. If extra work is done in night time, work points are to be given at progressive rate as a measure of reward.

(9) On the principle of coordination between industry and agriculture, small factories are to draw up both annual targets of struggle and seasonal targets of struggle.

Can it be said that what this cooperative is doing is actually an indication that our country can develop the productive forces of society at a rate unknown in history, can quickly eliminate the distinction between industry and agriculture and the distinction between mental and physical labor, thereby to open a road on which our country can smoothly pass over from socialism to communism? I think it can be said.

Over a hundred years ago, Engels stated in his "Communist Principles" that after the abolition of the private property, "overproduction that exceeds the immediate needs of the society will, instead of causing a disaster, ensure satisfaction of the needs of all citizens, will give rise to new needs and at the same time will create means to satisfy such new demands". "Production undertaken by the forces of the whole society and the new development of production arising therefrom will need new people and will create new people". "Industry undertaken by the whole society in the common interests according to plans will all the more need all-round men i.e. men versed in the whole system of production". "Education can speedily acquaint young people with the whole system of production and can enable them to get transferred from one production department to another according to the needs of the society and their liking". "... contradiction between town and country will disappear. Those performing agricultural and industrial labor will be the same persons instead of two different classes." What Engels said at the time was an ideal based on the law of development of society. Can it be said that illuminated by the general line of our Party for building socialism more, faster, better and more economically, the Hsukuang No. 1 cooperative is concretely and gradually realizing such an ideal of the founder of scientific communism? I think it can be said.

The titles of both news letters used modestly the words "small factories". But such "small factories" linked up with agriculture have infinite vitality because what they represent is invincible, new and progressive force, a communist force.

DOCUMENT 28

Resolution of the Central Committee of the Chinese Communist Party on the Establishment of People's Communes in the Rural Areas (Peitaiho Resolution), August 29, 1958.

The text used here is an official translation in a pamphlet entitled *People's Communes in China*, published by the Foreign Languages Press, Peking, 1958, pp. 1-8. The full Chinese version was first published by NCNA on September 9, 1958.

Comment. The general tone of this resolution is often extravagant—for example, "Since Right conservatism has been overcome ... the output of agricultural products has doubled or increased several-fold, in some cases more than ten times or scores of times." Communism, moreover, is said to be "no longer a thing of the distant future." Nevertheless, the text is reasonably cautious about detailed timetables, e.g., for the formation of communes throughout the country, the handing over of privately-owned plots of land, and the transition from "collective ownership" to "ownership by the whole people." For further examples of wild propaganda on the advance to Communism, see Document 30 below, also CB 517 (*People's Daily*, Aug. 6, 1958) and CB 520 (*People's Daily* on the Hsushui Commune, Aug. 23, 26, 27, 29, 30, and Sept. 1, 1958).

———————————TEXT OF DOCUMENT 28———————————

1. The people's communes are the logical result of the march of events. Large, comprehensive people's communes have made their appearance, and in several places they are already widespread. They have developed very rapidly in some areas. It is highly probable that there will soon be an upsurge in setting up people's communes throughout the country and the development is irresistible. The basis for the development of the people's communes is mainly the all-round, continuous leap forward in China's agricultural production and the ever-rising political consciousness of the 500 million peasants. An unprecedented advance has been made in agricultural capital construction since the advocates of the capitalist road were fundamentally defeated economically, politically and ideologically. This has created a new basis for practically eliminating flood and drought, and for ensuring the comparatively stable advance of agricultural production. Agriculture has leaped forward since Right conservatism has been overcome and the old technical norms in agriculture have been broken down. The output of agricultural products has doubled or increased several-fold, in some cases more than ten times or scores of times. This has further stimulated emancipation of thought among the people. Large-scale agricultural capital construction and the application of more advanced agricultural technique are making their demands on labour power. The growth of rural industry also demands the transfer of some manpower from agriculture. The demand for mechanization and electrification has become increasingly urgent in China's rural areas. Capital construction in agriculture and the struggle for bumper harvests involve large-scale co-operation which cuts across the boundaries between co-operatives, townships and counties. The people have taken to organizing themselves along military lines, working with militancy, and leading a collective life, and this has raised the political consciousness of the 500 million peasants still further. Community dining rooms, kindergartens, nurseries, sewing groups, barber shops, public baths, happy homes for the aged, agricultural middle schools, "red and expert" schools, are leading the peasants towards a happier collective life and further fostering ideas of collectivism among the peasant masses. What all these things illustrate is that the agricultural co-operative with scores of families or several hundred families can no longer meet the needs of the changing situation. In the present circumstances, the establishment of people's communes with all-round management of agriculture, forestry, animal husbandry, side-occupations and fishery, where industry (the worker), agriculture (the peasant), exchange (the trader), culture and education (the student) and military affairs (the militiaman) merge into one, is the fundamental policy to guide the peasants to accelerate socialist construction, complete the building of socialism ahead of time and carry out the gradual transition to communism.

2. Concerning the organization and size of the communes. Generally speaking, it is at present better to establish one commune to a township with the commune comprising about two thousand

peasant households. Where a township embraces a vast area and is sparsely populated, more than one commune may be established, each with less than two thousand households. In some places, several townships may merge and form a single commune comprising about six or seven thousand households, according to topographical conditions and the needs for the development of production. As to the establishment of communes of more than 10,000 or even more than 20,000 households, we need not oppose them, but for the present we should not take the initiative to encourage them.

As the people's communes grow there may be a tendency to form federations with the county as a unit. Plans should be drawn up right now on a county basis to ensure the rational distribution of people's communes.

The size of the communes and the all-round development of agriculture, forestry, animal husbandry, subsidiary production and fishery as well as of industry (the worker), agriculture (the peasant), exchange (the trader), culture and education (the student) and military affairs (the militiaman), demand an appropriate division of labour within the administrative organs of the communes; a number of departments, each responsible for a particular kind of work, should be set up, following the principle of compactness and efficiency in organization and of cadres taking direct part in production. The township governments and the communes should become one, with the township committee of the Party becoming the Party committee of the commune and the township people's council becoming the administrative committee of the commune.

3. Concerning the methods and steps to be adopted to merge small co-operatives into bigger ones and transform them into people's communes. The merger of small co-operatives into bigger ones and their transformation into people's communes is now a common mass demand. The poor and the lower-middle peasants firmly support it; most upper-middle peasants also favour it. We must rely on the poor and the lower-middle peasants and fully encourage the masses to air their views and argue it out, unite the majority of the upper-middle peasants who favour it, overcome vacillation among the remainder, and expose and foil rumour-mongering and sabotage by landlord and rich-peasant elements, so that the mass of the peasants merge the smaller co-operatives into bigger ones and transform them into communes through ideological emancipation and on a voluntary basis, without any compulsion. As to the steps to be taken, it is of course better to complete the merger into bigger co-ops and their transformation into communes at once; but where this is not feasible, it can be done in two stages, with no compulsory or rash steps. In all counties, experiments should first be made in some selected areas and the experience gained should then be popularized gradually.

The merger of smaller co-operatives into bigger ones and their transformation into communes must be carried out in close co-ordination with current production to ensure that it not only has no adverse effect on current production, but becomes a tremendous force stimulating an even greater leap forward in production. Therefore, in the early period of the merger, the method of "changing the upper structure while keeping the lower structure unchanged" may be adopted. The original, smaller co-operatives may at first jointly elect an administrative committee for the merged co-ops to unify planning and the arrangement of work, and transform themselves into farming zones or production brigades. The original organization of production and system of administration may, for the time being, remain unchanged and continue as before; and then later, step by step, merge, readjust and settle whatever needs merging or readjusting and whatever specific questions demand solution during the merger, so as to make sure there is no adverse effect on production.

The size of the communes, the speed of carrying out the merger of small co-operatives into bigger ones and their transformation into communes, and the methods and steps to be taken in this connection will be decided in accordance with the local conditions by the various provinces, autonomous regions and municipalities directly under the central authorities. But no matter when the merger takes place, whether before or after autumn, in the coming winter or next spring, the small co-operatives which are prepared to merge should be brought together from now on to discuss and jointly work out unified plans for post-autumn capital construction in agriculture and to make unified arrangements of all kinds for preparatory work for an even bigger harvest next year.

4. Concerning some questions of the economic policy involved in the merger of co-operatives. In the course of the merger, education should be strengthened to prevent the growth of departmentalism among a few co-operatives, which might otherwise share out too much or all of their income and leave little or no common funds before the merger. On the other hand, it must be understood that with various agricultural co-operatives established on different foundations, the amount of their public property,

their indebtedness inside and outside the co-operatives and so on will not be completely equal when they merge into bigger co-operatives. In the course of the merger, the cadres and the masses should be educated in the spirit of communism so as to recognize these differences and not resort to minute squaring of accounts, insisting on equal shares and bothering with trifles.

When a people's commune is established, it is not necessary to deal with the questions of reserved private plots of land, scattered fruit trees, share funds and so on in a great hurry; nor is it necessary to adopt clear-cut stipulations on these questions. Generally speaking, reserved private plots of land may perhaps be turned over to collective management in the course of the merger of co-operatives; scattered fruit trees, for the time being, may remain privately owned and be dealt with some time later. Share funds etc. can be handled after a year or two, since the funds will automatically become publicly owned with the development of production, the increase of income and the advance in the people's consciousness.

5. Concerning the name, ownership and system of distribution of the communes.

All the big merged co-operatives will be called people's communes. There is no need to change them into state-owned farms, for it is not proper for farms to embrace industry, agriculture, exchange, culture and education and military affairs at the same time.

After the establishment of people's communes, there is no need immediately to transform collective ownership into ownership by the people as a whole. It is better at present to maintain collective ownership to avoid unnecessary complications arising in the course of the transformation of ownership. In fact, collective ownership in people's communes already contains some elements of ownership by the people as a whole. These elements will grow constantly in the course of the continuous development of people's communes and will gradually replace collective ownership. The transition from collective ownership to ownership by the people as a whole is a process, the completion of which may take less time—three or four years—in some places, and longer—five or six years or even longer—elsewhere. Even with the completion of this transition, people's communes, like state-owned industry, are still socialist in character, where the principle of "from each according to his ability and to each according to his work" prevails. After a number of years, as the social product increases greatly, the communist consciousness and morality of the entire people are raised to a much higher degree, and universal education is instituted and developed, the differences between workers and peasants, town and country and mental and manual labour—legacies of the old society that have inevitably been carried over into the socialist period—and the remnants of unequal bourgeois rights which are the reflection of these differences, will gradually vanish, and the function of the state will be limited to protecting the country from external aggression but it will play no role internally. At that time Chinese society will enter the era of communism where the principle of "from each according to his ability and to each according to his needs" will be practised.

After the establishment of people's communes it is not necessary to hurry the change from the original system of distribution, in order to avoid any unfavourable effect on production. The system of distribution should be determined according to specific conditions. Where conditions permit, the shift to a wage system may be made. But where conditions are not yet ripe, the original system of payment according to workdays may be temporarily retained (such as the system of fixed targets for output, workdays and costs, with a part of the extra output as reward; or the system of calculating workdays on the basis of output). This can be changed when conditions permit.

Although ownership in the people's communes is still collective ownership and the system of distribution, either the wage system or payment according to workdays, is "to each according to his work" and not "to each according to his needs," the people's communes are the best form of organization for the attainment of socialism and gradual transition to communism. They will develop into the basic social units in communist society.

6. At the present stage our task is to build socialism. The primary purpose of establishing people's communes is to accelerate the speed of socialist construction and the purpose of building socialism is to prepare actively for the transition to communism. It seems that the attainment of communism in China is no longer a remote future event. We should actively use the form of the people's communes to explore the practical road of transition to communism.

DOCUMENT 29

Greet the Upsurge in Forming People's Communes, editorial in *Red Flag*, September 1, 1958.

The text used here is an official translation in a pamphlet entitled *People's Communes in China*, Foreign Languages Press, Peking, 1958, pp. 9-16.

Comment. Though the text is again cautious about the timetable of transition, the detailed examples given suggest a highly enthusiastic mood. For example, it mentions the abolition of the "last vestiges of private ownership" at the Weihsing commune, and the institution of the supply system for grain. Some of the caution about the premature use of the term "Communism" and "stretching the intensity of labor" is probably due to memories of the minor leap forward in 1956, when such things certainly occurred (see our General Introduction, part IV).

─────────────────────TEXT OF DOCUMENT 29─────────────────────

Following the great victories in agricultural production this summer and autumn, peasants over wide areas are becoming further organized: small co-operatives are being amalgamated into large ones, the agricultural producers' co-operatives are being transformed into people's communes where the township[1] and the commune become one entity and industry (the worker), agriculture (the peasant), exchange (the trader), culture and education (the student) and military affairs (the militiaman) merge into one. The establishment of people's communes is shaping up as a new, irresistible tide of mass movement on a nation-wide scale. In not a few places peasants of entire counties have organized themselves in people's communes in a very short period of time. In places where communes have not yet been set up, the broad mass of peasant activists are making preparations. They will strive to found communes through mass airing of views and debates around the time of the autumn harvest. The existing people's communes have shown even greater superiority over the farm co-operatives, in spurring the initiative of the masses in production, raising the rate of utilization of labour power and labour productivity, enlarging productive capital construction, accelerating the cultural and technical revolutions and in promoting public welfare.

The fact that the broad masses enthusiastically welcome the establishment of people's communes shows that this is the logical trend of development of the present situation. The main foundations of the development of people's communes are the all-round and continuous leap forward of China's agricultural production and the constantly growing political consciousness of the 500 million peasants. The Chinese peasants, having defeated capitalism economically, politically and ideologically and having overcome Right conservatism in agricultural production, have carried out agricultural capital construction on an unprecedented scale, adopted advanced technical measures in farming and thereby are doubling farm yields or increasing them by several, a dozen or scores of times. At the same time, small and medium industrial enterprises are being rapidly developed in the countryside (including county seats and towns) so as to develop agricultural production further, to develop industry over wide areas of the countryside, to promote the integration of industry and agriculture and to raise the standard of living of the rural population.

These changes in the countryside enable the peasants to see that the original organizational form of the agricultural producers' co-operative, which is relatively small in scale and has relatively few fields of operation, can no longer meet the requirements of the development of the productive forces. In fact, peasants in many places have already had to break down the demarcation lines between small co-operatives, between small townships and sometimes even between counties, in the course of constructing irrigation works, levelling and improving land, afforesting, struggling against natural calamities, mechanizing agriculture, building hydro-electric power plants and improving communications and living conditions in the countryside on a large scale. Besides, for the farm co-operatives to operate agriculture alone has become entirely backward. The farm co-operative not only has to become a unit for joint management of agriculture, forestry, animal husbandry, side-occupations

---

[1] The basic administrative unit in the countryside.

and fishery at one and the same time, but it also has to become a unified organizational unit where industry, agriculture, trade, education and culture, and military affairs merge into one. Thus, the merger of the township people's council[2] and the farm co-operative facilitates unified leadership and the rapid expansion of the social productive forces, while the separation of the township and the co-operative has become entirely unnecessary. To make full use of labour power, to enable women to play their full part in field work and to ensure that there is no waste of the labour time of men and women, the farm co-operatives must be not only organizers of production but also organizers of the way of life; not only do they have to collectivize labour further, but also to organize the collective way of life. On the basis of this urgent need, public canteens, nurseries, kindergartens, sewing teams, etc. are being formed in large numbers. All this demands that the agricultural producers' co-operatives take an additional step forward—to transform themselves into people's communes.

This transformation involves not only the enlargement of organization and the scope of management but also important changes in the relations of production. The people's communes in many places—for instance, the Weihsing (Sputnik) Commune in Suiping County, Honan Province, that is described in another article in this issue of *Hongqi*—have wiped out certain last vestiges of private ownership of the means of production (owing to the ever-growing need to work collectively and the extension of public canteen service to all the members, it becomes both impossible and unnecessary for them to keep small personal plots of land and breed their own pigs). And they have gone beyond the pattern of collective ownership in certain respects. Moreover, from such developments as the supply system of grain within the commune, people can easily see the budding sprouts of communism.

Of course, when the people's communes are established, it is not immediately necessary to transform collective ownership into ownership by the whole people and it is even less appropriate to strain to advance from socialism, i.e. the primary phase of communism, to its higher phase. The transition from collective ownership to ownership by the whole people is a process which may be fairly quick in one place and slower in another. After a period following the transition to ownership by the whole people, the productive forces of society will be expanded even more greatly; the products of society will become extremely abundant; the communist ideology, consciousness and moral character of the entire people will be raised immensely; and education will be universal and raised to a higher level. At the same time, differences between workers and peasants, between town and country as well as between mental and manual work—the remnants of old society that cannot but be retained during the socialist period—will gradually disappear; the remnants of unequal bourgeois rights which reflect these differences will also gradually disappear. Then the function of the state will only be to deal with aggression from external enemies; it will no longer be useful internally. By that time our country will enter a new era, from the socialist era based on the principle of "from each according to his ability and to each according to his work" to the communist era based on the principle of "from each according to his ability and to each according to his needs."

The present people's commune offers our country a good form of organization to accelerate socialist construction and the transition to communism. It will not only be the primary unit of our society at the present stage but will grow and become the primary unit of the future communist society.

The fact that the broad mass of working people, without any hesitation, accept this form of organization, the people's commune, and change some outdated relations of production, is due not only to the development of the productive forces of our society at a flying speed, but also because the Chinese people have grasped the guiding ideology of the Communist Party's Central Committee and Comrade Mao Tse-tung on uninterrupted revolution. The working people want no pause in the course of the revolution and they see that the more rapidly the revolution advances, the more benefits they will derive. In the course of their advance the working people have put forward these slogans which are full of revolutionary spirit: Get organized along military lines, do things the way battle duties are carried out and live collective lives. "Get organized along military lines" of course does not mean that they are really organized into military barracks, nor does it mean that they give themselves the titles of generals, colonels and lieutenants. It simply means that the swift expansion of agriculture demands that they should greatly strengthen their organization, act more quickly and with greater discipline and efficiency, so that, like factory workers and armymen, they can be deployed with

---

[2] Local government.

greater freedom and on a large scale. That is why they have come to the conclusion that they should organize along military lines. The peasant leaders who have put forward these slogans do not know perhaps that Marx and Engels in the *Communist Manifesto* had long since advanced a programme for the "establishment of industrial armies, especially for agriculture." But they and the broad mass of the peasants who have gone through the long years of the armed struggles of the people's revolution know perfectly well that military lines are nothing to be feared. On the contrary, it is only natural to them that the whole population should be citizen soldiers ready to cope with the imperialist aggressors and their lackeys. Although the organization of agricultural labour along military lines at present is for waging battles against nature and not human enemies, it is nonetheless not difficult to transform one kind of struggle into another.

While no external enemies attack us, the people's communes, in which the workers, peasants, traders, students and militiamen are merged into one, aim to storm the fortresses of nature and to march to the happy future of industrialization, urbanization and communism in the countryside. If and when external enemies dare to attack us, then the entire armed population will be mobilized to wipe out the enemies resolutely, thoroughly and completely.

Would this breed commandism? In our opinion, for the people's communes to be organized along military lines and to arm the entire population is a completely different matter from commandism. Without the people's communes, without the organization along military lines and without citizen soldiers, commandism can occur all the same. On the contrary, with the people's communes, with organization along military lines and with citizen soldiers, commandism can be avoided and the highest degree of democracy can be realized. Actually, as the productivity of labour is being constantly raised, as the mechanization and electrification of farm work is more and more developed, as there is a constantly increasing amount of social products and the people's cultural level is further raised, labour time will be gradually shortened, the intensity of labour will be gradually reduced and in this way the possibilities of overcoming commandism become greater and greater.

To organize along military lines, to do things the way battle duties are carried out and to live collective lives certainly does not mean that the intensity of labour should be infinitely stretched. As the Central Committee of the Party has pointed out, we should do our work rhythmically and combine hard battle with necessary rest and regrouping. Besides, discipline and centralization in work must be built on the voluntary and democratic basis of the masses.

The very establishment and development of the people's communes must go through the process of thorough mental ferment among the masses. Only through a full airing of views and debates, only when the people in a locality are willing to go in for it entirely out of their own accord, should the agricultural producers' co-operatives be transformed into people's communes. In the present conditions when the upsurge of our country's agricultural production is welling up so, when the revolutionary consciousness of our peasants is so mature and the cadres of our Party have become so closely knit with the masses in the course of leading the rectification campaign and production, we believe that the people's communes, with their inherent advantages, are sure to grow rapidly throughout the country.

DOCUMENT 30

Hold High the Red Flag of People's Communes and March On, editorial in *People's Daily*, September 3, 1958.

The text used here is an official translation in the pamphlet entitled *People's Communes in China*, Foreign Languages Press, Peking, 1958, pp. 17–25.

Comment. This *People's Daily* editorial is perhaps the most optimistic of all about the transition to Communism. The timetable for transition to "ownership by the whole people" remains "at most six years"; and the transition to Communism will take place "after another few years" only. On the question of industrial development, see our General Introduction, parts VII and VIII. For further typical accounts, see NCNA stories of August 18 and 21 from Chengchow about the targets of the Hsing-yang hsien, and of September 1 about the "ball-bearingization" of farm wagons in Tsinghai. Some of the most extravagant stories attracted criticism from the Party at the time. See URS, Vol. 14, No. 5 (*Liaoning Jih Pao*, Nov. 10, 1958), for an account of some local cadres who went too far in this direction.

In this document we have noted in square brackets three changes of wording supplied in an errata sheet included with the source pamphlet by the Foreign Languages Press. The footnotes were in the source pamphlet.

―――――――――――――TEXT OF DOCUMENT 30―――――――――――――

People's communes, which mark a new stage in the socialist movement in China's rural areas, are now being set up and developed in many places at a rapid rate.

This movement has been spontaneously started by the mass of peasants on the basis of great socialist consciousness. When a small number of people's communes were first established, their success at once inspired many of the agricultural producers' co-operatives to follow suit. The movement gradually gained momentum. Now, with the encouragement and guidance given by the Central Committee of the Communist Party and Chairman Mao Tse-tung, it is making even greater strides forward. *Tatsepao*[1] are appearing everywhere in the countryside, and a great number of applications have been made for the establishment of people's communes. Virtually all the peasants in Honan and Liaoning provinces are now members of people's communes and the movement is in high tide in the provinces of Hopei, Heilungkiang, and Anhwei. Meanwhile, preparations are being made in northwestern China, the Yangtse valley and provinces south of the Yangtse River to establish people's communes after the autumn harvest.

Where the people's communes have already come into existence, the peasants, beating drums and gongs, celebrated the occasion with great joy, and their enthusiasm for production has reached a new height. The poor and middle peasants, in particular, rejoice in the formation of the commune and regard it as the "realization of a long-cherished dream." [Errata sheet by Foreign Languages Press changes "middle peasants" to "lower middle peasants."]

The people's commune is characterized by its bigger size and more socialist nature. With big membership and huge expanse of land the communes can carry out production and construction of a comprehensive nature and on a large scale. They not only carry out an all-round management of agriculture, forestry, animal husbandry, side-occupations and fishery, but merge industry (the worker), agriculture (the peasant), exchange (the trader), culture and education (the student), and military affairs (the militiaman) into one.

People's communes so far established usually have a membership of 10,000 people each, in some cases 10,000 households. A commune generally corresponds to a township. If a township is too small, then several townships may be combined to form a commune.

Being big, they can do many things hitherto impossible to the agricultural producers' co-operatives, such as building medium-sized water-conservancy works, setting up factories and mines requiring complicated technique, carrying out big projects of road and housing construction, establishing secondary schools and schools of higher learning, etc. As a matter of fact, many of these undertakings are being carried out by the large communes and the matter of manpower shortage also becomes easier to tackle.

The people's commune represents a much higher degree of socialist development and collectivization than the agricultural producers' co-operative. Its massive scale of production requires organization with a higher efficiency and greater manoeuvrability of labour as well as the participation of all the women in production. Consequently more and more community canteens, nurseries, sewing groups and other kinds of establishments are being set up, and the last remnants of individual ownership of the means of production retained in the agricultural producers' co-operatives are being eliminated. In many places, for instance, the reserved plots, livestock, orchards and major items of production tools owned by individual peasants have been transferred to the people's communes in the course of their organization.

[1]Opinions and criticisms written out in bold Chinese characters on large sheets of paper and posted for everybody to see.

Ownership of the means of production by the whole people has been instituted by a few people's communes on the basis of the full agreement of their members. In the method of payment they are making experiments on both the wage and supply systems. These experiments are necessary because they help to point out the road to the further development of the relations of production in the countryside.

As the people's commune has for its membership workers, peasants, traders, students and militiamen it is no longer a solely economic organization—it combines economic, cultural, political and military affairs into one entity. There is, therefore, no longer any need for the separate existence of township governments. The management committees of the people's communes are in fact the people's councils of the townships. There is also a tendency for the federation of people's communes in a county to become one with the people's council of that county. This facilitates unified leadership, closely combines the collective economy of the agricultural producers' co-operatives with the state economy of the townships and counties and helps the transition from the collective ownership to ownership by the whole people.

For this reason the people's commune is the most appropriate organizational form in China for accelerating socialist construction and the transition to communism. It will become the basic social unit in the future communist society as thinkers—from many outstanding utopian socialists to Marx, Engels, and Lenin—had predicted on many occasions.

The transformation of agricultural producers' co-operatives into people's communes is the inevitable trend in the development of Chinese history.

China has now some 700,000 agricultural producers' co-operatives, mostly set up during the upsurge of socialism[2] in 1955 and later gradually transformed into advanced co-operatives. They are undoubtedly far superior to individual farming, mutual-aid teams, and even the elementary agricultural producers' co-operatives, and have contributed enormously to the steady increase of China's farm output in the past few years. With the growth of agricultural production, especially the great leap forward in agriculture since last winter, these co-operatives have, however, gradually become inadequate to meet fully the needs of the day. The reason is as follows. These co-operatives are comparatively small in size. Averaging less than two hundred [errata sheet by Foreign Languages Press changes this to "one hundred"] households in membership they have but a small amount of manpower. The amount of their public reserve funds is small and the rate of accumulation slow. With these handicaps it is difficult for them to engage in many kinds of production.

To achieve a high-speed advance in agriculture, enable the countryside to assume a new aspect at an early date, and improve the peasants' living standards as quickly as possible, as facts show, it is necessary to carry out large-scale capital construction that will fundamentally change the natural conditions; to apply new farming techniques; to develop forestry, animal husbandry, side-occupations and fishery side by side with agriculture; to build industries that serve agriculture and the needs of the peasants as well as big industries; gradually to carry out mechanization and electrification; to improve transport, communications and housing conditions in rural areas; and set up educational, health and cultural establishments—to do all this is beyond the power of an agricultural producers' co-operative consisting of a few dozens or hundreds of households.

The agricultural producers' co-operatives which merged into the present Chao Ying People's Commune in Shangcheng, Honan Province, previously had little industry though they abound in natural resources. After the formation of the commune 2,500 cadres and 17,500 members were allocated to the work and in ten days steel and iron plants, and factories making machinery, chemical fertilizer, cement, etc.—4,530 all told—were built, of which 3,250 enterprises soon went into operation. Here, the superiority of people's communes is clearly visible.

In the work of building water-conservancy projects, afforestation, combating drought, and flood prevention since last winter, the agricultural producers' co-operatives in many places acutely felt the inferiority of small co-operatives and the incompetency of their original labour organization to develop potential power and raise labour efficiency. Hence many small co-operatives spontaneously

---

[2]This refers to the upsurge of the agricultural co-operative movement in the latter half of 1955 and the first half of 1956, and, under its impulse, the nation-wide upsurge which swept individual handicraftsmen into co-operatives and transformed capitalist industry and commerce into joint state-private operation.

joined hands, and socialist co-operation between co-operatives of different townships, different counties, and even different provinces was carried out. A series of measures have also been taken to "get organized along military lines, work with a fighting spirit, and live in a collective way." This shows that the agricultural co-operatives, which are small in size, meagre in items of production and low in the degree of collectivization, are becoming handicaps to the further development of the productive forces.

It must be pointed out that the rapid growth of the people's communes definitely does not stem solely from economic causes. The keenness shown by the mass of peasants towards the people's communes speaks first of all of their greatly increased socialist and communist consciousness.

Through the 1957 debate among the rural population on the socialist and capitalist roads of development in the countryside, the Communist Party smashed the attack launched by the bourgeois rightists, landlords, rich peasants, and counter-revolutionaries, and overcame the capitalist trend among the well-to-do middle peasants. Later, through the rectification campaign, it fundamentally changed the relations between the cadres and the masses and eliminated the rightist conservative ideas in agricultural production. During the current leap forward in agricultural production and rural work the mass of peasants have witnessed not only a several-fold increase in agricultural production but also the happy future of industrialization and urbanization of rural areas. As a result, the prestige of the Party has become more consolidated than ever among the peasants. The peasants have shown an unprecedentedly firm determination to achieve socialism at an earlier date and to prepare conditions for the gradual transition to communism. While striving for the quickest advance in production and in culture and education, the peasants are trying to establish new relations of production and new organizational forms best suited to the development of the productive forces. Without political consciousness as a basis, development of the people's commune movement would be impossible and inconceivable.

The establishment of people's communes has provided good conditions for the further development of the relations of production in the countryside. The expansion of the people's communes and the merger of people's communes and townships into one entity, which facilitates the rapid advance of industry, mining, communications, culture and education in the rural areas, makes it possible gradually to eliminate the differences between rural and urban areas, between peasants and workers, between peasants and intellectuals, as well as between collective ownership and ownership by the whole people.

The present people's commune movement does not, however, require the immediate transformation, in all cases, of collective ownership into ownership by the whole people. Even less does it mean the transition from the lower stage of socialism which is based on the principle "from each according to his ability, to each according to his work," to its higher stage, i.e. communism, which is based on the principle "from each according to his ability, to each according to his needs."

Some people's communes may have gone farther than others, but generally speaking, the transformation of collective ownership into ownership by the whole people is a process that will take three or four years, even five or six years, to complete in the rural areas. After another few years [errata sheet by Foreign Languages Press changes this to "Then, after a number of years"], production will be greatly increased. The people's communist consciousness and morality will be highly improved. Education will be made universal and elevated among the people. Differences between workers and peasants, urban and rural areas, mental and manual labour—left over from the old society and inevitably existing in the socialist society—as well as the remnants of unequal bourgeois rights which are the reflection of these differences, will gradually vanish, the function of the state will be limited to protecting the country from external aggression; it will play no role in domestic affairs. By that time Chinese society will enter the era of communism, the era when the principle "from each according to his ability, to each according to his needs" will be realized.

Now the development of people's communes is growing into a mass movement more gigantic than the co-operative movement of 1955. The Party committees of various places must work out appropriate plans and give active guidance to the development according to local conditions. The development of people's communes will doubtlessly be different in time, scale, pace, and method in different places. Uniformity should not be imposed. People's communes must be set up on the basis of full discussion by the people concerned and it must be a matter of the people's own choice. No rash, impetuous, or domineering attitude should be taken, especially on the question concerning change in the ownership of the means of production.

At present, work in the autumn fields allows for no delay while preparations must be made for the farm work of the coming winter and the next spring. We must give first priority to work related to production in all places, regardless of the condition whether people's communes have or have not been established.

DOCUMENT 31

Tentative Regulations (Draft) of the Weihsing (Sputnik) People's Commune, August 7, 1958.

The text is an official translation in a pamphlet entitled *People's Communes in China,* Foreign Languages Press, Peking, 1958, pp. 61–80.

Comment. The regulations were first published in the *People's Daily,* September 4, 1958. In an annex were included alternative versions of articles 7 and 8 on marketing and credit which tempered somewhat the original draft's centralizing enthusiasm. The annex is printed here as a part of the document.

The *People's Daily* also introduced the regulations with a brief editor's note and discussed their significance in an editorial. The editor's note explained that the Weihsing commune (in Suip'ing *hsien,* Province of Honan) was established in April 1958 by the merger of twenty-seven agricultural producers' cooperatives in four *hsiang* (townships). CB 524 contains a translation of a report by Wu Chih-p'u, First Secretary of the Honan Provincial Committee of the Party, in which the popular origin of the Weihsing and other communes is emphasized. According to the *People's Daily,* the commune consisted of 9,300 households, comprising 43,000 people. It was thus one of the larger units. The newspaper said the draft regulations were being published in full as reference material for all other parts of the country, and it is clear from Document 42 below that the Weihsing commune had served as a model for study for some weeks before the Central Committee resolution on communes (Document 28) was adopted in late August. The Party committee of Hsinyang *hsien* had, for example, held a conference at the Weihsing commune from July 29 to August 4, 1958, on the management and control of communes (NCNA, Chengchow, Aug. 21, 1958).

Points emphasized in the *People's Daily* editorial of September 4 (not printed here, but available in English in the pamphlet *People's Communes in China,* pp. 81–90) include the following:

1. Communes will gradually, as production develops, substitute the wage system for the working and bonus system (the equivalent of piece-work pay in industry). The free supply of grain will be put into practice when "grain production is highly developed and when members of the commune unanimously agree to it." On this, see Documents 34, 35, and 36 below, with comments.

2. Plans should be made for the amalgamation of communes so as to coincide with the *hsien* (county) unit.

3. The merging of agricultural producers' cooperatives should be conducted so as to have the minimum effect on production. "The original small cooperatives may be changed into... production brigades. The original production organizations and management systems should remain unchanged for the time being and go on operating as usual... All the concrete problems that should be solved in the course of the merger may be dealt with step by step later so that production will not be affected." (This includes questions of land reserved for private use, small holdings of fruit trees, and the share funds of cooperatives.) There was probably some fear that blind imitation of the more "progressive" articles of the Weihsing draft (e.g., articles 4 and 5) might lead to chaos.

Other points of particular interest in Document 31 are contained in:

Article 6: The development of industry, especially ball-bearings, which received much publicity at this time (see comment on Document 30 above).

Article 9: "The commune should institute a system of universal, compulsory education combined closely with labour." See Document 26, above, and our comment in Chapter IX, below; also CB 539 and 540, which contain material on the institution of primary boarding schools within the communal framework. On this, see our General Introduction, part VIII, and our general comment in the present chapter.

Article 13: The division of responsibilities in a large commune between communal leadership and the "production brigade."

―――――――――――――――TEXT OF DOCUMENT 31―――――――――――――――

Article 1 The people's commune is a basic unit of society in which the working people unite of their own free will under the leadership of the Communist Party and the People's Government. Its task is to manage all industrial and agricultural production, trade, cultural and educational work and political affairs within its own sphere.

Article 2 The intent and purpose of the people's commune is to consolidate the socialist system and energetically create the conditions for the gradual transition to the communist system.

To this end, we must exert our utmost effort, and press ahead consistently to achieve greater, faster, better and more economical results in developing industry, agriculture and cultural and educational work, to carry through the technical and cultural revolutions, to gradually reduce the differences between town and country and between mental and manual labour.

As the social product becomes abundant and the people have high political consciousness, so will the transition from the principle of "from each according to his ability, to each according to his work" to the principle of "from each according to his ability, to each according to his needs" be gradually effected.

Article 3 Citizens who are over 16 years old are admitted as full members. Former landlords, rich peasants, counter-revolutionaries and other people deprived of political rights may be accepted as unofficial members and, when granted political rights according to law, may be accepted as full members.

All members have the duty to carry out the commune's regulations and resolutions, observe labour discipline and cherish and protect public property. Excepting mental defectives, full members have the right to elect, to be elected, to vote and to supervise the commune's affairs. Unofficial members have not the right to elect, to be elected or to vote in the commune, but they may enjoy the same economic treatment as full members.

Article 4 When the agricultural producers' co-operatives merge into the people's commune, they must, regardless of excess or deficiency, turn over all their collectively-owned property to the commune in the communist spirit of wide-scale co-ordination. Their former debts shall be paid off by the commune, excluding those for use in that year's production expenses, which should be settled by the co-operatives themselves. The share funds contributed by the co-operative members remain registered under their respective names, and bear no interest. Investments made by the co-operative members will be repaid by the commune.

Those who are accepted as commune members as having reached the age of 16, or after moving in from other parts of the country, need not make good the contribution of share funds. When a commune member moves away or dies, his share funds shall not be withdrawn.

Article 5 In changing over to the commune, the members of the co-operatives must turn over to the common ownership of the commune all privately-owned plots of farmland and house sites and other means of production such as livestock, tree holdings, etc., on the basis that common ownership of the means of production is in the main in effect. However, the co-operative members may keep a small number of domestic animals and fowls as private property. Privately-owned livestock and tree holdings when turned over to the common ownership of the commune should be evaluated and counted as the private investment of the co-operative members.

In applying for membership, the peasant households who work on their own should turn over to the common ownership of the commune all their means of production such as land, livestock, tree holdings, large farm tools, etc., with the exception of a small number of domestic animals and fowls. These means of production should be evaluated as share fund payments in accordance with the provisions of the former co-operatives, and the balance will then be regarded as investment by the owners concerned.

Article 6 To ensure a continuously expanding agricultural output the commune must continue to build irrigation works, apply more manure, improve the soil, use good strains of seed over large areas, breed draught animals, prevent and control insect pests and plant diseases, apply rational close-planting and practise deep ploughing and careful cultivation. It must make vigorous efforts to improve farm implements and carry into effect the mechanization of agriculture and the electrification of the countryside in the shortest possible time.

The commune must develop industry as rapidly as possible. The first things to be done in this field are to set up mines, iron and steel plants and factories for manufacturing ball-bearings, farm tools, fertilizer and building materials and for processing farm produce, repairing machinery, building hydro-electric power projects, installations for utilizing methane, and other enterprises.

The commune must, in a planned manner, build roads, dredge water-ways, improve the means of communications, install a telephone service and gradually build up a network of modern communications. Each production contingent must have one or two postmen to serve the commune members. The postmen shall be paid by the commune.

Article 7 The commune shall establish a supply and marketing department. The supply and marketing department is a basic organ of state trade. It receives funds from the higher state trading organs; its staff shall be paid by the commune. It shall deliver profits to the higher state trading organs, but the commune may retain a certain proportion of the profits. The commune must ensure that the supply and marketing department fulfil the tasks of state purchase and unified purchase[1] and implement the plan and system of the higher state trading organs, while at the same time it has the right to give concrete leadership over the business of the supply and marketing department.

The supply and marketing department should set up its branches in all production contingents, and retail departments in the community canteens of the production brigades which, so as fully to convenience the masses, are to render services at the dining hours. The supply and marketing branches shall keep their own accounts, while their gains and losses shall be managed by the supply and marketing department under a unified system. The funds of the supply and marketing branches shall be provided with the share funds contributed to the former supply and marketing co-operative by the members. The deficit shall be made up by the supply and marketing department. No dividends shall be given on the shares.

The supply and marketing department joins the county supply and marketing co-operative as a member organization.

Article 8 The commune shall establish a credit department. The credit department is an agency of the People's Bank. It receives funds from the People's Bank; its staff shall be paid by the commune. It shall deliver profits to the People's Bank, but the commune may retain a certain proportion of the profits. The commune must ensure that the credit department implement the plan and system of the People's Bank, while at the same time it has the right to give concrete leadership over the business of the credit department.

For the convenience of the people, the credit department should set up its branches in all production contingents and service centres in all production brigades. The credit branches shall keep their own accounts, while their gains and losses shall be managed by the credit department under a unified system. The funds of the credit branches shall be provided with the share funds contributed to the former credit co-operative by the members. The deficit shall be made up by the credit department.

As a cash treasury of the commune and the different production contingents, the credit department and its branches shall undertake the receipts and disbursement of cash in bulk. The credit depart-

---

[1] Grain, edible oil, mineral oil products [errata sheet by Foreign Languages Press changes this to "oil-bearing crops"], cotton and cotton piecegoods are five items earmarked exclusively for state purchase. Other commodities may also be purchased by the state in a unified way as determined by the condition of supply and demand on the home market.

ment shall undertake book settlement between the commune and other financial departments, and between the various departments in the commune which keep their own accounts. Book settlement is not to be practised among the commune members.

Article 9 The commune should, step by step, train its members to be cultured working people with professional skill and all-round qualifications.

The commune should institute a system of universal, compulsory education combined closely with labour. Primary schools and spare-time continuation schools should be set up on a wide scale so that by degrees all school-age children may attend school and all young people and the middle-aged may reach the educational level of senior primary school. Measures should be taken to ensure that step by step each production contingent will have a spare-time agricultural middle school to enable all young people and the middle-aged to attain the educational level of senior middle school. Conditions permitting, colleges or universities will be set up to meet the requirements of the commune. The working hours of the members may be duly reduced and their time for study increased when production reaches a higher level.

The commune should encourage and help its members to engage in scientific studies on a wide scale, first of all, studies and experiments in good-seed cultivation, soil improvement, tree planting, livestock breeding, elimination of insect pests and plant diseases, and the improvement of farming technique and tools.

Article 10 A system of citizen soldiery shall operate throughout the commune. The age-groups of young and middle-aged men as well as demobilized servicemen, should be organized into militia units that will undertake regular military training and fulfil tasks assigned by the state. The militiamen will be paid the usual wages when they undergo training and carry out tasks.

The commune shall undertake responsibility for compulsory military service and assign work to demobilized servicemen. Families of revolutionary martyrs, of disabled armymen and of armymen in active service that lack manpower should, to an appropriate extent, be given special consideration by the commune.

Article 11 As the commune has the same confines as a township, that is, one commune to a township, the township should be merged with the commune for the convenience of work. The deputies of the township people's congress will be concurrently representatives of the congress of the commune, members of the township people's council will be concurrently members of the management committee of the commune, the township head will be concurrently the head of the commune, the deputy heads of the township will be concurrently deputy heads of the commune, and the departments under the commune management committee will be concurrently the departments under the township people's council.

Article 12 The highest organization of management in the commune is the congress of the commune which will discuss and reach decisions on all important matters of the commune. The congress of the commune shall include representatives of all production brigades and all sections of the people, such as the women, youth, old people, cultural and educational workers, medical workers, scientific and technical workers, the personnel of industrial enterprises, traders and minority people.

The management committee shall be elected by the congress of the commune to take charge of the commune's affairs. It shall be composed of the head and deputy heads of the commune and committee members. Under it there shall be departments and commissions in charge of different jobs, such as agriculture, water conservancy, forestry, animal husbandry, industry and communications, finance and food supply, trade, cultural and educational work, armed defence, planning and scientific research, etc. The staffing of the departments and commissions shall be nominated by the management committee and be subject to the approval of the congress of the commune. The management committee may elect a group of standing members to handle its routine work.

A supervisory committee shall be elected by the commune congress to supervise the commune's affairs. It shall be composed of the chairman and vice-chairmen of the committee and committee members, and operates under the leadership of the state supervisory organs.

The term of office for the members of the commune's congress, its management committee and its supervisory committee shall be two years. Anyone seriously neglecting his duties may be dismissed by the electorate before the term of office expires.

Article 13 The commune shall institute a system of centralized leadership, with management organs at various levels, in order to operate a responsibility system in production. In accordance with the principle of facilitating production and leadership the commune shall organize its members into a number of production contingents which will divide up into a number of production brigades. The production contingent is a unit responsible for production and business accounting while its profits and losses are managed by the commune under a unified system. The production brigade is a basic unit for organizing labour. While ensuring the fulfilment of the general plan of the commune, the production contingent has, to a limited degree, the discretion of organizing production, undertaking capital construction, handling production expenses and distributing awards. The commune and production contingents should give an appropriate amount of award to those production contingents or brigades that have overfulfilled the planned production targets or economized production expenses. When agricultural mechanization is introduced, tractor teams should be organized with the production contingent as a unit. Bigger factories, mines, timber yards and livestock farms shall be run directly by the commune while the smaller ones may be left under the care of the contingents. Small machines and equipment such as sewing machines, methane pools and equipment for making granular fertilizer may be entrusted to the production brigades.

The production contingent shall have a representative conference, composed of the contingent's deputies to the commune congress. The conference shall elect a contingent leader, deputy leaders and a number of members to form the management committee of the contingent, and a chairman, vice-chairmen and a number of members to form a supervisory committee. The term of office for the members of these bodies shall be one year.

The general meeting of the members of the production brigade shall elect a brigade leader and deputy leaders to form a committee to lead the brigade's work.

Article 14 The commune shall operate a wage system when it acquires stability of income and adequate funds and when the members are able voluntarily to consolidate labour discipline. Wages of members will be fixed by the masses through discussion, taking into account the intensity and complexity of the work, physical conditions, technique and attitude towards work. Wages will be paid monthly. Technical allowances may be paid to those who have special skill. One month's wage may differ from another. In months when the commune gets more income and the members need more, the members may get more pay; in other months they may get less. In case of a serious natural calamity the commune may, according to circumstances, pay less to its members.

After the institution of the wage system, there must be periodic reviews and comparisons of work done by the various units and individuals. Those who work energetically and do well should be rewarded, while those who work in a slovenly way and failed to carry out their assignments may be penalized through deductions from their wages. Awards distributed in the commune in a year may amount to a maximum of one-fourth of the total basic wages. The awards are divided into three parts, respectively in charge of the commune, the production contingents and brigades. Assignment of work and reviews and comparisons of work done should be on the basis of the average advanced quota.

With the introduction of the wage system, deduction from his wage should be effected when a member absents himself from work. Every member may have two days' paid leave each month and women members three days' paid leave. Women members may have a month's maternity leave during which time they will be paid half wages. Anyone injured in the course of work will be paid full wages during the period of treatment and recovery. Subsidies will be given out of the public welfare funds to anyone whose livelihood is affected by disability due to chronic disease.

Until conditions are mature for the institution of the wage system, the system of piece-work wages may be introduced, with a fixed value calculated per workday. The members may be monthly, in part or in full, paid according to the number of workdays done.

The commune should take energetic measures to trim and simplify its administrative departments. The total wages of its administrative personnel should not exceed one per cent of the total wages of the members. Meetings should be short and fewer; they should take a minimum of work hours.

Article 15 A grain supply system should be operated when grain production reaches a higher level and all the members of the commune agree to it. All members as well as each person of their families will then be supplied with grain gratis in accordance with standards laid down by the state, irrespective of how many of the family can work. The institution of the grain supply system should ensure that families with more labour power get more income than before.

To reform those who work in a slovenly way and, despite repeated persuasion, persist in their mistakes, the commune may, with the discussion and approval of its members, exercise supervision over them in work.

Article 16 The principle "from each according to his ability" constitutes the basis for instituting the wage system and the grain supply system. All members shall voluntarily abide by the following disciplinary rules: (1) take an active part in labour; (2) cherish and protect public property; (3) ensure the quality of work; (4) obey orders and transference; and (5) voluntarily co-ordinate with one another.

The commune must strengthen political work and education in communist ideas and, relying on the activists among the poor and lower-middle peasants, initiate communist labour emulation campaigns and reviews and comparisons so that the principle "from each according to his ability" will gradually be executed by members of their own accord.

Article 17 The commune shall set up community canteens, nurseries and sewing teams to free women from household labour. To facilitate management, these canteens and nurseries shall in general be set up under each production brigade. Members need not use the canteen or nursery services if they do not want to. Those who use the canteen services may have dishes prepared by themselves. The staff of the canteens, nurseries and sewing teams shall be paid wages and supplied by the commune. The charges for the services they render to the members shall be paid in accordance with the principle of "no losses and no profits." The community canteens should keep kitchen gardens and raise pigs and chickens so as to consistently improve their food supply.

Article 18 The commune will gradually set up and improve the work of medical establishments so that step by step the commune will have a central hospital with in-patient wards for serious cases. Every contingent will have its own clinic for out-patients and every production brigade its own health officer and midwife for the prevention of illness and the care of patients, and a midwifery service. Sanatoria will be set up when conditions permit.

Medical care shall be given in the commune on a co-operative basis. Members will pay a yearly amount in accordance with the number in the family. No other fees will be charged for any benefits they get from the medical establishments. In exceptionally serious cases beyond the capacity of the central hospital, patients will be sent to the appropriate hospitals for cure, and travelling and medical expenses shall be paid by the central hospital. But this shall not apply, for the time being, to the cases arising from chronic diseases or diseases due to old age. The commune shall provide free medical care when the economic situation allows.

Article 19 The commune shall make necessary arrangements concerning production and living conditions for the aged, the bereft, the disabled members and people in bad health who have less or no ability to work and nobody to depend on, so that they can be ensured the means of living. It shall set up "happy homes for the aged" who have no children, help them take part in work within the limit of their physical strength and provide them with necessary supplies so that they can have a happy old age.

Public cemeteries shall be established by the commune. The graves may be removed, with the approval of the family concerned, as required by production and construction.

Article 20 To gradually improve the housing conditions of its members, the commune shall draw up and gradually carry out comprehensive, long-term plans for the lay-out of residential quarters and the building of housing estates. In accordance with the principle of facilitating production and leadership, smaller residential quarters may, gradually and in a proper way, be merged into bigger ones.

Material and manpower needed for the building of new houses under the plan shall be supplied by the commune. Existing houses of the members of the commune shall gradually be dismantled and the bricks, tiles and timber used by the commune as needed. Newly-built houses will belong to the commune. Their occupants shall pay rents equivalent to the cost of maintenance and repair.

Article 21 The commune shall encourage cultural, recreational and sports activities among the masses so as to bring forward communist people healthy in body and in mind. Steps should be taken to ensure that each commune has its own library, theatre and film projector teams; that each production contingent has its own club room, amateur theatrical troupe, choir and sports team; and that each production brigade has a small reading room and radio sets.

Article 22 The yearly income of the commune shall be distributed under the following heads:
(1) Production costs incurred for the current year;
(2) Depreciation of public property;
(3) State taxes;
(4) Grain supply for members of the commune;
(5) Basic wages and awards for members of the commune;

(6) Public welfare funds, in general not exceeding five per cent of the total income, to be spent on education, health facilities, culture and other welfare services; and

(7) Reserve funds, comprising all the remainder of the income, to be used for stockpiling and expanded reproduction (including the construction of transport facilities). The commune should gradually build up grain stocks sufficient for one to two years, and necessary wages funds.

The distribution of income shall be based on the principle of ensuring high speed in expanded reproduction. With the development of production, wages shall be increased every year, but the rate of increase must be slower than the rate of increase in production. When the average wages (including grain supply) of members of the commune rise to a level that guarantees a living standard equivalent to that of the well-to-do middle peasant, the rate of increase in wages should be reduced to ensure the rapid growth of industry, the mechanization of farming and electrification of the rural areas in the shortest possible time.

Article 23 The commune shall be managed according to plan. It shall work out long-term programmes and yearly plans of construction in accordance with the economic plan of the state and the specific conditions of the commune. So as to introduce a strict responsibility system in production and carry through the award and demerit system in a rational way, the commune should work out concrete plans for output, technical measures, production expenses and the use of labour power of the contingents, factories, mines, livestock farms and timber yards. The contingents should also work out similar plans for the different production brigades.

The commune's plans for production, capital construction, sales of products, circulation of commodities, purchase of machinery and equipment, financial affairs and wages must be submitted to the state planning organizations and other departments concerned for examination and balancing before being put into practice.

Article 24 Democratic management shall be exercised throughout the commune. A vigorous, regular democratic life must be ensured in the commune, and in all its production contingents, production brigades, factories, mines, timber yards, livestock farms, tractor teams, schools, hospitals, shops, banks, canteens and militia units. All organizations, which keep their own accounts, must publish their balance sheets and the accounts of awards distributed, regularly and in good time. All administrative staff must take part in productive labour as far as possible. The masses must be encouraged to carry out criticism and self-criticism, commend those who render meritorious service or put forward suggestions by way of *tatsepao*, so that defects in work can be overcome.

Article 25 The commune must carry out the policy of running the commune in the spirit of industry and thrift, encourage its members to work hard, make full use of its own potential to overcome difficulties, practise economy, lower production costs, oppose waste and extravagance, and, as far as possible, trim and simplify all buildings and equipment not connected with production.

Article 26 The commune must establish a strict system governing financial management. All organizations which keep their own accounts must work out income and expenditure budgets in good time, abide by the system and formalities governing the use of cash, and settle their accounts regularly.

Special persons should be appointed to take charge of all public property. Anyone causing loss to public property by negligence must be criticized, or dealt with by disciplinary measures by the commune. Cases of corruption, theft or destruction of public property must be handled in a serious manner; those involved in serious cases should be referred to the higher judicial departments to be punished according to law.

ANNEX

Alternative Articles Concerning the Supply and Marketing Department and of the Credit Department

Article 7 The commune will establish a supply and marketing department. The supply and marketing department will handle the sales of products and the supply of necessities of the commune under the guidance of state trading organs. The basic form of business of the supply and marketing department is to purchase and sell on behalf of state trading organs. In the purchase or sales of products it should stick to the price fixed by the state trading organs. The service charges for the supply and marketing department in purchasing and selling for state trading organs shall be fixed by the state trading organs in accordance with the principle that "the expenditure incurred plus a small amount of profits" be an allowable deduction. The supply and marketing department may sell in the commune the products left over after the commune has fulfilled the tasks of state purchase and unified purchase. The price and quantity of products sold shall be examined and approved by the state trading organs. The supply and marketing department may, with the approval of the state trading organs, sell to other quarters or buy in certain commodities that the state cannot purchase or supply.

The supply and marketing department shall keep its own accounts, while its profits and losses shall be managed by the commune under a unified system. Its funds shall be provided with the share funds contributed to the former supply and marketing co-operative by the members. The deficit shall be made up by the commune. No dividends shall be given on the shares.

For the convenience of the people, the supply and marketing department should set up its branches in all contingents and retail departments in the fairly distant and out-of-the-way areas. State trading organs should set up wholesale departments in appropriate places and gradually dismiss the retail departments.

The supply and marketing department joins the county supply and marketing co-operative as a member organization.

Article 8 The commune shall set up a credit department. The credit department shall handle the members' deposits, loans and the utilization of funds of the commune under the guidance of the state banks. The credit department is also an agency of the People's Bank, handling deposits and making loans on its behalf, and charges the latter for the service according to stipulations.

The credit department shall keep its own accounts, while its profits and losses shall be managed by the commune under a unified system. Its funds shall be provided with the share funds contributed to the former credit co-operative by the members. The deficit shall be made up by the commune.

For the convenience of the people, the credit department should set up its branches in all contingents and service centres in the fairly distant and out-of-the-way areas.

As a cash treasury of the commune and the different contingents, the credit department and its branches shall undertake the receipts and disbursement of cash in bulk. Under the leadership of the state banks the credit department shall undertake book settlement between the commune and other financial departments, and between the various departments in the commune which keep their own accounts. Book settlement is not to be practised among the members.

DOCUMENT 32

Directive of the Hopei Provincial Committee of the Party on the Building of People's Communes, August 29, 1958.

The English text is taken from CB 524, and is a translation by the U.S. Consulate General, Hong Kong, from *Red Flag*, September 16, 1958.

Comment. The first paragraph of the text makes it clear that the formation of communes had gone a long way before the publication of the Central Committee's resolution (Document 28 above). See our comment on Document 27. An editorial note in *Red Flag* said the rural areas of Hopei completed the building of people's communes during the early part of September. It said the directive was being published for the reference of other areas, and that "individual deletions from the original text have been made."

Special points of interest are:

1. Emphasis (in section I) on the mass demand for the formation of communes (see our comments on Documents 31 and 42).

2. Excessive optimism (section II) about the progress of semi-mechanization (to be completed in 1958) and full mechanization and electrification (to be realized in "three to five years"). On this, see ECMM 157 (*Planned Economy*, Oct. 22, 1958—the draft development program of the Hsushui *hsien* Party committee).

3. Plans to reduce acreage given to farm crops by 50 percent by achieving a yield of 2,000 to 3,000 *catties* per *mou* of grain. This is well ahead of the target set in the 12-Year Agricultural Plan (Document 5). In the summer of 1959, the proposed reduction of acreage had to be given up.

4. Extravagant plans for communications (section II). "Each commune must be accessible by highway, each household must have its own bicycles, and each commune must have its own automobiles. All *hsiang* (communes) must build a highway section which can be used for the landing and taking off of planes."

Lin T'ieh, First Secretary of the Hopei Provincial Committee, published an article in *Red Flag* of October 1 giving further details of the commune movement in Hopei. He emphasized popular initiative, as against the hesitations of "some comrades" who thought that production would be affected if communes were established before the autumn harvest.

───────────────── TEXT OF DOCUMENT 32 ─────────────────

I

Roused by the overall big leap forward in industrial and agricultural production and in various fields of socialist construction, in the rural areas of our province there has risen the new trend for the merger of small cooperatives into large ones for the building of people's communes. Particularly after Chairman Mao issued his important directive on the people's communes, the development of this situation has become all the more rapid. People's communes have been completely built in the two *hsien* of Hsushui and Changpai. By August 27, in the whole province the complete building of people's communes has been initially realized in more than 30 *hsien* and municipalities, a total of more than 200 communes having been formed. At the moment the broad masses of peasants have most enthusiastically taken up the task of building communes. A mass movement has been evolved for the merging of small cooperatives into big ones for the establishment of people's communes, and this movement is being universally developed. This movement must promote the further development of productive forces, promote the greater leap forward in industrial and agricultural production, and accelerate the mechanization, electrification of agriculture, further raise the Communist awakening of the masses, and accelerate the overall development of political, economic, cultural, ideological, and various socialist construction enterprises in the rural areas.

The emergence of the new situation of the movement for the building of people's communes has been no accident, for there are political, economic and other sources behind it. First, since the spring of 1956, our victory achieved successively victories in the socialist revolution on the economic, political and ideological fronts. The political awakening of the masses has been raised to unprecedented heights, productive forces have been greatly developed, and many high tides of agricultural production have arrived successively. Particularly since last winter and the spring of this year, under the illumination of the bright rays of the general line for socialist construction of the Party, the whole Party and the whole people in the province, through extensive efforts toward development of water conservancy and the fight against the serious drought, have achieved an unprecedented summer bumper harvest, so that the people have been ideologically liberated and their zeal for work has been further increased. At the moment the autumn farm crops are growing well, and it is quite possible that this year we shall realize the production targets for grain, cotton, and oilseed crops laid down in the Program for Agricultural Development, with each person getting on the average 1,000 catties of grain. The great achievements of the overall leap forward have educated the masses and educated the cadres. People now unrestrictedly place confidence in the correctness of the leadership of the Party and fully realize the superiority of the socialist system and the great prowess of the working people in the conquest of nature.

Second, in the midst of the big leap forward of agricultural production, and the struggle for the transformation of nature and for an overall big bumper harvest, among different *hsien*, different *hsiang* and different cooperatives, the people have universally adopted the form of socialist cooperation on a large scale, mutually supporting one another, and marching forward shoulder to shoulder, creating miracles the like of which were never seen in the past. The broad masses in their struggle for production have realized the great role of collective strength in the transformation of nature, the development of production, and the improvement of living standards. They feel that in the big leap forward in production, the original small cooperatives no longer meet the needs for manpower, material resources, financial resources, and technique. Very naturally they have brought forward the demand for the merger of small cooperatives into larger ones.

Third, the big leap forward in agricultural production has brought about, in its stride, the overall leap forward in industry, trade, culture, military affairs, and various socialist construction enterprises. The agricultural cooperatives in various areas have universally started nurseries and public mess halls, taken up the building of factories on a large scale, operating large numbers of middle schools and primary schools, and even universities, and further strengthened the armed forces of the people's militia. This new content of the inclusion of industry, agriculture, trade, culture, and military affairs, and the overall development of political, economic, cultural, and military enterprises has in effect exceeded the scope of the agricultural cooperatives, which are undergoing a change in their basic nature.

These conditions show that the merger of small cooperatives into large ones to form people's communes is the natural result of the development of productive forces, and it is an important transformation that promotes the still greater leap forward in production, accelerates the socialist construction of the rural areas. Party committees of all levels must actively take the initiative to step forward to lead the movement, so that the system of agricultural cooperativization may develop toward a higher stage, and the people's communes may be gradually developed into the best basic organizational form for the building of the Communist system in the rural areas.

II

The goal of the merger of small cooperatives into large ones for the building of people's communes is to make production relations suited to the productive forces which are being developed by leaps and bounds, to promote the development of production at a high speed, and to rapidly change the look of the countryside. For this reason, all tasks must be closely combined with production. At the moment, they must be centered round the strengthening of field management, autumn harvesting, manure collection, deep plowing, and wheat sewing. From the onset attention must be paid to the manifestation of the greater superiority of the people's communes, and especially we must ensure the fulfillment of the wheat sowing plans, guaranteeing both quality and quantity, to lay well the foundations for an even greater bumper harvest next year. At the same time, all tasks must also be combined with the formulation of plans for the development of the communes, showing the masses the great possibilities, increasing their confidence, and rousing them forward. As to the contents of the plans for the development of people's communes, various localities may take into account different conditions to make concrete provisions, but generally they should include the following targets.

In the field of agriculture, forces must be concentrated for the hard battle in the next three years to change the face of the countryside. This year semi-mechanization should be realized. In three to five years, mechanization and electrification should be realized. From deep plowing to sowing, irrigation, field management, reaping, and threshing, all the major farming operations should be carried out with the use of machinery, electricity or other motive power, to replace the old farm tools and manual labor, so as to achieve an even greater leap forward on the basis of the raising of the per unit area yield of different farm crops. Generally speaking, by achieving a per *mow* yield of between 2,000 and 3,000 catties for grain, 400 and 500 catties for ginned cotton, and 2,000 and 3,000 catties for oilseed crops (peanut), the existing acreage given to farm crops may be reduced by 50 per cent, and the land saved may be used for the development of forestry, orchards, sericulture, animal husbandry, fishery, and horticulture, thereby promote multiple economy. Each commune should have proper green belts, orchards, ranches, and vegetable gardens sufficient for its needs. All ditches and ponds should be used for raising fish and the planting of lotus plants, and the development of aquatic production. We must seek to realize the mechanization and electrification of agricultural production, the provision of all water conservancy projects possible, the achievement of high yield crops, and the operation of multiple economy, and to make the countryside look green with trees, beautiful and fragrant.

In the field of industry, we must uphold the spirit of the simultaneous development of industry and agriculture and realize the leap forward in the two fields shoulder to shoulder. Concrete conditions locally must be taken into account in deciding on the establishment of machinery repairing and assembly works, chemical fertilizer plants, brick and tile factories, cement works, timber yards, fodder processing works, cotton ginning and oil pressing mills, textile mills, tailoring and shoe-making works, paper mills, and food processing factories. To realize the industrialization of the rural areas, and to gradually eliminate the differences between workers and peasants and differences between cities and rural areas, the production value of industry must quickly exceed the production value of agriculture.

In the fields of culture, education, and public health, each commune must operate nurseries, kindergartens, primary schools, junior middle schools, senior middle schools, and universities and also establish an organ for scientific research, so that in 10 or 15 years, all people now below 25 may reach the cultural standards of a university student. All schools should practice part-time study and part-time work, or part-time study and part-time farming. Each commune must have its own library, club house, sports ground, choral group, drama group and motion picture theater. Each household must enjoy the facilities of wired broadcasting. Each commune must have its own hospital, each big company must have its own clinic, and each team must be staffed with health officer and midwife, and have its own bath house and barber shop, so that the promotion of public health may be placed on a regular basis. Sports must be popularized to improve the physical conditions of the people. All diseases must be gradually wiped out.

In the field of trade, each commune must have its own supply and marketing department, and establish a large-sized market. Each company must have its own store so that the circulation of supplies may be smoothly carried out.

In the field of military affairs, we must practice the combination of productive labor with military training. All young and able bodied persons of suitable age must be organized as militiamen or for reserve military service, to become the hard-core force or shock force of the relevant production companies. We must universally achieve the state in which youths of suitable age are peasants and workers and students and soldiers at the same time.

In the field of communications, each commune must be accessible by highway, each household must have its own bicycles, and each commune must have its own automobiles. All *hsiang* (communes) must build a highway section which can be used for the landing and taking off of planes. Each company must have its telephone. Each *hsien* must have a light railway and trains. We must gradually reach the state where all communication facilities are automatic.

In the field of mass life, with the development of production, all communes must strive to achieve, in two to three years, the state in which all are well clothed and well fed. Each person should on the average have 2,000 catties of grain, 200 catties of meat, 30 catties of vegetable oils, and 100 feet of cotton cloth a year. Living quarters must be improved in a planned manner, and new houses must be built. The operation of public mess halls must be universally realized. Happiness homes must be operated so that the old people may pass their last years happily. With the mechanization and electrification of the countryside, and under the premise of the great development of production, the working hours and rest periods of members of communes must be appropriately arranged.

In the field of political and ideological advancement, all Party member cadres must strive to become red and expert as soon as possible. The ideological state of the cadres and the masses must be communized, and they must possess a suitable level of political theory. All members of communes must become organized, disciplined, cultured, people with technical attainments and Communist awakening and moral character.

To make a good job of planning for overall construction, planning committees must rapidly be organized at the provincial, municipal, and *hsien* levels. Under the leadership of the corresponding level Party committees, they shall hold responsibility for drawing up the second Five Year Plan of development and the 10-year plan for construction for the rural areas (the plans for the next two years must be more concrete), in order to show the people the beautiful picture of the socialist and communist future, to clarify the direction of the struggle and to rouse the masses to march forward.

III

The people's commune is the further development of the agricultural cooperative. It is not merely an expansion in size, but also an improvement in quality. It will develop the hitherto simple agricultural production to include agriculture, forest, livestock, subsidiary productions and fisheries, and develop the overall combination of workers, peasants, merchants, students, and militiamen. It will further practice the integration of the government with the commune, and also gradually produce changes in the system of distribution.

At the present moment, the people's commune should more preferably adopt the system of collective ownership, and there should be no undue haste in making a change from collective ownership to ownership by the whole people, in order to avoid the incidence of unnecessary complications in the course of the change of the system of ownership. But in effect, the system of collective ownership in the people's commune already includes many components of the system of ownership by the whole people. This system of ownership by the whole people will be increased in the midst of continual development, to gradually replace the system of collective ownership.

After the building of the people's communes, there is also no need for undue haste in changing the original system of distribution, so as to avoid unfavorable effects on production. Our acts must stem from concrete conditions, and where conditions are ripe, we may change over to the wage system. Where conditions are not yet ripe, we may continue to use the original systems of the "three guarantees" and "one award", or the fixing of work according to production and payment of earnings according to labor days. When conditions are ripe, changes may then be made. Whether the wage system or the system of remuneration according to the number of labor days is adopted in distribution, it is still the principle of "to each according to his labor", and not "to each according to his need." However, the people's commune will be the best organizational form for the successful building of socialism and transition to communism, and it will develop into the basic unit of the future communist society.

As to the scale of the people's commune, plans should be made according to the principles of benefitting production and the willingness of the masses, so that it may suit the needs of the leap forward in industrial and agricultural production and suit the natural and communications conditions. At the same time, we must consider the needs of the development of socialist construction during a period to come. Generally, in the plains each commune should have about 10,000 households, in the hilly areas about 5,000 households, and in the mountain areas between 2,000 and 3,000 households. In some localities with a greater concentration of population and good communications facilities, should the masses desire, the commune may be a little bigger, to consist of not more than 15,000 households. In certain remote areas, mountain areas with a small population, a commune may also have less than 2,000 households, or several communes may be built in the same *hsiang*. Such scales will provide the necessary conditions for the reasonable regulation of manpower, the unified planning of land utilization, the large scale accumulation of capital, the operation of factories, and the running of schools. At the same time we may also avoid the need, within a short period, for further mergers occasioned by the rapid development of the situation.

The people's commune practices the integration of the government with the commune. The *hsiang* Party committee is also the Party committee of the commune; the *hsiang* people's council is also the administrative committee of the commune; and the deputies to the *hsiang* people's congress are also the delegates to the congress of the members of the commune. A single outfit may have two signboards. In the commune, specific personnel must be clearly provided for the implementation of the administrative duties of the *hsiang*.

The highest administrative machinery of the people's commune is the congress of its members. At such a congress, the administrative committee and the supervisory committee will be elected, responsible respectively for the administration of routine affairs and the supervision over the commune's activities. The administrative committee shall have a number of members. As to the management departments under the administrative committee of the commune, for the moment no unified provisions are laid down, and various localities shall decide on them according to local expediency. Generally, under the commune there may be a number of production companies, and under a production company a number of production teams. The production team shall be the basic unit for production. In a commune of a smaller scale, the production teams may be directly subordinate to the commune [administrative committee].

There shall be a Party committee for a people's commune (*hsiang*). Party general branches or branches may be established for the production companies and production teams in accordance with the numbers of Party members therein. Young Communist League organizations shall be established in accordance with the machineries of the Party committee and organizations. The commune shall have a representative conference of women and a federation of women. The commune (*hsiang*) shall have a department of armed forces, which is also the department of military affairs of the Party committee.

Cadres of a people's commune shall be suitably provided by the higher Party committee on the basis of cadres both within and outside the Party in the original *hsiang* and cooperatives. The organic machinery of the people's commune must be very simple, and the original structures must not be disturbed all of a sudden. On the original basis, increases or reductions of organizations may be carried out. The personnel establishment of the original cooperatives shall not be increased. In the provision of leadership cadres for a commune, attention must be given to arrangements for women cadres. Among ordinary cadres, a definite proportion of women cadres must be maintained. All the management personnel of a commune must participate in productive labor, and this must be made a regular system. Apart from cadres sent by the state for work in the commune who will be supported by the state, the subsidies in the form of wage points allowed all administrative personnel in a commune should in general be controlled at the level of not more than one percent of the total number of wage points for the year.

To meet the needs of the big leap forward in the socialist construction enterprises, to meet the new situation arising from the merger of small cooperatives into large ones to form people's communes and the integration of the government with the commune, all existing *ch'ü* organizations must be abolished, and existing *hsien* boundries should also be appropriately adjusted. In the plains, a *hsien* should generally be expanded to have a population of 800,000 (900,000 at most and 700,000 at least); in the hilly areas a *hsien* should be expanded to have a population of from 400,000 to 500,000; and in the mountain areas a *hsien* should be expanded to have a population of from 200,000 to 300,000. This will be comparatively appropriate.

Various localities may proceed with plans for the merger of *hsien* in accordance with the above principle. Such plans must be reported to and approved by the Provincial Party Committee, and at the same time be passed at the people's congresses of the *hsien* affected before they are implemented. Before the merger of *hsien*, the Party committee for the central *hsien* may first be organized, or else a joint council of the Party committees of the different *hsien* affected may be organized, to facilitate the unification of Party leadership, the unification of planning, and the unification of the direction of activities.

IV

In the merger of small cooperatives into large ones for the building of people's communes, the handling of various means of production must be carried out with attention to full consultation, the manifestation of democracy, the proper pursuit of the mass line, and in accordance with the spirit of the general line and upholding the principle of facilitating the development of socialist collective economy, all the public assets of the small cooperatives must be transferred to the collective ownership of the people's communes. In the spirit of Communism, generally those having assets in excess of the average shall not have the excess portions taken back, and those with assets less than the average shall not have to make good the deficiency. The original debts, excepting those incurred to finance production during the current year which should be liquidated by the original cooperatives themselves, shall all be taken over by the commune. The capital investments of the cooperative members shall remain under their names, but no interest shall be paid. Investments above the average shall not be refunded, and investments below the average shall not have to be increased. The commune will be responsible for the repayment of investments [in production] by members.

As to the self-retained land plots of the members, in the cases of the small cooperatives which had already established public mess halls, most members had already turned over such plots to the cooperatives or production teams for collective operation. In cases where the members still retained such plots to themselves, the masses must be mobilized for discussion, and with the agreement of the masses, such plots shall be taken over by the communes for collective operation. In a small number of mountain areas, large forests have not yet been turned over to the cooperatives, and in such cases persuasion and education must be developed to turn such forests into collective ownership. Draft animals still retained by members shall be turned over to the communes at prices decided. In addition to the above, the residences of the members, land inside the courts of their houses, small strips of land by the side of houses and certain small numbers of fruit trees, as well as the pigs, sheep, chickens, and ducks raised by the members shall remain their own private property, and shall not be touched. As to the members' bicycles, radio sets, house furniture, wrist watches, clothing, and bedsheets and such living needs, they shall all belong to the individuals themselves, for even in the communist society, these things shall remain private property. If these possessions of the members are taken over a mistake will have been committed, and they should be returned. Education in and propagation of this policy shall be developed among the masses. At the same time, we must exert vigilance against the sabotage activities and rumors of landlords, rich peasants, counter-revolutionaries, and bad elements.

V

The merger of small cooperatives into large ones for the building of people's communes is an important development in the system of agricultural cooperativization. It is an important economic and political movement in the rural areas today. The correct leadership of this movement will not only greatly rouse the revolutionary zeal of the masses of the people, and effectively push forward current production, but also will bring about a new look in rural construction in our province. For this reason, we must stress the strengthening of Party leadership, stress the combination of the movement with current production tasks, and from beginning to end properly pursue the mass line and make a good job of political and ideological work.

In the first place, Party committees of all levels must attach great attention to, and take the initiative to actively stand in the very forefront of the masses in leading the movement. The Party secretary shall assume command, the whole Party shall participate in the task, and special personnel shall hold responsibility under the system of the division of labor. We must strengthen investigation and research, acquire a timely control of the situation, strengthen the ties between the upper and the lower levels, and mutually supply information, so that the movement may develop rapidly and healthily.

The building of people's communes must be carried out with leadership, with preparation, and with measured steps. There must be speed and quality, and crudeness and rashness must be avoided. In the movement for the building of people's communes as a whole, during the period before wheat sowing and the period after wheat sowing, two separate steps may generally be taken. Before wheat sowing, the step taken should principally consist of two tasks. The first is to develop discussions among the cadres and masses, and in areas where conditions are ripe, the administrative machinery, or the preparatory committee, for the commune should be rapidly organized, building the framework of the cadres, putting up the bright sign of the people's commune, and announcing its inauguration. The second task is for the people's commune to unify the planning of wheat sowing, to unify the regulation of manpower and tools, to concentrate forces to make a good job of the autumn harvest, to deep plow off [sic] the land, to collect manure, and to complete the wheat sowing task.

In the second step to be taken after wheat sowing, the masses should be further mobilized for big blooming, big contending and big debate, and on the basis of the raised Communist awakening of the masses, various economic problems should be disposed of step by step. At the same time, attention should also be given to the establishment and consolidation of various organizations and systems. In the small number of areas where conditions are not yet ripe, the plans of the large cooperatives may temporarily be taken up, and, through organized cooperation, make a good job of autumn harvesting and wheat sowing, so that only after autumn may the task for the merger of cooperatives to build people's communes be taken. It is demanded that before the end of December this year, the building of people's communes and the merger of *hsien* will be completely carried out.

With the establishment of people's communes, new changes will take place in the economic base of society, and changes will also take place in the people's ideology. There must emerge the ideological struggle between socialism and capitalism, between the advanced and the backward, and between the collective body and the individual. Accordingly, in our own we must thoroughly implement the class line of the Party, and its mass line, and also strengthen political and ideological work. The building of people's communes is at the moment the common demand of the broad masses of the people. The poor peasants and the lower middle peasants resolutely support the movement, and the majority of the upper middle peasants also express agreement with it. We must rely on the poor peasants and lower middle peasants, fully mobilize the masses, unite with the majority of the upper middle peasants who support the building of communes, overcome the vacillating attitude of the other portion of the upper middle peasants, and expose and repulse the rumors and sabotage activities of the landlords and rich peasants, so that the building of communes may be smoothly carried out.

In the mobilization of the masses, we must extensively employ the methods of big blooming, big contending, and big-character bulletins, speak penetratingly and argue thoroughly, to enable the masses to understand that the form of one cooperative to each *ts'un* adopted in the past was suitable under former conditions, and this had promoted its role in the development of production. Now, however, under the situation of the overall leap forward in production and the further development of rural construction, the merger of small cooperatives into large ones for the building of people's communes is likewise completely necessary and correct. As to the various policies connected with the building of communes, they must be put into practice after thorough discussion by the masses. The movement for people's communes must be built on the foundation of the elevation of the political consciousness of the masses and made into a movement self-consciously promoted by the masses. Through the building of people's communes, we shall carry out a penetrating socialist and communist education among the whole Party and the whole people, to achieve the goal of the joint leap forward in the political and economic fields, so as to reap a double bumper harvest.

Chapter IX

PEOPLE'S COMMUNES: DISILLUSION AND CONSOLIDATION

(containing Documents 33, 34, 35, 36, 37)

General comment. The problems raised by the rapid formation of the communes and the unrestrained enthusiasms of local cadres soon began to make themselves felt. As usual, practical and ideological factors interacted closely. For some discussion of this and of the Central Committee's position in relation to it, see our General Introduction, part IX.

Problems arising in the economic and financial fields were discussed at an agricultural conference held in October 1958 by officials of eight provinces of Northern and Northeastern China. Li Hsien-nien, who had been on a tour of the newly-formed communes, and T'an Chen-lin were among those present. In Chengchow, from November 2 to 10, there was a meeting of prominent members of the Central Committee together with the first secretaries of the provincial committees of the Party.

Then, in the city of Wuchang—a part of the Wuhan metropolitan complex—the Eighth Central Committee of the Chinese Communist Party held its Sixth Plenary Session from November 28 to December 10, 1958. Three of our documents, 34, 35, and 36, derive from that meeting. The first is the communiqué which summarized the discussions. The second is the text of a brief statement in which the Central Committee approved Mao Tse-tung's plan to yield the office of Chairman of the People's Republic. But the most significant of the three is the so-called Wuhan Resolution on people's communes.

Though the meeting ended on December 10, the issuance of the three documents was delayed until December 17 in order that public opinion might be fully prepared by means of conferences and discussions at all levels. According to the NCNA on December 17, "It was envisaged during the nationwide discussions that the enemy both at home and abroad would certainly take the opportunity to disseminate rumors and slanders." It seems likely that the country was being prepared not only for the announcement on Mao but also for the disenchanting substance of the main Wuhan Resolution on communes.

The principal lines of publicity on the two items of news were indicated in further NCNA stories of December 18 and 19. The news agency said that the *People's Daily* ran the news under the banner headline "Chairman Mao Always Leads Us," and that many papers carried "headlines in red above the communiqué, and charts showing the figures of major industrial and agricultural output in 1957, the rocketing figures of estimated production in 1958, and the targets for 1959." In fact, for the casual reading public some effort was made to distract attention from the considerable amount of self-criticism in the resolution on communes and probably to mitigate the impression that failures in the commune experiment had had something to do with the change in Mao's position. The *People's Daily* postponed its main comment on the main resolution until December 21. The editorial of that date is adequately summarized by its own headline: "Skyrocketing Enthusiasm Should Be Combined with Scientific Analysis."

It is recorded in the communiqué that "the Plenary Session adopted a decision to improve the financial and trade administrative systems in the rural areas." The text of the Central Committee's decision on this subject (NCNA, Dec. 22) is given in SCMP 1929.

An appropriate preface to the three Wuhan documents is a *Red Flag* article published shortly before the Central Committee gathered in Wuhan.

DOCUMENT 33

Have We Already Reached the Stage of Communism? article by Hsu Li-ch'ün in *Red Flag*, November 16, 1958.

The English text is from ECMM 156, and is a translation by the U.S. Consulate General, Hong Kong, of the *Red Flag* article.

Comment. On "optimism and pessimism" about the transition to Communism, see commentary on Document 36 below. Further references are given there on the problem of wages versus free supply, which is discussed in the General Introduction, part IX. On the "bad elements employed to work in mess halls," see articles reproduced in CB 538 from the *People's Daily* and local press; some of these stress the need for great political vigilance in recruiting personnel for management of these. It seems likely that the mess halls afforded temptations for private sale of stores and similar forms of "preferring individual to collective interest." Such shortcomings, like "thefts from iron and steel factory sites" would normally be attributed by the Party to political sabotage rather than to original sin.

―――――――――――――――――TEXT OF DOCUMENT 33―――――――――――――――――

Under the central directive, the socialist and Communist education campaign has already been launched or is being prepared for launching in various places. In order to properly conduct this campaign, we must study the diversified ways the people look at the situation of our country's socialist construction.

ON WHETHER "WE HAVE REACHED COMMUNISM"

Some people now consider that "we have reached Communism" with the people's communes plus the supply system. Some people think that we will very shortly complete the transition to Communist society, and have therefore worked out detailed plans for their respective areas to realize Communism within two years. With this in mind, these comrades consider it quite "out of fashion" to propose to conduct the socialist education. This is apparently incorrect. But it reflects that people are eager to get, "faster and still faster", to Communism. Such a mood is understandable.

The development of our country's domestic situation is so fast that the people find it hard to get acquainted with. Productivity develops miraculously. Social productivity, being so fiercely developed, demands a production relation that is in line with our own development level. After the organization of people's communes, the people have set up *hsien* federations of communes in many places, thereby raising the level of collectivization still higher, and adopted the distribution system of combining grain supplies with wages in many other places, thereby starting to break through the scope of socialist distribution principle of remuneration according to labor. The attitude toward "voluntary", "non-quota" Communist labor "without caring for remuneration" and the coordination relations are all the more developing everywhere. These new deeds created by the masses are greatly beneficial to the development of productivity. They indicate that the development of Comrade Mao Tse-tung's theory of incessant revolution has greatly opened the people's vision and illuminated the road of our country's socialist construction and transition to Communism. This year's socialist and Communist education campaign is launched under such conditions. Of course, the higher we can raise the Communist red flag the better.

In conducting the education of Communist ideology for the masses, we will inevitably encounter one problem: how should we correctly handle the following two points? First, the ideal of the high-stage Communist society can only be realized in the future; and second, the present practice to pave the way for the realization of this ideal. These two are associated but different. It is incorrect to adopt any of the following two kinds of attitude. One is merely talking of the future ideal, not associating it with the present practice, and not actively preparing favorable conditions for its realization. Those people with this attitude are not enthusiastic and do not support the new deeds consisting of Communist factor which are created by the masses, and they even want to stop and threaten. This is a conservative attitude. The other is trying to work in the way of the ideal that can only be realized in the future. These comrades are enthusiastic but they may deviate from the present practice of the majority and achieve adverse results.

If we take the example of the distribution problem of the people's communes, to which the majority now pay special attention, there are also the two above-mentioned attitudes: One is to consider that the adoption of the distribution system that combines grain supplies with wages is "to favor the poor with what the rich is entitled to", "against the principle of giving more to whoever works more", and is divorced from the current level of productivity development and the degree of people's awareness. They fail to see how much the grain supply system has inspired the enthusiasm and production activism of the masses. They also fail to see that here is the young bud of the distribution system of "to each according to his needs" or a Communist element. In the present rural villages of our country, such kind of attitude in nature is the reflection of the ideology of well-to-do middle peasants' private ownership and it must be criticized. The other attitude, diagonally opposite to the one mentioned above, is the dissatisfaction toward the great victory of "having free meals" as practiced by us in many places. The comrades who take up such an attitude simply feel that the bigger the portion taken by the supply system, the nearer to Communism and the more "advanced" we are. Hence, they are eager to augment the scope of supply and to equalize the remunerations to those people with great and strong labor power and to those without. The result would be a great reduction of the wage portion or the portion of remuneration according to labor. These comrades are of the opinion that, in so doing, the remnant capitalist methods in the socialist society could rapidly be reduced or even eliminated.

If we say that the first attitude is not enthusiastic or even antagonistic to Communism, the second attitude is then "over-enthusiastic" to Communism with over-anxious demands. It is easily seen that the first attitude is wrong and we will not discuss it here. The cause for the emergence of the second erroneous attitude could be one-sided estimation of the current development level of productivity and the awareness of the masses. Naturally, it is incorrect to mystify the principle of "to each according to his needs" by some people. They do not believe that the principle of "to each according to his needs" can be gradually realized. They consider that only after the complete realization of "automation", "atomization", and other such conditions will its thorough enforcement be announced some day. However, it is also incorrect not to care for production developments and people's awareness and only to work subjectively according to "kind aspirations". When food takes up the major portion of the amount of individual consumption (the balance of the gross income after deducting all necessary expenditures and capital funds for enlarging reproduction), as furnished by the level of productivity, it is impossible to realize "to each according to his needs" in the various basic means of livelihood and other consumer goods. Here, let us take the example of people whose annual consumption amounts to ¥60 or ¥70. Their food and grain take up half or more than half of the amount. The remaining portion is not much. By relying on this little portion to ensure "to each according to his needs" of various consumer goods is apparently unrealistic. In this remaining portion, if the supply part is enlarged, the wage part will be reduced. Hence, the principle of remunerations according to labor will become more and more insignificant or non-existent. Some comrades of Peking municipality have made computations in a number of the suburban people's communes and conducted some investigation. They found that when more was supplied, the number of households whose income declined was increased. Furthermore, most of these households are those of poor and lower middle peasants with a strong labor power but few members. Here are the questions: Must we still adopt the principle of remunerations according to labor as the basis of the distribution system? Or must we reduce it to an insignificant position? If we now reduce the principle of remunerations according to labor to an insignificant position, is it beneficial or harmful to the development of production? Must we take the standard of whether it is beneficial to the development of production as a yardstick, or the standard of other factors as a yardstick? In answering these questions, we must not stem out solely from the abstract principles. In addition to conducting careful studies, we must also listen to the discussion of the masses as much as possible. The Hungkuang Commune of Sunho in Ch'aoyang ch'ü of Peking municipality achieved much increase in its grain and cotton production this year. The average per capita consumption was raised from ¥40 last year to ¥68.2 this year, showing an increase of 70 percent. This commune put forward three distribution programs for the masses to discuss. The first program was the same as last year's distribution according to wage points. The second program covered the supply of grain and wages according to labor contributed (the wages are higher). The third program guaranteed the supplies in seven fields (food, clothes, medical care, schooling, marriage, child birth, and burial) plus some allowance (the amount of which is much smaller than the wage portion of the second program). Many people spent whole nights discussing. The result was that the majority were in favor of the second program. They said, "With the problem of food solved, it gives much more conveniences to each individual by having more money on hand." Some also said: "It is 'capitalistic' to distribute according to last year's method. The third program seems a little bit 'over-hasty'. The second program is therefore the best." The situation is like that with this commune whose economic conditions are not considered bad. The situation can more apparently be seen in the few communes whose economic conditions are not as good, whose land is lean, or whose areas are affected by natural calamities. In these few communes, food occupies a very large portion of the gross income and, after deducting food, there is very little wage. If the supply is to be augmented, there will probably be no wage at all. Under such a situation, how can we consider the adoption of the system of "to each according to his needs"? In this manner, the people can see clearly that, without the high degree development of productivity, the Communist principle of distribution can not be realized. In order to enlarge the scope of the supply system under the present limited conditions, some people conceived two methods. One is to reduce the communal accumulation. This seems to reduce the scope of reproduction enlargement. The other is to request state subsidies or loans that are not required to be repaid. It is needless to say that these two methods are both inappropriate.

The distribution system that combines supply with wage is apparently a good system. It provides a good distribution method that facilitates the transition from the distribution principle of remunerations according to labor gradually to the distribution principle of to each according to his needs. Following the development of production and the elevation of awareness of the masses, the scope of supply system will grow and the supply standard will be raised. After a considerably long period, we will gradually enter the stage in which the basic means of livelihood are supplied to each according to his needs. However, as of the present development level of production and degree of awareness of the masses, the principle of remunerations according to labor should still be regarded as the nationwide basis of the distribution system.

This does not preclude the stress on the politics assuming command and the stress on the manifestation of the Communist spirit of "all for one and one for all". In the present socialist and Communist education campaign, the ideology of Communism should be fostered and the ideologies of individualism, departmentalism, and other various kinds of the capitalist class should be shattered with an all-out effort to promote a still faster forward development of our country. We want again to use the many new deeds (such as "having meals free of charge") that have emerged to indicate that the realization of the beautiful Communist future is not too distant away. While we point out the future, it is necessary to explain that to jump over the definite stage of development of objective conditions is impossible. The effect of man's subjective motivity can only, under the conditions that the objective development pattern is strictly adhered to, promote an early realization of the ideal. To respect materialism is not conservative.

ON SEVERAL CONTRADICTIONS IN RURAL VILLAGES

Here I would like to discuss another problem. It is the several comparatively important contradictions among the people which confronted the conduct of the socialist and Communist education campaign in the rural villages.

After the universal building of people's communes, the contradiction between landlords, rich peasants, remnant counter-revolutionaries, and all other kinds of bad elements and the masses of the people, or the contradiction between the enemies and ourselves, is not eliminated. On the contrary, these antagonists will make use of the opportunity in which the people are not accustomed to certain new deeds at the start of the universal building of people's communes to fabricate rumors or to carry out sabotage in production. Theft is often found at the construction sites of iron and steel industries. The enemies of socialism will not readily lay down their weapons. Attention should be paid to certain signs of relaxation in the vigilance of the masses following the universal building of people's communes. For example, some bad elements have been employed to work in the mess halls. This must be solved in the socialist and Communist education campaign.

Aside from the contradiction between the enemies and ourselves, I shall discuss the three aspects in the manifestation of the contradictions among the people.

First is the contradiction between some of the well-to-do middle peasants who have indulged in the ideology of the capitalist class and the poor and lower middle peasants who persist in taking the socialist road. Some well-to-do peasants cling to the stand of strong individualism and departmentalism. They are dissatisfied with turning their livestock and trees to the communes following the universal building of people's communes and they oppose the grain supply system. After the universal building of people's communes, some of them considered that since no work points are to be recorded they would simply "go slow" in labor. Some well-to-do middle peasants said: "Go slow with the work of the commune and then go our meals." After the adoption of the wage system, some said: "Work as much as we are paid for." They tried to sow the seed of discord between the commune members who are paid low and those who are paid high. In addition, they are often the representatives of the rightist conservative ideology in production. This is often the contradiction between the remnant capitalist spontaneous tendency of well-to-do peasants and the socialist direction.

Second is the firm support given by the masses of working people to the universal building of people's communes but there are the contradictions between the old and new ideologies and among other ideologies. Many among them harbor the doubt that large communes are hard to operate successfully, are not accustomed to the "collectivization of life, militarization of organization, and universal adoption of a combat spirit in production", and hesitate to send their children to nurseries. Furthermore, some people's communes include too much in their supply system so that the income of some poor peasants and lower middle peasants are reduced, thereby giving rise to new contradictions.

Third is the new situation emerged in the contradiction between the cadres and the masses following the universal building of people's communes. Of course, the absolute majority of the cadres are good and they emerge in an attitude of common workers. They take the initiative in all fields of work, forget to sleep and to eat. However, following the great victory won in the universal building of people's communes and the unprecedented heightening of the awareness and discipline observance of the masses of the people, some cadres neglect the working style of mass line, thus giving rise to simplification and commandism. Some of them regard the militarization of organization as a condition prepared for the adoption of commandism. They consider "debate" and "struggle" synonymous. The people get scared when they hear the word "debate". After realizing the collectivization of life, some new problems emerged in the life of the masses. (For example, after the establishment of mess halls, people need not to use stoves at home and this presents the problem of fire for heating in winter, which must be solved immediately.) Some cadres show disinterest in this. When the masses work with redoubled efforts and an over-strain of labor, some cadres fail to organize necessary rest to reduce the physical burden of the masses with all conceivable ways and means. Some of them are indulged in subjectivism and that must be rectified. In addition, there are very few cadres who could not negotiate the "pass" of the universal building of people's communes. They seriously resist the Party policies. Some want to lie down and not to work any more. In the present campaign, the "white flags" must be dug out.

Aside from the contradictions between the enemies and ourselves, the most important of the various contradictions among the people is the struggle between the two roads and two ideologies of capitalism and socialism which must not be taken up carelessly. Such a contradiction will continue to exist for a very long period. When they saw the awareness of the masses was greatly heightened after the universal building of people's communes, some people considered that "there are no more questions about the masses" and regarded the ideological struggle between the two roads unimportant. This way of thinking is erroneous. Here, attention should first be paid to strictly distinguish the methods of handling the contradictions between the enemies and ourselves from the methods of handling the contradictions among the people. In handling the contradictions among the people, which include the above-mentioned contradiction between the two roads, the method of persuasive education, not the method of high-handed suppression, should be adopted. Next, attention should be paid not to consider all erroneous ideologies as capitalist ideology and all contradictions as struggle between the two roads. Analysis is needed here. A clear distinction between the contradiction of the two roads of socialism and capitalism and the contradiction of the new and old ideologies of those people who are in favor of the socialist road or other ideological contradictions. Although the two are associated sometimes, yet the two are completely different in nature. Like what has been mentioned above, some poor and lower middle peasants may find it unsatisfactory to have reduced income because of expanded supply system. Such kind of dissatisfaction can not be categorically considered as a "capitalistic tendency". To settle such a contradiction, not only should they be guided to manifest the socialist and Communist spirit but the adjustment to the distribution system should also be considered. In addition, any one who has doubt about the collectivization of life should not be considered as "opposing to the collectivization of life". Or, this contradiction should not be categorically regarded as "the struggle between the two roads". The concrete cause for the outbreak of dissatisfaction should be carefully analyzed and it should not done in any simple way.

The central directive says: "The campaign from its beginning to its conclusion should be practiced in adherence to the principles of correctly handling the contradictions among the people by fully manifesting democracy, adopting the methods of big contention, big blooming, big debating, big-character wall newspapers, on-the-spot conferences, and exhibitions, so that all problems are really solved in an ideological way and that it becomes really a self-education campaign of the masses of the people." It is of utmost importance to implement this directive in earnest. While carrying out spot trials of the socialist and Communist education campaign in many places, a group of hard core cadres were first trained. In fact, the hard core cadres were first given a small-scale rectification campaign to heighten their Communist awareness and to enlighten their self-consciousness in listening to the opinions of the masses and in resolutely taking the mass line. This step will definitely offer many advantages to the launching of this great ideological education campaign.

DOCUMENT 34

Communiqué of the Sixth Plenary Session of the Eighth Central Committee, issued December 17, 1958.

The English text is taken from a pamphlet entitled *Sixth Plenary Session of the Eighth Central Committee of the Communist Party of China*, Foreign Languages Press, Peking, 1958, pp. 1-11.

Comment. The general significance of the Wuhan documents has already been discussed. The last paragraph of the communique printed below contains some deferential kowtows to the U.S.S.R., not only as head of the Socialist Camp but also as the author of a historically significant program for the construction of Communism, namely the 1959-1965 program proposed by the Central Committee of the Communist Party of the Soviet Union. The significance of this act of homage, coming after Chinese propaganda and Russian silence about the rapid advance of China to Communism, is discussed in our General Introduction, part IX.

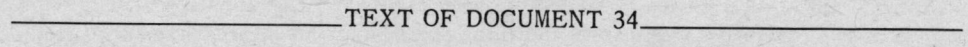

BRIEF SUMMARY OF THE COMMUNIQUE

The Session was held under the guidance of Comrade Mao Tse-tung and he made important speeches at the meetings.

The Plenary Session adopted a "Resolution on Some Questions Concerning the People's Communes." The resolution considered the movement of setting up people's communes in China's rural areas to be an event of great historic significance and elaborated a series of questions concerning the people's communes from the standpoint of theory and policy.

The Plenary Session summed up the main experiences of the unprecedented, great victory scored in the growth of China's national economy in 1958. It pointed out that the development of our national economy by leaps and bounds proved the correctness of the Party's general line of socialist construction and the whole group of policies of "walking on two legs."

The Plenary Session put forward the principle and some main targets for development of the national economy in 1959. It pointed out that for the fulfilment of the great leap forward plan in 1959 it is necessary to work fully in the spirit of the thesis consistently advocated by Comrade Mao Tse-tung that we should scorn difficulties strategically but pay full attention to them tactically, and that boundless enthusiasm should go hand in hand with scientific analysis.

The Plenary Session approved the proposal of Comrade Mao Tse-tung not to stand as candidate for Chairman of the People's Republic of China for the next term of office. It pointed out that working solely as Chairman of the Central Committee of the Party, Comrade Mao Tse-tung will be enabled to concentrate his energies all the better on dealing with questions of the direction, policy and line of the Party and the state; he will also be enabled to set aside more time for Marxist-Leninist theoretical work, without affecting his continued leading role in the work of the state. This will be in the better interests of the entire Party and of all the people of the country.

The Plenary Session pointed out that the general characteristic of the international situation is exactly as Comrade Mao Tse-tung stated at this Session: "The enemy rots with every passing day, while for us things are getting better daily." It noted with satisfaction that the socialist camp headed by the Soviet Union has grown even stronger and its unity has been consolidated even more firmly. It regarded the 1959-1965 programme for development of the national economy of the Soviet Union proposed by the Central Committee of the Communist Party of the Soviet Union as a programme for communist construction which is of great historic significance.

The Sixth Plenary Session of the Eighth Central Committee of the Chinese Communist Party was held in Wuchang from November 28 to December 10, 1958.

The Session was held under the guidance of Comrade Mao Tse-tung. It was attended by 84 members of the Central Committee including Liu Shao-chi, Chou En-lai, Chu Teh, Chen Yun, Lin Piao, Teng Hsiao-ping, Lin Po-chu, Tung Pi-wu, Peng Chen, Lo Jung-huan, Chen Yi, Li Fu-chun, Peng Teh-huai, Liu Po-cheng, Ho Lung, Li Hsien-nien, Ko Ching-shih, Li Ching-chuan and Tan Chen-lin, and 82 alternate members of the Central Committee. Leading comrades of various departments of the Central Committee concerned and first secretaries of the Party committees of various provinces, municipalities and autonomous regions, who are not members or alternate members of the Central Committee, were also present.

Between November 2 and 10, before the Sixth Plenary Session of the Central Committee was held, Comrade Mao Tse-tung had called a meeting in Chengchow which was attended by some of the leading comrades of the Party centre and some of the leading comrades in various localities. Later, between November 21 and 27, he called another meeting in Wuchang which was attended by some of the leading comrades of the Party centre and the first secretaries of the Party committees of the various provinces, municipalities and autonomous regions. These two meetings prepared for the Plenary Session.

The main items on the agenda of the Sixth Plenary Session of the Eighth Central Committee were: the question of the people's communes; the question of the national economic plan for 1959; and the question of not nominating Comrade Mao Tse-tung as candidate for Chairman of the People's Republic of China for the next term. In addition, the Session also discussed the question of improving the financial and trade administrative systems in the rural areas, and the international situation. After full and thoroughgoing discussions at group meetings and plenary meetings, the Plenary Session adopted the relevant resolutions. Comrade Mao Tse-tung made important speeches at the meetings.

The Sixth Plenary Session of the Eighth Central Committee adopted a "Resolution on Some Questions Concerning the People's Communes." The resolution evaluated very highly the movement to set up people's communes which has developed in China's rural areas in the past few months and considered this to be an event of great historic significance. The resolution elaborated a series of questions concerning the people's communes from the standpoint of theory and policy. It provided for the correct direction of the development of the people's communes, the principles of production of the communes, the introduction of a distribution system which combines the wage system and the free supply system, organizing the people's production and life, carrying through the organizational principle of democratic centralism and strengthening the Party's leading role and developing the mass line and a practical and realistic style of work. The resolution called on Party committees of various levels to make the best use of the five months from December this year to next April to check up on and consolidate the people's communes in their own areas in close integration with the production tasks for this winter and the coming spring.

The Sixth Plenary Session of the Eighth Central Committee summed up the main experiences of the growth of our national economy in 1958 and laid down the principles for development of the national economy in 1959. It pointed out that great victories without precedent has been scored in the development of China's national economy in 1958. According to present estimates of the output of industrial and agricultural products for 1958, steel will be increased from 5.35 million tons in 1957 to about 11 million tons; coal from 130 million tons in 1957 to about 270 million tons; machine-tools from 28,000 units in 1957 to around 90,000 units; grain from 185 million tons in 1957 to about 375 million tons; and cotton from 1.64 million tons in 1957 to about 3.35 million tons. The output of other important industrial and agricultural products will also register great increases.

It is estimated that the total value of industrial and agricultural output in 1958 will increase by about 70 per cent compared to 1957, while in 1957 it increased by only 68 per cent compared to 1952. The revenue in 1958 will increase by 14,000 million yuan compared to 1957, while the increase in 1957 was only 13,400 million yuan compared to 1952; investments in capital construction in 1958 will exceed 22,000 million yuan, nearly half of the total investment of 49,200 million yuan during the whole of the First Five-Year Plan.

The Plenary Session pointed out that the 1958 great leap forward in industrial and agricultural production and in the fields of science, culture and education, the great rise in the socialist and communist consciousness of the masses and the high tide of development of the people's communes during the summer and autumn of this year, are great victories for the Party's general line for socialist construction and the great fruits of the rectification campaign among the whole people. The achievements in economic construction in our country are inseparably linked with the assistance of the Soviet Union and other fraternal countries. The development of our national economy by leaps and bounds this year has proved the correctness of the whole group of policies laid down by the Party: the policy of simultaneous development of industry and agriculture on the basis of giving priority to heavy industry; the policy of simultaneous development of heavy and light industries; the policy of effecting an over-all leap forward on the industrial front with steel as the key link; the policy of simultaneous development of national and local industries; the policy of simultaneous development of large enterprises and medium-sized and small enterprises; the policy of simultaneously employing modern and indigenous methods of production, and the policy of combining centralized leadership with a full-scale mass movement in industry—in a word, the policy of walking on two legs and not on one or one and a half legs. The great leap forward in our industrial and agricultural production in 1958 is a great practice. Through this practice, we have not only found a broad way to build socialism with greater, faster, better and more economical results, but also gained rich experience in marching along this broad way. This will make it possible for us not only to continue the leap forward in 1959 but to do much better.

The Plenary Session pointed out that on the basis of the great victories and rich experiences gained in 1958, it is necessary in carrying on socialist economic construction in 1959 to continue to oppose conservatism, do away with blind faith, strictly carry out the Party's general line for socialist construction, continue to carry out the policies of simultaneously developing industry and agriculture, heavy and light industries, national and local industries, and large enterprises and medium-sized and small enterprises, of simultaneously employing modern and indigenous methods of production; to continue to carry out in industry the policy of achieving an all-round forward leap with steel as the key link and the policy of combining centralized leadership with a full-scale mass movement. At the same time, it is necessary to endeavour to put economic planning on a completely reliable basis, and to maintain suitable proportions between the various targets in accordance with the objective law of the proportionate development of the various branches of the national economy. In line with these policies and principles, the Plenary Session of the Central Committee put forward the following main targets for development of the national economy in 1959: steel output to be increased from the estimated amount of about 11 million tons this year to about 18 million tons; coal output will be increased from the estimated amount of about 270 million tons this year to about 380 million tons; grain output will be increased from the estimated amount of about 375 million tons this year to about 525 million tons; and cotton output will be increased from the estimated amount of about 3.35 million tons this year to about 5 million tons. The Plenary Session instructed the departments responsible to work out the 1959 plan for development of the national economy in the light of these main targets and in accordance with the needs of development of the national economy as a whole in 1959 and the material and technical conditions of our country, and to submit the plan to the First Session of the Second National People's Congress for discussion and adoption.

In the spirit of the thesis consistently advocated by Comrade Mao Tse-tung that we should scorn difficulties strategically but pay full attention to them tactically, and that boundless enthusiasm should go hand in hand with scientific analysis, the Plenary Session pointed out that to bring the 1959 national economic plan to realization, we must continue to oppose conservatism, get rid of blind faith and advocate boldness in thinking, speech and action; go all out, aim high and defy difficulties strategically. These are inflexible principles.

In the meantime, we must pay full attention to difficulties tactically and pursue a good, solid style of work that displays energy, perseverance and ingenuity, fix targets in a forward-looking way and take measures that will more than guarantee their fulfilment, insist on careful calculation of the facts, proper arrangements and practical inspection, guard against exaggeration and oppose concealment of shortcomings. Economic work must be done in an ever more thoroughgoing way and made to conform completely or as nearly as possible to reality.

The Plenary Session also pointed out that to carry out the plan for 1959, it is necessary to persist in putting politics in command, to rely on the masses, and to continue to follow the mass line and organize mass movements in construction; the entire Party and all the people must make concerted efforts, and all partial and local interests must be subordinated to the interests of the whole.

The Plenary Session considered that the national economic plan for 1959 worked out in the light of the above main targets will be a great leap forward plan. The Plenary Session called on the entire Party and all the people to unite as one, march heroically along the triumphant road of 1958 for the completion and overfulfilment of the national economic plan for 1959 and, in the decisive year of the three years' hard battle, achieve a greater leap forward than in 1958. The Plenary Session was confident that the people of our country will accomplish this glorious task.

After full and all-round consideration, the Sixth Plenary Session of the Eighth Central Committee decided to approve the proposal of Comrade Mao Tse-tung not to stand as candidate for Chairman of the People's Republic of China for the next term of office. The decision taken by the Plenary Session in this connection points out that this is a completely positive proposal. Because, relinquishing his duties as Chairman of the state and working solely as Chairman of the Central Committee of the Party, Comrade Mao Tse-tung will be enabled to concentrate his energies all the better on dealing with questions of the direction, policy and line of the Party and the state; he will also be enabled to set aside more time for Marxist-Leninist theoretical work, without affecting his continued leading role in the work of the state. This will be in the better interests of the entire Party and of all the people of the country.

The Plenary Session adopted a decision to improve the financial and trade administrative systems in the rural areas. This decision, after being discussed and approved by the State Council, will be published jointly by the Central Committee of the Communist Party of China and the State Council.

The Sixth Plenary Session of the Eighth Central Committee also discussed the international situation. It pointed out that recent developments in the international situation have further confirmed the fact that the forces of peace are stronger than the forces of war; that the progressive forces are stronger than the reactionary forces. These developments have further inspired the people all over the world and all who cherish peace, advocate peaceful co-existence and do not want war, and have isolated the war-makers more than ever. The imperialist camp is rent by many internal contradictions. Their so-called "unity" is now gradually heading towards its opposite; it is in the process of gradual disintegration. This process may extend over a fairly long period; but its general trend is inevitable.

Confronted with the forces of peace, of socialism and of national revolution which are growing stronger daily, the imperialists are panic-stricken. They are having a tough time of it. The general characteristic of the international situation is exactly as Comrade Mao Tse-tung stated at this Plenary Session: "The enemy rots with every passing day, while for us things are getting better daily."

The Plenary Session pointed out that the struggle of the people the world over for peace and liberation has made great progress in the past year. The struggle of the peoples in Asia, Africa and Latin America against colonialism and for national independence continues to surge ahead. The recent reactionary coups d'etat in France and certain other countries are by no means indicative of the reactionaries' strength, but of their decay and weakness. They are playing the role of "teachers by negative example" for the people; the people are enabled to draw lessons from their reactionary activities and are forced to raise their level of understanding and strengthen their unity. No adventures or struggles by the imperialist madmen of war and reactionaries can save them from final destruction. It will not do for the U.S. imperialists to try to hang on in Taiwan; if the American aggressive forces do not withdraw of their own accord, then the day will eventually come when the Chinese on the mainland and in Taiwan will unite to drive them out. Similarly, it also will not do for the U.S. imperialists to try to hang on in south Korea, south Vietnam, Japan, the Philippines, West Berlin, West Germany, Western Europe, North Africa, the Middle East and other foreign military bases; if the American aggressive forces do not withdraw of their own accord, then, similarly, the peoples of these countries will surely unite to drive them out.

The Plenary Session noted with satisfaction that in the past year the socialist camp headed by the Soviet Union has grown even stronger and its unity has been consolidated even more firmly. All the efforts of the imperialist reactionaries and revisionists to sow discord, to curse and to sabotage are doomed to failure. The Plenary Session was elated by the 1959-65 programme for development of the national economy of the Soviet Union proposed by the Central Committee of the Communist Party of the Soviet Union, and regarded this as a programme for communist construction which is of great historic significance. It represents the lofty aspirations and the splendid future of progressive mankind. Its realization will greatly change the balance of forces in the world and be of great benefit to mankind's cause of peace and the prevention of war. The Plenary Session expressed its firm conviction that in the peaceful competition between socialism and capitalism, socialism will surely emerge triumphant.

DOCUMENT 35

Decision Approving Comrade Mao Tse-tung's Proposal That He Will Not Stand as Candidate for Chairman of the People's Republic of China for the Next Term of Office, adopted by the Eighth Central Committee of the Party at its Sixth Plenary Session on December 10, 1958, and issued December 17.

The English text is taken from the pamphlet entitled *Sixth Plenary Session of the Eighth Central Committee of the Communist Party of China*, Foreign Languages Press, Peking, 1958, pp. 50-51.

———————————TEXT OF DOCUMENT 35———————————

In the past few years, Comrade Mao Tse-tung has more than once expressed to the Central Committee of the Party the wish that he should not continue to hold the post of Chairman of the People's Republic of China. Following full and all-round consideration, the Plenary Session of the Central Committee has decided to approve this proposal of Comrade Mao Tse-tung's, and not to nominate him again as candidate for Chairman of the People's Republic of China at the First Session of the Second National People's Congress. The Plenary Session of the Central Committee deems this to be a completely positive proposal, because, relinquishing his duties as Chairman of the state and working solely as Chairman of the Central Committee of the Party, Comrade Mao Tse-tung will be enabled all the better to concentrate his energies on dealing with questions of the direction, policy and line of the Party and the state; he may also be enabled to set aside more time for Marxist-Leninist theoretical work, without affecting his continued leading role in the work of the state. This will be in the better interests of the whole Party and of all the people of the country. Comrade Mao Tse-tung is the sincerely beloved and long-tested leader of the people of various nationalities of the whole country. He will remain the leader of the entire people of various nationalities even when he no longer holds the post of Chairman of the state. If some special situation arises in the future which should require him to take up this work again, he can still be nominated again to assume the duties of the Chairman of the state in compliance with the opinion of the people and the decision of the Party. Party committees at all levels should, in accordance with these reasons, give full explanations to the cadres and masses both inside and outside the Party at appropriate meetings of the Party, sessions of the people's congresses of various levels, meetings of workers in industrial and mining enterprises, and meetings in people's communes, offices, schools and armed units, so that the reasons for this may be understood by all and that there may be no misunderstanding.

DOCUMENT 36

Resolution on Some Questions Concerning the People's Communes (Wuhan Resolution), adopted by the Eighth Central Committee of the Party at its Sixth Plenary Session on December 10, 1958, and issued December 17.

The English text is taken from the pamphlet entitled *Sixth Plenary Session of the Eighth Central Committee of the Communist Party of China*, Foreign Languages Press, Peking, 1958, pp. 12-49.

Comment. There is a very large mass of detailed material available in translation on the problems discussed in the resolution on communes. This may be classified as follows (the order of headings corresponds to that in our General Introduction, part IX):

1. *Military style of work.* The sources here listed represent contemporary and of course mainly favorable accounts of the "military style," rather than explicit developments of the injunction given in the Wuhan Resolution against "commandism" and the confusion of military and Party chains of command. But these sources do illustrate the practices that were likely to give rise to complaints:

CB 517, especially the extract from *People's Daily*, Aug. 15, 1958, on militia activity in the "Firelight" cooperative in Shansi.

CB 530, containing an NCNA story from Peking, Oct. 19, 1958, which describes an "on-the-spot militia work conference" at Shihchingshan, near Peking, October 7-18. Even the "hard core" militia regiments are to be used for economic tasks as well as military training.

URS, Vol. 13, No. 2, a selection of articles about militia work from the *People's Daily*, Sept. 13, 14, and 16, 1958, and the *Kwang Ming Jih Pao*, Sept. 11, written at the height of the Offshore Islands crisis.

JPRS 666D, reprinting a pamphlet of questions and answers on communes, published at Canton in October 1958. There is an interesting answer to the question: "Does 'Everyone a Soldier' mean conscripted production?"

JPRS 1525N, reprinting a vivid account of militarization at the Weihsing commune from *Financial Research*, Sept. 15, 1958.

2. *Commune members to retain their own means of livelihood and personal possessions.* ECMM 154 (*China Youth*, Nov. 16, 1958), a vivid account of the fears aroused by the commune system and resulting action by individual members—withdrawal of savings deposits, a buying spree, and the hiding of such private consumer goods as sewing machines.

ECMM 161 (*Chinese Worker*, Dec. 27, 1958), a series of questions and answers on the Wuhan Resolution, "to be studied seriously by all workers." Conventional reassurances are given about the safety of private property (and the maintenance of family life) under the commune system. The Canton pamphlet already cited (JPRS 666D) contains similar reassurances.

SCMP 1902, reprinting an interesting item from NCNA, Nov. 12, 1958, on the question of remittances to commune members from overseas Chinese, and the preservation of property belonging to overseas Chinese.

3. *Communes in cities.* SCMP 1957, in which *Kweichow Jih Pao*, Aug. 31, 1958, shows that some urban communes had been set up at this time, and *Amoy Jih Pao*, Oct. 2 and 9, 1958, shows that the process had gone quite far.

SCMP 2009 (*Honan Jih Pao*, Feb. 22, 1959), describing the progress of communization in Kaifeng.

ECMM 155 (*Planned Economy*, Nov. 9, 1958), discussing problems of urban planning after the advent of Communism, and indicating that schools as well as factories may be units for communization.

ECMM 163 (*Teaching and Research*, Nov. 4, 1958), describing factory and street-type urban communes; the essential object of both is to increase production.

URS, Vol. 14, No. 2, items from the Shanghai *Wen Hui Pao* in October and November 1958, suggesting a drive to set up urban communes in Shanghai.

URS, Vol. 14, No. 14, quoting Shanghai papers on the Party's decision to "wait a little for them" (capitalists and intellectuals) before proceeding with urban communization.

4. *Importance of continued commodity exchange.* CB 548 (*Economic Research*, Oct. 17, 1958), discussing among other things the serious diminution in the returns of the industry and commerce taxes as a result of communization.

ECMM 157 (*Planned Economy*, Dec. 9, 1958), a report on the investigation of the market situation in Yaucheng *hsien*, Hupeh, indicating that commodity production would fall short by 20 percent of available purchasing power. ECMM 157 also contains a theoretical discussion from *Red Flag*, Dec. 14, 1958, on the need for continued commodity production and exchange, concluding that the "law of value" still operates, and that there is no "devil of capitalism" latent in the whole process.

URS, Vol. 15, No. 22, quoting a more theoretical treatment of the same theme from a Shanghai academic periodical of April 10, 1959.

5. *Payment according to work.* For some indications of the past history of this question, see:

URS, Vol. 13, No. 10, which quotes *People's Daily*, July 5, 1956, urging the extension of piece-work wages to all industries.

SCMP 1131, 1134, on the ratification by the State Council, 1956, of the decision to abolish the supply system for some government employees.

ECMM 67 (*Study*, Nov. 2, 1956), a strong attack on the "egalitarian" ideas implicit in the supply system.

ECMM 87 (*Finance*, April 5, 1957), stressing the disincentive operation of the supply system, where still in use.

ECMM 91 (*Study*, May 3, 1957), a theoretical discussion of the advantages and disadvantages of payment according to work.

ECMM 131 (*Study*, March 18, 1958), opposing the "egalitarian illusions" of some small peasants who wish to be paid as much as industrial workers.

ECMM 135 (*Planned Economy*, May 9, 1958), arguing for the reform of the wage allowance system—payment part in money and part in welfare services.

The problems of the fall of 1958 are discussed in:

CB 517 (*People's Daily*, Sept. 4, 1958), indicating that free supply of grain is contemplated at a later period.

CB 537, including correspondence and articles in the *People's Daily* and *Ta Kung Pao*, October 1958.

CB 538, articles mainly from the *People's Daily* in October and November 1958 on the importance of free supply and mess halls.

JPRS 623D, theoretical articles on the wage-and-supply issue from the *People's Daily* in November 1958.

ECMM 151 (*Political Study*, Oct. 13, 1958), remarks by Mao, on tour in Anhwei, in favor of extended supply system.

ECMM 153 (*Teaching and Research*, Sept. 4, 1958, and *Financial and Economic Research*, Sept. 15, 1958), on the negative effects of the piece-wage system.

ECMM 155 (*Red Flag*, Oct. 16, 1958), an investigation of the operations of the wage-and-supply system in a Shansi commune.

SCMP 1923, containing an article from *Kwang Ming Jih Pao* (Peking), Dec. 2, 1958, on "How to Understand Correctly the Question of Enforcing a Supply System on the Cadres." The general sense is that the vast majority of the cadres are in favor of a more progressive supply system, i.e., not a repetition but a development of what had been in operation.

6. *Transition to Communism*. Orthodox doctrine is explained, in much the same terms as those of the Peitaiho and Wuhan Resolutions (Documents 28 and 36) in the question-and-answer pamphlet and article already cited (JPRS 666D and ECMM 161). Practical difficulties of the changes of ownership already made or foreshadowed under the commune system are discussed in various articles from technical financial periodicals, October to December 1958, collected in CB 548 (see especially *Finance*, Oct. 9 and Dec. 24, 1958; and *Economic Research*, Oct. 17, 1958). More specific discussions may be found in:

ECMM 160 (*China Youth*, Jan. 1, 1959), on the long way ahead to Communism.

ECMM 161 (*New Construction*, Jan. 7, 1959), in which the Vice-Chairman of the State Planning Commission, Hsueh Mu-ch'iao, takes issue with comrades who want to hand communes over to the state and achieve Communism in three years.

ECMM 162 (*Financial and Economic Research*, January 1959), an interesting list of conditions for the transition to "ownership by the whole people" in communes.

ECMM 184 (*New Construction*, Aug. 7, 1959), in which it is said that the period of 15-20 years of transition to "ownership by the whole people" will be followed by a further long period of transition to Communism.

──────────────── TEXT OF DOCUMENT 36 ────────────────

I

In 1958 a new social organization appeared, fresh as the morning sun, above the broad horizon of East Asia. This was the large-scale people's commune in the rural areas of our country which combines industry, agriculture, trade, education and military affairs and in which government administration and commune management are integrated. Since their first appearance the people's communes with their immense vitality have attracted widespread attention.

The movement to set up people's communes has grown very rapidly. Within a few months starting in the summer of 1958, all of the more than 740,000 agricultural producers' co-operatives in the country, in response to the enthusiastic demand of the mass of peasants, reorganized themselves into over 26,000 people's communes. Over 120 million households, or more than 99 per cent of all China's peasant households of various nationalities, have joined the people's communes. This shows that the emergence of the people's communes is not fortuitous; it is the outcome of the economic and political development of our country, the outcome of the socialist rectification campaign conducted by the Party, of the Party's general line for socialist construction and the great leap forward of socialist construction in 1958.

Although the rural people's communes were established only a short while ago, the mass of the peasants are already conscious of the obvious benefits they have brought them. Labour power and the means of production can, on a larger scale than before, be managed and deployed in a unified way to ensure that they are used still more rationally and effectively, and consequently the development of production will be further facilitated. Under the unified leadership of the commune, industry, agriculture (including farming, forestry, animal husbandry, side-occupations and fisheries), trade, education and military affairs have been closely co-ordinated and developed rapidly. In particular, thousands and tens of thousands of small factories have mushroomed in the rural areas. To meet the pressing demands of the masses, the communes have set up large numbers of community dining-rooms, nurseries, kindergartens, "homes of respect for the aged" and other institutions for collective welfare, which have, in particular, completely emancipated women from thousands of years of kitchen drudgery and brought broad smiles to their faces. As the result of the bumper crops many communes have instituted a system of distribution that combines the wage system with the free supply system; the mass of peasants, both men and women, have begun to receive their wages and those families which in the past constantly worried about their daily meals and about their firewood, rice, oil, salt, soya sauce, vinegar and vegetables are now able to "eat without paying." In other words they have the most important and most reliable kind of social insurance. For the peasants, all this is epoch-making news. The living standards of the peasants have been improved and they know from practical experience and the prospects of the development of the communes that they will live much better in the future.

The development of the system of rural people's communes has an even more profound and far-reaching significance. It has shown the people of our country the way to the gradual industrialization of the rural areas, the way to the gradual transition from collective ownership to ownership by the whole people in agriculture, the way to the gradual transition from the socialist principle of "to each according to his work" to the communist principle of "to each according to his needs," the way gradually to lessen and finally to eliminate the differences between town and country, between worker and peasant and between mental and manual labour, and the way gradually to lessen and finally to eliminate the internal function of the state.

All this proves the correctness and historic significance of the Resolution on the Establishment of People's Communes in the Rural Areas adopted on the basis of the creativeness of the masses by the Political Bureau of the Central Committee of the Chinese Communist Party at its Peitaiho meeting in August 1958.

People's communes have now become the general rule in all rural areas inhabited by our people of various nationalities (except in Tibet and in certain other areas). Some experiments have also begun in the cities. In the future urban people's communes, in a form suited to the specific features of cities, will also become instruments for the transformation of old cities and the construction of new socialist cities; they will become the unified organizers of production, exchange and distribution and of the livelihood and well-being of the people; they will become social organizations which combine industry, agriculture, trade, education and military affairs, organizations in which government administration and commune management are integrated. There are, however, certain differences between the city and the countryside.

Firstly, city conditions are more complex than those in the countryside.

Secondly, socialist ownership by the whole people is already the main form of ownership in the cities, and the factories, public institutions and schools, under the leadership of the working class, have already become highly organized in accordance with socialist principles (with the exception of some of the family members of the workers and staffs). Therefore, the switch-over of cities to people's communes inevitably involves some requirements different from those in the rural areas.

Thirdly, bourgeois ideology is still fairly prevalent among many of the capitalists and intellectuals in the cities; they still have misgivings about the establishment of communes—so we should wait a bit for them.

Consequently, we should continue to make experiments and generally should not be in a hurry to set up people's communes on a large scale in the cities. Particularly in the big cities, this work should be postponed except for the necessary preparatory measures. People's communes should be established on a large scale in the cities only after rich experience has been gained and when the sceptics and doubters have been convinced.

The rural people's communes which have already been established have not had time to consolidate their organizations, perfect their working systems, or systematically settle the new questions concerning production, distribution, livelihood and welfare, management and administration which have arisen with the establishment of the communes. This is because the communes were only recently set up and most of them, immediately after their establishment, threw themselves into the heavy work of the autumn harvest, ploughing and sowing and the nation-wide campaign for iron and steel. There is as yet insufficient experience in successfully running and developing the people's communes. Different approaches to certain questions are unavoidable. The urgent tasks at present are to quickly achieve a unity of views on the communes among all members of the Party and among the people, strengthen the leadership over the communes, check up on and consolidate their organization, define and perfect their working systems, and improve the organization of production and life in the communes. Energetic efforts must be made to strengthen those communes which have already been set up, so that they will be in a position to carry out ever more successfully their great mission of promoting the development of the productive forces and the relations of production.

II

The people's commune is the basic unit of the socialist social structure of our country, combining industry, agriculture, trade, education and military affairs; at the same time it is the basic organization of the socialist state power. Marxist-Leninist theory and the initial experience of the people's communes in our country enable us to foresee now that the people's communes will quicken the tempo of our socialist construction and constitute the best form for realizing, in our country, the following two transitions.

Firstly, the transition from collective ownership to ownership by the whole people in the countryside; and,

Secondly, the transition from socialist to communist society. It can also be foreseen that in the future communist society, the people's commune will remain the basic unit of our social structure.

From now on, the task confronting the people of our country is: through such a form of social organization as the people's commune, and based on the general line for socialist construction laid down by the Party, to develop the social productive forces at high speed, to advance the industrialization of the country, the industrialization of the communes, and the mechanization and electrification of agriculture; and to effect the gradual transition from socialist collective ownership to socialist ownership by the whole people, thus fully realizing ownership by the whole people in the socialist economy of our country and gradually building our country into a great socialist land with a highly developed modern industry, agriculture, science and culture. During this process, the elements of communism are bound to increase gradually and these will lay the foundation of material and spiritual conditions for the transition from socialism to communism.

This is a gigantic and extremely complex task. In the light of experience already gained, as the concrete conditions now stand in our country, it is possible that socialist ownership by the whole people may be fully realized at a somewhat earlier date but this will not be very soon. Though the pace at which we are advancing is fairly rapid, it will still take a fairly long time to realize, on a large scale, the industrialization of our country, the industrialization of the communes, the mechanization and electrification of agriculture and the building up of a socialist country with a highly developed modern industry, agriculture, science and culture. This whole process will take fifteen, twenty or more years to complete, counting from now.

The imperialists and those who parrot them say that this is too short a time for us to build a highly developed modern industry, agriculture and science and culture, and that we won't be able to achieve our aim. We've got used to such tunes; we needn't pay any attention to them; the facts are bound to batter these people down time and time again. But there will be other people who will say that this time is too long. They are good-hearted people in our own ranks, but they are over-eager. They think that the building of a highly developed modern industry and so on, full realization of socialist ownership by the whole people, or even the attainment of communism, are very easy things. They think that ownership in the rural people's communes is even now of the nature of ownership by the whole people and that very soon or even now they can dispense with the socialist principle of "to each according to his work" and adopt the communist principle of "to each according to his needs." Consequently, they cannot understand why the socialist system will have to continue for a very long time. Their view, of course, is a misconception, which must be cleared up.

It should be pointed out that the switch from agricultural producers' co-operatives to people's communes, the transition from socialist collective ownership to socialist ownership by the whole people and the transition from socialism to communism are processes which are interconnected but at the same time distinct from each other.

First of all, the switch from the agricultural producers' co-operatives to the people's communes has expanded and strengthened the existing collective ownership and contains certain elements of ownership by the whole people. But this is not to say that collective ownership in the countryside has been transformed into ownership by the whole people. The whole Chinese countryside has now switched over to people's communes, but a certain time will have to pass before ownership by the whole people is realized throughout the countryside.

True, the establishment of the people's communes has added certain elements of ownership by the whole people to the collectively owned economy. This is because the rural people's communes and the basic organizations of state power have been combined into one; because the banks, stores and some other enterprises owned by the whole people, originally existing in the countryside, have been placed under the management of the communes; because the communes have taken part in establishing certain undertakings in industrial and other construction which are by nature owned by the whole people; because in many counties the county federations of communes, exercising unified leadership over all the people's communes in these counties, have been formed and have the power to deploy a certain portion of the manpower, material and financial resources of the communes to undertake construction on a county or even bigger scale (this has already started in many areas), and so on. But at the present time the means of production and the products of the rural people's communes are in the main still collectively owned by the communes and differ from those of the state-owned enterprises which belong to the whole people. Both collective ownership and ownership by the whole people are socialist ownership; but the latter is more advanced than the former because the state, representing the whole people, can directly make a unified and rational distribution of the means of production and the products of enterprises owned by the whole people according to the requirements of the national economy as a whole, while this cannot be done with regard to enterprises run under collective ownership, including the existing rural people's communes. To say that ownership now existing in the rural people's communes is already ownership by the whole people does not conform to reality.

To gradually promote the transition from collective ownership to ownership by the whole people, every county should set up its federation of communes. In coming years, on the basis of the energetic development of production and the raising of the people's political understanding, such federations should take suitable steps gradually to increase the proportion of their means of production that is owned by the whole people and the proportion of their products that is subject to unified distribution by the state, and, when conditions mature, should change collective ownership into ownership by the whole people. If timely steps are not taken to promote and complete this change and if the existing collective ownership is kept intact indefinitely with the result that commune members confine their attention to the relatively narrow scope of the interests of their collective, the continuous development of the social productive forces and the continuous raising of the people's political understanding will be impeded. This is not appropriate. However, it must be pointed out that collective ownership still plays a positive role today in developing production in the rural people's communes. How soon the transition from collective ownership to ownership by the whole people will be effected will be determined by the objective factors—the level of development of production and the level of the people's political understanding—and not by mere wishful thinking that it can be done at any time we want it. Thus this transition will be realized, by stages and by groups, on a national scale only after a considerable time. Those who, because they fail to understand this, confuse the establishment of people's communes with the realization of ownership by the whole people, making impetuous attempts to abolish collective ownership in the countryside prematurely, and trying hastily to change over to ownership by the whole people, will not be doing the right thing and therefore cannot succeed.

Furthermore, the change from socialist collective ownership to socialist ownership by the whole people is not the same thing as the going-over from socialism to communism. Still less is the change from agricultural producers' co-operatives to people's communes the same thing as the change from socialism to communism. The change from socialism to communism will require much more time than the change from socialist collective ownership to socialist ownership by the whole people.

True, the free supply system adopted by the people's communes contains the first shoots of the communist principle of "to each according to his needs"; the policy carried out by the people's communes of running industry and agriculture simultaneously and combining them has opened up a way to reduce the differences between town and countryside and between worker and peasant, and when the rural people's communes pass over from socialist collective ownership to socialist ownership by the whole people, the communist factors will grow further. All this must be acknowledged. Moreover, with social products becoming increasingly plentiful thanks to the continuous advance of industry and agriculture throughout the country; with the proportion of what is supplied gratis under the distribution system of the people's communes gradually growing larger and the standards of free supply being gradually raised; with the consistent raising of the level of the people's communist understanding; with the constant progress of education for the whole people; with the gradual reduction of the differences between mental and manual labour; and with the gradual diminution of the internal function of the state power, etc., the conditions for the transition to communism will also gradually mature. It is of course not proper to ignore or even impede this course of development and relegate communism to the distant future.

Nevertheless every Marxist must soberly realize that the transition from socialism to communism is a fairly long and complicated process of development and that throughout this entire process society is still socialist in nature. Socialist society and communist society are two stages marked by different degrees of economic development. The socialist principle is "from each according to his ability and to each according to his work"; the communist principle is "from each according to his ability and to each according to his needs." The communist system of distribution is more rational; but it can be put into effect only when there is a great abundance of social products. In the absence of this condition, any negation of the principle of "to each according to his work" will tend to dampen the working enthusiasm of the people and is therefore disadvantageous to the development of production and the increase of social products, and hence to speeding the realization of communism. For this reason, in the income of commune members, the portion constituting the wage paid according to work done must occupy an important place over a long period and will, during a certain period, take first place. In order to encourage the working enthusiasm of commune members and also to facilitate the satisfaction of their complex daily needs, the communes must strive gradually to increase the wages of their members and, for a number of years to come, must increase them at a rate faster than that portion of their income which comes under the heading of free supply. Even after the transition from collective ownership to ownership by the whole people, the people's communes will, during a necessary period of time, retain the system of "to each according to his work," owing to the fact that there is not as yet an abundant enough supply of social products to realize communism. Any premature attempt to negate the principle of "to each according to his work" and replace it with the principle of "to each according to his needs," that is, any attempt to enter communism by overreaching ourselves when conditions are not mature—is undoubtedly a Utopian concept that cannot possibly succeed.

Both the transition from socialist collective ownership to socialist ownership by the whole people and the transition from socialism to communism must depend on a certain level of development of the productive forces. Production relations must be suited to the nature of the productive forces and only when the productive forces develop to a certain stage will certain changes be brought about in production relations—this is a fundamental principle of Marxism. Our comrades must bear in mind that the present level of development of the productive forces in our country is, after all, still very low. Three years of hard battle plus several years of energetic work may bring about a great change in the economic face of the country. But even then there will still be a considerable distance to go to reach the goals of a high degree of industrialization of the entire country and the mechanization and electrification of our country's agriculture; and there will be an even longer distance to go to reach the goals of an enormous abundance of social products, of a great lightening of labour and of a sharp reduction of working hours. Without all these, it is, of course, impossible to talk about entering a higher stage of development in human society—communism. Therefore, since we are devoted to the cause of communism, we must first devote ourselves to developing our productive forces and working energetically to fulfil our plan for socialist industrialization. We should not groundlessly make declarations that the people's communes in the countryside will "realize ownership by the whole people immediately," or even "enter communism immediately," and so on. To do such things is not only an expression of rashness, it will greatly lower the standards of communism in the minds of the people, distort the great ideal of communism and vulgarize it, strengthen the petty-bourgeois trend towards equalitarianism and adversely affect the development of socialist construction.

On the question of transition from socialism to communism, we must not mark time at the socialist stage, nor should we drop into the Utopian dream of skipping the socialist stage and jumping over to the communist stage. We are advocates of the Marxist-Leninist theory of uninterrupted revolution; we hold that no "Great Wall" exists or can be allowed to exist between the democratic revolution and the socialist revolution and between socialism and communism. We are at the same time advocates of the Marxist-Leninist theory of the development of revolution by stages; we hold that different stages of development reflect qualitative changes and that these stages, different in quality, should not be confused. The Political Bureau of the Central Committee has pointed out clearly in its August Resolution on the Establishment of People's Communes in the Rural Areas: in the case of the people's communes, "the transition from collective ownership to ownership by the whole people is a process, the completion of which may take less time—three or four years—in some places, and longer—five or six years or even more—elsewhere. Even with the completion of this transition, people's communes, like state-owned industry, are still socialist in character, i.e. the principle of 'from each according to his ability and to each according to his work' prevails. Some years after that the social product will become very abundant; the communist consciousness and morality of the entire people will be elevated to a much higher degree; universal education will be achieved and the level raised; the differences between worker and peasant, between town and country, between mental and manual labour—the legacies of the old society that have inevitably been carried over into the socialist period—and the remnants of unequal bourgeois rights which are the reflection of these differences will gradually vanish; and the function of the state will be limited to protecting the country from external aggression; and it will play no role internally. At that time Chinese society will enter the era of communism in which the principle of 'from each according to his ability and to each according to his needs' will be practised." In order to clear up misconceptions about the people's communes and ensure the healthy development of the people's commune movement, extensive and repeated publicity and education based on this Marxist-Leninist point of view must be carried out seriously throughout the Party and among all the people of China.

III

The people's communes must plan their production, exchange, consumption and accumulation. Their plans should be subordinated to the state plans and to the administration of the state. In working out their plans, the people's communes should at the same time fully develop their own characteristic features and their initiative.

Development of production is the key to the consolidation and elevation of the people's communes. The correct policy of the people's communes for the development of production should be: to ensure the simultaneous development of industry and agriculture and of production for their own use and for exchange, in accordance with the principles of unified state planning, of adaptation to local conditions and of running the communes industriously and thriftily. In all fields of production and capital construction, strict economy must be practised; careful plans must be worked out; and manpower, material and financial resources must be used as rationally as possible; production costs must be reduced; expenditures must be cut down and income increased; extravagance and waste among some functionaries of the communes following bumper harvests should be prevented and opposed.

In agricultural production, shallow ploughing, careless cultivation, and "big acreage with low yield" should be gradually replaced by deep ploughing, intensive cultivation, and "small acreage with high yield." Farming should be carried on as meticulously as gardening, and agricultural production should be mechanized and electrified to bring about a big increase in per *mou*[1] yields and labour productivity and to gradually reduce the area under cultivation and manpower engaged in agriculture. We should strive to reach a yearly average of two to three thousand catties or one ton to one and a half tons of grain per capita within a comparatively short period. As the grain problem is solved, the proportion of the total agricultural output occupied by cotton, flax and jute, silk, soya beans, oil-bearing crops, sugar-bearing crops, tea, tobacco, medicinal and other industrial crops must be gradually increased. In addition, great attention should be paid to speeding the development of forestry, animal husbandry, farm side-lines and fisheries. In short, as on the industrial front, a great

---

[1] A *mou* is equivalent to 1/6 acre or 1/15 hectare.

revolution must be carried out on all the fronts of agriculture—farming, forestry, animal husbandry, farm side-lines and fisheries—so as to thoroughly change the face of agriculture.

People in the past often worried about our "over-population" and relatively small amount of available arable land. But this idea has been overturned by the facts of our 1958 bumper harvest. Insofar as we succeed in seriously popularizing the rich experience gained in getting high yields through deep ploughing, intensive cultivation, layer-by-layer fertilization and rational close planting, it will be found that the amount of arable land is not too small but very considerable, and that the question is not so much over-population as shortage of manpower. This will be a very big change. In a number of years to come, local conditions permitting, we should try to reduce the area sown to crops each year, say, to about one-third of what it is at present. Part of the land so saved can lie fallow by rotation or be used for pasturage and the growing of green manure; the rest can be used for afforestation, reservoirs and the extensive cultivation of flowers, shrubs and trees to turn our whole land with its plains, hills and waters into a garden. By these means:

Firstly, it will be possible to greatly economize the use of water, fertilizer and manpower, and to considerably increase the fertility of the soil;

Secondly, full use can be made of every mountain, river, forest and the pasture, and the comprehensive management of farming, forestry, animal husbandry, farm side-lines and fisheries can be greatly developed;

Thirdly, our natural environment will be transformed and the whole country beautified.

This is a great ideal that can be realized. People's communes throughout the countryside should work to realize this aim.

People's communes must go in for industry in a big way. The development of industry by the people's communes will not only accelerate the industrialization of the whole country but also promote the realization of ownership by the whole people in the rural districts, and reduce the differences between town and country. According to the differing conditions in each people's commune, an appropriate part of the labour force should be transferred, step by step, from agriculture to industry so as to develop, according to plan, the production of fertilizer, insecticides, farm implements and machinery and building materials; the processing and many-sided utilization of agricultural produce; the manufacturing of sugar, textiles and paper; the expansion of mining, metallurgy, electric power and other light and heavy industries. Industrial production in the people's communes must be closely linked with agricultural production; it should first of all serve the development of agriculture and the mechanization and electrification of farming; at the same time it should serve to meet the demands of commune members for staple consumer goods, and serve the country's big industries and the socialist market. The principles of adaptation to local conditions and obtaining raw materials locally should be fully taken into consideration; in order to avoid increased costs and waste of labour power, industries should not be set up in places where raw materials are lacking and have to be brought from very far away. With regard to production techniques, the principle should be carried out of linking handicraft with mechanized industry, and indigenous methods with modern methods of production. All handicraft industries which have good foundations and prospects for expansion must continue to be developed, and gradually carry through the necessary technical reform. The mechanized industries must also make full use of indigenous methods and iron, steel, machine-tools, other raw materials and equipment produced by indigenous methods; they will gradually advance from indigenous to modern, from small to large and from a low to a high level.

Whether in industry or agriculture, people's communes should develop production for their own use which directly meets their own needs, and they should also develop commodity production on as wide a scale as possible. Every people's commune according to its own characteristics and under the guidance of the state should carry out necessary division of labour in production and exchange of commodities with other people's communes and state-owned enterprises. Only in this way can the economy of our whole society expand at a faster rate, and every commune get through exchange the machinery and equipment required for the mechanization and electrification of farming, as well as the consumer goods and ready cash required to meet the needs of commune members and pay them wages, and make it possible to raise wages step by step. To ensure fulfilment of trading plans, a system of contracts should be extensively set up between the state and the communes and among the communes themselves.

It must be stressed that during the course of a necessary period of time commodity production by the people's communes and the exchange of commodities between the state and communes and among the communes themselves must be greatly developed. Such production and exchange of commodities are different from those under capitalism, because they are conducted in a planned way, on the basis of socialist public ownership and not in an anarchic way on the basis of capitalist private ownership. Continued development of commodity production and continued adherence to the principle of "to each according to his work" are two important questions of principle in expanding the socialist economy. The whole Party should have a common understanding of them. Some people, attempting to "enter communism" prematurely, have tried to abolish the production and exchange of commodities too early, and to negate at too early a stage the positive roles of commodities, value, money and prices. This line of thinking is harmful to the development of socialist construction and is therefore incorrect.

IV

The people's communes in rural districts should distribute their own incomes properly on the principle of running the communes industriously and thriftily. To speed up production, the proportion of accumulation should be appropriately increased after production costs, administrative expenses and taxes have been deducted from the gross income. But on the basis of the development of production, the portion of the income used to meet the individual and collective expenses of commune members (including the portion spent on public welfare, culture and education) should be increased annually in order to improve the livelihood of the people year by year.

The introduction of a distribution system which combines the wage system and the free supply system in the part of the commune's income allotted to its members for consumption is a form of socialist distribution created by China's people's communes, and at the present time it represents what the broad mass of members earnestly demand. As stated above, this distribution system includes the first shoots of communism but in essence it is still socialist—based on the principle of "from each according to his ability and to each according to his work."

The proportions of wages and free supplies in the total amount allotted to members should be determined in the light of the varying conditions of the development of production in the communes. At present, in fixing the ratio between wages and free supplies, care should be taken as far as possible to avoid reducing the income of households which have relatively few members but are strong in labour power; in general, it should be made possible for more than 90 per cent of the members to increase their income as compared with the previous year while the rest should get no less than in the previous year.

For the present, the scope of free supply should not be too wide. The application of the free supply system does not seek to make the life of the people uniform. Under socialism and communism, the needs of the people are on the whole similar while varying according to the individual. Therefore in the future as well as at present care should be taken to ensure, as far as possible, that members have suitable freedom of choice within the framework of the free supply system.

Wages must be increased gradually as production expands. For the present, except the items freely supplied, wage scales in the rural areas may, in general, be divided into six to eight grades, and the highest grade may be four or more times as much as the lowest grade. But the differences should not be too great; for if they were they would not conform to the existing differences in labouring skills in the rural areas. Certain differences between the wage levels in different areas are permissible. For the present differences between wage grades in the city are greater than those in the countryside, and this is necessary. In the future, as a result of the tremendous rise in production, everyone will be much better off and whether in city or countryside such differences between wage grades will be unnecessary and will gradually disappear. That will be nearing the era of communism.

The reasons why wage levels in the city are generally higher than those in the countryside are many-sided (including the factor of living costs being higher in the city), and this is also a temporary situation which should be explained to the peasants. Some commune members, apart from working in the villages, also receive money sent home by their relatives who are away in cities or elsewhere (such as workers, armymen, functionaries and Chinese living abroad). Work should be done to dissuade other members from wrangling about this. In distribution within the commune, members with such receipts should be treated the same as others without discrimination in regard to free supplies and wages, and they should not be urged to make special investments or contributions to the commune. If they rely on family members away from home for the whole of their livelihood, the commune should not interfere, but it may stop supplying them with the usual allotments. Those who leave home for study, apart from those whose needs are covered by the state or can be covered by their own families, should be supported by the county federation of communes according to the standards laid down by the schools.

The more socialism develops and the more abundant social products become, the more abundant will certainly become the means of livelihood allotted to each individual. Some people think that the switch to communes will call for a redistribution of existing property for personal use. This is a misconception. It should be made known among the masses that the means of livelihood owned by members (including houses, clothing, bedding and furniture) and their deposits in banks and credit cooperatives will remain their own property after they join the commune and will always belong to them. When necessary, the commune may borrow the surplus housing space of members with their consent, but the ownership still belongs to the owners. Members can retain odd trees around their houses, small farm tools, small instruments, small domestic animals and poultry; they can also continue to engage in some small domestic side-line occupations on the condition that these do not hamper their taking part in collective labour.

Debts incurred before the people's communes were established should not be declared cancelled irrespective of whether these are between individuals, between the commune and its members, or debts contracted by commune members with banks or credit co-operatives. These debts should be repaid where conditions permit and where the conditions do not allow repayment for the time being, they should be held over.

V

The people's commune is the organizer of the production and life of the people and the fundamental purpose of the development of production is to satisfy to the maximum extent the constantly growing material and cultural needs of all members of society. In leading the work of the commune, the Party must give all-round attention to the ideological development, production and livelihood of commune members. It must care for the people and correct the tendency to see only things and not human beings. The greater the working enthusiasm of the masses, the greater the attention the Party should pay to their well-being. The more attention the Party pays to the livelihood of the masses, the greater their enthusiasm will be in work. It is wrong to set production and people's livelihood against each other and to imagine that attention to the livelihood of the masses will hamper production. Of course, it is also wrong to put a one-sided or excessive stress on the improvement of the people's livelihood without regard to the raising of their level of political consciousness and the development of production, and not to advocate working hard for long-term interests.

Communists have always held that in a communist society labour will be changed "from a heavy burden into a pleasure" and will become the "primary necessity of life." There is no doubt that the working day will be greatly shortened in future. With the development of mechanization and electrification, we must strive to introduce the six-hour workday within a certain number of years. Our intensive work at the present time is precisely to create conditions for the six-hour workday and even shorter working hours in future. At present, the system of eight hours of actual work and two hours of study should be put into effect in both city and countryside. During the busy farm season or when other work in the rural areas is particularly heavy, working hours may be appropriately extended. But, in any event, eight hours for sleep and four hours for meals and recreation, altogether twelve hours, must be guaranteed every day and this must not be reduced. It is true that there is a labour shortage at present, but the way out must be found in stressing the successful implementation of the reform of tools and improvement of labour organization and not in extending working hours. Special attention must be paid to safety in production and labour conditions must be improved as far as possible in order to reduce to the minimum or completely eliminate work accidents. Adequate rest must be ensured to women both during pregnancy and after childbirth and they should also get the necessary rest during menstruation when they should not be asked to do heavy work, to get their feet wet in cold water or work at night.

Community kitchens should be well run. All commune members must be assured of plenty, good and clean food suited to their national and local habits. The communal eating establishments should have dining-rooms, and they should efficiently run their own vegetable gardens, beancurd mills, bean-noodle mills, and condiment shops; they should raise pigs, sheep, chickens, ducks and fish. The food should be varied and appetizing. Nutrition specialists should be consulted to make sure that the food contains enough calories and the nutriments needed by the human body. Where necessary and possible, special food should be provided for the aged, children, invalids, pregnant women, women who have just been confined, and nursing mothers. It is permissible for some commune members to cook at home. Community dining-rooms should be managed democratically. Their administrative staffs and cooks should be chosen from among those who are politically reliable. It is best that they be elected democratically.

Nurseries and kindergartens should be run well so that every child can live better and receive a better education in them than at home, and so that the children want to stay there and the parents want to put them there. The parents may decide whether it is necessary for their children to board there, and may take them home at any time. In order to run nurseries and kindergartens well, the communes should train a large number of qualified child-care workers and teachers.

The "homes of respect for the aged" should be run well so as to provide better dwelling places for those old people who have no children to take care of them (those who are eligible for the "five guarantees").[1]

Communes must ensure the successful running of primary and secondary schools and adult education. Universal primary school education should be instituted in the rural areas throughout the country. Full-time secondary schools and half-time secondary agricultural schools, or other secondary vocational schools, should be well run and universal secondary education should be introduced step by step. Earnest efforts should be made to wipe out illiteracy, organize various kinds of sparetime schools and conduct political education, cultural classes and technical education for adults. In reducing the differences between manual and mental labour, the institution of universal education among the working people and the gradual raising of their educational level is an important step which must be carried out conscientiously. The communes, in addition, must also select and send a number of young people to study in senior secondary schools, secondary vocational schools and institutions of higher learning in the cities so as to train fairly well educated working personnel for the state and the communes. The principle of combining education with productive labour must be carried out thoroughly in all schools, without exception. Children above the age of nine may take part in some labour to an appropriate extent so as to cultivate the habit of work in childhood and stimulate their physical and mental development; but full attention must be paid to the health of the children, they must only be given light work for short periods of time, suited to their physical strength and their aptitude.

Ideological and political work among the staffs in community dining-rooms, nurseries, kindergartens, "homes of respect for the aged," primary schools, public health centres, clubs and shops must be strengthened and efforts must be made to give positive guidance to public opinion so that the whole of society and the whole communes regard the successful running of community dining-rooms, nurseries, kindergartens and other collective welfare undertakings and satisfactory service work as noble work of service to the people. The attitude of the exploiting classes in looking down on work which concerns the daily life and welfare of the masses and work in the personal services, must be criticized and corrected.

The existing old-style houses must be reconstructed step by step; townships and village housing estates with parks and woods must be built by stages and in groups; these will include residential quarters, community dining-rooms, nurseries, kindergartens, the "homes of respect for the aged," factories, threshing floors, livestock sheds, shops, post and telecommunications offices, warehouses, schools, hospitals, clubs, cinemas, sports grounds, baths and public lavatories. The construction plans of townships and village housing estates should be thoroughly discussed by the masses. We stand for the abolition of the irrational patriarchal system inherited from the past and for the develop-

---

[1] The "five guarantees" represent the special help extended by the agricultural co-operatives to the aged, the weak, the orphaned, the widowed and the disabled, who lack labour power or are entirely unable to work, and who are without means of support. The co-operatives assure them a regular supply of food, clothing and fuel and see to it that the young have a chance of education and the aged a proper burial after death.—*Tr.*

ment of family life in which there is democracy and unity. This stand has been warmly received by the masses. Therefore, in building residential quarters, attention must be paid to building the houses so that the married couples, the young and the aged of each family can all live together.

There is now a big bunch of fools in the world who are attacking the people's communes with all their might and main and among them is Mr. Dulles of the United States. This Dulles knows nothing about things in our country but likes to pretend to be a China expert and madly opposes the people's communes. What breaks his heart especially is that we have supposedly destroyed the marvellous family system which has been handed down for thousands of years. True, the Chinese people have destroyed a feudal, patriarchal system. This patriarchal system, it must be noted, generally disappeared long ago in capitalist society and that was a progressive step in capitalist society. But we go a step further and establish a democratic, united family and this is generally rare in capitalist society. Only in the future, when the socialist revolution has been carried out and when the capitalist system of exploitation of man by man has been eliminated, will it be possible to establish such families there universally. As to nurseries, kindergartens and workers' canteens in the factories, these also first appeared in capitalist society. But under capitalism, all such undertakings established by the bourgeoisie are capitalist in nature and are aimed at facilitating the exploitation of men and women labourers by the capitalists. On the other hand, such undertakings run by us are socialist in nature and they facilitate the development of the socialist cause and the emancipation of the individual personality of man. They have truly and completely emancipated the mass of women and enabled the children to receive better education and care. That is why they are warmly welcomed by all the working people, and first of all by the masses of women.

VI

The organizational principle of the people's commune is democratic centralism. This principle must be thoroughly applied in the management of production, in the distribution of income, in the work concerning the life and welfare of commune members and in all other aspects of work.

Unified leadership as well as management at different levels should be put into effect in the people's commune. The administrative set-up of the commune may in general be divided into three levels, namely: the commune administrative committee, the administrative district (or production brigade) and the production team. The administrative district (or production brigade) is in general the unit which manages industry, agriculture, trade, education and military affairs in a given area and forms a business accounting unit, with its gains and losses pooled in the commune as a whole. The production team is the basic unit of labour organization. Under the unified leadership of the commune administrative committee, necessary powers should be given to the administrative district (or production brigade) and the production team over such matters as the organization of production work and capital construction, finances and welfare, in order to bring their initiative into full play.

The various levels of organizations of the county federation of communes and of the people's commune must learn to make reasonable distributions and deployments of manpower for the different branches of production (agriculture, industry, transport) and for routine production work, shock production tasks and service work, so as to avoid situations where there is work without men in one place and there are men without work in another. The organization of labour must be constantly improved, the system of responsibility for a given task at a given level must continue to be applied and reinforced in production and other tasks, the system of labour inspection and labour awards must be perfected in order to guarantee effectively the steady improvement of labour efficiency and the quality of work.

There must be both discipline and democracy in the organizations of labour in the people's commune. What we describe as getting organized along military lines means getting organized on the pattern of a factory. It means that the organizations of labour in the people's commune should be as organized and disciplined as in a factory or the army; this is necessary in large-scale agricultural production. The forces of large-scale agricultural production, like the forces of large-scale industrial production, constitute an industrial army. The modern industrial army was organized by the bourgeoisie, each factory being like a military camp. The discipline for the worker standing before the machine is as rigid as that in the army. The industrial army in socialist society is an industrial army of a single class, the working class, which has got rid of the capitalists who squeezed surplus value out of the workers and which has put into force in the working class a vigorous and lively democratic centralism based on the voluntary principle. We are now applying this system to the rural areas, thus establishing a socialist industrial army for agriculture based on democratic centralism, which is free from exploitation by the landlords and rich peasants and is elevated above the level of small-scale production.

Militia organizations should be set up at corresponding levels of the production organizations in the people's commune. The leading bodies of the militia and production organizations should be separate and, in principle, the commanding officers of the various levels of the militia such as regimental, battalion and company commanders, should not be concurrently directors of communes and administrative districts (leaders of production brigades) and leaders of production teams. These commanders should take part in the administrative organizations of the same levels in the commune as their members, and they will receive dual leadership: from the administrative organizations of the same level and the superior commanding organizations of the militia. The militia should be equipped with the necessary arms produced by arsenals set up locally. The basic units of the militia should undergo military training according to a set schedule, while the ordinary militiamen should also get appropriate training during the break of work; this is to prepare conditions for turning the whole nation into soldiers. The broad mass of working people in our country greet the militia system warmly, because, in the course of their protracted revolutionary struggle against imperialism, feudalism and their lackeys, the Kuomintang reactionaries, they came to realize that only by arming themselves would they be able to overcome the armed counter-revolution and become masters of the land of China. After the victory of the revolution, they have come to see further that there are still imperialist pirates abroad who are clamouring every day about wiping out this people's state. Therefore, the whole of our people are determined to continue to arm themselves, and they declare: Be warned, you pirates bent on plundering us; do not dare to make a vain attempt to harm our people engaged in peaceful labour; we are fully prepared! Should the imperialists dare to unleash an aggressive war against our country, then we will turn the whole nation into soldiers; the militia will co-operate with the People's Liberation Army and at any time replenish it to crush the aggressors utterly.

There should be both centralism and democracy in all organizations of the people's communes, including the militia organizations. The people's communes should not only organize the people's production work but the people's livelihood as well. In order to do their work well, the communes must practise a high level of democracy, consult the masses on all matters, faithfully represent their interests and reflect their will. Therefore, while "organizing along military lines, working as if fighting a battle and living the collective way," the communes must fully implement democratic management. It is absolutely impermissible to use "getting organized along military lines" as a pretext or to make use of the militia system—which is directed against the enemy—to impair, in the least, democratic life in the communes and the militia organizations. The people's commune is the basic organization of our country's state power; only by fully ensuring democracy in the commune will it be possible to create throughout the country a vigorous and lively political situation in which there are both centralism and democracy, both discipline and freedom, both unity of will and personal ease of mind.

VII

In running a people's commune well the fundamental question is to strengthen the leading role of the Party. It is only by strengthening the Party's leading role that the principle of "politics in command" can be realized, that socialist and communist ideological education among the cadres and commune members and the struggle against all kinds of erroneous tendencies can be conducted in a thoroughgoing way and that the Party's line and policy can be implemented correctly. There are some people who think that with the emergence of the commune the Party can be dispensed with, and that they can practise what they call "merging the Party and the commune in one." This kind of thinking is wrong.

In its work in the people's commune, the Party, besides its task of ensuring that the correct line and policy are put into effect, should also pay attention to educating the commune staffs to develop good styles of work—first of all the mass line and a practical style of work.

Following the 1957-1958 rectification campaign, the Party's mass line achieved a new, great victory. The great leap forward in socialist construction and the setting up of people's communes throughout the rural areas are two signal marks of this victory. The mass-line working method of the Party is the lifeblood of the people's communes. The setting up and consolidation of the people's communes is impossible without the mass line, without the full confidence of the people in the Party and in the People's Government and without an upsurge in the revolutionary zeal of the masses. Therefore, leading functionaries of all levels in the commune must put the mass line thoroughly into practice in every type of work tackled. They must look upon themselves as ordinary working people, and treat the commune members in a comradely way. Kuomintang and bourgeois styles of work which coerce the masses are strictly prohibited. Because of the big leap forward in production and the victory in setting up communes, some cadres are beginning to get dizzy with success and, unwilling to do the patient work of educating the masses by persuasion, they are exhibiting certain rude attitudes. Though these are individual cases, they should make us keenly vigilant.

In all its work, the Party should hold fast to the principle of combining revolutionary zeal with a scientific spirit. The great leap forward in 1958 has won an unprecedented victory for socialist construction in our country. Now even our enemies find it impossible to deny the significance of this victory. But we must never overlook our small weak points because of big achievements. On the contrary, the bigger the achievement the more we need to remind our cadres to keep cool-headed and not be carried away by the flood of news of victory and become unable or even unwilling to see the weak points in their work. One tendency which deserves our attention in the present work of socialist construction is exaggeration. This is incompatible with the practical working style of our Party, and is harmful to the development of our socialist construction. We must do our economic work in an ever more thoroughgoing way. Our leading personnel at all levels must be good at differentiating between the reality and false appearance of things and between demands which are justified and those which are not; in assessing conditions they must strive to keep close to objective reality. Only by doing so can we work out and carry through our plans on a reliable and solid basis.

VIII

In order to promote the consolidation of the people's communes and ensure an even bigger leap forward in industrial and agricultural production in 1959, the Party committees of the provinces, municipalities and autonomous regions should, in accordance with the requirements set forth in this resolution and in close integration with the production tasks of the winter and spring seasons, make full use of the five months from December 1958 to April 1959 to carry out, within the people's communes in their areas, educational work, overhaul and consolidation, that is the work of checking up on the communes.

In the course of checking up on the communes, it is necessary, in the first place, for leading personnel to make earnest self-criticisms and listen with modesty to the masses' opinions, and on this basis, mobilize the masses with great daring to air their views freely and frankly, carry out debates and post up *tatsepao*,[1] to commend good persons and deeds, criticize wrong ideas and bad styles of work, sum up experiences, clarify the line of work and develop a thoroughgoing socialist and communist ideological education movement.

In the course of checking up on the communes, it is necessary to carry out an over-all and thorough inspection of the production plan, distribution, welfare, management, financial work, organization and leadership in the communes. The organizations of the Party and communes should be carefully checked over at the same time to guarantee that leading personnel of the Party and communes at various levels are activists loyal to the interests of the people and to the cause of communism. In addition, the finest people who have been tested in the big leap forward and people's commune movement and are qualified for Party membership, should be enrolled in the Party.

Problems related to the style of work of Party members and cadres should be dealt with through Party education and frank airing of views by the masses. In dealing with these problems, attention should be paid to keeping up the zeal and initiative of the cadres and masses, and the principles of "unity—criticism—unity" and "taking warning from the past in order to be more careful in the fu-

---

[1] Written opinions in big Chinese characters posted publicly for everybody to read.

ture" and "treating the illness in order to save the man" must be observed. Those who have committed errors but are willing to correct them should be criticized seriously but treated with leniency. The masses should be mobilized to purge the leadership in the communes of those alien class elements who have smuggled themselves into the leadership and the very few who display a very bad style of work and have never corrected their errors even after being repeatedly admonished.

Complex class struggles not only develop sharply abroad, in the capitalist world, but also exist at home. It is necessary to educate the masses to increase their revolutionary vigilance to prevent disruptive enemy activities. Whether ex-landlords, rich peasants and counter-revolutionaries and other people deprived of political rights should be accepted as members or probationary members of the communes, or remain to work under the communes' supervision, should be discussed and decided by the masses dealing with each case on its merits in the course of checking up on the communes.

The work of checking up on the communes should first be carried out in one or two communes in each county as an experiment. That is to say, help should be given to the comrades in one or two people's communes to get things going well in a fairly short space of time, so as to acquire experience, set examples and then popularize the experience gained generally. Every province, municipality and autonomous region should organize its inspection teams consisting of a thousand, several thousands or ten thousand people for the check up, and the first secretaries of the Party committees at the provincial, regional and county levels should personally lead the work of checking up on the communes. These inspection teams should compare different special administrative regions, counties and communes, organize mutual visits, call on-the-spot meetings to develop the good points and overcome the shortcomings, rouse the drive of the people, and find ways of concretely solving current problems and promptly popularizing successful experience. In short, through these check-ups, the work of the people's communes in the country must be generally carried one step forward.

DOCUMENT 37

Report on Government Work, by Chou En-lai, delivered to the First Session of the Second National People's Congress, April 18, 1959.

The text is from the NCNA English-language release of April 18, 1959, as reprinted in CB 559.

Comment. For the political and economic context of this speech, see our General Introduction, part IX. The main emphasis is on the need for centralized leadership in addition to (or instead of) local initiative in the development of industry. The effect of the 1958 decentralization to local governments in the arrangement of industrial construction and production and of the encouragement of local industries at the communal level had been to produce chaos in planning and allocation of raw materials. For some time before Chou spoke, the Chinese leaders had been urging the institution of something like a system of priorities, under the slogan "The whole country a coordinated chess game." This slogan was launched in a *People's Daily* editorial of February 24 (SCMP 1970), which emphasized the need to distribute investment funds and construction projects around the country in an orderly way, to determine production targets, and to allocate raw materials according to a single plan. Each level of administration must produce its over-all plans; this concept is pushed very far by Chou En-lai in his mention of "10-day, monthly or quarterly time-tables" for the most important products and projects. The draft National Economic Plan for 1959, accepted by the Central Committee of the Party early in April of that year, was approved by the National People's Congress to which it was presented by Li Fu-ch'un on April 21 (CB 562).

The other primary domestic theme of Chou's speech was the consolidation of the communal system. The four-month period of examination and reorganization prescribed in the Wuhan Resolution (Document 36) was now almost over. As becomes apparent from the Lushan Resolution of the Central Committee (Document 40 below), this period had been marked by a resolution of the Politburo, which held a meeting in February at Chengchow, and by a series of directives covering: (a) business accounting at all levels; (b) the wage system "to each according to his work"; and (c) a three-level ownership system, with basic ownership at the production brigade level.

The process of consolidation was not at an end. Chou demanded, in his section II, that "every people's commune throughout the country should in the nearest future convene a representative conference of its members to sum up the results of the check-up" (p. 515 below). Teng Tzu-hui also spoke to the National People's Congress on agricultural themes (CB 575), and it is possible from his remarks to deduce some of the minor faults revealed by the check-up—over-close planting, over-hasty work in dam and irrigation projects, need to produce more subsidiary food. Two further themes mentioned by Chou in his section II were much discussed later: the need to keep manpower on agricultural rather than industrial tasks, and the need for production contracts between trading organizations on the one hand and the communes or production brigades on the other. Source material on these and cognate themes may be found as follows:

(a) *On consolidation of communes.* CB 575, containing speech by Teng Tzu-hui to the National People's Congress in April 1959.

SCMP 1975 (*Ta Kung Pao*, Feb. 18, 1959), communes not to aim at self-sufficiency.

SCMP 2013 (*People's Daily*, April 22, 1959), regulations on democratic management of communes.

SCMP 2059 (*Ta Kung Pao*, June 15, 1959), detailed production plan for Ch'ayang-shan commune.

SCMP 2066 (*People's Daily*, July 23, 1959), importance of restoring sown acreage.

JPRS 626D (*Masses Daily*, Feb. 12, 1959), draft regulations for reorganization of Shantung communes.

ECMM 158 (*Red Flag*, Feb. 16, 1959), Li Hsien-nien on improving rural administration.

ECMM 161 (*Red Flag*, Jan. 16, 1959), tidying up communes on a mass scale.

ECMM 174 (*Finance*, July 13, 1959), importance of correct accounting system.

(b) *On priorities for industry.* ECMM 166 (*Economic Research*, Feb. 17, 1959, on priorities in communes; and *Red Flag*, March 1, 1959, Ch'en Yun on problems of capital construction).

ECMM 176 (*Red Flag*, June 1, 1959), importance of improving quality.

SCMP 1970 (*People's Daily*, Feb. 24, 1959)—"The whole country a coordinated chess game."

(c) *On priority for agricultural work.* SCMP 2067 (*People's Daily*, July 26, 1959), communes to transfer hoarded industrial materials for immediate use.

Incidental points in Chou's speech may be mentioned as follows:

In his section I he discusses the "8-point constitution" for agriculture. This is described in ECMM 161 (*Current Events*, Dec. 1, 1958) as an 8-point measure for the increase of production, set out in the Revised 12-Year Agricultural Program and confirmed in October 1958 as the constitution for agriculture. Originally there were six points, attributed by Teng Hsiao-p'ing to Mao Tse-tung: water conservancy, application of fertilizer, soil improvements, deep plowing, close planting, and field management. These six points and two others were adopted by an agricultural conference at Sian in October 1958.

In his section V, Chou makes an extravagant reference to the Soviet Union's Seven-Year Plan, as signifying that "the Soviet Union has entered an important historical period—that of the all-out building of Communist society." This statement goes further than the terms of the Wuhan communiqué (Document 34). See also ECMM 159 (*Red Flag*, Feb. 16, 1959, lauding the Soviet Seven-Year Plan and quoting Khrushchev's remarks on the conditions for transition to Communism).

The effect of the establishment of communes on Chinese prestige in the doctrinal sphere, and on Sino-Soviet relations, is discussed in Zbigniew K. Brzezinski, *The*

Soviet Bloc: *Unity and Conflict* (Cambridge: Harvard University Press, 1960), pp. 366-370.

Chou's interesting passages on Tibet and on foreign relations fall outside the scope of this study. Our comment on Document 44, in Chapter XI, contains some brief notes on the Chinese treatment of national minorities as a whole. On Tibet, the CB series contains many collections of Chinese newspaper material (e.g., CB 564). For a short historical treatment, see Frank Moraes, *The Revolt in Tibet* (New York: Macmillan, 1960).

The parenthesized notes in Document 37 were in the NCNA release.

―――――――――――――――――TEXT OF DOCUMENT 37―――――――――――――――――

In accordance with the decision of the State Council, I will now report on the work of the government to the first session of the 2nd National People's Congress.

(1) THE GREAT ACHIEVEMENTS OF THE FIRST FIVE-YEAR PLAN PERIOD AND OF 1958—THE FIRST YEAR OF THE SECOND FIVE-YEAR PLAN

During the four years and more of the term of office of the first National People's Congress, a series of changes of great historic significance have taken place in our country.

When the first session of the 1st National People's Congress convened in 1954, the socialist sector already occupied a leading position in our national economy, but there still remained a large amount of capitalist industry and commerce and of individual agriculture and handicrafts. There was a widespread development of the mutual-aid movement in the rural areas, with about 60 per cent of all peasant households joining agricultural labor mutual-aid teams, but only about 2 per cent of all peasant households had organized themselves into agricultural producers' cooperatives. By that time our country had completed the tasks of the period of economic recovery, and begun large-scale, planned economic construction, but it remained to be seen whether we would be able in a fairly short period to lay a foundation for socialist industrialization in such a big country as ours with a population of more than 600 millions. How do things stand now? All of us can see what brilliant achievements in socialist revolution and socialist construction have been gained in just over four years by the Chinese people under the leadership of the Chinese Communist Party and Chairman Mao Tse-tung.

In 1955 and 1956, the country carried out the overall socialist transformation of capitalist industry and commerce, and of agriculture and handicrafts, thus accomplishing in the main the task of the socialist revolution in the sphere of ownership of the means of production. Now, with the exception of certain national minority areas, our country has in the main only two types of ownership of the means of production—socialist ownership by the whole people and socialist collective ownership. In 1957 and the first half of 1958, our people carried through the nation-wide rectification campaign and the struggle against the bourgeois rightists, linking a great victory for the socialist revolution on the ideological and political front. Thus, in the struggle between the two roads, socialism has now won a basic victory over capitalism on all fronts.

In our country socialist construction and socialist revolution are carried out simultaneously, with the one promoting the other. From 1953 to 1957, China implemented its First Five-Year Plan for development of the national economy. When we put forward this plan, the imperialists declared that it was all a dream foredoomed to failure. But the fact is that we overfulfilled the First Five-Year Plan in 1957 and, on this basis, began to implement the even grander Second Five-Year Plan in 1958.

As a result of the fulfillment and overfulfillment of the First Five-Year Plan, the total value of our industrial and agricultural output in 1957 amounted to 138,740 million yuan, an increase of 68 per cent compared with 1952 when it was 82,710 million yuan. The total output value of industry reached 65,020 million yuan, an increase of 141 per cent over 1952 when it was 27,010 million yuan; that of handicraft production reached 13,370 million yuan, an increase of 83 per cent over 1952 when it was 7,310 million yuan; and that of agriculture reached 60,350 million yuan, an increase of 25 per cent over 1952 when it was 48,390 million yuan.

(*Note*: In calculating the output value of industry and agriculture during the First Five-Year Plan period, prices were taken as being constant at the 1952 level. The output value of industry and agriculture in 1952 and 1957 was also calculated on the same basis. Because the prices of a certain number of industrial and agricultural products were adjusted in 1957, in calculating the output value of industry and agriculture during the Second Five-Year Plan period prices are taken as being constant at the 1957 price level. Therefore, when compared the output value in 1957 with those of the years of the Second Five-Year Plan period, all should be calculated taking prices as being constant at the 1957 price level. Thus, the total output value of industry and agriculture in 1957 should be 124,100 million yuan, that of industry and handicrafts, 70,400 million yuan, and that of agriculture, 53,700 million yuan.)

During the First Five-Year Plan period, capital investments made by the state in the economic and cultural fields totalled 49,300 million yuan, exceeding by 15.3 per cent the planned figure of 42,740 million yuan. During the five years under review construction started on more than 10,000 industrial and mining projects, of which 921 were above-norm ones, a total of 227 more than was envisaged under the plan. By the end of 1957, 537 above-norm industrial and mining projects had been completed or partially completed and had gone into production.

As a result of fulfillment of the First Five-Year Plan, we not only greatly strengthened those branches of industry which already existed, but created many new branches such as manufacturing industries for the production of metallurgical, mining and power-generating equipment, aircraft, motor vehicles and modern machine tools, as well as smelting industries for high-grade alloy steels and important non-ferrous metals. There was a big increase in our technical forces too. In 1957, industries throughout the country employed 175,000 engineers and technicians, a three-fold increase compared with 1952 when the number was 58,000; industries and capital construction projects employed 10,190,000 workers and staff, or 66 per cent more than in 1952 when the number was 6,150,000. As a result of the increase both in industrial output and the variety of industrial products, the rate of industrial self-sufficiency in both materials and equipment also went up. For example, in 1957 the rate of self-sufficiency in rolled steel reached 86 per cent, and in machinery and equipment, over 60 per cent.

At the same time, important changes took place in the ratio between industry and agriculture, and between heavy and light industries. Industry and handicrafts contributed 41.5 per cent of the combined output value of industry and agriculture in 1952, while in 1957 their share rose to 56.5 per cent. In 1952, capital goods accounted for 39.7 per cent of the total output value of industry; this proportion jumped to 52.8 per cent in 1957.

It may therefore be said that by fulfilling and overfulfilling the First Five-Year Plan, a preliminary foundation was laid for the socialist industrialization of our country.

In 1958, the first year of the Second Five-Year Plan, a big leap unparalleled in Chinese history took place in the development of our national economy.

In 1958 the total value of our industrial and agriculture output reached 205,000 million yuan; this was 65 per cent more than the 124,100 million yuan in 1957. The total output value of industry and handicrafts amounted to 117,000 million yuan, or 66 per cent more than the 70,400 million yuan in 1957. Compared with 1957, the outputs of pig iron, steel, coal, power-generating equipment, locomotives, motor vehicles, and motors more than doubled (part of the pig iron and steel output was produced by indigenous methods). The total value of agricultural output reached 88,000 million yuan, this was 64 per cent more than the 53,700 million yuan in 1957. Outputs of food crops, cotton and cured tobacco also more than doubled. Capital investments realized through the state budget totalled 21,400 million yuan, or 70 per cent more than the 12,600 million yuan in 1957.

In the case of many industrial and agricultural products increases in output in 1958 alone exceeded the increases of 1957 over 1952. For instance, compared with 1952, steel output in 1957 increased by four million tons; coal, by 64 million tons. Machine tools (here and below, excluding simple machine tools), by 14,300; food crops, by 16,200 million catties; and cotton, by 6.73 million *tan*. Compared with 1957, however, steel output in 1958 increased by 5.73 million tons; coal, by 140 million tons; machine tools, by 22,000; food crops, by 380,000 million catties, and cotton, by 33,580,000 *tan*.

Side by side with this leap forward in industry and agriculture, big advances were also made in transport, tele-communications and posts, in commerce, and in culture and education.

In the course of the big leap forward in 1958, the Chinese people made a great creation in social organization—the people's commune established in response to the demands of the broad mass of peasants in the rural areas throughout the country. On the basis of agricultural cooperation, 120 million peasant households in the country went on to organize themselves into over 26,000 large-scale people's communes in which industry, agriculture, trade, education and military affairs are combined and government administration and commune management are merged. This form of organization, the people's commune, has emerged to meet the needs of the big advance in our industry and agriculture. It will have vitally important significance for the development of our country's social economy. Under the conditions obtaining in our country, it is not only the best form for promoting the continued development of the productive forces and quickening the tempo of socialist construction, but is the best form for effecting the future transition of our entire countryside from socialist collective ownership to ownership by the whole people and the transition from socialist to Communist society.

The expansion of the national economy in 1958 is clearly not just an ordinary advance but a gigantic and all-round leap forward.

Our national economy has developed at a speed which has never been attained and cannot be attained, under the capitalist system. Take steel for instance. Britain's annual steel output exceeded 1.31 million tons as early as in 1880; but by 1935 it had only increased to 10.02 million tons. China's steel output was 1.35 million tons in 1952, but by 1958 it had already increased to 11.08 million tons. That is to say, it took us only six years to achieve in steel production what it took Britain more than fifty years to do. As regards coal, early in 1854 Britain was already able to produce 65.7 million tons, about as much as we produced in 1952, which was 66.49 million tons. It was not till 1907, after a lapse of more than fifty years, that Britain increased its coal output to 270 million tons; while it took our country only six years to reach that level in 1958. Twice in the early 20th century British coal output came close to 300 million tons, but it has declined and stagnated in the past 20-odd years. In 1958 it was only about 220 million tons, and lagged behind that of our country.

The imperialists, and in particular the U.S. imperialists, have done all they could to deny that this big leap has taken place in our national economy, because they know that this fact will inevitably strengthen the confidence of people the world over in the superiority of socialism and increase their doubts about the capitalist system. Since they have found it impossible to deny the facts about our big leap, they have resorted to every form of distortion and slander. No matter how they rack their brains, they will never achieve their ends. They allege that we are practicing slave labor. The work which the workers and peasants do voluntarily and conscientiously for their own well-being is described as "slave labor", while bitter toil for the capitalists and landlords in the face of the threat of starvation is called "free labor". And then how comes it that the masses of so-called "free" laborers in the western world live in sorrow and suffering while the so-called "slave" laborers under socialism are filled with joy and hope? They allege that the well-being of the people is sacrificed in this country. But while unemployment is spreading everywhere in the capitalist world, the socialist system not only has ended once for all the phenomenon of unemployment long inherited from the old society but also insures that the standards of living of our more than 600 million people rise steadily along with the growth of production. During the big leap forward of 1958, the year-round average figure of workers and employees in the country increased by about eight million compared with 1957. The number of people employed in cities has never been so large; while in the countryside the broad mass of women have been relieved of their household chores and joined agricultural production. However, as a result of the all-round leap in industrial and agricultural production and because mechanization cannot proceed so fast in our country, a shortage of manpower is still being felt in the cities and countryside. The incomes of our people have increased remarkably, and so has their purchasing power; the total retail sales of commodities increased by 16 per cent over 1957. Particular mention should be made of the fact that, while our capital goods industries spurted ahead, the output value of our consumer goods industries also increased by 34 per cent in 1958 alone. Has the capitalist world ever attained such rates of increase? The bosses of the western bourgeoisie can make as much noise as they like. Our workers and peasants have lost nothing but the "freedom" to be unemployed and starve.

The imperialists are unable to understand nor do they want to understand the reasons for our big leap. What are the reasons after all?

The big leap forward in 1958 was brought about on the basis of the victory of our socialist revolution and fulfillment of the First Five-Year Plan. The fact that for a long time in the past our country was "poor and blank", both economically and culturally, was not because we lacked manpower or natural resources but because we lacked a social system which could meet the requirements of the development of the productive forces. As you all know, ours is a country with a big population, rich natural resources and good climatic conditions, all of which are highly favorable to the growth of the productive forces. Old China had the same population and the same geographical conditions, but semi-colonial and semi-feudal as it was, it could never have brought about any leap forward. Even after liberation it would have been impossible to achieve such a big leap forward as that of 1958 before we had carried out the socialist transformation of capitalist industry and commerce, individual peasant economy and handicrafts, and won a revolutionary victory on the political and ideological fronts. Moreover, with fulfillment of the First Five-Year Plan, the building of a number of big, modern key enterprises, and the training of a body of personnel fully capable of mastering modern techniques, we were able to design and build on our own some fairly large and technically complicated industrial enterprises, such as integrated iron and steel works of an annual capacity of 1,500,000 tons of steel, coal mines of an annual capacity of 2,400,000 tons of coal, hydro-electric power stations of a generating capacity of one million kilowatts and steam power stations of a generating capacity of 650,000 kilowatts. Without this material and technical foundation, it would also have been impossible for us to achieve the big leap in 1958.

The most important reason for the 1958 big leap forward was, however, the fact that in the spring of 1958 we summed up the experience gained in carrying through the First Five-Year Plan, succeeded in finding out a better way of building socialism in our country, and worked out the general line of "going all-out, aiming high and getting greater, quicker, better and more economical results to build socialism." This general line, laid down by the Central Committee of the Chinese Communist Party and Chairman Mao Tse-tung, is a line which takes full account of the enthusiasm of more than 600 million people in building socialism after the victory of the socialist revolution, and mobilized all positive factors to the fullest extent. It was under the guidance of this general line that the big leap forward of 1958 was brought about.

Under the general line, we effected an overall leap forward in the industrial field with steel as the key link, following the policy of giving priority to heavy industry and simultaneously developing heavy and light industries. Steel is the most important material at the present stage of our industrial production and capital construction and an insufficient output of it hampers the growth of our entire national economy. In 1958, therefore, we mobilized the whole nation to increase the output of iron and steel, and so raised steel output from 5,350,000 tons in 1957 to 11,080,000 tons. The leap forward in steel output gave a direct impetus to a leap forward in the coal industry and created conditions for a simultaneous leap forward in the machine-building and other industries. How could the iron and steel and other industries develop at such high speed? This was because, on the industrial front, we implemented the policy of simultaneous development of national and local industries, the policy of simultaneous development of large enterprises and medium-sized and small enterprises, the policy of simultaneously employing modern and indigenous methods of production, and the working method of combining centralized leadership with a full-scale mass movement in industrial management, thus opening up the concrete way of developing our industry with greater, quicker, better and more economical results.

In 1958, we extended the powers of local governments in the arrangement of industrial construction and production. This gave a dynamic spur to the initiative of local organs of all levels and the working people in energetically building industry, greatly accelerated the tempo of construction and rapidly increased industrial output. More than 1,000 above-norm industrial and mining enterprises, either newly built or expanded, were started in 1958 by the Central Government and the provincial, municipal and autonomous regional governments; of these about 700, either completed or partially completed, went into operation. This exceeded the total of 537 industrial and mining enterprises which were put into operation, either completed or partially completed, during the First Five-Year Plan period. Large numbers of below-norm industrial and mining projects simultaneously employing modern and indigenous methods of production were started by different provinces, municipalities, autonomous regions, special administrative regions and *hsien*, and most of these, either completed or partially completed, were put into operation in 1958. In addition, the people's communes set up a host of industrial and mining units which in the main employ indigenous methods of production. Thanks to all this construction, our industrial production capacity has rapidly increased.

Of course, the big leap forward in industry in 1958 depended mainly on increased production in existing enterprises. By expanding equipment, increasing the labor force, improving management and the efficiency in the utilization of equipment and raising labor productivity, the existing enterprises greatly increased their production. Many enterprises put into effect the measures of workers' participation in management, cadres' participation in production, the welding of leading personnel, technicians and workers into a single entity, and launched a mass movement to improve working techniques, equipment and the design of products, make more rational use of materials, make fuller use of existing equipment, develop the trial manufacture and production of new products, improve labor organization, and reform irrational rules and regulations. As a result, full play was given to the productive potential of existing industrial enterprises.

The great achievements scored in 1958 on the agricultural front also testified to the power of the general line for socialist construction; they proved that industry and agriculture should and can be developed simultaneously and that agriculture, as well as industry, can be developed at top speed. As a matter of fact, the 1958 leap in industry and agriculture began with the latter. Our output of agricultural machinery and chemical fertilizer is still low, but once the initiative of the peasants is brought into full play farm yields per unit area can still be raised rapidly. The national program for agricultural development as revised in 1957 stipulates that by 1967 the per unit area yield of grain in the three regions into which the country is divided should reach the targets of 400, 500 and 800 catties respectively and in the case of cotton, 60, 80, and 100 catties respectively. As a matter of fact, by 1958 most *hsien* and municipalities throughout the country reached ahead of schedule the targets of grain production laid down for them in the national program for agricultural development, while most of the country's cotton producing areas also hit ahead of schedule the targets of cotton production set them by the program. In the same year, many places reported exceptionally high yields of grain and cotton reaped over wide area.

The measures taken by the peasant masses to raise per unit area yields are those covering soil improvement, fertilizer, water conservancy, seed selection, close planting, plant protection, field management, and tools reform, which are commonly called the "8-point constitution" for agriculture.

In the case of soil improvement, a great amount of work was done to deep plow the land, improve soil fertility and level the fields. In the case of fertilizer in 1958, sources of fertilizer were further expanded than in previous years and large numbers of small factories and workshops were built to make and process all kinds of fertilizer. In water conservancy, 480 million *mow* of irrigated area were added in 1958 compared with the preceding year, an increase of over 90 per cent. In seed selection, improved strains were in the main popularized for such major crops as rice, wheat and cotton and improved strains were exchanged between different areas. Close planting in varying degree was practiced extensively and much experience was gained in experiments with rational close planting. Much was also done in plant protection and elimination of plant diseases and insect pests. In 1958, notable achievements were registered in field management; high-yielding fields and experimental plots were popularized everywhere; and intensive and meticulous garden-style cultivation of farmlands was put into trial practice in some places. All this played a dynamic and leading role in reforming farming techniques. Tools reform made initial headway all over the country; the movement to use all sorts of vehicles to replace the shoulder-pole and the popularization of ball bearings were warmly welcomed by the peasants; new farm tools of all types were invented in large numbers.

The fact that the measures for increased industrial and agricultural production could be popularized and crowned with success was inseparably connected with the close ties existing between the Party and the masses and the raising of the socialist consciousness of the masses as a result of the rectification campaign. The principle of "Party secretaries assuming leadership and placing politics in command" was accepted by the broad masses of people. The measures of cadres participating in manual labor and cultivating experimental plots, transferring cadres to work at the grass-roots levels, and cadres eating, living and working with the masses, were carried out throughout the country; these measures greatly inspired the enthusiasm of the workers and peasants. In every sphere of endeavor, a series of measures was taken to overcome conservatism, topple old idols, promote a Communist style of doing things and the spirit of daring in thinking, speaking, acting, inventing and creating, to organize visits for study and make public appraisals of work done, and spread socialist emulation and cooperation. All this had great effect in pushing production and construction forward to an upsurge and insured the realization of the all-round big leap forward of the national economy.

The countries in the socialist camp headed by the great Soviet Union have given us many-sided assistance in our socialist construction. The 166 important projects which the Soviet Union helped us to build during the First Five-Year Plan period played a notable role in the development of our economic construction. The rich store of experience garnered by the Soviet Union since it was founded is another important base on which we draw up and carry out our economic construction plans.

Our achievements are phenomenal. But for a country with a population of over 600 million, the industrial and agricultural levels we have now reached are still very low. To meet the big requirements of our economic development and improvement of the people's livelihood, we must continue to work hard. Because the time is very short since we embarked on our socialist construction and even shorter since we put into effect the general line for socialist construction put forward by the Party, our experience is far from adequate and there are not a few shortcomings in our work. We must, therefore, continue to learn with modesty and we have no grounds whatsoever for self-complacency. On the basis of the great victories of 1958, we should continue to leap forward along the road opened up in 1958 and strive to win even greater victories on all fronts in 1959.

(II) OUR TASKS ON THE ECONOMIC FRONT IN 1959—THE SECOND YEAR OF THE SECOND FIVE-YEAR PLAN

1959 is the second year in which the Chinese people are implementing their Second Five-Year Plan for development of the national economy under the guidance of the general line for socialist construction. The 6th plenary session of the 8th Central Committee of the Chinese Communist Party, which convened in November 1958, discussed the major tasks and policy in developing the national economy in 1958 and put forward four targets—18 million tons of steel, 380 million tons of coal, 1,050,000 million catties of grain and 100 million *tan* of cotton. On the basis of these targets and the conditions of production and construction in the first quarter of this year, the 7th plenary session of the 8th Central Committee of the Chinese Communist Party in early April this year adopted the 1959 draft plan for development of the national economy. This draft has been adopted by the State Council and submitted for consideration and decision to the current session of the National People's Congress. We consider that the main task of the whole nation this year is to work energetically to fulfill and overfulfill the national economic development plan centering on the four major targets.

The 1959 plan for development of the national economy envisages a continued big leap forward. As we can see from the draft plan, the total value of industrial and agricultural output in 1959 will increase by 40 per cent over the 205,000 million yuan in 1958 and amount to 287,000 million yuan; of which the share of industry and handicrafts will be 165,000 million yuan and the share of agriculture 122,000 million yuan. Of 32 major industrial products, the output of 17 items will increase by over 50 per cent. These are pig iron, steel, crude oil, sulphuric acid, chemical fertilizer, antibiotics, power generating equipment, locomotives, freight wagons, tractors, grain combine harvesters, power-driven shellers, engines and motors, cotton spinning machines, paper making equipment, sugar refining equipment and sugar. With few exceptions, the output of the other major industrial products will also increase by more than 30 per cent. The output of certain products will be doubled or even increased several times. For example, in 1958 China produced power generating equipment with a total capacity of only 800,000 kilowatts, while the total capacity of such equipment produced in 1959 will be 2.8 to 3 million kilowatts, representing an increase of 250 to 275 per cent. Major items in agriculture whose output will increase by over 40 per cent include grain, cotton, jute, ambary hemp, sugar cane, sugar beet, ground-nuts, rapeseed and the number of pigs in the pig sties.

The total investment in capital construction for 1959 set out in the state budget is 27,000 million yuan, 26 per cent more than in 1958 when it was 21,400 million yuan. The number of above-norm projects under construction this year totals 1,092. They include 51 iron and steel enterprises, 33 non-ferrous metals enterprises, 154 engineering works, 184 power stations, 83 collieries, 19 oil-mining and oil-refining enterprises, 53 chemical enterprises, 105 building materials enterprises and lumbering enterprises, 161 light industrial enterprises, 28 water conservancy projects, and 5,500 kilometers of new railway trunk lines, double tracks, branch lines and special lines for various enterprises. Investments in these above-norm construction projects account for about two-thirds of the total capital investment this year. The remainder of the investment will be used to build large numbers of below-norm projects.

To provide the necessary transport facilities for the rapid development of industrial and agricultural production and capital construction, the plan sets the volume of railway freight at 520 million tons in 1959, an increase of 36 per cent over the 380 million tons in 1958; the volume of freight handled by enterprises directly under the Ministry of Communications will amount to 35 million tons, or 25 per cent over the 28 million tons in 1958. The plan lays it down that, on the basis of a continued leap forward in agricultural and light industrial production, the total retail sales in 1959 will amount to 65,000 million yuan, an increase of 19 per cent over the 54,800 million yuan in 1958.

The 1959 plan is drawn up in accordance with the Party's general line of "going all-out, aiming high, and getting greater, quicker, better and more economical results to build socialism"; it is drawn up on the basis of the set of policies included in the concept of "walking on two legs"—the policy of the simultaneous development of industry and agriculture on the basis of priority for heavy industry, the policy of the simultaneous development of heavy and light industries, the policy of the simultaneous development of national and local industries, the policy of the simultaneous development of large enterprises and medium-sized and small enterprises, and the policy of simultaneously employing modern and indigenous methods of production. The plan takes into account not only the objective possibilities presented by the material and technical conditions in our country but also the subjective driving force born of the revolutionary energy of the masses; it not only takes into account the requirement of mutual coordination between industry and agriculture, between heavy and light industries and between production and transport in the course of their development but also adheres to the principles of laying stress on the most important things in construction, giving priority to heavy industry, particularly to industries producing raw and other materials, and regarding steel as the key link. The production of 18 million tons of steel is the most important task on the industrial front. To accomplish this task, the plan has raised as far as possible the production targets for pig iron, coal and electric power as well as for transport, and given the engineering industry the task of speeding up production of equipment for mining, coal washing, coke making, steel rolling, power generation and transport. To alter the situation in which industries providing raw materials and other materials and power lag behind the processing industries, we have raised the rate of increase in the output of steel products, copper, aluminum, sulphuric acid and electric power. In accordance with the requirement of simultaneous development of heavy and light industries, the plan provides that in 1959 there will be an increase of 46 per cent in the output of capital goods and an increase of 34 per cent in the output of consumer goods. Provision has been made in the plan for increases in the output of certain industrial goods needed by the people in their daily life and especially those which were not produced in sufficient quantities for some time in the past. In accordance with the requirement of simultaneous development of industry and agriculture, the plan provides that the total value of industrial and handicraft output in 1959 will increase by 41 per cent over 1958 while the total value of agricultural production will increase by 39 per cent over 1958. To coordinate increases in the output of agricultural and animal products with light industrial development and the people's rising standards of living, the rates of increase for bast-fiber, sugar cane, rapeseed, pigs, cattle and horses will be raised in 1959 under the condition of insuring a continued big leap forward in grain and cotton production. Industrial support for agriculture will also be strengthened to supply the latter with more irrigation and drainage machines, tractors, grain combine harvesters, power-driven shellers, wheelbarrows with rubber tires, chemical fertilizers and farm insecticides.

Fulfillment of the magnificent 1959 plan for national economic development will further expand the material foundation of socialism in our country, provide better conditions for the continued leap forward in our industry and for agricultural mechanization, achieve ahead of schedule and overfulfill the targets for grain and cotton output set in the national program for agricultural development, and insure a continued rise in the people's material living standards.

The percentage increases in the targets of quite a number of products set in the 1959 plan compared with 1958, are higher than those achieved in 1958 compared with 1957. This is true in the case of such industrial products as electric power, sulphuric acid, chemical fertilizer, freight wagons, cotton spinning machines, cotton yarn, cotton cloth, paper, edible vegetable oils and sugar, as well as such farm produce as jute, ambary hemp, sugar cane, rapeseed, big livestock and pigs. There are also certain products whose planned percentage increases in 1959 output are lower than those achieved in 1958 but which will have increases in absolute output greater than in 1958. For instance, steel output in 1958 increased by 107 per cent or 5.73 million tons compared with 1957; the planned rate of increase in 1959, compared with 1958, is 62 per cent, but the planned increase in absolute terms is 6.92 million tons. This also applies to the total value of industrial and agricultural production: in 1958 it increased by 65 per cent compared with 1957, an increase of 80,900 million yuan; its increase in 1959 will be 40 per cent compared with 1958, but in absolute figures the increase will be 82,000 million yuan. Therefore, the rate of increase must not be measured only in percentages but at the same time in absolute figures. It is quite impracticable to regard the leap forward as meaning that the percentage increase of the total value of industrial and agricultural output and the output of every single product must be higher in each succeeding year.

Moreover, in the course of the leap forward it is also possible that output increases of certain industrial and agricultural products, particularly certain agricultural products, in one particular year may be lower than in the previous year. The 1959 plan schedules an increase of 40 per cent in grain production and this is undoubtedly a very high rate, rarely known in history. It should be remembered that an increase in grain output is to a great extent limited by natural conditions and it is impossible to double output year after year or send it up constantly by as much as the absolute increase registered in 1958. When there are still very few farm machines and very little chemical fertilizer, even an annual increase of between 10 and 20 per cent is a leap forward. The absolute increase in grain output in 1959 will be 300,000 million catties and this is an enormous figure. We all know that our total grain output in the highest pre-liberation year of 1936 was only 277,400 million catties. When the economy had recovered in the post-liberation year of 1952, it was still only 308,800 million catties. As a result of the efforts made during the First Five-Year Plan, it just reached 370,000 million catties in 1957. Now, on the basis of the increase of 380,000 million catties scored in 1958, we are going to raise the grain output by another 300,000 million catties. This, of course, is a plan for a leap forward which can be fulfilled only by a tremendous effort.

(*Note*: The output of soya bean is not included in the output of grain listed in this paragraph.)

To fulfill this big scale 1959 plan with its very high tempo, the whole nation must continue its heroic endeavors, work hard, perseveringly and resourcefully, and energetically overcome all difficulties. It is not possible that there should be no difficulties in the large-scale development of the national economy and this is especially true in our country which is economically backward and gave us little to start off with. In the present period, many important materials, electric power and transport capacity still lag behind the demands of national economic development, it is still not possible to bring about a quick and radical change in this respect and this is one of the difficulties we face. Besides, it is also possible that we may come up against certain difficulties that are hard to foresee, such as natural calamities seriously affecting agriculture. We should be fully prepared in our minds to face these difficulties and should strive to overcome them by every possible means. Provided we are prepared and work energetically to overcome it, no difficulty can prevent us from winning victories.

We have many favorable conditions insuring fulfillment of the 1959 plan. The big leap of 1958 created the general promise for our continued big leap forward.

We have a stronger material and technical basis than in 1958. We have the people's communes capable of promoting the expansion of the productive forces. Thanks to the victories gained on all fronts in 1958, our more than 600 million people have acquired greater confidence and energy, have more experience and learned new methods. Through practice in 1958, growing numbers of cadres and the masses have grasped the Party's general line for socialist construction and the whole set of policies known as "walking on two legs". All these are conditions which favor us.

What must we pay attention to if we are to fulfill the 1959 plan? The most important thing at present is to strengthen centralized leadership, make overall arrangements, look to our organizational work and concrete measures and vigorously develop the mass movement in all fields of economic endeavor.

On the industrial front it is particularly necessary to strengthen centralized leadership, so as to integrate fully the resources of the central authorities with those of the local authorities and the resources of the state with those of the masses, and make overall arrangements in the light of the country's unified plan. Here the needs of the key construction projects must be met first of all and fulfillment of tasks of an overall nature must be insured.

Thanks to the victory of the socialist revolution, the inspiration of the general line for socialist construction and the success of the people's communes, the initiative of the cadres and the masses all over the country and in every field of work has soared to new heights; all want rapid development of the projects that they need. It is quite natural for such desires to be expressed, they reflect the growing prosperity of our country. But our plan must base itself on objective possibilities. Our material and technical foundation is still very weak. While our material, financial and manpower resources go to satisfy the needs of certain key projects, we cannot meet the needs of other projects so satisfactorily. To resolve this contradiction, the interests of the parts must give way to those of the whole, and completion of the key projects must be insured in the first place. It was in accordance with this principle that we worked out the 1959 plan for industrial production and construction, and we must observe this principle in executing the plan. Readjustment in projects of production and capital construction, distribution and allocation of important materials and equipment, increasing and transferring administrative staff and workers in enterprises, changes in the labor and wages systems, and disposition of technical forces must be put under the full charge and united command of the central authorities as well as the provincial, municipal and autonomous regional authorities. As to specific production and construction tasks, a priority list should be worked out from higher to lower levels, taking into consideration their importance and urgency, and the availability of materials and equipment. For example, the most urgent task for the engineering industry at present is to produce rapidly the mining, coal dressing, coking, steel rolling, power, irrigation and draining equipment and locomotives and rolling stock stipulated in the plan. Materials which are under the unified allocation of the state must first of all go to meet the needs of producing such equipment. In arranging for the manufacture of such equipment, these enterprises should also work out an order of production covering types and models, so that the production and construction needs of the key enterprises will be met in good time and with the types and models they require.

It is necessary to strengthen leadership in organizational work, and constantly make a thorough check-up of the various links in production and construction, so that the tremendous work of accomplishing the 1959 tasks in industrial production and capital construction will be fulfilled according to schedule and satisfy all quantitative and qualitative requirements. As to the more important products and construction projects, it is necessary to draw up 10-day, monthly or quarterly time-tables and for the leading organs of the central governmental and the provincial, municipal and autonomous regional levels to send inspectors to make personal rounds of the workshops and construction sites to check up on progress and quality, and thus guarantee proper fulfillment of the planned targets.

As the experience of previous years, and that of 1958 in particular, shows the most fundamental guarantee of fulfillment of the industrial plan is the thorough application of the mass line in work, that is to say, the linking of centralized leadership with a vigorous mass movement. It is imperative that all industrial enterprises carry out the system whereby the director assumes full charge under the leadership of the enterprise' Communist Party Committee and that they observe thoroughly all rational and necessary rules and regulations; we will not countenance any lack of responsibility or violation of necessary rules and regulations in either production or construction work. But the centralism we need is that based on democracy; centralized leadership should not be such as to hinder the mobilizing of the masses, rather it must guarantee their unhampered mobilization. We should actively lead administrative staffs and workers to discuss tasks laid down in the state plan at staff and workers' representative conferences and at other meetings in the spirit of airing views and debating openly and freely to devise ways and means for fulfilling and overfulfilling the tasks set. Cadres of the basic units and activists from among the masses should be invited to participate on a broad basis in important meetings held by the enterprises, and their opinions should be canvassed when any important decision is made. Such methods as "Party secretaries taking command", leading cadres working on "experimental plots", the calling of on-the-spot conferences, the organization of visits for study and public appraisals of work done, the launching of emulation drives with red banners for the winners, cadres taking part in manual labor, workers participating in management, and closer coordination among the leading personnel, technicians and workers—all of which were found effective in the mass movement in 1958—must be strictly adhered to and continue to be developed and improved.

The mass movement on the industrial front to set up small enterprises and carry out production by indigenous methods should continue to be developed and steadily improved. Small enterprises employing indigenous methods will still play a great part in this year's industrial production, such as in mining, coal dressing, coke making, copper smelting and the production of building materials. After improving their techniques these enterprises will also play a certain part in iron and steel making. Although the quality of certain amounts of the iron, steel and other products manufactured by indigenous methods is not high enough and costs of production are relatively high, they are able to meet the immediate needs of our country in certain respects, particularly those of the vast countryside. Therefore, we should by no means belittle the role played by small enterprises and indigenous methods. If we do, we will commit mistakes. The simultaneous employment of modern and indigenous methods of production is a long-term policy for the development of our industry. The combination of modern and indigenous methods is a permanent feature, though both in content and in form what we signify by "modern" and "indigenous" will in the future be different from what they are now. It goes without saying, of course, that small enterprises employing indigenous methods of production, no matter to what branch of industry they belong, should improve their techniques, working methods and labor organization, endeavor to increase labor productivity, raise the quality and reduce the cost of their products. Through the gradual adoption of certain modern techniques such indigenous production in small enterprises will be transformed into modern production. This is an essential task. Those enterprises employing indigenous methods of production which consume comparatively more labor power and raw materials should tackle this task more urgently.

As on the handicraft front, it is necessary also to persist in the mass line as a working method and launch a vigorous mass movement to fulfill the 1959 plan in the fields of agriculture, transport, tele-communications and posts, and trade.

Last autumn and winter the mass of peasants on the agricultural front did a great deal of spade work for this year's production. To realize the big leap plan of this year, however, we must continue to mobilize the masses and unfold the mass movement for high yields on vast expanses of land. Cadres of the people's communes and *hsien* must go further into the fields and be as one with the commune members. They must work hard for rich summer and autumn harvests, for the realization of the ten proposals made by the national conference of representatives of advanced units in socialist agricultural construction in January this year, and for fulfillment and overfulfillment of this year's production plan for food crops, cotton, oil-bearing crops, bast-fibers, sugar crops, and various kinds of non-staple foods as well as in forestry, animal husbandry, side occupations and fishery.

Last year's great leap forward in agriculture brought us rich experience about the eight technical measures for increasing production, namely: soil improvement, use of fertilizer, water conservancy, seed selection, close planting, plant protection, field management and reform of farm tools. This experience enables us to see that we should apply different measures according to different natural conditions and crops and not apply the same measures indiscriminately, and that the various measures are related to, and dependent on, each other, so we should not rest content with applying one or several of them alone. We must do a good job in summing up this experience so that the people's communes and their production brigades can decide on and earnestly carry out the proper technical measures for increasing production according to their own concrete conditions.

To continue the great leap forward in agriculture before the mechanization of farming is realized, will need a lot of labor power. Although the emergence of people's communes, community dining rooms and nurseries has relieved women by tens of thousands from household chores, there is still a shortage of manpower in the countryside owing to the great increase of productive work. Under present conditions the number of people engaged in agriculture (including farming, forestry, animal husbandry, side occupations and fishery) should not, in general, be less than 80 per cent of the manpower available in the countryside. To insure the manpower needs of the countryside, factories and mines in the urban districts should within a given period of time stop recruiting workers from the countryside and send back their surplus irregular workers to the rural areas where they came from. The building of industrial and mining enterprises and other capital construction projects by the *hsien* and people's communes should, in general, be carried out with the farming season in mind, that is to say, more projects should be built during the slack farming season and less in the busy season. The number of administrative and service personnel in the people's communes must also be sharply reduced. Such jobs as can be done by people capable only of doing light or subsidiary work should, wherever possible, be done by them so that fully able-bodied men and women can be relieved, wholly or partially, from such jobs.

TEXT OF DOCUMENT 37

515

The fundamental way to end the manpower shortage in the countryside is to raise labor productivity in farming, to press ahead step by step with technical innovation and the technical revolution in farming and gradually semi-mechanize and mechanize farm tools. The farm tools reform movement started in 1958 must be continued and those reformed tools which have proved their worth in practice must be energetically promoted and popularized.

Consolidation of the people's communes is the prerequisite of the smooth growth of agricultural production. The resolution of the 6th plenary session of the 8th Central Committee of the Chinese Communist Party has enabled the broad masses of cadres and people to have a correct understanding of the nature of socialist collective ownership in the people's communes at the present stage and of the necessity of the people's communes practicing the principles of "to each according to his work" and of exchange on the basis of equal value; the administrative system of unified leadership for the commune as a whole while management and business accounting are done by the production units at different levels; and democracy and industry and thrift in running the commune. This has played a decisive role in consolidating the people's communes. The check-up in the people's communes in the past few months has gradually strengthened their administrative system and considerably improved their cadres' working style. Every people's commune throughout the country should in the nearest future convene a representative conference of its members to sum up the results of the check-up, review the work of production and make fresh assignments of work, check up on the commune's accounts, discuss the way to distribute the summer harvest and elect the leading bodies. We are confident that when all the work of checking-up and organization is well done, the people's communes will bring rank-and-file initiative into fuller play and further develop their energies; this will be a further guarantee for fulfilling the tasks of increasing agricultural production in 1959.

To realize the 1959 plan in the field of transport, first of all railway transport, we must strengthen organizational work in transport, fully tap the possibilities of existing transport facilities and, at the same time, fulfill the tasks of capital construction according to plan.

Transport departments should plan their work better, try to shorten loading and unloading time, speed up the turn around of freight vehicles and ships and economize on fuel consumption so that more goods can be carried with existing facilities. In transport, proper arrangements should be made depending on the importance and urgency of the goods to be carried so as to insure, in the first place, timely transport of such important consumer goods as grain and non-staple foods. Special attention should be paid to the integration of long-distance transport and of land and water transport. To reinforce short-distance transport, we should make a big effort to organize the use of the vehicles and junks of the rural people's communes so as to make up for the shortage of modern means of transport. All industrial and trading departments should give active help to transport departments in rationalizing their work, reducing and if possible eliminating such unreasonable phenomena as shipping the same goods from opposite directions, shipping goods over excessively long distances or by interrupted stages to their destination.

To insure supplies of essential materials and continued market stability, the trading departments face a heavy task in 1959. As I said before, total retail sales of commodities in 1959 will reach 65,000 million yuan, an increase of 19 per cent over 1958. This increase is 3.8 times the total retail sales figures of 17,000 million yuan of 1950, soon after the founding of the Republic. Compared with the 34,800 million yuan of 1953, the first year of the First Five-Year Plan, it is an increase of 87 per cent. As our country has a big population, a slight increase in each person's consumption means a phenomenally large total of additional consumption. Under the circumstances where the output of consumer goods cannot yet keep pace with demands, it is difficult to avoid completely the situation where one commodity or the other is temporarily in short supply. The important task of the trading departments at present is to make overall arrangements for the markets throughout the country; do the job of supplying consumer goods to the best of their ability and avoid and reduce as much as possible any discrepancy between supply and demand.

Trading organs at various levels should endeavor to improve the work of purchasing agricultural products and by-products and industrial goods for daily consumption. They should also see to it that the purchase of "waste materials" used as raw materials in industry is done well; promote agricultural production and sidelines and expand the interflow of commodities between the cities and rural areas by making purchase and marketing contracts. At the same time they must improve the administration of export trade so as to fulfill the state export plan on time and as regards quantity and quality.

No matter whether it is on the industrial, agricultural, transport, or trading front, the central aim of the mass movement should always be the raising of labor productivity, increased production, the strict practice of economy and opposition to waste. The scope of the 1959 national economic plan is very wide and the tasks involved are difficult, but it can by no means be said that there are no more potentialities to be tapped or that our planned targets cannot be overfulfilled. The possibilities of technical innovation and the technical revolution in both production and construction are unlimited. The improvement of tools and equipment, improved utilization of equipment, improvements in the design of products & projects & operating & building methods, economies in manpower and materials, the use of various substitutes and "waste materials", improvements in the quality of products and projects, reduction in the number of rejects and seconds—all these measures will help raise labor productivity and reduce costs. So long as we are determined to make politics take command, raise the political consciousness of the cadres and masses, make people realize the great political significance of the 1959 plan and the problems which lie ahead, and mobilize the masses to the fullest possible extent, we are sure to discover new ways and means for increasing production and practicing economy. For example, the average daily output of coal in all mines throughout the country was 960,000 tons in January and February this year, but after the emulation drive centering on technical innovation and revolution launched among the broad mass of the workers and staff in early March, the average daily output in March jumped to 1,130,000 tons, thus overfulfilling the task set for the first quarter of the year. A similar mass movement is beginning to make its appearance not only in the coal industry, but in other industries, and agriculture and transport as well. Now we are in the early part of the second quarter of the year, the decisive hour for fulfillment of the annual plan. We must mobilize ideologically and politically the energy of every worker, peasant, intellectual, and patriotic citizen in every part of the country for the immediate launching of a nation-wide movement for increasing production and practicing economy. We are confident that if we can develop such a movement in earnest and keep it going to the end, we will certainly be able to fulfill and overfulfill the 1959 plan for the national economy.

(III) OUR TASKS ON THE CULTURAL AND EDUCATIONAL FRONTS

Along with the upsurge in our socialist economy, there has started an upsurge in our socialist culture. Through the rectification campaign and following the struggle against the rightists, the leading position of the proletariat was firmly established and strengthened in the various branches and units of cultural and educational undertakings, thus providing the political guarantee for the upsurge of culture and education. In 1958, it was not only the cultural and educational undertakings run by the state which made rapid progress, masses of workers and peasants felt a pressing need to master culture and they too founded schools on their own, developed the sciences and culture and engaged in various spare-time literary and artistic activities, all combining into a panorama of a vast, mass cultural revolution. Most of the intellectuals on the cultural and educational fronts, in the course of self-remolding have enhanced their own socialist initiative, strengthened their ties with the workers, peasants and productive labor, and played an energetic part in popularizing culture and raising our cultural level. Our tasks are now to continue to mobilize all positive factors on the cultural and educational fronts, to push forward the cultural revolution, to popularize socialist culture and carry out the work of consolidating the positions gained and raising quality on the basis of popularization, so that cultural and educational work may meet the needs of socialist construction as a whole.

Education in our country has made tremendous progress in the last few years, and especially in 1958. In 1952, the number of students in higher educational institutions was 190,000; by 1957, it was already 440,000, an increase of over 100 per cent; in 1958, it again increased by 50 per cent compared with 1957, reaching 660,000. The number of middle school students in 1952 was over three million; in 1957 it was over 7 million, also an increase of over 100 per cent; in 1958, compared with 1957, it again increased by 70 per cent to 12 million. Primary school pupils in 1952 numbered over 51 million; in 1957 there were already over 64 million, an increase of 26 per cent; in 1958 there was another 34 per cent increase compared with 1957, bringing the total to 85 million. In 1958, spare-time school education for workers and peasants, including general, technical as well as political courses, given in varied forms, also made tremendous progress. Much has also been done in wiping out illiteracy.

But these quantitative increases are by no means the only manifestation of our achievements in the field of education. What is more important is the fact that, as the Party has greatly strengthened its leadership over the work of education, we have, based on the working class world outlook and the socialist and Communist principles of education, carried through the policy of making education serve working class politics and combining education with productive labor, thereby initiating a great and profound revolution in the educational field.

To serve working class politics and the cause of socialism is the basic starting point of our education. In our schools, socialist and Communist ideological and political education must be thoroughly well done to raise the socialist consciousness of the students; our children and youth must be educated in cultural knowledge and modern scientific achievements, step by step and in a systematic way, and form the habit of taking part in productive labor in the course of their schooling so as to fit them for not only mental work but also physical labor. Those who stick to the standpoint of the old society where education was run by the exploiting classes are, of course, opposed to our policy. In actual fact, the bourgeoisie and other exploiting classes introduce into their own schools political and ideological education aimed to bolster up their own class interests. The bourgeois society gives the workers only some rough, shallow and limited knowledge and makes every attempt to hoodwink, paralyze and corrupt them ideologically and politically. The bourgeoisie consistently trains intellectuals serving their system of exploitation in the spirit of separating theory from practice, and mental labor from physical labor. Our educational policy is the very opposite of this policy of the bourgeoisie. Our aim is to arm the workers, peasants and intellectuals with the scientific and revolutionary proletarian world outlook, to wipe out lock, stock and barrel, the ideological influences of the exploiting classes, to make education serve the working people, to put culture into their hands and to combine mental work with physical labor.

We have already begun officially to introduce productive labor into the educational program of our schools, and, in the light of varying conditions, to organize students to take part in productive labor for a specified period. Through engaging in productive labor, the mass of faculty members and students have acquired much more practical knowledge of production and love of labor and respect for the laborers have been fostered. In institutions of higher learning, practical work in production has also given a powerful impetus to scientific research. The facts show that properly integrating education with productive labor can assist in strengthening the ties between school and society, bringing about the integration of theory and practice and the gradual integration of mental and physical labor, and turning our schools day by day into a new type of school training new men with a Communist outlook. Of course, we have only gained a preliminary experience in this far-reaching revolution in education; there are still shortcomings in our work and questions that remain to be further studied and solved. We must continue to accumulate and sum up our experience, and constantly improve our work so as to carry out this policy of integrating education with productive labor still more effectively.

In developing education in our country we must adopt the method of combining popularization with a raising of quality. In order to popularize culture and meet the urgent needs of the current development of national construction, in addition to the existing full time, regular schools at all levels, we must also, in the light of actual possibilities, continue to develop half-day schools and spare-time schools in the countryside, factories and mines. The work of wiping out illiteracy must be energetically carried out with the participation of the masses. At the same time, we must also pay special attention to raising the quality of teaching and studying. Last year, schools at all levels all made great progress; now it is time to tidy up, consolidate and raise up their level on the basis of this great development. Full-time regular schools at all levels should make it their constant and fundamental task to raise the quality of teaching and studying; in the first place, we must devote relatively more energy to perfecting a number of "key" schools so as to train specialized personnel of higher quality for the state and bring about a rapid rise in our country's scientific and cultural level.

In 1958, great achievements were made in both the patriotic sanitation movement which centered on wiping out the "four pests" (rats, flies, mosquitoes and grain-eating sparrows) and the principal diseases and the athletic movement aimed at improving the physique of the people. We must continue these movements. In our public health work, we must continue to carry out the mass line and make specialists work in cooperation with the masses so as to rapidly and effectively improve the sanitary conditions of our people. We must get the doctors of the traditional school of Chinese medicine and doctors of the modern school to unite, organize joint efforts in serving the people's health work and developing the medical heritage of the motherland and medical and pharmaceutical sciences. In the field of athletics, it is necessary too to carry out the policy of combining popularization with a raising of quality, organize mass athletic movements on a wide scale and step by step raise our country's athletic level.

In the fields of science and technology, 1958 saw the start of a mass movement for scientific exploration in which thousands upon thousands of people took part. Research work in many fields was brought to fruition. The forces of scientific and technical work were also greatly expanded. In serving the cause of socialist construction, many scientific workers, engineers and technicians in scientific research institutes and institutions of higher learning and on the industrial and agricultural production fronts have displayed a very high degree of initiative.

We are still backward in science and technology and we will have to work still harder in these fields. Tasks directly serving production and construction must be given top priority. There are a thousand and one technical problems in every sphere of production and construction, and scientific workers should work hard to solve them through a division of labor and coordination of efforts. Attention must also be given to developing the most advanced branches of science and technology; as regards those branches in which we lack conditions for development, we must make all the necessary preparations now. Basic theoretic research exerts a far-reaching influence on scientific and technological progress, and we must pay sufficient attention to this field as well.

Theoretical studies in the social sciences must also be energetically developed and given better leadership. It is impermissible to ignore their importance. Theoretical workers in the social sciences must be encouraged to make long-term, systematic efforts under the guidance of Marxism-Leninism, to collect plenty of relevant material and undertake independent, creative studies.

There is lively movement on the literary and artistic fronts, both in the work of professional men of letters and artists and in the amateur literary and artistic activities of the workers and peasants. We must encourage professional men of letters and artists to work hard to educate the masses with works that are of a still higher ideological and artistic level and that answer the cultural needs of the people.

At the same time, we must give energetic leadership to the literary and artistic activities of the masses, and pay attention to training those with literary and artistic talents who appear among the working people.

To achieve a sound development in science and art, we must carry through the policy of "letting a hundred flowers bloom and a hundred schools of thought contend" on the basis of service to socialism. This policy has pointed out the way of flourishing and development for our science and culture, and given tremendous inspiration to the entire scientific and cultural circles. Soon after the Party put forward this policy in 1956, the bourgeois rightists distorted it. Pretending to be fragrant socialist "flowers" they attacked the Party and socialism in an attempt to seize the leadership in cultural affairs. Victory in the anti-rightist struggle smashed this reactionary attempt and favorable conditions for carrying out the policy were thus created. The leap forward in socialist construction and the upsurge of the mass cultural revolution have opened up a vast area for "a hundred flowers to bloom and a hundred schools of thought to contend" in the fields of science and art. Through free debates among different schools and views in science, through free competition between different forms and styles in art, we are confident that before long our scientific and cultural work will enter a prosperous era and achieve great successes.

The creation of an army of working class intellectuals numbered in millions is a great historic task on the cultural and educational front. It is by training new intellectuals and remolding old intellectuals that such an army will be created.

Happy results have been achieved in the self-remolding of the old intellectuals: many of them are not only sincerely willing to accept Party leadership and serve socialist construction, but have begun to go out among the masses, take part in physical labor in factories and villages at regular intervals, acquire new experience in living and working with the working people and raise their ideological level. Some bourgeois intellectuals after prolonged and serious self-remolding, have begun to transform themselves into working class intellectuals and among them some advanced ones have joined the Chinese Communist Party.

These facts show the complete correctness of the policy of uniting, educating and remolding the intellectuals consistently followed by the Party and the state. By coming over politically to the side of socialism and uniting with the masses, old intellectuals can use their knowledge and skill and give full play to their specialties in serving the cause of socialism, and so win the approval of the people. However, it will still take a fairly long time for them to go further and make a complete break with their bourgeois world outlook and really grasp the working class world outlook. It is wrong to think that old intellectuals no longer need to remold themselves or that they cannot work unless they complete their remolding in a very short time. All old intellectuals willing to take the socialist road must continue to exert themselves, and remold themselves step by step through their work for many years to come. We must make proper arrangements for their work, appreciate their initiative, and help them to achieve greater results in their work. At the same time we must help them study Marxism-Leninism, find more chances for them to go among the masses, learn about actual conditions and, of their own free will, take part to a suitable extent in physical labor.

Huge numbers of young intellectuals are sprouting up pretty fast, they are advancing bravely along the road of being "both red and expert", and have made their first contributions in various fields of work. We must lead them to strive for still greater achievements, encourage them constantly to scale the heights of scientific knowledge and teach them never to indulge in self-conceit. Young intellectuals too are faced with the task of constantly remolding themselves. Whatever post they may hold, they must, while striving to raise their vocational level, seriously study Marxism-Leninism, take part in the production and struggles of the masses, participate in physical labor, and be strict with themselves politically and ideologically as well as in work. They must learn with modesty from their learned elders who in turn should also learn from the strong points of the young intellectuals. All patriotic intellectuals must rally under the banner of socialism and work together to build our great motherland.

(IV) POLITICAL LIFE OF THE STATE

Since the decisive victory won in the socialist revolution on various fronts, the people's democratic dictatorship and the unity of our people have become more firmly consolidated than ever. The reasons for this are as follows:

(1) In the fields of industry and commerce, we have virtually replaced bourgeois ownership of the means of production with ownership of the means of production by the whole people, and at the same time pay a fixed rate of interest to the capitalists, thus basically resolving the economic contradiction between the working people and the bourgeois industrialists and businessmen.

(2) In the fields of agriculture and handicrafts, we have replaced the individual ownership of the peasants and handicraft workers with collective ownership of the means of production, thus resolving contradictions among the peasants and handicraft workers themselves, arising out of individual ownership, as well as the contradiction between individual economy and socialist planned economy.

(3) On the ideological and political fronts, we have waged the struggle against the bourgeois rightists, shattered their attack against the Communist Party, the people and socialism, heightened the socialist consciousness of the people in all social strata, and completely isolated the bourgeois rightists among the people.

(4) We have carried out the rectification campaign among the mass of people, and first of all, in the advanced section of the people, conducted debates and education on the question of the struggle between the socialist and capitalist roads, and launched the struggle against bureaucracy, sectarianism and subjectivism, so that the ties between the cadres and the masses have been greatly strengthened.

The remnant counter-revolutionaries in our country have in the main been weeded out and a stable social order is more than ever insured. There are, however, still a very small number of counter-revolutionaries whom we must continue to weed out. Towards the counter-revolutionaries who have been uncovered, we will continue to carry out the policy of combining punishment with leniency, which has proved its effectiveness in the past few years. Regarding the bourgeois rightists, we follow the lenient policy of helping them to remold themselves, not depriving them of their civil rights, and making appropriate arrangements for their work and livelihood, with a view to remolding gradually so far as possible all those who can be remolded into new men.

United States imperialism now occupies many places in the West Pacific, including our Taiwan, and is threatening us constantly. Therefore, we must continue to strengthen our defenses to safeguard our people's peaceful construction work.

As mentioned above, through the victory of the socialist revolution and particularly the deepening of the rectification campaign, and as a result of the steady implementation of the policy laid down by Chairman Mao Tse-tung for the correct handling of contradictions among the people, there has been a great development of people's democracy within the ranks of our people. From now on, all the good methods developed in the rectification campaign should be made a permanent feature of our political life. The masses should be consulted on problems that arise. Full discussions should be conducted if opinions differ. Cadres' meetings and mass meetings should be held regularly, "tatsepao" (posters written in big characters and posted up for everybody to see) encouraged and insisted on observing the principle of "not blaming him who speaks, but taking every criticism as a warning", so that everybody may speak out his mind freely. We should not fear the contention of different opinions; when contradictions are brought fully into the open, it becomes easier to find proper solutions fairly quickly to the problems raised. In both city and countryside, meetings must be held with cadres belonging to three, four, five or even six different levels of organs sitting together. Through these meetings participated in by cadres working in basic units and by both advanced and not so advanced elements of the masses, policies of the Party and state and decisions made at higher levels should be made known directly to cadres working in basic units and to the masses, and the opinions of the latter voiced face to face with the leading cadres. Experience has proved that these meetings are most convenient for pooling the wisdom of the masses and strengthening the unity of the people; they are an effective means of developing people's democracy.

In the past year, government workers have made remarkable progress in going deep among the masses. Vast numbers of cadres have corrected ways of thinking and working which estrange them from the masses in varying degrees, and have overcome the bureaucratic, lifeless, spendthrift, haughty and finicky airs with which they were infected in the old society, and now appear as ordinary laborers among the masses. Over a million cadres of state organs from the *hsien* level up have been sent to the countryside, to factories and mines to take part in manual labor and administrative work in basic units. At the same time, leading cadres in rural work and in the factories have gone at regular intervals to the people's communes or workshops as commune members or workers; commanders of the armed forces have similarly gone to the squads as privates, and all leading cadres who are physically fit have taken regular part in manual labor. This has begun to be a new social custom. This is a revolutionary and Communist custom.

It opens up a new way not only of linking the cadres and the masses but of integrating mental and manual labor. In 1959, state organs of all levels should, on the basis of summing up the experience gained in 1958, continue to organize the systematic and regular despatch of cadres to work in basic units and take part in manual labor.

The worker-peasant alliance is the foundation of the great unity of the Chinese people. This alliance has become more and more firmly consolidated as a result of the people's commune movement and the leap forward in the socialist cause as a whole. There are still some social strata who belong neither to the workers nor the peasants. Under the premise of continuing to strengthen the worker-peasant alliance, we will continue to maintain during the period of socialist construction the alliance of the laboring people with those non-laboring people who are willing to cooperate with the laboring people.

On the heels of the struggle against the rightists, a fairly thoroughgoing rectification campaign was also launched among the members of the democratic parties and groups and the national bourgeois elements. Through study, work and participation in manual labor, many of them have made varying degrees of progress. Except for a handful of rightists, most of those democratic party members and other democrats who take part in state work have fulfilled their duties at their posts. During the rectification campaign, the democratic parties tidied up their organizations. They still play a positive role in rallying the various social forces to serve socialism. In the future, it is still necessary in our country to continue to consolidate and develop the people's democratic united front on the basis of serving socialism. Under the premise of accepting the leading position of the Communist Party, long-term co-existence and mutual supervision between the Communist Party and the various democratic parties and groups is still beneficial to the people's cause. As for the capitalists, the state will pay them a fixed rate of interest for the period originally fixed, and will actively help them proceed with their self-education and self-remolding through participation in socialist construction.

In the work concerning nationalities, the government has had great success in the past four years in further promoting national regional autonomy on the principle of insuring the unity of the country and national equality in accordance with the stipulations of the Constitution. In addition to the Inner Mongolia Autonomous Region, the Sinkiang Uighur Autonomous Region, the Kwangsi Chuang Autonomous Region and the Ninghsia Hui Autonomous Region have been successively established. A Preparatory Committee for the Tibet Autonomous Region has also been established. Besides this, 29 autonomous *chou* and 54 autonomous *hsien* have been established in Tsinghai, Kansu, Sinkiang, Yunnan, Szechwan, Kweichow and other provinces and autonomous regions. These national autonomous areas comprise more than 30 national minorities.

In the national minority areas, with the exception of Tibet and a very few other places, democratic reforms have been carried out and socialist transformation has been accomplished in the main, and on this basis the switch to the people's communes has been realized. Many national minorities who only yesterday were still fettered by the feudal or even slave system have today taken the bright road of socialism. They are truly forging ahead in seven-league boots.

In 1958, a tremendous leap forward took place also in the economy and culture of the national minorities. Statistics show that in the four autonomous regions of Inner Mongolia, Sinkiang, Kwangsi and Ninghsia, the total value of industrial output increased 88 per cent in 1958 compared with the previous year, while the output of food crops shot up by 83 per cent. There has been a rapid increase in the number of national minority students throughout the country. In the first half of 1958, the enrollment of national minority primary school pupils reached 3,190,000; middle school students, 310,000; and students in higher educational institutions, 16,000. Of the country's national minority population of 36 million, the number of students totalled 3,510,000. Compared with pre-liberation days, the number of primary school pupils has increased over six times; middle school students, 79 times; and students in higher educational institutions, 27 times. Written language schemes have been devised for many national minorities who had no written language in the past, and they now have books and newspapers published in their own languages.

Because of the correct implementation of our policy on nationalities, the friendship and solidarity between the Han people and other brother nationalities and between the different national minorities have been greatly strengthened. In the past few years, a continuous struggle has been waged among Han cadres against the tendency toward Han-chauvinism. During the rectification campaign, struggles were also waged in many national minority areas against local nationalism of different forms and degree. The broad masses of national minority cadres and people, after tempering themselves in the rectification campaign and through practical work in economic and cultural construction, have steadily enhanced their political consciousness and large numbers of advanced elements are coming to the fore from among them. These constitute a reliable force for the further rapid advance of the socialist cause in the national minority areas.

The unity of our motherland is the paramount interest of all the nationalities in China. China as a united, multi-national country is the product of a long process of historical development. Ever since they began their invasions against China the imperialists have consistently tried to disrupt the unity of China and undermine the solidarity among its nationalities, but they have failed. On the contrary, imperialist aggression awoke the overwhelming majority of the people of China's many nationalities to the fact of their common destiny and the value of a united country. The victory of the Chinese people's revolution and the founding of the People's Republic of China brought all nationalities in the country closer together. The patriotic people of all the nationalities have realized, from the lessons taught by historical facts, that the nationalities can achieve prosperity only in the big united family of the motherland which has cast off imperialist oppression and taken the socialist path. They realize that the people's democratic state led by the Communist Party has uprooted national oppression and is striving to get rid of the last vestiges in ways of thinking connected with national discrimination which were inherited from the past. Under the capitalist system, a relatively developed and powerful nationality invariably does its best to keep other nationalities in a backward state so as to oppress and exploit them. But it is quite the reverse under the socialist system. In our country not only do all nationalities enjoy political equality but those nationalities which have bigger populations and are more advanced economically, politically and culturally have the duty to help the other nationalities which are smaller and relatively backward, so that all may progress and develop together.

The recent armed rebellion of the former Tibet Local Government and the reactionary clique of the upper social strata in Tibet, aimed at betraying the motherland and disrupting unity, has already met with ignominious defeat. Our government has ordered the dissolution of the former Tibet Local Government (the Kasha) and enjoined the Preparatory Committee for the Tibet Autonomous Region to exercise the functions and powers of the Local Government so that regional national autonomy may be speedily realized and democratic reforms instituted step by step in Tibet. This measure is warmly welcomed by the broad mass of patriotic people in Tibet, both ecclesiastic and secular. This is a great victory for our policy of national unity.

The policy of the Central People's Government in regard to the Tibet region has always been clear. In accordance with the stipulations of the Constitution, we have always adhered to the principle of unity of all the nationalities of our country and the unity of the Tibetan people themselves and stood for the institution of regional national autonomy in Tibet. The Central People's Government has always adhered to the policy of respecting freedom of religious beliefs and has taken various positive measures to help the economic and cultural development of the Tibet region. All this has been warmly welcomed by the Tibetan people. According to the 17-article agreement on the peaceful liberation of Tibet of 1951, the Tibet Local Government should unite the people and drive the imperialist aggressive forces out of Tibet; the backward social system in Tibet must be reformed. In view of the state of mind of the people of the upper social strata in Tibet, we agreed that the reforms there could come a little bit slow so as to allow time for the former Tibet Local Government and people of the upper social strata to give full consideration to the question. But the former Tibet Local Government and the reactionary clique of the upper social strata continued their collusion with the imperialists, the Chiang Kai-shek gang and foreign reactionaries on whose forces they attempted to rely to split the motherland, restore the imperialist aggressive forces in Tibet, and preserve a backward, dark, reactionary and cruel serfdom in Tibet. They did not want at all to put into effect a democratic regional autonomy with the participation of the people, but persistently obstructed the progress of preparatory work for setting up the Tibet Autonomous Region. Their activities seriously violated the interests of the Tibetan people and the common interests of all nationalities of the country. That is why, their rebellion was instantly and firmly opposed by the people of all nationalities throughout the country, and first and foremost by the broad mass of the Tibetan people including many patriotic and progressive people of the upper social strata. The reactionaries were totally mistaken in their appraisal of the situation. They failed to see that the days when imperialists could manipulate China's internal affairs have long since passed away.

The situation in Tibet is now completely under control by the Tibet Military Area Command of the People's Liberation Army and the Preparatory Committee for the Tibet Autonomous Region. The units under the Tibet Military Area Command of the People's Liberation Army, with the active support of the Tibetan people, both ecclesiastical and secular, are continuing to mop up some remnants of the rebels who have fled to remote areas. The Preparatory Committee for the Tibet Autonomous Region has begun to exercise the functions and powers of the Local Government. As for future social reforms in Tibet, the Central Government will conduct full consultation with the patriotic people of the upper and middle social strata and the masses of all walks of life in Tibet to decide on the time, steps and measures for their institution. In any case, the reforms will be carried out step by step with full regard for the specific conditions in Tibet, and in the course of the reforms the religious beliefs and customs and habits of the Tibetan people will be fully respected and the fine aspects of Tibetan culture will be upheld and developed. Although the Dalai Lama has been abducted to India, we still hope he will be able to free himself from the hold of the rebels and return to the motherland.

The Tibetan reactionaries often put on pious airs and express the hope that everyone will go to heaven, but they turned Tibet into a hell on earth; they want to force the Tibetan people to live perpetually in the abysmal darkness of a life of barbarism and cruelty worse than that of the Middle Ages in Europe. They also often pretended to be peace-loving, but in actual fact they directed bandits to wreak havoc among the people by committing arson, murder, rape and plunder, and in the end they themselves went to the length of madly launching the armed rebellion, thus bringing about their own destruction. Tibet consists of three parts: Chamdo, Chientsang and Houtsang. Its total population is 1,200,000. Only about 20,000 took part in the rebellion, a majority of these acted under coercion or were duped, and these further included part of the so-called Khambas, rebels who had fled to Tibet from the area to the east of the Kingsha River which used to belong to the now abolished province of Sikang. There are thus in Tibet over 1,100,000 people who are working people who demand reforms, progressives of the upper social strata who support reform and middle-of-the-roaders who can be won over. There are now some people abroad who are harping on their sympathy for the Tibetans. But they do not make clear which section of the Tibetans they sympathize with—the working people and progressives who demand and support reform and the middle-of-the-roaders who can be won over, amounting to over 1,100,000 people, or the handful of reactionaries. We hope that all well-intentioned friends—I refer to those who are willing to persist in practicing the five principles of peaceful co-existence with our country and have pledged not to interfere in China's internal affairs—will in the first place note this clear distinction between the overwhelming majority and the small handful. When one comes to understand the true conditions in Tibet, one ought to sympathize with the overwhelming majority of the Tibetan working people who are oppressed by an out-dated system, and with their demand for social reforms. With the defeat of the rebellion of the Tibetan reactionaries, the Tibetan people are now in a position to shake off the fetters of serfdom and realize their desire for democratic autonomy and social progress. With the help of other nationalities of the country, they will build the Tibetan Plateau step by step into a true paradise on earth. What a joyful thing this is for the Tibetan people, for the people of all nationalities of our country, and for all those abroad who genuinely sympathize with the Tibetan people!

Tibet is China's territory, and the rebellion of the Tibetan reactionaries and its suppression are China's internal affairs. Even the imperialists bent on carrying out aggression against Tibet cannot deny these facts. After the outbreak of the rebellion in Tibet, and after the Dalai Lama was abducted to India by the rebels, Prime Minister Nehru of our great friendly neighbor India issued successive statements on non-interference in China's internal affairs and in favor of continued consolidation of friendly Sino-Indian relations. We welcome these statements. There is a friendship over 2,000 years old between China and India, which are moreover the initiators of the five principles of peaceful co-existence. There is no reason at all why either of our two countries should let our mutual friendship and the principles in foreign relations adhered to by our two countries jointly be shaken on account of a handful of Tibetan rebels. It is true that before the defeat of the rebellion in Tibet, the Tibetan reactionaries and certain foreign reactionaries made use of certain areas on the Sino-Indian border to carry out activities designed to disrupt the unity of our country and undermine Sino-Indian friendship. The plans of those reactionaries however, have already fallen through. It is our hope that, with the suppression of the rebellion in Tibet and through the joint efforts of China and India, we will lay an even firmer foundation, and secure an even more flourishing development of friendly relations between our two great peace-loving Asian countries with their populations totalling more than 1,000 million people. All the ill-intentioned provocations of those who are deliberately seeking to disrupt Sino-Indian friendship will be in vain.

(V) FOREIGN POLICY

While winning great victories on all fronts at home, we have also made important progress in the field of foreign relations. Together with the other countries in the socialist camp headed by the Soviet Union and with all peace-loving countries and peoples, our country has made great efforts in the cause of defending world peace. The number of countries that have established full or partial diplomatic relations with us has, in the past four years, increased from 20 to 33; we have established economic relations with 93 countries and areas and cultural ties and exchanges of friendly visits with 104. The U.S. imperialists' attempt to isolate and ostracize new China in international affairs has suffered one defeat after another.

Chapter IX: COMMUNES (DISILLUSION)

The present overall international situation is characterized by the fact that the forces of socialism, the forces of the national independence movements and other peace-loving forces are growing rapidly while the imperialists' policy of aggression and war is beset with innumerable difficulties. Just as Chairman Mao Tse-tung puts it, the enemy rots with each passing day, while for us things are getting better daily.

The socialist camp headed by the Soviet Union is forging ahead rapidly. The Soviet people, under the leadership of the Communist Party of the Soviet Union, have achieved great successes in developing their national economy, improving the people's well-being, enhancing the might of the Soviet Union and the socialist camp and safeguarding world peace. After taking the lead in sending up man-made earth satellites, the Soviet Union was again the first to launch an artificial planet. Not long ago, the 21st Congress of the Communist Party of the Soviet Union adopted the grand 7-Year Plan for development of the national economy. This plan signifies that the Soviet Union has entered an important historical period—that of the all-out building of Communist society—and is announcing to mankind that the beauty and splendor of Communist society is not far off. The other socialist countries are also rapidly developing their own national economies. The entire socialist camp is in the midst of an upsurge of economic construction. It is quite certain that within a not very long historical period the Soviet Union will outstrip the United States in the level of per capita output, China will also become a great and advanced industrial power, and the entire socialist camp will markedly surpass the imperialist camp in material production, thus fully insuring world peace.

The unity of the socialist camp headed by the Soviet Union is even more firmly consolidated.

It is a fundamental policy of our country to strengthen our unity with the Soviet Union and with all other socialist countries. The fraternal relations of friendship and mutual assistance between our country and the Soviet Union and other socialist countries have greatly developed over the past few years. We have united as one and worked in close cooperation for the common cause of safeguarding world peace and promoting the progress of mankind. In the past year and more, our country has concluded with the Soviet Union three agreements on Soviet aid in our major items of scientific and technological research, in building 47 enterprises and in building another 78 enterprises, and a treaty on commerce and navigation; it has also concluded a series of agreements on the development of friendly cooperation and strengthening of economic trade and cultural ties with Albania, Mongolia, the German Democratic Republic, the Vietnam Democratic Republic, Poland, Czechoslovakia, Hungary, Rumania, the Korean Democratic People's Republic and Bulgaria respectively. The Soviet Union and other socialist countries have given us tremendous assistance in our socialist economic and cultural construction. Here I would like to express, on behalf of our government and people, our deep gratitude to the governments and peoples of the Soviet Union and other socialist countries. We are deeply aware from our own experience that mutual support and cooperation among the socialist countries is an important condition for their smooth development. In the future, we shall continue to strengthen actively our cooperation with the Soviet Union and other fraternal countries in the political, economic, technical, cultural and other fields, and continue to extend the education of our people in proletarian internationalism. The imperialists and the reactionaries in various countries always fear the unity of the peoples of various countries, and especially the unity of the peoples of the socialist countries. Recently, they have thought up all sorts of dirty tricks in their attempt to disrupt the friendship between the two biggest socialist countries, China and the Soviet Union. They are hostile to the friendship and unity between China and the Soviet Union and between all socialist countries, because this friendship and unity constitutes a strong bulwark for the cause of peace and progress of mankind, is in the interests of the people of the whole world and of world peace, and operates only to the disadvantage of the imperialist aggressors and reactionaries in various countries. But the steel bulwark of the friendship and solidarity between China, the Soviet Union and all other socialist countries is based on their common interests and ideals; it cannot be broken through by anybody, and never will be. The more the enemy seeks to undermine it, the more will the people of the world realize that mankind's bright future hinges on it and the more will they rally round it.

The socialist countries consistently support the endeavors of the people of the world and all peace-loving countries to safeguard peace, support the struggles of all oppressed nations against aggression and colonialism, and support the newly independent countries in safeguarding their national interests and developing their national economy. It is obvious that the more the forces of aggression are curbed, the more secure will be the cause of peace.

In recent years, the national independence movement has been rising to ever greater heights and the imperialist colonial system has continued to disintegrate. Asia, Africa and Latin America, which used to be the imperialists' rear, have now come to the forefront in the fight against aggression and colonialism. Even the spokesman of the U.S. Government has admitted that U.S. imperialism, which is the prop of modern colonialism, is already caught up in a "veritable whirlwind". Just as their previous aggression against Egypt and threat against Syria ended in ignominious defeat, the imperialists' subversive activities against Indonesia and their armed aggression against Lebanon and Jordan met with severe reverses in 1958. The national revolutionary movement in Iraq broke through the multiple oppression of the imperialists and the domestic reactionaries and won brilliant victories. The African people who have long been subjected to imperialist enslavement and plunder are rapidly awakening.

Many newly independent countries have emerged on the African continent. The Algerian people who are engaged in a heroic struggle have established their own government. The struggles for freedom and independence of the oppressed peoples of Congo, Cameroon, Nyasaland and other parts of Africa are growing vigorously. The day is drawing ever nearer when the African people will again be masters of the African continent. In Latin America the national independence movement goes hand in hand with the struggle for democracy and against dictatorship. The Cuban people after prolonged armed struggle have finally overthrown Batista's dictatorial regime fostered from first to last by U.S. imperialism. This marks a new upsurge in the national and democratic movements in Latin America.

The imperialist colonial forces will not step down from the stage of history of their own accord, and the struggle to achieve and safeguard national independence will not be all plain sailing. The imperialist colonial forces are trying hard to maintain or recover their control over those countries which have recently gained independence. Besides resorting to direct threats of force and armed suppression, they are also patching up military blocs, concluding military treaties, establishing military bases, stepping up economic aggression, engineering military coup d'etats and organizing subversive activities. It is particularly worth noting that the imperialists are lately trying by all possible means to undermine the internal unity of the newly independent countries and sabotage the solidarity among them and between them and the socialist countries, with the aim of defeating them one by one and playing the divide-and-rule game. In order to gain complete victory, therefore, all the countries striving to win and safeguard national independence not only have to defeat the armed intervention and aggression of the imperialists but also to smash their various underhand schemes and machinations.

The Chinese people have always expressed their sympathy for all struggles against imperialism, colonialism, aggression and intervention, because our country itself was not long ago a semi-colonial country suffering greatly from imperialist aggression, and even now imperialist forces are still occupying our territory of Taiwan. We are ready to give support and assistance to the full extent of our capabilities to all national independence movements in Asia, Africa and Latin America. In the Arab nation's anti-imperialist struggles over the past years we have always stood on the side of the Arab peoples. A complicated situation has arisen recently in the Arab national independence movement. Some people in power in the United Arab Republic have launched an attack on the Republic of Iraq, and then also attacked the Soviet Union, the great friend of the Arab peoples. Obviously, such actions are injurious to the cause of independence of the Arab nation and therefore cannot enlist the sympathy of the Arab people. Like all other friends of the Arab nations, we hope that a way may be found to overcome this difficulty now facing the Arab cause of national independence so that the imperialists will not succeed in their sinister scheme to harm the Arab nations.

Our country is developing good diplomatic relations with a number of countries in Asia and Africa which have newly gained independence. India, Indonesia, Burma, Cambodia, Ceylon, Nepal, Afghanistan and some Arab and African countries are pursuing a policy of peace and neutrality on international affairs. They oppose war and refuse to be drawn into aggressive military blocs. In the common struggle against the imperialists' policy of aggression and war, and in the common endeavor to uphold the five principles of peaceful co-existence and the ten principles laid down by the Bandung Conference, our country has established friendship with these countries on a broad basis. We hold this friendship very dear and are thankful to many friendly countries which have given our country support in international affairs. Since the beginning of 1958, our country has concluded treaties strengthening economic and trade ties and cultural cooperation with Yemen, Burma, Indonesia, the

United Arab Republic, Ceylon, Tunisia, Morocco and Iraq successively; at the same time, we have also increased our friendly contacts with other Asian and African countries. Many of the Southeast Asian countries are our next-door or nearby neighbors. We share common interests with these countries and there are no disputes between us which cannot be settled by peaceful means. We are, therefore, able to form, and indeed have already formed, together with these countries, a peace area in Asia. We hope that this peace area may last forever, and spread over the whole of Asia.

In order to poison the relations between many Southeast Asian countries and our country and cover up their own aggressive activities against those countries, the U.S. imperialists have deliberately spread the slander that our country will pose a "formidable threat" to our neighbors in Southeast Asia. The Yugoslav revisionist group, which has sold out to U.S. imperialism, is also trying hard to damage the friendly relations between the Asian and African countries and China and the other socialist countries after its activities to disrupt the solidarity of the socialist countries failed. But all these provocations and attempts at sowing dissension are fore-doomed to failure. It is known that our country has never encroached on the territory or interfered in the internal affairs of any neighbor and it will never do so in the future. The remnant Kuomintang bandits who fled to Burma have incessantly harassed our frontiers over the past ten years, endangering our security. Yet even in these circumstances our country has done no more than guard our frontiers and has remained patient, waiting for the government of Burma, our friendly neighbor, to handle the situation on its own. The undetermined boundary lines between our country and certain neighboring Southeast Asian countries and the nationality of Chinese nationals abroad have been used by mischief makers as propaganda material. But as is well known, the undetermined boundary lines between our country and certain neighbors are the results of many historical causes, first and foremost, prolonged imperialist aggression. Our country has always stood for a reasonable settlement of this question in accordance with the five principles of peaceful co-existence through peaceful negotiation with the countries concerned. Pending its settlement, we consider it to be in the interests of both parties to maintain the status quo and not to let the imperialists succeed in their scheme of sowing discord between us. As for the question of overseas Chinese, our government has always advised our nationals abroad to respect the laws and customs of the country of their residence, to refrain from participating in local political activities and to strive to help the local people in developing their economy. The voluntary choice by overseas Chinese of the nationality of the country of their residence has also the approval of our government. Certain Southeast Asian countries have adopted a wrong policy of discrimination against the Chinese. In doing so they are completely taken in by the imperialists' slanders and their treacherous attempts to sow dissension. It is our hope that this situation may be remedied and that the proper interests of the overseas Chinese will be protected.

The imperialists are furthermore spreading the rumor that our country is engaged in what they call "dumping" and "economic expansion" in Southeast Asia. But everybody knows, a socialist country has no need at all for so-called "economic expansion" or "dumping".

Our country has an immense domestic market. Our import-export trade with capitalist countries only accounts for 0.5 per cent of the total volume of imports and exports of the capitalist world. Our exports to the Southeast Asian countries make up one per cent of their total imports. There is no question at all of "dumping" or "grabbing foreign markets". Of course, there exists the possibility of developing economic cooperation between our country and those countries on a voluntary basis on the principle of equality and mutual benefit. We will in the future continue to develop such cooperation in the interest of both parties concerned.

The imperialists are always busy interfering in the internal affairs of all other countries and trying to bring the whole earth, and even the moon, under their armed control. Yet they are unable to run their own houses properly, the imperialist countries are being swept by an economic crisis. Their mutual contradictions are coming out in the open.

Although the imperialist countries are still looking for some way of compromise to ease their mutual conflict temporarily, their contradictions are irreconcilable and are growing more and more acute as the result of the unbalanced development of capitalism; their disintegration is inevitable as a general trend. Gloom and confusion reign throughout the entire imperialist camp, and the bourgeoisie of the west has lost their faith in the future.

The socialist countries have always advocated peaceful co-existence and peaceful competition

TEXT OF DOCUMENT 37   527

with the capitalist countries. The Soviet Union, China and other socialist countries have, over the past four years, made unremitting efforts to ease international tension and defend the peace and security of the peoples of the world; they have put forward important peace proposals for disarmament, the prohibition of tests of atomic and hydrogen weapons, the holding of an East-West Summit Conference and the establishment of atom-free zones and systems of collective security in Europe and in Asia and the Pacific region. These peace endeavors and proposals of the socialist countries have inspired the peace-loving countries and peoples of the world and become a decisive factor in easing the international situation. The warlike imperialist group, however, has all along rejected these peace proposals and attempted to turn back the wheel of history by means of a new war. The NATO bloc, the Baghdad Treaty bloc and the SEATO bloc are still stepping up their activities, and the United States is still expanding its network of military bases all over the world, and manufacturing atomic and hydrogen weapons and arming the forces of a number of countries with such weapons. The grave danger of war still exists. All peace-loving forces of the world must continue in a state of vigilance to defend peace and oppose war. Even relatively sober-minded people within the imperialist camp have begun to realize that, with the socialist camp mightier than ever and the broad masses in all countries firmly opposed to war, launching a new world war will not bring a favorable outcome to the imperialists but, on the contrary, will only accelerate the end of the whole imperialist system and the victory of socialism throughout the world.

For a long time since the conclusion of the Second World War, the U.S. imperialists have persistently prosecuted a policy of keeping Germany divided and reviving West German militarism. The Soviet Union and the German Democratic Republic have put forward a series of reasonable proposals and made unremitting efforts for the removal of the threat to peace in Europe and the world and to promote the fulfillment of the German people's national task of unifying their motherland through direct negotiations between the two German states. Not long ago, the Soviet government further proposed to terminate the occupation regime in West Berlin and convert West Berlin into a free city, and later proposed the holding of a peace conference of the countries concerned to discuss and conclude a peace treaty with Germany. The Chinese government supports these proposals made by the Soviet government. Thanks to the consistent efforts of the Soviet government and the pressing demand of the peace-loving countries and peoples of the world, the United States, Britain and France have had to agree to the Soviet proposal for holding a foreign ministers' conference and a conference of heads of government. We hope that these conferences will help settle the international issues that are ripe for solution, first of all the question of a peace treaty with Germany and the Berlin question, thereby paving the way for easing international tension.

In the East, the U.S. imperialists have persisted in reviving Japanese militarism. The Japanese monopoly capitalist group on its part is counting on the support of the United States to realize its lurking imperialist ambitions. Recently, the Kishi Government has again stepped up preparations for revising the Japan-U.S. "security treaty", entered into new military plots with the United States, and attempted to equip the Japanese armed forces with atomic weapons. This poses a serious threat to the security of the Asian countries, and that of our country in particular. The Chinese people have always supported the Japanese people's just demand to shake off U.S. control, follow a policy of peace and neutrality, and turn Japan into an independent, peace-loving and democratic country. To promote normalization of Sino-Japanese relations, the Chinese government, forgiving past misdeeds, has treated with leniency the overwhelming majority of the Japanese war criminals in the Japanese war of aggression against China and given active assistance in the repatriation of Japanese nationals from China, and the development of trade and friendly contacts between the two peoples. It was with such support of our government that the fourth non-official Sino-Japanese Trade Agreement was signed on March 5, 1958 after clearing away many obstacles. The Kishi Government, however, refused to grant the proper assurances, thus making it impossible to implement the agreement. In May, 1958 there occurred in Nagasaki the incident in which the Chinese national flag was insulted with the connivance of the Kishi Government. In October 1958, after our People's Liberation Army started shelling Quemoy, Kishi himself openly slandered our country as an "aggressor" and clamored that the Chinese people should not be allowed to liberate Taiwan. In this way, Sino-Japanese relations have been almost completely broken off. This reactionary policy of the Kishi Government aroused great indignation among the Japanese people. Although the Kishi Government cannot but profess willingness to resume Sino-Jananese trade in the face of the pressure of the Japanese people, in actual fact it has continued to follow the United States in its hostility of China and plotting to create "two Chinas", and has continued to obstruct normalization of Sino-Japanese relations, thus preventing up to now the realization of the Chinese and Japanese peoples' desire to improve relations and resume trade between the two countries. The Chinese people's interests accord with those of the Japanese people. The Chinese people cannot sit idly by while Japanese militarism is being revived, nor can they tolerate the continued hostile policy of the Kishi Government toward China. The Chinese people welcome the great efforts made by the Japanese people to advance friendly relations between the two peoples. We regard as being entirely correct the series of proposals for improving Sino-Japanese relations and resuming diplomatic relations between China and Japan which were put forward recently by the delegation of the Japanese Communist Party and that of the Japanese Socialist Party during their successive visits to China. We are confident that the Japanese people will ultimately break down all obstacles and develop peaceful and friendly relations with the Chinese people.

While further reviving Japanese militarism, the U.S. imperialists are stepping up their aggressive activities and war preparations in East Asia. The objective of the United States in ganging up the members of the SEATO bloc at the recent Wellington meeting was to plot new aggressive and subversive activities and create new tensions in the East Asian area, and to further tighten its control over the Asian members of the bloc. The U.S. imperialists are exerting their utmost efforts to obstruct the unification of Vietnam, reinforce their military establishments in South Vietnam and, in an attempt to turn Laos into their military base, instigate the Laotian authorities to repudiate the Geneva Agreements. The United States has engaged in flagrant subversive activities against the Kingdom of Cambodia through the instrumentality of countries under its control. While the Chinese People's Volunteers on their own initiative had completely withdrawn from Korea by the end of last year, the U.S. imperialists not only refused to withdraw their aggression forces from South Korea, but went even further in introducing large quantities of military equipment including nuclear and rocket weapons into South Korea and supporting the Syngman Rhee clique's clamorous demand to scrap the Korean Armistice Agreement as a whole. These aggressive activities of the United States in East Asia seriously endanger the security of the Vietnam Democratic Republic, the Korean Democratic People's Republic and the People's Republic of China as well as the peace of East Asia. As a party related to the Geneva Agreements and the Korean Armistice Agreement, we absolutely cannot allow the United States to violate these agreements and realize its scheme of extending aggression. We desire to establish and develop friendly, good-neighborly relations with all our neighbors in accordance with the five principles of peaceful co-existence. We advocate the establishment of an area free of atomic weapons, an area of peace, throughout the whole of East Asia and the Pacific region. We believe this is in conformity with the fundamental interests of the peoples of East Asia and the Pacific region. China does not want to threaten or harm anybody, nor ask anybody to change the socio-political systems they have chosen. But we want to remind those people who follow the U.S. imperialists in being hostile to and threatening our country that if they persist in this line of action they must bear all the consequences arising therefrom.

China is willing to establish diplomatic relations on an equal footing with all countries. There are now no diplomatic relations between China and the United States, and indeed their relations are very bad. As the whole world knows, responsibility for this state of affairs does not rest with us. We have not gone swash-buckling to the United States, we are not blockading the United States, occupying its territory or creating two United States of America. There is only one United States of America in the world. Likewise, there is only one China in the world. Taiwan is an inalienable part of Chinese territory. We are determined to liberate Taiwan, Penghu, Quemoy and Matsu. All U.S. armed forces in the Taiwan area must be withdrawn. No plot to carve up Chinese territory and create "two Chinas" can be tolerated by the Chinese people. In accordance with this principle, any country that desires to establish diplomatic relations with our country must sever so-called diplomatic relations with the Chiang Kai-shek clique and respect our country's legitimate rights in international affairs. We are willing to enter into contacts and cooperation with other countries in international organizations and conferences, but we will not participate in any international activities in which a situation of "two Chinas" may arise. The ways for the Chinese people to maintain and develop friendly relations with other peoples cannot be blocked. The intrigue of the U.S. imperialists and their followers of creating "two Chinas", like the "non-recognition policy" pursued by the United States toward China, will only lead them into a blind alley.

*

Fellow deputies! Both internally and internationally, the situation is favorable for our cause. Our cause is thriving and making great strides in every respect. This is because it is a just cause enjoying the support of the broad mass of the people.

Our country will mark its glorious 10th anniversary on October 1 this year. In reviewing the developments over the past ten years, we are all very happy and full of confidence. All our achievements have been gained through the concerted efforts of all our united patriotic people. We have in the past united with all those who could be united with; we will continue to do so in the future. The current session of our congress will adopt the 1959 plan for development of the national economy. All the forces of the entire nation need to be mobilized in order to fulfill this grand plan. The National Committee of the Chinese People's Political Consultative Conference is in session alongside our congress. We are convinced that the two sessions will contribute greatly to the fulfillment of our tasks under the 1959 plan. Under the leadership of the Chinese Communist Party and Chairman Mao Tse-tung and guided by the general line of going all-out, aiming high and getting greater, quicker, better and more economical results in building socialism, let us unite closely and greet the 10th anniversary of the founding of our great motherland—the People's Republic of China—with energetic efforts to fulfill and overfulfill the 1959 plan!

Chapter X

ANTI-RIGHTIST CAMPAIGN

(containing Documents 38, 39, 40, 41, 42, 43)

General comment. The longer-term significance of the campaign in August and September 1959 against "rightist-inclined opportunists" within the Chinese Communist Party is discussed in our General Introduction, part X.

The official version of preceding events—that there was a small temporary sag in morale and production during June and July—was given by Po I-po (NCNA, Oct. 27, 1959). It is very unlikely that this is the whole story, or that a minor economic shortfall would have been thought sufficient cause for a major propaganda campaign, particularly damaging to the government's prestige at a time when unity and achievement were the themes which the government wanted to impress on the outside world.

The *People's Daily* editorials of August 6 and 7 (the former is given as Document 38 below) were followed, or in some cases preceded, by:

1. Party meetings at provincial level and downwards to counter "rightist inclinations among the cadres." At most of these meetings Document 38 was made a compulsory text.

2. The Eighth Plenary Session of the Eighth Central Committee of the Party, at Lushan, August 2-16.

3. The publication by NCNA on August 26 of the communiqué and resolution of the Central Committee (Documents 39 and 40).

4. A report on the state of the Chinese economy by Chou En-lai, August 26, delivered on behalf of the State Council to the Standing Committee of the Second National People's Congress (Document 41).

5. An intense publicity campaign, of which Documents 42 and 43 are examples, defending the main achievements of the Government against the attacks of rightists within the Party.

6. Sporadic articles against "rightist-inclined opportunists" continuing at increasing intervals of time until December 1959.

The gap between the end of the Central Committee session on August 16 and the publication of the communiqué on August 26 suggested that a considerable interval was necessary for the proper instruction of the Party and preparation of the public. There had been a similar delay before publication of the Wuhan Resolution the previous December.

Supplementary material is found in CB 602 and 603, containing various speeches to the National Conference of Advanced Groups and Workers in Socialist Construction. See especially the speech of Po I-po (CB 602, from NCNA, Oct. 27, 1959) mentioning a "slight production dip" in June and July, and the speech of Lu Ting-yi (CB 603, from NCNA, Oct. 31, 1959) in which he said the political line of demarcation is whether to obey Mao or not. Other materials are in:

ECMM 189 (*Red Flag*, Oct. 1, 1959), an article by K'ang Sheng, an alternate member of the Politburo who has been prominent since the fall of 1959 for his theoretical pronouncements. This mentions rightist "fellow-travelers" within the Party who vaguely incline to socialism but oppose the general line.

ECMM 191 (*Red Flag*, Nov. 16, 1959), Ch'en Po-ta on rightists' demand for class equality.

ECMM 197 (*Red Flag*, Dec. 16, 1959), resistance within the Party to unity and discipline.

SCMP 2155 (*People's Daily*, Nov. 30, 1959), rightists' attacks on the Party's basic policies and leadership.

URS, Vol. 16, No. 24 (*People's Daily*, Aug. 30, 1959), on the "chronic disease of rightist deviation."

World Marxist Review, October 1959, Liu Shao-chi's historical review of rightist and leftist deviations in the Party from the 1920's on.

DOCUMENT 38

Overcome Rightist-Inclined Sentiment and Endeavor to Increase Production and Practice Economy, editorial in *People's Daily*, August 6, 1959.

The text is taken from SCMP 2074. The translation was made by the U.S. Consulate General, Hong Kong.

―――――――――――TEXT OF DOCUMENT 38―――――――――――

It is the urgent task today of industry, agriculture, transport, and commerce, and the economic front as a whole to carry forward still further a resounding campaign to increase production and practice economy during the months of August and September, take a determined stand against the rightist-inclined sentiment that has found its way into some of the cadres, and to endeavor to fulfill or overfulfill the forward leap plan for this year.

During the first half of this year, various branches of the national economy have, on the basis of last year's giant forward leap, scored another important new victory—the broad masses of workers, peasants, and cadres, vigorous and enthusiastic in labor, are driving hard to insure monthly increases in industrial production and a bumper summer harvest in agriculture. Despite the summer season, the people are working courageously and intensively in factories, mines, construction sites, and at the fields to surmount difficulties brought forth by material requirements and natural calamities of all kinds in order to fulfill the state plan and achieve a bumper autumn harvest.

The current economic situation is a situation for the continuous forward leap, presenting an extremely favorable condition for the fulfillment of the production and construction tasks for the second half of this year. However, while the broad masses of the people and cadres are pressing ahead consistently on the economic front, a tendency has emerged—an inclination to avoiding hardship has found breeding grounds among some of the cadres. These cadres exaggerated certain difficulties encountered in work and have either neglected or under-estimated the great achievements already scored or the conditions favorable to surmounting difficulties. They lack the confidence needed for overcoming difficulties, thus failing to employ all available means to fulfill those tasks which can be accomplished under existing objective conditions and with subjective efforts; to justify their rightist-inclined and conservative attitude, they maintained that it was better to have a simple plan and low targets. This is the rightist danger on the economic front today which should not be overlooked.

In order to fulfill or overfulfill the continuous forward leap plan for this year, this kind of rightist-inclined sentiment must be resolutely criticized and overcome. The Party's general line calls upon us to exert the utmost efforts, to press ahead consistently, and to achieve more, faster, better, and more economical results. This general line has armed the broad masses of the people and cadres and has been proven correct by the giant forward leap achieved last year and by the continuous forward leap this year.

In carrying out any undertaking, we must exert our utmost efforts instead of slackening in our endeavor; we must press ahead consistently instead of aiming low; we must achieve more, faster, better, and more economical results instead of doing less, at a slow pace, and turning out things of inferior quality, and at higher costs. Our Party has always upheld the spirit of practicality, putting the subjective initiative into full play based on objective requirements and capabilities in an effort to accomplish work in a more efficient manner, instead of putting off work which can be accomplished in keeping with both the subjective and objective conditions. Comrade Mao Tse-tung once said: "No one should build castles in the air, or make plans for action beyond the limit of objective conditions, or force himself to do things which cannot be done in any way. However, the question at present is that the rightist-inclined conservative idea is doing its foul play in many fields to such an extent that work in many fields has failed to conform to the development of the objective conditions.

"The current question is that things which can be done with effort are now considered by many people as impossible. Therefore, it is absolutely necessary to embark on unceasing criticism against the rightist-inclined conservative ideas now in existence." The above remarks made by Comrade Mao Tse-tung at the end of 1955 are indeed a good medicine for the disease applicable to the rightist-inclined sentiment among some of the cadres today. Of course, our road to the continuous forward leap is not entirely free of difficulties. However, these difficulties are but the temporary and sectional ones in the course of our forward leap. Ours is an earth-shaking revolutionary undertaking; it would be inconceivable if it does not encounter difficulties. Our Party has grown in strength in the course of overcoming difficulties of all kinds followed by one victory after another. The conditions we now face in surmounting difficulties are no worse than those in the past. In fact, they are far more favorable than before.

So long as we implement the directives of the Party Central Committee consistently and fully activate the masses, certain difficulties now in existence can be solved completely within a short period of time. Many localities, departments, and enterprises by so doing have stimulated the enthusiasm for work among the masses and solved difficulties in work, scoring new achievements. The tremendous strides made in industrial and agricultural production during the first half of this year are effective proof.

Communists and revolutionary cadres should not adopt such an attitude of having no confidence of overcoming difficulties, becoming dejected in face of hardships, and exerting no efforts to carry through an undertaking which can be accomplished. Evading difficulties, laxity in work, and dejection are extremely detrimental to the cause of socialism. It would be a crime to dampen the mass enthusiasm for labor. Seven months of this year have elapsed with only five months left. The tasks on the economic front demand still greater efforts for fulfillment. The months of August and September are the months which determine whether or not the plan for this year can be fulfilled; because, in industry, the raw materials, semi-finished materials, fuel, and finished products turned out during these two months will have a direct bearing on production and construction during the last three months of this year and on the needs of the people; in capital construction, construction projects completed during these two months can still be put into operation before the end of this year; in agriculture, these two months will see the deciding factors on the yield of the autumn crops; in commerce, these two months mean the arrival of a brisk season which requires great efforts in procurement as well as in marketing; in the field of transport, efforts should be exerted to transport more during these two months in order to minimize the load during the winter season.

Concrete measures should be adopted to surmount any rightist-inclined sentiment during these two months so as to stir up a high tide of a mass movement centering on increasing production and practicing economy in the fields of industry, agriculture, transport, and commerce, and on the economic front as a whole. In carrying forward this campaign, efforts should be made to grasp the production of iron and steel, coal, timber, cement, and machinery serving industry, and the production of daily necessities as well as handicraft products needed by the broad masses of the people. Steps must be taken to handle properly semi-finished products of all categories, and concentrate forces to complete important and urgently needed capital construction projects which can be completed sooner. Measures must be adopted to speed up loading and unloading in railway transport, and launch a short-distance transport emulation campaign without affecting the adequate coordination in the use of manpower.

In industry, transport, and capital construction, it is necessary to work hard with perseverance and resourcefulness, endeavoring to strengthen enterprise management, improve quality and quantity, increase variety, insure safety in operation, emphasize economic accounting, practice strict economy with accent particularly on the conservation of raw materials, materials, fuel, power, and manpower, and on reduction of production cost.

In agriculture, vigorous measures should be adopted to strengthen the management of autumn fields and wage a resolute struggle against drought, water-logging, and natural calamities in order to insure bumper grain crops and economic crops as well. Concrete steps must be taken to develop vigorously multi-productive activities and produce non-staple food including hogs, sheep, chickens, and ducks. In the field of commerce, vigorous efforts should be made to improve procurement and marketing work in order to ameliorate the marketing conditions.

All these tasks call for a strengthening of leadership on the part of the Party committees in various localities and at all levels. They must let politics take command and strictly adhere to the general line and the spirit of practicality, and activate the broad masses of the people to strive with full vigor for the fulfillment and overfulfillment of the continuous forward leap plan for this year. The tenth anniversary of the founding of the great motherland is approaching, let all cadres together with the people throughout the country increase their vigor and advance bravely with one heart and one aim under the beacon light of the Party's general line for socialist construction and celebrate the tenth anniversary by scoring spectacular achievements in the campaign to increase production and practice economy!

DOCUMENT 39

Communiqué of the Eighth Plenary Session of the Eighth Central Committee of the Chinese Communist Party, issued August 26, 1959.

> The English text is an official translation in a pamphlet entitled *Eighth Plenary Session of the Eighth Central Committee of the Communist Party of China*, Foreign Languages Press, Peking, 1959, pp. 1–7. (The same pamphlet contains Document 40.)

———————————————TEXT OF DOCUMENT 39———————————————

The Eighth Plenary Session of the Eighth Central Committee of the Chinese Communist Party convened at Lushan, Kiangsi Province, from August 2 to 16, 1959.

The Plenary Session was held under the guidance of Comrade Mao Tse-tung. Taking part in the session were 75 members and 74 alternate members of the Central Committee. Fourteen other comrades working in relevant departments of the Central Committee and in provincial, municipal and autonomous regional Party committees also attended the session.

The Plenary Session reviewed in detail the implementation of the 1959 plan for development of the national economy, fully discussed the existing economic situation and put forward the militant task of further developing the campaign to raise production and practise economy so as to fulfil ahead of schedule within this year the major targets of the Second Five-Year Plan (1958–1962). The control figures of the Second Five-Year Plan were adopted at the First Session of the Eighth National Congress of the Party in September 1956, and accepted by the State Council in February 1957.

The Eighth Plenary Session of the Eighth Central Committee noted with satisfaction that as a result of the thorough way in which the whole Party and the entire nation have carried out the Party's general line—go all out, aim high and get greater, quicker, better and more economical results to build socialism—the various branches of the national economy in the first half of this year continued to leap forward on the basis of the great leap forward in 1958 and won new, important successes. In the first half of this year the total output value of industry increased by 65 per cent and the volume of railway freight increased by 49 per cent compared with the corresponding period of last year. With respect to agriculture, although the sown acreage was somewhat reduced last winter and although not a few areas suffered from severe floods and drought, yet the average per *mou* yields of the summer crops have all registered an increase and the total output of wheat, early rice and rapeseed exceeded last year's exceptional bumper crops. The volume of retail sales of commodities in the first half of this year was 23 per cent higher than in the corresponding period of last year. Although the volume of retail sales expanded rapidly, the purchasing power of the people increased still more rapidly, so, for a time, there was a bit of a strain in the supply of a small number of commodities on the market. Thanks to the series of effective measures taken by the central and local authorities to step up the production of non-staple foods, manufactured goods and handicraft products for daily use and thanks to the marketing of the summer crops, the supply situation has taken a turn for the better. The economic situation in the first half of this year was on the whole good.

The Eighth Plenary Session of the Eighth Central Committee holds that in view of the achievements made last year and in the first half of this year, it is entirely possible to fulfil ahead of schedule within this year the main targets for the major industrial and agricultural products originally fixed for the last year (1962) of the Second Five-Year Plan. Fulfilment of the major targets of the Second Five-Year Plan ahead of schedule should be made the chief task of this year. This is a great and glorious task. Its fulfilment will raise the national economy of our country to a new and higher level.

On the basis of verified statistics on the national economy in 1958 compiled by the State Statistical Bureau, and in the light of the actual development of industrial and agricultural production in the first six months of this year and the recent occurrence of serious floods and drought over large areas of the country, the Eighth Plenary Session re-examined this year's plan for development of the national economy and found that the original targets set in this plan were somewhat too high and need to be appropriately adjusted.

Repeated check-ups made in the first half of this year show that the figures previously published on the 1958 agricultural output are a bit high. The bumper harvest in 1958 had no parallel in the history of our country. Owing to lack of experience in assessing and calculating the output of such an unprecedented bumper harvest, the agricultural statistical organs in most cases made an overassessment. Apart from that, the labour power allocated for the bumper autumn harvest was inadequate, with the result that reaping, threshing and storing were all done in a somewhat hurried manner. Verification shows that the actual amount of grain gathered in 1958 was 500,000 million catties (250 million tons), an increase of 35 per cent over that of 1957; the actual amount of cotton gathered in was 42 million *tan* (2.1 million tons), an increase of 28 per cent over that of 1957. This was obviously a great leap forward. But under these conditions, the original targets planned for grain and cotton this year require adjustment. Again, of the 11,080,000 tons of steel produced last year, 3,080,000 tons were made by indigenous methods and met the requirements of rural areas; the output of steel produced by modern equipment which met the requirements of industry totalled 8 million tons, an increase of 49.5 per cent over the 5,350,000 tons produced in 1957. In view of the fact that this year there is a certain shortage of labour power for agricultural production, it is suggested that the production of steel by indigenous methods for local use be decided upon by the local authorities in accordance with local conditions; it will no longer be included in the state plan. It was also decided that the output of coal be adjusted accordingly. The Eighth Plenary Session considers that this year's four major targets for steel, coal, grain and cotton should be readjusted as follows: steel, 12 million tons; coal, 335 million tons; grain and cotton, about 10 per cent respectively over the verified 1958 outputs. The Plenary Session recommends that the State Council, on the basis of these targets, submit a proposal on adjusting the 1959 plan for development of the national economy to the Standing Committee of the National People's Congress for examination and approval.

The Eighth Plenary Session of the Eighth Central Committee points out that the readjusted 1959 plan for development of the national economy remains a plan of continued leap forward. Steel output will be 4 million tons above last year's 8 million tons, an increase of 50 per cent; coal output will increase by 65 million tons, 24 per cent more; the rates of increase of grain and cotton output will both greatly exceed the average yearly rates of increase during the First Five-Year Plan period (grain 3.7 per cent and cotton 4.7 per cent). By fulfilling this year's readjusted national economic plan, we will have fulfilled, overfulfilled or nearly fulfilled the following targets originally set in the Second Five-Year Plan for fulfilment in 1962: steel, coal, timber, metallurgical equipment, power-generating equipment, metal-cutting machine tools, cotton yarn, machine-made paper, salt, grain and cotton. This will enable us, within the coming three years, to raise sharply the original targets of the Second Five-Year Plan and to devote greater efforts to strengthening certain weaker links in the national economy, and make it possible for us to strive to realize in the main, within about ten years, the slogan "catch up with Britain in the output of major industrial products within 15 years" and to overfulfil, at a much earlier date, the 12-year programme for agricultural development originally scheduled for completion in 1967.

The Eighth Plenary Session of the Eighth Central Committee points out that the present domestic and international situation is favourable for the realization of a continued leap forward in our national economy. Internally, industrial and agricultural production continues to grow; the people's communes in the countryside, following the check-up in the past months, are now advancing along the path of a consolidated and sound development; the labour enthusiasm of the mass of the workers and peasants continues to rise; the unity of the people of all nationalities in the country grows ever stronger; and science, culture and education continue their advance. Internationally, the strength of the socialist countries headed by the Soviet Union and their unity and cooperation are growing daily; the national independence movements and people's democratic movements in Asia, Africa and Latin America and the revolutionary struggles of the people in the other capitalist countries are expanding daily while the internal difficulties of the imperialist countries and the contradictions among them are daily increasing. The Plenary Session fully supports the efforts made by the Soviet Union at the Geneva Foreign Ministers' Conference and welcomes the announcements made by the Soviet Union and the United States on the exchange of visits between their heads of government. The Plenary Session holds that this is conducive to the further easing of international tension and helps the cause of defending world peace.

The Eighth Plenary Session of the Eighth Central Committee points out that the imperialists and their lackeys have, from the outset, viciously slandered and attacked our country's general line for building socialism, the great leap forward and the people's commune movements. But they have suffered ignominious defeat. The potency of our country's general line for building socialism is being demonstrated in ever greater measure. Under the guidance of the general line, the people of our country not only took a great leap forward last year, but are continuing to leap forward this year; the rural people's communes not only have taken firm root, but are displaying their advantages ever more clearly. The imperialists and hostile elements within the country will continue to slander and try to sabotage the socialist construction of our country, nevertheless this will only serve to stimulate all our people to raise their revolutionary enthusiasm to a still higher level, and impel our whole Party and the people of all our nationalities to strengthen unity, firmly uphold the brilliant banner of the general line, and carry forward the great socialist cause of our country steadily, but also by leaps and bounds.

After analysing the current situation, the Eighth Plenary Session of the Eighth Central Committee points out that the principal danger now facing the achievement of a continued leap forward this year is the emergence of Right opportunist ideas among some cadres. They do not try their best to accomplish tasks which, according to objective conditions and given subjective efforts, can be accomplished. They underestimate the great achievements made by the hundreds of millions of working people and the revolutionary intellectuals in the great leap forward movement and the people's commune movement and overemphasize the seriousness of certain defects which, owing to lack of experience, occurred in the two movements and which have been quickly overcome. They slander as "petty-bourgeois fanaticism" the great leap forward and the people's commune movements in which hundreds of millions of working people have been vigorously engaged under the leadership of the Party. This is utterly wrong. They fail to see that in all pursuits undertaken by the people under the leadership of the Party, the achievements are the main things, while defects and mistakes are secondary and are merely one finger out of the ten. The Plenary Session enjoins Party committees at all levels to criticize and overcome resolutely such erroneous Right opportunist ideas among some cadres, firmly put politics in command, fully mobilize the masses, go all out and strive to fulfil and overfulfil this year's leap forward plan.

The Eighth Plenary Session of the Eighth Central Committee points out that in order to fulfil this year's leap-forward plan, very arduous tasks must be dealt with on the economic front in the second half of this year. The Plenary Session calls on Party committees at all levels to make good use of the last month and more remaining of the third quarter to give vigorous leadership to the mass campaign for increasing production and practising economy which is in full swing on the industrial, agricultural, transport and trade fronts so as to greet the tenth anniversary of the founding of our People's Republic with even more brilliant successes.

The Eighth Plenary Session of the Eighth Central Committee calls on the whole Party and the people of all nationalities in the country to work with one will, to unite more closely and, under the leadership of the Central Committee of the Party headed by Comrade Mao Tse-tung, and with the beacon light of the general line, to forge ahead valiantly to carry out this year's national economic plan and fulfil ahead of schedule within this year the principal targets of the Second Five-Year Plan!

DOCUMENT 40

Resolution on Developing the Campaign for Increasing Production and Practicing Economy, adopted by the Party's Eighth Central Committee at its Eighth Plenary Session, August 16, 1959, and issued August 26.

The English text is taken from the pamphlet, *Eighth Plenary Session of the Eighth Central Committee of the Communist Party of China*, Foreign Languages Press, Peking, 1959, pp. 8-19.

―――――――――――――TEXT OF DOCUMENT 40―――――――――――――

I

The national economy of our country, on the basis of the unprecedentedly great leap forward in 1958, scored new great victories in the first half of 1959. Last year's and this year's victories fully testify to the absolute correctness of the Party's general line—go all out, aim high and get greater, quicker, better and more economical results to build socialism. To ensure this year's continued leap forward, great efforts have still to be made in the coming four months and more. The Eighth Plenary Session of the Eighth Central Committee of the Chinese Communist Party holds that the central task confronting the whole Party and the people of all nationalities throughout the country now is to develop intensively a vigorous mass campaign for increasing production and practising economy and strive for the fulfilment and overfulfilment of the production and construction plan of 1959. The precious time of the coming month or more should especially be made good use of to set going a new upsurge in production so as to win a decisive victory for industry, agriculture and transportation in the third quarter to greet the tenth anniversary of the founding of the great People's Republic of China.

II

The total output value of industry in the first half of this year was 65 per cent more than that in the corresponding period of last year. Pig iron reached 9.5 million tons; coal, 174 million tons and metal-cutting machine tools, 45,000 units. In each case output was more than double that in the corresponding period of last year. Steel (excluding steel made by indigenous methods) amounted to 5.3 million tons, an increase of 66 per cent over the corresponding period of last year. Cotton yarn amounted to 4,147,000 bales, and sugar, 780,000 tons; both represented an increase of 40 per cent and more over the corresponding period of last year. Other heavy and light industrial products also registered very great increases. The quality of various industrial products has improved from month to month. This is especially marked in the case of iron and steel. In iron smelting, small and medium-sized blast furnaces have quickly taken the place of small indigenous furnaces set up last winter in conformity with the conditions of that time. The technical level in operating such small and medium-sized blast furnaces, moreover, has been rapidly raised, thus not only saving a large amount of labour power and increasing their total output to approximately the same amount produced by all the large blast furnaces, but also improving the quality of their products and reducing coal consumption. The volume of railway freight reached 247 million tons, exceeding that of the corresponding period of last year by 49 per cent.

In agriculture, although the acreage planted to summer crops this year was somewhat reduced, and there were floods and drought, yet the average per *mou* yields of wheat, early rice and rapeseed greatly surpassed those of last year and their total outputs also exceeded those of last year.

A check-up has been carried out in the rural people's communes throughout the country in accordance with the resolution of the Sixth Plenary Session of the Eighth Central Committee of the Party adopted last December, the resolution of the Enlarged Meeting of the Political Bureau of the Central

Committee held in Cheng-chow in February this year and the series of directives issued by the Central Committee subsequently. During the check-up, the principles of management and business accounting at different levels, of "to each according to his work" and more income for those who do more work have been implemented. It has been decided that at the present stage a three-level type of ownership of the means of production should be instituted in the people's communes. Ownership at the production brigade level constitutes the basic one. Ownership at the commune level constitutes another part (in addition to ownership of the public economic undertakings run by the commune, the commune can draw each year a reasonable amount for its capital accumulation fund from the income of the production brigades). A small part of the ownership should also be vested in the production team. In this way, the people's communes, which are large in size, which integrate industry, agriculture, trade, education and military affairs and which combine government and commune administration into one, have overcome the tendencies which, owing to lack of experience, occurred during the initial period of their founding, such as the tendencies to over-centralization, to equalitarianism and extravagance, and have rapidly taken the road of sound and consolidated development. In this way, the advantages of the people's communes will come into play more and more clearly—being large in scale and having a wide range of activities, they can plan the production and distribution of the whole commune in a unified way; they can, more effectively than the agricultural producers' co-operatives, fully mobilize and rationally use labour power in the rural areas; they can undertake constructive tasks which the co-operatives could hardly handle; they can facilitate the speedy integrated development of agriculture, forestry, animal husbandry, side-occupations and fishery and also of industry, agriculture, trade, education and military affairs, the mechanization of farming, the steady increase of the incomes of the peasants, rapid progress in rural life as a whole, and the development of collective undertakings such as community dining-rooms and nurseries; and they can provide that a certain portion of their distribution system is in the nature of free supply, etc.

With regard to trade, the volume of retail sales in the first half of this year amounted to 29,600 million yuan, exceeding that of the corresponding period of last year by 23 per cent. The sale of grain was 12 per cent more than in the corresponding period of last year, while retail sales of other major consumer goods such as vegetables, cigarettes, cotton piece goods, knitwears, leather shoes [errata slip from Foreign Languages Press changes this to "rubber shoes"], soap, stationery and medicines also considerably exceeded those of the corresponding period of last year. But because the purchasing power of the people increased even more quickly, there was a bit of a strain in the supply situation on the market with regard to a small number of commodities. Thanks to the series of measures taken by the Party and the government, a change has rapidly taken place in the situation and a radical change will certainly take place in due time.

To sum up, the various branches of the national economy in the first half of this year was on the whole in good shape and the situation is favourable for the realization of this year's continued leap forward.

III

In the light of the verified figures on last year's agricultural output, the actual implementation of the national economic plan in the first half of this year and recent occurrence of natural calamities, the Eighth Plenary Session of the Eighth Central Committee recommends that the State Council submit to the Standing Committee of the National People's Congress a proposal for appropriate readjustment of the 1959 plan, fixing the following targets: steel (excluding that made by indigenous methods), 12 million tons (an increase of 50 per cent over last year's output of 8 million tons of steel produced with modern equipment; in view of the shortage of labour power in the rural areas, it is suggested that this year the production of steel by indigenous methods should be decided upon by the local authorities themselves in accordance with local conditions and will not be included in the state plan); coal, 335 million tons (an increase of 24 per cent over last year's coal output of 270 million tons); grain, about 10 per cent above last year's verified output of 500,000 million catties (250 million tons); cotton, about 10 per cent above last year's verified output of 42 million *tan* (2.1 million tons). It is quite clear that the readjusted national economic plan remains a plan for a continued leap forward; it is also one which can be overfulfilled and hence can all the more encourage the initiative of the working people.

As a result of the leap forward in 1958, we have fulfilled, four years ahead of schedule, the targets for coal, timber, salt and grain envisaged in the Second Five-Year Plan drawn up in 1956. After realizing this year's plan for a continued leap forward, we will have fulfilled or nearly fulfilled, three years ahead of schedule, the targets envisaged in the Second Five-Year Plan for such major industrial and agricultural products as steel, metallurgical equipment, power-generating equipment, metal-cutting machine tools, machine-made paper, cotton and cotton yarn. Thus it will be possible for us, within about ten years, counting from 1958, to realize the slogan "catch up with Britain in the output of major industrial products within 15 years." It will also be possible for us to overfulfil the 12-year programme for agricultural development (1956–1967) a long way ahead of schedule. Moreover, the successful fulfilment of this year's industrial production and construction plan and the winning this year of a bumper harvest in food and industrial crops will, to a large extent, determine the tempo of our industrial and agricultural development next year. Therefore, the whole Party and the entire nation must unite as one, go all out, develop a vigorous campaign for increasing production and practising economy in the coming four-odd months and strive by every means to fulfil and overfulfil this year's plan for a continued leap forward.

IV

Efforts must be made to increase production in industry, agriculture and transport; a socialist labour emulation campaign should be launched. This is, at the present time, the noblest task of the workers, peasants and revolutionary intellectuals throughout the country.

In industry, special attention should first of all be paid to the production of raw and other materials, fuel and electric power, and especially iron, steel, rolled steel, coal, timber, cement and raw materials for the chemical industry. Great efforts should be made to overfulfil the output targets in these industries. The machine-building industry should in the first place ensure the production of all equipment urgently required this year and deliver it in whole sets according to schedule. It should also promptly and properly handle the problem of semi-finished products. All key enterprises should fulfil and overfulfil the state plan according to required standards of quality, quantity and specifications and also according to monthly and ten-day schedules. Small and medium-sized local enterprises should also, in conformity with the requirements of the state plan, fulfil the targets for quality as well as for quantity. They should do their best to reduce the proportion of sub-grade products and eliminate rejects. Great efforts should further be made, in particular, to improve the quality of pig iron produced by small and medium-sized blast furnaces and of steel produced by converters. The production of light industrial and handicraft products for the daily use of the people should be increased as quickly as possible and all potentialities should be tapped to expand raw material resources for these products. All enterprises should improve management, maintenance and repair of equipment and ensure safety in production. In the field of capital construction, resources should be concentrated to guarantee swifter construction of important projects, particularly those which need to go into production this year, and see that capital investments yield quick results. Labour power throughout the country must be deployed more rationally by further transferring surplus labour power in industrial production and construction back to the rural areas so far as is possible or to other fields where labour power is urgently needed. Further efforts should be made to increase the productivity of labour.

In agriculture, great attention should be paid in the coming two months to the field management of food and industrial crops, weeding, dressing with fertilizer and the prevention and combating of plant diseases and insect pests so that a bumper harvest can be reaped. This year's autumn crops generally did well during the initial stage. But following the big floods in the south, the central areas of our country are now suffering from a serious dry spell and some areas in the north have been subjected to floods or water-logging. These natural calamities must be overcome before we can fulfil this year's plan for increased production. Man will conquer nature. Where natural calamities have occurred, the Party organizations must resolutely lead all people urgently to organize manpower and material resources, make full use of all existing water conservancy facilities and fight tenaciously to overcome the serious natural calamities, safeguard the autumn harvest and organize relief through production. In the coming two months, adequate preparations must also be made for autumn harvesting, ploughing and sowing. These include the allocation of labour power, readying of implements, autumn composting, etc. In autumn harvesting, last year's lesson must be borne in mind. Good work must be done in reaping, threshing, gathering, delivering, distributing and storing so that nothing is lost. After the autumn, labour power must be rationally deployed and diverse undertakings in forestry, animal husbandry, side-occupations and fishery strengthened. Meanwhile, no time should be lost in completing the check-up in the people's communes, in settling the remaining problems properly and building up the communes even better.

In transport, the primary emphasis must now be laid on the transport of coal, timber, grain, ores and building materials. After the autumn harvest, attention should at the same time be paid to the transport of autumn agricultural produce. All freight which can be handled earlier should, as far as possible, be transported during the third quarter, so that the burden of freight transport in the fourth quarter can be lessened. To improve short-distance transport, slack intervals in farming should be made use of everywhere to energetically organize rural manpower and means of transport and develop a mass campaign for short-distance transport.

Trade organizations should work energetically in conjunction with the campaigns on the various production fronts for increased production and make big efforts to organize a good supply of means of production to the cities and countryside and the purchase of agricultural, light industrial and handicraft products. Warehouse stocks should be carefully checked; commodities must be rationally allocated and distributed; and the supply of consumer goods must be organized systematically.

V

There must be a rigorous practice of economy while production is being increased vigorously. Increasing production and practising economy; building the country and running the people's communes, all enterprises and undertakings and homes industriously and thriftily—this is the way to make our country prosperous and strong; this is also the key to fulfilling and overfulfilling this year's plan.

All industrial enterprises must, while ensuring quality, make great efforts to economize raw and other materials, fuel and power. Metallurgical and power industries, railways, enterprises engaged in water transport and other industrial departments must work out strict plans to economize on the use of coal and enforce these plans resolutely. Heavy industrial enterprises and capital construction units must make great efforts to economize on the consumption of rolled steel and timber. Light industrial enterprises must make great efforts to economize on the consumption of agricultural raw materials. In agricultural production, good care must be taken of draught animals and implements. Water, manure and seeds must not be wasted. Attention must be paid to economizing labour power and circulating funds in industry, transport, agriculture and other enterprises and undertakings.

Education in economy should be carried out extensively in city and countryside throughout the land. State organs should first of all set an example of industry and thrift by reducing all expenses that can be cut. The economizing of grain, coal and other consumer goods which are not yet in abundant supply should be promoted among the people and waste combated. All rural people's communes must keep and use their grains well. Long-term overall planning should be worked out with regard to the production and consumption of grains, potatoes, vegetables, fodder and fuel in accordance with the need to provide against contingencies and make reserves last a long time. The people's communes should strive to increase the marketable part of their non-staple food products such as fish, meat, chickens, ducks, eggs and edible oil, so as to secure more income for the commune members, and increase the supplies for the cities and for export in support of the great cause of socialist construction. With regard to the community dining-rooms in the rural areas, the principle of making vigorous efforts to run them well and voluntary participation should be adhered to; grains should be distributed to each family on the basis of a fixed allocation for each individual; a food ticket system should be introduced in the community dining-rooms, with unconsumed food being returned to the person who saves it. The practice of saving should be vigorously promoted among the people of the cities and the countryside, so that money which the individual does not need to spend for the time being can be rationally and effectively used for construction in the interests both of the state and the family. The whole Party and the entire nation should be told that we should be skilled not only in handling production, but also in arranging our livelihood and house-keeping, making careful budgets and keeping reserves against need. As long as the government and the people work with one mind and vigorously increase production and practise economy, our country will certainly be able to surmount any obstacles in the way of our advance and grow with each passing day, to secure a thriving and prosperous life for the whole people.

VI

The general line, the great leap forward and the people's communes—these embody the great determination and wisdom of the 650 million industrious and brave people of our country; they are the products of the creative integration of the universal truths of Marxism-Leninism with the practical situation in China achieved by Comrade Mao Tse-tung, great leader of our Party and of the people of all nationalities in our country. We achieved great victories last year and in the first half of this year precisely because, in socialist construction, we strengthened the leading role of the Party, firmly put politics in command, resolutely adhered to the working method of the mass line and staunchly upheld the glorious banners of the general line, the great leap forward and the people's communes. In the future we will continue to advance valiantly along this glorious and victorious road and strive for great new victories.

The experience of 1958 very clearly proved that the wisdom and strength of the masses is unlimited. Enlightened and led by our Party and Comrade Mao Tse-tung, and inspired by and organized under our Party's general line, this wisdom and strength has become as irresistible as a mighty force under whose impact high mountains bow their heads and broad rivers make way. To our people, the great leap forward and the people's communes are new things which have no precedent in history. In the course of their advance it is naturally inevitable that certain difficulties are met with and that there are some shortcomings. But the masses of the people, under the close guidance of our Party and Comrade Mao Tse-tung, have quickly solved, or are quickly solving, these problems of a transient and local nature. Enemy elements hostile to the socialist cause of our country, both within our country and without, have seized the opportunity to slander us in an attempt to influence certain unstable elements within our ranks. But no reactionaries can in the least shake the great resolve of our Party and our 650 million people. On the contrary, the great mass of cadres and people are full of confidence that our achievements are exceptionally great and our future is extremely bright. The Eighth Plenary Session of the Eighth Central Committee of the Chinese Communist Party calls upon the whole Party and the people of all nationalities of the country, under the leadership of the Central Committee of the Party and Comrade Mao Tse-tung, to unite more closely, resolutely surmount all difficulties and correct all shortcomings in our work, overcome the Right opportunist sentiments among some unstable elements, deal telling blows to the disruptive activities of anti-socialist elements, fight for this year's great victories and strive to fulfil ahead of schedule within these two years (1958-1959) the major targets of the Second Five-Year Plan. In order to fulfil and overfulfil this year's plan, the third quarter is a crucial period. Each second is worth an ounce of gold. Let us act together at once to fulfil and overfulfil the plan for the third quarter and greet the tenth anniversary of the founding of our great People's Republic of China with a great, new upsurge in production!

DOCUMENT 41

Report on Adjusting the Major Targets of China's 1959 National Plan and Further Developing the Campaign for Increasing Production and Practicing Economy, delivered by Premier Chou En-lai to a plenary meeting of the Standing Committee of the Second National People's Congress, August 26, 1959.

The text is from the NCNA English-language release of August 28, 1959, as transcribed in CB 590 under the title "Premier Chou En-lai's Report on China's Economy."

Comment. For the parallels between the situations in 1956 and 1959, and between Chou En-lai's speech to the Eighth Party Congress in September 1956 (Document 11) and this speech of three years later, see our General Introduction, part IX. A fuller version of the criticisms leveled by rightists against the small iron and steel plants, and particularly of the allegations that "what you have lost [by building small-scale iron works] is more than what you have gained," is given in CB 590 (editorial from *People's Daily*, Sept. 1, 1959).

On Chinese exports of grain, see also CB 353 and 468, containing speeches by Yeh Chi-chuang, Minister of Foreign Trade, to the National People's Congress in 1955 and 1957.

TEXT OF DOCUMENT 41

The 8th plenary session of the 8th Central Committee of the Chinese Communist Party, held from the 2nd to the 16th of August, 1959, in the light of the implementation of the 1959 national economic plan and the analysis of the present economic situation, recommended to adjust the economic targets for this year and put forth the militant task of further developing the campaign for increasing production and practicing economy to fulfill ahead of schedule within this year the major targets of the Second Five-Year Plan. A plenary meeting called by the State Council on August 25 unanimously agreed to the appraisal of the present economic situation made by the 8th plenary session of the 8th Central Committee of the Chinese Communist Party and to its recommendation to adjust the major targets of the 1959 national economic plan and to further develop the campaign to increase production and practice economy. On behalf of the State Council, I shall now deliver a report to the Standing Committee of the 2nd National People's Congress on adjusting the major targets of the 1959 national economic plan and further developing the campaign to increase production and practice economy.

I. THE ECONOMIC SITUATION IN 1959

On the basis of the great leap forward in 1958, we won the victory of a continued leap forward in the national economy in the first half of 1959.

Industry: The total output value of industry in the first half of this year reached 72,900 million yuan, 65 per cent more than the 44,300 million yuan of the corresponding period last year. The outputs of some of the most important industrial products in the first half of this year and their increases over the same period of last year are as follows: iron produced by modern equipment, 9.5 million tons, 160 per cent; steel produced by modern equipment, 5.3 million tons, 66 per cent; coal, 174 million tons, more than 100 per cent; electricity, 18,400 million kilowatt-hours, 55 per cent; metal-cutting machine tools, 45,000 units, more than 100 per cent; cotton yarn, 4,147,000 bales, 46 per cent; and sugar, 780,000 tons, 43 per cent. The outputs of other products all surpassed those of the corresponding period last year to a greater or lesser extent, and among them only a few achieved an increase less than 20 per cent.

Agriculture: Although the sown acreage to summer crops was somewhat reduced and there were serious natural calamities in spring this year, thanks to the check-up and consolidation of the people's communes and the further display of the initiative of the broad mass of peasantry, the total output of wheat, coarse grains and early rice reached 139,000 million catties (69.5 million tons), even exceeding the 136,500 million catties (68.25 million tons) of last year's exceptional bumper summer harvest by 2,500 million catties (1.25 million tons).

Transportation: The volume of railway freight in the first half of this year was 247 million tons, increasing by 49 per cent compared with the same period last year; the freight volume of ships and barges 55 million tons, a 75 per cent increase; the freight volume of trucks 140 million tons, 94 per cent.

Capital construction: The total investment realized in the first half of this year reached 10,700 million yuan, a 54 per cent rise compared with the corresponding period last year. As a result of large-scale capital construction, many projects went into production as a whole or partially, and the production capacity of industry rose greatly.

Commerce: Retail sales in the first half of this year totalled 29,600 million yuan, increasing by 23 per cent compared with the corresponding period last year. The supply of most commodities in the same period surpassed that of the corresponding period last year in varying degrees.

It can be seen from the above that in the first half of this year industry, agriculture, transportation, capital construction and commerce have all continued to develop at a high speed. On the whole, the economic situation of our country is good, the achievement great and the whole picture one of continued leap forward. The broad masses of the people are satisfied with this situation and have full confidence in our right future.

But contrary to the overwhelming majority of the people, who are full of confidence and energy, there are a very small number of people who remain cold to our country's great achievements in socialist construction, they are pessimistic about the current economic situation and even try hard to spread their extremely erroneous ideas. This would, undoubtedly, dampen the enthusiasm of the masses and blunt their activeness. In the interests of the socialist cause, we must thoroughly repudiate these erroneous and harmful views. Here I would only refute their arguments on three questions about which they have talked about.

First, the massive campaign to make iron and steel.

Inspired by the general line—go all-out, aim high and get faster, greater, better and more economical results to build socialism—and the series of policies of "walking on two legs", our 600 million and more people, in high spirits, have ardently plunged themselves into the movement of building socialism. This has given rise to a large-scale mass campaign for economic construction unparalleled in China's history. One of the important aspects of this mass campaign was that tens of millions of people went in for mining ores and coal and making iron and steel. The mass of people understand that large-scale vigorous mass campaigns on the economic front will insure a high-speed development of the national economy so as the quicker to transform China's face of "poverty and blankness". They therefore display in work a boundless enthusiasm and even neglect sleep and meals. The reactionaries at home and abroad allege that this is "forced labor" and "depriving people of freedom". That is a shameless slander. It is the imperialist bosses who are accustomed to depriving people of freedom. Yet when in the western world has the magnificent feat happened to tens of millions of people going in for mining ores and coal and making iron and steel? Doubtless, such voluntary labor enthusiasm by the working people has been impossible and will remain impossible under the capitalist system. Our general line for building socialism is a true expression of the will of the working people throughout China. Therefore, once grasped by the masses, it has given forth such an unparalleled great force. The reactionaries at home and abroad can by no means understand this, nor do they wish to understand.

Some people hold that last year's massive campaign to make iron and steel was "more loss less gain" or at most "half loss half gain" because much manpower was used, much money was spent and among the products was some iron and steel made by local, simple methods. We regard this view as entirely wrong.

In 1958, we produced 13.69 million tons of pig iron (excluding the 4 to 5 million tons of pig iron suitable not for making steel, but for the manufacture of simple farm implements and tools), 2.3 times that of 1957; and 11.08 million tons of steel, more than doubling that of 1957. In iron and steel production the mass campaign to build small enterprises, use light equipment and employ local, simple methods gave impetus to a mass campaign for big enterprises, heavy equipment and modern methods and to mass campaigns on the entire industrial front. With steel as the key lever, there was brought about the big leap forward in industry, as a result the output of many important industrial products were doubled or went up several-fold and the 1958 gross industrial output value was 66 per cent higher than in 1957. Moreover, the mass campaign of making iron and steel has paved the way for the future development of the iron and steel industry and industry as a whole. In many places where there are suitable resources and local iron smelting furnaces and small blast furnaces were erected last year, groups of small blast furnaces have been developed and the output and quality of pig iron greatly raised after rational re-grouping, adding of equipment and improvement of technique during last winter and spring. The aggregate volume of small blast furnaces (between 6.5 and 100 cubic meters each) now in operation reached 43,000 cubic meters, nearly twice as much as the total volume of the large blast furnaces in the country—24,000 cubic meters. They are able to turn out about 10 million tons of pig iron this year. In the Second Five-Year Plan period, these small blast furnaces would produce a total of about 55 million tons of pig iron. Starting from 1963, they will turn out more than 15 million tons a year. It is completely worthwhile, and very important for us to allocate appropriate subsidies for the operation of the small blast furnaces in these five years. If we only build big blast furnaces, we would by no means be able, with the same or even a greater amount of investment, to produce so much pig iron in five years owing to the limitation of various conditions. The history of industrial development in all countries shows that given iron and steel, machinery can be made, and given iron and steel and machinery, it will be possible to develop rapidly industry as a whole and the entire national economy. It is therefore impermissible to slight in any degree last year's mass campaign to make iron and steel or the great significance of the large groups of small blast furnaces for iron and steel production in the future.

Considerable progress has been made in the past few months in raising the quality of products of the small blast furnaces and lowering coal consumption. By July, the proportion of pig iron produced by small blast furnaces which was up to standard had risen to about 75 per cent, the rate of coal consumption dropped to about 4 tons for a ton of pig iron and the utilization co-efficient approached 0.7 ton of pig iron per cubic meter of furnace volume every 24 hours. This proves that the mass campaign in the iron and steel industry has a tremendous vitality and has been raised to a new stage. It can be anticipated that even greater progress will be made in the near future in raising the output and improving the quality of the products of the small blast furnaces and lowering their coal consumption rate. The massive campaign of making iron and steel has also served to "temper people": enable the masses to acquire technical skill and knowledge and large numbers of cadres to gain experience.

Facts prove that the simultaneous development of large industrial enterprises and small and medium-sized enterprises and using integrated local and modern methods have the advantages of extensive distribution, quick completion, less strict demands as regards quality of raw and other material and convenience in supply. This is greatly conducive to our prospecting the resources extensively, deploying the productive forces rationally, making full use of the resources and economizing on the use of means of transportation. Of course, in our industrial construction, we must energetically build large and medium-sized enterprises using modern methods. This is the principal aspect. We must not, however, overlook the construction of small enterprises using local, simple methods or integrated modern and local methods. We must "walk on two legs", not on one alone.

In view of the above-mentioned facts, we must affirm that the mass campaign of making iron and steel has gained much; it has not resulted in "half loss half gain", even less in "more loss less gain". The iron and steel campaign constitutes an important aspect of the implementation of the general line for socialist construction and the series of policies of "walking on two legs". The attacks on the mass campaign of making iron and steel which distort the facts are in fact attacks on the general line for socialist construction and the policy of "walking on two legs". We must resolutely rebuff such attacks.

Second, people's communes and community dining rooms.

Alongside the great leap forward in the national economy, people's communes were set up throughout our countryside in 1958. The establishment of the people's communes represents the desire of hundreds of millions of peasants. In order to emerge from the state of poverty and backwardness more quickly and effectively, the broad mass of peasants were not content with the organizational form of the higher stage cooperative they already had and desired to organize communes much larger in scale and having a much wider scope of activities. As early as at the juncture of spring and summer of 1958, the organizational form of the people's commune actually appeared in many places in Honan Province and some other provinces. As soon as it came into existence, it had a host of followers and barely a few months had passed before our whole countryside was switched over to people's communes. Precisely because the people's communes represent the will of the great majority of the peasantry and play a great part in further emancipating and developing the social productive forces, they displayed a great vitality even in their initial stage. Everyone knows that the exceptionally big leap forward in the national economy last autumn and winter was inseparably connected with the setting up of the people's communes throughout the countryside.

Since the people's commune movement was a full-scale mass movement, and since the commune was a new thing, it is unthinkable that they were perfect and flawless from the very start and that there were no defects or difficulties at all. Some such phenomena as the over-centralization of some administrative powers, equalitarianism in distribution and extravagance did appear during the initial period of the people's commune movement because both the cadres and the masses lacked experience. But these defects were rapidly discovered and rectified by the Central Committee of the Party. The question of checking up the people's communes was already discussed at the meeting called by Comrade Mao Tse-tung at Chengchow in November last year which was attended by part of the leading comrades of the Central Committee and the local committees. Later, at the 6th plenary session of the 8th Central Committee of the Chinese Communist Party held at Wuchang and at the enlarged meeting of the Political Bureau of the Central Committee held at Chengchow in February and March this year, a series of important decisions on checking up the people's communes were made. In accordance with these decisions, local leading Party and government organs of various levels from last winter have conducted large-scale check-up in the people's communes, carried through the principles of management and business accounting at different levels, of "to each according to his work" and more income for those who work more; and laid it down that at the present stage a three-level ownership of the means of production should be applied in the people's communes, and that ownership at the production brigade level constitutes the basic one, part of the ownership is vested in the commune level and there should also be a small part of the ownership vested in the production team level. After the check-up and consolidation, the advantages of the people's communes have come into play more and more clearly and will do so even more clearly in the future in the comprehensive development of agriculture, forestry, animal husbandry, side occupations and fishery and also of industry, agriculture, trade, education and defense, the gradual mechanization of agriculture, increasing the peasants' incomes and ameliorating rural life, and developing collective undertakings such as community dining rooms and nurseries. The people's communes are now still of a collective ownership character, but, in the ownership at the commune level, there are already some rudiments of ownership by the whole people. It can be anticipated that the people's commune will provide a good organizational form and valuable experience for the future switch of the rural areas from collective ownership to ownership by the whole people and from socialism to Communism.

The emergence of the people's communes, the development of the commune movement, is an excellent thing and by no means a bad thing. The people's communes are the inevitable results of developing circumstances and their rise was not at all too early. Those who assert that the people's communes are very bad are none other than the imperialists who are extremely hostile to our country's cause of socialism, as well as some rightists and other reactionaries who are against the people and against socialism. Apart from these, there are some people who voice approval of socialism but find fault with this and that in the people's commune movement which has the active support of hundreds of millions of people and maintain that the people's communes have been set up too early and have gone wrong. We would ask: are you not afraid of being thrown over the border-line of the bourgeois rightists?

Here, I would like to say something about the community dining rooms. The community dining rooms established in the wide rural areas and run by some street communities in the cities are both undertakings of the masses. Many rural dining rooms are several years old and developed especially rapidly in the summer of last year; they suit the requirements of the masses and are thus welcomed by them. They are especially ardently welcomed by working women, because they relieve them to a great extent of heavy household chores and facilitate their taking part in production like the men. For the old folk and children they have at the same time the function of collective welfare and social insurance. In the initial period of their establishment, owing to lack of experience in management and to the influence of the bumper harvest and the mass campaigns for making iron and steel and for developing industry, some dining rooms failed to manage well their grain and other foods, so that a little too much was consumed. This is understandable. This defect has now been corrected. After the summer harvesting, such measures as distributing grain to each family, voluntary participation in dining rooms, rationing food according to each individual's capacity and returning unconsumed grain to the person who saves it have been applied in various localities, with the result that most of the dining rooms have been consolidated. We maintain that so long as the principles of active improvement and voluntary participation are adhered to, the community dining rooms will attain their aim of furnishing facilities to production and to the masses and thus will be warmly supported by the broad mass of working people. Therefore, it is obviously very wrong to exaggerate certain shortcomings of the community dining rooms in their initial stage, and find fault with and oppose them, or even close them down forcibly in contravention of the desire of the masses.

Third, the question of the market.

The market supply of most of the important commodities in the first half of this year increased by a wide margin over that of the same period of last year. According to statistics, the supply of grain, coal, silk, wine and matches increased by 10 to 30 per cent; cotton piece goods, table salt, soap, bicycles and cigarettes by 30 to 50 per cent; knit-wear, worsted, woollen cloth, rubber shoes and fountain pens by 50 per cent to more than 100 per cent; edible oils, paper, kerosene and tea by less than 10 per cent. Only the supply of about a dozen kinds of commodities dropped in the first half of this year, including pork, beef, mutton, egg products, aquatic products, sugar, cotton for domestic use, leather shoes, electric bulbs and watches. Reduction in the supply of these goods are not all due to decreased production. The cut in the supply of such commodities as meat, egg products, aquatic products and cotton for domestic use was because the consumption of these goods in the rural areas which

TEXT OF DOCUMENT 41 545

produced them had greatly increased. There is little justification for the urban inhabitants to blame our peasants, whose consumption level has always been rather low, for eating and using up a little more than usual for a period of time after the great expansion of production.

On the whole, there was no tension in the supply of the goods for wearing, most goods for daily use, grain and part of the subsidiary foodstuffs. Comparative tension was felt only in the supply of a small part of the subsidiary foodstuffs and a few consumer goods. Moreover, the supply of a number of consumer goods and subsidiary foodstuffs which was tense in the first half of this year has begun to improve in June and July. Some people claimed that there was an all-round tension in the market. This was a deliberate distortion of the fact. A handful of people even said that before liberation one could get anything in the market but now nothing was available. Everyone knows that this is not at all true, but a vicious distortion. To the working people who constitute 80 to 90 per cent of the population of the country, the fact is contrary to what these people asserted. The working people could not get anything they wanted before liberation, and now everything that is necessary is available. Those who make such assertions only show that they fail to see or are discontented with the rise of the working people's living standards. They still hanker after the luxurious and rotten life in the old society, led by only a very small number of people such as the aristocrats, officials, landlords, compradors and capitalists. Is it not quite clear what these people are after?

We should also see that the relative tension in the supply of certain commodities for a time was due to the particularly rapid increase in the purchasing power in the cities arising from the fast expansion of employment and the increase of large number of workers and staff, as a result of the fast development of production, capital construction and other work last year. According to estimates, the addition of new workers and staff last year, apart from those transferred from other jobs, have caused this year an increase in the purchasing power of more than 400 million yuan every month. Thus the purchasing power in the cities, including collective purchasing power, reached 14,300 million yuan in the first half of this year, 30 per cent higher than the 11,000 million yuan of the same period of last year. This is the main cause for the tension which occurred for a time in the supply of certain commodities in the cities, particularly subsidiary foodstuffs.

Some people suspect that the tension in the supply of certain commodities was due to excessive export. This conforms still less to the fact. The total volume of export this year is only 17.8 per cent higher than that of last year. Furthermore, there is no increase or very little increase in the quantity of export of grain and various subsidiary foodstuffs needed at home compared with last year. Up to August 15 this year, for instance, our total export of rice was only 792,000 tons and that of pork equivalent to only 1,400,000 pigs, each constituting less than one per cent of last year's output of rice and the total number of live pigs at the end of last year. To speed up socialist construction, it is absolutely necessary to exchange agricultural produce for materials needed by our country. This is in the interests of the development not only of industry but also of agriculture.

For a very short period in spring this year, grain was in short supply in areas amounting to less than 5 per cent of the expanse of the country. This was because last year there were natural calamities, but the household affairs of the peasants was not well managed, the grain crops were harvested in a somewhat crude way, there was lack of planning for consumption so that a little too much grain was used up, and because, on top of these there were new natural calamities in the spring of this year. But this was merely a local and temporary situation. With the energetic support and help of the Communist Party and the government, the grain shortage in those areas was soon solved. Difficulties were successfully overcome even in a place like Kwangtung Province which was seriously hit by flood and drought.

From the above analysis, we can definitely arrive at this conclusion: the big leap forward and the people's commune have registered great achievements, the present economic situation is favorable to us and our future is bright. This proves that the Party's general line for socialist construction and the series of policies of "walking on two legs" are entirely correct. We absolutely cannot allow reactionaries and the right opportunists among the ranks of the people to take advantage of the isolated and transient shortcomings in our practical work which have already been corrected to attack the big leap forward and the people's commune and to undermine and oppose the general line for socialist construction.

It must be pointed out that both the big leap forward and the setting up of the people's communes are revolutionary movements undertaken by the broad masses. How should one behave toward the revolutionary movements of the masses? Should one encourage the masses in their advance by actively supporting and leading them and enthusiastically identifying oneself with the masses; or should one stand outside the mass movements, arrogantly criticizing the masses, or even stand against the mass movements and oppose the masses? Here lies the fundamental difference between the proletarian revolutionary and the bourgeois and petty bourgeois revolutionary. The right opportunities are utterly wrong precisely because they have taken the attitude of a bourgeois master toward the mass movements.

II. ADJUSTMENT OF THE 1959 PLANNED TARGETS

The planned targets of 1959 require adjustment in the light of the problems discovered in the course of carrying out the plan for the first half of this year, in the light of the verified figures regarding the output of grain, cotton and other agricultural products of last year, and in the light of this year's serious natural calamities.

First of all, as already stated, industrial production in the first half of this year continued to leap forward on the basis of last year's great leap forward. The total industrial output value reached 72,900 million yuan. But, this comes to 44 per cent of the year's planned target as adopted by the first session of the 2nd National People's Congress and is below the percentage reached in the first half of any year in the First Five-Year Plan period when generally between 47 and 48 per cent of the year's plan of industrial output was fulfilled by the end of June. At the same time, in the second half of last year there was unusually rapid development in industrial production with the output value showing an increase of 64 per cent compared with the first half. This was mainly because of the running of large numbers of industrial enterprises by the *hsien* and the communes. As labor power now requires unified arrangement to reinforce the agricultural front, and the *hsien*-run and commune-run industries need to be adjusted and consolidated, and moreover, as there are certain limits of growth in the supply of raw and other materials and equipment, industrial output cannot grow in the second half of this year at as fast a rate in the second half of last year.

Taking the 33 main categories of industrial products, in the first half of this year 19 showed upward of 40 per cent fulfillment of the annual plan, namely, iron produced by modern equipment, electricity, coal, crude oil, timber, soda ash, caustic soda, antibiotics, metal-cutting machine tools, ships, combine harvesters, power-driven threshing machines, engines, cotton yarn, cotton cloth, paper, sugar, salt and cigarettes; and the other 14 showed below 40 per cent fulfillment, namely steel produced by modern equipment, rolled steel, cement, sulphuric acid, chemical fertilizer, power generating equipment, locomotives, freight wagons, automobiles, tractors, paper making equipment, sugar making equipment, cotton spinning frames and edible oils. Limited supplies of raw material and other material in these 14 categories, as matter stands, will make it impossible for them to show a very big increase in the second half of this year.

Second, due to our lack of experience in assessing harvests under the condition of a bumper harvest over large tracts of land and sudden great increase in the per hectare output, the relatively crude reaping, threshing, gathering in and storage in consequence of imperfect arrangement of labor power during the autumn harvest, and the under-estimation of the drop in output on the 400 million *mow* (26.6 million hectares) of farm land affected by natural calamities last year, the calculations made of last year's agricultural output were a bit high. The recent check-ups made by the State Statistical Bureau place last year's output of grain at 500,000 million catties (250 million tons), an increase of 35 per cent compared with the 370,000 million catties (185 million tons) of 1957, and cotton at 42 million *tan* (2.1 million tons), an increase of 28 per cent compared with the 32,800,000 *tan* of 1957. There were some over-estimates as regards certain other agricultural products and the products of side occupations. Check-ups have also been made on them this time. According to the verified figures of output, the total value of agricultural production last year was 67,100 million yuan, a 25 per cent increase compared with the 53,700 million yuan of 1957.

Taking the verified increase in agricultural production and output value last year, though the former estimate was rather high, this cannot shake the fact that a great leap forward took place in agriculture last year. Last year's agricultural production, in terms of the increase in the total output value, was still an unprecedented big leap forward.

The figures given earlier of last year's industrial output have been verified as correct. The figures of the total industrial output value remain at 117,000 million yuan, an increase of 66 per cent compared with the 70,400 million yuan of 1957. What should be noted here is that, of the 11,080,000 tons of steel produced last year, 8 million tons were produced with modern equipment, and the remaining 3,080,000 tons by simple, local methods. The 8 million tons of steel produced with modern equipment represent an increase of 49.5 per cent over the 5,350,000 tons produced in 1957. Of the 13,690,000 tons of pig iron included in the statistics last year, 9,530,000 tons were produced in modern installations and the other 4,160,000 tons by simple, local methods. The 9,530,000 tons produced with modern equipment represent an increase of 60 per cent over the 5,940,000 tons produced in 1957. This undoubtedly still represents the speed of a great leap forward.

Third, according to recent figures, this year a total of 510 million *mow* (34 million hectares) of farm land have been affected by flood, drought and insect pests, which form close to one-third of the total cultivated area. Of the 320 million *mow* (21.3 million hectares) stricken by drought, 200 million *mow* (13.3 million hectares) have been irrigated to varying degrees through the resolute efforts of tens of millions of people in the battle against the drought. This is one of the evidences of the superiority and strength of the people's communes. The water conservancy works built by the peasant masses in the last few years have played a great role this year in both beating off the drought and preventing waterlogging. The water conservancy works throughout the country can now irrigate some 1,000 million *mow* (66.6 million hectares) of farm land. Of this, 500 million *mow* (33.3 million hectares) are able to benefit fully from irrigation, and more than 300 million *mow* (20 million hectares) derive partial benefit. The remaining 200 million *mow* (13.3 million hectares) can also benefit from the irrigation works after the land is levelled and irrigation ditches are built. If it were not for the large-scale mass campaign to build water conservancy projects in the past few years, particularly the last two years, the damage done by this year's drought must have been many times more serious.

The 8th plenary session of the 8th Central Committee of the Chinese Communist Party took the above three aspects into consideration and recommended to the State Council an adjustment in the targets for this year. On the 25th of August, 1959, the 91st plenary session of the State Council unanimously agreed to the recommendation of the Central Committee of the Chinese Communist Party, regarding it as both realistic and showing responsibility to the people.

I now want to submit the adjusted figures of the major targets for the 1959 national economic plan as adopted by the 91st plenary session of the State Council to the Standing Committee of the National People's Congress for examination and approval.

The major targets are adjusted as follows:

Industry: Steel output from the original 18 million tons—(including steel produced by local, simple methods) to 12 million tons (not including steel produced by local, simple methods, which is at the disposal of the local authorities); coal—from the original 380 million tons to 335 million tons; and targets for other industrial products are adjusted accordingly.

Industrial production in terms of value is adjusted from the original 165,000 million yuan to 147,000 million yuan.

Agriculture: Grain output—from the original 1,050,000 million catties (525 million tons) to 550,000 million catties (275 million tons); cotton output—from the original 100 million *tan* (5 million tons) to 46.2 million *tan* (2.3 million tons); and targets for outputs of other agricultural and animal husbandry products are adjusted accordingly.

Agricultural production in terms of value is adjusted from the original 122,000 million yuan to 73,800 million yuan.

Capital construction: Total investment—from the original 27,000 million yuan to 24,800 million yuan; the number of above norm projects to be constructed from the original 1,092 to 788. This will insure the supply of materials necessary for the existing enterprises' production and, at the same time, by appropriately shortening the front of capital construction, important projects will be able to start production earlier.

With the targets readjusted, it should be pointed out, this year's plan remains one of a continued leap forward. The total value of industrial and agricultural production will be 20 per cent above 1958 when the exceptionally great leap forward was made. The value of industrial output will increase by 25.6 per cent. Steel produced with modern equipment will increase by 50 per cent and coal by 24 per cent. The total value of agricultural production will increase by 10 per cent, with grain and cotton each also by 10 per cent. Taking the rate of economic development in the socialist countries and our own experience in construction during the First Five-Year Plan, it should be said that a more than 20 per cent annual increase in industry is a leap forward, a more than 25 per cent increase is a big leap forward and a more than 30 per cent increase an exceptionally great leap forward. In agriculture, an annual increase of more than 10 per cent is a leap forward, more than 15 per cent is a big leap forward and more than 20 per cent is an exceptionally great leap forward. In my report on the work of the government, made to the first session of the 2nd National People's Congress on April 18 this year, I said: "For the production of grain, when there are still very few farm machines and very little chemical fertilizer, even an annual increase of between 10 and 20 per cent is a leap forward." Therefore, the adjusted targets for industry and agriculture in 1959 still maintain the speed of a leap forward.

It should also be pointed out that the 25.6 per cent increase in industry and the 10 per cent increase in agriculture this year are being achieved on the basis of last year's great leap forward in industry and agriculture. This is different from an ordinary year. The bigger the basic figure, as everyone knows, the bigger increase is required for every per cent rise, and the great efforts are needed to achieve this.

Given the all-out effort and aiming high by the masses, it is possible to overfulfill the adjusted targets for industry. As for agriculture, if there are no further serious natural calamities, the adjusted targets there, too, can be overfulfilled.

In fulfilling the adjusted targets, we will, in the output of major industrial and agricultural products, realize three years ahead of schedule the Second Five-Year Plan as proposed by the 1st plenary session of the 8th National Congress of the Chinese Communist Party and accepted by the State Council. Taking the four major targets as an example, the proposal of the Chinese Communist Party's 8th Congress envisaged a 1962 target for steel of between 10,500,000 and 12 million tons; for coal, between 190 million and 210 million tons; for grain, 500,000 million catties (250 million tons); and for cotton, 48 million *tan* (2.4 million tons). This year, output of steel made with modern equipment is to reach 12 million tons; coal, 335 million tons; grain, 550,000 million catties (275 million tons); and cotton, 46,200,000 *tan* (2.31 million tons). This means they will all reach, exceed or approach the targets proposed by the 8th Congress of the Chinese Communist Party. In addition, the output of 7 other major industrial products, namely, timber, metallurgical equipment, power generating equipment, metal-cutting machine tools, cotton yarn, machine-made paper and salt, is also due this year to reach or surpass the targets proposed by the 8th Congress of the Chinese Communist Party.

Since we shall in the main fulfill the five-year plan in two years, in the subsequent three years we shall be able to make further achievements in industry and agriculture and devote more effort to strengthening certain weaker links.

It can well be anticipated that in the Second Five-Year Plan period, our country's industry and agriculture will grow much faster than in the First Five-Year Plan period. The Second Five-Year Plan is surely a five-year plan of great leap forward. The realization of the great leap forward Second Five-Year Plan will make it possible for us to aim at fulfilling, in the main within about ten years, the slogan of "Catch up with Britain in the output of major industrial products within 15 years", and to overfulfill the 12-year program for agricultural development, originally planned for completion in 1957, at a much earlier date.

III. FIGHT AGAINST RIGHTWARD TENDENCIES, GO ALL-OUT, AND FURTHER DEVELOP THE INCREASE-PRODUCTION AND PRACTICE-ECONOMY CAMPAIGN

All rightward tending sentiments, thinking and activities must be opposed in order to uphold the general line and the great achievements gained through the great leap forward and the people's communes, to strive for a continued leap forward in the national economy.

Certain shortcomings and errors were made in the course of drawing up and implementing the 1959 national economic plan, in the upsurge of the great leap forward; mainly, the production targets were set rather too high, the scale of capital construction rather too large and the increase of workers and staff rather too fast; hence some problems in the deployment of labor power, the distribution of materials, the use of funds, and the improvement in the quality of products, giving rise to certain disproportions in some links of the national economy. This indicates that our organs in charge of planning and economic affairs are not yet adept at the work of coordination and equilibration under the conditions of a big leap forward in the national economy. We must sum up our experience in this regard, remember it and turn unfavorable factors into favorable ones. However, it is necessary to point out that the shortcomings occurred in the course of great development, mainly arising from our lack of experience of great leaps forward. They are shortcomings in practical work made while applying the general line for socialist construction, and not shortcomings in the general line. The general line itself demands that we exert to the utmost our subjective initiative on the basis of objective conditions and observe the objective economic laws and pay attention to the proportion among various branches. Our experience, whether of success or failure gained in the practice of the past year and more proves that the general line for socialist construction and the series of policies of "walking on two legs" are entirely correct. With our shortcomings in work overcome, their brilliancy will further shine forth. Moreover, these shortcomings and errors were local and temporary—"one finger among the ten"—and have been corrected immediately on being discovered. The broad mass of cadres and people have received a deep education and much valuable experience in this great practice. This is an important gain. We consider it an abiding principle in guiding mass movements that shortcomings must be corrected in a serious manner, and the initiative of the broad masses and cadres must be eagerly protected. At no time may there be any damping down of the spirit or discouragement of the masses.

In the correction of the shortcomings in practical work and in adjusting the economic targets in the light of realities, some people, taking the bourgeois stand, under-estimate and even deny the great achievements of last year's great leap forward and of the people's communes. They exaggerate certain shortcomings and errors in the work, taking the part for the whole, the tributary for the mainstream, and maintain that the lower the economic targets the better. This kind of sentiment and thinking has grown in the past two months. In fact, those who think this way at root are sceptical of the vigorous mass movements launched by our more than 600 million people to do away with "poverty and blankness". They are sceptical of the great leap forward, the people's communes, the general line for socialist construction, the series of policies of "walking on two legs", and even the socialist system. Obviously, if we allow such thinking to continue and grow, without firmly correcting it, we will do serious damage to the initiative of the broad masses, we will not be able to continue the leap forward and win victory in our socialist cause. This of course would only benefit the enemy at home and abroad and harm the workers, the peasants and the revolutionary intellectuals; it would serve the interests of capitalism but not those of socialism. Since this question concerns the future of more than 600 million people, we must set the task of opposing rightward tendencies and wage a serious struggle against all existing rightward sentiments, thinking and activities.

On the basis of overcoming rightward tendencies, of continuing to mobilize the masses fully and encouraging them to go all-out in their revolutionary enthusiasm, we deem it necessary to press on to further develop the campaign for increasing production and practicing economy decided on at the first session of the 2nd People's Congress.

The further development of the campaign to increase production and practice economy is the chief guarantee of all-round overfulfillment of this year's national economic plan. In the very short time since we put forward this slogan, a new situation has emerged on all fronts of the national economy. On the industrial front, the daily output of steel in the first half month of August rose to 34,100 tons (on August 13 it reached 38,800 tons), showing an increase of 17 per cent over the average daily output of 29,000 odd tons in the first six months of this year. On the agricultural front, the fight against drought, flood, waterlogging and insects has been waged in full measure. As regards the arrangement of manpower, by the end of July, more than 4 million workers and staff had gone back to the rural areas to help in agricultural production. On the trade front, stocks of commodities in July showed an increase of 500 million yuan above that of June. In finance, revenue exceeded expenditure by 2,000 million yuan in the state budget from January to the end of the first 10 days of August. We can also see that a labor emulation campaign to compete in the quantity and quality of work done, in labor productivity, low production costs and safety has been launched in quite a few enterprises, with the workers there full of vigor and enthusiasm. Many leading cadres in factories and the rural areas have gone to the production sites to give concrete guidance to production and fight alongside the masses. A new production upsurge has begun to appear. All this proves that the economic situation is continuing to develop along healthy lines, the more than 600 million people are full of confidence and our prospects are extremely bright.

To further develop the increase-production and practice-economy campaign, we ask all economic departments of industry, agriculture, transport and commerce, and all other departments without any exception to extend socialist emulation and exert great efforts to increase production and practice economy. All enterprises and undertakings should fulfill and overfulfill their tasks under the state plan, in quality, quantity and specifications, every month and every ten days. All the people's communes should strive to conquer natural calamities, use manpower and material resources rationally, strengthen field management and make adequate preparations to win a bumper harvest in the autumn. Alongside with efforts to increase production, all enterprises, undertakings and people's communes must give attention to economizing manpower, material resources and money and encourage savings, so that the slogans of building the country and running enterprises and undertakings, people's communes and homes with industry and thrift and budgeting well one's income and expenses become translated into action by every one. The leading organs at all levels must keep a tight rein on September's work and greet the great 10th anniversary of our National Day with outstanding achievements.

It is our firm belief that our more than 600 million people, under the leadership of our great Chinese Communist Party and our great leader Comrade Mao Tse-tung, will achieve new and still more brilliant successes along the road of socialist construction.

DOCUMENT 42

Long Live the People's Communes! editorial in the *People's Daily*, August 29, 1959.

The text is an official translation published in *Peking Review*, September 8, 1959.

Comment. This article is the principal source for the official version of how communes were born—that is, in accordance with the initiative of the masses. (See our general comment in Chapter VIII and our General Introduction, part VIII.) It looks from the text (p. 553 below) as if there has been a Marxist version of the criticism that communes were artificially imposed, in other words that the "material conditions" for these new "higher relations of production" had not existed in 1958. On the doctrinal point involved, see our General Introduction, part IV. The opposite criticism, that the reversion to the "production brigade" as the basic level involved a virtual return to the system of agricultural producers' cooperatives, is of considerable interest. On this doctrinal issue see General Introduction, part IX.

―――――――――――――――TEXT OF DOCUMENT 42―――――――――――――――

Today is the first anniversary of the adoption of the historic "Resolution on the Establishment of People's Communes in the Rural Areas" by the Political Bureau of the Central Committee of the Chinese Communist Party at its enlarged session held at Peitaiho. A year ago, the people's communes had only just begun to grow in a few areas in China. Now they have been established in all rural areas throughout the country (with the exception of a few national minority areas): they have taken firm root and are advancing along a road of sound development. The people's commune, this "morning sun rising above the broad horizon of east Asia," is radiating its great energy and light ever more strongly.

THE PEITAIHO RESOLUTION

The Peitaiho resolution made three outstanding contributions to history. First, it analysed the historical background against which the people's communes came into existence; it foresaw the inevitable trend of their development and laid down the correct policy that the Chinese Communist Party must warmly support and actively lead the people's commune movement. "The people's communes," the resolution pointed out, "are the logical outcome of the march of events. Large, comprehensive people's communes have made their appearance, and in several places they are already widespread. They have developed very rapidly in some areas. It is highly probable that there will soon be an upsurge in setting up people's communes throughout the country and their development is irresistible." History has proved that this estimate, and the positive policy adopted in accordance with this estimate, are absolutely correct.

Secondly, the resolution scientifically defined the economic character of the people's communes and their future development. Although it held that the people's communes were the best form of organization for transforming collective ownership into ownership by the whole people in the countryside and for the transition from socialism to communism, it also clearly pointed out that the people's communes in the present stage "are still socialist in character, where the principle of 'from each according to his ability and to each according to his work' prevails." It pointed out that ownership in the people's communes "is still collective ownership" and that "the transition from collective ownership to ownership by the whole people is a process" the completion of which would take a number of years; even after the people's communes switch over to ownership by the whole people, they will still be socialist in character for a fairly long time. To avoid misunderstanding, the resolution described in detail the conditions needed to bring about the transition from socialism to communism—conditions which do not yet exist in China.

Thirdly, the Peitaiho resolution laid down a series of appropriate measures to be taken in setting up people's communes. In particular it stressed that participation by the peasants must be voluntary and said "compulsion is to be avoided" and "no compulsory or rash steps should be taken." It also said that "in all counties, experiments should first be made in some selected areas and the experience gained should be popularized gradually"; "in the early period of merging agricultural co-operatives into people's communes the method of 'changing the upper structure while keeping the lower structure unchanged' may be adopted.... The original organization of production and the system of administration may, for the time being, remain unchanged and continue as before"; "it is not necessary to deal with questions of reserved private land plots, scattered fruit trees, share funds and so on in a great hurry; nor is it necessary to adopt clear-cut stipulations on these questions." "After the establishment of the people's communes it is not necessary to hurry the change from the original system of distribution, in order to avoid any unfavourable effect on production." These remarks clearly expose how utterly groundless is the ridiculous talk of the imperialists and a few other people opposed to the people's commune movement, who deliberately try to create an impression that the Central Committee of the Chinese Communist Party fanatically wanted to "march to communism in one step" by means of the people's commune movement, and had to "retreat step by step" in the face of difficulties.

The warm welcome given to the people's commune movement by the hundreds of millions of peasants who were making big advances in production and the positive support and correct guidance given to it by the Peitaiho resolution led to its rapid and great upsurge throughout the country following the publication of the resolution. In less than two months, the mass of the peasants, then organized in more than 700,000 agricultural co-operatives, set up more than 26,000 people's communes. The switch to the people's communes was carried out in the rural areas throughout the country. This was an epoch-making event in our country's history.

THE ADVANTAGES OF THE COMMUNE

Less than a year has passed since all this took place. But this new-born social organization— the people's commune—has already proved with irrefutable facts its immense vitality and incomparable superiority, and its great role in developing our rural economy and culture and in raising the living standards of our peasants.

An unprecedented bumper autumn harvest and the mass movement to produce iron and steel followed immediately on completion of the establishment of people's communes in the countryside. Though allocations of manpower during the harvesting were not so well arranged in many places, so that the crops there were gathered in a rather hurried manner, yet very much bigger crops of grain and cotton were harvested than in the previous year. And on top of this, several million tons of pig iron were turned out by small blast furnaces using modern methods of production and several more million tons of both iron and steel were produced by blast furnaces and puddling furnaces using indigenous methods. At the same time, a gigantic task was fulfilled in transporting over short distances both agricultural produce and the materials involved in iron and steel production. But for the people's communes, it would have been impossible to accomplish such heavy tasks at one and the same time.

COMMUNES SPUR PRODUCTION

During the summer harvest this year, the first since the people's communes were set up, though the weather was bad, we got an even bigger harvest than that of the summer of 1958, the year of the big leap forward. Preliminary figures from Shensi, Hopei, Honan and Kiangsu Provinces show that over 500 *jin* of wheat have been harvested per *mu* on more than 650,000 *mu*. In 1957, the year before the establishment of the people's communes, not a single province throughout the country ever achieved a yield of more than 200 *jin* of wheat per *mu*. But this year six provinces and municipalities have already gone beyond this level. This is how things stand in agricultural production. It is the same in industry, forestry, animal husbandry, side-occupations and fishery. Large numbers of plants have been set up throughout the countryside to make farm tools, produce chemical fertilizer by indigenous methods, or process agricultural products. A rough count in February of this year showed that the people's communes had set up more than 86,000 plants to manufacture and repair farm tools. The collective breeding of livestock was greatly developed during the time of the co-operatives but this cannot compare with what has been done by the people's communes. A recent survey in 21 provinces and autonomous regions shows that more than 80 million pigs are being collectively raised by the people's communes, an average of more than 3,000 to each commune. The number of pigs raised privately has also grown rapidly.

Similarly great achievements stand to the credit of the people's communes in the building of water conservancy projects. Apart from large numbers of small reservoirs with a storage capacity of less than 10 million cubic metres each, since last winter the people's communes have built 60 big reservoirs each with a storage capacity of more than 100 million cubic metres and over 1,200 medium-sized reservoirs with a storage capacity of between 10 million and 100 million cubic metres each. This year China has been attacked by the biggest drought and floods that have occurred for dozens of years past; more than 510 million *mu* of farmland have been affected. But thanks to the many water conservancy projects built by the people's communes, the full mobilization of men and women by the people's communes to fight natural calamities and the co-operation on a broad scale, more than 270 million *mu* of the land affected by drought have been irrigated and relieved from this serious menace. The community dining-rooms, the nurseries and the "homes of respect for the aged" which have been set up widely in the countryside have played an important role in freeing women for productive work and improving the living standards of the peasants.

In a mass revolutionary movement on such a big scale and advancing so rapidly as the people's commune movement it is, of course, inevitable that while there were great achievements, a few shortcomings should occur. In fact, what is surprising is not that a few shortcomings have occurred, but that the shortcomings have been so few compared with the achievements and have been overcome so quickly. The resolution on the people's communes was made public on September 10 last year. Early in November, the conference called by Comrade Mao Tse-tung in Chengchow already discovered that in certain respects and to a certain degree the movement was deviating from the correct lines laid down in the Peitaiho resolution, and remedial measures were taken. After that, the Sixth Plenary Session of the Eighth Central Committee of the Communist Party, held in late November and early December, and the second Chengchow conference (the enlarged meeting of the Party's Political Bureau) held in late February and early March this year, gave detailed instructions for the check-up in the people's communes. These were put into effect within two to three months and the problems that had cropped up in the earlier stages were completely solved. The result is that the overwhelming majority of the cadres and the masses who were for the people's communes right from the start have become more confident than ever, while those few in the rural areas who had previously been sceptical have also been fully won over and their minds put at ease. The masses of the Chinese peasantry rejoice over the people's communes from the bottom of their hearts and sing: "The people's communes are very good indeed! Long live the prosperity of the country and its peaceful people!"

A CONTINUATION OF SOCIALIST REVOLUTION

The people's commune movement is a continuation and development of the great socialist revolution in China's countryside. The socialist revolution, like the democratic revolution, must obviously be carried forward to its conclusion. Under the conditions prevailing in our country, the people's commune is a powerful instrument for quickening the growth of our collective economy in the rural areas and eradicating the possibility of any return of capitalism. Since it combines industry, agriculture, trade, education and military affairs and integrates government and commune administration into one, and while its ownership is still collective in character, it nevertheless has certain elements of ownership by the whole people (this is mainly seen in the integration of government and commune administration and the development of commune-run economic activity), and since this system which is socialist in character contains some first shoots of communism, the people's commune under the actual conditions in China is the best form of social organization not only for the transition from collective ownership to ownership by the whole people, but also for the transition from socialism to communism in the future. That is why the appearance of the people's communes in China instantly met with the virulent hatred and spite of all the hostile anti-socialist forces. From the very beginning the imperialists have used the most savage language and the foullest slanders in their attacks on the people's communes. In our own country, the remnants of the reactionary class who have been overthrown and the bourgeois rightists, seeing that their "good old days" are gone for ever, have also crudely slandered the people's communes in their bitter hatred. Nevertheless, the more they howl, the more the people's communes are proved right. No matter how they calumniate them, they cannot in the least prevent the people's communes from forging ahead.

At this time, when the anniversary of the resolution on the people's communes is being celebrated, when the shortcomings that cropped up in the earlier stages of the people's communes have been overcome and the people's communes are going ahead on a healthy basis, what is worth noting is that apart from the reactionaries at home and abroad there are certain people who are still dissatisfied with and opposed to the people's commune movement. They are those within the ranks of the Chinese people, including certain right-opportunists inside the Communist Party, who are influenced by bourgeois ideology to a rather serious degree. They fail to see that the people's commune movement is the product of a great social movement of the hundreds of millions of Chinese peasants, the product of the big growth of agriculture, the great extension of water conservancy work and the great upsurge of socialist understanding among the peasants which expressed itself in their demand for co-operation on a still broader scale. They cannot see that with the implementation of the principle of "to each according to his work" and with the basic ownership clearly defined as being vested in the production brigades of the people's commune, the organizational form of the people's commune is, in fact, a powerful instrument for the further advancement of socialist collective ownership. They babble that "the people's commune lacks objective material basis. It is not a natural product of objective reality but the fruit of the wishful thinking of a few who have cooked it up out of thin air." They say: "The people's communes were set up too soon and too fast and are in a mess." In a word, they fail to see the advantages of the people's communes and the revolutionary zeal of the hundreds of millions of peasants. They are only interested in the shortcomings of the communes though these were transient and local and have long since been overcome. They have thus placed themselves in opposition to the people, to the great socialist revolution and socialist construction.

Have the people's communes no objective material basis? Are they an unnatural trend in the march of events? Let history answer. The people's commune movement began to grow in certain parts of China in the summer of 1953. The reason why it did so at that particular time is that the rectification movement, the anti-rightist struggle and the education in socialism in 1957 led to an unprecedented upsurge of socialist consciousness and labour enthusiasm among the masses of cadres and people in the rural areas and to a determination to quickly change the economic backwardness of the rural areas and their state of "poverty and blankness." Therefore, since the winter of 1957 (for convenience sake, we will not here go back to the still earlier beginnings of the people's commune as a form of social organization) gigantic undertakings of production and construction developed very quickly, at the centre of which was the large-scale building of water conservancy projects. The preceding organizational form of the advanced agricultural producers' co-operatives, smaller in scale and confined to agriculture, could no longer meet the need to develop production quickly and on a big scale. In many places co-operatives began to merge into bigger ones.

INEVITABLE HISTORICAL DEVELOPMENT

At the meeting which was called in March of 1958 in Chengtu and attended by some leading members of the Central Committee and the local committees of the Chinese Communist Party, Comrade Mao Tse-tung took this into consideration and proposed appropriate amalgamation of smaller co-operatives in a planned way. This proposal was later formally approved by the Central Committee of the Chinese Communist Party. After that, in May, the Second Session of the Eighth National Congress of the Chinese Communist Party put forward the general line for building socialism. This general line gave boundless inspiration to the masses of cadres and people in the rural areas. Their morale and determination soared to unprecedented heights, and agricultural production and construction, industry, transport and communications in the service of agriculture, and rural commerce, cultural and educational work and militia activity all advanced rapidly. The peasants demanded a more rational and efficient organization of labour, and the integration of the basic organizations of state power with the economic organizations so as to achieve a stronger unified leadership. This was the very natural way in which a new, large-scale form of social organization was born in the rural areas, combining industry, agriculture, trade, education and military affairs and integrating government and commune administration. This new form of social organization was entirely a creation of the masses. In its earlier stages, it was given a number of different names. In June the Central Committee of the Chinese Communist Party and Comrade Mao Tse-tung selected the name "people's commune" as one that best expressed the essence of this form of organization and would be most welcome to the masses. It was unanimously adopted at the Peitaiho meeting of the Communist Party in August.

In fact, long before the Peitaiho meeting, some of the pioneering people's communes such as the Chayashan People's Commune in Suiping County and the Chiliying People's Commune in Hsinsiang County, Honan Province, were visited by hundreds of thousands of rural cadres from all parts of the country and an irresistible trend had already grown up to learn from these communes. It was in circumstances of a great development of rural economic activity and a great heightening of the peasants' political understanding that the upsurge to set up rural people's communes emerged. Therefore, only those who shut their eyes to facts can assert that this mass movement which conforms to the "course of nature and the ways of the people" was the result of the wishful thinking of a few people who "have cooked it up out of thin air" or that "the communes were set up too soon and too fast and are in a mess." The emergence of the people's commune and particularly its growth in the past year have demonstrated that it is an inevitable product of historical development. Though it has only a history of less than a year on a nationwide scale, it has ensured a general increase in per *mu* yield in agriculture, and made high yields on large tracts of farmland a widespread phenomenon. Not a single commune has collapsed under the rigid test of severe natural calamities. On the contrary, it has been during the battle against natural calamities that the peasants have understood more deeply the superiority of the communes compared to the agricultural co-operatives and have bound their destinies still more firmly to the communes. Marx wrote: "New, higher relations of production never appear before the material conditions of their existence have matured in the womb of the old society itself. Therefore mankind always sets itself only such tasks as it can solve; since, looking at the matter more closely, it will always be found that the task itself arises only when the material conditions for its solution already exist or are at least in the process of formation." Why don't those who have doubts about the people's commune movement make a serious study of the facts of history and this fundamental Marxist view of historical development?

WHAT IS THE NATURE OF THE COMMUNES?

At the present time in China there are two kinds of arguments which in essence deny the people's communes. One asserts that to establish people's communes, you must put communism into practice, otherwise you cannot establish them. The other believes that the people's communes are almost the same as the advanced agricultural producers' co-operatives and it was therefore quite unnecessary to set them up. Those who argue thus can be said to be ignorant of the realities of the people's communes. True, the name "commune" may be associated with communism, but on the other hand it may not; that is, there can be communes which are not, or are not yet, communist in character. We all know that in modern history there have been all kinds of "communes" of different characters. There have been not only "communes" which were not communist in character in the period of proletarian revolution; but "communes" of a bourgeois-democratic character in periods of bourgeois revolution and bourgeois-democratic revolution. The people's communes in China today are socialist in character. This has been clear and beyond doubt since the resolution of the Peitaiho meeting of the Communist Party a year ago. Is there anything wrong with organizing people's communes to promote the socialist collective economy more effectively?

As far as their socialist character is concerned the people's communes are the same as the advanced agricultural producers' co-operative. But there are differences between the two in many respects: the advanced agricultural producers' co-operative is a relatively small collective, the people's commune is a much larger collective; the co-operative manages agriculture only, the commune manages diversified economic activities; the co-operative is an economic organization, the commune is a unified organization embracing political, economic, military and cultural activities; the co-operative is only the organizer of collective production, while the commune is also the organizer of collective life. More important, in the people's communes as they stand now, even though the basic form of ownership is vested in the production brigade, which in general corresponds to the advanced agricultural producers' co-operative, part of the ownership is vested at the commune level; this did not exist before. Direct ownership by the people's communes, such as is exemplified in enterprises and undertakings run by the commune and the reserve and welfare funds controlled by the commune, does not so far amount to very much, but this represents a great and bright future for China's rural areas. As the commune is able every year to draw suitable sums for its accumulation fund from the income of the production brigades and also increases it with the profits of commune-run enterprises, in addition to any state investments it may get, there will be not a slow but a very rapid growth in the part that is owned by the commune. Ownership at the commune level already contains some elements of ownership by the whole people. With the development of production and the gradual enlargement of ownership at the commune level, the elements of ownership by the whole people will also grow steadily. Though the transition from collective ownership to ownership by the whole people is still a process that will take a number of years, the people's commune is undoubtedly the best form of social organization to carry out this transition.

At the same time, though the people's commune is still socialist in character, it already contains some rudiments of communism which the advanced agricultural producers' co-operative did not and could not possibly have. There are good reasons for affirming that the people's commune is not only a most powerful instrument for accelerating socialist construction, but also the best form of social organization for the future transition from socialism to communism. Since the new form of social organization, the people's commune, is able to develop fully the original advantages of the advanced agricultural producers' co-operative and overcome certain limitations of the co-operative, and since it contains the germ of even loftier ideals, is there any reason why it should not be set up to replace the advanced agricultural producers' co-operative? Why shouldn't we go one better when we can?

CORRECT ATTITUDE TO NEW THINGS

True, the history of the people's communes from its birth to the present is still a short one; its advantages are only just beginning to show themselves and it is only in the initial stages of developing its broad prospects, but can it be made light of merely because it is just in the budding stage? What tree has not grown from a young shoot? "Jeering at the feebleness of the young shoots of the new order, cheap scepticism of the intellectuals and the like—these are, essentially, methods of class struggle of the bourgeoisie against the proletariat, a defence of capitalism against socialism. We must carefully study the new shoots, we must devote the greatest attention to them, do everything to promote their growth and 'nurse' these feeble shoots.... The point is to foster each and every shoot of the new; and life will select the most virile." (From Lenin's "A Great Beginning") Here, then, is Lenin's attitude to such young shoots. This is the attitude of all Marxist-Leninists to new things. The Central Committee of the Chinese Communist Party and Comrade Mao Tse-tung regard the people's commune movement from this Marxist-Leninist viewpoint.

Exactly one year has passed since the Peitaiho meeting of the Communist Party. It is not yet a year since the people's commune movement spread through China's rural areas. But the people's commune, this newly born social organization, has already passed through serious trials and gathered rich experience. Despite the abuse and damage done them by hostile forces within the country and abroad, despite condemnation and opposition by the right opportunists within the Party, and the great onslaughts of natural calamities, the people's communes have not collapsed. We are, therefore, entitled to say that the people's communes will never collapse. The courageous and industrious Chinese people look to the future, confident of victory. We have every reason to proclaim: Long Live the People's Communes!

DOCUMENT 43

The Great Call, editorial in *Red Flag,* September 1, 1959.

> The text is a translation made by the U. S. Consulate General, Hong Kong, and issued in CB 590.

> *Comment.* The "ten sets of relationships" in connection with socialist construction, to which Mao is said to have proposed a solution at the beginning of the socialist construction period in 1956, are discussed in our comment on Document 25. The *Red Flag* editorial was later pronounced (along with Document 38) to be required reading for anyone wishing to be admitted to an institute of higher learning.

───────────────── TEXT OF DOCUMENT 43 ─────────────────

Shortly before the tenth anniversary of the founding of the great People's Republic of China, the Party convened the 8th plenary session of its 8th Central Committee. The 8th plenary session of the 8th Central Committee summed up the experiences in implementing the general line of the Party for going all-out, aiming high, and striving for more, faster, better, and more economical achievements in the socialist construction; and, in particular, reviewed the implementation of the 1959 plan for the development of the national economy. To the whole Party and the people of the whole country, the 8th plenary session of the 8th Central Committee clearly pointed out the economic situation at present, and also proposed the further development of the campaign for higher output and economy, and the militant task of fulfilling ahead of schedule within 1959 the major targets under the second Five-Year Plan (1958 to 1962). In order to fulfill this militant task, the 8th plenary session of the 8th Central Committee called on the whole Party and the people of all nationalities throughout the country, the workers, peasants, and revolutionary intellectuals of the whole country, to unite their hearts and efforts in one, and to move forward bravely under the leadership of the Party committee headed by Comrade Mao Tse-tung, and the brilliant illumination of the general line; to overcome the difficulties and shortcomings in our work; to smash utterly the attempts by imperialism and the antagonistic elements in the country to calumniate and sabotage our socialist construction; and also to overcome resolutely the rightist-inclined opportunist ideas which hinder our progress. This is a great call which correctly reflects the current situation, and a great call which inspires people. This great call will certainly enjoy warm response from the whole Party and the people of the whole country, thus transforming itself into an enormous force pushing forward the progress of our socialist construction. Facts will prove that the 8th plenary session of the 8th Central Committee is a conference of great historic significance during the period of the socialist construction in our country.

Our country began in 1953 the large-scale and planned socialist economic construction. The first Five-Year Plan, which started in that year, brought enormous achievements through its implementation. During the period of fulfillment of the first Five-Year Plan, the Party began to consider the second Five-Year Plan. In September 1956, the Party adopted at its first session of the 8th National Congress the proposal for the control figures of the second Five-Year Plan. In February 1957, the proposal was accepted by the State Council. According to this proposal, the national economy of our country during the period of the second Five-Year Plan from 1958 to 1962 would follow the example of the period of the first Five-Year Plan to continue maintaining a rather high speed of development. After the announcement of the control figures for the second Five-Year Plan, the imperialists and antagonistic elements in the country asserted that these figures were "unrealistic." According to them, the ratio of increase was rather high during the period of the first Five-Year Plan because the starting point was low; and it would be impossible to maintain such a high rate of increase during the second five years. They resorted vainly to such a view to shake our confidence, and they always hope in vain that the tempo of our progress will increasingly slow down, as they also hope that our undertakings will fail and collapse.

The liberated Chinese people have completely frustrated the wishes of the domestic and foreign enemies, and marched forward steadily and bravely under the leadership of their own Party, the Chinese Communist Party, and their own leader, Comrade Mao Tse-tung.

TEXT OF DOCUMENT 43   557

When the Chinese people had succeeded in freeing themselves thoroughly not only from the bondage of imperialism and feudalism, but also from the bondage of the capitalist system of ownership, and, particularly, following their subsequent achievement of the decisive victory of the socialist revolution on the political and the ideological fronts, the strong wishes of the 650 million people for the rapid transformation of their own country from the state of "poverty and blankness" and for speedy socialist construction poured out like Lava buried underground for millions of years in a volcanic eruption of tremendous force. The socialist system has enabled the 650 million people, who account for one-fourth of the population of the world, to achieve complete liberation and to use their own hands to change their own destiny. The enormous force thus produced and the subsequent great achievements in their undertakings will always remain beyond the comprehension of all the enemies of socialism.

The Central Committee of the Chinese Communist Party headed by Comrade Mao Tse-tung, the great leader of the people of all nationalities in China, is truly a Marxist-Leninist leadership, one of the principal characteristics of which is that it always holds in great esteem the spirit of revolutionary initiative and the revolutionary energy which emerge from the millions of people. Contrary to opportunist leadership of all descriptions, the Marxist-Leninist leadership, instead of using its own proposals and designs to restrain the hands and feet of the revolutionary masses, boldly joins the masses so as to move forward together with them, stands at the forefront of the masses, gathers together the wishes and will of the masses, and leads the masses by clear-cut, positive guiding principles aimed at seeking the truth through facts.

The general line for going all-out, aiming high, and striving for greater, faster, better, and more economical achievements in socialist construction, which the Central Committee of the Party and Comrade Mao Tse-tung formulated in the spring of 1958, is precisely an outstanding illustration of the revolutionary will and determination of the 650 million people of China, and a great guiding principle which combines the objective possibility and the revolutionary work enthusiasm of the millions of people.

Under the illumination of the general line of the Party for socialist construction, the people of our country brought forth in 1958 the big leap forward in socialist construction, and also established the people's communes in the countryside. Now, as everyone can see, the speed of development of socialist construction in our country has far exceeded the estimate in the past. Through the effort exerted in the two years of 1958-1959 alone, it will be possible to fulfill, overfulfill, or approach fulfillment of the targets for industrial and agricultural output originally scheduled for attainment in the five years beginning from 1958. In 1958, the tempo of output increase in major industrial and agricultural production was unprecedented in the history of our country. Judging by the verified actual output of food crops and cotton in 1958, the output increase during the year exceeded the total increase during the five years of the first Five-Year Plan. In the period of the first Five-Year Plan, the food crops increased by 20 per cent—in other words, increasing from 308.8 billion catties in 1952 to 370 billion catties in 1957, a total increase of 61.2 billion catties. The increase during the year 1958, however, was 35 per cent—in other words, from 370 billion catties in 1957 to 500 billion catties in 1958, a total increase of 130 billion catties. During the period of the first Five-Year Plan, cotton increased by 26 per cent, or from 26.07 million *tan* to 32.8 million *tan*, a total increase of 6.73 million *tan*. During the year 1958, however, the increase was 28 per cent, or from 32.8 million *tan* to 42 million *tan*, a total increase of 9.2 million *tan*.

From the verified, actual output of the two items of food crops and cotton, it is obvious that the year 1958 witnessed truly enormous leaping progress. The increase in the various industrial products during 1958 had been announced in the communique released in April this year by the State Statistics Bureau. Take the output of steel, as an example: in addition to the 3.8 million tons of "native steel" produced by local methods and suited to the needs in the countryside, 8 million tons of so-called "modern steel," suitable for industrial needs, were also produced in 1958, showing an increase of 49.5 per cent over the 5.35 million tons of steel produced in 1957. This tempo of increase considerably exceeded the average annual proportional increase by 31.7 per cent during the period of the first Five-Year Plan. The year 1959 is a year of continued leap forward on the basis of the big leap forward of 1958. According to the readjusted 1959 plan for the development of the national economy, the steel output (excluding "native" steel) is planned to increase by 50 per cent over that of 1958—an addition of 4 million tons to the 8 million tons to make a total of 12 million tons. This would amount to the output target between 10.5 million to 11 million tons originally scheduled for 1962 under the second Five-Year Plan.

The 1959 coal output is planned to increase by 24 per cent over that of 1958—or adding 65 million tons to the 270 million tons to reach 335 million tons. This would considerably surpass the original target for 1962 of reaching between 190 million to 210 million tons.

In agriculture, with a large acreage of 510 million *mow*—or nearly one-third of the total acreage of cultivated land—suffering from serious drought, flood, and infestation of insect pests, the planned output of food crops and cotton in 1959 is to be 10 per cent over that of 1958, or to reach about 550 billion catties of food crops, and more than 46 million *tan* of cotton. This tempo of increase also considerably exceeds the average annual proportional increase during the period of the first Five-Year Plan (that is 3.7 per cent in food crops and 4.7 per cent in cotton), as it also exceeds or approaches the original output target scheduled for 1962 (that is, about 500 billion catties of food crops, and about 48 million *tan* of cotton).

In addition to the four items of steel, coal, food, and cotton, other items, such as timber, metallurgical equipment, power-generating equipment, metal-cutting machine-tools, cotton yarn, machine-produced paper, and salt, are shown in the readjusted 1959 plan for the development of the national economy as fulfilling, overfulfilling, or near fulfilling in 1959 the output targets originally scheduled for attainment in 1962.

The fact that we are able to advance fulfillment by three years the major targets under the second Five-Year Plan is evidently of very great significance to the development of the national economy in our country and the improvement of the livelihood of the people. As stated in the communique of the 8th plenary session of the 8th Central Committee, "This will enable us, within the coming three years, to raise sharply the original targets of the second Five-Year Plan and to devote greater efforts to strengthening certain weaker links in the national economy." This will also enable us to win time in considerably shortening the period required for construction. It is possible to strive to realize in the main, within about ten years, or by about 1967, the slogan "Catch up with Britain in the output of major industrial products within fifteen years" suggested by Comrade Mao Tse-tung; and to overfulfill, at a much earlier date, the twelve-year program for agricultural development originally scheduled for completion in 1967.

In order to fulfill in advance the major targets of the 2nd Five-Year Plan within a period of two years, it is still necessary for us to render our utmost efforts in the next several months. However, with the victory of the big leap forward achieved in 1958 and the tremendous results scored in the first half of 1959, we are fully confident that we shall be able to obtain a new, great victory in the next few months of this year.

That such a victory can be achieved shows the complete correctness of the general line for socialist construction put forward by the CCP Central Committee and Comrade Mao Tse-tung and the policy of firmly maintaining politics in command and of fully mobilizing the masses of people to stimulate a leap forward in all fields in the course of economic construction. Meanwhile this victory also indicates that the people's communes have the tremendous vitality of promoting the socialist undertakings in our country. In the course of the big leap forward and the movement to establish people's communes in our country, the hostile elements within the country and abroad who are against our country's socialist construction undertakings have raised a great outcry. They have resorted to every form of vicious slander and distortion of our general line, the big leap forward, and the movement to establish people's communes. They have done so because under the banner of the general line a new future of great prosperity has unfolded in front of the people in our country and, also, because, under the leadership of the general line, the condition of "poverty and blankness" of our country both economically and culturally, inherited from the old China is being eliminated rapidly by the people of our country. This condition is what the reactionaries within the country and abroad have tried so hard to maintain in an attempt to again enslave the Chinese people in the future.

Exactly as the 8th plenary session of the 8th Central Committee of the Chinese Communist Party pointed out, the reactionaries within the country and abroad have attempted to influence some of the unstable elements among us, so as to sabotage our undertakings. However, no reactionaries have succeeded in shaking the great determination of our Party and the 650 million Chinese people. Keeping in mind our experiences accumulated during the past many years, we notice that since the enemy has shown such a hostile attitude toward our general line, the big leap forward, and the people's commune movement, this fact alone has proved that this is exactly the road which we must take.

The communique of the 8th plenary session of the 8th CCP Central Committee states: "After analyzing the current situation, the 8th plenary session of the 8th CCP Central Committee points out that the principal danger now confronting the achievements of a continued leap forward this year is the emergence of rightist opportunist ideas among some cadres." If we allow such rightist opportunist ideas to spread among us, they will seriously endanger our undertakings, after this point was clearly pointed out at the 8th plenary session of the 8th CCP Central Committee, there is no doubt that the entire Party and the people throughout the country will, under the leadership of the CCP Central Committee headed by Comrade Mao Tse-tung, resolutely struggle against such rightist opportunist ideas, and further realize the serious error of rightist opportunist ideas by taking part in this struggle, so that they will be able to further elevate their political consciousness and unite with one another closely to march forward under the banner of the general line.

The fundamental characteristics of the rightist opportunist ideas are as follows: overlooking the efforts of the people; denying the fact that revolutionary undertakings are the tasks of the masses of people; making criticisms without participating in the people's movements; discrediting the achievements; magnifying the shortcomings; and "they do not try their best to accomplish tasks which, according to objective conditions and given subjective efforts, can be accomplished. They underestimate the great achievements made by the hundreds of millions of working people and revolutionary intellectuals in the great leap forward movement and the people's commune movement and over-emphasize the seriousness of certain defects which occurred in the two movements owing to lack of experience and which have been overcome quickly."

The rightist opportunists even slandered as a "petty-bourgeois fanatic movement" the great leap forward and the people's commune movement. However, it is, in fact, the rightist opportunists themselves who have sunk into the bog of bourgeois pessimism. Such rightist viewpoints cannot exist together with the aspiration of proletarian revolution. Such rightist viewpoints reflect the anti-socialist ideas of the bourgeoisie among the rank-and-file of proletarian revolutionaries.

The historical task of the proletarians is to lead the entire body of people to engage in the reform of the old world and the establishment of a new world. In the course of launching such a great important task, if one holds the view that since "blueprints" have been made for carrying out every task, every task will be carried out smoothly without encountering difficulties and hardship—even though this is not the bourgeois viewpoint toward the people's movements—one will merely be indulging in the imagination of a fool who knows absolutely nothing about revolution. A proletarian revolutionary should never have such imagination and viewpoint. He must firmly march in the correct direction by relying on the efforts of the masses of people and estimating beforehand the many great difficulties and shortcomings which may occur on the road of development. As a result, he will not be scared by the difficulties and shortcomings, but, on the contrary, will bravely stand together with the masses of people to overcome all difficulties and shortcomings.

Let us see what Lenin said about this question. In his article "From the Destruction of the Ancient Social System to the Creation of the New" written in 1920, Lenin sharply criticized those who held a mocking attitude (or the attitude of being pleased at the calamities of others) at the certain short-comings and mistakes committed in the course of developing the new undertakings of socialism. Lenin said: "Those who are afraid of the difficulties in building socialism will be scared away by difficulties; those who become pessimistic or panicky in the face of difficulties are not socialists." Lenin also said: "We must use our full energy to carry out this work. We must have patience and firm determination, be skillful in repeatedly experimenting and improving, and never stop without reaching the aims. This fine quality of the proletarian is the guarantee of victory of the proletariat. What is lacking among the rightist opportunists is this quality of proletarianism.

In the course of our country's building of socialism, the construction experiences accumulated by the Soviet Union and other fraternal countries have been studied and utilized as reference material by us. This is an important factor in helping our country to develop her undertakings smoothly. However, what we intend to do is to build socialism in a country of more than 600 million people where the original economic foundation is extremely backward; in the course of our building of socialism, the question of how to combine the general principles of Marxism-Leninism with the actual conditions of

China must be solved by ourselves. This question has been solved by our Party and Comrade Mao Tse-tung, the great leader of the people of all nationalities in our country, who proposed the solution of the questions concerning the ten important relations in connection with socialist construction when the socialist construction had just begun in China. This proposal has provided our country with effective measures to carry out socialist construction. Furthermore, the general line for socialist construction was adopted at the second session of the 8th CCP Central Committee. This general line had achieved great results after it had been put into effect for a year or so. Compared with such great results, the temporary and partial shortcomings occurring in the big leap forward movement and the people's commune movement are merely one finger out of the ten. Facts have proved that, under the guidance of the Party and the great efforts of the masses of people struggling forward according to the general line, these shortcomings can be surmounted, and have been surmounted. The rightist opportunists stubbornly harped on these shortcomings which had been pointed out by us a long time ago. Since they have lost their confidence in all undertakings, then it is absolutely useless to talk about overcoming the shortcomings. From the very start, the aim of the rightist opportunists has not been to overcome the shortcomings. They have made strenuous efforts to collect and magnify the data of certain shortcomings which have been overcome and are being overcome rapidly, so as to dampen the spirit of the cadres and the masses of people, to slander against the people's movements, and to disseminate germs of pessimism among the masses of people. In fact, this is a criminal act against socialist construction.

That the revolutionary combatants of the proletariat are not afraid of difficulties is because that they believe in and rely upon the strength of the masses. Like all other revolutionary undertakings of the people, the socialist undertaking belongs to the millions of the masses of the people themselves. The Marxist-Leninists have always excluded the viewpoint which has regarded the revolution as a proposal first thought of by a small number of persons behind closed doors and then followed by the masses acting on orders. In essence, such a viewpoint is bourgeois. Lenin once said, "History generally, and the history of revolutions in particular, is always richer in content, more varied, more many-sided, more lively and 'subtle' than even the best parties and the most class-conscious vanguards of the most advanced classes can imagine.... Revolutions are made, at moments of particular upsurge and the exertion of all human capacities, by the class consciousness, will, passion and imagination of tens of millions, spurred on by a most acute struggle of classes."

How did such enormous achievements come about through the campaign of the big leap forward and the campaign for people's communes since 1958? The fundamental reason is that under encouragement from the general line of the Party millions of people freed themselves from the restriction imposed upon their thinking by all the old things, sufficiently demonstrated their will and wishes, sufficiently developed their wisdom and strength, and sufficiently enhanced the spirit of taking the initiative to think, speak, and work boldly. Without such initiative and enthusiasm on the part of the broad masses of working people and revolutionary intellectuals, it would have been impossible, to be sure, to have the enormous achievements since 1958.

There are two different attitudes toward such a mass movement. One is the attitude of constantly worrying and complaining, and even condemning the "excessive acts" which emerged from the mass movement; and of dreading the mass movement like a disastrous fire. This is the attitude of rightist-inclined opportunism. The other attitude is one of warmly upholding the creative move by the masses, of resolutely leading the mass movement, of carefully studying the experiences accumulated together with the masses, and of learning from these experiences together with the masses in order to raise the campaign to a higher level step by step. This is the attitude of Marxism-Leninism.

In the famous work of "Report on a Survey on the Peasant Movement in Hunan" over 30 years ago, Comrade Mao Tse-tung had called on the revolutionaries to adopt the Marxist-Leninist attitude toward the mass movement. In the undertaking of the socialist construction, this, likewise, is the only correct attitude toward the mass movement. Our revolutionary functionaries should all firmly establish this correct attitude toward the mass movement, and should all resolutely exclude that attitude of rightist-inclined opportunism.

All views which under-estimate the strength of the 650 million people under the leadership of the Chinese Communist Party are inevitably doomed in the face of facts. Under the great call issued by the 8th plenary session of the 8th Central Committee, a new upsurge in the mass campaign for higher output and economy has emerged on an imposing scale in all fields. The whole Party and people of the whole country will certainly unite closely as one to oppose the rightist tendency, and to raise fully their enthusiasm for work. They will first fulfill and overfulfill by a new great upsurge in production the plans for the third quarter of the year, and then fulfill and overfulfill the annual plans for the year, thus leading to advance fulfillment of the great task of meeting the major targets under the second five-year plan.

Chapter XI

CELEBRATION OF THE TENTH ANNIVERSARY

(containing Documents 44, 45, 46, 47, 48)

General comment. In most of the flood of propaganda celebrating the tenth anniversary of the assumption of power by the Chinese People's Government in late September and early October 1959, there is little of historical value—except perhaps to students of propaganda technique and of the cult of personality (the adulation of Mao was almost unlimited). From the mass of available material, much of which is translated in CB 595-600, the article by Li Fu-ch'un in *Red Flag* (Document 47) and the article by Teng Hsiao-p'ing in *Pravda* (Document 48) have been chosen as providing good surveys, designed by the Party leaders for home and Socialist Camp consumption. Wang Feng's article on the national minorities (Document 44) and Lin Piao's on the state of the army (Document 46), discussed in our General Introduction, part XI, have been included for the light that they shed on two important aspects of Communist policy which are dealt with only incidentally in our other documents. Only Liu Lan-t'ao's discussion of the Party as Supreme Commander (Document 45) bears directly on a main theme of this volume—the balance of political forces within the Party. This theme was also treated historically by Liu Shao-ch'i in *World Marxist Review*, October 1959. But in this connection perhaps the most interesting pronouncement of the anniversary celebration is one which falls outside the scope of this volume—Khrushchev's speech at the banquet given on September 30 by the Chinese People's Government to foreign delegations, in which he gave a blunt warning to whomever it might concern against "adventurism." This speech is reprinted in *Current Digest of the Soviet Press*, Vol. XI, No. 39, pp. 20-22.

DOCUMENT 44

The Great Victory in Our Nationalities Policy, article by Wang Feng, Vice-Chairman of the Nationalities Affairs Commission, in *People's Daily*, September 27, 1959.

The text used here is a translation made by the U.S. Consulate General, Hong Kong, and issued in CB 609.

Comment. Problems arising from the integration of the racial and religious minorities of Northwest, West, and Southwest China into a unitary Communist state have been the subject of much open discussion in political surveys by the Chinese Communist leaders—particularly Documents 9 (section IV), 14 (section 6), 19 (section V), and 37 (section IV), above. During the period 1955-1959 there was a considerable shift in the tactics of Communist policy toward the minorities, even apart from Tibet. As is clear from Wang Feng's article, down to 1957 the main effort was to avoid major clashes on racial and religious issues—or, in Party jargon, to overcome the tendency toward "great *Han* nationalism." From the time of the anti-rightist campaign of 1957, for reasons discussed in our General Introduction, the Communist leaders concentrated on overcoming "local nationalism."

For general surveys, see:

SCMP 1672, proceedings of the Nationalities Affairs Commission, Peking, November 19-20, 1957, marking the start of the campaign against local nationalism.

CB 494, report by Wang Feng to the fifth meeting of the Nationalities Committee of the National People's Congress, February 9, 1958.

ECMM 143 (*Study*, June 18, 1958), local nationalism exposed in rectification campaigns.

Further material on various regions may be found as follows (in all cases, unless otherwise indicated, it is the local press that is quoted in the series named):

Kansu: CB 528 and 533; URS, Vol. 10, No. 7, Party purges linked with racial feeling, December 1957 to August 1958.

Sinkiang: CB 512, 572, 574: SCMP 1998, attacks on local nationalism. SCMP 1917, 2167, local nationalism in Kashgar.

CB 521; URS, Vol. 12, No. 3, Vol. 13, Nos. 15-17, economic developments, summer and fall of 1958.

Szechuan: CB 407, rebellion in Western Szechuan, early 1956.

Tsinghai: CB 481, arrest of counterrevolutionaries, summer of 1957. CB 506; URS, Vol. 11, No. 6, Party purges, 1957-58. CB 549, counterrevolutionary activity, fall of 1958.

Yunnan: CB 519; URS, Vol. 9, No. 2, Vol. 13, No. 26, rightist activities, Party purge against localism, 1957-58.

―――――――――――――――TEXT OF DOCUMENT 44―――――――――――――――

Ten years ago today, the people of the various nationalities in China, led by the Chinese Communist Party and their great leaders, Comrade Mao Tse-tung, scored a decisive victory in the people's democratic revolution and brought forth the Chinese People's Republic.

The debut of the People's Republic ended the reactionary rule of imperialism, feudalism and bureaucratic capitalism, terminated the oppression of the nationalities, and ushered in a new age of equality, unity, cooperation and friendship among the people of China in the common cause of building socialism.

On the day of birth of the People's Republic, the country entered into a period of transition from capitalism to socialism. The principal mission confronting the country during that transitional period was to realize socialist industrialization and carry out gradually the socialist transformation of agriculture, handicraft trade and capitalist industry and commerce. As far as the question of the domestic nationalities was concerned, the policy of the Party and the People's Republic was: "To strengthen the unification of the motherland and the unity of the nationalities in order to build the country into a large family where there will be complete equality and regional autonomy for the nationalities, and the minorities people will be aided in undertaking social reforms and developing their economies, politics and cultures so that the backward may catch up with the advanced in the transition to socialism." This was a colossal historical mission and its realization would bring complete political, economic and cultural equality to the nationalities of China and lead them onto a higher stage of development —the stage of communism—thereby fundamentally solving the problem of nationalities.

Unification of the country, unity of the nationalities, complete equality, mutual assistance and common development are the fundamental principle on the basis of which we handle the relationship of our domestic nationalities. As Comrade Mao Tse-tung has justly pointed out, the unification of the country, the unity of the people, and the unity of the nationalities are the fundamental guarantee of success in our cause.

Equality is the political basis for the unification of the country and the unity of the nationalities and is also the fundamental principle the Party has followed in handling the nationalities problem. The Constitution of the People's Republic provides that citizens of China, regardless of their nationality or race, shall have equal rights and that oppression of or discrimination against any of the nationalities shall be strictly banned. In other words, it makes oppression or discrimination illegal and any nationality of the country no matter how small it is and regardless of its state of development will enjoy equal rights in the life of our country and society and will have the freedom of development as a master of the nation. In order to safeguard the rights of equality and autonomy for the minorities of our country, the Party and the Government have thoroughly carried out in the past ten years the policy of according full equality of all nationalities, educated the people of the country in the significance of that policy and have promulgated a series of laws and decrees in that respect. They saw to it that special provisions were written in the election law of the country for the minorities to participate in the people's congress at the different levels, with special arrangements made for them to have a voice in the running of the government. The Central People's Government sent a total of six delegations to the Northwest, the Southwest, the Middle South, the Northeast, Inner Mongolia and Tibet to sound the opinions of the nationalities as well as to convey the concern of the Government and Chairman Mao Tse-tung. All this has done much in insuring the full implementation of the Party's policy providing equality for all nationalities of the country, and in strengthening their unification and unity.

Regional autonomy for the nationalities is the Party's basic measure for solving the nationalities question of the country.

The Constitution of the People's Republic provides for autonomy to be instituted in the regions of the minorities, setting them down as an inseparable part of the Chinese People's Republic. On the basis of that provision, the minorities areas (autonomous regions, autonomous *chou*, autonomous *hsien*), aside from functioning as local government organizations under the unified leadership of the Central People's Government, have various rights of autonomy.

Autonomy for the nationalities means that each of the areas big enough to be a first-grade administrative autonomous unit has the right to administer its own local affairs in the big family of the motherland. It is intended to safeguard the equality of the minorities, increase their activism in the country's political life and socialist construction and increase the mutual trust and friendly cooperation among the various nationalities of the country.

The provision of regional autonomy as a basic means of solving the nationalities problem of China is based on the relevant theoretical principle of Marxism-Leninism with due regard for the historical background and the present situation of the various nationalities in China.

Lenin, in commenting on the question of autonomous right for nationalities, he said: "Marxism absolutely demands that in analyzing any question, we must bring it up with a certain historical scope, and then extend it to the country concerned (such as its nationalities principle), and in this connection, its concrete characteristics and the characteristics of the other countries in that historical period must be taken into full account.... Since the countries are different from one another in the speed of development and in the composition and the distribution of its nationalities, failure to pay due attention to those historical and the concrete conditions will prevent the formulation of a nationalities principle of the Marxist order."

China is a country composed of many nationalities with the Han people as the main constituent. It has a large population and vast land and has been existing in the world for a long time as a country of unified multi-nationalities. The following points are conspicuous in respect to the composition, distribution and relationship of its nationalities:

(1) The Han people account for 94 per cent of the national population with over 50 minority nationalities including the Mongol, Hui, Tibetan, Manchu, Chuang, Uighur, Miao, Yi, Puyi, Korean and other people making up the remaining six per cent. These nationalities are, nevertheless, widely distributed in the country, occupying from 50 to 60 per cent of its land. (2) The situation of commingling is most conspicuous. Most of the minorities mingle with the Han people in large or small communities where the latter serve as the main constituent with whom close economic, political and cultural ties are established. (3) In the long period of historical development, economic relations and cultural intercourse were developed among the people, forming a country of centralized power composed of various nationalities with the Han people acting as the main constituents. Under that feudal centralized power system, although there were wars between the nationalities resulting from oppression and discrimination with the Han rulers riding roughshod over the minorities or these treading the Han people underfoot, the economic and cultural relationships of the nationalities however developed unimpeded. This was the main current in the history of the relations of our nationalities.
(4) When the imperialists invaded China about 100 years ago, turning her into a semi-feudal and semi-colonial country, the existence of our minorities was, without exception, seriously threatened. Brought closer together by the common destiny, our people waged a long struggle against the domestic and foreign enemies, especially in the past 30 years in which the revolutionary struggle, led by the Chinese Communist Party, has forged an unbreakable relationship among our nationalities. (5) As a result of the historical development, the Han people have not only become the main constituents of our country,

but have led the other nationalities in economic, political and cultural development. (6) For a long period of time, the imperialists have launched sabotaging activities in an attempt to alienate the relationship of our nationalities, and to instigate the so-called "national independence" designed to enslave the people of China through the policy of "divide and rule".

Following the victorious conclusion of the people's democratic revolution, it was found necessary to rally the various nationalities of the country closer together to fight imperialist aggression and begin socialist construction under a unified government. The provision of regional autonomy for the minorities came pat as a true representation of the interests of the nationalities and a reflection of the natural tendency of our historical development. It therefore received the warm support of the people in general and the minorities in particular.

There are now in our country the Inner Mongolia Autonomous Region, the Sinkiang Uighur Autonomous Region, the Kwangsi Chuang Autonomous Region, the Ninghsia Hui Autonomous Region, and the Preparatory Committee for the Tibet Autonomous Region, 29 autonomous *chou,* and 54 autonomous *hsien.* With the establishment of these autonomous areas has ended the relevant mission of the Party and the Government. Nationalities cadres have grown up rapidly. Up to the end of 1958, there were in the country over 480,000 such cadres, being 40 times the number in 1949. In every nationalities autonomous organization, there are now a large number of such cadres, many of whom have assumed posts of responsibility and leadership.

Socialism is the common goal of the nationalities of our country and is also the road to prosperity. Only socialism can furnish the nationalities with a high degree of development and prosperity. And only socialism can solve our nationalities problem.

In the class society, the nationalities problem is invariably connected with the class problem. The nationalities problem is, in essence, though not in all its complexities, a class problem. The exploiting class and exploitation built on the system of private ownership of means of production is the social cause for oppression, discrimination and disputes between nationalities. So, China's job is to prosecute the socialist revolution among her nationalities to a successful finish, complete her democratic reform and socialist transformation, and eradicate the exploitative class and private ownership of means of production to solve her nationalities problem. Marx and Engels said in the Communist Manifesto: "With the elimination of exploitation of man by man, the exploitation of one nationality by another will be abolished. And with the elimination of class antagonism among the nationalities, the hostile relations will vanish." Lenin also pointed out: "It is not possible to eliminate the oppression of nationalities under the capitalist system. In order to eliminate that oppression, we must eliminate class and realize socialism."

There is no doubt that all nationalities must undergo social reform and take the socialist road, this being the universal law governing the development of human society. In our country, the social reform of the nationalities areas is divided into two stages—the stage of democratic reform and the stage of socialist transformation. The aim of democratic reform is to redistribute the land and abolish the oppression and exploitation which took shape before the commencement of the capitalist system. The aim of socialist transformation is to eliminate the exploitation existing under capitalism, change the system of private ownership of means of production and establish the system of socialist collective ownership and eventually the system of ownership by the whole people.

Social reform is an internal matter of the nationalities, and since their historical conditions are different, it must be carried out with due regard for the wishes of the people and the desire of the leaders who have strong ties with the people. In other words, there must be differences in the time, method, and speed of the reform for the various nationalities. As early as the time before the October Revolution, Lenin pointed out: "It is inevitable that all nationalities must take the socialist road. But they will differ in the method to be adopted. Each of them will have its own characteristics reflected in one way of democracy or another and in one method of dictatorship of the proletariat or another as well as in its social life and the speed of its socialist transformation."

Before our minorities were reformed, the feudal landlord economy persisted, in areas of close to 30,000,000 inhabitants among whom there were some who contained a high proportion of capitalist economic elements. These areas which included over 30 minority nationalities areas such as the Hui, Manchu, Chuang, Uighur areas and a large part of Inner Mongolia were the homes of the greater part of our minorities population. In addition, there were a number of minorities areas with a total population of 4,000,000 which retained the system of serfdom; in the Taliangshan and Hsiaoliangshan area on the borders of Szechwan and Yunnan provinces where the Yi nationality people lived, the peasants were bound to the soil, and in the Lisu, Kawa, Chingpo, Tulung, Nu and Pulang nationalities areas on the frontiers of Yunnan, in the Olunchun and Owenko areas of Inner Mongolia, in the Hoche nationality area of Heilungkiang, and among a small number of the Li nationality people on Hainan Island, vestiges of the primitive commune system which caused production to be low could still be found among the 600,000 inhabitants there.

The political and economic conditions of the minorities areas are complicated. Not only the stages of social development but also the inter-area social economic structures of a number of the minorities people are different. For example, while one part of the Yi nationality people are in the feudal state, the other part who live in the Taliangshan and Hsiaoliangshan area still in a slave society. In the Mongol, Tibetan, and Kaxak nationalities areas, the whole population of 2,200,000 are still engaged in backward animal husbandry and are widely different from the people of the agricultural areas in both production and livelihood. At the same time, the minorities people are highly religious and practically all of them are followers of Lamaism and Islamism. The upper strata of the minorities and the religious personages have a strong influence over the broad masses. Rooted in the policy of oppression and alienation carried out by the reactionary ruling class, certain misunderstandings persist among the nationalities. In many of the areas, contradictions exist and disputes are frequent between the sects and the tribes. The imperialists and the remnants of domestic counter-revolutionaries are sparing no effort to make use of these religious relations to sabotage our country.

In view of the foregoing situation, the Party and the people have mapped out active but cautious reform measures for the minorities areas in the light of their different conditions. In the socialist transformation of the areas, the Party and the Government have taken into full consideration the prevailing conditions and characteristics, respecting the popular wishes and withholding any decision until full discussions have been held with the public leaders who are connected with the broad masses. The social reform of the minorities areas has been carried out with the cadres and activists of the nationalities concerned as the hard core through whom the broad masses are mobilized. Party members and cadres of the Han nationality are placed under the unified leadership of the local Party Committees, and instead of command or compulsion, cooperation and help is given to the minorities people in their reform.

In accordance with the foregoing policy, the Party and the Government have adopted for the grazing areas of the minorities measures different from those applied to the agricultural areas. The social revolution for the agricultural areas generally starts with a land reform in which the lands of feudal lords and slave owners are seized and redistributed to the poor peasants who have little or no land, the privileges of the feudal lords and slave owners are abolished, and the toiling masses are liberated. Then on the basis of the successful land reform, the socialist transformation of the private ownership of the means of production is carried out to eliminate capitalist exploitation and ownership of means of production in order that the system of socialist collective ownership and ownership by the whole people may be established. However, in the social reform of the pastoral areas, cattle and sheep are not redistributed, but in its first step, the democratic reform, feudal privileges and exploitation are eliminated, and ranches are placed under public control, permitting, however, private grazing as a measure of mutual benefit to the herdowners and hired hands, and insuring the steady development of animal husbandry. On that basis, different measures are then adopted for the socialist transformation of the herdowners and hired hands in order to establish the system of socialist collective ownership and ownership by the whole people. As regards those minorities areas where class distinction is not very clear, production is low and the remnants of the primitive commune system still persist, the Party and the Government have helped them go gradually but directly on the socialist road through the institution of cooperativization and the necessary socialist transformation and social reform. As far as the method of reform is concerned, the peaceful way has been used not only in the socialist transformation of the minorities areas but also in the democratic reform of the nationalities areas of Sinkiang, Tibet, the pastoral area of Inner Mongolia, the frontier area of Yunnan, Szechwan, Kansu and Tsinghai as has been used for the Han people areas. In other words, with the full support of the masses, discussions are held from top to bottom on measures of reform best suited to the local conditions. So long as the upper strata of the minorities area to give up exploitation and accept reformation, the Government sees to it that they have the same political position and living standard after the reform and that the masses wage no intense struggles against them. For example, in the democratic reform of Tibet, we seized or confiscated no land or means of production of all those upper strata elements who refrained from participating in armed rebellion or in any other recalcitrant action; we pursued a policy similar to the buy-out measure adopted for capitalists in the Han people areas, allowing them to retain their civil rights and negotiating with their representatives on the time, steps and measures for reform. Though its concrete measures vary in the different areas, the essence of the peaceful way of "buying out" the upper strata of the minorities politically and economically is abided by. The peaceful reform is a revolution without bloodshed and is a special form of class struggle under specific conditions.

The success of the peaceful reform in many of our minorities areas can be attributed to the powerful support which the proletarian class has given to the nationalities people after seizing the rein of government, establishing the people's democratic dictatorship and completing the social changes in the majority of the areas of the country (principally the Han people areas). The comprehensive united front which our Party has established in the minorities areas with the participation also of the upper strata there has created conditions favorable to the realization of democratic reform in a peaceful way.

The Party has closely pursued the policy of a comprehensive united front with the worker-peasant alliance as the foundation and with the participation of the reformed upper strata of the minorities. It works and cooperates with any person who is against imperialism, willing to cooperate and supporting social reform. And as long as he does not change his mind, the Party will cooperate with him to the end. In reliance on this united front, we have strengthened the forces in the minorities areas who are opposed to imperialism, and support democracy and socialism, have successfully crushed and isolated the reactionary cliques of the minorities, and have smoothly developed our nationalities work. Its existence has facilitated the education of the upper strata of the minorities and the realization of reform through peaceful negotiations. But a word of caution is necessary. Whether or not peaceful reform can be successfully carried out can not be decided by the policy of the Party and the Government and the desire of the toiling masses alone. It depends much on the attitude which the upper strata of the exploitative class in the minorities areas adopt toward the reform. If elements of these strata follow the wishes of the people and accept the Party policy, then complete success will be possible. If they disregard the will of the people and the policy of the Party to such an extent as to put up resistance, then it will not be possible to continue the peaceful form and the alternative will be to crush this resistance in order that reform may go on. In either way (by force or through peaceful means), the masses must be fully mobilized and relied upon, and the Party's class line must be fully carried out to insure the successful realization of the reform. This is supported by the experience gained in the social reform of minorities areas.

In our numerous minorities areas, the upper strata of religious circles and the temples enjoy a wide range of feudal privileges, brutally exploiting and oppressing the people, and seriously obstructing development. The policy of the Party and the Government in this connection is to abolish the privileges and stop the exploitation. But where religious problems which the Party and the Government frequently meet in carrying out the reform are concerned, they are handled with caution and treated separately; clear lines of demarcation are drawn between the feudal privileges of the temples and religious habits, between normal religious activities and extortions and cruel treatment of followers, and between patriotic law-abiding religious workers and counter-revolutionaries operating under the cloak of religion. So, on the one hand, determined efforts are made to eradicate the feudal oppression and exploitation and suppress the counter-revolutionaries under the guide of religious workers, and on the other, care is taken that freedom of religion is fully safe-guarded, religious documents and structures are projected, and patriotic religious people are won over. The principle is to avoid any interference in the normal religious activities and to implement the Party's policy of freedom of religion.

In the past ten years, the Party and the Government have led the minorities in carrying out the complicated and arduous tasks of democratic reform and socialist transformation. Now, except for Tibet and some other areas with a small population, all the minorities areas of the country have completed their democratic reform and socialist transformation, their means of production being placed under collective ownership. The successful rectification campaign and the anti-rightist struggle carried out in 1957 and 1958 enabling a decisive victory to be won in the socialist revolution on the political and ideological front did much in freeing the greater number of our minorities people from the feudal system, the slave system and the primitive commune system and bringing into being the socialist system, thereby paving the way for the all-round development of China's nationalities people.

In the second half of 1958, on the foundation of the rapid development of our socialist revolution and socialist construction and under the illumination of the Party's general line for building socialism with greater, faster, better and more economic results, minorities areas which had completed the democratic reform and socialist transformation went together with the Han people areas on the road of the people's communes which wrapped up the roles of worker, trader, student, peasant and soldier into one and combined administration with business management. The people's commune is the basic-level organizational unit of our social structure. Since its universal establishment, it had demonstrated its great superiority in promoting the economic and cultural development of the people and in cementing their unity and cooperation.

The completion of the democratic reform and the victory of socialist transformation have opened the way to the prosperous development of China's nationalities. But the economic and cultural inequalities existing between the various nationalities resulting from their zigzag developments before the liberation can not be removed simply by the change of the ownership of means of production. And as long as the backward state of the minorities and the inequalities remain, our nationalities problem will stop short of complete solution.

For a complex of reasons mainly historical—sparse population, backward economy and culture, the absence of industrial workers and the dearth of cadres and intellectuals—our minorities areas, even after they have completed the socialist revolution in the system of ownership of means of production, cannot change their backward state by their own efforts. They must have regular and valid help from the state and the advanced people—the Han people—to solve this problem. Obviously, the state's help to the minorities areas can only be gradual, very much subject to its current capacity. But that there has been and will continue to be help for them is beyond any doubt.

Since the liberation, the state, despite the colossal work it has had to do in its economic rehabilitation, in the war to aid Korea against the United States, and in national construction, has given as much aid as it can to the minorities areas. This has been reflected in the following fields: (1) In accordance with the principle of the "nation operating as a coordinated game of chess" concerning economic and cultural construction, the state has given the minorities areas special consideration in investing money in capital construction projects. The rate of growth of state investments in the capital construction projects of the minorities areas has been faster than the national average in the past ten years, enabling them to develop at a pace faster than that of the other areas of the nation. (2) Financially, the state has provided the minorities areas with substantial subsidies each year in the form of loans, relief funds, production subventions, and subsidies for the establishment of educational institutions and medical organizations, in addition to granting tax exemption to the small number of areas which are extremely backward and to providing farm tools free of charge to those areas which are short of the basic means of production. As early as the initial stage of the liberation, the Party and the Government made arrangements for trade with the minorities areas to develop by pursuing a rational price policy and adjusting the price differential between industrial and agricultural products, thereby increasing the income of the people and spurring on the development of the areas. (3) The state has also provided the minorities areas with large quantities of materials including industrial and agricultural products and machinery and equipment. Take the Uighur Autonomous Region of Sinkiang for example. In the years 1949-1957, the state brought to Sinkiang 2,000,000 tons of materials but got out of it only 50,000 tons. (4) The Party and the Government have sent in the past years large numbers of cadres (including technical cadres) to the minorities areas and mobilized cadres and workers in other areas for work in the frontier areas. In addition, they had the troops of the Liberation Army stationed in the minorities areas participate in local industrial and agricultural production and transportation work. (5) Effective aid has been given in the development of the education and culture of the minorities areas. In the past years, the state has given written languages to over ten minorities including the Chuang, Puyi, Miao, Yi, Lisu nationalities.

Thanks to the leadership and help of the Party and the Government as a result of the close cooperation extended by the other areas, the economic and cultural aspects of the minorities areas have been markedly changed. The pace of improvement has been particularly rapid since 1958 when under the illumination of the Party's general line for socialist construction and with the sky-rocketing zeal of the people, a high tide in the general leap forward of socialist construction came into being. The economical and cultural inequalities between nationalities are being gradually but steadily driven into oblivion. A comparison of the production level and value in 1957, the last year in the first Five-Year Plan with those in 1949, the year marking the foundation of the Chinese People's Republic, shows that the grain production of the minorities areas rose by over 60 per cent and the gross industrial value product increased by over four times. Again in the leap forward year of 1958, grain production rose by 41 per cent and the gross industrial production value product by 84 per cent over the respective figures of 1957. The number of livestock in the pastoral areas of the areas more than doubled itself in the ten years up to 1958. Many of the areas previously short of grain had now surplus grain, industries, built from scratch, were steadily growing, and in some of the minorities areas, large modern industries were built up such as the Paotow iron and steel base in Inner Mongolia and the Karamai petroleum base in Sinkiang. The number of workers of the minorities increased in 1958 to 800,000, and the over 2,000,000 herdsmen forsook their nomadic life and stayed in fixed locations. Transportation and communications also developed fast. The aggregate length of highways opened to traffic reached 94,000 kilometers in 1958, being over eight times the total length in 1949, and that of railways reached 6,300 kilometers, being 80 per cent over the length in 1949. Aviation lines were set up in the year in 17 important cities of four autonomous regions, in Hsining and Yushu of Tsinghai, Kunming and Paoshan of Yunnan, and Lhasa of Tibet.

There was also a marked development in trade. State-owned and cooperative enterprises were established in all areas of the minorities, and usurious private merchants were driven out of sight. With the rapid development of production, the material and cultural life of the minorities was markedly improved, and the purchasing power of the urban and rural inhabitants rose in a conspicuous degree. The total sales value of the state-owned and cooperative-operated commercial enterprises rose in 1958 by four and a half times that in 1952. In the cultural and educational aspect, the number of school students increased to 4,650,000 which represented 12 per cent of the total population of the minorities. Compared with the numbers of students in the pre-liberation year of 1948, primary school students increased by eight times, secondary school students by 110 times, and college students by 35 times. In most of the minorities areas, universal primary education was carried out. It may be recalled that before the liberation, the population of the minorities had steadily declined owing to the rampancy of disease. On the liberation, the Party and the Government immediately took steps to remedy this situation. Up to 1958, they had established in the minorities areas a large number of health and medical organizations including 750 hospitals and 25 sanitariums with a total of 34,285 sick beds which was over nine times the number available in 1949. As a result of the betterment of livelihood and the rapid development of health and medical work, the population of the minorities has taken a swing upward. Take for example the Inner Mongolia Autonomous Region. In the years since its establishment in 1947 up to 1958, its population increased by over 300,000 or 36 per cent. All this bespeaks the superiority of our state and social system and the greatness and correctness of the Party's nationalities policy.

As early as 40 years ago, Lenin said that with the help of the advanced countries and people, and the proletariat, backward countries and people could obviate the stage of capitalist development and go directly on the road of socialism for ultimate transition to the communist state. The flying development of our minorities since the liberation has once again proved the brilliancy and correctness of this judgment.

In the course of the socialist revolution and socialist construction, mutual help is necessary between the minorities and the Han people in insuring a rapid advance to prosperity. On the road to socialism, help has to be mutual. It is because the Han people are relatively numerous and ahead of the other nationalities in economic, political and cultural development that they play the guiding role in the national life and have therefore the responsibility of giving more help than they can get in return.

The Party and the Government are opposed to chauvinism and local nationalism detrimental to the unity of our people, and make sure that Han cadres show no tendency toward greater Hanism. So, since the liberation, they have carried out broad education of the nationalities cadres and people in patriotism and socialism as well as in proletarian internationalism. They made a check each in 1953 and 1956 on the situation of the implementation of the nationalities policy, criticizing the tendency toward greater Hanism then existing among some of the Han nationality cadres. In the whole people's rectification campaign and anti-rightist struggle in 1957, they, while keeping up the fight against greater Hanism, also emphatically criticized tendencies toward local nationalism, dealing a heavy blow to a small bunch of bourgeois nationalities who had attempted to sabotage the unification of the nation and the unity of the people. The education greatly raised the socialist consciousness of the nationalities people and won for us a decisive victory in the socialist revolution on the political and ideological front. Experience proves that the nationalities problem, like other social problems, must be radically solved, and that in order to achieve that, the socialist revolution on the economic front alone is not sufficient; there must be a simultaneous revolution on the political and ideological front to criticize and overcome bourgeois nationalist tendencies. We feel that only by unflaggingly fighting the vestigial thought of bourgeois nationalism, can we consolidate the unity of our big national family, strengthen the cooperation among its members, and insure the successful development of our socialist construction.

With the rapid development of the socialist revolution and construction, the relationship of the socialist nationalist order featuring unity, cooperation, concerted action and joint development has come to be established in areas where socialist transformation has been completed. It has been inmeasurably consolidated since the victorious conclusion of the whole people's rectification campaign and anti-rightist struggle in 1957-1958, the appearance of the great leap forward in socialist construction and the institution of the commune system in 1958. All this has contributed to the consolidation of the big family of the Chinese People's Republic replete with freedom, equality, mutual help and friendship built in the past years on the solid foundation of socialism. Attempts of domestic and foreign reactionary forces to sabotage the socialist cause of our motherland are bound to fail in the face of the united might of China's nationalities.

The task confronting China's nationalities at the present stage is: On the basis of the Party's general line for socialist construction, and through this social organizational form of the people's commune, develop our social productive forces at a high speed in order to build our country into a socialist nation complete with highly developed modern industry, agriculture, and culture within a period of 15 to 20 years or even slightly longer. During that period, the task of the Party and the Government in respect to the domestic nationalities will be to diffuse the patriotic and socialist education, strengthen the unity of the motherland and the cooperation of the nationalities, develop the technical and cultural revolutions while helping the minorities complete their democratic reform and socialist transformation and consolidate their commune system, in order to speed up the progress of socialist construction thereby enabling the minorities people to catch up with the advanced Han people in the march toward socialism.

Encouraged by the great call of the Eighth Plenary Session of the Eighth CCP Central Committee, led by the CCP Central Committee headed by Comrade Mao Tse-tung, and holding aloft the banner of the general line and the commune system, the people of all nationalities in China are working in close cooperation for production increase and economy in an effort to fulfill the principal production targets of the second Five-Year Plan three years ahead of time.

The Chinese Communist Party is the organizer of the successful revolution of our people and the nucleus of leadership of our nationalities, and Comrade Mao Tse-tung is the greater leader of all our people. Only by following the instructions of the Party and proceeding in the direction which Comrade Mao Tse-tung has pointed out, can the people of China obtain true, thorough emancipation, social and national.

In order to strengthen the leadership of the Party over the minorities people, we must enlarge its organization and step up its ideological education in the areas, strengthening the political and ideological ties between the Party organs and the people, and preventing the spread of the baneful bourgeois nationalist thought within the Party. Unity is the Party's life where its strength lies. It is the sacred responsibility of every Party member to strengthen the Party's unity. Only when they can resist the encroachment of bourgeois nationalism, are the Party organs in the minorities areas worth the name of strong fighting unit.

In the past ten years, the Party has accomplished outstanding achievements in broadening its basis in the minorities areas. There are now over 500,000 minorities Party members and over 900,000 minorities League members. Generally, there are Party and League basic-level organs in all minorities areas. Minorities Party and League members, led by the local Party organs and in close touch with the masses, have played the role of hard core in leading the masses forward whether in the production field or in class struggle. Especially since the conclusion of the rectification campaign and the anti-rightist struggle in which local nationalism was severely criticized, the consciousness of the minorities Party and League members and cadres has been markedly raised. They are now the invincible forces in the struggle for the advancement of the socialist cause of the minorities people.

With the leadership of the Chinese Communist Party and our great leader, Comrade Mao Tse-tung, and with the unity of all China's nationalities, we shall certainly be successful in our cause.

DOCUMENT 45

The Chinese Communist Party Is the Supreme Commander of the Chinese People in Building Socialism, article by Liu Lan-t'ao, Alternate Secretary of the Secretariat of the Party's Central Committee, in *People's Daily*, September 28, 1959.

> The text is a translation made by the U.S. Consulate General, Hong Kong, and issued in CB 598.
>
> *Comment.* The claims of the Party to leadership are put very high. For example: "It is necessary to place all revolutionary organizations—be they governments, armed forces [or] people's organizations...—under the unified leadership of the Party's Central and Local Committees at the various levels, including the basic level..." (eighteenth paragraph of the document). The immediately following passage about some unit leaders who try to set up "independent kingdoms," relying on their own experts rather than on central directives, is particularly interesting; it confirms that there was technical criticism of Central Committee policies within the local organizations of the Party.

——————————————TEXT OF DOCUMENT 45——————————————

The founding of the People's Republic of China in 1949 marked the opening of a new epoch in China's history—the several hundred million exploited and oppressed Chinese working people were totally emancipated from the criminal rule of imperialism, feudalism, and bureaucratic capitalism and seized control of the country in its entirety for the first time in history, and the Chinese Communist Party became the first and only revolutionary political party to assume leadership of the state.

In the past 10 years our Party has traversed a tremendous, glorious path. It has led all the people in our country first to achieve a complete victory in democratic revolution and then a decisive victory in socialist revolution. As a result, the socialist system, which has held the imagination of the people of our country for many, many years, was established in the vast, rich land of our fatherland. This was a great victory of Marxism-Leninism in China. It was also a great victory of the leadership of the Chinese Communist Party.

During the 10 years since the founding of our country, the Chinese Communist Party has developed its organization on an unprecedented scale. The number of CCP members has increased from 4.5 million in 1949 to the present 13.96 million. The number of basic-level CCP organs has increased from the 250,000 in 1949 to the present 1.06 million. Basic-level CCP organs have been universally established in cities, towns, villages, industrial and mining enterprises, people's communes, government organizations, schools, and the combat units of the PLA. Party organs have been established even in the various minority nationalities areas in our country.

In the past 10 years, our veteran cadres, seasoned in revolutions and wars, have rapidly mastered the various skills needed for socialist construction. In the meantime, several million outstanding new cadres have been promoted from among the ranks of workers, peasants, and revolutionary intellectuals. These cadres have held glorious, responsible, and leading positions on the political, economic, national defense, foreign affairs, cultural, educational, science, and arts fronts.

In the past 10 years, the Party has carried out Party readjustment and rectification campaigns, has carried out thoroughgoing, systematic socialist and communist educational programs, has seriously criticized manifestations of subjectivism, sectarianism, and bureaucratism which are alien to reality and to the masses; has concentrated its force on the work of combating bourgeois ideology which hinders and undermines the cause of socialism, and has carried out resolute struggles against all violations of the line, policy, and principles of the Party. In the meantime, we have purged from our glorious Communist Party tens of thousands of counter-revolutionaries, class aliens, bourgeois rightists, elements guilty of grave breaches of law and violations of discipline, and other bad elements who infiltrated our Party. In this way, we have purified and consolidated the organization of our Party to an unparalleled degree, tremendously increased the communist consciousness of the great masses of our CCP members, and raised our Party to a high level of Marxism-Leninism.

In the course of prolonged revolutionary struggles, our Party has established a close relationship with the people of our country comparable to the relationship between flesh and blood and has enjoyed high prestige among the masses of the people. The leading cadres at the various levels and the members of the Party have demonstrated a selfless, altruistic spirit in labor, combat, and all types of work. They have shared the same happiness, bitterness, and difficulties with the masses, who accept them as close companions, good friends, and good comrades and treat them as brothers and sisters. From the prolonged revolutionary struggles, the masses of the people have heartily felt the CCP to be the great laboring masses' own Party, which alone represents the interests of the Chinese people.

The Chinese Communist Party constitutes the vanguard of the working class and the supreme form of class organization of the working class of China. It is composed of the most progressive, outstanding, courageous, and Communism-conscious elements. It is the sacred duty of our Communists to fulfill the great socialist and communist aims in China. Marxism-Leninism is our guide in all categories of our work. Under the leadership of its Central Committee headed by Comrade Mao Tse-tung, our Party has firmly adhered to the policy of combining Marxism-Leninism with the realities of the Chinese revolution. In this way, it has truly mastered the law of social development and the law of revolutionary struggles in China, correctly followed the development of the revolution, punctually submitted new historical tasks, adopted correct political and organizational lines, and led the Chinese people as a whole to advance from one revolutionary stage to another and from one victory to another.

History proves that the Chinese Communist Party is the greatest, the most glorious, and the most correct revolutionary Party in the history of our country; that it is a Marxist-Leninist Party completely mature politically, and that only the Chinese Communist Party is competent to be the supreme commander of the Chinese people in revolution and construction. Comrade Mao Tse-tung has long pointed out: "The Chinese Communist Party, and no other party—whether bourgeois or petty bourgeois—will be able to lead the two great revolutions, the Chinese democratic revolution and the Chinese socialist revolution, to a complete success." For this reason, firm and unremitting strengthening and consolidation of the leading role of the Party will fundamentally guarantee victory in the socialist cause of our country.

Clearly, the question of whether or not the Communist Party is needed is one of whether socialism is needed. This is a very important question having to do with the destiny of our country, a fundamental question in the "who will win" struggle between the bourgeoisie and the proletariat and between the capitalist and the socialist paths in the transitional period of our country. During the past 10 years, the various great mass revolutionary movements, particularly the experiences obtained in the struggle against the bourgeois rightists in 1957, have unfailingly borne out this truth on revolution. The attacks launched by the bourgeois rightists in 1957 were aimed mainly at the leadership of the Chinese Communist Party over the Chinese socialist program. However, in the course of the nationwide socialist revolution on the ideological and political fronts, the Communist Party did not retreat from "all positions" as the bourgeois rightists dreamed they would. On the contrary, the leadership of the Party was unprecedentedly strengthened on all fronts. Instead of a collapse of the proletarian dictatorship in China, the people's regime under the dictatorship of the proletariat, led by the Communist Party, became stronger and more consolidated. In a show of force against the Communist Party and the people, the bourgeois rightists met with ignominious defeat.

Although our socialist revolution has now won a decisive victory on the economic, ideological, and political fronts, the class struggle has by no means come to an end. There is still imperialism outside our country and there are still classes within. There are still bourgeois reactionary ideological and political activities in urban and rural areas which are trying to create great trouble in order to undermine the foundation of the dictatorship of the proletariat and the mansion of socialism. For this reason, the ideological and political struggle between the bourgeoisie and the proletariat will still be a prolonged, complex, and fluctuating one which may become quite acute at times. It may continue for scores of years, until the class struggle is completely ended.

The life-and-death struggle between the bourgeoisie and proletariat will inevitably be reflected in the Party. There is nothing surprising about this. The bourgeoisie is always trying to influence and corrode our Party with anti-socialist ideology from all sides and imperialism and the reactionary forces at home and abroad are always trying their best to secure agents within our Party in order to undermine the Party from within, even from within the core of leadership of the Party. Some wavering and unreliable elements within our Party are apt to be influenced by them.

The opportunists, class aliens, and ambitious individuals harboring bourgeois views of the world who infiltrated the Party are also liable to assume a bourgeois stand and make an effort to turn the Party into a Party of opportunism in accordance with the world views and desires of the bourgeoisie in order to achieve the aim of usurping the leadership of the revolution.

During the period of democratic revolution, a number of bourgeois agents including Ch'en Tu-hsiu and Chang Kuo-t'ao were discovered within our Party. In the period of the socialist revolution, at the time when the bourgeois and petty bourgeois ownership of the means of production was to be totally and completely liquidated, a number of the bourgeois revolutionaries and Marxist fellow-travelers who had joined our Party in the period of democratic revolution without mentally preparing themselves in the socialist revolutionary spirit at all, decided to put up a firm resistance to this action, as dictated by their reactionary bourgeois ideology. Echoing the reactionary forces at home and abroad, they carried out determined anti-Party activities. The anti-Party alliance of Kao Kang and Jao Shu-shih acted as the bourgeois agent within the Party in conformity with the wishes of the imperialists and bourgeois counter-revolutionaries.

At present, a number of rightist-inclined opportunist elements are opposing the general line of the Party, the tremendous leaps forward, and the people's communes. Their attacks on the Party are essentially aimed at advancing the interests of the bourgeoisie and undermining the socialist revolution and socialist construction. Very clearly, if these anti-Party activities are not completely smashed, the Party will be unable to defeat the bourgeoisie in the latter's resistance, to consolidate its leadership over the state, and lead all the people of our country to victory in the revolution and construction. A Marxist Party must be unified combat organ and it must be closely organized, with iron discipline. Unity and unification are the lifeline of the Party.

Absolutely no opportunist factions can be permitted and absolutely no views and activities aimed at splitting or usurping the Party are allowed within the Party. To be sympathetic to and to connive in these anti-Party activities and to show any compromising or wavering attitude in the course of the serious struggle against the anti-Party activities are, in reality, acts to help the bourgeoisie and to oppose the proletariat, regardless of the subjective desire.

To guarantee the unified leadership of the Party, it is necessary to place politics in command, to promote proletarian ideology and liquidate bourgeois ideology in society, and to guide all revolutionary tasks in accordance with a Marxist world view. Ideological and political work must forever be the soul and commander of all our tasks. It must be understood that if the proletariat fails to take command anywhere, the bourgeoisie will take command and if we give up or neglect ideological and political work anywhere, we will invariably be alienated from the masses, lose our bearings, and go astray.

There are persons who are determinedly opposed to placing politics in command, saying that as ideological and political work cannot yield grain or steel, this task is unable to solve any practical problem. This ideology, which tends to sever the political leadership of the Party from the practical work of the masses and political work from operational work, aims actually at weakening and even repudiating the role of leadership of the Party. May we ask, are the tremendous over-all leap forward and the great success of the people's communalization program in rural areas in 1958 not historic miracles achieved by placing politics in command and by adhering resolutely and completely to the mass line of the Party?

To insure the unified leadership of the Party, it is necessary to place all revolutionary organizations—be they governments, armed forces, and people's organizations; such political and legal organs as public security organs, courts, and procuratorates, or financial, economic, cultural, educational, science, and public health organs—under the unified leadership of the Party's Central and Local Committees at the various levels, including the basic level, so that they can carry out struggles for the realization of the general line and general tasks of the Party.

As the Chinese Communist Party is a Party which has undergone prolonged trials and which can most properly represent the interests of the people, all revolutionary organizations have accepted its leadership voluntarily, because only by so doing can their work be carried out correctly with a clear aim and play a positive part in fulfilling the common revolutionary cause.

In our actual work, however, we often come across some unit leaders who are so greatly interested in the "independent operations" of their own units that they attach an immoderately large importance to their operational chain of command and to the operational leadership between the upper and lower levels.

Some of them have even gone so far as to publicize the preposterous view that "laymen cannot assume leadership over the experts," in order to demand all sorts of power from the Party and turn the units under their leadership into "independent kingdoms." There are also cases where a unit is willing to accept operational leadership from departments at higher levels, but not the unified leadership of the CCP committee at a corresponding level.

Very clearly, these views and acts actually aim at repudiating the unified leadership of the Party as well as the role of the CCP committees at the various levels as organs of supreme power and as the core of leadership in the areas concerned under the leadership of the CCP Central Committee. These ideological tendencies are very dangerous. Many a comrade has let the work under his leadership be deprived of the leadership of the Party and the supervisions of the masses because of his insistence on this erroneous ideological view, thereby committing a serious political mistake.

A number of comrades, in spite of their verbal acceptance of the role of leadership of the Party, say that the Party should assume only political and ideological leadership but not organizational leadership over non-Party organizations; otherwise, the Party would be interfering in the "independence" of these organizations. As we all know, the Party depends for the fulfillment of its line, principles, and policies on its various organs (including the Party organs attached to state organs and to people's organizations) and on all Party members, who unite with and lead the great masses of the people. Only by assuming organizational leadership can political leadership be guaranteed.

May we ask how, without the benefit of actual organizational leadership and without the benefit of the leadership of the Party over Party organs and Party members in state organs and in people's organizations, fulfillment of the line, principles, and policies of the Party can be guaranteed and how the political and ideological leadership of the Party can be carried out with any effect to speak of.

It should be pointed out that the essence of the views of these persons who deny that Party members in non-Party organizations should unconditionally follow the organizational leadership of the Party is that they themselves are not Communist Party members assigned by the Party to work in non-Party organizations, but are instead representatives of their trades within the Communist Party, and that the Party is not an organ of supreme power of the proletariat, but rather a free federation of individual organizations.

Very clearly, this view is completely wrong. In reality, there is no "independence" on the part of any revolutionary organ from the leadership of the Communist Party. If they do not accept the leadership of the Communist Party, they must accept the leadership of the bourgeoisie. In refuting the slogan demanding the "independence" of trade unions from the leadership of the Communist Party, Lenin pointed out in 1919 that in a class struggle "all views on independence and on general democracy are great hoaxes and are anti-socialist, no matter under what cloak they appear." Do not the acts of those who are opposed to the assumption of leadership by the Party over non-Party organizations bear out this truth precisely?

Some may remark, by so doing are you not "mixing the Party with the government?" To this question, our reply is that we are, first, advocates of mixing the Party with the government, and, second, advocates of separating the Party from the government. In our socialist countries, under the leadership of the proletariat there can be only one "political planning department," not two. All the general line, general tasks, general policies, and general arrangements for all things can only be placed under the singular leadership of the Party under the unified leadership of the Party can all the non-Party organizations keep from going astray and fulfill their tasks properly.

It goes without saying, of course, that this is not intended to mean that the Party can take all the daily routine of such non-Party organizations as state organs and people's organizations completely into its own hand, thereby obscuring the difference in principle between the Communist Party and the non-Party organizations. Precisely the contrary—we hold that only when the Communist Party not only draws a line in principle between it and all other classes, but also stands at the forefront of the masses of its own class and resolutely plays the role of vanguard in ideological, political, and organizational work, will it be able to exercise better leadership over non-Party organizations and more efficiently raise the standards of ideological consciousness and the organization of the masses.

For this reason, it was wrong for a number of individual localities to practice "the merger of the Party with the commune" and "the merger of the Party with the government." These practices, in reality, amount to mixing the supreme form of organization of the working class with non-Party revolutionary organizations, thereby downgrading the Party's role as the vanguard of the proletariat. We have already criticized and corrected this mistake.

Our Party has consistently and resolutely followed the leadership system of combining collective leadership with the division of responsibilities. We hold that only through a collective body can the role of individuals be correctly played and that only by coordinating with responsible individuals will collective leadership be able to fully develop its required functions. Within a collective leadership, it is necessary not only to establish division of responsibilities, but also to have a person assume over-all responsibility. In the same way that it is necessary for a band to have a good conductor, and a squad to have a strong squad leader, CCP committees at the various levels must have their own leadership cores; otherwise, if each person is permitted to act on his own in the same way as a group of dragons moving about without a head dragon, it will be impossible to march forward in uniform steps and to take collective action. This is common sense, and there is truth in it.

The rightist-inclined opportunists know absolutely nothing about the harmonization between the collective leadership and the role of an individual (the harmonization of a CCP committee and its first secretary). They are opposed to the practice of placing the first secretary in command, regarding it as "dictatorship" and "undemocratic". In reality, they only aim at bringing down the "dictatorship" of the Party in order to establish their own dictatorship. This is a measure to usurp the leadership of the Party. We say that the core of collective leadership constitutes the center of collective wisdom. To place the first secretary in command on major tasks is to let him be a good squad leader so he can play a proper leading role in the work and is by no means to let him move away from collective leadership and practice personal "dictatorship."

The core of the leadership of the CCP committees at the various levels in general and of the leading Party organs in particular—loyal to Marxism-Leninism, seasoned in revolutions and wars, and in close contact with the masses—is a force guaranteeing that our Party will be able to stand all trials. By directing their spearheads at the leadership of the Party, the rightist-inclined opportunists are attempting to do nothing less than disintegrate the core of the masses and the vanguard of the proletariat. We must completely expose this point and deal a determined blow to them in return.

The aforementioned mistakes of opposing the practice of placing politics in command, opposing the role of the CCP committee at various levels as the core of leadership, opposing the leadership of the Party over non-Party organizations, and opposing the practice of placing the first secretary in command, in order to downgrade, weaken, and even discard the leadership of the Party, are essentially reflections of bourgeois individualism, liberalism, and anarchism within the Party. They run diametrically counter to the Party character of the proletariat.

The lessons learned from the long revolutionary struggles in the past, especially the lessons learned from the anti-rightist struggle and the rectification campaign, have imparted to us a simple but most fundamental principle, that is, a revolutionary organization of any kind, as soon as it divorces itself from the leadership of the Party, is liable to fall into great errors. It will only confuse things instead of improving them.

In order to demonstrate its positive role in revolutionary undertakings and avoid great errors, a revolutionary organization of any kind should place itself entirely under the leadership of the Party. Education on this question must be regularly and repeatedly carried out among functionaries and Party members. Similar lessons have told us that in the ranks of the proletariat, bourgeois individualism is the source of all evils and that if Communist Party members, especially high-ranking functionaries of the Party, fail to overcome individualism, dissension will inevitably take place within the Party, leading them to the evil anti-Party and anti-people's road.

Therefore, we must strengthen the Party's ideological work in close coordination with the strengthening of the Party's leadership in all revolutionary organizations and educate every Party member and functionary to strengthen his Party character and willingly become an obedient tool of the Party. Firm adherence to Marxism-Leninism, severe criticism and elimination of all erroneous tendencies to downgrade, weaken, or discard the leadership of the Party and continuous consolidation and strengthening of the Party's leadership in all fields of work constitute an important regular task in building our Party.

With a view to insuring the centralized leadership of the Party in all revolutionary organizations and all revolutionary tasks, the CCP Central Committee has formulated a series of systems of leadership for implementation of this fundamental principle. In the army, from its founding, our Party has instituted a system of division of responsibilities by the commanders under the leadership of CCP committees. In the recent years, in the administration of factories and enterprises, the system of responsibility of the director of each factory and enterprise under the leadership of the CCP committee has been instituted. In schools of higher learning, a system of responsibility of the school board headed by the principal and under the leadership of the CCP committee has been implemented. The implementation of these systems has not only insured the centralized leadership of the Party, but also enabled the leading administrative personnel to display their great sense of responsibility, as a result of which relations between the Party and the masses have been firmly cemented and the initiative and creativeness of the masses have been brought into fullest play.

This has been a creative development of our Party construction and of the mass line, attained by the CCP Central Committee headed by Comrade Mao Tse-tung on the basis of the revolutionary experience of our country.

In celebrating the great 10th founding anniversary of our country and hailing the Chinese Communist Party as the greatest, the most glorious, and the most correct revolutionary political party in the history of our country, our hearts are filled with great joy and boundless pride. It is very natural for us to associate the complete victory of our democratic revolution, the great victory of socialist revolution, the spectacular achievements of socialist construction, and the high international prestige of our country with the glorious name of our great leader, Comrade Mao Tse-tung, and his outstanding leadership inspired by invincible Marxism-Leninism. The high prestige of Comrade Mao Tse-tung, the great leader of our Party and the entire people, and the high prestige of the CCP Central Committee headed by Comrade Mao Tse-tung are an important guarantee of the centralized leadership of our Party in all revolutionary undertakings.

The history of China's revolution and construction has proved and will continue to prove that under the guidance of Comrade Mao Tse-tung and his thinking, our revolution will develop and achieve victory and our construction will progress at a high speed and that in the absence of the guidance of Comrade Mao Tse-tung and his thinking, our revolution will fail and our construction will meet handicaps. In the course of long revolutionary struggles, our Party and the people of the whole country have discovered Comrade Mao Tse-tung their own great leader. This is an indication that our Party has matured and also an indication of our Party's victory.

Comrade Mao Tse-tung is the most outstanding exponent of the heroic proletariat of our country, the most distinguished representative of our superior traditions in the entire history of our great nation, a beacon on our country's road to Communism, and the most outstanding contemporary revolutionist, statesman, and theoretician of Marxism-Leninism. He has creatively enriched the treasures of Marxism-Leninism on a series of important questions.

Looking back to the past and forward to the future, the Chinese Communist Party and the Chinese people, who have emerged victorious in their struggles against suffering under long, dark, reactionary rule and experienced hardships unparalleled in history, have been thinking of their own leader with great affection and boundless respect, as well as of the decisive role he played in bringing victory to our country's revolution and construction.

The 600 million or more people of our country have placed in his their hopes for their own happiness and future and considered him the incarnation of Communism and truth and the symbol of invincibility. The influence, wisdom, and experience of Comrade Mao Tse-tung and the system of thought created by him by combining Marxism-Leninism with the actual practices of Chinese revolution are the most valuable treasures of our Party and people. The warm affection for the Party leader is in full conformity with our ardent love for our Party, class, people, and great motherland.

Let us hold high the banner of victory of Comrade Mao Tse-tung, strengthen and consolidate our great glorious Party ideologically, politically, and organizationally, and unite and lead the 650 million people of our country under the leadership of the CCP Central Committee in braving the winds and waves, marching forward courageously, implementing the general line of socialist construction—go all out, aim high, and achieve greater, faster, better, and more economical results, and build our country rapidly into a strong socialist country with modern industries, modern agriculture, and modern science and culture!

DOCUMENT 46

March Ahead under the Red Flag of the General Line and Mao Tse-tung's Military Thinking, article by Lin Piao, Minister of National Defense, in *People's Daily*, September 27, 1959.

The English text of this document is taken from *Peking Review*, October 6, 1959, where it was published under the above title. The translation was made from *Red Flag* of October 1, 1959, which had reprinted the *People's Daily* article under its original title, "Take Giant Strides, Holding High the Red Flag of the Party's General Line and Military Thinking of Mao Tse-tung." The Foreign Languages Press published the article as a pamphlet, dated 1959, under the same title as that used by *Peking Review*.

Comment. Certain passages of Lin Piao's article give some support to the theories discussed in our General Introduction, part XI, about tensions between the Party and professional soldiers on military affairs. See especially his section II, where he argues that more ideological education is necessary in the army because most officers and soldiers are farmers and do not clearly understand the nature of socialist transformation in the countryside; his section III, where the opinion is noted that there should be a clear distinction between military training and economic construction work; and his section IV, in which "some comrades" are quoted as holding in esteem only machines and neglecting the factor of revolutionary initiative.

The "call of Comrade Mao Tse-tung" in 1958, for officers to serve one month a year as common soldiers, refers to a directive from the General Political Department of the People's Liberation Army on September 20, 1958 (URS, Vol. 14, No. 1).

Supplementary material may be found in Document 19 (Teng Hsiao-p'ing on rectification), section VI. See also:

CB 514, a speech by Chu Teh, July 31, 1958, on the importance of rectification and of the doctrine "politics in command."

CB 579, directives by the General Political Department of the People's Liberation Army, January 1959, on participation in socialist construction.

CB 596, Tenth Anniversary speech by Marshal Ho Lung.

Articles from the periodical *Soldier of the Liberation Army* in the URS series, as follows: Vol. 6, No. 2 (from the issue of Jan. 21, 1956—intensification of political indoctrination); Vol. 6, No. 6 (July 19, 1956—weaknesses in military training); and Vol. 8, No. 5 (May 25, 1957—rectification campaign to be pursued with due regard to discipline).

───────────── TEXT OF DOCUMENT 46 ─────────────

I

Ten years have passed since the founding of the People's Republic of China, our great motherland. All the officers and men of the Chinese People's Liberation Army join with the people throughout the land in joyful celebration of this great, historic festival of the entire nation.

Ten years are only a brief moment in the span of history. Yet in these ten years our country has achieved the great victory of the socialist revolution immediately after the victory of the new-democratic revolution. In the struggle between the two roads of socialism and capitalism, socialism has essentially defeated capitalism in all fields. The history of class exploitation of thousands of years has been ended in the main. The 650 million Chinese people, one-fourth of the world's population, have entered socialist society.

Following three years of economic rehabilitation, our country fulfilled the First Five-Year Plan for the Development of the National Economy (1953-1957) and thus laid the preliminary foundation for socialist industrialization. In 1958, on the recommendation of Comrade Mao Tse-tung, the Communist Party formulated the general line for building socialism—go all out, aim high and achieve greater, faster, better and more economical results. Under the guiding light of this general line, industry and agriculture, culture and education, began their great leap forward, making it possible for our country to fulfil the major targets of the Second Five-Year Plan three years ahead of schedule. Last autumn, in less than two months, people's communes were swiftly set up throughout our countryside. In less than a year they have consolidated themselves and embarked on the road of sound development and they are displaying their superiority with ever increasing clarity.

China's unparalleled speed in building socialism and her brilliant achievements testify eloquently to the inexhaustible power and wisdom of the industrious and courageous Chinese people in creating history, under the leadership of the great Chinese Communist Party and the great people's leader, Comrade Mao Tse-tung. Imperialism, however, has not stopped its sabotage against us for a moment and is still dreaming of overthrowing us. Not long after the founding of our Republic, U.S. imperialism launched the war of aggression in Korea and, at the same time, seized our Taiwan in a vain attempt to occupy Korea first and then strangle the new-born People's Republic of China. This attempt ended in ignominious defeat. Now China's great leap forward and the people's communes have thrown the imperialists into great fright and confusion and they have unleashed the most vicious smear campaign and attack against China. But again they have failed miserably. Despite all the obstruction and sabotage of imperialism and reaction, China's wheel of history is rolling forward at the speed of "twenty years concentrated in a day." The Chinese people have now grown strong!

Great achievements have been made on the national defence front, as on other fronts of socialist construction, in the past ten years. After the founding of the People's Republic of China, the Chinese People's Liberation Army rapidly mopped up the remnants of the Kuomintang reactionary forces and liberated the entire Chinese mainland. Together with the Korean People's Army, the Chinese People's Volunteers defeated the armed forces of the No. 1 imperialism of the world. U.S. imperialism was exposed before the peoples of the world as a paper tiger. In liberating the offshore islands, guarding the country's frontiers and its territorial waters and air, punishing Chiang Kai-shek's forces on Quemoy, preparing for the liberation of Taiwan and putting down the rebellion of Tibetan reaction, our army has been successfully discharging what is entrusted to it by the people of the country. Along the national defence frontiers and at strategic points in depth, modern, large-scale national defence projects have been undertaken, so that our country has begun to have a relatively complete network of modern defence installations. Guided by the correct line laid down by the Central Committee of the Party and Comrade Mao Tse-tung for building our army into a fine, modernized, revolutionary army, and with the assistance of the Soviet Union and other fraternal countries, the army itself has undergone a new major change in the history of its development. The technical equipment of the army has been improved and a series of reforms concerning the command, organization, training and other systems of the army has been effected. Now our army has developed from a single arm into a combined force of different arms. The major technical branches of the land forces have been strengthened markedly. A powerful air force has been built and the navy has grown correspondingly.

In the course of the modernization of the army, the Party's absolute leadership in the army has been consolidated, the glorious tradition of the unity between the army and the civilian population, between officers and men, has been developed and the mass line has been carried out in the various fields of work. Following the great rectification campaign, inspired by the Party's general line for building socialism and the nationwide big leap forward, the army has also taken an all-out, comprehensive big leap forward in its work. As part of our national defence forces, we have, in addition to a politically firm and technically modern standing army, built up a militia force of several hundred million people.

With this militia force, the entire population can be turned into a military force whenever imperialism dares to attack our country. In co-ordination with the standing army, this militia force can engulf the enemy in the flames of an all-out people's war. In addition to building itself up, our army has at all times taken a great part in national construction and social reforms. In the political report to the Second Session of the Eighth National Congress of the Party, delivered on behalf of the Central Committee, Comrade Liu Shao-chi pointed out that "the People's Liberation Army is the defender as well as the builder of the cause of socialism." Our army has in the past ten years faithfully carried out this honourable task.

In the past ten years our country has been undergoing a great change—the transition from the thorough victory of the democratic revolution to the carrying out of the socialist revolution and socialist construction. Militarily, our army has advanced from a single arm to a modern combined force of different arms; this is also a big leap forward. In these circumstances, we are confronted with a series of vital problems concerning the building up of the army. The main problem is: Is it still important for politics to be in command in the stage of the modernization of the army? Concretely speaking, what place has political and ideological work? What attitude should the members of the armed forces adopt towards the country's economic construction and the mass movements? What is the correct way to handle intra-army relations and to strengthen still further the Party's leadership in the army? All these questions must be settled in the new stage of the building up of the army. In the past ten years, we have achieved the successes and victories mentioned above because we have dealt with these vital problems quite correctly. Today, on the occasion of the tenth anniversary of the founding of our Republic, we would like to dwell mainly on some of our experiences relating to this.

II

The realization of socialism and communism is the lofty ideal for which the officers and men of our army have struggled heroically for many years. Even in the stage of the democratic revolution, the Party never relaxed in educating its armed forces in the ideals of socialism and communism. The great majority of the comrades of our army displayed resolution and courage in the period of the democratic revolution and, in the period of the socialist revolution, exerted their efforts heroically for socialism and showed themselves undaunted fighters in the cause. However, quite a number of comrades lack a high degree of socialist consciousness though they have certain aspirations for socialism and wish to see its fruition. Consequently, the thinking of some of them often remained at the stage of the democratic revolution while the socialist revolution had already begun. It is in the very course of the socialist revolution that quite a few of them gradually prepare themselves mentally for the socialist revolution. The socialist revolution is much broader and deeper than the democratic revolution. Its aim is to liquidate all systems of exploitation and the private ownership of the means of production. Each step in this revolution has a powerful impact on the life and thinking of the several hundred million people of our country, and the various ideological trends in society are inevitably reflected, directly or indirectly, in the army. If adequate mental preparation for the socialist revolution and serious self-remoulding are lacking, the revolutionary army man cannot possibly maintain a firm stand in the socialist revolution and, consequently, cannot possibly carry through the Party's general line for building socialism in a conscious, resolute manner. When socialism actually comes and private ownership of the means of production by the bourgeoisie and petty bourgeoisie is actually coming to an end, he will therefore be taken by surprise and even lose his bearings. Thus the germ of bourgeois ideology would spread in that section of our Party and army where resistance is weak and exercise a corrosive and splitting influence on our Party and army. Consequently, we would encounter internal resistance in the struggle for the realization of socialism.

Within our army, the two opposing classes, the bourgeoisie and the working class, do not exist, but the struggle between bourgeois and working-class ideology does exist. This ideological struggle is a reflection of the struggle between the two roads, socialist and capitalist, in the transition period. As the situation now stands, the transformation of the old economic system of society has been completed in the main, but not fully; the economic system of society has been changed, but remnant bourgeois ideological and political activities still remain and the social base for this, though shrinking, is still there to a certain extent. The force of habit of the bourgeoisie and small producers is a kind of social base of bourgeois ideology which still finds a place among a section of the people and would become active and cause trouble when the opportunity arises. Either socialist or capitalist ideology must predominate in the minds of the people. Therefore, in the transition period, the struggle to enhance proletarian ideology and liquidate bourgeois ideology remains vital at all times in building up the army.

None of the work of our army, including its modernization, can be divorced from this ideological struggle. This political and ideological struggle between the working class and the bourgeoisie rises and ebbs, rises again and ebbs again, like the tides; it is far from over to this day and will not be over until classes are finally and completely liquidated. Consequently, our work of socialist ideological education cannot be completed all at once. With the rise and ebb of the class struggle, it will necessarily be carried on sometimes steadily and evenly, in the form of long-term theoretical and policy education, and at other times in the form of large-scale rectification and ideological remoulding campaigns. Socialist ideology assumes its position and expands step by step through education and struggle. Every revolutionary must go through uninterrupted revolution ideologically. The *san fan* movement (against corruption, waste and bureaucracy), the movement to resist U.S. aggression and aid Korea, the movement to study the Party's general line for the transition period, the movement to clean out the counter-revolutionaries, the rectification campaign, the anti-rightist struggle, the great debate on socialism around the central question of agricultural co-operation, and the study of the Party's general line for building socialism with the people's communes and the great leap forward as its main content—all these things which we carried out during the past ten years represent highly successful political and ideological work. Of course we do not rest content with these successes and do not believe that the future tasks on the political and ideological fronts will be any lighter because of these successes.

In waging the struggle on the political and ideological fronts, we always maintain that as far as the overwhelming majority of comrades are concerned this is mainly a question of education and raising their level. The officers and men of our army ardently love socialism, fight for it resolutely and can withstand tests of great stress. Those who insist on taking the road of capitalism and are deliberately against socialism are merely a handful of individuals from alien classes who have sneaked into the army. However, since the overwhelming majority of the officers and men of our army come from the peasantry, unavoidably some comrades sometimes consider questions from the temporary, partial interests of small producers and do not clearly understand certain questions of socialist change; unavoidably, too, a small number of comrades are affected, in the great stress of socialist revolution, by bourgeois and petty-bourgeois, and especially well-to-do middle peasant, ideological influences and reveal an insufficiently resolute standpoint. This is the situation and, if allowed to develop, bourgeois ideology would spread in our army. Therefore, we must not slacken ideological work for a moment. These ideological questions belong to the category of contradictions among the people and cannot be solved by methods which are proper for contradictions between ourselves and the enemy or by coercive, high-handed methods; they can only be solved by democratic methods, the method of discussion, criticism, persuasion and education.

During the new historical period, political and ideological work in the army is very important and must never be slackened. "Political work is the life-blood of our army"—this is a truth which has been proved by decades of revolutionary practice of our army. Comrade Mao Tse-tung in one of his editor's notes in the book *Socialist Upsurge in China's Countryside* pointed out: "Political work is the life-blood of all economic work. This is particularly true at a time when the economic system of a society is undergoing a fundamental change." This statement, of course, applies equally to the army. In building up our army into a modernized army, we pay very much attention, of course, to improving equipment and mastering technique. But we must at the same time pay attention to the other side, which is indeed the predominant side, that is, we must not forget politics, we must emphasize politics. Our army is an army in the service of politics, in the service of socialism, and we must guide the military and day-to-day work with politics. Politics is the most fundamental thing; if political and ideological work is not done well, everything else is out of the question. The great achievements in the varied work of our army in the past ten years represent, first and foremost, the blossoming and fruition of socialist ideology. Henceforth it will still be a fundamental task in the building of our army to strengthen theoretical education in Marxism-Leninism, to strengthen education in socialism and the general line of the Party and to link this closely with the practice of the contemporary revolutionary struggle and the change in the thinking of the members of the army—so as continuously to eliminate from people's minds the vestiges of bourgeois and petty-bourgeois ideology and enhance their socialist consciousness.

III

The Chinese People's Liberation Army, which was born and grew up in the midst of the people's revolutionary struggles, has always regarded the revolutionary mass movement as its own affair. When the masses rise up and wage hard, bitter struggles against the old system and for the transformation of society and of nature, the People's Liberation Army always stands as one with the people and gives them wholehearted, powerful support; it participates directly in the seething, stirring mass movements in which, at the same time, it receives the greatest and best training. And whenever hostile forces attempt to obstruct and undermine the mass revolutionary movements, the People's Liberation Army always stands behind the masses. At the same time, the vast, surging mass movements, in turn, always inspire and educate the army greatly, serving as a revolutionary crucible in which the political consciousness of the army is tempered and raised. The reason why the People's Liberation Army, under extremely difficult conditions, has been able to defeat an enemy far superior both in equipment and numbers is precisely the fact that it is an armed force that has flesh and blood ties with the masses who, when fully mobilized, "create a vast sea and drown the enemy in it, remedy our shortage in arms and other things, and secure the prerequisites to overcome every difficulty in the war" (Mao Tse-tung: *On the Protracted War*). This relationship between the People's Liberation Army and the masses of the people is determined by the very nature of the People's Liberation Army and the very purpose for which it was founded. This was so in the period of democratic revolution and remains so in the period of socialist revolution. In March 1949, when the democratic revolution was attaining decisive victory and the new stage of socialist revolution was about to begin, Comrade Mao Tse-tung, at the Second Plenary Session of the Seventh Central Committee of the Chinese Communist Party, again issued a timely, great call to us—that the People's Liberation Army shall for ever be a fighting force and at the same time a working force.

After the liberation of the mainland, the major task of our army shifted from fighting to training; instead of living scattered in villages as before, it moved into regular barracks and had less opportunity for direct contact with the masses. At that time some comrades held that since there was a division of labour between economic construction and the building up of national defence and that since army training was very heavy work, it appeared as if there were no need for the army to take part in the revolutionary struggles of the masses of the people or in national economic construction, no need to take part in "civilian" business. We criticized this wrong view and firmly corrected it in time. We have continued to develop our army's long-standing, glorious tradition of simultaneously carrying out the three great tasks of fighting, mass work and production and we have launched various activities in support of the mass movements in line with the requirements of different stages of socialist transformation and socialist construction. During the past ten years, the People's Liberation Army has vigorously supported and enthusiastically joined in every major social reform and mass movement. The spokesmen of the imperialists who are violently hostile to our socialist cause describe our army's participation in the people's revolutionary movements as "armed suppression." Nothing, indeed, is more absurd. In fact, the imperialist bosses are accustomed to employing their reactionary armed forces in brutal suppression of the people of their own countries and of the national and democratic movements of the colonial peoples. Their slanders and calumnies against our army only show their mortal fear of the close unity between our powerful People's Liberation Army and the more than 600 million people, and their frantic attempts to cover up their own nefarious deeds with lies and fabrications.

The big leap forward in our national economy that began in 1958 along with the great upsurge to form the people's communes has shown the boundless vitality of our Party's general line for socialist construction. This line, which was readily grasped by the masses, has become a tremendous material force and brought about a vast mass movement unprecedented in history. What should be our attitude to this mighty mass movement? Should we plunge into it and support the masses with all our hearts? Or should we stand outside the movement and pick fault with the masses here and there, or even stand in opposition to the movement and against the masses? In sharp contrast to the right opportunists, the

People's Liberation Army, long brought up on the teachings of the Party and Comrade Mao Tse-tung and standing as one with the people, resolutely supports this great mass movement.

The officers and men of the People's Liberation Army fully understand from their personal experience that the big leap forward and the people's communes have their objective material base and are the inevitable products of China's historical development. The Party and Comrade Mao Tse-tung concentrated the will and creative energy of the masses and pushed this mighty movement forward. The mighty upsurge of revolutionary fervour and socialist consciousness manifested by the broad masses of the labouring people during the big leap forward and the people's commune movement is due precisely to their determination to change our backward economic situation as quickly as possible, to put an end to our state of being "poor and blank" and to build our country into a great socialist state with highly developed modern industry, agriculture, science and culture. All officers and men of the People's Liberation Army fully understand this lofty aspiration and burning enthusiasm of the people; they see eye to eye with the people and are deeply moved by their great determination. Our comrades in the People's Liberation Army know only too well that the imperialists and their henchmen are eyeing our socialist construction with hostility and will never miss a single chance to sabotage. This makes it all the more necessary for us to maintain constant vigilance and firmly carry through and defend our Party's general line for building socialism so as to develop our national economy at high speed. Only with our national economy developing at a rapid tempo can the modernization of our national defence be attained, and the happiness and tranquillity of our people be safeguarded.

Our comrades of the People's Liberation Army all realize that fear of the mass movement is in the ingrained nature of right opportunists and bourgeois revolutionaries. Confronted by the mass movement, they are only interested in picking faults and exaggerating them so as to spread slackness, despondency, dissatisfaction and pessimism, to negate our achievements and the Party's general line. We, on the other hand, are firmly for the full mobilization of the masses to carry the socialist revolution to its completion and to build socialism with great vigour and vitality. To reject the mass movement and oppose it by seizing upon some isolated, local and temporary shortcomings which have been quickly overcome, is to turn one's back upon progress, upon the revolutionary cause. Participating directly in the mass movement, the officers and men of the People's Liberation Army see, above all, the tremendous endeavours and magnificent successes of hundreds of millions of people. This is the main current, the essence of the mass movement. In the people's communes, for example, we see not only the powerful vitality and unparalleled superiority of this new-born social organization and the important role it plays in developing the national economy and culture and in raising the living standards of the people; we also come to realize that in the event of a war of aggression launched by imperialism against our country, the people's communes, in which township administration and commune management are merged into one and industry, agriculture, trade, education and military affairs are integrated into one, are the mighty prop for the task of turning the whole population into fighting men, of supporting the front, of defending the country and overwhelming the aggressors. Seeing this revolutionary creation of the masses of people which can accelerate the advance of the socialist cause and, at the same time promote the building of national defence, what else can anyone who genuinely desires a prosperous and powerful motherland do but support it wholeheartedly and praise it with deep emotion? Of course, it was inevitable that in the course of such a vast, rapidly growing, mass revolutionary movement as the establishment of the people's communes, lack of experience would result in some shortcomings. But what merits extraordinary attention is not at all that some shortcoming or another occurred but the fact that the shortcomings were so few and far between compared with the achievements, that the shortcomings were overcome so rapidly and that the skill with which our Party and Comrade Mao Tse-tung led the mass movement is so superb and so worthy of admiration and study.

As we have said, the People's Liberation Army is an instrument of political struggle and instead of standing aloof from politics, a revolutionary soldier must attach importance to politics and work hard at political study. And the practice of the mass movement and of social struggle is itself a rich political experience. We should at all times keep in touch with the masses and raise our own level by absorbing nourishment from the revolutionary mass movements. By vigorously and actively taking part in national construction and the mass movements, officers and men of the army can widen their breadth of vision, enrich their minds and fortify their own mass point of view and their love of labour, raise their theoretical level and deepen their understanding of policy through integration with rich practice. Furthermore, they can learn from the civilian cadres the methods of class analysis and the lively working methods of the mass line. Time and again, experience has shown that as far as the masses of officers and the rank and file are concerned, participation by the army in mass movements is a most vivid, fruitful and profound political schooling. Faster political and ideological progress is invariably achieved by the cadres and soldiers of any unit that pays attention to this; while the cadres and soldiers of any unit that neglects this become politically uninformed and narrow-sighted and their thinking lags behind events. Some years ago there were comrades who regarded it as an extra burden for the army to participate in mass movements and assist the people in production. They held that only drilling and lectures constituted training while participation in practical socialist struggles was not training but an obstruction to training which would bring "more loss than gain." Such a viewpoint is utterly wrong.

IV

In building a modernized army, when the technical equipment of our army is being constantly improved and the mastery of technique and the raising of the technical level of our army are more important than ever before, is man still the decisive factor? Some comrades take the view that modern warfare differs from warfare in the past, that since the weapons and equipment available to our army in the past were inferior we had to emphasize dependence on man, on his bravery and wisdom, in order to win victories. They say that modern warfare is a war of technique, of steel and machinery, and that in the face of these things, man's role has to be relegated to a secondary place. They attach importance only to machinery and want to turn revolutionary soldiers into robots without revolutionary initiative. Contrary to these people, we believe that although equipment and technique are important, the human factor is even more important. Technique also has to be mastered by man. Men and materiel must form a unity and men must be made the leading factor. What we have to consider constantly is how to mobilize all positive factors still better and bring the initiative of the mass of officers and men into full play. That is why in building up the army during the past ten years, we have paid special attention to creating close relations between the officers and men and between the men at the higher and lower echelons, and to applying the mass line thoroughly in all work.

The Chinese People's Liberation Army is an entirely new type of people's army. It began its work of building itself up by destroying the warlord system of the feudal, mercenary army and establishing the system of democratic unity. Our army has the most authoritative system of command but also the close relations of a great revolutionary family, with unity between the officers and men and between the higher and lower echelons. Our army is a fighting organization of the greatest centralism and the strongest discipline yet also an army with the richest democratic life. The members of our army work under a unified command from top to bottom yet are accustomed to applying the mass line in all spheres of work. Officers and men, centralism and democracy, unified command and the mass line, these seem to be diametrically contradictory yet they have been integrated excellently in our army. This is a Marxist-Leninist tradition which the Chinese Communist Party and Comrade Mao Tse-tung have long established in the Chinese People's Liberation Army. In the past ten years, regardless of the changes in our army's weapons and equipment and in its organizational systems, we have held fast to this glorious tradition and developed it incessantly.

Comrade Mao Tse-tung has long since pointed out that whether the relations between the officers and men are good or bad is not a question of technique or method but of attitude, it is a question of basic attitude as to whether or not the personality of the ordinary soldier is respected. We have always held that the only difference between the officers and men is one of division of labour within the revolutionary ranks and, politically speaking and as far as personality is concerned, there is no distinction of high and low. Officers are not special figures above the rank and file. Only when the officers have affection and solicitude for the rank and file, when the rank and file respect the officers and when they respect each other, can relations of equality and brotherhood be established and the aim of unity between the officers and men be attained. Such unity brings forth unlimited fighting strength. In 1958, our army responded to the call of Comrade Mao Tse-tung and began to put into practice the system of officers going down to the companies and serving as rank and file soldiers for a period of a month each year. Our comrade generals who are commanding officers and political commissars of the various military areas, services and arms, took the lead in putting this into effect.

The officers who join the companies as ordinary soldiers drill, do manual labour, live and spend their recreation time together with the rank and file. They do whatever the squad leaders order; what they do not know they learn from the squad leaders and the rank and file like pupils in school. Very soon they are united with the soldiers as one and become their bosom friends. The reports from the various units show that in companies which officers have joined as ordinary soldiers, political enthusiasm and morale is especially high. With the officers themselves setting examples, the rank and file show every possible concern for the officers. They pay great attention to their health and help them as much as they can so as to lighten their strain of physical labour. Serving as ordinary soldiers is also of great help to the officers themselves. In working and living with the rank and file, they are able to establish the communist style of treating others on an equal footing, guard against bureaucratic airs and raise the level of their mass outlook; they can examine the directives and decisions of the leading organizations and the style of work of the leadership from the angle of an ordinary soldier. Although only a year has passed since the introduction of the officers-serving-as-soldiers system, one can already see that it will enable the officers and the rank and file of our army to merge more closely into an integral body whose pulse and heart beat in unison, and to become an invincible force.

Comrade Mao Tse-tung has always attached great importance to the development of democratic life. He has instructed us many times on this. He has said that the army should practise a certain degree of democracy. This is the way to achieve unity between the officers and the men and hence increase the fighting strength of the army. He has said that every unit of the army should carry out campaigns to support the cadres and love the soldiers, calling on the cadres to have affection for the rank and file and at the same time calling on the rank and file to support the cadres. They should frankly explain their shortcomings and mistakes to each other and correct them quickly. This is the way the goal of internal unity can be properly achieved. He has also said that what is called the question of the correct handling of contradictions among the people is precisely one of the mass line, which our Party has often talked about. This democratic working method, the working method of the mass line which Comrade Mao Tse-tung taught us, was first carried out in the army and has provided us with rich experiences. In the Chinese People's Liberation Army, the rank and file are the ones to be governed and led, yet at the same time they are entitled to take part in the conduct of affairs, contribute their ideas and recommend ways and means in the course of the work. The cadres are the ones who govern and lead, yet at the same time they are subject to the supervision of the masses, depend on the masses and mobilize them in work. Where contradictions arise, the democratic method of persuasion and education is used to adjust them according to the unity-criticism-unity formula. In this way unity is strengthened, morale is raised, discipline is consolidated and the initiative and creative energy of the mass of officers and rank and file are developed. During the past ten years we have made great progress in all this. The Chinese People's Volunteers, too, scored outstanding achievements in applying democracy to the highly modern war of resisting U.S. aggression and aiding Korea. The "underground Great Wall," that is, the tunnel fortifications which played a very important role in this war, was the collective product of the wisdom of the masses gained through the joint efforts of the officers and the rank and file. We have also applied democracy to modern military training. The results prove that units which carry out the mass line well invariably score excellent achievements in training. In 1958, the mass campaign to master military technique under the slogan of "mastering many skills while specializing in one, every soldier capable of many uses" came into prominence. A technical innovation campaign that centred on improving technical equipment also developed on a large scale, resulting in many rationalization proposals and many valuable innovations and inventions. In addition, the democratic method of airing one's views, contending and debating to the fullest extent and publicizing one's views in *dazibao**—the method adopted throughout the country since the rectification campaign—has also been introduced in the army. This method is most suitable for mobilizing the masses for self-education, solving internal contradictions, bringing into full play mass initiative and increasing their sense of responsibility.

The democracy which we practise is democracy under centralized guidance and it is carried out under leadership. We are at all times opposed to anarchism and equalitarianism. While carrying for-

---

*Opinions written in bold characters and posted on walls for everybody to see—*Tr.*

ward democratic life in the army, we also consider and take into account the special features of an army at all times and places. We take democracy as a means whereas our end is to increase the army's unity, strengthen its discipline and raise its fighting strength. The officers and the rank and file of our army have the common political purpose and the common ideological basis of unity among themselves to defeat the enemy. Therefore, democratic life in our army has all along gone forward on a sound footing. We should firmly trust the majority of the masses. Should any people with ulterior motives try to use democracy to undermine our army, neither would the leadership at all levels tolerate them, nor would the mass of officers and men ever let them get away with it.

V

The Party's absolute leadership in the armed forces and the staunch Party character of the host of cadres of our army are the best guarantee for victory in the field of national defence in our country's socialist construction. We know full well that in the past ten years, as in the years of war before that, whenever we were confronted with crucial problems in the building of national defence and in military struggles, we always received our correct orientation from the Party and Comrade Mao Tse-tung and the problems were solved successfully. For example, the laying down of the policy for building a modernized revolutionary army, the correct handling of the relations between the building up of national defence and national economic construction, the wise policy decision on resisting U.S. aggression and aiding Korea and the correct strategic guidance, the decisions on the policies regarding the struggle for the liberation of Taiwan and the operations on the Fukien front, the introduction of the policy of combining the powerful regular forces, the special technical units and the armed militia in preparation for turning the whole population into fighting men, and so on—all these, without exception, are the result of leadership by the Party and by Comrade Mao Tse-tung personally.

In his article on "Problems of War and Strategy," Comrade Mao Tse-tung said: "According to the Marxist theory of the state, the army is the chief component of the political power of a state. Whoever wants to seize the political power of the state and to maintain it must have a strong army." He added in the same article: "Communists do not contend for personal military power (they should never do that, and let no one follow the example of Chang Kuo-tao), but they must contend for military power for the Party and for the people.... Our principle is that the Party commands the gun, and the gun will never be allowed to command the Party." The Chinese People's Liberation Army, in the ten years since the founding of the Republic, as in the time of war, has always resolutely supported the leadership of the Party and Comrade Mao Tse-tung, serving as a most faithful and dependable instrument in carrying through the line and policies laid down by the Party, as the staunchest defender of the people's democratic dictatorship under the Party's leadership and of the socialist cause. As a result, the masses of the people have always lavished great honours and love on the People's Liberation Army, whereas imperialism and all the reactionaries have invariably regarded the unmeasured loyalty of the People's Liberation Army to the Party and Comrade Mao Tse-tung as something that works to their greatest disadvantage. We cadres and Communists working in the army must be on the alert at all times against the intrigues of the enemy—both against invasion by the enemy with arms and against "sugar-coated shells" of all kinds and sabotage from within. The cadres and Communists in the army have an especially important duty in defending meticulously the interests of the people, the socialist cause and the leadership of the Party from assault and sabotage by any enemy whatsoever. This is a duty which, first and foremost, calls for conscientious study by the cadres and Communists in the army, for their self-remoulding so as to acquire a high degree of political consciousness and a staunch Party character.

Party character is not an abstract thing. The staunch Party character of a Communist and a cadre in the army should find expression, at all times and in all circumstances, in upholding the unity of the Party unswervingly and in wholehearted struggle for the programme and line of the Party. It is therefore constantly necessary for a Communist and a cadre to take interest in, and pay attention to, the political situation and to the policies, line and other issues concerning the direction to pursue, to maintain a firm stand, distinguish right from wrong and avoid wavering and loss of bearings when confronted with important problems of right and wrong. The position of the individual in relation to the Party must be placed correctly. The Party should be obeyed absolutely; no personal ambitions are permissible. Discipline should be strictly observed; in all circumstances importance should be attached to the unity of the Party and nothing should be done behind the back of the Party; one should be just, selfless and honest, and not chase fame hypocritically; modest and not conceited; courageous in accepting criticism and advice and active in combating all wrong tendencies, not rejecting criticism and persisting in mistakes. In short, individualism is the source of all evils. As soon as it sprouts, it must be criticized to the full and overcome by every effort, not a single bit of it must be allowed to get by. The Party character of the great majority of the cadres in our army has grown steadily stronger under the constant instruction of the Party and Comrade Mao Tse-tung. It is precisely because we have large numbers of cadres who are imbued with a staunch Party spirit that the Party's leadership in the army has been carried through and such great achievements have been made.

It has been pointed out time and again by the Party and Comrade Mao Tse-tung that in strengthening Party character, the basic question lies in using the proletarian world outlook of dialectical materialism to replace the bourgeois world outlook of idealism that exists in people's minds. This calls for stern effort over a long period of time. A Communist will inevitably commit mistakes so long as he does not thoroughly change his world outlook but observes things and handles problems with a bourgeois world outlook. A man cannot be very fully tempered and attain a high Party character without changing his world outlook. To study Marxist-Leninist theory and the writings of Comrade Mao Tse-tung conscientiously and to establish a proletarian world outlook firmly are the incumbent duty of every cadre and Communist in our army.

While we are celebrating our decade of brilliant achievements in the building of the country and the army, our socialist construction is continuing its leap forward at high speed and the international situation is developing in a direction all the more favourable to peace, democracy and socialism. The great Soviet Union and other fraternal socialist countries are flourishing in prosperity; the anti-colonialist liberation struggles are growing tempestuously all over the world; while the imperialist camp is ridden with internal contradictions and shrouded in grim shadows. The wise conclusions of Comrade Mao Tse-tung that "the East wind is prevailing over the West wind" and "the enemy rots with every passing day, while for us things are getting better day by day" are borne out by a growing volume of facts. The possibilities for the relaxation of international tension and the consolidation of world peace are increasing with each passing day. We should fight for peace resolutely. Though a handful of bellicose elements in the United States are still trying hard to continue to intensify the cold war, are repeatedly creating incidents to provoke the socialist camp and the national independence movements, and certain imperialist elements are unceasingly engaging in vicious instigations against the People's Republic of China—and we have to maintain full vigilance against all this— yet we are firm in our belief that the forces of the new are bound to defeat the forces of decay. The cause of world peace, democracy and socialism will continue to leap forward in mighty strides. All the circumstances are bright, both internally and internationally. Inspired by the brilliant achievements of our country during the past ten years and by the militant call of the Eighth Plenary Session of the Eighth Central Committee of the Party, and led by the great Chinese Communist Party and Comrade Mao Tse-tung, the great leader of all the nationalities of China, the 650 million Chinese people will certainly achieve new and still more brilliant successes in building socialism! In the years of the triumphant march to socialism, the Chinese People's Liberation Army, manning its battle stations, will resolutely carry out every mission entrusted to it by the Party and will fully live up to the expectations of the people throughout the country. Let us continue to hold high the red banner of the Party's general line and the military thinking of Mao Tse-tung, go all out, aim high and march forward courageously to consolidate our national defence, liberate Taiwan, uphold peace and build our motherland!

DOCUMENT 47

On the Big Leap Forward in China's Socialist Construction, article by Li Fu-ch'un in *Red Flag*, October 1, 1959.

> The text is a translation made by the U.S. Consulate General, Hong Kong, and issued in CB 598.

Comment. This article is particularly interesting for the broad sweep of its ideas. On the philosophy of the Great Leap Forward, see our General Introduction, part VII. At the beginning of Li Fu-ch'un's article the Great Leap is attributed to the scientific foresight of Chairman Mao Tse-tung in the winter of 1955. In section II of the article, very sweeping criticisms are said to have been made by the "right opportunists" within the Party, namely that the mass campaign, not only for iron and steel, but also for water conservancy projects, high-yield agricultural fields, and industrial capital construction, resulted in "more loss than gain." But the general tone of the survey is extremely optimistic (there is no mention of the revision of 1958 production and 1959 target figures), and the conclusion (in section IV) is that China should probably be able to catch Britain in the output of major products in about ten years, rather than in the previous target time of fifteen years.

As usual, the footnotes in Document 47 were not supplied by us, but by the Chinese.

———————————TEXT OF DOCUMENT 47———————————

I.

The question of how to integrate the universal truth of Marxism-Leninism with China's actual practice is one that our Party has to solve both in revolution and in construction. The complete victory of the democratic revolution and the all-round victory of the socialist revolution prove that our Party has creatively solved this question in revolution. Can it be said, then, that we have solved this question in construction?

The Question of Speed

The most important question in socialist construction is that of speed. Having achieved during the First Five-Year Plan a rate of growth unprecedented in China's history and seldom witnessed in the history of capitalist countries, the question of whether China's socialist construction could advance further at still higher speed became the central and most important question demanding solution in order to uphold resolutely the basic principle of integrating the universal truth of Marxism-Leninism with the actual practice of China's construction.

In the winter of 1955, when the socialist revolution in the ownership of the means of production was about to be completed in our country, Comrade Mao Tse-tung scientifically foresaw the possibility for the national economy to develop at still higher speed and put forward, in time, the slogan of achieving greater, faster, better and more economical results in developing socialist construction. Afterwards, he put forward a series of programmatic proposals for the realization of this objective possibility, including the draft 12-Year National Program for Agricultural Development (1956-1967) and the report on the "ten sets of relationships". On the basis of the practical experience in socialist construction in 1956 and 1957 and the development of Comrade Mao Tse-tung's thinking, the Second Session of our Party's 8th National Congress formally laid down the general line—to go all out, aim high and achieve greater, faster, better and more economical results to build socialism, and the set of policies of "simultaneous development". Thus, we have found a road which suits China's specific conditions to develop socialist construction at still higher speed.

Those who have right opportunist ideas, including the empiricists and dogmatists, fail to see the strong desire and firm will of the people throughout the country to get rid of poverty and backwardness rapidly, the great power and rich fund of wisdom of the hundreds, of millions of laboring people who have liberated themselves from the old system and have established the new system of socialism, and the role of the material and technical conditions created during the First Five-Year Plan. Bound by old ideas and old experiences, they are of the opinion that the speed achieved in the First Five-Year Plan was already very high, that the larger the base, the slower the rate of growth must be and that the tempo of the Second Five-Year Plan can only be slower, and not faster, than the First Five-Year Plan. Even when the general line, which embodies the will of more than 600 million people, has already been grasped by the broad masses and is displaying tremendous power when socialist construction has already achieved vigorous growth, the right opportunists are still sceptical of the general line, and try to find an opportunity to settle accounts with us and launch attacks against the general line.

Practice is the only criterion for judging truth. Is truth really on our side, or on theirs? Can the rate of growth in the Second Five-Year Plan exceed that of the First Five-Year Plan, or must it necessarily be slower? The big leap forward and the people's communes that have appeared since last year under the guidance of the general line have already definitely and unequivocally answered these questions. The facts show that we have essentially solved the question of developing socialist construction at a still higher speed not only in theory but also in practice.

II.

The big leap forward in 1958 enabled the rate of growth of our industrial and agricultural production and capital construction to exceed greatly the average annual rate of growth during the First Five-Year Plan and surpass the fastest annual rate of growth in that period.

During the First Five-Year Plan, the total value of industrial and agricultural production registered an average annual rate of growth of 10.9 per cent. The rate of growth of the total value of industrial production (including the output value of the handicrafts, as elsewhere) was 18 per cent, and that of the total value of agricultural production was 4.5 per cent. Whereas in 1958, the total value of industrial and agricultural production rose by 48 per cent compared with 1957, the rate of growth of the total value of industrial production was 66 per cent and that of the total value of agricultural production was 25 per cent. In terms of absolute figures, the increase in the total value of industrial and agricultural production during the First Five-Year Plan was 56,000 million yuan, whereas the increase in the single year of 1958 was 60,000 million yuan.[1]

During the First Five-Year Plan, total investments in capital construction amounted to 55,000 million yuan, 537 above-norm industrial projects[2] were completed or partially completed and commissioned and more than 218 million *mow* of land were brought under irrigation. In 1958, total investments in capital construction amounted to 26,700 million yuan, 700 above-norm industrial projects were completed or partially completed and went into production, and irrigation was brought to an additional 480 million *mow* of land.

Together with the big leap forward in industrial and agricultural production and in capital construction, other branches of the national economy also developed rapidly. Compared with 1957, total freight carried by modern means of transport increased by 220 million tons in 1958, 91 per cent of the total increase of 240 million tons during the previous five years; the total value of retail sales increased by 7,400 million yuan, 37 per cent of the total increase of 19,700 million yuan during the previous five years. In the field of culture and education, the colleges and universities in 1958 admitted 320,000 new students, 56 per cent of the total of 560,000 in the previous five years. The big leap forward in 1958 was not just a big leap in individual branches or individual fields. It was an all-round big leap forward of the national economy as a whole, an all-round big leap forward in socialist economic and cultural construction.

Special Features of the Big Leap

What were the special features of the all-round big leap forward in our national economy in 1958 compared with previous years?

---

[1] The absolute figure for the increase during the First Five-Year Plan is calculated in 1952 constant prices and that for 1958, in 1957 constant prices. Since the prices of heavy industrial products were gradually reduced during the First Five-Year Plan, the 1957 constant prices are generally lower than the 1952 constant prices. If we calculate in the same prices, the absolute increase in 1958 would be even more than 50,000 million yuan.

[2] The norm of investment in capital construction for heavy industry ranges from 5 million to 10 million yuan and that for light industry from 3 million to 5 million yuan.

First, during the First Five-Year Plan, industrial production registered an average annual increase of 18 per cent while agricultural production averaged an annual increase of 4.5 per cent. The rate of increase of industry was four times that of agriculture. In 1958, industrial production increased by 66 per cent and agricultural production by 25 per cent. The rate of increase of industry was 2.6 times that of agriculture. From this it is clear that an obvious change has begun to take place in the conditions that prevailed during the previous five years when the rate of agricultural development lagged behind the rate of industrial development. While industry forges ahead rapidly, our agriculture, with its productive forces greatly emancipated, is racing to catch up.

Secondly, during the First Five-Year Plan, production in heavy industry registered an average annual increase of 25.4 per cent and light industry 12.8 per cent. In 1958, production in heavy industry increased by 103 per cent and in light industry by 34 per cent. The rates of increase in heavy and light industries in 1958 were four times and 2.7 times respectively compared with the average annual rates of increase during the First Five-Year Plan. Production in heavy industry grew particularly rapidly in 1958, thus providing more means of production for the various branches of heavy industry and also for light industry and agriculture. This not only insured the rapid development of light industry and agriculture in 1958, but will also guarantee their quick growth in the years to come. With the rapid development of heavy industry and agriculture and with the steady increase in the supply of machinery and raw materials needed by light industry, it will be possible for light industry to continue to develop rapidly and at a rate corresponding more to the growth of heavy industry and agriculture. This trend has now become clearer.

Thirdly, the various branches of heavy industry developed greatly during the First Five-Year Plan. Among those branches with a higher speed of advance, steel, for example, had an average annual rate of increase of 31.7 per cent and the machine-building industry, 34.6 per cent. Among those with a lower speed of advance, coal had an average annual rate of increase of 14.4 per cent, electricity, 21.6 per cent and crude oil, 27.3 per cent. In 1958, the various branches of heavy industry developed at a still higher speed with the steel industry as the key lever. While steel produced by modern methods increased by 49.5 per cent and the output value of the machine-building industry increased by 204 per cent, the output of coal, electricity and crude oil, all of which increased relatively slowly in the past, rose 108 per cent, 42 per cent and 55 per cent respectively. Some originally weaker branches have radically changed for the better while others are changing gradually.

Fourthly, thanks to the great development of heavy industry in 1958, especially the iron and steel and machine-building industries, the rate of self-sufficiency in steel products rose from an average of around 75 per cent during the First Five-Year Plan to over 80 per cent, in machinery and equipment, from around 55 per cent to about 80 per cent. During the First Five-Year Plan, most of our important, large enterprises, either newly established or expanded on an old basis, were designed with the help of the Soviet Union which also supplied them with complete sets of equipment. They were built with the assistance of the experts of the Soviet Union and other fraternal countries. Thanks to the strenuous efforts of the masses of workers and employees to learn, we can now design many important enterprises ourselves and our achievements in this respect were most notable in 1958.

Comprehensive Industrial System

Fifthly, under the First Five-Year Plan, we built a series of large, modern enterprises which serve as the backbone of our socialist industrialization; we also began to build new industrial bases in North China, Central China, the southwest and northwest areas. In 1958, besides continuing the construction of close to 500 above-norm factories and mines started earlier, construction was started on more than 1,000 new, above-norm factories and mines; at the same time, we set up large numbers of small industrial units in medium-sized and small cities, in towns and in the countryside, totalling hundreds of thousands. In 1957, many provinces and autonomous regions did not produce a single ton of steel, including Inner Mongolia, Kiangsi, Chekiang, Fukien, Honan, Kwangsi, Kweichow, Kansu, Ninghsia, and Tibet. With the big leap forward in 1958, however, all the provinces, municipalities and autonomous regions in the country, excepting Tibet, began to produce steel. In that year, we not only expanded the existing 18 key iron and steel enterprises, but also established more than 20 new medium-sized iron and steel works and more than 300 small iron-smelting centers. In the machine-building industry, 220 large factories were either newly built or expanded and, in addition, tens of thousands of small and medium-sized ones were set up.

In 1958, those special administrative regions and counties which had no machine-building industry before and some of the districts and townships set up varying numbers of machine-building and repair shops of varying sizes. The great majority of the provinces, municipalities and autonomous regions can now produce some sort of metallurgical equipment, electrical motors, machine tools, engines, and agricultural machinery. All this shows that a nationwide, comprehensive industrial system, with iron and steel and machine-building as the key links, integrating large, medium-sized and small enterprises, more rationally distributed geographically, is being rapidly set up. In this way, the conditions are being created at the same time for the various economic areas,[3] many provinces and autonomous regions to build up their own industrial systems of different standards in the future, each with its own special features.

Sixthly, tempered in practice in the First Five-Year Plan and trained by the universities and specialized schools, the ranks of our technical personnel have greatly expanded. In 1958, thanks to the slogan put forward by the Party of "breaking down superstitions, emancipating the mind, promoting the Communist style of thinking, speaking and acting boldly," the spectacular scene of "a hundred flowers blooming" has become manifest in the technical innovations and in some fields of the technical revolution. New products trial-produced in 1958 equalled the total number manufactured during the First Five-Year Plan. In the agricultural field, typical examples of high yields were found in various farm crops. On the basis of summing up and developing the rich experiences accumulated by the broad masses of peasants over a long period of time, the "Eight-Point Charter for Agriculture," which has proved its effectiveness, was created.

Seventhly, inspired by the Party's general line and as a result of the tremendous development in rural production and construction, people's communes were set up in the countryside on the basis of the advanced agricultural producers' cooperatives. The people's commune, which merges township administration with commune management, combines industry, agriculture, trade, education and military affairs, and integrates farming, forestry, animal husbandry, side-occupations and fisheries, has displayed still greater superiority over the advanced agricultural producers' cooperative in the following respects: in bringing into fuller play the initiative of the masses for production, in more effective utilization of labor power and raising labor productivity, in expanding agricultural and water conservancy construction, in developing industries in the countryside, in carrying out technical reforms in agriculture and the rural cultural revolution, and in developing public welfare services, etc.

Eighthly, the big development in the various branches of our national economy has completely ended the unemployment in the cities, a legacy inherited from old China. The newly added labor power in the cities can no longer meet the needs of industrial production and the development of construction; in the countryside, a shortage of labor power is still felt although large numbers of women have been freed from household chores and have taken part in the production and construction in the rural areas since the establishment of the people's communes. That a shortage of labor power has begun to be felt in such a big country as ours with a population of more than 600 million is of course not a small event but a big one, not a bad thing but a good one. It shows that our socialist construction is expanding daily and flourishing in all fields. At the same time it also poses before us the task of speeding up technical innovation and technical revolution so as to steadily increase our labor productivity.

Rising National Income

Ninthly, on the basis of the big leap forward in industry and agriculture and the increase in social labor productivity, the national income for 1958 exceeded that of 1957 by 32,300 million yuan, an increase of 34 per cent. Whereas during the First Five-Year Plan, total national income only increased by 32,200 million yuan; the average annual increase was 6,440 million yuan, a rate of increase of 8.9 per cent. Reactionaries at home and abroad and their mouthpieces—the right opportunists—say that our mass campaigns last year to produce iron and steel, to build water conservancy projects, to cultivate high-yield fields and to undertake industrial capital construction resulted in "more loss than gain." But the increase in the national income for the single year of 1958 alone was even greater

---

[3] An economic area consists of several neighboring provinces. It is not an administrative unit. Its function is to coordinate and accelerate the economic development of the provinces in the given area. There are seven such areas in China.

than the total increase in the First Five-Year Plan. Isn't this single fact enough to tear all their slanders to pieces?

Tenthly, as a result of the increase in the national income, the accumulation in 1958 exceeded that of 1957 by 97 per cent, and was more than six times the average annual increase of 15 per cent for the First Five-Year Plan. The rapid increase in the accumulation makes possible a rapid expansion in the scale of capital construction, thereby creating extremely favorable conditions for expanded socialist reproduction in the future. The investment in capital construction in 1958 increased by 93 per cent as compared with 1957; this speed was unheard of in our country before. Owing to the fact that in 1958 the output of heavy industry increased by 103 per cent, capital construction is assured not only of funds but also of materials.

While the accumulation greatly increased, the proportion of consumption in the 1958 national income also increased at a rate faster than any year in the past. Though the amount of consumer goods that the peasants supplied themselves was much greater than in the past, the total retail sales of commodities in 1958 still registered an increase of 16 per cent as compared with 1957; and of this amount the increase for the countryside exceeded 20 per cent. The scale of city construction, including the building of housing for the workers and employees and public utilities in the cities, also exceeded any year in the past. With regard to cultural life in 1958, about 30 million school-age children entered the schools, and about 7 million pupils enrolled in the middle schools. At the same time, undertakings for public health and hygiene also developed accordingly. The imperialists slander us by saying that our big leap forward was obtained at the "expense" of the people's welfare. But the facts have completely exposed their lies. The big leap forward in our industrial and agricultural production has not lowered the standard of living of our people, but has rapidly raised the level of our people's material well-being and cultural life. The great increase in our accumulation was not obtained by reducing our consumption; it was realized on the basis of the tremendous increase in the national income, and under the circumstance of rapidly raising the standards of the people's consumption. Since 1958, in spite of the rapid increase in the production of consumer goods, the even more rapid increase in social purchasing power caused a temporary shortage in the supply of certain non-staple foods and a very few kinds of articles of daily use. There is nothing strange about this. This phenomenon does not show any lowering of the standard of living of our people, but, on the contrary, shows the rapid rise in their living standards.

All the above-mentioned features show that a new situation has come about in the development of our national economy, a new situation of both high-speed and balanced development. After the big leap forward in 1958 and under the conditions of greater harmony in the basic proportions between the various branches of the national economy, the proportion of industry in the total output value of industry and agriculture increased from 56.5 per cent in 1957 to 63.6 per cent in 1958, while the proportion of agriculture decreased from 43.5 per cent to 36.4 per cent; in the total output value of industry, the proportion of heavy industry rose from 48.4 per cent in 1957 to 57.3 per cent in 1958, while the proportion of light industry decreased from 51.6 per cent to 42.7 per cent. This shows that socialist industrialization took a great stride forward in 1958.

III.

It is, of course, not fortuitous that a big leap forward took place on all fronts in 1958. It came inevitably as a result of the growth of our economy. It was the natural outcome of combining the subjective activity of the more than 600 million people of our country with the objective possibility of high-speed economic development under the guidance of our Party.

Our socialist construction was able to advance in 1958 at a still higher speed than during the First Five-Year Plan period because we had still more favorable conditions and factors.

Firstly, as soon as we had carried through the democratic revolution, we pressed the socialist revolution to completion; after we had completed the socialist revolution in the ownership of the means of production, we also won a decisive victory in the socialist revolution on the political and ideological fronts. Moreover, during the big leap forward last year, people's communes were set up throughout the country on the basis of the agricultural cooperatives. These and other such factors have toppled all outdated systems without exception; they dealt telling blows to the timeworn ideas and conceptions which reflected these systems. This revitalized the social productive forces which had lain dormant for thousands of years.

Secondly, ours is a big country with a big population. Man is society's most precious asset. With the elimination of the system of exploitation and the roots of this system, it becomes possible to bring into full play the strength of more than 600 million people.

Thirdly, with the liberation of more than 600 million people from the old system and the consequent rapid growth of its industry and agriculture, our country has come to possess a bigger domestic market than any other country in the world. This domestic market offers enormous possibilities for an economic leap forward.

Fourthly, ours is a country with a vast territory and a good climate, a country with rich natural resources left untapped for centuries. Having become the masters of society, our people are gradually becoming the masters of nature. This has turned these rich natural resources into an important factor for a still more rapid development of our socialist construction.

Fifthly, the overfulfillment of the First Five-Year Plan and the setting up of a preliminary basis for socialist industrialization have prepared even better modern material and technical conditions for the further development of the national economy.

Sixthly, the international help given by the socialist camp headed by the Soviet Union was an important factor contributing to the success of our socialist construction. Now that the Soviet Union has embarked on its great seven-year construction plan, the other fraternal countries are all in the midst of an economic upsurge and all the socialist countries are gaining richer experience in socialist construction, it is possible for us to receive continued international help and to learn even better from the experience accumulated by the fraternal countries in their construction.

Those who have right opportunist ideas look on China's big population with its vast numbers of peasants as a heavy burden and advance it as a reason why our country's socialist construction cannot advance at a rapid speed, although, with the victory of the socialist revolution on all fronts, they have also perceived some of the favorable factors in a vague and superficial way. In contrast to the pessimistic views of these people, Comrade Mao Tse-tung has told us with the greatest militant fervor and revolutionary optimism: "The decisive factor, apart from leadership by the Party, is our six hundred million people. The more people, the more views and suggestions, the more intense the fervour and the greater the energy.... Apart from their other characteristics, China's six hundred million people are first of all, poor, and secondly, 'blank'. That may seem like a bad thing, but it is really a good thing. Poor people want a change, want to do things, want revolution. A clean sheet of paper has no blotches and so the newest and most beautiful words can be written on it, the newest and most beautiful pictures can be painted on it." He pointed out to us that the more than five hundred million peasants constitute a most powerful force both in revolution and in construction. The crux of the matter is that the working class and its vanguard—the Chinese Communist Party—should adopt a correct policy and suitable ways of bringing into fullest play the initiative and creative ability of our more than six hundred million people, of whom more than five hundred million are peasants.

It is with a firm understanding of these characteristics and by creatively applying the universal truth of Marxist-Leninist theories on socialist construction, that Comrade Mao Tse-tung put forward the Party's general line of going all out, aiming high and achieving greater, faster, better and more economical results to build socialism. To go all out and aim high is to place political leadership in command and give full play to human initiative on the basis of the objective laws of socialist economic development. To achieve greater, faster, better and more economical results means increasing the speed of production and construction as much as possible, reaping economic benefits from them to the full and continuously strengthening the material and technical basis. In other words, it means integrating politics with economics.

Basic Points of the General Line

Here are some explanations of certain basic points of the Party's general line.

Simultaneous development of industry and agriculture on the basis of giving priority to heavy industry is one of the important fundamentals of the general line. This includes the simultaneous development of heavy and light industries. Since heavy industry chiefly produces capital goods while agriculture and light industry chiefly produce consumer goods, this policy conforms to the objective law governing relations between the two major departments of production on the basis of priority for the development of the production of capital goods. It embodies the integration of the Marxist-Leninist principle of expanded reproduction with concrete practice in China. This policy makes it possible for us to avoid a one-sided emphasis on industry to the neglect of agriculture, and on heavy industry to the neglect of light industry. Thus we can bring into play at the same time the initiative of our tens of millions of workers and employees and of our more than five hundred million peasants, and at the same time the initiative of workers and employees in heavy industry and in light industry. Guided by this policy, we have broken away from the old idea that the cities should develop only industries and the rural areas should develop only agriculture. On the one hand, while the rural areas are devoting their efforts mainly to agriculture, within the limit of their capacity they also develop industries which serve the needs of agriculture. What should be stressed here is that we have found in the people's commune a form of social organization which is best suited for developing industry and agriculture in the countryside simultaneously. Thus, it is by no means fortuitous that there should be a simultaneous leap forward of industry and agriculture, and of heavy and light industries both in the cities and in the countryside.

Simultaneous development of large, small and medium-sized enterprises, simultaneous employment of modern and indigenous methods of production with large modern enterprises as the key lever—this is another important fundamental of the general line. The need to modernize industry and equip agriculture and other branches of the national economy with modern techniques is a universal law in socialist construction. The historical course of the development of capitalism shows that one of the important methods for less advanced countries to catch up with the more advanced is to hurry forward with the introduction of advanced techniques. The advantages of the socialist system make it all the more necessary and possible for a socialist country to use this method if it is to catch up with and surpass the well-developed capitalist countries. In order to change our condition of technical backwardness, we must build up a number of giant, modern, key enterprises and strive to make use of all the advanced techniques; this is a firm principle which we should stick to at all times. But the building of such big, modern enterprises needs large funds and takes time; it involves techniques not easily acquired all at once, and equipment whose supply is subjected to certain limitations; if we confined ourselves to developing only such enterprises, we would not be able to meet the needs of society fully, we could not make full use of the various resources at our disposal and would reduce the tempo of socialist construction. Thanks to the policy of simultaneous development of large, small and medium-sized enterprises, and of simultaneous employment of modern and indigenous methods of production, we have avoided one-sidedness in paying attention only to large enterprises to the neglect of small and medium-sized ones, and in paying attention only to modern methods of production to the neglect of indigenous methods. We have thus been able to mobilize not only the initiative of workers and employees with a relatively high technical level but also that of workers and employees with a relatively low technical level. We have thus not only inspired those who know how to run industry to run it still better, but also those who formerly did not know how to run industry to have the courage to run it. What is noteworthy here is that hundreds of thousands of small industrial units have already been established in the country's 24,000-odd people's communes. Though they are small in scale and are of a relatively low technical level, these industrial units actually form an important starting point for changing the poverty-stricken and backward face of China's vast countryside.

These commune-run industries have many outstanding advantages:

1. Built in the countryside, they directly serve the needs in production and in livelihood of the peasants who can see the advantages of such industries themselves; relatively small funds are needed to set them up; these factors help stir the initiative of the peasants in accumulating funds for the running of industry.

2. They can easily make use of China's fairly widely scattered local mineral and agricultural resources and get production to cater more satisfactorily to the concrete needs of the local peasants.

3. They help carry out technical transformation in the countryside and raise labor productivity in agriculture.

4. They can make full use of the old equipment of large and medium-sized enterprises that have been replaced by new equipment and thus prolong the service life of such equipment and save funds for society.

5. They can help provide reserves of technical forces for socialist industrialization and the modernization of agriculture.

Some people looked down upon these enterprises because in their initial stages, the quality of their products was fairly low, production costs were rather high and their rate of increase in labor productivity was relatively slow. They compared these industries built up in the early days of the communes only with modern large enterprises and not with the backward farming techniques in the nation's vast countryside. Their mistake lies in the fact that they know nothing about mobilizing the initiative of the more than 500 million peasants, that they are ignorant of the fact that the building of industry by the communes is the most suitable way of mobilizing this great force to take part in the socialist industrialization of the country; nor do they understand that the process of growth of things is always from small to large, from the elementary to the advanced stage. They slight new-born things. But new-born things have the greatest vitality and the most promising future. In 1958, it was exactly because we implemented the policy of integrating large enterprises with small and medium-sized ones, and of getting the whole population to run industry that we got that magnificent scene of small factories and mines using indigenous methods or modern methods spreading all over the country like stars in the sky. Isn't that a most powerful proof of the truth of this conception?

National and Local Industries

Another important fundamental of the general line is the simultaneous development of national and local industries under the principle of centralized leadership, over-all planning, division of work and coordination. The principle of management at different levels under central and local authorities must be applied not only in industry but also in other economic, cultural and educational undertakings. Without centralized leadership under the central authorities and without over-all planning, it is of course impossible to carry out planned socialist construction in such a large country as ours and to turn it in a relatively short time into a socialist state with a modern industry, agriculture, science and culture. Similarly, it also wouldn't do if there were only centralized leadership under the central authorities without proper decentralized leadership under the local authorities. The central authorities must pay attention to bringing the initiative of the provinces, municipalities and autonomous regions into play; the authorities of the provinces, municipalities and autonomous regions must also pay attention to bringing the initiative of the special administrative regions and counties into play; the authorities of the special administrative regions and counties must pay attention to bringing the initiative of the communes and enterprises into play; communes must also pay attention to bringing the initiative of production brigades and teams into play; enterprises must also pay attention to bringing the initiative of the workshops, shifts and teams into play. The practice of such a principle brings more people to share responsibilities in the work of the leadership, providing more ideas and ways and means of doing things. This enables the central authorities to concentrate their strength on administering matters of the greatest importance and what concerns the whole country; it also enables local authorities at all levels to do things that can and must be done by making adaptations to local conditions, in the light of specific conditions and circumstances, thereby raising efficiency and avoiding bureaucracy and different kinds of one-sidedness. Only in this way can we achieve an all-round and rapid development of our cause and get a general economic and cultural upsurge going in every part of the country.

All these basic points and the principles of effecting an all-round leap forward with steel as the key lever, of combining centralized leadership with the vigorous development of mass movements, of placing political leadership in command and combining political work with economic work and combining the political education for the masses with material encouragements, of leading production while making arrangements for the masses to live well, etc., have enabled us to mobilize the broad masses of people at the various fronts and posts of socialist construction, to mobilize all positive factors and useful forces and to get the people to keep up their labor enthusiasm and boundless energy.

IV.

Some people admitted that the occurrence of the all-round big leap forward in 1958 was inevitable but they believed that such a big leap forward could only be temporary, that it could not last long. We take an opposite view; we believe that it is not temporary and that it will last. The big leap forward in 1958 marked the beginning of the leap-forward stage of our socialist construction. This is because the Party's general line for socialist construction which reflects objective economic laws and the aspirations of over 600 million people will play its role for a long period and will show its strength in a more and more marked way; all the above-mentioned favorable conditions and factors which provide the possibility for our socialist construction to develop at a still higher speed will also make themselves increasingly felt. The all-round big leap forward in 1958 has not created difficulties for a future leap forward as the right opportunists allege but, on the contrary, prepared better material conditions for a continued leap forward in the days to come and given us a great deal of fresh experience.

Such are the facts. On the basis of the all-round big leap forward in 1958, new victories have been won in the continued big leap forward of the national economy in 1959. Between January and August this year, compared with the corresponding period of last year, the total value of industrial output increased by 48.5 per cent. Steel output increased by 66.6 per cent, coal 78.5 per cent, electric power 51 per cent, machine tools 49 per cent, cotton yarn 31.7 per cent. There was also a considerable growth in the production of other heavy and light industrial goods. In agriculture, despite serious natural calamities, the summer crops brought in this year were 2,500 million catties more than the extraordinarily rich harvest of last year. Railway freight increased by 46.8 per cent. The total volume of retail sales increased by 18 per cent. Following the directive of the 8th Plenary Session of the 8th Central Committee to oppose the right deviation and make an all-out effort, a new upsurge, a more vigorous development of the campaign to increase production and practice economy has appeared on various fronts of the national economy. Take the average daily steel output as an example. In the first ten days of August, it was 33,000 tons; in the second ten days, it was 37,000 tons; in the last ten days, it was 38,000 tons. In the first ten days of September, it was 41,000 tons, in the second ten days, it was 45,000 tons. That is, the daily output in the second ten days of September was 36 per cent greater than that in the first ten days of August. From this fact and facts in other fields, people can see and be confident that we shall be able to fulfill and overfulfill the goals set in this year's national economic plan and, thus, within this year, fulfill ahead of time the main targets of the Second Five-Year Plan. Accordingly, we shall be able to win three years and so carry on construction under the Second Five-Year Plan on a still larger scale and at still higher speed.

Higher Rate of Economic Growth Achieved

The successive big leap forward in the two years of 1958 and 1959 is proof positive that there is every possibility of developing the national economy at a still higher rate on the basis of the enormous progress made during the First Five-Year Plan. It also proves that it is wrong to imagine that the rate of national economic growth during the Second Five-Year Plan can only equal or even be less than that during the First Five-Year Plan. Of course, when the base figure grows, there is a certain limit to the continued increase of the rate of development. But, so far as the present situation of our country is concerned, there is still incalculable and powerful latent strength in raising labor productivity, tapping natural resources, carrying out the technical revolution, etc. Moreover, the more industrial and agricultural production grows, the bigger the material and technical basis gets and the more powerful is this latent strength. As long as we firmly and thoroughly implement the Party's general line and its several policies of simultaneous development, there is no doubt that our industrial and agricultural production will be able to maintain the rate of the leap forward over a long period.

When we say that our national economy will continue its leap forward, this does not imply an equal rate of development every year. Agricultural production which accounts for a considerable proportion of our national economy is still to a very large extent subject to the influence of natural conditions; sometimes harvests may be good while at other times they may be bad. The amount of new productive capacity cannot always be the same every year; it may be a little more in some years and a little less in others. There is also the possibility of some other factors emerging in national economic development which it is difficult to know fully about in advance. For these and other reasons, the national economy will inevitably advance in a wave-like manner; its rate of growth may be a bit higher at one time and a bit slower at another. This should be considered normal. But, taken as a whole, our economy has been growing steadily every year and construction has been going ahead at high speed. There is every possibility that we will be able to catch up with and surpass Britain in the output of major industrial products in about ten years.

The big leap forward is something new for us, and, of course, we have not yet acquired sufficient experience. To insure continuous and uninterrupted leap forward in the national economy, we must on the one hand overcome all sorts of rightist sentiments and ideas in good time and wage a resolute struggle against right opportunism, and, on the other hand, constantly gather and sum up experience, pay constant attention to the maintenance of the proper proportions between various branches of the national economy, and integrate subjective activity and objective possibilities to the best advantage, so that our economic planning can really embody the demands put forward by the Party's general line.

The Resolution on Developing the Campaign for Increasing Production and Practicing Economy adopted by the 8th Plenary Session of the Party's 8th Central Committee pointed out: "The general line, the great leap forward and the people's communes—these embody the great determination and wisdom of the 650 million industrious and brave people of our country; they are the products of the creative integration of the universal truth of Marxism-Leninism with the practical situation in China achieved by Comrade Mao Tse-tung, great leader of our Party and of the people of all nationalities in our country." In the periods of democratic revolution and socialist revolution, Comrade Mao Tse-tung, by taking into consideration the actual situation in China and using Marxist-Leninist principles in a flexible way, solved a series of problems arising out of the revolutionary process and further developed and enriched Marxism-Leninism in China. In the period of socialist construction, Comrade Mao Tse-tung made a timely summing up of the experience gained in construction, made great theoretical contributions, ideologically armed the whole Party and the people of the whole country and enabled us to gain continuous victories in our socialist construction. Numerous facts prove that the teachings of Mao Tse-tung are our invincible ideological weapon. Therefore, we must seriously study the works of Comrade Mao Tse-tung, and do our work and solve problems seriously and always according to Comrade Mao Tse-tung's principles for the correct handling of contradictions among the people. As long as we diligently study Marxism-Leninism and the teachings of Mao Tse-tung, we will be able to maintain a continuous and uninterrupted big leap forward in our national economy under the guiding light of the general line.

DOCUMENT 48

The Great Unity of the Chinese People and the Great Unity of the Peoples of the World, article by Teng Hsiao-p'ing, published in *Pravda* on October 1, 1959, and in the *People's Daily* on October 2, 1959, in celebration of the Tenth Anniversary of the Chinese People's Republic.

The text is the NCNA English-language release of October 2, 1959, as carried in CB 595 under the title "Article by Teng Hsiao-ping in Honor of National Day."

Comment. The main point of this article, written for *Pravda* and reprinted in Peking, is explanation and defense of mass movements. It seems possible that some of the criticisms attributed in Document 48 to "rightist opportunists" or to others unspecified within Chinese Communist ranks, about the efficiency and appropriateness of mass movements, had been voiced by Russian theoreticians. It is probably no accident that to a Russian audience the communes are asserted to be a creation of the masses. There is little emphasis on the transition to Communism in China, but also no mention of Soviet steps in this direction (see our comment on Document 37).

───────────────TEXT OF DOCUMENT 48───────────────

The Chinese people achieved the great victory of their revolution against imperialism, feudalism and bureaucrat-capitalism 10 years ago. Since then they have also won great victories in the struggle against enemies at home and abroad in the socialist revolution on the economic, political and ideological fronts, and in socialist economic and cultural construction. The Chinese people have succeeded in all this because they relied on the great unity of the entire people under the leadership of the Chinese Communist Party and also the great unity between the Chinese people and other peoples of the world.

On the eve of the birth of the Chinese People's Republic in 1949, Comrade Mao Tse-tung pointed out in his *On People's Democratic Dictatorship* that internally, we must unite with all forces that can be united with and establish the people's democratic dictatorship led by the working class and, externally, we must ally ourselves with the Soviet Union, the other socialist countries and the proletariat and the broad masses of people in all other countries. He said: "To sum up our experiences and bring them into focus, we must have the people's democratic dictatorship led by the working class (through the Communist) and based on the alliance of workers and peasants. This dictatorship must unite with all international revolutionary forces. This is our formula, our principal experience, our main program." We have consistently implemented this program during the past 10 years.

The revolution has united the hundreds of millions of people in China. The unity of the Chinese people has become more and more consolidated through the democratic revolution, through the socialist revolution, and with the uninterrupted development of the revolution in the protracted struggle, the broad masses of Chinese peasants have come to see the working class and the Communist Party as the only force which they can rely upon for ever. An indissoluble worker-peasant alliance has been forged under the leadership of the working class, and with this as the basis, we have united all forces that can be united with. The people of all nationalities in China stand united around the Chinese Communist Party, like a giant. In the past, the imperialists mocked the Chinese people by calling them "a heap of sand." Now they can only tremble in the face of the united Chinese people.

The Chinese Communist Party firmly upholds and believes in this Marxist-Leninist truth: The people are the creators of history. Only the masses themselves, with their own hands, can break the shackles of bondage; and only the masses themselves, with their own hands, can create their happiness. Proceeding from this truth, our basic method of work is as follows: To integrate the leadership with the masses, to pursue the mass line in all fields of work, to mobilize the masses boldly, to develop energetic mass movements under the guidance of the leadership, to sum up the views and pool the wisdom of the masses and rely on the strength of the masses to carry out the policies of the Party.

Before 1949, the Chinese Communist Party had already traversed a difficult and tortuous path for close to 30 years. What we did can be summed up in a nutshell:

We united and organized the broad masses of the people in the struggle against imperialism, feudalism and bureaucrat-capitalism under the leadership of the working class and thus created a broad mass movement for the democratic revolution. The people's revolutionary war was the concentrated expression of this mass movement. It was a people's revolutionary war in which hundreds of millions of impoverished peasants were mobilized and gave their all-out support. Thanks to this, we finally defeated the enemy and won complete victory.

What we have done inside China in the 10 years since 1949 can also be summed up as follows: In addition to completing thoroughly the tasks left over from the stage of the democratic revolution, we united and organized the broad masses of the people for the socialist revolution and construction and thus created a broad mass movement for socialist revolution and construction. We have already built up the dictatorship of the proletariat as our state power. This is a powerful weapon in all fields of our work. The strength of the proletarian dictatorship lies in the fact that it makes the broad mass of laboring people the real masters of the country and is built on the initiative of hundreds of millions of people. Hence it is obviously an erroneous view to ignore the initiative of the masses, to maintain that it is no longer necessary to organize mass movements since everything can be done from above by relying on the state apparatus.

In our country, the mass movements play their role in all phases of the socialist revolution and construction. The broad mass movement guarantees that the socialist revolution can be carried out thoroughly and speedily. It also insures that greater, faster, better and more economical results can be achieved in carrying out the socialist construction.

The socialist revolution in our country is the concentrated expression of the strong desire of the broad masses of people to eradicate bourgeois ownership, and ownership by small producers, and completely emancipate the social productive forces. Every important step in the revolution was made under the impetus of extensive mass movements. It was through broad mass movements that we speedily and successfully carried out the socialist transformation of agriculture, handicraft industry, and capitalist industry and commerce. Immediately following this, it was again through large-scale mass movements that we won decisive victories of the socialist revolution on the political and ideological fronts. All old relations of production and the superstructure which shackled the development of the productive forces collapsed rapidly under the impact of such great mass movements, while new relations of production and the superstructure befitting the development of the productive forces have grown up rapidly.

The socialist construction of our country has also been forging ahead under the impact of widespread mass movements. The 650 million Chinese people, completely liberated through socialist revolution, are confidently testing their strength on the truly gigantic tasks. They urgently desire to develop China's economy at high speed, to rid their country quickly of poverty and backwardness, and to catch up gradually with the imperialist countries which have always prided themselves on being "advanced." The Communist Party of China believes that it is its duty to support this entirely reasonable desire of the masses of the people enthusiastically and to lead them actively in organized actions. As early as 1949, the Party and Comrade Mao Tse-tung pointed out that the socialist construction of China, in accordance with our conditions, ought to be very fast, and not very slow. In the spring of 1958, after the overfulfillment of the First Five-Year Plan for the development of the national economy in 1957, the Party at the suggestion of Comrade Mao Tse-tung, mapped out the general line: "Go all out, aim high and achieve greater, faster, better and more economical results to build socialism." This general line has crystallized the great determination of the 650 million Chinese people to build a powerful nation, and has, in turn, played the role of setting the people in motion, mobilizing all the forces that could possibly be mobilized, thus creating a tremendous mass movement for socialist construction and the conditions for the uninterrupted leap forward of our national economy. Moreover, it has given rise to the historically significant movement to set up people's communes in the countryside.

The role of the mass movements in our socialist construction is being felt more and more clearly. The fact that hundreds of millions of working people have gone all out, aimed high, stepped up their enthusiasm for labor to the maximum, and developed the mass movements for technical innovation and technical revolution on a large scale, has guaranteed the continuous leap forward of our economy. We can say for sure that our technical revolution will be many times faster than the former industrial revolution of the capitalist countries. On the basis of giving priority to heavy industry, we simultaneously develop industry and agriculture, heavy and light industry, while strengthening the centralized leadership of the Central People's Government in economic construction, we also see to it that the initiative of the local authorities at various levels is encouraged; we also see to it that the development of large enterprises goes hand in hand with medium and small-sized enterprises; while developing the modern method of production, we see to it that indigenous methods are not ignored. The operation of the policy of "simultaneous development" serves to mobilize the masses on the broadest scale, and to bring into motion various positive factors so as to push forward our socialist construction most effectively and speedily. In steel making, in 1958, we launched a mass movement in the large enterprises and those using modern methods of production as well as in the medium and small-sized enterprises and those using indigenous methods. As a result, tens of millions of people jubilantly joined the movement and displayed boundless enthusiasm for socialist construction. All this led to the enormous leap forward in steel making and laid the basis for a rational distribution of the steel industry in our country, thus creating the important conditions for a speedy development of the steel industry in the future. At the same time, it was through large-scale mass movements that we made timely adjustments of human relations in labor, to adjust certain links in our economic and political set ups that were incompatible with the growth of the productive forces. As a result, our socialist relations of production have been improved steadily and the enthusiasm of the people for socialism was further enhanced. Clearly, it is only by relying on large-scale mass movements in our socialist construction that it will be possible to overcome our economic backwardness in a comparatively short period of time.

In our own ranks some people cannot see the socialist initiative of the masses and therefore entertain doubts about the mass movements. They always think that the masses are not conscious enough and that the mass movements are unreliable. The fact is, however, that the broad masses in China have very great initiative for socialist revolution and socialist construction. It is not the masses who lag behind, but those who entertain doubts of the masses that are lagging behind the masses. Of course, in keeping with the progress of socialism, it is necessary for the masses to educate themselves in order to raise their own consciousness continuously. The broad mass movements led by the Party have played a significant role in promoting the cause of socialism because through these movements the socialist initiative of the masses is fully developed and they serve as the best schools for the self-education of the masses. It is through a series of mass movements in the socialist revolution and construction that the Chinese people have received a profound socialist education which has rapidly raised their socialist consciousness.

In our own ranks some people consider mass movements necessary in the revolution but maintain that it is a different matter in construction. This view is also wrong. Certainly the forms of mass movements should be different in times of revolution and construction, in political struggles and economic work. But obviously our economic construction cannot be divorced from political work, and politics should be the soul and should be in command. To do economic work well, we must observe objective economic laws. The aim of large-scale mass movements is precisely the full application of the objective economic laws by bringing into full play man's subjective activity. Those who deny the role of mass movements in construction view political work and economic work as absolute opposites and therefore fail to see the very important part played by the socialist initiative of the broad masses in construction. They also view as absolute opposites two things in economic construction—reliance on the masses and reliance on technical personnel; they do not understand the vital significance of the practical experience of the masses in production for the development of science and technology. At present, there are not enough technical personnel as yet in our socialist construction, and a group of top-level, outstanding scientists, inventors and other technical experts are urgently needed. To develop their ability and the role they play, however, the experts have to work in close harmony with the masses and continuously absorb new experiences from the practical work of the masses. The view that in construction it is enough to have the management of the enterprises and a few experts issue orders, that the masses are negative or passive factors and that mass movements are not wanted, is obviously wrong.

The enthusiasm of the masses to create a new life and their spirit of initiative are inexhaustible resources for the development of the socialist cause. There can be no real socialist accomplishment which is divorced from the initiative and creative genius of the people. Lenin said: "Vital and creative socialism is created by the masses of people themselves." Marxism-Leninism always opposes the solution of new problems in life by resorting to ready-made formulas from books. In carrying out socialist construction in a country like ours, with a very large population and backward economy, we cannot possibly avoid a host of extraordinary difficulties and complicated problems. We must depend upon the living experience of mass struggles to overcome these difficulties and solve these problems. The Chinese Communist Party and Comrade Mao Tse-tung consistently maintain that the universal truth of Marxism-Leninism must be integrated with the practice of the Chinese Revolution, that is, applying and developing Marxism-Leninism through the practical struggles of the Chinese people. When hundreds of millions of people start to move under the Party's leadership, they not only rapidly accomplish those things which were once considered very difficult, but also break down the out-moded rules and regulations, go by the logic of life itself and discover various kinds of appropriate new forms for our cause. It is no accident that the broad masses of Chinese peasants have created a form of social organization, that is, the people's commune. The former agricultural producers' cooperatives, smaller in scale, could no longer meet the requirements of the leap forward in the productive forces of society. Consequently the large people's commune, which combines industry, agriculture, trade, education, and military affairs and combines the township administration with that of the commune, was born, and an upsurge of forming people's communes was soon apparent in the countryside throughout the country. The Chinese Communist Party and Comrade Mao Tse-tung gave timely, correct leadership of this mass movement. The people's commune has developed so widely and rapidly because it is a creation of hundreds of millions of the Chinese people. It plays a great part in developing the rural economy and culture and in raising the living standards of the peasants. Such a large-scale mass movement which conforms with historical laws cannot possibly rise all of a sudden under the orders of a few people, nor will it vanish in the face of opposition by a few. The people's commune has extraordinary vitality. The peasants say: "It can't be destroyed even by thunder!" Under the conditions in our country, the people's commune is a powerful weapon to accelerate socialist construction in the countryside; it will also be the best form of social organization for the future transition from collective ownership to ownership by the whole people, and from socialism to communism in the countryside.

It is inevitable, under any circumstances, that certain isolated, local and temporary shortcomings will crop up in great, new undertakings in which several hundreds of millions of people take part. But we cannot, as the saying goes, "refuse to take food because we fear choking," and we must not negate the mass movement because we fear these shortcomings. Our mass movement is conducted under the centralized leadership of the Party, with the leaders moving ahead along with the masses and learning together with them from practical experience; therefore, when defects crop up, they are easily detected and overcome. The handful of right opportunists within our Party do not see the great achievements made in the big leap forward movement and in the movement for people's communes since 1958; they spare no efforts to exaggerate certain shortcomings in the mass movements which have already been overcome so as to oppose the Party's general line for building socialism. The positive effect of the mass movement for more iron and steel on the rapid development of our national economy is becoming more and more evident in real life; but the right opportunists think that this movement can only play a destructive role. The people's communes, after summing up the experiences gained in the initial stage, are becoming more mature and sounder; but the right opportunists think that the people's communes are "moving backwards" and that the only way out is to dissolve them. The masses of the people look upon the leap forward in our national economy as something extremely good, but the right opportunists think it is all "in an awful mess." This right opportunist viewpoint is obviously nothing but a reflection within our Party of the reactionary viewpoint of the bourgeoisie which fears the masses and is antagonistic to the mass movement. Unlike the political parties of the bourgeoisie, the Marxist-Leninist party of the proletariat dares to bring into full play the creative power of the masses; it is for ever in the van of the mass movement; it continuously shows the masses the correct path to take, puts forward in time new tasks for which they should struggle, and leads them from victory to victory. That is what our Party has been doing. Our Party is a Marxist-Leninist party, a party of the masses of the people. The principles and policies for all our work are "from the masses, and back to the masses." Through the extensive mass movements, our Party has established intimate flesh and blood ties with the people. As a result of the victory of the Party's general line for the building of socialism, and as a result of the great leap forward in the national economy and the victory in the people's commune movement, these close ties have been further strengthened, and the prestige of our Party among the people has been further enhanced. The Chinese Communist Party has become the core of the great unity of the Chinese people in long years of struggle. This great unity is the fundamental factor that accounts for victories we have already won and victories we shall continue to win in the cause of socialism in our country.

The unity between the Chinese people and the peoples of the whole world is the essential international factor which enables us to score victories in our revolution and in our construction.

The revolutionary cause of the proletariat has always been international in character. The struggle of the proletariat of any country is a component part of the common struggle of the proletariat of the whole world. In this era of ours, the people throughout the world have united in a world-wide common struggle against imperialism for the lofty cause of peace, people's democracy and socialism. Every country in the world, whether big or small, and every nationality, whether advanced or backward, has its place in this common struggle. The people of any country or nationality, so long as they mobilize and organize themselves and are united as one, turning their might to full account, can carry on their struggles successfully, and thereby contribute to the common struggle of the people throughout the world; at the same time, they can obtain help and support in this common struggle.

The Chinese Revolution is a component part of the socialist revolution of the world proletariat. It is a continuation of the great October Revolution. The victory of the Chinese Revolution extended the tremendous influence of the October Revolution and is of great significance to world peace and human progress. The revolutionary victory in a country as big as China with a population of 650 million broke through the Eastern front of imperialism. It is an extremely heavy blow to the imperialist system. Victorious new China joined the socialist camp headed by the great Soviet Union and greatly added to the ascendancy of the world socialist system. The unity and growing strength of the big socialist family formed by the Soviet Union, China and other fraternal countries have fundamentally changed the relative strengths of the world's class forces. Under the leadership of the proletariat, the Chinese people have carried the anti-imperialist and anti-feudal democratic revolution to the end and, through the socialist revolution and construction, are rapidly getting rid of poverty and backwardness, providing an example of going over from the democratic revolution to the socialist revolution in a colonial and semi-colonial country and of the transformation of a backward agricultural country into an advanced industrial country. This cannot but tremendously inspire all the oppressed nations in their struggle for national liberation, people's democracy and a socialist future. The victory of China's revolution and construction is the result of integrating the universal truth of Marxism-Leninism with the realities of China by the Chinese Communist Party and Comrade Mao Tse-tung. It is the victory of Marxism-Leninism. The wide dissemination of Marxism-Leninism in a large country in the East and the continuous great successes it scores further prove the unlimited vitality of Marxism-Leninism, and hence all people of the world who want progress are more and more attracted by Marxism-Leninism.

The Chinese people have received broad sympathy and support from the great unity of the peoples of the world. We have never stood alone in our struggles. Under all conditions, the Chinese people have always carried on their struggle resolutely on their own; at the same time, the assistance and support from the world revolutionary forces are of great significance to the victory of our struggles. Comrade Mao Tse-tung said at the 8th National Congress of our Party: "Internationally, our victories are due to the support of the camp of peace, democracy and socialism headed by the Soviet Union and the profound sympathy of peace-loving people throughout the world." Our revolution and construction have received great, fraternal help from the Soviet Union, help from the other socialist countries, as well as help from the laboring people and all progressive forces of the various countries in the world. The Chinese people are sincerely grateful for this great international help.

Proletarian internationalism is an important condition for the victory of the revolution in all countries. It is an important weapon in the hands of the proletariat in liberating the whole of mankind. The Central Committee of the Chinese Communist Party and Comrade Mao Tse-tung have always educated the entire Party and the whole people in the spirit of proletarian internationalism and opposed all kinds of bourgeois reactionary ideologies of big-nation chauvinism and narrow nationalism. Bourgeois nationalism is an expression of the bourgeois world outlook. Starting from the selfish interests of the exploiting class, the bourgeoisie either places its own nation above the others under the banner of big-nation chauvinism in order to achieve the aim of oppressing and exploiting the other nations; or puts its own nation against the course of world human progress by spreading the ideology of narrow nationalism. Should the proletariat become contaminated with these reactionary bourgeois ideas, the cause of the revolution would be seriously impaired. The imperialists and the reactionaries of the various countries have always exploited national sentiments to spread the virus of bourgeois nationalism as an important means of undermining the cause of the proletarian revolution and disrupting the unity of the various nations of the world. The modern revisionists, as represented by the Yugoslav ruling clique, use bourgeois nationalism to oppose proletarian internationalism, use the nation as a cover to oppose international solidarity and have fully become an echo of imperialism. The Central Committee of the Chinese Communist Party and Comrade Mao Tse-tung have told the entire Party and people time and again that we must always unite with the proletariat and the peoples of the world and make proletarian internationalism our rules of conduct.

The great Soviet Union is the most faithful friend of the Chinese people. After the founding of the People's Republic of China, the two great socialist countries—the Soviet Union and China—formed a solid and close alliance. The unity of the Soviet Union and China plays an extremely important part in the unity of the peoples of the world. Comrade Mao Tse-tung said that the unity of the Soviet Union and China "will inevitably contribute not only to the prosperity of the two great countries—China and the Soviet Union—but also to the future of all mankind and the victory of peace and justice throughout the world." The Chinese Communist Party and the Chinese people have always regarded the strengthening of the friendly cooperation between China and the Soviet Union as our important internationalist duty.

The socialist camp headed by the Soviet Union is the reliable guarantee of world peace and human progress. The People's Republic of China has joined this camp, and shares the same destiny and lifebreath of this camp. In the big family of socialism, the national economies of all the socialist countries are surging forward together; the friendship and unity among us are being strengthened and consolidated day by day. The relations between the countries of the socialist camp are based on the proletarian internationalism of Marxism-Leninism. They are equal and fraternal relations of mutual respect, mutual encouragement and mutual assistance. These are the sincerest and most friendly international relations of a new type. The constant consolidation and promotion of the unity of the socialist camp conforms to the fundamental interests of the peoples of the socialist countries and of the peoples of the whole world.

The unity of the socialist camp headed by the Soviet Union and the unity of the International Communist Movement with the Communist Party of the Soviet Union at its center, form the core of ever more extensive international unity. With the holding of the historic Moscow Meeting of Representatives of Communist and Workers' Parties from all the countries of the world in 1957, this core has become even stronger and more consolidated. With such a strong core, the working class of the world, the laboring people of the world, the oppressed nations of the world, the world forces upholding peace and desiring progress, have united even closer, bringing boundless light and hope to mankind.

The great unity of the Soviet Union, China and all the socialist countries and the great unity of the peoples of the whole world are something imperialism and the reactionaries of all countries cannot disrupt. The more viciously imperialism and the reactionaries attack and try to disrupt our great unity, the harder we will work to consolidate and promote our unity. In the face of our great unity, any struggles on the part of imperialism and the reactionaries will not save them from inevitable destruction. The forces of peace will certainly triumph over the imperialist forces of war; the oppressed nations will certainly overthrow the reactionary rule of colonialism; the socialist system will certainly replace the capitalist system; these are irresistible historical laws. Our times are great times of the transition of mankind from capitalism to socialism. Our cause will surely advance from victories to bigger victories. No force on earth can prevent our victory.

NOTES TO GENERAL INTRODUCTION

1. Li Fu-ch'un, "Report on the Achievements of the First Five-Year Plan," in *Eighth All-China Congress of Trade Unions*, Foreign Languages Press, Peking, 1958; also CB 483.
2. See, for example, SCMP 1121 and 1123; and URS, Vol. 2, No. 16.
3. Teng Tzu-hui, "Report to the Rural Work Conference...New Democratic Youth League, July 15, 1954," reprinted in Chao Kuo-chün, *Agrarian Policies of Mainland China* (Cambridge, Mass.: Center for East Asian Studies, Harvard University, 1957), pp. 70–79.
4. Ch'en Yi, in *People's Daily*, Nov. 13, 1955 (SCMP 1177).
5. Li Choh-ming, *Economic Development of Communist China* (Berkeley: University of California Press, 1959), pp. 196–223.
6. Chu Cheng-ping, "Production and Consumption in China's First and Second Five Year Plans," *New Construction*, February 1957 (ECMM 81).
7. *People's Daily* editorial, May 19, 1955 (SCMP 1056).
8. NCNA, Peking, July 14, 1957 (CB 475).
9. The "hundred flowers" phrase in its present form is found in the popular nineteenth-century novel *Ching Hua Yüan*, in which the Empress Wu of the T'ang dynasty, in a state of drunkenness orders her fairies to make the flowers blossom in wintertime. For a further discussion of the slogan see Li Chi, *The Use of Figurative Language in Communist China*, Studies in Chinese Terminology No. 5 (Berkeley: Center for Chinese Studies, University of California, 1958), pp. 32–57.
10. CB 473.
11. *People's Daily* editorial, Dec. 19, 1957 (SCMP 1682). Several other articles in SCMP 1682 deal with the same problem.
12. Document 19, section I; see also Yu Wei, "Socialist Education Must Be Thoroughly Conducted in the Countryside," *Current Events*, Nov. 12, 1957 (ECMM 118).
13. Hsiao Ku, in *Finance*, Dec. 5, 1956 (ECMM 66).
14. Chu Cheng-ping, as cited in our note 6 (ECMM 81, pp. 22 ff.).
15. CB 464 and 465.
16. URS, Vol. 7, No. 13.
17. Published in *Eighth All-China Congress of Trade Unions*, Foreign Languages Press, Peking, 1958, pp. 21–65; also CB 482.
18. Roderick MacFarquhar, *The Hundred Flowers Campaign and the Chinese Intellectuals* (New York: Praeger, 1960), pp. 242–246.
19. Yeh Fei, in *People's Daily*, May 22, 1958 (CB 509).
20. Kwang Meng-chueh, in *New Construction*, July 1956 (ECMM 53, p. 13).
21. Li Hsüeh-feng, in *Red Flag*, Aug. 1, 1958, blames the failure of the 1956 leap on conservatism alone (ECMM 143).
22. *China Youth*, Dec. 1, 1956 (ECMM 64).
23. Yu K'e-hsing, "Two or Three Instances of Revisionism," *Study*, Jan. 8, 1957 (ECMM 74).
24. Chi Lu, "Some Questions on the Work Style Rectification Movement," *China Youth*, Jan. 16, 1957 (ECMM 70).
25. CB 452.
26. *New Observer*, May 16, 1957 (ECMM 97).
27. Lin Yen, in *Current Events*, May 21, 1957 (ECMM 96).
28. Lo Lung-chi, report to the National Committee of the Chinese People's Political Consultative Conference, March 1957 (CB 444).
29. *People's Daily*, May 31, 1957, as quoted in MacFarquhar, pp. 87–89.
30. Lin Yen, as cited in note 27 above.
31. Lu Ting-yi, "On Anti-Rightist Struggle," NCNA, Peking, Aug. 16, 1957 (SCMP 1958).
32. In SCMP 1618.
33. Mao Tse-tung, in *China Youth*, May 16, 1957 (ECMM 98).
34. Lo Jui-ch'ing, in *Study*, Jan. 3, 1958 (ECMM 118).
35. SCMP 1616.

36. "The Grain Question in the Countryside Is Mainly an Ideological Question," *Grain*, Aug. 25, 1957 (ECMM 106).

37. See *People's Daily* editorial, Dec. 7, 1957 (SCMP 1690).

38. URS, Vol. 8, No. 13, pp. 235–249, contains articles discussing cases of Ting Ling and Ch'en Ch'i-hsia. See also URS, Vol. 8, No. 18, pp. 331–336, and URS supplement to that issue (Aug. 30, 1957), p. 15.

39. For the official report on the conference, see NCNA, Peking, Dec. 13, 1957 (SCMP 1674).

40. CB 509.

41. CB 493.

42. T. J. Hughes and D. E. T. Luard, *The Economic Development of Communist China* (London: Oxford University Press, 1959), p. 67.

43. "Peking Scientists Plan Higher Goals," NCNA, Peking, June 6, 1958 (SCMP 1790, p. 5).

44. Tao Lu-chia, in *People's Daily*, May 16, 1958 (CB 509).

45. See URS, Vol. 12, No. 17.

46. See URS, Vol. 13, No. 3.

47. Po I-po, in *Study*, March 3, 1958 (ECMM 136); Wang Shih-han, in *Political Study*, May 13, 1958 (ECMM 139).

48. T'an Chen-lin, in *Second Session of the Eighth National Congress of the Communist Party of China*, Foreign Languages Press, Peking, 1958, p. 86.

49. See Chang T'se, in *China Youth*, Oct. 1, 1957 (ECMM 114).

50. See, for example, articles from *Political Study*, Feb. 13, 1957; *Study*, Jan. 18 and March 3, 1957; *Theoretical Study*, Feb. 16, 1957 (ECMM 73, 74, 82, 87, respectively).

51. Discussed by Li Kuo-tung, "How May We Understand the 'U-Shaped' Curve?" in *Study*, Aug. 3, 1958 (ECMM 145).

52. C. K. Yang, *A Chinese Village in Early Communist Transition* (Cambridge, Mass.: Technology Press, 1959), p. 238.

53. Tao Lu-chia, as cited in note 44 above.

54. See Party directive, "Overhaul of Agricultural Producers' Cooperatives," NCNA, Peking, Sept. 15, 1957 (SCMP 1618).

55. For a summary of these versions see A. V. Sherman, "The People's Commune," in Geoffrey Hudson, *et al*, *The Chinese Communes*, published by the magazine *Soviet Survey*, London [1959], pp. 20–21.

56. Sherman, in the essay just cited.

57. Sherman, p. 35.

58. *Liaoning Jih Pao*, Nov. 10, 1958 (URS, Vol. 14, No. 5, p. 70).

59. Translated in JPRS 666D, April 21, 1959. A discussion of the role of the militia is also in our Document 36, section VI.

60. *China Youth*, Oct. 28, 1958 (CB 540).

61. Wang Yen-cheng, "The Planning of the Suich'eng People's Commune...," *Architectural Journal*, November 1958 (ECMM 162).

62. NCNA, Peking, Oct. 19, 1958 (CB 530).

63. *People's Daily*, Oct. 6, 1958 (CB 530).

64. In JPRS 626D.

65. *Red Flag* editorial, Sept. 16, 1958 (CB 524).

66. CB 543 contains records of conferences on overseas Chinese affairs.

67. Cited in a Yugoslav radio broadcast, July 15, 1959.

68. Chin Jo-pi, in *Financial and Economic Research*, Dec. 15, 1958 (ECMM 156).

69. Tien Sheng, in *Political Study*, Oct. 13, 1958 (ECMM 151).

70. A number of these articles on the wage and supply controversy are collected in CB 537. This CB is the source of most of the discussion in our next few pages.

71. In *Ta Kung Pao*, Oct. 25, 1958 (CB 537).

72. Cheng Ssu, in *China Youth*, October 1958 (ECMM 155).

73. For example, *People's Daily*, March 7, 1959 (SCMP 1679).

NOTES TO GENERAL INTRODUCTION

74. "The People's Communes: Questions and Answers," in *Workers of China*, Dec. 27, 1958 (ECMM 161).

75. Chih Chung, *Financial and Economic Research*, Jan. 15, 1959 (ECMM 162).

76. Hsieh Li, "A Discussion on the Financial Problem of the People's Communes," *Economic Research*, Oct. 17, 1958; see also article in *Finance*, Dec. 24, 1958. Both items are found in CB 548.

77. *Finance*, just cited.

78. NCNA, Dec. 22, 1958 (SCMP 1929).

79. Issue of May 15, 1959, broadcast by Peking radio.

80. *People's Daily* editorial, March 13, 1959 (SCMP 1982).

81. *People's Daily*, July 1, 1959, broadcast by Peking radio.

82. *People's Daily* editorial, July 26, 1959 (SCMP 2067).

83. *People's Daily*, May 1, 1959 (SCMP 2009).

84. Pi P'ing-fei, in *Economic Research*, Feb. 17, 1959 (ECMM 166).

85. Wu Ch'uan-ch'i, in *People's Daily*, Aug. 30, 1959 (SCMP 2108).

86. Compare with a similar defense of export policy by Yeh Chi-chuang, "The Foreign Trade of China," *People's Daily*, July 13, 1957 (CB 468).

87. Ch'en Po-ta, in *Red Flag*, Nov. 16, 1959 (ECMM 191).

88. NCNA, Peking, Oct. 30, 1959 (CB 603).

89. Shang Chen, in *People's Daily*, Nov. 30, 1959 (SCMP 2155).

90. CB 533, entitled *Ma Chen-wu and Other Hui Rightists in Kansu*, and SCMP 1809 have a number of press articles on the Kansu controversy.

91. NCNA, Peking, April 23, 1959 (CB 574).

92. Some of these reports are collected in CB 549.

93. K'ang Sheng, "Communist Party Members Should Be Marxists...," *Red Flag*, Oct. 1, 1959 (ECMM 189).

INDEX

(NOTE: This index is designed to guide the reader to the principal places in the commentaries and documents where the important themes, events, ideas, and persons are discussed. The persistence with which the Chinese Communists repeat ideas and slogans makes it quite infeasible to refer to every mention. To have produced an exhaustive index of that kind for the forty-eight documents would have been to flood the reader rather than help him.)

Accumulation, see Capital accumulation
Acreage, in agriculture, 471, 472, 495, 541
Aged, happy homes for in communes, 468, 499
Agricultural cooperative movement, history of, 95–96
Agricultural middle schools, 439
Agricultural producers' cooperatives: advanced, 92 ff, 120; advantages of, 4, 65; animals and, 110–111; capitalist tendencies, 351–352; Central Committee directive on, 242–255; and communes, 457–458, 473, 474, 555; development of, 55, 92–93, 169; dissolution of, 8, 97; disturbances in, 291, 369; elementary, 56, 65, 109 ff; evaluated, 283–284; flaws of, 8, 15, 66, 103, 301, 367; and landlords, 114–115; leadership of, 251, 370; opposition to, 8, 96, 99–100, 103, 107, 114; organization of, 242 ff, 250–251; and production brigade, 31; and rectification, 370; second Five-Year Plan, 209; size of, 209, 250; speed-up, 3–5, 92 ff, 118; success of, 168, 352; and technical improvement, 114; and voluntariness, 174; and wealthy peasants, 349
Agriculture: acreage reduced, 471, 472, 541; close planting, 509; development of, 230–231; fundamental change in, 118; importance of, 3, 32, 65, 504; and industry, 224–225; mechanization of, 182, 432, 472; and prices, 251; priority of, 504; second Five-Year Plan, 208; socialist transformation of, 169
Ah Q, 163
All-round management, 454
Animals, and cooperatives, 110–111
Anshan steel works, 51
Antagonistic contradictions, see Contradictions
Anti-rightist campaign, 33–36, 530 ff. See also Rectification; Rightist conservatism
Apprentice system, 318
Army, 382–383; anti-rightist campaign, 357; and Chinese Communist Party, 38, 488, 576, 577 ff; and class struggle, 579–580; officers and men, 583–584; opposition to Chinese Communist Party, 38; politics in command, 580–581; rectification, 433
Automation, 480

Backyard furnaces, 540, 542–543
Birth control, 119, 240, 295–299, 496
Birth rate, 297
Blooming, see Hundred Flowers
Border disputes, 526
Bourgeois democracy, 277, 321
Bourgeois individualism, in Party, 358
Bourgeoisie, 171–173, 187–188, 276, 285; campaign against, 345–349, 520–521. See also Rectification; Rightist conservatism

Britain, 16, 401, 402
Bulganin, quoted, 139
Bureaucratism, 40, 133, 189–190, 223, 291, 323, 422, 433

Cadres: attitude toward communes, 31; and cooperatives, 94, 98, 105; fear of criticism, 398; and Hundred Flowers, 12, 15; lack of zeal, 520; and masses, 482; pressures on, 23; to countryside, 439; training of, 109
Cairo conference, 403–404
Capital accumulation, 205, 225–226, 435, 497, 591
Capital construction, 8; *1956*, evaluated, 306
Capital investment, 49–50
Capitalism, transformation of, 68; transformation to socialism, 47–48
Capitalist world, as a model, 162
Capitalists, 234–235; policy toward, 519, 521
Cash crops, and cooperatives, 244
Chang Kuo-t'ao, 150, 573
Chang-Lo alliance, 336, 337
Chang Po-chün, 2, 14, 330, 333; alliance with Lo Lung-chi, 336, 337; confession, 337–341
Chang Tsai, 443, 450
Chekiang, 8, 16; cooperatives in, 4; dissolution of cooperatives, 97; purge of rightists, *1957*, 363, 383
Ch'en Ming-shu, criticism of Mao, 5
Ch'en Po-ta, 4, 22, 23, 30, 35, 36; *New Society, New People*, 451–453
Ch'en Shao-yu, see Wang Ming (his pseudonym)
Ch'en Tu-hsiu, 150, 198, 573
Ch'en Yi, 3
Chengchow conference, November *1958*, 478, 484
Chiang Hua, *Adhere to the Correct Line of the Party and Win Victory of the Rectification Campaign on Every Front*, 363–388
Chiang Kai-shek, 24, 46, 54, 90
Child labor, 499
Ch'in Pang-hsien, see Po Ku (his pseudonym)
China: border disputes, 526; and Eastern Europe, 10, 11, 256 ff; and Japan, 527–528; compared to Soviet Union, 79, 139; and United States, 408–410, 523; compared to U.S., U.K., and Japan, 53; diplomatic relations, 523, 528 (see also International relations); exports, 35, 62–63, 241, 540, 545; unity of, 521
China's path to industrialism, 293–294
Chinese Communist Party, 197–203, 571 ff; and army, 488, 577 ff; and communes, 501; complacency in, 223; conservatives, see Rightist conservatism; counterrevolutionaries in, 342; criticism of, 13, 575; debate within, 16; fear of masses, 367; and govern-

606

CHINESE COMMUNIST PARTY (cont'd.)
ment, 325; growth of, 571; history of, 150, 198 ff; and intellectuals, 143; leftists, 16, 31, 366; and masses, 361; membership drive, 4; misunderstanding of theory of contradictions, 368; opposition to Hundred Flowers, 6, 7, 12; opposition to mutual supervision, 189; and peasants, 100; problems at local level, 386-387; purges in, 4, 16, 21, 383, 417, 572; rectification of, 2, 11, 12, 13, 162, 358 (see also Rectification); rightist opposition, 4, 5, 9, 10, 15, 34-36, 41, 107, 169, 358, 384, 387, 420. See also Rightist conservatism; Eighth Party Congress; Tenth Anniversary

Chinese Communist Party Rightists, victory of, 9, 27, 33

Chinese Communist Youth League, 202

Chinese path to socialism, 290

Ch'ing Dynasty, 46

Chou En-lai, April 1959 speech, 27, 32, 33; defense of Great Leap Forward, 35; June 1957 speech, 9, 299-329; on intellectuals, 5, 6, 127, 128-144, 158; on party control, 14; *The Present International Situation and China's Foreign Policy*, 401-410; *On the Question of Intellectuals*, 128-144; quoted, 158, 337, 416; *1959 Report on China's Economy*, 540-550; *Report on Government Work*, 503-529; *Report on the Work of the Government*, June 1957, 299-329; report to Eighth Party Congress, 8, 216-242; on Socialist Camp, 11; visit to East Europe, 256

Ch'u An-p'ing, 330, 340

Chu Yuan, 443, 449

Class struggle, 266-267, 288-289, 366, 396, 419-420, 579-580; in countryside, 4, 106, 108

Coexistence, see Peaceful coexistence

Cold war, competition, 391, 402

Collective leadership, 144, 148, 149, 200

Collective schools, 451

College graduates, manual work, 359

Commandism, 7, 9, 11, 25, 223, 373, 488; and cooperatives, 254

Commerce, 183-184; see also Free market; Free supply; Three fixes

Communes, 21-33, 451 ff, 478 ff, 503-504, 550 ff; August 1958 resolution on, 454-456; characteristics of, 460; and Communism (see Communism, and communes); consolidation of, 32, 504; difficulties, 24 ff; distribution problem, 480; and education, 466; experiments, 491; history of, 550-555; incentives, 482; inspection of, 502, 503; management, 466-467, 474; and militia, 24; opposition to, 558-559, 600; organization of, 454-455, 500; origin of, 8, 21 ff, 553-554; origin of name, 554; popular demand for, 463, 471-472; preparations for, 470-471; private ownership, 25, 26, 456, 458, 464-465, 475-476, 498; prospects, 476; and relations of production, 458 (see also Communism, transition to); reorganization of, 32; Wuchang resolution, summarized, 484-485; and small industry, 593; urban, 26, 489, 491

See also Aged; Agricultural producers' cooperatives; Communism; Family; Mess halls; Nurseries; Ownership; Private property; Wage system; Weihsing commune

Communism, 481; and communes, 22, 27, 438, 456, 458-459, 464, 490, 493, 544, 551, 554; productive base of, 30, 31, 481, 494; and Soviet Union, 487, 504; prospects for, 456; short cuts to, 19; transition

COMMUNISM (cont'd.)
to, 23, 28, 29, 30, 459, 461, 462, 479 ff, 490, 491, 493, 497

Communist Party, see Chinese Communist Party

Confucius, 449, 450; quoted on education, 443, 448

Conservatism, see Rightist conservatism

Consumer goods, 179, 205, 214-215, 316

Consumption, 78-79, 205, 226, 431, 480, 591

Contraception, 297

Contradictions, 148, 153, 258, 273-294, 420-421, 434; Mao Tse-tung, February 1957 speech on, 273-294

Counterrevolutionaries, 42, 192-193, 282-283, 303-304, 519-520; in cooperatives, 121, 251; in Party, 342; no leniency, 350-351; rounding up of, 381

Criticism, criteria for, 290

Cuba, 525

Cult of the individual, 144, 145; and economic development, 147

Decentralization, 40, 190, 211, 213, 216-217, 235-236, 320, 361, 416-417, 426, 434-435, 503, 508, 594

Democratic League, 332, 334, 339

Democratic parties, 5, 6, 13, 14, 188, 324, 347, 520-521

Departmentalism, 374, 482

De-Stalinization, 128, 263, 265; effect on China, 10, 11

Dining rooms, see Mess halls

Diplomatic relations, 523, 528; see also International relations

Division of powers, see Decentralization

Doctrinairism, 265, 266, 289-290, 437

Dogmatism, 7, 39

Down to the country, 18

Dulles, John Foster, and communes, 500; quoted, 258

Dumping, 526

East Europe, 10; and China, 256; economic aid from, 83-84, 215, 220; and Stalin, 270-271

Economic autarchy, 224

Economic development: decentralization, 213; financial limitations, 223; and personnel, 229; socialist and capitalist, 507; subjective factors, 511, 592; tempo of, 399, 425, 429, 453, 492, 587 ff

Education, 76-77, 184-185, 310-312, 440, 442, 516-517; and communes, 24, 466; and Great Leap Forward, 447-448; and productive labor, 18, 438-450

Eighth Party Congress, 7-9; 164 ff

Eisenhower doctrine, 403

Electoral system, 322

Empiricism, 437

Emulation drive, 422

Engels, F., quoted on authority, 268; *Communist Principles*, quoted on Communist production, 453; *The Housing Question*, quoted on leisure, 447; *Principles of Communism*, quoted on specialization, 444; *Socialism, Scientific and Utopian*, quoted, 394

Equalitarianism, 494

Experiments, communes, 491

Expert, red, see Red and expert

Experts, 143, 315, 325

Exports, see China

Family, 24, 451, 488, 499-500

Fan Chen, 443, 450

Fan Chih, 450
Fei Hsiao-t'ung, 339; quoted, 13
Five-Year Plan, first, 1–3, 42–43; 175–177; defects of, 8, 216, 218, 220–222; results of, 217 ff, 505–506, 557
Five-Year Plan, second, 216; industrial output, 548; and scientists, 212; tasks of, 177–179, 204–216, 223–225, 510–511
Fourier, Charles, on education, 448
Free distribution, and communes, 27
Free market, 7, 210, 216, 233–234, 252, 342; restricted, 378
Free supply, 29, 463, 467, 489; and communes, 28, 29, 497; and Communism, 493

General line, *1946–1949*, 166; *1952 ff*, 167
Geographical distribution of industry, see Industry
Gomulka, 256
Gradualness, see Voluntariness
Grain, free supply, 463, 467; shortages of, 16
Great-Han chauvinism, 256, 270, 287, 569–570; and rightist rectification, 356; in Soviet Union, 11; and Stalin, 270. See also Han
Great Leap Forward, 16–21, 389–393, 416; and Communism, 23; compared with leap forward, *1956*, 2, 5, 9, 21; criticism and opposition, 19, 35, 427, 429–430, 440, 542 ff, 587; general line, 428; international setting, 18–20; keynote speech of, 416–438; mistakes corrected, 549; national minorities, 521; origins of, 16 ff, 364, 422–423, 430; and rectification, 401; results of, 485, 506–507, 533–534, 536, 541, 588–591; and rightists, 531, 532; shortcomings of, 32, 546; targets, 510–511; targets reduced, 534

Han, importance of, 564–565, 569
Hanyang steelworks, 53
Heavy industry, 47, 48, 179, 226–227, 589; compared to Soviet Union, 59; importance of, 46–47, 179; priority of, 206, 375, 511, 592
Honan, 22, 31
Hopei, 29
Hsienchu county, dissolution of agricultural producers' cooperatives, 8
Hsinyang, 22
Hsu Hsing, 450
Hsu Li-ch'ün, *Have We Already Reached the Stage of Communism?* 479–483
Hsuanchuang commune, 29
Hsukuang agricultural producers' cooperative, 22, 23, 452–453
Hsun Tzu, 449; quoted, 443
Hu Feng, 2, 5, 42, 152, 154
Hu Shih, 152, 154, 162
Humphrey, Senator Hubert, 32
Hunan, 36, 40
Hundred Flowers, 5–7, 127, 151–163; after June *1957*, 314, 348, 434, 518, 590; attacks of intellectuals, 11, 13; and Chinese Communist Party, 9, 12; end of, 13, 14; defined, 153; fear of, 13; and Hungary, 14; in *1956*, 12; opposition to, 12; origins of, 2, 5, 7, 127, 288; rationalization of, 15; and science, 185; and second Five-Year Plan, 213; value of, 152 ff
Hungarian revolt, 257 ff, 277, 279, 328; and China, 11, 257, 277, 281–282, 401; lessons from, 279; and Lo Lung-chi, 333–334, 335; rightist attitude toward,

HUNGARIAN REVOLT (cont'd.)
346; and Soviet Union, 418; U.S. involvement, 392; Yugoslav role in, 415
Hungkuang commune, Peking, 481

Ideological work, 436–437; remolding, 299
Illiteracy, 319
Import-export problems, see China, exports
Incentives, 482
Income, peasants, 284, 301; see also Standard of living
Income distribution, in cooperatives, 248–249, 353
India: and Tibet, 523; on peace, 405
Individualism, 144, 482
Industrialization, subjective factors, 511
Industry: geographical distribution, 43, 60, 179, 180, 207–208, 227–228, 593; industrial quality, 61, 180–181, 210, 230, 306, 399, 538, 542, 594. See also Decentralization; Heavy industry; Light industry; Local industries
Inflation, 8
Intellectuals, 12–13, 128–144, 285–286, 332, 345–349, 420; Chou En-lai's report on, 128–144; class origin, 185; and economic development, 5, 129 ff, 286; improved conditions, 6, 7, 133–134; remolding of, 6, 14, 137–139, 346, 518–519. See also Hundred Flowers
International relations, 193–197, 401 ff, 486, 524–529. See also China
Internationalism, proletarian, 601
Investment, see Consumption; Accumulation
Iron and steel campaign of *1958*, 35
Iron and steel plants, small, 540, 542–543
Islam, 37

Jao Shu-shih, 90, 150, 573
Japan, 527–528

Kao Kang, 36, 43, 90, 144, 150, 573
Kardelj, on Hungary, 264–265
Khrushchev, 7, 10, 19, 32, 144, 562
Kiangsu, 17
Kirin, 22
Ko P'ei-ch'i, quoted, 13
Korea, 407–408
Kuan Han-ching, 443, 450
Kuang Ming Jih Pao, 340, 341, 556
Kuomintang, 43, 46, 55; science under, 313
Kwangsi, famine in, 7
Kwangtung, localism in, 16; rightists in, 4

Labor: and Communism, 498; child, 499; discipline, 500–501; manual, 359, 520; shortage, 496, 498, 507, 514–515, 590; slave, 507
Labor army, 21
Lai Jo-yü, 8
Land reform, stages of, 47
Landlords, and cooperatives, 114–115
Lao Tzu, quoted, 292
Laos, 408
Leadership, 181–182; centralization of, 324, 512; Party, 436; of cooperatives, 251; and physical labor, 355
Leap forward: *1955–56*, 2; *1956*, 4, 5, 7, 9, 42, 372, 426–427; defined, 548; uninterrupted, 596; *1958*, see Great Leap Forward

INDEX

Leftist mistake, 3
Legal system, 192, 320-321
Lenin: cited, 45, 144; cited on skipping of stage, 569; referred to by Mao Tse-tung, 390; quoted, 49, 145, 146, 147, 159, 391, 560, 599; quoted on Communism, 422, on democracy, 574, on dictatorship of proletariat, 187, 267, on heavy industry, 46, on nationalities, 270, 564, 565, on party leadership, 268, on state capitalism, 173; *A Great Beginning*, quoted, 555; *From the Destruction of the Ancient Social System to the Creation of the New*, quoted, 559; *Pearls of Narodniks' Hare-brained Schemes*, quoted on education and labor, 446-447; *What Is To Be Done?* quoted, 265, 266
Liang Sou-ming, 42, 154, 162
Liaoning, 23, 32, 33
Liberalization, 268; abandoned, 36-37, 300. See also Intellectuals; Hundred Flowers
Li Chu-ch'en, 27
Li Fu-ch'un, 1, 2, 4, 43; report on first Five-Year Plan, 42-91; *On the Big Leap Forward in China's Socialist Construction*, 587-596
Li Hsien-nien, 8, 17, 25
Li Li-san, 150
Li Wei-han, 335
Light industry, 2, 20, 59, 101, 179, 207, 226, 294, 375, 592-593
Lin Piao, 38; *March Ahead under the Red Flag of the General Line and Mao Tse-tung's Military Thinking*, 577-586
Li Teh-ch'üan, speech on *Birth Control and Planned Families*, 295-299
Liu Chieh-mei, 16
Liu Lan-t'ao, *The Chinese Communist Party Is the Supreme Commander of the Chinese People in Building Socialism*, 571-577
Liu Shao-ch'i, 9, 10, 12, 16, 19, 30, 39, 127; opposition to Hundred Flowers, 16; report to Eighth Party Congress, 164-203; *The Present Situation, the Party's General Line for Socialist Construction and Its Future Tasks*, 416-438; *The Significance of the October Revolution*, 393-400; quoted, 579
Liu Tsung-yuan, 443, 450
Lo Jui-ch'ing, 15
Lo Lung-chi, 2, 12, 13, 14; alliance with Chang Po-chün, 336-337; confession, 330-337
Local industries, 17, 21, 26, 62, 423, 594. See also Light industry
Local initiative, see Decentralization
Local nationalism, 356, 562. See also National minorities
Localism, 16, 21, 31, 32, 36, 40, 342, 364
Long-term coexistence, 290-291
Lu Hsun, 163; quoted, 159
Lu Ting-yi, 6, 14, 18, 22, 36; *Education Must Be Combined with Productive Labor*, 438-450; *Let a Hundred Flowers Blossom, a Hundred Schools of Thought Contend!* 151-163

Ma Chen-wu, 37
Ma Liang, 37
Machine-building and metallurgical industries, 226-227
Malenkov, quoted, 338
Malthusianism, 295

Management: communes, 474; industry, 64; managerial system, 435
Manpower, shortages of, see Labor
Manual labor, 359, 520
Mao Tse-tung: adulation of, 562; cited, 45; cited on transition to socialism, 48; and communes, 22, 554; contradictions, two types misunderstood, 368; and cooperatives, 3, 4, 92; criticized, 5; disillusionment of, 14; *Economic and Financial Problems during the Anti-Japanese War*, quoted, 79; free supply, 29; Great Leap Forward, 587; Hundred Flowers, 16; Hundred Flowers speech, 151; importance of, 201; as Marxist-Leninist theoretician, 576; *On Coalition Government*, quoted, 46; *On the Correct Handling of Contradictions among the People*, 8, 9, 11, 12, 14, 273-294, 425, 445; *On the People's Democratic Dictatorship*, quoted, 279, 597; *On the Protracted War*, quoted, 581; and Party rectification, 12; on passivity, 39; *Problems of War and Strategy*, 585; quoted against conservatism, 430, on counterrevolutionaries 381, on democratic methods 362, on education 446, on free supply 28, on industrialization 49, on knowledge 441, on rightists 532, on theory 441, on Sino-Soviet relations, *1950*, 400; quoted variously, 90, 91, 127, 144, 338, 437-438, 484, 487, 572, 580, 586, 592, 598, 601; *Rectify the Party's Style of Work*, quoted, 156, 441; *Report on a Survey on the Peasant Movement in Hunan*, referred to, 560; resignation, 478, 484, 486, 487-488; slogans, quoted, 422; *Socialist Upsurge in China's Countryside*, preface, 5, 117-119, 425-426; *Speech at Moscow Celebration Meeting*, 389-393; *Strategic Problems of China's Revolutionary War*, quoted, 58; *Ten Sets of Relationships*, explained, 426; *The Question of Agricultural Cooperation*, 94-105, 424, 425
Markets: competition for, 252-253; shortages, 544-545; stability of, 73
Marx: quoted, 393, 424, 554; *Capital*, quoted on education, 444; *Communist Manifesto*, quoted 565, on education and labor 447, and on industrial armies 459; *Critique of the Gotha Programme*, quoted on education and labor, 446; *The Directives to the Delegates of the Provisional Central Council on Some Questions*, quoted on education and labor, 448-449
Marxism, criticism of, 15, 289
Marxist quotations, referred to, 438
Mass line, 7, 22, 149, 255, 266-267, 322, 344, 353, 363, 386, 486, 513; conservative opposition to, 20; new form, 367
Masses: and leap in agricultural production, 372; role of, 366, 399, 436-437, 597-600; supervision by, 190
Matsu, see Offshore Islands
May 4 movement, 13
Mechanization, 182, 428, 432, 472, 492
Mencius, 449, 450; quoted on the people, 443; quoted on specialization, 448
Mess halls, 479, 482, 489, 498-499, 539, 543-544
Michurin, 157
Militarization of work, 25, 458-459, 482, 488, 501
Militia, 22, 24, 433, 473, 488, 501, 578-579
Minorities, see National minorities
Money, abolition of, 27
Moscow conference, 410-411
Moscow Declaration of November *1957*, 411 ff
Mutual supervision, 188, 290-291

National minorities, 36, 37, 190–192, 213–214, 236, 287, 420, 521–522; agricultural producers' cooperatives, 253–254; and army, 568; and Chinese Communist Party, 570–571; Great Leap Forward, 521; and Han, 568, 569; policy toward, 562–571; rectification of, 356–357, 565 ff; regional autonomy, 564
Nationalism, 601; narrow, 269
Nationalities, see National minorities
Natural calamities, 39, 301, 538, 547
Nehru, 523
New Democratic Youth League, 202–203
Ninghsia Hui autonomous region, 37
Non-antagonistic contradictions, see Contradictions
Nurseries, 468, 499

Objective laws, 599. See also Subjective factors
Offshore Islands, 22, 24, 38, 527
Overpopulation, 496. See also Birth Control
Overseas Chinese, 26, 489, 497–498
Owen, Robert, on education, 448
Ownership system, 493, 537, 555; see also Private ownership

P'an Fu-sheng, 21
Parochialism, 40, 385. See also Localism
Pavlov, 157
Peaceful coexistence, 19, 258, 391, 402, 405, 486, 586; five principles of, 90
Peasants: and agricultural producers' cooperatives, 107–108, 349; capitalism among, 103–104; economic position, 75–76, 99, 183, 238–239, 316, 317; enthusiasm of, 246; middle, 170, 482; and urban workers, 284; wealthy, against cooperatives, 349. See also Income; Standard of living
Peitaiho Resolution, 550–551; text, 454–456
Peking, Hungkuang commune, 481
P'eng Chen, 16, 18
P'eng Jui-lin, 363, 383, 384, 385
P'eng Teh-huai, 38
People, defined, 275, 327
People's communes, see Communes
People's democracies, see East Europe
Permanent revolution, see Uninterrupted revolution
Personnel: and agricultural development, 231; capitalists, 234–235; specialists in education, 442; technical, 76, 88, 125, 155; training of, 236–237. See also Red and expert
Physical labor, for leadership, 355
Piece-wage system, 28–29. See also Wage system
Planned childbirth, 297. See also Birth control
Planned purchase, 74, 75, 309
Planning, difficulties of, 502
Plow, two-wheel, two-share, 119, 123, 221
Po I-po, 8, 18, 33
Po Ku, 163, 199
Poland, 10. See also East Europe
Political leadership, and expertise, 315. See also Red and expert
Politics in command, 486, 501, 573; and army, 38, 580–581; and communes, 509
Population, see Birth control
Private property, compensation for, 249–250
Private ownership: in communes, 25–26, 456, 458, 464–465, 475–476, 498; peasants' attitude toward, 110; transformation of capitalism, 68; transformation to socialism, 47–48
Privilege, of Chinese Communist Party, 361
Production, and personnel, 371

Production brigade: and cooperatives, 31; and commune management, 467
Productive labor: and education, 18, 438–450; for bourgeoisie, 380
Productivity, and Communism, 30, 31, 481, 494
Professionalism, in army, 38
Pu Hsi-hsiu, 334
Purges, 4, 16, 21, 417, 572; Chekiang, 363, 383

Quality, industrial, see Industry
Quemoy, see Offshore Islands

Radical line, victory in 1957, 16
Rectification, 2, 12–16, 17, 273 ff, 341 ff, 344, 363 ff, 365, 516; effectiveness, 151, 419, 432; in Party, 2, 13, 273, 275, 333, 299–300; in Party, causes of, 11; of hard-core cadres, 483; speed-up of, 12; 1942–44, 160, 199, 278; of government, 323; periodic need for, 434; permanent, 520; workers, 353–354, 376. See also Rightist conservatism
Red and expert, 6, 16, 137, 341–342, 348, 379, 399, 400, 436, 439, 574; origins of, 14
Regional autonomy, 36, 564. See also National minorities
Regionalism, see Localism
Revisionism, 11, 19, 257, 266, 289–290, 389; and de-Stalinization, 265; Chinese view of, 411; danger to Communism, 413–414
Revisionists, 260. See also Rightist conservatism
Revolution, passim; see Uninterrupted revolution
Right deviation, see Rightist conservatism
Right opportunism, 260
Rightist conservatism, 3, 118, 129, 289, 347; and agricultural production, 370–371; and cadres, 531, 535; and Chinese Communist Party, 5, 11, 33, 40–41, 107, 200, 383–386, 420, 530 (see also Chinese Communist Party); criticisms of state system, 321; defect of, 16; defined, 2; and Great Leap Forward, 18, 19, 20, 542 ff, 559; leniency toward, 520; opposition to mass line, 20; among people, 327; strength of, 34; struggle against, 33, 128, 343, 352, 365, 530, 549; and unions, 8; victory of, 9, 27, 33. See also Rectification

Saifudin, 37
Science, 141–142, 313, 518; class character, 348; development of, 237–238, 313–314; no class character, 156–157. See also Personnel
Science and democracy, Chang Po-chün's view of capitalist countries, 338
Sectarianism, 324, 361, 385
Sha Wen-han, 363, 383, 384, 385
Shansi, 17, 18; commune experiment in, 21
Shih Nai-an, 443, 450
Sinkiang, opposition to Communism, 37
Slave labor, 507
Small enterprises, 513–514
Small industry, 17. See also Local industries; Light industry
Social sciences, 518; class character of, 313
Socialism, skipping of stage, 481, 494–495. See also Communism (transition to)
Socialist Camp, 10–11, 256–273 passim. See also East Europe; Soviet Union
Socialist development, compared with capitalism, 507
Socialist industrialization, see Heavy industry
Socialist transformation, 103, 168–175, 210–211, 303; of agriculture, 169; general line, 167; of industry, 68 ff, 171 ff

INDEX

Soviet Union: and China, 32, 35, 79, 132, 139, 483; Chinese exports to (see China); collectivization in, 3; and Communism, 487, 504, 524; dropped as only economic model, 6; as economic model, 1, 4, 54, 100–102, 140, 161, 294, 309; economic aid to China, 1, 3, 44, 45, 51, 52, 54, 58, 59, 83–84, 89, 132, 141, 215, 220, 241, 294, 307, 392–393, 510, 592; historic role of, 146, 259; and Hungary, 11; lessons from, 260. See also Communism; Khrushchev; Stalin
Specialists, in education, 442
Specialization attacked, 444. See also Personnel; Professionalism; Red and expert
Sputnik, 15, 19
Stages of development, see Socialism
Stalin: attacked, 144 (see also De-Stalinization); and East Europe, 270–271; errors of, 146, 147, 261 ff; evaluated, 146–147, 149, 150, 159; isolation from the masses, 262; quoted, 44, 45, 54; quoted on economizing, 79; Yugoslav attitude toward, 411
Stalinism, 11, 263. See also De-Stalinization
Standard of living, 8, 77–79, 238–240, 315–319, 435–436, 545; and first Five-Year Plan, 56; gains delayed, 498; and second Five-Year Plan, 214; workers, 176, 181. See also Peasants; Wages
Statistics, adjusted, *1959*, 546; problems of, 86, 374, 502
Steel, 547, 594, 600; iron and steel, 35, 540, 542–543
Strikes, 9, 291
Students: criticism of Chinese Communist Party, 13; and Hungarian revolt, 282; low standards, 237; political reliability, 312; and productive labor, 312
Su Yü, 38
Subjective factors, 436–437, 481, 511, 532, 599
Subjectivism, 199, 200
Suip'ing county, 22
Sun Chang-lu, 383, 384, 385
Sun Yat-sen, 443
Supply system, 480, 489. See also Free supply; Three fixes
Szema Chien (Ssu-ma Ch'ien), 443, 449

Taiwan, 193, 408–409, 410, 528
T'an Chen-lin, 18, 25, 33
Targets, adjusted, 534, 537, 541, 546, 547–548. See also Statistics
Tax, agricultural, 15, 219, 248–249, 252, 275, 284, 378
Teachers, shortage of, 237
Technical personnel, see Personnel; Red and expert
Tempo, see Economic development
Teng Hsiao-p'ing, 15, 39, 165; quoted, 386; *Report on the Rectification Campaign*, 341–363; *The Great Unity of the Chinese People and the Great Unity of the Peoples of the World*, 596–602
Teng Tzu-hui, on class struggle in countryside, 4; on Soviet Union as economic model, 3
Tenth Anniversary, 36–38; 562 ff
Terror, 300
Theft, 482
Third road, bourgeois democracy, 335
Three fixes, 4, 93, 219, 252
Tibet, 37, 38, 287, 505, 521, 523, 567; and communes, 491; revolt, 522–523
Ting Ling, 330
Tito, 10, 11, 19, 256, 257; on Hungary, 19, 264; quoted on Stalinism, 264
Trade unions, 8, 9, 202

Transition to Communism, see Communism
Tsao Hsueh-chin, 443, 450
Tsinghai, 37
Tsingtao conference, 343
Twelve-Year Agricultural Program, 5, 6, 18, 93, 119–126, 221
Twentieth Party Congress, Soviet Union, 193–194; effect on Chang-Po-chün, 338; effect on Lo Lung-chi, 335; lessons of, 144–145, 390
Two Chinas, 408–410, 528–529. See also Taiwan
Two-wheel, two-share plow, 119, 123, 221

U-shaped development, 9, 21, 427
Unemployment, 590
Uninterrupted revolution, 427, 458, 495, 580; theory of Mao Tse-tung, 479
Unions, 9, 202; rightists in, 8
United front, 187, 189, 324; national minorities, 567
United Kingdom, 16, 401, 402
United States: and China, 408–410, 523; depression, 19, 393, 404, 413, 418; foreign policy of, 405; way of life, 316
Unity, international Communism, 419
U.S.S.R., see Communism; Khrushchev; Soviet Union; Stalin
Utopian socialists, on education, 448

Vietnam, 408
Voluntariness, 3, 170; and cooperatives, 98, 174
Voluntary labor, 542

Wage system, 29, 318, 376; in communes, 27, 456, 463, 467, 469, 474, 480, 489, 497, 537; piece-wage, 28–29
Wages, as incentives, 181; in cities, 497; second Five-Year Plan, 214; workers, 219, 238, 306, 315
Wang Chung, 443, 450
Wang Feng, 37; *The Great Victory in Our Nationalities Policy*, 562–571
Wang Fu-chih, 443, 450
Wang Kuo-fan cooperative, 283
Wang Ming, 150, 163, 199
War, 292, 391, 418–419. See also Peaceful coexistence
Waste, economic, 80–83, 240–241
Water conservancy, 17, 66, 67, 85, 122–123, 176, 182, 209, 372, 547, 552
Weihsing (Sputnik) commune, 22, 457, 458; regulations of, 463–470
Wen Hui Pao, 334
West, as economic model, 6
Women, 124, 203, 475, 552
Work, and study, 439; voluntary, 507
Workers and peasants, 284. See also Standard of living; Income; Wages
Workers' Congress, 355, 378
Wu Cheng-en, 443, 450
Wuhan Resolution, 25, 29, 30, 39, 478, 488–503

Yang Ssu-yi, 363, 383, 384, 385
Yenan, 28, 29
Young Communist League, 360, 387
Yu Ping-po, 155, 162
Yugoslav League of Communists, 410–411, 414–415
Yugoslavia, 19, 256, 411; betrayal of, 414–415, 526; and China, 193; and November *1957* Moscow Declaration, 412; and Stalin, 147, 264

BOOKS FROM THE CENTER FOR INTERNATIONAL AFFAIRS

published by Harvard University Press

The Soviet Bloc, by Zbigniew K. Brzezinski, 1960 (jointly with the Russian Research Center).
Rift and Revolt in Hungary, by Ferenc A. Vali, 1961.
The Economy of Cyprus, by A. J. Meyer, with Simos Vassiliou, 1962 (jointly with the Center for Middle Eastern Studies).
Entrepreneurs of Lebanon, by Yusif A. Sayigh, 1962 (jointly with the Center for Middle Eastern Studies).

published by others

The Necessity for Choice, by Henry A. Kissinger, 1961. Harper & Brothers.
Strategy and Arms Control, by Thomas C. Schelling and Morton H. Halperin, 1961. Twentieth Century Fund.
United States Manufacturing Investment in Brazil, by Lincoln Gordon and Engelbert L. Grommers, 1962. Harvard Business School.

HARVARD EAST ASIAN STUDIES

1. *China's Early Industrialization: Sheng Hsuan-huai (1844-1916) and Mandarin Enterprise,* by Albert Feuerwerker, 1958.
2. *Intellectual Trends in the Ch'ing Period,* by Liang Ch'i-ch'ao, translated by Immanuel C. Y. Hsü, 1959.
3. *Reform in Sung China: Wang An-shih (1021-1086) and His New Policies,* by James T. C. Liu, 1959.
4. *Studies on the Population of China, 1368-1953,* by Ping-ti Ho, 1959.
5. *China's Entrance into the Family of Nations: The Diplomatic Phase, 1858-1880,* by Immanuel C. Y. Hsü, 1960.
6. *The May Fourth Movement: Intellectual Revolution in Modern China,* by Chow Tse-tsung, 1960.
7. *Ch'ing Administrative Terms,* translated and edited by E-tu Zen Sun, 1961.
8. *Anglo-American Steamship Rivalry in China, 1862-1876,* by Kwang-Ching Liu, 1962.
9. *Local Government in China under the Ch'ing,* by T'ung-tsu Ch'ü, 1962.